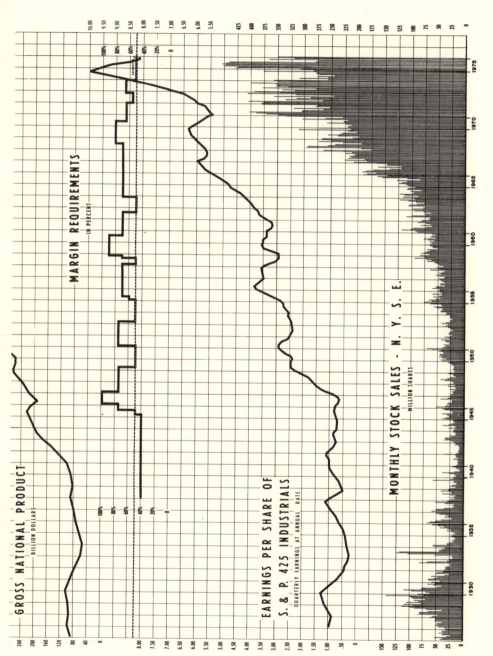

GROSS NATIONAL PRODUCT
—BILLION DOLLARS—

MARGIN REQUIREMENTS
—IN PERCENT—

EARNINGS PER SHARE OF S. & P. 425 INDUSTRIALS
QUARTERLY EARNINGS AT ANNUAL RATE

MONTHLY STOCK SALES - N. Y. S. E.
—MILLION SHARES—

Investment Analysis and Portfolio Management

Investment Analysis and Portfolio Management

Jerome B. Cohen
Professor of Finance and Dean (Emeritus)
Bernard M. Baruch College
The City University of New York

Edward D. Zinbarg
Vice President
Bond and Commercial Loan Department
The Prudential Insurance Company of America

Arthur Zeikel
Executive Vice President and
Chief Investment Officer
Merrill Lynch Asset Management, Inc.

1977 Third Edition

RICHARD D. IRWIN, INC. Homewood, Illinois 60430
Irwin-Dorsey Limited Georgetown, Ontario L7G 4B3

Third Edition

7 8 9 0 MP 5 4 3 2 1 0 9

ISBN 0-256-01883-9
Library of Congress Catalog Card No. 76–15739
Printed in the United States of America

To
Mina,
Barbara,
Terrie,
Carla,
Elizabeth,
Allison,
Jill,
Judith,

and Jeffrey

.

Preface

"Thrift is a wonderful virtue, especially in an ancestor" someone once said. If one of your forebears had bought 100 shares of IBM in 1913 for $44½ per share and held, it would, through stock dividends and stock splits, by mid-1976 have grown to 74,150 shares worth about $20.6 million. Or more recently, $1,000 invested in this stock in the mid-1950s would, by mid-1976, have increased to $88,790. Happy developments of this sort make investments a fascinating subject. On the other hand, there is a real danger of losing your slowly and painfully accumulated resources through ignorance and stupidity. Even the "pros" can stumble and fall. During the 1969–70 and 1973–75 market setbacks, over 125 brokerage houses and securities dealers went under, including a surprising number of well known and previously well regarded firms.

For the individual, investments is not only an intriguing subject, it is a very confusing and difficult one as well. There are so many choices. Whether you have $500 or $5,000, or $50,000 or $500,000 to place, the alternatives are so many and the decisions so perplexing that the process may become nerve-racking.

Is the time to invest now or should you wait? Should you plunge ahead and act on the tip you got yesterday, or should you try to check it out—or should you forget about it? Is this the time to buy stocks, or bonds, or nothing? Is real estate a better hedge against inflation than common stocks, or paintings, or oriental rugs, or postage stamps? Should you use analytic techniques to select and buy common stocks directly or should you buy mutual fund shares and let the professional money managers worry about investment selection and timing? But if it is to be mutual funds, then which one? There are now more than 500 of many varieties—stock funds, bond funds, money market funds,

index funds, growth funds, income funds. How do you find the limited number of effective ones among the many mediocre ones? Or, to be sure of preserving principal, should you play it safe and put your money in Treasury bills, or in a savings account? Should the savings account be in a commercial bank, in a savings bank, or in a savings and loan association? Or perhaps you should increase your life insurance or buy an annuity? But these are fixed dollar investments. What about inflation? Why the increased interest in bonds in the face of higher inflation?

Is this the time to buy common stock? What kind, in what industry, and in what company? What really are your investment objectives? Are you timid or aggressive; conservative or a speculator? Do you want safety of principal or appreciation of capital, or both? Should you choose blue chips or speculative options? Income stocks or growth stocks or performance stocks? Cyclical issues or defensive stocks? Should you invest in coal stocks, electronics, office equipment manufacturers, foods, or chain stores, or mobile homes or utilities? And when you decide upon an industry, then which company? For the professional money manager the questions may be somewhat different and more complex, but they are perplexing and involved, with no easy answers.

In the preface to the first edition we wrote of the book: "It starts out simply and then grows in complexity. It ends with the computer and a peering into the future." Our forecast was reasonably good. The field and subject has indeed become more quantitative and more theoretical. Our revision has attempted to reflect this, though we should make clear that the book is still intended for the first course in investments.

We have attempted to accomplish this in a rather unique manner. First, the new theory is presented primarily in what we hope is readable English rather than in mathematical terms. "I don't know math," a leading economist quipped, "so I am obliged to think." Second, the applicability of theory to portfolio management practices is treated at length. Third, there is a full discussion of risk and return.

We have tried to make this a practical, realistic book full of the sounds and sights of the real investment world. It tries to reflect what "Wall Street" is all about, what securities analysts and portfolio managers do. It has a full exposition of modern financial theory but this is not allowed to shut out the real world of finance, of which large sectors still remain unaffected by and unpersuaded of the usefulness of the theoretical innovations of the past decade. Institutional investment has come to dominate the financial scene and this book attempts to reflect the working activities and requirements of securities analysts and professional money managers.

This third edition now consists of 18 chapters, divided into four

parts. Part I, an *introduction*, surveys the *current investment scene*. Part II is on *security analysis* and *evaluation* and Part III covers *investment timing*. Part IV, which is devoted to *portfolio management*, has been largely reorganized and rewritten. The final chapter portrays the whole range and gamut of the professional security analysts' and money managers' handling of investment techniques by modern computer usage.

December 1976   JEROME B. COHEN
                                        EDWARD D. ZINBARG
                                        ARTHUR ZEIKEL

Acknowledgments

In our endeavor to explain the modern theory and its application to portfolio management practices we acknowledge most gratefully the past advice and help of Dr. Harry Markowitz, the pioneer in the field; Professor William F. Sharpe of Stanford University; Professor Irwin Friend and Marshall Blume of the Wharton School of the University of Pennsylvania; Charles D. Ellis, president of Greenwich Research Associates; Dr. Jack L. Treynor, editor of the *Financial Analysts Journal;* Professor Colyer Crum and Robert Glauber of the Harvard Graduate School of Business; Manown Kisor, Jr., director of research of Paine, Webber, Jackson and Curtis; Professor J. Peter Williamson of the Amos Tuck School of Dartmouth College; and Dr. Douglas A. Love, consultant to the Prudential Insurance Company of America.

We are grateful, too, to the Institute of Chartered Financial Analysts, and to its executive director, Professor W. Scott Bauman, C.F.A., to its education administrator, Dr. Hartman L. Butler, C.F.A., and its examinations administrator, Dr. O. Whitfield Broome, Jr., CPA, for their interest in our text and for permitting us to utilize sample problems from recent C.F.A. examinations.

Who else to thank? There are so many who have been helpful in so many ways that it is difficult to select, but a few must be singled out for special mention. They include Fred C. Cohn, Executive Vice President, Hugh Johnson & Co.; Ann V. Galvin of the Anchor Corp.; Dana H. Danforth, President, The Danforth Associates; Dennis A. Tito, President, Wilshire Associates, Inc.; Linda Lo Monaco, Centennial Capital Corporation; Stewart P. Zobian, Vice President, and Myra Drucker, Analyst, Philadelphia Investment Co.; David T. Wendell, Vice President, David L. Babson & Co.; Stanley Berkson, Editor, *Moody's Handbook of Common Stocks,* Moody's Investors Service;

xi

Fred Siesel, Weeden & Co.; N. Russell Wayne, Executive Editor, *Value Line;* Steven Lewins, and Mark K. Tavel, Associate Research Directors, Value Line Investment Survey; Dr. William Freund, Vice President and Chief Economist, New York Stock Exchange; Yale Hirsch, The Hirsch Organization, Inc.; Michael Culp, Analytical Department, Standard & Poor's Corp.; George A. Chestnutt, Jr., President Chestnutt Corp.; J. Edward McEntire, President, Investors Management Sciences, Inc.; Raphael Yavneh, C.F.A., President, Forbes Investment Advisory Institute, Inc.; Dr. Martin Leibowitz, Vice President, Salomon Bros.; Richard M. Hynes, Manager, Statistical Research Department, Standard & Poor's Corp.; Frederick P. Groll, Chief Statistician, Merrill Lynch, Pierce, Fenner & Smith; James Hunt, Kalb, Voorhis & Co.; Arnold B. Barach, Executive Editor, *Changing Times;* Joseph Naar, Director of Public Information, The Conference Board; Jerome Sterling, Vice President, M. C. Horsey & Co.; Lawrence Tint and Gilbert Hammer of Merrill Lynch, Pierce, Fenner & Smith, Inc.

We are indebted to Professor Stephen L. Hawk, chairman of the Department of Finance at the University of Wisconsin (Madison) for his account of the investment results of the Badgerfund and the Wiscofund under student investment management guidance.

Professor John A. Elliott of St. Lawrence University, Canton, New York, provided a ten year summary of student investment performance with monies provided as a gift from the Henry Crown Foundation. The Crown Foundation, 300 West Washington Street, Chicago, Illinois 60606, has made grants to a number of colleges and universities to enable investment students to gain actual experience in managing real portfolios.

We also wish to thank Professor Yvonne Knight of Colby College, Waterville, Maine, for her work on the Instructor's Manual which accompanies this text.

The previous editions were widely used in colleges and universities across the country. To the many adopters, especially to those who wrote to suggest additions, changes, corrections, we are especially grateful. Needless to say, for the numerous errors which doubtless will still be found we assume full and apologetic responsibility.

J. B. C.
E. D. Z.
A. Z.

Contents

PART II
SECURITY EVALUATION

PART IV
PORTFOLIO MANAGEMENT

PART I

INTRODUCTION

Chapter 1

The Investment Setting

October. This is one of the peculiarly dangerous months to
speculate in stocks. The others are July, January, September,
April, November, May, March, June, December, August and February.

—————————————————————————— *Mark Twain*

Investment has many facets. It may involve putting money into
bonds, Treasury bills, or notes, or common stock, or paintings, or real
estate, or mortgages, or oil ventures, or cattle, or the theater. It may
involve speculating in bull markets or selling short in bear markets. It
may involve choosing growth stocks, or blue chips, or defensive
stocks, or income stocks, or even penny cats and dogs. It may involve
options, straddles, rights, warrants, convertibles, margin, gold, silver,
mutual funds, money market funds, index funds, and result in accumulation of wealth or dissipation of resources. Diversity and challenge
characterize the field. For the able or the lucky, the rewards may be
substantial. For the uninformed, results can be disastrous.

Investment could mean buying 100 shares of IBM in 1913 for $44½
per share, and watching it appreciate, through stock dividends and
stock splits, to 74,150 shares by 1976, worth about $20.6 million. Or it
could have meant buying Du Pont in 1929 at $503 per share and
seeing it fall to $22 per share by 1932. It could mean buying Xerox at
$1⅞ per share and seeing it go to $171⅞ per share. Or it could mean
buying Brunswick at the peak of its popularity in 1961 at 74⅞ and
watching it fall to 6. In the raging bull market of the 1960s one could
have bought AT&T, the bluest of the blue chips, at 75 and seen it
decline from 75 to 40. In the past dozen years, Johnson & Johnson rose
from 6 to 133, while LTV Corporation common fell from 169½ to 7⅛.
Eastman Kodak rose from 20¼ to 151¾ but Litton Industries declined
from a high of 96¾ to a low of 2¾.

3

How Investment Alternatives Compare

How investment alternatives compare may be seen in Tables 1–1 and 1–2. All investment is a balancing of objectives and purposes. A very safe investment may not provide protection against inflation. An inflation resistant investment may not provide liquidity. And there is and has been an ongoing debate over the risk-return trade-off. It has been widely assumed that the higher the risk undertaken, the more ample the return and, conversely, the lower the risk, the more modest the return. But recent research has shown that this is often not the case.[1] Different investment media fit different investment objectives but the fit is seldom perfect.

The average investor seeks a safe, inflation resistant investment, which provides a good return, with capital gains opportunities, but which can be liquidated quickly if necessary. As the next 800 pages will make clear, there is no such animal.

COMMON STOCK INVESTMENT

Common Stock and Inflation

To most individuals investment means buying common stock. There are several reasons why this is so. First, the bull market over the 1949–72 period[2] provided substantial capital gains for many of those "in the market." The fever spreads, and the next fellow wants to duplicate the feat of his friend, who after all isn't any brighter or more knowledgeable.

In fact, over a longer period, a study[3] conducted by the Center for Research in Security Prices of the University of Chicago found that anyone who had invested in common stock broadly from 1926 on and had held through 1965 would have realized an average annual rate of return, compounded annually, of 9.3 percent. A study by Brigham and Pappas covering the years 1946–65 found that the average return for the entire period was 15 percent before taxes and 12 percent after tax on holdings of six or more years. Thirty-eight percent of this return was comprised of dividends while 62 percent was attributed to capital

---

[1] See, for example, "A High Beta Doesn't Always Mean a High Return," *Business Week*, March 15, 1976, p. 70.

[2] As measured by the Dow Jones Averages the market peaked in January 1973 when the DJIA reached 1051.

[3] Lawrence Fisher and James H. Lorie, "Rates of Return on Investments in Common Stocks," *Journal of Business*, University of Chicago, January 1964. See also Lawrence Fisher and James H. Lorie, "Rates of Return on Investments in Common Stock: The Year-by-Year Record, 1926–1965," *Journal of Business*, University of Chicago, vol. 39, no. 1, part II (January 1966).

TABLE 1–1
Markets of the Period

SECURITIES MARKETS OF THE PAST 20 YEARS
1956 - 1975

	Jan. 1 1956	Jan. 1 1961	Jan. 1 1966	Dec. 31 1975	% Change 10 Yrs. 1966-1975	% Change 15 Yrs. 1961-1975	% Change 20 Yrs. 1956-1975
Cost of Living Index	80.4	89.3	95.4	166.3	+ 74%	+ 86%	+107%
Value of the Dollar	124.4	112.0	104.8	60.1	− 43	− 46	− 52
Dow-Jones Industrial Average	488.40	615.89	969.26	852.41	− 12	+ 38	+ 75
Standard & Poor's 500 Stock Index	45.48	58.11	92.43	90.19	− 2	+ 55	+ 98
New York Stock Exchange Index	23.71	30.94	46.45	47.64	+ 3	+ 54	+101
Value Line Composite Average	−	−	135.11	70.69	− 48	−	−
S. & P. Utilities	31.70	51.76	75.51	44.45	− 41	− 14	+ 40
S. & P. Railroads	34.17	29.55	51.29	38.12	− 26	+ 29	+ 12
S. & P. High-Grade Corporate Bonds	112.4	95.1	90.7	56.50	− 38	− 41	− 50
S. & P. Municipal Bonds	108.1	108.1	106.3	68.05	− 36	− 37	− 37
S. & P. Long-Term Government Bonds	101.4	91.0	84.2	70.68	− 16	− 22	− 30
S. & P. Preferred Stocks	151.4	145.7	155.8	82.51	− 47	− 43	− 46
Savings Bank Deposit	100.0	100.0	100.0	100.0	0	0	0
Johnson Growth Fund Average	93.49	148.05	250.45	282.89	+ 7	+ 84	+183
Johnson Growth & Income Fund Average	91.70	123.80	193.20	211.00	+ 5	+ 63	+111
Johnson Income Fund Average	92.86	98.80	131.50	114.68	− 22	+ 5	+ 15
Johnson Balanced Fund Average	94.13	119.00	161.00	146.25	− 15	+ 15	+ 46

INVESTMENT YIELDS

Year End	Dow Jones Industrials	High-Grade Corporate Bonds	Municipal Bonds	Long-Term Gov't. Bonds	Preferred Stocks	3 Month Treasury Bills	Bank Prime Rate	*Savings & Loan Account
1975	4.39%	8.59%	6.99%	5.99%	8.48%	5.50%	7¼ %	5.25%
1974	6.12	8.65	6.95	6.72	8.89	7.18	10½	5.25
1973	4.15	7.67	5.14	6.13	7.90	7.36	10	5.25
1972	3.16	7.24	5.08	5.68	6.93	5.06	6	5.00
1971	3.47	7.14	5.19	5.72	6.79	4.02	5¼	5.00
1970	3.76	7.38	5.81	6.31	6.92	4.86	6¾	5.00
1969	4.24	7.76	6.93	6.91	7.16	7.72	8½	4.75
1968	3.32	6.51	4.93	5.83	6.01	5.92	6¾	4.75
1967	3.33	6.12	4.51	5.43	5.94	5.01	6	4.75
1966	4.06	5.39	3.78	4.63	5.24	5.01	6	4.75
1965	2.95	4.71	3.56	4.46	4.49	4.36	5	4.21
1964	2.90	4.35	3.13	4.17	4.21	3.86	4½	4.18
1963	3.04	4.36	3.32	4.18	4.32	3.52	4½	4.17
1962	3.39	4.20	3.11	3.85	4.42	2.86	4½	4.11
1961	2.91	4.44	3.44	4.11	4.64	2.62	4½	3.90
1960	3.32	4.41	3.73	4.02	4.84	2.27	4½	3.84
1959	2.85	4.59	4.05	4.42	4.85	4.57	5	3.50
1958	3.43	4.10	3.84	3.79	4.63	2.81	4	3.40
1957	4.96	3.81	3.47	3.07	4.49	3.10	4½	3.25
1956	4.60	3.80	3.44	3.41	4.63	3.23	4	3.20
1955	4.42	3.16	2.71	2.89	4.05	2.56	3¾	3.10

* From Savings & Loan League: 1966–1975 figures reflect maximum allowable rates on Regular Passbook Accounts.

Source: Johnson's Investment Co. Charts.

TABLE 1–2
How Investment Alternatives Compare

	Risk or Safety of Capital	Current Yield	Inflation Resistance	Liquidity	Additional Expense Involved
U.S. savings bonds:					
First year	Excellent	Poor	Poor	Excellent	None
Held to maturity	Excellent	Fair	Poor	Excellent	None
Insured savings accounts	Excellent	Poor	Poor	Excellent	None
Savings certificates	Excellent	Fair to good	Poor	Good	None
Government securities:					
Treasury bills	Excellent	Fair	Good	Excellent	May be a sales commission or bank charge
Medium-term notes	Excellent	Good	Fair	Good	
Long-term bonds	Excellent	Excellent	Poor	Good	
Common stocks	Fair	Poor	Good	Good	Sales commission
Preferred stocks	Fair	Excellent	Poor	Good	Sales commission
High-grade corporate bonds	Good	Excellent	Poor	Good	Sales commission or bank charge
Tax-exempt bonds	Good	Good	Fair	Fair	Sales commission or bank charge
Mutual funds:					
Growth stock funds	Fair	Poor	Good	Good	Management fee, may be a sales commission
Bond funds	Fair	Excellent	Poor	Good	
Money market funds	Good	Fair to good	Good	Good to excellent	Management fee, may be a sales commission
Real estate:					
Land	Good	None	Good	Poor	Maintenance and management costs (rental), taxes and interest
Rental property	Good	Varies	Good	Poor	
Gold:					
bullion	Fair	None	Good	Poor	Sales commission, storage fees, insurance
coins	Good	None	Good	Poor	
Art works	Good	None	Excellent	Good	Sales charge

Italics indicate authors' adaptations from *Changing Times* original.
Source: Adapted and reprinted from *Changing Times: The Kiplinger Magazine* (February 1976, p. 14) Copyright, 1976 by the Kiplinger Washington Editors, Inc., 1729 H Street, N. W., Washington, D.C., 20006.

gains. Of the amount contributed by capital gains 11 percent was caused by changes in the price-earnings ratio and 89 percent was caused by earnings per share growth.[4]

The most recent study, by Ibbotson and Sinquefield, found that over the 1926–74 period, common stocks far outperformed corporate and government bonds and Treasury bills, whether in current dollars, or adjusted for inflation.[5] (See Table 1–3.)

Over the 1926–74 period, common stocks returned 8.5 percent, compounded annually, compared with 3.2 percent for long-term U.S. government bonds, 3.6 percent for long-term corporates, and 2.2 percent for U.S. Treasury bills. On an inflation-adjusted basis, the returns were 6.1 percent for common stocks, 1 percent for long-term government bonds, 1.4 percent for long-term corporate bonds, and 0.1 percent for U.S. Treasury bills. The consumer price index rose 2.2 percent annually.

Fortune, commenting on the Ibbotson-Sinquefield study through 1975, noted that the traditional risk-return relationships were reversed over the 1965–75 decade.[6] Treasury bills fared much better than corporate bonds, corporates outperformed stocks, and growth-oriented mutual funds brought up the rear. But not even Treasury bills worked as a means of preserving purchasing power. One dollar invested in Treasury bills at year-end 1965 grew nominally in ten years to $1.72; but in 1965 dollars, that $1.72 was worth only 99 cents. Losses in purchasing power in the other media were much greater.

The debacle would have looked a lot worse had it not been for the big upswing in 1975. For 1975 alone, the total return to common stock investors was 37.1 percent. That record was good enough to make the year the sixth best among the last 50.[7] In constant dollars, the S&P 500—with dividends reinvested—was 20 percent lower at the end of 1975 than at the end of 1965.

---

[4] Summary from *The C.F.A. Digest,* The Institute of Chartered Financial Analysts, Charlottesville, Virginia, vol. 1, no. 2 (Fall 1972); see Eugene F. Brigham and James L. Pappas, "Rates of Return on Common Stock," *The Journal of Business,* University of Chicago, vol. 42, no. 3 (July 1969).

[5] See Roger G. Ibbotson and Rex A. Sinquefield, "Stocks, Bonds, Bills, and Inflation: Year by Year Historical Returns (1926–1974)," *The Journal of Business,* The University of Chicago, vol. 49, no. 1 (January 1976), pp. 11–47. In a subsequent updating, Ibbotson and Sinquefield found that over the 1926–75 period, common stocks returned 8.9 percent, long-term U.S. government bonds 3.3 percent, long-term corporate bonds 3.8 percent, and U.S. Treasury bills 2.3 percent. On an inflation-adjusted basis, the returns were 6.5 percent for common stocks, 1 percent for long-term U.S. government bonds, 1.5 percent for long-term corporate bonds, and 0.04 percent for U.S. Treasury bills.

[6] A. F. Ehrbar, "Looking Back on a Decade of Misery," *Fortune,* February 1976, p. 59.

[7] The highest total return, in the last 50 years (1925–1975), was 54 percent, in—believe it or not—the depression year of 1933.

TABLE 1-3
Rates of Return on Comparative Investment Media: Basic and Derived Series: Historical Highlights (1926–1974)

Series	Annual Geometric Mean Rate of Return	Arithmetic Mean of Annual Returns	Standard Deviation of Annual Returns	Number of Years Returns Are Positive	Number of Years Returns Are Negative	Highest Annual Return (and Year)	Lowest Annual Return (and Year)
Common stocks	8.5%*	10.9%	22.5%	32	17	54.0% (1933)	−43.3 (1931)
Long-term government bonds	3.2	3.4	5.4	37	12	16.8 (1932)	−9.2 (1967)
Long-term corporate bonds	3.6	3.7	5.1	39	10	18.4 (1970)	−8.1 (1969)
U.S. Treasury bills	2.2	2.3	2.1	48	1	8.0 (1974)	−0.0 (1940)
Consumer price index	2.2	2.3	4.8	39	10	18.2 (1946)	−10.3 (1932)
Risk premiums on common stocks	6.1	8.8	23.5	31	18	53.5 (1933)	−43.7 (1931)
Maturity premiums on long-term government bonds	1.0	1.1	5.6	25	24	15.7 (1932)	−12.8 (1967)
Default premium on long-term corporate bonds	0.3	.4	3.2	28	21	10.5 (1933)	−7.2 (1974)
Common stocks—inflation adjusted	6.1	8.8	23.5	31	18	53.3 (1954)	−37.4 (1931)
Long-term government bonds—inflation adjusted	1.0	1.3	8.0	29	20	30.2 (1932)	−15.5 (1946)
Long-term corporate bonds—inflation adjusted	1.4	1.7	7.7	31	18	23.5 (1932)	−13.9 (1946)
U.S. Treasury bills—inflation adjusted	0.1	0.2	4.6	29	20	12.6 (1932)	−15.1 (1946)

* The annual geometric mean rate of return for capital appreciation exclusive of dividends was 3.5 percent over the entire period.
Source: Robert G. Ibbotson and Rex A. Sinquefield, "Stocks, Bonds, Bills, and Inflation: Year-by-Year Historical Returns (1926–1974)," *The Journal of Business,* The University of Chicago. vol. 49, no. 1, January 1976, p. 40.

Yet, notwithstanding the poor record of the 1965–75 period, history suggests that the investor who complacently relies on bonds and T-bills for investment results is likely to be making a costly mistake. *Adjusted for inflation* and with dividends reinvested, the S&P 500 provided a 500 percent total return over the last 30 years—or a 6.2 percent annual rate of return. Over the same period, bonds and T-bills, even with the reinvestment of interest, failed to keep up with inflation. From the end of 1928, near the peak of the 1920s bull market, to the end of 1975, the inflation-adjusted value of a dollar invested in the S&P 500 grew to $10.28. Dollars invested in corporate bonds, government bonds, and T-bills grew, respectively, to $1.69, $1.38, and 88 cents.[8]

Ibbotson and Sinquefield not only studied the past; they also provided a startling forecast for the next quarter century. In their own words:

The compounded inflation rate is expected to be 6.4 percent per year over the period 1976–2000 compared to the historical compounded inflation rate of only 2.3 percent over the period 1926–75.

The expected compounded return on common stocks for the period 1976–2000 is 13.0 percent per year. . . . Stocks are expected to have a compounded return of 6.3 percent after adjustment for inflation. . . . The nominal compounded annual returns from maintaining either a 20-year maturity government bond or a 20-year maturity corporate bond portfolio are expected to be 8.0 percent and 8.2 percent, respectively, from 1976 to 2000. . . . The inflation adjusted returns are expected to be 1.5 percent per year for long-term government bonds and 1.8 percent per year for long-term corporate bonds. . . . The nominal Treasury bill rate is expected to be 6.8 percent per year, compared to the expected 6.4 percent compounded inflation rate, thus producing a very low inflation adjusted Treasury bill return (real interest rate).[9]

Looking backward, the value of the dollar has fallen steadily since the turn of the century and investment in common stock has appeared to be a good, *long-run* hedge against inflation. As Figure 1–1 shows, over the past 79 years, the value of the dollar fell by 85 percent while the Dow Jones Industrial Stock Average rose by 1,979 percent.

The extent of the deterioration of fixed dollar income may be shown in another way. Figure 1–2 shows "The Two-Way Squeeze" over the

---

[8] See *Fortune*, February 1976, p. 63.

[9] See Roger G. Ibbotson and Rex A. Sinquefield, *Stocks, Bonds, Bills, and Inflation: Simulations of the Future (1976–2000), The Journal of Business,* The University of Chicago, vol. 49, no. 3, (July 1976), pp. 334–35.

FIGURE 1–1
Common Stocks and the Cost of Living (1897–1975)

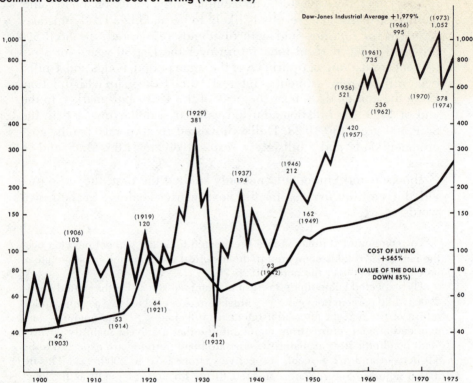

During this period of 79 years, common stocks as measured by the history of the Dow Jones Industrial Average increased 1,979 percent, while the cost of living, as measured by the consumers' price index of the Bureau of Labor Statistics, was up 565 percent. Over the very long term, common stocks provided an effective hedge against inflation, but there were shorter periods, during sharp declines in the market, where the opposite was true (1906–14, 1937–42, 1946–49, 1966–74).

Source: Johnson's Investment Co. Charts.

1960–76 period. The $10,000-a-year wage earner of 1960 would have had to earn $19,250 in 1976 to retain the same purchasing power as the 1960 income yielded after taxes. The $25,000-a-year wage earner of 1960 would have had to earn $49,225 in 1976 to retain the same purchasing power as in 1960. And the $50,000-a-year earner would have had to make $99,750 to keep the 1960 purchasing power. As you can see, of the 1976 income of $99,750 some $32,837 would have gone in federal income and social security taxes, compared to $14,396 in 1960, while $31,309 of purchasing power would have been lost due to

FIGURE 1–2
The Two-Way "Squeeze," 1976—Income Needed to Match 1960 Purchasing Power

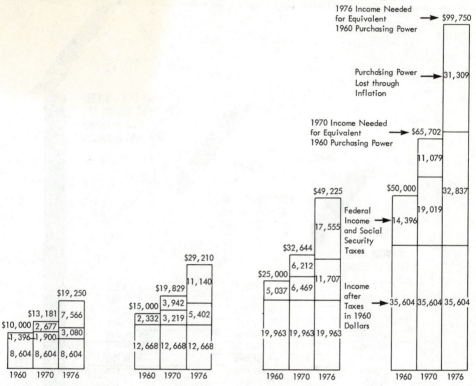

Source: The Conference Board, *Road Maps of Industry*, No. 1759, April 1976.

inflation. How income levels will have to change in your race with inflation can be seen in Figure 1–3.

What inflation will do to the value of the dollar *over the next ten years* may be estimated from the following tabulation:

	The Value of the Dollar
If the Cost of Living Increases	Will Be Down
4% annually	32.4%
5% annually	38.6%
6% annually	44.2%
7% annually	49.2%
8% annually	53.7%
10% annually	61.5%
12% annually	67.8%

Ours has not, fortunately, been the experience of some countries that have undergone hyperinflation. France, for example, experi-

FIGURE 1–3
In Your Race with Inflation*

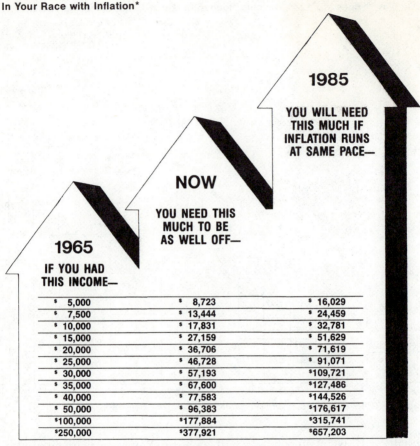

1965 IF YOU HAD THIS INCOME—	NOW YOU NEED THIS MUCH TO BE AS WELL OFF—	1985 YOU WILL NEED THIS MUCH IF INFLATION RUNS AT SAME PACE—
$ 5,000	$ 8,723	$ 16,029
$ 7,500	$ 13,444	$ 24,459
$ 10,000	$ 17,831	$ 32,781
$ 15,000	$ 27,159	$ 51,629
$ 20,000	$ 36,706	$ 71,619
$ 25,000	$ 46,728	$ 91,071
$ 30,000	$ 57,193	$109,721
$ 35,000	$ 67,600	$127,486
$ 40,000	$ 77,583	$144,526
$ 50,000	$ 96,383	$176,617
$100,000	$177,884	$315,741
$250,000	$377,921	$657,203

* Estimates by USN & WR Economic Unit, based on official data.

Note: These figures are for a married couple with two children and take into account federal but not state and local taxes. It is assumed that income is all from wages and salaries and prices will rise in the next decade by nearly 71 percent—as they did from 1965 to 1975.

Source: Reprinted from *U.S. News & World Report,* December 15, 1975, p. 74. Copyright 1975, U.S. News & World Report, Inc.

enced hyperinflation. In 1914 the French franc was worth 19½ cents (in U.S. currency). By 1920 it was worth only 7 cents. When France returned to the gold standard in 1928, the franc was worth only 4 cents. With the Nazi invasion of France in 1940, the franc went down to 2 cents. By 1946 the official rate was down to less than a cent: 0.84 cents. By 1948, in the free market, it had declined to less than one third of a cent. Just before General de Gaulle took over, the official value of the

franc was but 0.23 cents, less than a quarter of a cent, and in the free market it sold for less. Since 1914 the franc had lost 99 percent of its value.

How effective has the common stock hedge been over the long run? A study by the Anchor Corporation indicates that living costs rose in 62 percent of the one-year periods since 1871 and in 66 percent of the ten-year periods. When longer periods were tabulated, it was found that living costs increased in 73 percent of the 15-year periods, 80 percent of the 20-year periods, and in 95 percent of the 30-year spans. Whether they had invested for one year or longer, investors have had inflation in store for them more than half the time since 1871. Over 20-year spans they have experienced inflation three-quarters of the time; over 30-year spans nearly all the time.

Stock prices rose in 67 percent of the one-year inflationary periods and in 9 out of 10 of the longer periods of rising prices. Since 1871 common stock prices have increased in value in 96 percent of the 20-year periods and in all 30-year periods of rising living costs. Increases in stock prices matched or bettered increases in the cost of living in 72 percent of all 10-year periods, 83 percent of the 15-year periods, 90 percent of all 20-year periods, and 91 percent of all 30-year periods of inflation and rising stock prices. Clearly, over the long run, common stock prices, on the average, have more than kept pace with the rise in the price level.[10]

Yet the point should quickly be made that while common stock prices have more than kept pace with inflation over the long run, in shorter periods of rapidly rising prices and interest rates, common stocks have fared poorly. For example, between December 1965 and December 1975 the consumer price index rose 74 percent while common stocks, depending on how measured, declined as the following tabulation shows:

	12/65	12/75	Change
CPI	95.4	166.3	+74.3%
DJIA	969.26	852.41	−12.1%
S&P 500	92.43	90.19	− 2.4
Value Line	135.11	70.69	−47.7

Stock prices tend to decline when inflation exceeds a 3–3½ percent rate. This was particularly evident during 1965–66, 1969–70, and 1973–74. In each period, stock prices began to recover when inflation

[10] See *Common Stocks and the Cost of Living, 1871–1975* (Elizabeth, N.J.: Anchor Corporation, 1976).

abated.[11] In 1973 and 1974, when consumer prices rose at an annual rate in excess of 10 percent, and when interest rates rose sharply with the banks prime lending rate reaching 11 percent and the 3 months Treasury bill rate 8 percent, the Dow Jones Industrials fell from a high of 1,053 in January 1973 to a low of 577 in December 1974. When inflation abated and interest rates fell in 1975 and in 1976, stock prices rose again in 1976.

Types of Common Stock

There is a diversity in common stock which extends not only to industry and to company but to type of stock as well. In the loose and flexible language of the Street, it is customary to speak of blue chip stocks, of growth stocks, of cyclical stocks, of income stocks, of defensive stocks, and of speculative stocks—both high flyers and low-priced issues. Lines of demarcation between types are not precise and clear, but investors have a general notion of what is meant by each of these imprecise categories.[12]

Blue Chip Stocks. *Blue chip stocks* are high-grade investment quality issues of major companies which have long and unbroken records of earnings and dividend payments. Stocks such as American Telephone & Telegraph, General Motors, Du Pont, Exxon (Standard Oil of New Jersey), and Sears Roebuck are generally considered "blue chip." The term is generally used to describe the common stock of large, well-established, stable, and mature companies of great financial strength. The term was undoubtedly originally derived from poker, where blue chips (in contrast to white and red) had the greatest money value.

The financial press is replete with the term. "Blue Chips Losing Some Following. Stocks with More Potential for Growth Gain Favor," read one headline in the financial section of *The New York Times.* One mutual fund invests only in "The Royal Blue Chips," in contrast to its other series which are devoted to income stocks and speculative stocks.

The ability to pay steady dividends over bad years as well as good for a long period is, of course, an indication of financial stability. Some of the "blue chips" of yesteryear have fallen from greatness.

---

[11] See "An Inflation Hedge—For Those Who Wait," Citibank of New York, *Monthly Economic Newsletter,* September 1975, p. 12.

[12] Wall Street is given to colorful terminology. The billion dollar companies with unbroken growth records which dominated the market in the late 60s and early 70s, quickly became "glamour stocks," or the "nifty fifty," while the cyclical, or basic industry companies which led the 1975–76 bull market were dubbed "smokestack stocks."

What constitutes a blue chip does not change over time, but the stocks that qualify do. The railroad issues, once the bluest of the blue chips, no longer qualify. On the other hand, Minnesota Mining & Manufacturing and Johnson & Johnson which were not considered blue chips in the 1950s, do qualify today. Blue chips or high-quality companies, hold important, if not leading, positions in their industries where they are sometimes pacesetters and frequently determine the standards by which other companies in their fields are measured. The companies have foresighted managements that have taken steps to ensure future growth without jeopardizing current earnings. Such companies have the advantage of size—in a recession they should be able to hold their own and then record strong earnings gains in an economic upswing because they have the resources to capitalize on a recovery. By and large, however, investors who seek safety and stability and are conservative in their approach to the market turn to the blue chips.

Growth Stocks. Many of the blue chips may also be considered growth stocks. A *growth stock* is one of a company whose sales and earnings are expanding faster than the general economy and faster than the average for the industry. The company is usually aggressive, research minded, plowing back earnings to facilitate expansion. For this reason growth companies, intent on financing their own expansion from retained earnings, pay relatively small dividends and their yield is generally low. Over time, however, substantial capital gains may accrue from the appreciation of the value of the common as a result of the plowback and expansion.

Growth stocks are usually quite volatile. They go up faster and farther than other stocks, but at the first hint that the high rate of earnings is either leveling off or not being sustained, prices can come tumbling down. For example, Texas Instruments, a high-flying growth company of the late 1950s saw earnings fall from some $15 million in 1960 to about $9 million in 1961. The common price fell from $256 a share in 1960 to $95 a share in 1961. In 1966 Fairchild Camera fell from a high of 144½ to 64½; and after recovering somewhat in the 1967–68 boom fell to 18 in 1970. Polaroid fell from a high of 149½ to 14. From a high of 172½ Itek Corporation fell to a low of 4⅞ in 1974. Over the 1960–70 decade, IBM ranged from a high of 387 to a low of 72½ and in 1971–75 ran from a high of 426¾ to a low of 150½.

In an effort to define the term "growth" stock with more precision, several services have developed statistical tests to identify and select growth stocks. Standard & Poor's, for example, has developed a list of "140 Rapid Growth Stocks" by screening over 6,000 issues by electronic data processing methods. The resultant list of 140 stocks, obtained by a purely mechanical process, is not to be regarded as a "buy

list." The major criteria employed in selection are (*a*) if the growth in the share earnings over the previous five years is steady, it must have amounted to at least 7 percent per annum compounded; (*b*) if the trend had been interrupted in only one year and the decline was less than 5 percent, annual growth must have been at least 10 percent; (*c*) if growth had been interrupted in more than one year, or in one year the decline was more than 5 percent, annual growth rate must have been at least 12 percent. Selections are limited to issues with more than 750,000 shares outstanding and to those with earnings of at least $0.25 a share in the last full year. The screening is reported monthly. Thus the composition of the list changes from time to time as some stocks are added and others removed. At times companies are removed from the list even though they still qualify, if other firms with more desirable characteristics such as better marketability and/or better earnings records are unearthed. (See Table 1–4.)

Another service, John S. Herold's *America's Fastest Growing Companies*, uses somewhat different criteria. A company is listed as a growth company by Herold if its annual profits per share have grown without interruption over the most recent three years at a minimum compound rate of 10 percent a year and if there is evidence of continued growth at the time of listing. A company is removed from the list (*a*) when profits in any 12-month period decline more than 10 percent from its most recent fiscal year period or when a reliable forecast reveals that such a decline is in prospect or (*b*) if annual growth in earnings over the most recent two years averages less than 5 percent and growth in the latest reporting is less than 10 percent over the like period of the prior year.

The larger brokerage houses also publish lists of growth stocks from time to time. They do not always, however, explicitly indicate the statistical basis for their selection. Merrill Lynch, Pierce, Fenner & Smith, Inc., once issued an elaborate study of "101 Growth Stocks" and from time to time publishes select lists of growth stocks. An example may be seen in Table 1–5. By and large the Merrill Lynch growth stock selections are of the larger, more mature, and more conservative growth companies, whereas the list in *America's Fastest Growing Companies* tends more to the newer, smaller, and more obscure companies. For example, the Connecticut Capital Corp., an investment partnership managed by the officers of John S. Herold, Inc., publishes its holdings each month in AFGC. Holdings of AFGC stocks included Bandag, Dillon Companies, Franklin Mint, Lubrizol, Masco, Tampax, Wetterau, Inc.

Two leading, large no-load growth stock funds present an interesting contrast in growth stock investing. T. Rowe Price Growth Stock Fund, the larger, more mature fund, listed as its ten largest growth

TABLE 1–4. Standard & Poor's Rapid Growth Stocks

RAPID GROWTH STOCKS

This list of 140 stocks is the end product of screening the many thousands of issues in the Standard & Poor's data base. Through this process we have eliminated stocks with highly erratic earnings, and those with recent adverse trends, despite good over-all performance. While the process is intended to point out those stocks with strong growth trends, the results are not to be regarded as a "buy" list.

NOTE: Growth rates show the compounded annual rate of per share earnings for the past five years in Column A. Column B helps maximize the importance of the current earnings trend by substituting the last 12 months figure, if available, for the sixth or oldest year used in computing the five year trend.

Principal criteria used: (1) if growth in share earnings over the past five years has been steady, it must have amounted to at least 7% per annum, compounded; (2) if growth has been interrupted in only one year and the decline has been less than 5%, annual growth must have been at least 10%; (3) if growth has been interrupted in more than one year, or in one year the decline has been more than 5%, annual growth rate must have been at least 12%.

Selections have been limited to issues with more than 750,000 shares outstanding and to those with earnings of at least $0.25 a share in the last full year.

Range 1976 (Fractions in 8ths) Hi	Lo	Recent Price	P-E Ratio	Listed	Growth Stocks	Yr. End	Earnings $ Per Sh. 1974	1975	Last 12 Mos.	Gr Rate % See Note Above A	B
47^{4}	37^{6}	43	16	•	Abbott Laboratories	Dc	2.00	2.57	^{3}2.72	17	24
82^{7}	67^{2}	79	19	•	Air Prod. & Chem.	Sp	2.89	3.94	^{3}4.14	29	32
28	21^{3}	22^{7}	20	•	Alcon Laboratories	Ap	■0.83	■1.01	^{1}1.16	19	18
34^{5}	29^{1}	30	14		Alexander & Alex Sv.	Dc	1.72	2.01	^{3}2.17	14	13
15	10	12^{5}	7		American Family	Dc	□1.37	□1.58	^{3}1.80	23	16
27^{2}	20^{4}	25^{1}	12	•	Archer-Daniels-Midl	Je	1.19	1.40	^{3}2.08	28	33
34^{7}	27	34^{6}	15	•	Automatic Data Proc.	Je	1.66	1.98	^{3}2.37	25	23
54	40^{1}	51^{3}	15	•	Baker Int'l	Sp	1.68	3.23	^{3}3.45	29	34
46^{3}	33	39	26	•	Baxter Travenol Lab.	Dc	1.22	1.44	^{3}1.50	22	19
44^{6}	34	34^{4}	25		Betz Laboratories	Dc	1.04	1.28	^{3}1.37	26	24
81	58	71	20	•	Big Three Industries	Dc	2.37	3.31	^{3}3.56	25	29
49^{6}	38	40	7		Bird & Son	Dc	4.61	5.87	^{3}6.12	51	27
48^{4}	37^{3}	43^{6}	7	•	Blue Bell	Sp	3.26	4.19	^{3}6.44	15	21
29	15^{2}	28^{1}	8	•	Braun (C.F.) & Co.	Dc	1.64	3.14	^{3}3.75	32	64
79	66^{2}	77	17	•	Bristol-Myers	Dc	3.76	4.44	^{3}4.60	14	15
28^{1}	18	26^{4}	16	•	Bucyrus-Erie	Dc	1.15	1.53	^{3}1.67	18	20
29^{4}	22^{1}	26^{4}	12	•	Burndy Corp.	Dc	1.88	2.10	^{3}2.19	22	20
108^{4}	83^{1}	99^{7}	24	•	Burroughs Corp.	Dc	3.38	4.14	^{3}4.16	17	17
20	8^{7}	14^{7}	10	♦	C & K Petroleum	Dc	1.07	1.53	^{3}1.53	41	49
18^{6}	13^{2}	16^{4}	9		Cafeterias, Inc.	Au	0.89	1.32	^{5}1.79	31	30
30	23^{4}	27^{4}	10		Campbell Taggart	Dc	2.32	2.81	^{3}2.89	14	14
15	9^{2}	12^{2}	4		Campus Casuals Calif.	Au	2.14	3.06	^{2}3.39	69	75
19^{4}	12	16	10		Carboline Co.	Sp	1.03	1.47	^{3}1.60	33	32
29^{2}	19^{2}	25	11		Chart House	Dc	1.59	2.18	^{3}2.33	35	29
17^{7}	11^{3}	14^{6}	9		Child World	Ja^{76}	1.05	1.70	^{4}1.67	32	32
32^{6}	27	32^{6}	13		Citizens Util Cl A	Dc	▲2.26	2.54	^{3}2.60	16	13
95^{2}	77^{5}	81^{2}	19	•	Coca-Cola	Dc	3.28	4.00	^{3}4.18	9	8
24^{4}	12	18^{4}	11		Comtech Labor	Jl	0.45	0.94	^{4}1.67	71	91
56^{7}	37^{6}	45^{7}	5	•	Cone Mills	Dc	5.02	7.94	^{3}10.14	36	38
37^{4}	22^{7}	36	11	•	Cooper Indus.	Dc	2.44	3.03	^{3}3.33	29	40
18^{4}	12^{2}	17^{2}	7		Coquina Oil	Dc	1.96	2.49	^{3}2.55	105	61
22^{1}	16^{7}	17^{6}	7	•	Crown Cork & Seal	Dc	2.20	2.43	^{3}2.48	15	13
17^{5}	11^{1}	16^{5}	7	♦	Daniel Indus.	Sp	1.31	1.94	^{3}2.32	34	43
60^{6}	37^{3}	52^{1}	33	•	Data General	Sp	1.22	1.51	^{3}1.60	79	48
24^{4}	16^{6}	20^{4}	13		Datascope	Je	0.91	1.30	^{3}1.59	60	41
76^{6}	53^{1}	76^{1}	11	•	Diamond Shamrock	Dc	5.31	6.82	^{3}7.00	44	49
182^{4}	135^{4}	164^{2}	31	•	Digital Equipment	Je	3.80	3.85	^{3}5.29	29	39
37^{4}	29	29^{4}	12	•	Dillon Companies	Je	1.53	1.97	^{3}2.39	25	25
57^{2}	46	48^{4}	14	•	Dow Chemical	Dc	3.17	▲3.32	^{3}3.48	41	38
17^{4}	13^{2}	16^{2}	6	♦	Earth Resources	Au	1.68	2.31	^{5}2.58	183	97
40^{7}	23^{4}	40^{6}	9	•	Eastern Gas & Fuel	Dc	3.14	4.09	^{3}4.37	29	41
31^{5}	24^{2}	25^{2}	18		Economics Lab.	Jn	1.10	1.24	^{3}1.38	16	16
56^{2}	45^{4}	47	8	•	Edison Bros. Stores	Dc	4.10	5.94	^{3}6.21	23	23
28	21^{4}	27	7	•	Entex	Je	*2.60	3.09	^{3}4.04	20	27
46^{4}	36^{4}	45^{5}	13	•	First Int'l Bancshares	Dc	□3.10	□3.51	^{3}3.52	14	13
35^{6}	22^{5}	28^{4}	10	♦	Fluke (John) Mfg.	Sp	1.90	2.70	^{3}2.84	39	31
66	39^{4}	54	12		Food Town Stores	Dc	2.41	3.98	^{3}4.54	41	34

Range 1976 (Fractions in 8ths) Hi	Lo	Recent Price	P-E Ratio	Listed	Growth Stocks	Yr. End	Earnings $ Per Sh. 1974	1975	Last 12 Mos.	Gr Rate % See Note Above A	B
35^{6}	23^{2}	30^{6}	13	•	Franklin Mint	Dc	1.58	2.28	^{3}2.42	43	34
27^{2}	20	20	14		Friendly Ice Cream	Ap^{76}	1.06	1.38	1.38	21	
40^{1}	32^{2}	34^{2}	18	•	Gannett Co.	Dc	1.58	1.82	^{3}1.90	18	14
22	13	22	10	♦	Gearhart-Owen Ind.	Ja^{76}	1.39	2.21	^{4}2.19	47	46
17	10	14^{5}	11		Gelco Corp.	Jl	0.85	1.07	^{4}1.38	31	30
41^{3}	34^{6}	36	19	•	Genuine Parts	Dc	1.58	1.86	^{3}1.92	16	14
42	26^{4}	37	15		Goulds Pumps	Dc	1.46	2.12	^{3}2.42	23	26
19^{2}	13^{7}	18^{5}	6		Gray Tool	Sp	1.36	2.94	^{3}3.29	58	71
37^{6}	28^{1}	32^{4}	16	♦	Great Lakes Chemical	Dc	1.76	1.93	^{3}2.04	43	39
26^{7}	19^{5}	25	5	•	Gulf & West'n Indus.	Jl	2.69	4.08	^{4}5.18	32	35
63^{4}	44^{4}	62	15	•	Halliburton Co.	Dc	2.54	3.84	^{3}4.12	34	35
59^{2}	46^{4}	49^{6}	15	•	Heublein Inc.	Je	2.57	2.90	^{3}3.25	15	15
14^{5}	11^{6}	12	7	•	Hospital Affil Int'l	Dc	1.38	1.69	^{3}1.78	21	18
36^{5}	24^{3}	35^{6}	14	•	Houston Nat'l Gas	Jl	1.24	2.01	^{4}2.64	29	38
66	22^{1}	60^{2}	23	♦	Houston Oil & Mineral	Dc	1.37	2.14	^{3}2.65	77	80
93^{2}	70	92^{7}	14	•	Ingersoll-Rand	Dc	5.62	6.42	^{3}6.63	12	13
34	21^{4}	31^{7}	8	•	Inland Container	Dc	2.99	3.47	^{3}3.84	44	47
273^{2}	223^{3}	262^{4}	19	•	Int'l Bus Machines	Dc	12.47	13.35	^{3}14.03	15	14
44^{2}	32^{2}	39	19		Jerrico, Inc.	Je	0.73	1.25	^{3}2.07	61	58
33^{6}	13^{4}	23^{2}	7		Johnson (E.F.)	Dc	1.57	2.45	^{3}3.11	62	58
96^{4}	82^{2}	84^{6}	26	•	Johnson & Johnson	Dc	2.80	3.18	^{3}3.27	16	13
26^{3}	19^{2}	26^{2}	8	•	Kaneb Services	Dc	△2.70	3.11	^{3}3.19	31	30
24^{7}	20	24^{6}	16	•	Kellogg Co.	Dc	0.98	1.40	^{3}1.57	14	16
25^{4}	15^{4}	19^{6}	8		Keystone Int'l	Dc	1.60	2.31	^{3}2.41	40	39
59	35^{6}	57	11	•	Koppers Co.	Dc	4.08	4.98	^{3}5.41	36	30
33^{2}	16	27	17		Limited Stores	Jl	0.57	0.82	^{4}1.55	72	71
35	24	30^{4}	13		Liquid Air of N.A.	Dc	1.87	2.24	^{3}2.35	34	25
41^{4}	31^{4}	34^{6}	24	•	Longs Drug Stores	Ja^{76}	1.15	1.40	^{4}1.47	18	16
49^{6}	38^{6}	41	18		Mallinckrodt, Inc.	Dc	1.87	2.06	^{3}2.22	24	23
41^{7}	32^{6}	38^{7}	14	•	Mapco, Inc.	Dc	1.89	2.64	^{3}2.69	43	42
20	13	17^{2}	16		Mary Kay Cosmetics	Dc	0.92	1.04	^{3}1.11	34	25
31^{6}	23^{2}	26	17	•	Masco Corp.	Dc	1.09	1.32	^{3}1.50	27	24
39^{2}	32^{6}	33^{2}	14		McCormick & Co.	Nv	1.83	2.14	^{5}2.40	17	18
52^{4}	37^{7}	49^{4}	5	•	McDermott (J. Ray)	Mr^{76}	4.93	*9.79	9.79	86	..
66	51^{6}	56	24	•	McDonald's Corp.	Dc	1.64	2.17	^{3}2.29	34	28
40	30	34^{2}	15		Mervyn's	Ja^{76}	1.21	2.23	^{4}2.24	43	44
7^{2}	3^{1}	5	6		MFY Industries	Au	0.51	0.73	^{2}0.87	30	32
27^{6}	21^{4}	23^{4}	29		Millipore Corp.	Dc	0.64	△0.77	^{3}0.80	22	20
33^{6}	14^{7}	31^{7}	7	♦	Mitchell Energy & Dev.	Ja^{76}	2.29	4.10	^{4}4.42	45	41
24	12^{7}	19	9		Modern Merchandising	Je	1.08	1.29	^{3}2.12	54	44
33^{4}	21^{6}	33^{2}	16		Morrison, Inc.	My	1.34	1.65	^{1}2.08	23	24
23^{2}	14^{2}	19^{6}	11		Motion Indus.	Dc	1.23	1.63	^{3}1.72	37	35
36^{4}	30^{1}	34^{2}	19	•	Nalco Chemical	Dc	1.36	1.60	^{3}1.78	18	16
20^{3}	14^{1}	16^{6}	12	•	Nat'l Medical Care	Dc	0.68	1.30	^{3}1.45	74	43
34	27^{4}	32^{2}	8		Ocean Drill & Exp.	Dc	2.46	3.24	^{3}3.83	31	31
45^{1}	30^{2}	40^{7}	8	•	Olin Corp.	Dc	△4.10	5.03	^{3}5.37	35	40
13^{4}	9^{3}	10^{5}	10	•	Orange-co, Inc.	Au	0.67	0.92	^{2}1.02	41	29

Range 1976 (Fractions in 8ths) Hi	Lo	Recent Price	P-E Ratio	Listed	Growth Stocks	Yr. End	Earnings $ Per Sh. 1974	1975	Last 12 Mos.	Gr Rate % See Note Above A	B
33	22^{6}	29	13	♦	Pall Corp.	Jl	0.94	1.57	^{4}2.21	80	83
37^{7}	27^{4}	35^{2}	10	•	Pennwalt Corp.	Dc	2.81	3.25	^{3}3.55	25	25
76^{4}	69^{4}	73	16	•	PepsiCo., Inc.	Dc	3.69	4.41	^{3}4.61	12	12
80	67^{1}	68^{5}	16	•	Petrie Stores	Ja^{76}	2.89	3.95	^{4}4.22	25	22
84	66^{4}	67^{4}	17		Petrolite Corp.	Oc	2.90	3.23	^{4}4.00	19	25
59^{1}	50^{2}	53^{3}	14	•	Philip Morris, Inc.	Dc	3.15	3.62	^{3}3.80	16	14
35	24^{1}	35	10	•	Pioneer Corp.	Dc	2.16	3.03	^{3}3.48	29	32
42^{4}	31^{4}	36	12	♦	Pittway	Dc	2.02	2.78	^{3}3.00	21	24
31^{3}	20^{6}	27^{7}	13	•	Pizza Hut	Mr^{76}	1.47	2.10	2.10	47	
14	8^{4}	13^{2}	11		Presto Products	Sp	0.74	1.18	^{3}1.21	62	31
52^{2}	46^{4}	50^{4}	15	•	Ralston Purina	Sp	2.56	2.80	^{3}3.26	11	14
59^{7}	44^{6}	59^{7}	12	•	Raytheon Co.	Dc	3.85	4.69	^{3}4.81	15	16
27^{7}	16^{6}	17^{6}	6		Regency Electronics	Je	1.47	1.98	^{3}3.21	62	44
80^{6}	69^{6}	80	18	•	Revlon, Inc.	Dc	3.82	4.35	^{3}4.53	12	12
36	20^{2}	25	6		Rival Mfg.	Dc	2.07	3.69	^{3}4.03	79	74
16	11^{6}	12^{4}	8		RPM Inc.	My	1.27	1.45	^{2}1.66	24	20
19^{3}	14^{5}	15^{5}	10	♦	Sambo's Restaurants	Dc	1.09	1.48	^{3}1.57	45	36
33^{3}	20^{7}	33	10	•	Santa Fe Int'l	Dc	2.40	3.01	^{3}3.16	28	31
84^{5}	70	84^{1}	20	•	Schlumberger, Ltd.	Dc	2.68	3.92	^{3}4.14	34	36
17	10^{2}	13^{4}	4	♦	Scrivner Inc.	Je	2.18	2.59	^{3}3.40	23	27
22^{5}	10^{4}	18	9		Service Merchandise	Dc	0.78	1.78	^{3}1.93	65	58
32^{2}	26	29^{2}	20		Servicemaster Indus.	Dc	1.10	1.41	^{3}1.50	60	21
41	32^{2}	34^{4}	17		Seven Up	Dc	1.54	1.88	^{3}2.04	16	16
15^{7}	11^{6}	14^{4}	12		Shoneys Big Boy	Oc	0.85	1.03	^{4}1.22	22	21
38^{3}	28^{1}	37^{3}	9	•	Smith Int'l	Dc	1.85	4.06	^{3}4.32	47	50
32	23^{2}	29	8		Sonoco Products	Dc	2.86	3.06	^{3}3.55	18	18
38^{7}	28^{4}	32^{5}	14	•	Squibb Corp.	Dc	1.98	2.18	^{3}2.27	11	10
40^{5}	32^{3}	37^{5}	15	•	Standard Brands	Dc	2.02	2.40	^{3}2.48	11	12
49^{3}	37^{2}	39	21	•	Standard Brands Paint	Sp	1.45	1.68	^{3}1.87	19	17
36^{3}	24^{5}	34^{7}	10	•	Super Value Stores	Fb^{76}	2.88	3.60	3.60	17	
22^{7}	13^{5}	22^{7}	16		Taco Bell	Fb^{76}	0.77	1.45	1.45	60	
47^{3}	26	34^{2}	11	•	Tandy Corp.	Je	0.96	1.91	^{3}3.14	24	37
39^{7}	34^{4}	39^{5}	13	•	TexasCommerceBk'shr	Dc	△2.64	△3.09	^{3}3.12	15	14
38^{4}	28^{4}	35	6	•	Tidewater Marine	Mr^{76}	4.44	5.88	5.88	36	
19^{6}	12^{2}	16^{4}	12		Tri-Chem	Dc	0.79	1.30	^{3}1.43	35	37
18^{6}	13^{1}	17^{1}	5	•	Trinity Indus.	Mr^{76}	2.14	3.49	3.49	37	..
19^{1}	10^{2}	17^{6}	6	•	Tyler Corp.	Dc	2.31	2.76	^{3}2.81	27	20
27^{6}	18^{3}	25^{1}	19		Tymshare, Inc.	Dc	*0.85	*1.19	^{3}1.29	116	79
25	18^{4}	22^{2}	6	•	Universal Leaf Tobacco.	Je	2.40	2.97	^{3}3.82	14	18
30^{2}	14^{7}	26^{7}	9	♦	Vermont Amer'n A	Dc	1.70	2.31	^{3}2.87	29	27
26^{2}	19^{2}	20^{4}	13		Victoria Station	Mr^{76}	1.18	1.56	1.56	87	..
17^{3}	12^{5}	14^{4}	16	•	Wal-Mart Stores	Ja^{76}	0.48	0.83	^{4}0.92	37	31
38^{4}	29^{7}	31^{4}	15	•	Warner Lambert	Dc	1.88	2.08	^{3}2.13	10	9
39	24	35^{4}	26		Waters Associates	Dc	1.01	1.27	^{3}1.34	116	53
26	19^{1}	22^{6}	8	•	Weis Markets	Dc	2.17	2.55	^{3}2.70	12	13
24	15^{7}	24	11		Xomox Corp.	Mr^{76}	1.50	2.21	2.21	34	..

Superior numbers preceding Last 12 Mos. earnings indicate month where different from annual ([1]for Jan. [2]for Feb. etc.) Listed: •NYSE. ♦ASE.

Source: Standard & Poor's *Stock Summary*, July 1, 1976, p. 3.

TABLE 1–5
How Growth Stocks Grow*

	Mid-1953	Mid-1963	End 1966	End 1971	Mid-1976
American Cyanamid	$1,000	$ 2,610	$ 2,726	$ 3,038.82	$ 2,279
Bristol-Myers	1,000	15,671	34,727	36,857.96	50,196
Caterpillar Tractor	1,000	5,356	8,694	11,736.89	22,682
Corning Glass Works	1,000	5,548	10,033	6,023.04	6,089
General Electric	1,000	3,320	3,720	10,529.49	9,605
Grumman Aircraft	1,000	2,540	5,619	2,504.12	2,956
Gulf Life Holding	1,000	4,336	2,695	5,067.23	3,263
Honeywell Inc.	1,000	3,500	4,658	9,359.86	3,483
International Business Machines .	1,000	14,557	23,256	86,366.37	88,790
Minnesota Mining & Manufacturing	1,000	7,235	9,879	34,196.53	28,181
Pacific Gas & Electric	1,000	2,601	2,929	2,652.49	1,669
Pitney Bowes	1,000	7,557	7,442	15,154.61	10,361
Polaroid	1,000	33,777	137,700	308,795.00	140,953
Procter & Gamble	1,000	5,071	4,887	21,020.79	25,406
RCA	1,000	3,106	6,478	5,625.63	4,394
Safeway Stores	1,000	4,857	4,070	6,021.08	6,839
Texaco	1,000	5,646	6,012	11,561.53	9,460

* The table shows how a $1,000 cash investment in any of the above stocks regarded as growth stocks in 1953 would have grown since mid-1953. Full adjustment has been made in this tabulation for splits and stock dividends. But no account has been taken of cash dividends or rights offerings, and no allowance has been made for brokerage fees.
Source: Merrill Lynch, Pierce, Fenner & Smith, Inc.

stock holdings, IBM, Coca-Cola, Minnesota Mining & Manufacturing, S. S. Kresge, Avon Products, Merck, Burroughs, Johnson & Johnson, American Hospital Supply, and Warner-Lambert. On the other hand the ten largest growth stock investments of the newer, more volatile Rowe Price New Horizons Fund included Longs Drug Stores, Inc., American International Reinsurance Co., Inc., Millipore, Petrie Stores, Lowe's Companies, Inc., Intel, Tropicana Products, W. W. Grainger, Leaseway Transportation, and Wal-Mart Stores, Inc.[13] Thus growth stocks can mean different things to different people, and it makes a big difference whether psychologically you take a conservative or adventurous view of the market.

Income Stocks. Some people, particularly the elderly and retired, buy stock for current income. While in recent years stocks have yielded less, on the average, on current dividends, than bonds or the return on savings accounts, there are some stocks which may be classed as *income stocks* because they pay a higher than average return. Income stocks are those that yield generous current returns. They are often sought by trust funds, pension funds, university and college endow-

---

[13] For interesting, obscure growth companies, see *Over-the-Counter-Growth Stocks*, John S. Herold, Inc., 35 Mason St., Greenwich, Conn. 06830.

ment funds, and charitable educational and health foundations. Selecting income stocks can be a very tricky business. The stock may be paying a high return because price has fallen due to the fact that there is considerable uncertainty as to whether the dividend can be maintained in the light of declining earnings. Or the stock may be that of a lackluster company in an unpopular industry, with little future. Or the company may be located in a foreign area where there is a large risk due to political instability. On the other hand, there may be perfectly good overlooked stocks which are paying high yields because the public has not bid them up due to lack of knowledge. Some examples may be cited. Free State Geduld ADR, a South African gold producer, has a yield of 14.7 percent. Blyvoor Gold Mining ADR, another South African gold and uranium producer has a yield of 11.9 percent; Welkom Gold Mining ADR, 18.3 percent; and Telephonos de Mexico ADR provides a yield of 9.2 percent. These reflect the political factor of a foreign location.

Some real estate investment trusts provide a current return of 10 percent or better.

For example, North American Mortgage Inv. SBI yields 18.2 percent, United Realty Trust, 15.8, API Trust SBI provides 20.0 percent, Connecticut General Mortgage Real Estate Inv. Tr. 11.7, Continental Illinois Prop. SBI, 13, First Continental REIT, SBI, 12.8, ICM Realty SBI, 14.3, Lomas/Nettleton Mtg. Inv., SBI, 13.9, Mortgage Growth Investors, 10.7, and North American Mortgage Investors, 18.2. There are large elements of risk involved.

On the other hand, for the conservative investor a number of utility preferred stocks are available yielding 10 percent or more. These include Boston Edison 10.8 percent, Central Illinois Lt. 10.3 Cleveland Elec. Illum. 10.7, Columbus & Southern Ohio Edison 10.4, Indiana/Michigan El. 11.7, Consolidated Edison 11.6 and 11.8, Consumers Power 11.6 and 11.8, Dayton Pw. & Lt. 10.8 and 11.2, Detroit Edison 11.6.[14]

Focusing investment attention on *current income* is, of course, an inadequate approach in common stock selection. More properly, attention should center on *total return*, which is the addition of dividend income and capital appreciation over the holding period. Straining for maximum current return in stocks rather than for total return over time often involves greater risk and less capital appreciation. Often companies have high yields because their shares sell at low prices due to poor prospects and to doubts about continuation of dividends at the then current rate. (See Table 1–6.)

"Do 'Income' Stocks Provide a Higher 'Total Return'?", David L.

---

[14] Yields as of March 1976.

TABLE 1–6

The 100 Highest Dividend Yields (based upon estimated year-ahead dividends per share)

Page No.	Name	Recent Price	Performance Rank	Safety Grade	Percent Est'd Yield	Industry Rank
462	ALABAMA GAS CORP.	14	3	2	9.3	63
1963	ALLEGHANY CORP.	10	3	4	9.0	34
703	ALLEGHENY POWER SYS	17	3	2	9.6	74
1507	AMALGAMATED SUGAR	38	4	2	9.2	76
704	AMER. ELEC. POWER	22	4	2	9.1	74
1699	ARIZONA PUBLIC SERV.	15	4	2	9.5	75
465	ATLANTA GAS LIGHT	13	5	2	9.5	63
226	BALT. GAS & ELEC.	23	4	1	9.0	66
1781	BBDO INTERNATIONAL, INC.	20	3	3	9.0	39
227	BOSTON EDISON	23	5	2	10.6	66
705	BRASCAN LTD	11	4	3	9.1	74
466	BROOKLYN UNION GAS	18	3	2	9.6	63
672	CANAL-RANDOLPH CORP.	11	3	3	10.0	59
228	CAROLINA POWER & L'T	19	3	2	8.8	66
707	CEN. HUDSON G.& E.	18	4	2	9.7	74
708	CEN. ILLINOIS LIGHT	16	4	2	10.0	74
709	CEN. ILLINOIS PUB. SER.	14	3	2	9.1	74
711	CEN. MAINE POWER	15	3	1	9.1	74
712	CINCINNATI GAS & ELEC.	18	5	1	9.1	74
714	CLEVELAND ELECTRIC	28	4	1	9.3	74
468	COLUMBIA GAS	23	5	2	9.4	63
715	COLUMBUS & S. O. ELEC.	23	3	2	9.0	74
716	COMMONWEALTH EDISON	27	4	2	9.0	74
1233	CONN. GEN. MTG. & RLTY.	16	3	3	10.0	71
229	CONSOL. EDISON	17	2	3	9.4	66
717	CONSUMERS POWER	20	3	3	10.0	74
718	DAYTON POWER & L'T	18	4	1	9.2	74
230	DELMARVA POWER & L'T	13	4	1	9.3	66
719	DETROIT EDISON	14	4	2	10.4	74
720	DUQUESNE LIGHT	18	4	1	9.7	74
721	EASTERN UTIL. ASSOC.	15	3	3	10.0	74
722	EMPIRE DIST. ELEC.	15	4	1	9.1	74
1236	EQUITABLE LIFE MTG.	21	4	3	11.0	71
1920	FIDELCOR INC.	22	4	2	10.0	72
375*	FIRST BOSTON INC.	19	3	3	9.2	3
1928	FIRST NAT'L STATE BANCORP	22	4	2	9.1	72
1929	FIRST PENN. CORP.	15	5	3	8.8	72
477	GAS SERVICE CO.	13	5	2	9.2	63
723	GEN'L PUBLIC UTILITIES	16	5	2	10.9	74
1166	G'T NORTHERN IRON	15	5	2	11.0	80
724	GULF STATES UTIL.	12	3	2	10.0	74
1511	HOLLY SUGAR	42	3	3	10.5	76
727	ILLINOIS POWER	25	4	2	8.8	74
479	INDIANA GAS CO.	23	3	2	9.2	63
728	INDIANAPOLIS P'W'R & L'T	20	4	2	9.1	74
729	INTERSTATE POWER	16	4	1	9.1	74
730	IOWA ELEC. L'T & POWER	15	3	2	9.3	74
731	IOWA-ILL. GAS & ELEC.	19	5	2	9.1	74
733	IOWA PUBLIC SERVICE	19	4	2	9.1	74
1974	JOHN HANCOCK INVESTORS	21	3	2	9.0	34
735	KANSAS CITY POWER & L'T	26	4	1	9.1	74
736	KANSAS GAS & ELECTRIC	19	3	2	8.9	74
480	KANSAS-NEBR. NAT. GAS	15	4	1	8.8	63
737	KANSAS POWER & L'T	18	3	2	8.9	74
481	LACLEDE GAS	18	5	2	9.3	63
1937	LINCOLN FIRST BANKS	20	4	2	9.4	72
234	LONG ISLAND LIGHTING	17	3	2	9.3	66
1239	MASSMUTUAL MTG/R'LTY	10	4	3	11.5	71
1176	MESABI TRUST	9¼	4	3	13.2	80
483	MICHIGAN GAS UTILITIES	12	3	3	9.2	63
1512	MICHIGAN SUGAR	12	4	3	10.4	76
740	MIDDLE SOUTH UTILITIES	15	4	2	9.0	74
1240	MONY MTG. INVESTORS	8¼	3	3	10.7	71
1977	MUTUAL OF OMAHA INT. SHS	15	3	1	8.8	34
485	NATIONAL FUEL GAS	23	5	2	9.4	63
745	NEW ENGLAND ELECTRIC	19	4	2	9.9	74
746	NEW ENG. GAS & ELEC.	14	3	2	9.5	74
747	N.Y. STATE E. & GAS	26	4	1	9.2	74
748	NIAGARA MOHAWK	13	3	2	9.5	74
749	NORTHEAST UTILITIES	10	4	2	10.2	74
1241	NORTHWEST. MUTUAL LIFE	10	4	3	10.0	71
491	NORTHWEST NATURAL GAS	8¾	2	2	9.5	63
752	OHIO EDISON	18	3	2	9.2	74
754	ORANGE & ROCKLAND UTIL.	14	3	2	9.2	74
1702	PACIFIC GAS & ELECTRIC	21	4	2	9.3	75
493	PACIFIC LIGHTING	17	5	2	9.9	63
756	PENN. POWER & L'T	20	4	1	9.3	74
498	PIEDMONT NATURAL GAS	15	4	3	9.6	63
757	PHILA. ELECTRIC	16	3	2	10.3	74
235	POTOMAC ELEC. POWER	12	4	2	9.7	66
236	PUBLIC SER. ELEC. & GAS	19	3	2	9.5	66
759	PUBLIC SER. (N.H.)	21	4	1	9.0	74
761	ST. JOSEPH LIGHT & POWER	12	3	1	9.3	74
1708	SAN DIEGO GAS & ELECT.	13	3	2	9.2	75
1709	SIERRA PACIFIC POWER	11	3	1	9.1	75
237	SO. CAROLINA E. & GAS	16	3	2	9.5	66
1710	SOUTHERN CALIF. EDISON	20	3	2	8.9	75
763	SOUTHERN CO.	15	4	2	9.5	74
503	SOUTH JERSEY IND.	16	3	2	9.9	63
1951	STANDARD PRUD. CORP.	6	4	3	11.0	72
767	TOLEDO EDISON	23	4	1	9.3	74
1711	TUCSON GAS & ELECTRIC	12	5	2	9.0	75
510	UGI CORP.	15	3	3	9.3	63
768	UNION ELECTRIC	14	3	1	9.7	74
769	UNITED ILLUMINATING	24	4	2	9.8	74
1954	UNITED JERSEY BANKS	11	4	3	9.5	72
240	VA. ELECTRIC & POWER	13	4	2	9.5	66
512	WASHINGTON GAS LIGHT	19	3	2	9.9	63
689	WELLS FARGO MTG. INV.	6¼	3	5	9.8	71
514	WISCONSIN GAS CO.	18	4	3	9.4	63

Source: *Value Line Selection & Opinion*, June 25, 1976, p. 170.

Babson & Co., Inc., asked. Every so often the question is raised as to whether "growth" or "income" stocks produce the greater investment return over a period of years. Most shareowners assume that growth stocks create more in the way of capital gains. But some believe that income stocks—despite their more moderate appreciation—provide a higher "total return" when dividend income is added to the rise in market value.

Babson set out to find the answer. In 1951 its staff put together two $10,000 portfolios. Both contained ten issues with a market value of $1,000 each. One list consisted wholly of what Babson at the time considered to be "growth stocks," the other solely of "income" stocks. At that time, the growth stock idea was new, seldom discussed and misunderstood by many investors. At the time of selection, the average yield of the "income" stocks was 30 percent higher than that of the growth list. Large companies were picked for both lists so that the subsequent difference in results was not due to the selection of small, fast-growing firms in one case and large, mature companies in the other.

Selections were as shown in Table 1–7.

Obviously were the selections made today the choices would be different in many cases. However, no change was made in either list since 1951 in order to rule out the factor of hindsight.

As most investors would assume, the growth portfolio has shown

TABLE 1–7
"Income" and "Growth" Portfolios, December 31, 1950

"Income" Stocks	Industry Rank	Amount Invested	"Growth" Stocks	Industry Rank	Amount Invested
American Chicle*	Second	$ 1,000	Abbott Laboratories	Third	$ 1,000
American Telephone	Largest	1,000	Celanese	Second	1,000
American Tobacco	Largest	1,000	Corning	Largest	1,000
Beneficial Loan†	Largest	1,000	Dow	Fourth	1,000
Consolidated Edison	Largest	1,000	Eastman Kodak	Largest	1,000
Corn Products‡	Largest	1,000	Gulf Oil	Third	1,000
General American			IBM	Largest	1,000
Transport	Largest	1,000	Minnesota Mining	Largest	1,000
General Foods	Largest	1,000	Standard Oil (N.J.)#	Largest	1,000
International Shoe§	Largest	1,000	Union Carbide	Second	1,000
Woolworth	Largest	1,000			
Total		$10,000	Total		$10,000

Now: * Warner-Lambert. † Beneficial Corp. ‡ CPC International. § Interco. # Exxon.
Source: David L. Babson & Co.

more capital appreciation. Against the original $10,000 commitment, its market value by June 30, 1976 was $158,114. In contrast, the income list was worth $37,855. Over the same period, a $10,000 investment in the Dow Jones Industrial Average would have increased to $46,533.

Equally striking is the difference in the present income-paying ability of the two portfolios. The ten growth stocks, which back in 1950 yielded less, now provide an annual return on cost of 42.1 percent— over twice the 19.8 percent yield at cost of the income shares. Table 1–8 shows the investment progress of each list over the past 26 years.

Since 1950, the growth portfolio[15] has provided a total investment return of $192,212 ($148,114 in capital appreciation and $44,098 in dividends). This is over three times the income portfolio's overall return of $58,383 ($27,855 in appreciation and $30,528 in dividends).[16] Thus growth stocks over time may well outperform income stocks in both total return and yield at cost.

A Merrill Lynch study makes the same point. Often overlooked is the income potential of growth stocks (see Table 1–9). Merck provided a yield of 2.17 percent in 1960. The yearly dividend payments have more than quadrupled since then. The investor who bought it then would in 1975, be receiving $1.40 per share—an annual yield of 11.25 percent on the cost price.

---

[15] Two of the ten in the growth stock list of 1950—Celanese and Union Carbide failed to perform as might have been expected, while three of the income stocks—Beneficial Corp., General American Transport, and Warner Lambert (which acquired American Chicle in 1962), showed growth stock performance.

[16] *Weekly Staff Letter*, David L. Babson & Co., Inc., Boston, April 27, 1972, updated through the courtesy of Mr. David T. Wendell, vice president, and Ms. Mary J. Wilson.

TABLE 1–8
Comparative Performance of "Growth" versus "Income" Portfolios

Year-End	Market Value Growth	Market Value Income	Annual Income Growth	Annual Income Income	Yield at Market Growth	Yield at Market Income	Yield at Cost Growth	Yield at Cost Income
1976* ...	$158,114	$37,855	$4,212†	$1,940†	2.7%	5.1%	42.1%	19.4%
1975....	138,599	36,162	4,084	1,785	2.9	4.9	40.8	17.8
1974....	98,200	26,800	3,556	1,686	3.6	6.3	35.6	16.9
1973....	152,400	40,300	3,046	1,667	2.0	4.1	30.5	16.7
1972....	186,700	51,100	2,858	1,587	1.5	3.1	28.6	15.9
1971....	147,500	50,200	2,809	1,569	1.9	3.1	28.1	15.7
1970....	129,800	45,600	2,681	1,514	2.1	3.3	26.8	15.1
1969....	146,300	42,500	2,425	1,481	1.7	3.5	24.3	14.8
1968....	140,400	45,200	2,196	1,449	1.6	3.2	22.0	14.5
1967....	139,400	35,900	1,989	1,398	1.4	3.9	19.9	14.0
1966....	104,300	35,400	1,907	1,376	1.8	3.9	19.1	13.8
1965....	96,500	43,700	1,795	1,334	1.9	3.1	18.0	13.3
1960....	65,600	29,500	982	968	1.5	3.3	9.8	9.7
1955....	26,700	15,900	611	734	2.3	4.6	6.1	7.3
1950....	10,000	10,000	447	581	4.5	5.8	4.5	5.8

* As of June 30, 1976.
† Annual rate.
  Source: David L. Babson & Co.

TABLE 1–9
Dynamic Growth of Principal Value and Income Return

	1960			1976			
	Market Price* (January 31)	Dividend per Year* (cents)	Income Yield (percent)	Market Price (June 1976)	Dividend for Past Year (June 1976)	Present Income Yield on 1960 Price (percent)	Gain in Principal Value since 1960 (percent)
Avon Products	$12.88	$0.15	1.16	$ 47¼	$1.62	12.58	+ 267
Eastman Kodak.....	22⅝	0.49	2.17	100⅛	2.06	9.10	+ 343
IBM	57.70	0.42	0.72	276¾	7.00	12.13	+ 380
McDonnell-Douglas	2.92	0.11	3.87	24¼	0.41	14.04	+ 730
Merck & Co.........	12.44	0.27	2.17	72	1.40	11.25	+ 679
American Home Products	8.54	0.23	2.69	34¼	0.96	11.24	+ 301
AMP, Inc............	2.58	0.04	1.55	33¼	0.39	15.12	+1,189
CBS	14.90	0.54	3.62	58¾	1.60½	10.77	+ 294
Kerr-McGee	7.92	0.20	2.53	81⅛	1.00	12.63	+ 924
Nalco Chemical	4.75	0.13	2.74	32¼	0.71	14.95	+ 579

* Adjusted for stock splits and stock dividends.
  Source: Merrill Lynch, Pierce, Fenner, & Smith, Inc.

Cyclical Stocks. *Cyclical shares*, in Wall Street terminology, refer to stocks of companies whose earnings fluctuate with the business cycle and are accentuated by it. When business conditions improve, the company's profitability is restored and enhanced. The common stock price rises. When conditions deteriorate, business for the cyclical company falls off sharply, and its profits are greatly diminished.

Industries which may be regarded as cyclical include steel, cement, paper, machinery and machine tools, airlines, railroads and railroad equipment, and automobiles. Commenting on the two-tiered market, which placed growth stocks on one level and cyclical shares on a lower level, *Forbes* commented:

Probably never before in history has Wall Street had such a split personality. Call a stock a Growth stock and it sells for 40, 50, or even 60 times earnings. Call it Cyclical . . . and it sells for 10 times earnings or less. The market is saying that if General Motors earns $1, that $1 should be capitalized at only $10.90, but if, say, Johnson and Johnson earns $1, it is worth $64. This kind of disparity can go on for a long time, of course, but it can't go on forever.[17]

For example at a time when Ford was selling at 9 times earnings, Chrysler at 10 times earnings, Bethlehem Steel at 9.5 times earnings, U.S. Steel at 12 times earnings, Copperweld Steel at 8 times earnings, Kennecott Copper at 10 times earnings, Giant Portland Cement at 9.4 times earnings, Crane at 9.3 times earnings, Norfolk & Western Railway, at 10 times earnings, Mesta Machine at 9.9 times earnings, and so forth, Simplicity Pattern was selling at 51 times earnings, Winnebago Industries at 73 times earnings, Tropicana Products at 54 times earnings, Levitz Furniture 86 times earnings, Walt Disney Productions at 78 times, and McDonald's at 70 times earnings, to contrast but a few.

In the 1973–74 bear market the two-tiered market came apart as former favorites plunged. Polaroid fell from 149½ to 14, Avon Products from 140 to 18⅝, Xerox from 171⅞ to 49, Disney from 119 to 17, ARA Services from 187 to 46. But cyclical issues moved up as the economic recovery unfolded, U.S. Steel went from 25 to 89, International Paper rose from 28½ to 78¾, Du Pont from 84 to 161, General Motors from 28 to 70¼. *Cyclicals* surge in the early stages of recovery, tend to top out prior to the business cycle peak, and yield market leadership to the newly annointed "concept" stocks or "performance" issues of the period.

Defensive Stocks. At the opposite pole from cyclical stocks are the so-called *defensive* stocks; by *defensive stocks* are meant shares of a company which is likely to do better than average, from an earnings and dividend point of view, in a period of deteriorating business. If a

---

[17] "Statistical Schizophrenia," *Forbes*, August 1, 1972, p. 24.

recession is anticipated, a growing interest tends to develop in certain recession-resistant companies. While such stocks lack the glamour of the fallen market leaders, they are characterized by a degree of stability desirable when the economy faces a period of uncertainty and decline.

Utility stocks are generally regarded as defensive issues, since their slow (5 to 7 percent) but steady growth rate tends to hold up in recession years as well as in boom years. They are, however, very sensitive to interest rate changes, falling in price if interest rates rise sharply, and increasing in price if interest rates decline.[18] In addition to the electric and gas utilities, the shares of gold mining companies have tended to be effective defensive issues. The price of gold either rises or remains stable during recessions, while the cost of mining may decrease due to lower costs. Also the market demand for gold seems to hold up or even increase. Other defensive issues are found among companies whose products suffer relatively little in recession periods. These include shares in companies producing tobacco, snuff, soft drinks, gum, candy bars, and other staples. Also companies that provide the essentials of life, particularly food and drugs tend to hold up well. Packaged foods and grocery chain companies are examples.

Speculative Stocks. Webster defines "speculation" as a "transaction or venture the profits of which are conjectural. . . ." In this sense all common stock investment is speculative. When you buy shares you have no promise, no certainty that the funds you receive ultimately when you sell the stock will be more, less, or the same as the dollars you originally paid. Since they provide a variable rather than a fixed dollar outcome, common shares are speculative in Webster's sense. Yet in the accepted parlance of the Street, *speculative* shares or *speculative* stock has a more limited meaning. High-flying glamour stocks are speculative. Likewise, hot new issues and penny mining stocks are speculative. Other types could be identified as they come and go from time to time. Some are easy to identify, some more difficult. The high-flying glamour stocks can usually be identified by their very high price-earnings ratios. For example, at a time when the Standard & Poor's 500 were selling at 17 times earnings, leading glamour issues were selling at 68.8 times earnings for MGIC Investment, 68.6 for Walt Disney, 69.5 for McDonald's, 55.8 for Dr. Pepper, 65.7 for Automatic Data Processing, 51.8 for National Chemsearch, 46.5 for Schlumberger, 69 for Memorex, 94 for Meridan Industries, 60 for Marriott Corp., 53 times for Rite Aid and 66 for Baxter Laboratories. Speculative buying of these shares would appear to be discounting the future quite far ahead. As a famous

---

[18] Interest rates usually decline in recession periods but in 1973–74 they surged to very high levels reflecting the sharp inflation.

Dow Theory disciple, William P. Hamilton, wrote back in the 1920s: "A bull market runs until it outruns values: in the final stage it is discounting possibilities only."

There usually comes a point in a bull market when small, hitherto unknown companies go public, or little new companies are formed, and the offering of their low-priced shares finds a fierce speculative demand. Prices double, triple, or even quadruple within a few days after issuance. Dynatronics issued at 7½, went to 25 overnight. Cove Vitamin soared from 3⅛ to 60. Simulmatics, a two-year-old company with a net worth of minus $21,000 offered stock to the public at 2, and within a few hours it was quoted at 9. While stocks in companies with names ending in "tron" or "ics" were particularly coveted, even prosaically named issues like Leaseway Transportation and Mother's Cookie Company leaped 50 percent or more in price.

Playboy Enterprises came out at $23.50, but in a matter of weeks, like an aging "bunny," sagged to a price of 15½. National Video was issued at 3¾, soared to 120 and then went into bankruptcy. Four Seasons Nursing Homes was a hot new issue when it went public at $11 a share on May 10, 1968. It soared to more than $100 a share the same year. After a two-for-one split, this stock shot up again to $90.75 in 1969. It went into receivership in 1970 and in 1972 a number of those associated with the stock issue were indicted for alleged fraud.[19] Other examples of speculative issues which have had a sad demise are shown in Table 1–10, entitled the Klinker Index. Membership in *The Century Club*, as shown in Table 1–11, was not limited to obscure companies.

Business Week wrote of a new company devoted to ocean treasure hunts, Treasure Hunters, Inc., of Washington, which registered 1.9 million shares with the SEC. The company proposed to offer stock at $1 per share. According to its prospectus, the company "will primarily engage in the search for, and the recovery and sale of, sunken cargoes and buried treasure." Treasure Hunters' first project was to have been "to search for the unsalvaged silver, gold, and jewels that went to the bottom of Vigo Bay, Spain, in October, 1702." If all went well, its second undertaking was to have been a hunt for the "dozen wrecks of the Spanish treasure fleet which were lost during a violent storm off the Bahamas in November, 1643." In periods of intense excitement in the market, shares of this type sell readily, often soar in price, and then in due course, in most cases—but not all—fall drastically or disappear.

Perhaps the lowest level of speculative stocks are the penny mining and oil shares. A broker specializing in such shares circulated his

---

[19] Terry Robards, "Four Seasons Nursing Stock Rode Classic Wall Street Roller Coaster," *New York Times*, December 21, 1972; see also "Eight Are Cited in Four Seasons Fraud Indictment," *The Wall Street Journal*, December 21, 1972.

TABLE 1–10
Klinker Index

	Recent Price	High	Percent Decline	Former Business
Acme Missiles & Constr. . . .	.06	25	−100.0	Missile launching sites
AITS	0	93	−100.0	Travel agency
Airlift Int.	.19	12	− 98.4	Airfreight carrier
Alphanumeric	.10	84	−100.0	Computer peripheral equipment
Astrodata	.25	36	− 99.3	Electronic data equipment
Beck Indust.	.01	42	−100.0	Leased shoe departments
Bermec*	.05	31	−100.0	Truck leasing
Borne Chem.	1.12	27	− 96.0	Textile oils
Cognitronics	1.12	39	− 97.1	Optical scanning
Commonwealth United† . .	.25	25	− 99.0	Conglomerate/theaters
Corporation S	.38	64	− 99.4	Data services
Dolly Madison*	.13	47	−100.0	Ice cream, furniture
Elcor Chem.	3.38	80	− 96.0	New sulpher process
Energy Conver. Devices . . .	4.25	155	− 97.2	Electronic breakthrough
FAS Int.	.38	63	− 99.4	Famous artist schools
Farrington*	0	66	−100.0	Optical scanning
Fotochrome	.06	25	−100.0	Film processing
Four Seasons Equity	0	49	−100.0	Financing nursing homes
Four Seasons Nursing‡ . . .	3.38	91	− 96.3	Nursing homes
Gale Indust.	.50	26	− 98.1	Heat conductive windowpanes
R. Hoe	.06	60	−100.0	Printing presses
King Resources	.08	34	−100.0	Computerized oil development
Liquidonics	.06	155	−100.0	Magnetic door locks
Management Assistance . .	.50	46	− 99.0	Leasing data equipment
Nat'l Student Marketing . .	.30	36	− 99.1	Still trying to determine
Omega Equities	.05	36	−100.0	Questionable ventures
Panacolor	.06	40	−100.0	Color film processing
Performance Systems . . . . (i.e., Minnie Pearl)	.05	24	−100.0	Greasy chicken franchiser
Transitron	.50	60	− 99.0	Semiconductors
Viatron*	.10	62	−100.0	Computer systems

* In bankruptcy or receivership.
† Name change 1/73—Iota Industries.
‡ Name change 11/72—Anta Corp.
Source: Spencer Trask & Co., Incorporated, May 5, 1975.

market report and offers extensively by mail, and his combination packets read almost like a stamp dealer's. In one report he plugged Trans-Mountain Uranium Company, Globe Hill Mining Company, and Santa Fe International. His write-up on the first two companies was as follows:

Trans-Mountain Uranium Co.: Company has ore stockpiled at the Lucky Boy tungsten mine and are anxious to make shipments to the new Min-Con mill located about 14 miles distant. This mill is now in final stages of completion and am told they had expected to be ready for milling ores by October 15th. However, believe will take a little extra time before completed. We are all

TABLE 1–11

The Century Club: Common Stocks That Have Declined over $100 per Share from Their post-1960 High

Stock	High	Low	Stock	High	Low
Addressograph	$109	$ 3	Golden Cycle	$110	$ 9
ARA Svc	187	46	Harcourt Brace	121	12
Avon	140	19	Heath Tecna	325	6
Bio Medical	118	6	Honeywell	171	17
Boeing	112	11	IBM	366	150
Cinerama	112	1	Itek	173	5
Coca-Cola	150	45	KLM	156	13
Control Data	163	9	Leslie Salt	150	19
Corning Glass	156	25	Liquidonics	155	0.06
Disney	119	17	Litton Ind.	106	3
Du Pont	294	84	LTV	169	7
E-Systems	120	8	Possis Machine	124	1
Electronic Data			Prudential Funds	102	1
Systems	162	11	Raychem	323	147
Energy Conversion	155	4	Recognition		
Fairchild Camera	145	16	Equipment	102	1
Falconbridge Nickel	182	25	Scan Data	165	0.50
General Reinsurance	256	99	Superior Oil	358	134
McIntyre Mines	179	18	Tampax	136	22
Memorex	174	1	Wyly Corp.	187	1
Mohawk Data			Xerox	172	49
Systems	111	1			
National Video	150	0			
Norfolk & Western	151	50			
O'Okiep Copper	170	46			
Polaroid	149	14			

Source: Spencer Trask & Co., Incorporated, May 5, 1975.

hoping to hear soon that Trans-Mountain is again shipping tungsten ore. The shares of stock are low at present price of 2¢.

Globe Hill Mining Company: has been doing development work on their Beryllium claims located near the U.S. Beryllium mine at Badger Flats and are planning to make ore shipment in near future. A stockholder letter from the company is expected to be mailed out at any time and this report should carry much information as to development of properties. Globe Hill shares active and present price $6.00 a thousand.

The mail-order broker's packet offer read:

Combination Offer—Following combination orders will be filled for whatever number combinations desired while can locate stock in above 3 companies to fill at price shown below: (bonus 1000 United Empire Gold with each combination order)
1,000 Trans-Mountain, 1,000 Santa Fe and 5,000 Globe Hill Mining, $63.75.

Thus common stock investment can range from buying shares in the staid and stable Bank of New York which has paid dividends uninter-

ruptedly for the past 191 years, to buying Trans-Mountain Uranium at 2 cents per share. Obviously, with so wide a diversity in common stock, generalizations are both difficult and hazardous.

Of Random Walks and Efficient Markets

Before attempting to plumb the depths of common stock analysis, the aspiring security analyst must navigate the twin Scylla and Charybdis perils of two widely held academic concepts—the efficient market and the random walk. Both combined imply that the security analyst and the portfolio manager are engaged in futile exercises for their services can avail little.

According to one terse glossary, "an efficient market is one in which prices always fully reflect all available relevant information. Adjustment to new information is virtually instantaneous," while "a random walk implies that there is no discernible pattern of travel [of a drunk wandering in the woods—or of stock prices]. The size and direction of the next step cannot be predicted from the size and direction of the last or even from all the previous steps. . . . Random walk is a term used in mathematics and statistics to describe a process in which successive changes are statistically independent."[20]

Combined, in the words of another authority, "first, the theory [random walk and efficient markets] says that new information about a company, its industry, or anything that affects the prospects of the company is disseminated very quickly, once it becomes public. Second, the price of a stock at any particular time represents the judgment of all investors, based on all the information that is public. And third, new information about a company is disseminated randomly over time."[21]

Professor Malkiel points out, however, that there are two forms of random walk—narrow and broad. He says: "Thus, an accurate statement of the narrow form of the random-walk hypothesis goes as follows: The history of stock price movements contains no useful information that will enable an investor consistently to outperform a buy and hold strategy in managing a portfolio."[22] If this is correct then technical analysis (predicting future stock prices based on analysis of past stock prices and other internal market factors such as volume, breadth, highs, and lows) is about as scientific and useful as astrology.

[20] See James H. Lorie and Mary T. Hamilton, *The Stock Market: Theories and Evidence* (Homewood, Ill.: Richard D. Irwin, Inc., 1973), pp. 270, 273.

[21] See J. Peter Williamsom, *Investments: New Analytic Techniques* (New York: Praeger Publishers, Inc., 1970), p. 182.

[22] Burton G. Malkiel, *A Random Walk Down Wall Street* (New York: W. W. Norton & Co., Inc., 1973), p. 121.

Nor does fundamental analysis escape and survive. It is demolished by the broad form. Malkiel says:

The broad form states that fundamental analysis is not helpful either. It says that all that is known concerning the expected growth of the company's earnings and dividends, all of the possible favorable and unfavorable developments affecting the company that might be studied by the fundamental analyst, are already reflected in the price of the company's stock. Thus throwing darts at the financial page will produce a portfolio that can be expected to do as well as any managed by professional security analysts. In a nutshell, the broad form of the random-walk theory states: Fundamental analysis of publicly available information cannot produce investment recommendations that will enable an investor consistently to outperform a buy-and-hold strategy in managing a portfolio. The random-walk theory does not, as some critics have proclaimed, state that stock prices move aimlessly and erratically and are insensitive to changes in fundamental information. On the contrary, the point of the random-walk theory is just the opposite: The market is so efficient—prices move so quickly when new information does arise—that no one can consistently buy or sell quickly enough to benefit.[23]

Fischer Black has said:

My position has generally been even more extreme than the strong form of the random walk hypothesis. I have said that attempts to pick stocks that do better than others are not successful. Actively managed portfolios do not do better than buy-and-hold portfolios gross of expenses; and do worse than buy-and-hold portfolios when transactions and administrative costs are taken into consideration. This is particularly true when you adjust the performance of actively managed portfolios for the extra risk that they incur, because they tend to concentrate their investments in a relatively small list of stocks. Thus, I have said that it is better to buy a well diversified portfolio of stocks at a chosen risk level and hold it. An investor should change his list of stocks only to compensate for changes in the risk of stocks that he holds and to keep his portfolio well diversified.[24]

What does all this theoretic jargon mean for the aspiring security analyst? To many it may suggest that he or she is pursuing a career that has no real purpose or function. Why? Because in an efficient market buyers and sellers factor into their buying and selling decisions all known influences and knowledge, both public and private that has, is, or will impact on the price of a security. Since the current price reflects all the knowable, and since prices reflect swiftly any new

---

[23] Ibid., p. 168. In fact there are three forms of the efficient market-random walk hypothesis: the weak, the semistrong and the strong. See Charles D. Kuehner, "Efficient Markets and Random Walk," *Financial Analyst's Handbook*, vol. I (Homewood, Ill.: Dow Jones-Irwin, Inc., 1975), chap. 43, pp. 1226–95.

[24] Quoted in Arnold Bernhard, *How to Invest in Common Stocks* (New York: 1975), p. 61.

developments, all the digging by a securities analyst can add little or
nothing to the body of knowledge, which has itself determined the
current price of a security. In its strongest form the random-walk,
efficient market hypothesis maintains that past stock prices or earnings
cannot be used to forecast future prices or earnings since both series
behave randomly and already reflect all knowable facts and information about the market, an industry, a company, stock prices, or the
price of a single stock.[25]

Yet all is not lost! It is the thousands of trained security analysts who
are the eyes and ears of the efficient market. It is the industrious,
probing, prying analyst who ensures that relevant information, and
even rumor and hypothesis, is quickly reflected in the current price,
and who by the collective weight and chain reaction to prospective
trends helps determine the future price. It is the inquisitive analyst,
searching for all relevant factors to determine the intrinsic value of a
security, who by his (or her) actions or recommendations, helps bring a
momentarily deviant price to its intrinsic value level.[26]

One response of the investment community to the efficient market
concept, has been the development of "index" funds. A small but
growing number of money managers administering pension accounts
have placed part of their investment assets in so-called index funds.
These are common stock portfolios which either duplicate the structure of the S&P 500 or consist of 100 or more S&P issues selected to
"track" the overall index. The idea is that since the average money
manager can't do as well as the averages, the way to be sure of at least
keeping up with the averages is via the index fund approach. This has
the added advantage of doing away with so-called analytical judgment
and attendant investment fees. The portfolio manager is in essence
replaced by a computer. In the process brokerage fees are held down
since these funds have low portfolio turnover rates.[27]

Babson argues that index funds are a negative approach. The S&P
500 itself represents two thirds of the market value of all stocks and so
by definition cannot provide above-average results. The skilled money
manager, he urges, can do better than the market. He cites Table 1–12,

---

[25] Professor Fama defines an efficient market as "one in which prices always reflect
available information." See E. F. Fama, "Efficient Capital Markets: A Review of Theory
and Empirical Works," *Journal of Finance*, May 1970. See also Jack L. Treynor, "Efficient Markets and Fundamental Analysis," *Financial Analysts Journal*, March–April
1974.

[26] See Jerome B. Cohen, "Analysis of Common Stock," *Financial Analyst's Handbook*, vol. I (Homewood, Ill.: Dow Jones-Irwin, Inc., 1975), chap. 5, p. 135.

[27] See "Index Funds: Why Throw in the Towel," *Weekly Staff Letter*, David L.
Babson & Co., Inc., December 18, 1975; see also Robert Metz, "Debate over Market
Index Funds," *New York Times*, January 21, 1976.

TABLE 1–12
The Earnings and Dividend Record of the S&P 500 Compared with 12 Growth Companies, 1966–1975

| Index 1966 = 100 | In Current Dollars | | | | In Constant Dollars | | | |
| | Earnings | | Dividends | | Earnings | | Dividends | |
	S&P 500	12 Growth*	S&P 500	12 Growth*	S&P 500	12 Growth*	S&P 500	12 Growth*
1975	141	257	128	248	83	155	77	149
1974	160	244	125	224	105	161	82	147
1973	147	215	118	192	107	157	86	140
1972	116	182	108	177	90	141	84	137
1971	97	156	107	169	77	125	86	135
1970	91	139	109	153	76	116	91	128
1969	104	132	110	140	92	117	97	124
1968	104	119	107	123	97	111	100	115
1967	96	108	102	111	93	105	99	108
1966	100	100	100	100	100	100	100	100

* 12 Seasoned Growth Companies: American Home Products, Coca-Cola, Dow Chemical, Eastman Kodak, Honeywell, IBM, Merck, Minnesota Mining & Mfg., Procter & Gamble, Provident Life & Accident, Sears, Roebuck, and Xerox.
Source: David L. Babson & Co., Inc., January 30, 1976.

which compares the 1966–75 earnings and dividend record of the S&P 500 and his firm's index of 12 seasoned growth stocks. He notes that the S&P 500 have not kept pace with inflation, while the 12 growth companies have done so by a wide margin.

He notes that the 12 leading growth companies have had a better total investment return than either the S&P 500 or the DJIA 30, and have kept ahead of inflation since the end of 1965, as indicated in Table 1–13.

He maintains that better managed funds can "beat" the averages. (See Table 1–14.) Note that while the two funds did not do nearly as

TABLE 1–13
Total Investment Return*, 1966–1975

	10 Years	Annual Average
Dow 30	+29%	+2.6%
S&P 500	+33	+2.9
DLB 12 Growth	+97	+7.0
Corporate bonds	+15	+1.4
Treasury bills	+82	+6.2
Consumer price index	+70	+5.5

* Capital appreciation and dividends combined.
Source: David L. Babson & Co.

TABLE 1–14
Total Return of Investment of the S&P 500 and the Dow 30
Compared to Average of Two Mutual Funds, 1965–1975

	S&P 500	Dow 30	Average of Two Mutual Funds Total Return*
1975	+37.1%	+44.8%	+ 21.6%
1974	−26.3	−23.5	− 25.8
1973	−14.7	−13.3	− 12.4
1972	+18.9	+18.5	+ 27.0
1971	+14.2	+ 9.8	+ 18.2
1970	+ 3.9	+ 9.2	− 3.3
1969	− 8.4	−11.8	+ 3.6
1968	+11.0	+ 7.9	+ 12.8
1967	+23.9	+19.2	+ 25.9
1966	−10.0	−15.8	− 4.3
1965	+12.5	+14.4	+ 22.9
Total 1965–75	+55.1%	+49.1%	+101.1%

* The Chemical Fund and the David L.Babson Fund.
Source: David L. Babson & Co., Inc., January 30, 1976.

well as the averages in 1975, their return, over the whole period, had been twice as great.

Thus the debate continues.

Styles in Stocks

Fads and enthusiasms can be either very costly or very profitable to investors, or both, depending on their footwork. Or, as one Wall Street pundit put it, "If you want to make your pile, you got to be in style." Styles in common stocks, Eldon Grimm pointed out, change almost as rapidly as women's fashions. Reviewing past enthusiasms (which in due course faded), one can go back as far as World War I, during the course of which Bethlehem Steel was in high fashion. It jumped from $10 a share in 1914 to $200 in one year. In the 1920s talking pictures and radio swept the country. Warner Bros. Pictures soared from 9¾ in 1927 to 138 in 1928. RCA skyrocketed from 12½ in 1922 to 573 in 1929. Bank stocks took off in the mid 1920s. The ordinarily conservative First National City Bank of New York (now Citibank), for example, jumped from the equivalent of 131 in 1926 to 580 in 1929. In the ensuing collapse the bluest of the blue chips fell dismally. (See Table 1–15.) Even in the Great Depression there were fads and fancies. With the repeal of Prohibition, National Distillers became a magic word, and the stock jumped from 13 in 1932 to a peak of 124⅞ one year later and then went out of style.

In more recent years, aluminum stocks were very much in style in

TABLE 1–15
A Dozen Good Common Stocks, 1929–1932

Company	1929	1932
Anaconda Copper	174⅞	3
AT&T	310¼	70¼
Chrysler Corporation	87	5
Du Pont	503	22
General Motors	224	7⅝
Montgomery Ward	156⅞	3½
New York Central	256½	8¾
Standard Oil of New Jersey	83	19⅞
Standard Oil of California	81⅞	15⅛
Sears, Roebuck	197½	9⅞
U.S. Steel	261¾	21¼
Western Union	272¼	12⅜

Source: Jerome B. Cohen, *Personal Finance,* 5th ed., (Homewood, Ill.: Richard D. Irwin, Inc., 1975), p. 641.

the early 1950s. Alcoa went from 46 in 1949 to the equivalent of 352 in 1955. Reynolds Metals rose from 19 to the equivalent 300 over the same period. As a group, the aluminum stocks rose some 430 percent in the early 1950s and then fell out of bed in 1957, declining by more than 50 percent. The advent of the computers helped push IBM from 40 to over 600 and Control Data from 2 to over 100. The ephemeral popularity of Metrecal as a dieting fad sent Mead Johnson shares up by 230 percent, but when the style changed and sales fell 31 percent in 1962, net fell 90 percent to just 3 cents a share, and Mead Johnson stock went down to its 1958 pre-Metrecal level.

Electronics shares boomed in the late 1950s. For example, when Lehman Bros. decided to back Litton Industries and raise the $1.5 million needed, they created a unique financial package. They divided the sum into 52 units requiring a cash investment of $29,200 each. The makeup of each unit was:

20 bonds at $1,200 per bond	$24,000
50 shares of 5% preferred	5,000
2,000 shares of common stock (10 cents par)	200
	$29,200

The bonds were subsequently converted into common stock at $10.75 per share. The preferred shares were converted into common at $1 per share. There followed, after conversion, a 2½ percent stock dividend, a 2 for 1 stock split, and another 2½ percent stock dividend. When LIT common hit a high of $143 per share by 1961, each $29,200 unit had grown to 29,416 shares of common worth $4.2 million.

Other investors were not so fortunate. Toward the end of 1961 *Busi-*

ness Week reported "Glamour industry takes its lumps. Shakeout among electronics companies is starting as industry matures after a decade of fast, youthful growth. To survive, a company will need sharp management." *The Wall Street Journal* headed its story "Fading Glamour. Sales Growth Slows, Competition Tightens for Electronics Firms. Transistor Prices Drop 44%." Transitron Electronic Corporation shares fell from 60 to 4. Fairchild Camera, which had risen from 13¾ (adjusted) to 144½ per share, fell to 64½, though if investors held on during the deep gloom, the stock rose again during 1967 from 73 to 134. Then Fairchild ran into rough weather and by 1970 its stock reached a low of 18.

Conglomerates were all the rage in the late 1960s. Ling-Temco-Vought peaked in August 1967, selling at 169½. By 1970 it was down to 7. Litton hit a high of 120 in 1967, but was down to 10 in 1972. Monogram Industries reached a high of 81¾ in 1967, then fell to a low of 8½ in 1970. Gulf & Western peaked at 66⅛ in 1968 but then dropped to 11¾ in 1970. Comparable peaks and lows could be detailed for other conglomerates such as Fuqua Industries, National General, Bangor Punta, Whittaker, Ogden, AMK, Walter Kidde, and Northwest Industries. The average decline of the conglomerates from their 1967–68 highs to their 1970–71 lows was 85 percent.

Food franchisers captured the market's attention for a time in the late 60s Minnie Pearl (fried chicken), changed its name to Performance Systems, soared to a high of 67 in 1967, but by 1970 was selling for $0.50 a share. Other popular issues were Denny's Restaurants, Kentucky Fried Chicken, Lum's, Marriott, McDonald's Corp., and others. Some survived and prospered, others fell by the roadside.

Pollution control stocks waxed and waned. Buffalo Forge went to a high of 57 in 1970 then fell to 25 in 1972. Research-Cottrell rose from 4¾ to a peak of 84½ in 1972, then fell off to 54. Other companies in this volatile field, which surged and then faded, are Zurn Industries, Wheelabrator-Frye, Peabody-Galion, Marley, Joy Manufacturing, American Air Filter, Aqua-Chem, and Ecological Science.

Computer equipment and technology stocks rose spectacularly and some of them dropped sharply. For example, University Computing rose to a peak of 186 in 1967–68, but by 1970–71 was down to 12¾. Control Data went to 163½ and then fell to 28¾, but has since come back part way. Memorex reached a bull market high of 173⅞ and then fell to 14⅞. Telex ranged from a high of 159½ to a low of 20¾. Wall Street's penchant for stocks that end in an "x"—Xerox, Syntex, Ampex, Tampax, Tektronix, and so on, at least in the ascending phase—seemed to work for a time in the case of Memorex and Telex. The average decline of the computer stocks from their 1967–68 highs to their 1970–71 lows was 85 percent and the same was true of the so-called technology stocks.

When the dollar was devalued in 1971 and again in 1973, and the de facto price of gold rose from $42 an ounce to a high of $198 an ounce, gold shares zoomed. Dome Mines rose from a low of 17⅞ in the 1960s to 73 in 1971 and to 155 in 1973 and then fell back to 30 in 1975. Campbell Red Lake shot up from 9⅝ to 35 in 1971 and to 79 in 1973 and then fell to 17½ in 1975. Homestake Mining jumped from 8 to 31 in 1971 and then to 70⅞ in 1973, declining to 31 in 1975.[28]

After the oil embargo and the OPEC cartel price action in sharply raising oil prices, the spotlight in the United States turned onto coal, of which the United States has enormous reserves, totaling some 10,313,200 trillion BTUs, as compared to 277,500 trillion BTUs of oil and a mere 237 trillion BTUs of natural gas. Investors bid up the coal stocks rapidly, in 1975 and 1976. North American Coal rose from 24¼ to 49¾; Pittston Co. from 17⅞ to 46¼; Eastern Gas & Fuel from 16 to 40⅛; Westmoreland Coal from 18⅛ to 58¼; and St. Joe Minerals from 17⅛ to 50.

Keeping up with styles in stocks is, then, in many cases, an important part of the selection process.

Fundamental Analysis

The heart of the investment process is choosing what to buy and when to buy it, deciding what to sell and when to sell it. Coal and steel—seemingly both basic industries—why buy one and not buy the other? The choice to the casual investor may not have appeared very crucial or complicated but if you will look at Figure 1–4, you will see that over a recent decade coal shares were among the best performers of 50 industries while steel shares were among the poor performers. If you had bought Eastern Gas & Fuel you would have a 142 percent gain. The Pittson Co. shares rose 687 percent. On the other hand National Steel fell 39 percent, while Republic Steel declined 37 percent. By and large, investments in utilities, aerospace, automobiles, food and food chains, life insurance, cement, telephone, aluminum, and apparel would likely have had poor results, while, on the other hand, coal, gold mining, beverages (soft drinks), retail variety stores, office equipment, distillers, and drugs would have done well.

Even within a given industry selectivity was important and necessary. For example business equipment shares, on the average, performed well, but whereas Burroughs rose 572 percent, National Cash Register fell 39 percent. In cameras Eastman Kodak rose 81 percent while Polaroid fell 47 percent. In drugs, with relatively favorable performances, American Home Products rose 137 percent while Smith Kline dropped 24 percent. In oil, Phillips Petroleum rose 93 percent

---

[28] The price of gold fell sharply in 1975.

FIGURE 1–4
Stocks of Fifty Industries: January 1, 1966 to December 31, 1975

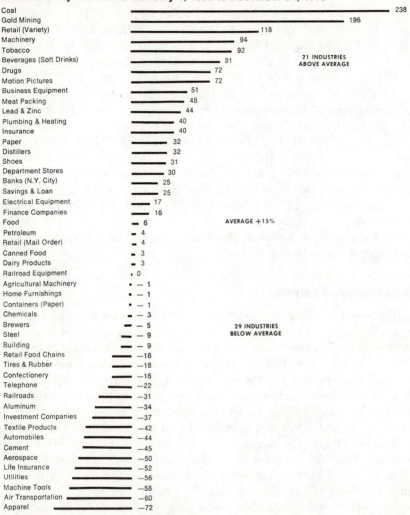

Coal	238
Gold Mining	196
Retail (Variety)	118
Machinery	94
Tobacco	92
Beverages (Soft Drinks)	81
Drugs	72
Motion Pictures	72
Business Equipment	51
Meat Packing	48
Lead & Zinc	44
Plumbing & Heating	40
Insurance	40
Paper	32
Distillers	32
Shoes	31
Department Stores	30
Banks (N.Y. City)	25
Savings & Loan	25
Electrical Equipment	17
Finance Companies	16
Food	6
Petroleum	4
Retail (Mail Order)	4
Canned Food	3
Dairy Products	3
Railroad Equipment	0
Agricultural Machinery	− 1
Home Furnishings	− 1
Containers (Paper)	− 1
Chemicals	− 3
Brewers	− 5
Steel	− 9
Building	− 9
Retail Food Chains	−18
Tires & Rubber	−18
Confectionery	−18
Telephone	−22
Railroads	−31
Aluminum	−34
Investment Companies	−37
Textile Products	−42
Automobiles	−44
Cement	−45
Aerospace	−50
Life Insurance	−52
Utilities	−56
Machine Tools	−58
Air Transportation	−60
Apparel	−72

21 INDUSTRIES
ABOVE AVERAGE

AVERAGE +15%

29 INDUSTRIES
BELOW AVERAGE

Source: Johnson's Investment Company, Charts.

while Ashland Oil fell 31 percent. In chain stores, Kresge rose 654 percent while W. T. Grant fell 96 percent. In tobacco Philip Morris rose 619 percent but Liggett & Myers fell 17 percent. In air transportation, Delta rose 58 percent, Eastern fell 90 percent. And in something as basic as chemicals, Dow rose 256 percent, while Du Pont fell 47 percent. The need for security analysis should be clear.

By security analysis we mean, of course, fundamental analysis. This is the basic process of the evaluation of common stock by studying

earnings, dividends, price-earnings multiples, economic outlook for the industry, financial prospects for the company, sales penetration, market share, and quality of management. Selecting the industry or industries which are likely to do best over the next three to five years and then choosing the company or companies within the selected industries which are likely to outperform their competitors—this is the essence of fundamental analysis.[29]

In general terms there are four aspects of any complete and concise analysis: (a) the sales analysis and forecast, (b) the earnings analysis and forecast, (c) the multiplier analysis and forecast, and (d) the analysis of management, a qualitative consideration.[30]

Basic to any estimate of earning power is a sales analysis and forecast. Growth of demand for a company's products is essential for common stock appreciation. While expanding production and sales do not guarantee rising profits, rising demand or the introduction of new products, at least give a company an opportunity to earn a rising profit.

What the analyst is seeking is a working forecast of sales in order to determine the profit implications of the sales forecast. But just as a sales forecast is essential to an effective profits forecast, an economic forecast is a preliminary prerequisite to the sales forecast. The starting point of an effective industry and company forecast may be a GNP forecast, with a breakdown of components. For example, a forecast of sales for the automobile industry may be tied to the growth of real GNP by using historic figures on the number of cars sold per billion dollar increase in real GNP. Or, the analyst may use estimates of prospective consumer durable goods expenditures, derived from an econometric model of the composite economy and use this to forecast automobile sales. Or, the estimate may begin with a forecast of personal disposable income for either the coming year or longer. Since expenditures on automobiles are a relatively stable percentage of disposable personal income, a reasonable estimate of expenditures for automobiles may be made. Since this will be an estimate for the entire industry, market shares must be allocated to companies.[31]

Having obtained an estimate or range of estimates of prospective sales growth rates, the next step is to proceed to obtain an estimate, or range of estimates, of prospective earnings growth rates. To achieve this an analysis of earnings is necessary. One approach is to start with

---

[29] For an elaboration, see Chapter 5. See also Leopold A. Bernstein, "In Defense of Fundamental Analysis," *Financial Analysts Journal*, January/February 1975.

[30] For a detailed discussion of (a) and (b), see Robert S. Schultz, "Sales Forecasting" and Edmund A. Mennis, "Forecasting Corporate Profits," in *Methods and Techniques of Business Forecasting*, eds. William Butler, Robert Kavesh, and Robert Platt (Englewood Cliffs, N.J.: Prentice-Hall, Inc., 1974).

[31] See Chapter 6.

the GNP forecast and derive from it a prospective corporate profits trend for all industry. Then factor out a profits trend for the particular industry under review, making such adjustments as special industry characteristics suggest a greater or lesser rate of growth than that of the total corporate profits series. From this develop a company estimate, again making adjustment for special company characteristics.

Or, one can start with the sales forecast developed earlier and relate this to the company's profit margin, operating income, equity turnover, rate of return on equity, earnings before interest and taxes, net income after interest and taxes, return on total capital, and net earnings per share. By dissecting the anatomical character of a corporation's profitability and measuring the impact of prospective changes on each element, it is possible to derive an estimate of a range of future earnings from one to three years ahead.[32]

Once an earnings forecast, or a range of forecasts, is derived, it remains to develop and apply a multiplier, the price-earnings ratio. A vareity of factors impinge upon and help determine a price-earnings ratio. Among these are the growth rate of earnings, actual and anticipated, the dividend payment, the marketability and volatility of the stock, the stability or volatility of earnings, and the quality of earnings and of management. Of these, perhaps, the growth rate of earnings is the most significant. In general, there seems to be a consensus that the higher the growth rate of earnings, the higher the p/e ratio.

From this brief summary of fundamental analysis, it should be clear that the modern approach to common stock, evaluation centers on a two-part question. What is the potential growth of earnings and dividends of a company whose stock is being analyzed and what is a reasonable price to pay for that potential?[33]

Investment Timing

Perhaps as important as the choice of what stocks to buy is the decision as to when to buy—and when to sell. Investment timing is possibly even more difficult a task than investment choice. But the competent analyst must constantly make a judgment as to the trend and level of the market as a whole to provide the appropriate environmental setting for portfolio additions or deletions. The level and

---

[32] See Chapter 7. Some newer analytic techniques for estimating earnings should be mentioned. They include probabilistic forecasting, conditional forecasts, and computer models for forecasting earnings. These have been excellently explained in J. Peter Williamson, *Investments: New Analytical Techniques* (New York: Praeger Publishers, Inc., 1970). See especially Chapter V on "Security Analysis," and Chapter VI on "Stock-Selection Techniques."

[33] For a more detailed exposition of fundamental analysis, see Samuel S. Stewart, Jr., "Corporate Forecasting," *Financial Analyst's Handbook*, vol. I (Homewood, Ill.: Dow Jones-Irwin, Inc., 1975), chap. 32.

trend of the market may be considered in three time dimensions: the secular, the cyclical, and the seasonal.

The secular trend is the long-run course of the market over a 20-, 25-, 40-, or 50-year period. Generally the trend has been upward for reasons indicated earlier—the continuing decline in the purchasing power of the dollar, the gradual inflation in the economy, the rise in demand for common stock as compared to a relatively limited supply, and the relatively steady growth in gross national product and corporate profits. The rising secular trend in common stock prices may be seen in Figures 1–5A, 1–5B and Table 1–16.

TABLE 1–16
Dow Jones Industrial Average: 41-Year Performance, 1935–1975

| | Market | | | | | | Yield | | P/E Multiple | | | Consumer Price Index (Annual |
Year	High	Low	Close	Yearly Change	Earn- ings	Divi- dends	High	Low	High	Low	Book Value	Average) 1967=100
1935	148.44	96.71	144.13	38.5	6.34	4.55	4.7%	3.1%	23½	15	80.42	41.1
1936	184.90	143.11	179.90	24.8	10.07	7.05	4.9	3.8	18	14	83.20	41.5
1937	194.40	113.64	120.85	− 32.8	11.49	8.78	7.7	4.5	17	10	86.48	43.0
1938	158.41	98.95	154.76	28.1	6.01	4.98	5.0	3.1	26	16½	87.38	42.2
1939	155.92	121.44	150.24	− 2.9	9.11	6.11	5.0	3.9	17	13	90.20	41.6
1940	152.80	111.84	131.13	− 12.7	10.92	7.06	6.3	4.6	14	10	92.39	42.0
1941	133.59	106.34	110.96	− 15.4	11.64	7.59	7.1	5.7	11½	9	95.45	44.1
1942	119.71	92.92	119.40	7.6	9.22	6.40	6.9	5.3	13	10	97.94	48.8
1943	145.82	119.26	135.89	13.8	9.74	6.30	5.3	4.3	15	12	101.68	51.8
1944	152.53	134.22	152.32	12.1	10.07	6.57	4.9	4.3	15	13	105.40	52.7
1945	195.82	151.35	192.91	26.6	10.56	6.69	4.4	3.4	18½	14	110.29	53.9
1946	212.50	163.12	177.20	− 8.1	13.63	7.50	4.6	3.5	15½	12	119.22	58.5
1947	186.85	163.21	181.16	2.2	18.80	9.21	5.6	4.9	10	9	126.65	66.9
1948	193.16	165.39	177.30	− 2.1	23.07	11.50	7.0	6.0	8	7	148.12	72.1
1949	200.52	161.60	200.13	12.9	23.54	12.79	7.9	6.4	8½	7	160.33	71.4
1950	235.47	196.81	235.41	17.6	30.70	16.13	8.2	6.9	7½	6½	186.11	72.1
1951	276.37	238.99	269.23	14.4	26.59	16.34	6.8	5.9	10½	9	197.05	77.8
1952	292.00	256.35	291.90	8.4	24.78	15.48	6.0	5.3	12	10	207.50	79.5
1953	293.79	255.49	289.90	− 3.8	27.23	16.11	6.3	5.5	11	9½	218.76	80.1
1954	404.39	279.87	404.39	44.0	28.18	17.47	6.2	4.3	14½	10	232.38	80.5
1955	488.40	388.20	488.40	20.8	35.78	21.58	5.6	4.4	13½	11	258.92	80.2
1956	521.05	462.35	499.47	2.3	33.34	22.99	5.0	4.4	15½	14	276.19	81.4
1957	520.77	419.79	435.69	− 12.8	36.08	21.61	5.1	4.2	14½	11½	283.49	84.3
1958	583.65	436.89	583.65	34.0	27.95	20.00	4.6	3.4	21	15½	292.45	86.6
1959	679.36	574.46	679.36	16.4	34.31	19.38	3.4	2.9	20	17	308.50	87.3
1960	685.47	566.05	615.89	− 9.3	32.21	20.46	3.6	3.0	21	17½	343.00	88.7
1961	734.91	610.25	731.14	18.7	31.91	21.28	3.5	2.9	23	19	356.96	89.6
1962	726.01	535.76	652.10	− 10.8	36.43	22.09	4.1	3.0	20	15	372.48	90.6
1963	767.21	646.79	762.95	17.0	41.21	23.20	3.6	3.0	18½	15½	377.10	91.7
1964	891.71	766.08	874.13	14.6	46.43	25.38	3.3	2.8	19	16½	405.98	92.9
1965	969.26	840.59	969.26	10.9	53.67	28.61	3.4	2.9	18	15½	446.23	94.5
1966	995.15	744.32	785.69	− 18.9	57.68	31.89	4.0	3.0	17	13	464.20	97.2
1967	943.08	786.41	905.11	15.2	53.87	30.19	3.8	3.2	17½	14½	467.12	100.0
1968	985.21	825.13	943.75	4.3	57.89	31.34	3.8	3.2	17	14	511.75	104.2
1969	968.85	769.93	800.36	− 15.2	57.02	33.90	4.2	3.3	17	13½	553.06	109.8
1970	842.00	631.16	838.92	4.8	51.02	31.53	5.0	3.7	16½	12½	584.54	116.3
1971	950.82	797.97	890.20	6.1	55.09	30.86	3.9	3.2	17	14½	600.28	121.3
1972	1,036.27	889.15	1,020.02	14.6	67.11	32.27	3.6	3.1	15½	13	634.32	125.3
1973	1,051.70	788.31	850.86	− 16.6	86.17	35.33	4.5	3.4	12	9	677.82	133.1
1974	891.66	577.60	616.24	− 27.6	99.04	37.72	6.5	4.2	9	5.8	730.00	147.7
1975	881.81	632.00	852.41	38.3	75.47E	37.46	5.9	4.2	12	8	746.95	161.2
Increase from 1935 to 1975	+494%	+554%	+491%	—	+1,090%	+732%	—	—	—	—	+829%	+292%

Source: Johnson's Investment Company, Charts.

FIGURE 1-5A

The Dow Jones Industrials—Price, Earnings and Dividend Trends 1946-1975

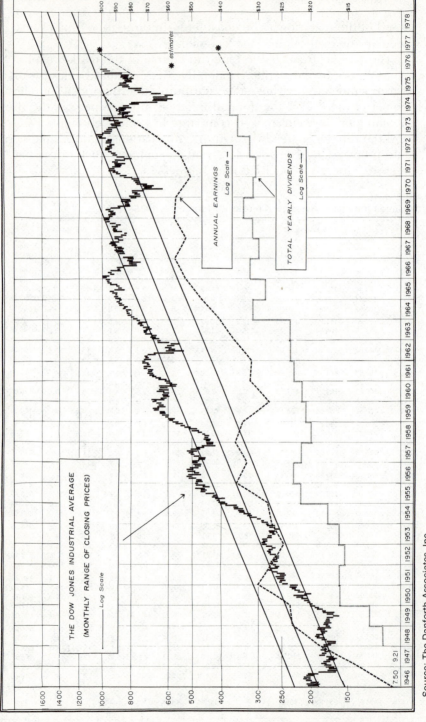

Source: The Danforth Associates, Inc.

FIGURE 1–5B
Dow Jones Industrial Average, 1926–1975

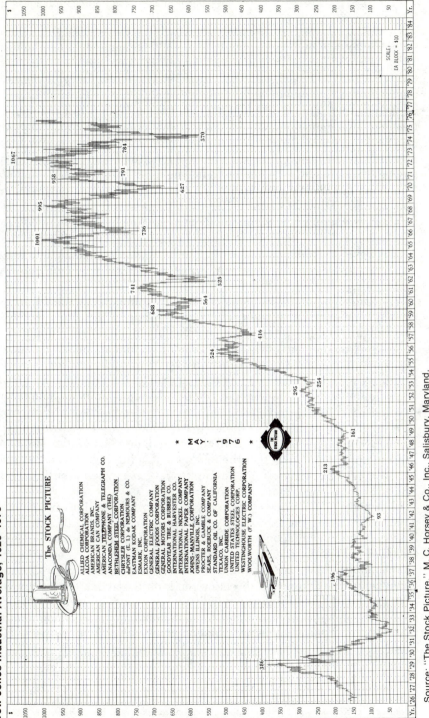

Source: "The Stock Picture," M. C. Horsey & Co., Inc., Salisbury, Maryland.

In 1898 the Dow Jones Industrials registered a low of 42 and a high of 60.97. By 1903 the high was 103, in 1916 it reached 110.15 and in 1919, 119.62. There followed a postwar setback but from 81.50 in 1921 the DJIA rose to a peak of 381.17 in 1929. The Great Depression saw the index fall to a low of 41.22 in 1932, back to the 1898 level. It then recovered to a peak of 194 in 1937, fell thereafter and did not regain this level again until it reached 195 in 1945. Thereafter it rose sharply to a peak of 995 in 1966. This postwar bull market far outshadowed anything in our history. Then the market remained on a plateau until a sharp setback in 1969–70, the DJIA falling to a low of 631 in May 1970. The years 1971 and particularly 1972 saw a resurgence with the DJIA piercing the 1,000 level in 1972, hitting a peak of 1,051 in January 1973. Then the market fell about 45 percent, touching a low at 577 in December 1974. Anticipating the economic recovery of 1975–76, the market rose sharply and reached 1,014 in September 1976. The long secular uptrend in the Dow Industrials is shown in Figures 1–5A and 1–5B.

The problem of investment timing, as opposed to selection, is mostly concerned with the *cyclical* dimension of the stock market. Ideally, the investor who can buy stocks when prices are cyclically low and sell when they are cyclically high, will, of course, greatly enhance his or her profits. Traditional value analysts approach the timing question in exactly the same way as they approach the selection process. They hold that in due course, despite possible temporary deviations or psychological pulls, stock prices anticipate and reflect basic economic trends and anticipate or respond to corporate profits, earnings per share, and dividends. Analysis of these fundamentals guides them in their judgment as to whether the market is in a buying (low) or selling (high) range. But they do not attempt to *forecast* when a bull market will turn into a bear market or vice versa.

Common stock prices are one of the 12 leading indicators developed during the course of years of business cycle study by the National Bureau of Economic Research (NBER). Leading indicators are those economic series, such as new orders for durable goods, commercial and industrial building contracts, and business failures, basic changes in whose trend or direction tend, on the average, to precede and signal basic cyclical changes in business activity as a whole. Based on a study of past business cycles from 1873 to date, it has been found that basic cyclical changes in common stock prices tend to precede cyclical changes in business as a whole by about five to nine months.[34]

---

[34] See Julius Shiskin, "The Best Economic Forecaster," *New York Times,* April 27, 1975; also Geoffrey H. Moore, "Security Markets and Business Cycles," *Financial Analyst's Handbook,* vol. I (Homewood, Ill.: Dow Jones-Irwin, Inc., 1975), chap. 27.

In a scoring plan developed by the NBER in evaluating indicators, the stock price series, scored 81, on a scale of 100, compared to 78 for the series on new orders for durable goods, its closest competitor as a leading indicator. In the NBER study the record of stock prices since 1873 was compared with peaks and troughs in general business conditions. During 43 expansions and recessions over this 100-year period, the movements of stock prices conformed in 33 instances, or 77 percent of the time. The same study showed that stock prices anticipated 33 out of 44, or 75 percent, of the business cycle turning points.

If the business cycle concept is broadened to include slowdowns in growth that did not qualify as recessions, then the record is even stronger. Thus, since 1948 stock prices show a one-to-one match at every peak and trough. They led at every turning point. They did not lag at any and they gave no false leading signals.

The designation of common stock prices as a leading indicator was based on performance on the average over preceding business cycles. It does not mean that common stock price trends by *themselves* forecast business changes, nor does it mean that a downtrend in stock prices preceded every recession since 1873. But the relationship between stock price cycles and business cycles has been close enough frequently enough to encourage investors to utilize the relationship for forecasting purposes. This effort will be examined at length in a later chapter.[35]

There is considerable debate as to whether there is a discernible seasonal pattern in the market. Financial writers speak of the traditional "summer rally" and "year-end rally." To a lesser extent there is a widespread impression that February and September are generally— but not always—poor months in the market. These impressions of financial writers and observers of the market are based upon tabulations of advances and declines, by months, of long past periods of time. A recent study, covering the 23-year period (May 1951–April 1974), found pronounced seasonal strength in January, March–April, July–August, and November–December, with weakness in February, May, June, and October (Figure 1–6).

Statistical analysts have taken issue with these conclusions on seasonality. Using a sophisticated technique, called spectral analysis, for examining economic time series, two experts found very little evidence of a seasonal pattern. They declared: "In general, the seasonal components, although just observable, are of no financial significance."[36]

---

[35] Chapter 12.

[36] Clive W. J. Granger and Oskar Morgenstern, *Predictability of Stock Market Prices* (Lexington, Mass.: D. C. Heath & Co., 1970), p. 131.

FIGURE 1–6

Market Performance Each Month of the Year (May 1951–April 1974)*

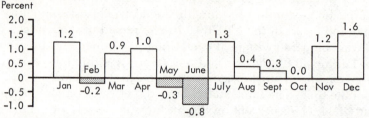

* Average month-to-month change in Standard & Poor's composite index (monthly average).

Source: The Hirsch Organization, Inc., *The 1976 Stock Trader's Almanac,* Old Tappan, New Jersey.

The folklore of the market refuses to die, however, and any practitioner will tell you that the professors are wrong—that there usually is a summer and end-of-year rally. Some will go even further and tell you that Friday morning trading is the strongest of the week; that Fridays rise 54 percent more than Mondays, that when the market is down on Fridays, chances are three to one that it will be down on Monday as well.

The market rises more often (64.5 percent) on the second trading day of the month than on any other. And a period of five consecutive trading days, the last, first, second, third, and fourth, distinctly outperforms the rest of the days of the month. In a 276-month study (May 1952–April 1975) the market was up 59.1 percent of the time on these five bullish days. (See Figure 1–7.) Perhaps most bizarre is the notion that what happens in the first five days of the calendar year is predictive of the market trend for that year.[37]

FIGURE 1–7

Market Performance Each Day of the Month (May 1952–April 1975)*

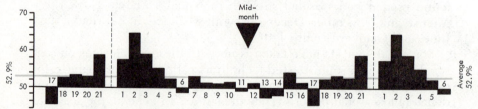

* Based on number of times S&P composite index closed higher than previous day.

Note: Trading days (excluding Saturdays, Sundays, and holidays).

Source: The Hirsch Organization, Inc., *The 1976 Stock Trader's Almanac,* Old Tappan, N.J.

---

[37] For an interesting presentation, see "Directory of Seasonal Trading Patterns," in Yale Hirsch, *The 1976 Stock Trader's Almanac* (Old Tappan, N.J.: 1976).

The Technical Approach

Some analysts do attempt to forecast changes in stock prices, including turning points in the market. They study the movements of stock prices themselves, past and present, and other technical data such as trading volume, number of stocks advancing and declining, and so on. They are the "technical analysts."

The tools of the technical analyst are numerous, and an elaborate and exotic jargon has been evolved. Technical factors examined and interpreted include odd-lot trading, the short interest, volume of trading indicators, breadth-of-market analysis, advance-decline lines, ratios and indexes, disparity measures, high-low indexes and ratios, moving average lines, the confidence index, and so on.[38] The complete market technician's kit would also have to include chart jargon involving support and resistance, heads and shoulders, double tops and bottoms, line and saucer formations, V formations, measured move, first leg, the corrective phase, second leg, the coil or triangle, continuation patterns, reversal days, gaps, islands, bear traps, bull traps, fulcrums, duplex horizontals, inverse fulcrums, delayed endings, saucers, inverse saucers, compound fulcrums, and so on.[39] A *Fortune* article on "The Mystique of Point-and-Figure" began "Question: Does this look like reaccumulation preparatory to a new upthrust? Answer: No—because fulcrum characteristics are not present."

This sort of jargon has convinced many observers that technical analysis is sheer rubbish. Indeed, as we have seen, a group of academicians has given prominence to a theory that short-term stock price movements are *random*, and that no amount of analysis of historical data on prices, volume, and the like can enable one to forecast future stock price swings around their long-term trends. On the other hand, large numbers of Wall Street practitioners are equally convinced that price movements are not random and that technical analysis can improve one's chances of making correct timing decisions.

Why, if stock prices are random in the short run, do so many brokerage houses employ technicians and analysts who profess to find meaningful patterns in the fluctuations of stock prices, patterns that may be discerned and utilized? Cootner suggests the answer when he quotes Julian Huxley to the effect that superstitions are always apt to flourish when men must make decisions about matters they cannot control, and he adds:

---

[38] For a detailed description, see Alan R. Shaw, "Technical Analysis," *Financial Analyst's Handbook*, vol. I, Homewood, Ill.: Dow Jones-Irwin, Inc., 1975), chap. 34.

[39] For a detailed description, see William L. Jiler, *How Charts Can Help You in the Market* (New York: Commodity Research Publications Corp., latest ed.).

Whether or not that is the reason, it is hard to find a practitioner, no matter how sophisticated, who does not believe that by looking at the past history of prices one can learn something about their prospective behavior, while it is almost as difficult to find an academician who believes that such a backward look is of any substantial value.

It should be noted that scholars holding the random-walk view usually qualify it by observing that the random movement takes place within the framework of a long-term "drift"—i.e., over long periods of time, stock prices do move higher; hence a belief in randomness is not inconsistent with a "buy and hold" policy for stocks.

No one analyst uses all of the technical approach methods. If he did he would be more confused than a psychiatrist. He becomes intrigued with several and comes to rely upon them. A more interesting approach, however, is that of the indicator consensus technique. Since individual technical indicators have given false signals from time to time in the past, the idea occurred to use a consensus of indicators for greater reliability. A number of services now use this technique. One of the more widely known is the *Indicator Digest*, which achieved some prominence as a result of the "sell" signal which it gave in January 1962, thereby correctly anticipating the subsequent sharp drop in the market in the spring of 1962. It also signaled the bear market of 1969–1970, 1973–74, and the upturn in 1975.

Indicator Digest, Inc., uses a composite index consisting of 12 technical indicators at any one time, varying several of them depending on whether a bull or a bear market is under way. These are then given weights of 1½, 1, or ½ for a total weight of 10. Whenever the composite total is 6 or more a favorable signal is given. If the score sinks to 4 or less, it is unfavorable. The 40 percent to 60 percent range is regarded as neutral.[40] (See Figure 1–8.)

Mechanical Timing Techniques

The limitations of the technical approach cause some investors to use mechanical timing techniques. Not only do the technical methods have varying degrees of effectiveness from time to time but they are often in conflict with respect to the signals they are exuding. Even the composite techniques, of which there are several, are not always in agreement. At such times an investor can well become confused.

Three varieties of mechanical timing techniques can be distinguished. There is dollar-cost averaging; there are formula plans, either

---

[40] Publication of the *Indicator Digest* was begun in May 1961. The composite index has been revised several times since then. For a sample copy of the semimonthly *Digest* as well as a copy of *The Directory of Indicators*, write to *Indicator Digest*, Palisades Park, New Jersey 07650.

FIGURE 1–8
Indicator Digest **Composite Index**

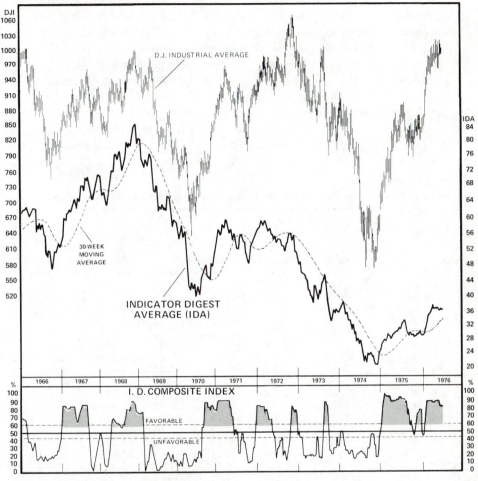

Source: *Indicator Digest,* Palisades Park, New Jersey.

constant dollar, constant ratio, or variable ratio; and there is automatic trend following. The broad purpose of these automatic techniques is to induce caution in bull markets and bravery in bear markets, to achieve the investor's long-sought but seldom achieved goal of buying low and selling high.

Dollar-cost averaging involves the regular purchase of securities—monthly or quarterly—in equal dollar amounts. The very obvious fact that the same amount of money will buy a greater number of shares of any stock when the price is low than it will when the price is high is the basis of the success of dollar averaging. You put the same

fixed amount of money periodically into the same stock or stocks regardless of the price of the stock. Your fixed amount of money buys more shares when the stock is low, less shares when it is high. The important thing is to stick to your schedule—to buy, even though the price keeps falling, which, psychologically, is usually hard to do. This brings your average cost down, and any subsequent rise will yield a significant capital gain. To engage in dollar-cost averaging successfully, you must have both the funds and the courage to continue buying in a declining market when prospects may seem bleak.

An example of a decade of dollar-cost averaging is shown in Table 1–17. It shows how you would have fared if you had bought the S&P

TABLE 1–17
Dollar Cost Averaging ($1,000 invested semiannually based on S&P 500 Index)

Date	Index First Trading Day	Cumulative Investment	No. Shares Bought	No. Shares Held	Accumulated Divds.	Mkt. Value and Divds. Received
1964 July	82.27	$ 1,000	12.16	12.16	$ 0	$ 1,000
1965 Jan.	84.23	2,000	11.87	24.03	16	2,040
July	84.48	3,000	11.84	35.87	47	3,077
1966 Jan.	92.18	4,000	10.85	46.72	99	4,406
July	85.61	5,000	11.68	58.40	164	5,164
1967 Jan.	80.38	6,000	12.44	70.84	250	5,944
July	90.91	7,000	11.00	81.84	351	7,791
1968 Jan.	96.11	8,000	10.40	92.24	474	9,339
July	99.40	9,000	10.06	102.30	611	10,780
1969 Jan.	103.93	10,000	9.62	111.92	773	12,405
July	98.08	11,000	10.20	122.12	946	12,924
1970 Jan.	93.00	12,000	10.75	132.87	1,143	13,500
July	73.04	13,000	13.69	146.56	1,352	12,057
1971 Jan.	91.15	14,000	10.97	157.53	1,582	15,941
July	99.78	15,000	10.02	167.55	1,823	18,541
1972 Jan.	101.67	16,000	9.84	177.39	2,081	20,116
July	107.49	17,000	9.30	186.69	2,352	22,149
1973 Jan.	119.10	18,000	8.40	195.09	2,654	25,889
July	102.90	19,000	9.72	204.81	2,966	24,041
1974 Jan.	97.68	20,000	10.24	215.05	3,331	24,337
July	86.02	21,000	11.63	226.68	3,701	23,200
1975 Jan.	70.23	22,000	14.24	240.92	4,127	21,047
July	94.85	23,000	10.54	251.46	4,568	28,419

Source: *The Outlook,* Standard & Poor's.

500 stock index on a dollar-cost averaging basis over the last eleven years. The tabulation assumes that $1,000 was invested each January and July. Through July 1975 you would have committed $23,000 and your portfolio would be worth $28,419. In addition, if you had regularly

reinvested the $4,568 of dividends as they were received, the value of your portfolio would have been even larger.

In a bull market investors hate to sell and take a profit both because they do not want to pay the capital gains tax and because they are afraid the market will continue to rise and they will, by selling, forego added gains. Thus they miss the top, for which most investors aim but rarely achieve, and continue to hold well into the downturn. They are reluctant to sell during the early stages of the downturn because they mourn the profits missed by not selling at or near the peak (which only hindsight now reveals as a peak), and they hold hoping the market will reverse itself and return to the peak. It usually does not, but they continue to hold until, well on the downside, patience is lost and the investors sell. In this way emotion and bad judgment play a real role in lack of investment success. Formula plans have been designed to overcome such human failing.

In the simple and somewhat naive constant dollar plan, you divide your funds between stocks and cash or savings. You keep the dollar amount in stocks constant. If the market rises you sell enough stock to hold your total dollar amount invested in stock to your predetermined level. If the market falls, you draw from cash or savings and buy stock. In the constant ratio plan you decide in advance what percent of your resources you want to keep in stocks—40 percent, 50 percent, 60 percent—and then at regular intervals, if the market rises, you sell stock so that your stock investments are maintained at the predetermined ratio to your total resources. If the market falls, you buy stocks out of your other resources to maintain the ratio. Under the variable ratio plan you change your ratio of stocks to cash, or stocks to bonds, or stocks to total resources as the level of the market changes. For example, toward the end or peak of a bull market, you hold 10 percent in stocks and 90 percent in other resources. If the market declines you increase your percentage of stocks until near the end of a bear market you are 90 percent in stocks and 10 percent in other resources.

There are tough problems to solve. How do you determine your bench marks? How often and by what magnitude do you determine your ratios? How often do you buy or sell? Some of the mutual funds have tried the variable ratio plan and have come up with different answers, which have been changed from time to time. One thing is obvious, however. The variable ratio plan can provide better results than the constant ratio plan because under the variable ratio plan you buy significantly more stock at low prices and sell substantially more at high prices than under a constant ratio plan. If you have the resources, can cope with the intricacies and problems of a variable ratio plan, can bring yourself to buy as the market slides, you can get close to the objective of buying low and selling high.

BOND INVESTMENT

When a bull market begins to near its peak, when blue chips begin to sag, when speculative high flyers and low-priced cats and dogs begin to get the play, when stock yields fall to 3 percent or less and the yield spread between stocks and high-grade bonds widens to 4 percent in favor of bonds, when business is booming and interest rates are tight, the shrewd institutional investment manager who has choice and flexibility will quietly withhold funds from new common stock commitments and place the funds in high-grade bonds.

When prosperity tops out into recession, when business and common stock prices begin to slide, high-grade bonds come into favor. As interest rates decline high-grade bond prices rise. High-grade bond prices tend to vary inversely with interest rates and with common stock prices. As recession turns into recovery, reverse trends set in. Interest rates and common stock prices which have fallen start to rise and high-grade bond prices tend to weaken. Generally speaking, by high-grade bonds are meant those rated AAA or AA by the rating services.

The primary investment interest in bonds comes from institutions such as banks and insurance companies which must pay obligations in fixed number of dollars. If you have a $50,000 life insurance policy, for example, at some point in the future—whether 5 years or 35 years hence—the company will have to pay $50,000. If it invests in securities—bonds—which will return it a fixed number of dollars—it is in a position to meet its obligation. It does not matter in this case whether the dollars it gets back buy half as little as when they were invested. It has a fixed dollar obligation, not a purchasing power obligation. The individual investor may shy away from high-grade bonds because of the purchasing power risk, but most institutional investors have less need to worry about this problem. Individual investors, particularly wealthier ones, find a special interest in several types of bonds, particularly tax-exempts and convertibles. As a hedge against recession and deflation, however, switching from common stock to highgrade bonds as a boom tops out may be an excellent, profitable move for any investor.

Bond Price and Interest Rates

The principal price risk in high-grade bonds is related to the trend of interest rates. If a commercial bank holds high-grade bonds, and interest rates, which had been low, start to rise, and the bank must sell its bonds because funds are needed for some other purpose, such as expanding business loans, then a capital loss results. Why? If the

bonds carry a coupon rate of interest of, say 6 percent, and similar quality bonds now are being issued with coupons of 7½ percent or higher, no one will be willing to purchase the 6 percent bond at par value. The unwillingness of buyers to pay the previously prevailing prices, coupled with the actual selling pressure of investors who are seeking to raise funds for other investments, forces the price of the old 6 percent issue down, and it will fall to the point where its price in the market yields the new purchaser approximately the same rate of return as the average new, higher level of rates in the market. Thus, as the boom moves ahead, the demand for funds expands, and interest rates rise, high-grade bond prices will fall as stock prices rise.

At the peak of the expansion, when the central banking authorities are pursuing a tight money policy, which has driven interest rates up, bond prices down, the institutional investment manager may start switching from common stocks to high-grade bonds. As expansion turns to recession, tight money will be relaxed, interest rates will be allowed to fall, and they will go down because the demand for funds slackens, and high-grade bond prices will rise. In fact, the deeper the recession, the higher will go the prices of high-grade bonds as institutional investment demand switches to them and thus bids up their prices. However, if inflation accelerates during a recession, as in 1973–74, interest rates will rise since lenders will demand a premium to cover the inflation. (See Figure 1–9.)

Types of Bonds

Bonds may be either secured or unsecured and may range from first-mortgage bonds on the one hand to subordinated debentures on the other. The security behind a bond, while important, is not crucial. The earning power, financial condition, and quality of management is vital. Because of this, one company's unsecured bonds may be rated higher than another company's secured obligations. For example, the debentures of AT&T are rated higher than the first-mortgage bonds of Indianapolis Power and Light. The debentures of Southern Bell Telephone have a higher rating than the first-mortgage bonds of Missouri Power and Light Company.

Mortgage bonds are secured by a conditional lien on part or all of a company's property. If the company defaults (fails to pay interest or repay principal), the bondholders, through the trustee appointed to represent them and look after their rights, may foreclose the mortgage and take over the pledged property. Some corporate mortgages have what is known as an *"after-acquired"* property clause, which provides that all property thereafter acquired will become subject to the mortgage and automatically be pledged to secure the bond issue.

FIGURE 1–9
High-Grade Corporate Bond Yields 1900–1975

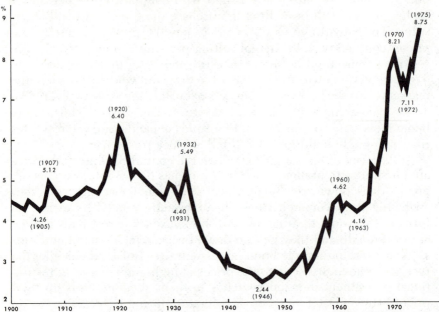

Bond yields in 1975 were the highest of the 20th century as shown by the chart. They were very likely the highest in our history, although Standard & Poor's Corporate Bond Yield Indexes only go back to 1900. Since bond prices fluctuate in inverse proportion to yields, high-grade bond prices in 1975 were the lowest on record. Major high and low points of bond yields and prices over the past 76 years were:

Year	Yield	Price Index	Year	Yield	Price Index
1902	4.29%	96.13	1960	4.62%	91.97
1907	5.12	86.09	1963	4.16	97.79
1920	6.40	73.14	1970	8.21	59.00
1931	4.40	94.72	1972	7.11	67.10
1932	5.49	82.05	1975	8.75	55.53
1946	2.44	124.60			

Source: Johnson's Investment Company Charts.

While this is not widely found, it is very favorable to the investor, and where it exists, if the company wishes to float another bond issue secured by a mortgage on its property, this *second* mortgage will be a *junior lien,* subordinate to the first mortgage or *senior lien* on the property.

Usually, when companies float junior issues, secured by junior liens, they do not clearly label them as such. They call them "general" or "consolidated," or some other ambiguous name, and the only way an

investor can determine the security status of the bonds exactly is to read the *indenture*. The *indenture* is the formal, and usually lengthy, legal contract between the borrowing company and the creditor bond-holders, spelling out all the detailed terms and conditions of the loan. The indenture will also indicate whether more bonds may be issued with the same security or under the same mortgage. If so, the mortgage is said to be *"open-end."* Additional issues of bonds under an "open-end" mortgage will naturally dilute the security available for earlier issues. If the mortgage is "closed-end," no additional bonds may be issued under the same mortgage, and the issue therefore has better protection.

A bond secured by a pledge of specific securities is known as a *"collateral trust bond."* These are issued mainly by holding companies, closed-end investment companies, and finance companies. They have not been popular in recent years, particularly after the passage of the Public Utility Holding Company Act in 1935. The *equipment trust bond or certificate* is usually used to finance the purchase of rolling stock by railroads. Under the Philadelphia Plan, title to equipment (freight cars, locomotives, passenger cars, and so on) being bought by a railroad rests in a trustee who holds it for the benefit of certificate holders. The railroad makes a down payment (perhaps 20 percent), and the trustee issues equipment trust certificates to cover the balance of the purchase price of the equipment. The trustee then leases the equipment to the railroad under an agreement whereby the railroad obtains title to the equipment only when all obligations have been met. Since the rolling stock can be moved anywhere in the country, should the railroad default, the equipment may be sold or leased to another railroad. Defaults have therefore been very rare in the case of equipment trust certificates.

Debentures are unsecured bonds protected only by the general credit of the borrowing corporation. They may contain a "covenant of equal coverage" which means that if any mortgage bond is issued in the future, which ordinarily would take precedence over the debentures, the issuer agrees to secure the debentures equally. In some states the law requires that this be done. All direct domestic obligations of federal, state, and municipal governments in the United States are debentures. This type of security is protected only by the general promise to pay; in the event of default, the debenture holder is merely a general creditor. The value of a debenture must be judged wholly in terms of the earning power and overall financial status and outlook of the issuer, which is the best basis for evaluating any bond. *Subordinated* debentures are very junior issues ranking after other unsecured debt, as a result of explicit provisions in the indenture. Finance companies have made extensive use of subordinated debentures. Be-

cause of these companies' high liquidity and their need for large sums of capital, they have tended to develop layers of debt of which subordinated debentures are the lowest. There are sometimes two layers of subordination.

Convertible bonds are bonds which may be exchanged, at the option of the holder, for a specified amount of other securities, usually common stock. Usually the bond is convertible into a fixed number of shares of common. For example, the Occidental Petroleum 7.5s of 1996 are convertible into 50 shares of common per $1,000 bond. The conversion price of the common is thus $20 per share. When the common sold above this price, the convertible bond would move up with the common. When the common sold below the conversion parity of $20 per share, the bond would rest upon its investment value as a bond without reference to the conversion feature.[41]

An *income bond* is a debt instrument whose distinguishing characteristic is that interest need be paid only if earned. Originally many income bonds arose out of railroad reorganizations and reflected the effort to reduce the burden of fixed charges to manageable proportions. Most income bonds require sinking funds; interest must be paid if earned, in contrast to preferred stock dividends; and interest is often cumulative for three years or longer, depending on the terms of the individual bond issue. Income bonds as an alternative to preferred stock have been taken up and utilized by some industrial companies. Interest payments are a deductible expense for corporate income tax purposes. The Atchison, Topeka, and Santa Fe Railroad adjustment 4s of 1995 issued in the railroad's reorganization of 1895 are rated A. This issue is an exception, however. Most income bonds are rated in the C category because as a group they are regarded as speculative.

Tax-exempt bonds are of special interest to wealthy investors and to certain institutional investors.[42] The income from state and municipal bonds is not subject to the U.S. federal income tax. This may mean that a nontaxable yield of 3.5 percent on a state or municipal bond may be equivalent to twice or three times as much as on a taxable security, depending on the investor's income tax bracket. Rules of analysis for bonds, which will be explored later,[43] vary somewhat for state and municipal issues. There is, however, a simple formula which will show an investor the percentage yield which a bond or other security with

---

[41] See *A Guide to Convertible Bonds* (New York: Kalb, Voorhis & Co., latest ed.); also *Understanding Convertible Securities*, New York Stock Exchange, (latest ed.). For a more detailed analysis, see Chapter 11.

[42] See *Municipal Bond Information Kit*, Lebenthal & Co., New York. For a free copy write to the firm at One State Street Plaza, New York, N.Y. 10004.

[43] See Chapters 9 and 10.

fully taxable income must give in order to provide an after-tax yield equivalent to a given tax-exempt yield. The formula is as follows:

Tax-exempt yield ÷ (100% − Tax bracket %) =

Taxable equivalent yield

Assume that an investor is in the 60 percent tax bracket. If he can buy a 5 percent tax-exempt, what would an alternate investment with fully taxable income have to yield to provide 5 percent after taxes?

$$5.00\% \div (100\% - 60\%) = ?$$
$$\frac{5.00\%}{40\%} = 12.50\%$$

A fully taxable investment would have to yield 12.50 percent to give an after-tax return of 5 percent for an investor in the 60 percent tax bracket.

Since trading costs are high and liquidity just fair, tax-exempts are usually bought by the individual investor for the long pull. Occasionally, shrewd investors will abandon a speculative stock commitment and seek the safety of municipals. *Fortune* cited the case of the Bakalar Brothers, original owners of Transitron Electronic Corporation. "After selling over $75 million of Transitron stock in 1959 and 1960, at around $34 a share, they put much of the money into municipal bonds; since Transitron later sold under $6 a share, and their bonds are intact, this surely rates as one of the great investment switches in history."

United States government securities include bills, notes, and bonds. Treasury bills have the shortest maturities—usually three-month or six-month bills. They are sold at weekly auctions by the Treasury. The smallest amount that can be purchased is $10,000. They are sold at a discount from par, the discount determining the yield, and are redeemed at par. Notes have a maturity of from one to seven years, and are thus an intermediate term security. Bonds generally have a range of maturity of from 7 to 25 years. Both notes and bonds can be purchased in denominations as low as $1,000. All these types of U.S. government securities are subject to federal income and capital gains taxes but not to state and local income or property taxes. When you buy Treasury bills, at say 96, and redeem them six months later at 100, the appreciation (for tax purposes) is regarded as interest income and not as a capital gain. A number of deep discount Treasury bonds are redeemable at par when used to pay federal estate taxes, and are known as "flower bonds." While the relative safety of U.S. government securities (although subject to interest rate and purchasing power risks) attracts conservative investors, speculators are frequently active in the

government securities market because the notes and bonds can be
purchased on very low margin—as little as 10 percent—thus giving
speculators the advantage of leverage.

Bond Analysis and Ratings[44]

For the individual investor and smaller institutional investor, an
initial step in bond analysis is to go to one of the financial services such
as Standard & Poor's or Moody's and see what rating they have assigned to the bond. While these financial services are not infallible,
their experts are accustomed to judging the relative merits of fixed
income securities, and the rating will give you a clear idea of the
approximate quality of the bond. It is a useful orientation for looking
further into the merits, or lack of them, of the proposed purchase. It
may be that when the rating assigned is seen, there may be no further
interest in the bond.

In one sense bond evaluation is not very different from stock evaluation. The real basis for evaluation lies in the financial status and earning power of the borrowing corporation or governmental unit.[45] The
far-sightedness and efficiency of management, the outlook for the industry, the position of the particular firm in the industry, the company's earning power and the soundness of its internal finances as
reflected in its balance sheet and income account, all must be carefully
considered.

The security behind a bond is, in itself, no guarantee of soundness,
since the value of the pledged property is usually dependent on earning power. If the company fails, its fixed assets may prove to be worth
very little. A good example is the Seaboard-All Florida Railway's first
mortgage 6s, which sold in 1931 at one cent on the dollar, soon after the
completion of the road. In selecting any security, but especially bonds,
it makes sense to try and choose a company which is likely to expand
and prosper rather than seek to protect yourself in the event of trouble.

OF RISK AND RETURN

Investors are subject to major types of investment risks. These include:

1. Business risk (i.e., a decline in earning power), which reduces a
   company's ability to pay interest or dividends.

---

[44] With the exception of the U.S. government.

[45] For an interesting discussion, see *The Rating Game* (New York: The Twentieth
Century Fund, (1974). See also Hugh C. Sherwood, *How Corporate and Municipal
Debt Is Rated* (New York: John Wiley & Sons, 1976).

2. Market risk (i.e., a change in "market psychology"), which causes a security's price to decline irrespective of any truly fundamental change in earning power.
3. Purchasing power risk (i.e., a rise in prices), which reduces the buying power of income and principal.
4. Interest rate risk (i.e., a rise in interest rates), which depresses the prices of fixed income type securities.
5. Political risk (for example, price-wage controls, tax increases, changes in tariff and subsidy policies).

Common stocks are most vulnerable to (1), (2), and (5). Bonds are most vulnerable to (1), (3), (4), and (5). No securities are free of all risks. Even U.S. government bonds are subject to (3) and (4).

"Keep your alpha high and your beta low," is a Wall Street slogan. It reflects increasing concern with how to measure risk, how to quantify this heretofore elusive factor, in order to compare it with the rate of return. It has long been apparent that the return achieved by an individual on a modest personal portfolio or by a money manager on a large investment fund is related to the degree of risk undertaken. But how to measure risk, for individual stocks as well as for the entire portfolio?

From the capital asset pricing model of the academic community, beta analysis swept through the financial world. The beta coefficient is a method of measuring risk. It relates the volatility of a stock to the volatility of the market as a whole.[46]

Beta seeks to anticipate what will happen to a stock or a portfolio of stocks given a change, up or down, in the total market. A high-risk stock, a volatile stock, has a high beta, a low-risk stock a low beta. If a stock moved exactly as the market moved it would have a beta of 1. If it was more volatile than the market its beta would be above 1. If less volatile than the market its beta would be below 1. For example, Columbia Pictures' beta has been measured as 1.8, General Foods' as 1.0, and AT&T's as 0.6.[47] But stocks seldom behave precisely as they are supposed to, which is where the alpha comes in. It is used to account for change in a stock's price not attributable to its beta.

For example, suppose that the market advances by 5 percent over a year's time. If a stock has a beta of 1.0, it should go up by 5 percent. If instead it went up 15 percent, the 10 percent difference between the anticipated and the actual performance would be the stock's alpha. If a

---

[46] Chris Welles, "The Beta Revolution: Learning to Live with Rish," *Institutional Investor*, September 1971; see also Franco Modigliani and Gerald A. Pogue, "An Introduction to Risk and Return," Part I, *Financial Analysts Journal*, March/April 1974; Part II May/June 1974.

[47] "Security Risk Evaluation: Beta Coefficients," Merrill Lynch, Pierce, Fenner & Smith, Computer Research and Applications Department, New York, August 1975.

stock had a beta of 2.0—meaning a more volatile stock—and it went up by 15 percent, it would have an alpha of 5 percent because, based on its beta, it should have gone up 10 percent.[48]

According to beta theory, there are two possible ways of achieving superior portfolio performance. One is to forecast the market more accurately and adjust the beta of your portfolio accordingly. If you foresee a substantial market rally, you might buy some high beta stocks and sell some low beta stocks to raise your portfolio to a beta level of say 2.0. If you are wrong, and the market drops, your portfolio will, of course, decline twice as much.

The second way of obtaining above average performance is to achieve a positive alpha, or "excess return." When one stock has a higher or lower rate of return than another stock with the same beta, when it does better or worse against the market than its beta would have predicted, this is said to be due to its alpha factor, or the various residual nonmarket influences unique to each stock. If you can select enough stocks with positive alphas, your portfolio will perform better than its beta would have indicated for a given market movement.[49]

But as you add more stocks to your portfolio you tend to diversify away both the chance of obtaining a positive alpha, as well as the risk of getting a negative alpha. Your portfolio's volatility will also become very much like the market as a whole. A fully diversified portfolio, if there is such, would have a beta of 1.0 and an alpha of 0. Interesting? If all this intrigues you and you want to know more about it, you will if you ever reach Chapter 15, wherein the subject is covered at length.[50]

SUGGESTED READINGS

Brealey, Richard A. *An Introduction to Risk and Return from Common Stocks*. Cambridge, Mass.: The M.I.T. Press, 1969.

———. *Security Prices in a Competitive Market: More about Risk and Return from Common Stocks*. Cambridge, Mass.: The M.I.T. Press, 1971.

---

[48] As will be seen in Chapter 15, this is a simplification. A more precise calculation would take into account the return on risk-free assets. The formula is:

Portfolio return = Risk-free rate + beta (market return − risk-free rate) + alpha

[49] See Jerome L. Valentine, *Investment Analysis and Capital Market Theory*, Occasional Paper No. 1 (Charlottesville, Va.: The Financial Analysts Research Foundation, 1975), pp. 31–38.

[50] For some well-founded empirical skepticism as to the value of beta, see Irwin Friend and Marshall Blume, "Risk and the Long-Run Rates of Return on NYSE Common Stock," *Working Paper* No. 18-72 (Philadelphia: Rodney L. White Center for Financial Research, The Wharton School, University of Pennsylvania, 1972); also, Robert A. Levy, "Beta as a Predictor of Return," *Financial Analysts Journal*, January/February 1974; Marshall Blume and Irwin Friend, "A New Look at the Capital Asset Pricing Model," *Journal of Finance*, March 1973.

Cootner, Paul (ed.). *The Random Character of Stock Market Prices*. rev. ed. Cambridge, Mass.: The M.I.T. Press, 1967.

Fisher, Lawrence, and Lorie, James H. "Rates of Return on Investments in Common Stock: The Year-by-Year Record, 1926–1965." *Journal of Business*, University of Chicago, July 1968.

Fisher, Lawrence, and Lorie, James H. "Some Studies of Variability of Returns on Investments in Common Stocks." *Journal of Business*, University of Chicago, April 1970.

Granger, Clive W. J., and Morgenstern, Oskar. *Predictability of Stock Market Prices*. Lexington, Mass.: D. C. Heath & Co., 1970.

Ibbotson, Roger G., and Sinquefield, Rex A. "Stocks, Bonds, Bills, and Inflation: Year by Year Historical Returns (1926–1974)." *Journal of Business*, University of Chicago, January 1976.

Ibbotson, Roger G., and Sinquefield, Rex A. "Stock, Bonds, Bills, and Inflation: Simulations of the Future (1976–2000)." *Journal of Business*, University of Chicago, July 1976.

Institute of Chartered Financial Analysts. *Supplementary Readings in Financial Analysis*, vol. 2, 1974. Homewood, Ill.: Richard D. Irwin, Inc., 1973.

———. *Supplementary Readings in Financial Analysis*, vol. 3, 1975. Homewood, Ill.: Richard D. Irwin, Inc., 1974.

Malkiel, Burton G. *A Random Walk down Wall Street*. New York: W. W. Norton & Co., Inc., 1973.

Modigliani, Franco, and Pogue, Gerald A. "An Introduction to Risk and Return." *Financial Analysts Journal*, Part I, March/April 1974, Part II, May/June 1974.

The Rating Game. New York: Twentieth Century Fund, 1974.

'Smith, Adam.' *The Money Game*. New York: Random House, Inc., 1967.

'Smith, Adam.' *Supermoney*. New York: Random House, Inc., 1972.

Valentine, Jerome L. *Investment Analysis and Capital Market Theory*, Occasional Paper No. 1. Charlottesville, Va.: The Financial Analysts Research Foundation, 1975.

Williamson, J. Peter. *Investments: New Analytic Techniques*. New York: Praeger Publishers, Inc., 1970.

REVIEW QUESTIONS AND PROBLEMS

1. How do you account for the decreased popularity of common stock investment over the years since 1969?

2. Explain each of the following: (*a*) "blue chips," (*b*) growth stocks, (*c*) income stocks, (*d*) defensive stocks, (*e*) cyclical stocks, (*f*) speculative stocks.

3. "If you want to make your pile, you've got to be in style," said Eldon Grimm, formerly of Walston & Co. Explain the relevance of this statement to investments.

4. Explain how stock prices exhibit (a) secular, (b) cyclical, and (c) seasonal patterns?

5. Explain the assumed relationship between bond prices, interest rates, and common stock prices.

6. How does the fundamental value approach differ from technical analysis of the market? What is the random walk? How does it apply?

7. Explain each of the following: (a) mortgage bonds, (b) indenture, (c) debenture, (d) equipment trust bond or certificate, (e) convertible bond, and (f) income bond.

8. Explain how an investor can calculate the percentage yield which a bond with fully taxable income must give to provide an after-tax yield equivalent to a given tax-exempt yield.

9. To what types of investment risks are (a) common stock investors subject? (b) bond investors subject?

10. What is the assumed relationship between risk and return? How does "beta analysis" attempt to measure a stock's volatility? How is beta used?

RESEARCH PROJECTS

1. Determine which of the following would have been the most effective hedge against inflation over the past decade: (a) gold stocks, (b) commodities, (c) growth funds (mutual), (d) common stocks generally, (e) growth stocks, (f) real estate, commercial and residential, (g) raw land, (h) old coins, (i) rare stamps, (j) old masters (paintings), (k) modern impressionists (art), (l) other (name and explain).

2. Select five brokerage houses or investment advisory services and ask each how it defines a "growth stock." Ask for a list of their recommended growth stocks. From the replies prepare a composite definition of a growth stock and develop a composite recommended list.

3. Select five brokerage houses or investment advisory services and ask each how it defines a "cyclical stock." From the replies prepare a composite definition of a "cyclical stock" and develop a composite recommended list.

4. Assume that you had invested $10,000 a decade ago in (a) a savings account, (b) long-term U.S. government bonds, (c) selected investment company growth funds, (d) the Dow Jones 30 Industrials, (e) U.S. Treasury bills, (f) S&P municipal bonds, (g) S&P high-grade corporate bonds. What would have been the percentage change over the decade (a) in absolute terms, (b) adjusted for the change in the purchasing power of the dollar?

5. You are the author of a monthly investment club commentary letter. In the light of current conditions in (a) the economy, (b) the stock market, (c) the bond market, (d) the money market, (e) corporate profits, prepare a draft of a monthly letter you would submit for possible publication, summing up current conditions and commenting on the investment outlook over the near future.

Chapter 2

Toward an Efficient National Market System

> Money doesn't bring happiness, but it calms the nerves.
> ——————————————————————— *French Proverb*

At a low point in the market two brokers were walking down the street commiserating with each other about market conditions:

One broker to the other: How are you bearing up under all this? Can you sleep nights?
Second broker: Sure, I sleep like a baby.
First broker: What do you mean, you sleep like a baby?
Second broker: I wake up every three hours and cry.[1]

Over the last decade a whole range of problems have confronted a changing financial marketplace. Disappearance and failure of some leading brokerage houses, the paper glut, the antiquated stock certificate, back office problems, the advent of extensive automation, the computer and the role of the specialist, a central marketplace, a composite tape, the rise of institutional trading, the question of institutional membership on exchanges, negotiated commission rates, block positioning, the proposed automated book, rule 394, the third market and the fourth market, members capital requirements, SIPC (Securities Investors Protection Corporation), box differences, disclosure, fails, give-ups, disintermediation, market governance and structure, the expansion of NASDAQ (National Association of Securities Dealers Automatic Quotation System)—these are but some of the issues and subjects that have received attention in recent years, and many still remain unresolved.

---

[1] Donald T. Regan, *A View from the Street* (New York: The New American Library Inc., 1972).

61

The investment process encompasses a number of markets and many institutions. There is a money market and a capital market. There are primary markets and secondary markets. There are organized exchanges and over-the-counter markets. There are both borrowers and lenders of short- and long-term funds. There are corporations and individuals with surplus funds who may decide either to invest, lend, or save them. There are a variety of financial intermediaries who facilitate the transfer of funds from those who have surpluses to those who need resources for a diversity of purposes, ranging from productive investment to speculative trading.

Sources and Uses of Funds

Perhaps the best overview of the flow of funds in financial markets is obtained from a sources-and-uses-of-funds analysis. One of the best of these is published each year by the Bankers Trust Company of New York.[2] The purpose of the detailed and elaborate analysis, which encompasses 31 tables covering different sectors, is to assess the investment outlook, to study demand and supply conditions in each of the sectors, and to form a basis for judging the probable trend of interest rates in various markets.

A summary of sources and uses of funds is given in Table 2–1. The volume of investment funds raised exceeded by far the volume of short-term funds. Savings institutions, both contractual type and deposit type, provided about 50 percent of the funds supplied; commercial banks were the next largest source. The commercial banks and business corporations channeled their funds into short-term uses in large part, although not wholly, while savings institutions, including life insurance companies, pension funds, savings banks, savings and loan associations funneled their resources largely into investment uses. As you can see it is a very complex structure.

Short-term funds change hands in the money market. It is customary to distinguish between the money and capital markets by saying that the money market is the arena in which claims to funds change hands for from one day up to one year, but not beyond. Money market instruments include promissory notes and bills of exchange, commercial paper, bankers' acceptances, Treasury bills, short-term tax-exempts, dealer paper, and negotiable time certificates of deposit. Institutions participating in the money market include the commercial banks, cor-

---

[2] See *The Investment Outlook for 1976.* A free copy may be obtained by writing to Economics Department, Bankers Trust Company, P.O. Box 318, Church Street Station, New York, N.Y. 10015. Salomon Brothers also publishes an excellent annual *Analysis.* See Henry Kaufman and James McKeon, "Supply and Demand for Credit in 1976."

TABLE 2–1
Summary of Financing—Total Funds (in billions of dollars)

	1970	1971	1972	1973	1974	1975 (est.)	1976 (proj.)
Funds raised							
Investment funds	66.4	101.1	114.7	113.4	111.4	112.3	113.1
Short-term funds	18.3	20.9	42.4	65.2	55.1	2.1	40.3
U.S. government and budget agency securities, privately held	6.9	16.7	20.5	−.4	10.2	77.6	66.5
Total uses	91.6	138.7	177.7	178.2	176.8	192.0	219.9
Funds supplied							
Insurance companies and pension funds							
Life insurance companies	9.0	11.9	13.4	15.9	15.2	17.3	18.6
Private noninsured pension funds	7.7	8.7	9.0	9.2	7.9	13.7	14.0
State and local retirement funds	6.1	6.8	6.8	6.9	7.2	9.2	10.4
Fire and casualty insurance companies	4.0	6.2	6.8	5.8	4.4	4.5	6.5
Total	26.8	33.6	36.0	37.8	34.7	44.7	49.5
Thrift institutions							
Savings and loan associations ...	12.5	28.9	35.8	25.4	18.7	35.1	38.4
Mutual savings banks	4.1	9.8	10.2	4.7	4.1	10.7	8.6
Credit unions	1.6	2.5	3.0	3.7	3.4	5.6	4.8
Total	18.2	41.2	49.0	33.8	26.2	51.4	51.8
Investment companies	1.9	.9	.7	.7	3.0	4.0	5.4
Other financial intermediaries							
Finance companies	.7	3.4	7.9	10.2	5.6	2.0	6.0
Real estate investment trusts	2.1	2.5	4.9	4.5	.9	−2.4	−2.7
Total	2.8	5.9	12.8	14.7	6.5	−.4	3.3
Commercial banks	36.5	49.8	74.6	78.2	59.3	31.0	55.5
Business							
Business corporations	1.9	7.1	6.6	10.0	13.9	15.2	16.8
Noncorporate business	.6	.7	1.1	1.3	.9	.9	1.1
Total	2.5	7.8	7.7	11.3	14.8	16.1	17.9
Government							
U.S. government	.4	.4	.1	−.3	2.4	4.0	2.0
Nonbudget agencies	8.4	3.0	4.5	7.7	12.8	6.8	8.4
State and local general funds	2.1	−1.7	6.9	4.4	2.8	5.8	4.2
Total	10.9	1.8	11.4	11.8	18.1	16.6	14.6
Foreign investors	11.0	27.1	10.6	3.4	10.9	8.8	15.5
Individuals and others	−7.4	−19.3	.9	19.1	28.3	25.7	25.2
Total gross sources	103.2	148.8	203.7	210.8	201.7	197.9	238.7
Less: Funds raised by financial intermediaries							
Investment funds	4.1	6.5	9.2	5.4	5.8	5.9	6.1
Short-term funds	−.8	3.0	13.9	11.2	5.5	−1.7	3.0
Nonbudget agency securities, privately held	8.3	.6	2.9	16.0	13.6	1.7	9.7
Total	11.6	10.1	26.0	32.5	24.9	5.9	18.8
Total net sources	91.6	138.7	177.7	178.2	176.8	192.0	219.9

Source: Bankers Trust Co., New York.

porations (large and small), the Federal Reserve, U.S. government securities dealers, and indeed anyone who lends or borrows on short term, including those who borrow on the collateral of securities to speculate. Activities in the money market range from a one-day loan of several millions by one commercial bank with surplus reserve funds to another which is short of reserves—the federal funds market—to an investor borrowing to buy securities on margin. Corporations with temporarily surplus funds may place them in Treasury bills for 91 or 182 days or in time certificates of deposit tailored to their financial time requirements. The money market is the vital arena in which the Federal Reserve influences the reserve positions of commercial banks, and therefore their capacity to lend, by engaging in open-market operations in U.S. government securities.[3]

In contrast, the capital market focuses on long-term funds. It is convenient to use the generally accepted demarcation line of one year or less maturity for the money market and over one year for the capital market. It is in the capital market that the demand for, and supply of, investment funds are brought together. Savings are converted into investments. The major supply of funds for the capital market is channeled through specialized financial institutions such as insurance companies, pension and retirement funds, and savings institutions. At times dealings between borrowers and lenders may be direct, but often transfers are effected through intermediaries such as investment bankers, stockbrokers, and securities dealers. Instruments in the capital market include, of course, bonds, notes, mortgages, stock, and warrants.

Like the money market, the capital market has many faces. A large corporation borrowing directly from an insurance company is participating in the capital market even though the whole transaction may be arranged by phone. Another corporation borrowing through the facilities of an investment banker who in turn makes use of a selling organization that spans the country is also participating in the capital market. There is a market for corporate bonds, a market for longer term U.S. government issues, a market for state and local bonds— "municipals," a market for corporate equities, and a mortgage market.

---

[3] For further information, see Wesley Lindow, *Inside the Money Market* (New York: Random House, Inc., 1972); also *Money Market Investments: The Risk and the Return* (New York: Morgan Guaranty Trust Co., latest edition); and *Instruments of the Money Market* (Federal Reserve Bank of Richmond, latest edition); *Money Market Investments* (Federal Reserve Bank of Cleveland, latest edition); *Money Market Handbook for the Short Term Investor* (New York: Brown Brothers, Harriman & Co., latest edition); and *The U.S. Government Securities Market*, Government Bond Division, Harris Trust and Savings Bank, (Chicago, latest edition); also Jerome B. Cohen, "Short-Term Investments," *Financial Analyst's Handbook* (Homewood, Ill.: Dow Jones-Irwin, Inc., 1975), chap. 15.

There is an active primary or new issues market as well as large secondary markets. For mortgages, for example, the new issue market is significant and substantial, while the secondary market is negligible. For equities, on the other hand, the new issues market is relatively limited, but the secondary market is large and active. For bonds there is both a large and active new issues market and a substantial secondary market.

Primary and Secondary Markets

Of total new corporate issues, in recent years, 70 percent to 80 percent consists of bonds. The percentage is even higher if U.S. government and state and municipal issues are included. The new issues market is therefore normally mainly a bond market. Securities in this market can be sold either through investment bankers or by private placements. About a third of all new corporate bond issues have been placed privately. Many of the largest firms with the best credit ratings have come to favor this quiet, unobserved method of financing. For large companies the method offers a variety of advantages, though investment bankers claim that the interest cost is somewhat higher than in a public offering. A private placement frees a borrower from the uncertainties of market conditions. Market fluctuations are avoided. For example, as IBM's computer program unfolded, it obtained a $500 million long-term credit from Prudential and drew down the funds from time to time as needed, without having to worry about changing conditions in the financial markets. Also, registration with the SEC was not necessary.

Investment bankers are, however, the traditional middlemen in the capital market. For the most part, they buy the new issue from the borrower at an agreed-upon price, assume a market risk, and hope to resell to the investing public at a higher price. In this respect, they differ from the stockbroker, who usually acts as an agent, earns a commission, and takes no risk. In the sale of certain issues, however, the investment bankers may function more as stockbrokers. Instead of buying the issue they may take it on a "best efforts" basis, accepting a commission for what they are able to sell but not buying the issue themselves. This type of arrangement occurs for the most part in cases that are poles apart. The seller may either be a small company whose securities are too unseasoned to warrant the investment banker's assuming the risk of purchase and redistribution. Or, on the other hand, the seller may be a very large corporation whose securities are so well known that it wants to pay the investment bankers only for their sales efforts and not for assuming the risks of distribution.

If an investment banker is used rather than a private placement,

there is a further choice between a negotiated transaction and competitive bidding. Or there could be a rights offering with or without a standby underwriting. Market risk is greater in competitive bidding. The negotiated transaction can be more readily postponed if a sudden dip in the market should occur. On the other hand, competitive bidding may be less costly to the borrower. In the negotiated transaction, the borrowing company calls in the investment banking house with which it has had favorable previous dealings and probably a long-standing relationship. The investment banking house then works up the issue, develops all the relevant facts, assembles a buying group, sets a price, and arranges to buy the issue. It subsequently forms a selling syndicate to resell or redistribute the issue. In competitive bidding, on the other hand, the borrowing company invites investment bankers to form syndicates to bid for the issue. Certain types of securities, such as state and municipal issues and interstate public utility and railroad securities, must be sold at competitive bidding.

Prices set in the primary market when the new issue appears may thus be negotiated prices, or competitive auction prices, or privately agreed-upon prices. Usually all three take into consideration prevailing prices for comparable or nearly comparable outstanding issues traded in secondary markets. Institutional investment managers are much more involved in prices and purchases in the primary market than are individual investors. While the value analysis of the individual investor is directed toward existing securities and secondary markets, institutional investment managers give substantial attention both to new issue markets and to secondary markets.

Secondary markets for securities—the organized exchanges and the over-the-counter markets—provide the trading forums, the liquidity, the familiarity with issues and companies, and the price and value determinations which encourage public interest in security investment and facilitate new financing. When individuals or institutional investors buy securities, they buy claims to assets or to future income, or to both, and faith in these claims are enhanced or diminished depending on the ease or difficulty of finding a ready market for the claim on short notice, if desired. No doubt many would hesitate to buy securities if they could not count on a ready market if needed. Clearly the development of the now elaborate machinery for trading in existing securities came about in response to a felt need.

The organized exchanges provide physical marketplaces where trading in existing securities occurs. They furnish facilities for the maintenance of a free, close, and continuous market for securities traded—free in that the trading price of any security, in the absence of now illegal manipulation, is governed by the forces of supply and demand; close in that the spread between the bid price for a security

and the price at which it is offered for sale is normally relatively narrow; and continuous in that successive sales ordinarily are made at relatively small variations in price, thus providing a liquid market. Organized exchanges are auction markets with prices set by thousands of buyers and sellers in numerous little auctions occurring daily on the floor of the exchange. The New York Stock Exchange is, of course, the most important, and accounts for about 80 percent of all trading on organized exchanges. The American Stock Exchange ranks next, with the Midwest and Pacific Coast and PBW (Philadelphia, Baltimore, Washington) exchanges of importance.

The over-the-counter market consists of a loose aggregation of brokers and dealers who make a market principally, though not exclusively, for securities not listed on organized exchanges. The term *over-the-counter market* itself is misleading. There are no counters and there is no market in the sense of a given place where buyers and sellers meet to dispose of wares. The over-the-counter market is rather a complex network of trading rooms all over the country, linked by telephone and electronic communications. The phrase is a carry-over from the past, when shares were literally sold over the counter of private banking houses.

Securities transactions on the over-the-counter market run about 60 percent of the volume on all organized exchanges. Most federal, state, and municipal securities, most bonds, and many bank and insurance company stocks are traded over the counter. There is also an over-the-counter market in exchange-listed securities, the so-called third market. Over-the-counter securities are traded in a negotiated rather than an auction market like the organized exchanges. The price at which a given security can be purchased or sold on the over-the-counter market is determined by bargaining, with the broker-dealer usually acting as a principal in the transaction, although sometimes asked to act as agent.

THE REGISTERED EXCHANGES

The New York Stock Exchange

The New York Stock Exchange is almost as old as the country. Established in 1792, it wasn't until 1863 that its name was changed to New York Stock Exchange. The exchange is now a corporation and has 1,366 members who have bought "seats" (memberships) on the exchange. Only members of the exchange are permitted to trade on its "floor." A seat, or membership, has sold for a high as $625,000 (1929) and for as low as $17,000 (1942). The price of membership since 1950 has ranged from $38,000 to $515,000 (1969). The current price is

around $100,000. The securities of more than 1,500 major companies are "listed" on the New York Stock Exchange, which means that they have been accepted for trading. Only those securities which have been accepted for listing may be traded on the exchange floor. Trading takes place between the hours of 10 A.M. and 4 P.M., New York time, Monday through Friday.

Located at the corner of Wall and Broad Streets, physically the exchange floor is almost the size of a football field. On the trading floor are 19 posts, at which some 2,000 listed stock issues are traded, and the "Bond Crowd," where 2,300 bond issues are bought and sold. Much more bond trading takes place in the over-the-counter market than on the floor of the New York Stock Exchange.

Automation has taken over at the Big Board but it is in such a state of flux that what is true today may be obsolete tomorrow. A high-speed ticker capable of printing 900 characters a minute now provides a "composite" tape carrying reports of trades in New York Stock Exchange listed stocks wherever traded, whether on the floor of the NYSE itself, or on the regional exchanges, or in the third market. There is also a "consolidated quotation system." Your broker, using a desk top electronic machine, can know immediately the state of the market in any listed security by simply punching in the stock symbol. Getting an immediate "quote" on a stock you are interested in can be done in a matter of seconds.

If you invest or trade you should learn the stock symbols. "T" stands for American Telephone and Telegraph; "A" for Anaconda Copper; "GE" for General Electric and "GM" for General Motors, but "N" is for Inco. Ltd., "NG" for National Gypsum, "X" for U.S. Steel; "Y" is Alleghany Corp.; and "Z" is F. W. Woolworth & Co. When a broker asks "how's Mickey Mouse?" he's referring to Disney (Walt) Productions (DIS) and if he asks "Knockout" he means Coca-Cola Co. (KO). There are some names derived from symbols that the listed companies themselves abhor—like Slob for Schlumberger (SLB). By logic that has nothing to do with the sound of their ticker symbols, Holiday Inns (HIA) is known as "Hot Beds" and Simmons Co. (SIM), the "world's playground." What the brokers call two AMEX stocks, Fluke Manufacturing Corp. (FKM), and Shaer Shoe Corp. (SHS) you can imagine.[4]

How does a transaction taking place on the floor of the Exchange get onto the ticker tape in seconds or minutes? There is an optical scanner or card reader at each trading post on the floor of the Exchange. The card reader scans optically the details of a transaction marked on a

---

[4] William G. Shepherd, "Playing the Nickname Game," *Business Week*, July 29, 1972, p. 37.

special IBM card by a reporter at the trading post and simultaneously transmits this information electronically—stock symbol, number of shares, and price—to the Exchange's computer center and in turn it is automatically printed on thousands of stock tickers and display devices.

The pneumatic tubes which were used formerly to convey completed transaction information from the trading posts to the ticker room have now gone the way of the horse and buggy and the trolley car. So also have the huge annunciator boards whose flashing or flapping numbers used to summon brokers from the trading posts to their phone and order booths lining the floor in the Exchange. Brokers no longer need to keep their eyes on the annunciator call boards because radio paging is now in effect. Members now carry five-ounce pocket radio receivers which audibly beep and indicate with lights which booth or booths are paging them.

Automated equipment has begun to be used, however, and in the coming central market system and certificateless society, vast changes are at hand. The NYSE and the AMEX have established a joint subsidiary, the Securities Industry Automation Corporation, and it is now engaged in a variety of experimental programs and techniques. Perhaps, just ahead, is the Consolidated Limit Order Book (CLOB), the electronic "black box," which may some day supersede the specialist.[5]

Under pressure from Congress and the SEC, the securities industry is now moving, or being pushed toward a computerized automated national market system. In a most perceptive book, Chris Welles traces past and prospective changes in the securities trading process and concludes that ultimately the NYSE, which has been fighting change at every step, will ultimately give way to an automated national market system. He says:

History, though, does not speak well of the ability of established institutions to achieve revolutionary renewal. As economist Joseph Schumpeter indicated, obsolete institutions afflicted with bureaucratic and ideological arteriosclerosis are seldom able to change; they must die in a "gale of creative destruction" and be replaced by wholly new institutions. It is possible that the New York Stock Exchange can survive the last days of the club. But that possibility is remote.[6]

---

[5] "A National Market System," *A Report by the National Market System Committee* (The Davant Committee) (The New York Stock Exchange, Inc., July 1, 1976), pp. 9–20. See also *Report of the National Market System Committee* (The Gustave Levy Committee) (New York: Securities Industry Association, June 10, 1976), pp. 3–11.

[6] Chris Welles, *The Last Days of the Club* (New York: E. P. Dutton & Co., 1975), p. 332.

There have been a number of proposals for an automated national trading system. One of the most complete is that advanced by Merrill Lynch, Pierce, Fenner and Smith, Inc.[7]

Functions of Members. A member of the New York Stock Exchange may be a general partner or holder of voting stock in one of the brokerage concerns which, by virtue of his or her exchange membership, is known as a member firm or member corporation. There are 508 such member organizations—247 partnerships and 261 corporations. About half the members of the New York Stock Exchange are partners or officers in member organizations doing business with the public— so-called *commission houses.* These members execute customers' orders to buy and sell on the exchange, and their firms receive negotiated commissions on those transactions. Many commission brokerage houses, particularly the larger ones such as Merrill Lynch, Pierce, Fenner & Smith; Bache Halsey Stuart Inc.; and Paine, Webber, Jackson & Curtis have more than one member.

About one fourth of all members of the exchange are *specialists,* so-called because they specialize in "making a market" for one or more stocks.

What exactly do the specialists do? How do they help provide liquidity in the central marketplace? Specialists have two jobs. First, they execute limit orders that other members of the exchange may leave with them. These orders are left with the specialists when the current market price is away from the prices of the limit orders, for instance, when a commission broker receives a limit order to buy at 55 a stock selling at 60. By executing these orders on behalf of other exchange members when the market price reaches the price stated on the orders, the specialists make it possible for these members to transact other business elsewhere on the exchange floor. In handling these orders the specialists act as brokers or agents.

The second, more complex role is that of dealers or principals for their own accounts. As dealers, the specialists are expected, insofar as reasonably practical, to maintain continuously fair and orderly markets in the stocks assigned to them. When there is temporary disparity, for example, between supply and demand, they are expected to buy or sell for their own accounts to narrow price changes between transactions and to give depth to the market. By doing this, they keep price

[7] See *Proposal for a National Market System* (New York: Merrill Lynch, Pierce Fenner & Smith, Inc. 1975); see also Gordon Platt, "Technology Catalyst for Change in the Markets," *The Money Manager,* Boca Raton, Fla., November 29, 1972; Morris Mendelson, "From Automated Quotes to Automated Trading: Restructuring the Stock Market in the United States," *The Bulletin,* Nos. 80–82 (New York: Institute of Finance, Graduate School of Business, New York University, March 1972); Fischer Black, "Toward a Fully Automated Stock Exchange," Part I, *Financial Analysts Journal,* July/ August 1971; Part II, *Financial Analysts Journal,* November/December 1971.

continuity more orderly than would otherwise be the case and contribute to the liquidity of the market. They thus usually make it possible for investors' orders to be executed at better prices when temporary disparity exists.

To maintain the market the specialists usually purchase stock at a higher price than anyone else is willing to pay. For example, let's assume that a stock has just sold at 55. The highest price anyone is willing to pay is 54¼ (the best bid), and the lowest price at which anyone is willing to sell is 55¼ (the best offer). The specialists, acting as dealers for their own accounts, may now decide to bid 54¾ for 100 shares, making the quotation 54¾–55¼, which narrows the spread between the bid and offer prices to ½ point. Now, if a prospective seller wishes to sell 100 shares at the price of the best bid, the specialist will purchase the stock at 54¾. By doing this, the specialist not only provides the seller with a better price, but also maintains better price continuity, since the variation from the last sale is only ¼ of a point.

Here on the other hand, is an example of how the specialists may sell stock for their own accounts to maintain a market. Let's assume that with the last sale in a stock at 62¼ the best bid is 62 and the best offer 63. The specialist offers 500 shares at 62½ for their own account, changing the quotation to 62–62½. A buyer enters the market and buys the stock from the specialist. Thus the buyer purchased the stock ½ point chaper than would have been the case without the specialist's offer.

Many times, when the specialists do not have sufficient stock in their inventories, they will sell "short" to maintain a market. In doing this, they must observe all the rules and regulations governing "short" selling.

Specialists enter limit orders on their "books" under each price category in the sequence in which they are received. For each order the specialists show the number of shares and from whom the orders were received. They represent these orders in the market, frequently competing against other members representing other customers. As they are successful in executing the orders on their books, reports are sent to the members for whom the specialists have acted according to the sequence of listing in their book.

Most of the orders received by brokers on the floor before the opening of the market are left with specialists. Using these orders and also dealing for their own accounts in varying degrees, the specialists arrange the opening price in each stock assigned to them. The opening is expected to be near the previous close unless some startling new development takes place in the interim after the previous close and the coming opening.

In arranging the opening the specialists must consider general market conditions and market conditions in the particular stock. Sometimes unusual situations arise which demand special treatment. Let's assume that XYZ Oil Company Common Stock closed at 39⅞. After the close of the market, however, announcement is made of a new oil strike on land owned by the XYZ Oil Company. This leads to a heavy influx of buy orders the following morning. One of the exchange's floor officials is called into the "crowd" to supervise the situation. All orders to buy and sell are given to the specialist.

Let's say that after a count is made the specialist has orders to purchase 15,000 shares at the market and orders to sell 3,000 shares at the market. (Usually there are also limited orders to buy, but for purposes of simplicity they are eliminated for this example.) The specialist also has limit orders to sell at the following prices:

$$
\begin{array}{r}
700 \text{ at } 40 \\
100 \text{ at } 40\tfrac{1}{8} \\
400 \text{ at } 40\tfrac{1}{4} \\
600 \text{ at } 40\tfrac{1}{2} \\
200 \text{ at } 40\tfrac{3}{4} \\
1{,}500 \text{ at } 41 \\
300 \text{ at } 41\tfrac{1}{2} \\
500 \text{ at } 42 \\
100 \text{ at } 42\tfrac{3}{4} \\
200 \text{ at } 43
\end{array}
$$

Thus an additional 4,600 shares are offered at prices ranging from 40 to 43. If it were decided to open the stock at 43, selling orders, including the market orders to sell, would supply only 7,600 shares of the 15,000 wanted—and at a price over three points higher than the previous close.

This might be considered too great a variation, and so an attempt would be made to narrow the gap between the large demand and the small supply.

To do this, the opening of XYZ Oil Company's stock is delayed, and notice of the delay is printed on the tape. Floor brokers who had left orders with the specialist and others ask, "How's XYZ?" The specialist replies that there are "buyers" in the stock. The floor brokers then relay this information to their member firm offices so that customers will know that XYZ is probably going to open at a higher price than the previous close. Similar information is also passed along by the specialist, to those firms known to have been interested in the security. Registered traders might also be consulted to see whether they wish to sell stock.

After the floor official in charge feels that the situation appears to have crystallized, a quotation is established even though the spread

between the bid and offer prices may be wider than usual. As a result of all this let's assume that 1,000 of the 15,000 shares to buy at the market are canceled. Sellers, however, are attracted by the bid price. They put in orders to sell totaling an extra 1,500 shares.

The floor official and the specialist now reappraise the situation and find that there are 14,000 shares to buy at the market and 4,500 shares to sell at the market, leaving 9,500 shares to buy on balance. The floor official notes that there are limited price orders in the specialist's possession to sell 3,500 shares up through 41. In other words, if the stock opens at 41, 3,500 shares could be sold on the orders limited at 41 or lower, reducing the on-balance amount to buy to 6,000 shares. The floor official learns that the specialist is "long" 2,200 shares, which if sold would reduce the amount to 3,800.

At this point, the specialist and the floor official decide on a quotation of 41 bid, offered at 43. This quotation is published on the ticker tape. It results in only one extra order—500 to sell at 41¼. The floor official then discusses the situation with the specialist to see at what price the specialist would be willing to supply the balance by going "short." As a result of this discussion then, 14,000 shares of XYZ Oil open at 41¼, up 1⅜ points from the previous close. Four thousand shares are sold on behalf of the orders held by the specialist to sell at limits of 41¼ or lower, 4,500 shares are supplied by the market orders to sell, and 5,500 shares by the specialist (known inventory of 2,200 shares and 3,300 shares sold "short").

The exchange sets specific requirements for specialists concerning market experience, their dealer function, and the amount of capital they must possess. Specialists are expected to subordinate their own interests in the market to the public's. Specialists, for example, cannot buy in the exchange market at any price for their own account until they have executed all public buy orders held by them at that price. The same rule also applies to sales by specialists. Specialists on the New York Stock Exchange must now be able to carry 5,000 shares of each stock handled, while on the American Stock Exchange, the specialist must either have a capital of $50,000 or be able to carry 1,000 shares of each stock, whichever is larger.

The specialists' business is concentrated in one or more stocks at one trading post. They "keep the books" in these stocks. They usually have associates or assistants, and one or the other is always at the post during trading hours. Thus the specialists can also act for other brokers who cannot remain at one post until prices specified by their customers' buy and sell orders—either purchases below or sales above prevailing prices—are reached. The specialists must assume full responsibility for all orders turned over to them. Part of the commission the customer pays his or her own broker goes to the specialists when their

services are used, and much of their earnings come from commissions on orders they execute for other brokers.[8]

Because the specialists keep the books in the stock and thus have advanced notice of prospective buy and sell orders at varying prices, and because they can also deal for their own accounts, suspicion has always been raised concerning their objectivity and impartiality and doubts have been expressed about their conflict of interest between making a market and making money for themselves. Their trading practices are carefully supervised but the supervisors, exchange officials or other members, are either their employees[9] or associates. As one of the basic steps toward a national automated market system, competing market makers (another term for specialists) has been started on the NYSE. Also proposed is that an automated computer maintained book, open to the scrutiny of all traders be established. The Merrill Lynch Proposal for a National Market System provides for the latter.

Other members serve as *floor brokers,* assisting busy commission brokers to ensure swift execution of orders. Investors complain if their orders are not handled rapidly and efficiently. Commission brokerage houses are very sensitive to this. One large house advertises:

Unsurpassed floor coverage for fast and efficient executions. Twelve brokers on the floor of the New York Stock Exchange, each with an intimate feel for the market in the stocks he handles because he covers only two trading posts, an average of 125 stocks.

Smaller houses, which have only one member of the firm on the floor of the exchange, need help when orders flow in rapidly or in bunches. They can call upon the floor brokers to take over some of their volume and by this means secure quick execution of orders which might otherwise be delayed. The commission brokerage houses which utilize the services of floor brokers share commissions with them. Floor brokers are still popularly known as "$2 brokers," although the commission they receive for their services has long been above that amount.

There are some 90 members of the New York Stock Exchange, now known as *registered traders,* who use their privilege of being able to engage in transactions on the floor of the exchange, simply to buy and sell for their own accounts. Their transactions must meet certain exchange requirements and must contribute to the liquidity of the mar-

---

[8] For more information, see *The Specialist,* the New York Stock Exchange. For a free copy write to the Publications Division of the New York Stock Exchange, 11 Wall Street, New York, N.Y. 10005. It has been proposed that a system of "competing" specialists be established. See "Mitchum Jones Asks Big Board Approval to Compete as a Specialist in 23 Stocks," *The Wall Street Journal,* June 24, 1976, p. 2.

[9] In the broad sense that as a member of the Exchange, exchange officials are the employees of members, who collectively own the Exchange, which is in effect a private club.

kets in the stocks in which they trade. Registered traders may also be called upon to help expedite the handling of blocks of stock bid for or offered on the exchange.

Listing Requirements. To be listed on the New York Stock Exchange, a company is expected to meet certain qualifications and to be willing to keep the investing public informed on the progress of its affairs. In determining eligibility for listing, particular attention is given to such qualifications as: (*a*) whether the company is national or local in scope; (*b*) its relative position and standing in the industry; (*c*) whether it is engaged in an expanding industry, with prospects of at least maintaining its relative position.

While each application for *initial listing* is judged on its own merits, the exchange generally requires the following as a minimum:

a. Demonstrated earning power under competitive conditions of $2.5 million annually before taxes, for the most recent year and $2 million for each of the two preceding years.
b. Net tangible assets of $16 million, but greater emphasis will be placed on the aggregate market value of the common stock.
c. A total of $16 million in market value of publicly held common stock.
d. A total of 1,000,000 common shares publicly held.
e. 2,000 holders of 100 shares or more.

As a matter of general policy, the exchange has for many years refused to list nonvoting common stocks, and all listed common stocks have the right to vote.

There is no absolute right of *continued listing*. The exchange may at any time suspend or delist a security when it feels that continued trading is not advisable. For example, the exchange would normally give consideration to suspending or removing from a list a common stock of a company when there are:

a. Less than 1,200 round-lot shareholders.
b. 600,000 shares or less in public hands.
c. $5 million or less aggregate market value of publicly held shares.
d. $8 million or less in aggregate market value of all outstanding common stock or net tangible assets applicable thereto, combined with an earnings record of less than an average of $600,000 after taxes for the past three years.

Of the approximately 1,700,000 publicly and privately held corporations filing reports with the U.S. Treasury, 30,000 have their shares quoted over-the-counter; about 11,000 have sufficiently wide ownership to be considered publicly owned; and 2,900 are listed or traded on stock exchanges. The NYSE currently lists the common

stock of 1,500 corporations but these include most of the larger, nationally known companies. They earn about 90 percent of total corporate income.

The American and Regional Stock Exchanges

AMEX, sometimes called the "Little Big Board," is located a few blocks away from the NYSE. Founded in the 1850s, it was known as the New York Curb Exchange until its name was changed in 1953. Its earlier name resulted from the fact it was an outdoor market from its origin until 1921, its members conducting trading along the curb on Broad and Wall Streets. Brokers' clerks sat or leaned out of second-story windows of office buildings lining the street and by the use of hand signals conveyed orders and messages to their brokers on the street down below. The brokers wore picturesque hats of various bright multicolored hues, so they could be distinguished from each other and recognized by their clerks in the second-story windows. Occasionally a clerk, in eagerness to attract the attention of his broker, gestured so vigorously that he lost his balance and fell out of a window, but the market went on, grew and prospered, and finally moved into its own building in 1921. One of the most colorful sights of old New York disappeared. Yet even today the hand signals survive, and a visitor to the American Stock Exchange can watch the rather esoteric. hand signals between the telephone clerks in tiers around the floor of the exchange and brokers milling around the various trading posts.[10]

Basically procedures on the American Stock Exchange are much like those on the New York Stock Exchange. The listing requirements follow those of the NYSE but are not as stringent. While some stable old-line companies are listed on the AMEX, generally the companies listed are less mature and seasoned than those listed on the NYSE. Indeed, the AMEX has served as a kind of proving ground for newer companies, many of which, as they grow and expand, transfer their listing to the NYSE. Thus, for example, both Du Pont and General Motors were in their earlier days first traded on the AMEX. Starting in 1976, dual listing of shares on both NYSE and AMEX was permitted in yet another move toward a central market system.

Many of the stocks on the AMEX are low priced (the average is about $15 per share versus approximately $55 on the Big Board), and many trade in round lots of 10, 20, and 50 shares, instead of the customary hundred. Unlike the New York Stock Exchange, the AMEX permits trading in some 60 unlisted companies. Specialists are granted the right by the American Stock Exchange to make a market in certain

---

[10] See Robert Sobel, *The Curbstone Brokers: The Origins of the American Stock Exchange* (New York: The Macmillan Co., 1970).

issues, even though the companies have not applied for listing privileges. There is also considerable trading in foreign securities on the AMEX. The AMEX, in fact, originated the ADR—American Depositary Receipts—by means of which American investors can trade in claims to foreign securities, the shares themselves being held by U.S. banks abroad. Many large commission brokerage houses hold membership on both the AMEX and the NYSE.

The AMEX has been automating as rapidly as the NYSE and in cooperation with it and the Securities Industry Association has suggested that the two exchanges merge both for enhanced efficiency and as an economy measure to cut costs. Such a move would be one of the logical steps toward the desired central marketplace for securities.[11]

The Regional Exchanges. Over the last decade the regional exchanges expanded their proportion of total shares sold on registered exchanges. By 1975 their share of total volume traded was a little more than 11 percent, while their proportion of total value of shares traded reached 12 percent.

The three principal regional exchanges are the Midwest Stock Exchange (MSE), the Pacific Coast Stock Exchange (PCSE), and the Philadelphia-Baltimore-Washington (PBWSE) exchange. The Midwest Stock Exchange is the result of the consolidation of former exchanges in Chicago, Cleveland, St. Louis, and Minneapolis–St. Paul. Its trading floor and principal office are in Chicago with branches in Cleveland and St. Louis connected to Chicago by wire. Over a third of the member organizations of the MSE are also members of the NYSE, and over 90 percent of the issues traded on the MSE are also traded on either the NYSE or the AMEX.

The Pacific Coast Stock Exchange resulted from a consolidation in 1957 of the San Francisco and Los Angeles Stock Exchanges. It has two divisions, one in San Francisco and one in Los Angeles, each with its own trading floor, interconnected by an extensive communications system. The PCSE has the largest volume of shares traded of all regional exchanges. About one third of the PCSE member firms are members of the NYSE, and over 90 percent of its stocks are those traded on either the NYSE or the AMEX. Because of the time differential, the PCSE provides trading facilities after the close of the NYSE and AMEX.

Generally the larger regional exchanges list some 600 to 900 companies each, while the smaller ones list about 100 companies each.

---

[11] "Brokers' Group Urges Big Board and Amex Merge," *The Wall Street Journal*, December 1, 1972. For further information on the operation of the American Stock Exchange, see its publications "Market for Millions," "The American Investor," and "Amex Databook." Copies can be obtained by writing to the American Stock Exchange, 86 Trinity Place, New York, N.Y. 10006.

The companies listed are for the most part regional or local concerns, but there is extensive trading in securities listed on the NYSE or the AMEX. Such shares usually enjoy unlisted trading privileges on the regional exchanges. Odd lots are a larger part of total trading volume on regional exchanges than on the NYSE. For dually traded issues, transactions on the regional exchanges are usually based on the prices and quotations of the NYSE or the AMEX. The NYSE, AMEX, MSE, PCSE, and PBWSE account for 99 percent of the dollar volume and 99 percent of the share volume of securities traded on all exchanges.[12]

EXECUTION OF TRANSACTIONS ON THE EXCHANGES

Types of Orders

Most generally used is the *market* order. When a customer places an order "at the market," it means that the commission broker is authorized to execute the order at the best possible price that can be obtained at the time the order reaches the post at which the stock is traded: in brief, at the then prevailing market price or close thereto. Probably about 75 percent to 85 percent of all orders are market orders. They can be executed very quickly. Market orders are perhaps more common in sales than in purchases, since the seller is usually more anxious to obtain action than the buyer.

When the buyer or seller wishes to specify the price at which the order is to be executed, a *limit order* is placed. The broker is expected to execute it at the limit set or better. If it is a buy order, this means either at the price specified or lower, while if it is a sell order, at the price specified or higher. It may be that the order cannot, at the time given, be executed at the price specified. In that case the customer will have to wait until the market gets around to that price. Naturally the floor member of the commission brokerage house given the order to execute cannot wait at the trading post until the market moves to the specified price. This may take days, or weeks, or may never occur at all. Instead of waiting, the commission broker gives the order to the specialist in the stock. It is immediately entered in the specialist's book. If and when, minutes, or hours, or days, or weeks, or months later, the market price moves to the price specified in the limit order, and it is still in effect, the specialist will execute the order at the price specified and notify the commission broker, who in turn will notify the customer.

---

[12] For further information, see *Regional Stock Exchanges in a Central Market System*, Occasional Paper of the National Bureau of Economic Research, vol. 2, no. 3 (*New York*, Summer 1975); also *Institutional Investors Study Report of the Securities and Exchange Commission*, vol. 4 (92d Cong., 1st sess., House Document No. 92–64, Part 4 [Washington, D.C., March 10, 1971]).

How an Order is Handled

Perhaps routine auction market operations will be clearer if we trace a typical order. Assume that Anne Wilton of New Orleans decides to buy 100 shares of American Telephone and Telegraph Company. She asks the member firm's registered representative to find out for her what AT&T shares are selling for on the exchange. Employing an electronic interrogation device which has instant access to a computer center that receives current market data from the Exchange, the representative reports that "Telephone" is quoted at "50 to a quarter." This means that, at the moment, the highest bid to buy AT&T stock is $50 a share, the lowest offer to sell is $50.25 a share. Ms. Wilton thus learns that a round lot—100 shares—will cost her about $5,000 plus commission. She decides to buy. The registered representative writes out an order to buy 100 shares of T "at the market." This is transmitted to the New York office at once and phoned from the firm's New York office to its clerk in a phone booth on the floor of the exchange. The clerk summons the firm's member partner and gives him the order. Each stock listed on the exchange is assigned a specific location at one of the trading posts, and all bids and offers must take place at that location. The floor partner hurries over to Post 15 where T is traded.

About the same time a Minneapolis grain merchant, Edward Hardy, decided he wants to sell his 100 shares of Telephone. He calls his broker, gets a "quote," tells his broker to sell. That order, too, is wired or phoned to the floor. Hardy's broker also hurries to Post 15. Just as he enters, the AT&T "crowd," he hears Ms. Wilton's broker calling out, "How's Telephone?" Someone—usually the specialist—answers, "50 to a quarter."

Ms. Wilton's broker could, without further thought, buy the 100 shares offered at 50¼, and Mr. Hardy's broker could sell his 100 at 50. In that event, and if their customers had been looking over their shoulders, they probably would have said, "Why didn't you try to get a better price for us?" And they would have been right. Ms. Wilton's broker should reason: "I can't buy my 100 shares at 50. Someone has already bid 50, and no one will sell at that price. I could buy at 50¼ because someone has already offered to sell at that price but no one has come forward to buy. Guess I'd better try 50⅛." Mr. Hardy's broker reasons: "I can't sell my shares at 50¼ because someone has already tried and no one will buy them. I could sell at 50 but why don't I try 50⅛?" At that moment he hears Ms. Wilton's broker bid 50⅛ and instantly he shouts: "Sold 100 at 50⅛." They have agreed on a price and the transaction takes place.

The two brokers complete their verbal agreement by noting each other's firm name and reporting the transaction back to their phone

clerks so that the respective customers can be notified. At the moment the transaction took place, an exchange reporter noted it on a card and placed the card in the optical card reader at the post. This transmitted the report of the transaction to the exchange's Computer Center and to the ticker. Automatically in a few seconds it appears as T 50⅛ on some 12,000 tickers and display devices all over the United States and Canada. In two or three minutes the buyer in New Orleans and the seller in Minneapolis are notified of the transaction. In a transaction on an organized exchange when you buy, you buy from another person. When you sell, you sell to another person. The exchange itself neither buys, nor sells, nor sets prices. It merely provides the marketplace, the physical setting, and the equipment. Prices are determined in "double auction," a number of prospective buyers and a number of prospective sellers bidding in an active market.

Special Types of Orders

Do you know what a W.O.W. order is? It is one of the numerous special types of orders, but you won't need to know about it until you buy your seat on the exchange. There are a few special types of orders, however, that are important.

Stop orders may be used in an effort to protect a paper profit or to try to limit a possible loss. There are stop orders to sell and stop orders to buy. They are essentially conditional market orders. They go into effect if something happens. For example, you bought IBM at 150 and now it is 300. You want to continue to hold it as long as it keeps going up, but you want to protect your gain in case the market turns down. You place a stop order to sell at, say, 290, 10 points below the current market. If the market turns down and goes to 290 or lower, your stock will be sold. Though you lose the last 10 points of your stock's climb, you preserve all the rest of the gain.

Or, to take another use, you note that General Motors is selling at 62. You think and hope it's going up farther and then split. You buy 100 shares at 62 but at the same time place a stop order to sell at 60. If your guess is incorrect and GM falls instead of rising, you will be out of it with a 2-point loss, plus commissions.

The stop order to buy is used in a short sale to limit losses. You sell Celanese short at 60. You expect and hope that it will decline to 40. If it does, you will cover at that time and have a 20-point gain. But there is also the possibility that it may go up farther. To cut your possible loss, if it does, you place a stop order to buy at 65. Thus if the stock goes up contrary to your expectation, you will have bought back and covered at 65, and your loss will be held to 5 points.

The investor is not assured of getting the exact price designated by the stop order. If the market takes a sudden drop, the specialist sells the stock at whatever can be obtained; and that might be somewhat below the stop price. If you place a stop-loss order at 50, an accumulation of prior sell orders at this price, or a sharp drop in the market, may prevent the specialist from executing your order until the price is somewhere below 50. There is, however, a hybrid version called the *stop-limit order*. This enables the investor to stipulate the maximum or minimum price acceptable for purchase or sale. If the specialist cannot execute at that price or better, no transaction takes place.

At times the New York Stock Exchange has become worried about stop-loss orders in high-flying glamour stocks, because a downward dip in the market could set off a chain of stop orders and by enlarging sales cause a sharp break in the given stock or stocks. It has, therefore, from time to time, suspended the placement of stop orders in designated stocks to prevent undue market repercussions.

Both stop-limit and stop-loss orders may be day, week, month, or "open" (GTC) orders. A market order is always a day order, good until the close of trading on the day it is written. When you give your broker a limit or stop order, you can specify that it is to be good for only one day—or for a week—or for a month. If the order is not executed during the period designated, it automatically expires. An open or GTC order is one that holds good indefinitely. The order holds until either the broker executes it or the customer cancels it. GTC means "good till cancelled."

A discretionary order is one which allows the broker to determine when to buy and when to sell, what to buy, what to sell, in what volume and when. This is a complete discretionary order. It must be given in writing by the customer and approved by a member of the firm. A limited discretionary order permits the broker to determine only the price and timing. Discretionary orders are used by those who are ill, aged, or off on a prolonged vacation. A long and close relationship with a reputable broker is a basic requirement for the use of such orders.

What It Costs to Buy and Sell Stocks

Until 1971–72 the NYSE was able to maintain a fixed rate structure for all transactions regardless of amount. Membership was limited and it was able to require all members to charge fixed rates depending on the price of the stock and the number of shares involved. Pressure on the fixed-fee system came from Congress, from the SEC, and especially from institutional investors. Institutions have pressed either for

membership on exchanges or for negotiated commissions. Obviously an order that is 10 times as large as a round lot (100 shares) does not involve 10 times as much overhead—telephoning, bookkeeping, execution, and delivery costs. Yet until recently, commission charges on a 1,000-share order were 10 times as large as the fees on the 100-share (round-lot) order. As a result of institutional pressures commissions became competitive (negotiated) on transactions of $500,000 and over in 1971 and this was lowered to $300,000 or more in 1972. On May 1, 1975 all fixed commission rates were abolished and commissions became competitive (negotiated).

With the move to competitive rates in 1975 the chief beneficiaries were the institutional investors. Discounts of up to 60 percent off the old fixed rates were granted on large transactions, according to the financial press.[13]

In its first report to Congress on changes in commission rates, the SEC noted that "rates paid by institutions are lower for each order size category, declining about 15 percent for small orders and about 28 percent for the largest orders. . . . In contrast, rates paid by individuals have changed relatively little . . . rates remain relatively stable except on the very largest orders. Rates have increased on small orders by about 4 percent and are down almost 44 percent for orders of 10,000 or more shares."[14] Examples of reductions in commission rates may be seen in Figure 2–1.

The small investor was benefited by the rise of the retail discount house. Prior to May Day (May 1, 1975) discounters offered substantial reductions from fixed rates and since then they have made their rates even more attractive.

Settlement

After a transaction has taken place on the floor of the exchange, shares must be delivered from seller or buyer, and funds must pass the other way. The customary standard procedure in the absence of any agreement to the contrary is for delivery of certificates and cash to be made by noon of the fifth business day following the day of the transaction. Thus, transactions on Tuesday require delivery by noon on the following Tuesday, since Saturday and Sunday are not counted as they are not business days. Holidays are not counted either.

[13] "Cutting of Brokerage Rates on Big Trades Escalates into All-Out War among Firms," *The Wall Street Journal*, May 23, 1975, p. 30; "Rate War Rages among Brokers," *New York Times*, May 30, 1975, p. 1.

[14] Securities and Exchange Commission, *Report to Congress on the Effect of the Absence of Fixed Rates of Commissions* (Washington, D.C., February 5, 1976); see also A. B. Lechner and D. J. Londoner, "Brokerage Profits after May Day," *Financial Analysts Journal*, January/February, 1976.

FIGURE 2–1
Effective Commission Rates for All Trades since April 1975
(NYSE member-firms—overall)

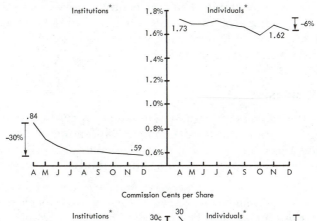

Commissions as Percent of Principal Value

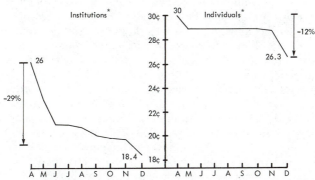

Commission Cents per Share

* Where institutional and individual customers cannot be precisely
identified, COD business is defined as institutional, and all other business
as individual.
    Note: Data for December are preliminary.
    Source: Survey of Commission Charges on Brokerage Transactions,
Branch of Securities Industry and Self-Regulatory Economics, Directorate
of Economic and Policy Research, Securities and Exchange Commission,
March 29, 1976.

In addition to *regular way* settlements, there are two other principal
forms, *cash contracts* and *seller's option*. A *cash contract* calls for
immediate delivery. A transaction for cash made before 2 P.M. on a
given day requires delivery before 2:30 P.M. on the same day. If the
transaction occurs after 2 P.M., delivery must be made within a half
hour. There are a variety of special circumstances which dictate a cash
contract, but three are recurrent. They involve expiration of tax years,
rights, and conversion privileges. To establish a capital loss on December 30 or 31, a cash transaction is required, because a regular way

contract would bring delivery and settlement into the following year. A cash contract is necessary to acquire rights on the last day of the period for which they run. When convertible securities are called for redemption, cash contracts are necessary the last three days the conversion feature is available. The cash contract must be specified at the time the transaction occurs and calls for same day settlement. *Seller's option* is a form of settlement contract which gives the seller, at his or her option, up to 60 days to deliver.

Recent Problems

While the various rules and regulations regarding delivery and clearance are straightforward enough, conforming to the rules has been quite a problem in recent years. Donald Regan, the chairman of America's largest brokerage firm has described it this way.[15]

The Street was caught in a paper blizzard. Paper came in through the doors and windows, and sometimes seemed to come down through cracks in the ceiling and up through the floor as well. . . . Fails were only one of the results.[16] Serious as they are, most fails do get straightened out in time. The resolution of a fail may take weeks or months and may raise the blood pressures of broker, transfer agent, and customer, but still, most fails are cleared up eventually, usually within 30 days.

A couple of other complications are graver and even harder to resolve. These are shortages of securities, called "box differences"[17] and the cousin of box differences, "dividend differences."[18] No one will ever know the precise value of missing securities in these [1969–1970] days of crisis and chaos. The record keeping was so complex and was so incredibly tangled at the time that quantities of securities missing simply can't be determined.

But in my judgment there was at least one day in 1969 when, if you had taken all the securities in all of the vaults in all of the member firms and banks on the Street and counted them, and checked the count against the record, you would have found differences in the range of half a billion dollars.

Automation of back offices finally brought the problem under control. Trading volume in January–February 1976—by far the busiest

---

[15] Regan, *A View from the Street*, pp. 105–6.

[16] A fail to deliver occurs when a broker does not deliver the certificate representing a stock or a bond sold for a customer within the required time period (now five business days). A fail to receive occurs when a broker does not receive the securities bought for a customer within the period. An aged fail is one 30 or more days old. Total fails reached their peak of $4.1 billion in December 1968.

[17] "Box differences" are shortages (or overages) in the inventory of securities in a broker's vaults. Box differences arise when the securities in the broker's possession differ from the securities that his records indicate should be there.

[18] The usual reasons for dividend differences are that the securities deposited with the broker have not been transferred into the broker's name, or that the broker or paying agent has inaccurate records on the amount of stock the broker should be holding.

ever—soared to over 700 million shares. All prior trading records were broken on February 20, 1976 when volume rose to 44.5 million shares in one day. Wall Street took it all in stride and managed the paperwork without noticeable difficulty.

The paper glut of 1968–69 was followed by a capital crisis in 1970 and again in 1973–74. More than 160 NYSE member organizations— and an undisclosed but presumably large number of non-NYSE brokerage firms—went out of business. Most of the NYSE firms either merged with or were acquired by other NYSE firms—quite often through arrangements facilitated or initiated by the Exchange itself. Some 80 firms dissolved, retired from the securities business or self-liquidated. A number of well-known brokerage houses disappeared.[19]

To meet the crisis a number of steps were taken. Prior to the revision of the Exchange's capital rules in 1971, member firms carrying public accounts were required to have at least $1 of net capital for every $20 of aggregate indebtedness—i.e., a "net capital ratio" of 20:1. In 1971 this was changed to 15:1, which meant that a NYSE member organization had to maintain a minimum of $1 of net capital for every $15 of aggregate indebtedness. Also the *minimum* net capital which must be maintained by firms carrying public accounts was doubled—from $50,000 to $100,000. *Initial* net capital required of firms seeking to carry public accounts was raised from $60,000 to $200,000, or to 200 percent of the amount that must be maintained. Additionally all capital contributed to member firms must remain at the firm's disposal for at least one year and six months' notice was required of a contributor's intention to withdraw.[20]

The Security Investors Protection Act of 1970 established the Security Investors Protection Corporation (SIPC, pronounced Sipic) to cover certain investors' losses should it again become necessary to liquidate broker-dealer firms. Generally speaking, the corporation will protect customers against losses of up to $50,000 of securities held for them by a broker-dealer, and $20,000 of cash. Where both are involved and the claim is over $50,000, only $50,000 will be paid. The securities industry, through assessments by SIPC on its member firms, is the principal source of SIPC funds. However, SIPC may borrow up to $1

---

[19] See Welles, *The Last Days of the Club*, especially Part II, Chapter 5: "The Great Crisis: How the Club Nearly Destroyed Itself through Incompetence, Inefficiency, and Resistance to Change Induced by Monopoly Profits"; Chapter 6: "Case Studies of the Great Crisis: The Rise, Decline, and Fall of McDonnell and Dempsey-Tegler"; Chapter 7: "The Rescuers, the Rise and Fall of Ross Perot and du Pont, the Fall of Weis, the Great Malaise"; and Chapter 8: "The Struggle over the New Marketplace: The Exchange's Fight to Preserve Itself against Economic Change, the Determination of Reformers, and the Onrush of Technology," pp. 125–334.

[20] "Net Capital Rules to Be Uniform under SEC Plan," *The Wall Street Journal*, December 6, 1972.

billion from the U.S. Treasury through the SEC if the Commission determines that such a loan is necessary for the protection of customers and the maintenance of confidence in U.S. securities markets.[21]

BUYING ON MARGIN AND SELLING SHORT

Pay Cash or Buy on Margin?

Stock can be purchased for cash or on margin. When you buy on margin, you put up only part of the purchase price, and the broker lends you the remainder. What part you put up and what part you can borrow is not a matter of negotiation. It is determined by the Federal Reserve System, but the New York Stock Exchange also has its own requirements in addition. The Federal Reserve is involved because it is charged with control and regulation of the volume of credit. Under Regulation T, it controls the initial extension of credit to customers by members of national securities exchanges and by other brokers or dealers. Under Regulation U, the Federal Reserve regulates loans by banks for the purpose of purchasing and carrying stocks registered on national securities exchanges. Most unregistered securities can only be purchased on a cash basis.

Since the Federal Reserve Board first set margin requirements in 1934, the amount of margin which a purchaser of listed securities has been required to deposit has ranged from 40 percent to 100 percent of the purchase price. Today the margin rate is 50 percent.

To understand margin fully you must know the difference between *initial* margin and *maintenance* margin, *debit balance* and *equity*, *undermargined* and *restricted* account. The Federal Reserve's present 50 percent requirement is an *initial* margin. It applies only to the day of purchase. The *maintenance* margin applies to the account after the day of the transaction. The New York Stock Exchange has both an initial and a maintenance margin. The former is very simple. There must be an initial equity or $2,000 in the account, not to exceed the price of the shares purchased. The maintenance margin requirement is 25 percent of the current market value of the securities long in the account. When a customer buys securities on margin, puts up part of the purchase price and borrows the remainder from his broker, the securities bought become *collateral* for the loan and must be left with the broker. The collateral is normally carried in the broker's (Street) name but is the purchaser's property. He is entitled to receive dividends and to vote the stock.

---

[21] For a brochure entitled "An Explanation of the Securities Investor Protection Act of 1970," write to Securities Investors Protection Corporation, 485 L'Enfant Plaza, S.W., Suite 2150, Washington, D.C. 20024.

By *debit balance* is meant the net amount owed to the broker. At the outset it is usually the amount of the loan. Interest is charged on the debit balance. *Equity* is the value of the collateral minus the debit balance. Margin then can be described as the equity expressed in dollars or as a percentage of the current market value of the securities. For example, if you purchase 100 shares at $100 per share, or a total of $10,000 worth of stock on margin, assuming a 70 percent margin you put up $7,000 and you borrow $3,000 from the broker. Your margin is $7,000 or 70 percent. Your debit balance is $3,000 (ignoring commissions). Equity is the current market value ($10,000) minus the current debit balance ($3,000) which is $7,000. In percentage terms, then, margin can be expressed as:

$$\text{Margin} = \frac{\text{Value of collateral} - \text{Debit balance}}{\text{Value of collateral}}$$

or

$$\text{Margin} = \frac{\text{Equity}}{\text{Value of collateral}}$$

Now, suppose that the stock falls to 80. The value of the collateral is now $8,000 instead of $10,000; equity is $5,000 ($8,000 − $3,000); the margin has fallen to 62½ percent, the debit balance remaining at $3,000, of course. If the stock falls to 40, the value of the collateral becomes $4,000, the equity shrinks to $1,000, the margin falls to 25 percent, with the debit balance remaining at $3,000. Thus in this case the stock can drop 60 percent in market value before the New York Stock Exchange's maintenance margin is reached.

A simple method of determining the minimum security position in the account is 4/3 rds of the debit balance.[22] This applies only to long positions. Thus:

$$\text{4/3 rds of } \$3,000 = \$4,000$$

On a market value of $15,000 and a debit balance of $4,500, the equity would be $10,500. Applying the 4/3 rds method to $4,500, we get $6,000. This is the security value to which the account could fall without requiring additional equity. And 25 percent of the $6,000 security value is $1,500, which is the minimum maintenance margin.

An *undermargined* account is one which falls below the New York Stock Exchange's maintenance margin requirements. It results in a call for more margin. While brokerage practice varies, it is customary

---

[22] According to the New York Exchange staff.

to call for an increase in the equity to about 35 percent of the then current market value of the collateral. An *unrestricted* account is one in which the equity equals or exceeds the Federal Reserve's initial margin requirement. The excess equity can be withdrawn in cash or in securities of equivalent loan value. To revert to our previous example. If the market price of the shares went from the initial purchase price of 100 to 120, the value of the collateral would be $12,000, the debit balance $3,000, the equity would thus be $9,000, or $600 more than 70 percent of $12,000. For the customer to make a withdrawal, the broker must refigure the account, and the 70 percent margin applies to the $12,000 market value to determine the excess margin for the purpose of making the withdrawal. Thus the customer could withdraw $600 in cash from his account or could use it as margin to buy an additional $857 worth of stock.

A *restricted* account is one that has less equity than the Federal Reserve's initial margin requirement demands. In our earlier case, where the price of shares dropped from 100 to 80, the margin at 80 was 62½ percent. Since this was less than the assumed Federal Reserve's requirement, the account became restricted. The Federal Reserve has no objection to restricted accounts, but certain limitations on additional transactions are applied to them. The difference, then, between an undermargined account and a restricted account should be clear. The undermargined account is one that has fallen below the New York Stock Exchange's maintenance margin requirement. It results in a margin call. The restricted account, on the other hand, is one that has fallen below the Federal Reserve's initial margin requirement. It results in certain restrictions on subsequent transactions in the account.

Margin requirements also apply to short sales. The Federal Reserve's initial margin requirement applies to both long and short transactions. Under a 70 percent margin requirement, therefore, if you want to sell $8,000 worth of stock short, you must provide $5,600. Contrary to what happens in a long margin transaction, when the percentage margin decreases as the price of the stock falls, in short selling margins, as the price of the stock falls, the percentage margin increases. Thus, if you sold 100 shares short at 80 and put up $5,600 and the shares fall to 68, your margin rises to 100 percent. A formula has been developed which will help to explain this.[23]

$$\text{Margin} = \left(\frac{\text{Net proceeds of sale + Initial margin}}{\text{Current market value of stock}} - 1.00 \right) \times 100$$

[23] See Edward Willett, *Fundamentals of Securities Markets*, rev. ed. (New York: Appleton-Century-Crofts, 1971).

Therefore, at a current market price of 68, the $5,600 deposited at the time of sale at 80, will bring your margin to 100 percent:

$$\text{Margin} = \left(\frac{8,000 + 5,600}{6,800} - 1 \right) \times 100 = 100\%$$

Conversely, as the stock price rises, margin in a short sale falls percentagewise. Thus, if the stock price goes up to 100, the margin drops to 36 percent as follows:

$$\text{Margin} = \left(\frac{8,000 + 5,600}{10,000} - 1 \right) \times 100 = 36\%$$

Should the stock rise above 104, at which point the margin would have fallen to 30 percent, the New York Stock Exchange's maintenance margin requirements for short sales would come into play, resulting in a call for more margin.

The purpose of buying on margin, of course, is to stretch your funds. You can command more shares on margin with a given amount of funds than if you pay cash. If the stock rises in price, your profits are enhanced. On the other hand, if the stock goes down and you cannot put up more margin, assuming that you are long, and you are forced to sell, or are sold out, you can lose more than you would if you had used the same amount of money to buy the stock for cash. With a 50 percent margin you can buy twice as many shares as in a cash transaction. With a 25 percent margin you can buy four times as many. The principle of leverage comes into play. By operating with other people's money, the opportunity for profit or loss is magnified. This may be seen in Table 2–2. Keep in mind, however, that if the chance for profit is increased two- or fourfold, the change for loss also increases too.

TABLE 2–2
Relative Gain or Loss under Different Margin Requirements

Requirement for Margin	Funds Advanced by Buyer	Amount of Credit Needed	Number of Shares Purchased at $50 Each	Per Share Change in Market Value	Profit (+) or Loss (−) Involved
10%	$1,000	$9,000.00	200.00	±$5	±$1,000.00
20	1,000	4,000.00	100.00	± 5	± 500.00
50	1,000	1,000.00	40.00	± 5	± 200.00
75	1,000	333.33	26.67	± 5	± 133.33
100	1,000	0.00	20.00	± 5	± 100.00

Bull or Bear: Long or Short?

Where the expressions first arose we don't know, but a "bull" market is a rising market; a "bear" market is a falling market. A "bull" in

Wall Street is an optimist, one who expects the market to go up. A "bear" is, of course, just the opposite, a pessimist who expects stock prices to decline. To take advantage of his forecast, a bull buys stock today in the hope of selling it later at a higher price. He goes *"long."* The bear, on the other hand, expecting the market to go down, *"sells short"*; that is, he sells stock today in the hope of buying it back at a lower price, thus profiting from the decline.

Short selling in the securities market basically is selling shares you don't own and borrowing the same number of shares to deliver to the purchaser. When you buy the stock later to return to the lender, you hope to do so at a lower price, thus making a profit. How is it possible to sell something you don't own and buy it back later? In securities markets the short sale is possible as long as you can borrow the shares you have sold and deliver them to the buyer. Almost always you can do this, because your broker can borrow the stock either from some left in "Street names" with him, from some of his other customers, or from some other broker. Why are these people willing to lend? Because it is usually to their financial advantage. When you sell short and borrow a hundred shares, say of General Motors, to deliver to the purchaser, he, in turn, pays for the stock. You, the short seller, receive payment. If General Motors was selling at 100, you receive $10,000 (less costs). But you can't keep this $10,000.[24] You have to give it to the person or firm that loaned the 100 shares of General Motors. They hold it as collateral for the loan. When you return the shares, you get your funds back. Meanwhile they can use the money, lend it out at short-term and get the prevailing interest, or use it to buy more stock, or for any other purpose. Since stock involved in a short sale now usually lends "flat," no fee attached, no charge, whereas the use of the cash turned over as collateral may bring a return, it is financially advantageous to lend stock, and that is why short sellers can function. The loan can be "called" at any time by either side. The borrower of the stock can ask for his funds back and return the shares, or the lender of the stock can ask for the shares back and return the funds, at any time.

If you are alert, several possible dilemmas may have suggested themselves. What, for example, if the lender of the stock wants his shares back, and you are not yet ready to close the short sale? Very simple. You borrow 100 shares of General Motors from someone else. Suppose that General Motors rises to 110 and thus the stock is worth $11,000, but the money collateral given was only $10,000. The lender of the shares will call for more money collateral to support the loan. This is called "mark to the market." You, the short seller, will have to

---

[24] The short seller must also provide the prevailing percentage margin.

provide an additional $1,000, either from your own resources or by borrowing it. Conversely, if the stock price falls to $90 from the original $100—the short seller can and will ask for $1,000 of his cash collateral back. Both sides must "mark to the market."

Another problem may occur to you. Suppose that a dividend is declared while the short sale is underway. Who is entitled to the dividend? It would seem as if two parties are, since seemingly two parties "own" the shares—the party to whom you sold the shares and the lender from whom you borrowed the shares you sold. Actually, both parties get the dividend. General Motors pays the dividend to the registered owner, and the short seller pays the dividend to the lender. Usually, this is not an extra cost to the short seller because when the stock goes "ex-dividend," the market price of the stock drops by an amount approximating the dividend and when the short seller covers later, it will be at a lower price than if the stock had not gone ex-dividend.

In addition to short sales for speculative purposes, there are various technical types of short sales. One variety is known as a "sale against the box." This occurs when the short seller does actually own the stock, has it in his or her safe deposit box, but prefers to sell short "against the box." For example, an investor bought General Motors at $50, has watched it go to $100. She hears rumors that at a forthcoming directors' meeting a week later the stock may be split. She reasons that if the stock is in fact split, it will continue to rise and she will want to hold it. If it is not split, she knows that a number of disappointed speculators will sell and the stock may decline. She wants to hold if the stock is split but avoid losing part of her profit if the stock is not split and declines. She sells General Motors short at $105, a point to which it has risen in anticipation of a split. The directors meet but do not vote a split. The stock declines to $95. Our seller against the box closes her short sale by delivering her own shares. She has gained time, bridged the directors' meeting, and kept her gain from $50 to $105 intact, and now is out of the stock, as she wanted to be if there was no split, but at $105 instead of at $95.

A second use of a sale against the box is for tax purposes. A short sale can be used to carry over a capital gain from one year to the next. Mr. Astute bought Eastman Kodak at 50 and it's now 110. He has had a very good year—incomewise—and doesn't want to take his capital gain this year. He wants to carry it over to next year, which he estimates will not be as good for him or for the stock market as was the year just ending. Keeping his long position in Eastman Kodak, he sells short, against the box, at 110. At the end of the year he has two outstanding positions. He is both long and short Eastman Kodak. Neither transaction has been concluded, but by his short sale, he has ensured

his gain in his long position. In January, he concludes his short sale. He covers by delivering the Eastman Kodak stock which he owns. He is out of Eastman Kodak, both long and short. He has his gain, and it has been taken in the year he preferred.

In a declining market, extensive short selling might cause a panic drop. Both the SEC and the exchange have been determined that short selling not be used to depress security prices artificially. There are rules to enforce this. No short sale of a stock is permitted except on a rising price. One can sell short at the price of the last sale providing that price was above the next preceding different price. For example, two sales of ZXY occur: the first at 44⅛, the second at 44. You cannot sell short at this point. You must wait for an uptick. The next transaction is at 44. You cannot sell short yet. The next price is 44⅛. Now you can sell short. The next transaction is also at 44⅛. You can sell short. As long as this price lasts, you can sell short, since the next preceding different price was lower. The market uses the terms "plus tick," "minus tick," and "zero plus tick," to indicate subsequent transactions. Dials at each post for each stock indicate the last sale and by + or −, whether a plus tick or minus tick. You can sell short on a plus tick. You cannot sell short on a minus tick. You can sell short on a zero plus tick. The prices 44, 44⅛, 44⅛ in succession provide an example of a zero plus tick.

Short selling is done mainly by professionals. The small investor seldom engages in short selling. The risk is very much greater than in a long transaction. If you buy 100 shares of a stock at 30, the worst that can happen, if the company goes bankrupt, is that you can lose $3,000. But if you sell short at 30 and sit mesmerized and watch the stock go up to 70, 80, 90, 100, and so on, your potential loss is open-ended. It depends on your stubbornness and upon your financial resources. To engage in short selling, resources should and must be very ample and your temperament should include a quick capacity to admit a mistake.

THE OVER-THE-COUNTER MARKET

As former SEC chairman William Casey said: "There has been an erosion of trading on the New York Stock Exchange, a drifting away to the over-the-counter markets, the third markets[25] and regional stock exchanges. If you like this you call it competition. If you don't you call it fragmentation."

"The over-the-counter markets are large and important, they are

---

[25] Over-the-counter trading in securities listed on registered exchanges.

heterogeneous and diffuse, they are still relatively obscure and even mysterious for most investors, and they are also comparatively unregulated." This is the way the *Report of the Special Study of the Securities Markets* characterized the over-the-counter market.[26]

Transactions in securities not taking place on an exchange are referred to as over-the-counter transactions. The over-the-counter market, unlike the exchanges, has no centralized place for trading. There are no listing requirements for issues traded, and all registered broker-dealers are entitled to participate. The broker-dealers vary in size, experience, and function; the securities differ in price, quality, and activity. While the OTC market includes from 30,000 to 40,000 common stocks of public corporations, only about 10,000 to 12,000 issues trade with any regularity within a given year and only 5,000 of these could be described as actively traded.

It is generally agreed that the over-the-counter market is the biggest securities market in the world—but exactly how big nobody knows. In a year's time, the National Quotation Bureau quotes prices on approximately 40,000 securities: 26,000 stocks and 14,000 bonds.

The over-the-counter market encompasses all securities not traded on national securities exchanges. Securities traded over the counter are quite diverse in kind, price, quality, and activity, reflecting the free entry of securities into the over-the-counter market. Most of the trading in government and municipal bonds, bank and insurance company stocks, and common and preferred stocks in some seasoned industrial companies as well as in thousands of newer or smaller industrial companies, takes place in the over-the-counter market. The SEC Special Study estimated that $556 billion out of a total of $1,092 billion in securities outstanding in the United States were not listed on any national securities exchange. There is also an active over-the-counter market in exchange-listed securities.

The issues of corporate stocks traded over the counter vary considerably in asset size, number of shareholders, and shares outstanding. There are substantial numbers of over-the-counter companies that cannot be distinguished from companies with securities listed on exchanges. Many others, however, are small companies, often speculative ventures in the promotional stage which have recently obtained public financing.

OTC securities had an aggregate minimum value of $125 billion as of June 30, 1975. About 16 companies showed a market value in excess

---

[26] See *Report of Special Study of the Securities Markets of the Securities and Exchange Commission*, part 2, chap. vii on Over-the-Counter Markets, p. 669, (88th Cong. 1st sess., House Document No. 95, Part 2 [Washington, D.C.: U.S. Government Printing Office, 1963]).

of $500 million, while another 127 companies topped 100 million. Among the better known companies whose securities are traded in the OTC market are American Express, Anheuser-Busch, Connecticut General, and General Reinsurance. There are also unproven companies that require more careful consideration.

Just as there is an unlimited right of entry of securities into the over-the-counter markets, there is also virtually free access of persons into the over-the-counter securities business. There are about 5,000 active broker-dealers registered with the SEC. By comparison, approximately 1,200 member firms participate in trading on the securities exchanges. There is a high concentration of over-the-counter business within a few large firms. Fifty-six broker-dealers, or less than 2 percent of the total number, accounted for half the dollar volume of over-the-counter sales.

Activity in the over-the-counter market breaks down into two general categories—wholesale and retail. The wholesale dealers "make markets" by standing ready to buy or sell securities for their own accounts from or to professionals who act for themselves or for the public. There are about 1,100 broker-dealer firms who "make markets" in OTC securities. The retail firm, on the other hand, is engaged in selling securities to public customers and buying or finding buyers when its customers wish to sell. Sales efforts are extensive and have been greatly facilitated by the development of NASDAQ.

In executing OTC transactions a firm may act either as principal or as agent for a public customer. If the firm owns the securities that the customer wishes to buy, it may sell them from its own account at a "net" price. The confirmation which the customer receives does *not* disclose the cost of the security to the firm, or its markup or profit.

If the broker-dealer does not own the security at the time of a customer's inquiry, it may buy the security from another broker-dealer (a wholesale dealer), place the security in its own account, and immediately resell it to the customer on a principal basis. Again the difference between the firm's cost (the price paid to the wholesale dealer) and the net price to the customer, known as the "markup," is *not* disclosed to the customer.

Alternatively, the transaction may be consummated on an agency basis. In this event the customer's firm buys the security from the wholesale dealer on behalf of its customer without placing the security in its own account. It charges a commission, which is disclosed to the customer in the confirmation. If the customer's broker-dealer uses the services of another firm to communicate with the wholesale dealer, or to "shop around," this second firm may also charge a fee for this service, in which case it is said to be "interpositioned." Although this fee may be passed on to the customer it is *not* disclosed.

NASDAQ

The over-the-counter market faced a special problem. The old system for obtaining quotations in this negotiated market necessitated a broker-dealer checking with several dealers by telephone in order to develop reasonably accurate bid and asked figures. Even then the broker couldn't be sure he had the correct range unless he checked all market members and this often wasn't practicable. As volume reached record heights, the system which had worked for years reached its limits. It became saturated with more trading activity and more demand for quotes than it could handle effectively. Stockbrokers were having difficulty securing bid and asked prices for their clients. And the clients were becoming disillusioned with the inadequate service.

The National Association of Securities Dealers (NASD) set out to correct the situation. After much study and discussion the NASD signed a contract with the Bunker-Ramo Corporation to build an electronic communication system to tie the OTC segment of the industry into one vast electronic stock market. The result was NASDAQ, the NASD's automated quotation system which became operative in February 1971 and drastically changed and modernized the OTC market.[27]

NASDAQ is a computerized communications system that collects, stores, and displays up-to-the-second quotations from a nationwide network of OTC dealers making markets in stocks which have been approved for inclusion in the NASDAQ system. At present there are about 2,600 companies listed on NASDAQ. The companies are required by the NASD to have $1 million in total assets, 300 or more shareholders, a minimum of 100,000 shares outstanding and at least two broker-dealers registered as market makers and continually quoting the stock in the system. NASDAQ companies must also meet the same SEC reporting and disclosure standards as established for exchange listed stocks.

Serving as an electronic link between almost all of the major retail firms and OTC market makers, NASDAQ made trading more efficient because the best market for a security, no matter where it was, could be located instantly. Because each dealer could see competitors' quotations, price spreads (the difference between bid and asked quotations) narrowed. With accurate and timely trading information, and with heightened competition narrowing spreads, the NASDAQ dealer

---

[27] See "NASDAQ & the OTC: How the NASDAQ System Creates an Electronic Stock Market in Over-the-Counter-Securities." Prepared by the OTC Information Bureau in cooperation with the National Security Traders Association and the National Association of Security Dealers. For a free copy write to the NASD at 1735 K Street, N.W., Washington, D.C. 20006.

market seemed a significant alternative to the exchange-listed auction market.

Market makers are, in effect, the trading sponsors of OTC securities. They stand ready to buy and sell as individual and institutional orders appear. A market maker's role is similar in many ways to that of a stock exchange specialist. An important difference, however, is that often only one specialist makes a market in an exchange listed stock, while a half-dozen or more market makers may compete in a particular NASDAQ/OTC security.[28]

NASDAQ operates on three separate levels to meet the needs of investors, OTC traders, and OTC market makers.

As the system is organized, *Level 1 service* is designed to serve individual investors who are clients of the retail branches of brokerage firms. It takes the quotations of all dealers making a market in a stock and delivers current representative bid and asked prices. This is actually a median quote representing the middle point of the quotes of all the dealers. Since any NASDAQ stock has a minimum of two market makers and some as many as 25 or 30, this quotation will fairly reflect the existing market. As of May 1976 there was an average of 6.1 market makers per security.

The representative quote is transmitted electronically from the computer center and is received on about 28,000 standard desk top quotation units that are familiar pieces of equipment in most brokerage firm offices.

What is of key importance with Level I service is the fact that quotations are current, accurate, and visible. All market makers in a particular stock are obligated to feed changes in bid or asked prices into the system immediately. These changes appear on terminals within five seconds.

Thus, with stocks in the NASDAQ system, you can call your broker for a quote, receive it immediately, make your decision to buy or sell then and there, while you are still on the telephone.[29]

Level II terminals are specially designed units with TV-type screens to serve the needs of two kinds of users: (1) Broker-dealers retailing OTC securities to the public and (2) large-scale professional order executers. By pressing a few buttons on the keyboard of the Level II unit, the trader can see immediately all the current quotations

---

[28] See "The Market Maker System," and "The Features of the NASDAQ System," in *NASDAQ and the Listing Dilemma*, National Association of Securities Dealers, Washington, D.C. 20006, 1975.

[29] See "The NASDAQ Revolution: How Over-the-Counter Securities Are Traded," Merrill Lynch, Pierce, Fenner & Smith. For a free copy write to the firm at One Liberty Plaza, New York, N.Y. 10006.

of the market makers in a specific stock in the NASDAQ system. The quotes of only five market makers, ranked according to the best prevailing bids or offers at that time, are displayed on the screen. If there are more, the balance can be retrieved in groups of five by pressing a special "more" button.

NASDAQ eliminates literally thousands of telephone calls that were formerly made in an effort to determine which dealer was making the best market. The system also enables brokerage firms and institutional investors to gain prompt execution of orders since the trader can directly contact the dealer showing the best market to complete the transaction.

NASDAQ does not change the actual trading process. Once they know what the quotations are, the traders must still telephone or activate a direct wire to the market makers.

Some 600 market making dealers are equipped with *Level III units* that are similar to Level II equipment except that they have added features which enable the dealers to enter and change or update quotations on the stocks in which they make markets. Entries and changes are fed into the computer system and within five seconds the current figures will appear on all Level II and III terminals everywhere in the country. In addition, the representative bid and asked price showing on Level I units will also be automatically adjusted.

Dealers cannot make markets in any stocks without prior authorization from the NASD. Dealers must meet and maintain certain capital standards and they must agree to make markets on a regular basis. Only when they have been approved as market makers can a dealer enter quotations and changes into the NASDAQ system, and then only for those stocks in which they have authority to act as market makers. It is physically impossible for them to enter or change the quotes of any stocks but their own.

In accordance with NASD rules, market-making dealers are required to execute transactions for at least 100 shares of stock upon the request of other NASD members at the dealers' prevailing quotations in the NASDAQ system.

The NASDAQ system now provides OTC stock price indexes as well as volume reports. NASDAQ-OTC trading has been as high as 14.5 million shares per day. Since the NASDAQ quotations are not the record of actual transactions themselves but only the offers and bids of dealers and brokers, the next step that remains to be taken is for the NASD to require that everyone using NASDAQ report the actual transactions that result so that completed trades are publicly announced as on organized exchanges.

NASDAQ has given impetus to the so-called third market since it

facilitates trading in "listed stocks" by broker-dealers who are not members of organized exchanges.[30] If this movement grows it could lead, in the opinion of some observers, toward the formation of a central market, encompassing the organized exchanges, the OTC, and the third market. Pressure for such a major restructuring of the stock market mechanism has been growing as a result of increased institutional trading.

Anticipating steady progress in the trend to a central market system under pressure from Washington, the NASD early in 1976 took the lead in developing a workable communications system for the envisioned national market, by announcing plans to begin offering by midyear a composite stock quotation service over its NASDAQ quote system. The NASD said its system, which currently carries just over-the-counter quotes, will provide buy and sell prices from *all* stock exchanges and the so-called third market over the counter transactions in listed securities. The composite quotations service will be available to NASDAQ subscribers on the same terminal on which they currently receive over the counter bid and asked quotes.[31]

THE IMPACT OF INSTITUTIONAL TRADING

Block Transactions

Block transactions and block positioning have now become a way of life in the securities markets. A Salomon Bros. transaction, detailed by *Fortune,* provides an insight into how it's done.[32]

The moment of highest excitement on the stock desk came with a big trade. Take that American Airlines block in January. It came on a day in which the stock desk had opened with a $30-million inventory, all of it left from positions taken in previous days. A level of $30-million is about average; Salomon's all-time high was $58 million.

The first call about American Airlines (AMR) came in the morning when the stock was trading at 30½. The institution calling (Salomon never identifies a customer, but newspapers next day guessed that this one was Massachusetts Investors Trust) allowed that it might be a big seller of American Airlines. "How big," Perry demanded.[33] Around 650,000 shares, the trader answered,

---

[30] *The NASDAQ—Third Market Study,* National Association of Securities Dealers, Washington, D.C., April 1972.

[31] "NASD Will Offer Composite Stock Quotes over Its NASDAQ System by Middle of 1976," *The Wall Street Journal,* February 10, 1976.

[32] Carol J. Loomis, "Living It up in a 'Salomon-Sized World'," *Fortune,* April 1970; see also Newton W. Lamson, "Block Trader at Salomon," *The New York Times,* November 9, 1975.

[33] Jay Perry, partner in charge of block trading, at that time.

but maybe not all at once. From there on, Perry was determined to get the full block.

He did, too. An hour and fifteen minutes later, after countless phone calls to countless people, a flash to Salomon's Branch offices, and a staccato conversation between Perry and Gutfriend[34] about price, Perry offered to buy 650,600 shares at 29. The seller deliberated, then accepted. Behind Perry's bid was a skein of buyers. One institution, already a large holder of AMR, took 300,000 shares. Another 284,600 shares were accounted for by eight other institutions, a competing but friendly broker buying for its own clients (on that part of the block Salomon collected no commissions), and by the specialist on the floor. The specialist, when he learned about the trade, a few minutes before it occurred, took shares for his own account and for the accounts of investors who had buy orders on his book at prices of 29 or higher. That left 66,000 shares for Salomon itself to buy, and of these 25,000 went to the arbitrage desk, which was short that amount of AMR shares and was willing to cover. So, in the end, 41,000 shares, purchased for $1,189,000 went into position at the stock desk.

Over the next few days, Salomon sold its 41,000 AMR shares at prices that probably averaged around 27, which (not counting execution costs) would have given it a positioning loss of about $80,000. Against that, Salomon took in commissions on 650,600 shares on the sell side and 457,600 shares on the buy side. These commissions amounted to nearly $200,000 leaving Salomon about $120,000 ahead. It was a better than average experience, for in the recent past Salomon has typically seen more than half of its commissions on large blocks eaten up by positioning losses.

A new record was set in 1972 when Kaiser Industries Corp. sold 5,245,000 shares of the American Motors Corp. in the largest trade ever executed on the New York Stock Exchange, in terms of shares. It topped the previous record block of 3.25 million shares of the Allis-Chalmers Manufacturing Co. traded in 1971. However, the value of the Kaiser-AMC transaction was less than the record of $76,135,026 paid for 730,312 shares of American Standard, Inc., earlier. A close runner-up was the $72,512,000 paid for a block of IBM in 1971.

The expanding role of institutions in the securities markets has resulted in their dominance of NYSE trading activity in recent years. At the end of 1960, major financial institutions (excluding bank-administered personal trust funds) held an estimated 17.8 percent of the market value of NYSE stock; by year-end 1975, this figure had grown to 33 percent. However, the shift in trading patterns of individuals and institutions has been much more dramatic than the increase in institutional ownership. According to a NYSE study, during 1974, *institutions and intermediaries* (including personal trusts) accounted for 59 percent of NYSE public share volume and 69 percent of public

---

[34] John H. Gutfriend, partner in charge of syndicate department, at that time.

dollar volume on the Exchange.[35] This is a reversal from 1960, when *individuals* accounted for 69 percent of public share volume and 61 percent of public dollar volume on the Exchange. Although many policy and regulatory issues yet to be decided, such as the establishment of a new central market, may substantially alter the trading pattern of financial institutions, it is clear that they have become the major factor in the market and will become increasingly dominant.

Major financial institutions held an estimated $169 billion, or 33 percent of all NYSE-listed stocks at year-end 1974. These institutions are projected to hold about 39 percent of the NYSE list in 1980. (See Table 2–3.)

TABLE 2–3
Estimated Holdings of NYSE Listed Stocks by Selected Institutional Investors (excluding bank-administered personal trust funds—billions)

	1964	1974	1980	Average Annual Growth Rates 1964–74	Estimated Annual Growth Rates 1974–80
Insurance companies:					
Life insurance companies	$ 5.4	$ 16.8	$ 53.5	12.0%	21.3%
Nonlife companies	9.5	11.0	28.5	1.5	17.2
Investment companies:					
Open-end	23.2	28.0	92.8	1.9	22.1
Closed-end	6.6	4.4	7.8	−4.2	10.0
Private noninsured pension funds	29.7	62.1	197.0	7.7	21.2
State and local pension funds	1.1	14.0	54.6	29.0	25.6
All other	29.6	32.3	68.6	0.9	13.4
Total	$105.1	$168.6	$ 502.8	4.8%	20.0%
Market value all NYSE stock	$474.3	$511.1	$1,300.0	0.8%	16.9%
Estimated percent held by institutions	22.2%	33.0%	38.7%	—	—

Source: New York Stock Exchange, 1976.

It is expected that institutions and intermediaries will account for about 72 percent of the *public* share *volume* in 1980.[36] (See Figure 2–2.) This compares with just under 59 percent during 1974. On a *value* basis, institutions are expected to comprise about 78 percent of

---

[35] William C. Freund and David F. Minor, "Institutional Activity on NYSE: 1975 and 1980," *Perspectives on Planning*, No. 10, New York, June 1972; see also Frank K. Reilly, "Block Trades and Stock Price Volatility," Faculty Working Paper, College of Commerce and Business, University of Illinois at Urbana–Champaign, October 19, 1975.

[36] Public share volume is defined as total volume excluding members trading for their own accounts. See NYSE, *Public Transaction Study*, April 1972. PTS volume is defined as purchases plus sales in round and odd lots.

FIGURE 2–2
Distribution of NYSE Public Volume

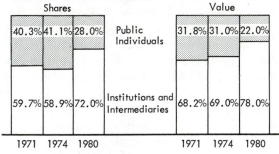

Source: New York Stock Exchange, 1975.

public dollar amount in 1980. In 1974, they were responsible for 69 percent of public dollar volume.

The average size of institutional orders has been growing, as has large block activity. Block activity of 10,000 shares or more on the NYSE has grown over 55 percent annually since full-year data were first collected in 1965. While block volume may not continue to expand at this dynamic rate, stronger specialist capital requirements, block positioning, as well as potential technical advances should assure an increase in trades of 10,000 shares or more. (See Figure 2–3.)

"One of the most dramatic impacts of institutionalization on the securities markets has been the growth of block trading," the Institu-

FIGURE 2–3
Block Share Volume as Percent of Reported Volume

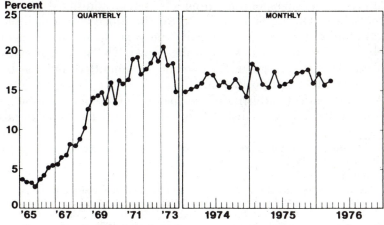

Source: New York Stock Exchange.

tional Investor Study of the SEC noted.[37] Theoretically, a block trade is a securities transaction that cannot be executed in the exchange auction market in the normal course. Nevertheless, the Institutional Investor Study noted that about 65 percent of the total volume in transactions of 10,000 or more shares of common stocks listed on the NYSE is executed on that exchange. As an important market factor on the NYSE, block trading is a relatively recent phenomenon.

Block trades on the NYSE usually involve numerous participants. There are usually fewer participants on the side that initiates the trade ("active side") than on the other side ("passive side"). The broker-dealer primarily responsible for assembling the orders of the different participants ("block trade assembler") handles the active side and all or almost all of the passive side in about one third of all such transactions, particularly the larger ones. In block trades of $1 million or more the assembly process usually takes place initially over the upstairs communications network of the block trade assembler. There is some indication that the negotiation process by which smaller block trades of some size are assembled is somewhat more related to the floor of the NYSE, particularly to the specialist.[38]

A typical block trade is initiated by an institution that wishes to purchase or sell a large quantity of stock and will accept a discount from the current market price or pay a premium in order to do so. The key to assembling a block trade is to find the orders on the passive side. The SEC study found that to offset the order of the institution initiating the trade in the median block, the block trade assembler finds one institution and five to nine other parties. On the average, the institution accounted for 39 percent of shares on the passive side; other customers for 3 percent. By further upstairs communications the block trade assembler finds other broker-dealers, primarily representing institutions, with orders for something less than an additional 14 percent of the shares. On the floor of the NYSE the block trade assembler is able to find orders for an additional 7 percent among the specialist's book, and other broker dealers in the crowd. The specialist takes 14 percent. This leaves about 23 percent uncommitted and the block trade assembler must position it.

At times conflict and irritation seems to develop between the block positioner and the specialist.[39] The former wants the latter to take a

---

[37] *Institutional Investor Study Report of the Securities and Exchange Commission, Summary Volume,* Part 3.

[38] Ibid., pp. 87–88.

[39] For an excellent discussion of the relative roles and views of the block positioner and the specialist, see Heidi S. Fiske, "Can the Specialist System Cope with the Age of Block Trading?" *Institutional Investor,* August 1969. See also Alan F. Kay, "Block Trading for Best Execution," *Trusts and Estates,* October 1975.

larger position and the specialist at times is either unwilling or unable to do so. The SEC study found that the specialist's relatively low-participation rate in block trades of $1 million or more seems to reflect the orientation to the exchange floor away from the upstairs communications network. On the other hand, in the smaller block trades, whose assembly is more related to the floor, the specialist's participation rate on the passive side is substantially larger while the block trade assembler's is significantly smaller. Positioning by the block trade assembler, then, performs part of the market-making function when, for whatever reason, the specialist does not offset fully the imbalance in a potential block trade.

In all, about 70 percent of the shares positioned appear to be laid off to institutions or their brokers as a result of upstairs communications, and the remaining 30 percent appears to be laid off to the specialist or to brokers representing individuals or institutions in the regular round-lot market on the NYSE floor. "Thus, the block positioner," the SEC study declares, "is highly dependent upon efficient and inexpensive access to that market."

Almost as dramatic as the growth of block trading has been the *decreasing* concentration of the volume in NYSE-listed stocks that has resulted. Although 65 percent of the volume in transactions of 10,000 or more shares is executed on the NYSE, the 35 percent that is not, is quite important. Moreover, the proportion of the block volume that is executed in other markets has been growing rapidly.

Indeed one authority feels that the development of block trading has undermined the supremacy of both the NYSE and the AMEX. Charles Ellis writes:

> The classic description of the New York Stock Exchange as a perfect auction market with both buyers and sellers openly bidding with each other is as passé as the idea that the specialist on the floor of the Exchange can provide "continuous markets" and smooth out the "ripples" in prices caused by large irregularities in buying and selling interests. The specialist who could buy 1,000 or even 10,000 shares is simply unable to cope with the capital required to digest block transactions of 100,000 or 500,000 shares—nor can such volume be absorbed readily by the classic auction market still conducted on the exchange floor for investors who want to buy or sell 100 or less shares.
>
> Today, the market for large transactions between institutions is *not* an auction, is *not* conducted on or even very near the exchange floor, and is *not* made public until after the transactions are fully settled as to amount and price. Block trades are privately negotiated transactions. They do not depend to any substantial degree upon either the facilities or the procedures of the stock exchanges. As a result of this remarkable difference between the new institutional transactions and the customary individual transactions, the regular exchanges no longer have full control over trading in the shares they list. This is because such transactions can be executed on regional exchanges which du-

ally list the stocks involved or can be executed in the so-called third market which operates on an over-the-counter basis. With the recent automation of the over-the-counter markets, another challenger is in the lists against the traditional exchanges. The primacy of the New York and American Stock Exchanges is being challenged because institutional investors have different needs than individual investors and are pressing inevitably for changes that will meet their new needs.[40]

The potential depth of the auction market however, is often greater than may appear on the surface. Through a member firm, an institutional investment manager can go beyond the "quote." This, after all, is simply a report of the highest bid to buy and the lowest offer to sell. It frequently is given in terms of a single round lot, or a few hundred shares. At the time a 150,000 share block transaction order was placed, the quoted market was rather thin—66¾ bid for 200 shares; 500 shares offered at 67 (the price of the last sale). The broker, knowing the full size of the order, was able to enlist the assistance of other commission brokers, floor traders, and, of course, the specialist. Despite the thin quote, within a few hours the selling team rounded up enough buy orders to take care of the entire block. With the last sale at 66½, most of the block was sold at 66. In a 192,000 share block transaction, the selling broker was able to develop offsetting buy orders for 7,000 shares within his own organization. Orders of the specialist's book ultimately accounted for another 15,000. The specialist not only provided information which led to orders for 28,000 shares among three commission brokers on the floor, but he bought 141,811 shares—nearly $8 million worth—for his own account.

The Exchange and Block Transaction Techniques

There are now a number of special methods for buying and selling large blocks on the NYSE. On the buy side, there is the specialist block sale, the exchange acquisition, and the special bid; on the sell side the specialist block purchase, an exchange distribution, a special offering, and a secondary distribution. The specialist block purchase or sale is simply a situation where a commission broker or a floor broker with a large block to buy or sell approaches the specialist in the stock to see if the specialist wishes to, and is able to, absorb the entire block, usually at a price very close to the market but with a slight concession to the specialist. The trade is made privately. There is no notice on the ticker, no announcement of any kind before or after, and no entry in the specialist's book.

---

[40] Charles D. Ellis, *Institutional Investing* (Homewood, Ill.: Dow Jones-Irwin, Inc., 1971), pp. 228–29. See also Nicholas Close, "Price Effects of Large Transactions," *Financial Analysts Journal*, November/December 1975.

For larger sized blocks the exchange distribution or acquisition may be used. It involves a large member firm (commission brokerage house) using its private communications system to generate buy or sell orders in sufficient volume to take up the block amount, with the block seller or buyer paying all brokerage costs. When sufficient orders have been accumulated, these are crossed with the block order on the floor, within the current auction market "bid-and-asked" range. Only after a "cross" has been executed does the ticker disclose that an acquisition or distribution has been accomplished. No prior public announcement of a forthcoming acquisition or distribution is made.

The special offering or bid now seldom used, involves appealing to the combined resources of the stock exchange community by announcing an attractive fixed, net price over the exchange's nationwide ticker system. The ticker message, appearing simultaneously across the country, sums up the terms of the special offering. An incentive commission is offered to induce brokerage interest. This is paid by the block seller or buyer. Customers responding to the special offer or bid pay no brokerage commission.

Secondary distributions usually involve blocks exceedingly large in relation to the current market. The institutional investment manager agrees on a net price per share for his block, somewhat under the current auction market. A selling group is formed to handle the distribution. It offers the stock to buyers at a net price reflecting the current auction market level. Buyers are attracted by the fact that the price is net—that is, they pay no commission.

Sometimes when a block is very large and offsetting interest cannot readily be located either on the trading floor or among other institutions, the broker handling an institutional order may recommend the use of "flow-in, flow-out" trading, providing the institutional investment managers are willing and able to spread their purchases or sales over a longer period of time. The brokers make their bids or offers in such a way as to execute the order within a specified price range, with the least possible impact on the market and at the best possible average price for the institutional client. In one case, in one month's time 87,000 shares of a given stock were purchased for an insurance company at an average price of 39—less than the offer side of the market when the order was first placed. An estimated 250 sellers—institutions as well as individuals—had supplied the stock in 73 separate transactions. The specialist contacted the broker wherever selling interest appeared. In addition, the specialist, given specific limit orders by the broker, acquired more than 30,000 shares as the broker's agent.

Still another way a specialist can accommodate an institutional order is by "stopping" stock, as in the case of a recent bank order to sell 500 shares of a petroleum issue. The current market was 49¼ to

49½, 100 shares wanted, 1,000 offered. The bank's floor broker sold 100 shares at 49¼. The market became 49 bid (by the specialist), offered at 49½ (by the broker). The broker then asked if he could be "stopped" at 49, and the specialist agreed to "stop" the remaining 400 shares at that price. Thus, the broker was guaranteed at least 49 for the 400 shares and was assured that the specialist, now representing the order as a broker, would try to do better. As it turned out, a buyer appeared, and the specialist sold 200 shares at 49¼. Because sellers entered the market it became necessary for the specialist to buy the remaining 200 shares himself at 49. Even so, the "stop" had secured an extra ¼ point on 200 shares.

Generally, however, the NYSE is not effectively structured to handle large blocks, and the illusion of extensive block activity on the Exchange results from large block houses crossing orders on the floor of the Exchange so as not to run afoul of Rule 394, which prohibits members from engaging in off-board trading of NYSE listed shares.

Chris Welles says:

The rise of the block houses (Salomon Brothers, Goldman Sachs, Oppenheimer, Bache, Smith Barney, Shields Modell Roland, and Blyth Eastman Dillon) is the direct result of the deficiencies of the Exchange floor. Since its founding the NYSE has been a creature of the individual investors who were its principal customers. To function efficiently, the Exchange's auction-trading system requires a large and continuous flow of small buy and sell orders which can be matched relatively easily with one another. The penchant of Gerald Tsai and his followers for trading in blocks of 10,000 shares and more produced on the Exchange floor the equivalent of a blown fuse. When Tsai decided, for instance to unload 50,000 shares of Polaroid only the remotest chance existed that the floor could match it with 50,000 shares worth of buy orders. Such large orders simply overload the auction system. . . .

When blocks such as 50,000 Polaroid began arriving on the floor regularly, specialists were reluctant to become involved. If no buyer for such a block could immediately be located, the specialist would have had to risk $1 million or more of his own capital. Second, the specialist lacked an efficient means of finding buyers. The likeliest buyer for a big institutional block is another institution, but due to a typically monopolistic market-sharing arrangement, specialists are prohibited from soliciting business directly from institutions. If this prohibition did not exist a good deal of institutional trading would bypass NYSE brokerage houses, thus depriving them of commissions. Specialists, though, are compensated for acquiescing in this arrangement. NYSE rules also prohibit other members from disrupting the specialist's monopoly by formally advertising lower prices and luring business away.

When specialists proved both unwilling and unable to accommodate block trading, several NYSE firms established new facilities to handle the business. To a block house such as Salomon Brothers, a 50,000 share sell order is as routine as a 100-share sell order to a specialist. Block houses rely not on an

auction-style order matching but on an aggressive solicitation-and-trade-assemblage procedure. Block houses maintain direct communications and close working relationships with all major institutions from whom sufficient buying interest can usually be elicited within minutes. If buyers cannot be located immediately, the block house, which is usually much more highly capitalized and willing to take risks than specialists, will often "position" the block—that is, it will buy some or all of the block for its own portfolio, usually in the hopes of selling it shortly thereafter. Salomon Brothers, which has a net worth of $123 million, carries an average daily inventory of securities worth $1.8 billion, which may include $50 million in common stocks.[41]

Most blocks are bought and sold upstairs and only brought to the Exchange floor to be crossed in order to appear on the tape and comply with Rule 394. Were it not for Rule 394 they would probably not be brought to the Exchange floor.

Automation and Block Trading

Three major systems were planned primarily to facilitate institutional trading in common stocks, particularly block trading. They were AutEx, the NYSE's Block Automation System (BAS), and Instinet.

AutEx was the first to start operations (in August 1969).[42] It is solely a communications and information retrieval system. Its subscribers include broker-dealers and institutions. Only broker-dealer subscribers may broadcast indications of interest to all other subscribers to the AutEx system. These indications set forth the side and size[43] of the interest and the broker-dealer's own name. The AutEx System is a real-time network enabling brokers to flash their block trading buy and sell interests, as well as indications of availability of market and research information to an audience of subscribing institutions. The system also carries to all subscribers reports of current block trades executed on the various exchanges and OTC. Brokers enter messages and receive reports through teletypewriters connected by a private wire network to the system computer and to special TV screen displays and keyboards provided to subscribing institutions. Information is visibly displayed on the terminals of all or selected other subscribers, who may contact the broker-dealer named either directly or through their own brokers or may notify the broker-dealer to contact them. Once an initial contact has been made, all future communications are by ordi-

---

[41] Welles, *The Last Days of the Club*, pp. 43–44.

[42] See *AutEx Equity Trading Information System*, AutEx, Inc. 90 Broad Street, New York, N.Y. 10004. AutEx is derived from *Aut*omated *Ex*change.

[43] Actual share amounts are not entered. Rather, three categories are used: small for 1,000 to 5,000 shares, medium for 5,000 to 20,000 shares, and large for 20,000 shares and over.

nary telephone or teletype. The transaction may therefore be executed on a stock exchange, or over-the-counter, according to the desires of the purchasers and sellers and the rules of any stock exchanges to which the brokers belong. AutEx requests that transactions resulting from contacts established on the system be voluntarily reported to it. Those transactions that are so reported without a request for confidentiality are in turn reported to all subscribers. In addition to its communication function, AutEx also provides for the retrieval of messages previously entered.

The New York Stock Exchange's *Block Automation System* (BAS) was also primarily a communications and information retrieval system. BAS began operations in February 1970. Again membership by subscription was available to both brokers and to institutions. Its director explained:

> You've got to envision three circles of activity; there's the pre-trade circle; the execution circle which is the floor of the NYSE; and the post-trade circle which is the confirmation activities. It is ATS or Automated Trading Systems which shall handle by the computer the 100-share market orders on the floor. BAS is involved in the first and third circles of activity, pre-trade and post-trade. . . . BAS was not established as a trading system. It was designed to facilitate the exchange of information between brokers and institutional clients about the availability of large blocks of stock. The principal function of BAS is to get the two sides—buyer and seller—together. The trade is not executed in the system. It is executed on the floor of the NYSE by the members.[44]

BAS, however lasted only briefly; terminating in the fall of 1973. A number of things went wrong. Technical computer competence seemed to be lacking. Day after day, BAS would be inoperative for significant stretches of time and sometimes the system would be down for the whole day. BAS was designed as an exclusive NYSE system for NYSE members to trade NYSE stocks. Non-NYSE blocks and non-NYSE firms were not permitted to participate. By excluding OTC stocks, third market dealers and other nonmembers, BAS severely reduced the number of potential trades it could facilitate and institutional traders naturally tended to favor AutEx, the more comprehensive system.

Instinet, owned by the Institutional Networks Corporation is the only one of the three that performs execution as well as communications and information retrieval. Instinet is a system which enables institutions to trade directly via the computer terminal. It is designed to perform the execution function at costs that are generally less than stock exchange commissions. Instinet began operations in December 1969. All subscribers may make entries in the Instinet system. They

---

[44] "Liquidity Key to Growing Role of Block Trading," *Trusts & Estates*, March 1972.

may enter indications of interest stating the side and either the number of shares or the price. They may also enter firm orders stating all three. The information may either be broadcast to all or selected other subscribers, or it may be placed in the "book" maintained in the system. A code to preserve anonymity is specified for the subscriber making the entry. Other subscribers may either communicate with the former by teletype, negotiate with it by means of programmed messages and/or accept firm bids or offers thereby executing transactions. Reports of all executions are disseminated to all subscribers at the end of the day. Since it involves institution to institution dealing, Instinet's activity has been labeled the "fourth market."[45] This contrasts with the "third market," in which institutions deal with each other but use broker-dealers as intermediaries or deal with block positioning houses.

The "Third" Market

The growth of institutional transactions in large blocks of securities and the rigidity of certain NYSE rules particularly Rule 394 resulted in a rapid expansion of the so-called third market. This is the off-board market for exchange-listed securities. It is a negotiated market rather than an auction market; yet as a general rule the price of a stock on the third market rarely deviates from the price on the NYSE by more than the exchange commission. The larger the block traded, however, the more room for negotiation. The market appears to have developed to service the special needs of two groups: (a) institutional investors who have increasingly become large holders of, and traders in, common stock; and (b) broker-dealers, not members of an exchange and therefore without direct access to the trading of listed stocks.

The old NYSE fixed rate structure did not provide for volume discounts. Institutional investors dealing in large blocks of stock on the NYSE paid the same commission, computed on the dollar value of each round lot, as other public customers. For a long time, they received no adjustment or graduated discount for the number of round lots in multiple round-lot transactions. The commission charged on an order for 10,000 shares was 100 times that on an order for 100 shares at the same price. Such inflexibility led to the rise of the third market. Institutions found that they could deal as principals on the third market and pay (or receive) a price net of commission fixed by a broker-dealer (nonmember of the NYSE) who adjusted his markup to shade the NYSE commission.

---

[45] See "Instinet an Institutional Marketplace That Lowers your Transaction Costs," Institutional Network Corporation, 122 East 42nd Street, New York, N.Y. 10017; see also "Fourth-Market Business Swells Sharply Following End of Fixed Brokerage Rates," *The Wall Street Journal*, May 5, 1975.

The NYSE did not permit its members and member firms to trade or execute orders in NYSE-listed issues off the NYSE floor, except on other organized exchanges, or with special permission. It viewed the growth of the third market with alarm. Corporate bond trading, which was once centered on NYSE, is now conducted almost entirely over the counter. Indeed, NYSE has a special rule allowing member firms to trade over the counter in listed bonds whenever the transaction involves ten bonds ($10,000) or more. A long list of high-grade preferred shares and rail stocks with guaranteed dividends, all fully listed on the NYSE, are also exempt from the usual requirement that a NYSE member firm must trade in listed securities on the floor. It did not, however, want to be forced to exempt block transactions in common stock from trading on the floor, too.

Firms dealing in the third market operate in two ways. A number of large firms maintain continuous trading markets in a number of listed stocks—meaning that they inventory these stocks and stand ready to buy or sell them at a quoted price. They make markets in the same fashion as the wholesalers in the OTC market. Most often, there is no commission charged on such deals. The dealers' profit lies in the spread between the bid and offered prices. These firms also (along with some firms that don't maintain continuous trading markets) act as agents in bringing together buyers and sellers—almost always institutions—with big blocks to trade. They may aim for a profit on the spread but, more often, they charge a commission on such deals, usually less than the NYSE commission. Where formerly off-board markets were made in listed utility stocks or others of comparable stability, today the market encompasses a wide variety of industrials and other equities.

The third market offers certain advantages. Institutions deal directly with market makers on the third market and do not need the services of a broker. Their market interest and trading receive no publicity. Their transactions, which tend to be large, are not likely to affect prices on the exchange in a way detrimental to the satisfactory completion of the remainder of a large-block transaction. The off-board market maker has considerable latitude in quoting prices to institutions net of commissions that are better than the combination of exchange price and commission. Depth of market, which is important to institutions in large transactions is easily and definitely ascertainable on the third market. The market makers, such as Weeden & Company, Blyth Eastman Dillon, First Boston Corporation, American Securities Corporation, Chicago's H. S. Kipnis & Company, and San Francisco-based J. S. Strauss & Company, generally possess the capability of taking large positions.

A description of the "third market" by its leading proponent Donald E. Weeden, chairman of the board of Weeden & Co. is as follows:

Let me briefly describe the Third Market. It is the over-the-counter marketplace dealing in exchange listed stocks, predominantly those issues listed on the NYSE. It consists of some dozen or so well capitalized firms who maintain markets in anywhere from a few to over 200 listed issues. By maintaining markets it is meant that a firm stands ready to buy and/or sell for its own account in sizes ranging from an odd lot to large blocks. In the process, it is putting its capital at risk in taking on inventory—both long and short—until such time in the future when another inquiry from another customer allows it to even out its position. The role of the Third Market maker is thus similar to that of the specialist on the floor of an exchange or that of the dealer in government, corporate and municipal bonds. These market makers also may act as agents bringing together a buyer and seller at the same time and charging a nominal commission for this service. But normally their profit is derived from the difference between the price at which they buy shares and the price at which they eventually sell them. Our firm's experience over the years shows an average gross profit per share-turned-over of around 20¢. This cost divided between the buyer and seller who use the Third Market approximates 25% of the minimum cost of processing similar priced stocks in similar amounts through the exchange structure. This fact represents one compelling reason for the growth of the Third Market over the years.

In general, the customers of the Third Market are institutions, such as bank trust accounts, mutual funds, corporate pension funds, and corporations who buy for treasury stock or employee stock purchase plans. They find it advantageous not only in terms of cost but in terms of size, convenience, and efficiency.

In addition, there are the thousands of broker/dealers who are not members of any exchange but who desire to merchandise quality issues to their accounts and who receive orders from these customers in exchange listed stocks. The Third Market allows them to charge a full or at least a partial commission and still remain competitive with the member firm down the street.

Recently, there has been a growing use of the Third Market by member firms who find that in many cases the off-board market maker can not only compete with the specialist in price but is willing to deal in larger amounts. This type of trade is normally executed through the facilities of a regional exchange.[46]

The NYSE reported that third market volume in NYSE-listed common stock reached a record 7.3 percent of total NYSE volume during 1972, compared to 6.5 percent in 1970 and only 2.7 percent in 1965. The value of these issues also rose to a new high—8.5 percent of NYSE

[46] Donald E. Weeden, "The Central Market vs. The Single Market," a speech before the National Investor Relations Institute, Washington, D.C., November 5, 1970. See also his "The Securities Industry: A Copernican View," remarks before the Securities Traders Association of Los Angeles, Palm Springs, Calif., May 20, 1972.

value, from 3.5 percent in 1965. For 1975 comparable percentages were 4.6 percent for volume and 6 percent for value.

Rule 394—The Controversy

The NYSE's Rule 394 requires members to expose customers' orders to the auction market before they can take a trade in a listed stock off the Exchange floor to get a better price for the customer. It restricts the ability of member firms to trade in the third market. James J. Needham, former chairman of the board of the New York Stock Exchange, has said:

> Because of Rule 394, NYSE member brokerage firms who do business with the public must first bring their customers' orders in NYSE stocks to a stock exchange[47] so they can meet the thousands of other orders present in an auction market setting to determine stock prices.
>
> If Rule 394 is repealed, it will only be a matter of time and economic pressure before major securities firms, now members of the NYSE, will start making dealer markets in the most active stocks in their own offices. Today, some 250 stocks, 15% of those listed for trading on the NYSE, account for 53% of the exchange's volume. These stocks have a high flow of orders. Markets can be made in them at little risk and at high profit. Instead of one market and one price for these really active issues there will be several markets and several prices.
>
> How the individual investor will be able to compete against the large institutional professional trader in getting the best price in this new "competitive" environment might best be illustrated by noting the huge discounts large institutions—but not individual investors—have been able to bargain off commission rates since the advent of "competitive" commissions last May 1.
>
> Be that as it may, some attention should now be focused on what will happen to the 1,300 less active NYSE-listed stocks in the "competitive" over-the-counter market of the future. With the cream of the flow of orders in the active stocks being skimmed off by dealers in the back offices of brokerage firms, there will be little incentive for specialists to remain on an exchange floor, risking their own market-making capital in the many hundreds of less active stocks. The flow of orders will be elsewhere, and that is where the market-making capital will go.[48]

Donald Weeden has a different point of view. He has written:

> Rule 394 is to the investing public what the Blackout Rule was to the sports viewing public-league sponsored rules, erected to assure a full house for club owners. Both were collective boycotts pure and simple and both worked very effectively. But neither were remotely in the public interest. . . .

---

[47] It need not be the NYSE. It can be any of the regional exchanges.

[48] James J. Needham, "Rule 394 and the Public Interest," *The Wall Street Journal*, October 16, 1975; see also Larry Friedman, "Needham's Last Stand," *Finance*, January 1976.

In clear language the Congress has directed the Commission [SEC] to expedite the bringing about of a national market system by eliminating barriers to competition. Rule 394 is such a barrier. Ergo Rule 394 must go.

The New York Stock Exchange's submission of July 2, 1975 cunningly argues for retention of Rule 394 until a national market system comes into existence. The argument is utterly circular. What the Stock Exchange knows all too well is that there will never be, there can never be, a national market system so long as Rule 394 exists. . . .

Stripped of all its cloying cotton candy references to protecting the public interest in the auction market, the New York Stock Exchange's real pitch is for government intervention to keep it "the chosen instrument" of the securities industry. Like Pan American embracing the CAB to avoid the rigors of competition from charter flights, the Stock Exchange wants the Commission to protect it from the Third Market which despite its name is now the second largest market in listed securities—larger than the Amex or any of the regionals. So far, the Stock Exchange has succeeded, but to those of us who see the future possibilities of a national market system complete with an automated book and competing market makers, the Stock Exchange resembles not so much a chosen instrument as another Penn Central, remarkable only because of its size. In this computer age with enormous daily volumes in listed stocks, the Stock Exchange's arguments in favor of its beloved crowd are largely a myth.[49]

The Securities Acts Amendments of 1975 called for remolding the nation's securities markets into single competitive arena, linked by an electronic communications system. The SEC's authority to regulate the stock exchange was expanded. Although the legislation did not outlaw the off-board trading rule, the SEC was ordered to report to Congress in six months whether it viewed Rule 394 as anticompetitive and whether the rule should be modified or abolished entirely.[50]

On December 19, 1975 the SEC acted. It ruled that starting April 1, 1976 exchanges must drop present restraints on member's ability to execute customers trades in exchange-listed stocks through over-the-counter or other off-board transactions. Rule 19C–1 states that:

. . . on and after March 31, 1976, the rules of each national securities exchange shall provide that no rule, stated policy or practice of that exchange

---

[49] Donald E. Weeden, Letter to the Securities and Exchange Commission, August 14, 1975.

[50] The House Subcommittee took a much stronger stand. Its report declared: "In a central market system whose objectives are that customers should receive the best possible execution of their orders in any market wherever situated and that such orders be transacted at the lowest possible cost, rule 394 has no justification. Accordingly, the New York Stock Exchange should immediately rescind the rule. If this is not done the Subcommittee will introduce legislation which will have the effect of abrogating the rule."

Subcommittee on Commerce and Finance, House Committee on Foreign Commerce, *Securities Industry Study Report*, H. R. Rep. 92–1519, 92d Cong., 2d sess. (Washington, D.C., 1976), p. viii.

shall prohibit or condition, or be construed to prohibit, condition, or otherwise limit, directly or indirectly, the ability of any member acting as agent to effect transactions on any other exchange or over-the-counter with a third market maker or nonmember block positioner in any equity security which is listed on that exchange or to which unlisted trading privileges on that exchange have been extended.

After March 31, 1976, and until January 2, 1977, exchange rules may not prevent a member of an exchange, acting as an agent, from effecting transactions in listed securities on other exchanges, or over-the-counter, with a third market maker or nonmember block positioner, except that exchange rules may require members effecting such transactions to satisfy limit orders left with a specialist or represented through any other limit order mechanism. After January 2, 1977, such requirements that limit orders be satisfied will cease to be in effect. Unaffected, for the time being are bans on "principal" transactions off the Exchange floor. However, the Commission strongly suggested that ending exchange restrictions on such trades would promote competition and benefit investors, and it stated that it will "reconsider" the continuance by March 1, 1977 at the latest.[51]

Toward a Central Market

With change creeping at a glacial pace through the securities markets, the consensus of informed opinion seems to be that we are headed for an automated central marketplace, but having agreed on this the experts then part company. Each seems to have his own view of the shape and form, inclusiveness or exclusiveness of a "central marketplace," and the degree of automation which should accompany it. The SEC has declared:

The term "central market system" refers to a system of communications by which the various elements of the marketplace, be they exchanges or over-the-counter markets, are tied together. It also includes a set of rules governing the relationships which will prevail among market participants. To mandate the formation of a central market system is not to choose between one auction market and a dealer market. Both have an essential function and both must be put to work together and not separately in the new system.[52]

---

[51] See "SEC Orders Exchanges to End Most Curbs on Off-Board Stock Trades by April 1," *The Wall Street Journal*, December 22, 1975. See also Securities Exchange Act of 1934, Release No. 11942, December 19, 1975, "Adoption of Rule 19c–1 under the Securities Exchange Act of 1934 Governing Off-Board Trading by Members of National Securities Exchanges" (Washington, D.C.: Securities and Exchange Commission, 1975), p. 54 et seq.

[52] *Statement of the SEC on the Future Structure of the Securities Markets*, Washington, D.C., February 2, 1972.

But this was not Mr. Martin's view. William McChesney Martin, Jr., the highly respected former chairman of the Federal Reserve Board, declared:

To serve the interests of the public and the nation, as well as the interests of the securities industry itself, a national exchange system must be developed to provide a single, national auction market for each security qualified for listing. Such a system would integrate the New York Stock Exchange, the American Stock Exchange and the regional exchanges. Because of their geographical locations and their identification with local needs, the regional exchanges have a vital role to play in making a truly national system. To accomplish this, the structure of the market mechanism must be redesigned and modernized.[53]

But many have taken issue with his proposed redesign.[54] Perhaps the organization choices were best posed by Dr. Farrar, who headed the Institutional Investors Study.

Fundamentally, three alternatives have been put forth to date for the organization of the nation's securities markets:

1. *A Single, Central Marketplace from Which Competition Is Excluded by a Variety of Devices.* Supported vigorously by the New York Stock Exchange, this alternative includes the package of prohibitions contained in the Martin report. Its effect would be to return the NYSE to the position it once enjoyed as the exclusive market for securities of major corporations.

2. *A System of Separate but Competing Markets.* Supported by some of the regional exchanges, this proposal includes maintenance of fixed-minimum commissions, institutional membership, and opportunities for the regionals to compete with the NYSE through differences in rules regarding the recapture, use, and distribution of excess commissions. Its effect would be to preserve, if possible, the multiple trading structure in which regional exchanges and third markets have flourished.

3. *A Single, Central Market System That Eliminates Barriers to Access.* Supported by various reformers, major third-market firms, some of the larger NYSE houses, many institutional investors, leading economists, and a virtually unanimous business press, this alternative embodies the operational provisions advocated by the IIS. Its effect would be to create a marketplace in which competitive forces are accorded the widest latitude.[55]

---

[53] William McChesney Martin, Jr., *The Securities Markets: A Report with Recommendations*, submitted to the Board of Governors of the New York Stock Exchange, New York, August 5, 1971.

[54] See Donald M. Feuerstein, "Toward a National System of Securities Exchanges," *Financial Analysts Journal*, Part I, May/June 1972; July/August 1972; Donald E. Farrar, "The Martin Report: Wall Street's Proposed 'Great Leap Backward'," *Financial Analysts Journal*, September/October 1971.

[55] Donald E. Farrar, "The Coming Reform on Wall Street," *Harvard Business Review*, September-October 1972.

Some highlights of the historical development of the central market concept are the following:

The Securities Amendments Act of 1975 ordered the SEC to appoint a board to advise the Commission on "steps to facilitate the establishment of a national central market system for the trading of securities." Congress directed that the National Market Advisory Board submit a report to it by December 31, 1976. The SEC named a 15-member board, with John J. Scanlon, formerly vice president and chief financial officer of AT&T, as chairman.

Congress instructed the SEC to use its authority to "facilitate the establishment of a national market system" by expanding the Commission's authority over a number of matters including automated systems providing last sale and quotation information, unjustified competitive restraints, market makers, exchange trading of unlisted securities, off-market trading in listed securities, commission rates, and rules of self-regulatory organizations.[56] The new national market system is to

---

1. *Institutional Investor Study.* This March 1971 report by the SEC was perhaps the first published mention of the central market concept.
2. *Martin Report.* Published in August 1971 by the NYSE, this was the first attempt at a reasonably complete description of a central market approach.
3. *SEC Policy Statements.* These early 1972 and early 1973 reports spelled out in some detail the SEC's thinking about the central market.
4. *NYSE Study. A Staff Analysis of Issues Affecting a Central Exchange Market for Listed Stocks* was published in 1973 as a discussion paper.
5. *Yearly Committee.* Established in early 1974 as an advisor to the SEC, it completed its work with two reports in July and September 1975.
6. *Composite Tape.* Introduced in mid-1975, this was the initial step in the actual development of a central market.
7. *Composite Quotation System.* The SEC, under proposed Rule 17a–14, required all issuers of quotations, including stock exchanges, to make such information available to any organization desiring to disseminate quotations.
8. *Securities Act Amendments of 1975.* Following studies by subcommittees of both houses of Congress, enactment of this legislation laid the groundwork for the central market. While the legislation does not clearly mandate such a development, "It direct(s) the Commission to facilitate the establishment of the system in accordance with enumerated Congressional findings and objectives. . . ." Thus, the system is considered as evolving with the cooperation of the securities industry, under SEC oversight.
9. *National Market Advisory Board (NMAB).* Established by the 1975 legislation as an advisory body to the SEC, this group is now deliberating upon the many aspects of the central market. It has been meeting once a month since October 1975 and is to report by the end of 1976. One of its first acts was to request others to submit plans or sketches of a possible system—in response to which the Davant and the Gustave Levy reports were developed.
10. *Limit Order Book Proposals.* On March 2, 1976, the SEC released a request for proposals regarding a consolidated limit order book (CLOB). However, the release left open the possibility of alternatives to the CLOB and the central market itself.
11. To immobilize the cumbersome stock certificate the NYSE created the Central Certificate Service (CCS). This was converted into the Depository Trust Co. (DTC) in May 1973. Its function was to hold stock certificates for banks, brokerage houses, depositories, in order to develop a national clearance and depository system.

[56] See Walter Werner, "Adventure in Social Control of Finance: The National Market System for Securities", *Columbia Law Review*, vol. 75, no. 7, November 1975.

be "fair and orderly," "in the public interest," for the "protection of investors," and "efficient." The latter term can have several meanings.[57] "An economically efficient execution of securities transactions" can mean that the cost of transferring securities should be reasonable. Markets may be structured so as to secure an efficient allocation of scarce resources (capital).[58] Or the term "efficient markets" may be used in the way economists use it to mean markets in which prices respond quickly to new information.[59]

No blueprint for a national market system was given in the 1975 Amendments Act. Earlier the Senate Committee had said that no definition was needed because "the general concept is sufficiently clear from the words themselves and it is best to allow maximum flexibility in working out specific details."[60]

There have been a number of reports[61] and a variety of proposals.[62] More are due.[63] That compromise and modern technology will play a part in the evolving outcome and that it will take time, seems apparent but that is about all that is clear at this writing.

The last word may be left to SEC Commissioner Philip A. Loomis, Jr.:

Perhaps the cornerstone of a national market system is the creation of a mechanism by which all, or at least most, of the orders for securities traded in the system are channeled into the system rather than being fragmented and dispersed. This concentration of the order flow has at least two important consequences. It provides a maximum opportunity for such orders to interact and to be matched, and it enables market professionals, particularly market makers, to have access to the entire order flow and this in turn greatly improves their ability to perform their functions effectively and efficiently.[64]

---

[57] Richard R. West, "Two Kinds of Market Efficiency," *Financial Analysts Journal*, November/December 1975.

[58] See James H. Lorie, *Public Policy for American Capital Markets*, Report to the Secretary of the Treasury, February 7, 1974.

[59] Burton G. Malkiel, *A Random Walk down Wall Street* (New York: W. W. Norton & Co., Inc., 1973).

[60] Senate Committee on Banking, Housing and Urban Affairs, *Report on National Securities Market System Act of 1974 to Accompany S.2519*, Report No. 93-865 93d Cong., 2d sess. (Washington, D.C., 1974).

[61] See, for example, "Securities and Exchange Commission, Advisory Committee on the Implementation of a Central Market System," (Alexander Yearly IV, Chairman), *Summary Report*, July 17, 1975, *Full Report*, October 23, 1975.

[62] See, for example, *Proposal for a National Market System*, Merrill Lynch, Pierce, Fenner & Smith, Inc. New York, 1975. Weeden & Co. has produced a somewhat similar proposal called WHAM, for Weeden Holding Corporation's Automated Market. See *New York Times*, August 20, 1976.

[63] The Scanlon Committee Report, the Davant Committee Report, the Gustave Levy Committee Report.

[64] See *The CFA Digest*, The Institute of Chartered Financial Analysts, Charlottesville, Va., vol. 6, no. 1 (Winter 1976), p. 37.

SUGGESTED READINGS

Barnea, A., and Loque, D. E.   "Risk and the Market Maker's Spread." *Financial Analysts Journal*, November/December 1975.

Black, Fischer.   "Toward a Fully Automated Stock Exchange." *Financial Analysts Journal*, Part I, July/August 1971; Part II, November/December 1971.

Farrar, Donald E.   "The Coming Reform on Wall Street." *Harvard Business Review*, September-October 1972.

Hayes, Douglas A., and Bauman, W. Scott.   *Investments: Analysis and Management*, 3d ed. New York: Macmillan Publishing Co., 1976. Chapter 4.

Institutional Investor Study Report of the Securities and Exchange Commission: Summary volume. 92d Cong., 1st sess., House Document No. 92–64, Part 8, Washington, D.C., March 10, 1971.

Lechner, A. B., and Londoner, D. J.   "Brokerage Profits after May Day." *Financial Analysts Journal*, January/February 1976.

Martin, William McChesney, Jr.   *The Securities Markets: A Report with Recommendations*, submitted to the Board of Governors of the New York Stock Exchange, August 5, 1971.

Mendelson, Morris.   "From Automated Quotes to Automated Trading: Restructuring the Stock Market in the U.S." *The Bulletin*, Nos. 80–82. New York: Institute of Finance, Graduate School of Business Administration, New York University, March 1972.

Mendelson, Morris, and Robbins, Sidney.   *Investment Analysis and Securities Markets*. New York: Basic Books, 1976. Chapters 1 and 2.

Merrill Lynch, Pierce, Fenner and Smith, Inc. *Proposal For a National Market System*. New York, 1975.

New York Stock Exchange.   *Crisis in the Securities Industry: A Chronology, 1967–1970*. July 30, 1971.

———.   *A Staff Analysis of Issues Affecting the Structure of a Central Exchange Market for Listed Securities*, July 1973.

———.   *A National Market System: A Report by the National Market System Committee*. July 1, 1976.

Regan, Donald T.   *A View from the Street*. New York: The New American Library Inc., 1972.

Securities and Exchange Commission. *The Future Structure of the Securities Market*. Statement of the SEC. Washington, D.C., February 2, 1972.

———.   *White Paper on the Structure of a Central Market System*. Washington, D.C., March 30, 1973.

———.   Advisory Commission on the Implementation of a Central Market System.   *Summary Report*, Washington, D.C., July 17, 1975; *Report* October 23, 1975.

Securities Industries Association.   *Report of the National Market Systems Committee*. June 1976.

Sobel, Robert. *N.Y.S.E.: A History of the New York Stock Exchange, 1935–1975.* New York: Weybright and Talley, 1975.

Welles, Chris. *Last Days of the Club.* New York: E. P. Dutton & Co, Inc., 1975.

Werner, Walter. "Adventure in Social Control of Finance: The National Market System." *Columbia Law Review,* vol. 75, no. 7 (November 1975).

West, Richard R. "Two Kinds of Market Efficiency." *Financial Analysts Journal,* November/December 1975.

REVIEW QUESTIONS AND PROBLEMS

1. How do primary markets for securities differ from secondary markets?

2. Explain the economic and financial role of specialists on the New York Stock Exchange.

3. Explain each of the following: (*a*) market order, (*b*) limit order, (*c*) stop order, (*d*) open (G.T.C.) order, (*e*) discretionary order.

4. With respect to margin, explain what is meant by (*a*) initial margin, (*b*) maintenance margin, (*c*) debit balance, (*d*) equity in the account, (*e*) undermargined account, (*f*) restricted account.

5. Explain the various special methods for buying and selling large blocks (*a*) on the New York Stock Exchange, (*b*) off the New York Stock Exchange. What is block positioning?

6. How does the over-the-counter market differ from the organized exchanges? What is NASDAQ? How does it work on three levels?

7. What is meant by "the Third Market"? Who uses it and why? What are its advantages? Its disadvantages? What is the significance of Rule 394?

8. What is the "efficient market" theory? What are its implications for securities analysis and portfolio management?

9. Should institutions be allowed to purchase memberships on organized exchanges? Why? Why not?

10. A recent monograph was entitled "From Automated Quotes to Automated Trading: Restructuring the Stock Market in the United States." How has automation changed securities trading over the last decade? How is it likely to do so over the next decade?

RESEARCH PROJECTS

1. Prepare a report on "the development of a national market system" for securities. What have been the various recommendations of governmental agencies, congressional committees, special surveys, and so forth, with respect to a "national market system"? As of this date, indicate the degree to which the various recommendations have been implemented. What are the next likely steps in your judgment?

2. Several interesting articles have appeared in the *Financial Analysts Journal*, entitled "Toward a Fully Automated Stock Exchange." Assume that you were trying to rewrite and update these articles to appear under the title "Toward a Fully Automated Central Marketplace for Securities." Prepare a draft of an article on the latter subject for possible submission to the *Financial Analysts Journal*.

3. Assume that you are a public member of the board of directors of the New York Stock Exchange. Draft a report listing and explaining the steps you think the Exchange should take (*a*) for the protection of investors, (*b*) for greater efficiency in market operations, (*c*) for improvement in the financial condition of member firms, (*d*) for the better accommodation of institutional traders, (*e*) to ensure fair and reasonable commission rates for both small and large investors.

4. Visit a member firm of the National Association of Securities Dealers, having a NASDAQ installation. Study its operation. Prepare a report to summarize what you saw and what you heard. How did it operate? At what level? How could the operation be extended? To serve what purposes?

5. Assume that you are the portfolio manager of a large mutual fund, and that you want to dispose of 200,000 shares of a growth stock, whose earnings you estimate are about to level off. What channel or channels do you propose to use and what are the costs involved? Compare and contrast the various alternatives, indicating which you have chosen and why.

Chapter 3

Obtaining Investment Information

> "Investigate before you invest."
> —— *Better Business Bureau*

The "Bawl Street Journal" comes out once a year. In it many a true word is said in jest. "We sincerely hope the market catches up with our predictions before the SEC does," advertised one brokerage house specializing in growth stock recommendations. "Now that logical reasoning is no longer required in this crazy market we have more confidence in our recommendations," announced another large firm. "Let us review your holdings with an aim at increasing our commissions," suggested another jokingly. "If you're looking for laughs come in and see us! Some of our offerings are hilarious," said a new issue house. "Get our research bulletin: Rarely do so many who know so little say so much," advertised another firm. Wall Street poking fun at itself but highlighting a real problem—which of many, many sources of information to rely upon? Where to go for unbiased, accurate information?

For the small, inexperienced investor, the vast outpouring of investment information, advice, alleged facts, and recommendations can be bewildering and confusing. Even the skilled analyst can be misled. For example, one large investment advisory service was sued by an irate investor who had lost a large sum in a land company, whose stock had been recommended by the advisory service. In pretrial discovery and examination it developed that the service had made its recommendation based, in part, on a forecast of earnings. To develop this forecast the securities analyst of the investment advisory service had made a trip to Florida, talked with company officials, including the president and financial vice president. The information they provided turned out to be incorrect, and changes they had made in accounting

techniques gave an artificially favorable cast to current and prospective earnings. Instead of the expected and forecasted increase in earnings per share over the next two years, losses developed.

The Individual Investor

No one invests in a vacuum. We act on some type of information, whether it be a tip from a friend, advice from a banker, a broker's recommendation, a newspaper report, or a magazine article. Not knowing which of the many sources of information to rely upon, one investor hit upon a simple expedient which may yield substantial returns in bull markets. He watched the most active list in the daily paper, and whenever a stock, which had not previously been on the list, appeared twice and each time showed an increase in price, he bought, held six months and a day, and then sold, regardless of where the stock was at that time. He was getting his investment advice and suggestions from the market itself, reasoning that whatever was being bought in large volume had many favorable judgments behind it, some carefully considered and reasoned, others possibly less well based, but all, on the whole, serving as an evaluation and recommendation.

Individual investors have a difficult time. They don't usually have the facilities, resources, or time to research a stock in depth before making their investment decision. They have a business life, a family life, a social life, and the time remaining from these pursuits, if any, is likely to be very limited. What they read, what they look into, must be most judiciously selected because it can't, by definition, be very extensive. For the small investor, investment selection may become almost a hit-and-run operation.

Ideally the intelligent investor should ask and obtain answers to at least four basic questions: (1) What is the state of business and the economy? In the light of such conditions is it a favorable time to invest? Where are we in the business cycle? Is the boom likely to top out shortly? Is a recession near at hand? Questions in this area will vary with the stage of the business cycle. (2) What is the state of the market? Are we in the early stages of a bull market? Has the low point of a bear market about been reached? Is the bull market about to top out? Questions to be asked will vary with the state of the market. (3) If answers to the preceding two questions seem favorable, then there must be an investment selection. What industries are likely to grow most rapidly? Are there any special factors which favor a particular industry? (4) Which company or companies within the industry are likely to do best? Which companies are to be avoided because of poor prospects?

While small investors may not be able to devote the time to answer

all these questions in depth, they must spend some time, with one or more sources of information, to come to an investment decision. Which source or sources should they choose? Reliance on a broker, on the financial press and on one or more investment services seem minimal.

The Financial Analyst and the Institutional Investor

The financial analyst and the institutional investment manager have both the time and the resources to dig deeper than the individual investor. Increasingly, they also have the capacity. Financial analysts, or securities analysts, organized in a national federation, have introduced a professional qualification examination leading to a C.F.A. designation—Chartered Financial Analyst. A formal training program with three stages of examinations lead to this designation. It requires not only a thorough knowledge of accounting, balance sheet and income statement analysis, of economics and finance, but also competence and maturity in investment management and securities analysis.[1]

Institutions are able to employ skilled economists, financial analysts, and investment managers. They are able to mesh economic forecasts with investment research.[2] They can study SEC filings and SEC Form 10–K's for detailed financial information about companies in which they have an interest.[3] They can purchase copies of registration statements and read them with understanding. Where published financial information is not clear or adequate, or where questions arise about the financial affairs of a company, or about its management or management policies, the institutional investment manager or the financial analyst can afford the time and expense of calling upon the company at its home office and putting the questions privately before making an investment decision or judgment. Not only is the initial investment commitment a considered one but there is usually continuous review and scrutiny of issues held. When and if conditions develop which are adverse, securities are eliminated from the portfolio on the basis of facts, research, and experienced evaluation. Many small investors tend to put securities away and forget about

---

[1] See W. Scott Bauman, "The C.F.A. Candidate Program," *Financial Analysts Journal*, November/December 1974.

[2] Harvey M. Spiro, "Use of Economics in Portfolio Decisions," *Journal of Portfolio Management*, Spring 1976; Roy E. Moor, "Economic Disciplines for Economic Disciples," *Journal of Portfolio Management*, Winter 1975; and Arthur Zeikel, "Random Walk and Murphy's Law," *Journal of Portfolio Management*, Fall 1974.

[3] See "Securities and Exchange Commission," and "Form 10–K," *Financial Analyst's Handbook*, vol. I (Homewood, Ill.: Dow Jones-Irwin, Inc., 1975), chaps. 3 and 26, respectively.

them. Institutional investors seldom do this. The institutional investors usually has a great advantage over the average individual investor.

Brokerage Houses

Brokerage houses with research departments provide much information for both individual and institutional investors. Most large brokerage houses maintain substantial research staffs. They publish market letters or market reviews. They provide individual company analyses and recommendations. They undertake portfolio reviews. They provide industry studies. If you tell them the approximate amount you wish to invest, they will provide a suggested portfolio in line with the investment objective you have indicated.

Leading brokerage houses with competent research departments include:

Oppenheimer & Co., One New York Plaza, N.Y. 10004
Bache Halsey Stuart Inc., One Gold Street, New York, N.Y. 10038
Loeb, Rhoades & Co., 42 Wall Street, New York, N.Y. 10005
Kidder, Peabody & Co., 10 Hanover Square, New York, N.Y. 10005
Merrill Lynch, Pierce, Fenner & Smith, One Liberty Plaza, New York, N.Y. 10006
Reynolds Securities, Inc., 120 Broadway, New York, N.Y. 10005
Paine, Webber, Jackson & Curtis, Inc., 140 Broadway, New York, N.Y. 10005
Hornblower & Weeks-Hemphill, Noyes, 8 Hanover Street, New York, N.Y. 10005
E. F. Hutton & Company Inc., One Battery Park Plaza, New York, N.Y. 10004
Smith Barney, Harris Upham & Co., 1345 Avenue of the Americas, New York, N.Y. 10019
L. F. Rothschild & Co., 99 William Street, New York, N.Y. 10038
Shearson Hayden Stone Inc., 767 Fifth Avenue, New York, N.Y. 10022
Blyth Eastman Dillon & Co., One Chase Manhattan Plaza, New York, N.Y. 10005

The largest brokerage house, Merrill Lynch, Pierce, Fenner & Smith, has a huge research department, as might be expected. They have published extensively.[4]

Other large brokerage houses publish similar material. Most firms issue weekly or monthly "market" letters as well as "recommended" lists from time to time covering selected companies in favored industries. Almost without exception the brokerage houses make their re-

---

[4] Free copies of any of their reports may be obtained by writing Merrill Lynch, Pierce, Fenner & Smith, at One Liberty Plaza, 165 Broadway, New York, N.Y. 10006.

search bulletins and reports available to investors without charge. They will analyze and evaluate an existing portfolio, provide sample portfolio suggestions for given investment objectives such as growth, capital gains, income and stability, or they will develop an individually tailored portfolio to meet age, amount, and investment objective requirements. Smaller brokerage houses which do not have research departments of their own sometimes buy their "research" from "wholesale" organizations like Argus Research or Data Digests, or else obtain it from large houses through which they clear.

The Financial Press

The intelligent investor and the professional securities analyst generally browse through, read, or study a significant part of the financial press each week, ranging from the financial section of a large metropolitan daily newspaper, or *The Wall Street Journal* to the *Financial Analysts Journal* (published every two months) or the *Journal of Finance* (published quarterly). The financial section of a newspaper can range from the elaborate and informative pages of *The New York Times* to a mere listing of daily stock quotations.

The Wall Street Journal is a daily, published every weekday by Dow Jones & Co. in New York, Chicago, San Francisco, and Los Angeles. It provides full coverage of business and financial news, including special news of companies, corporate profits reports, new issues, bond financing, national and local over-the-counter quotations and NYSE and AMEX stock prices, and CBOE option quotations.

The Wall Street Journal each day contains the Dow Jones Industrial stock price average, the most widely quoted and extensively used stock price average, though not the most accurate. The Dow Jones Industrials consist of 30 blue chip stocks. There is also an average of 20 transportation stocks, 15 utility stocks, and a composite average of the 65. The DJI goes back a long way; originally it was published in 1897 based on 12 stocks. In 1916 it was broadened to 20, and in October 1928, it was raised to 30. From time to time over the years, individual stocks have been dropped from the list and replaced by others. There have been some 30 such substitutions since October 1928. The 30 at present are: Allied Chemical, Aluminum Co. of America, American Can, AT&T, American Brands, Bethlehem Steel, Chrysler, Du Pont, Eastman Kodak, General Electric, General Foods, General Motors, Goodyear, International Harvester, International Nickel, International Paper, Johns-Manville, Minnesota Mining and Manufacturing (3M), Owens-Illinois, Procter & Gamble, Sears Roebuck, Standard Oil of California, Exxon (Standard Oil of New Jersey), Esmark (Swift & Co.), Texaco, Union Carbide, United Technology (United Aircraft),

United States Steel, Westinghouse, Woolworth. The only names in the above group that appear in the original 12 are American Tobacco (now American Brands) and General Electric.[5]

The first computations were quite simple. The prices of the 12 stocks were added and the result divided by 12. That was the average. Complications developed when some stocks in the average split their shares. Some sort of compensation had to be made to avoid distorting the average. To cite an example given by Dow Jones & Co., take, for example, a three-stock average. One sells for $5, another for $10, a third for $15 a share. The average price is $10. Then the $15 stock is split three for one, automatically reducing the value of each share to $5. The day of the split the $5 stock advances to $6, the $10 stock to $11, and the split stock to $6—an average of $7.67 a share, down sharply from the preceding day's average of $10 a share despite the fact that the market actually advanced. To correct for this distortion, Dow Jones came up with a solution which has been in effect since 1928. They changed the divisor to reflect the split. Instead of dividing by 30, when a stock split they divided by a lesser divisor. Over the years each new split within the 30-stock group dropped the divisor lower. Thus now, when the Dow Jones Industrial average is computed, the total of the 30 stock prices isn't divided by 30 but rather by 1.504.

There is, of course, a tremendous disparity, as a result of the way the average is derived, between DJI points and dollars and cents. This has led to some highly misleading descriptions of the market. The DJI advances 10 points, for example, and immediately there are reports that the market is soaring; the fact is that the stocks in the DJI have moved up an average of 55 cents a share. If the DJI declines 15 points, the market is said to have plunged; again the fact is that the stocks in the DJI have lost an average of 83 cents a share. With a divisor of 1.504, a 1-point change in the DJI equals about 6 cents in the arithmetical average of the stocks in the DJI. A 10-point decline is the equivalent of a dip of 55 cents per share in the dollar value. A 20-point decline represents $1.11 in dollar value.

In the light of the excitement about the DJI finally breaking through 1,000 in 1972–73, it is interesting to note that but for one substitution, the DJI would have broken through the 1000 level in December 1961. In 1939 IBM was removed from inclusion in the DJI 30 and AT&T was

---

[5] The other ten were American Cotton Oil, American Sugar, Chicago Gas, Distilling and Cattle Feeding, Laclede Gas, National Lead, North American, Tennessee Coal and Iron, U.S. Leather Preferred, and U.S. Rubber. At various times the following were included: Victor Talking Machine, Standard Rope and Twine, Pacific Mail, Central Leather, Amalgamated Copper, Famous Players Lasky, Baldwin Locomotive, Studebaker, Hudson Motors, Nash Kelvinator, and Wright Aeronautical.

substituted. Had IBM remained, the DJI would have reached a December 1961 high of 1017.39 instead of 734.91.[6]

". . . It's *Catch-22*. Everyone looks at the Dow because it's prominently displayed. Its displayed because everyone looks at it. . . ."[7]

After the Dow Jones Industrial average, probably the most widely known market barometer is the index prepared by Standard & Poor's Corporation based on 400 industrial stocks. It also has a 40 stock financial group, a 20-stock transportation index, a 40-stock utility index, and a 500-stock composite of the four, as well as other individual industry stock price indexes.[8] Standard & Poor's, in arriving at an index figure, doesn't just add up per share prices and divide. It starts by multiplying the price of each share by the number of shares in that issue; for example, in the case of a stock selling at $10 a share with 10,000 shares outstanding, it would get $100,000. These market value figures are then added, giving the aggregate market value of the issues covered. This aggregate is expressed as a percentage of the average market value during the years 1941–43. Then, finally, this percentage figure is divided by 10. There is no need for a changing divisor. Adjustment for stock splits is made automatically—because each stock enters the index not as a per share price but as a market value figure covering all the shares in the issue. Take the $10 stock with 10,000 shares outstanding and a consequent market value of $100,000. If that is split two for one, the result is 20,000 shares of $5 stock—still worth $100,000. It's the $100,000 not the $10 or the $5 that goes into the index.

The S&P 400 industrial stock price index is numerically far down the ladder from the DJI. At the time that the latter was about 900, the S&P index was about 90. This was not an accident. When a prior S&P industrial index was discontinued in 1957 and the present new index inaugurated, the old index was at around 370 on a 1935–39 equals 100 base. When the new index was launched on a 1941–43 base, it was made equal to 10 not to 100. This, in effect, divided the index by 10. The new Standard & Poor's index started in 1957 at 47. That was

---

[6] The DJIA has in recent years been criticized as not accurately reflecting the market. See, for example, Wyndham Robertson, "The Trouble with the Dow-Jones Average," *Fortune*, March 1972, David T. Wendell, "The Dow Average: Its Make-Up and History," *Weekly Staff Letter*, David L. Babson & Co. Inc., Boston, Mass., January 15, 1976. See also Alan R. Shaw, "How Now Dow Jones?" *Financial World*, November 5, 1975.

Dow Jones & Company publishes a brochure entitled "The Stock Averages: Here's How the Major Market Indicators Are Computed to Make Sure They Have Valid Historical Perspective." For a copy write to Public Relations, Dow Jones & Company, Inc., 22 Cortlandt Street, New York, N.Y. 10004.

[7] Andrew Tobias, "The Decline and Fall of the Dow Jones Industrials," *New York Magazine*, November 13, 1972.

[8] "Standard & Poor's Revises 500 Index, Adds Fourth Group: Financial Concerns' Stocks Make Up New Category; OTC Issues Are Included," *The Wall Street Journal*, July 1, 1976.

almost precisely the same as the then average price of $45.23 for all common shares listed on the NYSE. The DJI 30 stocks represent about 25 percent of the market value of all NYSE listed stocks. Standard & Poor's index of 500 stocks accounts for about 74 percent of the market value of all listed shares.

In mid-1966 both the American and the New York Stock Exchanges developed and introduced their own stock price indexes. The AMEX average is computed by adding all of the plus net changes and minus net changes above or below previous closing prices. The sum is then divided by the number of issues listed and the result added to or subtracted from the previous close. For example, on a given day, the sum of all price changes was an increase of $170.94. Dividing by 952, the number of common stocks and warrants then listed, produced a result of $0.18, which, added to the closing value of the index on the previous day—$13.15—produced a price level index of $13.33.

Changes in the number of issues used as a divisor will be made when new stocks are listed or existing ones removed; adjustments in the previous day's closing index will be made in the case of stock splits, stock dividends, and cash dividends. Since the AMEX index considers net price changes only, no consideration is given to the importance of the relationship of the net change to its price. This means that a $1 move in a $5 stock receives the same weight as a $1 change in a $100 stock.

The NYSE Common Stock Index is a composite index of all the equity issues listed on the Exchange. In addition the NYSE also publishes four separate indexes as follows:

a. The Finance Index includes 75 issues of closed-end investment companies, savings and loan holding companies, real estate holding and investment companies, and others in commercial and installment finance, banking, insurance, and related fields.

b. The Transportation Index is based on 76 issues representing railroads, airlines, shipping, motor transport, and other operating, leasing, and holding companies in the transportation field.

c. The Utility Index includes 136 issues of operating, holding, and transmission companies in gas, electric, power, and communications.

d. The Industrial Index comprises the nearly 1,000 NYSE-listed stocks not included in the other three subgroup indexes. These, of course, represent a wide variety of industrial corporations in many fields of manufacturing, merchandising, and service.

The Composite Index takes into consideration the total market value of every common stock traded on the exchange. To compute the Common Stock Index, the market value of each common share is multiplied by the number of shares of that issue which are listed. The

results are added to obtain total market value. The index is a number that expresses simply the relationship between total current market value and a base market value (as of December 31, 1965) after necessary adjustments have been made.

To establish a close relationship at the outset between the Common Stock Index and the actual average price of all listed common stocks, a figure of 50 as of December 31, 1965, was selected as the base for the index. The actual average price on that date was about $53. The sub-indexes are also based on 50 as of December 31, 1965. If the index gets too far away from the actual average price of listed stocks, the exchange plans to bring it back in line by changing the base date or splitting the index.

All the indexes are expressed in points. Point changes in the all-stock index are also converted into dollar and cent changes in the average price per share, which many investors may find more meaningful than points and easier to relate, in terms of actual market value, to the particular issue in which they may be interested.[9]

Computers of the Stock Exchange's Market Data System calculate the new indexes throughout the trading day. Each half hour the exchange's international ticker network carries the Common Stock Index, with its net change in points from the previous day's close, and the net change in the average price of NYSE common stocks. The Industrial, Transportation, Utility, and Finance Indexes, with net changes, are reported hourly in points. Final results for the day are printed on the tape after the close of the market. The index, computed back to 1940, is shown in Figure 3–1. Statistical aspects of its computation are shown in Figure 3–2.

There are other stock price averages or indexes such as the Value Line Average of 1,600 stocks. (See Figure 3–3.) It should be noted that in the Value Line Composite, prices are not weighted by the number of outstanding shares as in the case of the NYSE and S&P averages. From the viewpoint of investment analysis, the Standard & Poor's indexes with their 97-category industry breakdown would appear to be the most useful. These indexes are published weekly in *The Outlook*. (See Figure 3–4.)

The Standard & Poor's Stock Price Indexes have been steadily expanding their coverage over the years, to supply a dependable measure of the composite price pattern of the majority of stocks. Currently the coverage is 500 stocks, broken down into 97 individual groups, which include the four main groups; i.e., industrial composite (400), financial (40), transportation (20), utilities (40), and the 500 composite.

---

[9] The Research Department of the New York Stock Exchange has published a monograph entitled *New York Stock Exchange Common Stock Indexes*. For a copy of the latest edition write to Research Department, New York Stock Exchange, 11 Wall Street, New York, N.Y. 10005.

FIGURE 3–1
New York Stock Exchange Common Stock Index

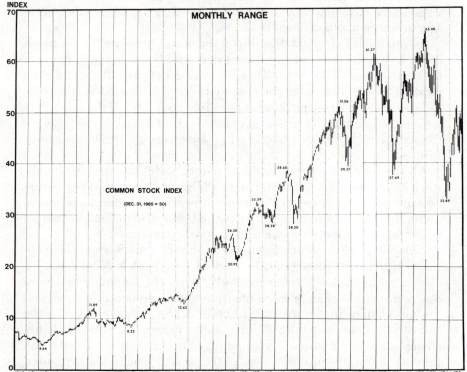

January 1940 to May 1964 based on weekly closing prices.
June 1964 to date based on daily closing prices.
Source: Research Department, New York Stock Exchange.

There are also four supplementary group series, namely Capital Goods Companies, Consumer Goods, High-Grade Common Stocks, and Low-Priced Common Stocks.

The changes made in the S&P index in 1976 are described on page 131.

To increase the usefulness of these price indexes, Standard & Poor's computes companion series of *per share data* by industry groups, all related to the stock price indexes, including per share earnings, dividends, sales, operating income, depreciation, taxes, book value, working capital, and capital expenditures, and significant ratios and yields. These data are published in Standard & Poor's *Analysts Handbook* annually, back to 1946. The *Analysts Handbook* is kept current through a monthly supplement, which also contains S&P's official group earnings estimates and indicated dividend rates.

Dow Jones & Co. publishes *Barron's National Business & Finan-*

Major Changes in S&P 500

Major revisions in the S&P 500 stock price index which will make it more representative of the over-all market have been made, effective July 1. The changes, explained below, are the most comprehensive since the index was introduced.

The 500 had previously been made up of 425 Industrials, 15 Railroads, and 60 Utilities. Now it comprises 400 Industrials, 20 Transportation, 40 Utilities, and 40 Financial.

The new Financial main group includes bank, insurance and other categories which had previously been tracked by means of indexes outside the 500. In replacing Railroads with the broader Transportation group, we now provide readings for rails, airlines, truckers and an air freight issue combined, as well as continuing the sub-indexes. Some of these Transportation sub-indexes had been in the Industrials group, which was streamlined and improved in

other ways as well, as was the Utilities group.

Thanks to recent improvements in technology, we have been able to include 12 major over-the-counter issues in the 500 for the first time. In all, 45 stocks have been added and 45 deleted.

Calculations of historical data indicate that these changes would have resulted in no statistically significant deviations. Earnings, P/E ratios and dividend yield data on the new Financial and Transportation groups will be available in our statistical page in the near future. Our next cumulative (blue) index will show all the individual stocks in the revised S&P 500.

The 500 is not only a widely followed measure of stock market movements. As one of the Commerce Department's 12 leading business indicators, it is also an accepted barometer of economic conditions.

Source: Standard & Poor's, *The Outlook,* July 5, 1976, p. 675.

cial Weekly as well as *The Wall Street Journal. Barron's* usually may be viewed as having three categories: leading articles in depth; departments such as The Trader, Up & Down Wall Street, Investment News & Views, Capital Markets, "The Striking Price" (Options), and "Market Laboratory" as well as a substantial statistical section which includes "new highs and lows in stocks," "mutual funds," "short interest," "stock quotations," "over-the-counter market," "bond quotations," and "pulse of trade and industry." The market laboratory section contains a wealth of basic figures on the Dow Jones averages, price-earnings ratios, odd-lot trading, stock yields and bond yields, the 20 most active stocks of the week, and the Confidence Index.[10]

---

[10] The Confidence Index is the ratio of the yield on *Barron's* high-grade bond (10) average to the yield on the broad Dow Jones (40) bond average. The ratio generally ranges in the 80s and 90s. It is supposed to reflect the "smart money" judgment of institutional portfolio managers. As the Confidence Index moves down, some observers of the market believe that stock prices will reflect this "smart money" judgment and sentiment and turn downward from two to four months after the turn in the Confidence Index. Those who follow the Confidence Index also believe that a rise in it will be reflected in a rise in stock prices two to four months later. The timing has varied substantially in the past, however.

FIGURE 3–2
Computation of the NYSE Indexes

For the benefit of the statistically minded, here is a capsule description of how the New York Stock Exchange Indexes are calculated.

Assume that on January 10 this year the Current Market Value of all listed common stocks was $550 billion at the close of the market. The Base Market Value on the base date (December 31, 1965) was $500 billion. The Index on the base date, of course, is constant at 50. Then we have:

$$\frac{\$550 \text{ B}}{\$500 \text{ B}} = 1.1; \ 1.1 \times 50 = 55, \text{ the Index.}$$

If the Current Market Value should increase to, say, $600 billion and the Base Market Value remains at $500 billion, we would have:

$$\frac{\$600 \text{ B}}{\$500 \text{ B}} = 1.2; \ 1.2 \times 50 = 60, \text{ the new Index.}$$

In actual practice, the Base Market Value changes daily to reflect capitalization and other changes. If a stock is delisted, for example, Current Market Value is decreased by the market value of the delisted issue. To keep the Index on a comparable basis, Base Market Value is decreased by a proportionate amount.

The adjusted or new Base Market Value must bear the same relationship to the new Market Value as the old Base Value has to the old Market Value. These ratios are expressed as follows:

$$\frac{\text{New Market Value (after change)}}{\text{New Base Value}} = \frac{\text{Old Market Value (before change)}}{\text{Old Base Value}}$$

Let's assume that a new issue with a market value of $1.2 billion is added to the Exchange's list. The old Market Value is $600 billion and the new Market Value is $601.2 billion. The old Base Value is $500 billion. Applying the formula, we have:

$$\frac{\$601.2 \text{ B}}{\text{New Base Value}} = \frac{\$600 \text{ B}}{\$500 \text{ B}}$$
$$\text{New Base Value} \times \$600 \text{ B} = \$601.2 \text{ B} \times \$500 \text{ B}$$
$$\text{New Base Value} = \$501 \text{ B}$$

So the new Index is figured as follows:

$$\frac{\$601.2 \text{ B}}{\$501 \text{ B}} \times 50 = 60$$

Converting a point change in the Index to a dollar and cent change is done on a similar proportionate basis. The relationship of the new average price per share to the new Index must be the same as the relationship of the change in the average price per share to the change in the Index, or:

$$\frac{\text{New Average Price}}{\text{New Index}} = \frac{\text{Change in Average Price}}{\text{Change in Index}}$$

Assume that the new average price is $55 a share. The Index declines .60 to 59.40, so:

$$\frac{\$55}{59.40} = \frac{\text{Change in Average Price}}{.60}$$
$$\text{Change in Average Price} \times 59.40 = \$55 \times .60$$
$$\text{Change} = 56 \text{ cents a share}$$

Source: The New York Stock Exchange.

FIGURE 3–3
The Value Line Average

Reprinted by permission of Arnold Bernhard & Co., Inc., publisher of *The Value Line Investment Survey.*

Forbes is published twice monthly. It features articles on industry and company financial developments and trends. There are regular columns on "The Market Outlook," on "Stock Analysis," "Investment Pointers," "Market Comment," and "Technician's Perspective." The January 1 issue each year is devoted to rating companies within industries, comparing and contrasting profitability and performance. The August 15 issue each year contains the *Forbes* evaluation and rating of comparative mutual fund performance. It is one of the better tools available for mutual fund evaluation.

Billed as the "world's most expensive weekly newspaper," *The Wall Street Transcript,* is published every Monday and costs $10 a copy. This is clearly for professional analysts and money managers. It reproduces complete texts of top-management speeches and interviews at meetings of 35 security analysts societies. *The Transcript* is hundreds of information sources in a single publication. In a year of issues some 2,000 company analyses, 300 industry surveys, and 500 management reports are reproduced. Features include a "Technical Corner," which reproduces technical analysis of leading brokerage

FIGURE 3–4

S&P Indexes of the Security Markets (weekly stock price indexes—1941–1943 = 10)

	Close July 7	Close June 30	% Change	1976 Range High	1976 Range Low
500 Stocks, Combined	103.83	104.28	− 0.4	104.28	90.90
400 Industrials	116.66	117.38	− 0.6	117.49	101.64
20 Transportation [g]	14.81	14.91	− 0.7	[q]14.91	12.63
40 Utilities	47.34	46.37	+ 2.1	48.37	44.70
40 Financial [g]	11.68	11.69	− 0.1	[q]11.69	10.21
109 Capital Goods	120.09	121.14	− 0.9	121.14	102.68
190 Consumer Goods	92.55	92.76	− 0.2	96.61	87.46
*25 High Grade Common	83.72	84.07	− 0.4	85.14	78.98
*20 Low Price Common	135.09	136.29	− 0.9	136.74	101.14

INDUSTRIALS

	Close July 7	Close June 30	% Change	1976 Range High	1976 Range Low
7 Aerospace	71.34	71.67	− 0.5	71.67	49.74
4 Aluminum	103.27	106.89	− 3.4	107.89	81.43
*2 Atomic Energy [e]	100.26	106.08	− 5.5	106.08	59.78
4 Automobile	83.66	85.85	− 2.6	88.54	72.00
Excl. General Motors	28.92	29.67	− 2.5	31.25	22.76
4 Auto Parts—After Market [g]	15.02	14.77	+ 1.7	16.02	13.67
5 Auto Parts—Orig. Equipment [g]	14.96	15.01	− 0.3	15.01	11.35
3 Auto Trucks & Parts	43.78	44.98	− 2.7	46.40	32.33
4 Beverages: Brewers	55.64	52.65	+ 5.7	61.15	47.97
4 Distillers	151.62	156.91	− 3.4	171.21	147.89
5 Soft Drinks	110.24	110.71	− 0.4	117.94	102.94
Building Materials Composite	49.11	49.08	+ 0.1	54.24	42.03
4 Air Conditioning [b]	23.52	23.76	− 1.0	25.01	17.75
6 Cement	20.81	21.29	− 2.3	22.93	18.52
2 Heating & Plumbing	61.08	60.77	+ 0.5	62.94	41.91
6 Roofing & Wallboard	61.89	61.46	+ 0.7	70.89	58.21
7 Chemicals	76.37	79.20	− 3.6	89.70	76.06
4 Coal: Bituminous	581.31	601.32	− 3.3	602.66	437.18
3 Confectionery	39.90	40.02	− 0.3	40.02	32.30
*10 Conglomerates [e]	16.83	16.55	+ 1.7	•16.83	12.04
5 Containers: Metal & Glass	38.01	38.35	− 0.9	38.35	34.23
7 Paper Containers	139.24	140.53	− 0.9	151.84	124.97
5 Copper	39.67	38.94	+ 1.9	39.87	33.27
6 Cosmetics [b]	62.20	62.06	+ 0.2	•62.20	52.21
11 Drugs	183.51	183.68	− 0.1	197.73	171.02
5 Electrical Equipment	288.37	290.05	− 0.6	294.91	250.45
4 Major Electrical-Electronic	93.02	92.87	+ 0.2	•93.02	77.80
4 Household Appliances	204.17	204.65	− 0.2	238.98	188.57
8 Electronics	705.44	709.26	− 0.5	709.26	579.29
6 Entertainment	117.19	118.15	− 0.8	132.67	106.77
4 Fertilizers [h]	12.15	12.36	− 1.7	14.75	11.39
Food Composite	77.04	76.50	+ 0.7	•77.04	70.75
5 Canned Foods	88.66	85.89	+ 3.2	91.54	83.09
4 Dairy Products	96.54	96.49	+ 0.1	•96.54	87.49
3 Meat Packing	56.14	57.20	− 1.9	61.33	50.71
7 Packaged Foods	111.11	110.36	+ 0.7	112.25	98.36
7 Forest Products [e]	25.44	26.17	− 2.8	28.46	22.96
4 Gold Mining	80.86	77.72	+ 4.0	93.90	76.58
4 Home Furnishings	29.21	29.56	− 1.2	33.74	28.16
4 Hospital Supplies [e]	38.94	38.71	+ 0.6	44.05	35.84
4 Hotel-Motel [e]	27.86	27.86	0	35.87	24.77
3 Lead & Zinc	35.02	34.57	+ 1.3	35.67	27.14
5 Leisure Time [e]	25.86	26.18	− 1.2	29.59	20.67
6 Machine Tools	33.73	34.59	− 2.5	34.59	22.79
3 Machinery: Agricultural	74.86	76.08	− 1.6	76.08	58.25
Machinery Composite	238.31	240.43	− 0.9	240.43	196.97
5 Construction & Materials Hand.	421.93	427.34	− 1.3	427.34	327.27
5 Industrial	144.22	146.80	− 1.8	146.80	118.17
6 Oil Well Equip. & Services	812.20	816.92	− 0.6	816.92	663.01
5 Specialty	38.50	38.06	+ 1.2	•38.50	30.70
3 Steam Generating	199.04	203.53	− 2.2	203.53	131.29
3 Metal Fabricating	102.21	99.26	+ 3.0	107.41	84.78
5 Metals—Miscellaneous	73.97	74.24	− 0.4	74.60	58.50
3 Mobile Homes [e]	76.77	77.43	− 0.9	86.80	63.55
7 Office and Business Equip.	1171.54	1169.26	+ 0.2	•1171.54	965.56
Excl. IBM	259.18	259.68	− 0.2	265.04	215.21
4 Offshore Drilling [e]	44.42	44.63	− 0.5	44.92	31.96
Oil Composite	158.87	159.31	− 0.3	159.31	133.18
3 Crude Producers	219.33	217.14	+ 1.0	•219.33	187.77
9 Integrated: Domestic	171.59	171.38	+ 0.1	•171.59	137.07
6 International	148.87	149.72	− 0.6	149.72	128.18
8 Paper	283.41	298.21	− 5.0	312.97	242.40
5 Pollution Control [e]	20.22	20.15	+ 0.3	20.48	16.54
6 Publishing	167.86	168.45	− 0.4	181.46	155.16
3 Publishing (Newspapers) [g]	19.25	18.75	+ 2.7	19.61	17.06
6 Radio-TV Broadcasters	361.12	364.67	− 1.0	364.67	282.40
4 Railroad Equipment	55.30	55.85	− 1.0	55.85	41.59
4 Real Estate [e]	13.28	13.67	− 2.9	16.15	11.33
6 Restaurants [e]	27.09	27.87	− 2.8	30.86	24.77
Retail Stores Composite	102.63	102.73	− 0.1	118.51	98.64
9 Department Stores	155.63	159.81	− 2.6	190.02	151.92
*3 Discount Stores [b]	10.62	10.50	+ 1.1	12.87	9.30
3 Retail Stores (Drug) [g]	18.41	18.47	− 0.3	21.55	17.37
8 Food Chains	53.44	53.22	+ 0.4	58.55	51.93
2 Mail Order & Gen. Chains	166.98	165.68	+ 0.8	195.05	159.66
3 Variety Stores	71.59	70.33	+ 1.8	77.49	65.29
3 Shoes	44.51	44.85	− 0.8	49.66	41.43
5 Soaps	183.00	179.25	+ 2.1	184.10	165.11
9 Steel	77.55	79.66	− 2.6	82.80	64.39
Excluding U. S. Steel	70.90	72.50	− 2.2	73.21	56.33
3 Sugar-Beet Refiners	39.46	37.97	+ 3.9	40.66	33.75
7 Textiles: Apparel Mfrs.	24.30	24.98	− 2.7	28.12	20.87
2 Synthetic Fibers	67.26	70.28	− 4.3	78.60	63.45
6 Textile Products	54.85	56.63	− 3.1	67.34	54.34
4 Tires and Rubber Goods	181.01	180.58	+ 0.2	194.98	168.47
4 Tobacco	64.77	63.03	+ 2.8	70.58	63.03
3 Toys [e]	9.75	9.79	− 0.4	11.47	7.06
4 Vending & Food Service [b]	26.96	26.94	+ 0.1	29.64	23.91

PUBLIC UTILITIES

	Close July 7	Close June 30	% Change	1976 Range High	1976 Range Low
22 Electric Companies	31.24	30.53	+ 2.3	32.52	29.44
8 Natural Gas Distributors	69.06	67.60	+ 2.2	69.30	64.16
6 Pipelines	128.49	128.00	+ 0.4	•128.49	104.44
5 Telephone	25.43	25.30	+ 0.5	25.83	23.17
Excluding AT&T	36.47	35.60	+ 2.4	38.55	34.35

[p]TRANSPORTATION

	Close July 7	Close June 30	% Change	1976 Range High	1976 Range Low
5 Air Transport	48.01	48.58	− 1.2	48.58	38.89
10 Railroads	47.73	48.03	− 0.6	48.03	38.71
4 Truckers [a]	122.20	121.02	+ 1.0	134.72	115.26

[p]FINANCIAL

	Close July 7	Close June 30	% Change	1976 Range High	1976 Range Low
6 New York City Banks	55.72	56.84	− 2.0	56.98	47.34
10 Banks, Outside N.Y.C.	105.12	105.50	− 0.4	105.50	84.52
6 Life Insurance	177.12	174.73	+ 1.4	179.18	157.23
4 Multi-Line Insurance [f]	10.98	10.92	+ 0.5	11.86	9.57
6 Property-Casualty Ins.	99.37	97.89	+ 1.5	103.22	90.84
3 Sav. & Loan Holding Cos. [c]	18.26	18.15	+ 0.6	20.22	15.36
2 Finance Companies	64.80	65.99	− 1.8	69.68	59.53
2 Small Loans	83.32	82.88	+ 0.5	85.14	71.58
*3 Real Estate Inv. Trust [g]	1.84	1.85	− 0.5	2.04	1.73
*8 Investment Cos. (Closed-End)	47.37	48.83	− 3.0	49.71	44.89

THE MARKET LAST WEEK

Daily Stock Price Indexes (1941-43 = 10)

	July 9	July 8	July 7	July 6	July 2	July 1
400 Industrials						
H...	n118.46	117.72	117.10	117.63	117.50	118.10
L...	116.66	116.26	115.50	115.96	115.95	116.01
C...	•117.95	116.85	116.66	116.33	117.01	116.47
20 Transportation						
H...	15.11	14.99	14.84	14.92	14.95	15.04
L...	14.84	14.76	14.68	14.72	14.72	14.81
C...	15.06	14.88	14.81	14.74	14.85	14.83
40 Utilities						
H...	47.68	47.64	47.44	47.29	46.99	46.81
L...	47.03	46.96	46.74	46.58	46.26	46.07
C...	47.48	47.20	47.34	46.97	46.85	46.37
40 Financial						
H...	11.90	11.76	11.76	11.85	11.84	11.82
L...	11.70	11.62	11.60	11.68	11.66	11.63
C...	11.87	11.70	11.68	11.72	11.80	11.72
500 Composite						
H...	n105.41	104.75	104.23	104.67	104.53	104.98
L...	103.80	103.44	102.80	103.19	103.13	103.14
C...	•104.98	103.98	103.83	103.54	104.11	103.59

n-Indicates new intraday high.

	July 7	June 30	1976 High	1976 Low	1975 High	1975 Low
400 Industrials						
P-E Ratio	12.86	12.94	14.06	12.23	12.44	7.63
Yield (%)	3.35	3.34	3.58	3.25	4.89	3.59
**Range of Price Index			n118.46	100.45	108.51	76.54
20 Transportation						
P-E Ratio			m			
Yield (%)	3.30	3.28				
**Range of Price Index						
40 Utilities						
P-E Ratio	8.16	7.99	8.38	7.79	8.31	6.75
Yield (%)	7.85	8.07	8.35	7.61	9.55	7.89
**Range of Price Index			48.80	44.28	46.13	33.79
40 Financial						
P-E Ratio			m			
Yield (%)	3.76	3.75				
**Range of Price Index						
500 Composite						
P-E Ratio	12.29	12.34	13.37	11.69	11.87	7.54
Yield (%)	3.62	3.67	3.91	3.59	5.25	3.92
**Range of Price Index			n105.41	89.81	96.58	68.65

Preferred Stocks	Close as of July 7	Close as of June 30	1976 High	1976 Low	1975 High	1975 Low
Price, Dollars per share	86.5	86.5	88.5	83.1	88.4	80.4
Yield, Per Cent	8.09	8.09	8.42	7.91	8.70	7.92

Weekly Bond Yields %

	July 7	June 30	1976 High	1976 Low		July 7	June 30	1976 High	1976 Low
[k]Composite					**Industrials**				
AAA	8.54	8.57	8.68	8.26		8.33	8.36	8.47	8.06
AA	8.54	8.52	8.68	8.29		8.40	8.43	8.63	8.12
A	8.90	8.91	9.25	8.82		8.81	8.83	8.89	8.49
BBB	9.62	9.64	10.12	9.41		9.70	9.71	10.13	9.39
Railroads					**Utilities**				
AAA	—DISCONTINUED—					8.75	8.77	8.88	8.46
AA	8.14	8.04	8.46	7.99		9.08	9.10	9.19	8.72
A	8.57	8.55	9.38	8.45		9.32	9.35	9.56	8.99
BBB	9.27	9.32	9.79	9.18		9.87	9.90	10.44	9.52

	Yields July 7	Yields June 30	Yields 1976 High	Yields 1976 Low	†Prices July 7	†Prices June 30	†Prices 1976 High	†Prices 1976 Low
Corp. AAA	8.54	8.57	8.68	8.26	56.88	56.63	58.66	55.97
Government:								
Long Term	5.67	5.68	5.92	5.40	73.27	73.19	75.54	71.23
Intermediate	6.95	7.02	7.05	6.47	77.22	76.87	79.63	76.73
Short Term	6.93	6.96	7.34	6.35	87.97	87.88	89.64	86.82
Municipal	6.73	6.81	6.98	6.58	70.27	69.59	71.56	68.14

Miscellaneous Indexes

	Latest Week	Week Ago	Year Ago	1976 High	1976 Low
[1]Industrial Raw Material Prices	211.0	206.0	170.8	•211.0	183.1
[2]Weekly Business Index	124.9	124.9	110.5	124.9	108.5

•Indicates a new high or low. **Range for 500 stocks, 400 Industrials, 20 Transportation, 40 Utilities and 40 Financial is based on daily closing indexes. †Converted from average yield to maturity, assuming an appropriate coupon and maturity. *Not included in composite indexes. [a]1955 = 10; [b]1957 = 10; [c]1959 = 10; [e]1965 = 10; [f]1968 = 10; [g]1970 = 10; [h]1973 = 10. [k]AAA composite bond yields based on average of industrial and utility bond yields, while other composite bond yields are based on average of industrial, rail and utilities bond yields. [m]Missing data on these new major groups will be available shortly. [p]Transportation group also includes Emery Air Freight; Financial group also includes American Express. [q]Ranges based on weekly indexes. **Based on intraday high and low prices. [1]BLS Index (1967 = 100). [2]Business Week Index (1967 = 100).

Source: Standard & Poor's, *The Outlook*, July 12, 1976, p. 664.

houses and financial services; "Executive's Corner" covering speeches of company officials at company annual stockholders' meetings, or at financial analyst society meetings; "New Issue Corner," which presents summaries of new issue prospectuses; "Connoisseur's Corner," which each week has a long article on valuation of art or antiques, or wines.

The Media General Financial Weekly, published in Richmond, Virginia, covers the financial waterfront each week. In addition to a series of feature articles and columns, it provides financial and statistical facts on 3,400 common stocks, including 720 OTC issues; indicator charts on every NYSE and AMEX common stock plus 720 OTC issues. It has "Stocks in the Spotlight," the 40 leading and lagging issues in six major price categories and 40 leading issues in six-volume categories. There are two pages of charts showing the performance of all 60 major industrial groups, compared with Media General's Composite Market Index. There are a long series of fundamental and technical indicators, shown in both charts and figures. This too is a publication primarily for the security analyst and the professional money manager.

The Money Manager is a weekly, edited exclusively for the investment professional. It is a source of financial intelligence on the Money Market, the Government, Municipal and Corporate Bond Markets, the Stock Market, the Mortgage Market, Foreign Finance and developments in the economy.[11]

The *Financial World,* published weekly, and the *Magazine of Wall Street,* published biweekly, both feature articles on the trend of the market, industry evaluations, and individual company analyses. The *Financial World* has a monthly supplement in which common stocks are rated. Comparable data on preferred stocks and mutual funds are published quarterly. The publisher of the *Magazine of Wall Street* issues weekly a separate "Investment and Business Forecast." This is in the nature of an investment advisory report.

The *Financial Analysts Journal* is published every two months by the Financial Analysts Federation, an association devoted to the advancement of investment management and security analysis. Each issue features 7 to 12 articles on varying phases of investment analysis and portfolio management. For example, topics covered have included: "Valuing Quality Growth Stocks," "The Trouble with Earnings," "The Efficient Market Model," "Stock Prices and the Money Supply," "Profile of the Financial Analyst," "Financial Forecasting by

---

[11] For a free sample copy write to Albert Kraus (ed.), *The Money Manager,* 77 Water Street, New York, New York 10005.

Corporations," "Minimax Portfolio Policies," "The Third and Fourth Markets," "How Willing Is Management to Disclose," and "How Good Is Institutional Research." In addition each issue reports current developments in "Securities Law and Regulation," "Accounting for Financial Analysis," and "Corporate Information and Disclosure."

The Institutional Investor is a monthly journal published for professional money managers. It also features articles on investment analysis and portfolio management but there is more emphasis on money manager personalities, and the articles are often grouped about a theme such as "Wall Street's Search for Leadership." Its more learned and academic counterpart is the *Journal of Portfolio Management*.

The *Journal of Finance* is published quarterly by the American Finance Association. It is much more academically and theoretically oriented than the *Financial Analysts Journal*. In recent years it has attempted to cover not only all phases of finance—banking, investments, international finance, real estate finance, corporate finance, but monetary and economic theory as well.

Even more mathematical and theoretically oriented is the *Journal of Financial and Quantitative Analysis*, published quarterly. Other publications of possible interest include *The Chronicle, Finance, Financial Executive, Financial Management, Investment Dealers Digest, Journal of Commerce, Money, Trusts and Estates,* and *Wall Street Letter*.

The Investment Advisory Services

A wealth of information is available in the publications of the investment advisory services. The major services are:

Moody's Investor Services, Inc. (owned by Dun & Bradstreet)
99 Church Street
New York, N.Y. 10007

Standard & Poor's Corporation (owned by McGraw-Hill)
345 Hudson Street
New York, N.Y. 10014

The Value Line Investment Survey (owned by Arnold Bernhard & Co.)
5 East 44th Street
New York, N.Y. 10017

A comprehensive and copious flow of bulletins and reports emerge daily, weekly, and monthly from these services. It is possible to subscribe to part or all of the publications. The annual cost of any of the services is a properly deducted expense from investors' income under the personal income tax regulations. A well-stocked college or univer-

sity library will have one or more of these services, and the larger public libraries also make them available.

A basic part of both the Moody's and the Standard & Poor's services are the reference volumes: Moody's *Manuals* and Standard & Poor's *Corporation Records*. Moody's *Manuals* are big thick volumes published each year and issued for various fields—industrials, OTC industrials, public utilities, transportation, municipal and government, and banks and finance. Each volume contains reports on thousands of corporations (or governmental bodies), giving the financial history and full investment data for a period of years. Standard & Poor's *Corporation Records* are continuous and alphabetical regardless of field. The volumes are kept up to date by current supplements. Standard & Poor's six-volume *Corporation Records* are augmented by a daily bulletin, while the six Moody's *Manuals* are kept up to date by a semiweekly report. Most large brokerage offices will have one or the other of these basic services.

Standard & Poor's issues a weekly magazine, *The Outlook*, while Moody's issues a weekly *Stock Survey*. Both review market conditions and recommend investment choices in common stock. *The Outlook* generally contains an overall market forecast and policy recommendation, a list of the ten best performing groups of the week, and ten poorest performing groups, an occasional "Stock for Action" recommendation, stocks in the limelight, on-the-spot reports on individual companies, a report on business, and special articles, such as "Stocks with Tax Exemption on Dividends," "Portfolio for New Investors," "Low-Priced Speculations," and "Buys among Institutional Favorites." A master list of recommended issues is maintained, classified into: "Group 1—Foundation Stocks for Long-Term Gain"; "Group 2—Stocks with Promising Growth Prospects"; "Group 3—Cyclical/Speculative Stocks"; and "Group 4—Liberal Income with Inflation Protection." The annual forecast of *The Outlook* features ten stocks for action in the year ahead, industries best situated for the year ahead, speculative stocks for aggressive investors, candidates for dividends increases, and stocks to outrun inflation.

The Standard & Poor's *Stock Guide* is a pocket-size condensed handbook, issued monthly, containing a thumbnail sketch of essential facts about some 5,000 common and preferred stocks, listed and unlisted. Two pages of one of these monthly guides are shown in Figure 3–5. Most of the 5,000 stocks are rated for earnings and dividend stability and growth.

Each month the *Stock Guide* also contains a list of "stocks for potential price appreciation" and another list of "stocks for good income return." There is one feature article such as "Cyclical Buys Offering Sound Values," and "Electronics-Electrical Prospects Brighter." At

FIGURE 3–5

Sample Pages from Standard & Poor's *Stock Guide*

INDEX	Ticker Symbol	STOCKS NAME OF ISSUE (Call Price of Pfd. Stocks)	Market	Earns &Div Rank-ing	Par Val.	Inst. Hold Cos	Inst. Hold Shs. (000)	PRINCIPAL BUSINESS	PRICE RANGE 1960-74 High	1960-74 Low	1975 High	1975 Low	1976 High	1976 Low	Apr. Sales in 100s	April, 1976 Last Sale Or Bid High	Low	Last	% Div. Yield	P-E Ratio
1	GCN	General Cinema	NYS,Bo	A—	1	34	998	Theatre chain:soft drinks	55½	1½	24	7½	26¼	18½	1005	21¼	19¾	19¾	2.7	7
2	GDV	General Development	[1]NYS,Bo,MW,PB,PS	NR	1	3	2048	Florida real estate developm't	38⅛	2⅛	6½	2¾	6⅞	3¾	944	6½	4¾	5¼	...	5
3	GD	General Dynamics	[2]NYS,Bo,Ci,De,MW,PB	B—	1	33	2648	Aircraft/subs,bldg mater'ls	79	13½	56¼	19	58	37¼	7269	58	50	57¼	...	7
4	GED	Gen'l Educational Sv	ASE,Bo	NR	70¢	1	7	Book mfr:vocation schools	287	8¾	21⅞	7	17	13¼	24	14¼	13½	14B	...	8
5	GE	General Electric	NYS,Bo,Ci,De,MW,PB,PS	A+	2½	667	17016	Lgst mfr electrical equipment	75⅞	27⅛	52⅞	32⅜	56¾	46	20088	56	51¼	53¾	3.0	15
6	JOB	Gen'l Employ Enterpr	ASE	B—	No	...	...	Personnel placement service	24¼	1½	2⅞	1⅛	2	1⅜	41	1¾	1½	1⅝	...	d
7	GNLE	General Energy	OTC	NR	1	7	461	Coal mining	17¼	1/16	19¼	7⅞	14⅜	9⅛	1682	10¾	9⅛	10¾ B	3.7	16
8	GEX	General Exploration	PS	B—	1	2	24	Coal:oil & gas:earth mov'g	18¼	2	10⅛	2⅜	6½	4	404	5⅜	4½	4⅝	...	7
9	GF	General Foods	NYS,Bo,Ci,De,MW,PB,PS	A	1	179	3224	Leading mfr packaged foods	53⅞	16	29⅜	18⅜	31¼	27	8047	29⅞	27¾	28½	5.3	9
10	GGP	Gen'l Growth Prop SBI	NYS	...	1	31	876	Real estate investment trust	27¾	6¾	18⅜	12½	20½	15⅜	390	20	19	19½	6.8	18
11	GHEL	General Health Serv	OTC	B	1	...	...	Acuté gen'l hospitals: labs	36½	1⅜	3¾	1½	5⅞	3¼	1324	5⅞	4⅞	5⅛ B	...	11
12	GHOB	General Hobbies	OTC	NR	1¢	...	...	Hobby mdse: model RR eq	10	¾	1⅜	⅜	1⅝	⅜	45	1¼	1	1B	...	d
13	GH	General Host	NYS,PB,PS	B	1	2	107	Meat packer, bakery,food sv	45⅜	4¼	13⅜	4⅞	14⅞	9⅞	766	12⅜	9⅞	10⅛	5.9	5
14	WS	Wrrt (Purch 1 com at $40)	PS	...	...	2	174	convenience foods & stores	12½	¼	1¼	¼	1⅜	⅝	969	1	⅝	¾	...	..
15	GHW	General Housewares	ASE	NR	33⅓¢	...	...	Cookware, giftware, leisure pr	20¼	¼	1⅞	½	4¼	1¼	522	4	3⅛	3⅛	...	7
16	GRL	General Instrument	[3]NYS,Bo,Ci,De,MW	B	1	20	612	Electronic components & eq,	72	4¼	14	4¾	13⅜	8⅛	4890	13	10¾	11¾	s...	15
17	Pr	$3.00 cm Cv A Pfd ([59]62)vtg	NYS,MW,PS	B	No	14	36	data collect eq: CATV eq	72½	23½	31½	24½	32½	27¾	91	30¾	30	30¼	9.9	..
18	GMD	General Medical	NYS	B+	1	10	228	Dstr hospital & med supplies	49½	3⅜	20	6⅛	21	14¾	476	18⅛	15⅜	16	1.2	10
19	GIS	General Mills	NYS,Bo,Ci,De,MW,PB,PS	A	75¢	120	5477	Consumer foods,apparel,toys	33 11/16	5⅜	30½	20 1/16	34⅛	27⅝	5411	29⅞	27⅝	28¼	2.4	14
20	GM	General Motors	[4]NYS,Bo,Ci,De,MW,PB,PS	A—	1⅔	682	14448	Largest mfr automotive prods	113¾	28⅞	59⅛	31¼	72¾	57¾	36630	72¾	67	71	3.4	10
21	Pr B	$5.00 cm Pfd (120)	NYS,MW,PB,PS	AAA	No	72	351	cars, trucks, buses: diesel,	118¾	55½	68¾	59	73¼	65	145	72¾	68¾	71	7.0	..
22	Pr A	$3.75 cm Pfd (100)	NYS	AAA	No	56	313	aircraft engines:appliances	95½	43½	51¾	45½	53¾	49¼	116	53¾	50½	52¾	7.1	..
23	GPT	General Portland	NYS,Bo,MW	B—	1	32	1267	Cement producer	42½	4⅛	8⅜	4	7⅝	5	2197	7⅝	6¾	6⅞	...	d
24	GPU	General Public Util	[5]NYS,Bo,Ci,De,MW,PB	B+	2½	64	801	Util hldg co: N.J. & Penna.	40¾	9½	17½	10⅜	18¾	15⅝	4495	17¾	16¾	16¾	10.0	9
25	GER	General Recreation	ASE	NR	1	...	...	Outdoor recreational prod	13½	1	2⅜	1	2¼	1⅛	152	1⅞	1⅝	1¾	...	d
26	GRX	Gen'l Refractories	NYS,PB	B	5	...	...	Fire-brick for steel industry	33¾	3¾	11¼	5⅞	11⅛	7¾	359	10	9⅛	9⅜	3.2	4
27	GREI	General Reinsurance	OTC	...	2	50	613	Reinsurance exclusively	256½	11½	188	129	168	144	1162	162	148	160B	0.2	23
28	GRS	General Research	ASE,PS	B—	10¢	...	...	Systems research: tech: lab	29	⅞	4⅜	1⅛	4¼	1⅞	134	3⅜	2¾	3¼	...	5
29	GEN	General Resources	ASE	C	50¢	...	...	Mfr prefinished plywood:R.E.	24	⅜	1¼	½	1¼	⅝	265	1⅛	¾	⅞	...	d
30	GSEM	Gen'l Semiconductor	OTC	NR	1	...	...	Semiconductor devices	7⅜	1⅜	7	2	8	3⅜	129	7¼	6⅝	6¾ B	3.1	7
31	GSHL	General Shale Prods	OTC	B+	No	1	14	Face brick & concrete blocks	28⅜	3	11½	7	13¾	9½	142	12⅜	11¾	12B	s6.7	8
32	GSX	General Signal	NYS,PB,PS	A—	1	50	1411	Electrical & electronic prods	59¼	10⅝	42⅜	23⅞	45⅞	34¼	1299	43	39⅜	39⅝	2.1	12
33	GSI	General Steel Ind	NYS	B—	1	...	...	Metal process: constr:safety	32¾	1⅞	5⅜	2⅛	5¾	3⅛	419	5⅛	4⅜	4⅝	...	5
34	GTELO	Gen'l Tel Cal 4½%Pfd(23½)vtg	OTC	A	20	28	95	Largest sub Gen Tel system	20¼	8½	10½	8½	10½	8¾	26	10½	9¾	10¼ B	8.8	..
35	GLF.B	Gen Tel Fla $1.30cmB Pfd[66]	NYS([10])	A↓	25	15	44	Tel. service in Fla., Tampa	28⅛	12½	16	13	16½	14½	19	16	14¾	14¾ B	8.8	..
36	Pr A	$1.25 cm Pfd (25½)	NYS([10])	A↓	25	20	175	largest community served	28	12½	15½	12½	16	14	24	16	14¾	14½ B	8.6	..
37	Pr C	8.16% cm Pfd ([67]108.16)	NYS([10])	A↓	100	68	326		100	67	85½	76	89	87	6	89	87	88B	9.3	..
38	GTE	General Tel & Electr	[6]NYS,Bo,Ci,De,Ho	A	3⅓	351	12935	2d lgst tel sys-TV sets,	55	16⅛	26	16⅞	28¼	25⅛	12438	27	25⅛	26	6.9	9
39	Pr	5% cm Cv Pfd ([68]55)vtg	NYS	BBB	50	16	52	tubes: elec control eq	58	25¼	33½	25⅝	35¾	31¼	57	34	32½	34	7.4	..
40	GY	Gen'l Tire & Rubber	[5]NYS,Bo,De,MW,PB	A—	30¢	39	132.9	Tires, plastics, chemicals:TV	32⅝	9⅜	18	10¼	23½	17⅝	2337	22⅜	19⅞	20⅞	s5.3	6
41	GCO	Genesco Inc	NYS,Bo,De,MW	C	1	5	165	Mfr, retail: apparel/footwear	58¼	2⅝	6¼	2⅞	9	5⅜	1714	8¼	7	7	...	d
42	GENBB	Genesee Brewing[71]	OTC	NR	50¢	2	5	Beer and ale	14⅝	6¼	10½	6¼	13¾	10	30	13½	11¾	12B	†7.7	6
43	GII	Genge Inc	ASE,Bo,PB,PS	B—	50¢	1	47	Architect,engr'g,design sv	56	½	4¼	1	3¾	1½	116	3⅜	2¾	2¾	...	8
44	GES	Genisco Technology	ASE,PS	B—	50¢	...	...	Aerospace, electronic test eq	19¼	½	2⅝	1	2	1¼	95	1¾	1½	1¾	...	8
45	GNVA	Genova, Inc	OTC	NR	1	...	...	Plumbing mfr: pipe/fittings	14⅜	2½	6½	2⅞	7¼	3¾	102	4½	3¾	4¼ B	...	d

Uniform Footnote Explanations—See Page 1. Other: [1]TS. [2]PS,MS. [3]PB,PS. [4]TS,MS. [5]PS. [6]MW,PB,PS. [51]®$1.02,'75. [52]®$0.58,'75. [53]$0.9594 non-taxable'75. [54]Plan fiscal yr change to Dec. [55]△$8.06,'74. [56]△$3.27,'75,®$1.64,'75. [57]Accum on Pfd. [58]®$0.43,'75. [59]To 8-31-76, scale to $60 in'77. [60]®$1.32,'74. [61]Estimate 2%,'75 non-taxable. [62]Subsid. Pfd. Stk.. [63]®$2.41,'74. [64]△$0.27,'75. [65]□$12.37,'72. [66]Callable at $26¼. [67]To 8-1-78:scale to $102.04 in'88. [68]®$2.72,'75. [69]To 6-30-77, then $52½. [70]□$4.45,'73. [71]Cl B,non-vtg.

FIGURE 3-5 (continued)

COMMON AND PREFERRED STOCKS

Index	Same Div. Ea. Yr. Since	DIVIDENDS — Latest Payment Date	Ex. Div.	Total Ind. Rate	So Far 1976	Paid 1975	FINANCIAL POSITION — Cash & Equiv.	Mil-$ Curr. Assets	Curr. Liabs.	Balance Sheet Date	CAPITALIZATION Lg Term Debt Mil-$	Shs. 000 Pfd.	Com.	EARNINGS $ Per Shr 1971	1972	1973	1974	1975	Last 12 Mos.	INTERIM EARNINGS OR REMARKS Period	1975	1976	Index
1♦	1953	Q0.13½ 4-26-76	3-30	0.54	0.27	0.46¾	18.9	46.9	41.5	10-31-75	74.1	...	5517	△1.62	0.96	△1.03	*1.93	f2.68	2.74	3 Mo Jan	0.35	0.41	1
2♦		2%Stk 6-27-72	5-22	Nil	2%Stk		Equity per shr $11.74		555.	12-31-75	74.9	...	9230	0.90	0.96	1.18	1.18	1.04	1.05	3 Mo Mar	0.27	0.28	2
3♦		0.25 6-10-76	5-5	Nil			30.9 788.		810.	3-31-75	119.	...	10819	△1.96	△2.47	△3.81	△4.88	△7.62	7.90	3 Mo Dec△	1.31	1.59	3
4♦		None Paid		Nil	...		0.7 14.2		8.8	3-31-75	13.4	22	224	△1.19	5.25	3.81	3.20		1.73	3 Mo Dec△	*3.83	*2.36	4
5♦	1899	Q0.40 4-26-76	3-3	1.60	0.80	1.60	853. 5566		3963	12-31-75	1038	...	18427	2.60	2.91	3.21	3.34	3.17	3.49	3 Mo Mar	0.41	0.73	5
6♦	1973	0.04 12-20-75	12-1	0.40	0.10	0.20	0.66 1.74		1.69	12-31-75	1.21	48	980Sp	d0.65	d0.29	d0.30	d0.52	d0.15	d0.32	6 Mo Mar	d0.09	d0.26	6
7♦	1974	0.10 3-1-76	2-6	Nil		0.40	6.20 10.8		14.9	12-31-75		225	4419Dc	△0.33	d0.01	△0.45	*3.91	s11.05	0.66	6 Mo Mar	0.50	0.11	7
8♦		None Since Public		Nil			6.74 15.5		566.	12-31-75	19.5		3631Dc	△0.33	△1.27	d0.37	△0.46	*52.67	0.63	3 Mo Mar	*0.21	0.17	8
9♦	1922	Q0.37½ 3-5-76	2-11	1.50	0.37½	1.40	187. 1164			12-27-75	242.		49776	2.26	2.21	2.40	2.00	E3.05	2.51	9 Mo Dec△	1.76	2.27	9
10♦	1971	Q0.33 4-20-76	3-22	1.32	0.66	1.22	Equity per shr $5.52			9-30-75	191.	...	57055p	△0.40	0.55	0.77	0.93	1.01	1.11	6 Mo Mar	0.48	0.58	10
11♦	...	None Paid		Nil			4.29 18.9		12.8	8-31-75	35.1	...	2004Au	0.93	0.90	0.87	0.90	0.02	0.47	6 Mo Feb	0.01	0.46	11
12♦	...	0.05 5-1-74	3-26	Nil			24.5 25.4		17.7	7-31-74	4.05	...	2375II	0.26	0.45	0.53	△0.50	0.53	E△0.82	6 Mo Dec△		0.01	12
13♦	1974	Q0.15 5-7-76	4-20	0.60	0.30	0.45	101.		47.3	12-27-75	114.	...	1616Dc	△1.01	△1.21	△1.79	55△1.11	56△2.47	1.87	3 Mo Mar	△0.04	d0.56	13
14♦	...	Terms&trad basis should be checked in detail					Cash on 7% Deb '94						6636Dc	can reduce pur price temp periods							Warrants expire 1-31-77			14
15♦	...	*Nil			*Nil		5.76 27.7		18.8	12-31-74	12.4	127	2180Dc	d0.93	△1.07	d3.71	d0.64	P△0.45	0.48	3 Mo Mar	*0.16	0.19	15
16♦	...	2%Stk 5-28-76	4-27	Stk	2%Stk	2% Stk	16.3 230.		49.0	8-31-75	p137.	520	7322Dc	△0.55	1.04	1.71	1.36	P△0.76	0.76				16
17♦	...	Q0.75 3-12-76	2-24	3.00	0.75	3.00	2.29 55.4		13.5	12-31-75	14.3	520		10.39	16.80	26.82	22.63		Fb			1.17	17
18♦	1967	Q0.05 5-5-76	4-14	0.20	0.10	0.18¼	78.8 668.		356.	2-22-76		2836	2620Mr	1.02	1.15	1.25	r60 1.35	f11.60	1.67	9 Mo Dec△	0.85	1.63	18
19♦	1898	Q0.075 5-5-76	4-5	0.68	0.10	0.60	3767 14397		7371	3-31-75	294.	49233		0.99	1.18	1.40			1.96	39 Wk Feb	1.27	1.19	19
20♦	1915	Q0.60 3-10-76	2-5	2.40	0.60	2.40				3-31-75	1194	287643		6.72	7.51	8.34	3.27	4.32	6.90	3 Mo Mar	0.20	2.78	20
21♦	1930	Q1.25 5-1-76	3-30	5.00	5.00	5.00	7.64 60.5		21.4	12-31-75	50.9	1836	6800Dc	682.6	762.7	845.7	335.0	441.9	d0.05	3 Mo Mar	0.38	0.26	21
22♦	1947	Q0.93¾ 5-1-76	3-30	3.75	1.87½	3.75	35.4 197.		255.	12-31-75	1659	1000		682.6	762.7	845.7	335.0	441.9	1.85	12 Mo Mar	2.39	1.85	22
23♦	1947	Q0.20 3-10-75	2-7	Nil		Nil	0.78 141.		20.5	12-31-75	6242			1.61	1.65	0.88	0.26	0.07	2.63	3 Mo Mar	0.03	0.04	23
24♦	1942	Q0.42 5-26-76	1-19	0.84	0.84	*1.68				12-31-75	4.41	20	1640Dc	2.08	2.21	2.25	△2.25	2.00	d2.64	3 Mo Mar			24
25♦		None Paid												0.31	0.56	0.36	0.44						25
26♦	1974	Q0.10 5-25-76	3-15	0.30	0.10	0.30	9.09 14.1		68.3	12-31-75	29.9	49	3798Dc	0.01	△0.28	*0.80	43z1.97	P*2.21	1.97	3 Mo Mar	△1.23	△1.91	26
27♦	1934	Q0.10 4-6-76	3-16	0.40	0.10	0.40	Equity per sh $36.54		11.2	12-31-75	20.0		5445Dc	55.59	0.80	*7.02	*5.93	*6.27	6.95	3 Mo Mar	0.11	0.48	27
28♦		None Paid		Nil			n/a 17.3			12-31-75	4.24		1121Dc	d0.67	0.80	0.94	d1.32	0.32	0.69	9 Mo Jul△	0.30	0.22	28
29♦		0.01 9-10-73	8-27	Nil	0.15		1.84		0.33	12-31-75	3.43	80	3098Dc	d0.69	d40.40	0.10	d0.33	0.16	3 Mo Jul△	0.30	0.13	29
30♦	1976	0.03 4-23-76	4-5	0.21	5%Stk	5%Stk	0.32 1.78		0.33	11-30-74	0.55		474Nv	d0.22	0.44	0.54	0.66	d0.89	0.91	3 Mo Feb	0.19	0.21	30
31♦	1951	Q0.20 4-5-76	3-15	0.80	s0.39	s0.752	n/a 14.7		4.12	12-31-75	6.04		2008Dc	△1.17	1.66	1.72	1.24	△41.11	1.46	3 Mo Mar	d0.14	0.21	31
32♦	1940	Q0.21 7-1-76	6-1	0.84	0.63	0.76	16.4 263.		94.3	12-31-75	50.9		7798Dc	1.39	2.40	2.51	2.71	3.18	3.33	3 Mo Mar	0.65	0.80	32
33♦		0.10 9-30-70	9-14	Nil			4.45 217.		11.1	12-31-75	12.3	2999	2519Dc	d3.49	d2.02	*0.60	*0.94	*0.96	0.97	3 Mo Mar	*0.22	0.13	33
34♦	1945	Q0.22½ 5-1-76	4-2	0.90	0.45	0.90	11.6 116.		196.	12-31-75	789.	24500	14000Dc	17.60	20.04	21.35	15.42	16.02		3 Mo Mar		0.20	34
35♦	1959	Q0.32½ 5-15-76	4-20	1.30	0.65	1.30	8.39 116.		56.3	12-31-75	580.	±1580		28.58	20.04	14.50	12.38	9.25		3 Mo Feb			35
36♦	1961	Q0.31½ 5-15-76	4-20	1.25	0.62½	1.25	Red restr (8.16%) to 8-1-78			1-8-78	...	400		14.50	32.65	14.50	12.38	9.25					36
37♦	1973	Q2.04 5-15-76	4-20	8.16	4.08	8.16	182. 2319		2586	12-31-75	5210	400		58.01		58.01	49.50	36.99			0.59	0.64	37
38♦	1936	Q2.04 7-1-76	5-18	1.80	1.35	1.80	Conv into 0.95 to 777,then 0.81			12-31-75	6085	453	126760	2.86	2.58	2.86	2.02	*2.88	2.93				38
39♦	1967	Q0.62½ 5-18-76	5-18	2.50	1.87½	2.50	n/a 617.		245.	2-29-76	351.	109	22395	△2.24	△3.12	△3.50	3.53	2.82	3.32	3 Mo Feb	0.18	d0.68	39
40♦	1937	Q2%Stk 3-15-76	1-29	1.10	s1.072					1-31-76			12488							3 Mo Mar			40
41♦	1934	0.17 4-30-73	4-9	Nil	0.17		21.3 321.		192.	4-6-76	173.	2118		1.84	0.72	d0.09	1.07	△1.41	d0.82	6 Mo Jan	0.15	0.74	41
42♦		†0.47¼ 4-1-76	3-16	0.92½	†0.60	†0.81	5.24 16.9		6.40	4-30-75	0.69		1980Dc	0.41	†1.55	†1.56	*152	†1.64	2.12	6 Mo Jan	±1.09	†1.57	42
43♦		h: Nil		Nil			0.74 12.4		8.69	9-30-75	1.29		1511Sp	0.41	0.62	0.77	d2.03	0.31	0.35	6 Mo Mar	0.05	0.09	43
44♦		5% Stk 12-15-67	11-28	Nil			0.15 3.99		2.28	9-30-75	5.16		1434Sp	d0.16	*d0.09	*0.15	*0.09	0.20	0.21	6 Mo Mar	0.10	0.11	44
45♦		None Since Public					0.30 8.83		4.30					0.60	0.76	0.13	1.00	0.32	d0.20	6 Mo Mar	*0.15	d0.03	45

♦ Stock Splits & Dvrs By Line Reference Index [1] 3-for-2,'71. [2] Adj to 2%,'72. [3] Adj to 2%,'72. [4] 1-for-7 Reverse,'75. [5] 3-for-1,'71. [6] Adj to 2%,'76. [7] Adj to 2%,'76. [8] Adj to 2%,'76. [9] 2-for-1,'75. [10] 2-for-1,'72. [11] Adj to 5%,'74. [12] 2-for-1,'75. [13] 2-for-1,'75.
[14] 5-for-2,'71. [15] 2-for-1,'73. [16] Adj to 5%,'75. [17] Adj to 5%,'76. [18] Adj to 5%,'75. [19] Adj to 2%,'76. [20] 2-for-1,'71. [21] Adj to 4%,'73. [22] 2-for-1,'72. [23] 2-for-1,'71. [24] 2-for-1,'71. [25] 2-for-1,'72. [26] 2-for-1,'72. [27] 2-for-1,'75.

FIGURE 3-6
Sample Page from Moody's *Handbook of Common Stocks*
AMERICAN HOME PRODUCTS CORPORATION

LISTED	SYMBOL	INDICATED DIV.	RECENT PRICE	PRICE RANGE (1975)	YIELD
NYSE	AHP	$0.92			

INTRINSIC INVESTMENT QUALITY: HIGH GRADE. A BROAD BASE OF CONSUMER PRODUCTS HAS
GENERATED PERSISTENT GROWTH.

CAPITALIZATION:	(12/31/74)	
	(000)	(%)
Minority int.	$ 22,904	2.8
$2cv.pfd.	a 1,246	0.2
Com. & Surp.	799,130	97.0
Total	$823,280	100.0%

Shs. ($0.3333)-(5/31/74)-156,170

INTERIM EARNINGS:

Qu.	3/31	6/30	9/30	12/31
72g	0.28	0.24	0.29	0.26
73	0.32	0.28	0.34	0.31
74	0.37	0.32	0.38	0.35
75	0.41	0.36	0.42	

DIVIDENDS:	RECORD	PAYABLE
0.20Q	8/13/74	9/1/74
0.20Q	11/13	12/1
0.22Q	3/13/75	3/1/75
0.22Q	5/13	6/1
0.23Q	8/13	9/1

EARN. | DIV. line (under chart):

	1961	1962	1963	1964	1965	1966	1967	1968	1969	1970	1971	1972	1973	1974
EARN.	0.36	0.38	0.41	0.44	0.52	0.61	0.67	0.73	0.80	0.87	0.95	1.08	1.25	1.42
DIV.	0.24	0.26	0.27	0.28	0.32	0.35	0.38	0.42	0.47	0.52	0.57	0.59	0.63	0.78

BACKGROUND:

American Home is a well-diversified producer of consumer products. Its Prescription Drug div. is comprised of four units: Wyeth Labs., Ayerst Labs., Ives Labs. and Fort Dodge Labs. The Food div. probably is best known for its Chef Boy-ar-dee line. Houseware is marketed under such labels as Ekco and Country Kitchen. The Packaged Drug Div. makes Anacin and Dristan and a wide variety of other proprietary drug items. Major products in the Household Products div. are Woolite, Easy-Off oven cleaner, Black Flag and Wizard air fresheners. The candy div. consists of the E.J. Brach line. In 1974, sales were as follows: prescription drugs, 38%; packaged drugs, 14%; food products, 23%, housewares and household products, 25%. Foreign operations were 30% of sales.

RECENT DEVELOPMENTS:

Despite the recession, good growth continued in the first nine months of 1975 as sales rose 11% to $1.8 billion, boosting net income proportionately to $191.2 million. In 1974, on a 15% sales increase, net income rose 13%. There has been significant pressure on margins as a result of rising raw material costs and large merchandising expenses, particularly for food and household products. However, the substantially higher margin on drugs has helped the Company maintain a good level of profitability.

PROSPECTS:

The Company's broad sales base provides good protection against adverse developments in any one area. Strong consumer orientation also provides for stable growth with good defensive characteristics. Historically, profit margins have been well maintained and this pattern is expected to continue. Further good earnings growth is expected in 1976, although some softness may continue in some areas. Over the longer term, good growth should continue and dividends should be liberalized further.

STATISTICS:

YEAR	GROSS REVS. ($ MILL.)	OPER. PROFIT MARGIN%	NET INCOME ($ 000)	WORK CAP. ($ MILL.)	SENIOR CAPITAL ($ MILL.)	NO. SHS. OUT. (000)	EARN. PER SH. $	DIV. PER SH. $	DIV. PAY. %	PRICE RANGE	PRICE X EARN.	AVG. YIELD %
65	751.0	21.0	76,495	162.4	21.8	137,382	0.52	0.32	61	15¹ - 10⁶	24.9	2.5
b66	909.6	20.1	93,809	212.3	23.1	142,150	0.61	0.35	57	15¹ - 10²	20.8	2.8
c67	987.3	20.2	104,072	249.5	22.5	144,018	0.67	0.38	57	20 - 13²	24.8	2.3
68	1,085.6	20.4	111,868	266.6	20.2	144,276	0.73	0.42	57	22⁴ - 16⁷	27.0	2.1
69	1,193.0	20.2	123,287	278.2	16.3	148,635	0.80	0.47	59	24 - 17³	25.8	2.3
70	1,294.3	20.2	135,422	320.0	13.6	151,635	0.87	0.52	60	24¹ - 17	23.6	2.5
71	1,429.3	20.0	g151,301	399.0	11.5	155,037	g0.95	0.57	60	31³ - 23³	28.8	2.1
72	1,587.1	21.6	g172,703	456.0	11.0	156,831	g1.08	0.59	55	40⁵ - 28⁵	32.1	1.7
73	1,898.0	20.9	199,155	480.9	Nil	156,376	1.25	0.63	50	48⁶ - 36³	34.1	1.5
74	2,183.0	25.2	225,642	558.5	1.2	156,937	1.42	0.78	55	44⁷ - 26¹	25.0	2.2

Note: Adjusted for 2-for-1 stock split, 5/67, and 3-for-1, 5/73. a-512,767 shares each convertible into 4½ common shares b-Incl. E.J. Brach (acquired 5/20/66) for entire period, 1965 comparison: Sales, $834.2 mill.; net, $83.3 mill., per share $1.55. c-Incl. Luck's, Inc., acquired during year for entire period. g-Before special items: 1971, $8.7 mill.(16c a sh.) gain; 1972, $2.7 mill. (5c a sh.) gain.   TAX FREE IN PENNA.

INCORPORATED: Feb. 4, 1926 - Delaware	TRANSFER AGENT: Manufacturers Hanover Tr. Co., N.Y. Continental Illinois National Bank & Trust Co., Chicago, Ill.	OFFICERS
PRINCIPAL OFFICE: 685 Third Avenue New York, N.Y. 10017		CHAIRMAN: W.F. Laporte
	REGISTRAR: Manufacturers Hanover Tr. Co., N.Y. Continental Illinois National Bank & Trust Co., Chicago, Ill.	PRESIDENT: J.W. Culligan
ANNUAL MEETING: Fourth Wed. in April		SECRETARY: M.E. Schmalzried
NUMBER OF STOCKHOLDERS: 72,759	INSTIT. NO.: 342 HOLDINGS: SHS.: 12,383,764	TREASURER: R.G. Blount

Source: Moody's *Handbook of Common Stocks*, 1975.

the back of the *Guide* each month are to be found "quality ratings of utility preferred stocks" and a section on the performance of 400 mutual funds.

Both Moody's and Standard & Poor's publish compendiums on individual companies. Moody's *Handbook of Common Stocks*, first published in 1964, is issued quarterly. It covers over 1,000 companies. For each one it has a chart, showing the years 1953 to date, the industry group stock price trend, and the company's stock price performance. Basic financial statistics for the past decade are given. The written analysis covers the company's financial background, recent financial developments, and prospects. An example of a typical page is shown in Figure 3–6. The Standard & Poor's compendium is called *Standard N.Y.S.E. Stock Reports*. It covers about 1,850 stocks. Full financial facts are given for each company. A chart shows the market performance of the stock, the average performance of stocks in its industry, and the performance of the stock market as a whole, in addition to showing the trading volume of the stock. Each report carries a Standard & Poor's opinion of the investment merits of each stock.

Both Standard & Poor's and Moody's publish weekly and monthly bond guides. Standard & Poor's issue a weekly *Bond Outlook*, Moody's a weekly *Bond Survey*. Each issue discusses new offerings in the corporate and municipal markets, opportunities in convertibles, changes in bond ratings, new issue ratings, bonds called for payment. Both services issue one-page summaries of individual bond situations.

The extensive nature of the many services provided for investors and for security analysts may be seen from the following list of publication services provided by Standard & Poor's:[12]

Analysts Handbook	*Earnings Forecaster*
Bond Guide	*Fixed Income Investor*
Called Bond Record	*Industry Surveys*
Compmark Data Services	*International Stock Report*
Convertible Bond Reports	*Investment Advisory Survey*
Corporation Records	*Municipal Bond Selector*
Daily Stock Price Records	*Opportunities in Convertible*
Dividend Record	*Bonds*

---

[12] A booklet describing these services entitled "Standard & Poor's Services and Publications Cover Every Financial Information Need' may be obtained by writing to Standard & Poor's at 345 Hudson Street, New York, N.Y. 10014. Moody's comparable services are described in a booklet entitled "How Moody's Can Help You." A copy may be obtained by writing to Moody's Investor Service, Inc., 99 Church Street, New York, N.Y. 10007.

The Outlook	*Security Dealers Directory*
Poor's Register of Corpora-	*Statistical Service*
tions, Directors, and	*Stock Guide*
Executives	*Stock Reports*
Registered Bond Interest	*Stock Summary*
Record	*Transportation Service*
The Review of Securities	*Trendline Charts*
Regulation	

Of particular interest are the *Analysts Handbook* and the *Earnings Forecaster*. The former provides composite corporate per share data on a true comparison basis. It maintains the best possible continuity since 1946 for 95 industries and the S&P 400 Industrial Index, making possible a great variety of significant per share comparisons. It is available annually with monthly updatings. The latter provides weekly new and revised earnings estimates on the 1,800 companies prepared by S&P and other leading investment organizations and brokerage firms. Continuously updated, this 40–52 page summary offers at-a-glance check of the various estimates against one another. For each company, listings include identification of source of estimates, per share earnings for the past full year, and where possible, for the next year. (See Figure 3–7.)

In addition to their own extensive use of computers in investment analysis, portfolio selection, and financial information retrieval, the major services provide security analysts, financial institutions, and money managers with computerized data banks and computer developed reports and tabulations. A major data compiliation, first developed by Standard & Poor's and now lodged in the hands of a subsidiary, Investors Management Sciences, Inc., is Compustat. Many quantitative-oriented research organizations rely on Compustat tapes as the financial data base for computerized financial analysis.[13] Compustat is available via magnetic tape directly from Investors Management Sciences, Inc., or remotely through a number of time-sharing systems, one of which, Interactive Data Corporation, has taken over a number of electronic services from Standard & Poor's and provides access to additional financial data banks.[14] The Compustat tapes contain 20 years of annual data for approximately 2,200 listed industrial companies, 900 OTC companies, 155 utilities, 115 banks, and 500 Canadian companies. Quarterly data are also available for the past 10

---

[13] For a descriptive brochure of Compustat and other Investors Management Sciences' products, write to Investors Management Sciences, Inc., P.O. Box 239, Denver, Colorado 80201.

[14] For a description of Interactive Data Corporation financial services, write to company at 486 Totten Pond Road, Waltham, Massachusetts 02154.

FIGURE 3–7
Standard & Poor's Earnings Forecaster

COMPANY & FISCAL YEAR / ESTIMATOR	APPX. PRICE $ / EST. DATE	P/E RATIO	A1974	E1975	E1976
›INLAND STEEL (Cont'd)					
Standard & Poor's				5.75	---
•INMONT CORP (Dec)	7	7	$1.74		
Hornblower & Weeks	Sep 17			1.00	---
Standard & Poor's	*			1.00	
•INSPIR'N CON COPPER (Dec) 23		92	3.92		
Standard & Poor's				0 25	---
•INTEGON CORP (Dec)	8	8	w0.97		
Standard & Poor's	*			1.00	
INTEL CORP (Dec)	74	31	2.96		
Bache & Co.	**			2.45	---
Herzfeld & Stern	Sep 22			2.60	
Shearson Hayden Stone Inc	Jul 3			2.40	---
Sutro & Co.	***			2.35	---
United Business Serv.	Jun 16			2.00	---
•INTERCO, INC (Feb)	35	8	4.60 Q4.47		
A.G. Edwards & Sons	Aug 15			Q4.25	---
•INTERLAKE, INC (Dec)	24	5	6.97		
Standard & Poor's	*			4.66	---
INTERMOUNTAIN GAS (Sep)	12	6	1.80 Q1.69		
Willamette Management Associates,	Jun 30			Q1.90	---
•INT'L.BUS.MACHINES (Dec) 188		15	12.47		
Bache & Co.	Jul 16			12.50	13.25
Hardy & Co.	Jul 1			12.80	---
Herzfeld & Stern	Sep 22			12.60	---
Shearson Hayden Stone Inc	Jul 3			13.20	---
United Business Serv.	Sep 2			12.75	---
Standard & Poor's				12.25	---
•INT'L FLAVORS/FRAGR (Dec) 23		28	0.88		
United Business Serv.	Aug 25			0.85	---
Standard & Poor's				0.80	---
›INT'L FOODSERVICE (Dec)	2	20	†d2.08		
Alex Brown & Sons	Aug 25			0.10/0.20	---
†Incl. $1.42 loss on sale					
•INT'L HARVESTER (Oct)	23	4	s4.24		
Robert W. Baird & Co.	Aug 13			6.25	6.00
Drysdale & Co.	Aug 29			5.25	---
E.F.Hutton & Co,	Aug 4			6.00	4.50
Piper,Jaffray & Hopwood,	Sep 16			5.00	---
Standard & Poor's				5.00	---
•INT'L MINERALS/CHEM (Jun) 44		4	ws3.59	wA9.91 QwA8.90	
Bache & Co.	Aug 19			12.00	
Piper,Jaffray & Hopwood,	Sep 16			Q10.00	
				11.00	
•INT'L MULTIFOODS (Feb)	22	5	3.88		
Piper,Jaffray & Hopwood,	Aug 14			4.30	---
Standard & Poor's				4.15	---
•INT'L NICKEL CAN. (Dec)	25	8	4.11		
Standard & Poor's				3.00	---
•INT'L PAPER (Dec)	52	12	5.95		
Bache & Co.	**			4.00	---
Robert W. Baird & Co.	Aug 13			4.50	5.00
Piper,Jaffray & Hopwood,	Aug 18			4.35	---
Shearson Hayden Stone Inc	Jul 3			4.50	---
United Business Serv.	Sep 22			4.00	---
Standard & Poor's				4.50	---
•INT'L TEL & TEL (Dec)	19	6	3.63 Q3.57		
United Business Serv.	Jul 14			3.60	---
Standard & Poor's	*			3.30	---
›INTERPOOL LTD (Nov)	11	4	2.52		
Frederick Research	Jun 30			3.00*	3.60*
Hornblower & Weeks	Sep 17			2.40	---
INTERSIL, INC (Dec)	5	15	0.05		
Sutro & Co.	***			0.35	---
•INTERSTATE BRANDS (Dec)	14	5	1.14 Q1.09		
Standard & Poor's	*			3.00	---
•INTERSTATE POWER (Dec)	14	9	1.67		
Standard & Poor's	*			1.65	---

COMPANY & FISCAL YEAR / ESTIMATOR	APPX. PRICE $ / EST. DATE	P/E RATIO	A1974	E1975	E1976
•INTERSTATE UNITED (Jun)	4	3	1.22	P1.04	
Lamson Bros.& Co.	Jul 1				1.25
Standard & Poor's	*				1.15
›INTERWAY CORP (Dec)	7	--	3.41 Q3.09		
Hornblower & Weeks	Sep 17			B.E.	---
•IOWA BEEF PROCESSORS (Oct) 24		3	5.94		
Piper,Jaffray & Hopwood,	Aug 14			7.25	---
Standard & Poor's	*			7.00	---
•IOWA-ILL GAS & ELEC (Dec) 16		7	2.03		
Lamson Bros.& Co.	Jul 1			2.30	---
Standard & Poor's	*			2.30	---
•IOWA POWER & LIGHT (Dec)	20	7	2.63		
Lamson Bros.& Co.	Jul 1			2.80	---
Standard & Poor's	*			2.85	---
•IOWA PUBLIC SERVICE (Dec) 16		7	2.06		
Lamson Bros.& Co.	Jul 1			2.25	--
•I-T-E IMPERIAL (Dec)	16	8	2.50		
Standard & Poor's	*			2.10	---
•IU INT'L (Dec)	10	4	2.77 Q2.50		
Shearson Hayden Stone Inc	Jul 3			Q2.25/2.50	---
Standard & Poor's				2.50	---
›JACLYN, INC (Jun)	7	4	1.20	P1.50	
Frederick Research	Sep 11				1.65
•JAMES (FRED S) & CO (Dec) 11		8	1.36		
E.F.Hutton & Co,	Aug 4			1.40	1.55
Standard & Poor's	*			1.45	---
•JANTZEN INC (Aug)	13	5	2.85		
Piper,Jaffray & Hopwood,	Mar 4			2.55	---
United Business Serv.	Aug 25			2.40	---
Standard & Poor's	*			2.40/2.50	---
JASON EMPIRE (Jan)	5	7	0.85		
B. C. Christopher & Co.	Sep 23			0.75	---
•JEFFERSON-PILOT (Dec)	27	11	w2.41		
Alex Brown & Sons	Aug 25			2.60	---
E.F.Hutton & Co,	Aug 4			2.50	2.80
Shearson Hayden Stone Inc	Jul 3			2.50	---
Standard & Poor's	*			2.50	---
•JEWEL CO'S (Jan)	18	7	2.65		
Standard & Poor's	*			2.75	---
•JEWELCOR, INC (Jan)	4	5	0.02		
Drysdale & Co.	Jun 30			0.75	---
•JIM WALTER (Aug)	29	7	3.65 Q3.48		
Bache & Co.	Aug 26			4.00	---
Josephthal & Co.	Sep 22			4.00	---
Raymond,James & Associates,	Aug 8			4.20	5.00
Wm.C.Roney & Co.	Jun 30			Q4.00	---
Standard & Poor's	*			4.00	4.50
›JOHNS-MANVILLE (Dec)	20	10	z w2.73		
Bache & Co.	Sep 15			2.00	---
Josephthal & Co.	Sep 22			2.00/2.25	---
Standard & Poor's	*			2.00	---
z w $1.15,*74					
JOHNSON (E.F.) (Dec)	28	6	3.14 Q2.90		
Piper,Jaffray & Hopwood,	Sep 12			4.50	6.00
•JOHNSON CONTROLS (Dec)	12	8	w0.80		
Robert W. Baird & Co.	Aug 13			1.50	1.75
The Milwaukee	Jun 30			Q2.00/2.35	Q2.50
•JOHNSON & JOHNSON (Dec)	79	25	2.80		
Bache & Co.	**			3.30	---
Heine,Fishbein & Co.	Jul 2			3.10	---
Shearson Hayden Stone Inc	Jul 3			3.11	---
Thomson&McKinnon,					
Auchincloss Kohlmeyer	Apr 24			3.15	3.50
United Business Serv.	Aug 25			3.30	---
Standard & Poor's	*			3.30	---
›JOHNSON PRODUCTS (Aug)	19	14	1.24		
United Business Serv.	Aug 25			1.35	---
•JORGENSEN, (E.M.) (Dec)	29	5	8.08		
Standard & Poor's	*			5.50/6.00	---

Source: Standard & Poor's, October 3, 1975.

years for the 2,200 listed industrial companies and 12 years of quarterly data for the banks and utilities. The Compustat tapes are updated regularly.

Each subscriber is provided with a *Compustat Manual* which covers usage, accessing, programming, definition of accounting items, explanation of financial ratios available. By screening for financial criteria, the different groups of companies that can be extracted from the Compustat tapes, based on various selected financial criteria are

almost infinite. The different criteria used are primarily a function of the investment concepts and objectives of the user. For example, the following set of criteria, over a one-, five-, or ten-year period, might be used to select a group of companies from the total industrial file deserving further investigation by the analyst:

a. Price-earnings ratio above (or below) a specified value.
b. Dividend yield above (or below) a specified value.
c. Operating profit margin above (or below) a specified value.
d. After-tax margin above (or below) a specified value.
e. Return on stockholder's equity above (or below) a specified value.

In addition to *Compustat*, other computerized Investors Management Sciences services include: *Comparative Analysis; Financial Dynamics, DataScan; Financial Summary*, and *Portfolio InSight, Comparative Analysis* is a custom computerized service that generates financial reports according to the analyst's specifications. It produces computer-generated reports for any combination of the following elements specified: (1) companies, (2) time periods, and (3) data items and ratios. Applications of this service include (but are not limited to) the following frequently requested reports: (*a*) company screenings and rankings, (*b*) company and industry comparisons, (*c*) profitability and growth analysis, and (*d*) merger and acquisition studies. A multimillion dollar data base consisting of over 3 million raw data items can be utilized in any way desired.

Financial Dynamics is a comprehensive statistical service incorporating all the traditional ratios. These, combined with many unique investment concepts, provide an extensive library of financial facts. *DataScan* is a weekly report detailing important quarterly financial trends of 1,500 companies. It is a powerful time-saving tool. You can scan a large number of companies quickly. By checking only three or four columns per report (such as rate of change in sales or earnings per share, or P/E), you can identify companies which deserve additional examination. *Financial Summary* is a fixed format financial service designed for the smaller user. The reports are one page per company and contain ten years of annual data. Seven categories are given: (1) total dollar amounts for principal income account items; (2) per share dollars and cents for selected income account items; (3) operating profit margins; (4) price and related ratios; (5) growth analysis of sales, earnings and common equity; (6) capitalization ratios; and (7) total dollar amounts for key balance sheet items. *Portfolio InSight* was created to provide busy portfolio managers and others responsible for asset management with an incisive method of monitoring portfolio performance and analyzing portfolio structure. Each weekly *Portfolio InSight* report is organized into the following major sections:

1. Portfolio changes for the week.
2. Schedule of investments and time weighted rate of return.
3. Portfolio summary and five largest equity investments.
4. Performance of equity investments sold.
5. Relative portfolio performance.

Some of the electronic services developed by Standard & Poor's were transferred to the Interactive Data Corporation, a time-sharing computer service company, specializing in the financial field and originating by a merger of the Interactive Data Services Division of White, Weld & Company and the Computer Communications Center. This consolidation brought together important competences in financial data and languages, and in the design, development, and operation of large-scale, time-sharing systems. Today, IDC maintains, or makes available, a number of large-scale financial data bases and a variety of product programs to access them. These data bases include:

The Security Master Data Base.
The Prices Data Base.
The Split and Dividend Data Base.
The Compustat Data Bases.
The Value Line Data Bases.
The I/B/E/S Summary Statistic Data Base.
The FDIC Data Base.
The Edie Economic Data Base.

IDC also provides a number of processing programs and systems, including Analytics, Xport, and XPM.

Analytics is a computer system providing a comprehensive data retrieval and report generation service for the financial community. It consists of two major components: the data itself and the processing systems which generate the analyses and reports.

Xport is a Portfolio Management Information and Performance Measurement Service for money managers. *Xport* gives the user immediate on-line access to all portfolio data from a time-sharing terminal and optionally provides a low-cost scheduled production service where *Interactive* performs all updating and report generation tasks for the user. *XPM* provides the capability to measure a portfolio's performance against standard market indices or user-defined model portfolios. It provides dollar- and time-weighted rates-of-return as prescribed by the Bank Administration Institute.

The Value Line Investment Survey covers 1,640 stocks in 75 industries. It is essentially a reference and current valuation service. Each stock in the list is reviewed in detail once every three months. Interim reports are provided in weekly supplements on any new devel-

opments between the time of the regular quarterly reports. Each week the new edition of *The Value Line Investment Survey* covers four to six industries on a rotating basis. Each industry report contains full-page reports on individual stocks. About 125 stocks are covered every week in the order of their industries. After all 1,640 stocks have been covered in 13 weeks, the cycle starts over again.

Each week there are three or four parts to the survey. Part I is the "Weekly Summary of Advices and Index." It provides an average of estimated yields for the ensuing 12 months; the estimated average price-earnings ratio for the period 6 months past and 6 months future; the average appreciation potentiality of all 1,640 stocks in an hypothesized economic environment three to five years ahead; a rank of industrial groups according to probable market performance over the next 12 months; a rank for each stock's safety (total risk); and the beta based on 5 years of weekly price fluctuations. Part II is the "Selection & Opinion" section. It covers topics such as "Business and the Stock Market," "Recommended Stock," "Inflation and Common Stocks," and presents computer screens for stock selection. Part III, "Reports and Ratings," provides the industry and company analyses described above.

Value Line has developed statistical techniques designed, in each stock report, to answer five questions:

1. How safe a stock is it in relation to 1,640 others?
2. How well can it be expected to perform in the market during the next 12 months compared to other stocks?
3. How attractive is it over a three- to five-year pull?
4. How much will this stock yield over the next 12 months?
5. How suitable is the stock for the individual investor in the light of his or her investment objectives?

In addition to The Investment Survey, *Value Line* also has a Special Service and a Convertible Survey on Convertible bonds, preferred and warrants.

See Figure 3–8 for the *Value Line* individual company analysis.

The Value Line Data Base contains historic annual and quarterly financial records for 1,500 industrial companies, finance companies, and savings and loan associations. The annual data begin in 1954, quarterly figures in 1963. The Data Base contains the following information.

1. Comprehensive income statements.
3. Comprehensive balance sheets.
3. Source and uses of funds statements.
4. Sales and income as reported.

FIGURE 3—8
Value Line Individual Company Analysis

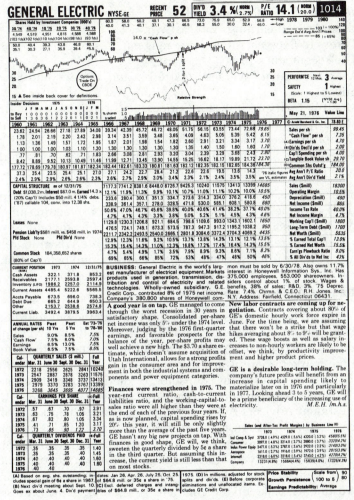

Reprinted by permission of Arnold Bernhard & Co., publisher of *The Value Line Investment Survey*.

5. Sales and income restated for merger.

6. Restated sales and earnings by product line.

7. Precalculated ratios, return rates, per share data.

8. Measures of earnings predictability.

9. Stock price characteristics including beta, and R-square.

10. Identification of key accounting methods for inventories depreciation, tax credits, and leases.

11. Footnote information including pension liability and debt due in five years.
12. Year-ahead dividend estimates.
13. Calendarized earnings forecasts.
14. Three- to five-year stock price ranges.
15. The recent stock price.
16. Average annual, average quarterly, and quarter ending stock prices.
17. Monthly high and low stock prices.
18. Monthly trading volume statistics.
19. Composite record for individual industries.
20. A composite file combining the historic annual and quarterly results of U.S. industry.

Another service, Computer Directions Advisor, Inc. (Silver Spring, Maryland), provides a *Composite Filter Report* for screening all NYSE and AMEX common stocks by such factors as dividend yield, absolute earnings growth, relative earnings growth, absolute P/E ratio, relative P/E ratio, relative price strength, price volatility, and beta coefficient.

Investment Counseling Services

For the well-to-do investors who want to avoid the burdensome and often time-consuming chore of digging up facts for themselves, following industry and company trends, and judging the state of the economy and of the market, there is an easy and relatively inexpensive "out." They can use an investment counselor, or the investment counseling department of a bank, or of one of the large investment services. Under the Investment Advisers Act of 1940, independent (nonbank) investment counseling firms must be registered with the SEC. Busy professional people, active business executives who have little or no time to do the digging involved in managing their own investments, or widows or widowers who have no knowledge whatsoever of finance and investments, make up the clientele, in general, of the professional money managers.

The usual annual fee charged by an investment counselor is 0.5 percent of the value of the portfolio being managed. For a $200,000 portfolio this means an annual fee of $1,000. Most of the larger investment counseling firms will not take accounts with portfolios of less than $100,000. The largest firms in the business—Scudder, Stevens & Clark; Loomis-Sayles; Lionel D. Edie;[15] Calvin Bullock; Stein, Row & Farnham; Van Strum & Towne; Eaton & Howard, Inverness Counsel—maintain professional staffs of security analysts and portfolio

---

[15] Now a Merrill Lynch subsidiary.

managers to assist clients. They do the investment research and make recommendations to customers. The counselors prefer to have discretionary accounts in which they have the legal power to manage the client's funds. In almost all cases, of course, the client is informed of portfolio changes, proposed or accomplished. Many clients prefer to retain final authority for passing upon a proposed change. In some cases the investment counselors have custody of the client's securities, since this makes for more expeditious purchasing and selling; a number of clients prefer to retain possession of their own securities and turn them over to the investment counselor only to effectuate a transaction.

Some of the large investment counselors have their own mutual funds which they manage. Others advise corporate pension funds or college or university endowment funds. The mutual funds are for the investors whose assets are nowhere near the $100,000 minimum level. It has been estimated that the investment counselors' clients' average portfolio is about $250,000. Since investment counselors publish no records of performance, selecting a firm is usually an act of faith based on someone's recommendation or on the firm's general reputation.

Banks provide investment advisory services, sometimes on a formal, fee basis, sometimes on an informal customer-relations complimentary basis. A wealthy individual who wants investment help from the bank can usually obtain it without formally turning funds over to the bank's trust department. An investment officer in the trust department, or in the investment advisory department, if the bank has one, will serve as an investment counselor to those with portfolios of $100,000 and over. The investment officer ascertains the client's investment objectives and attempts to tailor his or her recommendations to meet the objectives. Again the account may be discretionary or nondiscretionary, custodial or the customer may retain possession of the securities. While the portfolio is reviewed regularly, the customer usually receives a quarterly report from the bank on his or her portfolio. The investment officer makes recommendations and in the case of the discretionary account arranges portfolio changes. For wealthier investors who wish to be free from money-management problems and are comfortable in conservative investment hands, this is a handy arrangement. In the discretionary account the owners do not surrender title to their own securities. The bank acts only as their agent. This is in contrast to the more formal trust arrangement.

Bank administered trusts may be either living trusts (*inter vivos*) set up during an individual's lifetime or testamentary trusts set up at death by will or other prior arrangement. There are individual trusts or common trust funds. The common trust fund, akin to a mutual fund, is gaining in popularity and is designed to appeal to smaller investors,

those with from $5,000 to $75,000 to invest, but some accounts go up to $100,000 and more. You set up a trust, name the bank as trustee, and the bank, in turn, mixes or pools your funds with other small individual trust accounts for investment in a common portfolio of securities. In a common trust fund, investments are spread far more widely than would be possible in an individual trust. Also, the cost is lower.

Banks offer several types of common trust funds. If you set up the trust without specifying the type of investment you want, the bank is required by law to put you into what is called a legal investments fund. This is a conservative type, about 65 percent bonds and 35 percent stock. But if you give the bank discretion, you may be placed in one of four types of funds: the balanced fund, about 60 percent common stock, 40 percent bonds; the 100 percent common stock fund; the tax-exempt bond fund (a rapidly growing type); or finally a taxable corporate bond and preferred stock fund for income. When you establish the trust, you can name the type of fund you want. Thus banks have increasingly developed flexibility in serving investors.

Recently there has been a trend toward accommodating the small investor, both on the part of banks and of financial services.[16] Citibank (of New York) will accept investment advisory accounts with a $10,000 value minimum. The cost of its advice is 1 percent a year on the market value of the investment, with a $250 minimum charge. The Marine Midland banks will give investment advice on accounts as low as $8,000. The fee is 0.75 a year with a $160 minimum charge. Danforth Associates, of Wellesley Hills, Massachusetts, takes clients with as little as $5,000, charging a fee of 2 percent a year on portfolios up to $25,000 in value and 0.25 percent on additional amounts over that, with a $100-a-year minimum fee.[17]

Business Conditions and Corporate Profits

If the security analyst's starting point is an examination of business trends, including a forecast of the outlook for business, the economy, and corporate profits, it is not difficult to find material. Indeed, the real problem may be choosing from among the multiplicity of sources. A number of the leading banks publish monthly reports or surveys dealing with the business outlook and other topics. The First National City Bank of New York publishes a *Monthly Economic Letter*. The leading article is always on "General Business Conditions." The *Morgan Guaranty Survey* is published monthly by the Morgan Guaranty Trust

---

[16] "Now the Small Investor Can Have an Adviser," *Business Week*, February 23, 1974, p. 75.

[17] W. Scott Bauman, "The Investment Management Organization," *Financial Analyst's Handbook*, vol. I (Homewood, Ill.: Dow Jones-Irwin, Inc., 1975), chap. 41.

Company of New York. The first article always covers "Business and Financial Conditions." The Bank of New York issues *General Business Indicators* which is a statistical tabulation of selected economic indicators. It provides the bank's forecast of prospective gross national product, disposable personal income, index of industrial production, corporate profits, and earnings of the Dow Jones Industrials, over the coming year. The Chase Manhattan Bank publishes *Business in Brief,* issued bimonthly by its Economic Research Division. The first article usually covers an analysis of the business outlook.

The 12 Federal Reserve Banks publish monthly bulletins devoted to banking, economic, and financial topics. The Federal Reserve Bank of New York, for example, publishes a *Monthly Review,* which always includes an article on "The Business Situation." The Federal Reserve Bank of Philadelphia publishes the *Business Review,* monthly. The Federal Reserve Banks of Chicago and St. Louis also issue excellent monthly reviews. In addition to its monthly review, the Federal Reserve Bank of St. Louis issues a number of other publications, monthly, including *National Economic Trends, Monetary Trends, Federal Budget Trends,* and so forth. The Board of Governors of the Federal Reserve System in Washington, D.C., publishes the *Federal Reserve Bulletin,* monthly. It contains a "National Summary of Business Conditions." This can be obtained as a separate release, monthly, as can "Money Stock Measures," a statistical release covering trends in M_1, M_2, and M_3. The Federal Reserve also publishes a *Chart Book on Business, Economic, and Financial Statistics,* monthly, as well as an annual *Historical Chart Book.*

The library of the Federal Reserve Bank of Philadelphia has issued an excellent index, *Federal Reserve Bank Reviews Selected Subjects 1950–1970.* This is kept current by a quarterly index, *The Fed in Print,* which may be obtained free of charge from the Federal Reserve Bank of Philadelphia.

The federal government provides a number of useful sources of information on developing business trends. The *Survey of Current Business* is published monthly by the U.S. Department of Commerce. It has two principal parts. The first deals with basic business trends and starts with an article on "The Business Situation" which reviews recent developments, pointing out underlying strengths or weaknesses. The second section is an elaborate compilation of basic statistical series on all phases of the economy. There is also a weekly supplement in which the indexes of business activity, prices, production, and so forth, appearing in the *Survey of Current Business* are kept up to date. The President's Council of Economic Advisors publishes the monthly *Economic Indicators* and the *Annual Economic Review,* which deal with the state of the economy and the outlook.

For economic forecasting purposes, perhaps the most useful publication of the government is *Business Conditions Digest,* issued monthly by the Bureau of the Census of the U.S. Department of Commerce.[18] This report brings together many of the available economic indicators in convenient form for analysis and interpretation. The presentation and classification of the series follow the business indicator approach of the National Bureau of Economic Research (NBER). The classification of series and business cycle turning dates are those designated by NBER, which, in recent years, has been the leader in this field of investigation. About 90 principal indicators and over 300 components are included in the report. Among others there are the NBER leading indicators, the NBER roughly coincident indicators, the NBER lagging indicators, and series for international comparisons. The movements of the series are shown against the background of the expansions and contractions of the general business cycle so that "leads" and "lags" can be readily detected and cyclical developments spotted.[19]

A private source provides data on the NBER indicators weekly. This is the Statistical Indicator Associates of North Egremont, Massachusetts, directed by Leonard H. Lempert. These weekly reports include both current statistics and interpretive text and forecasts. *Business Week,* in its "Business Outlook" section reviews the indicators from time to time and regularly provides an analytic review of changing business and economic developments. Published by McGraw-Hill, Inc., and written in a lively and interesting style, *Business Week,* provides coverage of major developments in many areas of business and finance. Two other journals which provide somewhat similar coverage are *Nation's Business* and *Dun's Review. Fortune* magazine has a section each month entitled "Business Roundup." This is a monthly report on the economic outlook. The Conference Board issues a monthly *Record,* a weekly *Desk Sheet of Business Indicators,* and a chart service, *Road Maps of Industry.*

The federal government's influence in shaping the American economy is inescapably a factor in investment decisions. As a result, a

---

[18] This was revised in 1975. See May 1975 issue of *Business Conditions Digest,* and "Questions and Answers about the Revision of the Composite Index of Leading Indicators," Bureau of Economic Analysis, U.S. Department of Commerce, Washington D.C., May 28, 1975.

[19] For a further discussion of the use of this tool in investment analysis and portfolio management, see Chapter 12. See also selections 12, 13, 14, and 20 in Institute of Chartered Financial Analysts, *1973 Supplementary Readings in Financial Analysis,* vol. 1 (Homewood, Ill.: Richard D. Irwin, Inc., 1972); and Geoffrey H. Moore, "Security Markets and Business Cycles," and Nathan Belfer, "Economic Indicators," *Financial Analyst's Handbook,* vol. I (Homewood, Ill.: Dow Jones-Irwin, Inc., 1975), chaps. 27 and 28, respectively.

number of private services have been established with Washington as their base of reporting. These include, among others, "Research from Washington," a subsidiary of Smith, Barney, & Co., Inc.; "Washington Service," prepared by the Government Research Corporation, a subsidiary of E. F. Hutton & Co.; and "Washington Economist" by Bradley, Woods, & Co., Inc.

On corporate profits, overall trends can be seen in the *Quarterly Financial Report for Manufacturing Corporations,* published jointly by the Federal Trade Commission and the Securities and Exchange Commission. The purpose of this survey is to produce, each calendar quarter, an income statement and balance sheet for all manufacturing corporations, classified by both industry and asset size. Profitability is reported in two ways—"profits per dollar of sales" and "annual rate of profit on stockholders' equity at end of period." The quarterly summaries may be used to measure efficiency and appraise costs by comparing a company's operating results with the average performance of companies of similar size or in the same line of business.

Each year, in the April issue of its *Monthly Economic Letter,* the Citibank (of New York) publishes the results of its survey of the profits performance of almost 4,000 U.S. corporations, not only in manufacturing lines but also in trade, transportation, utilities, services, real estate, and banking. Profits are reported, for the two prior years, on two bases, as "percent return on net worth" and as "percent margin on sales." The detailed industry classification and breakdown permits an investor or a securities analyst to compare a given company with the reported industry average.

The outlook for corporate profits is usually tied to a forecast of business conditions.[20] While securities analysts may occasionally undertake their own forecasts, individual investors usually are not equipped, nor do they have the time, to make independent forecasts on their own. They must rely on one or more of the estimates of the business outlook described previously. There are, of course, many sources in addition to those mentioned. Competent investors will absorb as much material as their time and energies permit. The wider their reading, the better equipped they will be to assess the outlook.

The professional analysts usually have available probably more sophisticated sources of economic forecast data, certainly more expensive, than the individual investor can afford. For example, for $3,000 per annum they may subscribe to the Chase Economic Consulting Service, provided by the economics and research staff of the Chase Econometric Associates, Inc., a subsidiary of the Chase Manhattan

---

[20] See Samuel S. Stewart, Jr., "Corporate Forecasting," and Robert A. Kavesh and Robert B. Platt, "Economic Forecasting," *Financial Analyst's Handbook,* vol. I (Homewood, Ill.: Dow Jones-Irwin, Inc., 1975), chaps. 32 and 33, respectively.

Bank. For this fee, one receives (*a*) monthly forecasts and analyses for the next eight quarters, and (*b*) once a year, a ten-year forecast. You also receive the privilege of consulting the Chase Econometric Research staff at Bala Cynwyd, Pennsylvania. From time to time, on an unscheduled basis you receive special in-depth reports on the latest developments in the U.S. economy.

Projections from other econometric services, such as Data Resources, Inc., of Lexington, Massachusetts are also available at substantial fees.[21] Or, if you are willing and able to generate brokerage commission in a range of $12,000–$25,000 a year you can get the *Quality of Earnings Report,* which analyzes individual company's corporate reporting practices and interprets the reality of the reported earnings behind varying accounting techniques.[22]

Another service which is intended for the professional institutional investor, both because of its complexity and its cost, is William O'Neil & Co.'s *Datagraphs.* It provides complex charts on major companies in major industry categories, each chart carrying 75 items of financial information. For example, item 1 is *Industry Group Rank* which is derived by calculating the percentage price change for the past six months of each stock in a particular group, and then averaging these individual percentage changes for an overall industry group average. Item 2, the *Relative Strength of Each Stock* is the result of calculating price changes over the last 12 months, with more weight given for the recent three months' period. All stocks are arranged in order of price change and assigned a percentile from 99 to 1. There are 73 other items of financial information.

The Securities Markets

The competent analyst must constantly make a judgment as to the trend and level of the market as a whole to provide the appropriate environmental setting for selection and timing of portfolio additions or deletions.

On an elementary level, one can keep abreast of the market by

---

[21] See "Figuring the Future: Econometricians Seek Answers by 'Building' Models of the Economy," *The Wall Street Journal,* May 23, 1972; also Leonall C. Andersen, "The St. Louis Econometric Forecasting Model," *Business Economics,* September 1971; and Joseph Zeisel, "Forecasting at the Federal Reserve," *Business Economics,* September 1971. See also Michael W. Keran, "An Econometric Approach to Analysis of the Stock Market," in Institute of Chartered Financial Analysts, *Supplementary Readings in Financial Analysis,* vol. 3 (Homewood, Ill.: Richard D. Irwin, Inc., 1975), chap. 3.

[22] Issued by the Reporting Research Corporation, 560 Sylvan Avenue, Englewood Cliffs, New Jersey 07632. See Michael Clowes, "Coenen's Quality of Earnings Reports Warn Funds of Corporate Problems," *Pensions & Investments,* February 17, 1975, p. 3.

reading the financial section of a daily newspaper such as *The New York Times* or *The Wall Street Journal*. On a weekly basis, review of *Barron's*, Standard & Poor's, *The Outlook*, and the Sunday financial section of *The New York Times*, will provide basic data on stock market action and trends. Looking daily at the *Times* market summary story and tabulation page and at *The Wall Street Journal* "Abreast of the Market" "Heard on the Street" columns and Dow Jones index page, and weekly at *Barron's* "Study of Price Movement—Market Laboratory" page, and at *The Outlook's* "Forecast and Policy" page and at its "Indexes of the Security Markets" page, will build a continuing awareness of price trends. (See Figure 3–9.)

FIGURE 3–9
***The Outlook's* Forecast and Policy Page**

UPTREND RESUMED

FORECAST AND POLICY

The market finally seems to be responding to the increasingly favorable economic and technical conditions that have been accumulating during its extended stalemate. We would maintain a positive approach, while exercising discrimination in making new commitments.

• • •

MARKET MEASURES			
	*Price/Earn.		
July 7	Ratios	Yields	
Industrials	12.86	3.35%	
Transportation	†	3.30	
Utilities	8.16	7.85	
Financial	†	3.76	
500 Stocks	12.29	3.62	

INDUSTRIAL PRICE INDEXES (1941-43 = 10)			
July	High	Low	Close
9	118.46	116.66	117.95
8	117.72	116.26	116.85
7	117.10	115.50	116.66
6	117.63	115.96	116.33
2	117.50	115.95	117.01
1	118.10	116.01	116.47

*Based on preliminary earnings for 12 months through the first quarter of 1976, adjusted to the price indexes: Industrials 9.07; Utilities 5.80; 500 Stocks 8.45. †P/Es on these two new groups will be available in the near future.

Industrials Last Week Rose 0.8%, Transportation 1.4%, Utilities 1.3% and Financial 0.6%.

BEST ACTING GROUPS	
	Change From Prev. Wk.
Brewers	+5.7%
Gold Mining	+4.0
Sugar-Beet Refiners	+3.9
Canned Foods	+3.2
Metal Fabricating	+3.0
Tobacco	+2.8
Publishing (Newspapers)	+2.7
Electric Utilities	+2.3
Natural Gas Distributors	+2.2
Soaps	+2.1

Ten Groups Reached New 1976 Highs in the Week Ended Wednesday.

POOREST PERFORMERS	
	Change From Prev. Wk.
Atomic Energy	−5.5%
Paper	−5.0
Synthetic Fibers	−4.3
Chemicals	−3.6
Aluminum	−3.4
Distillers	−3.4
Coal	−3.3
Textile Products	−3.1
Investment Companies	−3.0
Real Estate	−2.9

There Were No 1976 Group Lows in the Week Ended Wednesday.

Despite earlier selling pressure concentrated in basic industrial blue chips, notably the autos and papers (see facing page), the stock market scored a good advance on Friday, buoyed by the release of surprisingly good news on the inflation front. As a result, the S&P 500, which had been hovering just below the upper limits of its long consolidation zone, moved decisively into new recovery high ground.

It has done this before, most recently in early April, only to fall back into and extend its earlier trading area. But this time the breakout has been reinforced by favorable breadth and volume characteristics, and it therefore holds greater promise of resolving the five-month impasse.

To the extent that political uncertainties may have been a restraining influence, this week's Democratic National Convention may shed some light on the policy views of the likely nominee. Certainly, the stock market has not been reassured by Mr. Carter's reported plans to concentrate economic policy on reducing unemployment to the 3% level in the near term, a move that would almost surely crank up the engines of inflation and would probably be accompanied by economic control machinery.

Meanwhile, the economic background remains broadly favorable for the security markets. Bond prices, like those of utility and other interest-rate-sensitive stocks, have benefited from news that the Federal deficit for the fiscal year ended June 30 was well below earlier expectations, and that the U. S. Treasury ended the year with a comfortable cash balance of $14.7 billion. As a result, the Treasury will have to borrow less in the capital markets in the months ahead, thereby reducing competitive pressures on interest rates. Moreover, the monetary aggregates continue to respond favorably to the earlier braking actions by the Federal Reserve, with the result that an easier tone has prevailed in the money market.

Business activity continues to show satisfactory progress. As expected, preliminary retail trade data for June show that the post-Easter slowdown was a temporary phenomenon, and indications for the fall are highly encouraging. And second-quarter earnings reports, now starting to appear, support our expectations for excellent full-year gains.

The market's long consolidation has absorbed a lot of nervous selling and should now be able to support another upleg of the ongoing bull market. The going will not be easy, however; rather, it is likely to be quite selective and subject to frequent reactions.

• • •

Wholesale prices rose at a surprisingly moderate 4.8% annual rate in June, despite the initial impact of earlier increases in metal and fuel prices. The resulting bulge in industrial commodity prices was offset by slower gains in prices of farm products, notably produce, cattle and eggs.

Source: Standard & Poor's, *The Outlook,* July 12, 1976, p. 655.

On an intermediate level, fundamental and technical analysis may help to provide a perspective of where the market is and where it is likely to go. Fundamental market analysis involves the use of composite stock yields, composite price-earnings ratios, and the yield spread between stocks and bonds as market indicators. For example, the level of the market may be judged by yields on the Dow Jones Industrials. At major bull market peaks in the past, the DJI and yields on its 30 stocks were as follows:

Date	DJI	Yield
September 3, 1929	381.17	3.33%
March 10, 1937	194.40	3.76
May 29, 1946	212.50	3.23
January 4, 1960	679.06	3.07
December 13, 1961	734.91	3.03
February 9, 1966	995.15	2.92
December 3, 1968	985.21	3.22
January 11, 1973	1,051.70	3.07

It would appear that when the DJI yields approach the 3 percent level, at least in the past, major bull markets have tended to peak. The record at bear market lows is not as clear:

Date	DJI	Yield
July 8, 1932	41.22	10.40%
April 28, 1942	92.92	7.58
June 13, 1949	161.60	6.84
April 3, 1958	440.50	4.89
October 25, 1960	566.05	3.78
June 26, 1962	535.76	4.32
May 26, 1970	631.14	4.62
December 6, 1974	577.60	6.52

The price-earnings ratio on the DJI has often, in the past, been used to judge the level of the market. At previous bull market highs, for example, the record was as follows:

Date	DJI	Earnings	P/E Ratio
September 3, 1929	381.17	$19.94	19.1
March 10, 1937	194.40	11.12	17.5
May 29, 1946	212.50	10.24	20.8
January 4, 1960	679.06	33.82	20.1
December 13, 1961	734.91	31.91	23.0
February 9, 1966	995.15	53.67	18.5
December 3, 1968	985.21	57.89	17.0
January 11, 1973	1,051.70	62.80	16.7

In the past, at least, one could say that when the DJI–P/E went into or above the 17–19 average, bull markets tended to top out, but again the record at bear market lows is not consistent, the P/E ratio at selected lows ranging from 7 to 16 approximately. See Figure 3–10 and Table 3–1.

FIGURE 3–10
Dow Jones Price/Earnings Ratio

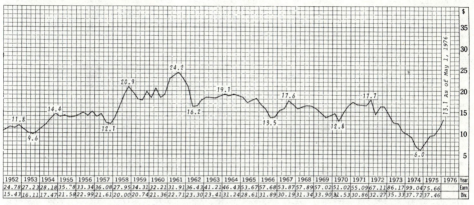

Source: Adapted from M. C. Horsey & Co., Inc., "The Stock Picture," Salisbury, Maryland, 1976.

This is a rudimentary approach, of course. Whether stock prices respond to or anticipate changes in earnings, in inflationary expectations, in the money supply, in consumer outlook and sentiment, in investment in capital goods, or to a combination of all or of several of those or other factors, or to none at all, is a matter of continuing debate and dispute among financial economists. For example, in a pioneering study Beryl Sprinkel found that broad changes in the money supply preceded broad changes in the direction of stock prices. He was quite specific and formulated an investment rule that, "a bear market in stock prices was predicted 15 months after each peak in monetary growth and that a bull market was predicted two months after each monetary growth trough was reached."[23] A study by Mascia confirmed that a relationship between monetary changes and stock prices does exist and that such relationship is not "a mere statistical quirk." But doubt remains that a causal relationship exists between the two.[24]

---

[23] Beryl W. Sprinkel, *Money and Stock Prices* (Homewood, Ill.: Richard D. Irwin, Inc., 1964); see also his subsequent *Money and Markets* (Homewood, Ill.: Richard D. Irwin, Inc., 1971).

[24] Joseph S. Mascia, "Monetary Change and Equity Values," *The Bankers Magazine*, Summer 1969; see also Michael S. Rozoff, "The Money Supply and the Stock Market: The Demise of a Leading Indicator," *Financial Analysts Journal*, September/October 1975.

TABLE 3–1

Selected Financial Indicators

	Index of Prices, 500 Stocks 1941-43=10	Dow-Jones Industrial Averages				# Federal Funds Rate	U.S. Treas. #3 Mo Bills New Issues	#Long Term Bonds	Bond Buyer 20 Mun.#	Moody's Corporate Bonds		#Yield on S&P 500
		Price Range	Earns.	Divs.	*P-E Ratio					Aaa#	Baa#	
		------------Per Share----------				------------------------Percent----------------------						
1976												
July							5.28					
June P	101.77					5.48	5.44	6.92	6.87	8.62	9.72	3.75
May	101.16	1011-958		$10.19		5.29	5.19	6.99	6.87	8.58	9.76	3.76
April	101.93					4.82	4.88	6.73	6.60	8.40	9.83	3.66
March	101.08					4.84	5.05	6.87	6.92	8.52	9.99	3.65
Feb.	100.64	1009-859	$23.12	9.23	12-10	4.77	4.85	6.92	6.94	8.55	10.10	3.67
Jan.	96.86					4.87	4.96	6.94	7.02	8.60	10.24	3.80
1975												
Dec.	88.70					5.20	5.50	7.17	7.31	8.79	10.35	4.14
Nov.	90.07	861-784	23.34	9.63	11-10	5.22	5.47	7.21	7.43	8.78	10.33	4.07
Oct.	88.57					5.82	6.08	7.29	7.39	8.86	10.37	4.22
Sept.	84.67					6.24	6.38	7.29	7.44	8.95	10.38	4.39
Aug.	85.71	882-792	18.37	9.05	12-10	6.14	6.46	7.06	7.17	8.95	10.35	4.36
July	92.49					6.10	6.16	6.89	7.07	8.84	10.33	4.02
June	92.40					5.55	5.19	6.86	6.95	8.77	10.40	4.02
May	90.10	879-743	17.04	8.97	11-7	5.22	5.31	6.99	6.97	8.90	10.46	4.08
April	84.72					5.49	5.69	7.03	6.95	8.95	10.34	4.34
March	83.78					5.54	5.54	6.73	6.74	8.67	10.29	4.42
Feb.	80.10	787-632	16.91	9.81	8-7	6.24	5.58	6.61	6.39	8.62	10.43	4.61
Jan.	72.56					7.13	6.49	6.68	6.82	8.83	10.62	5.07
1977E		$118.00										
1976E		103.00										
1975	86.16	882-632	75.66	$37.46	12-8	5.82	5.82	6.98	7.05	8.83	10.39	4.31
1974	82.85	892-578	99.04	37.72	9-6	10.50	7.87	6.98	6.17	8.57	9.50	4.47
1973	107.43	1052-788	86.17	35.33	12-9	8.74	7.04	6.30	5.19	7.44	8.24	3.06
1972	109.20	1036-889	67.11	32.27	15-13	4.44	4.07	5.63	5.26	7.21	8.16	2.84
1971	98.29	951-798	55.09	30.86	17-14	4.67	4.35	5.74	5.48	7.39	8.56	3.14
1970	83.22	842-631	51.02	31.53	17-12	7.17	6.46	6.59	6.35	8.04	9.11	3.83
1969	97.84	969-770	57.02	33.90	17-14	8.22	6.68	6.10	5.77	7.03	7.81	3.24
1968	98.70	985-825	57.89	31.34	17-14	5.66	5.34	5.25	4.46	6.18	6.94	3.07
1967	91.93	943-786	53.87	30.19	18-15	4.22	4.32	4.85	4.44	5.51	6.23	3.20
1966	85.26	995-744	57.68	31.89	17-13	5.11	4.88	4.66	3.77	5.13	5.67	3.40
1965	88.17	969-841	53.67	28.61	18-16	4.07	3.95	4.21	3.54	4.49	4.87	3.00
1964	81.37	892-766	46.43	31.24	19-16	3.50	3.55	4.15	3.12	4.40	4.83	3.01
1963	69.87	767-647	41.21	23.41	19-16	3.18	3.16	4.00	3.26	4.26	4.86	3.17
1962	62.38	726-536	36.43	23.30	20-15	2.68	2.78	3.95	3.05	4.33	5.02	3.37
1961	66.27	735-610	31.91	22.71	23-19	1.96	2.38	3.90	3.42	4.35	5.08	2.98
1960	55.85	685-566	32.21	21.36	21-18	3.22	2.93	4.01	3.38	4.41	5.19	3.47
1959	57.38	679-574	34.31	20.74	20-17	3.30	3.41	4.07	3.77	4.38	5.05	3.23
1958	46.24	584-437	27.95	20.00	21-16	1.57	1.84	3.43	3.38	3.79	4.73	3.97
1957	44.38	521-420	36.08	21.61	14-12	3.11	3.27	3.47	2.97	3.89	4.71	4.35
1956	46.62	521-462	33.34	22.99	16-14	2.73	2.66	3.08	3.21	3.36	3.88	4.09
1955	40.49	488-388	35.78	21.58	14-11	1.78	1.75	2.84	2.56	3.06	3.53	4.08
1954	29.69	404-280	28.18	17.47	14-10	–	0.95	2.55	2.38	2.90	3.51	4.95
1953	24.73	294-256	27.23	16.11	11-9	–	1.93	2.94	2.54	3.20	3.74	5.80
1952	24.50	292-256	24.78	15.43	12-10	–	1.77	2.68	2.38	2.96	3.52	5.80
1951	22.34	276-239	26.59	16.34	10-9	–	1.55	2.57	2.11	2.86	3.41	6.13
1950	18.40	235-197	30.70	16.13	8-6	–	1.22	2.32	1.66	2.62	3.24	6.57
1949	15.23	201-162	23.54	12.79	9-7	–	1.10	2.31	2.07	2.66	3.42	6.59
1948	15.53	193-165	23.07	11.50	8-7	–	1.04	2.44	2.19	2.82	3.47	5.54
1947	15.17	187-163	18.80	9.21	10-9	–	0.59	2.25	2.35	2.61	3.24	4.93
1946	17.08	213-163	13.63	7.50	16-12	–	0.38	2.19	1.89	2.53	3.05	3.85
1945	15.16	196-151	10.56	6.69	19-14	–	0.38	2.37	1.42	2.62	3.29	4.17
1944	12.47	153-134	10.07	6.57	15-13	–	0.38	2.48	1.62	2.72	3.61	4.86
1943	11.50	146-119	9.74	6.30	15-12	–	0.37	2.47	1.77	2.73	3.91	4.93
1942	8.67	120-93	9.22	6.40	13-10	–	0.33	2.46	2.17	2.83	4.28	7.24
1941	9.82	134-106	11.64	7.59	12-9	–	0.10	1.95	2.24	2.77	4.33	6.82
1940	11.02	153-112	10.92	7.06	14-10	–	0.01	2.21	2.14	2.84	4.75	5.59

Source: S&P   ---------Dow Jones and Co.----------   F.R.B.   F.R.B.   F.R.B.   B.B   --Moody's--   S&P
        Corp.   Corp.

* - Based upon High & Low Prices.
\# - Average for the period.
d - Deficit.
E - Bank of New York Estimate.

Source: The Bank of New York, August 1976.

Other observers have stressed the relationship between the trend of corporate profits and the trend of stock prices.[25] That a close relationship exists may be seen in Figure 3–11.

By looking at both fundamental indicators[26] and at the host of tech-

FIGURE 3–11
Corporate Profits and Stock Prices

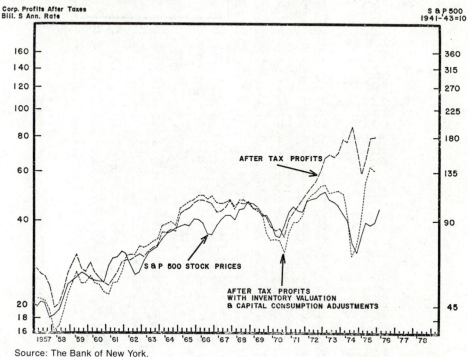

Source: The Bank of New York.

nical indicators,[27] it is possible to gain relative bearings in the market and thus make more intelligent judgments as to approximate values.

Industry Analysis

Generally, after examining the state of business and corporate profits and the condition of the market, security analysts make industry-to-industry comparisons to select those industries whose growth and profitability outlook is most favorable. The importance of

---

[25] Charles P. Jones and Robert H. Litzenberger, "Quarterly Earnings Reports and Intermediate Stock Price Trends," *Journal of Finance*, March 1970.

[26] See Chapter 12.

[27] See Chapter 13.

FIGURE 3–12

Stock Group Performances in 1975

Rank	1974 Dec. 31	1975 Dec. 31	% Change	1975 Range High	Low
1 Hotel/Motel	10.57	26.51	+150.8	29.06	11.44
2 Leisure Time	8.22	19.89	+142.0	20.79	8.88
3 Motion Pictures	49.54	110.19	+122.4	140.31	50.99
4 Pollution Control	7.03	15.42	+119.3	21.51	7.65
5 Restaurants	12.59	27.51	+116.8	27.51	12.41
6 Shoes	17.99	38.50	+114.0	39.84	18.87
7 Publishing	78.30	157.01	+100.5	157.01	90.87
8 Retail Stores (Drug)	9.23	17.78	+ 92.6	18.40	9.45
9 Textiles-Apparel Mfrs.	10.59	19.89	+ 87.8	21.29	11.84
10 Household Appliances	98.54	179.76	+ 82.4	192.19	110.66
11 Low Priced	53.23	95.87	+ 80.1	120.69	65.50
12 Confectionery	17.75	31.93	+ 79.9	31.93	19.10
13 Auto Parts-Orig. Equip.	35.04	62.99	+ 79.8	62.99	38.80
14 Toys	3.82	6.72	+ 75.9	7.93	3.90
15 Heating & Plumbing	22.91	40.28	+ 75.8	40.65	23.23
16 Department Stores	95.15	165.83	+ 74.3	172.87	105.61
17 Textile Products	31.67	55.15	+ 74.1	57.27	32.69
18 Lead & Zinc	14.67	25.51	+ 73.9	28.93	15.13
19 Textile-Synthetic Fib.	35.73	61.87	+ 73.2	63.33	39.00
20 Conglomerates	6.55	11.31	+ 72.7	13.24	7.15
21 Automobile	40.61	69.70	+ 71.6	70.03	46.00
22 Home Furnishings	15.48	26.40	+ 70.5	26.61	16.67
23 Specialty Machinery	17.24	28.98	+ 68.1	33.64	18.36
24 Publishing (Newspapers)	9.70	16.24	+ 67.4	17.86	11.07
25 Truckers	64.65	108.06	+ 67.1	113.14	62.81
26 Radio-TV Broadcasters	158.94	265.15	+ 66.8	294.20	159.48
27 Real Estate	6.49	10.72	+ 65.2	14.86	8.27
28 Air Transport	23.73	38.44	+ 62.0	38.44	24.10
29 Tires & Rubber Goods	102.63	165.33	+ 61.1	170.24	112.36
30 Soft Drinks	66.35	105.60	+ 59.2	115.19	68.10
31 Variety Stores	41.90	66.67	+ 59.1	68.32	41.89
32 Discount Stores	5.64	8.92	+ 58.2	9.51	5.91
33 Paper	146.01	230.25	+ 57.7	231.04	150.19
34 Metal Fabricating	51.61	80.95	+ 56.8	86.62	54.98
35 Air Conditioning	10.12	15.82	+ 56.3	19.19	11.11
36 Packaged Foods	66.80	104.21	+ 56.0	106.66	70.14
37 Forest Products	13.97	21.47	+ 53.7	23.54	15.23
38 Meat Packing	31.78	48.53	+ 52.7	48.53	32.82
39 Air Freight	17.23	26.28	+ 52.5	28.78	16.03
40 Retail Stores Comp.	67.85	101.89	+ 50.2	108.37	72.82
41 Vending & Food Serv.	15.61	23.39	+ 49.8	27.42	16.74
42 Chemicals	48.22	72.06	+ 49.4	74.63	48.76
43 Atomic Energy	40.30	59.76	+ 48.3	75.01	41.09
44 Aerospace	31.57	46.58	+ 47.5	55.24	33.83
45 Paper Containers	81.07	119.30	+ 47.2	120.54	88.19
46 Electrical Equipment	166.28	243.35	+ 46.3	265.22	177.29
47 Food Composite	49.36	72.10	+ 46.1	73.68	51.60
48 Dairy Products	61.83	87.88	+ 42.1	91.32	63.53
49 Major Electronics	41.30	58.65	+ 42.0	83.28	52.04
50 Electronics	389.68	550.54	+ 41.3	687.28	382.51
51 Steel	43.40	60.73	+ 39.9	66.38	44.81
52 Coal: Bituminous	306.06	424.65	+ 38.7	593.28	314.20
53 Electric Companies	22.03	30.56	+ 38.7	30.56	24.56
54 Building Composite	28.16	39.03	+ 38.6	45.45	30.48
55 Con. & Mat. Hand. Mach.	225.39	312.15	+ 38.5	333.78	231.88
56 Cosmetics	38.04	52.24	+ 37.3	65.07	39.44
57 Mail Ord. & Gen. Chains	117.29	161.04	+ 37.3	180.88	124.24
58 Telephone—excl. AT&T	24.97	34.22	+ 37.0	35.92	27.24
59 Auto Parts—After Mkt.	31.04	42.41	+ 36.6	45.26	32.07
60 Consumer Goods	63.33	86.04	+ 35.9	89.45	65.18
61 Auto—excl. Gen. Mot.	16.14	21.54	+ 33.5	21.76	17.01
62 Food Chains	41.11	54.77	+ 33.2	60.39	43.90
63 Oil Integ. International	92.94	123.48	+ 32.9	129.54	96.47
64 60 UTILITIES	33.54	44.45	+ 32.5	45.61	35.31
65 Capital Goods	74.50	98.28	+ 31.9	105.04	74.07
66 425 INDUSTRIALS	76.47	100.88	+ 31.9	107.40	77.71
67 Aluminum	55.78	73.55	+ 31.9	89.32	56.85
68 500 COMPOSITE	68.56	90.19	+ 31.5	95.61	70.04
69 Steam Generating Mach.	94.37	123.45	+ 30.8	197.82	98.03
70 Small Loans	51.66	67.33	+ 30.3	76.90	56.78
71 Roofing & Wallboard	41.91	54.43	+ 29.9	64.95	45.32
72 Brewers	39.39	50.56	+ 28.4	74.27	45.63
73 Office & Bus. Equip.	739.54	943.97	+ 27.6	1035.58	716.62
74 Sugar Beet Refiners	28.10	35.80	+ 27.4	41.37	28.07
75 Real Estate Inv. Trust.	1.28	1.63	+ 27.3	2.07	1.39
76 Canned Foods	70.59	88.97	+ 26.0	93.15	75.13
77 Banks, Outside N.Y.C.	64.29	80.98	+ 26.0	93.02	67.59
78 Cement	13.36	16.81	+ 25.8	22.70	15.12
79 Railroad Equipment	31.30	39.32	+ 25.6	50.20	34.74
80 Mobile Homes	50.12	62.85	+ 25.4	83.93	46.66
81 High Grade Common	60.77	75.71	+ 24.6	81.44	61.35
82 Invest. Cos (closed end)	33.82	41.98	+ 24.1	47.62	36.72
83 Multi-Line Insurance	7.53	9.32	+ 23.8	10.14	7.15
84 Auto Trucks & Parts	24.30	29.97	+ 23.3	34.46	26.53
85 Agricultural Mach.	45.35	55.92	+ 23.3	56.59	44.09
86 S & L Assn. Hold. Cos.	11.87	14.62	+ 23.2	18.09	11.26
87 Metals Misc.	45.37	55.66	+ 22.7	63.33	45.61
88 Steel—excl. U.S. Steel	43.61	53.34	+ 22.3	62.16	44.94
89 Machinery Composite	155.52	187.49	+ 20.6	214.26	149.50
90 Hospital Supplies	31.28	37.59	+ 20.2	44.77	32.68
91 Oil Composite	109.12	131.16	+ 20.2	144.78	109.64
92 Machine Tools	17.69	21.13	+ 19.4	27.12	19.58
93 Industrial Mach.	93.31	111.26	+ 19.2	125.27	92.03
94 Metal & Glass Cont.	27.92	33.03	+ 18.3	33.93	28.87
95 Telephone	19.68	22.94	+ 16.7	23.20	20.40
96 Soaps	149.22	173.46	+ 16.2	188.28	146.28
97 Tobac.-Cigarette Mfrs.	56.70	65.56	+ 15.6	66.35	54.80
98 Nat. Gas Distributors	52.46	60.54	+ 15.4	66.07	55.89
99 Property-Liability Ins.	81.98	94.34	+ 15.1	99.59	75.50
100 Nat. Gas Pipelines	87.84	99.34	+ 13.1	112.41	89.74
101 Office & Bus. Equip.—excl. I.B.M.	186.24	207.77	+ 11.6	302.55	178.85
102 Distillers	124.47	138.60	+ 11.4	159.53	130.50
103 Mach.—Oil Well Equip. & Serv.	616.84	677.37	+ 9.8	811.30	535.08
104 15 RAILROADS	35.59	38.12	+ 7.1	40.18	34.02
105 Oil-Integ. Domestic	133.51	140.66	+ 5.4	166.68	119.21
106 Copper	30.13	31.53	+ 4.6	37.08	29.02
107 New York City Banks	44.69	46.66	+ 4.4	60.91	41.04
108 Life Insurance	144.05	148.98	+ 3.4	182.26	138.70
109 Drugs	177.05	181.97	+ 2.8	216.12	159.67
110 Oil-Crude Producers	185.26	179.68	− 3.0	244.98	171.12
111 Finance Companies	66.02	62.10	− 5.9	76.08	55.79
112 Gold Mining	93.71	81.02	− 13.5	123.17	75.35
113 Offshore Drilling	35.47	30.16	− 15.0	50.19	28.88
114 Fertilizers	16.46	13.43	− 18.4	18.57	12.23

ANNUAL RANGES AND CLOSES

	425 Industrials High	Low	Close	Rails High	Low	Close
1975	107.40	77.71	100.88	40.18	34.02	38.12
1974	111.65	69.53	76.47	47.36	29.38	35.59
1973	134.54	103.37	109.14	49.80	32.50	45.80
1972	132.95	112.19	131.87	48.31	40.50	44.26
1971	115.84	99.36	112.72	48.32	35.03	44.61

	Utilities High	Low	Close	500 Stock Composite High	Low	Close
1975	45.61	35.31	44.45	95.61	70.04	90.19
1974	49.44	29.37	33.54	99.80	62.28	68.56
1973	61.57	43.91	46.91	120.24	92.16	97.55
1972	62.99	52.95	61.05	119.12	101.67	118.05
1971	64.81	54.48	59.83	104.77	90.16	102.09

Source: Standard & Poor's *The Outlook*, January 12, 1976, p. 987.

industry analysis may be seen from Figure 3–12 and from the Appendix to this chapter.

To secure data for industry studies and comparisons, the analysts may either research an industry in depth, using a variety of sources, or if they have less time available and wish compact and concise information, they may turn to one of the investment services. Standard & Poor's issues an excellent series of *Industry Surveys,* covering 45 industries. In each case a *Basic Analysis* is issued, usually annually, followed by supplementary sections entitled "Current Analysis and Outlook," issued at varying intervals, usually quarterly, during the year. The *Basic Analysis* contains a wealth of data, which would require an extensive expenditure of time by individual analysts if they

were to attempt to gather it themselves. In the report on the container industry, for example, the *Basic Analysis* includes:

The Outlook.	Ecology.
Paper.	Financial.
Packaging.	Composite industry data.
Metal containers.	Company analysis.
Glass containers.	Market action.
Plastic packaging.	Statistical data.
Closures.	

Where the industry is more homogeneous, as in the case of automobiles, the content of the *Basic Analysis* will reflect more internal operational data. Thus the automobile industry survey contains:

The Outlook.	Imports-exports.
Sales and production.	Financial.
Technology.	Composite industry data.
Auto parts.	Comparative company analysis.
Market action.	Statistical data.

In most of the industry surveys, data are provided for forecasting purposes. For example, as shown in Figure 3–13 in the electronics-electrical equipment *Basic Analysis,* a line of average relationship, or least squares line, has been fitted to show the relationship between electrical appliance sales production and disposable personal income, a component of gross national product. Using a GNP and DPI estimate for the ensuing five years, a forecast can be obtained for electrical appliance sales, and this in turn can be brought down to profitability to determine an earnings-per-share estimate for the forecast period.[28]

The "Current Analysis and Outlook" updates the figures in the basic survey, provides a short-run forecast, gives brief analyses of representative companies in the industry, and provides updated data on the comparative statistical position of leading common stocks in the industry.

Forbes publishes an "Annual Report on American Industry" at the beginning of each calendar year. It covers each of the major industries and within the industry makes comparisons of companies based on two yardsticks of performance: growth (five-year compounded rate for both sales and earnings) and profitability (five-year average for return on equity, and on total capital). See Figure 3–14 for an example cover-

---

[28] Such techniques will be considered in detail in the Appendix to Chapter 5.

FIGURE 3–13
Electrical Appliance Sales versus Disposable Income

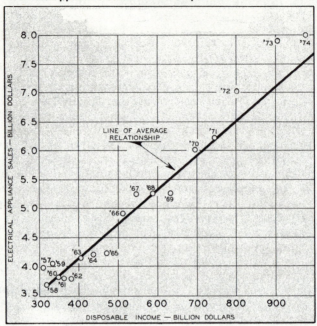

Year	Electric Appliance Sales	Total Retail Sales	Disposable Income
1974	8.01	537.8	979.7
1973	7.90	503.3	903.7
1972	7.03	448.4	802.5
1971	6.22	408.9	746.4
1970	6.07	375.5	691.7
1969	5.69	357.9	634.4
1968	5.41	341.9	591.0
1967	5.25	313.8	546.3
1966	4.91	304.0	511.9
1965	4.22	284.1	473.2

Source: Department of Commerce and Standard & Poor's *Basic Analysis*.

ing the electronics industry. Each industry reviewed is analyzed for both past and prospective performance.

For the analyst who wishes to do an industry study in depth, a variety of sources are available. Various trade journals covering different industries include *Chemical Week; Drug and Cosmetic Industry; Modern Plastics; Computer Age; Pulp, Paper and Board Quarterly,*

FIGURE 3–14

Electronics and Electrical Equipment—Yardsticks of Management Performance

| | PROFITABILITY | | | | | | | | GROWTH | | | |
| | Return on Equity | | | | Return on Total Capital | | | | Sales | | Earnings/Share | |
Company	5-Year Average	5-Year Rank	Latest 12 Months	Debt/Equity Ratio	Latest 12 Months	5-Year Rank	5-Year Average	Net Profit Margin	5-Year Average	5-Year Rank	5-Year Average	5-Year Rank
ELECTRICAL EQUIPMENT												
Schlumberger	20.8%	1	28.6%	0.2	24.8%	1	17.4%	13.7%	18.8%	2	22.3%	1
Avnet	19.0	2	18.2	0.4	12.6	6	12.6	5.1	14.6	3	9.6	7
Hewlett-Packard	17.4	3	18.2	0.0	17.7	2	17.2	8.6	19.6	1	19.3	2
Texas Instruments	15.8	4	11.6	0.1	10.6	3	13.6	4.5	11.4	8	15.5	3
Raytheon	14.6	5	17.0	0.2	14.7	5	12.7	3.2	8.3	15	9.9	6
Perkin-Elmer	12.9	6	12.5	0.0	12.3	4	12.8	6.3	9.3	14	12.4	4
General Tel & Elec	12.3	7	12.5	1.5	5.7	17	6.0	6.2	10.9	9	3.6	11
Motorola	12.2	8	5.7	0.3	5.3	8	10.8	2.6	10.4	11	11.7	5
Fairchild Camera	11.5	9	8.2	0.3	7.0	9	9.0	4.5	5.7	19	D-P	
Tektronix	11.3	10	14.2	0.2	13.4	7	11.2	7.9	10.5	10	3.8	10
Corning Glass Works	10.3	11	3.6	0.3	3.7	10	9.0	2.0	11.4	7	-1.8	15
Teledyne	10.0	12	13.5	0.7	7.5	13	7.1	3.1	12.4	6	9.0	8
American Tel & Tel	10.0	13	10.1	0.9	5.9	14	6.4	11.3	10.2	12	4.3	9
North Amer Philips	9.3	14	6.5	0.4	4.1	11	7.6	1.5	13.9	4	0.7	13
Honeywell	9.2	15	6.0	0.4	4.8	16	6.3	2.1	12.4	5	3.0	12
Lear Siegler	8.6	16	12.7	0.6	8.3	12	7.3	3.1	5.5	20	-9.4	17
RCA	8.3	17	8.0	1.0	5.6	18	5.5	2.0	6.6	18	-13.9	20
Harris Corp	7.6	18	1.7	0.3	2.2	15	6.3	0.7	7.8	16	-5.9	16
General Instrument	5.9	19	3.4	1.0	3.9	19	5.0	1.8	9.4	13	-1.2	14
Varian Associates	3.1	20	6.0	0.2	5.5	21	3.1	2.5	7.6	17	-9.5	18
Bunker-Ramo	3.0	21	def	0.5	1.0	20	4.4	def	3.3	21	-12.2	19
Ampex	def	22	1.0	2.3	3.3	22	def	0.2	1.9	22	P-D	21
Medians	10.2		9.2	0.4	5.8		7.5	3.1	10.3		3.6	
ELECTRONIC EQUIPMENT												
AMP	21.5%	1	13.1%	0.2	12.1%	2	19.6%	7.3%	15.8%	4	13.8%	2
W W Grainger	21.0	2	16.5	0.3	13.6	3	17.5	5.2	17.9	3	16.7	1
Square D	20.6	3	17.0	0.3	14.0	1	19.6	7.3	12.0	7	4.4	11
Fischbach & Moore	19.4	4	16.7	0.6	11.5	5	14.6	1.8	19.8	2	12.5	3
Emerson Electric	19.1	5	18.0	0.1	17.3	4	17.1	7.7	13.2	6	9.5	7
Reliance Electric	18.2	6	26.1	0.3	16.0	7	12.1	5.4	14.9	5	5.8	9
General Electric	17.6	7	14.9	0.3	11.7	6	14.4	4.1	7.5	11	10.3	5
UV Industries	15.5	8	15.1	0.8	8.1	12	7.7	5.6	22.6	1	11.2	4
Eltra	12.7	9	13.4	0.2	10.8	8	11.2	4.7	9.4	10	7.5	8
Cutler-Hammer	11.8	10	11.3	0.5	9.3	9	9.3	3.7	7.1	13	9.9	6
I-T-E Imperial	11.3	11	9.3	0.5	7.0	11	8.5	3.5	10.9	8	5.0	10
McGraw-Edison	8.9	12	8.4	0.2	7.6	10	8.6	3.4	7.3	12	-3.7	12
Westinghouse Elec	6.9	13	1.8	0.4	2.3	13	5.9	0.7	9.8	9	-3.9	13
Medians	17.6		14.9	0.3	11.5		12.1	4.7	12.0		9.5	
Industry Medians	11.8		12.5	0.3	8.1		9.0	3.7	10.5		5.4	

P-D = Profit to deficit.
D-P = Deficit to profit; not ranked.
def = Deficit.
Source: *Forbes*, January 1, 1976, p. 147.

Coal Mining; Mining Journal; Electrical World; Electrical Week; Drug and Cosmetic Industry; Electronics; Food Industries; The Timberman; Iron Age; Paper Trade Journal; Oil and Gas Journal; Petroleum Times; Ward's Auto World; Airline Management & Marketing; Airline Newsletter; Brewers Digest; Textile World; Automotive News; Ocean Oil Weekly Report; Metals; and so on. The *Business Periodicals Index* and the *Science and Technology Index* list articles in all trade journals. In addition, each industry has one or more trade associations with specialized libraries and books, bulletins and monographs on industry developments.[29]

The analyst specializing in a particular industry will wish to review all relevant industry publications on a regular, recurring basis. The New York Society of Security Analysts has published *A Guide to Industry Publications for Securities Analysts,* covering 41 industries.

---

[29] For an extensive listing, see James Woy, *Investment Methods: A Bibliographic Guide* (Ann Arbor, Mich.: R. R. Bowker Co, 1973); "A Guide to Industry Publications," *Financial Analyst's Handbook,* vol. II (Homewood, Ill.: Dow Jones-Irwin, Inc., 1975), chap. 34; also *Encyclopedia of Associations 1975,* Gale Research Company, Book Tower, Detroit, Michigan 48226.

Under "electronics industry," it listed, for the interest of the security analyst specializing in this area, title, source, address, and annual charge for selected publications.

Among the publications listed were *Aviation Week & Space Technology; IEEE Spectrum; Electronics Buyers' Guide; Electronic Design; Electronic Distributing & Marketing; Electronic Industries; Electronic Industries Yearbook; Electronic News; Electronic News Financial Fact Book & Directory; Electronic Procurement; Electronic Trends—USA; Electronic Trends—International; Aerospace International; Air Force & Space Digest; American Aviation; Aviation Daily; Computers & Automation; Datamation; EDP Industry and Market Report;* and *Information and Records Management.*

There are a number of services available to professional analysts and money managers, too involved for the nonprofessional, or too costly, which provide useful analysis along industry lines. Brown Brothers Harriman & Co., issues *Institutional Investment Guides,* while Crandall, Pierce & Co. (of Chicago) publishes *Crandall's Business Index* which title is not fully descriptive of the extent of the industry and company data provided.

The U.S. Department of Commerce publishes a number of industry reports such as *Chemicals; Containers and Packaging; Copper; Construction Review; Printing and Publishing; Pulp, Paper and Board,* some monthly, some quarterly. The Department of Commerce industry reports include a full series entitled *Current Industrial Reports,* as well as the *Industry Trend Series.* Also the Commerce Department issues an annual volume, *U.S. Industrial Outlook,* with forecasts for 100 specific industries.

Many of the trade associations issue annual reports or compilations. For example, in one field, the American Iron and Steel Institute issues an *Annual Statistical Report.* The American Metal Market, Inc., issues an annual *Metal Statistics.* The American Bureau of Metal Statistics issues a *Yearbook.* The U.S. Bureau of Mines releases the *Minerals Yearbook,* and McGraw-Hill publishes *The Engineering Mining Directory,* an annual.

Studies of various industries are available (to the professional analyst) from Predicasts, Inc. (Cleveland, Ohio), Frost & Sullivan (New York, N.Y.), Arthur D. Little, Inc. (Cambridge, Mass.), and Stanford Research Institute (Menlo Park, California).

Data Resources, Inc. (Lexington, Mass.) provides the *DRI Economic Information System* designed to facilitate industry analysis. It provides macroeconomic estimates and forecasts for some 79 industries. Its databank includes nearly 7,000 economic and industry time series.[30]

---

[30] See Chapter 18 which covers, among other matters, computer data sources utilized by professional money managers and securities analysts.

The deeper analysts dig into a given industry, the more likely they are to find a superabundance of information, rather than a paucity. Selecting, organizing, and analyzing the information may become a major task. The economy and usefulness of the financial services will become apparent in the course of the process.

Company Analysis

After industry analysis comes company selection within the chosen industry or industries. The most obvious source of information about a company is its own annual reports, including balance sheets and income accounts.[31] Frequently these are not as informative as they might be, and the analyst may wish to look at various reports filed with regulatory agencies.

In addition, the various investment services publish individual company reports. Standard & Poor's covers both listed and unlisted companies. An example of both sides of an S&P individual company report is shown in Figure 3–15. These reports provide, in capsule form, much of the relevant information the analyst seeks. They provide data on sales, operating revenues, common share earnings, recent developments, fundamental position, dividend data, prospects, finances, capitalization, and pertinent balance sheet and income account statistics for the prior ten years. In addition, the investment service recommendation is given. The individual company reports are dated and are revised every three or four months or more often as developments require.

Extensive sources of company data and information are to be found in the registration statements, prospectuses, proxy statements, and other reports resulting from SEC, ICC, FPC, FCC, CAB, NYSE "full disclosure" philosophy. SEC filings, for example, contain much essential information that may be generally omitted from voluntary reports. To be specific, the following are subjects about which there is important information commonly found in SEC filings but not in voluntary reports or the principal manuals—detail which may not interest a casual unsophisticated investor but which may be highly significant to a professional security analyst—expenses (rentals, maintenance, repairs, royalties, interest), receivables, inventories (classification, method of valuation), source and application of funds, depreciation,

---

[31] For those who are not fully acquainted with balance sheet, income account, and financial ratio analysis, the following are recommended: "How to Read a Financial Report," Merrill Lynch, Pierce, Fenner & Smith, New York, current; "Understanding Financial Statements," New York Stock Exchange, latest edition; J. A. Mauriello, *Accounting for the Financial Analyst*, rev. ed., C.F.A. Research Foundation (Homewood, Ill.: Richard D. Irwin, Inc., 1971), chap. 4; Erich A. Helfert, "Analysis of Financial Statements," and "Evaluation of Financial Statements," *Financial Analyst's Handbook*, vol. I (Homewood, Ill.: Dow Jones-Irwin, Inc., 1975), chaps. 21 and 22, respectively.

FIGURE 3–15
Individual Company Report

T[1] **American Tel. & Tel.** 182

Stock—	Price Jun. 7'76	[6]P-E Ratio	Dividend	Yield
COMMON	54⅛	10	[2]$3.80	[2]7.0%
$4 CONV. PREFERRED	57⅞		4.00	6.9

SUMMARY: AT&T is dominant in communications, not only through its telephone subsidiaries but also through Western Electric and Bell Telephone Laboratories. The Justice Department filed an antitrust suit in 1974 charging AT&T with monopolizing the market for telecommunications services and equipment, and seeking the break up of the company. The ultimate resolution of the suit should not impair shareholders' interests. The quality of the company's earnings is high owing to the use of conservative accounting; nevertheless, continuing rate relief will be needed to maintain long-term share earnings progress.

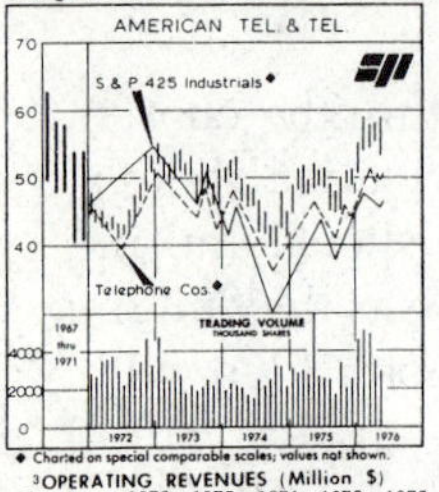

◆ Charted on special comparable scales; values not shown.

[3]OPERATING REVENUES (Million $)

Quarter:	1976	1975	1974	1973	1972
Feb.	7,678	6,694	6,234	5,511	4,884
May		7,117	6,514	5,815	5,139
Aug.		7,300	6,588	5,915	5,262
Nov.		7,504	6,677	6,044	5,417

Revenues for 1975 rose 11% from those of 1974, reflecting rate increases. Operating income was up 9.3%. After 42% lower other income (Western Electric income dropped 66% because of the recession) and 12% heavier interest charges, net income was down nominally (less than 1%). Earnings equaled $5.13 a share on 1.8% more shares, compared with $5.:8 (restated). Earnings for 1975 included $0.15 per share of rate increases subject to refund in California and $0.12 subject to refund in other states.

For the three months ended March 31, 1976, revenues advanced 15%, year to year. After a 70% drop in Western Electric income but only 4.8% larger interest, net income rose 21%, to $1.39 a share from $1.17.

[3,4]COMMON SHARE EARNINGS ($)

Quarter:	1976	1975	1974	1973	1972
Feb.	1.33	[5]1.13	[5]1.26	1.16	0.97
May		1.34	[5]1.39	1.28	1.07
Aug.		1.36	[5]1.31	1.28	1.10
Nov.		1.30	[5]1.32	1.27	1.15

PROSPECTS

Share earnings for 1976 should show a good increase from 1975's slightly reduced $5.13, reflecting rate relief and the favorable impact of the economic recovery on toll call volume. The dividend was raised to $0.95 quarterly, from $0.85, with the payment on April 1, 1976.

Long-term prospects point to continued growth in operations. Long distance calls are expected to rise to about 18 billion annually by 1980 from 10.2 billion in 1974, and the number of telephones served should approach 150 million, against 114 million.

RECENT DEVELOPMENTS

AT&T received a $218 million interstate rate increase ($137 million after taxes and adjustments) effective February 29, 1976, subject to refund, following $365 million on March 9, 1975. The case was filed on January 3, 1975, and $1,025,000,000 (later updated) was requested.

On November 20, 1974, the Justice Department filed an antitrust suit charging AT&T with monopolizing the market for telecommunications services and equipment through the use of illegal methods against competitors, mainly in the area of business services. The suit sought divestiture of Western Electric and its division into two or more companies, and the divestiture of AT&T's Long Lines Department or the sale of some or all of the 23 local telephone companies served by Long Lines. The suit may not come to trial until 1977 or 1978, and court proceedings could continue for many more years unless a negotiated settlement is reached. AT&T has indicated that it will contest the suit with all its resources.

DIVIDEND DATA

A dividend reinvestment plan is available. Payments in the past 12 months:

Amt of Divd $	Date Decl	Ex divd Date	Stock of Record	Payment Date
0.85...	Aug. 20	Aug. 22	Aug. 28	Oct. 1'75
0.85...	Nov. 19	Nov. 24	Dec. 1	Jan. 2'76
0.95...	Feb. 18	Feb. 25	Mar. 2	Apr. 1'76
0.95...	May 19	May 24	May 28	Jul. 1'76

[1]Listed N.Y.S.E.; com. also listed Boston, Midwest, Pacific & Philadelphia S.Es. & traded Cincinnati S.E.; pfd. also listed Philadelphia S.E. [2]Indicated rate. [3]Consol. [4]Based on avge. shs. [5]Restated to reflect revised depr. rates. [6]Based on latest 12 mos. earns.

182 **AMERICAN TELEPHONE & TELEGRAPH COMPANY**

[1]INCOME STATISTICS (Million $) AND PER SHARE ($) DATA

Year Ended Dec. 31	Revenues Local	Revenues Toll	[3]Gross	% of Gr. Revs. Depr. & Maint.	% of Gr. Revs. Oper. Taxes	[2]Oper. Ratio	[7]Fxd. Chgs. & Pfd. Divs. Tms. Earns.	[8]Net Inc.	Common Share ($) Data [4,9]Earns.	Divs. Paid	Price Range	Earns. Ratios HI LO
1976--	------	------	------	---	---	---	---	-----	----	2.75	58⅞-50⅞	-----
1975--	14,027.8	13,925.2	28,957.2	34.6	17.5	82.3	2.18	3,147.7	5.13	3.40	52 -44¾	10- 9
1974--	12,812.8	12,460.9	26,174.4	34.6	18.2	82.1	2.31	3,169.9	[9]5.27	3.16	53 -39⅝	10- 8
1973--	11,418.5	11,278.5	23,527.3	34.7	18.5	82.2	2.47	2,946.7	4.98	2.80	55 -45⅜	11- 9
1972--	10,362.9	9,771.4	20,904.1	35.1	18.2	82.9	2.50	2,532.1	4.34	2.65	53½-41⅛	12- 9
1971--	9,135.5	8,632.8	18,442.1	35.5	18.0	83.4	2.66	2,202.0	3.92	2.60	53⅞-40¼	14-10
1970--	8,456.0	7,874.1	16,954.9	34.8	19.3	83.4	3.25	2,192.2	3.99	2.60	53⅞-40⅜	14-10
1969--	7,774.4	7,297.8	15,683.8	33.5	22.3	83.6	4.70	2,198.7	4.00	2.40	58⅛-48⅛	15-12
1968--	7,184.1	6,341.2	14,100.0	32.7	23.4	83.3	5.34	2,051.8	3.75	2.40	58⅜-48	16-13
1967--	6,737.7	5,737.9	13,009.2	32.5	22.1	82.2	5.95	2,049.4	3.79	2.20	62¾-49¾	17-13
1966--	6,354.7	5,274.4	12,138.3	32.3	22.4	82.2	6.76	1,978.9	3.69	2.20	63½-49¾	17-13

[1]PERTINENT BALANCE SHEET STATISTICS (Million $)

Dec. 31	Gross Prop.	Capital Expend.	%Depr. of Gross Prop.	[6]%Earn. on Net Prop.	[5]Long Term Debt	% Long Term Debt of— Net Prop.	Gross Rev.	Invest. Cap.	Total Invest. Cap.	[6,7]%Earn. on Inv. Cap.	Net Inc. per Tel.	($) Book Val. Com. Sh.
1975--	87,621	9,329	19.6	7.3	31,793	45.1	109.8	43.5	73,172	7.5	26.57	64.46
1974--	81,146	10,074	20.0	7.2	32,308	49.8	123.4	46.4	69,575	7.6	27.69	59.74
1973--	74,005	9,322	20.9	7.1	28,371	48.4	120.6	45.2	62,748	7.6	26.71	55.08
1972--	67,082	8,306	21.6	6.8	26,020	49.5	124.5	45.7	56,969	7.2	24.05	50.95
1971--	60,568	7,564	22.1	6.5	22,828	48.4	123.8	44.7	51,112	7.0	21.96	47.36
1970--	54,813	7,159	22.4	6.6	20,454	48.1	120.6	44.2	46,286	7.0	22.70	45.53
1969--	49,244	5,731	22.8	6.8	15,868	41.7	101.2	38.9	40,792	7.1	23.72	43.96
1968--	44,975	4,742	22.7	6.8	13,430	38.8	95.2	36.0	37,366	7.0	23.31	42.24
1967--	41,476	4,310	22.1	7.2	11,901	36.8	91.5	34.1	34,905	7.3	24.46	40.63
1966--	38,354	4,193	21.7	7.2	10,352	34.5	85.3	32.2	32,178	7.4	24.77	38.91

[1]Data for 1973 & thereafter as originally reported; data for each yr. prior to 1973 as taken from subsequent yr.'s Annual Report. [2]After depr. & taxes. [3]Aft. deduct. uncollectible revs. [4]Based on avge. shs. [5]Incl. interim debt to be refinanced prior to 1975. [6]Based on bk. value, may differ from return on rate base. [7]Fixed chgs. only prior to 1971; aft. 1969 reflects change in FPC method of accounting for allowance for funds used during construction. [8]Bef. spec. cr. of $0.08 a sh. in 1973. [9]As restated to reflect 1975 elimination of provisions for certain contingencies sh. earns. were $5.28.

Fundamental Position

A holding company, American Telephone & Telegraph, through its telephone subsidiaries comprising the Bell System, controlled 118,464,000 phones at year-end 1975, about 80% of the U.S. total. Noncontrolling interests are held in other telephone operating companies. The parent directly operates long-distance lines connecting regional units and independent systems.

Of 1975 revenues, local and toll each accounted for 48%. Telephones in service rose 3.5% in 1975, versus 3.7% in 1974 and 4.8% in 1973; toll calls were up 5.2% in 1975, 7.5% in 1974 and 10.8% in 1973.

Equipment is purchased largely from 100%-owned Western Electric Co., an important contributor to earnings. Research is done for AT&T and Western Electric on a non-profit basis by Bell Telephone Laboratories.

Auxiliary services of AT&T include private line telephone services, and transmission of data and radio and TV programs. Overseas service to over 235 countries is provided through cable, radio, and satellite circuits.

Rapid depreciation is used for tax purposes with normalization. Savings from investment tax credits are amortized.

During 1975 AT&T received state rate increases totaling $1,420 million annually ($556 million accrued in 1975); some $1.2 billion of requests was pending at March 31, 1976.

The FCC in its January, 1976 decision authorized a 9.5% investment return (to a maximum of 10% through efficiencies), versus 8.74% previously authorized and 10.5%-11% requested.

Dividends paid in each year since 1885, averaged 62% of earnings in 1971-75.

Employees: 937,000. Stockholders: 2,921,-735.

Finances

Capital outlays for 1976 are estimated at $10.2-$10.4 billion, versus the $9.3 billion (cut from $10.5 billion) of 1975. Up to $2.5 billion of financing is planned for 1976, against $2.8 billion in 1975. About 12 million common shares are to be offered on or about June 16, 1976. The previous common offering was 12 million shares on October 1, 1975.

At 1975 year-end common equity per share was $52.86 and the 1975 return thereon 9.5%. For 1975 the Federal income tax rate equaled 40.3%, and construction credits 8% of common earnings.

CAPITALIZATION

LONG TERM DEBT: $32,193,326,000.
MINORITY INTEREST: $870,602,000.
$4 CUM. CONV. PREFERRED STOCK: 27,-080,000 shs. ($1 par; $50 stated value); red. at $50.50 thru July 31, 1976, then $50; conv. into approx. 1.05 com.
$77.50 PREFERRED STOCK: 625,000 shs. ($1 par; $1,000 stated value). Privately held.
$3.74 CUM. PREFERRED STOCK: 10,000,000 shs. ($1 par; $50 stated value).
$3.64 CUM. PREFERRED STOCK: 10,000,-000 shs. ($1 par; $50 stated value).
COMMON STOCK: 584,249,000 shs. ($16,-2/3 par).

Incorporated in N.Y. in 1885. **Office**—195 Broadway, NYC 10007. **Tel**—(212) 393-9800. **Pres**—W. L. Lindholm. **Secy**—F. A. Hutson, Jr. **VP-Treas**—W. L. Mobraaten. **Dirs**—J. D. deButts (Chrmn), W. M. Batten, C. L. Brown, E. W. Carter, C. B. Cleary, A. K. Davis, W. M. Ellinghaus, E. B. Hanify, W. A. Hewitt, J. H. Holland, R. K. Johnson, J. R. Killian, Jr., W. L. Lindholm, D. S. MacNaughton, W. J. McGill, J. I. Miller, W. B. Murphy, E. B. Speer, R. Warner, Jr. **Transfer Offices**—Company's offices: 180 Fulton St., NYC; New England Tel. & Tel. Co., Boston; Illinois Bell Telephone Co., Chicago; Pacific Tel. & Tel., San Francisco. **Registrars**—Bankers Trust Co., NYC; First National Bank, Boston; First National Bank, Chicago; Wells Fargo Bank, San Francisco.

Source: Standard & Poor's *Standard N.Y.S.E. Stock Reports*, June 11, 1976.

depletion, amortization, tax accounting (accounting for the investment credit, information on loss carry-overs, deferred taxes), employment costs (pensions), backlogs, information on significant unconsolidated subsidiaries, additions and retirements of fixed assets, treatment of nonrecurring "special items," commitments (for capital expenditures, guarantees, long-term leases), investments in subsidiaries, reserves, management (direct and indirect compensation, options, bonuses, pensions), and wasting assets. These subjects relate principally to financial statement disclosures. Of course, there is a great deal of other material in SEC filings, not found in any other source. For example, the filings may be the exclusive source of information on control, background of management, and stockholdings of, and transactions with, insiders.[32]

[32] See *C.F.A. Readings in Financial Analysis*, The Institute of Chartered Financial Analysts, Part II, Chaps. 23 and 24 (Homewood, Ill.: Richard D. Irwin, Inc., 1970). Also "Form 10–K," *Financial Analyst's Handbook*, vol. I, chap. 26.

The registration statement is the basic disclosure document in connection with a public distribution of securities registered under the Securities Act. It is made up of two parts. The prospectus, the first section, is the only part which is generally distributed to the public. Part II of the registration statement contains information of a more technical nature dealing with such matters as marketing arrangements, the expenses of the distribution, relationships between the registrant and certain experts, sales of securities to special parties, recent sales of unregistered securities, a list of subsidiaries, and treatment of proceeds from stock being registered. In addition, Part II contains signatures, financial schedules, and historical financial information not required in the prospectus. Filed with the registration statement are exhibits such as contracts relating to the underwriting; the charter and bylaws of the registrant, specimen copies of securities; instruments relating to long-term debt, option agreements, pension plans, retirement plans, and deferred compensation plans; an opinion of counsel; material foreign patents; and certain material contracts not made in the ordinary course of business.

The Exchange Act has four types of disclosure requirements relating to registration, periodic reporting, proxy solicitation, and insider trading. Listed and OTC-registered companies are required to file certain periodic reports. The three most important of these reports are Forms 8–K, 10–K, and 10–Q.

Form 8–K is a current report which is filed for each calendar month during which an event occurs which requires reporting. The report is due by the tenth day of the following month. The various events to be reported on Form 8–K include the following: (a) changes in control of registrant; (b) acquisition or disposition of assets; (c) interest of management and others in certain transactions; (d) legal proceedings; (e) changes in securities; (f) changes in security (i.e., collateral) for registered securities; (g) defaults upon senior securities; (h) increase in the amount of securities outstanding; (i) issuance of debt securities by subsidiaries; (j) decrease in the amount of securities outstanding; (k) options to purchase securities; (l) revaluation of assets or restatement of capital share account; (m) submission of matters to a vote of security holders; (n) newly enacted requirements affecting registrant's business; (o) other materially important events; and (p) financial statements and exhibits. When a business of significant size is acquired, the registrant is required to file financial statements of the acquired business.

Form 10–K is an annual report which is due 90 days after the end of each fiscal year. The SEC's Regulation S–X governs the form and content of most of the financial statements, including 10–K, required to be filed with the Commission. Financial statements prepared in compliance with Regulation S–X, and particularly the notes to the state-

ments, often give substantially more information than other financial statements distributed by companies. For instance, Regulation S–X requires the notes to contain certain details on long-term leases, funded debt, management stock options, classification of inventories, and basis for computing depreciation which often do not appear in other financial statements. Regulation S–X also requires supplemental schedules to complete the financial statements. The information in these schedules almost never appears in financial statements generally distributed to the public. The Form 10–K report contains certified financial statements, including a balance sheet, a profit and loss statement for the fiscal year covered by the report, an analysis of surplus and supporting schedules. Form 10–Q, replaced Form 9–K. It is a quarterly report calling for summarized financial information.

A new and tougher set of disclosure requirements were stipulated for all 10–K filings on or after December 31, 1970. The SEC ordered companies to break down both sales and earnings for each major line of business. Under the new rules, however, a company with sales greater than $50 million does not have to carry an individual breakdown unless a product line contributes 10 percent or more to total volume or pretax profits. For smaller companies, the disclosure point is 15 percent. While companies must break out such product line data on their annual 10–K reports to the SEC, they need not disclose it in the annual report to the shareholder, though more companies are now beginning to do so. Also according to this new ruling on 10–K content, companies are required to reveal the dollar amount spent on R&D in the preceeding year. Again it need not be revealed to the stockholders unless it is "material." Also where it is "material and applicable" additional information must be disclosed on the 10–K, such as dollar amount of order backlogs; availability of essential raw materials; competitive conditions in the industry; and financial statements of unconsolidated majority-owned subsidiaries.

In 1973, the SEC ruled that companies must disclose in the 10–K, any leasing and rental commitments and their dollar impact on both present and future earnings. They must also explain any differences between the effective tax rates that they report to shareholders and the statutory corporate income tax rate. They must also spell out in the footnotes to the 10–K statements any compensating balance arrangements they have with banks and other lenders.[33]

The SEC has warned publicly held companies that the quarterly 10–Q financial reports they file with the commission must be "complete, accurate, and timely." Although the 10–Q is a condensed, unau-

---

[33] "New Rules to Keep Investors in the Know," *Business Week*, January 5, 1974, p. 47.

dited interim financial report and isn't legally considered to be a "filed" document for purposes of the liability provisions of the Securities Exchange Act of 1934, the SEC said this doesn't "mean that such reports shouldn't be carefully reviewed by the management, and to the extent necessary by a company's independant public accountants and counsel." The Commission noted that the reports are subject to the general antifraud provisions of the 1934 Act.[34]

But not all that is now found in a 10–K finds its way into the company's annual report to its shareholders. Thus the careful analyst must work with the 10–K and not with the annual report.[35] Continuing difficulties of the analyst with accounting practices are reviewed in Chapter 4.

Because of microfiche, the 10–K enjoys widening circulation. Under a contract with the SEC, Disclosure, Inc. of Bethesda, Maryland, microfilms all the basic reporting documents a corporation must submit to the Commission. Depending on the company, this can run to 11 documents a year or more; counting the 10–K, the stockholder's annual, proxies, quarterly reports (the official version is the 10–Q), any registration statements or prospectuses, and the 8–K form. Large public libraries, larger financial houses, and leading business school libraries subscribe to and make available all or part of the Disclosure, Inc. microfiche service. It is a useful tool for the practicing securities analyst.[36]

---

[34] "SEC Warns Public Firms That 10Q Filings Must Be 'Complete, Accurate, and Timely'," *The Wall Street Journal*, December 13, 1973. See also "SEC Moves to Force Corporations to Put More Financial Data in Their Annual Reports," *The Wall Street Journal*, January 11, 1974.

[35] For a further discussion, see "Selective Reporting?" *Forbes*, March 15, 1971; also "Annual Reports Bare Long-Hidden Facts," *Business Week*, April 3, 1971; "New Accounting Rules to Broaden Scope of Quarterly Reports Are offered by SEC," *The Wall Street Journal*, December 20, 1974; "Disclosure Rules Widened by SEC," *The New York Times*, November 1, 1974; David F. Hawkins, "Accounting Dodos and Red Flags," *Financial Executive*, May 1974; also "It's Not Material," *Forbes*, April 15, 1971. See also a speech by William C. Foster of the New York Stock Exchange before the Advanced SEC Seminar; *Accounting Newsletter*, The New York Society of Security Analysts, Inc., no. 19, August 7, 1972; "Adoption of Revised Form 10–K," *SEC Release No. 9000*, October 21, 1970; Notice of Adoption of Amendments to Regulation S–X," *SEC Release No. 9648*, June 23, 1972.

For a penetrating account of deficiencies of corporate financial reporting and disclosure (or nondisclosure), see Abraham J. Briloff, *Unaccountable Accounting* (New York: Harper & Row, Publishers, 1972), and his *More Debits Than Credits* (New York: Harper & Row, 1976). See also David F. Hawkins, *Financial Reporting Practices of Corporations* (Homewood, Ill.: Dow Jones-Irwin, Inc., 1972), and *Objectives of Financial Statements*, American Institute of Certified Public Accountants, October 1973.

[36] For the most current *Disclosure* information, write to Disclosure, Inc., 4827 Rugby Avenue, Bethesda, Maryland 20014, or 1450 Broadway, New York, N.Y. 10018.

Forms, publications, and reports may be consulted at the Commission's main and regional offices.[37] All officially filed forms may be consulted and photocopied. In similar fashion, official filings of certain types of companies may be consulted at the offices of the Interstate Commerce Commission (railroads and trucking companies), Federal Communications Commission (telephone and broadcasting companies), Federal Power Commission (electric and gas utilities), Comptroller of the Currency, and Federal Deposit Insurance Corporation (commercial banks). A vast array of data on individual companies can be found in official filings with governmental agencies. Increasingly these data are being made available to the public in accordance with the SEC's "full disclosure" concept. They are, of course, of great value to the professional securities analyst.

The careful securities analyst may wish to know more about the company's competitive position, its financial condition and profitability, its operating efficiency and management, its outlook and prospects, than published data and statistics provide. It has been routine procedure for analysts to invite company officials to address meetings of analysts at which an opportunity is afforded to ask questions and receive company replies.

It has also become standard procedure for an analyst doing a report in depth to visit the company's plant or main office and talk with top management. Homework needs to be done carefully prior to such visits. All available published data about the company should have been reviewed, an initial analysis undertaken, and a list of questions for management prepared. The competent analyst will approach visits and interviews as thoroughly prepared as possible from external sources. Complete security analysis usually requires discussion with top management and involves much more than mere financial ratio analysis, a somewhat mechanical technique largely carried over from the old days when corporations regarded their financial and industrial position and prospects as closely guarded company secrets unavailable to the public.

---

[37] Regional offices (and branches of regional offices) are maintained in New York City, Boston, Atlanta (Miami), Chicago (Cleveland, Detroit, St. Paul, St. Louis), Fort Worth (Houston), Denver (Salt Lake City), San Francisco (Los Angeles), Seattle, and Arlington, Virginia.

SUGGESTED READINGS

"An Open Door Policy for Annual Reports." *Business Week*, May 12, 1975.

Baker, H. Kent, and Haslem, John A. "Information Needs of Individual Investors." *The Journal of Accountancy*, November 1973.

Chandra, Gyan. "Information Needs of Security Analysts." *The Journal of Accountancy*, December 1975.

Farrell, Maurice L. (ed.). *The Dow Jones Investor's Handbook.* Princeton, N.J.: Dow Jones Books, 1976 edition.

Financial Analyst's Handbook, vol. II. Homewood, Ill.: Dow Jones-Irwin, Inc., 1975, chaps. 31–34.

Herman, Edward S., and Safanda, Carl F. "Allocating Investment Information." *Financial Analysts Journal*, January/February 1973.

Institute of Chartered Financial Analysts. *1975 Supplementary Readings in Financial Analysis*, vol. 3. Homewood, Ill.: Richard D. Irwin, Inc.; see also vol. 2, 1974 and vol. 1, 1973.

Mauriello, Joseph A. *Accounting for the Financial Analyst*, C.F.A. Research Foundation. Rev. ed. Homewood, Ill.: Richard D. Irwin, Inc., 1971.

Merrill Lynch, Pierce, Fenner, and Smith. *How To Read a Financial Report.* Latest edition. A free copy can be obtained by writing to this firm at One Liberty Plaza, New York, N.Y. 10006.

Nevans, Ronald. "The Market Opinion Letters: How Good Are They?" *Financial World*, July 16, 1975.

Woy, James. *Investment Methods. A Bibliographic Guide.* Ann Arbor, Mich.: R. R. Bowker Co., 1973.

APPENDIX: INDUSTRY GROUP PERFORMANCE, 1970–1975

The importance of industry analysis may be seen in the following charts, one for each of the years 1970–75 inclusive. These are reproduced with the kind permission of George A. Chestnutt, Jr. They are to be found in *Stock Market Analysis: Facts and Principles*, latest edition, by George A. Chestnutt, Jr., copyright by the Chestnutt Corporation, 88 Field Point Road, Greenwich, Connecticut 06830.

FIGURE A3–1
Industry Group Performance Charts, 1970–1975

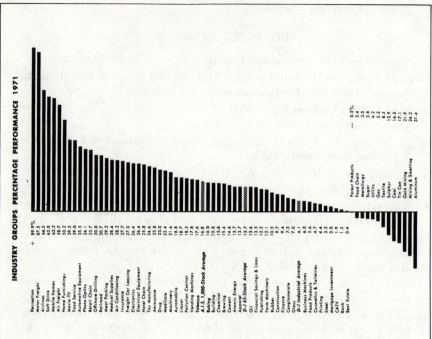

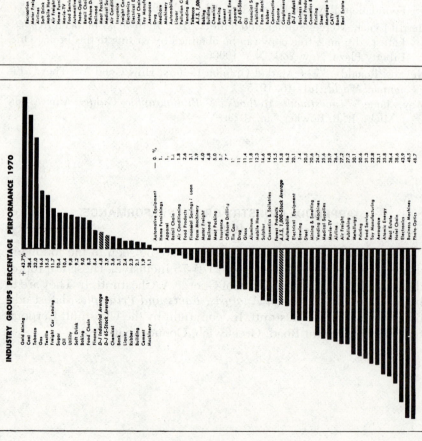

FIGURE A3-1 (continued)

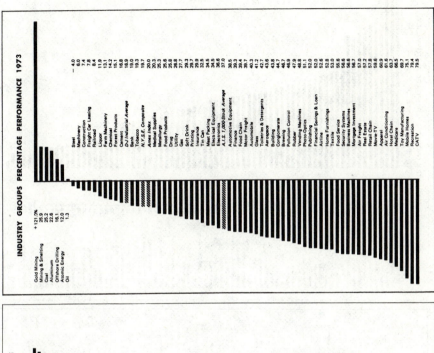

PROGRESS OF INDUSTRY GROUPS – PERCENTAGE PERFORMANCE
December 31, 1971 to December 29, 1972

Farm Machinery	+36.8%
Medical Supplies	35.4
Gold Mining	29.6
Offshore Drilling	28.1
Construction	25.5
Financial Savings & Loan	23.2
Bank	21.2
Drug	20.0
Oil	19.4
Electrical Equipment	18.7
Insurance	17.8
Liquor	17.7
Soft Drink	16.8
Toiletries & Detergents	16.0
Movie-T.V.	16.0
Gas	15.1
Aerospace	14.8
D-J Industrial Average	14.6
Machinery	14.6
NYSE Composite	14.3
Steel	13.0
Food Service	11.9
Electronics	10.5
Mining & Smelting	9.7
Chemical	8.9
Recreation	6.8
Tin Can	6.5
Finance	6.3
Automotive Equipment	4.9
Food Products	4.2
A.S.E. Price Level Index	3.0
Pollution Control	3.1
Metallurgy	1.2
Tobacco	1.1
Hotel Chain	0.9
A.S.E. 1,000-Stock Average	0.6
Aluminum	0.0
Freight Car Leasing	0.2%
Automobile	0.4
Utility	0.8
Vending Machines	1.4
Mortgage Investment	2.9
Forest Products	3.0
Rubber	4.0
Railroad	4.2
CATV	4.2
Printing	6.3
Atomic Energy	6.9
Conglomerates	7.6
Cement	8.6
Glass	8.8
Coal	9.7
Photo Optics	10.0
Home Furnishings	10.6
Brewing	10.8
Air Freight	12.2
Baking	12.2
Sugar	12.3
Motor Freight	12.6
Business Machines	12.6
Air Conditioning	12.8
Building	12.8
Meat Packing	13.6
Real Estate	16.7
Apparel	17.9
Publishing	20.1
Textile	20.4
Toy Manufacturing	20.4
Retail Chain	21.4
Food Chain	25.2
Medicare	26.8
Mobile Homes	29.5

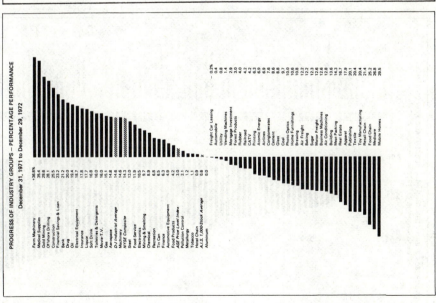

INDUSTRY GROUPS PERCENTAGE PERFORMANCE 1973

Gold Mining	+121.2%
Mining & Smelting	25.9
Coal	25.2
Aluminum	22.6
Offshore Drilling	18.1
Atomic Energy	12.0
Oil	1.3
Steel	– 4.0
Machinery	6.0
Construction	7.4
Freight Car Leasing	7.8
Railroad	8.4
Farm Machinery	11.9
Chemical	13.1
Forest Products	14.2
Cement	15.1
Bank	16.8
Tobacco	18.9
D-J Industrial Average	19.0
N.Y.S.E. Composite	19.3
Amex Index	19.7
Medical Supplies	20.0
Metallurgy	20.3
Food Products	25.3
Drug	25.8
Utility	25.8
Gas	26.8
Soft Drink	27.7
Printing	29.3
Insurance	29.7
Tin Can	29.9
Meat Packing	32.5
Electrical Equipment	34.5
Electronics	34.5
A.S.E. 1,000-Stock Average	36.6
Automotive Equipment	37.0
Finance	38.5
Food Chain	39.3
Motor Freight	39.4
Automobile	39.7
Glass	40.3
Toiletries & Detergents	41.2
Aerospace	42.7
Building	43.6
Conglomerates	43.8
Brewing	44.7
Pollution Control	46.7
Rubber	46.9
Vending Machines	47.9
Photo-Optics	48.8
Publishing	51.1
Financial Savings & Loan	52.0
Textile	52.0
Home Furnishings	52.8
Food Service	53.0
Security Systems	55.6
Business Machines	56.6
Mortgage Investment	56.6
Air Freight	56.7
Real Estate	57.0
Retail Chain	57.2
Food Chain	57.8
Apparel	59.6
Air Conditioning	60.9
Hotel Chain	61.6
Medicare	63.7
Toy Manufacturing	66.5
Mobile Homes	69.7
Recreation	75.1
CATV	79.4
	79.5

FIGURE A3–1 *(concluded)*

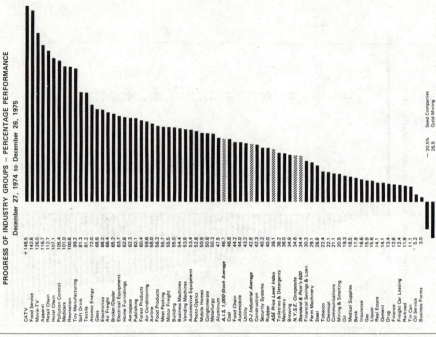

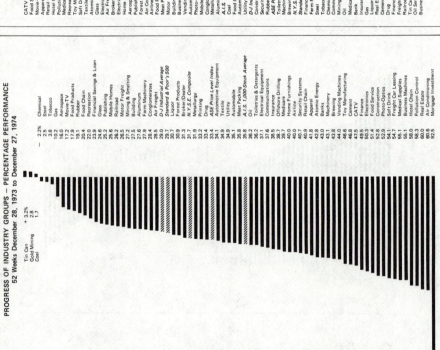

Source: George A. Chestnutt, Jr., Chestnutt Corp., Greenwich, Conn.

REVIEW QUESTIONS AND PROBLEMS

1. Contrast the sources of investment information open to the individual investor as compared to the institutional investment manager.

2. What types of investment information can (a) the individual investor, (b) the institutional investment manager, expect to obtain from (c) a commission brokerage house and from (d) the computerized financial services?

3. Explain how the Dow Jones Stock Price Averages are constructed.

4. Explain how the Standard & Poor's Stock Price Indexes are constructed.

5. Explain how the New York Stock Exchange stock price indexes are constructed.

6. Which do you think most accurately reflects the trend of stock prices? Why?

7. If someone recommends a small, obscure growth company to you and you wanted to obtain more information about it and its prospects how would you go about getting such information?

8. If your broker recommended a large listed company which he claimed was the most profitable in its industry, how would you go about checking out his recommendation? What sources would you use?

9. If you were trying to decide whether or not this was an appropriate time to switch out of stocks and into bonds what factors would you consider and what sources of information would you use?

10. Since the competent securities analyst must make a judgment as to the outlook for the economy as well as the outlook for the market as a whole, in addition to selecting industries and companies, what sort of a reading program would you recommend? What should be read (a) each day, (b) each week, (c) each month?

RESEARCH PROJECTS

1. You are a junior securities analyst and your firm has just assigned you to specialize in the "electronics" industry. Prepare a report for your firm's librarian indicating the publications you would like to have acquired (a) weekly, (b) monthly, (c) quarterly, (d) semiannually or annually. Develop a plan for becoming familiar with all phases of the industry.

2. You are in charge of computer services for a large financial firm. It utilizes the data bases of both Interactive Data Corporation and Investment Management Sciences, Inc. You are asked to prepare an orientation brochure for your firm's junior analysts indicating the nature and extent of the data available and the ways in which they may be used in securities analysis and portfolio management. Prepare a draft of such an orientation brochure.

3. You are asked to develop a survey of professional forecasts of earnings for the leading firms in the office equipment industry for the coming 12-month period, giving sources of data and bases for estimates. Prepare such a report in accordance with these instructions.

4. For your investment service's annual forecast issue you are asked to prepare an article estimating the 10 industries which are likely to show the best composite market price performance over the coming calendar year. You are additionally asked to give the reasons for your selections and the sources utilized in your estimates. Prepare a draft article in accordance with these instructions.

5. You are an account executive and a wealthy client asks you to give her a report on the five leading no-load growth funds and the five leading growth (load) funds, which showed the best performance over the past year. She also asks that you provide her with a composite list of the ten best performing stocks most popular with the ten best performing funds. Prepare such a report indicating sources utilized.

PART II

SECURITY EVALUATION

Chapter 4

Deficiencies of Financial Statements

> We can easily represent things as we wish them to be.
> ————————————————————————— *Aesop*

Of all the sources of investment information discussed in the previous chapter, a company's financial statements are among the most vital. They are indispensable ingredients of any effort to determine the value of a corporate stock or bond. They are the principal reference we turn to for information on the level and trend of a company's earning power and debt repayment ability. But they leave much to be desired.

Many years ago, security analysts had to guard against the possibility that corporate financial statements might be fraudulent. Today, however, regulations of the Securities and Exchange Commission, the New York and American Stock Exchanges, the American Institute of Certified Public Accountants (AICPA), and the Financial Accounting Standards Board (FASB) have all but eliminated this problem except in the case of small, closely owned corporations. Nevertheless, a security analyst cannot accept at face value the figures designated by a company as net income or net worth.

The net income and net worth figures shown in a company's annual report may be given a "clean opinion" by the independent auditors. This means they certify that:

a. No circumstances precluded the application of reasonable auditing procedures.

b. The accounts are a fair and adequate representation of the company's financial position and of the results of its operations, conforming to "generally accepted accounting principles" (GAAP).

c. No substantive uncertainties exist which cannot be reasonably provided for in the accounts.

179

Notwithstanding the clean opinion, "generally accepted accounting principles" are neither unambiguous, nor uniformly interpreted and applied, nor completely useful from an *investment* point of view.[1] Moreover, the figures reported on an interim basis, usually quarterly, are not audited by independent accountants, although they must conform to GAAP. The purpose of this chapter is to provide students of investments with some guides to help them through the financial statement maze.

Income Statement Format

For purposes of security analysis, it is convenient to adopt as an income statement format something similar to the following:

	Sales		xxx
Minus:	{ Cost of Goods Sold	xxx	
	{ Selling and Administrative Expenses	xxx	
	{ Depreciation and Depletion*	+xxx	
			−xxx
Equals:	Net Operating Income		xxx
Plus:	Nonoperating Income		+xxx
			xxx
Minus:	{ Nonoperating Expenses	xxx	
	{ Interest on Loans	+xxx	
			−xxx
Equals:	Net Income before Taxes		xxx
Minus:	Federal and State Income Taxes		−xxx
Equals:	Net Income		xxx
Minus:	Dividends on Preferred Stock		−xxx
Equals:	Net Income on Common Stock Equity		xxx
Minus:	Dividends on Common Stock		−xxx
Equals:	Net Income Transferred to Surplus or Retained Earnings		xxx

* In many income statements, depreciation is not shown separately in the body of the report, but is allocated to Cost of Goods Sold ("product costs") and Other Expenses ("period costs"). In such reports, depreciation will be given either in a footnote or in the Statement of Changes in Financial Position.

---

[1] The noted critic of misleading accounting, Abraham J. Briloff, supplements the term GAAP with CRAP—"Cleverly Rigged Accounting Ploys." See his article, "Prescription for Change," *Management Accounting,* July 1974, as well as his recent books cited in the "Suggested Readings" at the end of this chapter. An interesting concept has been proposed by Mlynarczyk and Treynor, which they refer to as the "GAAP Range." This range is the highest and lowest earnings number which could be produced by using the least and most conservative accounting treatments sanctioned by GAAP. The analyst could then compare companies in terms of where their reported earnings lie within the range. See "Materiality, Body Counts, and GAAP Range," *Financial Analysts Journal,* March/April, 1976.

Problems of interpretation are involved in almost every item of this sample income statement. Among the most common problems are the following, which we shall examine in detail:

1. Even so apparently simple an item as "sales" causes difficulty. For example, when a company sells merchandise on an installment payment plan, questions arise as to *when* the sale should be recorded as revenue in the income statement—at the time of sale or as payments are received? Similar questions arise when a company fills an order on a gradual basis because a long production process is involved, or when a company leases merchandise rather than sells it outright.

2. Cost of goods sold is affected by a company's method of evaluating ("costing") inventories. Different companies use different methods. Furthermore, a breakdown of the materials versus labor cost components of cost of goods sold is of vital interest to the investor, but information providing such breakdowns is seriously deficient. Of particular concern are intercompany differences in accounting for obligations under employee pension plans.

3. Depreciation and depletion charges are subject to a great deal of managerial discretion and are further affected by legislative changes.

4. Problems are caused by the need to distinguish between the basic profitability of a firm's primary activities—manufacturing, wholesaling, retailing, and the like—and profits or losses resulting from "nonoperating" transactions or "extraordinary" occurrences.

5. Many companies report to the Internal Revenue Service one way and to stockholders another way.

Sales

A noted authority on accounting theory has stated that revenue (and related expenses) should be recognized only when it is "captured," "measurable," and "earned."[2] Revenue is said to be "captured" when the company is reasonably certain that it will be paid for what it has sold, or when it is clear that the portion which might be lost is small and can be estimated as to amount. But this innocent-sounding phrase can create problems, as has been illustrated dramatically in the case of land development companies. These companies sell parcels of land to buyers who pay in periodic installments over a period of many years. After how many payments can it be assumed that the buyer has a sufficient stake to be likely to continue his payments? Accounting guidelines have been issued on minimally acceptable standards, but

---

[2] A. L. Thomas, "Revenue Recognition," in S. Davidson, ed., *Handbook of Modern Accounting* (New York: McGraw-Hill Book Co., 1970), chap. 10.

some companies choose a more conservative accounting policy than suggested by the guidelines while others follow only the minimally acceptable standards.

Revenue is said to be "measurable" if the medium of payment can be valued without serious difficulty. Clearly, cash payment presents no difficulties at all. Nor do accounts receivable if the terms of trade are the typical 60 or 90 days. But what if the terms are, as in the case of the land companies noted above, 10 or 12 years? The "value" of such long-lived receivables should be "discounted" at a rate which reflects appropriately the credit worthiness of the buyer.[3] But what should this discount rate be? Some companies are likely to be more liberal than others in choosing a rate.

Finally, revenue is said to be "earned" when no significant activities remain to be performed for the customer. But it is not uncommon for revenue to be "captured" and "measurable" but not fully "earned." For example, machinery companies usually undertake substantial potential future costs in connection with service contracts and warranties. This may create an important element of noncomparability among companies which use different methods of providing for such possibilities.

Another way of viewing the problems inherent in revenue recognition is to consider a company's schedule of activities: marketing, production, delivery, collection. There are various points in this cycle when reasonable men can differ as to whether revenue should be recorded. Among the obvious possibilities are: (a) at the time the company *produces* the product or service which it has agreed to sell; (b) at the time the company *delivers;* and (c) at the time it *receives payment*. Among the major questions which arise in this context, and which have caused numerous problems in comparing the income of firms in similar industries but using different methods of revenue recognition, are the following:

1. Many products have a very long production period—ships, planes, buildings, process-control systems, and so on. Some companies, such as General Electric, follow a conservative policy of refraining from recording revenues on the income statement until an order has been completed and delivered. Many other companies, however, record revenues on a "percentage of completion" basis. That is, as each critical phase of the production process is completed, a percentage of the final value of the product is recorded as a sale. But how are these critical phases to be determined objectively? And what happens if, after booking 80 percent of the value of, say, an order of

---

[3] The discounting of future dollars to a "present value" basis is discussed in Chapter 5.

aircraft, some serious design defect is discovered which causes the entire project to fail or to require renegotiation?

2.   Some products, such as computers, may be either sold outright or leased. Leasing involves some extremely complex problems of revenue recognition because of the many varieties of lease terms. In some cases, the leased product is viewed as remaining the property of the lessor (the party who receives the rental payments). This results in a straightforward procedure whereby each payment is income to the lessor and expense to the lessee. But in other cases, the lease is viewed as a method of financing an acquisition of the property by the lessee— i.e., as a *sale* by the lessor. This creates problems for the lessor company similar to those described above for the land development companies. *When* is the sale assumed to be consummated? Should the future payments be discounted and, if so, at what rate?[4]

Additional difficulties are presented because the mix between outright sale and leasing, and among the different types of leases, varies both among companies and, for any given company, from one year to the next. This creates very erratic movements in trends of income over time.

While one may find it frustrating that we have enumerated many questions and problem areas without offering solutions, it is a fact of life that there are no clear solutions. But the analyst who recognizes the existence of the problems should be better able to make at least qualitative adjustments to net income when evaluating, say, two companies, one of which follows very conservative practices in recording revenues and one of which typically opts for the most liberal treatment available under GAAP. Moreover, the analyst who is aware of the problems should be better able to comprehend the implications of *changes* in GAAP via a continuing stream of new rulings by the Financial Accounting Standards Board. With this as our guiding premise—i.e., that an understanding of the questions is necessary even though this is a field where there are few firm answers—we turn from revenue recognition to the multifaceted subject of expenses.

Cost of Goods Sold

Accountants calculate cost of goods sold in an indirect manner. At the beginning of an accounting period, the value of the firm's inventories on hand is ascertained. The sum of this value plus the value of goods subsequently acquired for sale equals the cost of all goods *available* for sale during the period. By subtracting from this sum the value of inventories on hand at the *end* of the period, a determination is

---

[4] The most recent effort to cope with this problem is "Exposure Draft (Revised)" of the Financial Accounting Standards Board, *Accounting for Leases*, July 22, 1976.

made of the cost of what was actually sold. For wholesale and retail firms, this is simply the value of merchandise which they bought from others. For manufacturing firms, cost of goods sold includes not only merchandise—i.e., raw material—costs, but also wage and other costs directly associated with the manufacturing process (e.g., depreciation of owned plants and rents on leased plants).

Inventory Accounting.   If prices were unchanging, the method of determining cost of goods sold would involve no problems. It would merely be a matter of counting the *number of units* in inventory at the start of the period, adding the number purchased or produced during the period, and subtracting the number on hand at the end of the period. But the fact is that prices do change. And this means that the number of units is only one variable in determining cost. To illustrate, suppose that a retailing firm begins the year with no inventory, and during the year buys three lots of 1,000 units of an item at successive prices of $15, $16, and $17 per unit. Its purchases, then, will be:

1,000 units at $15 = $15,000
1,000 units at $16 =   16,000
1,000 units at $17 =   17,000
Total purchases $48,000

Assume now that during this same year the firm sold 2,500 of the 3,000 units purchased. This being the case, it will end the year with 500 units of inventory. A key question is how to value these 500 units. The traditional rule is "lower of cost or market," which usually means cost in a period of rising prices. But what is the "cost" of the 500 units on the shelves?

On the one hand, the firm can assume that units were sold in the same order as they were purchased. This is the so-called first-in-first-out method of inventory accounting, referred to in brief as Fifo. Using Fifo accounting, final inventory will have a unit cost equal to the most recent price—$17—and will be worth $8,500. On the other hand, it can be argued that when prices are trending up (or down), Fifo does not properly match current costs with current selling prices. Those holding this view prefer so-called Lifo (last-in-first-out) accounting, whereby the most recent purchase costs are charged against sales before earlier costs. Under this method, the unit cost of the final inventory in our example would be the earliest price—$15—and the total inventory value would be $7,500.

Thus, both accepted accounting procedures produce different inventory "costs"—$8,500 and $7,500.[5] When final inventory is sub-

---

[5] Other inventory valuation methods are in use, including a moving average basis which produces results in between Lifo and Fifo.

tracted from the $48,000 of purchases, cost of goods sold becomes either $39,500 or $40,500. But the value of *sales* during the period was what it was, regardless of the method of inventory accounting. Therefore, the *gross profit* on these sales will be highest under Fifo accounting (sales minus $39,500), and lowest under Lifo accounting (sales minus $40,500). This occurs during a period of rising prices. During a period of falling prices, Fifo would produce the lowest profits and Lifo the highest.

In other words, Fifo accounting causes reported profits to move in the direction of price changes as compared with Lifo accounting. Stated another way, Fifo accounting incorporates inventory profits and losses while Lifo accounting does not.

Since Fifo incorporates inventory gains and losses, it usually causes profits to be more volatile during the course of the business cycle than Lifo. During prosperous periods, when profits are normally rising, prices also frequently rise, and Fifo accounting causes inventory profits to be recorded on top of regular operating profits. Lifo does not. The opposite often occurs during recessions, when normal operating profit declines are augmented by inventory losses under Fifo but not under Lifo.

During the highly inflationary environment of recent years, many companies have switched from Fifo to Lifo in order to avoid having to pay income taxes on inventory profits.[6] The 1975 edition of *Accounting Trends and Techniques*, published annually by the AICPA, reveals that of the 600 companies surveyed, 51 percent used Lifo in 1974 versus 25 percent in 1973. Included among the companies shifting to a Lifo basis were such giants as Du Pont and Eastman Kodak, which had previously carried only a portion of their inventories on Lifo. In all cases, the shift to Lifo reduced reported profits during the year of the shift. Indeed, one company, A. O. Smith, went from an $8.5 million profit under Fifo to zero profit under Lifo.

Unfortunately, the tax savings achieved by the switches to Lifo accounting had an offsetting cost to investors in terms of their ability to understand the financial statements produced. In the first place, Lifo makes the inventory figures shown on the *balance sheet* almost meaningless during a period of inflation. In our example, if inventory remained stable at 500 units for many years, it would always be carried on the balance sheet at $7,500, even though its market price might have risen to $25 or $30 per unit.

Second, and perhaps more important since the current replacement

---

[6] The IRS allows companies to make one inventory method change without asking permission. A second switch, however, would require approval. This is to prevent companies from constantly changing to whatever method will produce the lowest taxes.

value of Lifo inventory may be shown in a footnote to the balance sheet,[7] is the fact that profits under Lifo can be greatly influenced by reducing the level of year-end inventory below the level of inventory at the start of the year. This can be seen in Figure 4–1 which is, admittedly, complicated, but which should help clarify the entire sub-

FIGURE 4–1

Illustrative Costs and Profits

Lifo versus Fifo (inventory unchanged)

Assumptions:

   a. Moderate inflation in 1975, speeding up in 1976.
   b. Company A is on Fifo both years; Company B switches to Lifo at end of 1976.
   c. Both companies have closing inventory of 10 units at year-ends 1974 through 1976; have the same unit costs and sales; and selling prices are double concurrent costs.
   d. Purchases and sales of both companies are:

	Purchases		Sales	
1974				
4th quarter	10 units at $48 =	$ 480		
1975				
1st quarter	10 units at 50 =	500	10 at $100 =	$1,000
2nd quarter	10 units at 51 =	510	10 at 102 =	1,020
3rd quarter	10 units at 52 =	520	10 at 104 =	1,040
4th quarter	10 units at 53 =	530	10 at 106 =	1,060
	40	$2,060	40	$4,120
1976				
1st quarter	10 units at 54 =	$ 540	10 at 108 =	$1,080
2nd quarter	10 units at 56 =	560	10 at 112 =	1,120
3rd quarter	10 units at 59 =	590	10 at 118 =	1,180
4th quarter	10 units at 62 =	620	10 at 124 =	1,240
	40	$2,310	40	$4,620

	Company A		Company B		Comment
Cost of Sales Analysis—1975:					
Closing inventory 12/31/74	10 at $48 =	$ 480	10 at $48 =	$ 480	Fifo cost of sales is $50 less
Plus: 1975 purchases	40	2,060	40	2,060	than purchase amount of
	50	$2,540	50	2,540	$2,060—10 units × $5 in-
					crease in carrying value of
Less: Closing inventory 12/31/75	10 at $53 =	$ 530	10 at $53 =	530	inventory.
Equals: 1975 cost of sales	40	$2,010	40	$2,010	
Cost of Sales Analysis—1976:					
Closing inventory 12/31/75	10 at $53 =	$ 530	10 at $53 =	$ 530	B's switch to Lifo causes its
Plus: 1976 purchases	40	2,310	40	2,310	cost of sales to be higher
	50	$2,840	50	$2,840	than A's by $90—10 units × $9
					difference between $62 and $53
Less: Closing inventory 12/31/76	10 at $62 =	$ 620	10 at $53 =	$ 530	inventory carrying value. B's
Equals: 1976 cost of sales	40	$2,220	40	$2,310	cost of sales is equal to its
					purchases; this will always be
					the case under Lifo if be-
					ginning and ending inventory
					levels are the same.
Gross Profit Analysis—1975:					
Sales	$4,120		$4,120		Fifo profit includes $50 in-
Less: Cost of sales	2,010		2,010		ventory gain—10 units × $5
Equals: Gross profit	$2,110		$2,110		increase in carrying value.
Gross Profit Analysis—1976:					
Sales	$4,620		$4,620		A's profit (Fifo) includes $90
Less: Cost of sales	2,220		2,310		inventory gain—10 units × $9
Equals: Gross profit	$2,400		$2,310		increase in carrying value. B's
					profit (Lifo) includes only the
					100 percent markup of selling
					price over cost.

---

[7] Indeed, it *must* be shown in the SEC 10–K report.

FIGURE 4–1 (continued)

Lifo versus Fifo (inventory reduced)

Assumptions:

    a. Continued inflation in 1977.

    b. Company A continues on Fifo and Company B on Lifo.

    c. Both companies again sell 40 units, but instead of purchasing 40 units they purchase only 35, allowing inventory to run down from 10 units to 5 units.

    d. Purchases and sales of both companies are:

		Purchases			Sales	
1977						
1st quarter	10 at $63 =	$ 630		10 at $126 =	$1,260	
2nd quarter	10 at 64 =	640		10 at 128 =	1,280	
3rd quarter	10 at 65 =	650		10 at 130 =	1,300	
4th quarter	5 at 66 =	330		10 at 132 =	1,320	
	35	2,250		40	5,160	

	Company A		Company B	
Cost of Sales Analysis—1977:				
Closing inventory 12/31/76	10 at $62 =	$ 620	10 at $53 =	$ 530
Plus: 1977 purchases	35	2,250	35	2,250
	45	2,870	45	2,780
Less: Closing inventory 12/31/75	5 at 66 =	330	5 at 53 =	265
Equals: 1977 cost of sales	40	2,540	40	2,515
Gross Profit Analysis—1977:				
Sales		$5,160	$5,160	
Less: Cost of sales		2,540	2,515	
Equals: Gross profit		2,620	2,645	

ject of Fifo versus Lifo—a subject which often is made to sound simple but which really is quite complex.

Discussion of Figure 4–1. It will be seen that, despite continued inflation, Lifo profits in 1977 were *higher* than Fifo profits. Insight into why this happened can be gained by considering what the figures would have been if purchases had been 40 units and inventory had remained at 10 units.

Purchases would have been:

$$
\begin{array}{ll}
10 \text{ at } \$63 = & \$\ 630 \\
10 \text{ at } 64 = & 640 \\
10 \text{ at } 65 = & 650 \\
10 \text{ at } 66 = & 660 \\
\hline
 & \$2,580 \\
\end{array}
$$

Cost of sales would have been:

	Company A		Company B	
Closing inventory 12/31/76	10 at $62 =	$ 620	10 at $53 =	$ 530
Plus: 1977 purchases	40	2,580	40	2,580
	50	$3,200	50	$3,110
Less: Closing inventory 12/31/77	10 at $66 =	660	10 at $53 =	530
Equals: 1977 cost of sales	40	$2,540	40	$2,580

And gross profit would have been:

	Company A	Company B
Sales	$5,160	$5,160
Less: Cost of sales	2,540	2,580
Equals: Gross profit	$2,620	$2,580

Thus, Fifo profits would have been $2,620 whether or not inventories had been reduced. This would have consisted of $2,580 of regular markup (the profit under Lifo with unchanged inventory level) plus $40 of inventory profit (10 units × the $4 increase in carrying value). But Lifo profit is seen to be $2,645 with the inventory reduction versus $2,580 with constant inventory. The extra $65 represents a $13 per unit gain ($66 − $53) on the 5 unit reduction of inventory.

Clearly, if reductions in inventory levels from one year-end to the next can have such an impact on reported earnings under Lifo, that accounting method provides management with a tool for manipulating its earnings reports. If, during an inflationary period, the results of operations are not as good as management would like to present to the shareholders, an improvement can be made simply by letting the level of (low-cost) inventory run down, thus taking inventory profits into the accounts at the sole discretion of management. Since the details underlying the inventory figures are not available to the analyst,[8] this method of earnings manipulation may not be detectable. At the very least, however, the analyst should be suspicious if the dollar value of Lifo inventory shown on the balance sheet declines during a period of rising prices.

Another disadvantage of Lifo, in terms of investor understanding, follows from this discussion of the impact on profits of reductions in inventory levels. Lifo is a concept which is applied only to the evaluation of year-end inventories. Therefore, *quarterly* earnings reports to shareholders are based on management's *estimate* of year-end inventory levels. That being the case, quarterly earnings can be altered simply by altering the estimate—but the estimate is not shown in the report.

Finally, although it is generally true that profits tend to be more volatile under Fifo than under Lifo, this is not true in all cases. Under

---

[8] By a perverse sort of logic, the rules of the Internal Revenue Service severely limit the ability of Lifo companies to inform investors what their results would have been under Fifo. Curiously, during the year in which a switch is made from Fifo to Lifo, the IRS says that a company *must* show its results on both bases; but in subsequent years, the company *may not* make public any income figure other than on a Lifo basis. This latter rule is in direct opposition to the SEC's philosophy of full disclosure. See C. L. Schaefer, Jr., "Lifo-tax Conformity and Report Disclosure Problems," *Journal of Accountancy*, January 1976.

some circumstances, Fifo can be a stabilizing influence. For example, meat-packing companies' selling prices to wholesalers and food chains tend to be less flexible than their raw materials prices (i.e., the prices of freshly slaughtered animals). Therefore, when meat prices in general are falling, total packing company costs often fall far more than dollar sales, and as a result profits rise. The contrary often occurs when meat prices are rising; costs tend to rise faster than sales, and profits fall. In this type of environment, Fifo accounting can be a stabilizer and Lifo a destabilizer. For under Fifo accounting, inventory losses during downward price cycles would tend to offset rising operating profits, and inventory gains during upward price cycles would tend to offset falling operating profits. Under Lifo accounting, on the other hand, there would be no inventory gains and losses to smooth out total net profits.

Wage and Pension Costs.   As noted earlier, the cost of goods sold in a manufacturing firm includes not only raw materials, but also the wages of employees and other expenses directly associated with the manufacturing process. An unfortunate aspect of most income statements received by stockholders is that cost of goods sold is shown as a single item with no breakdown of the cost components. Such breakdowns are provided in accounting schedules contained in the 10–K reports to the SEC, but even here the details are usually inadequate to enable the investor to determine, for example, the likely impact of a new contract between the company and the labor unions representing its employees.[9]

One aspect of labor cost reporting which is particularly inadequate, despite efforts to make improvements, relates to employee pension plans. A company's financial obligations under such plans can be divided into two major segments. One part, the "past service liability," stems from the fact that when a company adopts a pension plan it has a large number of old hands among its employees. Thus, if a worker with, say, 25 years of service is 50 years old when the plan is adopted, the company will have to begin paying him a pension in 15 years. But the amount of his pension will be based on as much as 40 years of service. Therefore, the company starts right out with a "past service liability" to which is added the "current service liability" for service rendered after the adoption of the plan. Past service liabilities are also incurred when benefits under an existing plan are improved.

There are various legal, tax, and personnel relations reasons for putting money aside in advance to provide for these liabilities, usually

---

[9] The 10–K requires details only on depreciation, amortization of intangibles, maintenance, taxes other than on income, rents, royalties, advertising, and research and development—and only to the extent that each one of these expenses exceeds 1 percent of sales.

with a commercial bank or life insurance company. This is known as "funding." But the rate at which pension liabilities are funded, and reflected in current net income, is a matter of managerial discretion, within the following guidelines:

1. Pension costs must be charged each year even if no cash contributions are made by the company to the pension fund. Differences between charges and funds actually set aside are shown on the balance sheet as accrued or prepaid pension costs.

2. At a minimum, the accountant must charge (a) the current service cost plus (b) interest on the unfunded past service cost. The maximum which may be charged in one year is the minimum plus 10 percent of the past service cost.[10]

3. A footnote in the annual report must state the pension accounting and funding policy of the company, the pension charge for the year, the remaining balance of unfunded *vested* liabilities (i.e., liabilities which will remain even if the employer goes out of business or the employees quit their jobs), and matters significantly affecting comparability with prior years.

It will be noted that there is a very broad range of discretion between the minimum and maximum charge. Given this range of discretion, some companies have manipulated their pension charges in such a way as artificially to smooth reported earnings by increasing charges in good years and reducing them in poor years. Furthermore, the absence of a requirement to state the total amount of unfunded past service liability, as opposed to merely the vested portion, is regrettable since, for many companies, this sum exceeds the entire net worth of the firm.[11] In addition, there is no requirement to state the interest rate which the company's actuaries are assuming will be earned on the investments of the pension fund, or the rate which the fund actually has earned. If the assumed rate is unrealistically high, the calculated unfunded liability may be far too low and the company may be faced in the future with a need for large additional cash contributions to the fund. With the available information, the investor has little basis for assessing such risks.

Depreciation and Depletion

When a company acquires a plant or machinery, or other fixed asset, it obviously expects to use the asset for many years. Consequently, it would not be appropriate to charge the full cost of the asset against the

---

[10] ERISA, the Employee Retirement Income Security Act, requires past service costs to be amortized within at least 40 years.

[11] "When Pension Liabilities Dampen Profits," *Business Week*, June 16, 1975, pp. 80–81.

income of the year in which it was acquired. Instead, the asset is recorded on the balance sheet at cost (which is what is meant by "capitalizing an expense"), and each year thereafter, for the duration of the asset's estimated life, a portion of the cost is charged against income. At the same time, the balance sheet value of the asset is lowered by the amount of the depreciation charge.

Thus, one function of depreciation charges is gradually to write off the cost of a fixed asset as its economic value shrinks due to wear and tear and obsolescence. The term "amortization" refers to essentially the same procedure, except that it involves the charging off of the cost of an *intangible* asset such as a patent or "goodwill". Finally, the term "depletion" refers to the literal physical exhaustion of an asset, such as a mine or oil well, during the process of conducting the business.

The Rate of Charge-Off. In connection with the expense-charge-off function of depreciation and depletion, a problem of interpretation arises for security analysts. This results from the fact that management has considerable leeway in the *rate* at which it depreciates assets. There are many acceptable accounting techniques, and the Internal Revenue Service sanctions several of them. For example, under "straight-line" depreciation the charge-off occurs in equal annual installments. But under other methods, a greater proportion of an asset's cost is charged off in the earlier years of its life. And the specific proportion varies with the method—"double-declining balance," "sum-of-the-years'-digits," and so forth.[12]

Moreover, different companies may depreciate the identical type of asset over a different number of years. For example, at the time Honeywell Information Systems was formed through the combination of Honeywell's computer division and certain segments of General Electric's computer operations, Honeywell was depreciating its rental equipment on a six-year straight-line basis whereas G.E. used five-year straight-line abroad and five-year "modified sum-of-the-years'-digits" domestically. Further complicating things is the fact that Congress and the Internal Revenue Service change the depreciation rules every so often. As a result, depreciation charges are difficult to compare not only among companies at any instant of time but also for a single company over a span of many years.

Depletion is an even more complex matter. As with depreciation,

---

[12] The double-declining balance method reduces each year's asset value by twice the straight-line percentage. For example, a 10 percent straight-line rate (i.e., an asset with ten-year life) results in a $1,000 per annum depreciation charge on a $10,000 machine. Under double-declining balance, the first year charge is 20 percent of $10,000 = $2,000; the second year charge is 20 percent of $8,000 = $1,600; and so forth. Under sum-of-the-years'-digits, in this illustration, one first calculates "10 factorial" (i.e., $10 + 9 + 8 . . . + 1 = 55$). The depreciation schedule which is then applied to each year's asset value is $10/55$, $9/55$, $8/55$, . . . , $1/55$.

differences arise among companies because of managerial judgment. But, in addition, depletion has become a political football. Under the guise of encouraging certain lines of mineral exploration, Congress has legislated different depletion bases and rates for different mineral industries. Indeed, in some industries, the original cost of obtaining a raw material may be recovered many times before the resource is exhausted.

Interyear and intercompany variations in depreciation and depletion accounting can severely distort profit comparisons. Many differences are more apparent than real. Ideally, the security analyst should restate all income accounts, putting them on a consistent depreciation basis. For example, all depreciation might be stated on a straight-line basis (with an appropriate adjustment of the income tax liability). In practice, however, available data are not usually adequate to make such adjustments. The analyst knows little about the true economic life of various types of assets or about the age composition of a particular company's assets at a given time.

Cash Flow. Many security analysts have tried to cope with these problems by, in effect, ignoring depreciation and depletion altogether. Against the advice of the SEC,[13] the accounting profession, and many of their own colleagues, they have used a concept known widely as "cash flow"—defined as net income plus depreciation and depletion. Thus, it supposedly represents the difference between sales and all expenses (including taxes) *other than* depreciation and depletion.

Security analysts who use the cash flow concept, if they are intelligent, do not consider cash flow to be a measure of the *level* of profits. For they recognize that depreciation and depletion should be deducted from revenues in determining profits. What they do argue, however, is that differences in depreciation-depletion accounting procedures can so distort reported net income that if the analyst hasn't the data with which to restate the account, cash flow often is more useful than reported net income in comparing the *trends* of profitability among companies and over time.

To be sure, the practice of simply adding depreciation to net income after taxes is not wholly satisfactory. A company's income tax liability is greatly affected by its depreciation policies. Other things being equal, the higher the depreciation the lower the income tax. By adding depreciation back to net income after taxes, to derive "cash flow," the problem of depreciation noncomparability is not completely sidestepped, because net income reflects the tax liability which, in turn, reflects depreciation policies. If it is truly desired to put all companies

---

[13] Securities and Exchange Commission, *Accounting Series Release No. 142*, March 15, 1973.

on a comparable predepreciation basis, it might be better to add only half of depreciation (and depletion) to net income, assuming a 50 percent tax rate for simplicity. Another alternative would be to use "*pre-tax* cash flow"—i.e., net income before deducting either federal income taxes or depreciation.

Furthermore, it must be recognized that "cash flow" is a poor descriptive phrase for the sum of net income plus depreciation and depletion. For it implies that this sum is a correct representation of the amount of *cash* generated by operations during the accounting period. That is, depreciation does not involve a cash outlay; it is a noncash expense. So, by adding it back to net income, the implication is that the resulting figure equals the difference between cash income and cash outlays. But this is not true at all. As will be discussed later in this chapter, there are many transactions which increase or reduce cash but do not affect reported net income. Thus, a distinction should be made between cash flow as an attempt to determine the true *trend* of profits, and cash flow as a sources and uses of funds network. The former would be better referred to as "profit before depreciation."

Expensing versus Capitalizing. Another aspect of intercompany differences in depreciation policies concerns "intermediate-term expenses." Some items purchased by a company are so obviously short lived that they are almost invariably charged against income during the year in which they are acquired. Examples of such items are pencils, pads, drill bits, light bulbs, and so forth. Other items are so obviously long lived that they are capitalized (set up on the balance sheet as assets) and charged off gradually—for example, buildings, lathes, and office furniture. But many companies incur expenses which cannot be clearly labeled as short or long term in nature. Some of these companies follow a policy of "expensing" such items immediately, while others capitalize them and charge them off over several years.

Examples of intermediate-term expenses are numerous. Automobile companies, for example, spend huge sums for dies when they make basic style changes in their cars. These dies are usually used on a few years' models thereafter, but it is not too long before a major restyling is underway again. Should these dies be expensed or capitalized? Oil companies are constantly exploring for new wells. Should the drilling expenses of each year be attributed to that year's operations, or should such expenses be considered in the nature of long-term capital outlays? Should a distinction be made between expenses incurred in actually bringing in wells versus drilling "dry holes"? For many years, Texaco followed a practice of capitalizing many outlays which other major oil companies expensed. In 1975, Texaco changed its accounting policy to conform to that of the other majors. But smaller, independent oil companies remained staunch ad-

vocates of capitalizing. Similar questions have applied to research and development expenses, to the initial marketing expenses of introducing a new product, and to interest charges paid during the construction phase of a new plant. And what about the costs of producing a motion picture? If a movie is good, it may run for two or three years, and it may be rerun several years later, or sold to television. Should the production costs be charged to the year in which incurred or spread over a period of several years?

There are no right or wrong answers to these questions. They are largely matters of managerial discretion, although the FASB has been moving in the direction of requiring expensing in the year incurred.[14] For the security analyst, management's discretion in this regard creates a problem in comparing the level and trends of profitability among companies.

Evidence that expense items are being capitalized, rather than charged against income as incurred, may be found in the item labeled "deferred charges," which is in the "other asset" section of the balance sheet. A deferred charge is a corporate outlay which has not yet been charged against net income. If deferred charges are growing abnormally, therefore, security analysts had better ask questions of management.

Price-Level Accounting. In addition to posing an analytical problem because of *differences* in accounting treatment, depreciation also causes a problem because of one outstanding similarity of treatment. Regardless of the rate of depreciation, accepted accounting practice and tax regulations allow only the original cost of the asset to be written off during its useful life.[15] The reason this is significant to security analysts is that there is a second function of depreciation. The first function, as we have seen, is to allocate the cost of a capital asset over its useful life. But a second, indirect, function is to provide a fund for the replacement of the assets after they have worn out, either physically or technologically. Of course, depreciation per se does not provide a company with cash. It is an expense. Cash is generated primarily by making sales. But by deducting depreciation from sales revenues in computing net income, the company withholds cash which might otherwise be paid out in the form of higher wages, dividends, and taxes.

The function of depreciation as an (indirect) source of funds for asset replacement creates analytical problems during inflationary periods.

---

[14] For example, a recent ruling banned capitalization of research and development outlays, and sentiment is growing for a prohibition against capitalizing unsuccessful drilling expenditures.

[15] As noted previously, this is not true of depletion.

For having charged off the original cost of assets, companies find that the costs thus recovered are inadequate, because replacement cost has risen far above original cost.

Many economists and accountants have advocated the adoption of "price-level accounting," at least as a supplement to "historical cost accounting."[16]

There are two approaches to price-level accounting. One substitutes estimates of the *specific current replacement cost* of each financial statement item for the recorded historical cost. The other adds an increment to each item for changes in the *overall level of prices* since the item was initially recorded. Under both approaches, however, the following principles apply to the construction of the financial statements:

1. With regard to the balance sheet:
    a. "Monetary assets and liabilities" (cash, receivables, and most current and long-term payables) are not adjusted.
    b. "Nonmonetary" items (mainly inventory and plant and equipment) are adjusted.
    c. Net worth is, as usual, a residual item.
2. With regard to the income statement:
    a. All items are adjusted. This means, in general, that during inflation a company's depreciation and cost of goods sold will be much higher than under historical cost accounting.
    b. Net income is equal to the difference of the adjusted income and expense items in (2a), *plus* the "gain in purchasing power" achieved by "net debtors" (i.e., firms whose monetary liabilities exceed their monetary assets) or the "loss in purchasing power" suffered by "net creditors" (monetary assets exceed monetary liabilities). For example, if a firm begins its accounting period with $1,000,000 of receivables and $2,000,000 of payables, and prices rise 10 percent by the end of the period, the firm is said to have gained $100,000 of purchasing power during the period because it paid out more cheapened dollars than it received cheapened dollars (10 percent multiplied by the "net debt" of $1,000,000).

The most controversial aspects of price-level accounting are:

1. It requires a total change in the customary way of thinking about financial positions and earnings.

---

[16] See, for example, Financial Accounting Standards Board, *Financial Reporting in Units of General Purchasing Power*. Exposure Draft dated December 31, 1974. In March 1976, the SEC announced a new requirement of footnote disclosure of replacement cost values of inventories and plant and equipment, at least by large-size companies.

2. Specific replacement cost is an easier concept to understand than general price-level adjustment, but is more subjective and, therefore, more likely to result in earnings "manipulation."
3. "Monetary gains" attributable to long-term indebtedness are of questionable value because they are not realizable in the near-term. Indeed, firms which are near bankruptcy because their liabilities are about to overwhelm their liquid (monetary) assets, can report very large profits due to "purchasing power gains" under this accounting system.

Studies of the probable impact of price-level accounting have compared:

a. Adjusted profit, before monetary gains and losses.
b. Adjusted profit, after monetary gains and losses.
c. Historical cost profit.

These studies indicate[17] that (a) generally is considerably lower than (c), but (b) may well be higher than (c) for net debtors.

In view of these controversies, it is doubtful that price-level accounting will become more than a supplement to traditional historical cost accounting in the near future. In any event, analysts may find that the best way to understand the impact of inflation on the companies they study is to engage in a thorough sources and uses of funds analysis, such as will be described later in this chapter. This type of analysis downplays reported income and reported net worth, and focuses instead on the *availability of cash* for dividend payment and capital expansion purposes.

Extraordinary Items, Contingencies, and Discontinued Operations

One of the main reasons for studying corporate income statements in security analysis is to estimate and forecast the "normal" earning power of the companies being studied, as to both level and trend. To the extent that reported net income reflects debits and credits attribut-

---

[17] See, for example, two articles by S. Davidson and R. L. Weil, "Inflation Accounting," *Financial Analysts Journal*, January/February 1975 and "Impact of Inflation Accounting on 1974 Earnings," *Financial Analysts Journal*, September/October 1975. An accounting issue quite related to the problem of adjusting for changes in the purchasing power of the dollar is the problem of adjusting the financial statements of foreign subsidiaries of U.S. corporations for changes in the exchange rate of foreign currencies versus the dollar. Space constraints preclude a discussion of this subject, but the reader is referred to D. Norr, "Currency Translation and the Analyst," *Financial Analysts Journal*, July/August 1976; also "FASB 8: A Spirited Accounting Controversy," *Morgan Guaranty Survey*, July 1976.

able to transactions which are not part of a company's everyday operations, normal earning power may be obscured.

Under recent accounting regulations, companies must make separate disclosures of: (a) realized income or expense items which are *both* unusual in nature *and* infrequent of occurrence—so-called extraordinary items; (b) realized income or expense items which are unusual *or* infrequent, but not both—known as "special items"; (c) charges to income for expenses not yet incurred but which are probable and can be reasonably estimated—so-called contingency reserves, which after being charged against income are set up as liabilities on the balance sheet to be debited when the contingency does, in fact, occur; and (d) the results of operations which used to be a regular part of the business but are in the process of being discontinued. Thus, it is possible for a single year's income statement to look somewhat as follows:

    Results of Continuing Operations
        Sales
        Cost of Sales and Operating Expenses
        Nonoperating Items (e.g., royalties earned by a manufacturing company)
        Special Items (enumerated)
            Net before Extraordinary Items
        Extraordinary Items (to be described in detail in SEC Form 8–K)
        Provision for Contingencies (to be described in detail in SEC Form 8–K)
            Net from Continuing Operations
    Results of Discontinued Operations
        Sales
        Cost of Sales and Expenses
            Net from Discontinued Operations
    Net Income from Continuing and Discontinued Operations

Faced with this display, which figure represents "normal" earning power? On the surface, it would appear that the figure labeled "Net before Extraordinary Items"—sometimes called earnings "above-the-line"—should be considered most representative. And that is probably a correct interpretation in most cases. However, four observations are in order before reaching such a conclusion:

1. With the trend toward corporate diversification, it is quite difficult to distinguish between a company's ordinary versus extraordinary activities.

2. Accounting principles give management a good deal of discretion in deciding which items are extraordinary, although the range of discretion has been steadily narrowing. Being only human, there is a tendency for management to treat unusual expense items as extraordinary more readily than unusual income items.

3. There are so many varieties of unusual items that one may occur one year, another a second year, and another a third year. While their timing and magnitude cannot be predicted, they are likely to occur

and reoccur. Therefore, items which in prior years might have been labeled extraordinary are now identified as special items, above-the-line, and there is a discontinuity in the figures over time.

4. It is quite common for a new management, either after a merger or takeover of a company, or after the board of directors ousts the existing management, to make huge "extraordinary" write-offs of unproductive assets or unsuccessful projects. For example, in 1975 the A&P (Great Atlantic and Pacific Tea Co.) took a $200 million extraordinary write-off associated with the new management's store closing program. In the same year, a $400 million write-off occurred at the Singer Co., where new management discontinued the company's unsuccessful business machines division. These write-offs "clean the slate" and often permit the new management to report remarkable profit improvements in the years following its ascendancy to power. Or a company may use contingency reserves to smooth artificially the trend of total reported earnings—holding down the reported profits of prosperity years and bolstering those of recession years. Alternatively, the opposite practice may be employed, namely, deliberately to *destabilize* reported earnings in the hope that stock prices will rise more on good profit reports than they will fall on poor reports.

Having made these observations, many security analysts argue that extraordinary items, provision for contingencies, and results of discontinued operations should not be excluded from the determination of the level and trend of earnings. These analysts agree that straightforward inclusion of such items may be a distorting factor because they may be very large in one year and very small in the next. But their inclusion on some sort of smoothed basis, such as a three-year or five-year moving average, may present a more realistic picture of the results of corporate activities than would be presented by pretending that they never occurred.

Income Tax Reconciliation

A simple test can be very rewarding in security analysis, and indeed is now required in annual reports. It is to compare reported net income with the reported income tax. Since most publicly owned corporations are subject to a 48 percent tax on regular income, their reported net income and income tax should be roughly equal in amount. If they are not, an explanation is in order. Among the reasons for a lack of equivalence between net income and income taxes, the following are particularly important.

1. A significant portion of the company's income may not have been taxable at regular income rates; for example, capital gains, earnings from foreign operations, dividends from affiliates, and so on. It is

important for the analyst to be aware of the magnitude of these low-taxed earnings in order to be able to judge the probable impact of proposed changes in the tax law—e.g., proposals to tax unrepatriated foreign earnings more heavily.[18]

2.   The company may have been the beneficiary of a significant tax credit. Two types of credits may be noted here.

   a.   The tax law provides that when a company operates at a net loss it can, in effect, merge the losses with earlier or later years of profits (three-year "carry-back" or five-year "carry-forward") in order to determine its tax liability on profits. This means that a company may report substantial profits in some years yet pay little or no income tax. Investment analysts, however, should not permit the incidence of tax credits to distort their views of earnings *trends*. They should reallocate the tax credits to the years to which they apply. That is, they should impute a tax, at the company's typical rate, to the profit years, and reduce the losses of the loss years by the amount of tax credit generated by such losses. Ordinarily this would be about half the loss, but in some cases a part of the tax credit might go unused because there are not sufficient profits against which to offset the entire loss. Analysts always should keep track of unused, but still available, tax loss credits.

   b.   The Congress periodically has legislated an "investment credit," whereby companies making specified types of plant and equipment expenditures may credit a percentage of such outlays against their income tax. Companies have an option of reporting such credits to stockholders in full during the year taken (known as "flow-through" accounting), or of spreading them over the lifetime of the capital assets whose purchase generated the credits. Clearly, problems of interfirm and interperiod comparability can arise from investment credits. In the first quarter of 1975, for example, Ford Motor Company reduced its reported loss from $106 million to $11 million by switching its accounting for investment credit from a spreading basis to flow-through.

3.   The company may have reported different income and expense items to stockholders than it reported to the Internal Revenue Service. Prominent in this connection is the reporting of depreciation. Despite all of the complaints by business executives regarding the inadequacy of historical-cost depreciation during periods of inflation, the 1975 edition of *Accounting Trends and Techniques* reveals that most companies report depreciation to shareholders on a straight-line basis even though they charge depreciation at the most rapid rate possible on their income tax returns. This creates a lower pretax profit on the tax return than on the stockholder report, and therefore the income tax

---

[18] Some companies already set up a liability for taxes that may have to be paid on foreign earnings not yet repatriated to the United States.

actually paid is a good deal less than 48 percent of the pretax profit reported to stockholders.

A similar problem may arise with regard to companies that sell on an installment payment basis. If they report the full amount of sales and related expenses in their stockholder reports during the years in which shipments are actually made, but report to the Internal Revenue only as payments are received, the amount of taxes actually paid will be less than the amount which would be expected based on income reported to stockholders.

Finally, some companies fully expense certain outlays on their tax returns, but capitalize them on reports to stockholders. Examples include exploration costs of natural resource companies and interest costs incurred during the period of construction of a new plant.

Generally accepted accounting principles (GAAP) adopt the position that if such "tax savings" are allowed to "flow through" to net income reported to stockholders, the investor may be misled. For the tax saving may be only temporary. In the case of accelerated depreciation, the tax-reported assets will become fully depreciated faster than under a straight-line basis. Therefore, the firm's tax bill ultimately will be higher than 48 percent of stockholder-reported pretax profit, unless new capital spending keeps filling the void. Likewise, in the case of installment sales, unless the volume of sales and accounts receivable grow continuously, payments received on account—and the corresponding taxes—ultimately will exceed stockholder-reported sales and taxes. GAAP, therefore, requires that income be charged with a "deferred tax," which deferral also is to be shown in the balance sheet as a liability.

To illustrate, suppose we assume that the pretax, predepreciation income of a company is $100,000,000 and that it records accelerated depreciation of $4,000,000 in its tax return but straight-line depreciation of $2,000,000 in its stockholder report. Its tax statement net income and its stockholder-reported net income, without any adjustment (i.e., on a "flow-through" basis), would be as follows:

	Tax Statement	Flow-Through
Pretax, predepreciation income	$100,000,000	$100,000,000
Less: Depreciation	4,000,000	2,000,000
Equals: Net before taxes	$ 96,000,000	$ 98,000,000
Less: Taxes (assume 50% rate)	48,000,000 ——→	48,000,000
Equals: Net Income	$ 48,000,000	$ 50,000,000

If the company had reported to both the tax authorities and the stockholders on a straight-line basis, its net income would have been:

Pretax, predepreciation income	$100,000,000
Less: Depreciation	2,000,000
Equals: Net before taxes	$ 98,000,000
Less: Taxes	49,000,000
Equals: Net Income	$ 49,000,000

GAAP requires that the "flow-through" report be adjusted to produce the net income which would have been reported had straight-line depreciation been used on the tax return as well as on the stockholder report. This is accomplished, in effect, as follows:

Pretax, predepreciation income	$100,000,000
Less: Depreciation	2,000,000
Equals: Net before taxes	$ 98,000,000
Less: Taxes paid	48,000,000
Deferred taxes	1,000,000
Equals: Net Income	$ 49,000,000

This required accounting treatment has caused a great deal of controversy. Opponents argue that many, if not most, large corporations do, indeed, have steadily expanding capital expenditures and accounts receivable. For such companies, the "deferred tax" is really a remote contingency, payable in the distant indeterminable future. The "present value" of such a distant liability is negligible, they argue,[19] and to charge current income as if it were a current liability is greatly misleading. For example, a study done several years ago by the accounting firm of Price Waterhouse estimated that the reported earnings of Sears Roebuck were understated by one-third because of this aspect of GAAP.[20]

Income Manipulation—A Summary

As has been shown throughout this discussion, the accounting rules governing the calculation of net income permit a great deal of managerial discretion. While honest managers may have honest differences in the accounting treatment they accord similar types of transactions, the investment analyst must be wary of managers whose motives are less pure, and who are quite willing to puff up current reported earnings even though such puffery ultimately will result in diminished

---

[19] See Chapter 5, for a discussion of present-value calculations.

[20] Some public utility commissions insist on "flow-through" accounting for rate-setting purposes. Obviously, higher reported profits mean less justification for rate increases.

future earnings. Generally, such managers will engage in one or more of the following practices:

1. Recognize sales as having occurred long before final delivery has been made to the customer's satisfaction, and paid for.
2. Select inventory valuation methods which minimize cost of goods sold.
3. Accrue pension expenses at the lowest possible rates.
4. Charge depreciation and amortization at the lowest permitted rates.
5. Capitalize all manner of "intermediate-term" expenses.
6. Classify numerous outlays as extraordinary expenses.
7. Flow through to earnings all available income tax benefits.
8. Manipulate quarterly earnings by:
   a. Varying the intrayear allocation of such expenses as depreciation, pension charges, and executive bonuses.
   b. Varying assumed closing inventory levels under Lifo accounting.

Calculation of Earnings per Share

Whatever dollar figures the analyst ultimately accepts as indicative of a company's earnings, it is customary to express those figures in "per share" terms. Similarly, dividend and stock price information is expressed in per share terms. In view of the importance of per share calculations, an extended discussion of the subject is warranted at this point.

To begin with an example, suppose that in 1975 Company A had 1 million shares of common stock outstanding and had net income available to common (i.e., net income minus preferred dividends) of $2 million. In 1976 Company A decided to expand its business by acquiring another company. To consummate the deal, Company A issued 250,000 shares of its stock in exchange for the other company's stock. Thus, Company A now had 1¼ million shares of stock outstanding.

Suppose that the acquisition raised 1976 earnings on common stock to $2½ million from the $2 million earned in 1975. From the point of view of the individual stockholder, earnings did not rise at all. The 25 percent increase of total dollar earnings was accompanied by a 25 percent increase in capital stock *held by others*. From the point of view of individual investors, progress means higher earnings on each ownership interest so that the individual can look forward to higher dividend payments or to a higher market value on the stock.

In our example the dividend potential of the individual shareholding did not increase at all. This can be shown by dividing each year's net income (after deducting any preferred stock dividend obligations)

by the number of shares outstanding *that year*. Thus 1975's earnings of $2 million, divided by the 1 million shares outstanding in 1975, produces earnings per share of $2. And 1976's earnings of $2½ million, divided by that year's 1¼ million shares outstanding, also produces per share earnings of $2. No progress is indicated for the individual investor.

Stock Splits and Stock Dividends.   In the above example, the 25 percent increase in outstanding shares reflected new capital invested in the business. Many times, however, the number of shares rises because of stock splits and stock dividends. The holders of a corporation's stock are often given additional stock certificates to represent their ownership interest. Technically, there is a difference between a stock split and a stock dividend. In the case of a split, the capital account is maintained at a constant amount and the par or stated value per share is reduced. In the case of a stock dividend, the par value per share is maintained and a transfer is made from the earned surplus account to the capital account. For purposes of the present discussion, these accounting differences are unimportant. Both a 100 percent stock dividend and a two-for-one split cause the owner of 100 shares to end up with 200. Both a 20 percent stock dividend and a six-for-five split cause the owner of 100 shares to end up with 120.

Companies have various reasons for splitting their stock or paying stock dividends. The principal reason for large percentage increases in number of shares (say 20 percent or more) is to broaden the market for the stock. Most small investors have an aversion to very high-priced stocks, notwithstanding their apparent willingness to buy a few shares of IBM or Du Pont at prices above $100 a share. Thus, a two-for-one split of, say, an $80 stock cuts its price to $40, other things being equal, and makes it more attractive to a wider group of investors.

The reasoning behind *small* stock dividends is not as clear. The public seems to like stock dividends, according to various surveys which have been taken. Some of this attitude is probably due to the fact that stock prices seem to respond favorably when stock dividends are declared. On the other hand, there is considerable statistical evidence to suggest that the favorable price response is not due to the stock dividend per se, but rather to the fact that the *cash* dividend per share is usually maintained on the greater number of shares, so that the stock dividend really means an effective increase in the cash dividend.[21]

The effective increase in the cash dividend also raises questions about another alleged reason for small stock dividends, namely the

---

[21] Price may rise in response to a dividend increase either because the original dividend payout rate was less than optimum or because the market takes the increase as a sign that earning power has significantly improved.

desire to conserve cash. The argument is that if a company wants to retain cash in the business, payment of periodic small stock dividends enables it to do so, but at the same time gives the recipient of the stock dividend the opportunity to realize cash by selling any extra shares. Proponents argue that periodic stock dividends are more efficient than the practice in the electric utility industry, for example, of paying large cash dividends, on the one hand, but then taking the cash back by selling new stock to existing stockholders in a "rights offering."[22] The rebuttal to the cash-retention argument is that (a) the total cash dividend may really be increased, as noted above; (b) the company could retain earnings without paying a stock dividend; (c) stock dividends involve the company in a large clerical expense; (d) stockholders have to pay odd-lot commissions to sell their shares; (e) if stockholders want cash they can always sell off a part of their original holdings; and (f) uninformed stockholders are deluded into thinking that they're getting something for nothing.

Whatever the reason, let's assume that Company A, in our example, split its stock two for one in 1977, at a time when earnings had risen to $5 million. That is, total dollar earnings had doubled without any additional capital being raised. But since there were 2½ million shares outstanding, instead of 1¼ million, earnings per share remained at $2. Thus, no progress is indicated in the per share data when, in fact, there was great progress. The dividend potential of each individual investor's holdings had doubled. He had twice as many shares, and earnings on each share remained constant.

In order to make the series of per share earnings meaningful, we must go back and adjust all the *presplit* data. What we want to do is put the presplit data at the level they would have been had the stock always been split. Thus, in 1975, when earnings were $2 million on 1 million shares, per share earnings on a split basis were $2 million divided by 2 million shares, or $1 per share instead of $2. And in 1976, $2½ million of earnings should be divided by 2½ million shares instead of 1¼ million, for per share earnings of $1 instead of $2. Accordingly, per share earnings for 1975, 1976, and 1977, on an adjusted basis, would be $1, $1, and $2, respectively. No progress would be shown from 1975 to 1976, as before, but a doubling would be shown from 1976 to 1977.

A simpler method of adjusting presplit per share data is to apply the following formula: Divide presplit per share data by 100 percent plus the percentage stock dividend or split. Thus, with a two-for-one stock

---

[22] In addition to the company's extra work in paying cash and then selling new stock, the stockholder has to pay an income tax on the cash dividend. If he sells a stock dividend, he merely pays a capital gains tax on the difference between the selling price and his adjusted cost price.

split, divide presplit data by 100 percent + 100 percent. Dividing by 200 percent is the same as dividing by $^2/_1$, which is the same as multiplying by ½. So $2 presplit, times ½, equals $1 adjusted.

Likewise, with a 20 percent stock dividend we would divide presplit data by 100 percent + 20 percent. Dividing by 120 percent is the same as dividing by $^6/_5$, which is the same as multiplying by $^5/_6$. Conversion to fractions, however, is inconvenient for small stock dividends. Therefore, with a 2 percent stock dividend we would divide presplit data by 100 percent + 2 percent, or 1.02. It should be noted that while we have been discussing *earnings* per share, the same comments apply to price per share, sales per share, and dividends per share.[23]

Potential Dilution. During the 1960s, a large number of mergers occurred involving the exchange of convertible debentures, convertible preferred stocks, warrants, and other "equity-type" securities, some of a rather exotic nature which came to be called "Chinese money." Since these securities were not actually common stock, their existence was not directly reflected in earnings per share calculations. Yet they had the potential for being converted into common stock and "diluting" earnings per share. Sophisticated analysts would calculate the potential for dilution, but most investors did not. The widespread

---

[23] A shortcoming of some published per share data is that they may not be adjusted for stock dividends of less than 10 percent. This is not too bad if a company has only an occasional 2 percent or 5 percent stock dividend. But it can result in severely distorted data where a company pays a whole series of small stock dividends. Furthermore, the daily newspapers publish year-to-date high- and low-price ranges of listed stocks which are not adjusted at all for stock dividends. Thus, a high-low range of 60–30 may be shown. But if the high of 60 occurred before a 20 percent stock dividend, while the low occurred afterward, the true price range is really 50–30 on an adjusted basis, not 60–30 ($^5/_6 \times 60 = 50$).

Because of the similarity, noted above, between a small stock dividend and a rights offering which recoups money previously paid out in cash dividends, some analysts believe that past per share data should be adjusted to reflect rights offerings as well as stock dividends. The procedure suggested is to divide by 100 plus the number of shares which could be bought by selling enough rights to raise the necessary subscription price (thus obviating the need to invest additional capital). The formula for determining this number (X) is:

$$X = \frac{T(P - S)}{S + NP}$$

Where

T = Number of rights received
P = Price of common, with rights
S = Subscription price
N = Number of rights to purchase one share

For further discussion, see S. L. Hawk and L. W. Thatcher, "The Treatment of Rights Offerings in Common Stock Valuation," *Public Utilities Fortnightly*, November 11, 1971.

ignorance of the potential for dilution resulted in a requirement of greater disclosure on the subject, as follows:

1.   Earnings per share, or net loss per share, must be shown on the face of the income statement, separately for ordinary items, extraordinary items, and total earnings. All historical earnings covered in the statement, likewise, must be shown in per share terms, adjusted for stock splits and stock dividends and adjusted for dilution as described below.

2.   The number of shares used in the divisor should be a weighted average of the number of shares outstanding during the statement period. For example, suppose that a company has 20 million shares outstanding at the start of the year and then sells 1 million shares of new stock on October 1. For purposes of calculating per share earnings, the company had 20 million shares outstanding for nine months and 21 million shares outstanding for three months, a weighted average for the year of 20,250,000 shares.

3.   Where there is potential dilution in excess of 3 percent, the earnings per share must be shown on two bases, "primary" and "fully diluted." The principal definitions and procedural requirements are stated below, followed by an illustrative set of calculations.[24]

a.   Primary earnings per share must give effect to "common stock equivalents." These include all options and warrants and any convertible securities which, *at the time of their issuance,* provided a cash yield of less than two thirds of the then current commercial bank prime interest rate. (Convertibles issued in mergers are not subject to this rule.)

In the case of the convertibles, the procedure is to calculate what the net income available for common stock would have been without interest or dividends on such convertible securities, taking into account any income tax effects of such adjustments. This net available figure is divided by the actual weighted average number of common shares which were outstanding *plus* the number which would have been outstanding if the conversion features had been exercised.

In the case of the options and warrants, it is to be assumed that they were exercised and that the proceeds were used to retire outstanding stock at the average market price of the reporting period. For example, suppose that a corporation has 1,000,000 warrants outstanding, exercisable at $27 (i.e., the warrant holder can buy a share of stock from the company for $27 plus one warrant), and the market price of the stock during the year is $30. If all the warrants are assumed to have been

---

[24] Also, see Chapter 11 for an in-depth discussion of convertible securities and warrants.

exercised, the corporation would have received $27,000,000 and could have repurchased 900,000 shares for that sum of money. Therefore, the warrants are equivalent to 100,000 "common stock equivalents" (1,000,000 minus 900,000).

b. Fully diluted earnings per share must give effect to *all* securities which could be converted into common stock.

c. Footnotes should explain the bases upon which these calculations are made, and should describe, in summary form, the pertinent rights and privileges of the various securities outstanding.

To illustrate, assume that the following securities of a corporation were outstanding during a reporting period:

Common stock	15,000,000 shares
3% convertible debentures, sold when the prime rate was 5%, and convertible into 50 common shares per $1,000 of debenture	$10,000,000
4% convertible debentures, sold when the prime rate was 5%, and convertible into 40 common shares per $1,000 of debenture	$20,000,000
$3 convertible preferred stock, $100 par value, sold when the prime rate was 6%, and convertible into common stock share for share	1,000,000 shares
Warrants exercisable at $27 (average price of common during period is $30)	1,000,000 warrants

Next, assume the following income data for the period:

Net before interest and income taxes	$97,100,000
Less: Interest (3% × $10 million and 4% × $20 million)	1,100,000
Equals: Net before taxes	$96,000,000
Less: Income taxes (assume 50% rate)	48,000,000
Equals: Net income...	$48,000,000
Less: Preferred dividends ($3 × 1 million shares)	3,000,000
Equals: Net Available for Common	$45,000,000

Prior to the regulations being discussed, earnings per share would have been reported as $3 ($45 million of net available for common divided by 15 million shares). Under the revised rules, however, this company has three issues of "common stock equivalents": the 3 percent convertible debentures, whose yield at time of issue was only three fifths of the prime rate; the $3 convertible preferred, whose yield was only one half of the prime rate; and the warrants. Note that the 4 percent convertible debentures are not common stock equivalents because their yield at time of issue was four fifths of the prime rate.

Primary earnings per share would be calculated as follows:

Net before interest and income taxes $97,100,000
Less: Adjusted interest (4% × $20 million) 800,000

Equals: Adjusted net before taxes $96,300,000
Less: Adjusted income taxes 48,150,000

Equals: Adjusted net income $48,150,000
Less: Adjusted preferred dividends .... none

Equals: Adjusted Net Available for Common........................ $48,150,000

Adjusted shares outstanding:
Common stock 15,000,000
Plus: 3% debenture "equivalent" (50 × 10,000) 500,000
$3 preferred "equivalent" 1,000,000
Warrant "equivalent" 100,000

Equals: Total Common and Common Equivalents.................. 16,600,000

Primary earnings per share ($48.15/16.6) $2.90

Fully diluted earnings per share would be calculated as follows:

Net before taxes $97,100,000
Less: Adjusted income taxes 48,550,000

Equals: Adjusted Net Available $48,550,000

Adjusted shares outstanding (as above) 16,600,000
Plus 4% debenture "equivalent" (40 × 20,000) 800,000

                                                             17,400,000
Fully diluted earnings per share ($48.55/17.4) $2.79

Confronted with alternative calculations of earnings per share, the analyst must decide which to use. Generally, the decision should be based on the probability of a company's warrants actually being exercised, or its convertibles actually being exchanged for stock, in the near future.

Balance Sheet Format

Prior to the depression of the 1930s, the balance sheet—the statement of a company's assets and liabilities—was the financial statement on which security analysts focused their attention. During the depression, however, it became apparent that the book values at which a company's assets were carried were quite meaningless unless the operations of the company were generating a commensurate level of earnings from those assets. Gradually, the focus of analytical attention shifted to the income statement and, like most such shifts of attention, it carried too far. For it is not an exaggeration to state that most security analysts who received their training during the 1950s and 1960s were so concerned with earnings per share, and the growth thereof, that they forgot about the necessity of a sound financial structure to support

the growth. And it is the balance sheet to which one must turn when evaluating financial structure.

The principal items to be found in a balance sheet are shown below. A number of them call for extended discussion in the context of the ambiguity of accounting principles and the relationship between the income statement and the balance sheet. As with the income statement, future chapters will consider methods of *analyzing* the data once the analyst is convinced that the underlying accounting principles are understood.

Assets	Liabilities and Capital
Current Assets:	Current Liabilities:
Cash and short-term marketable securities	Trade accounts payable
Accounts receivable	Taxes payable within one year
Inventories	Bank loans payable within one year
Prepaid expenses	Portion of long-term debt due in one year
Plant and Equipment (net of depreciation)	Other short-term accruals
Other Assets:	Other Liabilities:
Investments in affiliates and in nonconsolidated subsidiaries	Deferred taxes
Other securities held for long-term investment	Reserve items
	Minority interest in consolidated subsidiaries
Intangibles:	Capital:
Patents	Long-term debt (due in over one year)
Goodwill	Preferred stock (par or stated value)
Deferred charges	Common Equity:
	Par or state value of common stock (net of Treasury stock)
	Paid-in surplus
	Retained earnings

Current Assets

This is the section of the balance sheet to which one is supposed to be able to turn for evidence regarding a company's liquid resources. Unfortunately, it is too often the case that only the cash and short-term obligations (such as Treasury bills, commercial paper, and certificates of deposit at commercial banks) are liquid—and sometimes even some of these obligations, such as commercial paper, are of questionable liquidity.[25]

Receivables. In the earlier discussion of the item labeled "sales" in the income statement, it was noted that considerable discretion

---

[25] FASB rules now require equity securities held for short-term investment to be carried at the lower of cost or market, with writedowns (or writeups) to be charged (or credited) to net income. Equities held for long-term investment are to be written down to market if the value of the entire portfolio drops below cost. These writedowns are to be charged to surplus unless the value impairment is permanent, in which case income is to be charged.

exists regarding the timing of revenue recognition. Since every credit to the sales account carries a concurrent debit to accounts receivable (except in cash-and-carry businesses), the same doubts to which the sales figures are subject also apply to receivables. *When* are the receivables due to be paid? Have adequate allowances been established for returns or other customer credits? Has adequate allowance been made for bad debts? For example, in 1975 Beckman Instruments, Inc. lowered its allowance for doubtful accounts from 1.9 percent to 0.9 percent, in the face of a bad economic environment. Was this change justified? Unfortunately, information that would be helpful in answering these questions is not usually available in published financial statements.

Inventories.   It already has been shown that the same physical volume of inventories can be carried on the balance sheet at a variety of values. Under Lifo accounting, the balance sheet value of inventories typically is vastly understated. With Fifo accounting, the balance sheet value of inventories reflects current prices. But the amount that actually could be realized from the forced sale of the inventories usually is considerably less.

Other Assets

*Investments (**Principles of Consolidation**).*   When a company owns more than 50 percent of the common stock of another company, a parent-subsidiary relationship is said to exist (although the most typical ownership percentage in such cases is 100 percent or close to it). If the ownership proportion is substantial, but less than 50 percent, the owned company is referred to as an "affiliate." When ownership is split 50–50 between two companies, a "joint venture" exists.

Historically, stock ownership of affiliates and joint ventures was carried as an asset on the balance sheet at cost, and labeled "Investments." Dividends received on such stock was recorded in the income statement as a nonoperating—but not extraordinary—item. However, problems of interpretation often arose in the treatment of investments in, and dividends received on, stock ownership of "subsidiaries."

When a subsidiary exists, the parent, by definition, controls it and could compel it to pay out 100 percent of its earnings as dividends. (An obvious exception would be the case of a subsidiary located in a foreign nation which restricts repatriation of earnings.) Since the parent could compel full payment, it can be considered more realistic to "consolidate" the financial statements. In a consolidated statement, the parent and subsidiary are looked upon as one big company, with the subsidiary being treated as a division of the parent. All sales, expenses, assets, and liabilities are added together, except that transac-

tions between the parent and subsidiary are netted out. If a minority ownership in the subsidiary is held by other parties, the minority percentage of the subsidiary's net income is deducted in computing the consolidated net income, and the "Other Liabilities" section of the consolidated balance sheet shows the "Minority Interest" in the subsidiary's net worth.

Most parent companies report on a consolidated basis, but for various reasons one or more subsidiaries may not be consolidated. Where this was the case in the past, the practice was to use the same accounting treatment as for affiliates. That is, the balance sheet showed the cost of the "Investment in Nonconsolidated Subsidiaries" as an asset, and the income statement showed dividends received. However, footnotes were added to the financial statements showing "equity in undistributed earnings" and "equity in net worth" of the nonconsolidated subsidiaries. These footnotes permitted analysts to calculate the net income and net worth which would have been shown in fully consolidated statements.

While footnote disclosure of equity in undistributed subsidiary earnings and net worth was better than no disclosure at all, the relegation to footnotes caused many investors (including many professional security analysts) to overlook these items in evaluating the securities of parent companies. This provided an opportunity for managements to abuse unconsolidated statements in several ways. First, they could utilize dividends from unconsolidated subsidiaries as a device for smoothing earnings artificially—transferring larger amounts of dividends from subsidiary to parent when the parent's own earnings were depressed, and transferring smaller amounts when the parent's earnings were very high. Second, they could create the illusion of greater parent company profitability than would be shown in a consolidated statement by selling goods or services to the subsidiary at inflated prices. In a consolidated statement, of course, the excessive profits of the parent would be offset by abnormally high costs of the subsidiary, so there would be no incentive for such maneuvers. Finally, they could obscure losing operations by keeping them in unconsolidated subsidiary form, thus submerging the losses in footnotes.

A further complication was presented by the convention of distinguishing between subsidiary and affiliate status on the basis of a majority ownership level. For it is quite possible for one corporation to own considerably less than 50 percent of the stock of another corporation yet to "control" it just as effectively as if majority ownership were held.

In an effort to overcome these difficulties, the Accounting Principles Board ruled in 1971 that henceforth the operations of all unconsolidated subsidiaries, all joint ventures, and all 20 percent or more owned

affiliates, were to be reflected by the so-called equity method.[26] Under this method, a company's equity in the total net income of such interests is shown as a single-line entry in the body of the income statement, and the balance sheet "Investment" item is carried at cost *plus equity in the earnings or losses* of the investees since the ownership interests were acquired. In other words, the method is designed to produce the net income level and to approximate the net worth level that would be shown in statements which consolidated all substantial equity interests, even though the individual sales, expense, asset, and liability items are not themselves consolidated.[27]

While this rule represented an improvement in that it removed a large discretionary element from financial statements, it clearly introduced a discontinuity into trend analysis of these statements. In addition, there are a number of limitations of consolidated financial statements—or their approximation via equity accounting—of which analysts should be aware. The most significant limitations are as follows:

1.   The financial statements of the individual companies of the consolidated group may not be prepared on a comparable accounting basis. For example, the year-end dates of the individual members of the group may vary by as much as 90 days. Thus, consolidation often represents an "adding of apples and oranges."

2.   By consolidating all members of a group in a single statement, the analyst is unable to determine whether some of the components are operating at losses and in poor financial condition, while others are profitable and sound.[28]

3.   It is quite important, *especially in analyzing the credit status of the parent,* to know what the assets and liabilities of the individual subsidiaries are. Creditors of a subsidiary have a claim against *its* earnings and assets which is superior to the claim of the creditors of the parent. The latter can look only to the *residual* earning power and assets of the subsidiary; in other words, to the value of the parent's stock ownership in the subsidiary. And this value, of course, could be wiped out by the claims of the subsidiary's creditors. Yet analysts

---

[26] Certain exceptions were permitted, however. For example, if there is doubt about the ability to repatriate earnings from a foreign land, or if the holder of the equity interest contemplates selling it, or if the holder of the interest cannot exercise a "significant influence" over the policies of the company in which it has the interest, the equity method need not be used.

[27] If an affiliate's stock is publicly traded, the market value of the parent's interests should be shown in a footnote.

[28] Moreover, management has discretion in making current provision for taxes that would have to be paid in the future if the profitable subsidiaries or affiliates distribute their earnings to the parent in the form of dividends. The issue turns on management's judgment as to whether these earnings are to be permanently retained in the subsidiary or affiliate.

confronted with consolidated financial statements only know the aggregate assets and liabilities of the entire group. They cannot determine where the assets are lodged, the extent to which different sets of creditors have claims against different sets of assets, or, as noted above, the earning power of each component company.[29]

The only way to retain the benefits of the concept of consolidation, while avoiding these significant limitations, is to obtain *consolidating* statements. These present, in columnar form, the individual income statements and balance sheets of the component companies, followed by a column showing the intercompany netting items, and concluding with a column representing the consolidated amounts. Unfortunately, consolidating statements are rarely made available to the investment community.[30]

Intangibles (Accounting for Mergers). The problem of accounting for mergers has been at the heart of a bitter controversy among accountants and corporate financial executives. Some background on this controversy should be helpful to an understanding of the current status of the subject.

The two principal methods of accounting for mergers are "purchase of assets" and "pooling of interests." The purchase method always is used when the acquiring company (which will be referred to as "A") pays *cash* to the owners of the acquired company ("B"). If the amount of cash paid by A exceeds the book value of the net assets acquired from B, as is often the case, the excess may be handled in two ways. It may be set up as an intangible asset labeled "goodwill,"[31] or it may be added to the book value of the physical assets, plant and equipment. Either way, it should subsequently be charged against earnings, gradually over a period of years—i.e., as amortization of goodwill or depreciation of plant and equipment. (These generally would not be *tax deductible* expenses, however.[32])

Although many mergers are accomplished via cash payments, a

---

[29] Similarly, to the creditors of subsidiaries, a consolidated statement is not relevant. Because of the limited liability of corporations, each subsidiary of a group under common control is legally responsible only for its own liabilities. Unless there are cross-guarantees, creditors of any one subsidiary have no recourse to the assets or earning power of the parent or the sister corporations.

[30] Nonpublic investors—e.g., commercial bank lenders and private placement lenders—usually insist on receiving consolidating statements as a condition of their investments.

[31] Recently, the label "cost in excess of book value" has been used instead of "goodwill."

[32] The higher depreciation might be tax deductible if an independent appraiser verified the higher asset value. If the purchase price is *below* the book value of the acquired assets, the assets are written *down* and depreciation is *reduced*. The potential for higher reported earnings through reduced depreciation may be a motive in recent takeovers of companies whose stock is selling well below book value. See "Gimmick for All Seasons," *Forbes*, October 1, 1975, p. 60.

more common practice is for A to exchange an agreed upon number of its common shares for the shares of B. Until fairly recently, managements had considerable leeway to decide whether to account for such exchanges of shares as purchases or as poolings. If purchase accounting was chosen, the entries would be analogous to those described above, except that it would be the market value of the shares given up by A which would determine whether any goodwill or asset revaluation was needed—along with the consequent future charges against earnings. But if the pooling method was chosen, a quite different result would be obtained.

Under pooling of interests, the existing book values of the assets of the merging companies are added together and the liabilities are added together. The difference between the new asset total and the new liability total is the new "equity" of the merged enterprise. Thus, if A gave up more "value" than it received from B, the excess would be charged, in effect, in one fell swoop *against equity in the balance sheet* and never would show up as a charge *against earnings in the income statement*. There are two other important differences between purchase and pooling accounting. First, under pooling, the earnings of the acquired company are included for the full year, even if the acquisition took place late in the year, whereas under purchase accounting, earnings are included only from the date of acquisition. Second, under pooling, but not under purchasing, the earnings of prior years are restated on a pro forma basis—that is, to show what the earnings would have been if the merger had been in effect during those earlier years.[33]

Critics of pooling raised the following major objections:

1. It permits "excessive" payments for acquisitions to be submerged in the balance sheet rather than exposed to all investors via charges against earnings.

2. It permits slow growth companies to acquire rapid growth companies and, by restating historical earnings, to create an "artificial appearance of growth." Indeed, some acquisitive companies might (and did) treat slow growth acquisitions as purchases and rapid growth acquisitions as poolings.

3. It permits acquiring companies to "manufacture" future profits almost at will by selling off some of the acquired assets at prices in excess of book value.

Defenders of pooling offered the following major rebuttals:

1. If, indeed, A pays "too much" for B, its error will be reflected in a subsequent slowdown of the growth rate of its earnings per share.

---

[33] It should be noted, however, that good purchase accounting procedures call for *footnotes* showing results on a pro forma basis from the beginning of the year and for the immediately preceding year.

Investors, after all, are not concerned so much with aggregate dollars of earnings as with earnings per share of stock outstanding. If A gives up "too many" shares to acquire B, its future per share earnings growth will be diluted rather than enhanced.

2. The pro forma restatement of historical earnings is quite relevant to the analysts who are trying to appraise the value of the present shares of the merged enterprise. If they were trying to understand the historical pricing of A's shares in the marketplace, the restated earnings would not be a good guide. In the past, A's shares were priced on the basis of A's earnings and not on the basis of the earnings of A plus B. But now that the merger has taken place, it is quite appropriate for the analysts to want to know what the past record would have been had the merger always been in effect.

3. Any "manufactured" profits would be separately identified and investors would be on notice to evaluate them accordingly.

4. If purchase accounting results in the upward revaluation of assets of firms which happen to merge, what about the assets of firms in the same industry which do not happen to merge? Comparability among firms is diminished.

5. Although "goodwill" is supposed to be amortized under purchase accounting, many firms have failed to carry out this requirement, so that the end result may be the same as under pooling.

These critiques and rebuttals were not mere academic argument. Indeed, some critics urged total abolition of pooling and some defenders came near to urging abolition of purchase accounting, even where cash was the merger vehicle. Finally, a compromise was reached, the critical elements of which were as follows:

1. *All* business combinations having certain characteristics *must* be treated as poolings. The major characteristics are: (a) the combining companies have been completely autonomous during the past two years, with no intercorporate stockholding in excess of 10 percent *and* (b) the combination occurs through exchange of at least 90 percent of the acquired company's stock for stock of the acquiring company, with resulting stockholders all having the same rights and with no contingent payments called for.

2. Any combination not a pooling, as thus specified, *must* be treated as a purchase, with goodwill to be amortized in *no more than 40 years*.

Despite this accounting ruling, goodwill remains a controversial subject, especially among security analysts. Many analysts will assign a value of zero to goodwill (as well as to all other "intangibles" and deferred charges) in appraising a company's financial structure. At the other end of the spectrum, goodwill may not only be taken into account at its balance sheet value, but a strong effort may be made to deter-

mine if its true current market value is substantially higher. That is, just as the balance sheet values of plant and equipment may be totally unrepresentative of inflated current market values, so may this be true of the balance sheet values of intangibles.

Liabilities

Turning from the asset to the liability side of the balance sheet, several questions need to be explored. Among them are:

1. When is debt a "current" liability and when should it be considered a "long-term debt?"
2. Are deferred taxes debt, or equity, or neither?
3. Does the balance sheet reflect all of a firm's liabilities?

Current versus Long-Term Debt. When a company issues bonds or notes having a maturity in excess of one year, there is generally no question that the obligation would be considered a long-term debt, with any amortization of principal required within one year considered a current liability. However, it has become quite common for companies to enter into so-called revolving credit agreements with commercial banks. Under such an arrangement, a company is given a line of credit for, say, three or four years, which may be drawn down in whole or part at any time at the company's option. Each draw-down is repayable in installments over the life of the agreement. But the company may repay in advance at any time without penalty, and may borrow again and again *at its option* for the life of the agreement. Moreover, the company may have an option to convert the line into a true long-term loan. Under current accounting rules, considerable leeway is permitted in the treatment of such borrowing as either current or long term. As will be seen in a later chapter dealing with bond analysis, the treatment which is chosen can have a significant impact on credit evaluation.

Deferred Taxes. It was noted earlier that a company may report lower earnings to the Internal Revenue Service than to its stockholders, and that when this occurs the company is required to set up a deferred tax liability in its balance sheet (and to charge this amount against stockholder-reported earnings). But it was also noted that these deferred taxes may never, in fact, have to be paid, or may be payable so far in the future that their "present value" is negligible. As a result of this ambiguity, there may be times when the deferred tax amount on the balance sheet should be considered as true long-term debt; there may be times when it should be considered simply as an "other" liability; and there may be times when its payment is so unlikely that it really should be added to stockholders' equity.

"Off-Balance Sheet" Liabilities.   One of the most difficult tasks of balance sheet analysis is to determine the nature and extent of liabilities which are not shown on the face of the balance sheet. Probably the most significant of these obligations is the long-term lease. The FASB has written:

Leasing as a means of acquiring the right to use property has proliferated markedly throughout the post-war period. However, it was the decade of the 1960's that saw the greatest expansion, not only in the volume of leasing transactions, but also in the variety of application and degree of sophistication of the techniques employed. . . . Accounting for leases is a subject which has been thoroughly studied over a long period of time and on which numerous pronouncements have been made. . . . Still, inconsistencies remain in the accounting practices for leases, and the polarization of views as to what should be done about it has not abated.[34]

The controversy revolves around several major issues, including:

1.   Is a long-term lease, in general, analogous to other long-term debt?
2.   Are some kinds of leases more analogous to long-term debt than others?
3.   If leases are analogous to debt, what mathematical procedures should be used to determine what the debt equivalent of a lease is?
4.   When debt equivalents are determined, should they be shown in the body of the balance sheet or in footnotes? And how should they be reflected in income statements?

Those who answer question (1) affirmatively argue that long-term leases, just like ordinary long-term debt, create an obligation for future payments which cannot be canceled, a default on which may result in bankruptcy or the loss of essential operating properties. The opposing argument is that in actual bankruptcy cases, the courts have limited the lessee's liability to, at most, a few years' rental payments.

As for question (2), some leases provide for a rental amount which returns to the lessor the full amount invested after only a few years, followed by a sharply reduced rental amount thereafter or an option which enables the lessee to take title to the property for a relatively low price. Other leases provide for a much more even stream of rental payments over a longer period of time, with no option to buy. And there are hybrids in between. Some analysts argue that the former type of lease is really a disguised debt-financed purchase and, therefore, should be treated as debt. Others acknowledge the difference in form but ask, "so what?"

---

[34] Financial Accounting Standards Board, "An Analysis of Issues Related to Accounting for Leases" (discussion memorandum dated July 2, 1974), pp. 1–2.

The method of determining the debt equivalent amount of a lease is fairly simple in concept but not in practice. One should determine: (a) the portion of the rental payments which represents interest and amortization *on the debt which the lessor undertook* (in fact or on an imputed basis) to acquire the property; and (b) the interest rate *which the lessee would have had to pay* had he chosen to borrow and buy the property himself. The debt equivalent is the present value of the amounts determined in (a), discounted at the rate determined in (b).

While the mathematical concepts underlying these procedures, known as "capitalizing lease payments," are clear, the problem is that the determination of (a) and (b) is easier said than done. Only the lessor really knows what portion of the rent he is charging represents interest and amortization, and what portion represents his profit and any expenses he undertakes to service the property.[35] Perhaps the lessee and his auditors also know, but unless they reveal it in footnotes to the lessee's financial statements, the investment analyst surely does not know. As for the hypothetical interest rate which the lessee would have had to pay had he borrowed and bought, rather than leased, the property, this surely is a judgment subject to a wide variety of answers.[36]

Finally, even if agreement could be reached on how to determine debt equivalents, it has been difficult for the accounting profession to decide whether these amounts should be shown in footnotes or directly on the liability side of the balance sheet, together with an offsetting fixed asset representing the value of the property acquired with the debt equivalent issue. If the latter method is chosen, moreover, the income statement would need to be recast. Instead of rental expense, there would have to be shown the debt equivalent interest expense plus a depreciation expense representing the writeoff of the asset.

The SEC and the FASB have clearly been leaning in the direction of showing in the body of the balance sheet the *auditor's estimate* of the capitalized value of leases which have the characteristics of purchases.[37] But while this approach may solve the controversy in the sense of setting up a few rules, it will not eliminate the many subjective, and arbitrary, judgments outlined above.

There are many other types of "off-balance sheet" liabilities which

---

[35] Under a so-called gross lease, his obligation to keep the property in good condition is extensive. Under a "net lease," this becomes the lessee's responsibility.

[36] Absent good answers to these problems, various rule-of-thumb procedures have been devised. For one such rule of thumb, see the revised edition of this text (1973), p. 388.

[37] See "Exposure Draft (Revised)" of the Financial Accounting Standards Board, *Accounting for Leases*, July 22, 1976.

pose analytical problems almost as complex as long-term leases. Space constraints dictate only a brief enumeration of some of them:

1. It is fairly common for a large corporation to guarantee payment of the debt of one or more of its smaller (nonconsolidated) affiliates or of supplier companies, because the latter may have difficulty raising debt capital without the guarantee. Outright guarantees usually are reported in footnotes to the balance sheet. Questions which arise are: Should analysts consider these guarantees to be debt equivalents? If yes, should the debt equivalent be the full amount of the guarantees or an amount reduced in proportion to the probability that the guarantor will never have to make good on the guarantees because the debtors will pay their debts as they come due?

2. While outright guarantees are supposed to be footnoted, there are many disguised guarantees which may be hidden. Typical are so-called take-or-pay contracts whereby a company agrees to purchase the output of a supplier at a price sufficient to service the supplier's debts. Such contracts may require payments to be made even when the supplier is unable to produce the output contracted for. Also common are "working capital maintenance" agreements, whereby a corporation agrees to put sufficient funds into another corporation such that the latter's working capital never falls below a specified amount. The potential liability under such an agreement can be open-ended, yet not show up in the balance sheet. Mention should also be made of companies which "factor" their receivables (i.e., sell the receivables at a discount), giving the factor "recourse" (i.e., the right to demand payment from the seller of the receivables) if the receivables turn bad.

3. Where subsidiary corporations are consolidated, any debts which they have are included in the consolidated liabilities, even though they are not separately identified. This lack of separate identification is bad enough, but consider the case where subsidiaries or affiliates are accounted for by the equity method, discussed earlier. Here, the owner's equity in the net worth of the subsidiary or affiliate appears as an asset. Nowhere is there a public record of whether the net worth is net of a small amount of liabilities or of a huge amount. If the subsidiary's liabilities are very large, it may be quite unrealistic to view its residual net worth as a meaningful asset of the owner.

4. Preferred stock is shown on the balance sheet at par value—e.g., $100 per share. In some cases, however, the par value is nominal (e.g., $1) but the *liquidating value* in the event of corporate dissolution is much higher. In such cases, the net worth of the issuer is much lower than is readily apparent.

The many problems involved in understanding both income statements and balance sheets have caused analysts to turn their attention
increasingly to a financial statement commonly referred to as "sources
and uses of funds," or "funds flow." More technically, it is known as
the "Statement of Changes in Financial Position."

Cash versus Accrual Accounting

To the unsophisticated observer who has not studied accounting,
net income represents the difference between what a business "takes
in" during a period and what it "pays out." If it takes in more than it
pays out, it has "earned a profit"; if it pays out more than it takes in, it
has "suffered a loss." Most individuals think of their own personal
transactions in these terms, and many businesses and nonbusiness organizations, in fact, keep their books on this basis, known as
"cash accounting." Net income for a period is equal to the increase
in the cash balance for that period; net loss is equal to the cash
reduction.

Most modern accounting is done on an accrual basis, rather than a
cash basis. Accrual accounting seeks to match the recording of expenses and income on a basis which represents the economic process
rather than the timing of receipts and disbursements of cash. Thus, for
example, a current outlay of cash for machinery is reflected by the
recording of an asset on the balance sheet rather than a current charge
against income, and the charge is recorded gradually over the future
useful life of the machinery. On the other hand, pension costs are
charged against current income (and recorded as liabilities on the
balance sheet) even though the actual cash outlays to pay pension
benefits will not occur until many years in the future.

While accrual accounting surely makes more economic sense than
cash accounting, it permits positive net income to be recorded year
after year in the face of a progressive depletion of liquid resources
which ultimately may result in bankruptcy. The sources and uses of
funds statement focuses on changes in liquid resources. It is, in many respects, wider in scope than either the income statement or the balance
sheet and, indeed, integrates the two statements, as will be shown.

Noncash Income.   There are a number of items which are recorded
as revenue or other income on the income statement, but which do not
necessarily generate cash. For example, when a company sells goods
or services it credits income. But its customers may not pay all the bills
during the accounting period. As a result, accounts receivable rise,
rather than cash, to the extent of the uncollected income. As another
illustration, the equity method of accounting records the total proportionate ownership of nonconsolidated subsidiary or affiliate earnings

as income of the parent; but if these earnings were not distributed as dividends, they do not generate cash for the parent.

Noncash Expenses. As has been noted earlier, depreciation is a charge against income which does not represent a current cash outlay, but rather represents a gradual apportionment of an earlier lump-sum cash outlay for the purchase of capital assets. Amortization and depletion are similar noncash charges. Likewise, a deferred tax charge against income reflects income tax which may have to be paid at a future date, but does not reflect a current cash outlay. The same is true of any other "reserves" which may be established by charges against current income. Finally, cost of goods sold and other operating expenses may be accompanied by a build-up of accounts payable. To that extent, these costs are not cash outlays. Note that this is the opposite of the case where sales do not reflect *cash income* to the extent of a buildup of *accounts receivable*.

Cash Items Not Recorded in Income Statement. While many income statement items do not reflect cash inflow or cash outgo, many receipts or outlays of cash do not appear in the income statement. Among the cash receipts not recorded as income are: proceeds from new debt or stock issues; proceeds from the sale of capital assets (only the net gain or loss over book value is recorded in the income statement); and payments received from customers in advance of delivery (e.g., when a fire insurance company receives a premium covering the next three years; generally, only one third of the premium is recorded as income and two thirds is recorded on the balance sheet as a deferred credit). Among the cash outlays not recorded as expenses are: capital expenditures; stockpiling of inventory; repayment of debt or repurchase of stock; dividends paid on stock; and items referred to earlier as "intermediate-term expenses" which may be "capitalized" and gradually amortized rather than expensed as incurred (examples of such deferred charges, cited earlier, were tool and die expenses of an auto company and outlays of oil drilling companies).

Sources and Uses Format. It should be clear from these illustrations that a company's flow of cash is very difficult to trace from its published income statements and balance sheets. There is a complex interaction whereby some transactions involving cash (e.g., purchase of materials) appear in part in the income statement (cost of goods sold) and in part in the balance sheet (cash and accounts payable). Other cash transactions (e.g., capital expenditures) appear entirely in the balance sheet (debit assets, credit cash); while still others are reflected in the balance sheet but are not shown as specific line entries (e.g., when a dividend is paid on common stock, earned surplus grows only by the amount of *retained* earnings; this is not shown directly in the balance sheet, but rather in a supplementary schedule known

as "Reconciliation of Surplus"). Because the cash flow network is so varied and complex, there is no uniform format used by accountants to present it. However, three basic types of format can be discerned.[38]

· The first type of format might be called "Reconciliation of Cash." Here, the effort is to show how the cash balance at the start of the period changed to the cash balance at the end of the period. For example:

	Starting Cash Balance		$ 2,000,000
Plus:	Reported Net Income	$10,000,000	
	Noncash Charges (depreciation, deferred taxes, etc.)	2,000,000	12,000,000
Plus:	Increase in Accounts Payable	1,000,000	
Less:	Increase in Accounts Receivable	750,000	250,000
Less:	Capital Expenditures	5,000,000	
	Inventory Accumulation	1,000,000	
	Common Stock Dividends	5,000,000	(11,000,000)
Equals:	Ending Cash Balance		$ 3,250,000

The second type of format might be referred to as "Reconciliation of Working Capital." Here, the focus is on changes in total working capital (current assets minus current liabilities) and in the components of working capital. For example:

	Reported Net Income		$10,000,000
Plus:	Noncash Charges (components would be shown)		2,000,000
Equals:	Working Capital Provided by Operations		$12,000,000
Less:	Capital Expenditures	$5,000,000	
	Common Stock Dividends..............	5,000,000	(10,000,000)
Equals:	Increase in Working Capital		$ 2,000,000
	Consisting of: Increase in Cash	$1,250,000	
	Increase in Inventory	1,000,000	
	Increase in Accounts Receivable	750,000	
	Increase in Accounts Payable	(1,000,000)	
		$2,000,000	

The third type of format is less common but, from the viewpoint of the investment analyst, probably most meaningful. It might be called "Reconciliation of Cash Available for Growth and Providers of Capi-

[38] In considering these formats, it is helpful to bear in mind with regard to balance sheet items that decreases in noncash assets and increases in liabilities generally represent cash inflows, while increases in noncash assets and decreases in liabilities represent cash outflows.

tal." It focuses on the generation of funds available for dividends, capital expenditures, and debt reduction. For example:

	Reported net income	$10,000,000
Plus:	Noncash charges (components would be shown)	2,000,000
Less:	Increase in working capital (components would be shown)	(2,000,000)
Equals:	Cash Available for Growth and Providers of Capital....	$10,000,000

Used for:	Capital expenditures	$ 5,000,000
	Common stock dividends	5,000,000
		$10,000,000

Whichever of these formats is chosen, it is certain that analysts who pays attention to the Statement of Changes in Financial Position will have a far deeper understanding of a company's operations than if they focus only on the Income Statement and Balance Sheet. Indeed, the best way to be sure you really understand a company's financial statements is to:

1. Be sure you can trace through the integration of Income Statement and Balance Sheet through the Statement of Changes in Financial Position.
2. Be sure you read and understand all of the footnotes to the various statements.
3. Be sure you review the auditor's opinion and are alert for unusual wording, unusual length, and references to changes in accounting policies.

SUGGESTED READINGS

Alexander, Michael O. *Accounting for Inflation: A Challenge for Business*. Toronto: Maclean-Hunter, Ltd., 1975.

APB Accounting Principles. Rev. ed., two vols. Chicago: Commerce Clearing House, Inc.

Bernstein, Leopold A. *Financial Statement Analysis: Theory, Application, and Interpretation*. Homewood, Ill.: Richard D. Irwin, Inc., 1974.

Briloff, Abraham J. *Unaccountable Accounting*. New York: Harper & Row, Publishers, 1972.

―――. *More Debits Than Credits*. New York: Harper & Row, Publishers, 1976.

Burton, John C. (ed.) *Corporate Financial Reporting: Ethical and Other Problems*. New York: Financial Analysts Federation, 1972.

Copeland, Ronald M., and Dascher, Paul E. *Managerial Accounting*. New York: John Wiley & Sons, Inc., 1974.

Davidson, Sidney; Stickney, Clyde P.; and Weil, Roman L. *Inflation Accounting*. New York: McGraw-Hill, Inc., 1976.

Dearden, John, and Shank, John. *Financial Accounting and Reporting: A Contemporary Emphasis*. Englewood Cliffs, N.J.: Prentice-Hall, Inc., 1975.

Hawkins, David F. *Financial Reporting Practices of Corporations*. Homewood, Ill.: Dow Jones-Irwin, Inc., 1972.

Kripke, Homer. "A Search for a Meaningful Securities Disclosure Policy." *The Business Lawyer*, November 1975.

Lev, Baruch. *Financial Statement Analysis: A New Approach*. Englewood Cliffs, N.J.: Prentice-Hall, Inc., 1974.

Mauriello, Joseph A. "Effect of Taxes on Earnings and Earnings Estimates," *Financial Analyst's Handbook*, vol. I. Homewood, Ill.: Dow Jones-Irwin, Inc., 1975, chap. 23.

Norr, David A. *Accounting Theory Illustrated*. A series of booklets published in 1975 by First Manhattan Company, a New York brokerage firm.

O'Malia, Thomas J. *Bankers' Guide to Financial Statements*. Boston: Bankers' Publishing Co., 1976.

Symonds, Curtis W. *Profit Dollars and Earnings Sense*. New York: American Management Association, 1975.

REVIEW QUESTIONS AND PROBLEMS

1. In what ways can inflation distort the interpretation of financial statements? What remedies have been proposed?

2. Illustrate the impact of Lifo versus Fifo inventory accounting during a period of *falling* commodity prices.

3. What are the advantages and disadvantages of the "cash flow" concept in financial statement analysis?

4. What are some problems of implementing the principle that revenue should be recognized only when it is "captured, measurable, and earned?"

5. What problems are created for security analysts by corporate tax laws and regulations, and by changes in these?

6. What problems of financial statement analysis are created by pension plans?

7. What arguments can be offered in favor of or against capitalizing versus expensing various corporate outlays?

8. What analytical problems may the existence of subsidiaries and affiliates give rise to?

9. Discuss the pros and cons of pooling of interests versus purchase accounting.

10. Describe the various types of off-balance sheet liabilities for which the analyst should be alert.

RESEARCH PROJECTS

1. Assume that you are the research director of the Financial Accounting Standards Board. Prepare a review of unresolved issues which deserve the board's attention, with an indication of the priority you would assign for considering these issues. Select two of the issues and prepare a paper on the alternatives available to the board.

2. Compare and contrast the methods of recording revenues and expenses for one of the following pairs of companies:
   a. IBM versus Control Data
   b. General Electric versus Westinghouse
   c. Textron versus Gulf & Western

3. Pick a company which has long had extensive foreign operations and trace the history of that company's accounting treatment of these operations.

4. From data in Annual Reports, 10–Ks, and so on, determine the wage and fringe benefits bill, as a percentage of sales, for the leading three companies in any industry of your choice.

5. Find five annual reports in which the auditors gave "qualified opinions." Discuss the circumstances which gave rise to the qualifications, and suggest how the companies might have changed their policies to obtain "clean opinions."

C.F.A. QUESTIONS

1. *From Exam III, 1976*

FASB Statement No. 8, Accounting for the Translation of Foreign Currency Transactions and Foreign Currency Financial Statements, effective January 1, 1976, requires multinational companies to adopt the so-called temporal method (similar to the former monetary/non-monetary method) for purposes of translating foreign assets and liabilities, and it also imposes rules on the reporting of gains and losses from such translation.

Explain briefly how this new rule is likely to affect the volatility of profits and losses of multinational companies.

2. *From Exam III, 1974*

Early in 1974 the following comments appeared in a bulletin sent to clients of a prominent investment firm:

> Some companies have found it difficult to show profit improvements in 1973. It can be anticipated that many more companies will find it increasingly harder to maintain profits in 1974, let alone show growth. Another expectation is that if a company had trouble improving or maintaining its position in its operating and financial fundamentals in 1973, it will have an even harder time in these areas during 1974. A third proposition is that it is going to be difficult to detect from 1973 financial reports whether or not a company's fundamentals are deteriorating since there

are many accounting, operating, and financial gimmicks that managements can use in the short-run to hide the effect on profits of a deterioration in fundamentals.

Discuss briefly five different methods commonly used by some managements
to maintain earnings that may indicate operating problems or deterioration in
fundamentals.

3. *From Exam I, 1973*

Company A's common stock had a market value of $72.00 immediately
prior to the announcement of a merger with Company B. There were 6,100,000
shares outstanding and earnings just reported were $3.50 per share.

Company B had 800,000 shares of common stock outstanding. Immediately
prior to the merger announcement, its stock sold at 10 times most recent
earnings per share.

Company A acquired Company B on a pooling of interests basis with Company A being the surviving corporation. Company A exchanges one share of its
stock for three shares of B's stock. The exchange ratio was determined solely
on the basis of the market prices of the two stocks immediately prior to the
merger announcement.

a. Calculate the per share earnings of Company A after the merger.
b. Based on your calculation in (a) for Company A, explain why post-merger
    EPS for Company A differs from its pre-merger EPS.

Chapter 5

Evaluation of Common Stocks: A Framework

> The greatest of all gifts is the power to estimate things at
> their true worth.
> —————————————— *La Rochefoucauld*

The object of common stock evaluation is to obtain standards against which prevailing prices of stocks may be judged. It is assumed that investors as a whole are essentially rational over the long run (although their actions occasionally seem to border on the insane), and that rational individuals attempt to measure the economic, or "going-concern" values of the corporations whose stocks they buy and sell. Since there are millions of investors, there will exist vastly different ideas about the value of any given stock at any given time, and purchases and sales of the stock will be made in accordance with this multitude of ideas. Therefore, over an extended period of time, prices will fluctuate in a wide range, *but they will tend to fluctuate around some concensus of value.*

The Rationale

The normal tendency of the marketplace, it is assumed, is to drive prices to extremes. When optimism is dominant, conceptions of value are liberalized, and prices rise steadily. Ultimately, it is recognized that the optimism was excessive, and prices react downward. As prices fall, caution turns to fear, and the price decline snowballs until it is finally recognized that the pessimism was overdone. At this point a price reversal occurs once again. Successful evaluators of common stocks, therefore, will try to avoid becoming overly optimistic or overly pessimistic. They will attempt to determine the approximate level around which the price tides will swell and ebb.

227

The evaluation process can be described graphically, as follows:

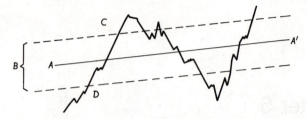

Where: *AA'* is an objectively determined value line; *B* is a range allowed for errors which may have been made in the determination of *AA'*; *C* represents an area where prices would be considered too dear; and *D* represents an area where prices would be considered bargains. With regard to *AA'*, we do not mean to imply that an evaluation must necessarily cover an extended span of time. The analyst may be content to make an estimate of any *point* on the line, near or distant.

The Sources of Common Stock Value

Readers who ponder the problem for a while will realize that a common stock has value for only three possible reasons. First, the ownership of common stock confers a claim to a corporation's net income. This claim bears fruit when the corporation's board of directors declares dividends. Second, if the corporation enjoys growing success, earnings and dividends will rise, and the price of its stock may rise also. The third, and least significant, source of common stock value is that if a corporation is liquidated, the common stock owner has a pro rata claim to any asset value that may remain after all creditors and preferred stockholders have been paid. This claim, therefore, may give the common stock some value. But it is not a very important source of value as a rule, because an efficiently operating corporation is not usually liquidated. And if it is liquidated because it is not operating efficiently, the asset value is not likely to be high enough to leave much of a residual for the stockholders.[1]

---

[1] Nevertheless, asset values can, in some cases, be of significance. A corporation may have *net current assets* per share (cash, receivables, and inventories minus all liabilities and preferred stock, divided by number of common shares) in excess of the market price of its stock. It will thus be "worth more dead than alive," for which reason another corporation or syndicate of investors may be willing to pay a sizable premium over the current market price of the shares in order to acquire control.

In addition to this "special situation" (see Chapter 11) reason why asset values may influence stock values, some corporations have as their principal earning asset money or other liquid resources. For such corporations—banks, insurance companies, investment companies, and so on—stock prices are frequently closely geared to asset values. In actuality, however, to say that the prices are geared to asset values is a bit of a semantic trick. What we are really saying is that the assets provide the basis for *earnings*, and in fact it is earning power which causes assets to have a value that can be transmitted to stock prices.

The juxtaposition above of earnings and dividends in the context of common stock value gives rise to an interesting question on both a practical and a philosophical plane. Often the argument will be heard that dividends are distinctly subordinate to earnings as a determinant of stock values. The evidence offered in support of this argument is the activity of thousands, perhaps millions, of investors whose dominant objective in buying common stock is to sell it to someone else at a higher price rather than to collect dividends.

It is, of course, true that many individual stockholders do not intend to hold their stocks for dividends, hoping instead to sell the stocks to others at capital gains. But to conclude from this observation that "dividends don't count" would be quite mistaken. In the first place, it is a frequent occurrence for the price of a stock to change substantially when a dividend increase or dividend reduction is announced. One likely explanation for this is that since reported earnings do not necessarily represent "true" earnings (see Chapter 4), investors look to dividends for an indication of what management really thinks earnings are, or are going to be.[2]

On a more theoretical plane, the significance of dividends has sometimes been illustrated by hypothesizing the existence of a corporation which has written into its bylaws a perpetual prohibition of dividend payments or of return of capital to stockholders via sale of assets or by any other means. With these bylaws, no rational investor should be willing to purchase the corporation's stock, no matter how high its earnings or how low the asking price. (We exclude from consideration purchasing the stock in order to become an operating officer and thus receive a salary, or purchasing the stock in the hope of changing the bylaws.) Of course, people sometimes become irrational or follow the "greater fool theory," whereby each buyer assumes that he or she will be able to sell at a higher price to a "greater fool." For example, in the tulip mania in Europe a few centuries ago, people bought and sold tulip bulbs at fantastic prices without the vaguest intention of actually planting the bulbs to get flowers.[3] But such bubbles must inevitably burst. Our hypothetical corporation's stock might trade for a while, but people must eventually recognize that they are buying and selling a mere piece of paper, without any *value* in the absence of an ability to

---

[2] See R. Richardson Pettit, "Dividend Announcements, Security Performance, and Capital Market Efficiency," *Journal of Finance,* December 1972. For data showing that, even over long time periods, stock prices may be more closely related to dividend growth than to earnings growth, see L. M. Wagley, "Questionable Performance Pattern Shows Investment Concept Errors," *Pensions & Investments,* December 8, 1975, pp. 23–24. A debate on the subject of the information content of dividends is contained in four articles in the January 1976 *Journal of Business.*

[3] For a fine account of this and other speculative manias, see Charles Mackay, *Extraordinary Popular Delusions and The Madness of Crowds.* Originally published in 1841; reprinted by Investors Library, Inc., Palisades Park, N.J.

pay dividends or liquidate.[4] Thus, while much of a stock's value to an investor undoubtedly lies in the prospect of price appreciation, prices cannot be divorced from dividend prospects any more than they can be divorced from prospective earning power.

The Concept of Present Value of Future Dividends

Those who recognize the significance of dividends as a determinant of stock values can understand the reasoning behind a widely accepted tenet of investment theory. The tenet is that a common stock is "worth" the *present value* of all future dividends.

The concept of present value is really quite simple and can be prosaically illustrated. Assume that Mr. A wants to borrow money from Mr. B, repayable at a future date. Mr. B is willing to make the loan, but feels that, considering the risks involved, he is entitled to a 10 percent annual rate of return. This being the case, how much money will B advance to A on A's IOU for $10 payable one year hence? The answer is $9.09, because the $10 paid next year provides 91 cents interest, which is 10 percent of a $9.09 loan. Thus, $9.09 is the "present value" of $10 payable one year hence at a "discount rate" of 10 percent.

Likewise, if A offers a $10 IOU payable *two* years hence, how much will B be willing to lend? Answer: $8.26. Ten percent of $8.26 is 83 cents (first year's interest); $8.26 plus $0.83 = $9.09. Ten percent of $9.09 is 91 cents (second year's interest); $9.09 plus $0.91 = $10. The present value of $10 payable two years hence is $8.26 at a discount rate of 10 percent.[5]

It will be obvious to the reader that the concept of present value is the reverse of compounding.[6] Table 5–1A shows the *future* values

---

[4] Prior to the securities legislation of the 1930s, there was a good deal of outright *manipulation* of stock prices. Stocks often were, indeed, mere pieces of paper being bought and sold without regard to "intrinsic values." While it cannot be denied that manipulative practices still exist, particularly in the new issues market, such practices seem to be less prevalent than in earlier years.

[5] The generalized formula is:

$$P = V/(1 + i)^n$$

where:

P = Present value.
V = Terminal value being discounted.
i = Rate of discount.
n = Number of years being discounted.

Our illustration assumes the discount rate reflects interest which is compounded once a year. For more frequent compounding, the formula is:

$$P = V/[1 + (i/m)]^{mn},$$

where m = number of times per year compounding takes place (e.g., monthly, quarterly, semiannually).

[6] Where $V = P(1 + i)^n$, with the symbols having the same meaning as before.

TABLE 5-1

A. Compound Future Value of $1

Year	5%	6%	7%	8%	9%	10%	12%	15%
1	1.050	1.060	1.070	1.080	1.090	1.100	1.120	1.150
2	1.102	1.124	1.145	1.166	1.188	1.210	1.254	1.322
3	1.158	1.191	1.225	1.260	1.295	1.331	1.405	1.521
4	1.216	1.262	1.311	1.360	1.412	1.464	1.574	1.749
5	1.276	1.338	1.403	1.469	1.539	1.611	1.762	2.011
6	1.340	1.419	1.501	1.587	1.677	1.772	1.974	2.313
7	1.407	1.504	1.606	1.714	1.828	1.949	2.211	2.660
8	1.477	1.594	1.718	1.851	1.993	2.144	2.476	3.059
9	1.551	1.689	1.838	1.999	2.172	2.358	2.773	3.518
10	1.629	1.791	1.967	2.159	2.367	2.594	3.106	4.046
11	1.710	1.898	2.105	2.332	2.580	2.853	3.479	4.652
12	1.796	2.012	2.252	2.518	2.813	3.138	3.896	5.350
13	1.886	2.133	2.410	2.720	3.066	3.452	4.363	6.153
14	1.980	2.261	2.579	2.937	3.342	3.797	4.887	7.076
15	2.079	2.397	2.759	3.172	3.642	4.177	5.474	8.137
16	2.183	2.540	2.952	3.426	3.970	4.595	6.130	9.358
17	2.292	2.693	3.159	3.700	4.328	5.054	6.866	10.761
18	2.407	2.854	3.380	3.996	4.717	5.560	7.690	12.375
19	2.527	3.026	3.617	4.316	5.142	6.116	8.613	14.232
20	2.653	3.207	3.870	4.661	5.604	6.728	9.646	16.367
25	3.386	4.292	5.427	6.848	8.623	10.835	17.000	32.919
30	4.322	5.743	7.612	10.063	13.268	17.449	29.960	66.212

B. Present Value of $1

Year	5%	6%	7%	8%	9%	10%	12%	15%
1	.952	.943	.935	.926	.917	.909	.893	.870
2	.907	.890	.873	.857	.842	.826	.797	.756
3	.864	.840	.816	.794	.772	.751	.712	.658
4	.823	.792	.763	.735	.708	.683	.636	.572
5	.784	.747	.713	.681	.650	.621	.567	.497
6	.746	.705	.666	.630	.596	.564	.507	.432
7	.711	.665	.623	.583	.547	.513	.452	.376
8	.677	.627	.582	.540	.502	.467	.404	.327
9	.645	.592	.544	.500	.460	.424	.361	.284
10	.614	.558	.508	.463	.422	.386	.322	.247
11	.585	.527	.475	.429	.388	.350	.287	.215
12	.557	.497	.444	.397	.356	.319	.257	.187
13	.530	.469	.415	.368	.326	.290	.229	.163
14	.505	.442	.388	.340	.299	.263	.205	.141
15	.481	.417	.362	.315	.275	.239	.183	.123
16	.458	.394	.339	.292	.252	.218	.163	.107
17	.436	.371	.317	.270	.231	.198	.146	.093
18	.416	.350	.296	.250	.212	.180	.130	.081
19	.396	.331	.276	.232	.194	.164	.116	.070
20	.377	.312	.258	.215	.178	.149	.104	.061
25	.295	.233	.184	.146	.116	.092	.059	.030
30	.231	.174	.131	.099	.075	.057	.038	.015

of $1 *compounded* annually for 1 to 30 years at various interest rates from 5 percent to 15 percent; B shows the *present* values of $1 *payable* in 1 to 30 years, *discounted* at annual rates of 5 percent to 15 percent.[7] Most readers are well aware of the fact revealed by the A portion of Table 5–1; namely, that $1 grows to a very large sum when compounded at high rates for long time periods. They may be less aware, however, of the fact revealed by the B portion of the table; namely, that $1 payable in the distant future is worth a good deal today if discounted at fairly low rates, but is worth very little if discounted at higher rates. For example, $1 payable 30 years hence is worth 23 cents today at a 5 percent discount rate, but less than 6 cents at 10 percent.

Returning to the matter of future dividends on common stock, suppose we estimate that dividends on Standard & Poor's Stock Price Index will grow at a rate of 7 percent per annum far into the future. Suppose we estimate that "the market"—not any individual investor but all investors as a group—will always demand a 10 percent rate of return in order to undertake the risks of common stock investment. Recognizing that these assumptions are made purely for illustrative purposes, what is the value of the S&P Index today?

There is a simple formula for approximating the present value of perpetual dividend growth, at a constant discount rate. The formula is:[8]

$$\text{Present value} = \frac{\text{Current dividend rate}}{\text{Discount rate minus Growth rate}}$$

Under our illustrative assumptions, this works out as:

$$\frac{\text{Current dividend rate}}{0.10 \text{ minus } 0.07}$$

Thus, the formula and the illustrative assumptions tell us that the appropriate current dividend "yield" of the S&P Index is 3 percent. To derive the value of the Index, under these assumptions, we would divide the current dividend rate by 0.03. For example, early in March, 1976, the indicated dividend rate on the S&P Industrials Index was

---

[7] More detailed tables are available. For example, *Financial Compound Interest and Annuity Tables* (Boston: Financial Publishing Co.).

[8] The formula is a reduced form of the equation:

$$\text{Present value} = \frac{D}{(1+i)} + \frac{D(1+g)}{(1+i)^2} + \frac{D(1+g)^2}{(1+i)^3} + \cdots \cdot \frac{D(1+g)^{n-1}}{(1+i)^n}$$

Where:

D = Dividend paid at end of first period.
g = Growth rate of dividends.
i = Discount rate to be applied to dividend stream.

about 4.00. Dividing by 0.03 produces a "value" of about 133. Since the actual level of the Index was about 113 at the time, we can say that, under our illustrative growth and discount rate assumptions, which will be reconsidered and altered at a later point, stocks were priced too cheaply in relation to their "fair value."

But does this all mean that today's investors actually have to estimate dividend growth and discount rates to *perpetuity* in order to utilize the theoretical concept of present value of future dividends? Not really, because the proportion of the total value represented by distant years' dividends diminishes rapidly unless the discount rate is quite close to the growth rate. Under most reasonable discount and growth rate assumptions—e.g., where the discount rate is at least several percentage points higher than the growth rate—two thirds or more of the total "value" is accounted for by the first 30 years of dividends. (Note that if one assumes a growth rate equal to, or greater than, the discount rate, a nonsense "value" results.[9])

Of course, 30 years is by no means a short period for estimating either growth rates or discount rates. Indeed, most security analysts consider themselves fortunate if their growth rate estimates for the companies they follow hold good for five years.[10] On the other hand, while long-term estimates are highly uncertain for individual stocks, the potential errors are diminished when considering all stocks in aggregate, the subject to which we turn next.

ESTIMATING THE VALUE OF "THE MARKET"

Dividend Growth Prospects for Stocks in Aggregate

As economists, the authors have a proclivity to relate most economic variables to gross national product, which they feel can be forecast more accurately than most other variables. The question of aggregate dividend growth, therefore, is broken into three parts. First, what rate of GNP growth can be expected in the years ahead; second, will earnings per share of common stock keep pace with GNP; and third, will dividend growth keep pace with earnings growth? It should be emphasized at the outset that our main purpose is to provide a framework for thinking about these problems rather than to argue that our specific answers are correct.

---

[9] Using actual discounting, the present value would be infinite if the growth rate exceeded the discount rate. Using the short-cut formula, the divisor would be a negative number. Either way, the result is nonsensical.

[10] Even shorter term estimates have a high degree of error. See, for example, E. J. Elton and M. J. Gruber, "Earnings Estimates and the Accuracy of Expectational Data," *Management Science*, April 1972; also S. S. Stewart, Jr., "Corporate Forecasting," *Financial Analyst's Handbook*, vol. I (Homewood, Ill.: Dow Jones-Irwin, Inc., 1975), chap. 32.

GNP Growth. The growth of gross national product can be conveniently divided into four variables for analytical purposes: the growth of the employed labor force, the trend of average hours worked per week, the trend of output per hour worked ("productivity"), and the rate of change in the price level. By combining forecasts of the first three of these variables, a forecast of growth of so-called *real* GNP is derived—that is, growth of physical output of goods and services excluding the effects of price changes.

The three determinants of real GNP have had a stable enough history during the past century to enable us to make some long-term estimates with a fair degree of confidence. Without outlining their views in detail, it can be said that the estimates of most economists fall within the following ranges: approximately 1.5–2 percent per annum growth in the employed labor force; stability or up to a 0.5 percent per annum decline in hours worked per week; and 2–3 percent per annum growth of output per hour worked. These elements combine to produce a 3–5 percent range of real GNP growth possibilities, with about 3.5–4 percent being the most common forecast. To put this range in historical perspective, consider these past growth rates of real GNP: 1900–75: 3.25 percent; 1900–29: 3.75 percent; 1947–75: 3.75 percent.

To the 3.5–4 percent physical growth rate, we must add an allowance for inflation. Here the "experts" have developed a much wider range of views than with regard to real GNP. Two contrasting quotations will illustrate this diversity. The first[11] is typical of those who equate the rate of inflation with speedups and slowdowns in the nation's utilization of its physical and human resources, and who foresee a return to a relatively low rate of inflation because they expect significant underutilization of resources to be characteristic of the years ahead.

The major worldwide recession that is now ending has left more unemployed men and idle machines in the U.S. and in other countries than have been seen since the 1930's. This economic slack is unlikely to be dissipated any time soon. Businessmen and consumers throughout the industrialized world are likely to remain cautious and more concerned with rebuilding liquidity than with embarking on spending sprees. More important, massive governmental monetary and fiscal stimulus seems unlikely since voters now appear to want less government involvement in their economies than earlier, and seem more willing to accept higher unemployment as a trade-off for lower inflation.

History suggests that in this environment, inflation should not be a major problem in the years ahead, and a consumer price inflation rate of 2% to 3% in the U.S. seems likely. Other major industrial countries with greater commitments to maintaining full employment will probably have somewhat higher inflation rates, but still well below recent levels.

---

[11] *Economic Comment* (New York: White, Weld & Co., Inc., November 14, 1975), p. 1.

The second quotation[12] reflects a view that modern inflation is essentially different from historical inflation, having its roots in the changed sociopolitical environment known as the "welfare state." While the particular quotation cited here does not specify an inflation rate, most proponents of this view believe that the nation will be lucky if inflation can be held to a 5 percent rate, and believe that a 6–8 percent range is more likely.

Starting shortly after the middle Sixties, the United States (along with much of the rest of the world) has experienced an inexorable uptrend in prices. This new inflation does not appear to be fundamentally cyclical; rather, it looks like a new strain, highly resistant to conventional anti-inflationary policy, and flagrantly in violation of the theoretical explanations of price behavior that were part of the consensus of 1965. The inflation has proceeded with and without high unemployment, before and after devaluation, before, during and after a frantic experiment with direct controls. And it seems to draw in its wake a suspiciously persistent stream of inflationary accidents that augment the general rate of inflation and seem to imbed themselves irremovably in the price structure.

If we take these two statements as representative of the alternative future paths of inflation, the growth rate of "current dollar" GNP can be projected on the low side at about 6 percent (3 to 4 percent real growth plus 2 to 3 percent inflation), and on the high side at over 10 percent (3 to 4 percent real growth plus 7 percent or higher inflation).

Earnings per Share Relative to GNP.   Turning to the question whether earnings per share will keep pace with GNP, a look at the past is in order. Figure 5–1 shows the ratio of earnings on the Standard & Poor's Industrials to GNP for the post–World War II period. For comparison purposes, the average ratio for 1923–29 is also shown.[13] The chart indicates clearly that over the past several decades, earnings per share have *not* kept pace with GNP. There has been a steady deterioration of profit margins, by this and other measures, with earnings per share growing about 1.5 percent per annum *slower* than the growth rate of current dollar GNP. In our view, there are few persuasive reasons for believing that the historical erosion of profit margins will be reversed, particularly in view of the increasingly "politicized" economy which has evolved in recent years.

Dividends Relative to Earnings.   Except during periods of recession, when dividend payout ratios rose sharply because managements

---

[12] A. T. Sommers and L. R. Blau, *The Widening Cycle* (New York: The Conference Board, August 1975), p. 3.

[13] Postwar data are as published by Standard & Poor's; prewar data are derived from Alfred Cowles, III, *Common Stock Indexes*, 2d ed. (Chicago: Principia Press, 1939), and also reflect certain estimates by the present authors and by Mr. Kerwin Stallings, assistant vice president, Morgan Guaranty Trust Company of New York. The ratio method of analysis is described at length in the statistical appendix to this chapter.

FIGURE 5–1
Ratio of After-Tax Earnings (S&P Industrials) to Current Dollar GNP

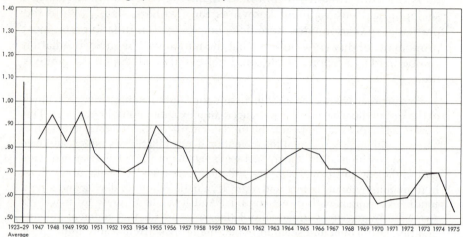

tried to maintain payments to stockholders even in the face of declining earnings, dividends on the S&P Industrials averaged about 55
percent of reported earnings for several decades—*until 1970.* Since
then, there has been a persistent reduction in payout ratios, to less than
40 percent in 1974. Even in 1975, when earnings declined sharply
while dividends were maintained, the payout ratio was less than the
long-term 55 percent central tendency.

Part of the reduction in payout ratios reflected temporary federal
controls on corporate dividend payments. But much more important
was the fact that "generally accepted accounting principles" tend to
overstate reported earnings during periods of strong inflation such as
were witnessed during the early 1970s. As discussed in Chapter 4,
original cost-based depreciation does not reflect the inflated replacement cost of fixed assets, and Fifo accounting understates cost of goods
sold without making provision for the inflated replacement costs of
inventory. Given the need to finance these high replacement costs,
managements reduced dividend payout ratios to supplement the use
of borrowed funds.

Looking to the future, it seems appropriate to argue that if the optimists on inflation are correct, the pressure on managements to retain
more earnings will abate and dividends will once again grow in line
with earnings. On the other hand, if the pessimists are correct, further
reductions in payout ratios would not be surprising. In summary, if the
rate of inflation returns to a fairly low level and current-dollar GNP
grows at a 6 percent rate, earnings can be expected to continue the
historic pattern of growth at a slower rate—about 5 percent—and divi-

dends can be expected to grow at approximately the same rate as earnings. But if the rate of inflation persists at a high level, not only are earnings likely to grow more slowly than GNP, but dividends probably will grow more slowly than earnings. With a 10 percent rate of GNP growth, earnings growth might be only 8 or 9 percent and dividend growth might average only some 7 percent. We have, then, two estimates of long-term dividend growth: 5 percent in a low-inflation economy and 7 percent in a higher inflation economy. The higher rate of inflation is associated with a higher rate of dividend growth—but not *proportionately* higher.

Choosing an Appropriate Discount Rate

To discount the estimated stream of future dividends on the S&P Industrials, we must have some idea of the rate of return that investors will demand in order to take the risks of common stock investment. Bear in mind that we are speaking of investors in aggregate, not any single investor, and that we are considering all stocks in aggregate, not any specific stock.

We cannot go out and ask millions of investors what their yield demands are. Even if it were physically possible to do so (for example, using a sampling technique), it is doubtful that we would get very reliable answers. But there are at least three independent items of indirect evidence which seem pertinent:

1.   The annual return on stockholders' equity in American industry has typically been about 11 percent–13 percent.[14] But *stockholders* should not expect this whole rate to be passed on to them. The marketability and diversification potential inherent in share ownership justifies a somewhat lower rate of return than that earned by corporations directly.

2.   During the past 20 years, the rate of return on the *safest* kinds of long-term, fixed-income securities, U.S. government bonds and "triple-A" corporate bonds, has been about 5–6 percent in periods of low inflation and about 8–9 percent in periods of greater inflation. Clearly, the added risk of owning common stocks justifies a higher rate of return than can be earned on high-quality bonds.

3.   During the past half century, the compound rate of return (including dividends and price appreciation) on broad, market-value-weighted, indexes of common stocks, such as the S&P Industrials, was about 9 percent.

---

[14] See annual earnings compilations prepared by Citibank of New York, or earnings and book value data for the S&P Industrials published by Standard & Poor's. Frequency distributions for large cross sections of individual corporations confirm these data.

These three items of evidence are suggestive of appropriate discount rates to be applied to estimated dividend growth. The first bit of evidence suggests a discount rate below 12 percent. The second item of evidence suggests a discount rate greater than 6 percent during low-inflation periods and greater than 9 percent during higher inflation. The third piece of evidence suggests a discount rate not too different from the historical 9 percent. All three criteria would be met reasonably well by applying a discount rate of 8 percent during periods of low inflation and 11 percent during periods of higher inflation.

Estimated Value of the S&P Industrials

It will be recalled that the formula for calculating the present value of perpetual dividend growth, at a constant discount rate, is:

$$\frac{\text{Current dividend rate}}{\text{Discount rate minus Growth rate}}$$

Our analysis has indicated that reasonable parameters for the denominator of this formula are as follows:

		Low Inflation	Higher Inflation
	Discount rate	8%	11%
Minus:	Growth rate	5	7
Equals:	Fair value current yield ..	3	4

Using these parameters, the value of the S&P Industrials Index at a time of fairly low-inflation expectations would be the then-current dividend rate divided by 3 percent; and at a time of fairly high-inflation expectations, the divisor would be 4 percent. Actually, since our dividend growth rate estimates refer to *trends,* the dividend rates which should be used in the numerator of the formula should be trend levels rather than actual current dividends, since the latter may be cyclically high or low.

Figure 5–2 is a reproduction of a chart utilizing these concepts. It superimposes a "value range" on the monthly movements of the S&P Industrials Index since 1959. The value range is derived as follows: (1) Define dividend trend amount each year as the average dividend of that year plus the immediately preceding and succeeding years (i.e., a three-year moving average).[15] (2) Center the dividend trend amount on

---

[15] Except for retrospective calculations, this procedure requires the analyst to estimate dividends for the current and succeeding years.

FIGURE 5–2
Standard & Poor's Industrials: Actual Prices* versus Estimated Values†

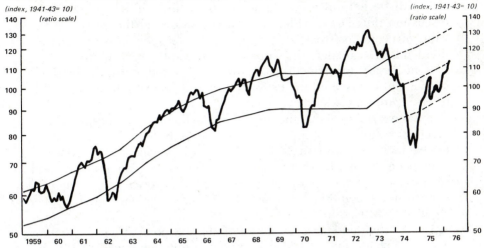

* Monthly average of daily close.
† See text for derivation of values.
Source: Prudential Insurance Company of America and Loeb, Rhoades & Co.

June 30 and divide by 3 percent and 3.5 percent to derive upper and lower points, respectively, of the range of stock "values" for periods of low- or moderate-inflation expectations. For periods of high-inflation expectations such as 1974–75, derive a lower value range by dividing dividends by 4 percent.[16] (3) Connect the June 30 values with freehand curves. The chart is drawn on semilogarithmic graph paper, which is scaled to make equal vertical distances represent equal percentage changes.[17]

It will be observed that the chart has been most useful in putting the swings of the market into broad perspective. The areas above and below the "band of value" have been opportune selling and buying zones. For example, the chart suggested quite clearly in 1972, and during the early months of 1973, that the stock market was seriously overpriced. Similarly, in late 1974, the chart strongly suggested that the stock market decline had carried too far.

---

[16] The negative impact on stock values of a shift from lower to higher inflation expectations is discussed from a theoretical viewpoint in J. Lintner, "Inflation and Security Returns," *Journal of Finance*, May 1975. Also, see P. Cagan, *Common Stock Values and Inflation–The Historical Record of Many Countries* (New York: National Bureau of Economic Research, 1974).

[17] The use of this type of graph in growth analysis is described in detail in the statistical appendix to this chapter.

Recapitulation

It will be helpful to pause at this point for a brief review of the discussion thus far. A widely accepted investment theory is that the value of a common stock is equivalent to the *present value* of all future dividends. To calculate the value of a stock on the basis of this theory, it is necessary to estimate the growth rate of the stock's dividend stream and to discount the estimated dividends at a rate which is felt to be appropriate.

It has been shown that the present-value theory can be applied with practical results to an appraisal of a general index of common stock prices such as Standard & Poor's Industrials. Specifically, reasons have been given why dividends on a broad cross section of common stocks can be expected to exhibit a long-term growth rate of about 5 percent under conditions of low inflation and 7 percent at higher rates of inflation. In addition, a case has been made for discounting an aggregate dividend series at a rate of about 8 percent when inflation expectations are low and 11 percent when inflation is expected to be more rapid. Finally, it has been shown that these assumptions produce a "fair value dividend yield" of between 3 percent and 4 percent.

No one can be so presumptuous as to claim that a set of economic assumptions will remain valid forever. Thus, it is not claimed that a 3 or 4 percent dividend yield will be an effective basis for evaluating the Standard & Poor's Industrial Stock Price Index for all time to come. However, a chart has been presented which illustrates the usefulness of the assumptions herein described, and it is hoped that the assumptions will continue to be useful in appraising the level of stock prices in general. In any event, an analytical framework has been presented which can provide the basis for any revisions that seem called for due to changed circumstances.

ESTIMATING THE VALUE OF INDIVIDUAL STOCKS

Since the concept of the present value of future dividends has proven to be useful in estimating the value of common stock prices in aggregate, it is reasonable to try to apply the concept to the evaluation of individual common stocks. In the pages which follow, the present-value approach will be examined for its applicability to individual stock appraisal, and a supplementary—more pragmatic—approach will be outlined as well.

Estimation Problems

In several respects, the present-value concept is more difficult to apply to individual common stocks than to stocks in the aggregate.

First, it is much more difficult to project the growth rate of an individual company than it is to project total corporate growth. Second, it is much more difficult to select an appropriate discount rate for an individual company's estimated dividend stream than it is to select a rate for all corporations combined. Finally, the discounting approach has been framed in terms of dividends rather than earnings, making it difficult to deal with companies which do not pay cash dividends.

Extraordinary Growth.   Theoretically, a corporation cannot grow indefinitely at a faster rate than companies generally, because it would ultimately swallow up the entire economy. But there are many companies which have managed for a decade or longer to outperform the average company by a wide margin. International Business Machines Corporation is probably the foremost example of such a company. With occasional interruptions, its earnings and dividends have grown at a rate of 10 percent–20 percent per annum for many years. If we try to derive a value for IBM by discounting its annual dividend growth potential during the next 25 years or more, we know that an ultimate slowdown in its growth rate must be assumed. But the specific pattern of this projected slowdown will have a great impact on the calculated value.

Some proponents of the discounting technique of evaluation have attempted to avoid making long-term dividend growth estimates by assuming a selling price some years in the near future and discounting it in lieu of a stream of dividends. For example, they may project dividend growth for five years and assume some dividend yield at that date.[18] Then, to calculate present value, they discount the 5 dividend payments and the assumed ultimate selling price. In reality, however, this procedure merely disguises the problem without overcoming it. For the assumed future dividend yield must explicitly or implicitly incorporate an estimate of dividend growth beyond that point.

Uncertainty.   An estimate of the growth potential of a company should be considered in light of the probability of its being accurate. Clearly, one is likely to feel more confident of an estimate of the future growth of stocks in the aggregate than of a single company's growth. An estimate of the future behavior of a broad aggregate contains a built-in protection against error—the protection of diversification. An estimate of the future behavior of a single component of the aggregate does not have this hedge and is less likely to be correct, particularly if the estimate is that the component will grow more or less rapidly than the aggregate. Furthermore, the projected growth of a company whose

---

[18] An alternative is to project earnings, assuming a constant dividend payout ratio, and hypothesize an ultimate price-earnings multiple. Some analysts project earnings and also allow for changes in dividend payout ratios.

past earnings have fluctuated violently usually contains a greater element of uncertainty than the projected growth of a company with a
history of stability.

Present-value theory adjusts for uncertainty via the discount rate.
The more uncertain the growth projection, the higher the discount rate
should be.[19] But the appropriate relationship between uncertainty and
discount rate is not at all apparent. Thus there are grave difficulties
posed by the need to select different discount rates for different
stocks[20]—and even to select different discount rates for different time
periods in the growth cycle of any individual stock. In the case of IBM,
for example, we might be more certain about an above-average growth
rate projected for, say, the next five years than for an above-average
growth rate projected for, say, the ten years thereafter. This means that
we might select two, three, or even more different discount rates in
evaluating IBM stock by the method of discounting future dividends.[21]

Nondividend Payers. Many rapidly growing companies, especially young ones, plow all of their earnings back into the business,
paying no cash dividends to their common stockholders. Ultimately, of
course, a dividend-paying policy may be instituted. But if the company's stock is to be valued by discounting its future dividends, a
rather precise estimate must be made of when the policy will
commence—quite a difficult task when there is no history of management's attitude toward dividends.

Illustration of Present-Value Analysis Applied to an Individual Stock

To illustrate the application of present-value theory to the evaluation of an individual stock, let us use the case of IBM, since we have
had occasion to refer to that company so frequently. In the fourth
quarter of 1974, IBM's net income declined 5 percent from a year
earlier, the company's first profit decline since 1969. Earnings remained level to slightly down in the first and second quarters of 1975.
On June 24, 1975, the board of directors raised the quarterly dividend

[19] Of course, it might be assumed that some investors prefer uncertainty—placing a
higher value on the chance of doing very well than they deduct for the chance of doing
very poorly. But most theoreticians believe that investors, in general, are "risk averters."

[20] The discount rates might also be different because of differences in the marketability of the two stocks. Other things being equal, the less marketable a stock, the
higher its discount rate should be.

[21] If interest rates are expected to fluctuate sharply during the forecast period, different discount rates technically should be used for different time periods to reflect this
expectation (to the extent it can be quantified). Such adjustments of the discount rate
should be made for evaluations of the market as a whole as well as for evaluations of
individual issues.

to $1.75 per share from $1.50. Some analysts argued that the dividend increase was a sign of the directors' confidence in the future; that the earnings slowdown merely reflected the end of IBM's latest product cycle, and that new product cycles—and, indeed, new ventures such as the company's recently announced entry into the communications satellite field—would restore the company's traditional vigorous growth. Other analysts argued, on the other hand, that the dividend increase reflected a diminishing of high-profit outlets for retained earnings, and that the company's growth curve was in the process of tapering off. The price of IBM's stock at the time was about $200 per share.

Based on these two views of IBM's future, let us hypothesize two alternative dividend growth paths for the 20 years, 1975–95, and see what the implications were for the value of IBM's stock in relation to its then-current price of $200. Specifically, let us assume an optimistic "Path A," by which dividends grow at a rate of 15 percent per annum for 5 years and then gradually slow down until, at the end of 20 years, they grow at the same rate as dividends of the S&P Industrials. Alternatively, suppose the pessimists were correct and dividends follow "Path B," growing at only 10 percent per annum for five years and fairly quickly slowing down to the growth rate of the average company. The two growth paths are as follows:

	Path A: Rapid (percent per annum)	Path B: Slow (percent per annum)
1975–1980	15	10
1980–1985	12	8
1985–1990	10	*
1990–1995	8	
1995 and beyond	*	

* Assume that growth will be equivalent to the broad average of between 5 percent and 7 percent (see the preceding analysis of the S&P Industrials).

As for the discount rate to be applied to these dividend paths, let us assume that the market demands a 12 percent per annum rate of return as long as IBM's growth rate is above average. Once the growth rate becomes average, however, assume that the dividend rate which then prevails is "capitalized" at 3.5 percent, similar to the dividend yield used earlier in estimating the value of the overall market.

Admittedly, these are heroic assumptions, but the present-value technique requires that assumptions of this character be made. Indeed, the very fact that the assumptions are so heroic illustrates the

difficulty of applying the present-value technique to individual stock appraisal. The effort may be worthwhile, but it is not easy.[22] In any event, given the stated assumptions the following calculations can be made:

1.   The first two columns of Table 5–2 show the progression of dividends under the two growth paths.

TABLE 5–2
Present Value of IBM Dividend Stream during Above-Average Growth Period (based on assumptions outlined in text)

Year	Mid-Year Rate of Dividends		Discounted Value of Dividends in Mid-1975 at 12 Percent	
	Path A	Path B	Path A	Path B
1975	$ 7.00	$ 7.00	—	—
1976	8.05	7.70	$ 7.19	$ 6.88
1977	9.26	8.47	7.38	6.75
1978	10.65	9.32	7.58	6.64
1979	12.24	10.25	7.78	6.52
1980	14.08	11.27	7.98	6.39
1981	15.77	12.18	7.98	6.18
1982	17.66	13.15	7.98	5.94
1983	19.78	14.20	7.98	5.74
1984	21.15	15.34	7.98	5.54
1985	24.81	16.56	7.98	5.33
1986	27.29		7.83	
1987	30.02		7.72	
1988	33.03		7.56	
1989	36.33		7.45	
1990	39.96		7.31	
1991	43.16		7.04	
1992	46.61		6.80	
1993	50.34		6.54	
1994	54.37		6.31	
1995	58.72		6.11	
Sum 1976–1995			$148.48	
Sum 1976–1985				$61.91

2.   The third and fourth columns of Table 5–2 show the present values, in mid-1975, of each dividend during an above-average growth year, discounted at a 12 percent rate. The sum of these present values is about $148 for Path A and $62 for Path B.

---

[22] For evidence that practicing security analysts generally consider the present-value technique to be either too difficult, or not worthwhile, see R. A. Bing, "Survey of Practitioners' Stock Evaluation Methods," *Financial Analysts Journal,* May/June 1971. For a contrary view, see W. P. O'Connor and S. A. Ferrer, *Dividend Stock Monitor* (New York: The Fourteen Research Corporation November 14, 1975), in which results are presented of applying this technique to 170 stocks of major companies.

3. The growth and discount rates beyond 1995, for Path A, and beyond 1985, for Path B, are assumed to be those of the average company. Therefore, we "capitalize" the dividend of the terminal growth year by 3.5 percent to arrive at hypothetical selling prices of IBM stock in that terminal year. Dividing $58.72 (for Path A) by 0.035 produces a price of $1,678 in 1995; and dividing $16.56 (for Path B) by 0.035 produces a price of $473 in 1985.

4. Discounting these terminal prices of IBM stock at 12 percent produces present values, in mid-1975, of $175 for Path A and $152 for Path B.

5. Summing the present values of future dividends and the present values of the terminal selling prices produces a value range of between $214 (for Path B, $62 + $152) and $323 (for Path A, $148 + $175).

Thus, IBM's actual price of $200 in June 1975, represented "fair value" under the slow-growth assumptions we have used. But under the rapid-growth assumptions, IBM was worth at least 50 percent more than its selling price. An analyst should not have stopped at this point, however. A fruitful next step would have been to see if assumptions could be made which seemed reasonable and yet which produced a value substantially *below* $200. If not,—i.e., if the assumptions necessary to produce so low a value were unrealistic—the analyst could feel rather confident that buying the stock at $200 would, at worst, produce merely an average return, and, at best, an extraordinarily high return. (As it turned out, IBM's stock had risen to $280 by July 1976. On July 27, 1976, as this book was being prepared for press, IBM increased its quarterly dividend by almost 30 percent, from $1.75 to $2.25 per share. This was the largest dividend increase in over a decade, and was concurrent with a rebound in earnings. The debate continued as to whether the sharply higher dividends were an indication of the company's confidence in the future or whether they reflected a diminishing of high-profit outlets for retained earnings.)

A More Pragmatic Approach—
The Price-Earnings Ratio

As discussed above, the application of the concept of present value of future dividends to individual stock evaluation requires many assumptions about developments in the quite distant future. In addition to the difficulties posed by the need for such assumptions, there is the further problem that some companies follow a policy of paying little or no dividends as long as highly profitable reinvestment opportunities are plentiful. Practicing security analysts generally overcome the latter problem by evaluating stocks in terms of price-earnings multiples

rather than dividend yields. The problem of detailed assumptions usually is attacked by devising various rules of thumb for selecting an appropriate price-earnings ratio which can be applied to a company's existing level of earnings per share. The basis for these rules of thumb may range from the purely intuitive to elaborate statistical analysis.

Price-Earnings Ratio of "the Market" and the Industry. Most security analysts begin their attempt to select an appropriate price-earnings ratio (often referred to simply as P/E) for an individual stock with a judgment regarding the appropriate price-earnings ratio for the market as a whole—i.e., for one of the popular stock price indexes. In addition, they usually take into consideration the typical P/E ratio of the particular *industry group* in which the stock is classified, in relation to the P/E ratio of the market averages.

Figure 5–3 traces the price-earnings ratio of Standard & Poor's

FIGURE 5–3
P/E Ratio of Standard & Poor's 500 Stocks, 1950–1975

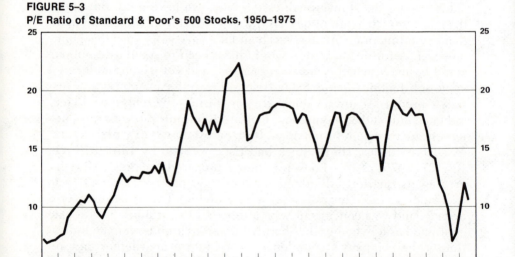

Source: Loeb, Rhoades & Co.

Composite Stock Price Index (Industrials, Finance, Utility and Transportation stocks) since 1950. Note the steady rise from 10 to 20 between the early 1950s and 1961. From 1962 through 1972, the P/E had a steady central tendency of about 17. Thereafter, it dropped back to the lower levels of the 1950s.[23]

[23] The point has been made often that changes in price-earnings ratios, rather than changes in earnings, account for the major portion of fluctuations in stock prices. See, for example, J. R. Holmes, "100 Years of Investment Experience with Common Stocks," *Financial Analysts Journal,* November/December 1975.

The central tendency of about 17 for the market's price-earnings ratio during the decade 1962–72 relates directly to an earlier finding. As illustrated in Figure 5–2, the "fair value" of the market can be derived, during periods of modest inflationary expectations, by dividing the trend amount of dividends by 3–3.5 percent. It also has been indicated that companies in the S&P Index typically distributed about 55 cents of dividends, on average, for every dollar earned. Given this information, a simple algebraic transformation can be made. Letting D equal dividends and E equal earnings:

$$\frac{D}{.03} = \frac{.55E}{.03} = 18E$$

$$\frac{D}{.035} = \frac{.55E}{.035} = 16E$$

In other words, a 3–3.5 percent yield on the trend amount of dividends—i.e., on "normalized" dividends—is equivalent to 16–18 (averaging 17) times *normalized* earnings.[24]

Similarly, the sharp decline in the market's price-earnings ratio during 1973–75 also relates directly to our earlier discussion. With the dividend payout ratio dropping to about 40 percent in reflection of inflation's impact on reported earnings, and with the "fair value dividend yield" rising to 4 percent, the algebraic transformation works out as follows:

$$\frac{D}{.04} = \frac{.40E}{.04} = 10E$$

That is, a 4 percent dividend yield is equivalent to only ten times normalized earnings if the dividend payout ratio drops to 40 percent because of inflation. Or, putting it another way, a rise in dividend yield produces a more than proportionate decline in price-earnings ratio if the dividend payout ratio is declining at the same time.

Table 5–3 offers some perspective on the P/E ratios of groups of companies, classified by industry. The data are shown both in absolute terms and as a percentage of the P/E of the S&P Industrials on the

---

[24] The stress on the word "normalized" is important, particularly when dealing with individual stocks rather than the market as a whole. For if actual earnings rather than normalized earnings are used as the divisor of a P/E ratio, the ratio may appear to be very high or very low, or can rise and fall sharply, not primarily in reflection of the valuation process, but rather because earnings are abnormally depressed or inflated. Of course, actual earnings usually are easier to work with because there is no generally accepted method of normalizing earnings. The concept involves a large element of subjective judgment. One way of at least partially overcoming this difficulty is to calculate a P/E ratio by relating price to the nearest four-quarter earnings total which is unaffected by recession or boom conditions in the economy and unaffected by special occurrences such as strikes.

TABLE 5–3. Industry Group Price/Earnings Ratios, 1970–1975

	1/2/70* S&P Industrials P/E 16.3x		9/1/72* S&P Industrials P/E 20.8x		10/1/74† S&P Industrials P/E 7.2x		12/31/75† S&P Industrials P/E 12.2x	
	Average	Relative	Average	Relative	Average	Relative	Average	Relative
Aerospace	9.9x	0.61	14.6x	0.70	4.07x	0.57	5.84x	0.48
Airlines	16.1	0.99	19.3	0.93	5.92	0.82	12.46	1.02
Aluminum	12.5	0.77	26.9	1.30	5.29	0.74	10.06	0.83
Automobiles	9.0	0.55	11.2	0.54	7.00	0.97	16.45	1.35
Automobile parts	10.4	0.64	13.3	0.64	6.85	0.95	12.73	1.05
Banks, N.Y. and other	11.5	0.71	13.3	0.64	5.13	0.71	5.99	0.49
Beverages	23.1	1.42	29.9	1.44	7.78	1.08	12.06	0.99
Chemicals	13.2	0.81	18.0	0.86	6.67	0.93	15.18	1.25
Coal	31.1	1.91	18.2	0.88	5.73	0.80	7.89	0.65
Construction supplies	16.4	1.01	15.5	0.75	5.33	0.74	9.91	0.81
Containers	14.6	0.90	13.2	0.64	4.38	0.61	6.20	0.51
Copper	9.7	0.60	12.8	0.62	3.45	0.48	19.04	1.56
Cosmetics	29.8	1.83	31.7	1.53	9.10	1.27	16.38	1.35
Drugs	34.4	2.11	34.9	1.68	15.84	2.20	18.26	1.50
Electric equipment	19.8	1.21	22.6	1.09	7.52	1.05	12.52	1.03
Foods	16.1	0.99	14.8	0.71	6.77	0.94	10.23	0.84
Forest products	19.1	1.17	17.8	0.86	4.87	0.68	12.77	1.05
Home furnishings	14.7	0.90	17.6	0.84	4.34	0.60	11.74	0.96
Hotel and motel	36.3	2.23	36.7	1.76	5.50	0.76	10.63	0.87
Machinery	11.6	0.71	17.4	0.84	7.53	1.05	8.75	0.72
Metal fabricating	13.9	0.85	16.5	0.79	4.54	0.63	8.91	0.73
Office equipment	33.3	2.04	32.4	1.56	8.41	1.17	14.49	1.19
Oils	12.2	0.75	16.7	0.80	5.38	0.75	8.28	0.68
Paper	13.9	0.85	20.5	0.98	5.66	0.79	9.65	0.79
Publishing	21.8	1.34	19.5	0.94	4.23	0.59	7.24	0.59
Railroads	8.9	0.55	10.3	0.49	5.42	0.75	8.83	0.73
Railway equipment	12.6	0.77	15.8	0.76	6.03	0.84	6.33	0.52
Real estate	24.0	1.47	20.3	0.97	2.75	0.38	0.68	0.06
Restaurant	29.2	1.79	25.6	1.23	9.10	1.27	17.45	1.43
Retail trade	14.8	0.91	14.6	0.70	8.89	1.24	10.24	0.84
Rubber	11.4	0.70	9.8	0.47	4.77	0.66	8.89	0.73
Shoes	12.8	0.79	15.1	0.73	5.21	0.72	10.39	0.85
Soap	16.4	1.01	27.2	1.31	9.65	1.34	13.90	1.14
Steel	12.0	0.74	14.8	0.71	3.97	0.55	5.14	0.42
Textiles	10.8	0.66	11.6	0.56	3.99	0.55	11.54	0.95
Tobacco	12.3	0.75	13.8	0.66	7.68	1.07	9.78	0.80
Utilities								
Electric power	12.3	0.75	10.9	0.52	5.98	0.83	8.16	0.67
Gas	11.3	0.69	11.8	0.57	6.24	0.87	7.22	0.59
Telephone	15.7	0.96	14.7	0.55	6.36	0.88	9.14	0.75
Vending	18.6	1.14	21.4	1.03	5.96	0.83	8.25	0.68

* For each company, and for the S&P Industrials, price was divided by earnings per share of the latest four quarters reported as of the date shown. The dates chosen for this particular illustration were selected so that the earnings used in the calculations were not recession-level earnings. Aggregation of the company data into industry groupings was done in two steps, the objective being to minimize the influence of companies with abnormal P/E ratios: (1) An average was computed only for those companies in the industry whose P/E was greater than zero (thus eliminating companies with deficit earnings) and less than 100 (thus eliminating companies with only nominal earnings). (2) Each remaining company's P/E was compared with the preliminary industry average calculated in (1). Those companies whose P/E was more than double the preliminary average were also eliminated, and a final average was computed. Each industry average P/E was divided by the S&P P/E to derive the relative P/E.

† The P/E ratios presented here are also based on latest-12-month earnings. However, a less detailed procedure was followed to eliminate distortion. Data exclude stocks with P/Es that are negative or abnormally high (75 times or more). The average multiple for the particular industry is the arithmetic average of the P/E ratios of stocks comprising the respective group; the relative multiple is obtained by dividing the industry group multiple by the multiple of the S&P.

Source: First Boston Corporation.

corresponding dates. They are compiled in such a way as to minimize the impact of abnormal earnings (see the footnote to the table for a description of the methodology). The dates chosen for the illustration occurred during both bull and bear phases of the stock market.

The Stock's Typical Price-Earnings Ratio. The analyst's next step is to make a judgment as to whether the particular stock under study usually will sell at an equivalent, a higher, or a lower P/E than that of the averages and of other companies in its industry group. Frequently, this judgment is basically an intuitive one, based on the analyst's experience and an examination of the historical record of the stock's P/E in relation to that of the market and the industry. It is clear, however, that a more analytical approach than mere extrapolation of past relative P/E's can be employed.

During the past 15 years, there has been an outpouring of scholarly research on the determinants of differences in the price-earnings ratios of different companies at any given point in time.[25] The most definitive finding of these studies is that the principal reason for P/E differences during most of the postwar period was the expectation of differences in the future normal trend of growth in earnings per share. Consider, for example, Figure 5–4(a), which is based on data shown in Table 5–4. The scatter diagram, and the line of regression drawn on the diagram,[26] illustrate the relationship, at the end of 1971, between the price-earnings ratios and the expected earnings growth rates of 30 well-known companies in a wide variety of industries. The definitions and sources of the P/E and growth rate data are given in a footnote to Table 5–4.

The equation of the line of regression is: P/E = 2.3 (Growth) + 4. This means that on the bull market date represented by the diagram (December 31, 1971), an average growth rate of around 6 percent commanded a P/E of about 18 (2.3 × 6, + 4 = 13.8 + 4 = 17.8). This figure is in line with the chart presented earlier on "the market's" P/E ratio. Likewise, a stock with an expected growth rate of 15 percent commanded a P/E, on average, of about 38.

Of course, the relationship was not perfect; all of the points did not fall on the line of regression.[27] For example, both IBM and Texas In-

[25] The more recent articles include: B. G. Malkiel and J. G. Cragg, "Expectations and the Structure of Share Prices," *American Economic Review*, September 1970; S. Cohen and D. J. Smyth, "Some Determinants of Price/Earnings Ratios of Industrial Common Stock," *Quarterly Review of Economics and Business*, Winter 1973; and F. W. Bell, "The Relation of the Structure of Common Stock Prices to Historical, Expectational and Industrial Variables," *Journal of Finance*, March 1974.

[26] Scatter diagrams and regression techniques are described in the statistical Appendix to this chapter.

[27] The Appendix to this chapter contains a calculation of the coefficient of determination (r^2) for this set of data. It works out to 90 percent, which is unusually high in this type of analysis. Nevertheless, it is far from perfect.

TABLE 5–4
P/E Ratios versus Expected Growth Rates (data for Figure 5–4)

Company (in order of growth rate)	Col. 1 Bull Market P/E*	Col. 2 Bear Market P/E†	Col. 3 Expected Earnings Growth‡
U.S. Steel	10	8	0
American Metal Climax	11	10	2
Ingersoll-Rand	13	8	3
Standard Oil of N.J. (now Exxon)	10	9	3½
General Motors	12	10	4
Johns-Manville	15	11	4
American Telephone	10	11	4
Time Inc.	16	10	5
Federated Department Stores	21	13	5½
General Foods	14	15	5½
Clark Equipment	16	8	6
Firestone Tire	12	9	6
Dow Chemical	21	12	7½
Texas Utilities	16	16	7½
Magnavox	18	10	8
Upjohn	25	14	8½
Carrier	24	19	9
Sears, Roebuck	27	18	9½
Eastman Kodak	32	23	10
Merck	33	28	11
Emerson Electric	29	20	12
Perkin-Elmer	38	18	12½
Anheuser-Busch	31	30	13½
Coca-Cola	39	29	13½
Hewlett-Packard	42	27	14
Texas Instruments	35	28	15
International Business Machines	33	29	15
Avon Products	46	44	16½
Xerox	40	34	16½
Johnson & Johnson	46	35	18

* Prices of December 31, 1971 divided by 1972 earnings per share as estimated by analysts of Prudential Insurance Company of America.
† Prices of May 26, 1970 divided by 1969 reported earnings per share.
‡ Estimates of basic growth rate (e.g., five years forward) made by "Comparative Values" service of Cowen & Co., New York City. While the estimate for any given company may be subject to argument, conversations with other analysts suggest that there would be general agreement as to the relative magnitudes of the investment community's expectations regarding these companies.

struments had indicated growth rates of 15 percent, yet both carried P/E ratios below the calculated 38 (33 and 35, respectively). On the other hand, Hewlett-Packard's estimated growth rate was 14 percent, yet its P/E was 42—well above the 36 indicated by the line of regression.

Next, examine the P/E versus growth relationship some 18 months earlier than the previous example—at the depths of the 1969–70 bear market. This is shown for the same sample of companies in Figure

FIGURE 5–4
P/E Ratios versus Expected Growth Rates*

(a) 1971-72 Bull Market

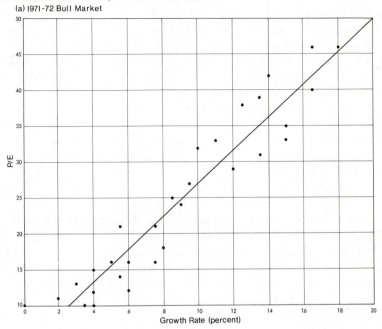

(b) 1970 Bear Market

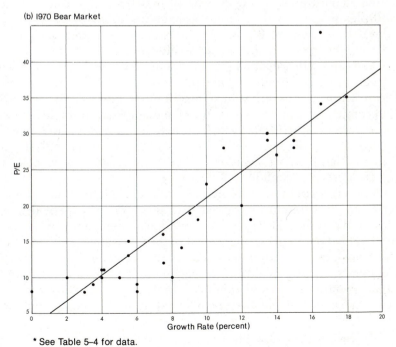

* See Table 5–4 for data.

5–4(b). The equation of this relationship is: P/E = 1.8 (Growth) + 3, and there is a somewhat wider scatter of the individual points around the line of regression.[28] This is typical of the findings of other researchers on the subject. During traditional bear markets, the growth factor commanded a lower premium than during bull markets (in our two illustrations, a "growth coefficient" of 1.8 as opposed to 2.3) and, in addition, growth explained less of the P/E behavior while other factors, to be discussed below, became increasingly important. The equation suggests that an average growth rate of around 6 percent commanded a P/E of about 14 on the bear market date represented by the diagram (May 26, 1970). This figure also is in line with the chart presented earlier on the range of P/E ratios for a broad market index such as the S&P Industrials.

The massive bear market of 1973–75 repeated the pattern of earlier bear markets in that the P/E premium for growth was reduced. In addition, however, the relationship became vastly more fragmented. As shown in Figure 5–5, one could not characterize the market as having a describable relationship between P/E and expected earnings growth. Whereas Figure 5–4(b) indicates that stocks of companies with expected growth in excess of 10 percent sold at price-earnings ratios of between 20 and 35, a relatively narrow range, during the 1970 bear market, Figure 5–5 shows some growth stocks selling at multiples as low as 8 or 10 in 1975, while others were at multiples near 30. This enormous range highlights the need to consider determinants of P/E other than expected earnings growth.

It will be recalled that present-value theory contains two major elements, growth rate and discount rate. The discount rate is the mechanism used to adjust for risk. Correspondingly, in analysis of price-earnings ratios, allowance must be made for differences in risk. Two companies can be expected to have approximately the same future earnings growth rate, yet there may be important differences in the degree of confidence with which this expectation is held. It stands to reason that higher P/E ratios should be associated, in general, with higher degrees of confidence.

One may hypothesize numerous additional determinants of P/E. For example, it might be argued that, given equal expected growth rates held with equal degrees of confidence, companies with higher dividend payout ratios should sell at higher P/Es than companies with lower payout ratios. Frequent reference also is made in the investment community to the "quality of management." That is, apart from the actual quantitative record produced by a given company's management, the management may be viewed as highly competent in its

---

[28] r^2 is equal to 84 percent, still quite high for this type of analysis.

FIGURE 5–5
P/E Ratios versus Expected Growth Rates, 1975

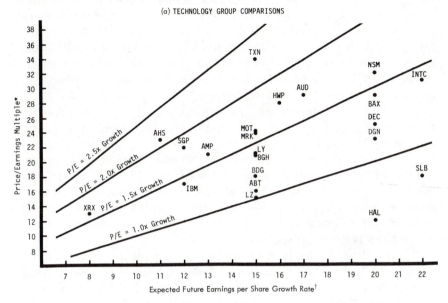

(a) TECHNOLOGY GROUP COMPARISONS

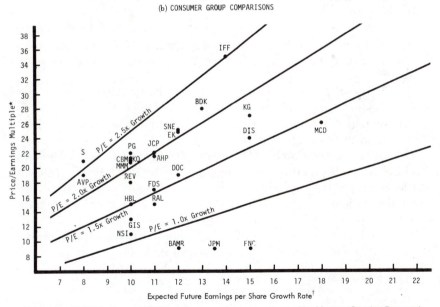

(b) CONSUMER GROUP COMPARISONS

* Based on 11/4/75 price and 1975 earnings per share as estimated by Morgan Stanley Research.
† Based on 1975–79 projected earnings growth assuming 6 percent inflation.
Source: Morgan Stanley & Co. Inc.

ability to cope with unexpected developments, or it may be viewed as mediocre—one which produced a good record only because external conditions were favorable. This quality, or "image," factor is difficult to express quantitatively,[29] but there is good reason to believe that it influences price-earnings ratios among different companies. Other factors which have been alluded to in the literature include differences in: financial leverage, stock price volatility, corporate size, and accounting practices ("quality of earnings").[30]

Just as "simple regression" can be used to analyze the relationship between P/E and a single determining factor, such as expected growth, so "multiple regression" techniques can be applied when one is considering the more complex relationship between P/E and a number of hypothesized determining factors in addition to growth. We have cited previously several landmark articles which explore these more complex relationships. Rather than attempt a detailed summary of findings here, suffice it to say that the most important additional explanatory factors appear to be:

1. *Stability* of sales and earnings around their trend paths. Companies which are relatively immune to fluctuations in the overall business cycle tend to sell at P/Es 2 or 3 points higher than companies with equal expected growth rates but which likely to be more vulnerable to cyclical fluctuations.

2. Management and product *image*. Companies with the admittedly nebulous, and perhaps ephemeral, characteristic of being "quality" firms tend to sell at P/Es 2 or 3 points higher than companies not so endowed.

3. *Dividend payout* and *debt* policies. Particularly in bear markets, investors appear to pay a premium of 1 or 2 P/E points for an above-average dividend payout ratio, or below-average leverage, given equal growth expectations.

Deviations of the Stock's P/E around Its Typical Level. Thus far, we have been discussing differences among the P/E ratios of different stocks at a point in time. This is known as cross-sectional analysis. But what about changes in the relative price-earnings ratio of a particular stock *over time?* This is known as time-series analysis.

Obviously, the relative P/E of a stock should be expected to change if the investment community's appraisal of its basic growth potential,

---

[29] The Fourteen Research Corp., a New York brokerage firm, has made some interesting attempts to quantify the quality factor. See W. P. O'Connor, Jr., *The 14 Point Method for Beating the Market* (Chicago: Henry Regnery Co., 1972), chap. 3. This study is updated and revised each year in supplements issued by the firm. Also, see Chapter 8 below for further discussion of the subject.

[30] William O'Connor, *The 14 Point Method for Beating the Market*, has put forth the interesting suggestion that the quality of earnings may be quantified by determining the percentage of reported earnings which actually is available for dividend payments or expansion of operating assets.

or stability, or "quality" changes. But what if these basic appraisals do not change? What causes short-term P/E fluctuations? At least a partial answer seems to be that P/Es move up and down in response to acceleration and deceleration of earnings. That is, the basic earnings growth rate (or "velocity," to use a physical analogy) is usually the prime determinant of the normal P/E of a stock. But shorter term movements of earnings around the basic trend (acceleration and deceleration) seem to cause shorter term movements of the stock's P/E around its own norm.

Conclusion. It is clear that one can determine a reasonable value level for a stock (or for "the market") in a variety of ways. These range from the rather theoretical approach of discounting long-term projections of dividends to the very simplistic approach of assuming that a stock's recent price-earnings ratio history represents a norm which can be applied to current earnings estimates. Our own preference is to adopt an eclectic approach in which the results of different procedures are compared and inconsistencies are reconciled. In any case, estimating a growth rate of earnings and dividends is usually crucial to the valuation process, and to this we turn next.

SUGGESTED READINGS

Bell, Frederick W. "The Relation of the Structure of Common Stock Prices to Historical, Expectational and Industrial Variables." *Journal of Finance.* March 1974.

Brealey, Richard A. *Security Prices in a Competitive Market.* Cambridge, Mass.: The M.I.T. Press, 1971.

Cagan, Phillip. *Common Stock Values and Inflation–The Historical Record of Many Countries.* New York: National Bureau of Economic Research, 1974.

Cohen, Jerome B. "Analysis of Common Stock," *Financial Analyst's Handbook,* vol. I. Homewood, Ill.: Dow Jones-Irwin, Inc., 1975, chap. 5.

Elton, Edwin J., and Gruber, Martin J. (eds.) *Security Evaluation and Portfolio Analysis.* Readings 7–12. Englewood Cliffs, N.J.: Prentice-Hall, Inc., 1972.

Huang, Stanley S. C. *Techniques of Investment Analysis.* Scranton, Pa.: Intext Educational Publishers, 1972.

Lintner, John. "Inflation and Security Returns." *The Journal of Finance.* May 1975.

Lorie, James H., and Hamilton, Mary T. *The Stock Market: Theories and Evidence.* Homewood, Ill.: Richard D. Irwin, Inc., 1973, chaps. 6–9.

McCarthy, George D., and Healy, Robert E. *Valuing a Company.* New York: The Ronald Press Co., 1971.

Williamson, J. Peter. *Investments: New Analytic Techniques.* Chaps. V–VI. New York: Praeger Publishers, Inc., 1970.

APPENDIX: SOME USEFUL STATISTICAL TECHNIQUES
FOR ANALYSIS OF GROWTH

Clearly, analysis of growth is critical to common stock evaluation. And growth analysis requires an understanding of certain elementary statistical techniques. Most readers of this text have had a formal course in statistics. For those who have not had such a course, or who have had one but have forgotten much of its content, this appendix is designed to outline some *mechanical* techniques for measuring and analyzing growth trends. Readers desiring greater detail than can be provided in the space available here should consult one of the statistics textbooks recommended at the end of this appendix.

Semilogarithmic Charts

There is an old saying that "one picture is worth a thousand words." This saying has a counterpart in statistical analysis. A well-drawn *chart* usually leads to far greater understanding than the *tabulation* on which the chart is based. A well-drawn chart reveals at a glance important trends, cyclical swings, and relationships among different series of data (if all are drawn on the same chart). A table of data *can* reveal the same facts, but usually only with a good deal of further processing by the analyst (for example, via calculation of percentage changes).

To be most useful in studying growth over a span of years, a chart usually should be drawn on semilogarithmic rather than arithmetic graph paper. On arithmetically ruled paper, equal distances represent *equal absolute quantities.* For example, if from 196X to 197X Company A's sales grew from $10 million to $20 million, while B's grew from $50 million to $60 million, and C's from $90 million to $100 million, an arithmetic chart of these three companies' sales would show three parallel lines. This is illustrated in Figure A5–1a.

But for growth analysis, Figure A5–1a presents a most deceiving picture. For the three companies have in fact had quite different *rates* of progress. Company A's sales have doubled during the period, while B's have increased only 20 percent and C's only 11 percent. Semilogarithmic graph paper is designed to show comparative growth more meaningfully.

The horizontal scale of semilogarithmic graph paper is ruled arithmetically. In our example, each equal horizontal distance represents an equal time period. The vertical scale, however, is ruled so that equal distances represent not equal *amounts* of change but equal *percentage* changes. This is the same type of scale utilized on a slide rule.[31] Each ruling of 1 through 10 is known as a "cycle." Thus, any

---

[31] The scale is called "logarithmic" because when two pairs of figures have the same percentage relationship, the differences between the logarithms of each pair are equal. A logarithmic scale is often refered to as a "ratio scale." The paper is called "semilogarithmic" because only one of the two scales is logarithmic.

FIGURE A5–1
Sales Growth of Three Companies

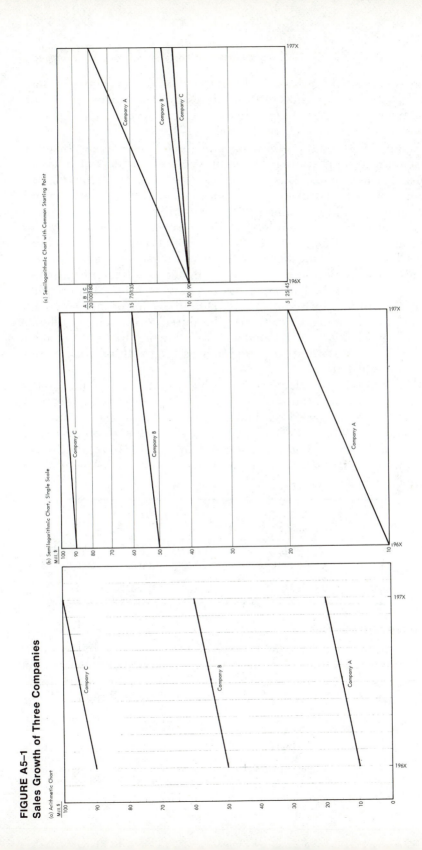

(a) Arithmetic Chart

(b) Semilogarithmic Chart, Single Scale

(c) Semilogarithmic Chart with Common Starting Point

increase of tenfold or less can be graphed on one-cycle paper. Two-cycle paper has two banks of 1–10 rulings, and thus covers a hundred-fold increase (1–10; 10–100). Likewise, three-cycle paper covers a thousandfold increase (1–10; 10–100; 100–1,000).

Figure A5–1b portrays the sales growth of Companies A, B, and C on semilogarithmic scaling. The improvement it renders in an ability to make visual comparisons is obvious. Moreover, by imaginative handling of the scales, even greater visual comparability can be achieved. One of the possible variations will be described.

Although a cycle on semilog paper represents a change from 1 to 10, the starting point need not be 1 or 10 or 100. It can be *any* number—other than zero or a negative value.[32] In fact, it can be several numbers simultaneously, with each number applying to a different line to be drawn on the graph. This fact permits a very useful type of presentation, as exhibited in Figure A5–1c. Here the sales of the three companies are all brought together at the initial year, using a different numerical scaling for each company. By allowing the lines to fan out from a common starting point, differences in growth rate can be dramatically illustrated.

Figure A5–1c in effect, is a graphic counterpart of the "index number" technique. Index numbers are constructed by choosing some year(s) as a "base period" and making each value of the original data series equal to a percentage of the base period value. Returning to our three companies, and adding another year of data, 196Y, for illustrative purposes, if 196X is set as the base period the following index numbers result:

Year	Actual Data (million $)			Index Numbers (196X = 100)		
	A	B	C	A	B	C
196X	10	50	90	100.00	100.00	100.00
196Y	15	50	81	150.00	100.00	90.00
197X	20	60	100	200.00	120.00	111.11

Relative Growth Ratios

When differences in growth rates are quite pronounced, as in the illustrations used thus far, a semilogarithmic chart with one line for each series of numbers portrays those differences quite clearly. Lines with equal slopes—parallel lines—have equal growth rates.[33] Where

[32] The inability to plot negatives can be a handicap in portraying an earnings record—i.e., if there are years of deficits.

[33] It might be noted that although equal slopes imply equal percentage changes, a given vertical distance in an *upward* direction represents a greater percentage change than the same vertical distance in a *downward* direction. Thus, an increase from 4 to 5 is a change of +25 percent but a decrease from 5 to 4 is a change of −20 percent.

the slope of one line is steeper than the slope of another line, a more rapid growth rate is indicated. Where the slope is shallower, a slower rate is indicated. Moreover, the *curvature* of a line indicates whether its growth rate is accelerating or decelerating.

However, when differences in growth rates are not pronounced, semilog charting of each series may be inadequate for visual analysis. This is because the eye cannot perceive small differences in slope.

A handy device for overcoming the difficulty of comparing similarly sloped lines is to calculate and plot the *ratio* of one series relative to the other. (Arithmetic scales can be used to draw ratio lines, except for certain specialized purposes.) For example, Figure 5–1 of the main text of this chapter plots the ratio of earnings on the S&P Industrial Stock Price Index to gross national product.

When a ratio line rises, it indicates that the numerator of the fraction (in our example, S&P earnings) is rising faster or falling slower than the denominator (in our example, GNP). Likewise, a declining ratio line indicates that the numerator is rising slower or falling faster than the denominator. A horizontal ratio line, of course, means that both numerator and denominator are changing at equal rates. Note that the numerator and denominator do *not* have to be expressed in similar units to make the ratio calculation meaningful. Tons of one commodity, for example, can be compared with pounds—or even bushels—of another. In Figure 5–1, index units of earnings are compared with billions of dollars of GNP, but the ratio line makes quite vivid the point that earnings have grown more slowly than GNP, except for brief periods such as 1953–55, 1961–65, and 1970–73.

Growth Rate Calculations

Suppose, now, that more than simply a quick visual image of differences in growth is desired. After all, a ratio line merely indicates that the numerator of the ratio has grown faster or slower than the denominator. It indicates nothing about *how much* faster or slower.

The term "growth rate" is most meaningful in the context of *compound* interest. If a quantity grows from 2 to 3 over a ten-year period, for example, the total growth is 50 percent, or a *simple average* per annum rate of 5 percent. But 5 percent is not the most meaningful expression of the growth rate, because it ignores compounding—i.e., the accrual of interest on interest as well as on the original value. Assuming annual compounding, 2 grows to 3 in 10 years at a rate of 4.1%.

How do we know the rate is 4.1 percent? One way is to use logarithms. First divide the terminal value by the starting value: (3/2 = 1.5). Then look up the logarithm of the ratio: (log 1.5 = 0.17609). Then divide the logarithm by the number of years involved: (0.17609/10 = .017609). Look up the antilog of this value: (antilog

.017609 = 1.0414). Subtract 1.00, and we have the answer: 0.0414, or 4.1 percent per annum.

If the reader is confused by the use of logarithms, or if he will be satisfied with an approximate answer, Table A5–1 should prove useful.

TABLE A5–1
Growth Rates Indicated by Ratio of Terminal to Initial Value

Growth Rate %	Number of Years														
	1	2	3	4	5	6	7	8	9	10	11	12	13	14	15
−15	0.85	0.72	0.61	0.52	0.44	0.38	0.32	0.27	0.23	0.20	0.17	0.14	0.12	0.10	0.09
14	0.86	0.74	0.64	0.55	0.47	0.40	0.35	0.30	0.26	0.22	0.19	0.16	0.14	0.12	0.10
13	0.87	0.76	0.66	0.57	0.50	0.43	0.38	0.33	0.29	0.25	0.22	0.19	0.17	0.15	0.13
12	0.88	0.77	0.68	0.60	0.53	0.46	0.41	0.36	0.32	0.28	0.25	0.22	0.19	0.17	0.15
11	0.89	0.79	0.70	0.63	0.56	0.50	0.44	0.39	0.35	0.31	0.28	0.25	0.22	0.20	0.17
−10	0.90	0.81	0.73	0.66	0.59	0.53	0.48	0.43	0.39	0.35	0.31	0.28	0.25	0.23	0.21
9	0.91	0.83	0.75	0.69	0.62	0.57	0.52	0.47	0.43	0.39	0.35	0.32	0.29	0.27	0.24
8	0.92	0.85	0.78	0.72	0.66	0.61	0.56	0.51	0.47	0.43	0.40	0.37	0.34	0.31	0.29
7	0.93	0.86	0.80	0.75	0.70	0.65	0.60	0.56	0.52	0.48	0.45	0.42	0.39	0.36	0.34
6	0.94	0.88	0.83	0.78	0.73	0.69	0.65	0.61	0.57	0.54	0.51	0.48	0.45	0.42	0.40
− 5	0.95	0.90	0.86	0.81	0.77	0.74	0.70	0.66	0.63	0.60	0.57	0.54	0.51	0.49	0.46
4	0.96	0.92	0.88	0.85	0.82	0.78	0.75	0.72	0.69	0.66	0.64	0.61	0.59	0.56	0.54
3	0.97	0.94	0.91	0.89	0.86	0.83	0.81	0.78	0.76	0.74	0.72	0.69	0.67	0.65	0.63
2	0.98	0.96	0.94	0.92	0.90	0.89	0.87	0.85	0.83	0.82	0.80	0.78	0.77	0.76	0.74
1	0.99	0.98	0.97	0.96	0.95	0.94	0.93	0.92	0.91	0.90	0.89	0.88	0.87	0.86	0.85
+ 1	1.01	1.02	1.03	1.04	1.05	1.06	1.07	1.08	1.09	1.10	1.12	1.13	1.14	1.15	1.16
2	1.02	1.04	1.06	1.08	1.10	1.13	1.15	1.17	1.20	1.22	1.24	1.27	1.29	1.32	1.35
3	1.03	1.06	1.09	1.13	1.16	1.19	1.23	1.27	1.30	1.34	1.38	1.43	1.47	1.51	1.56
4	1.04	1.08	1.12	1.17	1.22	1.27	1.32	1.37	1.42	1.48	1.54	1.60	1.67	1.73	1.80
5	1.05	1.10	1.16	1.22	1.28	1.34	1.41	1.48	1.55	1.63	1.71	1.80	1.89	1.98	2.08
+ 6	1.06	1.12	1.19	1.26	1.34	1.42	1.50	1.59	1.69	1.79	1.90	2.01	2.13	2.26	2.40
7	1.07	1.14	1.23	1.31	1.40	1.50	1.61	1.72	1.84	1.97	2.10	2.25	2.41	2.58	2.76
8	1.08	1.17	1.26	1.36	1.47	1.59	1.71	1.85	2.00	2.16	2.33	2.52	2.72	2.94	3.17
9	1.09	1.19	1.30	1.41	1.54	1.68	1.83	1.99	2.17	2.37	2.58	2.81	3.07	3.34	3.64
10	1.10	1.21	1.33	1.46	1.61	1.77	1.95	2.14	2.36	2.59	2.85	3.14	3.45	3.80	4.18
+11	1.11	1.23	1.37	1.52	1.69	1.87	2.08	2.30	2.56	2.84	3.15	3.50	3.88	4.31	4.78
12	1.12	1.25	1.40	1.57	1.76	1.97	2.21	2.48	2.77	3.11	3.48	3.90	4.36	4.89	5.47
13	1.13	1.28	1.44	1.63	1.84	2.08	2.35	2.66	3.00	3.39	3.84	4.33	4.90	5.53	6.25
14	1.14	1.30	1.48	1.69	1.93	2.19	2.50	2.85	3.25	3.71	4.23	4.82	5.49	6.26	7.14
15	1.15	1.32	1.52	1.75	2.01	2.31	2.66	3.06	3.52	4.05	4.65	5.35	6.15	7.08	8.14
+20	1.20	1.44	1.73	2.07	2.49	2.99	3.58	4.30	5.16	6.19	7.43	8.92	10.70	12.84	15.41
25	1.25	1.56	1.95	2.44	3.05	3.82	4.77	5.96	7.45	9.31	11.64	14.55	18.19	22.74	28.42

It covers periods from 1 through 15 years, and growth rates from −15 percent through +25 percent. To use the table, divide the terminal value by the starting value, as before (e.g., 3/2 = 1.5). Then locate the column that covers the number of years involved (e.g., 10). Search down the column for the ratio that is closest to the ratio just calculated (it is 1.48 in the table), and run your finger to the far left column to find the growth rate (4 percent).

Users of the "terminal/initial method" of calculating growth rates must be wary of a serious potential distorting factor. If either the initial or terminal values are atypical—unusually high or unusually low—the resulting growth rate will not truly reflect developments during the period. For example, if the initial year happens to be one of recession and the terminal year one of boom, the indicated growth rate will be unrealistically high.

Distortion can be avoided in one of two ways: (1) Choose initial and terminal years that have similar economic characteristics. (2) Do not use single years' data, but rather the *averages* of the first few (e.g., three) and last few years' data. Actually, the second method seems preferable because it involves less subjective judgment.

A more sophisticated method of calculating a growth rate is to fit a "least squares line" to the logarithms of all the data in the series. A description of this method can be found in most standard statistics texts. However, while the method is more precise, especially in that it includes *each* observation of the period rather than merely the initial and terminal values, our experience suggests that unless the growth rate is quite high the additional precision is not worth the considerable extra calculation effort.[34]

Regression Analysis

Regression analysis, or correlation, is another statistical technique which can be applied to a comparison of the growth paths of two series—e.g., sales of IBM versus total equipment outlays of American industry, or annual changes in earnings of the S&P Industrials versus annual changes in U.S. industrial production. Regression can be applied to an even wider variety of problems, however. For example, it was employed in our earlier comparison of the price-earnings ratios of different stocks with the expected growth rates of earnings per share of those stocks.

Table 5–4 showed, in column 1, the price-earnings ratios of 30 stocks on December 31, 1971, and, in column 3, the expected earnings growth rates of these stocks. In regression analysis, the P/E variable would be referred to as Y, the "dependent" variable (the variable we seek to "explain"), and the growth rate variable would be referred to as X, the "independent" variable (the explanatory variable). Figure 5–4(a) was a "scatter diagram" of these data—a series of dots, with each dot representing a pair of X and Y data for a specific stock. For example, to plot the IBM data ($X = 15$ percent; $Y = 33$ P/E), run your finger along the horizontal X-axis to 15, then move vertically until you are alongside 33 on the vertical Y-axis. A dot is placed at that point.

If the P/E of any given stock was higher (or lower) by some constant amount each time the growth rate was higher (or lower) by some constant amount, the dots would fall in a straight line. This is known as "perfect linear correlation." If the dots all fell on a smooth *curved* line, we would have a case of "perfect curvilinear correlation." Perfect correlation is, of course, rare, and our example is no exception. But the

---

[34] The calculation effort can be reduced, however, by the use of Glover's *Tables*. See J. W. Glover, *Tables of Applied Mathematics*. . . . (Ann Arbor, Mich.: George Wahr Publishing Co., 1951).

"line of regression" drawn on the scatter diagram indicates that the relationship, while not perfect, is fairly close. The dots do not all fall on the line, but most dots are not very far from the line.

How was the line of regression derived, and what does it tell us? Although the availability of modern computer programs eliminates the need for any manual calculations, it helps to understand what regression analysis is all about if we briefly outline the principal arithmetic procedures.

The equation form of any straight line is $Y = bX + a$. The b value represents the "slope" of the line—i.e., how much change in Y is associated, on average, with a change in X. The a value is known as the Y intercept. It sets the *level*, as opposed to the *slope*, of the line. It is the value of Y when X is equal to zero.[35]

From a theory known as "least squares," we can derive a straight line (or a curve) which will pass through the individual observations (the dots) in such a way that the sum of the differences between the Y values of the dots (the P/Es in our case) and the Y values of the line will be zero and that the squares of the differences will be minimized. To do this, two equations (in the case of a straight line) must be constructed from the basic data. The equations are:

$$(\text{Sum } Y) = (\text{Sum } X)\, b + (N)\, a \qquad (1)$$
$$(\text{Sum } XY) = (\text{Sum } X^2)\, b + (\text{Sum } X)\, a \qquad (2)$$

Each of the values in parentheses can be calculated quite easily from the raw data in Table 5–4, and the equations can be solved to derive a and b. The resulting line of regression is:

$$\text{P/E} = 2.3\ (\text{Growth rate}) + \quad 4$$
$$(Y) = \quad (b) \qquad (X) \qquad\quad + (a)$$

Once the regression equation has been developed, the regression values of each stock's price-earnings ratio can be computed readily. Table A5–2 shows the regression values (rounded to the nearest whole number) and the differences between the actual and the regression values.

A further sequence of calculations produces some very useful additional information about the nature of the relationship between the dependent and independent variables. The steps are as follows:

1. Square each difference between the actual and regression values of Y (P/E).
2. Sum the squared differences. (In our example, the sum is 369.)

---

[35] Modern portfolio theory makes great use of the b (beta) and a (alpha) values derived from regressions of individual stock price changes against the corresponding changes of a stock market index such as the S&P 500 (see Chapter 15).

TABLE A5–2
Actual versus Regression Values

Company	X (growth rate)	bX (2.3 × growth rate)	Regression Values of P/E (bX + 4, rounded)	Actual P/E	Difference, Actual minus Regression
U.S. Steel	0	0	4	10	6
American Metal Climax	2	4.6	9	11	2
Ingersoll-Rand	3	6.9	11	13	2
Standard Oil of N.J.	3.5	8.0	12	10	−2
General Motors	4	9.2	13	12	−1
Johns-Manville	4	9.2	13	15	2
American Telephone	4	9.2	13	10	−3
Time Inc.	5	11.5	16	16	0
Federated Department Stores	5.5	12.6	17	21	4
General Foods	5.5	12.6	17	14	−3
Clark Equipment	6	13.8	18	16	−2
Firestone Tire	6	13.8	18	12	−6
Dow Chemical	7.5	17.2	21	21	0
Texas Utilities	7.5	17.2	21	16	−5
Magnavox	8	18.4	22	18	−4
Upjohn	8.5	19.5	24	25	1
Carrier	9	20.7	25	24	−1
Sears, Roebuck	9.5	21.8	26	27	1
Eastman Kodak	10	23.0	27	32	5
Merck	11	25.3	29	33	4
Emerson	12	27.6	32	29	−3
Perkin-Elmer	12.5	28.7	33	38	5
Anheuser-Busch	13.5	31.0	35	31	−4
Coca-Cola	13.5	31.0	35	39	4
Hewlett-Packard	14	32.2	36	42	6
Texas Instruments	15	34.5	38	35	−3
International Business Machines	15	34.5	38	33	−5
Avon	16.5	37.9	42	46	4
Xerox	16.5	37.9	42	40	−2
Johnson & Johnson	18	41.4	45	46	1

3. Divide this sum by N. (369 divided by 30 = 12.3.)
4. Take the square root of the number obtained in the previous step. (The square root of 12.3 is 3.5.) This number is referred to as the "standard error of estimate." Generally, about two thirds of the actual values of the dependent variable, Y, will fall within the range of the regression value plus or minus one standard error. Ninety-five percent of the actual values usually will fall within the range of the regression value plus or minus two standard errors.
5. Compute the "variance" of the actual values of Y. This is done by calculating the arithmetic average of Y; calculating the difference between each individual value and the average; squaring the differences; summing the squared differences; and dividing the sum by N. (In our example, the variance of Y is 133.)

6. Divide the number obtained in step (3)—i.e., the square of the standard error—by that obtained in step (5)—i.e., the variance—and subtract this percentage from 100 percent. (12.3 ÷ 133 = 9 percent, which subtracted from 100 percent = 91 percent.) This number is referred to as the "coefficient of determination." It is a direct measure of how closely X and Y are associated. With most economic data, a coefficient of 80 percent or more (it cannot exceed 100 percent) can be considered very high, 60 percent to 80 percent fairly high, and 40 percent to 60 percent moderate. The higher the coefficient of determination, the more confidence one can have in using the line of regression as a predictor of the dependent variable.[36]

The statistical procedures we have been describing relate to "simple regression"—that is, regression involving only one independent variable, in this case the impact of expected earnings growth on P/E ratios. When a problem involves the simultaneous impact of several different independent variables on a dependent variable, such as the discussion in Chapter 5 of the impact of expected growth, dividend policy, financial leverage, and earnings stability on P/E ratios, "multiple regression" techniques are employed. The result of applying these techniques is an equation of the form $Y = a + b_1X_1 + b_2X_2 + b_3X_3 + b_nX_n$, where the various b-values indicate the influence of each of the independent variables (X_1, X_2, X_3, X_n) on the dependent variable. As with simple regression, an overall standard error and coefficient of multiple determination can be calculated to test the "goodness of fit" of the equation.

Perhaps the greatest difficulty encountered in the use of multiple regression analysis is described by the term "multicollinearity." This term refers to the fact that the independent variables may not really be *independent of each other*. For example, it will be shown in Chapter 7 that growth of a company's earnings per share is greatly influenced by the company's policies regarding dividend payment versus earnings retention. Similarly, earnings stability is greatly influenced by the degree of financial leverage. Consequently, a multiple regression analysis of the influence on P/E of earnings growth, dividend policy, financial leverage, and earnings stability, must confront the multicollinearity problem. For when multicollinearity exists, the b-values derived from the analysis are far less reliable than if the independent variables were truly independent. Textbooks on econometrics devote considerable space to methods of trying to overcome or minimize the multicollinearity problem.

---

[36] The standard error of estimate and coefficient of determination are measures of the reliability of the regression line as a whole. It also is possible to measure the reliability, or "statistical significance," of the a and b coefficients individually. The methods are described in the texts cited at the end of this appendix.

Mention should also be made of a technique known as "discriminant analysis," which is being used increasingly in econometric research. The objective of discriminant analysis is similar to that of multiple regression analysis; namely, to quantify the influence of a group of variables on another variable. Discriminant analysis is used, however, when the dependent variable cannot itself be quantified. For example, if the problem is to determine the impact of financial leverage, cash flow, and company size on the probability of whether or not a company will go bankrupt, the dependent variable is qualitative in nature—yes or no; bankrupt or not bankrupt—rather than the more typical type of variable which can be measured on a quantitative scale. The independent variables in discriminant analysis may be either quantitative or qualitative.

Seasonal Adjustment

Most companies report sales and earnings quarterly, and monthly sales data are available in many industries. The security analyst studies these interim data for an indication of recent trends and as a basis for estimating full-year data. Most analysts recognize that it may be misleading to compare directly the results of any given month or quarter with the results of the previous month or quarter. This is because many companies are influenced by a recurring seasonal pattern in the demand for their products or in their mode of production. Two traditional solutions to the problem of seasonality have been (1) to compare the results of any given month or quarter with the results during the *same period of the previous year,* or (2) to examine 12-month or 4-quarter moving totals instead of individual monthly or quarterly data.

Economic statisticians are in widespread agreement, however, that both of these "solutions" can themselves produce distorted impressions of current trends. This is particularly likely to happen when a cyclical turning point is taking place after an extended period of upward or downward movement. A far better resolution of the problem is the statistical technique of seasonal adjustment, whereby mathematical manipulations produce a series of factors which can be used to adjust the raw data. The "seasonally adjusted" data purport to represent the probable pattern of movement of the data if no seasonal influences were present.

Seasonal adjustment techniques range from very simple calculations which can be performed with pencil and paper, to more complex methods requiring electric calculators, to extremely sophisticated procedures requiring electronic computers. Even the crudest techniques, however, ordinarily produce more meaningful data than the raw unadjusted data which many security analysts persist in using. Space does

not permit an elaboration of the mathematics of seasonal adjustment in this appendix, but perusal of one of the texts included in the bibliography is strongly recommended.

SUGGESTED READINGS (APPENDIX)

Bonini, Charles P., and Spurr, William A. "Statistical Concepts," *Financial Analyst's Handbook*, vol. I. Homewood, Ill.: Dow Jones-Irwin, Inc., 1975, chap. 37.

Elton, Edwin J., and Gruber, Martin J. "Time Series Analysis." *Financial Analyst's Handbook*, vol. I. Homewood, Ill.: Dow Jones-Irwin, Inc., 1975, chap. 39.

Jedamus, Paul; Frame, Robert J.; and Taylor, Robert. *Statistical Analysis for Business Decisions*. New York: McGraw-Hill Book Co., 1976.

Merrill, William, and Fox, Karl A. *Introduction to Economic Statistics*. New York: John Wiley & Sons, Inc., 1970.

Milne, Robert D. "Regression Analysis." *Financial Analyst's Handbook*, vol. I. Homewood, Ill.: Dow Jones-Irwin, Inc., 1975, chap. 38.

Valentine, Jerome L., and Mennis, Edmund A. *Quantitative Techniques for Financial Analysis*. Homewood, Ill.: Richard D. Irwin, Inc., 1971.

REVIEW QUESTIONS AND PROBLEMS

1. Discuss the significance of earnings, dividends, and asset values as sources of common stock values.

2. Chapter 5 discussed the application of present-value calculations to the evaluation of common stocks. What differences would there be in applying such calculations to the evaluation of *bonds?*

3. What are some of the practical difficulties encountered in applying present-value calculations to the evaluation of common stocks?

4. What considerations are important in choosing an appropriate discount rate in present-value calculations?

5. Why may there be differences in the price-earnings ratios of different companies in the same industry?

6. What differences may there be between price-current earnings ratios and price-normalized earnings ratios?

7. Illustrate algebraically the relationships between price-earnings ratios, dividend payout ratios, and dividend yields.

8. If you were doing a multiple regression analysis of price-earnings ratios, what variables might you study in addition to those discussed in Chapter 5?

9. What charts might you draw to study the sales growth of General Motors? Be specific as to the type of information you would show on the charts and the arrangement of the scales.

10. What statistical analyses, other than charting, would you undertake to study the growth of total profits of American corporations?

RESEARCH PROJECTS

1. Prepare a paper which considers various national economic developments that could invalidate the evaluation of the Standard & Poor's Industrial Stock Price Index presented in this chapter.
2. Apply the IBM present-value analysis illustration to two other "quality growth companies."
3. Select three industries with similar potential growth rates. Compare their price-earnings ratio histories and attempt to explain any observed differences.
4. Identify the three leading companies in an industry of your choice. Review their price-earnings ratio histories and attempt to explain any observed differences.
5. Figures 5–4 and 5–5 are used to study the relationship between price-earnings ratios and earnings growth. Using this same approach, describe the relationship at the present time.

C.F.A. QUESTIONS

1. *From Exam I, 1973*

Shown are financial data for three corporations. Select the most attractive investment under stated assumptions. Dividend payout ratios and P/E ratios will remain constant. The growth rate in earnings per share from 1967 through 1972 is presumed to continue indefinitely. Investor's required rate of return is adjusted for the different risk characteristics of each security. Show all calculations.

	Albemarle Co.		Nelson Co.		Orange Co.	
	1967	1972	1967	1972	1967	1972
Earnings per share	$2.00	$ 2.94	$2.30	$ 3.70	$1.20	$ 2.10
Current market price		40.00		60.00		40.00
Current dividend rate		1.60		1.80		1.00
Investor's required rate of return		10%		12%		14%

Compound sum of $1 for N years	6%	7%	8%	9%	10%	12%	14%	16%
4	1.26	1.31	1.36	1.41	1.46	1.57	1.69	1.81
5	1.34	1.40	1.47	1.54	1.61	1.76	1.93	2.01
6	1.42	1.50	1.59	1.68	1.77	1.97	2.20	2.44
Compound sum of an annuity of $1 for N years								
4	4.64	4.75	4.87	4.99	5.11	5.35	5.61	5.88
5	5.98	6.15	6.34	6.52	6.72	7.12	7.54	7.98
6	7.39	7.65	7.92	8.20	8.49	9.09	9.73	10.41

2. *From Exam I, 1975*

Using the dividend valuation model $P = D/(k - g)$, explain how inflation affects prices of common stocks where:

P = Market price.

D = Dividends per share.

k = Investor's discount rate.

g = Expected growth rate of dividends (and earnings) per share.

3. *From Exam III, 1974*

You are head of security analysis in the Trust Department at Metropolitan Bank which has an Approved List of about 125 rather well-known common stocks. Top management of the bank has become very "quality-minded' as a result of recent market swings and has asked you to give each stock on the Approved List a quality rating (A, B, C, D) for the guidance of portfolio managers.

List six major criteria you would use in assigning stocks to your A, B, C, D classes and discuss two in detail.

Chapter 6

Analysis of Growth I: Sales Growth

> Observe always that everything is the result of a change.
> ———————————————————————— *Marcus Aurelius*

Virtually any logical approach to the evaluation of a corporation's common stock requires as primary information an estimate of the corporation's probable growth in earning power—either in absolute terms or relative to the growth of all corporations in aggregate. So important is the estimate of earning power that three chapters, of which this is the first, will be devoted to a survey of techniques that can assist the analyst in making such estimates.

Why Start with Sales?

Since the mid-1920s, when common stocks first attained a degree of respectability as a sound investment vehicle,[1] security analysts have stressed growth of demand for a company's products as a keystone of investment success. Why the emphasis on growing demand? On growing sales? Probably the main reason is that overhead has been a factor of steadily increasing importance in American industry. Except during depressions, the U.S. economy has always had a shortage of skilled labor. Pressure has therefore constantly been in the direction of increasing utilization of laborsaving plant and equipment. But capital equipment carries a heavy fixed overhead in the form of interest on debt incurred to buy it, depreciation, maintenance, insurance, taxes,

---

[1] A thin volume by Edgar L. Smith, *Common Stocks as Long-Term Investments*, 2d ed. (New York: Macmillan Co., 1928), is widely regarded as a prime mover in gaining respectability for common stocks.

supervisory salaries, and so forth. This raises the "break-even point" of companies—that is, the number of units which must be produced and sold in order to cover costs. In order for a company to operate profitably under conditions of increasing mechanization and skilled-labor shortage (with consequent high wages), it is essential that its market expand so that its plants can operate at a high percentage of capacity.

Not that expanding production and sales *guarantee* rising *profits*, which in the final analysis is what investors are after. But rising demand does, at least, give a company an *opportunity* to earn a rising profit. In many cases, rising demand can even absorb losses from managerial errors that must be expected to occur from time to time. Indeed, without the cushion of rising demand, management may be loathe to take risks, and without risk-taking little should be expected in the way of rising profits.

History as a Guide

Experience indicates clearly that the best way to begin to estimate future developments is to examine what has happened in the past. Analysts first become familiar with the historical data—with the actual record of sales growth. They then try to learn *why* the past record was what it was. For example, if sales growth had been exceptionally rapid relative to the sales of competitors, analysts might want to find out the extent to which exclusive patent rights accounted for the competitive advantage.

As they begin to understand the conditions that created the past trends, analysts question whether these conditions are likely to persist in the future. Continuing the above illustration, analysts would investigate whether any basic patents were nearing expiration or whether any other companies had developed some improvements that would render the existing product technologically obsolete. If the conditions that created the past trends seem likely to persist in the future, analysts can simply project the past trends forward. But if, as is more likely, analysts believe that certain past conditions will probably be altered in form, or disappear entirely, they will try to estimate the impact of the changes and make allowance for them in their projections of the past record. In either event, however, the key to the future lies in an understanding of the past.

If possible, analysts should try to gather data for a period which encompasses a variety of economic conditions. In this way they have an opportunity to observe the impact of changing conditions on the company's sales (and on its prices, labor costs, raw material supplies, and other profit determinants). They also can examine management's response to change more adequately than if they have only a few years of data available.

The Industrial Life Cycle

An analysis of the sales growth record and growth prospects of an industry or a company frequently can be conducted within the framework of the so-called industrial life cycle. Many students of economic history have argued that industries, like people, go through a few fairly well-defined stages of development. In the early part of their lives they grow at a very rapid rate. After a time the growth rate slows down; they continue to expand, but at a more moderate pace. Finally, they stop growing and either live a relatively stable existence for a long time—or die. The "industrial life cycle," visualized from an investment perspective, is illustrated in Figure 6–1.

FIGURE 6–1
The Industrial Life Cycle

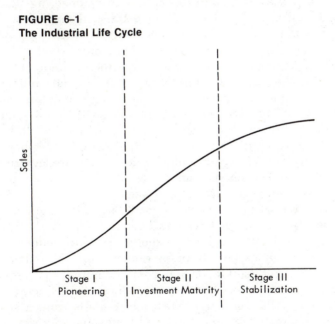

| | Stage I | Stage II | Stage III |
| | Pioneering | Investment Maturity | Stabilization |

Pioneering Stage. Exponents of the industrial life cycle concept, such as the late Professor Julius Grodinsky of the Wharton School of Finance and Commerce, see the "pioneering stage" of an industry's development as being characterized by rapid expansion of the market with concomitant opportunities for large profits. These opportunities, however, give rise to fierce competition and high risk of bankruptcy. The automobile industry provides a dramatic example of this phenomenon. Between 1900 and 1908, more than 500 automobile companies were organized. Of these, about 300 quickly went out of business, either voluntarily or involuntarily. By 1917, 76 companies were active in the industry, but 10 produced three quarters of the

total output. Today, of course, only three companies dominate the U.S. auto industry.[2] More recent examples of rampant competition in new fields include air conditioners, television manufacturing, and electronic components such as semiconductors.

Some investment authorities recommend that the best way to participate in the pioneering phase of the industrial life cycle is to buy the stocks of several competing companies. By thus spreading risks, investors take the position that even if only one of the several companies survives, the profits on that one will more than make up for the losses on the others.

Investment Maturity and Stabilization Stages. Most of the discussion in the balance of this chapter, and in those which follow, will focus on the phases of growth that follow the pioneering stage. The second stage of growth is labeled "investment maturity" on Figure 6–1. It refers to the fact that after some years, through consolidations and internal expansion, a relatively few companies usually take over a fairly large percentage of a young industry's total volume of business. They broaden the market by improving the quality and reducing the price of the product or service. They establish a strong financial position and a record of dividend payments—even if the dividends are quite modest. Growth of the industry's market continues to be quite rapid. It is not as rapid as in the pioneering stage, but neither are the risks as great. The air conditioning, television manufacturing, and semiconductor industries all can be said to have passed from the pioneering to the investment maturity stage.

Gradually, however, even this second stage of growth begins to slow down. Technological advances become fewer and occur after longer time lags. Unit costs become more difficult to reduce, and the ability to broaden markets through reduced prices is thereby restricted. The market itself tends to become saturated, a process which is aggravated by the inroads of newer products and services.

The theory of the industrial life cycle departs from a strict anthropomorphic analogy at this point. Although the industry may, in fact, die, it is not argued that an aging industry necessarily must ultimately die. Indeed, in absolute terms its sales may continue to grow. But the growth may be below average. The industry's sales may expand less rapidly than the economy during periods of general prosperity, and they may decline more rapidly during recessions. This stage in the evolution of an industry is labeled "stabilization" in Figure 6–1. Of the three industries referred to above, perhaps television manufacturing is closest to this stage.

To many proponents of industrial life cycle concept, the investment

---

[2] Automobile Manufacturers Association, *Automobile Facts and Figures* (Detroit: latest edition).

implications of the stabilization stage are quite bleak. In their view, investors should dispose of their stockholdings in the industry *before* stabilization takes hold. If they wait until it is common knowledge that the industry is leveling off, it may be too late. Stock prices may decline, and opportunities for a good rate of return may disappear. According to this approach, investment success will be achieved by (*a*) detecting growth industries that are about to emerge from the pioneering phase; (*b*) investing in the stocks of the dominant companies in those industries; and (*c*) selling the stocks just before the industries enter the stabilization phase. Typifying this approach was a study released in 1973 by the investment firm of Lehman Brothers. They noted that during 1967–72, industry groups which had above-average sales growth recorded an average stock price gain of 57 percent, while groups with below-average sales growth had a stock price gain of only 4 percent. To underscore these data, Lehman Brothers commented: "As important as growth selection is to performance, [*avoiding*] *the selection of non-growth companies is almost as important.*"[3]

Critique.   In many respects, the life cycle approach offers a convenient method of classifying the growth patterns of different companies. But while the industrial life cycle concept is useful, several criticisms can be leveled at the concept and at its investment implications. First, it is not necessarily true that a new industry is pioneered by large numbers of small companies which kill each other off in a bitter competitive struggle. The synthetic fiber industry, for example, was largely pioneered by a single giant company—Du Pont—and vigorous competition did not emerge until many years *after* the original introduction of nylon. Electrostatic copying of documents (Xerox) and instant photographic processing (Polaroid) are other illustrations.

Furthermore, the latter years of an industry's life are not necessarily characterized by permanent stagnation. Many industries go through a long period of oscillation between prosperity and recession. This type of oscillation may be noted in the cement and copper industries, for example.

Finally, the most important criticism of the life cycle approach to investment analysis is that to equate automatically each growth stage with a different degree of investment attractiveness is to overlook the factor of security *prices* and *values*. A major premise of this text is that it is possible to pay too much for growth and that at the right price even a no-growth situation can be attractive. Surely, the disastrous price declines which befell the stocks of many growth companies in 1974–75, in spite of continued above-average sales gains, attests to the importance of being careful not to pay too much for growth.

Illustrations.   For all of its deficiencies, the life cycle framework does provide an interesting basis for at least an initial review of an

---

[3] Lehman Brothers, *A Rationale for Growth* (New York, October 10, 1973), p. 9.

industry's sales history. To illustrate, the aluminum and semiconductor industries have been chosen as examples.

The history of the American aluminum industry is a long one. Aluminum production was begun in 1888 by the Pittsburgh Reduction Company, a predecessor of the Aluminum Company of America. As shown in Table 6–1, the industry's growth rate in its formative years was in excess of 20 percent per annum, and a 15 percent growth rate was maintained from 1910 to 1920. As its markets became increasingly saturated, the growth rate slowed markedly in the 20s, but evidence of the continued vitality of the industry was the 6 percent growth rate achieved during the years of the Great Depression. World War II gave rise to major new aluminum-consuming industries such as mass-produced aircraft, and the industry's growth rate accelerated. Since 1960, a slowing has taken place once again, but a rate well in excess of aggregate real economic growth has been maintained. Thus, one might categorize the aluminum industry as having been in its pioneering phase until about 1920, and in an extended investment maturity phase since then. A question emerging from this view is whether the stabilization phase was approaching as the decade of the 1970s unfolded. A closer examination of aluminum sales in recent years will be made in the pages which follow in order to attempt an answer to this question.

In contrast to the long history of the aluminum industry, the semiconductor industry was born in the early 1950s, although research in this field can be traced to the 19th century. Another significant difference is that semiconductors are not a homogeneous product like aluminum. One major segment of the market, "discrete" devices such as transistors, exhibited ten years of explosive growth (see Table 6–1)

TABLE 6–1
Life Cycle Patterns of Aluminum and Semiconductors

		U.S. Factory Sales of Semiconductors		
U.S. Primary Aluminum Production			Transistor Growth Rate (percent)	Integrated Circuit Growth Rate (percent)
Period	Growth Rate (percent)	Period		
1900–1910	21			
1910–1920	15			
1920–1930	5			
1930–1940	6			
1940–1950	13	1955–1960	100	
1950–1960	11	1960–1965	37	
1960–1970	7	1965–1970	10	100
1970–1976	5	1970–1976	13	25

Source: Underlying data from Aluminum Association, Electronic Industries Association, and Dataquest.

and then entered an investment maturity phase which, as will be shown in succeeding pages, exhibited many of the characteristics of the stabilization phase. The other major segment of the market, integrated circuits, arose early in the 1960s and since then has exhibited the same explosive growth as in the early years of transistors. Whether a rapid maturation process will similarly occur will be considered below.

Relative Growth in Recent Years

Having examined the historical record of the aluminum and semiconductor industries from a broad life cycle perspective, we turn next to a more intensive study of the recent history of these industries. An adequate study should include:

1. A comparison of the dollar sales of the industry with the dollar sales of competing industries if such can be identified (e.g., aluminum competes with copper but semiconductors have no direct competition), and with one or more broad economic measures such as gross national product, personal consumption expenditures, and durable goods manufacturing.

2. Similar comparisons to those above, but in physical unit rather than dollar terms—pounds, tons, ton-miles, and so on. Sole reliance on *dollar* sales data is inadvisable. Dollar sales are equal to the number of *units* sold multiplied by the sales price per unit. But as is well known, the prices of different commodities, such as aluminum, copper and steel, do not change uniformly. Differences in price movement exist both in timing and in magnitude. Thus it is quite possible to conceive of the following situation. Industry A expands its unit sales faster than competing Industry B. In order to accomplish this, Industry A has gradually reduced its prices relative to those of Industry B. As a result, the *dollar* sales of A have expanded less rapidly than those of B.

Analysts who concern themselves solely with *dollar* sales comparisons in this example would miss an opportunity to gain real insight into the competitive forces at work. If they project future sales relationships on the basis of the past without recognizing that the past record reflects sharply contrasting price-volume patterns, their projections probably will turn out to be quite inaccurate. For it is most unlikely that the past price-volume patterns will remain unchanged. Accordingly, it is strongly recommended that interindustry and industry-economy sales comparisons be carried out in terms of volume in addition to dollars.

To illustrate a portion of such a study, Figure 6–2 shows the ratio of annual aluminum and semiconductor dollar sales to gross national product since 1953. Figure 6–3 presents the same comparisons in unit

FIGURE 6–2
Dollar Sales of Aluminum and Semiconductors Relative to GNP

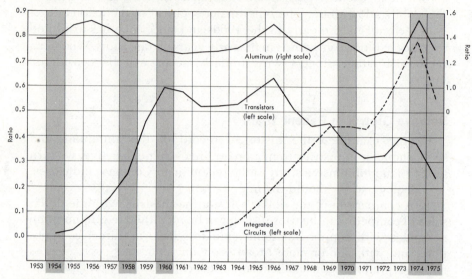

Recession years indicated by shading.

FIGURE 6–3
Unit Sales of Aluminum and Semiconductors Relative to "Real" GNP

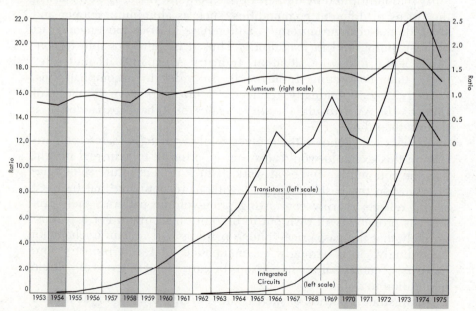

Recession years indicated by shading.

terms. Before examining these charts, let us analyze the derivation of the underlying data.

Industry Dollar Sales. The aluminum sales figures are the summation of the reported annual revenues of the four leading companies in the U.S. aluminum industry—Alcoa, Alcan, Kaiser, and Reynolds (Alcan is a Canadian company but is a major competitor of the three leading U.S. companies). Admittedly, a summation of leading companies' revenues usually is not equivalent to aggregate U.S. industry sales, because (*a*) there are other firms in each industry,[4] and (*b*) the sales of most large companies are not exclusively concentrated in the products of a single industry and often include foreign operations. (In September 1975, the FASB proposed rules which will be very helpful to analysts in this connection. The rules require fairly detailed breakdowns of sales and earnings by major product line and distinctions between domestic and foreign operations.) However, up-to-date aggregate industry data, in dollar amounts, usually are available only for broader categories than we are interested in—for example, all nonferrous metals[5]—and summations of leading companies' revenues generally serve as a convenient and useful substitute. Until recently, the semiconductor industry was an exception to this generalization. Aggregate dollar sales data were published for each major product line of the industry by the Electronic Industries Association. In 1971, however, a major producer stopped submitting its data, and it became necessary to rely on "expert opinion" for such information. It should be noted that almost every important industry in the United States has at least one trade association publication, and these often serve as valuable data sources for industry analysis.

Industry Unit Sales. For both aluminum and semiconductors (until 1971), unit volume data have been published by the respective trade associations. Interestingly, volume data are often available for industry aggregates while they may be unavailable for individual companies. The situation is quite the opposite from that of dollar sales. Sources of industry volume statistics often are found in the *Statistical Abstract of the United States,* together with summary data for selected years. The Conference Board and trade journals are other excellent sources of statistics. In addition, one of the several dozen industry subgroups of the Federal Reserve Board Index of Industrial Produc-

---

[4] For example, in addition to the "big four" aluminum companies, a sizable amount of aluminum is produced by Conalco, Anaconda, Howmet, Martin Marietta, Revere, and other companies. The names of the leading companies in most major industries can be obtained from the relevant Standard & Poor's *Industry Survey,* among other sources.

[5] For current sales data on broad manufacturing industry groupings see the FTC-SEC's *Quarterly Survey of Manufacturing Corporations.* Narrower groupings are presented in the *Census of Manufactures,* and *Census of Mineral Industries,* but there is a considerable time lag in the availability of these data.

tion may be used. Many of these subindexes are published monthly in the *Federal Reserve Bulletin*, and additional details are contained in monthly releases by the Board, which are kept on file at most business libraries. (The fact that these are index numbers rather than actual volume data makes no difference for our present purposes.)

Of course, production volume is not synonymous with sales volume—the difference being inventory accumulation or liquidation.[6] However, while the short-term movements of production can differ markedly in amplitude from sales movements, over a period of several years the trends of the two series usually will be quite similar.

If physical volume data are not available from any of the above-indicated sources, an approximation can often be calculated by the analyst. Since dollar sales are equal to volume multiplied by price, it follows that volume equals sales *divided by* price. Thus, if analysts have a series of dollar sales for their industry, or for the leading companies in the industry, they can try to obtain a statistical series which reflects reasonably accurately the price history of the industry. Then, by dividing each year's dollar sales by the corresponding prices, they can obtain a reasonable estimate of annual volume.[7]

Where can price data for an industry be obtained? Probably the most convenient source is the Bureau of Labor Statistics' Wholesale Price Index (or Consumer Price Index if the industry is one of the relatively few that deal directly with the public). Like the Industrial Production Index, the Wholesale Price Index is broken down into a large number of product group subindexes. These subindexes are published in the *Monthly Labor Review* and similar government periodicals, with greater detail being presented in monthly releases sent to libraries all over the country.

To illustrate the procedure of approximating volume data—a procedure known as "deflating"—consider the processed foods industry. The companies in this industry produce cans of peas, boxes of corn flakes, packages of bacon, bottles of mayonnaise, containers of milk, and thousands of other items with no common unit denominator. Yet there *is* a wholesale price index component labeled "processed foods." Assume that the value of this index rose from 94 to 101 (1967 = 100)[8] over a ten-year period, and that a representative sample

---

[6] In the case of metal industries, moreover, production of primary metals is supplemented with secondary production—i.e., the reprocessing of scrap.

[7] In many instances this indirect measure of volume may, in fact, be more satisfactory than actual unit data because of the possibility of changes in the nature of the unit. For example, a million cars means something quite different when a large percentage are compacts from when most are full size or when they are equipped with air conditioners, power steering, and other expensive accessories. In other words, when the quality of the product-mix changes significantly, unit measures can become obsolete.

[8] The base year of the index numbers has been changed from time to time, but this is of no consequence in terms of the final results.

of companies in this industry reported a rise in dollar sales from \$1.25 billion to \$1.90 billion over the same ten years. Dividing these dollar sales figures by the corresponding price indexes we get, respectively, 1.33 and 1.88 "billions of 1967 dollars," otherwise referred to as "billions of dollars of constant purchasing power," or simply as "constant dollars" or "real dollars." Regardless of the label attached to the data, they can be used just like any actual physical volume data in measuring growth patterns. The percentage changes are significant, not the terminology employed. Thus, the growth of "current dollar" sales of these companies during the decade was 52 percent (1.90/1.25), but the growth of "constant dollar" sales—or volume—was only 41 percent (1.88/1.33).

Figure 6–4 offers another illustration of the approximation of volume data by deflating dollar sales. Here, the sales of various segments of the retailing industry are decomposed into price and volume components at key points during the 1973–75 business cycle. Note how many cases exhibited new highs in dollar sales in 1975, yet with volume well below that of earlier years. Note, also, the lack of uniformity of price/volume behavior in the different retailing sectors.

Aggregate Economic Data. Industry dollar sales of aluminum and semiconductors are compared in Figure 6–2 with gross national product. Industry unit sales, on the other hand, are compared in Figure 6–3 with "constant dollar" or "real" gross national product. The constant dollar data for GNP and its major components are published regularly along with the current dollar data in the Department of Commerce's *Survey of Current Business.* They are derived by the "deflating" procedure described above.

Ratio Analysis of the Data. Figures 6–2 and 6–3 are in ratio form. That is, industry sales are divided by GNP and the resulting quotients, or ratios, are plotted on a graph. This method of analyzing data visually was described in the Appendix to Chapter 5, where it was noted that the underlying data need not be expressed in similar units (e.g., dollars versus dollars) to make ratio analysis possible. Pounds of one product can be compared with bushels, or quarts, or, as in Figure 6–3, with "constant dollars." The absolute amounts of the ratios are not significant; the *changes* in the ratios are.

In examining each ratio line, answers should be sought to four questions:

1. Is the line rising or falling—that is, is the numerator of the ratio growing more or less rapidly than the denominator—over the whole length of the period (from initial to terminal years)?
2. Has the relative growth (or relative decline) of the numerator been fairly uniform or has it occurred in fits and starts? The less the variability around trend, the more confidence one can have in

FIGURE 6–4
Retail Sales by Type of Store (comparison of price and quantity components at 1973–1975 cyclical turning points and recovery, in billions of dollars)

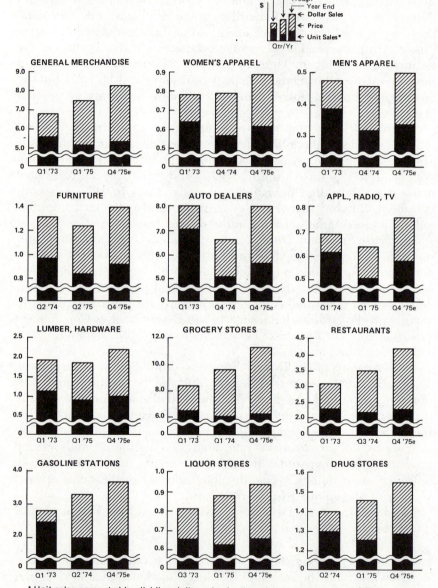

* Unit sales computed by dividing dollar sales by the relevant component of CPI.
Source: Sanford C. Bernstein & Co., Inc.

using the past trend as the starting point of an analysis. Indeed, if the variability is slight it may be possible to use some type of *mechanical* trend projection technique. (It also will be recalled from Chapter 5 that stability is an important determinant of a stock's price-earnings ratio.)

3. Is there any sign that the overall trend of the ratio line has been leveling off in recent years?
4. What has been the behavior of the line during years of general economic recession? Has the numerator been more or less vulnerable to economic adversity than the denominator? To facilitate this comparison it is convenient to shade in the years of recession, as indicated on the charts for the years 1954, 1958, 1960, 1970, and 1974–75 (See Chapter 12 for a detailed chronology of modern business cycles.) It is even more helpful to examine the data on a quarterly or monthly basis since the impact of recessions usually overlaps calendar year-ends.

When these questions are applied to the charts at hand, some interesting observations emerge. Taking Figure 6–3 first, it can be seen that over the full period shown, unit sales of aluminum and of both major types of semiconductors rose much more rapidly than total economic output. The relative growth of aluminum, however, did not proceed steadily from year to year, and the relative growth of the transistor segment of the semiconductor industry was very volatile during several years of the period. In each recession year, aluminum was more vulnerable than the overall economy (the ratio line declined). Transistor growth was not greatly impeded by most recessions, but it was hit hard by the 1970 recession and by the continued economic decline in 1975. The relative growth of integrated circuits was not stopped by the 1970 recession, but there was a noticeable slowdown, and in 1975 the industry experienced its first downturn in volume. Thus, unit sales of these industries have strong secular growth trends, but they are substantially affected by movements in the general business cycle.

When *dollar* sales are examined relative to gross national product (Figure 6–2), the impact of the business cycle becomes more pronounced, especially for the semiconductor industry, and the secular trend of relative growth also takes on a different configuration. The growth in dollar sales of the four leading aluminum companies was no greater over the full period than GNP—the ratio line fluctuated cyclically around a fairly horizontal trend. Transistor dollar sales grew relative to GNP until 1960; the ratio line then flattened for several years, and then trended downward. Relative growth of dollar sales of integrated circuits was rapid until 1968, flattened in 1969–71, and then

resumed an uptrend, but not as steep, with cyclical vulnerability showing up clearly in 1975. The weaker showing of these industries when examined in dollar terms as opposed to unit terms suggests the possibility of underlying weakness in the price structure. This aspect of the history of these industries will be considered next.

Prices

There are two price factors which should be distinguished because they may have different implications for the future. One is the natural secular price decline of growth products; the other is the erratic price movement of industries whose productive capacity periodically spurts far ahead of immediate sales potential.

Think of an industry which has grown rapidly in sales volume for a period of 10 or 20 years, and then think of what has happened to its selling prices relative to the general price level. Almost invariably, the selling price of a growing product has shown a secular downtrend— either in absolute terms or at least relative to other prices. Aluminum and semiconductors both are examples; nylon, the miracle drugs, television, and air transport are others.

Where the basic demand for a product is strong, managements try to tap and expand the market by reducing cost and improving quality. Productivity gains are used, in part, to lower selling prices. On the other hand, in nongrowth industries, like steel and railroad passenger transport, selling prices tend to be raised whenever possible, instead of lowered to broaden markets. When prices do get cut in nongrowth industries, it usually takes the form of price warfare rather than secular price reduction. Price warfare refers to intraindustry price cutting in an attempt to capture a larger share of a relatively fixed market. But secular price reduction is designed to enlarge the total effective demand for a product or service. (It is assumed, of course, that demand for the product is "price elastic.")

Frequently, however, situations are encountered where an industry exhibits the price characteristics of a stagnant market and yet demand for the industry's product is, in fact, growing at an above-average rate. Typically, the cause of this peculiar behavior is excess capacity. Although demand for the product is rising, productive capacity may be rising much more rapidly.[9] As a result, the companies in the industry engage in extremely vigorous price competition in order to build up their sales relative to capacity. Then, when a better sales/capacity

---

[9] Capacity can rise sharply not only through the deliberate construction of new facilities but also through the chance discovery of new sources and through the development of major new productive processes which substantially increase output per dollar of cost.

balance is achieved, they attempt to restore their previous prices. Perhaps as good examples as any of this pattern have been the aluminum and semiconductor industries.

Overcapacity of primary aluminum ingot plagued the industry from 1957 to 1963, and had a depressing impact on price. Moreover, in the fabricating end of the aluminum business (the major aluminum companies fabricate the bulk of their ingot output into finished or semifinished products), the overcapacity problem was even more severe. By the second half of the 1960s, however, the industry once again was operating at capacity, and sometimes above. Indeed, aluminum shortages in some European nations were made up by imports from Communist countries. A firm price structure accompanied the return to high utilization of capacity.

With the recession of 1970–71, demand for aluminum dropped both in the United States and in Europe, which also experienced a recession. Meanwhile, a rash of new aluminum smelters had been opened, many in nations new to the industry and built with government subsidies. Aluminum prices declined sharply in the face of the renewed overcapacity.

This experience caused the industry to curtail expansion of capacity. In the United States, for example, primary aluminum capacity rose only 5 percent in the three years, 1971–74. But production rose 25 percent and the utilization rate rose from 84 percent to 100 percent. As a result, prices soared. From a realized price level of 24 cents a pound in 1971, the price of aluminum rose to 34 cents in 1974 and to 40 cents in 1975—the latter increase coming in the face of the worst worldwide economic recession of the postwar years.

The unprecedented strength of aluminum prices during a severe economic recession caused many analysts to proclaim that a new era had arrived for the metal, and, indeed, for many other raw materials whose prices showed similar strength. Their argument was that the costs of building new capacity had risen to such high levels (e.g., from about 20 cents per pound of aluminum in 1971 to about 35 cents in 1975) that without high selling prices no new capacity would be built. But while this argument perhaps had *long-run* merit, the fact was that by late 1975, with production slowing markedly in lagged response to the recession, price-cutting reappeared in the industry.[10] Although the renewed price weakness may, in retrospect, be viewed as a temporary aberration (by the summer of 1976, the price had risen to another new high), the long history of aluminum prices just recited suggests two conclusions regarding the years ahead. First, aluminum prices are more likely than not to decline secularly relative to other prices, in

---

[10] "The Price War in Aluminum," *Business Week*, November 17, 1975, pp. 151–53.

line with the industry's expansion of markets (see further discussion below). Second, this secular trend is likely to be punctuated by periodic episodes of overexpansion and cyclical price reductions—perhaps from a higher *level* of price than earlier, but substantial nevertheless.

The semiconductor industry presents another interesting illustration of the interaction between secular, market-expanding, price reduction, and cyclical price warfare. Figure 6–5 shows the relationship

FIGURE 6–5
Semiconductor Price/Volume Relationships

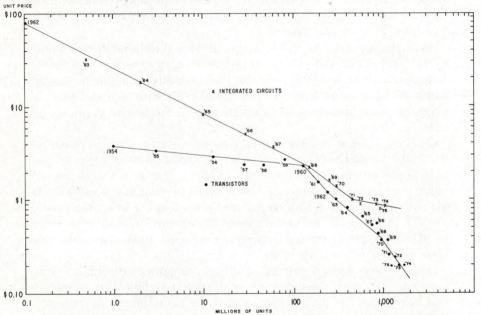

between price and volume for both transistors and integrated circuits since the beginning of their life cycles (note that both the horizontal and vertical axes are on logarithmic scales). Turning first to the price/volume relationship for transistors, it can be seen that from 1954 to 1960 there was a smooth progression of declining prices and rising volume. From 1960 to 1962, the slope of the price/volume line changed sharply, with prices falling 50 percent on a relatively modest volume increase. This drastic price decline reflected distress selling due to widespread overcapacity in the industry. With hindsight, the industry leaders determined that the reason for the severe overcapacity was that they had not reduced prices sufficiently during the industry's formative years. This provided a "price umbrella" which allowed hundreds of small firms to enter the transistor business profitably—

many of which subsequently went bankrupt during the 1960–62 shake-out. This experience, as we shall see, taught the industry a lesson which was applied to integrated circuit pricing policy. In any event, after 1962, a new price/volume relationship was established, with substantial price reductions accompanying volume growth.

The price/volume relationship for integrated circuits has had a rather different shape from that of transistors. Learning from their experience with transistors, the industry leaders dropped prices substantially in the early years of the life cycle of integrated circuits.[11] This made it difficult for marginal firms to enter the business, with the consequent hope that serious supply/demand imbalances could be prevented. To date, this hope has been justified and, in the most recent years, the industry has been able to maintain prices at a higher level in relation to volume than was the case earlier.

As for the future of semiconductor prices, there is every reason to expect continued secular price reduction. Whether this will be accompanied by periodic price warfare, as occurred in the transistor sector in 1960–62, depends importantly on the ability of the producers to differentiate their products. The transistor has become a standardized "commodity-type" product, like aluminum, and periodic recurrences of rampant price-cutting would not be surprising. Several varieties of integrated circuits—even of advanced versions known as microprocessors and microcomputers—also have become highly standardized, posing a similar risk. But to the extent that producers of integrated circuits can custom-design products, and become producers of "subsystems" (e.g., subsystems of computers) or of final products rather than producers of mere "off-the-shelf components," the risk will be lessened. While it would appear that the odds favor avoidance of the price warfare type of behavior, the odds in this direction are not very great, as suggested by the price-cutting which has occurred among producers of hand-held calculators and, more recently, digital watches.

Market Analysis

Thus far, our examination of aluminum and semiconductor sales has been in aggregate terms. This is insufficient for an in-depth understanding of either the history or the future prospects of an industry. A study of the individual markets for the industry's output is extremely helpful.

An industry can grow at an above-average rate in three ways: (1) by supplying a stable share of rapidly growing markets; (2) by supplying

---

[11] Since the number of circuits per unit has increased steadily over time, the price *per circuit*, or *per function*, has declined even more sharply relative to volume than indicated on the chart.

a growing share of markets having only average growth; and (3) most dynamically, by supplying a growing share of rapidly growing markets.

There are many ways to delineate an industry's markets—for example, by geographic area, by age or income bracket of individual consumers of its products, by the various "life styles" of consumers, or, most commonly, by *consuming industry*. Market analyses which focus on consuming industries have been facilitated by the development and improvement of a social accounting system known as input-output analysis. This accounting system, which is still in the process of evolution and expansion, divides the economy into dozens of industrial groupings. The sales volume of each of these industries to each of the other industries—thousands of purchase and sale entries—is shown in the input-output tabulations, and the whole network of data is tied to the well-known gross national product figures. A more detailed description of input-output, and a discussion of its use in sales forecasting, is presented in the Appendix to this chapter.

The various trade associations are also important sources of information on markets. For example, Table 6–2 summarizes the Aluminum

TABLE 6–2
Estimated Distribution and Growth of U.S. Aluminum Shipments, by Market

Market	Percent of Total Shipments			Growth Rate (percent)
	1960–1965	1966–1970	1971–1974	
Construction	25	22	25	7
Transportation	21	19	18	7
Packaging	7	11	15	15
Electrical	12	13	13	10
Consumer durables	11	10	9	6
Machinery and equipment ...	7	7	7	6
Exports	8	8	6	5
Other	9	10	7	7
	100	100	100	7

Source: The Aluminum Association.

Association's estimates of the end-user markets for its industry since 1960. It will be noted that the most rapid growth areas for aluminum have been packaging (cans and foil) and electrical (wire and cable). These two markets now account for about 30 percent of the aluminum industry's total shipments. Shipments to each other identified major market—construction, transportation, consumer durables, and industrial machinery—have grown at a rate of at least 6 percent, and as high as 8 percent, well in excess of "real GNP" growth; and export growth

also has been above average. Strong growth in various "other" markets reflects the increasing substitution of aluminum for copper, steel, and other metals.

Having determined the major markets which have accounted for aluminum's *past* growth, the next questions are: (1) What are the growth prospects of these markets themselves? (2) What is the likelihood that the penetration of these markets by aluminum will rise?

A detailed discussion of question (1) is beyond the scope of this chapter, but some brief observations can be made regarding the growth prospects of each major market in the foreseeable future.

Construction. The residential portion of the construction market can be expected to grow at a rate no faster than GNP. Two opposing forces are at work in this market. On the one hand, increases in the cost of private housing have outstripped the income growth of "middle America." On the other hand, a continuation can be expected of governmental efforts to improve the nation's housing conditions. As for commercial and industrial construction, this sector, too, should be merely an average growth market, with cyclical variations around trend in response to shifts in business capital spending budgets.

Transportation. As with construction, this market can be expected to grow at about the same rate as GNP, with crosscurrents within the market. Passenger automobile growth prospects are generally conceded to be, at best, average, and more likely slightly below average, while truck, trailer, and railroad car prospects appear somewhat better than average. Aircraft growth will depend in large measure on the willingness and ability of the airline industry to undertake another major expansion program in connection with supersonic aircraft. Their unhappy earnings experience following the introduction of "jumbo-jets" has, for the time being, caused a major cutback in capital programs.

Electrical. Growth of electric generating and transmission facilities long seemed certain to be well above average, but the "energy crisis" and resulting soaring costs of electricity have caused consumers to cut back their usage of electricity. Therefore, average, rather than above-average growth seems the safest prediction.

Packaging. A continuation of the postwar trend toward convenience foods makes this a likely above-average growth market.

Consumer Durables and Industrial Machinery. Combined growth of these two markets is generally expected to be about average or slightly above-average.

Exports. The potential growth of foreign markets for aluminum is quite high. The Aluminum Association estimates per capita consumption in the United States at over 60 pounds, compared with 40 pounds in West Germany, over 30 in Japan, 25 in Great Britain and France,

and only 5 or 10 in underdeveloped countries. However, as was noted earlier, there has been considerable expansion of overseas smelting capacity in recent years, so the actual export market for U.S. companies may not be as great as these comparative consumption data suggest.[12]

The subject of per capita consumption of aluminum turns us from the question of the growth prospects of aluminum's markets to the second question; namely, the intensity of aluminum's use in those markets. In residential construction, for example, the quantity of aluminum used to build a house has more than tripled during the past 15 years. Aluminum's corrosion-resistant qualities make it ideal for roofing, siding, windows, doors, and ornamental uses. It is replacing increasingly expensive wood products, particularly in low- and moderate-income conventional housing and in mobile homes.

The amount of aluminum used in the average American passenger car doubled during the 1950s, but the growth rate of aluminum use per car then slowed. However, the energy crisis has given rise to a demand for lighter cars, which use less fuel, and this, in turn, suggests a major effort to replace steel with lighter metals such as aluminum.

In the nonautomotive segment of the transportation market, increased use of aluminum for mass transit systems can be expected. On the other hand, the relative use of aluminum in the aircraft industry has declined due to the Defense Department's emphasis on missiles, which require much less aluminum than manned fighters and bombers. In other markets for aluminum, further penetration is likely in packaging and electrical products. For example, 32 percent of beverage cans in the United States in 1974 were all-aluminum versus 10 percent in 1969, and the growth seems to be continuing.

Yet, further market penetrations by aluminum cannot be taken for granted. While aluminum has obvious advantages over other metals, its competition is not inherently limited to other metals. Since World War II, plastic technology has progressed by leaps and bounds. Plastics are being used for pipes, walls, auto parts, containers, and countless other products formerly made of metals. In the packaging field, aluminum has benefited mightily from the inventiveness of housewives and package designers in finding uses for aluminum foil and thin sheet. But plastic and paper producers have not lacked for inventiveness themselves. Goods are being packaged in plastic film, squeeze bottles, rigid containers, and semirigid coated paper containers. In addition, the steel industry itself has counterattacked with such products as "thin tin" and vapor-coated aluminum steel for canneries.

---

[12] For a possible new source of export demand, see "The Chinese Quest for Foreign Aluminum," *Business Week*, October 6, 1975, pp. 28–29.

And the glass industry has countered with less expensive bottles. In short, steel, copper, aluminum, wood, and glass are not clearly defined materials with clearly defined markets. They must face the competition of substitute materials and of refined versions of the old standbys.[13] Moreover, if the predictions of permanently high aluminum prices prove correct, the metal may find itself priced out of markets it otherwise could capture.

Analysis of markets leads to a reasonable basis for estimating the growth in physical volume of aluminum sales during the next five to ten years. The sum total of the markets which use aluminum seems likely to grow at a rate slightly above that of aggregate economic activity. Within these markets, the penetration of aluminum should grow, but one's confidence in this judgment must be tempered by a recognition of the dramatic changes that are taking place in the materials field. Assuming that "real" gross national product grows at a 3.5 percent–4 percent per annum rate, as suggested in Chapter 5, a 6–7 percent growth rate of unit sales volume of the major aluminum companies can be used as a working hypothesis. But we also have noted that aluminum prices are likely to decline relative to the overall price level. Adding price and volume gains produces total dollar sales gains for the major aluminum companies which is modestly higher than total GNP growth—perhaps 8 percent in a low-inflation environment and 12 percent if inflation is more severe (versus GNP growth of 6 percent or 10 percent, depending on the rate of inflation).

Turning just briefly to semiconductors, since the basic approach to market analysis has now been outlined, information available from the Electronic Industries Association and other sources permits us to make the following estimate of U.S. market distribution[14] in the mid-1970s:

	Total Semiconductors (percent)	Integrated Circuits (percent)
Computers	30	40
Products for government	15 ⎫	
Auto and industrial	25 ⎬	60
Consumer products	15 ⎪	
Exports*	15 ⎭	
	100	100

* Excludes output of foreign facilities of U.S. manufacturers.

---

[13] Indeed, producers of primary aluminum may have to face increasing competition from scrap reprocessors as the flow of scrapped aluminum products increases.

[14] Data exclude "captive production" of firms such as Western Electric, which produce semiconductors as components for their own products rather than for sale to others. The distribution is of dollar values; unit distribution is not available.

In terms of market growth, clearly computers are a well above-average market. Home entertainment and other consumer luxury products are generally expected to show moderately above-average growth, auto and industrial products average growth and government products below-average growth because of decreasing military and space procurement. (It should be noted, however, that defense cut-backs have been mainly in personnel. Advanced electronic equipment purchases have not been cut.) Export markets for advanced technological products doubtless have great growth potential, and U.S. companies appear to have a decided competitive advantage over foreign producers.

Regarding market penetration by semiconductors, some quite dramatic statistics can be cited. In the late 1950s and early 1960s, about 4 percent of the dollar value of U.S. electronic equipment represented semiconductor content. This percentage rose to 5 percent by the end of the decade of the 60s, to about 7 percent by 1976, and probably will continue growing. Some of the reasons for the expectation of continued market penetration are as follows:[15]

In computers—development of semiconductor memories and microprocessors (densely packed integrated circuits which can permit full-fledged computers to be assembled on 8 × 10-inch circuit boards).

In industry—increasing need to reduce labor costs in distribution, communication, testing and measurement, and clerical work via automated processes using increasing amounts of electronic devices.

In autos—electronic ignitions, fuel injectors, antiskid devices, and equipment monitors.

In other consumer products—low-cost electronic devices for television, video tape, washing machines, wrist watches, and so forth.

With end-use markets growing at an above-average rate, and penetration of those markets increasing steadily, unit sales growth of semiconductors can be estimated at about 15 percent per annum over the next ten years. But this will consist of 10 percent or less for transistors and other "discrete" products and about 20 percent for integrated circuits and related devices, as the latter continue to make inroads into transistor markets.

As discussed earlier, we expect prices of both major types of semiconductors to continue to decline—possibly at a 5 percent average

---

[15] Interesting articles illustrating the broad range of possibilities include: G. Bylinsky, "Here Comes the Second Computer Revolution," *Fortune*, November, 1975; "Digital Watches," *Business Week*, October 27, 1975; A. G. Vacroux, "Microcomputers," *Scientific American*, May 1975.

annual rate. This would put the dollar growth rate of sales at somewhat under 10 percent for the industry, with transistors showing only nominal growth and integrated circuits about 15 percent growth.

Market Share of Competing Companies

Once an estimate is made of industry sales growth, analysts turn to a study of the sales growth of the company in which they are interested, compared with the sales pattern of its principal competitors. For example, sales data for the leading North American aluminum companies—Aluminum Company of America, Reynolds Metals, Kaiser Aluminum, and Alcan Aluminum—can be gathered readily from their annual reports or from the manuals of the investments services. But while the data thus gathered will be reliable, they may not be appropriate for comparative growth analysis.

The problem that frequently arises is that mergers or acquisitions introduce discontinuities into sales totals for a company. When two companies merge, the sales of the surviving company will be larger than they were before the merger. But this sales increase does not necessarily represent "growth" in a meaningful sense. "Growth" means doing more with the same resources; increasing the output per unit of input. To the shareholder, sales growth means increasing sales (output) per unit of capital (input).[16]

It is advisable to convert total dollar sales into per share form for intercompany sales comparisons (and also, for that matter, in examining the sales trend over time for an individual company in isolation). Only if complete "pro forma" data are available, or if there were no mergers or acquisitions, is the use of total dollar sales advisable. Table 6–3 presents per share sales data for the four major aluminum companies. The data are fully adjusted for all stock splits and stock dividends.[17]

Generally speaking, there is little point in gathering physical volume data when comparing different companies in a homogeneous type of industry such as aluminum. This is because their price movements usually will be quite similar. Of course, where the *product mix* varies considerably from company to company, as in the case of semiconductor producers, even though they are in the same

---

[16] Mergers also may distort data on industrywide sales trends, when industry sales are measured as the sum of individual company sales. But the problem is less acute in interindustry comparisons than in intercompany comparisons, because the impact of a merger is more diffused in the industry data.

[17] Some analysts supplement sales per share data with sales per dollar of *total capital*, thus washing out the influence of changing debt-equity ratios in the capital structure.

TABLE 6–3
Sales per Share—Four Major Aluminum Companies

Year	Alcan Aluminum Ltd.	Aluminum Co. of America	Kaiser Aluminum & Chemical	Reynolds Metals
1955	$13.78	$27.64	$22.50	$ 25.03
1960	16.71	26.94	27.08	25.75
1965	26.63	36.27	36.96	44.50
1970	41.52	47.19	46.27	61.14
1971	43.43	44.60	47.48	63.34
1974	69.99	82.10	90.57	115.23
1975	63.63	68.60	82.11	97.36

"industry" it would be quite informative to have comparative volume data. But companies that handle a broad product line usually do not publish volume data, and rarely can the analyst obtain price indexes that adequately enough reflect the differences in product mix to permit a meaningful approximation of the different companies' volumes. Obviously, if the same price index is used for each company, the deflated figures will bear the same relationship to each other as the actual dollar amounts.[18]

Table 6–4 relates per share sales of Alcoa to the sales of the other three companies. The table reveals that Alcoa's sales per share

TABLE 6–4
Ratios: Alcoa's Sales per Share to Competition

Year	Alcoa/Alcan	Alcoa/Kaiser	Alcoa/Reynolds
1955	2.0	1.2	1.1
1960	1.6	1.0	1.0
1965	1.4	1.0	0.8
1970	1.1	1.0	0.8
1971	1.0	0.9	0.7
1974	1.2	0.9	0.7
1975	1.1	0.8	0.7

declined markedly relative to the sales of the three other major aluminum producers until 1971, and since then have stabilized. To some extent the decline was merely a reflection of the fact that Alcoa was a giant when the others were just being born. In this light, a decline in Alcoa's market share was inevitable. But there also was some evidence over the years of a lack of competitive vigor on the company's part.[19]

---

[18] $\frac{B}{X}$ is to $\frac{A}{X}$ as B is to A.

[19] One possible reason for the company's lack of aggressiveness may have been a fear of antitrust litigation, since the company has had several serious encounters with the government on this subject.

Since the general subject of marketing philosophy and strategy is discussed in Chapter 8 (although not with specific reference to Alcoa), we will not elaborate here. It may be noted, however, that Alcoa's marketing policies have become more aggressive over the last several years.[20] Futhermore, the company has done a more extensive job of "vertical integration" than its competitors. Alcoa fabricates a higher percentage of its ingot production than most other companies. This capacity will aid Alcoa in its fight to maintain its market share. Thus, there would appear to be a fairly good chance that the earlier erosion of Alcoa's market share has ended. It seems reasonable to assume for the company the same growth rate of dollar sales that is assumed for the entire aluminum industry.

Unlike the case of the aluminum companies, product mix is crucial in comparing the sales of semiconductor producers. A company can be a high-growth company or a declining company, depending on its particular product lines. Thus, semiconductor producers whose major product is transistors can be expected to have much slower sales growth than companies whose major product is integrated circuits. And among integrated circuit producers, those specializing in microprocessors and other advanced devices can be expected to grow the most rapidly. Of course, product mix does not tell the entire story of a company. Marketing and production skills are extremely impor- tant, as are financial strength and technological expertise. For example, Motorola is heavily engaged in transistor production but manages to increase its transistor sales at an above-average rate and earn a good profit in the process. The reason is that it has developed an outstanding mass-production capability in what is now a commodity- type product.

In recent years, over 100 companies in the United States and about 15 companies abroad have produced semiconductors of one type or another. Of these, more than 20 companies can be considered substantial producers. Market shares of even the largest companies are relatively small compared with the aluminum industry, and many large companies have been unsuccessful in the business (e.g., United Technologies, Sylvania, and Philco-Ford in transistors and General Electric and Westinghouse in integrated circuits). The four leading U.S. producer/marketers (to distinguish from producers for internal use such as IBM and Western Electric), and some relevant data on product mix in 1974, are shown in Table 6–5.

One of the more interesting aspects of the tabulation is that the two largest producers of semiconductors have substantial other activities. Thus, if you were to do a thorough analytical study of Texas Instruments, you would have to examine not only the semiconductor

---

[20] See *Business Week*, October 28, 1972, p. 39.

TABLE 6–5
Product Mix for Semiconductors in 1974 (shown in percent)*

	Texas Instruments	Motorola	Fairchild	National Semiconductor
Approximate market share				
United States	16	15	13	10
Worldwide	15	11	6	4
Semiconductor sales as percent of total company sales	45	35	85	85
Semiconductor product mix				
Discrete	35	65	35	15
Integrated circuits	65	35	65	85

* Data obtained from company reports and estimates by electronic industry specialists.

industry, but also radar and other electro-optical defense systems (about 15 percent of sales); hand-held calculators (15 percent); high-purity chemicals, clad-metals, and control devices (almost 15 percent), and oil exploration and other geophysical services (10 percent). The task obviously is not an easy one, especially for amateurs. Yet Texas Instruments is clearly an outstanding candidate for investment consideration by amateurs as well as professionals. The company is generally considered to be the "premier" firm in the semiconductor industry, with the largest penetration of the rapidly growing European and Japanese markets and with advanced in-house capability in computer technology. The company's management has set a sales growth goal in excess of 15 percent per annum through the late 1980s. This goal seems overly ambitious. But, given our earlier projections of the semiconductor market, and assuming that the company's nonsemiconductor activities can produce sales growth at a rate of about 12 percent, aggregate sales growth of close to 15 percent per annum seems attainable.

SUGGESTED READINGS

Bolt, Gordon J. *Marketing and Sales Forecasting: A Total Approach.* New York: John Wiley & Sons, Inc., 1972.

Butler, William F.; Kavesh, Robert A.; and Platt, Robert (eds.). *Methods and Techniques of Business Forecasting.* Englewood Cliffs, N.J.: Prentice-Hall, Inc., 1974.

Carter, Anne P. *Structural Change in the American Economy.* Cambridge, Mass.: Harvard University Press, 1970.

Chambers, John C. *An Executive's Guide to Forecasting.* New York: John Wiley & Sons, Inc., 1974.

Chisholm, Roger K., and Whitaker, Gilbert R., Jr. *Forecasting Methods.* Homewood, Ill.: Richard D. Irwin, Inc., 1971.

Cleaver, George H. "Nonferrous Metals," *Financial Analyst's Handbook*, vol. II. Homewood, Ill.: Dow Jones-Irwin, Inc., 1975, chap. 21.

Copulsky, William. *Practical Sales Forecasting*. New York: American Management Association, 1970.

Goodman, Sam R. "Product Life Cycles and the Sources of Profit." In *Techniques of Profitability Analysis*. New York: John Wiley & Sons, Inc., 1970. Chap. 4.

Hughes, G. David. *Demand Analysis for Marketing Decisions*. Homewood, Ill.: Richard D. Irwin, Inc., 1973.

Levitt, Theodore. *Marketing for Business Growth*. New York: McGraw-Hill Book Co., 1974.

Rosen, Benjamin. "Electronics," *Financial Analyst's Handbook*, vol. II. Homewood, Ill.: Dow Jones-Irwin, Inc., 1975, chap. 15.

Smallwood, John E. "The Product Life Cycle: A Key to Strategic Market Planning," *M.S.U. Business Topics*, Winter 1973.

APPENDIX: INPUT-OUTPUT ANALYSIS

The system of "social accounting" which gives us the gross national product and its components deals with expenditures for *finished* goods and services. For example, consumer expenditures for automobiles appear in the GNP tables. But the tables do not show explicitly the value of, say, the steel used to make the autos, or the coal used to make the steel. These values are, of course, included implicitly in the value of the autos shown in the GNP tables, but one cannot identify the steel or coal specifically. Input-output is designed precisely to trace these "interindustry flows" and to tie these intermediate flows to the final product GNP data.

Description of Input-Output

The most recent input-output tables published by the Department of Commerce are for the year 1967 and tables for 1972 will be published in 1977[21] (the long time lag will be discussed at a later point). They contain data on over 300 "industries." This coverage, and that of the 1963 tables, represented a dramatic increase from earlier tables. The 1958 tables, for example, included less than 100 industries. To illustrate, aluminum is now separately identified whereas it was earlier lumped together with copper and other metals in a broad "nonferrous metals" category.

Industry definitions used in input-output follow the Office of Management and Budget's *Standard Industrial Classification Manual*, the latest version of which was published in 1972. This is a

---

[21] They are published in condensed form periodically in the *Survey of Current Business*, with additional detail published in supplementary volumes of statistics.

four-digit code wherein the first two digits represent a "Major Group" (01 through 89). The third digit represents the most important subdivisions of the major group, and the fourth digit represents specific product lines within each subdivision. For example, the code number 28 refers to Chemicals and Allied Products. Under number 28 there are subdivisions 281 through 287, representing, respectively, industrial inorganic and organic chemicals; plastic and synthetic materials; drugs; soaps and cosmetics; paints and allied products; gum and wood chemicals; and agricultural chemicals. There is also a "miscellaneous" subdivision, 289.[22] Taking subdivision 281 for an example of the four-digit breakdown, we find alkalies and chlorine (2812), industrial gases (2813), coal tar crudes (2814), dyes (2815), inorganic pigments (2816), miscellaneous industrial organic (2818), and miscellaneous industrial inorganic (2819).

For purposes of our discussion, the industries represented in the input-output tables can be thought of under three broad headings, although the Commerce Department does not actually "tag" each industry this way. The headings are: (1) raw materials, which have no use per se other than as components of more finished products; (2) semifinished products—e.g., electric motors—which can either be used directly or can become components of more advanced products; and (3) finished products, such as automobiles.

On the left-hand side of an input-output table, a listing of industries appears. These may be labeled "selling industries," as follows:

Selling Industries
  Raw Materials
    Copper
      •
      •
      •

  Semi-Finished
  Products
    Motors
      •
      •
      •

  Finished
  Products
    Autos
      •
      •
      •

This listing of industries is then repeated as the headings of columns, which may be labeled "buying industries." The result, shown in Table A6–1, is a grid or matrix which, when filled in, will

---

[22] There is no subdivision 288. Miscellaneous subdivisions normally end with the number 9.

TABLE A6–1
Input-Output Table

Selling Industries	Buying Industries				Total Intermediate Sales
	Copper	Motors	Autos	···	
Copper					
Motors					
Autos · · ·					
Total Purchases					

show how much each industry named at the head of a row sold to each industry named at the head of a column during the time period covered by the table. It is the *intermediate product grid*. The final column of this grid shows total sales of the industry named at the head of the row which went to other industries rather than to ultimate consumers of final products. The final row of the grid shows total purchases by each industry named at the head of the column.

For the purpose of illustration, and using *purely hypothetical* numbers, suppose that the copper industry sold $10 million of copper wire to itself (transactions among companies in the same industry are included in the tables), and $10 million each to the motor and auto industries. And suppose that $50 million of motors were sold to the auto industry. The intermediate product grid would look as shown in Table A6–2 (note that there are no intermediate sales of autos because autos are a finished product).

TABLE A6–2
Input-Output Table—Intermediate Product

Selling Industries	Buying Industries				Total Intermediate Sales
	Copper	Motors	Autos	···	
Copper	10	10	10		30
Motors			50		50
Autos · · ·					0
Total Purchases	10	10	60		80

We can now consider sales of final products to ultimate consumers. Following the GNP accounts, input-output tables subdivide ultimate purchases into personal consumption, investment (business plant and equipment outlays and housing), government purchases, and exports. Suppose we assume that copper is bought directly only by the housing component of these ultimate consumer groups, but that some motors and all autos are bought directly by several sectors in the amounts shown in the Table A6–3, the *combined intermediate and final product grid*.

TABLE A6–3
Input-Output Table—Combined Intermediate and Final Product

Selling Indus-tries	Buying Industries				Total Inter-mediate Sales	Final Sales Sectors				Total Inter-mediate and Final Sales
	Copper	Motors	Autos	...		Per-sonal	Invest-ment	Govern-ment	Ex-port	
Copper	10	10	10		30		10			40
Motors			50		50	5	10	5	5	75
Autos · · ·					0	100	40	25	20	185
Total Pur-chases	10	10	60		80	105	60	30	25	300

We can now add a final row to the table which performs the function of tying input-output to gross national product. If we subtract from the cells of the final column—*total intermediate and final sales* of each industry—the corresponding cells of the *total intermediate purchases* row, the difference represents the so-called value added by each industry. Value added, the difference between an industry's sales and its purchases from others, represents the contribution of that industry's "factors of production" to the gross national product. Specifically, it represents that industry's wages, interest, rents, profits, depreciation, and taxes. And, by definition, gross national product is the sum of all such values added in the entire economy. That is, gross national product can be viewed either as the value of all final sales of goods and services or as the sum of all payments to factors of production (plus depreciation and taxes).

Thus, returning to our table, the final "value added" row would be as follows:

	Copper	Motors	Autos	Total
Sales − Purchases =	40 − 10 =	75 − 10 =	185 − 60 =	300 − 80 =
Value Added	30	65	125	220

The sum of all the values added (GNP) is 220. And this is the same sum as the value of final sales to each sector:

Personal Consumption	105
Investment	60
Government	30
Export	25
	220

To summarize, gross national product in this highly simplified, hypothetical, illustration was 220. To bring this GNP into being required 300 of interindustry and final transactions. The input-output tables detail the distribution of the interindustry transactions.

Uses of Input-Output for Industry Sales Analysis

Among the industries discussed in this chapter was aluminum. Input-output tables can assist analysts of the aluminum industry in the following ways:

1. By locating the *aluminum row* in the recent input-output tables, we can determine which industries were the major purchasers of aluminum that year, and the absolute and relative magnitudes of such purchases. We can determine, for example, the percentage of total aluminum sales that was absorbed by the automotive industries; and by examining the *automotive columns* in the table, we can determine the percentage of total automotive purchases that was represented by aluminum. Thus, we can derive detailed data on markets and market shares in a given year.

2. If the aluminum industry had been separately identified in the 1947 and 1958 tables, we could determine whether there had been significant *changes* over time in the proportionate relationships between the aluminum and automotive or other industries. Unfortunately, the 1947 and 1958 tables did not separately identify aluminum, but included it in a broad "nonferrous metals" category. Lack of disaggregation and long delays in the publication of updated tables are the principal drawbacks to the widespread use of input-output at the present time.

3. In addition to enabling us to trace interindustry flows, the input-output tables permit us to trace the relationship between an industry's sales and the major GNP final sale sectors. An industry's

sales can enter GNP either directly or indirectly. For example, aluminum siding would be a direct sale to the housing sector of GNP whereas the aluminum in an aluminum automobile engine would enter GNP only indirectly. Fortunately, by a process known as "matrix inversion," it is possible to determine from the basic input-output tables described above, the amount of aluminum accounted for, both *directly and indirectly* by, say, personal consumption expenditures.[23]

4. Actually, the recent tables permit us to trace each industry's direct and indirect sales to not only the four GNP sectors illustrated in the hypothetical tables of this appendix, but to almost 20 GNP sectors. For example, personal consumption expenditures is divided into durables, nondurables, and services, and each of these subdivisions is further divided (e.g., durables is divided into autos and parts; furniture and household equipment; and "other"). The availability of such detail can be of extreme value in sales forecasting, particularly when the Commerce Department shortens the time lag between the occurrence of the sales transactions and the publication of the input-output tables. One interesting method of using such data for forecasting purposes will be described here in outline form.[24]

a. Compile annual historical data, in current dollars and in "constant dollars," for each GNP sector represented in the latest available input-output tables.

b. Determine by matrix inversion the "coefficients" applicable to each GNP sector for the industry under analysis. For example, a coefficient will indicate how many dollars of aluminum sales were associated directly and indirectly with a billion dollars of durable personal consumption expenditures in the latest year.

c. Multiply each historical GNP sector amount by the aluminum coefficient for that sector, as derived in (*b*). This will produce two historical series of *hypothetical* aluminum sales. They show what aluminum sales *would have been* in the past had the latest input-output coefficients been constant throughout time. (The series resulting from multiplying current dollar GNP data by the coefficients represents hypothetical *dollar* sales of aluminum, and the series resulting from multiplying constant dollar GNP data by the coefficients represents hypothetical *unit* sales of aluminum.)

d. Compile historical *actual* sales of aluminum and calculate the annual differences between actual and hypothetical.

---

[23] Clopper Almon, Jr., *Matrix Methods in Economics* (Reading, Mass.: Addison Wesley Publishing Co., Inc., 1967). Also see M. F. Elliott-Jones, *Input-Output Analysis: A Nontechnical Description* (New York: The Conference Board, 1972).

[24] Perhaps the most prominent forecasting service utilizing this method is Data Resources, Inc., of Lexington, Mass.

e. Try to explain these differences. Among the possible explanations consider: changes in relative prices (e.g., the use of aluminum in autos may appear different in earlier years in part because the price relationships between aluminum and autos were different); technological changes (e.g., substitution of plastics and aluminum for steel); changes in consumer tastes (e.g., small cars do not use materials in the same proportions as large cars); inventory adjustments (this is a key problem in using input-output for analysis of short-time spans).

f. Using either a standard forecast of GNP and its major components, or the analyst's own forecast,[25] multiply each *forecasted* GNP sector amount by the latest aluminum coefficient for that sector, as done in (c) with *historical* GNP sector amounts.

g. Adjust the forecasted aluminum sales to the extent that the explanations derived in (e) for historical differences in actual versus hypothetical sales are applicable to the future. This gives the analyst his working forecast of sales, and can be the basis of a subsequent effort to determine the profit implications of the sales forecast (see Chapter 7).

REVIEW QUESTIONS AND PROBLEMS

1. List ten factors which might cause the future sales pattern of any given company to differ significantly from past results.

2. Discuss the trend toward corporate diversification in the context of the industrial life cycle.

3. What are the many different perspectives of a thorough analysis of sales growth?

4. Why should a security analyst pay careful attention to trends in the selling prices of a company's products?

5. Distinguish between market growth and market penetration.

6. What data-gathering problems arise in studying an industry's dollar sales?

7. What data-gathering problems arise in studying a company's sales volume?

8. Assume that two companies have had identical rates of sales growth. Why might an analyst nevertheless consider the sales record of one to be superior to that of the other?

9. What factors might cause two different large companies in the same industry to experience different sales growth patterns?

10. Comment on the following statement: "It is highly probable that a large company's sales will represent a gradually diminishing share of the market."

---

[25] See Chapter 12.

RESEARCH PROJECTS

1. Trace the "life cycle" of one of the following industries: automobile, tele-vision, hotel/motel, air conditioning, airline, plastics, antibiotics, photog-raphy, soft drink, computer.
2. For one of the above industries, gather data for at least ten years on the relationship between unit sales and selling price (e.g., as illustrated in Figure 6–5).
3. What industries are most likely to benefit (or suffer) from international trade developments during the next five years?
4. What industries are most likely to benefit (or suffer) from U.S. population and income trends during the next five years?
5. Analyze the changing market shares of two different industries utilizing the two most recent input/output tables published by the U.S. Department of Commerce.

C.F.A. QUESTIONS

1. *From Exam I, 1975*

Based solely on the data in the accompanying table, which shows ship-ments of chemicals and allied products compared to U.S. gross national prod-uct for the years 1960–73, how would you characterize the growth and stability of the physical volume of shipments of chemical and allied products for the period shown. Illustrate by making statistical analyses for the years 1961, 1969, 1970, and 1973.

	U.S. GNP (billions of 1958 dollars)	Shipments of Chemical and Allied Products (billions of current dollars)	Index of Wholesale Prices	
Year			Chemical and Allied Products (1967 = 100)	All Industrial Commodities (1967 = 100)
1973	839.2	67.0	110.0	125.9
1972	792.5	57.4	104.2	117.9
1971	746.3	52.2	104.2	114.0
1970	722.5	48.8	102.2	110.0
1969	725.6	48.7	99.9	106.0
1968	706.6	46.5	99.8	102.5
1967	675.2	42.3	100.0	100.0
1966	658.1	38.7	99.4	98.5
1965	617.8	36.0	99.0	96.4
1964	581.1	33.6	98.3	95.2
1963	551.0	30.8	97.9	94.7
1962	529.8	28.5A	99.1	94.8
1961	497.2	26.5A	100.7	94.8
1960	487.7	25.7A	101.8	95.3

A-Adjusted to newer series beginning 1963.

2. *From Exam III, 1974*

"As the full effect of the high price of Middle East oil works its way through the world economy the U.S. dollar is expected to strengthen further. Another

fundamental factor favoring the dollar outlook is the recent improvement in the U.S. trade balance."

Assume that the above statement is correct. Explain in detail three ways in which this strengthening of the dollar is likely to affect the profits of U.S. multinational companies. In each instance indicate whether profits would be increased or decreased. ("Multinational companies" may be interpreted as companies obtaining at least 20 percent of revenue from foreign sources.)

Chapter 7

Analysis of Growth II: Earnings Growth

> Shallow men believe in luck, wise and strong men
> in cause and effect.
> —————————————— *Ralph Waldo Emerson*

Since stock values ultimately are dependent upon prospective earnings and dividends, the analysis of sales growth is merely the starting point of a broader investigation. To understand adequately the forces influencing profit growth, it is helpful to break down the past earnings growth record into several key component parts. It is the objective of this chapter to illustrate the analysis of earnings by component parts. (Unless otherwise indicated in the discussion which follows, references to net income should be taken to mean income "available to common stockholders"—i.e., after deducting preferred dividends, if any. Furthermore, for simplicity of exposition, financial data are taken directly as reported by the companies, without making allowance for the many accounting problems described in Chapter 4.)

THE SOURCES OF EARNINGS GROWTH

Net income per share of common stock is equal to the rate of return on stockholders' equity multiplied by the per share value of stockholders' equity. This can be shown algebraically, as follows:

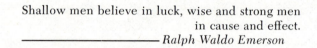

$$\frac{\text{Net income}}{\text{per share}} = \frac{\text{Net income}}{\text{Stockholders' equity}} \times \frac{\text{Stockholders' equity}}{\text{Number of common shares}}$$

Note that stockholders' equity appears in the denominator of one fraction and in the numerator of the other, thus canceling out and

304

leaving Net income/Number of common shares, or net income per share. Stockholders' equity, also referred to as book value, equals the balance sheet value of common stock plus surplus items, which is the same as total assets minus liabilities and preferred stock.

It follows from this relationship that *growth* of net income per share can stem from either an increase in stockholders' equity per share, or from an increase in return on stockholders' equity,[1] or from some combination of the two. (Actually, a sufficient increase in one can offset a reduction in the other.)

Growth of stockholders' equity per share has two principal sources. First, and foremost, is the plowback of earnings into the business—i.e., paying out only a portion of net income in cash dividends to common stockholders and retaining and reinvesting the balance. The contribution of earnings retention to growth of net income per share can be illustrated by a numerical example. Assume that a company is earning 10 percent on stockholders' equity—that is, $1 of net income per common share for every $10 of stockholders' equity per share. And assume, further, that the company has a dividend payout ratio of 40 percent—that is, it pays dividends of $0.40 per share for every $1 of available earnings. Its "retention rate," then, is 60 percent—$0.60 plowed back into the business out of every $1 earned.

Now, if the company continues to earn 10 percent on the old capital and, in addition, is able to put the new, plowed-back funds to work at a 10 percent return, its earnings per share will grow by 6 percent. This may be shown as follows:

Previous stockholders' equity
    per share (old capital) $10\% \times \$10.00 = \$1.00$ Earned per share
Retained earnings
    per share (new capital) $10\% \times \$\ 0.60 = \underline{\ \ 0.06}$ Earned per share
             New level of earnings $= \$1.06$ Earned per share
Growth rate of earnings per share $1.06/1.00 = 6\%$

It should be noted that the percent growth rate is equal to the rate of return on stockholders' equity (10 percent) multiplied by the retention rate (60 percent). That is, $60\% \times 10\% = 6\%$. This algebraic function is of great significance in security analysis.

---

[1] We wish to make it clear at the outset of this discussion that by defining "rate of return" simply as each year's net income divided by the same year's capital investment we are not using the term in its modern capital budgeting theory context. In modern capital theory, which we accept as valid, "rate of return" refers to the discount rate that equates all future cash flows from an investment with the original cost of the investment. Our only reason for not defining rate of return in this way is that the *external* analyst rarely, if ever, has available the information necessary to make the calculation.

In the preceding illustration it was assumed that the growth of stock-holders' equity per share came from earnings retention. But stock-holders' equity per share also can grow in another way—by the company selling additional shares of common stock at a price per share which is higher than the existing book value per share. For example, if book value is $100 million and 10 million shares are outstanding, book value per share is $10. If 1 million additional shares are sold at 2 times book value, or $20 a share, total book value rises to $120 million and total shares outstanding to 11 million. Book value per share thus is raised to $120/11, or $10.91 per share. This provides a basis for growth in earnings per share if the rate of return on stockholders' equity can be maintained.

Sale of common stock at a "premium over book value" traditionally has been an important source of growth for public utility companies. (However, this source of growth has been largely unavailable in recent years because most utility stocks no longer sell at premiums.) In addition, *mergers* often result in a rise in book value per share of the surviving corporation. This comes about when the acquiring corporation exchanges its shares for those of the acquired corporation and the book value of the acquired shares is greater than the book value of the shares given in exchange. We shall return to this aspect of earnings growth at a later point in the chapter. For the time being, suffice it to note that most industrial corporations do relatively little new common stock financing, so that earnings retention is the major source of growth of stockholders' equity per share.[2]

To summarize, growth of net income per common share can be looked upon as stemming from two sources: growth of stockholders' equity per share and/or improvement in the rate of return on stockholders' equity. Since the former source of growth is primarily a reflection of earnings retention, it may be stated as a generalization that the growth rate of earnings per share is a function of the product of the rate of return on stockholders' equity multiplied by the retention rate. Algebraically, this can be expressed as:

$$\frac{\text{Net income}}{\text{Stockholders' equity}} \times \frac{\text{Net income} - \text{Dividends}}{\text{Net income}}$$

It should be noted that in applying this expression, general practice is to use the average of beginning-of-the-year and end-of-the-year

---

[2] In recent years, much of the common stock financing which has been done by industrial corporations has been done indirectly, through the medium of convertible debentures. Such financing initially has its impact on earnings growth through the leverage influence on return on equity—to be discussed below—rather than through growth of equity per share. In later years, if conversion takes place, equity per share is affected.

stockholders' equity, to allow for the gradual plowback of earnings during the year and for any new common stock financing that may have been done during the year.[3]

Illustration. Table 7–1 shows the rates of return on equity and the retention rates of Aluminum Company of America and Texas Instru-

TABLE 7–1
Return on Equity and Retention Rates of Alcoa and Texas Instruments

| Year | Rate of Return on Average Stockholders' Equity | | Retention Rate | |
	Alcoa (percent)	Texas Instruments (percent)	Alcoa (percent)	Texas Instruments (percent)
1965	8.9	20.4	59	80
1966	11.7	19.4	67	83
1967	11.0	10.1	63	62
1968	10.1	10.8	62	67
1969	11.0	12.5	68	74
1970	9.7	10.2	65	70
1971	4.4	10.7	26	74
1972	8.1	13.8	61	81
1973	7.8	19.8	58	83
1974	12.1	17.7	74	74
1975	4.2	11.0	27	63

ments, Inc., since 1965. Some marked contrasts are apparent. Alcoa's rate of return has been substandard more often than not in comparison with the typical 11 percent to 13 percent return on equity of industrial corporations. On the other hand, although Texas Instruments' rate of return has been highly variable, it has not dropped below 10 percent and usually has been well above average.

With regard to retention rates, Alcoa appears to have a long-run "target" dividend payout ratio of about 40 percent, with a 60 percent retention rate. (The low rates in 1971 and 1975 reflect sharp declines in earnings rather than increased dividends.) Texas Instruments has followed a policy of retaining a higher percentage of earnings—about 75 percent—paying out about 25 percent in dividends.

Based purely on this historical record, one might conclude that the most probable future rate of return for Alcoa is about 10 percent and for Texas Instruments about 15 percent. Multiplying these rates of

---

[3] It will be observed that the expression reduces to Retained earnings/Stockholders' equity, which is equivalent to the growth rate of stockholders' equity if no new stock is sold (or if stock is sold at a price equal to prevailing book value). In other words, if no new stock is sold, and if there are no accounting adjustments made to book value of equity, growth rate of earnings per share and growth rate of book value per share will be equal.

return by each company's typical retention rate (60 percent and 75 percent, respectively), the earnings growth potential would appear to be about 6 percent for Alcoa (10% × 60%) and about 11 percent for Texas Instruments (15% × 75%). For both companies, this would imply earnings growth at a considerably lower rate than the sales growth estimates made in the preceding chapter (8 percent to 12 percent for Alcoa, depending on future inflation, and 15 percent for Texas Instruments). Before accepting either figure, however, an examination of the components of return on equity is essential.

ANALYSIS OF RETURN ON EQUITY

Additional insight into the factors underlying a company's record of earnings growth can be gained by examining the components of its rate of return on common stock equity. By examining the trends in each component, the analyst can isolate the principal causes of a decline or rise in return on equity, which gives him a sounder basis for determining whether past rates of return will persist or change during the years ahead.

Return on common stock equity can be viewed as the product of the "profit margin" on every dollar of sales multiplied by the "equity turnover," or number of dollars of sales per dollar of stockholders' equity. This can be expressed algebraically as follows:

$$\underset{\text{(Profit margin)}}{\frac{\text{Net income}}{\text{Sales}}} \times \underset{\text{(Equity turnover)}}{\frac{\text{Sales}}{\text{Stockholders' equity}}} = \underset{\text{(Rate of return on equity)}}{\frac{\text{Net income}}{\text{Stockholders' equity}}}$$

To illustrate the significance of this equation, assume that a company's return on equity declined from 15 percent to 12 percent between the years 1965 and 1975. This might have occurred in one of several ways, as shown.

	Year	Profit Margin (percent)	×	Equity Turnover	=	Rate of Return on Equity (percent)
Case A	1965	5		3		15
	1975	4		3		12
Case B	1965	5		3		15
	1975	5		2.4		12
Case C	1965	5		3		15
	1975	4.8		2.5		12
Case D	1965	5		3		15
	1975	3		4		12
Case E	1965	5		3		15
	1975	6		2		12

In Case A, the problem was a reduced profit margin, and the analyst who knows this can proceed to find out why. For example, was the price structure of the industry upset? Were the operating expenses of the company out of control? Were there heavy, but temporary, start-up expenses attributable to the launching of a new plant or of a new product? How does the trend of this company's profit margin compare with that of its competitors?

In Case B, the profit margin was maintained, but turnover declined. Why? Was the problem a declining sales trend due to the inroads of competing products? Or were sales being maintained, but with overly large capital investment?

In Case C, both ratios deteriorated, so joint problems must be explored, while in Cases D and E, one of the ratios actually rose but was accompanied by a more than offsetting decline in the other. With regard to Case D, it might be noted that a decline in the profit margin on sales need not necessarily be undesirable. If turnover can be improved sufficiently, it may pay to follow a deliberate policy of trimming profit margins to expand sales and improve the ultimate return on equity. Indeed, this is the principle underlying, for example, mass-retailing operations such as food chains or discount department stores. Of course, in Case D the rise in turnover was not adequate to offset the profit margin decline.

Turning to Alcoa and Texas Instruments again, Table 7–2 provides

TABLE 7–2
Profit Margins and Equity Turnover of Alcoa and Texas Instruments

| Year | Net Income/Sales | | Sales/Average Stockholders' Equity | |
	Alcoa (percent)	Texas Instruments (percent)	Alcoa	Texas Instruments
1965	6.3	5.7	1.4	3.6
1966	7.5	5.9	1.6	3.3
1967	7.7	4.0	1.4	2.5
1968	7.6	3.9	1.3	2.8
1969	7.8	4.0	1.4	3.1
1970	7.3	3.6	1.3	2.8
1971	3.7	4.4	1.2	2.4
1972	5.7	5.1	1.4	2.7
1973	4.7	6.5	1.7	3.0
1974	6.3	5.7	1.9	3.1
1975	2.7	4.5	1.5	2.4

some interesting insights into the operating characteristics of the two firms. Alcoa typically has had higher profit margins than Texas Instruments but much lower equity turnover. Except for a few years, Alcoa's margins typically range between 6 percent and 8 percent. Texas Instruments' margins, on the other hand, typically range be-

tween 4 percent and 6 percent. Alcoa's turnover has oscillated around a 1.4 level (1974's turnover of 1.9 was most unusual) whereas Texas Instruments' turnover has averaged almost 3.

Multiplying Alcoa's 6–8 percent margin range by an equity turnover of about 1.4 produces a return on equity of 8 percent under relatively poor conditions and 11 percent under more favorable conditions. This would suggest that the previous section's estimate of about 10 percent as Alcoa's "most probable" rate of return was reasonable.

In the case of Texas Instruments, there is no reason in the history of the company to assume that margins will be much different from 4–6 percent. If turnover can be maintained at a level of 3, a 12–18 percent return on equity can be expected, with a mean equal to the 15 percent estimated in the previous section.

This examination of the interaction between net profit margin and equity turnover provides useful insight into the sources of rate of return on equity. But it is too broad brush for a deep understanding and a confident estimate of the future. For example, the net profit margin reflects not only the basic operating efficiency of a firm, but also its *nonoperating* income and expense and its income tax rate. These factors should be examined separately in an intensive analysis. Similarly, equity turnover reflects not only the degree of utilization of the company's assets but also the method of *financing* those assets—debt versus equity. Since a company's asset utilization and its financial policies are two quite different factors, they should be examined separately.

Following this line of reasoning, it is instructive to approach the interaction of margin and turnover from a somewhat different angle than we have just done. First, we shall focus on the interaction of the *operating margin (pretax)* and the *turnover of operating assets*. The product of these two ratios is the *return on operating assets (pretax)*:

$$\frac{\text{Operating income}}{\text{Sales}} \times \frac{\text{Sales}}{\text{Operating assets}} = \frac{\text{Operating income}}{\text{Operating assets}}$$

$$\text{(Operating margin)} \times \frac{\text{(Turnover of}}{\text{operating assets)}} = \frac{\text{(Return on}}{\text{operating assets)}}$$

We shall also examine the components of the operating margin. That is, to what extent are changes in the margin attributable to changes in specific cost components—labor, materials, selling and administrative expenses, depreciation? Likewise, we shall examine the main components of turnover of operating assets—turnover of receivables, inventories, and plant.

Following this study of operating margin and turnover of operating assets, we shall consider the influence of nonoperating income and

expense, of leverage (the relationship of debt to equity), and of tax rate. This entire network of interrelationships is presented schematically in Figure 7–1.

Return on Operating Assets

Table 7–3 presents the history of Alcoa's and Texas Instruments' operating margin (pretax), turnover of operating assets, and rate of

FIGURE 7–1
Components of Return on Equity

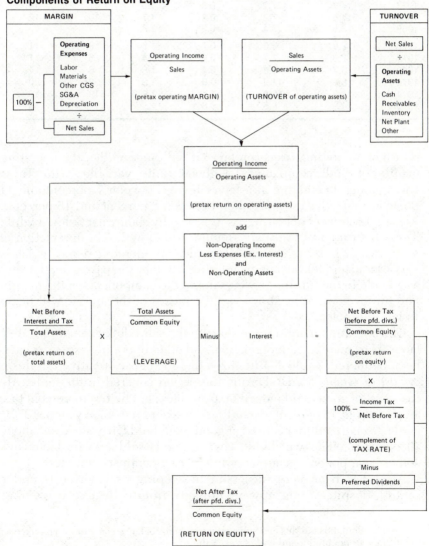

TABLE 7–3
Components of Return on Operating Assets of Alcoa and Texas Instruments

	Operating Margin (operating income/ sales)		×	Turnover of Operating Assets (sales/ operating assets)		=	Return on Operating Assets (operating income/ operating assets)	
Year	Alcoa	Texas Instruments		Alcoa	Texas Instruments		Alcoa	Texas Instruments
1965	11.8%	10.6%		0.8	1.9		9%	20%
1966	14.5	11.2		0.9	1.8		13	20
1967	14.7	7.2		0.8	1.5		12	11
1968	14.5	7.3		0.7	1.7		10	12
1969	13.5	7.4		0.8	1.8		11	13
1970	12.9	6.6		0.7	1.6		9	11
1971	7.9	7.7		0.6	1.4		5	11
1972	8.4	8.8		0.8	1.6		6	14
1973	8.8	11.3		0.9	1.8		8	20
1974	11.8	10.8		1.1	1.8		13	19
1975	4.9	8.5		0.8	1.5		4	13

return on operating assets (pretax).[4] It will be seen that the operating margin of both companies has been quite variable, with Texas Instruments' fluctuating at a lower level (between 7 percent and 11 percent) than Alcoa's (most often between 8 percent and 15 percent). Alcoa's turnover of operating assets is usually somewhat below 1 while Texas Instruments' is usually somewhat below 2. The interaction of these two factors has produced a return on operating assets which is very erratic and leaves one wondering whether the past is at all useful as a guide to the future. As we examine the components of the margin and turnover variables, however, the pieces of the mosaic will begin to fall into place.

The operating margin is the share of the sales dollar remaining after labor costs, materials, depreciation, and other operating expenses have been deducted. Table 7–4 itemizes these expenses relative to sales.

Cost of Goods Sold. During the period covered in the table, Alcoa's cost of goods sold moved up from a level of below 70 percent to a level of about 75 percent (excluding the severe recession year of 1975), while Texas Instruments' cost of goods sold held fairly steady at about 70 percent. When we divide cost of goods sold into its labor and "other" components, some very interesting contrasts emerge.

Alcoa has been very successful in keeping its labor costs under control, despite strong upward pressure from collective bargaining

---

[4] In all calculations in this and subsequent sections, balance sheet items are taken as the average of beginning-and-end-of-year values.

TABLE 7–4
Operating Expenses of Alcoa and Texas Instruments as Percent of Sales

Year	Labor		Materials and Other Costs of Goods Sold		Total Cost of Goods Sold		Selling, General & Administrative		Depreciation and Depletion	
	Alcoa	T.I.	Alcoa	T.I.	Alcoa	T.I.	Alcoa	T.I.	Alcoa	T.I.
1965	37	n.a.	33	n.a.	70	71	11	14	7	4
1966	36	n.a.	33	n.a.	69	69	10	15	7	5
1967	36	n.a.	31	n.a.	67	71	10	15	8	7
1968	35	n.a.	32	n.a.	67	72	10	14	8	6
1969	34	n.a.	35	n.a.	69	71	9	15	8	6
1970	36	n.a.	33	n.a.	69	72	10	15	8	7
1971	37	n.a.	35	n.a.	72	71	10	15	10	7
1972	34	n.a.	40	n.a.	74	70	9	16	9	5
1973	33	40	43	29	76	69	8	15	7	5
1974	30	38	45	31	75	69	7	15	6	6
1975	36	38	44	30	80	68	8	17	7	7

n.a. = not available.

agreements. Labor costs exceeded 40 percent of sales prior to 1964, and in recent years have been in the 30–35 percent range. This has been accomplished by holding the work force fairly constant and securing productivity gains which offset the rising wage rates. Sales per employee rose from under $25,000 in 1965 to over $30,000 in 1970, $40,000 in 1972, and over $50,000 in 1974. Labor cost data did not become available for Texas Instruments until 1973, so we cannot be sure what the trend has been. However, it can be seen that the level of labor costs was much higher than Alcoa's in 1973 and 1974 (near 40 percent). Moreover, while Texas Instruments' sales per employee have grown, the improvement has not been as dramatic as Alcoa's, and are at about half of Alcoa's level: $13,000 in 1965, $18,000 in 1970, and $24,000 in 1974.

Concurrent with Alcoa's control of labor costs has been a surge in its costs of raw materials and other direct manufacturing expenses, including taxes other than income tax. These costs, which were less than 30 percent of sales in 1962 and 1963 (not shown in the table) have risen fairly steadily, reaching 45 percent in 1974. Among the most important causes of this rise have been steadily escalating electricity rates, which bulk very large in aluminum production, and, more recently, sharp rises in the cost of the prime raw material for aluminum, bauxite. Texas Instruments, on the other hand, is a high technology company in which raw material costs are negligible and other manufacturing costs can be kept under tight control. Thus, its level of nonlabor costs is fairly low (about 30 percent) and, although we do not have enough data to prove the point, probably has been rather stable over time.

Hopefully, Alcoa can continue to keep a tight rein on labor costs, and the escalation of electricity and raw material costs may not be as steep in the future. (The U.S. aluminum industry had pledged to reduce energy consumption per unit of product by 10 percent by 1980, in comparison with 1972.) Therefore, it seems reasonable to forecast that Alcoa's cost of goods sold will recede a bit from the 75 percent level of recent years, although probably not back to the 70 percent and lower levels of earlier years. Texas Instruments' cost of goods sold are most likely to continue to represent about 70 percent of that company's sales dollar.

Other Expenses. Selling, general, and administrative expenses (known among analysts as S.G.&A.) have been kept under very strict control by Alcoa. Indeed, they have tended to decline as a percentage of sales—from 13 percent in 1962 (not shown in the table) to 10 percent in 1966 to 1971, and, more recently, to well under 10 percent. However, it seems doubtful that this figure can continue for long at less than about 9 percent without damaging Alcoa's marketing and administrative capabilities.

Texas Instruments also has kept its S.G.&A. under careful control, in the sense of not permitting much variation, but at a considerably higher level than for Alcoa. Given the company's need to spend heavily for research (7 percent or more of sales versus 2 percent for Alcoa) in order to keep at the forefront of technology, the 15 percent figure seems likely to continue, and perhaps even grow somewhat larger.

The final component of operating expense, depreciation and depletion, does not usually fluctuate very much over time because the level of depreciable plant and equipment tends to grow at a rate similar to sales. The level of Texas Instruments' fixed assets relative to sales is very much lower than Alcoa's, as will be described shortly. But Texas Instruments' fixed asset *mix* is more toward equipment than plant, while Alcoa's is more "brick and mortar." Since equipment has a shorter life-span than plant, its depreciation rate is higher. Consequently, Texas Instruments' depreciation/sales ratio is not too different from Alcoa's, typically about 6 percent versus about 8 percent, despite the very great difference in the fixed asset/sales ratio of the two companies.

Summary of Operating Margin Components. Pulling together the various elements of the preceding discussion, we can estimate the future operating margins of Alcoa and Texas Instruments as shown.

	Alcoa	Texas Instruments
Expenses as percent of sales		
Labor	29 ⎫72	40 ⎫70
Other cost of goods sold	43 ⎭	30 ⎭
S.G.&A.	9	15
Depreciation	8	6
Total operating expense	89	91
Operating income/sales	11%	9%

Turnover Analysis. It was noted earlier that Alcoa's turnover of operating assets is usually somewhat below 1 while Texas Instruments' is usually somewhat below 2. Let us, first, consider the significance of the turnover figure, since it is perhaps a less familiar concept than profit margin. Following that, we will examine the key components of turnover and attempt to estimate the future figures for the two companies.

In order to exploit effectively a growing demand for a company's output, the company must expand its productive assets and working capital so as to keep it in a balanced relationship with demand. If demand rises much faster than productive capacity, or than the com-

pany's willingness to finance larger receivables or larger inventories, the company may find itself in the position of being unable to satisfy its customers to the full extent of their demands. If this results in the customers turning elsewhere for supplies, it may represent a permanent loss of markets. Thus, a steadily rising ratio of sales to operating assets may be a sign of unbalanced growth. On the other hand, it may reflect the fact that some newly acquired plant and equipment is technologically more advanced than older facilities and is capable of carrying a higher sales load.

While a steadily rising sales/operating assets ratio may be a warning of trouble ahead, so too may a steadily falling ratio. If expansion of productive facilities is rapidly outpacing the expansion of sales, the usual result is a weakening in the product's price structure until a better balance is achieved. The aluminum and semiconductor industries, among others, have been affected by this type of imbalance between sales and capacity in recent years.

A few caveats are in order regarding the interpretation of changing ratios of sales to operating assets.[5] In the first place, capital is a "lumpy factor of production," in economists' jargon. New plants usually cannot be built in installments. Consequently, when a company expands its facilities, some time usually elapses before sales rise sufficiently to use the full new capacity. In the meantime the sales/operating assets ratio is likely to fall. But the falling ratio, in such cases, should not be interpreted pessimistically unless there is reason to doubt that sales will shortly justify the expansion.

A second source of difficulty relates to rising sales/operating assets ratios, and is caused by a change in company "lease versus buy" policies. A company which has been buying most of its physical facilities may begin increasingly to lease them. Leased facilities (unless capitalized; see Chapter 4) do not show up in the company's property accounts, but they do result in sales. Thus, a rising sales/operating assets ratio will result, and the rise may be interpreted favorably by the analyst when, in fact, if the leased facilities were taken into account the inference might be quite the opposite. A similar problem may be caused if a company sets up an unconsolidated subsidiary to finance its receivables. Sales will rise relative to the

---

[5] Most analysts also keep track of the relationship of *unit* sales to plant capacity if the data are available. Problems of data nonavailability are least existent in the raw materials and public utilities industries, where capacity data—in tons, barrels, kilowatts, and so forth, are published frequently in company annual reports and, on an industry-wide basis, by trade associations and government agencies. It should be recognized, however, that although the data *look* precise, the concept of capacity is inherently imprecise. Most capacity measures are based on existing technology and customary methods of operation. But these are both subject to changes that can have a significant impact on the potential output of existing facilities—for example, adding a third shift of workers, or using oxygen in blast furnaces, or thermal recovery methods in oil pumping.

indicated working capital of the parent company, but the rise will be more apparent than real.

Making allowance for these caveats, it can be concluded that the most desirable trend for the sales/operating assets ratio is for it to be stable at a high level. The high level tends to assure optimum efficiency of operation,[6] and the stability tends to assure that the market will neither be unsatisfied nor glutted. For greater insight, as will be shown below, the analyst should examine separately the relationship between sales and each individual component of operating assets—net plant, cash, receivables, and inventories. In addition, since depreciation accounting practices can cause severe distortions in intercompany and intertemporal comparisons, it may also be useful to look at the trends of sales/gross plant and depreciation/gross plant ratios in connection with asset turnover analysis.[7]

Turnover Statistics. If the ideal is for operating asset turnover to be stable at a high level, how do Alcoa and Texas Instruments rate versus the ideal? Clearly, Texas Instruments is superior in terms of level. Both leave something to be desired in terms of stability, although far worse examples can be cited.[8] To determine the sources of both level and variability, as the basis for a forecast, it is necessary to examine the components of turnover. To do this, it is helpful to think of the *reciprocal* of turnover, or assets per dollar of sales.

A turnover of 1 would mean that a company requires a dollar of assets to generate a dollar of sales, while a turnover of 2 would mean that only 50 cents of assets is needed per dollar of sales. Let us, then, examine the left-hand side of Alcoa's and Texas Instruments' balance sheets to see how many cents of each major asset category have been needed to generate each dollar of sales. The data are shown in Table 7–5.

The first two columns of Table 7–5 show that both companies have been very inconsistent in their *cash* management policies. Alcoa has kept much less liquid, on average, than Texas Instruments, but cash has varied from as low as 2 cents per dollar of sales to as high as 7 cents. Texas Instruments' cash management has been even more erratic, varying between 7 and 20 cents per dollar of sales.

Both companies have had stable, and similar, records in terms of

---

[6] *Too* high a level, however, can be inefficient because obsolete facilities have to be brought into use. McGraw-Hill's *19th Annual Survey of Business Plans for New Plants and Equipment* revealed that manufacturers prefer to operate, on average, at a rate of about 93 percent of physical capacity.

[7] In some industries, trends of operating assets per se, in addition to asset *turnover*, are of interest. For example, in setting electric utility rates, public regulatory commissions seek to allow utility companies to earn a "fair" rate of return on investment. The investment, or "rate base," to which this "fair return" is applied, is largely a function of the book value of the plant.

[8] The airline industry provides good illustrations of highly erratic turnover.

TABLE 7–5
Major Operating Assets of Alcoa and Texas Instruments—Cents per Dollar of Sales

Year	Cash and Equivalents		Accounts Receivable		Inventories		Net Plant and Equipment	
	Alcoa	T.I.	Alcoa	T.I.	Alcoa	T.I.	Alcoa	T.I.
1965	4	11	16	14	23	10	83	16
1966	4	13	15	15	22	10	76	18
1967	5	14	16	17	24	12	83	23
1968	7	11	16	15	24	12	85	21
1969	6	7	17	16	22	13	80	20
1970	6	10	18	17	23	13	90	21
1971	5	20	18	16	28	11	100	21
1972	3	20	16	15	25	10	86	16
1973	3	15	16	15	20	11	70	15
1974	2	11	14	17	18	12	60	16
1975	2	15	17	20	26	12	79	20

accounts receivable per dollar of sales—maintaining about 16 cents of receivables per dollar of sales (also referred to as a "receivables turn-over" of about 6 times). With regard to inventories, however, Texas Instruments has had much better control than Alcoa. Whereas Alcoa has carried inventories of about 22 cents per dollar of sales, on average, there has been a range of 18 cents to 28 cents. Texas Instruments, on the other hand, has kept inventories at half of Alcoa's average level in relation to sales, with fairly little variability from year to year.

The final columns of Table 7–5 reveal dramatically the fact, referred to earlier in the comments on the depreciation/sales ratio, that Alcoa has a much greater investment in plant and equipment per dollar of sales than Texas Instruments. Until very recently, Alcoa typically had 80 to 90 cents of fixed assets per dollar of sales while Texas Instruments has had a fourth or less of that amount. The sharp decline in Alcoa's plant and equipment ratio in 1973–74 probably will not be permanent since it reflects soaring aluminum selling prices in those years, and consequently soaring dollar sales, rather than a fundamental change in the technology of producing aluminum which would require less fixed assets relative to *unit* sales. In the future, as Alcoa adds capacity, the cost of those additions will be very high compared with historical costs, and the ratio probably will move upward again. On the other hand, the company has demonstrated an ability to im-prove labor productivity, and it may be on the verge of some significant improvements in capital productivity. Alcoa has developed a continuous casting process and a new smelting process, both of which show considerable promise of productivity gains. Therefore, we

shall assume that while plant and equipment per dollar of sales will not equal the 60 cent level reached in 1974, it will average less than 75 cents.

The range of Texas Instruments' fixed assets/sales ratio was 15 percent to 23 percent during the period covered in the table. Recalling the discussion in Chapter 6 of trends in the semiconductor industry, with companies increasingly *integrating forward* to produce microprocessors and even final consumer products such as electronic calculators and wrist watches, it seems probable that more fixed assets will be needed in the future. Therefore, the higher end of the historical range seems a more likely precursor of the future than the lower end.

Summary of Turnover Components.   As with the operating margin components, we can now pull together the various threads of the turnover discussion, and estimate the future as shown.

Operating Assets per Sales Dollar	Alcoa	Texas Instruments
Cash and equivalents...........	3	12
Accounts receivable............	16	16
Inventories....................	22	11
Net plant and equipment	72	20
Total	113	59

The turnover implied by Alcoa's 113 cents of operating assets per sales dollar is 0.9, and Texas Instruments' is 1.7. Having previously estimated the two companies' operating margins at 11 percent and 9 percent, respectively, their implied returns on operating assets (pre-tax) are:

$$\text{Alcoa: } \quad 11\% \times 0.9 = 10\%$$
$$\text{Texas Instruments: } \quad 9\% \times 1.7 = 15\%$$

Nonoperating Items, Leverage, and Taxes.   In addition to earning a return on assets in "regular operations," many companies have a considerable degree of "nonoperating" activity. Alcoa is such a company; Texas Instruments is not.

Of Alcoa's total assets, about 85 percent can be classified as "operating" and 15 percent as "nonoperating"—a distribution which has held fairly constant for many years. Alcoa's nonoperating assets consist of real estate ventures, minority investments in affiliated companies related to Alcoa's regular aluminum activities, and various deferred charges and other intangibles. On the whole, the company's real estate ventures have been unsuccessful and have pulled down the earnings flowing from the company's other investments.

If we divide Alcoa's net nonoperating income (before interest and

taxes) by nonoperating assets, we derive a return on nonoperating assets which has ranged between 3 percent and 15 percent, with a mean of about 8 percent. Since there has been no consistent tendency for this return to either improve or deteriorate, it seems reasonable to assume that the mean return of about 8 percent will persist. And since an 8 percent return (on 15 percent of assets) is close to the 10 percent we have estimated as the most probable return on the 85 percent of *operating* assets, we can estimate the return on *total* assets (before interest and taxes) at 10 percent as well.[9] Of course, for Texas Instruments, we need not be concerned about the impact of nonoperating items since they are negligible. Therefore, we can estimate its return on total assets at the same 15 percent we have estimated for return on operating assets. (As an interesting aside, it may be noted that in the jargon of Wall Street, net income before interest and taxes is referred to as EBIT, and, as will be discussed in Chapter 9, EBIT is the amount considered to be available for payment of fixed charges in bond analysis.)

Leverage. The return on operating assets and on total assets can be viewed as a measure of a management's effectiveness in developing, producing, and marketing goods or services. Another key dimension of management policy is the *financing* of the business. While common equity is the principal source of long-term capital for most firms, another important source is funded debt—bonds and other long-term loans. In addition, some companies, especially public utilities, use preferred stock as a financing vehicle, and many use "off-balance sheet" financing such as leasing and guarantees of third-party debt. Only some 10 percent of the 500 companies in Standard & Poor's Composite Stock Price Index have capital structures consisting of common equity only.

Notwithstanding the frequent comments one encounters regarding the virtues of a "clean balance sheet"—i.e., one where common stock is the only source of long-term capital—the judicious use of leverage can be very advantageous to the common stockholder. For if a corporation sells bonds on which it pays an interest rate of, say, 7 percent (which is really an effective after-tax rate of only 3.5 percent),[10] and if it can earn, say, 12 percent after taxes on the funds so secured, the differential accrues to the benefit of the stockholders. This is often referred to as "trading on the equity." Moreover, if the rate of return on total funds used in the business rises, the rate earned on stockholders'

---

[9] $(10\% \times 85\%) + (8\% \times 15\%) = 9.7\%$

[10] Preferred stock dividends are not tax-deductible expenses, hence the relative paucity of new preferred stock issues.

equity alone will rise at an even faster rate, because the charges on the senior issues remain fixed.[11]

These observations can be illustrated with a hypothetical example. Let us assume two companies, each with $50 million of capital in 197X and $60 million in 197Y. However, assume that one of these companies (Company A) has all of its capital in common stock, and one (Company B), has four fifths in common and one fifth in 7 percent bonds. Let us also assume that both companies have annual sales of $200 million in 197X and $250 million in 197Y and that net income before taxes and before interest expense equaled 5 percent of sales in 197X and 6 percent in 197Y. The statements of these two companies would appear as shown in Table 7–6.

TABLE 7–6
Income Statements (in millions of dollars)

	Company A		Company B	
	197X	197Y	197X	197Y
Income account				
Sales	200	250	200	250
Net before taxes and interest (5% of sales in 197X and 6% in 197Y)	10	15	10	15
Interest (7% on Company B's $10 million in bonds in 197X and $12 million in 197Y)	—	—	0.7	0.84
Net before taxes	10	15	9.3	14.16
Income taxes (at 50% rate)	5	7.5	4.65	7.08
Net income available to common	5	7.5	4.65	7.08
Capital account				
Long-term debt	0	0	10	12
Stockholders' equity	50	60	40	48
Total Capital	50	60	50	60
Rate of return				
Return on total capital*	10%	12.5%	10%*	12.5%*
Return on stockholders' equity	10%	12.5%	11.6%	14.8%

* The components of return on total capital are defined as follows:

Total capital = Common stock + Surplus + Preferred stock + Long-term debt

Income earned on total capital = Net available for common + Preferred dividends + 50% of interest on long-term debt. The reason for using one half of interest rather than the full amount is that since interest is a tax-deductible expense, "the government pays half of it." For companies with low effective tax rates, use [(Interest) (1.0 − Tax rate)].

---

[11] In addition to fixed interest charges, there also may be heavy fixed charges related to a large capital investment—for example, depreciation and maintenance expenses. The latter give rise to what is known as "operating leverage," while the former relate to "financial leverage." "Break-even" analysis is used to study operating leverage. The subject is discussed in detail in textbooks on managerial economics.

Note that although both companies earned the same return on total capital, the leveraged company's rate of return on stockholders' equity was higher than that of the unleveraged company in both years, and it increased by over 3 percentage points between 197X and 197Y, compared with a gain of 2.5 percentage points for the unleveraged company.

Of course, as the past history of the railroads and the recent history of the airlines suggests, stockholder profits are also made more vulnerable by leverage. For in a period of poor business the existence of heavy fixed charges causes the return on equity to fall faster than the rate on total capital. Clearly, what is necessary from the stockholder's point of view is a sensible balancing of debt and equity in relation to the risks of the specific business at its particular stage of development. Moreover, debt can be both short- or long-term, and a sensible balancing of maturities can be equally crucial, as the sad experience of New York City and the W. T. Grant Co. attested in 1976.

Table 7–7 provides the basis for understanding the leverage policies of Alcoa and Texas Instruments. The first ratio, total assets to common equity, measures the *total leverage* of the two companies; that is, the extent to which assets are financed by *all funds other than common equity*—including accounts payable, short-term bank loans, the current portion of long-term debt, and preferred stock. The second measure reflects a more traditional view of leverage; namely, the percentage of the total capital structure represented by long-term debt and preferred stock. The final columns indicate the percentage of assets being financed by current liabilities, on the one hand, and by long-term debt and preferred stock, on the other.

The total leverage measure indicates that Alcoa relies a bit more on external (nonequity) funds than does Texas Instruments. Alcoa uses about $1.10–$1.20 of external funds per dollar of common equity while Texas Instruments uses $0.70–$0.80. This relatively minor difference in *overall* leverage, however, is the result of some major differences in type of external funds utilized, as shown by the other columns of Table 7–7. Alcoa has consistently relied heavily on long-term debt. (The company also has an old $66 million issue of preferred stock, which is shrinking rapidly as a percentage of a total capital base now near $3 billion). Texas Instruments, on the other hand, has used little long-term debt, and even that has been shrinking as a percentage of capital and of assets. Moreover, Texas Instruments' comparatively high usage of short-term funds has been mainly in the form of accounts payable rather than bank loans. Instead, all of its bank loans represent borrowings by *foreign* subsidiaries, which do not have access to a long-term debt market. As a result of these differences in the form of external funds, Alcoa's interest expense is more than 5 times that of

TABLE 7–7
Leverage Measures of Alcoa and Texas Instruments

Year	Total Assets/ Common Equity		Long-Term Debt plus Preferred Stock/ Total Capitalization		Current Liabilities/ Total Assets		Long-Term Debt plus Preferred Stock/ Total Assets	
	Alcoa	T.I.	Alcoa	T.I.	Alcoa	T.I.	Alcoa	T.I.
1965	2.0	1.9	40%	18%	11%	34%	33%	12%
1966	2.1	1.9	42	22	11	31	34	15
1967	2.1	1.7	43	19	9	27	36	14
1968	2.1	1.7	43	18	9	27	35	13
1969	2.1	1.8	42	22	11	28	35	15
1970	2.2	1.8	44	24	11	27	35	17
1971	2.2	1.7	45	22	10	27	37	17
1972	2.2	1.7	45	19	9	28	37	14
1973	2.1	1.7	42	14	10	32	35	10
1974	2.1	1.8	41	12	13	35	32	8
1975	2.2	1.7	44	10	13	34	35	6

Texas Instruments (almost $60 million in 1974 and over $80 million in 1975 for Alcoa versus $11 million in both years for Texas Instruments) while its assets are only some 3 times as large ($3.5 billion versus $1 billion).

The impact of these leverage policies on rate of return can now be brought into focus. If return on total assets (before interest and taxes) is multiplied by the total leverage ratio, and then we subtract interest expense (expressed as a percentage of common equity to make the arithmetic symmetrical), we have the pretax return on common equity. Thus:

$$\left[\frac{\text{Net before interest and tax}}{\text{Total assets}} \times \frac{\text{Total assets}}{\text{Common equity}} \right] - \frac{\text{Interest}}{\text{Common equity}} = \frac{\text{Net before tax}}{\text{Common equity}}$$

We have already estimated the return on total assets at 10 percent for Alcoa and 15 percent for Texas Instruments. Our analysis of the leverage policies of the two companies reveals patterns so persistent that simple extrapolation into the future seems warranted. That is, Alcoa can be predicted to have a total leverage ratio of about 2.1, with a heavy reliance on interest-bearing debt. Texas Instruments probably will continue to have a total leverage ratio of about 1.8, with a low reliance on interest-bearing debt.

Next, let us assume that interest-bearing debt in relation to equity will be in a ratio of about 45 : 55 for Alcoa and about 20 : 80 for Texas Instruments. Let us further assume an average future interest rate on all debt, old and new, short-term and long-term, of 8 percent. If so, interest costs will be about 6.5 percent of equity for Alcoa (.08 × 45/55) and about 2 percent for Texas Instruments (.08 × 20/80). Putting it all together, we have:

		Alcoa	Texas Instruments
	EBIT as percent of total assets	10%	15%
Times:	Total leverage	2.1	1.8
Equals:	EBIT as percent of common equity	21%	27%
Minus:	Interest as percent of common equity	6.5	2
Equals:	Pretax return on common equity..............	14.5%	25%

Tax Rate. We now have only to consider the rate of income tax likely to prevail for each company and we will have the final piece of the return on equity mosaic. Alcoa's effective tax rate (income tax as percent of net before tax) has ranged between 30 percent and 45 percent, averaging about 38 percent. This low rate in comparison with

the statutory rate of 48 percent reflects the "tax shelter" aspects of depletion allowances, foreign operations, and real estate activities. With Congress continuously reviewing such shelters, some increase in Alcoa's average tax rate, say to 40 percent, will be assumed in our projections of future rates of return. Texas Instruments has had a more normal tax rate of about 45 percent, benefiting to some extent from low-taxed unrepatriated foreign earnings, and we shall assume a continuation of its historical average rate.

In the previous section, it was concluded that Alcoa's pretax return on equity will be about 14.5 percent and Texas Instruments' will be about 25 percent. Applying a 40 percent tax rate to Alcoa's estimated return (and making no allowance for preferred dividends, which are negligible), leaves an after-tax return on equity of about 8.5 percent ([100% − 40%] × 14.5%). Applying a 45 percent tax rate to Texas Instruments' estimated return leaves an after-tax return on that company's equity of about 14 percent ([100% − 45%] × 25%).

Summary of Return on Equity Analysis

When we looked at the raw data on Alcoa's and Texas Instruments' return on equity over the past decade (Table 7–1), we surmised that if the future resembles the past Alcoa will have a rate of return of about 10 percent and Texas Instruments about 15 percent.

We then divided return on equity into two components, net profit margin on sales and turnover of common equity. Examining the history of these two components (Table 7–2), we concluded that the 10 percent and 15 percent rate of return estimates for Alcoa and Texas Instruments, respectively, still looked reasonable.

But a more in-depth analysis leads us to suspect that a 10 percent rate of return estimate for Alcoa may be much too optimistic, and a 15 percent estimate for Texas Instruments may be a shade too optimistic. Table 7–8 presents a summary of this in-depth analysis. We turn next to the implications of these estimates for the future earnings growth of the two companies.

GROWTH OF EQUITY PER SHARE

As demonstrated at the outset of this chapter, the basic growth potential of earnings per share can be estimated by multiplying the anticipated rate of return on stockholders' equity by the proportion of earnings expected to be retained in the business. Studies of corporate dividend and retention policies suggest that many interacting factors are at work in any given situation. Among these factors, the following

TABLE 7–8
Summary of Return on Equity Analysis, Alcoa and Texas Instruments

		Estimates Made for:	
Component		Alcoa	Texas Instruments
1. Pretax operating margin (Tables 7–3 and 7–4):		11%	9%
a. Labor costs	⎫	29	40
b. Other costs of goods sold ⎰ Percent		43	30
c. S.G.&A. ⎱ of sales		9	15
d. Depreciation and depletion	⎭	8	6
2. Turnover of operating assets (Tables 7–3 and 7–5):		0.9 times	1.7 times
a. Cash and equivalents	⎫	3	12
b. Accounts receivable ⎰ Percent of Sales		16	16
c. Inventories ⎱		22	11
d. Plant and equipment	⎭	75	20
3. Pretax return on operating assets (lines 1 × 2):		10%	15%
4. Nonoperating return, before interest and taxes:		8%	Not applicable
5. Return on total assets before interest and taxes:		10%	15%
6. Total leverage (total assets/equity—Table 7–7):		2.1 times	1.8 times
7. Interest/common equity		6.5%	2.0%
8. Pretax return on common equity (lines 5 × 6 − 7)		14.5%	25.0%
9. Tax rate		40%	45%
10. Return on equity [line 8 × (100% − line 9)]		8.5%	14%

may be listed, although not necessarily in order of importance: (1) an effort to project systematically future financial requirements, rates of return, and costs of alternative sources of funds; (2) subjective attitudes of the executives toward debt; (3) a weighing of the desires and tax status of the principal stockholders against the desires and tax status of the "typical" stockholders; (4) the policies of competing companies; and (5) a reluctance to set dividends at a rate that may later have to be cut back.

In general, the result of all these crosscurrents is a relative stability of dividend payout ratios. While payout ratios vary considerably from company to company, (e.g., Alcoa usually has paid out a much higher percentage of earnings than Texas Instruments) any one corporation's average dividend payout ratio tends to remain fairly stable for extended periods of time—Alcoa at about 40 percent; Texas Instruments about 25 percent. On a year-to-year basis, of course, payout and retention ratios may fluctuate considerably because dividends—the numerator of the dividend payout ratio—tend to be kept relatively stable while earnings—the denominator—fluctuate cyclically. Therefore, reference must be made to *average* payout ratios. It also may be helpful, in this regard, to examine the ratio of dividends to *cash flow* (net available for common plus depreciation, amortization, and depletion), since this figure tends to be more stable from year to year than the more traditional payout ratio.

Of course, security analysts cannot simply assume that the average historical payout and retention rates will be maintained in the future. They must try to determine whether any changes in policies are underway or forthcoming. Evidence of such changes might be present in the payout data themselves (e.g., the analyst may observe a gradual increase or reduction in the payout percent), or in statements made by management in stockholder reports or at annual meetings, or in the analyst's projections of future capital expenditures and capital requirements. Indeed, just as corporations are now required by the SEC to include a statement of sources and application of funds along with their income statements and balance sheets, so too is it becoming increasingly common for security analysts to make projections of future sources and application of funds along with their projections of future sales and earnings. In the case of Alcoa and Texas Instruments, a skeletal sources and application of funds projection for the total of the five years, 1976–80, might look as shown in Table 7–9.

TABLE 7–9
Skeletal Funds Projections (in millions of dollars)

	Alcoa	Texas Instruments
Application of Funds		
Capital expenditures and other investments	$1,900	$ 850
Increase in net working capital	150	150
Common stock dividends.........................	350	150
	$2,400	$1,150
Sources of Funds		
Net available for common	$ 950	$ 650
Depreciation, etc.	1,000	500
Net change in long-term debt	450	0
	$2,400	$1,150
Memo: Dividends as percent of net available	37%	23%

Effects of Selling New Stock. While earnings retention is the principal source of growth of equity per share, it also was noted at the outset of this chapter that growth can be achieved by selling new shares at a price higher than the existing equity per share (i.e., at a "premium over book value"). Let us consider a simple example of how this might occur.

Suppose we are dealing with a company that has $400 million of total capital, on which it is able to earn 15 percent before interest and taxes. Suppose that half the capital is represented by 6 percent bonds and the other half by 10 million shares of common stock. We shall consider the impact on this company's earnings per share of a 25 percent increase in capital funds employed. We shall assume that the

TABLE 7–10
Starting Position (in millions)

Capital structure:		Earnings:		
6% Bonds	$200	15% Pretax preinterest return		$ 60
Common equity		Less: Bond interest		12
(10 million shares)	200	Net before Taxes		48
	$400	Less: Income taxes (at 50 percent		
		rate)		24
		Net available for common		$ 24
		Earnings per share (24/10)		$ 2.40
		Source of earnings per share:		
		Book value per share (200/10)		$20
		Times: Return on common equity		
		(24/200)		12%
		Equals: Earnings per share		$ 2.40
		The capital increase would be:		
		6% Bonds	$ 50	
		1.25 million shares at $40	50	
			$100	

additional $100 million of capital is evenly divided between 6 percent bonds and common stock, and that the pretax preinterest return on total capital continues to be 15 percent. However, we shall assume that the new shares of common stock are sold at a price of 2.0 times book value.

The starting position of this hypothetical company would be as shown in Table 7–10 and the ending position in Table 7–11.

TABLE 7–11
Ending Position (in millions)

Capital structure:		Earnings:	
6% Bonds	$250	15% Pretax preinterest return	$75
Common equity		Less: Bond interest	15
(11.25 million shares)	250	Net before Taxes	60
	$500	Less: Income taxes	30
		Net available for common	$30
		Earnings per share (30/11.25)	$ 2.67
		Source of earnings per share:	
		Book value per share (250/11.25)	$22.22
		Times: Return on common equity (30/250)	12%
		Equals: Earnings per share	$ 2.67

Thus, the book value per share increased by 11.1 percent (22.22/ $20) and the earnings per share increased by the same percentage (2.67/2.40). This increase was *not* attributable to any change in leverage (which remained at 50 percent), or in return on equity (which remained at 12 percent). It was attributable solely to the fact that new stock was sold at a premium over book value. This can be proven algebraically, as follows:

1. Let *P/BV* equal the ratio of the selling price of the new shares to the book value of the existing shares.

2. The percentage growth in *dollar book value* equals the percentage growth in number of shares multiplied by *P/BV*. In our example, there was a 12.5 percent increase in number of shares (from 10 million to 11.25 million) at a *P/BV* of 2.0. This resulted in a 25 percent increase in dollar book value (from $200 million to $250 million).

3. The percentage growth in *per share book value*, and therefore of earnings per share if rate of return on equity remains constant, equals:

$$\left[\frac{1 + \text{Percent growth in dollar book value}}{1 + \text{Percent growth in number of shares}}\right] - 1.0$$

In our example, this works out to:

$$\left[\frac{1 + 25\%}{1 + 12\frac{1}{2}\%}\right] - 1.0 = \left[\frac{1.25}{1.125}\right] - 1.0 = 1.111 - 1.0 = .111$$

4. Substituting statement (2) in the numerator of statement (3), we have the growth rate of book value and earnings per share equal to:

$$\left[\frac{1 + (\text{Percent growth in number of shares})(P/BV)}{1 + \text{Percent growth in number of shares}}\right] - 1.0$$

In our example, this works out to:

$$\left[\frac{1 + (12\frac{1}{2}\%)(2.0)}{1 + 12\frac{1}{2}\%}\right] - 1.0 = \left[\frac{1 + 25\%}{1 + 12\frac{1}{2}\%}\right] - 1.0$$

as in (3).

It should be borne in mind that while we have been discussing the sale of new stock *for cash*, the same type of analysis is applicable to a *merger* in which the book value of the assets received by the acquiring company exceeds the book value of the shares given to the stockholders of the acquired company. The result is to increase the book value per share of the surviving company. Whether the earnings per share of the surviving company also increase depends, of course,

on the rate of return of the surviving company. But the potential for increasing earnings via exchanges of stock in a merger should be apparent to the reader from this discussion.

Furthermore, it should be noted that book value per share also can be increased by *retiring shares at a discount* from existing book value. For example, suppose that a company has 10 million shares outstanding with a book value of $50 per share. And suppose that the company's stock is selling in the open market for $30 (a *P/BV* of 0.60). If the company has $60 million of excess cash which it uses to buy in 2 million shares at $30, the book value per share will be increased from $50 (500/10) to $55 (440/8), or by 10 percent. This can be shown, using our formula, as follows:

$$\left[\frac{1 + (-20\%)(.60)}{1 + (-.20\%)}\right] - 1.0 = \left[\frac{1 - 12\%}{1 - 20\%}\right] - 1.0 = \left[\frac{.88}{.80}\right] - 1.0 =$$
$$1.10 - 1.0 = .10$$

Table 7–12 shows the average price/book value ratio of Alcoa and Texas Instruments each year from 1965 to 1975. It will be seen that

TABLE 7–12
Average Price/Book Value Ratio, Alcoa and Texas Instruments

	Alcoa	Texas Instruments
1965	1.3	5.5
1966	1.9	5.5
1967	1.8	5.7
1968	1.5	4.3
1969	1.4	4.6
1970	1.1	3.6
1971	1.0	3.5
1972	0.8	4.6
1973	1.0	5.2
1974	0.9	3.7
1975	0.9	3.5

Alcoa's stock price dropped from a substantial premium over book value to below book value. On the other hand, Texas Instruments consistently sold at a very large premium. It would not be surprising, therefore, to see Texas Instruments gain a bit of extra earnings growth—over and above earning a high rate of return on a high percentage of retained earnings—by issuing additional shares of common stock during the years ahead, either in cash sales to the public or in exchange for an attractive merger candidate. This route to earnings

growth would appear closed to Alcoa, however, at least in the foreseeable future.[12]

Summary: Earnings Growth Forecast. We have estimated that Alcoa's rate of return on stockholders' equity will be about 8 to 10 percent and that Texas Instruments' return will be close to 15 percent. We also have estimated that Alcoa's retention rate would be about 60 percent (a dividend payout of 40 percent) and Texas Instruments' about 75 percent (a payout of 25 percent). Multiplying rate of return by retention rate produces "internal growth rate" estimates of about 5 to 6 percent for Alcoa and about 10 to 11 percent for Texas Instruments. No additional growth from sale of new stock at a premium seems likely for Alcoa, but this does seem a likely source of extra growth for Texas Instruments. Although the magnitude and timing of such growth is not possible to estimate with any degree of precision, an additional 10 percent over five years—or 2 percent per annum—would appear to be easily achievable.

Thus, our estimated earnings growth rate for Alcoa is considerably below the sales growth estimate arrived at in the preceding chapter. Our estimated earnings growth rate for Texas Instruments is also below the sales growth rate estimate of the preceding chapter, but not by as large a margin as Alcoa's. It is, perhaps, significant that these earnings shortfalls in relation to sales are consistent with the belief expressed in Chapter 5 that earnings *in aggregate* (and therefore dividends) are not likely to keep pace with the growth of gross national product. These shortfalls probably have much to do with the weak stock markets we have experienced since the mid-1960s.[13]

SOME ADDITIONAL ASPECTS OF EARNINGS ANALYSIS

Marginal Analysis. Readers who have studied economics will be acquainted with the concept of marginal rate of return, in contrast to *average* rate of return. Let us hypothesize a company whose total capital, from all sources, increased by 5 percent from 1970 to 1971, and by 10 percent, 0 percent, 20 percent, and 5 percent in each of the following four years, respectively. Assume also that the company's rate of return on total capital is 10.5 percent, 10 percent, 10.5 percent,

---

[12] A contrary view of this subject has been expressed by Theodore Levitt in "Dinosaurs among the Bears and Bulls," *Harvard Business Review*, January–February 1975. In this article, Levitt argues that conditions are always right (the state of the stock market, notwithstanding) for giant single-industry companies ("dinosaurs," he calls them) to diversify into related businesses via acquisition.

[13] A recent study of 631 companies during the period, 1956–70, shows that earnings per share grew at a rate of only 4 percent. Moreover, this growth was the result of a 7 percent rise in book value per share and a 3 percent *decline* in rate of return. See R. A. Larsen and J. E. Murphy, Jr., "New Insight into Changes in Earnings per Share," *Financial Analysts Journal*, March/April 1975.

10 percent, 11 percent, and 11 percent in each of the six years, 1970 to 1975, respectively. The average rate of return in this series is 10.5 percent, and the individual figures are so close to the average that most analysts would be willing to assume it as a "normal" rate of return on *increments* of capital in trying to estimate the company's growth potential. But further analysis would reveal that the return on increments of capital—the "marginal" rate of return—has been considerably higher than 10.5 percent. The tabulation shown in Table 7–13, which is not strict marginal analysis but yet is simple and useful,

TABLE 7–13
Marginal Return Analysis

Year	(1) Total Capital (1970 = 100)	(2) Earnings on Total Capital (percent of column 1)
1970	100	10.5 (10½%)
1971	105 (+5%)	10.5 (10%)
1972	115.5 (+10%)	12.1 (10½%)
1973	115.5 (no increase)	11.6 (10%)
1974	138.6 (+20%)	15.3 (11%)
1975	145.5 (+5%)	16.0 (11%)
5-year increment	45.5 (145.5 − 100)	5.5 (16.0 − 10.5)
	Incremental return: 5.5/45.5 = 12.1%	

suggests that the increments to capital have actually been invested at a rate of about 12 percent.[14]

Thus, really incisive analysts have reason to suspect that the company's potential earnings growth rate may be greater than surface data indicate. Before jumping to that conclusion, however, they should try to determine why the marginal return on capital has been significantly different from the average return. Among the possibilities are: introduction of new and more efficient equipment; a new product line; or a particularly advantageous merger. Once the major reason is isolated, a judgment must be made as to whether its effects are likely to persist and whether the event itself is likely to be repeated in the future. It usually will help in this connection to examine marginal returns over *successive* three-year or five-year periods instead of just a single period. Care should be taken that the initial and terminal years of each period are not too dissimilar in economic characteristics.

---

[14] Actually, there is some evidence that marginal rates of return may be more typically below rather than above average rates of return. See W. J. Baumol et al., "Earnings Retention, New Capital and the Growth of the Firm," *Review of Economics and Statistics*, November 1970; also, G. Whittington, "The Profitability of Retained Earnings," *Review of Economics and Statistics*, May 1972.

Product-Line Disclosure and Other Supplementary Informa-
tion. Corporations are now required by the SEC to report sales and
earnings of their major product lines as supplementary information to
the regular income statement. In addition, the FASB has proposed that
companies be required to allocate operating assets to major product
categories. Where such detail is available, the security analyst should
be sure to calculate profit margins and turnover ratios by product line,
since these data will provide valuable insight into the determinants of
observed trends in overall margins and turnover rates.

While on the subject of product-line data, it may be noted that
attempts have been made to integrate the concept of industrial life
cycles, described in the previous chapter, into the analysis of earnings.
For example, Figure 7–2 repeats the illustrative life cycle of sales used
in the earlier discussion, and adds curves of profit margins and dollar
profits.[15] The following characteristic relationships can be observed in
the chart:

FIGURE 7–2
Relationship between Sales and Profit Cycles

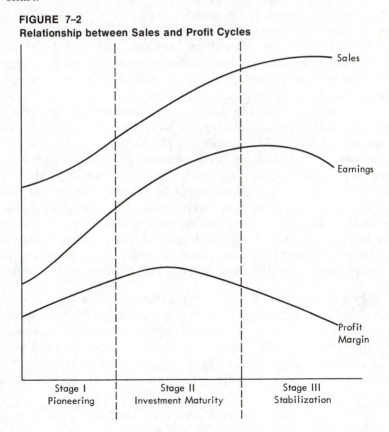

---

[15] The profit curves are based on an analysis by Sam R. Goodman, *Techniques of
Profitability Analysis* (New York: John Wiley & Sons, Inc., 1970), chap. 4.

1. The profit margin rises during the early period of sales growth, but begins to decline before sales growth levels out. This decline probably reflects such factors as the price reductions made in order to expand the market for the product, and a gradual slowing down of productivity gains as full efficiencies of scale become utilized.

2. Although margins decline, dollar profits continue to rise as long as the growth of sales is sufficient to offset the decline of margins.

3. Finally, sales growth becomes insufficient to offset declining margins, and dollar profits fall.

If this sequence of events is typical of most products, it implies that continued growth of dollar profits for a corporation requires the periodic introduction of *new products*. Moreover, if the new product introductions can be timed appropriately to overlap the life cycles of the old products, dollar profits can grow along a smooth path (for example, as in the case of Minnesota Mining & Manufacturing—the 3M Corp.). On the other hand, if the new product introductions cannot be so carefully timed, profit growth will occur in spurts, followed by leveling periods, followed by renewed spurts (for example, as in the case of Polaroid Corp.). The discussion also implies that the larger a corporation becomes, the more difficult it may be to generate new products with large enough market potential to make a meaningful impact on the total profit.

In addition to requiring disclosure of product-line data, the SEC now requires all 10–K (annual) and 10–Q (quarterly) reports to include a section entitled, "Management's Discussion and Analysis of the Summary of Earnings." These comments by management are supposed to get away from the puffery which often typifies the "Letter to Stockholders" appearing at the front of most Annual and Interim Reports, and to indicate in specific terms why earnings of the period just ended changed in the way they did. It is to be hoped that there will be regularly included in such analyses facts not previously made available by many companies, such as price versus volume components of sales, more detailed expense breakdowns, and productivity data.

But while management's analysis of changes in *actual earnings* will doubtless be very helpful to analysts, great controversy surrounds the question of whether management should be allowed to, or should be required to, *forecast* earnings.[16] Some observers believe that management forecasts will be more misleading than helpful. Indeed, there is a fair amount of evidence that management forecasts are little,

---

[16] See, for example, Financial Analysts Federation, *Disclosure of Corporate Forecasts to the Investor* (New York, 1973); and Financial Executives Research Foundation, *Public Disclosure of Business Forecasts* (New York, 1972).

if at all, more accurate than simple extrapolations of past data.[17] Nevertheless, many observers believe that management has a duty to disclose its planning assumptions, for better or worse. Should this point of view prevail, analysts will be well advised to use the earnings component framework presented in this chapter to test the consistency of the forecasts published by companies.

Profitability and Market Share. A major research project carried out at the Harvard Business School concluded that: "Under most circumstances, enterprises that have achieved a high share of the markets they serve are considerably more profitable than their smaller share rivals. . . . On the average, a difference of 10 percentage points in market share is accompanied by a difference of about 5 points in pretax return on investment."[18] The data also revealed that the rate of return improvement associated with higher market shares is attributable to higher profit *margins* on sales rather than higher asset *turnover*.[19]

The directors of the research project believe that in most industries there is a minimum market share which is necessary for a company to be viable. They do not offer a basis for determining what that minimum share is, but presumably an in-depth "break-even analysis" would help answer the question. Unfortunately, investment analysts do not usually have access to the detailed data needed for break-even analysis because most of it falls under the heading of "inside information."[20] In the absence of such information, a worthwhile alternative approach is to study the behavior of the key profitability ratios discussed in this chapter under conditions of economic adversity, for five or six leading competitors in an industry, each of which has a different market share. The lowest market share associated with minimally acceptable profitability ratios during such a period might be viewed as the "break-even market share." In any event, the project directors try to hypothesize reasons why market share and profitability are associated. They focus on three:

1. Economies of scale—in procurement, manufacturing, marketing, and other cost components.

---

[17] Illustrative of such evidence is R. M. Copeland and R. J. Marioni, "Executives' Forecasts of Earnings per share versus Forecasts of Naive Models," *Journal of Business,* October 1972.

[18] R. D. Buzzell, B. T. Gale, and R. G. M. Sultan, "Market Share—a Key to Profitability," *Harvard Business Review,* January–February 1975, p. 97.

[19] The greater importance of margin than of turnover also showed up in the study by Larsen and Murphy, "New Insight into Changes in Earnings Per Share."

[20] If the information is available, a good presentation of the *technique* of break-even analysis is contained in L. A. Bernstein, *Financial Statement Analysis* (Homewood, Ill.: Richard D. Irwin, Inc., 1974), chap. 21.

2. Market power—the ability to bargain more effectively and "administer" higher prices than competitors.
3. Quality of management—which succeeds both in gaining and retaining market share, and in controlling costs.

It is the third factor, management quality, which many observers believe lies at the heart of all corporate success stories. We turn to that factor in the next chapter.

SUGGESTED READINGS

Bernstein, Leopold A. *Financial Statement Analysis: Theory, Application and Interpretation.* Homewood, Ill.: Richard D. Irwin, Inc., 1974.

Buzzell, Robert D. et al. "Market Share—A Key to Profitability." *Harvard Business Review,* January–February 1975.

Goodman, Sam R. *Techniques of Profitability Analysis.* New York: John Wiley & Sons, Inc., 1970.

Helfert, Erich A. *Techniques of Financial Analysis.* 3d ed. Homewood, Ill.: Richard D. Irwin, Inc., 1972.

Larsen, Robert A., and Murphy, Joseph E., Jr. "New Insight into Changes in Earnings per Share." *Financial Analysts Journal,* March/April 1975.

Levitt, Theodore. "Dinosaurs among the Bears and Bulls." *Harvard Business Review,* January–February 1975.

Vancil, Richard F., ed. *Financial Executive's Handbook.* Parts III, VIII, IX. Homewood, Ill.: Dow Jones-Irwin, Inc., 1970.

Weiss, Leonard W. *Case Studies in American Industry.* 2d ed. New York: John Wiley & Sons, Inc., 1971.

Weston, John F., and Brigham, Eugene F. *Management Finance.* 5th ed. New York: Holt, Rinehart & Winston, Inc., 1975.

Whittington, Geoffrey. *The Prediction of Profitability and Other Studies of Company Behavior.* London: Cambridge University Press, 1971.

REVIEW QUESTIONS AND PROBLEMS

1. What are the two primary sources of growth of net income per share?
2. Discuss the interaction of profit margin and equity turnover.
3. What factors can cause profit margins to change?
4. What factors can cause asset turnover to change?
5. How can leverage improve or impair the position of the common stockholder?
6. In what ways can the issuance of new shares influence growth of earnings per share?
7. What is the influence of a company's dividend policy on its growth of earnings per share?

8. Distinguish between average return and marginal return on capital.
9. Discuss the interrelationships between the growth rate of sales and the growth rate of earnings.
10. What corporate data not normally available to the security analyst might enable him to make better earnings forecasts?

RESEARCH PROJECTS

1. Select an industry in which the two leading companies have had substantially different rates of return on equity during the past ten years. How do you account for the differences in terms of the profit margin, turnover, and other ratios discussed in the text?
2. Select three companies which have issued bonds during the past three years. Compare the interest rate paid by each company with its *marginal* rate of return on capital during this period.
3. Mergers often result in increased earnings per share simply because of the relative price/book value ratios of the acquiring and acquired companies. Prepare a paper describing a recent merger which illustrates this phenomenon.
4. Do a comparative sources and application of funds analysis for the two leading companies in an industry of your choice.
5. Compare and contrast the availability of product-line breakdowns of income for two multiproduct corporations.

C.F.A. QUESTIONS

1. *From Exam II, 1974*

Rate of return (percent earned) on book value of the common equity is often regarded as the ultimate test of the profitability or earning power of a company.

State the qualifications you would attach to the use of this measurement. Explain.

2. *From Exam II, 1974*

A major component of cost to many corporations is raw materials that are characterized as commodities with volatile prices. List and explain two steps which corporations may take in a period of rising prices to protect their unit profit margins.

Chapter 8

Management: The Qualitative Factor

> The wise man does no wrong in changing his habits
> with the times.
> ————————————————————————————————*Cato*

Ever hear of Midvale Steel & Ordinance, Central Leather, International Mercantile Marine, Cambria Steel, Consolidation Coal, Chile Copper, Magnolia Petroleum, American Woolen, Ohio Cities Gas, Virginia Carolina Chemical, Prairie Oil and Gas, Atlantic Gulf & West Indies, American Locomotive, Cuba Cane Sugar, Baldwin Locomotive, Associated Oil, Greene Cananea Copper, American Cotton Oil, United Verde Extension Mining? They were among the top 100 industrials in 1917. For its 50th anniversary issue, *Forbes* studied "Corporate Mortality, Corporate Vitality: Which companies have had outstanding top management? Which have been run by second raters or worse? The answers show up in the changes in relative rank among the top 100 companies over the last five decades." *Forbes* said "Of the top 100 [industrials] in 1917, only 43 are among the top 100 today. Twenty-eight of 1917's companies have disappeared entirely. Of the top 20 in 1917 only seven remain in that corporate eminence."[1]

The Quality of Management

One obvious reason why so many companies "fall from grace" is that the growth of the industries of which they are members slows down relative to the growth of other industries. This is a natural

---

[1] The *Forbes* 50th anniversary issue appeared September 15, 1967. See also "The Fortune Directory of the 500 Largest Industrial Corporations," and "The 500: A Report on Two Decades," *Fortune*, May 1975.

concomitant of a healthy and growing competitive economy. But interindustry competition is far from a complete explanation, although it is an important factor. Intraindustry competition is also crucial. *Forbes* asks, for example, "why did American Locomotive and Baldwin Locomotive fight progress by sticking too long with the steam locomotive, while General Motors' diesels rode away with the markets?"

Why do some companies in the same industry have better growth records than others? Sometimes it is because they possess an unduplicatable characteristic such as a unique geographic location or a patented production process. More often, however, it is because they are *better managed*. For example, the difference between the dynamic S. S. Kresge and the now bankrupt W. T. Grant may be attributed to differences in the caliber of their management.[2] This may also account for the difference between Ford and Chrysler.[3]

Differences in management ability also can explain why the same company may have a better relative growth record within its industry in one period than in another. For example, in the four years after Rodney C. Gott took over the helm of bowling-battered AMF, earnings increased 70 percent on a sales increase of 33 percent in the perilous leisure market.[4] Under a new president and chief executive officer, William G. Meese who replaced veteran Walter L. Cisler, Detroit Edison sought retrenchment, a new image and better profitability. Moreover, examples can be cited of companies whose executive recognized the onset of industrial stagnation and shifted part or all of their operations into completely new lines, while the heads of similarly situated companies rested on their laurels.

National Cash Register was for years number one in its field.

It failed, however, to apply electronics to its traditional markets. Big retailers, J. C. Penny, Sears, Kroger, pounded on NCR's door trying to get the company to experiment with computerized point-of-sale systems. But NCR failed to listen. They were all bound up in cement with their mechanical cash registers.[5]

---

[2] "The Orchestrated Growth of S. S. Kresge," *Duns Review*, December 1975, pp. 46–47.

[3] See Peter Vanderwicken, "What's Really Wrong at Chrysler?" *Fortune*, May 1975, pp. 176–77.

[4] "The Cool World of Rodney Gott," *Dun's Review*, May 1972. See also "Man on the Spot: Tough Salesman Shuts Stores, Cuts Jobs to Save W. T. Grant," *The Wall Street Journal*, December 4, 1975. See also: "Meet Your New Partner—What Happens to an Overextended Company When the Bankers Finally Move in? Ask W. T. Grant," *Forbes*, June 1, 1975, p. 36; see also "W. T. Grant: Ripples from a Collapsing Giant," *Business Week*, October 20, 1975, pp. 98–100.

[5] "What Happened at NCR after the Boss Declared Martial Law," *Fortune*, September 1975, p. 102; see also "The Coming Battle at the Supermarket Counter," *Fortune*, September 1975, p. 105; also "Point of Sale Cash Registers Are Becoming a Growth Industry," by Gene Smith, *The New York Times*, July 7, 1976.

Meanwhile Burroughs was nibbling away at NCR's banking markets and Singer and Pitney-Bowes at its retail markets. NCR's bank sales began to dwindle but still the company failed to introduce new systems to halt Burroughs and other competitors' advances.

Fortune noted:

Puzzled critics attributed NCR's inertia to a "Dayton" mentality. With a long record of corporate success to look back on, the company's top managers often tended to look backward instead of forward. To visitors' eyes, the NCR complex in Dayton seemed old-fashioned in appearance, customs, and style. "We had a living retirement program going on here," one vice president recalls.

NCR spun such a tight cocoon around its Dayton operations that employees in other cities were called "outsiders." The computer division in California seemed to bear little relation to the electromechanical cash registers and accounting machines manufactured in Dayton. No one seemed able to muster the vision to connect the two.

As late as 1970, Wall Street regarded NCR as a glamour stock, and it commanded a price-earnings multiple of 63 that year. But shortly after, profits fell sharply and the company had to fight for its life. The directors decided they had no choice but to intervene. The outcome was the selection of a new president with full authority to clean house. From a peak of 15,700 workers in Dayton, the number was reduced to 2,000 by the end of 1976. Five high executives took early retirement; seven others found new jobs, and seven others were demoted. NCR entered the electronic age.

The most obvious way of measuring the management process is by the quantification of the results of operations. A number of services and sources present comparative data. For example, *Fortune* in its "Annual Survey of the 500 Largest Industrial Companies," uses sales, assets, net income, stockholder's equity, earnings per share, total return on investment, sales per dollar of stockholders' equity, and return on sales.

Forbes, in its "Annual Report on American Industry," uses return on stockholders' equity, return on total capital, sales growth, earnings per share, debt-to-equity ratio, net profit margin, and stock market performance.

The caliber of management, however, is often not fully amenable to quantification. To a certain extent it is true that management can be judged by its statistical record—the growth of sales and earnings which it was capable of generating. But frequently it is impossible to separate the causes of the growth record into specific managerial decisions, on the one hand, and external factors over which management had little or no control, on the other. Moreover, the statistical record does not necessarily reveal very well management's

capacity for coping with change. And if anything is certain about the future of most companies, it is that changes will occur with increasing rapidity. Thus, a thorough analysis of a company's growth prospects must go beyond the quantitative approach which has been discussed in the previous chapters. It must take into account the *quality* of management.

Factors Which Give Management a Quality Reputation

A Louis Harris & Associates survey of the decision criteria used by major institutional portfolio managers, in the selection of individual common stock, found that the single most important criterion was *the quality of management*.

Six factors were selected as very important by at least three out of four portfolio managers. At the top of the list—as it had been in each of the three previous surveys—was the quality of management, considered very important by 85 percent (see Table 8–1).

Since the preeminent criterion in evaluating a company continued to be quality of management, various facets of this general criterion were examined by asking each portfolio manager how important each of a series of 12 factors was in determining the quality of management. (See Table 8–2.)

The first factor on this list is to some extent an expression of distrust of the concept of interchangeable, all-purpose management. Eighty-five percent felt that it is very important for management to have "extensive experience and knowledge of the specific business in which the company is involved." This item also has overtones of an anticonglomerate attitude. At the same time this does not imply that it is necessarily desirable for management to grow from within the company rather than being brought in from outside—only 17 percent feel such internal development of management is very important.

Modern management science teaches that good managers will be effective in almost any company. This is because they are masters, not of a particular business, but rather of the critical *managerial functions:* setting objectives, formulating plans to achieve these objectives, organizing and inspiring subordinates to carry out the plans, and innovating when previous methods seem outmoded. Thus, the present chapter is concerned with the way people—management people—do their work.

It is recognized, of course, that an outsider is at a great disadvantage in trying to assess the caliber of a company's managers, for the outsider usually does not have an opportunity to observe them in their day-to-day work. The disadvantage is particularly pronounced for the small, individual investor. A professional security analyst, however, may gain

TABLE 8–1
Importance of Various General Criteria in Stock Selection (base: total portfolio managers)

	Total			
	1975	1974	1973	1972
Very important:				
Quality of management	85%	86%	91%	91%
Return on shareholders' equity	83	75	72	68
Rate of return on total invested capital	78	75	72	65
Accounting policies	76	70	76	68
Ratio of debt to equity	76	n.a.	n.a.	n.a.
Earnings growth rate	75	77	77	n.a.
Predictability of earnings (i.e., likelihood				
earnings estimates will be met)	71	73	83	85
Level and type of fixed debt	69	62	55	56
Operating profit margins	68	70	75	78
Cash flow generated	65	57	48	41
Interest coverage	60	60	46	45
Long-term general economic projections	59	66	74	71
Capital needs over next five years	58	60	52	46
Level and type of other debt	55	58	40	44
Price/earnings ratio relative to other				
comparable companies	55	53	54	60
Dividend history (consistency of payment)	55	53	45	38
Amount of liquid working capital	54	57	43	n.a.
Cyclical nature of the company	48	55	59	n.a.
Level of capital expenditures	43	43	40	43
Frequency of dividend increases	40	40	32	31
Level of research and development	38	38	41	n.a.
Dividend yield	34	39	30	24
Reputation of management with the public ...	33	45	48	51
Price/earnings ratio in absolute magnitude ...	32	35	31	n.a.
Short-term general economic conditions	32	32	22	24

n.a. = not asked.
    Source: *Major Institutional Investors, The Fourth Survey, Summary,* conducted by Louis Harris & Associates, Inc., New York, November 1975, p. 81.

some understanding of a company by personally visiting both its corporate headquarters and its outlying plants. These trips afford the analyst a chance to speak with the company's managers face-to-face, to speak with the managers' subordinates, and to wander about the company's plants (preferably unescorted) and observe the attitudes of the workers, the condition of the equipment, the smoothness of the work flow, and similar clues to management's efficiency. Over and above these surface indications of the quality of management, however, the analyst should search for more subtle clues.

The Best-Managed Companies. Each year *Dun's Review* selects what its editors consider to be the five best-managed companies

TABLE 8–2

Importance of Factors in Determining Quality of Management (base: total portfolio managers)

	Total		
	1975	1973	1972
Very important:			
Top management has extensive experience and knowledge of the specific business in which the company is involved..........................	86%	85%	n.a.%
Management is willing to admit its mistakes..........	64	75	79
There are identifiable successors to the top executive.......................................	53	60	66
Management has a strong incentive compensation program	41	50	n.a.
Top executives have a strong financial background	39	35	33
Top management is concentrated in the hands of a few strong executives	21	20	23
Top management has a significant ownership position or stock options in the company	18	21	24
Top management comes from within the company rather than being brought in from outside	17	17	n.a.
Top management receives a high level of compensation................................	15	25	31
Top management creates a high-pressure performance-oriented environment................	12	9	n.a.
Top management has a real social awareness	9	22	23
Top management is relatively young	2	3	3

n.a. = not asked.

Source: *Major Institutional Investors, The Fourth Survey, Summary,* conducted by Louis Harris & Associates, Inc., New York, November 1975, p. 87.

in the United States. For 1975, *Dun's* picked Dow Chemical, Hewlett-Packard, S. S. Kresge, Merrill Lynch, and Procter & Gamble. It declared:

But the exceptionally well-managed companies somehow performed their own magic, chalking up earnings gains even in troubled times—and in troubled industries. The ultimate five presented in *Dun's Review,* and the most outstanding management trait of each one: Dow Chemical Co., sophisticated financial management; Hewlett-Packard Co., technological innovation; S. S. Kresge Co., controlled corporate growth; Merrill Lynch & Co., strategic corporate planning; and Procter & Gamble Co., management depth.

Like P&G, the other masters of management in 1975 found that it is continuity of effort that really pays off. The companies that managed best this year have managed well for a long time. As a top executive at Dow puts it: "You had to come into the year in real good shape in terms of your people and your money—or you could get killed."

Kresge Chairman Robert E. Dewar explains the challenge of 1975 this way:

"It was a year when companies needed confidence—confidence in their own organizations and in their decisions." And in this toughest year of all, every one of the five had the confidence to keep on leading from strength. P&G, to beef up its management, kept on hiring new people even as other companies were laying them off; Merrill Lynch kept on hammering out new plans—including one of the most revolutionary in the history of the securities business—while other Wall Street firms closed their doors; Hewlett-Packard, in an industry wracked by severe price competition and eroding profits, kept shoveling in more R&D dollars while competitors cut back; Dow's illustrious financial system kept earnings rising even after its spectacular showing in 1974; and Kresge, methodically expanding in an industry where others were going bankrupt, far outperformed its major competitors."[6]

In 1974 it selected AT&T, R. J. Reynolds, Merck, Southern Railway, and Kerr-McGee, stating:

The five best-managed outran adversity because their own goals, their targets, were set beyond normal corporate reach. True, each company's goals were different. But their ability to keep on course toward a goal—and then, finally, to hit the target—was the thread that tied the *Dun's* five together in 1974. For deButts, it meant that in a cash-scarce year, AT&T could maintain a sharply competitive posture in a market where hardly any other company could raise capital. For Chairman Colin Stokes, it meant that R. J. Reynolds, facing up to mounting costs and a government dam on its mainstream business, was able to generate additional earnings from a base-broadening—and, in many respects, daring—diversification program. In Stokes' view: "A sense of urgency is the best thing for a business. For only when a company is tested in the crucible can its fundamental strengths be measured."

At Merck, Chairman and President Henry W. Gadsden's primary goal in a drug industry under fire from consumers and government alike has been to position his company for future discoveries. The way: more dollars into research and development, even if profit margins were narrowing. At the Southern Railway, serving the South with one of the nation's most efficient railroads, the boxcars were laden with freight in a flat year because of long-term modernization and marketing goals. Chairman Dean McGee's goal of developing a solid foothold in every source of energy, from oil to uranium, has brought Kerr-McGee to a unique position at just the right time.[7]

Its choices for 1973 were:

The five companies chosen by *Dun's* editors as the U.S. five best managed companies in 1973—Citibank, J. C. Penney, Exxon, Monsanto and Weyerhaeuser—had one special quality in common: a unique ability to see the

[6] "The Five Best-Managed Companies," *Dun's Review*, vol. 106, no. 6 (December 1975). Reprinted with special permission of *Dun's Review*, Copyright 1975, Dun & Bradstreet Publications Corp.

[7] "The Five Best-Managed Companies," *Dun's Review*, vol. 104, no. 6 (December 1974). Reprinted with special permission of *Dun's Review*. Copyright 1974, Dun & Bradstreet Publications Corp.

future. Call it perspicacity. Call it long-range planning. In each case, the five companies recognized their problems years ago and determinedly took the steps that finally bore fruition in 1973. While many companies performed well in a difficult year, without exception *Dun's* choices out-performed their major competitors.

At Monsanto, it was recognition of an unwieldy corporate structure that caused the company to reorganize in 1971 and bring in a new president, John Hanley, to reshape its directions. At Weyerhaeuser, it was a realization that it had to respond to changes in the marketplace and break out the cyclicality of the housing market. As George Weyerhaeuser puts it, "This year is the culmination of five years of careful planning."

That J. K. Jamieson's Exxon could produce record results in a testy year for the oils owes much to management's foresight and in undertaking a decade ago an ongoing exploration program that effectively lessened its dependence on Arab oil. Nor could Exxon be faulted as a marketer; with everything else, it also managed to change its name "without losing a customer."

Walter Wriston's Citibank was years building up not only its assets (which have doubled since 1968), but its managers as well. As the result of establishing its foreign beachheads early and experimenting with every kind of financial service before diversifying at home, Citibank developed the know-how—and the executives to write banking's biggest growth story. And while most other companies were hard put to sweeten the executive compensation pot under restrictive government controls, William Batten's J. C. Penney could go on doing what it has done for years: keeping and attracting top retailing executive talent with one of the best long-range compensation packages in industry.[8]

Management's Motivation

One thing the analyst should try to ascertain is whether the senior officers of the company have a strong desire, perhaps drive is an even better word, to make their company grow. Without the presence of such ambition among the key personnel, "competence" usually will not suffice.[9]

In business, at least, it is a fairly valid generalization that a firm must either grow or lose its market share. A firm whose essential philosophy is to preserve the status quo soon becomes unable to attract or retain capable young personnel, for whom the death or retirement of existing officers is the only route to promotion. Preservation of the status quo tends to be an unattainable goal because the firm's products become

---

[8] "The Five Best-Managed Companies," *Dun's Review*, vol. 102, no. 6 (December 1973). Reprinted with special permission of *Dun's Review*. Copyright 1973, Dun & Bradstreet Publications Corp.

[9] See Harold Koontz, *Appraising Managers as Managers* (New York: McGraw-Hill Book Co., 1971); also *The Chief Executive Office and Its Responsibilities* (New York: AMACOM, 1975); Lee Grossman, *The Change Agent* (New York: American Management Association, 1974).

displaced by the newer and better products of expansion-minded competitors. A policy of nonexpansion incurs grave risks of loss of markets through technological obsolescence and consumer withdrawal.

It is true, of course, that growth-oriented managers may pose another risk for investors in their enterprises. For they may seek growth at the expense of *profit*. This risk, however, appears less serious than the risks posed by managers of opposite temperament. Whether the managerial drive is share of the market, power, prestige, public approval, or "the mere love of the game," it usually gets reflected on the bottom line. And there are various diverse ways of motivating management by rewarding executives for their performance. Analysts in judging probable management performance should examine companies' management motivation techniques.[10]

Management's "Grand Design"

Conception of the Market. History suggests that if managers are to bring their desires for growth to fruition, they should have a rather broad conception of their company's "natural" product line. Few successful companies have continued to produce the same type of product throughout their lifetime. Successful companies are usually market oriented rather than product oriented, and the type of product demanded by the *relevant market* tends to undergo radical changes as time passes. Unless a company's product mix is restructured to meet the market's changing demands, growth is impeded, if not prevented.

Consider the contrast between IBM and Underwood prior to the Olivetti takeover of the latter. Here is a classic example of the difference between a well-conceived and an ill-conceived product line. For almost 50 years, until World War II, Underwood was the premier business machine company in the nation. During this period, the word "business machine" was virtually synonymous with "standard manual typewriter," and Underwood was the typewriter king.

But a new business machine technology was developed during and after the war. For one thing, manual typewriters were increasingly displaced by electric typewriters. When Underwood failed completely to make the shift, IBM virtually took over the market. Furthermore, typewriters became only a small segment of a much broader office equipment market, which included electric calculators, punched card

---

[10] See "Evaluating Results" in *AMA Management Handbook*, ed. Russell F. Moore (New York: American Management Association, Inc., 1970); see also Oscar Grusky, "Evaluating Organizations" in *Large Corporations in a Changing Society*, ed. J. Fred Weston (New York: New York University Press, 1975); and Merritt L. Kastens, *Long-Range Planning for Your Business: An Operating Manual* (New York: American Management Association, 1976).

equipment, electronic computers, and duplicating devices. Underwood waited to move into electronic computers—long after its competitors—and was hopelessly outclassed. IBM, on the other hand, maintained a consistent technological lead in punched card equipment and computers, and more recently has moved into the duplicating machine field.

Significantly, IBM itself might not have made the move into electronic computers if the elder Mr. Watson had not turned the company's leadership over to his son. This points up all the more strongly the dangers of a management resting on its laurels, continuing to do that which it has always done best but overlooking newer aspects of the relevant market.

"Developing basic business missions is a fundamental step in corporate planning," according to George A. Steiner, one of its leading proponents. "If the Baldwin Locomotive Works had said its mission was to make traction power for railroads, instead of sticking with steam locomotives, it would probably still be in business." He notes, however, that "there is no such thing as a single goal or objective of a company. Each firm has a network of aims which includes the basic socio-economic purpose of the company, value objectives of top managers, business missions, long-range objectives, and short-range targets and goals."[11]

Plan of Action. Even a broad conception of the market is not a sufficient precondition for rapid growth. The security analyst should inquire whether management has specific objectives, and specific plans and timetables for achieving those objectives. "We're keeping a watchful eye on things" is not very convincing evidence that management is doing its job.

"The essence of long-range planning," Steiner declares, "is a systematic identification of opportunities and threats that lay in the future which, in combination with other relevant data, provide a basis for a company's making current decisions to exploit the opportunities and avoid the threats."[12] The management experts, who have suggested ways of auditing management for security analysts, advise a careful review of the planning ability. One, for example, states: "The third matter to be explored is the chief executive's plan for the company's future. What results does he plan to achieve and how? Do his plans capitalize on the company's strengths? Do they take proper account of environmental forces impinging on the business, and the key factors

---

[11] George A. Steiner, *Comprehensive Managerial Planning* (Oxford, Ohio: Planning Executives Institute, 1972), p. 13.

[12] Steiner, *Comprehensive Managerial Planning*, p. 4. See also Richard M. Osgood, "Strategic Planning for Large Corporations," *Managerial Planning*, September/October 1972.

affecting its profitability? Do they sound realistic, or are they pie in the sky?[13] Heneman suggests that the analyst ask: "Is there sound medium and long-range planning to assess the validity of established objectives? Has proper provision been made for the flow of information to the long-range planning function? Do the results of the work of the planners get to the decision makers and to the doers? Objectives must be reviewed continuously in order to make certain that they are in accord with actual conditions. The production of unwanted or outmoded products should not be started or allowed to continue. Not every corporation can afford an Edsel."[14] The planning that went into the Edsel wasn't effective. The planning that went into RCA's commitment to and development of color television was effective, as was IBM's pouring of vast resources into the third generation computer—the 360 and 370 series—but the planning that got RCA involved in computers was not. It had to write off $490 million and get out of a business that had lost $90 million after taxes over five years.[15] Effective planning turned CIT, the onetime auto financing firm, into a big bank holding company.[16] Planning for diversification pulled Pullman from the role of a tired old giant onto a fast new track.[17]

Planning led General Electric to establish a wholly owned subsidiary, Business Development Services, Inc., the biggest and most active of the new corporate venture groups.[18] The *Du Pont Guide to Venture Analysis* has been made available outside the company, and it provides massive insights into the elaborate planning process at Du Pont.[19] Raytheon Co. has become so confident about its corporate planning that it even makes public its long-term goals.[20]

Organization. "We think management is the cause, and everything else is the effect," said the president of a leading, well-organized company. The giant General Motors made the list of the ten best man-

---

[13] William E. Rothschild, *Putting It All Together: A Guide to Strategic Thinking* (New York: American Management Association, 1976). See also N. D. Modak, "Corporate Planning and Security Analysis," *Financial Analysts Journal,* vol. 30, no. 5 (September/October 1974), p. 51.

[14] Harlow J. Heneman, "The Financial Analyst and Management," Institute of Chartered Financial Analysts, *C.F.A. Readings in Financial Analysis,* Reading 38, 2d ed. (Homewood, Ill.: Richard D. Irwin, 1970).

[15] Allan T. Demaree, "RCA after the Bath," *Fortune,* September 1972.

[16] "CIT: The Tactics of a Major Turnaround," *Business Week,* June 17, 1972.

[17] "Pullman: Its Best Businesses Look Queasy, but Some of Its Poorest Are Doing Fine," *Forbes,* November 1, 1975; see also "The Big Switch at Pullman," *Dun's Review,* December 1971.

[18] "Venturing Out: Corporate Giants Now Providing Some Capital for Risky New Business," *The Wall Street Journal,* February 1, 1972.

[19] *Du Pont Guide to Venture Analysis: A Framework for Venture Planning* (Wilmington, Del.: E. I. du Pont de Nemours & Co., Inc., 1971).

[20] "Raytheon's Five-Year Plans That Work," *Business Week,* July 14, 1975, p. 113.

aged companies for organization. How has this multibillion dollar enterprise, with its 29 separate divisions, kept its lead in the intensively competitive automobile industry? In a word: organization. Onetime chief executive Alfred P. Sloan developed for GM the policy of "decentralization with coordinated control." Said one former GM chairman: "We've had good products and good people. But the management philosophy of decentralization to the fullest possible extent but with central policy control has, I think, allowed us to build each one of our divisions, each one of our activities, into an entity that is responsive not only to the needs of the public but to the growth, development and success of General Motors."

Each of GM's 29 divisions is headed by a general manager who functions relatively independently in running his operation. He has authority, for example, whether to add or reduce products in his line, how to formulate marketing strategy, where to buy his components and supplies, including going outside the company itself if he can get a better product or a better price. Each division general manager reports to a group vice president who in turn reports to top management. Policy making, however, is really the prerogative of two top committees, the executive committee and the finance committee. The operating side of GM is controlled by the five-member executive committee. It is the executive committee that makes final decisions on proposed innovations and decides how much control will be exercised over the operating divisions. The 12-man finance committee wields the most power, however, with control over major expenditures. It sounds cumbersome, but for General Motors it has worked well over the years. Executive succession has been smooth and there have been no major organizational crises.

Marketing Strategy. Some 2,300 top executives placed Procter & Gamble among the best-managed companies because of its marketing prowess. Yet its president voiced a seemingly heretical idea about marketing. "There is no such thing as marketing skill by itself," he said. "For a company to be good at marketing, it must be good at everything else, from R&D to manufacturing, from quality controls to financial controls." Yet it's not so heretical when you think about it because the best managed companies must be good, if not superb, at all corporate functions. For example, when one thinks about IBM one thinks of growth and innovation. Yet IBM is an outstanding marketing organization. It backed the 360 and the 370 with a marketing and service organization that became legendary in the industry. Its roughly 250 branch offices in the United States give it a capability its competitors cannot match. "When I entered the company in 1937," Watson recalls, "we had only 200 salesmen, and they dealt with some rudimentary punch card equipment. But in retrospect, in working

with that equipment they were developing an expertise upon which we built a large sales force able to market the much more complex computer when it came along." When the 360 began to saturate the U.S. market, IBM made its big thrust abroad at just the right time. And at home, it introduced its System 370, a computer that uses the same software as the 360 but is a step forward in its technology. Instead of using the core memories—the heart of the computer—of the 360, the 370 is designed around much faster monolithic integrated circuits. There is no doubt that IBM's success is as much attributable to the excellence of its service and marketing strategy as to the excellence of its product.[21]

The outstanding marketer, however, is Procter & Gamble; 95 out of every 100 American homes has at least one P&G product in bath or kitchen. While thousands of products battle for the consumer's attention, P&G manages to get itself heard and known in practically any market it chooses to enter. Each new product is test marketed and if successful backed by a huge advertising budget. Each P&G brand has its own budget but its total advertising budget is estimated to be in excess of $250 million. Its president noted, however, that "The only real measure of our efficiency is that we spend less per dollar of sales than any of our competitors." Backing up the enormous advertising effort is P&G's famed sales staff.[22] Over 3,000 salesmen fan out over the country making sure that P&G products are highly visible on supermarket shelves from Portland, Maine, to Portland, Oregon. Its president attributes P&G's success to a lot more than marketing, however. "No amount of marketing skill," he said, "can sell a product that is no good. . . . A good marketing organization can help, but without all the other skills, you're wasting a lot of money and effort."

Looking at another phase of marketing, for most of a decade, S. S. Kresge has been the fastest growing retailer in the country, outpacing even Sears, Roebuck and J. C. Penney. How did it accomplish this feat? The answer is discounting. The company all but abandoned the oldtime five-and-dime store concept and began building—at the astonishing rate of more than 50 a year—large, one-level, full-line discount department stores in which a customer selects her own

[21] See "IBM after Watson: Tougher Than Ever," *Business Week*, January 22, 1972; also Gene Bylinsky, "Vincent Learson Didn't Plan It That Way, But IBM's Toughest Competitor Is—IBM," *Fortune*, March 1972.

[22] "Procter & Gamble: We Grow Our Own Managers." *Dun's Review*, December 1975 pp. 48–49. See also Brenda J. Gall, "The Product Life Cycle and Its Relevance to an Analysis of Procter & Gamble," *Institutional Bulletin*, Merrill Lynch, Pierce, Fenner & Smith, Inc., New York, December 12, 1975. See also "Procter & Gamble Eyes the Soft Drink Business," *Industry Review*, Faulkner, Dawkins & Sullivan, September 10, 1975, and "All Those Leaky Diapers," *Forbes*, February 15, 1976.

merchandise and takes it to a checkout counter just as she does in a food supermarket. These are the Kresge "K Marts." Less than a generation ago such stores did not exist. But then along came Kresge's "K Marts," F. W. Woolworth's "Woolco's," Federated Department Stores' "Fedways," Allied Stores' "Almart," and Zayre's. A marketing innovation caught on and blanketed the country. Whether Kresge is better managed than Federated, or Sears or Penney you prospective analysts can attempt to judge as you examine marketing strategy and marketing effectiveness as one phase of your evaluation of management performance.[23]

Research and Development

Nowhere, perhaps, is the innovative spirit of a company's managers more discernible than in the conduct of its research and development activities. R&D has become of such critical importance to modern security analysts that the subject warrants some extended discussion.

Corporate growth is greatly dependent on the development of new products and the improvement of existing products and processes of production. Product and process development and improvement, in turn, can be shown to be directly related to the scale of a company's R&D expenditures. Manufacturers expect 14 percent, or $187 billion of 1978 sales to come from products introduced since 1974, according to a recent McGraw-Hill survey.[24]

In 1975, U.S. businesses and government spent about $34 billion on research and development, making R&D one of the nation's largest "industries," larger than steel ($27 billion in sales) or automobiles ($30 billion). R&D has been, and continues to be, a major source of economic growth. Whole new industries have been created in the electronics, chemical, and computer areas. The accelerating returns from R&D can be illustrated by countless examples. Recently IBM announced that while in 1952 it cost $1.18 for an IBM computer to perform 100,000 multiplications, by 1964 the cost had been reduced to 11 cents and today it is down to 1 cent.

From an investment viewpoint, R&D is very important. Companies that are outstanding in this field tend to be outstanding in their growth and earning power as well. Minnesota Mining & Manufacturing, for instance, one of the nation's leaders in R&D, obtained more than 85

---

[23] "The Orchestrated Growth of S. S. Kresge," *Dun's Review*, December 1975, pp. 46–47.

[24] *Business' Plans for Research and Development Expenditures, 1975–1978*, 20th Annual McGraw-Hill Survey (New York: McGraw-Hill Book Co., 1975).

percent of its growth in the past five years from products developed in its own laboratories.[25]

Minnesota Mining & Manufacturing (MMM) is a good example of a company which has grown on the research and development of new products. On sales of over $2 billion, it expends $120 million annually for R&D, of which 90 percent is applied and 10 percent basic. The quality of management is high and it is especially oriented to the management of R&D.[26]

But while it is clear that the magnitude of research outlays is related to successful product development and improvement, it is not crystal clear that there is a direct connection of R&D with *profitability*. Some studies do suggest that there is a connection; other studies suggest that the connection is tenuous at best. The highly profitable pharmaceutical industry spends heavily for R&D.[27] A recent study by the Food and Drug Administration concluded that: "the heavy spenders for research and development are responsible for the marketing of the significant new single chemicals." The FDA's ranking of leading drug firms according to the number of important therapeutic advances made during a recent decade is: Merck, 14; Lilly, 12; Pfizer, 7; Abbott, 6; American Home, 5; Bristol, 5; Roche, 5; Squibb, 5; Parke, Davis, 4; Schering, 4; Sterling, 4; and Upjohn, 4.

In the *Fortune* "Directory of the 500 Largest U.S. Industrial Corporations," of the ten highest in return on sales, 3 were pharmaceutical companies: Merck (15.4 percent), Schering-Plough (17.5 percent) and Eli Lilly (14.7 percent).[28]

Perhaps the most spectacular drug industry R&D development has been Upjohn's breakthrough with prostaglandins, the hormonelike substances that play a role in regulating many body functions. Over 15 years it has committed millions of dollars to research in this area, without a commercial product until 1972. In anticipation of success with prostaglandins, its stock rose from 46 in 1971 to 132 in 1973. *Fortune* declared: "the prostaglandins could turn into the biggest pharmaceutical windfall since the steroids and antibiotics, which

---

[25] "Research and Development Vital to Growth of Major Industries," David L. Babson & Co., Boston, September 18, 1975; see also Nestor E. Terlecky, *Effects of R&D on the Productivity Growth of Industries: An Explanatory Study* (Washington, D.C.: National Planning Association, 1974); and Nestor E. Terlecky, *State of Science and Research: Some New Indicators*, prepared for the National Science Foundation, and summarized in National Planning Association, "Looking Ahead and Projection Highlights," vol. 1, no. 12, March 1976.

[26] Alfred Bennett, "Quality of Management Study on Minnesota Mining & Manufacturing," Rosenkrantz, Ehrenkrantz, Lyon & Ross, New York, December 1974.

[27] "The Pharmaceutical Industry," David L. Babson & Co., Boston, May 18, 1972; see also "Pharmaceutical Companies Again Report Excellent Earnings Progress," David L. Babson & Co., Inc., May 20, 1976.

[28] *Fortune*, May 1976, p. 339.

helped propel worldwide sales of the U.S. drug industry from slightly more than $100 million in 1950 to $7.6 billion last year."[29]

For the security analyst the problem is not so much to determine whether or not a firm is actively engaged in research. Almost every modern firm is as a matter of survival. What the security analyst really has to do is distinguish between the sheer *volume* of research and the *quality* of research.

The growth in R&D spending over the past two decades may be seen in Table 8–3. Note that the growth in spending slowed

TABLE 8–3
Research and Development Spending (billions)

	Total	Basic	Applied	Development
1975E	$34.3	$4.1	$8.0	$22.3
1974	32.0	4.0	7.5	20.6
1973	30.4	3.8	6.8	19.8
1972	28.4	3.7	6.3	18.4
1971	26.7	3.5	6.0	17.2
1970	26.0	3.5	5.9	16.6
1965	20.1	2.6	4.5	13.0
1960	13.6	1.2	3.1	9.3
1955	6.2	0.5	1.5	4.1
Average Annual Growth				
1970–75	6%	3%	6%	6%
1965–70	5	6	6	5
1955–65	12	18	8	12

Source: National Science Foundation as quoted in *Weekly Staff Letter*, David L. Babson & Co., Inc., Boston, September 18, 1975.

significantly after rapid expansion from a small base in the early 1950s. In the 1955–65 period the average annual spending for research and development grew at a 12 percent annual rate, while in the 1966–75 decade the growth rate fell to an annual rate of 5–6 percent. When R&D spending is adjusted by the GNP price deflator to allow for inflation it is clear that real R&D expenditures are slowing down.[30]

The average manufacturing company which has a research program, budgets 3–4 percent of its revenues for this purpose. By this yardstick, the biggest spenders are the aircraft and electronics producers—or rather the Department of Defense and NASA—and the

---

[29] "Upjohn Puts the Cell's Own Messengers to Work," *Fortune*, June 1972; see also Jerome Schnee and Earl Caglarean, "The Changing Pharmaceutical R&D Environment," *Business Economics*, vol. xi, no. 3, May 1976.

[30] The GNP deflator (used by the National Science Foundation to adjust R&D spending for inflation) increased at 2 percent rate between 1955 and 1965, 4 percent between 1965 and 1970, and 7 percent in the last five years.

drug firms, who pay for most of their R&D out of their own pockets; Table 8–4 shows total R&D spending as a percent of sales in 11 industries.

The lion's share of industrial R&D is performed by the largest

TABLE 8–4

	R&D as Percent of Sales		R&D as Percent of Sales
All industries	3.4%	Chemicals	3.6%
Aircraft and missiles	16.3	Drugs	7.5
Electrical equipment	7.2	Motor vehicles	3.1
Communications	8.3	Petroleum	0.8
Scientific instruments	5.4	Food	0.5
Machinery	3.9	Textiles and apparel	0.4

Source: National Science Foundation as quoted in *Weekly Staff Letter,* David L. Babson & Co., Inc., Boston, September 18, 1975.

companies. Four dollars out of $5 are spent by firms with 10,000 employees or more. When companies are ranked by the size of their R&D programs, the top 20 account for 54 percent of all R&D spending. One reason for this concentration is the rising cost of research. Both inflation and increasingly complex technology have contributed to this trend. It now costs about $65,000 per year, on an average, to support one full-time scientist, compared to $47,000 only five years ago.[31]

There is no doubt that defense-oriented research contributed importantly to the introduction and improvement of products for civilian use. Notable examples are jet aircraft, electronic computers, atomic energy, and antibiotics. Moreover, defense research has added significantly to the general know-how of the companies conducting the research, even where no specific civilian applications of the research can be cited. But while it may be granted that defense-oriented research spills over into civilian technology, it is doubtful whether security analysts should equate a dollar of federally sponsored research with a dollar of company-sponsored research.

Basic and Applied Research. Hand in hand with the decidedly "practical" distinction that should be made between defense-oriented and civilian-oriented research, it often seems that both business executives and security analysts give far too little weight to that most "impractical" aspect of R&D, *basic research.* Basic research has no specific commercial objective. It seeks knowledge for knowledge's

---

[31] "Halting the Drift in R&D Policy," *Business Week,* March 3, 1975. See also "The Silent Crisis in R&D," *Business Week,* March 8, 1976; and "How GM Manages Its Billion Dollar R&D Program," *Business Week,* June 28, 1976.

sake. As such, it has been pretty well confined to universities and nonprofit research foundations. Yet some of the most dramatic commercial innovations in such fields as communications, energy production, and chemicals can be traced directly to the research findings of "pure scientists" who did not initially envision specific commercial applications of their work.

Admittedly, the "payoff period" is longer for basic than for applied research. Only 3 percent of industry's estimated R&D outlays in 1970–75 were for basic research. This is chiefly a luxury that can be afforded only by such giants as AT&T and General Electric. Even Du Pont, whose past discoveries include cellophane and nylon shies away from basic research. Of course, applied research is not an automatic source of profits, as Du Pont discovered when it was unable to market successfully its Corfam artificial leather. But there can be no doubt that the mental cross-fertilization of pure and applied scientists working side by side in an industrial research laboratory—even one of modest size—can produce eminently practical, and profitable, results.

In probing the quality of a company's research effort, the analyst also must make sure that the management envisions research as a continuing program. If a company expects to make continuing profits from innovation, it must continually innovate. Otherwise, its profit potential will be exhausted when the market for a particular product becomes exhausted. Too often research is treated as a variable, rather than a fixed, cost. Thus, when business is good, research outlays are expanded, only to be cut back when hard times hit. Such programs are likely to fail, if only because capable research personnel will not stay with the company.

A further clue to the quality of research lies in the actual record of product and process developments and improvements, and the number and significance of ideas on the drawing boards or in pilot plants. In examining the record, the analyst should recognize that a steady stream of new ideas, each of which makes only a modest contribution to the company's total activities, is probably more symptomatic of high-quality research than a single "blockbuster" invention that transforms the entire character of the company. Of course, foreknowledge of the latter can be enormously profitable to the investment sleuth who ferrets out the information. Think of those who bought Xerox at 1⅞ or Polaroid at 10.[32]

The drive to protect the environment has introduced a new aspect of R&D. The nonmanufacturing industries such as mining, utilities, and railroads, used to depend mostly on their suppliers to develop

---

[32] See John H. Dessauer, *My Years at Xerox* (Garden City, N.Y.: Doubleday & Co., Inc., 1971). Also, Dan Cordtz, "The Two Faces of Xerox," *Fortune*, September 1974.

new techniques. Now, however, they are coming directly to grips with pollution control. Industry's R&D spending for pollution control was $1.2 billion in 1975 and is expected to rise to $1.5 billion in 1978. Energy-related R&D expenditures by industry reached $4 billion in 1975 and is expected to increase 51 percent by 1978 to $6.1 billion. For the most part, antipollution devices are simply an expense for the polluting industries, but they are a windfall for the companies that make the equipment.

Management's Willingness to Take Large Risks

Few companies will grow at an above-average rate if their managers are not willing to eliminate obsolete product lines, add completely new lines, make large commitments to research and to the marketing of research output, go into debt, or slash prices to broaden markets or meet competition. Each such action carries the possibility of serious, even catastrophic mistakes, and the growth-oriented manager must be prepared to risk making serious mistakes.

A review of the history of Sears, Roebuck & Co., one of America's great growth companies, reveals a number of strategic decisions during the past 40 years which shaped that company's growth path. Those decisions are outlined here, because they are illustrative of a management which had the courage to take the risks involved in radically altering a company's character.[33]

1. In the mid-1920s, retail stores were added to Sears' original mail-order business. Farmers, the backbone of the mail-order business, now had cars and wanted to drive into town to shop. Sears obliged.

2. But a large chain of retail stores posed new problems of managerial control. Sears responded by centralizing buying and promotional functions in Chicago, while actual store operations were decentralized territorially. Moreover, contrary to traditional retailing practice, it was decided that the bulk of Sears' merchandise would be manufactured to its own specifications. In addition, Sears invested heavily in the stock of its supplier corporations, which both strengthened supply channels and paved the way for large capital gains.

3. After World War II an aggressive store expansion program was launched, while Sears' chief competitor, Montgomery Ward, decided to wait for the "typical" postwar economic depression. Sears moved with its customers westward and into the suburbs, preempting the best store locations.

4. Beginning in the mid-1950s the image of the company's stores

---

[33] See Peter F. Drucker, *Management: Tasks, Responsibilities, Practices* (New York: Harper & Row, 1974), pp. 56–57. See also "Sears' Identity Crisis," *Business Week*, December 8, 1975.

was drastically changed from hardware-oriented to full-line department stores. Style and fashion were emphasized along with economy.

5.   Operations also were diversified during the 40-year period into insurance and other financial services. In 1931 the company decided to sell low-cost auto insurance by mail, and in 1934 insurance sales were moved into Sears' stores as well. Both moves were startling innovations in the staid insurance industry. One out of every three American families now carries a Sears credit card. The company also operates a motor club, a tourist agency, and two savings and loan associations. Sears, Roebuck Acceptance Corporation is a giant installment finance company; and Sears operates a fleet of several thousand service and installation trucks to back up its durable goods sales.

6.   The company also has been an innovator in personnel relations. It has instituted college training programs for young employees, established a practice of promoting from within the organization, and set up a generous profit sharing plan which has been invested in Sears' own stock, thus giving its employees part ownership of the company.

7.   More recently Sears has been reaching out to move up from the low-price field and broaden its price range and appeal.

8.   Since World War II, Sears has depended on three factors: explosive population growth in the suburbs, a high homebuilding rate, and a burgeoning automotive market. Perhaps Sears can no longer count on these factors. If not, it can be expected to change in response to newer trends.

Are the managers of all large companies willing to take large risks? No, they are not. A long-entrenched management frequently becomes so personally committed to doing things a given way that it is unwilling to risk doing them any other way. It even may be literally unable to see the possibility of doing things differently. How common it is to see a new management take over a company and, within a short period of time, dramatically improve profits by slashing unnecessary costs and enabling the company to compete more effectively.

Consider, as an example of risk aversion, the steel industry in the 1950s and 1960s. Facing the competition of substantial imports of steel and steel products, at lower than domestic prices, the large, integrated steel companies preferred in many instances to abandon whole product lines rather than figure out how to sell in a market where their tidy price structure had been upset. Only recently have the managers of the top steel companies begun to be oriented toward growth rather than maintenance of the status quo in setting their research, production, and marketing policies.[34]

---

[34] See Arthur Zeikel, "On the Threat of Change," *Financial Analysts Journal,* November/December 1975.

Management's Delegation of Authority
and Responsibility

Decentralization. In most modern large enterprises, the "one-person show" has given way to some form of decentralized operation. On paper, a decentralized organization typically has the following characteristics: Each major product line, or each major geographic area, of a company is headed by a different vice president and is run as if it were a separate company. That is, the vice president of the "division" supervises a number of functional officers—production, marketing, finance, research, and so forth—and this team makes the decisions for that division. These decisions, however, are made within a broad framework of corporate policy established by the highest echelon of management—the chairman, president, and one or more executive vice presidents—acting in concert with both the divisional vice presidents and a group of vice presidents in the "corporate home office" who have *functional* rather than divisional responsibilities. For example, there will usually be a vice president–marketing at the corporate level, and a number of lower echelon marketing managers at the divisional level. The marketing managers are responsible to their respective divisional vice presidents, but the decisions of the latter are made within an overall corporate sales policy framework which is strongly influenced by the vice president–marketing. In addition, at the corporate home office level there usually will be a group of vice presidents and "staff" personnel whose authority and responsibilities cut across divisional lines—for example, in the financial and legal areas.

Thus, most large firms nowadays are decentralized, *at least on paper.* What the security analyst must be concerned with, however, is whether the paper surface is truly reflective of the underlying substance. All too frequently it is not. What occurs in some cases is that the divisional vice presidents' authority is severely limited by the "home office" superstructure, with corporate people interfering with, instead of supporting, divisional activities. When this condition is present, there is a grave danger that the vitality of the entire organization will eventually be sapped—if it is not already—and the security analyst must be alert to sense this.

To understand the seriousness of the problem, it is necessary to understand the presumed benefits of truly effective decentralization—which is really just an extension of the age-old concept of delegation of authority and responsibility. Simply stated, the idea is that the best efforts of people are forthcoming when they are given wide latitude to exercise their own discretion and are then rewarded or penalized on the basis of their performance. Pride of accomplishment

comes to the fore, "buck-passing" is minimized, innovation is encouraged, and executive development takes place in the best possible atmosphere. Moreover, members of top management are freed from most of the day-to-day chores involved in running a business and can concentrate on planning for the future.

Beatrice Foods markets 8,000 dairy and food products, runs a $1 billion business abroad and—because of its acquisition binge—is deep into leisure goods (Samsonite luggage, Airstream travel trailers), agriproducts and insurance. "It's a simple company to manage," said its new president, who believes success lies in giving autonomy and big rewards to his 382 profit-center managers. "You can't wind up each manager every morning. He has to do it himself."[35]

Limitations of Decentralization. To be sure, decentralization is not entirely free from criticism. For example, in the 1960s U.S. Steel Corporation found it necessary to reorganize drastically because its decentralization had gotten completely out of hand. Multiple layers of supervisory personnel had evolved, and too many independent production divisions and overlapping sales, accounting, and engineering offices were operating with inadequate policy guidelines. The most vivid way of illustrating the extent of this corporate sprawl is to cite some of the changes that were made over a five-year period:

1. About 3,000 management-level people—more than 10 percent of all the managers—were released or retired.
2. Seven production divisions were consolidated with larger units.
3. All research, development, and facility planning operations were coordinated under the direction of a single executive vice president.
4. Twenty-five district sales offices were closed and more than 50 others were consolidated. New area sales vice presidencies were established to direct and coordinate the activities of the district sales offices.

Even GM found it necessary to recentralize. It set up a new GM Assembly Division. Its assignment was to tighten and revamp assembly operations that GM believed had become seriously deficient under divisional direction. The new division engineered impressive cost reductions and quality improvements and in due course was given responsibility for about 75 percent of the company's domestic output.[36]

Thus, it is possible for decentralization to run rampant and for top management to lose control—much the same as in an improperly

---

[35] "Some Farm Boy," *Forbes*, October 15, 1975, p. 116.

[36] "The GM Efficiency Move That Backfired," *Business Week*, March 25, 1972.

executed merger program. The numerous executives "in the field" lack a sense of overall corporate purpose and are unwilling to sacrifice their own immediate goals, on occasion, to the overriding long-term goals of the entire enterprise. Furthermore, recent technological breakthroughs in the areas of automated information retrieval and data processing have led some management experts to call for a movement back toward centralization.

One compromise solution has been the renewed interest in group management. *Business Week* noted:

> The group executive—the manager who sits between a president and his operators—has not always been a popular figure in American business. To some, in fact, he seems worse than useless, more an obstruction than an expediter. But for better or worse, when companies reach a certain size (normally about $500 million in sales) and complexity (three or four distinct kinds of business), they begin to look at the group structure as one way out of the managerial morass. And these days, with companies preoccupied with pruning costs, an increasing number of corporations are adopting the group setup for cost effectiveness.[37]

Hewlett-Packard, Chemetron, Whittaker Corp., CBS, General Electric, General Foods, and Textron, all have group executives.

Another effort at solving the problem is to rotate top executives. Union Carbide recently began rotating the assignments of three executive vice presidents in an effort to broaden their management capabilities. *Business Week* reported:

> Union Carbide Corp. is not the first diversified corporation to discover that some of its most senior managers know much about their own piece of the business, but not enough about the rest of the company. But at the chemicals and metals giant, which last year boosted sales 36% to $5.3 billion, the problem was deep seated and long standing.
>
> We were a holding company until the mid-1950's, and you could count on your fingers the number of people who moved from division to division, explains Executive Vice President Warren M. Anderson. You grow up in a division, and you get about four miles tall but not very broad.[38]

Now the three executive vice presidents are being rotated, as part of a broadening program that will not only test their mettle and give them a chance at the presidency but is also likely to bring about fundamental management changes in the company.

Management Information Systems

Machines have been developed, and are now being improved and brought down in cost, which "read" printed characters, "understand"

---

[37] "Group Management to Control Diversity," *Business Week*, September 15, 1975, pp. 98–100. See also "Aetna: When Group Management Didn't Work," *Business Week*, February 16, 1976.

[38] "Rotating Top Jobs at Union Carbide," *Business Week*, July 14, 1975, p. 82.

human speech, and "simulate" human thought processes. Under recently developed management information systems, the following is now feasible for a large corporation: (1) Vast quantities of information regarding current operations in hundreds or thousands of scattered plants and offices are fed into a home office computer installation. (2) This information is rapidly processed to prepare reports for management which indicate the current status of operations, alternative courses of action, and the probable results of these alternative actions. (3) Management then makes its decisions—i.e., chooses among the alternatives—and immediately transmits instructions to the field. (4) Soon after these decisions have been implemented, the rapid information retrieval system enables management to learn whether its decisions are having the expected results (known as "feedback"). If not, modifications are instituted before errors begin to accumulate.

All of this is not science fiction. On-line management information systems are now widely used in American enterprise. The concept is very simple: "A management information system is one that supports managerial decision-making by supplying relevant information when required."[39] While in simpler applications a computer may make a decision such as to replenish inventory in an inventory control system, or to say, "no," don't extend credit because the relevant programmed factors come out negatively, in the broader managerial decision-making process, the hardware and the software add up to providing relevant information and no more. Basic decision making is still the province of the human mind in complex, policy situations.[40]

While managers may be helped, therefore, it is their competence and their judgment which still governs. There are three purposes of an efficient management information system. The first is to provide timely relevant information to managers; the second to aid in the allocation of resources; and the third to aid in the selection of alternatives. In evaluating management the security analyst needs to be able to recognize an effective management information system and to be able to judge whether the top managers are capable of taking advantage of it and are in fact doing so. This suggests some analysis of the training of managers. How well have they been trained? Are they effective users of the new decision-making tools and of the new managerial information systems?

Executive Development. A Washington regulatory official paid AT&T a backhanded compliment when he said: "If the entire Bell top

[39] Kit Grindley and John Humble, *The Effective Computer* (New York: AMACOM, 1974); see also David M. Ahlers, "Management Information Systems, from Spyglass to Pocket Calculators," *Financial Executive,* July 1976.

[40] S. R. Mixon, *Handbook of Data Processing, Administration, Operations and Procedures,* (New York: American Management Association, 1976); see also Charles F. Axelson, "How to Avoid the Pitfalls of Information Systems Development," *Financial Executive,* April 1976.

management were snapped off the earth, the system would continue operating without a detectable tremor." In more positive fashion, the head of the American Management Institute has said: "If I were allowed only one question by which to evaluate an executive, this one would suffice: *Has he developed an adequate replacement for his own job?*" Perhaps this question can serve as a useful guideline to the security analyst seeking to appraise the quality of a company's management team.

When a company begins to lose its market share, or stagnate, it may be time for a change in management. Some companies guard against staleness of top management by early retirement. More and more companies are turning to this, some now retire top executives at 55 or 60 in order to move up able younger personnel.[41] Others have no effective succession plans and in desperation the board of directors has to go outside the company for a new chief executive officer.[42]

One of the main purposes of highly touted internal management development programs is to ensure effective succession in the company. Since the Sloan management days at GM a primary duty of any top manager is to develop an able successor. The candidate is supposed to be selected from inside the company and then groomed and guided for the top role. Such has been the practice followed by GM, GE, IBM, AT&T, U.S. Steel and scores of large companies.[43] But of late there have been a number of companies that failed to provide for effective internal succession. Recent examples include Columbia Broadcasting System, Inc., Dictaphone Corp., Johns-Manville Corp., Monsanto Chemical, White Motor Corp., Mack Truck, Pan American World Airways, Rockwell Manufacturing, United Aircraft Corp., and UAL.[44]

Frequently, a company's compensation system can serve as evidence of its policies regarding executive development. The analyst should be wary of an organization whose chief executive earns several times as much as the three or four closest subordinates, or whose junior officials have impressive titles but unimpressive material rewards.

[41] William F. Lucas, "Lessons of Leadership," *Nation's Business*, March 1975; see also "Is Management Really an Art?" *Harvard Business Review*, January–February 1975; also "How Companies Raise a New Crop of Managers," *Business Week*, March 10, 1975, p. 44.

[42] "Why Companies Go outside for New Bosses," *Business Week*, February 26, 1972.

[43] "The Succession Plan at I.T.&T.," *Business Week*, April 22, 1972.

[44] "A Tough New Boss at Monsanto," *Business Week*, November 4, 1972; Rush Loving, Jr., "How a Hotelman Got the Red out of United Airlines," *Fortune*, March 1972; "Pan Am Gives Seawell a Clear Path," *Business Week*, April 1, 1972; Making a Sick Company Healthy," *Nation's Business*, November 1975; see also X. R. Srinivas Murthy and Malcolm S. Slater, "Should CEO Pay Be Linked to Results?" *Harvard Business Review*, May–June 1975.

High salaries and fringe benefits for the whole spectrum of managers are necessary if the participants in the executive training are to remain with the company. At the same time, capable, high-spirited, hard-working executives are not retained by a policy of guaranteed job security. Junior executives should be challenged to make decisions which will be backed up by company funds, and they should be held accountable for those decisions.

Is the Board of Directors Being Used Wisely?

It is sometimes said that the function of a company's board of directors is to set basic policies, which management is then charged with executing. This is an overly idealized conception. Actually, management both sets and executes policy in most companies, and the principal function of the board is to review and appraise management's decisions. If the appraisal is favorable, the board ratifies the decisions. If the appraisal is unfavorable, the board suggests that management try a different course, or, in a crisis, replaces the management. A recent example was the replacement of Robert Sarnoff as head of RCA. "Inside and outside directors united to dump Sarnoff because of his poor record," reported *Business Week*.[45] Another example was the replacement of Donald P. Kircher as head of Singer by Joseph Flavin. "After diversifying far afield from sewing machines, it ran into a multitude of troubles. Members of the board came to see that they had to find the company [Singer] a new boss," reported *Fortune*.[46] Still another was the Chessie System's board's ouster of John Hanifin.[47]

Generally, the only time the board is the prime policy maker is when there is a conflict among the managers themselves, in which case the board serves as a superior court of appeal.

In carrying out its functions of review, appraisal, and appeal, a board of directors can be independent and objective or a mere rubber stamp. It can be a truly valuable and useful corporate asset, or a mere public relations showpiece. A security analyst is not usually privy to the inner workings of a company's board and must judge it on the basis of indirect evidence.

Foremost among the pieces of evidence is whether or not a majority of the board members are drawn from outside the management.

---

[45] "Why Robert Sarnoff Quit at RCA," *Business Week*, November 24, 1975, pp. 76–81.

[46] "How the Directors Kept Singer Stitched Together," *Fortune*, December 1975, pp. 100–103.

[47] See "The Golden Racket: Did Chessie's President Really 'Resign'," *Forbes*, November 15, 1975, p. 20; also "Why TWA's Board Wanted a New President," *Business Week*, July 7, 1975, pp. 52–53.

Although it is acknowledged that some companies have done very well with "inside" boards, it would seem that they have done well *in spite* of the system rather than because of it. For an inside board—even if composed of full-time directors in the manner pioneered by Exxon (Standard Oil Company of New Jersey)—tends to be too parochial in perspective and too much under the thumb of the chief executive. On the other hand, outside board members can provide the operating managers with new insights based upon their diversified experience and knowledge.[48]

A management consultant, maintaining that the outside directors are the only real safeguard stockholders have against incompetent management, developed a method for scoring top management. The scorecard has two parts: general factors and personal factors. The directors are urged to evaluate executive performance from both angles. The general factors include development of sound organizational structure, of successors, of products, of organizational morale, of the corporate image. The personal scorecard covers topics such as interlocking directorships, outside business activities, health, development of promising young managers, decisiveness, and trading in company stock.[49]

Criticism of Boards. Of late there has been growing criticism of boards of directors. Spurred by the Penn Central disaster critics inside and outside of business are demanding that directors do a far better job or else resign.[50] In a survey of corporate boards Professor Myles L. Mace of the Harvard Business School found an enormous gap between what the consultants and professors say boards should do and what they in fact do, or neglect to do. They are, he concludes, "powerless men in seats of power." The chief executive officer usually calls the shots and the directors discuss and ratify. They seldom provide more than advice and prestigious window dressing. In most large and medium-sized companies directors are usually rubber stamps.[51] As a result of stinging criticism and lawsuits, boards are now changing, the composition and public representation is being broadened and in the shadow of "The Wreck of the Penn Central" new dimensions of responsibility are being assumed or recognized.

---

[48] Mortimer M. Caplin "Outside Directors and Their Responsibilities: A Program for the Exercise of Due Care," *The Journal of Corporation Law*, 57 (Fall 1975); See also "The Hot Seat: Outside Directors Get More Careful, Tougher after Payoff Scandals," *The Wall Street Journal*, March 24, 1976.

[49] "A Scorecard for Rating Management," Edward McSweeney, *Business Week*, June 8, 1974, pp. 12.

[50] John G. Gillis, "Responsibilities of Outside Directors," *Financial Analysts Journal*, vol. 31, no. 6 (November/December 1975), p. 12.

[51] Myles L. Mace, *Directors: Myth and Reality* (Boston: Harvard Business School, 1971); see also Courtney C. Brown, *Putting the Corporate Board to Work* (New York: Macmillan, 1976); and "Will the Directors Speak Up," *Forbes*, May 15, 1976.

In a court-approved settlement of a class-action stockholder suit stemming from illegal campaign contributions by Phillips Petroleum Co. the big oil concern agreed to turn over control of its board to independent outside directors. The outside directors would also have sweeping powers over the company's audit function and any further nominations to the board. The agreement stipulates that future vacancies on the newly reconstituted board be filled by independent outside directors until at least 60 percent of the members are outsiders.[52]

Management and the Financial Analyst

"Perhaps the most important responsibility of a financial analyst, however, is to evaluate the quality of company management," declares the Institute of Chartered Financial Analysts.[53] For the most part, relationships between analysts and management are cordial, occasionally they are not. As *Business Week* noted:

> Philip K. Wrigley, the crusty, autocratic, 76-year-old chairman of the chewing gum empire founded by his father, William Wrigley, Jr., really got mad at the security analysts last week. On Monday the price of his company's stock dropped by more than 30 points on the New York Stock Exchange, although earnings for the first three quarters were up by more than 19% over the same period in 1970. Wrigley was quick to blame Wall Street security analysts. . . . In Wrigley's view, some analysts made earnings projections for 1971 that he considers unreasonably high, then turned bearish when earnings failed to measure up—thus triggering a selling wave by institutions holding large blocks of Wrigley stock.[54]

In a biting attack on analysts, J. B. Fuqua of Fuqua Industries, Inc., told a group of Atlanta analysts that they were too much concerned with "the numbers game"—that is, with estimating earnings per share. "Perhaps your real job is to evaluate management," Fuqua told the analysts—a task that he feels has been largely ignored. Most top managers feel otherwise, however, complaining that they are flooded at times by requests from analysts for information and interviews.

"How to Interview a Corporate Executive" was the subject of a publication prepared by the New York Society of Security Analysts for

---

[52] "Phillips Petroleum to Turn over Control to Outside Directors in Settlement of Suit," *The Wall Street Journal*, February 19, 1976; see also Michael C. Jensen, "Corporate Boards Rise to Challenge," *The New York Times*, December 28, 1975.

[53] *The Profession of Financial Analysis and the Chartered Financial Analysts*, The Institute of Chartered Financial Analysts, Charlottesville, Va., 1976–1977.

[54] "Why Security Analysts Irk Management," *Business Week*, November 6, 1971, p. 96. See also Everett Mattlin, "Are the Days of the Numbers Game Numbered?" *Institutional Investor*, November 1971. See also John G. Gillis, "Corporate Disclosure," *Financial Analysts Journal*, vol. 30, no. 4 (July/August 1974).

a training program for its junior analysts. Some of the main points
suggested were:

1.   The analyst is advised to observe the C.F.A. code of ethics (see
Appendix to this chapter).

2.   Upon initiating a corporate contact, the analyst is advised to
identify who he or she is, nature of affiliation, some indication of what
information is desired, and the reasons for which it is requested.

3.   Prepare for the interview or interviews. Have a topical outline
and a list of questions.

4.   To develop such questions and outline, review all available
background material, 10–K's, annual reports, proxies, quarterly reports
(gingerly), prospectuses, file clippings, and so on.

5.   Organize the background data for the interview so you have
data sheets of facts for various phases to be covered, company's market
share, old products, new products, competition, labor situation,
operating costs and operating results, trends of sales, prices, costs,
margins, financial condition, debt structure, cash position, cash flow,
capital expenditures, mergers and acquisitions, R&D, management
and corporate policies and goals.

6.   Take time to tour the plant or plants and see as much of the
company in action as possible.

7.   Don't just go on a fishing expedition and don't waste
management's time with random conversation.

8.   Find out if anyone else in your firm or institution has visited the
company. Who did they see? For what purpose? What did they learn?
Try not to duplicate a prior effort and if possible keep your firm's or
institution's contacts limited to one person, yourself, if possible.

9.   Don't ask for information which management should not be
giving you. Don't ask for "inside information." As Mr. Peter De
Angelis, C.F.A., of the New York Society of Security Analysts put it:

The analyst does not seek to obtain information that is not permitted by law.
Now, what am I referring to? I'm referring to monthly shipments, monthly
earnings, figures, earnings announcements before they are announced. This
sort of matter. We analysts shouldn't seek this type of information. If it's offered
or available, Beware! While it may help you for a short period of time, in the
long run, you pay the price. Number one, it's illegal. And number two, that
information is often misleading, unreliable and only available, typically,
during favorable periods. It is usually unavailable during adverse periods of
operation. So the analyst should not seek this information. If it is forthcoming,
the analyst should not use it under any circumstances, and should advise
management that this information should not be given.[55]

---

[55] "How to Interview a Corporate Executive," New York Society of Security
Analysts, August 7, 1972; for an interesting description of the work of a senior analyst,
see "To Buy or Not to Buy," *The Wall Street Journal*, May 3, 1972. See also Alfred S.
Rudd, "Site Visits," *Financial Analyst's Handbook*, vol. II (Homewood, Ill.: Dow
Jones-Irwin, Inc., 1975), chap. 31.

Inside Information. There have been a number of cases involving illegal use of "inside information," violation of the SEC's rule 10b–5. One disclosure case making the headlines involved an especially delicate area—earnings—in which the chairman of Bausch & Lomb, Inc., allegedly gave to an analyst of Faulkner, Dawkins & Sullivan Securities, Inc., information regarding a quarterly earnings report that had not yet been made public. Class actions against these two organizations were filed in federal district courts, charging violation of securities laws.[56]

A day before the company disclosed the facts publicly, the B&L chairman allegedly told an FDS analyst that first quarter profits would be between 65 cents and 75 cents a share. FDS had expected 85 cents to 90 cents, and some other analysts had estimated $1 or more. The word apparently got around quickly and in two trading days the stock fell 31 points, and over a two-month period was nearly 90 points off its high.[57]

John G. Gillis of Hill & Barlow, Boston, general counsel to the Financial Analysts Federation, said that "The Bausch & Lomb case is likely to become the newest of the landmark cases on the law of inside information. To a degree unmatched by predecessor cases, its issues will involve vital aspects of the research process followed by security analysts."

The major issue that emerges, according to Mr. Gillis, "is whether the analyst acted on analytical judgment resulting from the collection and analysis of information and facts, which, though undisclosed, were not material, reaching a determination on those coupled with his experience and knowledge of the company, or whether he was the recipient of material, non-public, inside information and acted on it. The SEC, courts, and others have repeatedly stated the former is permissible, while the latter is not."[58]

The SEC and "Inside Information." There have been earlier cases on "inside information" but none so directly involving a financial

---

[56] "Research vs. Inside Information," *Newsletter*, The Financial Analysts Federation, vol. 10, no. 5 (September 1972). See *Hawk Industries Inc., et al. v. Bausch & Lomb, Inc. et al.* 59 F.R.D., 619 (S.D., N.Y. 1973).

[57] "The Analyst as Insider," *Business Week*, March 25, 1972; see also "Analysts Closed Talks with Firms Are Called Unfair by the Press," *The Wall Street Journal*, March 31, 1972; and "New Guidelines on Inside Information," by the Inside Information Committee of the Financial Analysts Federation, *Financial Analysts Journal*, vol. 30, no. 1 (January/February 1974). See also John G. Gillis, "Inside Information: Are Guidelines Possible?" *Financial Analysts Journal*, vol. 30, no. 3 (May/June 1974); and John G. Gillis, "Responsibilities of Professionals under Securities Law," *Financial Analysts Journal*, vol. 30, no. 2 (March/April 1974).

[58] John G. Gillis, "Bausch & Lomb and Analytical Judgment," *Financial Analysts Journal*, May/June 1972, p. 10; see also "Loomis on Inside Information," *Financial Analysts Journal*, May/June 1972; and Arlene J. Lurie and Victor S. Pastena, "How Promptly Do Corporations Disclose Their Problems?" *Financial Analysts Journal*, vol. 31, no. 5 (September/October 1975).

analyst. In *Cady Roberts*,[59] the SEC disciplined a broker who received and acted upon information from a director that the board had just voted a dividend cut. This had not been made public at the time and the broker had sold for discretionary accounts. The broker said he had a duty to his discretionary accounts to act on the information. The SEC said that, while he certainly had an obligation to his discretionary accounts, the obligation did not extend to violating federal law for their benefit. In the *Texas Gulf Sulphur* case,[60] the SEC found that some officials and employees of the company, plus some outsiders who had been tipped off, had bought stock in Texas Gulf Sulphur while they had inside information (not yet made public) about the importance of the firm's discovery of a rich ore vein. Eventually the courts deprived some of the insiders of their profits. Merrill Lynch and several of its employees consented to disciplinary sanctions for allegedly divulging to some of its customers undisclosed information of a sharp drop in current and projected earnings of Douglas Aircraft.[61]

The SEC has brought a significant number of cases against companies, securities firms, and others for alleged violations of the "inside information" doctrine under Rule 10b–5. These include, among many others, Faberge, Glen Alden, Lum's, Mattel, Bausch & Lomb, Avis, Liggett & Myers, Equity Funding, and Celanese.[62]

An area of rapidly growing concern for the analyst is liability under the various antifraud provisions of the federal securities law and in particular Rule 10b–5, writes William E. Chatlos. "Applications of Rule 10b–5 now appear quite frequently in reported cases and represent about one third of all current cases, both public and private, under the whole array of SEC statutes. This dramatic increase in the number of cases being brought before the courts or the commission is attributable, in significant part, to the loss of investor confidence in the market system due to repeated violations of the rules covering material nonpublic information."[63]

The Equity Funding case was an astonishing example of an alleged infraction of the 10b–5 rule. An analyst, Raymond Dirks, received a

---

[59] *Cady Roberts & Co.*, 40 SEC 907 at 912 (1961).

[60] See *SEC v. Texas Gulf Sulphur*, 401 F. 2d 833 (2d Cir. 1968); also *SEC v. Texas Gulf Sulphur*, 312 F. Supp. 77 (S.D.N.Y. 1970).

[61] *Merrill Lynch, Pierce, Fenner & Smith, Inc. et al.*, Securities Exchange Act, Rel. No. 8459 (November 25, 1968); see also Les Gapay, "Rise Detected in Use of Inside Information to Make Stock Profits," *The Wall Street Journal*, October 31, 1972; and *Investors Management Company et al.*, Securities Exchange Act, Rel. No. 9267, (July 29, 1971).

[62] John G. Gillis, "Trends in Disclosure," *Financial Analysts Journal*, vol. 31, no. 1 (January/February 1975).

[63] William E. Chatlos, "Inside Information and the Analyst," *Financial Analyst's Handbook*, vol. I (Homewood, Ill.: Dow Jones-Irwin, Inc., 1975), chap. 2.

phone call from a disgruntled former employee of Equity Funding saying that at least two thirds of the total of the company's insurance underwriting was bogus. While starting to investigate this "sensational rumor," he allegedly discussed the matter with various clients, who then proceeded to unload their stock. News of the scandal did not break publicly until some three weeks later. Dirks was charged with violating Rule 10b–5.[64] He was, in effect, caught in a strange predicament. He was trying to get the full facts of the fraud and expose it, which he did. He also wanted to protect his clients. He contended that unsubstantiated rumors cannot be considered inside information and that to disseminate such "hearsay" information publicly would have been irresponsible and improper. Partly as a result of his activity, the New York Stock Exchange stated that analysts have "an obligation to the public which must take precedence over the duty to clients or to employers."[65]

The various cases suggest that analysts should be very wary of using any *material nonpublic* information, given to them by corporate management and, indeed, any such information which comes to them from outside the company but which they have reason to believe, or may suspect, emanated from the corporation itself.

The information disclosed in these cases met the SEC *test of materiality* because it "was of such importance that it could be expected to affect the judgment of the investors whether to buy, sell or hold the stock, and if generally known to affect materially the market price of the stock."[66]

Three elements establish corporate intelligence as inside information, according to Commissioner Loomis of the SEC. These are:

1. Materiality of the information to the corporation's immediate financial situation as reflected by changes in the company's common stock price.
2. Undisclosed nature of the information in relation to the investing public.
3. Confidential nature of the information in relation to how it was acquired.

---

[64] See *Securities and Exchange Commission* v. *Equity Funding Corporation of America* (C.D.C.1973) 73 Civ. 714, CCH #79417.

[65] New York Stock Exchange release dated, May 10, 1973.

[66] For a discussion of "Materiality" in securities cases, see John G. Gillis, "The Tippee in Transition," *Financial Analysts Journal*, January/February 1971, p. 11. See also John G. Gillis, "Mandatory Use of Inside Information," *Financial Analysts Journal*, vol. 31, no. 2 (March/April 1975).

Possession of corporate information with these characteristics presumably precludes the possessor from trading in its securities or inducing others to do so.[67]

Thus both the financial analyst and management must now be cautious about disclosing, receiving, and using "material inside information." And this applies to the entire financial community. It should not, however, inhibit the careful analyst in the search for a totality of data to evaluate the quality of management and its impact on the financial prospects of the company.[68]

Management and Social Responsibility

Shareholders who attended Continental Oil Co.'s annual meeting in May 1972 were surprised to be handed two annual reports as they filed into the hall. One was the traditional report of corporate achievements and goals; the other was a stinging indictment of the social ills allegedly caused by a subsidiary of Conoco, Consolidated Coal Co., the country's largest coal producer.[69] The "counter" report pointed to mine disasters and environmental pollution. Of course, it caused quite a stir at the annual meeting.

Most large corporations have now faced up to social responsibilities in many areas—environmental improvement, pollution control, reducing ecological damage, greater opportunities for minorities, community development and involvement, and so on. Indeed, *Business Week*, which, for a time, made annual awards for business citizenship, declared: "The U.S. Corporation's involvement in social projects is attaining maturity. . . . corporate social responsibility is no longer unique, startling, or, in most cases, controversial. Social responsibility has become part of the business of business."[70] Its 1972 awards went to Dow Chemical Co. of Midland, Michigan, and Hallmark Cards, Inc., of Kansas City, Missouri, for improving the physical environment, to International Business Machines Corp. of

---

[67] As stated by Howard B. Bonham, Jr., "When a Creditor Has the Right to Inside Information," *Financial Analysts Journal*, January/February 1970, p. 116; for a discussion of the "law of inside information," see John G. Gillis, "Securities Law and Regulation," *Financial Analysts Journal*, May/June 1972, p. 12.

[68] For an excellent statement of what the financial analysts seek in the way of comprehensive financial information from management (and its accountants), see William C. Norby and Frances G. Stone, "Objectives of Financial Reporting," *Financial Analysts Journal*, July/August 1972; see also David Norr, "What a Financial Analyst Wants from an Annual Report," *Financial Executive*, August 1970.

[69] "Dissenters Compose an Annual Report," *Business Week*, May 6, 1972, p. 24–25.

[70] "How Business Tackles Social Problems," Special Report, *Business Week*, May 20, 1972. See also "Disclosing Social Data," *Business Week*, April 14, 1975, p. 76.

Armonk, New York, and the Colorado Economic Development Association of Denver for developing human resources; and to the Reverend Leon Sullivan of Philadelphia, for exceptional leadership.

Dow Chemical spent millions to clean up the river alongside of which its plant was situated, as well as to reduce the air pollution from its chemical operations. Hallmark undertook a $200 million, 85-acre major office residential development called Crown Center to improve the rundown urban area around its headquarters building in downtown Kansas City. In Denver, the Colorado Development Association has helped to get financial aid, totaling more than $15 million, for more than 500 minority businessmen. IBM located and successfully maintained a plant, employing 400 minority workers, in the Bedford-Stuyvesant area of Brooklyn. By training workers and then funneling them to other of its plants, it created jobs for far more residents than it currently employed. The Rev. Sullivan, the first black director on General Motors' board, started the Opportunities Industrialization Center in Philadelphia in 1964. It was successful in providing job training and basic skills and OIC's are now operating in 105 cities. At General Motors, Sullivan persuaded the company to increase the number of black dealers, to train more black workers, to develop black managerial talent and to place funds in black banks and black insurance companies.[71]

Company annual reports now highlight social responsibility accomplishments and a new magazine, *Business and Society Review*, publishes a "Company Performance Roundup." It commended S. C. Johnson & Sons (Johnson's wax) for removing all fluorocarbon propellants from its production line. It noted that Kroger & Co., the nation's third largest supermarket chain, had granted discount coupons to senior citizens. It called attention to the fact that five stewardesses of Continental Airlines had filed a $5 million class action suit charging that Continental's new ad slogan, "We really move our tail for you," humiliates them and creates a public view of them as sex objects.[72]

Each year it presents corporate responsibility awards to outstanding corporate performances in this field. In 1974–75 it commended Bank of America, The Citizens & Southern National Bank, Consolidated Edison Company of New York, Control Data Corporation, Ford Motor Company, Lowe's Companies, Inc., Mobil Oil Corporation, Phillips-Van Heusen Corporation, J. C. Penney Company, Ralston Purina Com-

---

[71] See Christopher Stone; *Where the Law Ends: The Social Control of Corporate Behavior* (New York: Harper & Row, 1975); also Neil H. Jacoby, *Corporate Power and Social Responsibility* (New York: Macmillan, 1973).

[72] "Company Performance Roundup," *Business and Society Review*, Fall 1975, p. 96.

pany, and Standard Oil (of Indiana).[73] Its "Case History File: Corporate Social Responsibility at Work, No. 1," cited IBM for its "Fund for Community Service." All employees of the company have been alerted that there are corporate funds available to community groups in which IBM employees themselves are active. IBM also grants paid leaves to its employees for public service.[74]

Eastman Kodak's annual report contains a section called "The Corporate Role in Society." "Activities at Prudhoe Bay continue to reflect the company's basic concern for conservation of the Arctic environment," wrote Exxon in its annual report. Baltimore Gas & Electric postponed indefinitely its plans to build a nuclear plant in Maryland, due in part to growing opposition of environmentalists to nuclear plants.

Both on their own and prodded and pushed by organizations such as "Project on Corporate Responsibility," "Nader's Raiders," "National Affiliation of Concerned Business Students," and "Council on Economic Priorities," companies are facing up to and meeting their social responsibilities in new and often ingenious ways. A new dimension has been added to the financial analyst's evaluation. How effectively is the company responding and what are the costs and benefits involved?[75]

SUGGESTED READINGS

Ansoff, H. L.; Hayes, R. L.; and Declerck, R. P. *From Strategic Planning to Strategic Management*. New York: John Wiley & Sons, Inc., 1975.

Boettinger, Henry M. "Is Management Really an Art?" *Harvard Business Review*, January–February, 1975.

Brown, Courtney C. *Putting the Corporate Board to Work*. New York: Macmillan, 1976.

Burton, John C. (ed.) *Corporate Financial Reporting: Ethical and Other Problems*. (Second Seaview Symposium.) New York: American Institute of Certified Public Accountants, 1972.

Couger, J. D., and McFadden, F. R. *Introduction to Computer Based Information Systems*. New York: John Wiley & Sons, 1975.

Drucker, Peter F. *Management: Tasks, Responsibilities, Practices*. New York: Harper & Row, 1974.

---

[73] "Business and Society Review Corporate Responsibility Awards: This Year's Good Guys," *Business and Society Review*, Winter 1974–75, pp. 12–20; see also Milton Moskowitz, "Profiles in Corporate Responsibility: The Ten Worst, The Ten Best," *Business and Society Review*, Spring 1975.

[74] "Case History File: IBM's Fund for Community Service," *Business and Society Review*, Spring 1975, pp. 92–93.

[75] Stanley G. Karson, "The Social Responsibility of Management," *Nation's Business*, July 1975.

Harvard Business Review—On Management. New York: Harper & Row, 1976.

Hawkins, David F. *Financial Reporting Practices of Corporations.* Homewood, Ill.: Dow Jones-Irwin, Inc., 1972.

Head, Robert V. *Managers' Guide to Management Information Systems.* Englewood, N.J.: Prentice-Hall, Inc., 1972.

Karson, Stanley G. "The Social Responsibility of Management." *Nation's Business,* July 1975.

Kastens, Merritt L. *Long-Range Planning for Your Business: An Operating Manual.* New York: AMACOM, 1976.

Louden, J. Keith. *The Effective Director in Action.* New York: AMACOM, 1974.

Mueller, Robert K. *Board Life: Realities of Being a Corporate Director.* New York: American Management Association, 1974.

New York Society of Security Analysts. "How to Interview a Corporate Executive," August 7, 1972.

Norby, William C., and Stone, Frances G. "Objectives of Financial Reporting," *Financial Analysts Journal,* July/August 1972.

Rothschild, William E. *Putting It All Together: A Guide to Strategic Thinking.* New York: AMACOM, 1976.

Seidler, Lee J., and Seidler, Lynn L. *Social Accounting: Theory, Issues and Cases.* Los Angeles: Melville Publishing Co., 1975.

APPENDIX: I.C.F.A. CODE OF ETHICS[76]

WHEREAS, the profession of financial analysis has evolved because of the increasing public need for competent, objective and trustworthy advice with regard to investments and financial management; and

WHEREAS, The Institute of Chartered Financial Analysts was organized to establish educational standards in the field of financial analysis, to conduct examinations of financial analysts and to award the professional designation of Chartered Financial Analyst, among other objectives; and

WHEREAS, despite a wide diversity of interest among analysts employed by banks, brokers and security dealers, investment advisory organizations, financial relations counselors, insurance companies, investment companies, investment trusts, pension trusts and other institutional investors and corporate bodies, there are nevertheless certain fundamental standards of conduct which should be common to all engaged in the profession of financial analysis and accepted and maintained by them; and

WHEREAS, The Institute of Chartered Financial Analysts adopted a Code of Ethics on March 14, 1964; and

---

[76] The Institute of Chartered Financial Analysts, *The Profession of Financial Analysis and the Chartered Financial Analyst,* Revised January 15, 1976, "Fifteenth Annual Announcement of C.F.A. Programs" (Charlottesville, Va.: 1976–77), pp. 17–20.

WHEREAS, it is now deemed appropriate to make certain amendments to this Code;

NOW, THEREFORE, The Institute of Chartered Financial Analysts hereby adopts the following Code of Ethics and Standards of Professional Conduct:

A Chartered Financial Analyst should conduct himself with integrity and dignity and encourage such conduct by others in the profession.

A Chartered Financial Analyst should conduct himself and encourage the practice of financial analysis in a manner that would reflect credit on himself and on the profession.

A Chartered Financial Analyst should act with competence and strive to maintain and improve his competence and that of others in the profession.

A Chartered Financial Analyst should use proper care and exercise independent professional judgment.

THE I.C.F.A. STANDARDS OF PROFESSIONAL CONDUCT
(Revised January 15, 1976)

A. Compliance with Governing Laws and Regulations

1. The Chartered Financial Analyst shall have and maintain knowledge of and shall comply strictly with all applicable federal, state, and provincial laws as well as all applicable rules and regulations of any governmental agency governing his activities. The financial analyst shall also comply strictly with applicable rules and regulations of the stock exchanges and of the National Association of Securities Dealers if he, or his employer, is a member of these organizations.

2. The Chartered Financial Analyst shall take steps to assure that his employer is aware of the existence and content of the Code of Ethics and of these Standards of Professional Conduct.

3. The Chartered Financial Analyst shall not knowingly participate in, assist, or condone any acts in violation of any statute or regulation governing securities matters, nor any act which would violate any provision of the Code of Ethics or these Standards of Professional Conduct.

4. A Chartered Financial Analyst having supervisory responsibility shall exercise reasonable supervision over subordinate employees subject to his control, with a view to preventing any violation by such persons of applicable statutes, regulations, or provisions of the Code of Ethics or Standards of Professional Conduct.

5. The Chartered Financial Analyst shall not communicate or act on information if to do so would violate the laws and regulations relating to the use of material inside information. When the Chartered Financial Analyst acquires inside information, unless the analyst is in a special or confidential relationship with the issuer and receives the information in that capacity, which in his judgment is of a material nature, he shall, when appropriate, make reasonable effort to achieve public dissemination of such information by the issuer involved.

6. When in the course of practice, the Chartered Financial Analyst has encountered evidence that illegal acts have occurred, he is encouraged to report such evidence to an appropriate governmental or self-regulatory authority.

B. Investment Recommendations and Actions

1. The Chartered Financial Analyst shall have a reasonable and adequate basis for investment recommendation and action. He shall maintain appropriate records to support the reasonableness of such recommendation and action. He shall distinguish between facts and opinions in the presentation of investment recommendations.

2. The Chartered Financial Analyst, in making an investment recommendation or taking investment action, shall exercise diligence and thoroughness in the analysis of relevant investment risks and the valuation of, or the expected return from, investment securities. Any such recommendation or action shall be supported by appropriate research and investigation.

3. The Chartered Financial Analyst shall not, in the preparation of material for distribution to his employer, associates, customers, clients, or the general public, copy or use in substantially the same form material prepared by other persons without acknowledging its use and identifying the name of the author or publisher of such material. The analyst may, however, use without acknowledgment factual information published by recognized financial and statistical reporting services or similar sources.

4. The Chartered Financial Analyst shall scrupulously avoid any statements, oral or written, which guarantee any investment.

5. The Chartered Financial Analyst, in making an investment recommendation or taking investment action for a client, shall make reasonable efforts to be aware of and consider the appropriateness and suitability of such recommendation or action for such client.

6. The Chartered Financial Analyst shall act in a manner consistent with his obligation to deal fairly with all customers and clients when (a) disseminating investment recommendations, (b) disseminating material changes in prior investment advice, and (c) taking investment action.

C. Compensation

1. The Chartered Financial Analyst shall inform his customers, clients, and employer of compensation arrangements in connection with his services to them which are in addition to compensation from them for such services.

2. The Chartered Financial Analyst shall make appropriate disclosure of any consideration paid to others for recommending his services.

3. The Chartered Financial Analyst shall not undertake independent practice for compensation in competition with his employer unless he has received written consent from both his employer and the person for whom he undertakes independent employment.

D. Disclosure of Conflicts

The Chartered Financial Analyst, when making investment recommendations, or taking investment actions, shall disclose to his customers, clients, and employer any material conflict of interest relating to him and any material beneficial ownership of the securities involved which could reasonably be expected to impair his ability to render unbiased and objective advice. The financial analyst shall also comply with all requirement as to disclosure of conflicts of interest imposed by law and by rules and regulations of organizations governing his activities and shall comply with any prohibitions on his activities if a conflict of interest exists.

E. Priority of Transactions

The Chartered Financial Analyst shall conduct himself in such manner that transactions for his customers, clients, and employer have priority over personal transactions, that personal transactions do not operate adversely to their interests, and that he act with impartiality with respect to customers and clients. Thus, if an analyst has decided to make a recommendation as to the purchase or sale of a security, he shall give his customers, clients and employer adequate opportunity to act on such recommendation before acting on his own behalf.

F. Relationships with Others

The Chartered Financial Analyst shall act in a highly ethical and professional manner in his dealings with the public, his clients, his employees, his associates and fellow analysts. The Chartered Financial Analyst shall conduct himself in a fair and businesslike manner in all competitive business situations and shall adhere to the high standards of business conduct expected of all Chartered Financial Analysts. The Chartered Financial Analyst shall not use his business position to influence fellow analysts improperly on matters relating to their professional analysts organizations and shall respect the right of individual analysts to hold varying viewpoints.

G. Use of Professional Designation

The Chartered Financial Analyst may use the professional designation Chartered Financial Analyst, or the abbreviation C.F.A., but only in a dignified and judicious manner. The only proper use of the professional designation in advertising media shall be the designation itself. In printed advertising media, the professional designation shall be used only after the name of the holder of such designation appearing in such media and in type no larger than the type used in his name. The professional designation shall not be used in the text in such advertising. The term advertising media used herein shall not apply to promotional booklets, annual reports and similar publications that

may be published from time to time by various financial institutions for limited distribution.

REVIEW QUESTIONS AND PROBLEMS

1. What criteria can a securities analyst apply in judging the quality of management?
2. How should a securities analyst prepare for an interview with management?
3. What questions may a securities analyst properly ask mangement? What should not be asked?
4. What specific plans should a securities analyst inquire about in order to determine whether management has a broad concept of its market and its potential?
5. Contrast product differentiation and market segmentation? Should management attempt both? Why?
6. What are the pros and cons of heavy expenditures by industry for research and development?
7. What evidence should a securities analyst look for in trying to decide whether a company's management is willing to take large risks? Is such willingness favorable or unfavorable?
8. "There have been a number of cases involving illegal use of 'inside information', violations of the SEC's rule 10b–5." Outline the leading cases and summarize the current position of the securities analyst under Rule 10b–5.
9. What are the pros and cons of decentralization as a management technique?
10. What is your concept of an effective board of directors? What are the responsibilities of outside directors?

RESEARCH PROJECTS

1. As a junior securities analyst you are asked to accompany a senior analyst on a visit to top management at IBM headquarters. Since you will be away from your office and your files, the senior analyst asks you to prepare an essential minimum data summary to take along to the interviews and also to prepare a list of questions which your review of the data suggests should be asked of management. Prepare a report carrying out these instructions.
2. The AT&T management is to make a report before the New York Society of Security Analysts, of which you are a member. They have indicated in advance that they will be willing to answer questions after their presentation. The chairman of the meeting asks you to prepare a list of relevant, useful, and permissible questions which can be asked of management. Comply with his request.

3. A leading financial magazine asks you to prepare a brief article listing your choices for the ten best managed U.S. companies. You are also asked to give the reasons for your selections in each case. Prepare a draft of such an article.

4. You are asked to undertake a "corporate social audit" of the companies you cover as a senior analyst, for a university endowment fund. Prepare a list of topics you would wish to cover in such a social audit and also a list of questions you would want to put to management for each major company to be reviewed.

5. Assume that you are a practicing securities analyst. Arrange to visit two leading industrial or public utility companies in your area. Examine, through interviews, their management organizational structures and their management information systems. Prepare a brief report on your findings comparing and contrasting the two companies.

C.F.A. QUESTIONS

1. *From Exam I, 1975*

George Jones, C.F.A., is a senior analyst in the investment research department of Ballard and Company, an investment banking and brokerage firm specializing in large institutional accounts. Ballard was recently approached by Apex Corporation to act as soliciting agent in the acquisition of the stock of Campbell Company. Both Apex and Campbell are publicly listed companies manufacturing complementary lines of products.

Apex had retained Davis and Company, a financial consulting firm, to prepare a report recommending that stockholders of Campbell agree to the acquisition. The report also led to a recommendation on the ratio of exchange for the stocks of the two companies. Apex made this report available to the Ballard officers who were involved in negotiations on behalf of Apex. This report was given to Mr. Jones.

Mr. Jones reviewed the report of Davis and Company together with other material on the Apex and Campbell companies in his office and other information available to him based on his familiarity with the industry involved. From his analysis, Mr. Jones concluded that the common stock of Campbell Company represented extremely good value at its current price but that Apex Corporation common was considerably overvalued at its current price. In his opinion, Campbell Company stockholders would be ill-advised to accept the Apex offer based on the proposed terms.

Mr. Jones reported the results of his study to the partner in charge of new business. The partner said in reply: "Use the research report of Davis and Company, add a few words, sign your name, and get the report out. We need it right away."

a. If Mr. Jones does as requested, what provisions of the *I.C.F.A. Code of Ethics* and *The I.C.F.A. Standards of Professional Conduct* are involved? Discuss.

b. What should Mr. Jones do and why?

2. *From Exam I, 1976*

Mr. Jack Jones is a C.F.A. and security analyst at Hedy brokerage company, following the banking industry. At a cocktail party last weekend, Jack ran into Mr. Smith, a former loan officer of the Lamar Bank Corporation. Mr. Smith left Lamar six months ago because he was unhappy with the bank's management. After a few drinks, Mr. Smith tells Jack about some of the problems of Lamar Bank Corporation. In particular, he relates that Lamar has made massive loans to several large REITs which he believes must be written off as bad debts. In addition, Mr. Smith tells Jack of a large loan to a small developing country which currently is experiencing severe balance of payment deficits.

While Lamar Bank Corporation has never been one of Jack's favorite stocks for purchase, he knows that a number of Hedy's institutional clients hold large positions in the stock. While he had been aware of some bad real estate loans at Lamar, he never thought they amounted to very much. Also, Jack had never heard any discussion about sizable loans by Lamar to developing countries.

a.   List the provisions of *The I.C.F.A. Standards of Professional Conduct* that apply to this case.
b.   Discuss the pertinent elements of the above situation, using the information in the articles, "The Tippee in Transition," *Financial Analysts Journal*, January/February 1971 and "Mandatory Use of Inside Information," *Financial Analysts Journal*, March/April 1975 both by John Gillis and the appropriate sections of *The I.C.F.A. Standards of Professional Conduct*.

Summary of Chapters 5–8:
Evaluation of Common Stocks

The modern approach to common stock evaluation revolves around a two-part question: What is the potential growth of earnings and dividends of a company whose stock is being analyzed? What is a reasonable price to pay for that potential? Chapter 5 dealt with the growth potential of all corporations combined, and with various methods of determining the appropriate price to pay for growth—both in terms of stocks in the aggregate and in terms of individual stocks. Chapters 6 and 7 considered some of the problems and techniques involved in estimating the growth potential of individual companies and industries.

The approach to growth analysis that has been presented in these chapters proceeds from the general to the specific, and from the retro-spective to the prospective. First, an appraisal of total economic activity and total corporate profits is undertaken. Next, the role of the industry within the economy is examined; and, finally, attention is focused on the position of the company within its industry. In each of these steps, an analysis is made of the factors responsible for the past record of growth. By considering possible *changes* in these factors, a basis is provided for an estimate of future developments. Although heavy emphasis is placed upon the marketing aspects of growth, sales are not equated automatically with profits, as is all too frequently the case among common stock analysts. Rather, a method is presented for appraising in depth the growth of profits in relation to the growth of sales.

The determination of a reasonable stock price, given an estimate of growth prospects, can take several forms. A relatively abstract and theoretical—but nonetheless useful—approach is to discount the pro-

jected income stream from a stock to a present-value basis, at a discount rate which seems appropriate in relation to the risks involved and in relation to yields available on alternative investments. More pragmatic approaches are based upon analyses of current and past price-earnings ratios. The method of analyzing price-earnings ratios may vary from simple calculations of average P/E ratios in recent years to elaborate multiple regression studies. Chapter 5 suggests that the most desirable approach is an eclectic one in which the results of different procedures are compared and inconsistencies are resolved.

Although specific analytical procedures are presented in these chapters, it would be a serious error for the reader to come away with the impression that the process of common stock evaluation is somewhat analogous to a recipe for baking a cake. One cannot simply mix together a number of statistical ingredients in accordance with a fixed formula and produce an acceptable result. For example, Chapter 8 stressed the importance of appraising the *quality* of a company's management as distinct from the company's statistical record. And Chapter 4, which is relevant both for common stock and bond evaluation, indicated that even the statistical record cannot be accepted at face value—that what is reported as net income by a company may be a far cry from its "true" earnings.

Thus, a good securities analyst must combine a firm grasp of technical skills with a large element of imagination, creativity, and intuition. Without a spark of ingenuity, statistical techniques are likely to prove sterile.

Chapter 9

Bonds and Preferred Stocks I: Quality Analysis

> It's better to be safe than sorry.
> ——————————— *Proverb*

The subject of bond and preferred stock analysis often has been viewed as highly academic and even rather a waste of time. This attitude has stemmed from an overriding concern with common stocks as a rewarding and exciting investment medium. But interest in fixed-income security analysis has been growing as a result of the disappointing performance of the stock market and the high interest rates available on bonds. Indeed, in recent years there have been more new career opportunities for imaginative bond analysts and traders than for common stock analysts and traders.[1] Moreover, a knowledge of corporate bonds and preferreds is very useful even to an investor whose interest is exclusively in common stocks. A company with a high credit standing can finance growth more readily and more efficiently than a company whose senior securities are held in low esteem. Therefore, in evaluating the common stock of a company which has senior securities outstanding, it is usually well worthwhile to examine the merits of the latter. Similarly, it is worthwhile to examine the *potential* credit standing of a company which does not currently have senior securities outstanding.

---

[1] In his article, "New Fashions in Bonds," *Finance Magazine*, February 1976, C. C. Hardy notes that "Wall Street firms are scrambling to offer a wide range of services in bonds."

Principles

Except in the case of convertible securities and certain other investment outlets, which will be discussed at length in Chapter 11, investors in bonds and preferred stocks sacrifice most of the benefits that may ensue from a company's future growth.[2] In exchange for this sacrifice, bondholders get a promise by the company to pay a fixed amount of interest on specified dates, and to repay the principal at a specified time. Investors in preferred stocks do not get a promise, but they do get a *prior claim* on income and assets ahead of the common stock.

Since bond or preferred stock investors forego the benefits of growth, they must try to assure themselves that the issuers will be able to fulfill their obligations. Analytical procedures must be more concerned with the issuer's probable earnings under adverse circumstances than under favorable circumstances. Moreover, the bond investor will pay more attention than the common stock investor to balance sheets—to the legal and institutional nature of a company's liabilities, to its off-balance sheet obligations, and to *realization* values of assets as opposed to book values. Finally, more weight must be given to the possibility of a bear market for fixed income securities (i.e., a rise in interest rates[3]) than of a bull market (falling interest rates)—not because a bear market is more likely, but because risks should be more emphasized than opportunities in this area of investment.[4]

A logical approach to bond and preferred stock evaluation would proceed along the following lines:

1. Establish standards of quality which will not be compromised readily.
2. Determine whether the outlook for interest rates militates against the purchase of fixed-income securities generally. That is, determine whether an extended uptrend of interest rates is in prospect.

---

[2] Some benefit may accrue if the growth raises the senior security's credit standing, thereby lowering its yield in the market and raising its price.

[3] Rising interest rates mean declining prices of fixed-income securities. If you buy a 5 percent coupon bond at par, and two years later newly issued bonds of the same quality carry a higher coupon, no one will pay you par for your bonds. The price you can get will decline until the yield is competitive with new issues. At a later point, yield calculations are discussed more precisely.

[4] *Falling* interest rates also can pose a risk for investors in fixed-income securities. Although the market prices of such securities tend to rise when interest rates fall, unless their terms include nonrefunding clauses they may be called by their issuers, thus confronting investors with the problem of reinvesting at lower interest rates than originally anticipated. If the "call premiums" are inadequate to compensate for the lower reinvestment rates, significant losses may be suffered. The subject of callability will be considered at greater length in Chapter 10.

3. If the time is ripe, compile a list of securities meeting the quality standards, and choose the most attractive securities on the list. Frequently this means the highest yielding securities on the list, but not necessarily, as will be shown.

Step 1—the establishment of quality standards—is the subject of this chapter.

The Rating Agencies

One way of judging the quality of a bond is to examine the unbiased opinions of informed and experienced professionals. Bond rating agencies, such as Moody's, and Standard & Poor's, provide the investment community with an up-to-date record of their opinions on the quality of most large, publicly held corporate and governmental bond issues. These rating organizations are not in the business of selling bonds. Moreover, their ratings are made by committees rather than by single individuals. Thus, there is a minimal possibility that ulterior motives will cause one bond to be more highly rated than another. Indeed, agency ratings are held in such high regard that official regulatory commissions utilize them in evaluating the safety of the securities held by banks and insurance companies. The ratings and descriptions of the rated bonds are made available in a variety of publications which are sold on a subscription basis. For example, the indexes at the front of Moody's Manuals indicate Moody's ratings of the bonds of the indexed corporations or governments.

Bond ratings are designed essentially to rank issues in order of the probability of default—that is, inability to meet interest or sinking-fund payments or repayment of principal.[5] Only issues of the federal government carry no risk of default, because Congress has the power to issue money to pay its debts.[6] Thus, "triple-A" bonds (Aaa using Moody's designation, AAA using S&P's) are those judged to have a negligible risk of default and therefore to be of highest quality. "Double-A" bonds are of high quality also but are judged not to be quite as free of default risk as triple-A. Bonds rated A and BBB (Baa is Moody's designation) are generally referred to as medium-quality obligations, with the latter possessing a higher risk of default than the former. Bonds not falling within the first four rating categories are believed to contain a considerable "speculative" element.

Rating Statistics. Some 4,000 corporate bond issues are rated by the agencies. Of these, about 60 percent are the bonds of utility com-

---

[5] The word "essentially" is used in this sentence because the ratings also on occasion have given weight to marketability factors in addition to default risk per se.

[6] However, government bonds do entail a risk of loss of purchasing power, and marketable government bonds entail an "interest rate risk"—i.e., risk of capital loss due to rising interest rates.

panies, 25 percent are industrial issues, 12 percent are finance company issues, and the balance are bonds of transportation companies (railroads, airlines, and shipping).

Table 9–1 shows the distribution of ratings on outstanding corporate

TABLE 9–1
Rating Distribution of Agency-Rated Corporate Bonds* (percent of par value outstanding, December 31, 1975)

	Total Corporate	Utilities	Industrial	Finance	Transportation
AAA	23%	26%	21%	19%	7%
AA	26	25	26	33	10
A	33	32	34	34	27
BBB	13	16	10	5	18
BB	2	1	3	1	8
B	1	—	2	1	8
CCC and lower	2	—	4	7	22
	100%	100%	100%	100%	100%

* Convertible bonds are not included in the data.
Source: Salomon Brothers.

bonds in terms of par value. The table indicates that about 15 percent of utility and finance company bonds are of BBB quality or lower. Of industrial bonds, about 20 percent of the par value (and a much larger percentage by number, not shown in the table) are BBB or lower. Lower quality bonds were about 50 percent in the transportation sector.

While there is a substantial percentage of lower rated corporate bonds *outstanding*, the percentage of *new issues* in the lower rated categories has been declining during the past ten years. The bond markets' desire for quality is reflected in the data shown in Table 9–2. Indeed, between the spring of 1974 and the winter of 1975, lower rated corporations were virtually closed out of the public bond market. (They continued to be able to sell their issues in the private placement market, however. See pages 405–8 for a discussion of private placements.)

Of the bonds rated by several agencies, perhaps half are rated identically. Where differences exist, they usually are not in excess of one rating category. That is, a bond rated, say, Aa by Moody's is most unlikely to be rated BBB by Standard & Poor's. While cynics may suspect collusion from the fact that such similarity exists, a more reasonable conclusion is that bond quality evaluation has become a rather precise art. This will become clearer as we examine the factors that the rating agencies take into consideration.

Statistics on ratings of state and local government bonds are not

TABLE 9–2
Credit Ratings of New Corporate Bonds Publicly Offered (dollar data in billions)

Rating	1966	1967	1968	1969	1970	1971	1972	1973	1974	1975*
AAA	$1.9	$ 3.0	$ 2.5	$2.1	$ 6.2	$ 5.9	$ 5.3	$ 3.7	$ 7.9	$ 8.1
AA	1.9	3.2	2.7	3.0	5.3	5.4	4.2	3.8	8.1	8.4
A	1.5	2.8	1.9	2.6	8.8	6.8	4.5	3.6	7.1	10.9
BBB and below ...	2.1	4.4	2.5	1.8	2.5	2.4	1.1	0.6	1.5	2.2
Not rated	0.4	1.4	1.3	0.0	0.3	0.8	0.6	0.6	0.2	0.8
Total	$7.8	$14.8	$10.9	$9.5	$23.1	$21.3	$15.7	$12.3	$24.8	$30.4
AAA	24%	20%	23%	22%	27%	28%	34%	30%	32%	27%
AA	24	22	25	31	23	25	26	31	32	27
A	19	19	17	27	38	32	28	29	29	36
BBB and below ...	27	30	23	20	11	11	8	5	6	7
Not rated	6	9	12	0	1	4	4	5	1	3

* Estimated.
Source: Salomon Brothers data, as quoted in R. E. LaBlanc and M. D. Luftig, "What Are the New Market Prospects for Raising Utility Capital?" *Public Utilities Fortnightly,* February 26, 1976.

available in as fine detail as corporate bond data. From what is available, however, it appears that about two thirds of the value of rated bonds of such governments are in the top three rating categories, but that this percentage has been declining rather steadily in recent years. In terms of number of issues, moreover, a considerably smaller portion is in these categories. Furthermore, there are a vast number of relatively small issues (around $1 million to $5 million in value) that are unrated, even though publicly held.

Default Record.   One argument for the use of agency ratings as a guide to bond quality is their record of correlation with actual default experience during the first half of this century. The National Bureau of Economic Research made an exhaustive analysis of investor experience with corporate bonds sold during the period 1900–43. Among the data compiled were the following, which show the percentage of bonds in each rating category at the time of offering which subsequently defaulted:[7]

Rating Category (composite of ratings of various agencies)	Default Rate (percent of par value)
1	6%
2	6
3	13
4	19
5–9	42

---

[7] W. Braddock Hickman, *Corporate Bond Quality and Investor Experience* (New York: National Bureau of Economic Research, 1958), p. 10. These data cover "regular issues" only, excluding bonds issued as part of a reorganization.

Thus, during the more than 40 years covered, including the greatest depression in history, only 6 percent of the par value of bonds originally rated in the top two categories subsequently defaulted. Twice as high a percentage of third-category bonds defaulted, and three times as high a percentage of fourth category. Over 40 percent of the bonds classified as speculative subsequently defaulted.

Since these default percentages reflect the impact of the Great Depression, they should not be considered representative of conditions during the years ahead. Indeed, during the prosperity of the 1950s and 1960s, there was virtually no default on any bonds rated BBB or better.[8] But while the specific default rates of the early 1900s may be unrepresentative, the agencies' accuracy in *ranking* issues by probability of default was impressive.[9]

Inadequacies of Ratings. Although agency ratings should be held in high regard, investors in fixed-income securities should go beyond mere examination of ratings in evaluating the quality of various issues. Agency ratings should be used primarily as a tool for quickly eliminating obviously unsuitable issues from consideration. For example, the investor may say: "Any issues rated lower than BBB/Baa (less than 10 percent of the par value of all rated corporate bonds) are probably too risky for me. Maybe a few *would* be suitable, but the effort involved in ferreting them out is very great, and I'll always have doubts. It's just not worth it to me."

But having said this much, the investor is still left with an enormous range of issues from which to choose. And four ratings categories is not a very detailed classification system for 90 percent of all rated bonds. Every AAA bond is not necessarily of equal quality; and it may well be that a given investor may think that a particular A bond is really as good as many AA issues. For example, a corporation's debentures will almost automatically be rated one category lower than its mortgage bonds. Yet the quality of the debentures may be so high that for practical purposes they can be considered as good as the mortgage bonds. Moreover, even the rating agencies often differ in evaluation by one rating category.

Nor are these the only reasons why it is important to go beyond the ratings. *Privately* placed bonds, 25–50 percent of all corporate bond issues in recent years, are rated only on request—for a fee, of course. Preferred stocks and small bond issues are also unrated.[10] Finally,

---

[8] G. Pye, "Gauging the Default Premium," *Financial Analysts Journal*, January/February 1974, p. 52.

[9] However, a different interpretation of the National Bureau data, with less favorable implications for the rating agencies' skills, is contained in J. S. Ang and K. A. Patel, "Bond Rating Methods: Comparison and Validation," *Journal of Finance*, May 1975.

[10] Standard & Poor's *Stock Guide*, and other investment services, contain ratings for preferred stocks which appear similar to bond ratings. In fact, however, preferred stocks are not rated on a basis consistent with bond ratings.

there are the frequently voiced criticisms that ratings are not comparable over time—that A, for example, does not connote the same risk
today as it did 20 years ago—and that the agencies do not *change* their
ratings quickly enough when underlying conditions change. This latter comment warrants more extended discussion at this point.

Ask a member of an agency rating committee what factors go into
making the rating. The answer will surely be similar to that given by a
senior vice president of Moody's, who said that bond rating ". . . is not
a number game. You couldn't rate bonds on a computer. It would blow
a gasket. Bond rating is a comprehensive analysis of the position of a
company in whatever industry it is in."[11] This is certainly true. There
is no set formula for rating a bond. Nevertheless, certain of the more
important yardsticks are well known because they are in common use
by all bond analysts. Indeed, the agency ratings can be simulated
quite well by reference to these yardsticks.[12] In the next section, the
yardsticks will be examined. But for the subject at hand, the significant
point is that they are very heavily weighted by past developments.

The National Bureau study shows (see Table 9–3) that 43 percent of

TABLE 9–3
Revisions of Agency Ratings of Corporate Bonds, 1900–1943

Rating Category at Time of Issue	Rating Category at Time of Extinguishment (percent)						
	1	*2*	*3*	*4*	*5–9*	*Unrated*	*Total*
1	57	21	7	6	9		100
2	9	56	13	7	13	2	100
3	2	12	45	18	21	2	100
4	1	2	15	43	35	4	100
5–9	1	1	3	14	75	6	100

Source: W. Braddock Hickman, *Corporate Bond Quality and Investor Experience* (New York: National Bureau of Economic Research, 1958), p. 158. Ratings are a composite of the ratings of various agencies.

the value of bonds which were highest rated at the time of issue were
subsequently downgraded; 44 percent of the second-category issues
later had their ratings raised or lowered, as did 55 percent of the
third-category, and 57 percent of the fourth-category issues. Clearly,

---

[11] Quoted in "The Men Who Make Treasurers Tremble," *Forbes*, September 1, 1970, pp. 19–20. Also see I. Ross, "Higher Stakes in the Bond-Rating Game," *Fortune*, April 1976.

[12] For evidence, see G. E. Pinches and K. A. Mingo, "A Multivariate Analysis of Industrial Bond Ratings," *Journal of Finance*, March 1973; R. R. West, "An Alternative Approach to Predicting Corporate Bond Ratings," *Journal of Accounting Research*, Spring 1970; and E. I. Altman and S. Katz, "An Analysis of Bond Ratings in the Electric Public Utility Industry," Working Paper #21, Salomon Brothers Center for the Study of Financial Institutions, New York University.

ratings are not frozen once made. Nevertheless, they tend to be reexamined mainly at the time a company issues new bonds,[13] and are changed only when the agencies feel confident that changes in the factors which influence them are not just temporary aberrations. Since these factors are largely *historical* balance sheet and income ratios,[14] it usually takes some time before changes can be viewed as nontransitory.

While it is perfectly sound analytical procedure to wait for proof before revising a rating, the investor who reviews the ratings at times other than when a new issue is being offered, with its attendant publicity, and who can detect fundamental changes (as opposed to purely cyclical changes) before they are conclusively proven can gain an advantage over other investors. For when a change in an agency rating is publicly announced, the price of the bond in question almost always reacts sharply to the announcement.[15] Thus, an understanding of the important yardsticks of bond quality is valuable because it may be possible to anticipate changes in agency ratings and take advantage of the implied price change which should be forthcoming.

Analysis of Corporate Bonds and Preferred Stocks

While astute bond analysts take "everything" into account, it is clear, as noted above, that some factors are more important than others. They are:

1. The level and trend of "fixed charge coverage," which is the relationship between earnings and interest charges (or, in some cases, between earnings and total debt service requirements, including both interest and sinking funds).

2. The level of long-term debt in relation to equity, with debt measured both by the amount shown on the balance sheet and the amount represented by off-balance sheet obligations.

3. The debtor's liquidity position, current and prospective.

4. The size and economic significance of the company and of the industry in which it operates.

---

[13] H. W. Long, in "An Analysis of the Determinants and Predictability of Agency Ratings of Domestic Utility Bond Quality," a Ph.D. dissertation abstracted in the *Journal of Finance*, December 1974 notes that "well over 80 percent of rating change announcements coincide with the subject company's issuance of new, rated bonds."

[14] For a view that inflation is causing the rating agencies to take a more forward-looking, less historical, view, see *What's in a Utility Bond Rating* (New York: Salomon Brothers, December 17, 1975).

[15] S. Katz, "The Price Adjustment Process of Bonds to Rating Reclassifications," *Journal of Finance*, May, 1974. This and similar findings have been used as evidence that the bond market is not as "efficient" as the stock market, a subject which will be discussed further in Chapter 10 and Chapter 15.

5. The standing of the specific debt issue in the hierarchy of priorities in bankruptcy (e.g., secured versus unsecured, senior versus subordinate) as well as the overall "protective provisions" of the issue.

Fixed Charge Coverage

The concept involved in fixed charge coverage (also referred to as "times charges earned") is quite simple to grasp, for it is analogous to a measure used by banks and finance companies in judging applications for consumer credit. The lending officer considering the application will examine the relationship between the applicant's normal monthly or annual income and the size of the required monthly debt payments. The higher the income relative to debt service liabilities, the safer it is to extend credit, other things remaining equal. It is precisely the same with a bond.

Charges. In corporate bond analysis, the amount of charges to be covered usually is equal to the item "interest on loans," which appears on the income statement. Typically, the bulk of this item equals the par value of outstanding funded debt times the coupon rate, although it also includes interest on short-term bank loans, and may include amortization of debt discount. In addition, the interest component of rentals under long-term leases should be included as a fixed charge.

If a corporation has more than one class of bonds outstanding—say first-mortgage bonds and debentures—the pertinent figure is usually the sum of the annual interest charges on *all* of the debt. This is because all the bonds are legally enforceable claims; a default on any one of them can put the company into bankruptcy, thus jeopardizing the holders of the other issues as well. Therefore, we do not usually speak of coverage of mortgage bond charges and coverage of debenture charges, but rather coverage of total debt charges. However, there may be some justification for evaluating senior mortgage bonds separately. Senior mortgage bondholders generally receive better treatment in reorganization than other bondholders. For example, in the event of bankruptcy the courts may allow a well-secured issue to continue to receive interest payments even though payments on other issues are suspended.

Sinking-fund requirements—i.e., amortization of principal—usually are not included in the definition of fixed charges when analyzing corporate bonds, although they are included in appraising consumer credit and municipal revenue bonds (often they also are included in railroad bond analysis). There are two main reasons for the omission: (1) Although sinking-fund default is an act of bankruptcy, creditors usually are willing to waive payments for a year or two if the company

is temporarily embarrassed. (2) Sinking-fund payments are presumed to be covered by depreciation charges.

Earnings Available. A convenient working definition of the amount of earnings available for the payment of bond charges is: net income before taxes, before interest, and before the interest component of rents under long-term leases. The use of pretax earnings is suggested in preference to after-tax earnings even though many analysts and investment services use the latter. Since interest is a tax-deductible expense, it is logical to compare it with net *before* taxes. Earnings are taken before deduction of interest, since we want to know how much is available for payment of interest. If it is felt desirable to include sinking-fund requirements in fixed charges, earnings available for payment should be defined as *predepreciation* pretax earnings. Moreover, if the *total* amount of rentals is included in fixed charges, rather than just the interest component of these rentals, earnings available should be defined as pretax earnings before interest and before rent.

Coverage Ratio. After calculating (*a*) earnings available for payment of bond charges, and (*b*) the amount of bond charges, the earnings coverage ratio is calculated by dividing (*a*) by (*b*). An example will clarify the procedure. Suppose that a corporation's income account shows net income before taxes equal to $30 million. And suppose that its balance sheet shows $20 million of 5 percent first-mortgage bonds, $8 million of 6.25 percent second-mortgage bonds, and $6.25 million of 8 percent debentures. Therefore, interest payments on the first-mortgage bonds would be 5% × $20 million, or $1 million; interest on the second-mortgage bonds would be 6.25% × $8 million, or $0.5 million; and interest on the debentures would be 8% × $6.25 million, or $0.5 million. Assuming there are no significant long-term leases, earnings coverage would be calculated as follows.

If the so-called *overall method* were being utilized—i.e., if the analyst took the usual view that a default on junior bond issues is just as serious as a default on senior mortgage bonds—then a single coverage ratio for all three classes of bonds would be computed. Earnings available for payment of charges would be equal to net income before taxes ($30 million), plus bond interest ($2 million), or $32 million. Bond charges would be equal to $2 million; and the coverage ratio would be 32/2, or 16.

As noted earlier, however, there may be some justification for evaluating the first-mortgage bonds and the junior issues separately. In this case, three coverage ratios would be calculated, using the so-called *cumulative deductions method*. Earnings available for paying interest on the first mortgage bonds would be the full $32 million of

net income before taxes and before interest; but charges would be only $1 million, and the coverage ratio would be 32. To calculate coverage on the junior issues, earnings available for all interest charges ($32 million) is divided successively by interest charges on each junior issue *plus* interest charges on issues senior to it. Thus, the coverage ratio of the second-mortgage bonds would be 32/1.5, or 21⅓. The coverage ratio of the debentures would be 32/2, or 16.

Although the overall method of calculating earnings coverage ratios generally is preferble to the cumulative deductions method, in no case should the so-called *prior deductions method* be utilized. Under this method, earnings available for payment of charges on each particular bond being analyzed is determined by deducting prior interest charges from total earnings available for all interest charges. This amount, in turn, is divided by only the charges on that particular bond. Thus, the coverage ratio of the first-mortgage bonds under this method would be $32 million divided by $1 million, or 32, while the coverage ratio of the second-mortgage bonds would be $32 million, minus $1 million, divided by $0.5 million, or 62 (31/0.5 = 62). But this is patently absurd. The second-mortgage bonds cannot be safer—better covered by earnings—than the first-mortgage bonds.

In spite of its obvious inadequacy, a version of the prior deductions method frequently is encountered in connection with preferred stock analysis. Many investment services calculate "earnings per preferred share" by dividing net income (after bond interest as well as other expenses) by the number of preferred shares outstanding. When this figure is divided by the dividend rate on the preferred stock, a coverage ratio results which is analogous to coverage calculated by the misleading prior deductions method. In the following section, a more meaningful approach to coverage of preferred stock dividends is presented.

Coverage Ratio–Preferred Stock.   In earnings coverage analysis of preferred stocks, the overall and cumulative deductions methods are identical. Preferred dividend requirements are added to interest charges, if any, in calculating charges to be covered, and this sum is divided into total "available earnings."

The preferred stock dividend requirement is equal to the par value of the outstanding preferred times the percentage dividend rate, or the number of preferred shares times the dollar dividend rate. But a complication arises. We cannot simply add preferred dividends to interest charges because the latter are tax deductible whereas the former are not. At a tax rate of almost 50 percent, a corporation has to earn $2 before taxes to pay $1 of preferred dividends, but need earn only $1 before taxes to pay $1 of interest.

In order to equate preferred dividends and interest charges when

comparing them with earnings available for payment of charges, the preferred dividends ought to be doubled at a 50 percent tax rate. As a generalized formula, to take account of other tax rates, preferred dividends should be divided by 100 percent minus the tax rate. For example, assume a tax rate of 48 percent and preferred dividend obligations of $1 million. Dividing $1 million by 0.52 (1.00 − 0.48 = 0.52) produces adjusted preferred dividends of $1,923,000 (rounded). That is, at a 48 percent tax rate a company has to earn $1,923,000 before taxes to pay $1 million of preferred dividends.

Once preferred stock dividends have been adjusted for the tax factor, earnings available for payment of *interest charges plus preferred dividends* can be defined identically to earnings available for payment of interest charges alone—i.e., net income before taxes and before interest. Note that preferred dividends are not added back to net income before taxes, as are interest charges, because they were not deducted in calculating net before taxes whereas interest was.

To illustrate the coverage calculations, assume that a company's net income before taxes amounts to $33 million. And assume that its balance sheet shows:

5% First-mortgage bonds	$20,000,000
6¼% Debentures	16,000,000
7½% Preferred stock	20,000,000

Total charges to be covered, adjusted for the preferred stock tax factor (assuming a 50 percent tax rate for simplicity), are as follows:

Preferred dividends:	7.5% × $20,000,000 =	$1,500,000
Times: Adjustment factor		×2
Equals: Adjusted preferred dividends		$3,000,000
Plus: Interest on bonds:	5% × $20,000,000 =	1,000,000
	6.25% × $16,000,000 =	1,000,000
Equals: Total charges, adjusted		$5,000,000

Earnings available for payment of the $5 million of charges equal net income before taxes ($33 million), plus bond interest ($2 million), or $35 million. The coverage ratio of the preferred stock, therefore, is 35/5, or 7. On the other hand, the overall coverage of the two bond issues is 35/2, or 17½. Note that where a company has both bonds and preferred stock in its capital structure, the coverage of the preferred always will be lower than the coverage of the bonds. Thus it is entirely possible that the bonds will be of acceptable quality whereas the preferred stock will not.

Standards. The next logical question is whether 7 times charges or 17½ times charges should be considered high or low, good or bad. It is

impossible to be dogmatic in answering this question. Different investors have different safety standards. However, we would suggest the following guidelines:

1.   Compute a coverage ratio whose numerator is *average* earnings available for the payment of charges during at least the past five years, or as many years as necessary to include periods both of prosperity and recession. It often is misleading to use recent earnings only, since a bond's quality can appear high during prosperity and low during recession. What is desired is a conception of quality which holds good over extended periods of time.

2.   The denominator of the coverage ratio should be the amount of charges at the time the analysis is being made. Average charges of the historical period usually should not be used because the object of the analysis is to determine whether the company has a demonstrated ability to earn enough to cover today's charges not yesterday's. Only in the case of very rapidly growing companies should an average of past charges be used. In such cases, earnings and indebtedness usually grow together, and it would be unreasonable to expect yesterday's earnings to be adequate relative to today's interest charges.[16]

3.   In evaluating the coverage ratio which results from dividing (1) by (2), a distinction should be made between companies whose earnings are very vulnerable to economic recessions (for example, steel), and companies which are more stable (for example, utilities). A better historical coverage record of the former should be demanded than of the latter. By demanding a higher average coverage for cyclical companies, the investor is better protected against an unusually severe recession.

4.   The National Bureau of Economic Research study of bond default experience, referred to earlier in this chapter, revealed a sharp difference between the default rates of bonds with coverage ratios of less than 4, as defined above,[17] and bonds with higher coverage ratios. Bonds with coverage ratios of 6 and over proved particularly safe. Based on these statistics, and upon the standards we have observed

---

[16] A somewhat related aspect of this subject has to do with the timing of a corporation's borrowing. It often develops *quite fortuitously* that one corporation borrows at a time when interest rates are fairly high while another similar corporation borrows when rates are low. Other things being equal, this causes the coverage ratio of the former company's bonds to be lower than the coverage ratio of the latter's bonds. Recognizing this possibility, some bond analysts relate earnings to the principal amount of debt rather than to the interest charges.

[17] The NBER study defined earnings coverage as average annual income *after taxes*, but before interest charges, over the five-year period preceding the offering date, divided by fixed charges for the first full year following offering. Since the coverage ratio recommended in this chapter is based on *pretax* earnings, the NBER ratios should be approximately doubled for comparability. The default rates referred to were as follows

among large institutional investors, it is suggested that coverage ratios of fixed income securities, whether bonds or preferred stocks,[18] may be graded in accordance with the standards shown in Table 9–4, in conjunction with all of the other quality tests discussed in this chapter.

TABLE 9–4
Standards for Grading Coverage Ratios of Fixed-Income Securities

Coverage Ratio	Characteristic of Company	Relative Quality of Issue
6 and over	Cyclical	Very high
4 and over	Stable	Very high
3–6	Cyclical	Medium to high
2–4	Stable	Medium to high
Under 3	Cyclical	Low
Under 2	Stable	Low

These suggested standards are formed in terms of the *average level* of fixed charge coverage. In addition, analysts should be concerned with the year-to-year *trend*. Indeed, the analyst may well view a lower-than-desired level of coverage as more satisfactory than a higher level of coverage if the former is accompanied by a rising trend while the latter is accompanied by a declining trend.

Capital Structure

Another quality measure which almost all bond analysts stress is the proportion of total capitalization represented by debt versus equity. The individual bond or preferred stock owner would be best off if the certificate were the only senior security outstanding, because earnings coverage then would be at a maximum (assuming that the corporation could raise elsewhere the funds necessary to operate a prosperous

---

for large new offerings during 1900–1943 (from Hickman, *Corporate Bond Quality and Investor Experience*, p. 413):

	Coverage Ratio, after Taxes				
	Under 1.0	1.0–1.4	1.5–1.9	2.0–2.9	3.0 and over
All industries	35.0%	34.1%	17.9%	4.0%	2.1%
Railroads	55.2	49.9	28.0	15.1	5.5
Public utilities	41.8	11.5	9.3	0.1	0.2
Industrials	9.7	16.0	16.5	7.4	4.0

[18] Since we have suggested that coverage ratios of preferred stocks be adjusted to a tax basis comparable with bonds, there is no need to establish separate sets of standards for the two types of fixed-income securities.

business). Thus, to the bondholder or preferred stockholder, the greater the junior capital as a percent of total capitalization the better. An analysis of the corporation's capital structure is, therefore, a sort of "asset coverage" measure which supplements the earnings coverage measure previously discussed.

Unfortunately, the components of a company's capital structure cannot simply be read off the balance sheet. While the outstanding amount of bonds and bank loans due in more than one year appear clearly on the balance sheet, the analyst must determine whether there are additional debt-equivalent items not identified. As discussed at length in Chapter 4, such off-balance sheet debt may include long-term lease obligations, guarantees of the debt of other parties, and "take-or-pay" contracts. Furthermore, amounts borrowed under revolving credit agreements with banks usually appear on the balance sheet as *current* notes payable. But if the company continuously utilizes these credit lines, the analyst probably should treat such "current" borrowings as the equivalent of long-term debt.

Another complication can arise when a company has preferred stock outstanding which is shown on the balance sheet at a nominal par value (e.g., $1 per share), but which has a much higher liquidating value in the event of corporate dissolution (e.g., $100 per share). In such cases, the analyst must use the liquidating value as the amount of preferred stock in the capital structure, deducting the added amount from surplus.[19]

Finally, common stock and surplus accounts shown on the balance sheet represent the difference between the book value of all the assets and the sum of all liabilities plus preferred stock. But plant and equipment is carried on the books at original cost less depreciation, and this may or may not be realistic in view of current reproduction costs or earning power. Moreover, as discussed in Chapter 4, there may be questions regarding the value of inventories, patents, subsidiary assets, "goodwill," and other intangibles. Furthermore, various "reserve" accounts and deferred tax liabilities may or may not represent real liabilities. Consequently, the balance sheet summation of common stock plus surplus accounts does not necessarily reflect the true asset value of the common equity.

Although it would be nice to send out teams of industrialists, engineers, and real estate appraisers to evaluate corporate assets, this usually is not feasible. Accordingly, the practice has developed among security analysts of using two measures of common stock equity: (1) the book value as shown on the balance sheet, and (2) the market

---

[19] No reduction of surplus need be made when capitalizing rentals, or accounting for other off-balance sheet debt, because an offsetting amount must be assumed to exist on the asset side of the balance sheet.

value, derived by multiplying the number of shares outstanding by current market price, or by an average of recent high and low market prices. Where the two measures produce quite different results, the analyst must use his judgment as to which is more representative of realistic asset values.

Illustration. Assume that the following information was derived from a company's year-end balance sheet (in million dollars):

Long-term debt (excluding due in 1 year)		$ 500
Preferred stock ($100 par)		150
Common stock (20,000,000 shares no par)		20
Capital surplus		50
Retained earnings		780
Total Long-Term Capital		$1,500

The capital structure can be stated as:

Long-term debt	33%	(500/1,500)
Preferred stock	10	(150/1,500)
Common stock and surplus	57	(850/1,500)
Total	100%	

Assume that during the most recent two years, the high-low price range of the company's common stock was 60–90. If the mean of this range, 75, is taken as a reasonable approximation of the market's appraisal of the company's stock value, the total market value of the common equity works out to $75 × 20 million shares, or $1.5 billion. Thus, the capital structure, with common equity at market value, is as follows:

	Million Dollars	Percent of Total
Long-term debt	500	23
Preferred stock	150	7
Common equity	1,500	70
Total	2,150	100

If the company's bonds were being analyzed, the debt ratio would be 33 percent or 23 percent, depending on whether book or market value of common stock were being used. If the company's preferred stock were the focus of interest, the debt-plus-preferred ratio would be 43 percent or 30 percent.

Standards. Again the question arises: Are these ratios high or low? Again, one cannot be dogmatic, especially since the NBER study of bond default experience, which provides some objective data on earnings coverage ratios, does not provide similar data on capital structure. Some guidelines may be offered, however, on the basis of general observation (see Table 9–5).

TABLE 9–5
Maximum Percent of Senior Capital for Security Quality Classifications

Company Characteristic	Quality		
	Very High	Medium to High	Low
Cyclical	30	40	60
Stable	50	60	70
Public utility*	50–60	60–75	75

* Separate standards are given for public utility companies, as distinct from stable companies generally, and are given as a *range*, because the subject of optimal leverage is even more controversial for public utility companies than for corporations in aggregate.

Liquidity

Some companies may appear to have satisfactory earnings and capital yet be "cash poor." That is, their earnings look satisfactory relative to obligations and they do not seem to be overly leveraged, yet bondholders or preferred stockholders may not be sure that enough cash will be on hand to pay their claims as they come due. This condition may have several causes. For example:

1. The company may be "pushing sales" (and thereby increasing reported earnings) by extending unusually long credit terms to its customers, thus tying up its resources in receivables which are not very liquid.

2. The company may be tying up resources in excessive inventories in order to be able to respond promptly to all incoming orders.

3. The company may be relying heavily on trade payables and short-term bank borrowings to provide its working capital needs, rather than building up its long-term capital base, and in a period of general economic difficulty may find that its vendors and bankers are reluctant to continue being as liberal in extending credit.

Ideally, the appraisal of a company's liquidity position should encompass the type of sources and uses of funds analysis described in Chapter 4. Such an analysis will highlight the past and probable future *sources of cash* available to the enterprise, and the probable *uses of cash* for both mandatory and discretionary corporate purposes. Since this type of analysis is extremely complex,[20] various financial ratios have been used as a substitute for the more rigorous analytical effort. The principal ratios in common use are outlined below.

1. Receivables Collection Period. This ratio measures the

---

[20] See the revised edition of this text (1973), pp. 395–404, for a probabilistic approach to cash flow analysis.

number of days it takes, on average, to collect accounts and notes receivable. To do the calculation, first determine the average daily selling rate (usually taken as annual sales divided by 360, or quarterly sales divided by 90). Then determine the average amount of accounts receivable outstanding during the year, or the quarter, being measured (usually taken as one half of beginning and ending receivables). Finally, divide average receivables by average daily sales. For example, suppose annual sales of a company are $180 million, receivables at the start of the year are $24 million, and receivables at year-end are $36 million. The receivables collection period would be 60 days:[21]

$$\frac{24 + 36}{2} \div \frac{180}{360} = 30 \div 0.5 = 60 \, \text{days}$$

If the analyst in this case determined that the typical "terms of trade" in the industry were 2/10 : net/30, and that competing companies have a collection period of, say, 45 days or less, it would be clear that some sleuthing is needed to find out why this particular company has a 60-day collection period. The reason could be, as noted above, that the company is "pushing sales" by extending unusual credit terms; or the company might be doing a poor collection job; or the company might have a number of customers who are in financial difficulty.

2. Number of Days to Sell Inventory. This is a variation of the inventory turnover ratio which was discussed in Chapter 7. Instead of relating inventory to sales, however, inventory usually is related to cost of goods sold, since inventory is essentially valued at cost.[22] Analogous to the prior ratio described, this ratio is derived by dividing average daily cost of goods sold into the average of beginning and ending inventory. The resulting figure should be compared with similar calculations for other firms in the same industry, both in the current period and in prior periods, to judge whether the company in question is operating with especially sparse or especially heavy, and possibly obsolete, inventory.

An interesting additional insight can be gained by adding together the receivables collection period and the number of days to sell inventory.[23] Suppose the figures are 60 days and 90 days, respectively. One might say that it takes 150 days to convert inventory into cash—90 days

---

[21] Note that if we divide 60 days into 360 days, we derive the "receivables turnover" (6) discussed in Chapter 7.

[22] It should be recognized, however, that Lifo accounting may render the inventory valuation meaningless, in which case these ratios would be meaningless.

[23] This concept is discussed in Leopold Bernstein, *Financial Statement Analysis* (Homewood, Ill.: Richard D. Irwin, Inc., 1974), p. 393.

to sell what is produced and 60 days to collect from the customers. The 150-day period has been referred to as the "operating cycle."

3. Number of Days' Bills Outstanding. Here, the average daily cost of goods sold is divided into average accounts payable. The resulting number is compared with that of other firms in the same industry, and is also tracked over time in comparison with the receivables collection period. Though days receivable and days payable can be quite different magnitudes, generally speaking one would expect to find a fairly *constant relationship* between the two. If they begin to depart from their customary relationship, further investigation is called for.

4. Working Capital Ratios. Whereas the prior three ratios dissect working capital (current assets minus current liabilities) into its major components—accounts receivable, inventory, and accounts payable—analysts like to take an overall view of a company's ability to meet current liabilities. The most common measures, in this regard, are:

a. Current Ratio. Current assets divided by current liabilities.
b. Quick Asset, or Acid-Test, Ratio. Current assets exclusive of inventory, divided by current liabilities.
c. Cash Ratio. Bank deposits plus liquid securities owned, divided by current liabilities.

It is even more difficult to generalize about what constitutes a high- or low-working capital ratio than it is to generalize about earnings coverage or capitalization ratios. Although a current ratio of at least 2 to 1 often is set as a standard (1 to 1 for the acid test), liquidity requirements are very much a function of the nature of a company's business. For example, a telephone company can operate with a very low current ratio because there is a relatively short time lag between the provision of services to subscribers, the billing, and the receipt of payment. On the other hand, a machinery company faces a long time span between the acquisition of raw materials, the construction and shipment of machines, and the receipt of payment. This is particularly true if the machine is leased rather than sold. Consequently, the only feasible procedure is to compare the working capital ratios of the company under analysis with the ratios of other similarly situated companies, although there is an obvious element of circular reasoning in an approach where everyone looks at what someone else is doing.

In judging all the ratios described in this section, the analyst should examine not only the most recent data, but also the data for a period of at least five years, preferably including at least one year of recession. This will give a better "feel" of the company's working capital policies. If possible, the analyst also should obtain working capital

data at quarterly intervals rather than at year-ends only, since many companies follow a policy of "window dressing"—squeezing receivables and inventory to below-normal levels in order to pay off their short-term bank loans at year-end, and then borrowing again after the turn of the year and rebuilding receivables and inventory. Even though debt repayment depletes current assets by an amount equal to the reduction of current liabilities, the current ratio will be improved. For example, suppose that current assets are $5 million and current liabilities $2 million, for a current ratio of 2½ to 1. The simultaneous reduction of both the numerator and denominator of the ratio, by, say, $1 million—to $4 million and $1 million—increases the current ratio to 4 to 1.

A clue as to whether a company may be engaging in window dressing can be found in an annual statement footnote which is now required by the SEC. This footnote indicates the company's maximum borrowing position during the year. The maximum borrowing figure may be a better indication of the company's true short-term debt position than the year-end figure. The analyst should seek to determine if it is out of line with the prior year's maximum borrowing and is not explained by any normal seasonal pattern in the company's business.

The footnote containing the maximum borrowing figure also will indicate how much of the company's cash balances are "compensating balances" with its bank creditors. The fact that these balances are not available for corporate uses should be taken into account when appraising a company's liquidity.

A good rule of thumb in analyzing liquidity is that a company should have enough of its capital needs provided by long-term debt, by revolving credit bank agreements which are convertible into three- to five-year term loans, and by equity money so that it can be free of current notes payable for at least 30 to 90 days each year without an inordinate buildup in its trade payables (i.e., without substituting trade credit for bank credit). In this connection, analysts should be wary of companies which continually postpone long-term financing because short-term interest rates are below long-term rates or because the stock market is depressed. While it is incumbent on the chief financial officer to try to achieve the lowest cost of capital, too many companies overestimate their ability to forecast interest rates and/or stock prices, and wind up with an inadequate long-term capital base.

The *cost* of short-term borrowing is also presented in the same footnote. If this cost is higher than the company's past credit rating might warrant, or higher than the rates paid by other companies in its industry, it suggests that the company may have deteriorated financially. It is an indication of the bankers' appraisal of the company's creditworthiness.

Bond analysts must be very cautious in appraising companies which make persistent use of short-term bank borrowing or issuance of commercial paper for purposes other than financing seasonal sales patterns. The high risk in current debt is apparent in the bankruptcies and companies having financial difficulties in recent years. In most of these cases, short-term creditors lost confidence and demanded payment, which precipitated the same demands by funded-debt holders.

Finally, analysts should keep a wary eye on the amortization schedule of a company's long-term debt. Frequently, there are large repayments due within the next few years, and the analyst must be sure that the resources to meet these obligations will be available, or that the company's borrowing capacity will be adequate to refinance them before they come due.

The significance of a careful analysis of liquidity, in addition to fixed charge coverage and capital structure, is perhaps most apparent in the data compiled by the investment banking firm, Salomon Brothers, shown in Table 9–6. It documents a "startling cycle-to-cycle

TABLE 9–6
Some Measures of Aggregate Corporate Liquidity in the Postwar Period
(cyclical year-end highs and lows, ratios of outstanding amounts)

	Bond Debt to Short-Term Debt		Liquid Assets to Short-Term Debt	
	High	Low	High	Low
1945–48	2.11	1.54	3.47	1.98
1949–53	2.09	1.63	2.41	1.85
1954–57	2.04	1.67	1.97	1.38
1958–60	1.93	1.70	1.45	1.19
1961–70	1.75	1.25	1.23	0.63
1971–74	1.42	1.05	0.69	0.56

Source: Salomon Brothers, *Supply and Demand for Credit in 1975*, p. 6.

deterioration in both short-term ratios and the debt maturity structures of nonfinancial corporations" during the postwar years. The same point was emphasized in a recent *Business Week* survey of the capital needs of 550 of the nation's largest corporations.[24] The article makes the following observation: "In the face of record-high interest rates, many corporations are reluctant to make long-term commitments, and the level of short-term borrowing has burgeoned. As of the end of 1975's first quarter, one-third of the companies in BW's survey had

[24] "How 550 Companies Face the Capital Gap," *Business Week*, September 22, 1975, pp. 65–82.

doubled the percentage of short-term debt in their capital structures compared with their most recent 10-year averages."

Economic Significance

Bond analysts place heavy emphasis on the size and trade position of the issuing company and on the nature of the industry. They are inclined to look most favorably upon companies which are in industries that are considered "indispensable." Similarly, large corporations which represent a substantial share of their industries' output are believed to involve less risk to creditors than smaller corporations with less entrenched trade positions. The National Bureau study, to which frequent reference has been made in this chapter, contains clear evidence of a correlation between size and default rate.[25] This aspect of bond quality analysis is indirectly reflected in the fact that in 1974, the average size of outstanding AAA bonds in the marketplace was $80 million, the average AA bond amounted to $43 million, A's were $31 million, and BBB's were $25 million.[26] While size of issue and size of issuer are not necessarily perfectly correlated, there is a close enough relationship to infer that bond quality ratings and size of issuer go hand in hand.

Protective Provisions of the Issue

The rights of bond and preferred stock owners are spelled out in detailed legal instruments—bond indentures and preferred stock contracts. The specifics of these instruments are important ingredients of quality estimates although, as will be stressed below, continuance of the issuer's earning power is more significant than the contractual provisions of the issue.

With regard to contractual provisions, there is, first, the question of collateral. A corporate *mortgage bond* provides that in the event of bankruptcy the bondholders have first claim on the value of specified corporate assets. Where a bond is not secured by a mortgage, it is referred to as a *debenture*. Unless they are explicitly *subordinated* by the terms of the indenture (as is common, for example, with convertibles), debentures are like accounts payable. They are general liabilities of the corporation which have a claim on the value of corporate assets, in the event of bankruptcy, that precedes the claim of preferred and common stock owners (and of subordinated creditors)

---

[25] Hickman, *Corporate Bond Quality and Investor Experience*, chap. 8.

[26] Salomon Brothers, *Anatomy of the Secondary Market in Corporate Bonds: Update.* See the studies cited in footnote 12 for further evidence of the relationship between quality rating and size of issuer.

but comes after the claim of mortgage bondholders, corporate employees (for unpaid wages), the government (for unpaid taxes), and other claims to which the bankruptcy statutes give priority. The claim of preferred stockholders may be exercised after the general creditors have been satisfied and before the common stockholders receive anything.

Various clauses may be inserted into the indenture of a bond to protect its priority position vis-à-vis other creditors. For example, an *equal-and-ratable-security* clause specifies that if a prior lien subsequently is placed on corporate assets, the bond in question will have an equal and pro rata share in the lien. *Open-end* mortgage clauses provide that additional bonds may be issued with an equivalent lien, but only if the additional debt does not cause the total to exceed a specified percentage of the mortgaged assets. Other limitations on the issuance of additional debt may be that earnings have to bear a minimum relationship to the amount of debt or to the amount of interest charges, and that working capital has to be maintained at some minimum level. *After-acquired-property* clauses state that if property is acquired after the issuance of a first-mortgage bond, it automatically will fall under the lien of that mortgage unless waived by the existing mortgage bond owners. In the case of preferred stock contracts, it usually is provided that subsequent issues of stock with a priority over the preferred are not permitted unless approved by the holders of a certain percentage of the preferred stock outstanding.[27]

Collateral De-Emphasized. The collateral provisions of bonds used to be very heavily stressed by investment analysts. They are much less emphasized today. Not that they are ignored—indeed, the rating agencies usually grade a corporation's debentures one notch lower than the same corporation's first-mortgage bonds, and subordinated debentures generally are rated lower than senior debentures.[28] But collateral and priorities are less emphasized than in earlier days.[29]

The reasons for the de-emphasis of collateral are quite clear. Property value is a function of the earnings which the property can produce. Most property which serves as bond collateral is in the form of specialized plant and equipment—for example, a steel mill. When the economics of the issuing company deteriorate to the point of bankruptcy, the likelihood is that its property is incapable of earning a decent rate of return and is therefore not worth very much.

---

[27] These provisions may not be too strict with regard to unsecured debt however.

[28] See G. E. Pinches and K. A. Mingo, "The Role of Subordination and Industrial Bond Ratings," *Journal of Finance*, March 1975.

[29] For example, only some 40 percent of corporate bond issues during the postwar years have been secured bonds, compared with some 75 percent during the prewar years. See T. R. Atkinson, *Trends in Corporate Bond Quality* (New York: National Bureau of Economic Research, 1967), p. 67.

In some cases, the property may be convertible into some other use, or may be made more profitable by more efficient managers. Such property can have an intrinsic worth sufficient to meet the claims of secured creditors. But in bankruptcy cases involving truly valuable property, the courts have been extremely reluctant to allow secured creditors to exercise their lien and sell the property to meet their claims. Typically, reorganization proceedings are ordered, the end result of which is to liquidate existing claims by issuing new securities to the claimants. The trouble is that the more valuable the property, the more strenuously the junior claimants will fight to keep from being left out of the reorganized company.

Under the Supreme Court's "doctrine of absolute priority," each rank of securities must be compensated for the full amount of its claim before anything can be alloted to a junior claim. However, determination of the value of the assets of the bankrupt company, and of the manner in which the claims are to be satisfied, are subject to debate and interpretation.[30] Court proceedings can last for years. A classic example of the extremes to which debate can be carried is that of the Missouri Pacific Railroad. Trustees in bankruptcy were appointed in 1933, and reorganization was not achieved until 1956—23 years later. In the end, even if the senior creditors emerge without a loss of principal, they may well have lost a substantial amount of interest payments, and they may have been locked into their investment for an extended period of time, because the market value of even first-mortgage bonds usually is very depressed during reorganization proceedings.

Private Placements. About 25 percent of all long-term debt issued by U.S. corporations takes the form of so-called private placements rather than publicly issued bonds. The percentage of debt represented by private placements is considerably higher for industrial, as opposed to utility, companies, and higher still for companies with credit ratings lower than A. Since private placements are a rather specialized market in which investors are limited mainly to large life insurance companies and pension funds, most investment texts contain little, if any, discussion of them. But in view of their significant magnitude, this is an unfortunate oversight which we shall attempt to remedy here. It is particularly appropriate to discuss private placements in the context of protective provisions, since there generally are much more complex provisions in privately placed debt than in public issues.

Private placements are either made exclusively by a single lender such as a large life insurance company, or by a small group of institutional lenders wherein one of them takes the lead and the others participate. In general, a loan is deemed a private placement, and therefore

---

[30] For a discussion of reorganization procedures, see L. S. Forman, *Compositions, Bankruptcy, and Arrangements* (Philadelphia: Joint Committee on Continuing Legal Education, 1971).

exempt from SEC registration requirements, if the following characteristics are present:

1. The lenders have access to information equivalent to that found in
    an SEC registration statement, have the knowledge and experi-
    ence enabling them to evaluate the information and determine the
    risks, and have the financial capability of bearing the risks.
2. There is no general advertising of the issue prior to placement, and
    no widespread solicitation of unsophisticated lenders.
3. The lenders have no intention of reselling their participation to
    others, although they reserve the right to do so.

Companies may find private placements to be a better method of
debt financing than public offerings when one or more of the following
conditions are present:

1. If the borrower wishes to avoid the expense and time involved in
    an SEC registration, while minimizing investment banking ex-
    penses, or for competitive reasons desires that a great deal of con-
    fidentiality be maintained for a period of time, a private placement
    is clearly desirable.
2. If interest rates are fluctuating violently and the borrowing com-
    pany does not want to risk an adverse change in the market be-
    tween registration of a public issue and its ultimate sale, a private
    placement minimizes such risks because once the borrower and
    lender have "shaken hands," they stick with the rate negotiated.
3. If the funds to be raised are for a project which is to be completed
    over a long period of time rather than at once, a private placement
    can provide for an advance commitment by the lender, to be fol-
    lowed by a series of future takedowns of funds. This may be more
    desirable to the borrower than a single lump-sum borrowing in the
    public market at the outset of the project.
4. If the financing involves complex features, such as guarantees of
    other parties, these may be too difficult to explain in a prospectus
    prepared for public investors, many of whom are relatively un-
    sophisticated. Similarly, if the borrowing company is in an indus-
    try which is unfamiliar to public investors, or has less than an A
    credit rating, a private placement may be easier to accomplish
    than a public offering.
5. If the company is likely to have major changes in its operating or
    financial structure which will require periodic renegotiation of the
    terms of its debt, private financing is ideal because public bond
    indentures are extremely difficult to modify after issuance.

Unlike the holders of the typical publicly issued bonds, the holders
of privately placed notes, despite the recent development of a modest

secondary market in such notes, must consider themselves locked into their investments. Hence, it is imperative that they be in a position to review proposed actions by the borrower and to exercise a veto when they feel strongly that these actions will impair the credit. While private placements invariably differ in certain particulars, the following "negative covenants" are contained in most loan agreements.[31]

1. Working capital is prohibited from falling below a specified dollar amount or, alternatively, current assets are prohibited from falling below a specified percentage of current liabilities.[32]

2. Certain types of corporate outlays are defined as "restricted payments," and the aggregate of such payments is then limited to a specified percentage of cumulative net income of the borrower from a specified date. The obvious purpose of this provision is to require some portion of net income to be reinvested in the business, thus building up the equity base behind the debt obligation. Restricted payments typically include dividends on common and preferred stock; stock repurchases (net of new issues); discretionary payments to holders of subordinated debt; and loans to, or investments in, unconsolidated subsidiaries and affiliates.

3. A series of limitations is placed on the indebtedness of the borrower and its consolidated subsidiaries, and on liens securing such debt. The most common limitations are as follows:

   a. There is a general prohibition of liens against corporate assets, followed by an enumeration of exceptions to the general prohibition. The exceptions cover liens in existence at the time the private placement is negotiated, tax and similar legal priorities, and may provide for some amount of future purchase-money mortgages.

   b. There is a limitation of aggregate funded debt to either a specified dollar total or a specified percentage of net worth (usually defined to exclude intangibles). Funded debt under this limitation may be defined broadly to include off-balance sheet debt, or it may be defined to include only long-term notes and revolving bank credits, with off-balance sheet indebtedness limited by specific reference to those items.

   c. In addition to the limitation of aggregate consolidated funded debt, there usually is a separate limitation on debt incurred by consolidated subsidiaries to anyone other than the parent.[33]

---

[31] This section is based on E. D. Zinbarg, "The Private Placement Loan Agreement," *Financial Analysts Journal*, July/August 1975.

[32] Publicly issued bonds typically do not make failure to maintain a specified working capital level an act of default, but merely restrict a company's right to issue new debt or pay stock dividends.

[33] See Chapter 4, for a discussion of the complexities of parent-subsidiary relationships.

    d. Short-term notes payable are limited to a specified dollar total (or are limited via some ratio requirement), with a further requirement that the borrowers must "clean up" their short-term borrowings (or "clean down" to some low level) for, say, 60 consecutive days every 12 or 18 months.

4. Finally, a common provision limits the borrower's ability to sell or dispose of a significant part of the company's assets.

The Preferred Stock's Priority. While investors often have given too much weight to the collateral features of bond contracts, they often have paid too *little* heed to the nature of preferred stock contracts.[34] Preferred stock is classified legally as equity, but investors traditionally have looked upon preferreds as almost the same thing as bonds. The reasoning has been as follows.

The major legal difference between a bond and a preferred stock lies in the nature of the holder's claim. Bondholders get a legally enforceable claim while preferred stockholders do not. Legally, they get only a priority above common stockholders. Failure to pay bond interest is an act of bankruptcy; failure to pay a preferred stock dividend is not. But practically speaking, when a corporation is operating profitably, the claims of both bond and preferred stock owners usually will be met. And when a corporation is in serious trouble, it isn't too much comfort that you're a bondholder rather than a preferred stockholder; you're in trouble either way. This very practical observation has led many investors to believe that a preferred stock is, by its nature, just about as good as a bond.

The conclusion that preferred stocks are inherently as investment worthy as bonds is faulty, however. It omits consideration of the great number of corporations which are neither so consistently profitable that there is no question of omitting interest or preferred dividend payments, nor in such dreadfully poor condition that the bankruptcy courts loom ahead. Such corporations will make every possible effort to meet their bond obligations as they come due but often will not be nearly as diligent in paying preferred stock dividends. Numerous instances can be cited of companies whose earnings were high enough to pay preferred dividends but whose directors chose to keep the money in the business to build up future earning power. True, the inclusion of a cumulative dividend feature in most preferred stock issues acts as a deterrent to the promiscuous passing of dividends. (An unpaid dividend on a cumulative preferred stock is carried as an "ar-

---

[34] A recent upsurge of small investor buying of preferred stocks (many *without* sinking funds which, as noted in the next section, can be vital to sound investment in such securities) is described in "The New Preference for Preferred Stock," *Institutional Investor,* December 1975.

rearage" which must be cleared before common stock dividends can be paid.) Nevertheless, when management thinks it is to the company's long-term advantage to pass preferred dividends, it will do so. Unfortunately for the preferred stockholders, even if management is right about the long-term merits of its action, passing a dividend invariably depresses the market price of the preferred stock considerably.

Sinking Funds. Virtually all private placements, about 80 percent of publicly issued industrial bonds, about 20 percent of utility bonds, and some preferred stocks require an annual "sinking-fund" payment by the corporation in order gradually to retire the issue.[35] The specific bonds or preferred stock certificates to be retired at any given time may be selected at random and "called" at a specified price,[36] or they may be bought in the open market if a sufficient supply is available at below the call price. In rare cases nowadays, are the annual sinking-fund payments left in an escrow account (earning interest) for eventual retirement of the entire issue at once.

Sinking funds are disadvantageous to investors in one significant respect. After they have gone to all the trouble of evaluating and purchasing a security at what they consider to be an attractive rate of return, the investors may find the security snatched away from them by a sinking-fund call. And at that time interest rates may be considerably lower than when they purchased the issue, so that reinvestment in an equally attractive issue may not be possible. But there are several advantages of sinking funds to investors, and these are generally considered to outweigh the disadvantage:

1. Sinking funds for bonds, like amortization provisions in home mortgages, give the lender greater assurance that the principal amount of the debt will be repaid by the maturity date. Chances of the borrower being embarrassed are much greater when a huge principal balance suddenly comes due. If the original proceeds of the issue had been used to acquire plant and equipment, as is likely, sinking fund payments as the property depreciates help maintain a healthy balance between fixed assets and long-term liabilities.

2. With preferred stocks, a sinking fund compensates for the fact that such securities have no maturity dates as bonds do. This can be particularly important in a period of persistently rising interest rates

---

[35] Salomon .Brothers, *Anatomy of the Secondary Market in Corporate Bonds.* It should be noted that while private placement sinking funds retire most of the original issue by maturity, publicly issued bond sinking funds usually retire only 70–80 percent, leaving fairly large "balloon payments" due at maturity.

[36] The sinking-fund call price is usually par, or a very small premium above par, unlike an "optional" call price, which is usually par plus one or more years' coupon. Optional call privileges are strictly devices to protect the corporation—mostly to enable it to refinance its debt in a period of low interest rates. For this reason, the investor gets a sizable premium. The subject will be treated in greater detail in the next chapter.

and resulting declining prices of fixed-income investments. The owner of a preferred stock which has no sinking fund is doomed to a capital loss, whereas the owner of an issue which has a sinking fund knows that eventually the par value will be returned.[37]

3. If the company's earnings hold steady, the retirement of a portion of its bonds or preferred stock leaves the remaining investors better protected.

4. If the price of the bonds or preferreds falls below par, the company will use the sinking fund to buy up securities in the open market rather than call them at par, or par plus a premium. This provides some price support for the issue, although it by no means constitutes a floor. Of course, the other side of the coin must also be recognized, namely that call price tends to set a ceiling on market price. Since an investor who pays more than the call price will suffer a loss if his holding is called, he is reluctant to pay the high price.[38]

Analysis of Municipal Bonds

Since the focus of this text is on corporate securities, we will not dwell at length on the techniques employed in analyzing the bonds of states, municipalities, and other local subdivisions, all of which are classified under the broad heading, "municipals." Nevertheless, some discussion is in order in view of their important role in the securities markets.

There are two general types of municipal bonds—general obligations (also known as G.O.s or full-faith-and-credit bonds), and revenue bonds (or assessment bonds). The former are backed by the total taxing power of the issuer,[39] while the latter are backed only by specific revenues, usually those derived from the facilities which are constructed with the proceeds of the bonds, such as turnpikes, dormitories, and sewers. With municipal bonds, even more than with corporates, the bondholder's security lies in the *income* potential of the community or facility rather than in *asset* values. For courts certainly will not allow vital public facilities to be seized by creditors.

In the analysis of general obligations, three ratios are perhaps most widely used.[40] They are:

---

[37] This is not to suggest that the owner should necessarily sit and wait for the stock to be called. It may well pay to sell at a loss and reinvest in something else.

[38] The situation is somewhat different in the case of *convertibles*, as will be discussed in Chapter 11.

[39] The recent failure of New York City to honor some of its general obligations has cast serious doubt on the real investment significance of such backing. An excellent discussion of the subject by the president of Standard & Poor's, Brenton Harries, is contained in the December 22, 1975 issue of *The Money Manager*, beginning on page 6.

[40] A good source of statistical data is Moody's *Governments Manual*.

1. Principal amount of tax-dependent debt as a percent of the assessed valuation of taxable real estate. This measure is used because property taxes are the key revenue-raising devices of most local governments, and property values are a good indirect measure of the wealth and income of a community. In comparing the level of this ratio among different communities, allowance must be made for differences in assessment methods. For example, one community may assess property at, say, 70 percent of estimated market value, while another may assess at full value. Another complication stems from the existence of overlapping debt, which occurs when the same piece of property is taxed by different governmental units.

After making allowance for these analytical problems, a ratio of 8 percent of debt to property values for smaller governments, and 10 percent for larger ones, traditionally has been considered a practical maximum in order for their bonds to be rated high quality.

2. Debt per capita. Small cities with good credit ratings generally do not have more than $250–$350 principal amount of debt per resident. For larger cities, the figure may run to $500 or more before their bonds get accorded less than highest ratings.

3. Debt service (annual interest and debt retirement obligations[41]) as a percent of the community's budgeted operating expenses. If debt service begins to approach 20 percent of the budget, a clear warning signal usually can be inferred.

In addition to these ratios, municipal bond analysts also place heavy emphasis on the amount of debt maturing within five years (when it exceeds 25 percent of total debt, caution is advisable), on the prospective capital expenditures of the governmental unit, on the unit's ability to avoid persistent deficit financing, and, in recent years, on broader "sociological" trends.[42]

Revenue bonds are very much like the bonds of business corporations. Their quality depends largely on the "profitability" of the facilities whose revenues are pledged to support the bonds. Therefore, the key ratio in revenue bond analysis is earnings coverage. Since civic facilities are not profit-making operations in the business sense—fees are usually designed to meet only operating expenses and debt service, with a small addition for contingencies—coverage ratios are not expected to be as substantial as for corporate bonds. Ratios of 1½ to 2 times charges are common for good quality obligations.

---

[41] Most municipal bonds are issued in so-called serial maturity form. Under this procedure, a portion of the issue actually matures each year, so the holder knows precisely when the bonds will be retired as opposed to the holder of a sinking-fund bond. Different maturity dates of the serial issue usually carry different interest rates.

[42] See Chapter 13, "How Municipal Bonds Are Rated," in Hugh C. Sherwood, *How Corporate and Municipal Debt Is Rated* (New York: John Wiley & Sons, 1976).

SUGGESTED READINGS

Calvert, Gordon L.   "State and Municipal Obligations," *Financial Analyst's Handbook*, vol. I. Homewood, Ill.: Dow Jones-Irwin, Inc., 1975, chap. 12.

First Boston Corporation.   *Handbook of Securities of the United States Government.* New York, issued biennially.

Hempel, George H.   *The Postwar Quality of State and Local Debt.* New York: Columbia University Press, 1971.

Merrill Lynch, Pierce, Fenner & Smith, Inc. *The Bond Book.* New York, latest edition.

Phillips, Jackson.   "Analysis and Rating of Corporate Bonds," *Financial Analyst's Handbook*, vol. I. Homewood, Ill.: Dow Jones-Irwin, 1975, chap. 8.

————.   "Analysis and Rating of Municipal Bonds," *Financial Analyst's Handbook*, vol. I. Homewood, Ill.: Dow Jones-Irwin, Inc., 1975. Chap. 13.

Reilly, James F.   *Too Good for the Rich Alone.* Englewood Cliffs, N.J. Prentice-Hall, Inc., 1975.

Salomon Brothers.   *The Anatomy of the Secondary Market in Corporate Bonds.* New York, 1973 and Updates.

Securities Industry Association.   *Fundamentals of Municipal Bonds.* Washington, D.C., 1972.

Shapiro, Eli, and Wolf, Charles R.   *The Role of Private Placements in Corporate Finance.* Boston: Harvard Graduate School of Business Administration, 1972.

Sherwood, Hugh C.   *How Corporate and Municipal Debt Is Rated.* New York: John Wiley & Sons, 1976.

REVIEW QUESTIONS AND PROBLEMS

1. What basic differences exist between the approaches of the bond analyst and the common stock analyst? What similarities exist?
2. In what ways are agency ratings of bonds deficient?
3. Discuss various protective provisions of bonds in the context of the following statement: "It is more important for a bond investor to avoid trouble than to protect himself in the event of trouble."
4. What are some important differences between the analysis of corporate bonds and the analysis of municipal bonds?
5. Contrast fixed-charge coverage ratios and capital structure ratios as measures of corporate bond quality.
6. In what ways can balance sheet accounting practices distort capitalization ratios?
7. How can you determine whether a company is "cash poor"?

8.   In what way may the size and economic importance of a company influence its bond rating? Give illustrations.

9.   Under what circumstances might a company choose to issue bonds through a private placement rather than a public offering?

10. Compare and contrast bonds and preferred stocks as fixed-income investments.

RESEARCH PROJECTS

1.   Select a company which presently has relatively little long-term debt outstanding. Assume that the company now increases its total 10 percent by selling bonds. Make appropriate analyses to determine: (a) the interest rate it would currently have to offer on such debt; (b) the earnings which could be produced by investing the proceeds in new facilities (or, in the absence of expansion opportunities, the impact on earnings of retiring common stock through repurchase in the open market); and (c) the resulting change in earnings per share.

2.   Select two retailing companies and compare their policies regarding ownership versus leasing of stores. Indicate how the capital structure of each would change if rentals under long-term leases were appropriately capitalized.

3.   Do a comparative financial ratio analysis for a major U.S. city's bonds and the bonds of a much smaller, more rural town.

4.   Using an actual company to illustrate, show how it is possible for a company's bonds to be an acceptable risk but for its stock to be an unattractive investment (even aside from market price considerations).

5.   Compare the bond indenture provisions of three different companies in each of three different industries.

C.F.A. QUESTIONS

1.   *From Exam I, 1975*

The financial data and information shown pertains to Saginaw Corporation for 1974.

	(dollars millions)
Sales	$100.0
Cost of sales and operating expenses	81.0
Taxes on income—50% rate	7.6
Earnings available to common	7.2
Common dividends	1.8
Assets	$ 80.0
Current liabilities	5.0
Long-term debt:	
8%, First mortgage bonds, 2000	15.0
10%, Sinking-fund debentures, 1995	20.0
6%, Convertible debentures, 1984	10.0
Preferred stock, 8% ($25 par)	5.0
Common equity (10 million shares)	25.0

Both the mortgage bonds and the sinking-fund debentures are immediately callable at 108. A 2 percent sinking fund on debentures begins in 1980. First mortgage bonds and sinking-fund debentures currently sell to yield 9 percent to maturity.

Convertible debentures are convertible into common stock at $12.50.

a. Calculate the pretax earnings coverage for the preferred stock.
b. Cite and explain the advantages of holding either the First Mortgage Bonds or the Sinking-Fund Debentures given the information above.
c. Calculate fully diluted earnings per share for 1974.

2. *From Exam III, 1976*

Financial publications frequently carry articles similar to the one from *Forbes,* from which excerpts are quoted below:

> "The Supersolvent"—No longer is it a mark of a fuddy-duddy to be free of debt. There are lots of advantages to it. One is that you always have plenty of collateral to borrow against if you do get into a jam. Another is that if a business investment goes bad, you don't have to pay interest on your mistake.
>
> Debt-free, you don't have to worry about what happens if the prime rate goes to 12% again. You might even welcome it. You could lend out your own surplus cash at those rates.

The article then went on to list 92 companies which reported on their balance sheets no more than 5 percent of total capitalization in noncurrent debt.

Give examples, and explain, why so-called debt-free companies in the sense used by this article may actually have long-term debt or other long-term liabilities.

Chapter 10

Bonds and Preferred Stocks II: Selection among Qualifying Issues

> Every prudent act is founded on compromise.
> ————————————— *Edmund Burke*

The previous chapter described the methods by which a fixed-income investor can establish quality standards to use in compiling a list of "eligible" bonds or preferred stocks. We turn, now, to the *evaluation* (i.e., the attempt to determine *proper prices*) of issues on the list, so that they can be ranked in order of attractiveness for purchase or sale at any given time. The problem of whether to buy or sell fixed-income securities generally, as opposed to common stocks or other assets, is reserved for Parts III and IV.

Yield Mathematics

The first step to an understanding of bond evaluation is an understanding of yield mathematics. When a bond is priced at par, it is customary to refer to its coupon rate as its yield. At prices above or below par, however, yield and coupon rate are not synonymous.

Yield to Maturity. When a bond is selling at a premium (above par) or discount (below par), yield is sometimes defined as "current yield." This is simply the coupon rate expressed in dollars, divided by the price. Thus, an 8 percent coupon bond selling at 90 (i.e., $900 per $1,000 bond) has a current yield of 80/900, or 8.89 percent. This is the same type of calculation used in determining the yield on a common

415

stock—dividend divided by price—and is applicable to preferred stocks as well.

For most purposes, however, current yield is an inadequate measure of a bond's rate of return. It fails to reflect the fact that unless the issuer defaults, the holder will receive the par value at maturity. (In a subsequent section we discuss the possibility of the issue being "called" before maturity.) In addition to annual coupon payments, therefore, allowance must be made for the ultimate appreciation in value of bonds purchased at a discount or the ultimate depreciation of bonds purchased at a premium. Even if the individual investor has no intention of holding the bond to maturity, it ultimately will be sold to a party who does so intend. And more important than the personal predilections of investors is the need for a common denominator in expressing the yields on different bonds of varying maturity. Obviously, a discount of, say, $100 per $1,000 bond is worth more if the bond will mature in 5 years than if it will mature in 20 (assuming that it will, in fact, be paid off at maturity). For these reasons, the concept of "yield to maturity" is the accepted common denominator in the financial community.

A simple analogy should make the yield-to-maturity concept clear. Assume that you are examining an 8 percent coupon bond, with ten years remaining to maturity, selling at a price of 90. The yield to maturity in this situation is equivalent to the rate of interest, compounded semiannually, which a savings bank would have to guarantee to enable you to deposit $900 today, withdraw $40 every half year (bond interest usually is paid semiannually), and have $1,000 in your passbook ten years hence. In more technical terms, it is that discount rate which will cause the present values of (a) $1,000, ten years hence plus (b) a ten-year semiannual annuity of $40, to total $900.[1]

Those conversant with mathematics will realize that yield to maturity cannot be precisely derived algebraically. It would have to be found by trial and error. In practice, however, there are published

---

[1] The generalized formula for the present value (price) of a bond is given below. For simplicity of exposition, the formula assumes annual (rather than semiannual) compounding, and an even number of years to maturity (rather than years, months and days).

$$V = \left(\sum_{n=1}^{N} \frac{I_n}{(1+i)^n} \right) + \frac{P_N}{(1+i)^N}$$

where:

V = Present value.
I = Annual interest ($).
i = Required rate of interest (%).
P = Principal value at maturity.
N = Number of years to maturity.

tables which can be used to find the answer, or, lacking tables, an approximation formula is available which can be applied.

Yield Tables. Table 10–1 is excerpted from a book of bond value tables. It is a relatively simple matter to find one's way through such a

TABLE 10–1
Excerpt from Bond Value Table.   8%

Price	Years to Maturity 10	Years to Maturity 20	Price	Years to Maturity 10	Years to Maturity 20
90	9.58	9.09	100	8.00	8.00
91	9.41	8.98	101	7.85	7.90
92	9.24	8.86	102	7.71	7.80
93	9.08	8.75	103	7.57	7.70
94	8.92	8.64	104	7.43	7.61
95	8.76	8.53	105	7.29	7.51
96	8.60	8.42	106	7.15	7.42
97	8.45	8.31	107	7.01	7.33
98	8.30	8.21	108	6.88	7.24
99	8.15	8.10			

book, despite its forbidding appearance. In the upper right- or left-hand corner of each page a percentage figure appears—in our example 8 percent. This represents the coupon rate of the bond under study. Having turned to the appropriate page, move to the column which corresponds to the number of years (and months) remaining to maturity, as indicated by the column heading—ten years in our example. Then scan the price column to locate the price of the bond under consideration. The yield to maturity will be found at the intersection of the price row and the maturity column—9.58 percent in our example.[2]

Suppose, however, that the price of the bond is 90¼ (i.e., $902.50 per $1,000 bond), and that the available tables do not show small fractional prices. A simple interpolation can be performed to find the yield. Note that the table shows a yield of 9.58 percent at a price of 90, and 9.41 percent at a price of 91, a drop of 0.17 percent, or 17 "basis points" (each 0.01 percent yield is known as a basis point; 100 basis points equals 1 percent) for a $10 increase in the price of the bond. Therefore, a $2.50 price increase should cause a yield decline of about four basis points; which means that a price of 90¼ produces a yield of about 9.54 percent.

---

[2] While Table 10–1 shows yields in the body of the table, with price shown in the first and fourth columns, many such tables show prices in the body, with yield shown in the initial columns. The underlying principles of interpreting the tables are the same, however.

Yield Formula. When yield tables are not handy, an approximation formula can produce fairly satisfactory results. The formula is:

$$\frac{\text{Annual coupon interest} + (\text{Discount/Number years to maturity})}{(\text{Current price} + \text{Par value})/2}$$

or

$$\frac{\text{Annual coupon interest} - (\text{Premium/Number years to maturity})}{(\text{Current price} + \text{Par value})/2}$$

The reasoning behind this formula will be explained in a moment, but as applied to our example it would produce this result:

$$\frac{80 + 100/10}{(900 + 1,000)/2} = \frac{80 + 10}{950} = \frac{90}{950} = 9.47\%$$

Our answer would thus be 0.11 percent away from the correct yield. Now suppose that the same bond were selling for 108 instead of 90. Applying the formula, we would get:

$$\frac{80 - 80/10}{(1,080 + 1,000)/2} = \frac{80 - 8}{1,040} = \frac{72}{1,040} = 6.92\%$$

Turning back to Table 10–1, it will be noted that a price of 108 produces a yield of exactly 6.88 percent. Our estimate is off by only four basis points.

The same formula can be used in reverse. Instead of calculating the approximate yield based on a known purchase price, we can calculate the approximate purchase price which would produce a desired yield. Continuing the previous example, suppose that we want to find the price necessary to provide a yield to maturity of 9 percent. Since the coupon rate is 8 percent, we know that the bond must sell at a discount to produce 9 percent yield. Therefore, letting X = purchase price and $1,000 - X$ = discount, we have the following:

$$0.09 = \frac{80 + (1,000 - X)/10}{(X + 1,000)/2}$$

This reduces to:

$$0.09 = \frac{80 + 100 - .1X}{.5X + 500}$$

Cross-multiplying, we get:

$$0.09(.5X + 500) = 180 - .1X$$

or

$$.045X + 45 = 180 - .1X$$

Transposing, we have:

$$.145X = 135$$

thus

$$X = 135/.145$$

or

$$X = \$931 \text{ (Interpolating from the bond table produces a price of } \$935)$$

In the same way, if we wanted to find the price that produces a 7 percent yield, we know that a premium bond is involved. Let X = purchase price, $X - 1,000$ = premium. Therefore:

$$0.07 = \frac{80 - (X - 1,000)/10}{(X + 1,000)/2}$$

$$0.07 = \frac{80 - .1X + 100}{.5X + 500}$$

$$0.035X + 35 = 180 - .1X$$

$$0.135X = 145$$

$$X = \$1,074 \text{ (Interpolated price from bond table is } \$1,071)$$

Regarding the derivation of the formula, the numerator assumes that each year from the date of purchase the bondholder will receive: (a) $80 of coupon interest, plus (or minus) (b) a pro rata portion of the appreciation (or depreciation) attributable to the purchase at a discount (or premium) of a bond which will be paid off at par at maturity. Obviously, the appreciation or depreciation will not be *realized* until maturity, but an annual amortization of the amount makes good sense.

The denominator of the formula represents the average "true" investment during the period to maturity. On an amortized basis, a bond purchased at a discount or premium appreciates or depreciates in value each year. It would, therefore, be unrealistic to assume that the investor has a constant commitment throughout the life of the bond, equal to his purchase price. What he really has committed is the average of each year's amortized value. This average is approximated by the expression ½ (Purchase price + Par value). It is, in effect, the amortized value in the middle year of the bond's remaining lifetime.

Maturity and Risk. A comparison of the 10- and 20-year maturity columns of Table 10–1 brings out another very significant fact to bond investors. Note that a 10 point price rise from 90 to 100 is associated

with a 158 basis point yield decline (from 9.58 percent to 8 percent) for a 10-year maturity bond, but with only a 109 basis point yield decline for a 20-year bond. Similarly, a yield increase of 55 basis points (from 6.88 percent to 7.43 percent) produces a price decline of 4 points (from 108 to 104) on a 10-year bond; but a yield increase of 56 basis points (from 7.24 percent to 7.80 percent) drops price 6 points (from 108 to 102) on a 20-year bond. It is usually the case that fluctuations in the general level of interest rates cause long-term bonds to fluctuate more in price than shorter term bonds. When interest rates rise, long-term bonds fall more sharply in price than shorter term bonds; when interest rates fall, long terms rise faster in price. Reference to the yield approximation formula will demonstrate more clearly why this is so.

Let us assume the existence of three bonds of identical quality and identical coupon rate—say 6 percent. All are selling at par. The only difference among the bonds is maturity. Bond A has a 1-year maturity; Bond B has a 20-year maturity; and Bond C has a 40-year maturity. Let us next suppose that a rise in the general level of interest rates causes all three bonds to go to a 7 percent yield basis. To what price will each fall? The following calculations show the approximate answers (numbers at left are steps in calculation).

Bond A (1 year)

$$(1) \qquad\qquad 0.07 = \frac{60 + (1{,}000 - X)/1}{(X + 1{,}000)/2}$$

$$(2) \qquad\qquad 0.07 = \frac{60 + 1{,}000 - X}{.5X + 500}$$

$$(3) \qquad 0.035X + 35 = 1{,}060 - X$$

$$(4) \qquad\qquad 1.035X = 1{,}025$$

$$(5) \qquad\qquad X = 990$$

Bond B (20 years)

$$(1) \qquad\qquad 0.07 = \frac{60 + (1{,}000 - X)/20}{(X + 1{,}000)/2}$$

$$(2) \qquad\qquad 0.07 = \frac{60 + 50 - 0.05X}{.5X + 500}$$

$$(3) \qquad 0.035X + 35 = 110 - 0.05X$$

$$(4) \qquad\qquad 0.085X = 75$$

$$(5) \qquad\qquad X = 882$$

Bond C (40 years)

$$(1) \qquad 0.07 = \frac{60 + (1,000 - X)/40}{(X + 1,000)/2}$$

$$(2) \qquad 0.07 = \frac{60 + 25 - 0.025X}{.5X + 500}$$

$$(3) \qquad 0.035X + 35 = 85 - .025X$$

$$(4) \qquad 0.06X = 50$$

$$(5) \qquad X = 833$$

Thus, with the same 1 percent yield increase, the 1-year issue drops 1 percent in price ($10 per $1,000), the 20-year issue drops 11.8 percent and the 40-year issue drops 16.7 percent. The reason may be inferred directly from the formula. The additional 1 percent yield to maturity must be derived from the discount since, as will be seen in calculation step (1), every other value in the formula is identical. But as maturity increases, the discount is being amortized over an increasing number of years. Therefore, in order for the discount to produce an extra 1 percent *per annum*, it must be progressively larger in dollar amount as maturity increases.

Even if account is taken of the fact that *yields* on short-term securities typically fluctuate more violently than on long-term securities, it remains true that *price* typically fluctuates more on long-term issues. For example, suppose that the one-year security in our example rose in yield, not to 7 percent, but to 9 percent. Solving for price, we have:

$$0.09 = \frac{60 + (1,000 - X)/1}{(X + 1,000)/2}$$

$$0.09 = \frac{60 + 1,000 - X}{0.5X + 500}$$

$$0.045X + 45 = 1,060 - X$$

$$1.045X = 1,015$$

$$X = 971$$

A yield increase of three full percentage points from a 6 percent level causes the price of the 1-year issue to fall only 3 percent, compared with 12 percent and 17 percent price declines on 20- and 40-year issues, respectively, when yield rises 1 percent from a 6 percent level. Clearly, then, bond risk is in large part a function of maturity. Indeed, long maturity increases risk not only because of the interest rate factor but also because it increases the time available for unex-

pected occurrences, such as obsolescence of the borrower's product line, general economic dislocations, or severe depreciation in the value of the dollar.

The Coupon Factor. In the illustrations of the previous section, it was assumed that the coupon rates of the various issues were identical (6 percent), and that only the maturities were different. What if the maturities were the same but the *coupons* were different? Suppose, for example, that two different bonds of equal quality both have 25-year maturities and are priced to yield about 7.5 percent, but that one has a 4 percent coupon (selling at 550) and one has a 9 percent coupon (selling at 1,200).[3] What is likely to happen to the price of each bond if the general level of interest rates either rises sharply or falls sharply?

The answer is that the lowest coupon bond will have the greatest price change and the highest coupon bond will have the least, other factors remaining equal. For example, if the yield on the two bonds cited above rose from 7.5 percent to 9 percent, the 4 percent coupon bond would drop about 27 percent in price from 550 to 400, while the 9 percent coupon bond would drop about 17 percent from 1,200 to par (1,000). The reason for the greater volatility of the low coupon bond is that a large portion of its yield to maturity represents capital gain which will not be realized until a distant date, while the yield of the high coupon bond will be realized much earlier in the form of large semiannual interest payments. Therefore, to obtain a yield improvement, a larger proportionate increase in capital gain component (i.e., a larger proportionate price decline) is required from the low coupon bond than from the high coupon bond. Similarly, a *yield decline* is associated with a larger proportionate *price improvement* on the low coupon bond.[4]

Thus, we have seen that bond price responses to changes in yield levels tend to vary directly with maturity and inversely with coupon.[5] Another important consideration in trying to determine the appropriate price of a bond is its callability feature.

---

[3] In actuality, two bonds with very different coupons would not sell at the same yield to maturity because of the different impact of taxation. Coupon income is taxed differently from capital gains and losses arising from discounts and premiums. The tax factor is discussed later in more detail.

[4] Like all generalizations, this one has exceptions. In its December 3, 1975 *Comments on Values*, for example, Salomon Brothers noted that traditional buyers of deep-discount issues had little need for tax-preference income at the moment and such bonds, therefore, were not participating in the ongoing price rally to the extent that might normally have been expected.

[5] The mathematically-inclined reader should be aware of the concept of "duration," which is the weighted average life of all coupon, sinking-fund, and final principal payments, where the weighting factors are the present values of each payment. Bonds of equal duration respond identically to a given change in interest rates. The concept was first developed by F. R. Macaulay. His work has become a classic in the field, entitled

Taking Account of the Call Privilege.   Some bonds are fully callable at their issuer's option (usually with 30 days' notice). Others are not callable for any purpose other than sinking-fund requirements. Between these extremes, some bonds are callable for other than refunding purposes. That is, they cannot be called with the intent of replacing them with new bonds at lower yields, but they may be called to be retired or replaced with stock, or in a debt consolidation move, or because of a merger, or for some similar reason. Still other issues are nonrefundable for a specified number of years, but are refundable thereafter.

When a bond is callable for refunding purposes, the yield-to-maturity calculation may not be an appropriate measure of the issue's expected rate of return. For if there is a significant chance that interest rates will fall to a level which makes refunding attractive to the issuers, they may exercise their call privileges. If they do, the investors will be faced with the necessity of reinvesting their money— presumably at lower interest rates if they do not reduce quality. In addition to reinvesting at lower rates, they will incur the expense and bother of making a new search for an acceptable issue. An offset against this expense will be the "call premium" which the issuers are required to pay in order to exercise their call privileges. The end result of all these factors may be a realized yield that is substantially different from the originally calculated yield to maturity.

Bond investors have typically been unduly lax in taking call features into account when calculating yields.[6] Occasionally, reference will be made to the "yield to first call date." This calculation is usually made on high coupon bonds selling at a premium during a period of low interest rates. In terms of the yield formula described above, instead of amortizing the premium over the number of years remaining to maturity, the number of years to the earliest date at which the bonds may be called for refunding is used in the numerator. In the denominator, the call price is substituted for the par value. An analogous calculation may be made to reflect the possibility of sinking-fund calls, if the investor owns a large block of a given bond issue. For example, suppose that a bond issue has 20 years left to maturity when a major financial institution buys a large amount at a premium. If the bond has

---

Some Theoretical Problems Suggested by the Movements of Interest Rates, Bond Yields and Stock Prices in the United States Since 1856 (New York: National Bureau of Economic Research, 1938). Also see J. B. Yawitz, G. H. Hempel, and W. J. Marshall, "Is Average Maturity a Proxy for Risk?" *Journal of Portfolio Management*, Spring 1976. In this article, duration is defined as the period of time which elapses before a stream of payments generates one half of its present value.

[6] E. J. Elton and M. J. Gruber, "The Economic Value of the Call Option," *Journal of Finance*, September 1972.

a regular annual sinking-fund requirement, the actual "average life" of this institution's block is likely to be closer to 10 than to 20 years. Accordingly, in calculating yield the premium may be amortized over a shorter number of years.[7]

But this is a faulty method of taking the call feature into account when calculating the expected yield from a bond. For it gives no weight to the *probability* of call, nor, more important, does it take into account the yield on the resulting *reinvestment*. Moreover the yield to first call date is usually calculated only after interest rates already have fallen.

To illustrate with a simple example what an investor ought to do, suppose that a 20-year bond with a 9 percent coupon is being considered for purchase at par, and assume that the bond is refundable at any time at 109 (i.e., a 9 percent premium[8]). The first step should be to estimate the amount of interest rate decline which would persuade the issuer to call and refund. Bearing in mind that refunding costs him a premium and may involve him in substantial underwriting expenses on a new issue, suppose we decide that rates would have to fall 1.5 percentage points, to 7.5 percent, to make refunding attractive.[9] Also assume that if he refunded at that lower level of rates, the investor would reinvest for the balance of the period at that level—i.e., in 7.5 percent coupon issues—and would incur credit investigation and brokerage expenses of 1 percent.

Next, an estimate should be made of the probability that interest rates will, in fact, fall 1.5 percent sometime during the next 20 years. Suppose historical evidence suggests a 50 percent chance that they will and a 50 percent chance that they will not. Taking the midpoint of the 20-year period as the probable time to call in the case where call is assumed to occur, the following calculation can be made:

(1)   Final principal value of investment = $1,080
      (Note the $1,080 results from the 9 percent call premium minus the 1 percent reinvestment expense.)
(2)   Interest received for first 10 years = 9% × $1,000 = $90 per year

---

[7] Indeed, this may also be the best procedure for the individual buyer of even a single bond. Since there is an equal chance of his bond being called for redemption in any one of the 20 years, the "most probable" date of call is in 10 years. Note that this procedure should not be applied to discount bonds, since the issuing company is likely to exercise the sinking-fund requirement by purchasing bonds in the open market rather than by calling them and paying a premium.

[8] The fact that call premiums are so frequently equal to one years' coupon, regardless of maturity or level of rates at time of offering, is prima-facie evidence that the market is not doing much sharp-penciled calculation.

[9] Much smaller declines might be sufficient. See M. L. Leibowitz, *The Timing of Corporate Refundings* (New York: Salomon Brothers, April 1975).

(3)   Interest received for last 10 years = 7.5% × $1,080 = $81 per year
(4)   Discount rate equating $1,000 today with 10 years of income at $90 per year, 10 years at $81 per year, and a final value of $1,080 is approximately 8.70 percent (arrived at by a trial and error procedure).

Thus, there is a 50 percent chance of an 8.70 percent realized yield and a 50 percent chance that it will be 9 percent. The "probability weighted yield," therefore, is 8.85 percent. In a more sophisticated analysis, of course, the number of possibilities would not be limited to two in a 50–50 ratio.

Realized Compound Yield.   The concept of incorporating into a yield calculation the *reinvestment rate* on the principal of a called bond can be broadened to include consideration of the reinvestment rate on the semiannual coupon payments of a bond. This broadened concept has been emphasized by the investment banking firm of Salomon Brothers in its advice to institutional portfolio managers. The firm points out that most financial institutions do not utilize their entire stream of interest income for current outlays, but reinvest all or a portion of the income. Thus, if an investment is made in, say, 9 percent bonds, the long-run rate of return will be 9 percent only if the flow of income can be reinvested at 9 percent. Indeed, it is implicit in the mathematics of yield to maturity calculations on discount or premium bonds that the coupons will be reinvested at the rate indicated by the yield to maturity. For example, when a 9 percent coupon 25-year bond priced at 1,200 is said to have a 7.5 percent yield to maturity, it is implicit in the calculation that the coupons will be reinvested at 7.5 percent during the life of the bond (or, alternatively, that they will not be reinvested at all).

Recognizing this aspect of yield mathematics, Salomon Brothers has cited many cases of misleading conclusions which result when yield to maturity is used to compare bonds with different coupons. For example,[10] consider two 30-year bonds, one with 4 percent coupon and one with 8 percent, selling at prices which produce a 6.5 percent yield to maturity on each issue. If future reinvestment rates approximated 6.5 percent, an investor could view the two bonds as being equivalent in yield. But if future reinvestment rates were to fall to 4 percent, the aggregate rate of return on all dollars invested and reinvested during the life of the bonds would be 5.36 percent on the 4 percent coupon issue and 5.19 percent on the 8 percent issue, a 17 basis point advan-

---

[10] S. Homer and M. L. Leibowitz, *Inside the Yield Book: New Tools for Bond Market Strategy* (Englewood Cliffs, N.J.: Prentice-Hall, Inc., 1972), p. 178.

tage for the low coupon issue. On the other hand, if future reinvestment rates were to rise to 9 percent, the aggregate return would be 7.86 percent on the 4 percent coupon issue and 8 percent on the 8 percent issue, a 14 basis point advantage for the high coupon issue. Salomon Brothers refers to this aggregate return as *"realized compound yield."*

Thus, future changes in interest rates are important to bond investors for two reasons. First, they cause the prices of outstanding bonds to change, thus creating capital gain and loss opportunities and risks. Second, they cause the total return on bonds held to maturity to be different from the expected yield to maturity because of the impact of the reinvestment rate.

Tax Factors. In comparing the yield of a tax-exempt security with the yield of a fully taxable issue, allowance should be made for the investor's tax bracket. For example, if an individual in the 50 percent tax bracket buys a 5 percent coupon tax-exempt issue *at par,* the same after-tax return as a 10 percent coupon taxable bond *bought at par* is received. The formula for calculating "taxable equivalent yields" is: tax-exempt yield divided by 100 percent minus the tax rate. This is akin to the formula used to adjust preferred stock dividends for tax factors in calculating earnings coverage.

Stress is placed on purchase at par value in the preceding paragraph, because yield to maturity of a bond purchased at a discount or premium includes not only regular income but also a capital gain or loss component. Gains and losses are taxed differently from regular income. Suppose that the same 5 percent municipal bond is purchased by the same 50 percent bracket individual, but at a discount to yield 6 percent to maturity. As a crude rule of thumb,[11] the following calculation can be made:

	Pretax Yield (percent)	Tax Rate (percent)	After-Tax Yield (percent)
Coupon income	5.00	0	5.00
Capital gain	1.00	25*	0.75
Total	6.00		5.75

* The regular rate on one half the gain.

If a 5 percent coupon *taxable* bond were available at a discount to yield 9 percent to maturity, we can assume (again, very crudely) that 5 percent of the 9 percent total yield is taxed at regular rates, and 4

---

[11] More precise measures are discussed in M. L. Leibowitz, *Total After-Tax Bond Performance and Yield Measures* (New York: Salomon Brothers, 1974).

percent is taxed at capital gains rates. The calculation for the same individual would be:

	Pretax Yield (percent)	Tax Rate (percent)	After-Tax Yield (percent)
Coupon income	5.00	50	2.50
Capital gain	4.00	25	3.00
Total	9.00		5.50

Thus, one might have thought that a taxable bond must sell at twice the yield of a tax-exempt bond to equalize the after-tax returns to a 50 percent bracket investor. In this case, however, it is shown that the taxable bond's yield to maturity (9 percent) is nowhere near twice that of the tax-exempt issue (6 percent). Yet, when the differences between coupon and capital gains, and the related taxes, are considered, the taxable bond's net yield to the 50 percent bracket investor is only 0.25 percent lower than the tax-exempt issue.

Yield Changes

Having considered the *measurement* of bond yields and the mathematics of bond price changes, we turn next to the *economics* of yield changes over time. Bond investors have to concern themselves with three types of changes: (1) changes in the level of yields; (2) changes in the "yield curve"—which refers to the relationship among yields on short-maturity, intermediate-maturity, and long-maturity bonds; and (3) changes in "yield spreads"—which refers to the relationships among bonds of different quality, different coupon, different call features, or different tax status.

Yield Levels. Figure 10–1 portrays the movement of yields on corporate bonds of highest quality since 1900. Three features of the data stand out:

1. There was no overall trend in bond yields during this period, taken as a whole.
2. Although there was no overall trend, bond yields have moved in "long cycles." Thus they rose from 1900 to 1920, declined from 1920 to 1946, and climbed steadily back to the level of the 1920s from 1946 to 1965. Thereafter, they moved sharply higher, to levels not seen since the Civil War.
3. Superimposed on the long cycles have been cycles of shorter duration.

While it is not possible to specify with precision the causes of long and short cycles of interest rates, the most important factors can be

FIGURE 10–1

Yields of Prime Long Corporate Bonds Since 1900 (annual averages based on Durand basic 30-year yields)

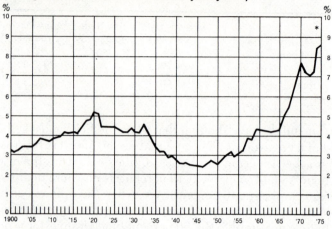

* 1974 monthly high.
Source: Salomon Brothers.

outlined briefly.[12] First, there has been increasing acceptance, in recent years, of a theory of interest rates which was propounded more than 40 years ago by Professor Irving Fisher.[13] This theory states that interest rates contain a premium for inflation expectations. That is, when borrowers and lenders expect a rising rate of inflation, lenders demand higher interest rates to compensate for the expected loss of purchasing power of their investments, and borrowers are willing to pay higher rates because they expect to be able to pay their debts with "cheaper money."

There is much debate over the proper way to measure inflation expectations.[14] Nevertheless, when the expected rate of inflation is deducted from observed, or "nominal," interest rates, the differences are referred to as "real" interest rates. Fluctuations in real interest rates are most often analyzed in terms of the relative strength of supply and demand for loanable funds. When lenders have more funds and are more anxious to lend than borrowers need or want to borrow, interest rates fall. When the tables are turned, interest rates rise.

---

[12] The eclectic theory outlined here is supported by much empirical research. See, for example, M. Feldstein and O. Eckstein, "The Fundamental Determinants of the Interest Rate," *Review of Economics and Statistics*, November 1970.

[13] Irving Fisher, *The Theory of Interest* (New York: Macmillan Co., 1930).

[14] *The Federal Reserve Bank of St. Louis Review* has had many articles on the subject.

The demand for funds has two major components: demands from private borrowers—businesses and consumers—and demands from government—federal, state, and local. The supply of funds likewise has two major components—individuals' savings and, at least in the shorter run, extension of credit by the commercial banking system.

Private demands for funds are largely a function of the actual and expected level and growth rate of economic activity. Government demands are determined by the socioeconomic philosophy of the electorate and its chosen representatives. As for the supply of funds, over the long run a remarkably steady percentage of disposable personal income has been saved by the private sector of the economy. But short-run cyclical changes in the savings-to-income ratio are common. Commercial bank credit extension also is cyclically volatile, hinging largely on Federal Reserve policy, which, in turn, is geared to the outlook for business activity and international capital flows.

Thus, the level and trend of economic activity is a common denominator on both the supply and demand sides of the interest rate equation.[15] Governmental fiscal philosophy is a second major factor, and international economic relationships a third. These subjects will be discussed at length in Chapter 12.

Yield Curves. Regardless of the specific causes of changes in interest rate levels, it is clear that if, at a given point in time, most fixed-income investors expect a substantial rise in rates, they will tend to avoid buying long-term bonds. This is because such bonds will fall substantially in price if the investors are correct and the level of rates does, in fact, rise. Investors will prefer to keep funds in shorter term securities, awaiting a more opportune time for switching into long terms. On the other hand, if investors expect a substantial decline in rates, long-term bonds will appear to be very attractive investments from two points of view: (1) they can provide a high level of income for many years; (2) they will rise in price if rates fall, and can be sold at a profit if a holder so chooses.

Thus, a general expectation of rising interest rates will cause lenders (bond investors) to prefer shorter maturity to longer maturity issues, and a general expectation of falling interest rates will lead to a greater relative desire for longer maturity than for shorter maturity

---

[15] These paragraphs illustrate the simultaneity of economic phenomena. The level of economic activity affects the levels of saving and investing; but the levels of saving and investing also affect the level of economic activity. Furthermore, investment affects income, which affects saving; and saving is the reverse side of consumption, which affects the incentive to invest. Thus savings and investment affect each other. Interest rates are said to be *caused* by the supply and demand for funds, yet changes in interest rates also *affect* supply and demand by affecting saving and capital investment. No wonder a famous physicist is said to have given up the study of economics because he considered it too difficult.

issues. On the borrowing side of the market, however, the relative desires tend to be the opposite. A general expectation of rising interest rates will encourage borrowers to rush their offerings of long-term bonds to market in order to minimize the rise in their cost of capital. An expectation of falling rates, on the other hand, will encourage them to delay their bond offerings and to do as much financing as possible in the short-term market.

In sum, expectations regarding future interest rate levels give rise to differing supply and demand pressures in the various maturity sectors of the bond market. These pressures are reflected in differences in the yield movements of bonds of different maturity. If borrowers prefer to sell long-term bonds at the very time lenders prefer to invest in shorter maturity issues, as is the case when interest rates are expected to rise, longer maturity issues will tend to carry higher yields than shorter maturity issues. The "term structure of interest rates," or "yield curve," will be "upward sloping." Likewise, if borrowers prefer to sell short-maturity issues at the time lenders prefer to invest in longs, as is the case when interest rates are expected to fall, longer maturity issues will tend to yield less than shorter maturity issues. The yield curve will be "downward sloping." This expectations theory of yield curve determination[16] is illustrated in Figure 10–2.

FIGURE 10–2
Yield Curve Determination

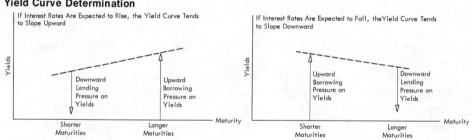

Yield Spreads. A yield curve expresses the relationship, at a point in time, between yield and one vital characteristic of bonds—maturity.

---

[16] It must be noted that many large institutional investors, such as life insurance companies, find themselves forced to buy long-term bonds even when they anticipate an extended rise of interest rates. Likewise, other institutional investors, such as commercial banks, have to keep most of their security investments in relatively liquid (short-maturity) form even if they expect rates to fall. Thus, there exists an element of "market segmentation" which makes the expectations theory of yield curve determination not completely satisfactory. The literature on the subject is vast. See, for example, J. C. Dodds and J. L. Ford, *Expectations, Uncertainty and the Term Structure of Interest Rates* (New York: Barnes and Noble, 1974); also, C. R. Nelson, *The Term Structure of Interest Rates* (New York: Basic Books, Inc., 1972).

Also of great interest to investors are the relationships between yield and other characteristics of bonds, such as quality, coupon, call features, and tax status. These relationships are referred to as yield "spreads." For example, one would naturally expect the yield of Baa bonds to be higher than the yield of Aaa bonds; lower quality gives rise to a "risk premium" in yield. But the magnitude of the difference—the yield spread between Baas and Aaas—is variable. One factor explaining yield spreads among issues of different quality, other characteristics held equal, is investors' expectations regarding economic prosperity. If a recession is expected, a Baa bond will appear to be riskier than that same bond at a time when continuous prosperity is expected. The riskier the bond appears to be, the higher will its yield tend to be relative to very high grade bonds, such as Aaas or U.S. government bonds.

Of course, yield spreads are not determined solely by investors' preferences. Borrowers' activities also are vital. Thus, a major new financing program by the U.S. Treasury may cause the spread between yields on corporate bonds and yields on Treasury bonds to narrow. The corporate yields will still be higher than the Treasury yields because of the quality difference, but the yield spread may be narrower than usual because the large increase in offerings of Treasury bonds causes their yields to be forced upward.

Changes in expectations also cause changes in the yield relationships among bonds of equal quality but carrying different call provisions. Thus, if interest rates are expected to fall, callable bonds become relatively less attractive to investors than bonds with nonrefunding features. Other things being equal, therefore, yields on callable bonds will be higher in relation to yields on nonrefundable bonds than would be the case if interest rates were expected to rise. Similarly, assume two bonds of equal quality, equal maturity, and similar call provisions, but with different coupons—for example, an 8 percent coupon Aa callable bond, selling at par, versus a 4 percent coupon Aa callable bond, selling at a deep discount. Which bond is more likely to be called if interest rates fall sharply? Obviously, the 8 percent coupon bond is more likely to be called. Therefore, if rates are expected to fall, the high coupon bond is less attractive relative to the low coupon, deep discount bond, than it would be if rates were not expected to fall. Accordingly, the yield spread between the two issues depends in large measure on the market's expectations regarding future interest rate levels.

Continuing with the previous example, the yield spread between the two issues is not solely a function of the market's expectations regarding future interest rate levels. As discussed earlier, there is a tax difference between the two bonds. The yield on the 8 percent bond,

selling at par, is taxed at regular income tax rates. But the yield on the 4 percent discount bond has two components, a regular income component and a capital gains component. Since these components are taxed differently, the yield relationship between the two issues will reflect in part the tax bracket of the investors in those issues. High-tax-bracket investors may prefer as much capital gain relative to coupon income as they can get, whereas nontaxable investors may be more indifferent regarding the source of the income. They may not be completely indifferent, however, since they may be dependent on coupon income to cover their day-to-day operating expenses, as is the case, for example, with many college endowment funds. The point to be made is that yield spreads change as investors with different tax considerations enter the market and drop out of the market.

Selecting among Qualifying Issues

At this point, let us assume that the investors have decided that neither the interest rate outlook nor any other portfolio considerations militate against the purchase of fixed-income securities and that they wish to buy some bonds. Let us also assume that they have a clear conception of the minimum bond quality which is acceptable to them and that they have compiled a list of issues meeting their quality standards. For example, such a list may include all long-term U.S. government and government agency bonds, all corporate and municipal bonds carrying agency ratings of "triple A" through A, and several lower rated bonds which pass various ratio tests established by the investors. They must now choose from among the issues on the list, and therefore a consideration of relative yields *finally* is in order.

Safety First. The word "finally" is stressed in the previous sentence because we believe strongly that for most investors the proper order of investigation is to consider the quality of a bond or preferred stock before considering its yield. For most investors, if quality is inadequate, yield is irrelevant. Too many bond buyers reverse the order, looking first at yield and then deciding whether sufficient extra yield is being offered to compensate for extra risk. While it is easily possible to exaggerate the need for high quality, the primary objective of bond and preferred stock investment is, after all, a *steady flow of income*. Consequently, a cavalier attitude toward quality can be disastrous.

It is true that *some* investors—notably very large financial institutions—have the resources to diversify sufficiently so that aggressive trade-offs can be made between below-average quality and above-average yield. What is most significant to them is the anticipated net yield after allowing for probable defaults. In this section, however,

we are concentrating on the more typical individual and moderate-size institutional investors, who are not in a position to diversify their risks broadly, who would be badly hurt by large-scale defaults, and for whom minimum quality standards should, therefore, have precedence over yield.[17]

If one's philosophy is "safety first," then selection even from a list of qualifying issues should not be dictated solely by the determination of which issue has the highest relative yield. While high yield is undoubtedly a plus factor, one should ask the question, even among qualifying issues: Is the yield *enough* higher relative to other qualifying issues to justify any extra credit risk that may be present? Even though one is prepared to assume the risks inherent in, say, "A" quality, if the yield on such issues at a particular time is not substantially higher than, say, Aa yields, one might be better off buying the higher quality issues.

Consider Table 10–2, where the average spreads among long-term bonds of different quality are shown for a long time period. Note that

TABLE 10–2
Yield Spreads on Long-Term Bonds of Different Quality

Year	U.S. Govern- ments	Utilities* New Aa	Utilities* New A	Municipals New Aaa	Municipals New Aa and A	New Aa Utilities versus U.S. Govern- ments	New A versus New Aa Utilities	New Aa–A versus New Aaa Municipals
1962	4.06%	4.36%	4.43%	3.00%	3.20%	0.30%	0.07%	0.20%
1963	4.08	4.33	4.37	3.00	3.20	0.25	0.04	0.20
1964	4.21	4.46	4.53	3.05	3.30	0.25	0.07	0.25
1965	4.26	4.57	4.65	3.10	3.25	0.31	0.08	0.15
1966	4.72	5.45	5.59	3.65	3.85	0.73	0.14	0.20
1967	4.94	5.87	6.02	3.75	3.90	0.93	0.15	0.15
1968	5.40	6.61	6.77	4.20	4.40	1.21	0.16	0.20
1969	6.28	7.75	7.99	5.45	5.65	1.47	0.24	0.20
1970	6.82	8.83	9.18	6.10	6.30	2.01	0.35	0.20
1971	6.12	7.74	7.99	5.25	5.40	1.62	0.25	0.15
1972	5.95	7.45	7.58	4.95	5.05	1.50	0.13	0.10
1973	7.00	7.74	7.93	5.00	5.10	0.74	0.19	0.10
1974	8.01	9.27	9.79	5.70	5.80	1.26	0.52	0.10
1975	8.25	9.51	10.33	6.29	6.42	1.26	0.82	0.13

* With deferred call features.
Source: Salomon Brothers, *An Analytical Record of Yields and Yield Spreads,* October 1971, and December 1975.

---

[17] Violations of the "safety first" doctrine have been particularly noticeable in many recent purchases of preferred stocks by unsophisticated individuals. Other departures from the "safety first" doctrine are discussed in S. White, "Reaping the Reward of 'Junk' Bonds," *Institutional Investor,* March 1976.

from 1962 to 1965, there was only a 0.25 percent yield advantage obtainable by purchasing Aa utility bonds in preference to U.S. government bonds, and almost no yield advantage obtainable from A versus Aa utilities. Clearly, this was a period when investors might have been well advised to sacrifice some yield and buy highest quality issues.[18] On the other hand, from 1969 to 1971, and again in 1974–75, when the *level* of interest rates soared to unprecedented heights, yield spreads widened dramatically, and investors who were willing to move down the quality spectrum (provided they did not violate their minimum quality standards) were well rewarded for doing so. Note also that in the tax-exempt ("municipals") market, quality spreads remained fairly constant throughout the period shown, with little incentive offered to investors for reducing the quality of their portfolios.

Active Bond Portfolio Management. Our discussion of the "safety first doctrine" should not be taken to imply that, once having determined which category of bonds represents the best trade-off between risk and reward, the investor should simply buy a representative sample of that category of bonds and put them in a vault until they mature. Not at all. There are many opportunities, within the confines of the safety first doctrine, to "swap" one bond for another—i.e., to sell bonds which appear to be overpriced and buy others which appear to be underpriced, and later even to reverse the transaction if a more normal relative pricing structure reappears. Indeed, one of the deans of bond portfolio management, Mr. Sidney Homer, has written:[19] "While most long-term bonds purchased should be appropriate for holding to maturity, none should be held to maturity. This is because the best bond values today will not be the best bond values next year and certainly will not continue to be the best bond values until maturity." Mr. Homer's statement is, perhaps, too extreme. Nevertheless, the basic idea warrants some extensive comment.

There are three basic types of active bond management, which may be referred to for convenience of exposition as (1) arbitrage, (2) security analysis, and (3) interest rate forecasting. Arbitrage refers to swapping among issues which are essentially identical in quality, maturity, and coupon, but whose yields differ because of temporary supply/demand conditions. Obviously, the lower yielding issues should be sold and the higher yielding issues purchased. Security analysis refers to swapping among issues which are *dissimilar* in some important characteristic, basing the swaps upon one's judgment as to what kind of yield spreads *should* exist among such issues in comparison with the *actual* yield spreads at a given moment of time. Finally, interest rate

---

[18] That is, to the extent that they bought any long-term bonds. In retrospect, of course, the subsequent rise in interest rate levels gave rise to huge discounts on bonds purchased in the early 1960s.

[19] S. Homer, *Total Money Management* (New York: Salomon Brothers, 1973), p. 11.

forecasting refers to the effort to predict major and minor interest rate cycles and to alter the maturity or coupon structure of one's portfolio in conformity with the forecast.

Arbitrage. Opportunities to improve yield by swapping among virtually identical issues arise fairly often. For example, it has been observed frequently that the yields (prices) on "seasoned" issues—i.e., issues which have been outstanding for some time—do not adjust quickly and completely to changes in interest rate levels on new issues. Thus, it would not be at all surprising to find in one's portfolio a 25-year bond with coupon of, say, 8.5 percent, selling at par when a new issue of the same quality and maturity appears on the market with an 8⅝ percent (8.625 percent) coupon. Clearly, it would be advantageous to sell the seasoned issue and buy the new issue.

Yield aberrations among comparable issues exist *within* the seasoned market as well as between the seasoned and new issue markets. For example, on December 19, 1974, a prominent bond management organization sold $1 million of Smith Kline Corp. 8.15 percent AA rated bonds, with 1984 maturity, at a price of 100⅛ (a yield to maturity of 8.13 percent). Simultaneously, they purchased $1 million of CIT Corp. 8.85 percent AA rated bonds, with 1982 maturity, at a price of 100 (a yield to maturity of 8.85 percent). In summarizing the transaction for its client, the organization said:

While maintaining the same quality (AA), the following was accomplished:

1. Yield to maturity increased 72 basis points.
2. Current yield increased 71 basis points.
3. Current income increased $7,000 per year ($88,500 instead of $81,500).
4. Cash was withdrawn of $1,250 (sales proceeds were $1,001,250 while purchase price was $1,000,000).
5. Maturity was shortened by two years (normally shorter maturities reduce rather than increase yield).

Security Analysis. Astute bond portfolio managers are always on the lookout for abnormal yield spreads among issues of different quality, different coupon, different maturity or different market sector. Purchases of the issues selling at abnormally high yields in relation to other issues will be rewarded if the spreads return to a more normal relationship. If the overall level of interest rates subsequently declines, the prices of the issues which had been trading at abnormally high relative yields should rise more steeply than the prices of the issues which were trading at abnormally low relative yields. If the overall level of interest rates rises, capital losses should be less on the abnormally high-yielding issues than on the abnormally low-yielding issues. If the overall level of rates hold steady, the prices of the relatively high yielders should rise in relation to other prices. A number of different illustrations should make the concept clear.

Consider, first, issues of different quality. Daniel Ahearn, a prominent bond manager, has cited the following example.[20] In July 1973, 7.5 percent coupon long-term U.S. Treasury bonds were selling at 95 to yield 8 percent, while Aa rated long-term 8.625 percent electric utility bonds (lower quality than Treasuries) were selling at 101.3 to yield 8.5 percent. This 50 basis point spread was abnormally narrow; it compared with average spreads during the prior six years of 100–200 basis points (see Table 10–2). A year later, overall interest rates had risen sharply. The Treasury bonds were trading at 90 to yield 8.5 percent while the utility bonds had declined to 72 for a yield of 12 percent, a 350 basis point spread. A price decline of 5 points on the Treasuries, which had been selling at abnormally high yields in relation to the utilities, was accompanied by a price decline of 29 points on the latter.

Next, consider issues of different coupon. As noted earlier, tax factors and better protection against refunding cause low-coupon issues to trade at significantly lower yields to maturity than high-coupon issues, even if the latter are of identical quality and maturity. The magnitude of the difference varies from time to time, but almost always within a defined range. For example, in most years since 1968 new issue (high-coupon) utility bonds have yielded at least 30 basis points more than deep discount (low-coupon) utility bonds, and typically about 50 basis points more. But in October of 1973, the spread was only 12 basis points. The discount bonds, therefore, were clearly the better buys at that time if one could assume a return to more normal spreads. And, indeed, not only did the spread subsequently widen, it reached 90 basis points in July 1974 and 127 basis points in May 1975. Similarly, new issue *industrial* bonds yielded only 20 basis points more than seasoned industrials early in 1973, but yielded 100 basis points more in the summer of 1974. So, while the low-coupon discount bonds were the better buys in 1973, high-coupon new issues were the better buys in 1974.

Turning to maturity considerations, the expectations theory of yield curve determination, cited earlier, suggests that investors can infer from the shape of the yield curve whether "the market" expects the general level of interest rates to rise or fall in the future. This knowledge can be useful if the investor is trying to pit his or her own interest rate forecasts against those of the market and to shorten or lengthen the maturity structure of the portfolio accordingly. But a study of yield curves is important for reasons beyond the measurement of expectations. Although a yield curve is represented as a fairly smooth, con-

---

[20] D. S. Ahearn, "The Strategic Role of Fixed Income Securities," *The Journal of Portfolio Management*, Spring 1975, p. 16.

tinuous curve, it is a *hypothetical* curve which attempts to portray the *average* relationship between yield and maturity. However, just as a line of regression has a scatter of individual observations above and below it, so too does a yield curve. Figure 10–3, for example, is a

FIGURE 10–3
Yields of Treasury Securities, July 31, 1975 (based on closing bid quotations)

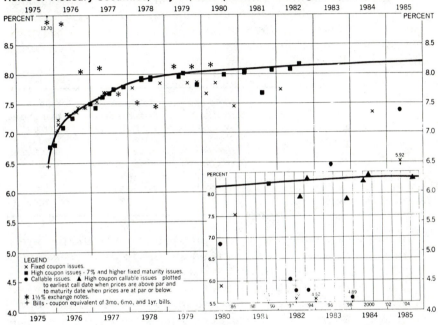

Note: The curve is fitted by eye. Market yields on coupon issues due in less than three months are excluded.
Source: *Treasury Bulletin*, August 1975.

recent yield curve of government securities. Note the number of individual issues above and below the curve—i.e., yielding more or less than their maturity suggests they should. These issues should be investigated further to see if their above-average or below-average yields can be explained by other factors. For example, an above-average yield might be attributable to poor marketability because the outstanding amount of the issue is fairly small; or the issue may have disadvantageous call features. If an above-average yield cannot be fully explained by such factors, the issue may represent a bargain relative to other available issues. A similar type of analysis should be applied to issues with below-average yields. For example, the low yields of several long-maturity government bonds can be explained by their preferential status for estate tax purposes; but the amount of yield

reduction for such preferential status may be unusually large for a specific issue at a given point in time, and this may represent a *selling* opportunity.

Another way to utilize yield curves is to compare them at different points in time when their *general* shape is similar, but their *specific* shape is not. For example, in its June 4, 1975 issue of *Comments on Values,* Salomon Brothers pointed out that the yield curve on municipal bonds had developed some unusual characteristics. The shape of the curve, they noted, is almost always upward sloping, and the typical spreads between longer maturity and shorter maturity issues during the previous five years had been as follows:

	Yield on 5-Year Issues versus Yield on 1-Year Issues (basis points)	Yield on 15-Year Issues versus Yield on 5-Year Issues (basis points)	Yield on 30-Year Issues versus Yield on 15-Year Issues (basis points)
Maximum yield spread	105	160	85
Minimum yield spread	50	105	45
Average yield spread	80	125	65

In comparison with these typical spreads, on June 1, 1975 the 5-year versus 1-year spread was 100 basis points, the 15-year versus 5-year spread was 120 basis points, and the 30-year versus 15-year spread was 40 basis points. The authors of the *Comments* concluded: "Thus, at present the municipal investor has an unusually large yield inducement to extend from 1 to 5 years, but at the same time a very small yield incentive to extend from 15 years to 30 years."

Our illustrations thus far have shown how yield spreads change among issues which are basically similar in type, but which differ in either quality, coupon, or maturity. Another fruitful place to search for bargains is across sectoral lines. For example, Martin Leibowitz has written:[21]

One of the classic situations arose in the Fall of 1973 when the yields on GNMA Pass-Throughs [bonds issued by the Government National Mortgage Association secured by portfolios of insured mortgages] rose to unprecedented levels relative to both corporate and other Government Agency issues. Delving behind the statistics, the underlying cause could easily be traced to a drying up of new investable funds among thrift institutions. These had been the primary buyers of the then relatively new Pass-Through instrument. Because of their apparent complexity relative to straight bonds, the Pass-Throughs had not yet established a wide following among pension fund managers. . . . However, at the extraordinarily attractive nominal yields that then

[21] In "Bond Portfolio Split into Three Parts Advised to Circumscribe Risks," *The Money Manager,* December 2, 1974.

prevailed (and the even more attractive probable cash flow yields), it was fairly likely that some major pension fund managers would soon overcome their initial problems with GNMA Pass-Through analysis and accounting. In fact, this is precisely what occurred. The bond manager who moved quickly and massively into Pass-Throughs reaped considerable rewards as the spread relative to corporates narrowed by over 75 basis points in the course of the next 6 months.

Cross-sectoral opportunities became very prevalent in the summer of 1975, when New York City found itself in a desperate financial bind and generated a bad market psychology for *all* municipal bonds. The June 30, 1975 *Schroder Report* commented:

Yield relationships between markets in the current recession are in many cases substantially different from past recessions. The question that arises therefore is whether the most recent experience represents a new "normal" or just an aberration. Unfortunately, thinking in such simple either-or terms frequently gets the analyst into trouble because the answer is usually more complicated than these two alternatives allow. What is needed is to fully understand what factors caused the historical relationships to arise and then to determine how these factors have changed and how yield spreads will be altered as a result. One of the most interesting of these changes is in the relationship between corporate and municipal bond rates. Past experience would suggest that in comfortable money times, the Bond Buyer Index (BBI) on municipals should decline to about 5% while high grade corporate rates should fall into the 7% to 8% area. At the present time—the bottom of the latest recession—the BBI is up around 7% while in the corporate market the highest grade industrials are returning about 8½%. The much smaller differential this time around primarily results from three factors, all on the municipal side. First, we have seen some State and local Government units in grave financial difficulty because of budget deficits and past financing improprieties. Second, banks have little need for tax-exempt income this time around. Finally, because of their own cash flow problems, fire and casualty companies have not been significant buyers of municipals.

An important message conveyed by this comment, in addition to the implication that the municipal market was a very good place to search for bargains at the time, is that it is not enough simply to calculate past yield spreads and look for current spreads which depart from past experience. The investor must try to determine *why* a spread is atypical. This emphasis on analysis brings us to a further illustration of opportunities to improve bond portfolio performance. In Chapter 9, it was stressed that traditional methods of evaluating bond quality, especially on the part of the rating agencies, give very heavy weight to historical coverage and related data as opposed to projected future data. This emphasis on the past causes the market to be slow to recognize when a company's credit-worthiness has improved or deteriorated. As a result, the bond yields of such companies tend to reflect the historical state of affairs and then, when the market suddenly recog-

nizes the new status, the yields (and prices) change abruptly.[22] Clearly, then, a careful analyst who is quicker than the market to recognize an improvement or deterioration in a bond's quality can make some very profitable shifts in a portfolio.

As interest in active bond management has grown in recent years, many investment firms have developed services which alert investors to the existence of abnormal yield spreads in one or another sector of the bond market. Among the more creative such services is that prepared under the direction of Paul Reilly, of Loeb, Rhoades & Co. This service classifies individual bond issues, of $100 million or more in outstanding amount, into categories having similar industry, coupon, maturity, and quality characteristics. For example, on February 20, 1976, the Loeb, Rhoades data base contained the following information:

Rating	Issuer	Coupon	Maturity	Yield on Bid Price
Aaa	General Motors	8.050%	4/ 1/85	7.93%
Aaa	Merck & Co.	7.875	6/15/85	7.87
Aaa	MMM Co.	8.200	4/ 1/85	7.89
Aaa	Sears, Roebuck	7.750	3/ 1/85	7.95

These bonds were all classified as "Aaa Industrial 8 percent Short Maturity." The average yield for this market "sector" on February 20, 1976, was therefore calculated to be 7.91 percent. The Loeb, Rhoades service contained data on 64 such sectors, each identified by an alphabetic code, as shown in Table 10–3. The table also gives representative yields for each sector during two weeks in early March 1976.

Yield spreads between each sector are calculated weekly, and a range of "normal spreads" is created on a moving average basis in such a manner that extreme values are excluded (extreme is defined as the outer 20 percent of the observations). When an observed spread for any sector lies outside the normal range thus calculated, it is identified as a possible buying or selling opportunity. This is shown in Table 10–4, which is a printout of yield spreads existing on March 12, 1976 among long-maturity bond sectors having coupons between 8 percent and 10 percent. The top number in each box is the current spread. The bottom two numbers are the normal spread range. Abnormal spreads are indicated by asterisks.

The service has another interesting way of spotting abnormal yield spreads, and of concurrently gaining an overview of the changing state of the bond market. The procedure begins by noting the current yield

---

[22] For evidence, see S. Katz, "The Price Adjustment Process of Bonds to Rating Reclassifications: A Test of Bond Market Efficiency," *Journal of Finance*, May 1974.

TABLE 10-3
Sector Yields

Sector Code	Sector Description	March 5, 1976	March 12, 1976	Sector Code	Sector Description	March 5, 1976	March 12, 1976
AA	Agency, 8–9%, Long	8.27	8.22	IM	Aa Industrial, 8–9%, Short	7.97	7.94
AB	Agency, (TVA 7.35%), Long	8.45	8.37	IN	Aa Industrial, 7–8%, Long	8.29	8.21
AC	Agency, 7%, Long	8.37	8.37	NA	Treasury, 7½%, Long	7.84	7.86
AD	Agency, 9%, Short	7.94	7.97	NB	Treasury, 7%, Long	7.79	7.80
AE	Agency, 7%, Short	7.80	7.77	NC	Treasury, 9%, Short	7.55	7.44
AF	Agency, World Bank, 8.375%, Int.	8.36	8.30	ND	Treasury, 8½%, Long	8.19	8.07
BA	Aaa Bank, 8%, Long	9.05	8.98	OA	Aaa Oil, 7–8%, Long	8.34	8.24
BB	Aaa Bank, 6–7%, Short	7.95	7.93	OB	Aaa Oil. 6–7%, Long	8.18	8.15
CA	Aaa Finance, 7½%, Long	8.60	8.51	OC	Aa+ Oil, 8%, Long	8.35	8.22
CB	Aaa Finance, 8–9%, Long	8.80	8.71	OD	Aa+ Oil, 5–6%, Long	7.94	8.02
CC	Aaa Finance, 4–5%, Short	8.08	8.05	OE	Aaa Oil, 4–5%, Short	7.42	7.50
CD	Aaa Finance, 7–8%, Long	8.79	8.76	OF	Aaa Oil, 9%, Long	8.79	8.70
CE	Aa Finance, 7%, Short	8.00	8.04	PA	Aaa SubTel, 8–9%, Long	8.65	8.56
CF	Aa Finance, 8–9%, Long	8.93	8.90	PB	Aaa SubTel, 7½%, Long	8.67	8.58
CG	Aa Finance, 8–9%, Short	8.26	8.27	PC	Aaa SubTel, 9–10%, Long	9.05	9.00
CH	Aa/A Finance, 9½%, Short	8.79	8.79	PD	Aaa SubTel, 6–7%, Long	8.55	8.52
GA	Aa/A Gas, 7–8%, Long	8.68	8.65	PE	Aaa SubTel, 8–9%, Short	7.93	7.90
GB	A Gas, 9–10%, Long	9.30	9.25	TA	Parent Tel, 7%, Long	8.35	8.28
GC	A Gas, 4–5%, Short	8.07	7.99	TB	Parent Tel, 4–5%, Long	8.20	8.09
GD	A Gas, 9⅝%, Long	9.18	9.18	TC	Parent Tel, 8–9%, Long	8.68	8.56
GE	A Gas, 7⅝%, Long	8.73	8.67	TD	Parent Tel, 7–8%, Short	7.80	7.75
GF	A Gas, 8½%, Long	8.75	8.75	UA	Aa Electric, 7½%, Short	8.65	8.56
GH	A Gas, 6¾%, Long	8.51	8.47	UB	Aa Electric, 7½%, Long	8.85	8.81
GI	A Gas, 9–10%, Long	9.20	9.26	UC	Aa Electric, 9–10%, Long	9.12	9.00
GJ	Baa/A Gas, 6⅝%, Long	8.95	8.78	UD	Aa Electric, 8–9%, Long	8.92	8.90
IA	A Industrial, 7–8%, Long	8.62	8.53	UE	BBB Electric, 9–10%, Long	9.66	9.62
IB	Aaa Industrial, 8%, Long	7.95	7.90	UF	Aa/A Electric, 10%, Short	8.26	8.23
IC	Aa Industrial, 5–6%, Long	7.76	7.72	UG	Aa Electric, 9½%, Short	8.35	8.30
ID	A Industrial, 9%, Long	9.06	9.03	UH	A Electric, 8–9%, Long	9.11	9.08
IE	A Industrial, 8%, Long	8.61	8.58				
IF	A Industrial, 6–7%, Long	8.34	8.34				
IG	Aa Industrial, 8–9%, Long	8.61	8.52				
IH	Aaa Industrial, 8–9%, Long	8.45	8.37				
IK	Aaa Industrial, 6–7%, Short	7.44	7.42				
IL	A Industrial, 8–9%, Short	8.20	8.18				

Source: Loeb, Rhoades & Co.

TABLE 10–4
Matrix of Sector Yield Spreads (long-maturity; 8–10 percent coupon; March 12, 1976)

OUT OF (Sell) →

Each cell shows the main spread (with `*` where outside established limits) followed by the pair of range values `(low, high)`.

INTO (Buy) ↓	BA	CF	ID	IE	IG	IH	ND	PA	PC	UD	UE	UH
Aaa Bank 8% — BA	—	8 (0, 15)	-4* (3, 15)	42 (39, 51)	46* (50, 64)	61* (62, 82)	91* (92, 112)	43 (38, 58)	-1* (1, 16)	8 (5, 20)	-63* (-129, -79)	-9 (-53, -3)
AA Finance 8½% — CF	-8 (-15, 0)	—	-13* (-8, 12)	34 (29, 44)	38* (43, 57)	53* (57, 72)	83 (82, 107)	35 (33, 49)	-10* (-6, 9)	0 (-5, 15)	-72* (-136, -86)	-18 (-56, -16)
A Industrial 9% — ID	4* (-15, -3)	13* (-12, 8)	—	46* (25, 45)	50 (40, 55)	66 (55, 70)	95 (80, 105)	47 (26, 51)	3 (-8, 7)	13 (-12, 18)	-59* (-138, -88)	-5* (-67, -7)
A Industrial 8% — IE	-42 (-51, -39)	-34 (-44, -29)	-46* (-45, -25)	—	4 (3, 23)	20 (15, 40)	49 (45, 70)	1 (-6, 14)	-43 (-46, -26)	-34 (-42, -22)	-105* (-173, -123)	-51 (-98, -48)
AA Industrial 8½% — IG	-46* (-64, -50)	-38* (-57, -43)	-50 (-55, -40)	-4 (-23, -3)	—	16	45 (37, 52)	-3 (-19, 1)	-47 (-54, -42)	-38 (-55, -35)	-109* (-191, -131)	-55* (-110, -60)
Aaa Industrial 8½% — IH	-61* (-82, -62)	-53* (-72, -57)	-66 (-70, -55)	-20 (-40, -15)	-16	—	30 (20, 40)	-19 (-34, -14)	-63 (-69, -57)	-53 (-70, -50)	-125* (-206, -146)	-71 (-130, -70)
Treasury 8½% — ND	-91* (-112, -92)	-83 (-107, -82)	-95 (-105, -80)	-49 (-70, -45)	-45 (-52, -37)	-30 (-40, -20)	—	-48 (-66, -41)	-93 (-103, -83)	-83 (-110, -70)	-154* (-236, -176)	-100 (-160, -100)
Aaa SubTel 8½% — PA	-43 (-58, -38)	-35 (-49, -33)	-47 (-51, -26)	-1 (-14, 6)	3 (-1, 19)	19 (14, 34)	48 (41, 66)	—	-44 (-47, -32)	-35 (-46, -26)	-106* (-172, -132)	-52 (-101, -51)
Aaa SubTel 9½% — PC	1* (-16, -1)	10* (-9, 6)	-3 (-7, 8)	43 (26, 46)	47 (42, 54)	63 (57, 69)	93 (83, 103)	44 (32, 47)	—	-10 (-14, 7)	62* (93, 133)	8* (57, 117)
Aa Electric 8½% — UD	-8 (-20, -5)	0 (-15, 5)	-13 (-18, 12)	34 (22, 42)	38 (35, 55)	53 (50, 70)	83 (70, 110)	35 (26, 46)	10 (-7, 14)	—	72* (86, 146)	18 (16, 66)
ESB Electric 9½% — UE	63* (79, 129)	72* (86, 136)	59* (88, 138)	105* (123, 173)	109* (131, 191)	125* (146, 206)	154* (176, 236)	106* (132, 172)	62* (93, 133)	72* (86, 146)	—	54 (51, 101)
A Electric 8½% — UH	9 (3, 53)	18 (16, 56)	5* (7, 67)	51 (48, 98)	55* (60, 110)	71 (70, 130)	100 (100, 160)	52 (51, 101)	-8* (-117, -57)	18 (16, 66)	-54 (-101, -51)	—

* Indicates spread is outside established limits.
Source: Loeb, Rhoades & Co.

on U.S. Treasury securities. Next, the normal spreads between Treasuries and each other sector are added to the current Treasury yield. This gives an "expected sector yield." The ratio of the Treasury yield to the expected sector yield is defined as "expected sector performance." "*Actual* sector performance" is then compared graphically with expected performance, as illustrated in Figure 10–4 for ten differ-

FIGURE 10–4

Comparison of Expected and Actual Yield Relationships, Selected Sectors

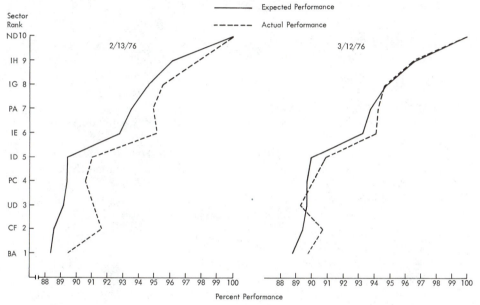

Source: Loeb, Rhoades & Co.

ent long-maturity market sectors on two different dates. Note the large number of abnormal relationships existing on February 13, 1976, followed by a return to more normal relationships by March 12, 1976. (The sectors are aligned on the graph according to a ranking from lowest to highest "expected performance.")

Interest Rate Forecasting. Just as bond investors can improve their performance by perceiving changing quality more quickly than other investors, they can further improve performance by perceiving the development of new trends in the movement of interest rates. As indicated in the section on yield mathematics, a prediction of rising interest rates should logically lead one to emphasize shorter maturities and higher coupons, thus minimizing downward price volatility, while a prediction of falling interest rates should lead one toward longer maturities and low-coupon deep-discount, or noncallable issues, thus maximizing upward price volatility.

In Chapter 12, we consider many techniques utilized to make economic forecasts, including the forecasting of interest rates. However, it should be understood that while the rewards of acting on accurate forecasts can be great, the penalties of acting on inaccurate forecasts can be equally great. In laymen's language, those who "bet the bank" on the basis of a forecast should be prepared to accept the consequences if the forecast is wrong.

SUGGESTED READINGS

Ahearn, Daniel S. "The Strategic Role of Fixed Income Securities." *The Journal of Portfolio Management*, Spring 1975.

Darst, David. *The Complete Bond Book*. New York: McGraw-Hill Book Co., 1975.

Fiske, Heidi S. A series of four articles on professional bond management. *Institutional Investor*, August 1973.

Homer, Sidney. *Total Money Management*. New York: Salomon Brothers, 1973.

Homer, Sidney, and Leibowitz, Martin L. *Inside the Yield Book: New Tools for Bond Market Strategy*. Englewood Cliffs, N.J.: Prentice-Hall, Inc., 1972.

Kaufman, Henry. *The Anatomy of the Secondary Market in Corporate Bonds*. New York: Salomon Brothers, 1973 and Updates.

Leibowitz, Martin L. *Total After-Tax Bond Performance and Yield Measures*. New York: Salomon Brothers, 1974.

Nelson, Charles R. *The Term Structure of Interest Rates*. New York: Basic Books, Inc., 1972.

Spence, Bruce et. al. *Standard Securities Calculation Methods*. New York: Securities Industry Association, 1973.

Williamson, J. Peter. *Investments: New Analytic Techniques*. New York: Praeger Publishers, 1970, chap. VIII.

REVIEW QUESTIONS AND PROBLEMS

1. What is meant by "yield to maturity"?
2. Explain the derivation of the formula for approximating yield to maturity.
3. Under what circumstances may the yield-to-maturity figure be misleading?
4. In appraising the investment attractiveness of two bonds, what should one study in addition to their relative yields at the time of the appraisal?
5. Distinguish between "real" and "nominal" interest rates.
6. How is a "yield curve" constructed?
7. Why does the shape of the yield curve change from time to time?
8. Why do "yield spreads" among different types of bonds change from time to time?

9. What is the relationship between coupon and maturity to price volatility?

10. How can capital gains-oriented investors trade in bonds to achieve their objectives?

RESEARCH PROJECTS

1. Prepare a paper which demonstrates the circumstances under which the approximation formula for calculating yield to maturity does not produce very accurate results.

2. Assume that you are an investor considering the purchase of (a) a newly issued bond which is callable at any time at a premium equal to one year's interest, or (b) a newly issued bond which is noncallable for refunding purposes. Given current interest rate levels and your opinions regarding future changes in interest rates, determine how much yield sacrifice you would be prepared to make to purchase the noncallable bond.

3. Prepare a review of the literature on "real" versus "nominal" interest rates.

4. Contrast the yield curves on U.S. government versus high-grade municipal securities at the present time. What interest rate forecasts, if any, seem implicit in these yield curves?

5. Examine current and historical yield spreads among various categories of bonds. Do any issues seem particularly "out of line" at present?

C.F.A. QUESTIONS

1. *From Exam II, 1975*

In *Inside the Yield Book*, Homer and Leibowitz make the statement "For most long-term bonds, the interest-on-interest is a surprisingly important part of the total compounded return to the bondholder: typically over half." The following three available corporate bonds are being considered for purchase:

> 8% noncallable 20-year bond priced at 100.
> 5% noncallable 20-year bond with 17 years remaining to maturity, priced at 72⅜.
> 9½% noncallable 20-year bond with 19 years remaining to maturity, priced at 114½.
> All three issues have a yield to maturity of approximately 8%.

Assume that the bond selected will be held to maturity.

a. Assume that interest is to be reinvested in a growing tax-free pension account.
   1. Which security would be most attractive if it is presumed that interest rates will decline steadily for the next two decades to a level of approximately 4 percent? Explain and justify.
   2. Which security would be most attractive if interest rates were to increase steadily for the next two decades to a level of approximately 10 percent? Explain and justify.
b. As the fiduciary of a college endowment fund that must distribute all income (tax-free), which security would you select? Explain and justify.

2. *From Exam I, 1976*

a. Given the data on U.S. Treasury Securities shown, construct a yield curve.

b. Describe what this yield curve indicates as to investors' and borrowers' expectations about the future course of interest rates.

c. On the basis of your answer to (*b*), state how you expect that investors and borrowers will react.

Issue	Yield to Maturity
91-day bills	4.80%*
182-day bills	5.10*
365-day bills	5.50*
6¼% 2/15/78	6.35
7⅞% 5/15/79	7.00
6⅞% 5/15/80	7.15
7⅜% 2/15/81	7.40
8% 5/15/82	7.70
7⅞% 11/15/82	7.70
8¼% 5/15/05-00	8.00

*Approximate bond equivalent yield.

3. *From Exam III, 1974*

As senior investment officer for the Street Insurance Company, you have been asked by the president to justify the increased turnover rate over the past year in the debt portfolio. You have been given examples of transactions which were executed by your staff as shown.

Month		Rating	Issue	Price	Yield
January	Sold:	Aaa	Standard Oil of California 7% due 4/1/96	91¼	7.83%
	Bought:	—	U.S. Treasury Bonds 7% due 5/15/98	92⅛	7.72
June	Sold:	—	U.S. Treasury Bonds 7% due 5/15/98	97	7.26
	Bought:	Aaa	Standard Oil of California 7% due 4/1/96	93⅞	7.57
July	Sold:	Aaa/AA	Pacific Telephone & Telegraph 7⅝% due 6/1/09	100	7.625
	Bought:	Aa/AA	Illinois Power 7⅝% due 6/1/03	99¾	7.65
October	Sold:	Aa/AA	Illinois Power 7⅝% due 6/1/03	99	7.71
	Bought:	Aaa/AA	Pacific Telephone & Telegraph 7⅝% due 6/1/09	98¾	7.73
March	Sold:	Aaa	General Electric 7½% due 3/1/96*	104⅞	7.07
	Bought:	Aaa	Short-term investment yielding an average of 8.25%		

*At the end of September the price of the General Electric, 7½ percent due 3/1/96 was 97, yielding 7.78 percent.

a. Describe the bond portfolio management methods illustrated by the transactions above.

b. Discuss the desirability of the results obtained.

Chapter 11

Convertibles, Options, and Special Situations

> One cannot eat one's cake and have it too.
> ——————————————— *T. H. Huxley*

The investment counterpart of Huxley's famous expression is that substantial opportunities for capital gains can be achieved only at the risk of substantial losses. In this chapter, we shall discuss some investment media which are used in an attempt to refute the notion that large gains involve large risks of loss. We also shall discuss some investment vehicles which are quite the opposite in nature—"go for broke" investments, in which the investors accept the possibility of losing 100 percent of the principal in exchange for the chance of multiplying the principal severalfold.

CONVERTIBLE SECURITIES

The term "convertible security" usually implies a preferred stock or a debenture which may be exchanged for common stock at the owner's discretion on specified terms.[1]

Many investors see in convertible securities "the best of all possible worlds." As debentures or preferreds, they offer stable income as opposed to the variable income of common stocks. This stable income appears to make them relatively less vulnerable to price decline dur-

---

[1] A bond or preferred stock with warrants attached is not a convertible in this sense because the exercise of the warrants does not extinguish the issues to which they were attached. Nevertheless, much of the following discussion on analysis of convertibles applies implicitly to issues bearing warrants, where the warrants have not been detached. Detached warrants will be considered in a subsequent section.

ing a stock market downturn. At the same time, the conversion privilege appears to offer most of the prospects for capital gain which are offered by common stocks.

Why They Are Issued.   Prior to World War II, the convertible feature was used to make offerings of senior securities more attractive than they would be as "straight" (i.e., nonconvertible) issues. In other words, the issuing corporation wanted to float debt or preferred securities, but its credit standing was not the highest and it had to add a "sweetener" in order to sell the issue at a reasonable interest or dividend rate. Since World War II, however, convertible securities have been issued by companies of the highest credit standing as well as by companies with lesser credit ratings. For these companies, convertible securities are primarily a tool for acquiring equity capital rather than senior capital.

There are several reasons why corporations may issue convertible securities rather than sell common stock directly. Since this is not a text in corporation finance, it is not our intention to present an exhaustive list of these reasons. Instead, we shall concentrate on what appears to be the typical situation. An understanding of the issuer's principal motive sheds light on the analysis of convertibles from the investor's point of view.

Suppose that Company X is earning $50 million a year and has 10 million shares of common stock outstanding. Thus it is earning $5 per share. Suppose further that the stock is selling at 15 times earnings, or $75 a share. The market value of the company's common stock, therefore, is $750 million.

At this point, the management decides to expand productive capacity by building a major new facility which will cost $75 million. This $75 million, moreover, will have to be raised externally. That is, retained cash flow is adequate to replace obsolete existing facilities but is not deemed adequate to expand capacity. Furthermore, it is management's opinion that the company's capitalization is already top heavy with debt and preferred stock and that the $75 million of new capital should be in the form of common stock.

The problems in this situation are these. A $75 million common stock offering represents 10 percent of the company's total common stock market value. An offering of such magnitude could not possibly be put across at $75 per share, the present price of the stock. Let us say the stock would have to be offered at $70 (net to the company). Thus, the company would have to sell almost 1,100,000 shares, raising outstanding stock to 11.1 million shares. But even after the company has raised the money by selling its stock at a discount from the going price, it will take a long time—say a year or more—before the new facility is constructed, equipped, and running efficiently. In the meantime, per share earnings will have declined from $5 to about $4.50—the same

$50 million of earnings divided by the new number of shares, 11.1 million. (Actually this is probably an overstatement, since the overhead of a partly completed plant would tend to reduce profits additionally; but there is no need to complicate the example.) Assuming the price-earnings ratio remains at 15, the market price of the shares will fall to about $68. Under these circumstances, the original stockholders may well be annoyed at management's "dilution" of their equity.

A convertible issue may be a convenient alternative for management in this example. Suppose that the company sold $75 million of 5 percent subordinated debentures,[2] convertible "at 75." In other words, each $1,000 bond could be converted by the holder into 13$\frac{1}{3}$ shares of the company's common stock.[3] Interest payments on the debenture would amount to 5 percent of $75 million annually, or $3.75 million. After tax, this would come to about $2 million, cutting net income to $48 million before the new facility was contributing to profits (again assuming no further reduction due to uncovered new overhead). But there still would be only 10 million shares of common outstanding, so earnings would fall to only $4.80 instead of $4.50.

After the new facility comes into operation, earnings and dividends should rise, and the market price of the stock should do likewise. When dividends on 13$\frac{1}{3}$ shares exceed $50 annually (the interest per $1,000 bond), original purchasers of the debenture will be encouraged to convert. But they may prefer to stay with their bonds, feeling that the greater safety is worth a somewhat lower income as long as the value of the bonds is rising in line with the price of the stock (a point which will be discussed at greater length below). In this event, management can "call" the bonds at a price which will have been specified in the bond indenture, say 105.

If the market value of the company's stock at the time of call is $80

---

[2] Convertible debentures usually are subordinated to other debt of the corporation.

[3] The conversion terms may be expressed as a ratio (i.e., 13$\frac{1}{3}$ shares per $1,000 of face value) or as a price (i.e., convertible at 75). Occasionally the investor may have to put up additional cash when converting (for example, various American Telephone & Telegraph issues).

The conversion price may be set at, or higher than, the going price of the stock at the time of issue. The investor should be sure that the issue has an "antidilution" clause which proportionately lowers the conversion price if a stock split or stock dividend is subsequently declared. (This and other types of antidilution clauses are described at length in S. A. Kaplan, "Piercing the Corporate Boilerplate: Anti-Dilution Clauses in Convertible Securities," *University of Chicago Law Review*, Autumn 1965.)

Conversion may be permitted immediately, or not until some stated period of time has elapsed. Also, there may be a cutoff date after which the conversion privilege expires. Or there may be a series of dates on which the conversion price gradually increases (i.e., fewer shares can be obtained by converting after each date passes). Managements try to tailor the terms of the issue in line with their expectations of future conditions. See Martin L. Leibowitz, "Analysis of Convertible Bonds," *Financial Analyst's Handbook*, vol. I (Homewood, Ill.: Dow Jones-Irwin, Inc., 1975), chap. 10.

or higher, the value of the shares which can be obtained on conversion ($13\frac{1}{3} \times \$80 = \$1,067$) will be significantly higher than the call price ($1,050). This being the case, the bondholders will convert, albeit involuntarily.[4] But whether conversion takes place voluntarily or involuntarily, management will have achieved its goal of financing the new facility with common stock. And the stock will, in effect, have been sold at 75—a better price than could have been obtained on a direct offering at the outset. Furthermore, the original stockholders are likely to have been much more satisfied by the introduction of new stock *after* the company had built up its earning power.

There are a few other important reasons why corporations sell convertible securities, two of which may be briefly noted at this point:

1. Many institutional investors, such as banks and life insurance companies, either are prohibited legally from buying common stock or are severely restricted in the amounts which they may buy. However, they have greater leeway in buying convertible securities. Commercial banks cannot buy preferreds, straight or convertible, but can buy convertible bonds of reasonably high quality if their yields approximate those on nonconvertibles of similar quality. Life insurance companies can buy either convertible preferreds or convertible bonds of good quality.

2. Convertible preferred stocks have become an important medium for financing corporate mergers.[5] For example, Company A wants to acquire Company B by purchasing B's outstanding stock. If stockholders of B take cash or notes for their stock, they incur an immediate capital gains tax liability, assuming they receive an amount in excess of their original investment. But if they exchange their stock for Company A's common or preferred stock, the transaction is regarded as a tax-free exchange of assets. Only when the newly acquired shares ultimately are sold is any capital gains tax payable, again assuming that the proceeds of the sale exceed the original cost of the Company B shares.

This being the case, Company A can make a very tempting offer to Company B's stockholders. Company A can offer convertible preferred stock in exchange for shares of B. If the dividend rate on the convertible is set at least as high as the rate on B's common, the selling stockholders will have a more *secure* income than they had formerly. And if the conversion price is close to the current market price of A's shares, they also will be able to participate in the future growth of the merged

---

[4] The main reason for inserting a "sliding scale" conversion price—i.e., one which rises over time—is to encourage *voluntary* conversions.

[5] See G. E. Pinches "Financing with Convertible Preferred Stock," *Journal of Finance*, March 1970; also "Understanding Convertible Securities," (New York: New York Stock Exchange, latest edition).

company via the conversion privilege. This attractive package may encourage B's holders to ratify the merger, and may enable A to consummate the merger with a minimum dilution of its own equity, since on a straight common for common exchange it might have had to offer a good deal more stock than it is offering via conversion.

Analytical Procedures. While it would appear that convertibles are an ideal investment medium—providing stable income, capital gains potential, and resistance to stock market declines—the case is not so certain. In the first place, analysis of the investment merits of convertibles is quite complex. Since the issuer has to consider a large number of factors in deciding what terms to place on the issue— coupon rate, conversion price, time span of conversion privilege, and call price—the investor also has to consider this large number of variables. Second, since the form of convertibles is inherently attractive to investors, one should not expect to find them generally selling at bargain prices.

The following hypothetical example can be used to illustrate the method of evaluating a convertible security. A 6 percent coupon debenture, with 20 years remaining to maturity, is convertible at any time into common stock at $50. It is currently selling at 90 (i.e., $900 for a $1,000 debenture),[6] and the stock into which it is convertible currently is selling at $42.

The first phase of the analysis is to evaluate the issue as if it were a "straight" (i.e., nonconvertible) debenture. As indicated in the earlier discussion of bond and preferred stock analysis, this involves a determination of quality of the issue, a decision as to whether the quality is satisfactory, and a judgment as to whether the time is propitious for buying fixed-income securities in general. Suppose it is concluded that the issue is of medium quality, that this estimate is confirmed by the rating agencies (assume Moody's rates it Baa),[7] and that the investor's standards permit the purchase of securities of such quality. Suppose it also is concluded that interest rates may rise a bit, but not substantially enough to militate against the purchase of fixed income securities.

---

[6] In this example, and those that follow, we assume that the investor is evaluating a convertible issue which has been outstanding for some time and which has a market price above or below par. The principles discussed, however, are equally applicable to the evaluation of a new issue being offered at par.

[7] A representative cross section of convertible debentures at any given time is likely to include 25 percent—50 percent with ratings of Baa or better and at least 50 percent with lower ratings.

In considering ratings of convertible debentures, it should be borne in mind that the agencies almost automatically downgrade subordinated issues by one rating category. Therefore, the proportion of truly lower grade issues is probably considerably less than indicated by the data. See Thomas C. Noddings, *The Dow Jones-Irwin Guide to Convertible Securities* (Homewood, Ill.: Dow Jones-Irwin, Inc. 1973).

Next, a calculation is made of the price the debenture would carry in the absence of a conversion feature—i.e., its "bond value." Since it is of Baa quality, the yield at which *straight* Baa issues currently are selling is determined. Suppose Moody's weekly *Bond Survey* shows that such issues currently yield 7.5 percent. The question, then, is: At what price must a 6 percent coupon, 20-year issue, sell to yield 7.5 percent to maturity? The answer can be obtained readily from a set of bond tables, or by the approximation method described in the previous chapter. Thus, letting X = purchase price, and $1,000 - X$ = discount:

$$0.075 = \frac{60 + (1,000 - X)/20}{500 + 0.5X}$$

$$= \frac{60 + 50 - 0.05X}{500 + 0.5X}$$

Cross-multiplying, we get

$$0.075 (500 + 0.5X) = 110 - 0.05X$$

or

$$37.50 + 0.0375X = 110 - 0.05X$$

thus

$$0.0875X = 72.50$$

and

$$X = 829$$

In other words, the debenture would have to fall in price from $900 to $829 to yield 7.5 percent.[8] But some allowance also must be made for the fact that a moderate rise in interest rates is believed to be possible. Suppose it is thought that Baa issues can rise 0.5 percent to an 8 percent yield basis. If this were to occur, the debenture could decline in price to $778, derived as follows:

$$0.08 = \frac{60 + (1,000 - X)/20}{500 + 0.5X}$$

$$40 + 0.04X = 110 - 0.05X$$

$$0.09X = 70$$

$$X = 778$$

The conclusion of the first phase of the analysis, therefore, is that when the straight bond value can be taken as a given, the purchase of

---

[8] At $900 its yield to maturity is:

$$\frac{60 + 1/20 (1,000 - 900)}{500 + 1/2 (900)} = \frac{65}{950} = 6.8\%$$

the convertible debenture entails a price *risk* relative to its straight bond value, of about $120 per $900 invested ($900 purchase price less $778 minimum price), or about 13 percent. Of course, changing credit perceptions and interest rates can lead to declines in the straight bond value. This constitutes a further element of risk. The second phase of the analysis is designed to determine how much an investor stands to *gain* from the conversion privilege.

The first concept to be understood is that of the "conversion parity price" of the common stock. The debenture is convertible into common stock "at 50." This means that each $1,000 of par value can be exchanged for 20 shares of common stock (1,000/50 = 20). By paying $900 for the bond, therefore, the investor can be viewed as in effect buying the company's stock at $45 per share (900/20 = 45). This price is the conversion parity price of the stock.[9]

The conversion parity price, then, is different for different investors, depending on the price paid for the convertible security. Conversion parity price is equal to the purchase price of the convertible security divided by the number of common shares into which it is convertible. This price is highly significant analytically. For, as will be demonstrated, once the actual market price of the stock rises to the investor's conversion parity price, any further rise is certain to increase the value of his convertible security at least as rapidly percentagewise.

The minimum price of a convertible security, regardless of the level of interest rates or any other considerations, is equal to the current price of the common stock multiplied by the number of shares into which it can be converted. In our example, the current price of the stock is $42 and the debenture is convertible into 20 shares of common. Therefore, the minimum price of the debenture is $42 × 20, or $840. Any lower price would have to be temporary, because it would give rise to "arbitrage" transactions which would restore the balance. For example, if the debenture sold at, say, $800 when the stock's price was $42, a guaranteed profit could be made as follows. Buy the debenture for $800. Simultaneously sell short 20 shares of common for $840. Then convert the debenture into 20 shares with which to cover the short sale, and make a $40 profit, less brokerage commissions and transfer taxes. The existence of the profit guarantee would cause enough such transactions to drive the debenture price up to $840.[10]

If the logic presented above is understood, the significance of the "conversion parity price" of the common should begin coming into

---

[9] Fifty is the "conversion price," and 45 is the "conversion parity price." The two terms are equivalent in value only for an investor who buys the issue at par.

[10] It need not go to precisely $840 for two reasons. First, brokerage commissions would have to be allowed for; and second, the short selling could depress the price of the common to below $42.

focus. If the stock in our example rose from its present price of $42 to its conversion parity price of $45, the minimum price of the debenture would be 20 × $45, or $900, which is the purchase price. Every additional $1 rise in the stock would increase the debenture's price by at least $20. The actual price of the debenture might well rise more than proportionately if buyers became enthusiastic enough. Indeed, in strong markets, convertible issues often sell at high and rising premiums over conversion value.

Thus, the conversion parity price can be viewed as a break-even point. Once the common stock attains that value, the investor is assured of at least getting his money back; and any further rise in the price of the common guarantees him at least a proportionate profit. In our example, the $45 conversion parity price is only $3, or 7 percent, away from the current $42 price of the common.

Having considered the relationship of the conversion parity price to the current price of the common stock, the next step of the analysis is to consider the *potential price* of the common stock. To make such a determination, of course, the investor would have to apply all of the evaluation techniques which were discussed in earlier chapters. Suppose the investor decides that the stock is worth $65.

If the stock were to go to $65, the convertible debenture would be worth at least 20 × $65, or $1,300. Thus, there exists a potential gain, based on the debenture's conversion feature, of $400 per $900 invested, or 44 percent.

All of these facts now can be brought together in a simple summary statement. The convertible security under analysis offers a potential gain of 44 percent at a maximum risk of 13 percent. If a mistake has been made regarding the value of the stock, and its price declines sharply, the bond value of the security should prevent the loss from exceeding 13 percent.[11] But the investor does not have to be completely right about the stock to earn a profit. A price advance of only 7 percent, to $45, will mean breaking even, because the minimum price of the convertible would then be 20 × $45, equal to the $900 purchase price. A further advance in the price of the stock will produce a profit. Furthermore, while waiting for the capital gain the investor will be earning a *current* yield on the bond of 60/900, or almost 6.75 percent. This may be above the dividend yield on the stock.

Thus, our example represents an ideal convertible situation—significant profit potential with small loss possibility and high proba-

---

[11] However, the stock's decline may be due to circumstances which also have the effect of lowering the bond's quality from Baa to, say, Ba. In that case, the maximum loss would be a function of yields on straight bonds of this lower quality. On the other hand, if the stock's price declines because of a general economic recession, falling interest rates actually may cause the price of the bond to rise.

bility of at least breaking even. It is useful to state formally the characteristics of an attractive convertible. Ideally, six tests must be passed:

1. The issue must meet the investor's minimum quality standards.
2. The long-range outlook for interest rates should be fairly stable or down.
3. The minimum value of the issue as a straight bond or preferred stock must not be too far below the current selling price (not more than, say, 15 percent below), taking into account any expected rise in the level of interest rates.
4. The current price of the common stock must not be too far below conversion parity (say a maximum of 20 percent).
5. The potential price of the common stock must be well above conversion parity (say 25 percent or more).
6. The *current* yield on the bond or preferred stock should compare favorably with the dividend yield on the common stock.

Illustrative Applications of the Tests. We now set forth a number of cases which are typical of the convertibles usually available. That is, most fall short of the ideal by at least one of the tests. Brief analysis of each case should make clear the practical application of the procedures which have been discussed.

In each of the cases, it will be assumed that the quality level of the convertible issue is satisfactory. It also will be assumed in each case that straight issues of comparable quality are likely to yield a maximum of 8 percent.

Case 1. A 6 percent, 20-year debenture, convertible at $50, is selling at $1,500. The common stock is selling at $70 and is likely to rise substantially.

Analysis. The bond is yielding 2.8 percent to maturity and could fall almost 50 percent in price if the stock declined sharply and the bond had to sell strictly on its merits as a bond. The conversion parity price of the common is $75, which is $5 above the going price of $70. Since it is assumed that the stock has much further to go, the investor should, if anything, buy the stock directly rather than the convertible debenture. By selling at so high a premium above its *bond* value, the convertible provides no protection against a decline in the stock market. Suppose that the stock drops 20 percent to $56. The debenture easily could drop an equal 20 percent, to $1,200, and it still would be yielding only 4.6 percent to maturity. Therefore, if the stock is believed to be very attractive, why pay $75 for it in effect, when it can be bought at $70?

Case 2. A 6 percent, 20-year debenture, convertible at $50, is selling at $850. The common stock is selling at $20 and is likely to rise substantially.

Analysis. The bond is yielding 7.3 percent. To yield 8 percent, it would have to sell at $778, a maximum downside risk of only 9 percent. But the conversion parity price of the common stock is $50, which is more than double the present market price. Although a substantial rise in the stock's price can be expected, conversion parity is so far away that most of the stock price rise would not have a counterpart in the bond. It would be wiser to buy the stock directly, since the debenture is selling almost as if it were a straight bond and is quite lacking in appreciation potential from its common stock element. (In Case 1 the debenture was selling as if it were strictly a stock. It lacked price protection from its bond element.) Commercial banks are probably the only investors for whom this type of investment might have attraction. Although the appreciation potential of the bond may be remote, something is better than nothing if close to full bond value also is obtained, since commercial banks may not in some states be permitted to buy stocks directly.

Case 3. A 6 percent, 20-year debenture, convertible at $50, is selling at $850. The common stock is selling at $40, but already has risen sharply above a normal value range, and seems to be settling at this new plateau.

Analysis. As in Case 2, the bond feature provides a limited (9 percent) price risk. In addition, the conversion parity price of the common stock ($42½) is only 6 percent above the present market price ($40), which is an attractive spread. But the potential price of the stock is quite limited.

A purist would not buy this convertible bond. It provides good protection against a stock market decline but little appreciation potential. On the other hand, a reasonably good argument can be made for buying the issue. The estimate of the stock's value may be overly conservative. A modest further price rise would provide a profit on the convertible debenture, while a stock market reversal might have little or no impact on the debenture. Indeed, if a market reversal were caused by an economic recession, a fall in the level of interest rates could cause the debenture to rise in price. Moreover, the current yield of 7 percent on the debenture probably is higher than the dividend yield on the stock into which it is convertible and above that of most other stocks as well.

Case 4. A 7 percent, 19-year debenture, issued one year ago, is convertible at $25 and is selling at $1,200. The common stock is selling at $28 and is expected to rise to $60.

Analysis. The bond is yielding about 5.5 percent to maturity at its current price. To yield 8 percent, it would have to sell at about $880, so its risk as a bond is about 25 percent ($320 on a price of $1,200). While this risk is higher than our ideal criterion, the conversion parity price of the common stock is $30, or only 7 percent above the present

price of $28. Moreover, the potential price of the stock is double the conversion parity level. Therefore, despite the 25 percent downside bond risk, this convertible debenture would appear to be an attractive investment for high current income and large potential appreciation. However, there is a possible drawback which must be considered.

Suppose that the debenture in our example is callable at 107 (one year's interest is a common call premium). If the bond were called, what would happen?

With the stock selling at $28, the bond has a conversion value of 40 times $28, or $1,120. Thus, as long as the stock's price stays at $28, a bondholder would be better off converting into stock (or selling to someone else who will convert) than turning the bond in for $1,070. Those investors who bought the bond at par at original issue, one year earlier, would have a 12 percent profit. But those who bought at $1,200 would have a loss of $80, or 7 percent. And if the call announcement depressed the price of the stock because of the imminent addition to the number of outstanding shares, the loss would be greater.[12]

The moral of this example is that even when a convertible security meets most or all of our rules, if it is selling above call price there is a risk present. The risk is that the security will be called before the stock's price rises to conversion parity (once it reaches conversion parity, the investor will at least break even). Therefore, the investor has also to consider the situation from the corporation's point of view as well.

In this particular example, it seems unlikely that the company would call the bonds for the purpose of forcing conversion. For a call at this time might easily boomerang. Suppose that the call announcement depressed the price of the stock to $26. At this price, the debenture would have a conversion value of only $1,040. People would not convert but would turn the bonds in for $1,070 in cash. But this is not what the company wanted. It wanted more common stock in the business, and instead would be faced with a huge depletion of cash and capital.[13] Thus, a call for the purpose of forcing conversion is unlikely, given the set of facts in this case, and purchase of the debenture is probably a wise move.

---

[12] In March 1972, for example, Western Union called a convertible issue and the company's stock declined 10 percent in price within two days. It should be noted that the announcement of the call is made in the financial press several weeks before the actual call date. Since the decision to sell the issue, or to convert it, must be made within this short time period, it is imperative that the investor be aware of the call announcement. One can keep track of such announcements by reading the newspaper carefully or by regularly perusing one of several published financial services which report corporate developments of this type.

[13] A number of companies have hedged against this risk by entering into an underwriting agreement when calling convertible issues. Under such an agreement, an investment banker, for a fee, agrees to buy any unconverted securities and to convert them. Thus, the underwriter rather than the company takes the risk of a sharp decline in the stock's price during the call period.

FIGURE 11-1. Sample of Standard & Poor's Convertible Bond Report

CONVERTIBLE BONDS — Issue, Rate, Interest Dates and Maturity	S&P Quality Rating	B/O d	F/O m	Outstg Mil-$	Conv. Expires	Price per Share	Div. Income per Bond	Shares per $1,000	1975 Range Hi	Lo	Curr Bid Sale(s) Ask(A)	Curr. Return	Yield to Mat	Stock Value of Bond	Conv. Parity	STOCK DATA Curr. Price / P/E Ratio	Yr. End	EPS 1973	EPS 1974	EPS Last 12 Mos	Dil-u't'n 1974
Whittaker Corp ...4¾s Mn15 1987	B		R	1.64	1987	17.00	….	58.82	47	35	47	10.1	14.1	17⅜	8	●3	23 Oc	d0.19	0.44	[7]0.13	n/r
Whittaker Corp ...4½s sJl 1988	B		R	11.8	1988	47.00	….	21.28	48¾	37	46	9.78	13.4	6⅜	21⅜	●3	23 Oc	d0.19	0.44	[7]0.13	n/r
Wickes Corp ...5⅞s Mn 1994	BB		R	11.7	1994	19.93	….	50.17	55	46¾	54⅞	10.7	12.4	44½	23⅞	8⅞	10 Ja	2.20	[10]1.54	[10]1.54	n/r
Wickes Corp ...9s Mn 1999	BB		R	19.1	1999	50.17	….	19.93	91	68¾	80	11.2	11.4	17¾	20	8⅞	10 Ja	2.20	[10]1.54	[7]0.90	n/r
¹Will Ross ...4¼s mS 1987	A		R	5.92	1987	31.04	16.75	32.22	82	63	64	6.64	9.31	47⅞	19⅞	14⅞	10 Dc	1.21	1.41	[6]1.53	n/r
¹Will Ross ...5¾s fA 1989	A		R	19.9	1989	43.96	11.83	22.75	83½	67	s73¼	7.84	9.61	33⅞	29⅜	14⅞	10 Dc	1.21	1.41	[6]1.53	n/r
¹Will Ross ...4¼s mS 1992	A		R	25.0	1992	45.83	11.35	21.82	74	59¾	55	8.18	10.1	32½	25¼	14⅞	10 Dc	1.21	1.41	[6]1.53	n/r
◆Wilshire Oil, Tex ...6s mS 1995			R	4.75	1995	6.64	7.53	150.60	101½	76¾	s91	6.59	6.83	80⅞	6	◆5⅜	7 Dc	0.47	0.77	[6]0.75	0.72
Witco Chemical ...4½s sJD15 1993	BBB		R	15.0	1993	50.00	24.00	20.00	66½	59¾	61	7.38	8.85	38¾	30¾	19⅜	6 Dc	△3.05	4.44	6.19	3.95
Wometco Enterpr ...5¾s Ms15 1994	BB		R	13.3	1994	23.20	24.14	43.10	83	55	s77	7.14	7.88	57⅝	17⅞	13⅜	6 Dc	1.33	1.51	[9]1.86	1.44
◆Work Wear ...4¾s mS 1985	B		R	2.09	1985	14.25	42.11	70.18	69½	47	^64¾	7.34	10.5	47⅜	9¼	◆6¾	5 Dc	*1.95	[10]1.41	[6]1.31	n/r
◆Wyle Laboratories ...5¾s fA 1988	B		R	14.6	1988	22.75	10.55	43.96	60	45	^54¼	9.68	12.4	15⅜	12½	▲3½	6 Ja	*0.77	0.87	[7]0.62	0.83
²Wyly Corp ...7¾s Ms15 1995	CCC		R	39.2	1995	45.00	….	22.22	40¾	24⅛	34	21.3	22.0	6⅜	15¼	◆2⅞	7 Dc	d0.42	d1.08	[6]d2.24	n/r
Xerox Corp ...6s mN 1995	A		R	155	1995	92.00	10.87	10.87	117	89½	^90¾	6.61	6.85	58⅜	83½	d53¾	17 Dc	3.80	4.18	[6]3.18	n/r
Zapata Corp ...4¾s Fa 1988	B		R	14.9	1988	26.50	11.32	37.74	76¾	61	63	7.92	10.6	50½	15¾	13⅜	3 Sp	△2.06	3.15	[6]4.25	2.52
Zapata Corp 'B' ...4¾s Fa 1988	B		R	14.7	1988	26.50	11.32	37.74	76¾	61	s61	7.54	10.0	50½	16¾	13⅜	3 Sp	△2.06	3.15	[6]4.25	2.52
Zapata Corp 'C' ...4¾s fA 1988			R	37.5	1988	26.50	11.32	37.74	76¾	61	81	7.79	10.2	50½	16¾	13⅜	3 Sp	△2.06	3.15	[6]4.25	2.52
Zapata Explor ...5½s sJD 1979	B		R	14.9	1979	5.71	….	175.13	89	70	s46	6.79	11.3	63½	4⅝	3⅝	8 Sp	▣0.15	0.09	[6]0.37	0.07
Zayre Corp ...5¾s jD15 1994			R	18.0	1994	40.00	….	25.00	48½	32	46	12.5	13.8	13⅜	18¾	5⅜	d Ja	1.84	d0.04	d0.04	0.14
Zurn Indus ...5¾s mN 1994	BB		R	17.9	1994	28.50	11.23	35.09	68¾	44	63½	9.06	10.1	32⅞	18¾	9⅜	11 Mr	△0.64	0.83	[9]0.90	0.83

Uniform Footnote Explanations—See Page XVI. Other: ¹Subsid. of & conv. into Searle (G.D.) & Co. ²Was University Computing.

EXPLANATION OF COLUMN HEADINGS AND FOOTNOTES

MARKET: Unlisted except where symbols ● or ◆ are used.
● –New York Stock Exchange   ◆ –American Stock Exchange

ISSUE TITLE: Name of Bond at time of offering; otherwise issue footnoted with name change of obligor. Minor changes with old title indicated in brackets, i.e. Gen Tel (Corp) & Elec.
Prin & int payable in U.S. funds. § Int. and/or prin. in default.

FORM OF BOND: Letters are used to indicate form of bond: C–Coupon only; CR–Coupon or Registered, interchangeable; R–Registered only.

CONVERSION EXPIRES: Footnote keyed to bottom of page when conversion price changes during life of the privilege; also noted on conversion price.
⊚ Indicates a change in next 12 months. a–No fractional shs. issued upon conversion; settlements in cash.

DIVIDEND INCOME PER BOND: If $1,000 Bond were converted, the annual amount of dividends expected to be paid by the company on the stock based on most recent indication of annual rate of payment.
t–Less tax at origin. g–in Canadian funds less 15% or 10% non-residence tax.

STOCK VALUE OF BOND: Price at which bond must sell to equal price of stock, i.e., number of shares received on conversion times price of the stock.

CONVERSION PARITY: Price at which stock must sell to equal bond price, i.e., price of bond divided by number of shares received on conversion.

P–E RATIO: (Price–Earnings Ratio) Represents market valuation of any $1 of per share earnings i.e., the price of the stock divided by estimated or latest 12 months per share earnings.

EARNINGS, in general, are, per share as reported by company. **FOR YEAR INDICATED:** Fiscal years ending prior to March 31 are shown under preceding year. Net operating earnings are shown for **banks**; net earnings before appropriation to general reserve for **savings & loan associations**; net investment income for **insurance companies**; **railroads'** earnings are as reported to ICC. **Foreign** issues traded **ADR** are dollars per share, converted at prevailing exchange rate. Specific footnotes used:

△ Excl extra-ord income	j–Currency at origin	†–Partial Year
▲ Incl extra-ord income	P–Preliminary	‡–New Year Earns
■ Excl extra-ord charges	p–Pro forma	b–Before depletion
▣ Incl extra-ord charges	R–Fully diluted	d–Deficit
* Excl tax credits	n/r–Not reported	E–S&P Estimate
	∫–1972 dilution	

LAST 12 Mos. indicates earnings through period indicated by superior number preceding figure: for Jan. for Feb. etc. Figure without superior number indicates fiscal year end.

DILUTION: Earnings on a fully diluted basis, as reported in accordance with Accounting Principles Board opinions.

Source: Standard & Poor's *Convertible Securities Reports*, October 13, 1975.

FIGURE 11–2
Convertibles in the Oil Industry

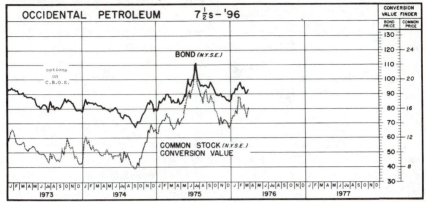

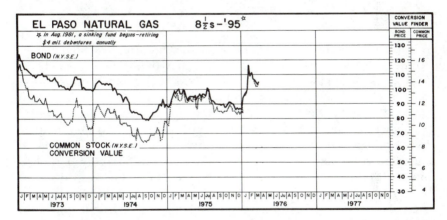

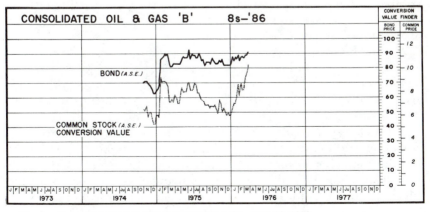

Source: *Convertible Fact Finder*, Kalb Voorhis & Co., April 26, 1976.

On the other hand, suppose the company has found a merger partner. And suppose this partner has ample equity capital and can borrow
at 6.5 percent. In this situation, a 7 percent *convertible* debenture has
less place in the merged company's capital structure than, say, a 6.5
percent straight debenture. A call might well be at hand, and purchase
of the debenture would be quite risky.

Sources of Information.   Several investment service organizations
publish data on convertible securities in tabular or graphic forms
which are convenient for quick screening preliminary to an in-depth
analysis. Among these are the weeklies of Goldman Sachs; Value Line;
Kalb, Voorhis & Co.; R.H.M. Associates; and the convertible bond
section of Standard & Poor's *Bond Reports*. A sample of the latter
tabular service is reproduced as Figure 11–1, while Figure 11–2 shows
the chart section of the Kalb, Voorhis survey.

OPTIONS

"Option" is a broad term encompassing a variety of financial instruments. At least four types of options may be distinguished. There
is the stock option for corporate executives. This is a form of executive
compensation, the right given a company official to purchase company
shares at a given price usually below market, thus providing a capital
gain when exercised and sold. There are qualified and nonqualified
stock options. The former has government-mandated requirements
concerning option price, length of exercise period, holding period required. It permits the executive to defer most or all tax liability from
the time of option exercise to the time when the stock is actually sold.
Then, if the required holding period has been met, the profit above the
original exercise price is taxable at long-term capital gains rates. A
nonqualified stock option, on the other hand, has few restrictions but
does not receive favorable tax treatment.[14]

A second type of stock option is the warrant. A warrant is an option
issued by a corporation giving the buyer the right to purchase a
number of shares of its common stock at a given exercise price for a
given period of time. Warrants offer extensive investment and speculative opportunities.

A third type is the call (or put) option. A call is an option written by a
broker or an investor granting the buyer the right to purchase a
specified number of shares at a specific price for a given period of
time. The seller of a call option may or may not own the stock against
which the call is sold. If he does not own it, the option he sells is a

---

[14] See Graef S. Crystal, "The Qualified Stock Option: R.I.P.," *The New York Times*,
November 17, 1974.

"naked call," and if it is exercised he will have to buy or borrow the stock for delivery. A put option is one which allows the purchaser to "put" (sell) the stock to the writer of the put option for a specified period of time, at a specified price.[15]

The fourth type, "rights," or "preemptive rights," are short-term options, usually for 30, 60, or 90 days, granted to existing shareholders, to enable them to purchase a new issue of the company's stock, usually at a favorable price.

Warrants

Warrants are issued by corporations in conjunction with senior security financing (as "sweeteners"), or as part of "units" of new common stock plus warrants, or independently as compensation to underwriters and others. They became truly "respectable" securities in April 1970, when they were issued as part of a major financing program by AT&T[16] and were accepted for trading on the New York Stock Exchange after a ban of many years. (The American Stock Exchange did not have such a ban, and has many warrant issues listed.)

Warrants give their holders an option to purchase the corporation's securities, usually its common stock, at a stated price. While so-called rights offerings of new stock to existing owners are a form of warrant, the exercise period is only a month or two. "Rights," therefore, are not included in this discussion. Most warrants may be exercised over a period of many years, sometimes at a price which increases the longer the investor waits to exercise. Occasionally, a warrant may be a perpetual option. The holder of a warrant has no voting rights and receives no dividend income. Care must be taken to assure that the warrant has antidilution provisions which cause the exercise price to be reduced and the number of shares under the warrant to be increased in line with any stock dividends or stock splits.

Warrants may provide for the purchase of one share per warrant or more than one share; frequently, fractional share purchases are in-

---

[15] For an excellent discussion, see Daniel Turov, "Warrants and Options," *Financial Analyst's Handbook*, vol. I (Homewood, Ill.: Dow Jones-Irwin, Inc., 1975), chap. 17.

[16] The company issued 31 million of five-year warrants to purchase one share each, at a price of $52. The stock's market price at the time was $42. The warrants were attached to 8.75 percent debentures, two warrants per $100 par value, and became detachable after six months. They traded initially at a price of $8, a "premium" of $18 (see following discussion of premiums). The AT&T warrants were exercisable at any time after November 15, 1970, expiring on May 15, 1975. For most of the period AT&T stock was below $52 a share. By May 15, 1975, 3,058,320 warrants were exercised providing total proceeds to the company of $169 million, but the bulk of the warrants—28,135,649—expired unexercised. See Sanford L. Jacobs, "Sizeable Amount of New Common Created for AT&T," *The Wall Street Journal*, May 16, 1975; also Dan Dorfman, "Who Goosed Ma Bell," The Bottom Line, *New York Magazine*, June 2, 1975, pp. 11–12.

volved. Whereas short-term "rights" options carry an exercise price below the prevailing market price, the typical warrant carries an exercise price well above the prevailing market price at the time the warrant is issued. To begin to understand the speculative attraction of warrants, assume that a new warrant is issued which gives the holder a ten-year option to buy one share of stock for $30. This price will be referred to as (EP), the exercise price. Assume that at the time the warrant is issued, the market price of the stock (MP) is $20. Assume also that a particular investor believes there is a good probability that the stock's price will rise to $40 within the next several years.

Minimum Values. If the investors buy the stock for $20 and it rises to $40, they will have earned 100 percent plus any dividends received. Suppose, instead, that they could have purchased the warrant for $5. If the stock reaches $40, the *minimum value* of the warrant will be $10 $(MP$ of $40 less EP of $30). It cannot be less than $10 because, if it were, arbitrageurs would buy the warrant and sell the stock short for a guaranteed profit, in a manner exactly analogous to that discussed earlier in connection with convertible securities.[17] Obviously, if the warrant goes to just $10, the investors will have doubled their investment, no more than they could have achieved with the stock, and indeed less because of the absence of dividends on the warrant. But if, when the stock is $40, investors expect it to rise further, the warrant will sell at some premium over minimum value. Suppose that the premium is $5—i.e., the warrant sells for $15. In that case, investors, who bought at $5, will have tripled their investment instead of doubling it.

Now consider another investor who comes along when the stock is $40 and the warrant is $15. This one thinks the stock will keep rising to at least $50. Purchase of the stock would bring a 25 percent profit (plus dividends), whereas the warrant would be expected to rise *at least* to $20 ($50 minus $30), and probably more, for a profit of more than one-third. So this investor buys the warrant for $15. But suppose that the analysis of the stock was incorrect and it *falls* 30 percent to $28 instead of rising to $50. The warrant has no minimum value $(MP$ is below $EP)$, but merely a speculative value reflecting the possibility that the stock will rise again. Suppose that the warrant price declines to $8. Our second investor will have lost almost 50 percent on the warrant but would have lost 30 percent on the stock.

Finally, suppose that a third investor buys the warrant for $8, but by this time it has only a few years left before expiration. And suppose the

---

[17] If a warrant entitles the holder to purchase more or less than one share of stock, the minimum value is $N (MP - EP)$, where N is the number of shares that can be bought. The transaction costs of arbitrageurs are omitted from the calculation for simplicity of exposition.

stock never does rise above $30. At the expiration of the warrant, it will be worth zero, and the investor will have lost his entire principal—a vastly different result than if he had bought the stock instead. Clearly, there is a lot of speculative leverage in warrants. For example, in the last two weeks of 1971, AT&T common stock rose 12 percent from 41 to 46, while AT&T warrants rose 50 percent from 6 to 9. On the other hand, from August 1969 to January 1972, Atlantic Richfield stock declined 40 percent while its warrants, approaching expiration, dropped from 47 to 1½ during the same period.[18]

A historic example of the speculative leverage of warrants may be seen in the case of the Tri-Continental perpetual warrant. In 1942, at the bottom of the market, Tri-Continental (a well-known, closed-end investment trust) common was selling on the New York Stock Exchange for 75 cents a share. The Tri-Continental warrant provided the right to buy 1.27 shares of the common stock for $17.76 per share, or $22.55 for the 1.27 shares. Since the $17.76 seemed so far away from the 75 cents per share, the warrants were then considered almost worthless and were selling for but 1/32nd, or 3⅛ cents per warrant.

From 1942 on, the market price of Tri-Continental stock rose. Had you invested $500 in Tri-Continental stock in 1942, at 75 cents a share you would have been able to buy 666 shares of the common. In contrast, $500 invested in the warrants (at 3⅛ cents per warrant) would have purchased 16,000 warrants. By 1969, with the common stock at an adjusted high of 72¾, the 666 shares were worth $48,451 (72¾ × 666).

Since each warrant represented the right to buy 1.27 shares of common at $17.76 per share, or $22.55 for the 1.27 shares, those 1.27 shares, when the common touched 72¾ were worth 1.27 × $72.75, or $92.39. The right to buy $92.39 worth of common for only $22.55 had to be worth at least $92.39 − 22.55, or $69.84.

The actual high for the TRC warrants on the American Stock Exchange in 1969 was $75¾, the 16,000 warrants (bought for $500 in 1942) were worth $1,212,000.

If you had bought the common in 1942, and held to 1969, you $500 would have appreciated to $48,451. Had you used the $500 to buy the warrants and held them until 1969, your $500 would have appreciated to $1,212,000. Probably no one bought the warrants and held for 27 years from low to high, but the figures do illustrate the leverage possibilities of warrants.[19]

What goes up usually comes down again and in the 1973–74 stock

---

[18] Data from R.H.M. Associates, publishers of the weekly *R.H.M. Warrant and Stock Survey*.

[19] See Sidney Fried, *Fortune Building in the 70's with Common Stock Warrants and Low-Price Stocks* (New York: RHM Associates, 1975).

market debacle. Tri-Continental warrants fell sharply to 23 in 1974. The toboggan slide of a list of representative warrants during the 1973–74 market setback was as follows:

Avco warrants	$18.00 to $0.56
Carrier Corp. warrants	$13.00 to $0.75
Cott Corp. warrants	$ 4.00 to $0.31
Cont. III & Rlty warrants	$14.00 to $0.31
Holiday Inns warrants	$31.00 to $0.31
Instrument Syst. warrants	$ 3-⅛ to $0.10
IT&T warrants	$12.00 to $0.25
Jones & Laughlin warrants	$ 3.00 to $0.13
LCA warrants	$18.00 to $0.50
Loew's warrants ...., ...	$39.00 to $2.25
Natl Indust warrants .... , ...	$16.37 to $0.50
Ozark Airlines warrants	$ 7.00 to $0.38
Rollins Intl warrants	$ 6-¾ to $0.13
Starr Bdcstg warrants	$20.00 to $0.25
Triangle Pacific warrants	$ 8.00 to $0.25
United Brands warrants	$56.00 to $0.43
Zayre warrants	$12.00 to $0.25

Warrant Premiums.   Thus far our discussion has focused mainly on the minimum value of warrants ($MP - EP$). But just as a convertible security tends to sell at some premium over its pure stock value, so too will a warrant tend to sell at a premium over its minimum value. Indeed, when there is a "negative minimum value" ($MP < EP$), the premium is quite pronounced. The size of the premium will reflect expectations of future increases in MP, plus other factors which will now be examined.

Letting P = premium; WP = warrant price; MP = market price of the stock; and EP = exercise price,[20] we can state the following relationship:

$$P = WP - (MP - EP)$$

In the tabulation below, several illustrations of this relationship are given, building upon the earlier example. These illustrations reflect one major characteristic of warrant pricing; namely, the higher the ratio MP/EP the lower the premium. This is because the speculative leverage available in a warrant diminishes as the price of the underlying stock rises relative to the exercise price. Recall that the warrant's minimum value rose from $10 to $20, or 100 percent, as the stock's price rose 25 percent from $40 to $50. The minimum value would rise 50 percent from $20 to $30 if the stock's price rose 20 percent from $50 to $60. But suppose that the stock was $100, with minimum warrant

---

[20] Some warrants provide that the exercise price may be paid by turning in the company's bonds. Since the bonds are accepted at par value, if they trade in the open market at below par the *effective* exercise price is lower than it appears to be.

TABLE 11–1
Illustrative Relationship of Premium to *MP/EP*

Stock Price MP	Exercise Price EP	Minimum Value MP − EP	Illustrative Warrant Price WP	Premium WP − (MP − EP)	MP/EP	P/EP
20	30	−10	5	15	67%	50%
30	30	0	10	10	100	33
40	30	10	15	5	133	17
50	30	20	24	4	167	13
60	30	30	33	3	200	10
70	30	40	42	2	233	7
80	30	50	51½	1½	267	5
90	30	60	61	1	300	3
100	30	70	70½	½	333	2
110	30	80	80	0	367	0

value of $70. A 10 percent rise in the stock to $110 would lead to only a 14 percent rise in the warrant's minimum value, from $70 to $80. Taking account of the lost dividends, and of the downside risk on the warrant if the stock declines, the warrant becomes unattractive and will command little or no premium over its minimum value. Indeed, were it not for arbitrage opportunities, the warrant might sell at a discount at this point.

What factors other than the relationship *MP/EP* affect the size of the warrant premium? Empirical investigations suggest that the following are important considerations:[21]

1. Vitally important, of course, is the investment community's expectations regarding the future price of the stock. If the price is expected to fall, the premium will shrink, and may even disappear. (In this connection, it should be noted that if we express *P* as a percent of *MP*, instead of as a percent of *EP*, the percentage tells us by how much the stock must rise in price to assure that we will break even on the warrant.)

2. The time remaining to expiration of the warrant also is very important. Warrants begin to lose their premiums when the expiration date becomes less than two years. On the other hand, warrants with

---

[21] See, for example, Daniel Turov, "Dividend Paying Stocks and Their Warrants," *Financial Analysts Journal*, March/April 1973; and Constantine Kalogeras, "A Primer on Warrants," *Baylor Business Studies*, vol. 105 (August/October) 1975, pp. 25–41; see also S. T. Kassouf, "Warrant Price Behavior, 1945–1964," *Financial Analysts Journal*, January/February 1968; and J. D. Miller, "Longevity of Stock Purchase Warrants," *Financial Analysts Journal*, November/December 1971; New Life for Old Warrants," *Forbes*, July 1, 1974.

very long lives—e.g., over ten years—do not appear to command extra premiums over warrants with lives of three to five years.

3.   The higher the dividend yield on the underlying common stock, the lower the warrant premium, other things being equal, because the lost dividend income becomes more significant to the investor.

4.   Warrants trading on organized exchanges tend to have higher premiums than those trading over-the-counter.

5.   Small size issues, or inactively traded issues, tend to have smaller premiums.

An investor should ask eight questions before purchasing any warrant:

1. Is the underlying common stock attractive? Don't ask which warrants are attractive now. Examine the outlook for the underlying common stock first and then study the warrant related to that common.

2. When does the warrant expire? Do not buy unless the warrant has three or four years to run. If you must buy a short-term warrant be sure the premium, if any, is very low.

3. Is the warrant protected against dilution? Is there provision for the adjustment of the warrant terms in case of stock splits, stock dividends, or issuance of additional stock below the warrants exercise price?

4. Is the warrant protected against call? Some warrants can be called by the issuer at will and at nominal prices. Others can only be called at prices significantly above current prices.

5. Is the premium sufficiently low so that if the stock advances the warrant will increase by a greater percentage amount? That is, is the leverage ratio favorable?

6. Is the premium reasonable in light of the expected volatility of the underlying common as well as in terms of normal value?

7. Is the premium reasonable in terms of the normal trading pattern for this particular warrant? Differing levels of institutional sponsorship may cause warrants of equal volatility to trade at different levels.

8. Is the premium reasonable in the light of aberrations which may occur to warrant premiums in general during a specific market period?[22]

Puts and Calls

Whereas warrants are options written by corporations on their own stock, puts and calls are options written by security dealers and by

[22] See Daniel Turov, "Warrants and Options," *Financial Analyst's Handbook*, vol. I, pp. 473–74.

other investors on any stock they care to write an option on, as long as they can find an investor willing to buy the option. A put gives the holder the right to *sell* 100 shares of the specified stock to the writer of the option (via a registered stockbroker) at a specified price. A call gives the holder the right to buy 100 shares at a specified price. The time period of the option may be as short as 30 days, or as long as 9 months. Thus, calls are attractive to investors who think a near-term rise in price is in store for a stock, but who prefer not to buy the stock itself. Likewise, puts are attractive to investors who anticipate a near-term price decline, but who prefer not to sell short.

Various combinations of options may be purchased, such as "straddles" (a combination of a put and a call on the same stock at the same price), "spreads" (a straddle where the call price is greater than the put price), and "straps" (one put and two calls), but these are not used frequently. Indeed, puts and calls in general were not a very active business in comparison with direct trading in common stocks. However, the Chicago Board of Trade starting in 1973 developed a regular auction market in call options in contrast to the traditional over-the-counter negotiated market. The success of this option market has made the option a more widely used trading vehicle.

The Listed Exchange Traded Option

. . . Scratch an options trader, a broker or an investor . . . and you'll find an optimist. The euphoria on Wall Street over options trading rivals the light-headedness found at the height of the growth stock craze of the late nineteen sixties or any other example of mass enthusiasm that Wall Streeters care, or don't care to remember.[23]

Since option trading started on the Chicago Board Options Exchange in the spring of 1973, the growth in trading has run far beyond anyone's expectation. On the sidelines a few voices can be heard cautioning the optimists. "I've seen the 'hottest new game in town,' trotted out too many times before," one critic said. "But down in the arena, options appear to be the closest that Wall Street will come to offering a repeal of the there's-no-such-thing-as-a-free-lunch law."

The major innovations introduced by the Chicago Board Options Exchange revolutionized option trading. The old O-T-C conventional options market gave way to listed trading in standardized options on a wide list of first-class stocks. Transactions costs were reduced and a secondary market developed. Standardized listed call options are now traded on the American Stock Exchange, the Chicago Board Options Exchange, and the Philadelphia, Baltimore, Washington Stock Ex-

---

[23] Newton W. Lamson, "Wall Street Is Just Wild about Options," *The New York Times*, May 25, 1975.

change. Trading is likely also on the Pacific Coast, The Midwest, The Montreal, and the Toronto Stock Exchanges. Plans are underway for trading in standardized put options.

Call options that are traded on the exchanges have certain common characteristics that make it possible for investors to trade in options in a more flexible and convenient manner than is possible in the prior over-the-counter market for puts and calls. The striking price or exercise price, the price per share at which the option buyer may purchase a call is now standardized. On option exchanges the exercise price is set in advance and does not change during the life of the option. If the underlying stock price changes appreciably, new exercise prices will be introduced for trading to reflect more closely the price of the underlying stock.

In contrast to the older put and call market where it was possible to buy or write an option with practically any striking price or expiration date, the striking price of listed options almost always end in $5 or $0, unless a stock dividend or other capital change occurs after trading in the options has begun. If AT&T is selling at $51 a share at the time options for a new expiration month are being listed for trading, the new AT&T option will have a striking or exercise price of $50 per share. If the stock price closes above $52.50 for two consecutive days, the exchange will add $55 contracts for each expiration date beyond 60 days.

Exercise prices are generally fixed at 5-point intervals for securities trading below 50, 10-point intervals for securities trading between 50 and 200, and 20-point intervals for securities trading above 200. When trading is introduced in a new expiration month, the exercise price selected will ordinarily be the one closest to the market price of the underlying security. For example, if the underlying security is selling at 27 when trading is introduced in a new expiration month, the exercise price will customarily be set at 25.

In addition to the standardized exercise price the listed options have standardized expiration dates.

Under present practices, the expiration months of certain classes of options are January, April, July, or October, while for other classes the expiration months are February, May, August, or November. In the old option market expiration was any date the buyer and the writer negotiated. Now it is the third Friday of the month of expiration.

This standardization has made possible the development of a secondary market. Each listed option with a common expiration date and striking price is interchangeable with any similar listed option. In contrast the old conventional option is a direct contract between a particular writer, or his brokerage firm, and a particular buyer. One

conventional option contract is not interchangeable with another. Moreover, as Gastineau explains, because of the direct tie between buyer and writer, it is frequently difficult for the owner of a conventional option to sell or exchange the option privilege for a price in excess of the intrinsic or exercise value of the option.[24] And more importantly, it is impossible for an option writer (old style) to terminate his obligation except through direct negotiation with the buyer of the specific contract he wrote. With listed options, however, the writer's obligation is to the Options Clearing Corporation,[25] and not to the buyer. The buyer and writer in a listed option transaction have no direct connection. Each has a contract only with the Options Clearing Corporation which is the issuer of listed options. Either the option buyer or the writer can close out their positions by closing purchases or closing sales.

This standardization allows the option to trade in much the same manner as common stocks are traded and it has resulted in a high degree of liquidity which has made the old traditional options market almost obsolete. Open trading and continuous price reporting of op-

---

[24] Gary L. Gastineau, *The Stock Options Manual* (New York: McGraw-Hill Book Co., 1975). There is now an extensive literature on options. See Fischer Black, "Fact and Fantasy in the Use of Options," *Financial Analysts Journal*, July/August 1975; "Options—A New Lure for Investors in Stocks," *U.S. News and World Report*, May 26, 1975; "New Game in Town," *The Wall Street Journal*, April 22, 1974; Robert G. Merton, "Theory of Rational Option Pricing," *Bell Journal of Economics and Management Science*, Spring 1973; Burton G. Malkiel and Richard E. Quandt, *Strategies and Rational Decisions in the Securities Options Market* (Cambridge, Mass.: The M.I.T. Press, 1969); Lawrence R. Rosen, *How to Trade Put and Call Options* (Homewood, Ill.: Dow Jones-Irwin, Inc., 1974); Kenneth B. Platnick, *The Option Game* (New York: CommuniConcepts, 1975); Thomas C. Noddings and Earl Zazove, *CBOE Call Options: Your Daily Guide to Portfolio Strategy* (Homewood, Ill.: Dow Jones-Irwin, Inc., 1975); Practising Law Institute, *Option Trading*, Course Handbook Series, no. 146 (New York, 1974); Leroy Ross, *The Stockbrokers Guide to Put and Call Option Strategies* (New York: New York Institute of Finance, 1974); Robert Reback, "Risk and Return in Option Trading," *Financial Analysts Journal*, July/August 1975; G. W. Hettenhouse and D. J. Puglisi, "Investor Experience with Options," *Financial Analysts Journal*, July/August 1975; "Some New Approaches to Playing the Options Game," *Institutional Investor*, May 1975; "Limitless Options: Spreads May Appeal to Bulls and Bears Alike," *Barron's*, June 23, 1975.

[25] The Options Clearing Corporation is jointly owned by the Chicago Board Options Exchange, The American Stock Exchange, and the PBW Exchange. A call option traded on any of the exchanges gives the holder the right to buy the number of shares of the underlying security covered by the option from the Options Clearing Corporation at the stated exercise price by the proper filing of an exercise notice with the Options Clearing Corporation at any time prior to the fixed expiration time of the option. Every option issued by the Options Clearing Corporation is registered under the Securities Act of 1933, and all purchasers (but not the writers) of such options are entitled to the protection of that act. See *Prospectus of the Options Clearing Corporation: Exchange Traded Call Options*, October 30, 1975. As the table of contents of the Prospectus indicates it provides an excellent summary of fact and procedures for exchange traded options.

FIGURE 11–3
How Options Trades Are Reported

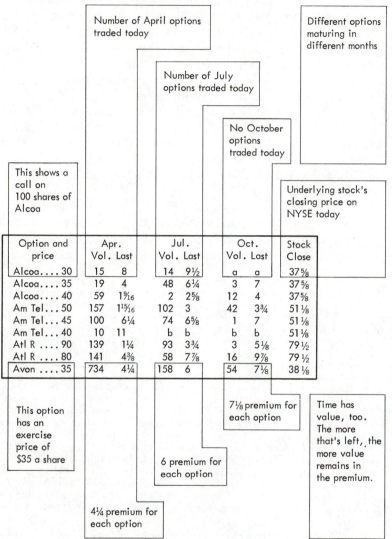

Number of April options traded today		Different options maturing in different months

Number of July options traded today

No October options traded today

This shows a call on 100 shares of Alcoa

Underlying stock's closing price on NYSE today

Option and price	Apr. Vol. Last	Jul. Vol. Last	Oct. Vol. Last	Stock Close
Alcoa.... 30	15 8	14 9½	a a	37⅝
Alcoa.... 35	19 4	48 6¼	3 7	37⅝
Alcoa.... 40	59 1⁹⁄₁₆	2 2⅝	12 4	37⅝
Am Tel... 50	157 1¹⁵⁄₁₆	102 3	42 3¾	51⅛
Am Tel... 45	100 6¼	74 6⅝	1 7	51⅛
Am Tel... 40	10 11	b b	b b	51⅛
Atl R 90	139 1¼	93 3¾	3 5⅛	79½
Atl R 80	141 4⅜	58 7⅞	16 9⅞	79½
Avon 35	734 4¼	158 6	54 7⅛	38⅛

This option has an exercise price of $35 a share

7⅛ premium for each option

Time has value, too. The more that's left, the more value remains in the premium.

6 premium for each option

4¼ premium for each option

This is how trading in options is reported in the financial pages of newspapers. Look under Chicago Board Options Exchange and American Exchange Options.

The explanation of each item is contained in the box surrounding it.

Source: From *Merrill Lynch Guide to Writing Options,* Merrill Lynch, Pierce, Fenner & Smith, Inc., New York, N.Y.

tions transactions show both buyer and writer where they stand at any given moment. The liquidity allows both parties to close out, or offset, their original transactions at a time of their own choosing.

The standardization and price reporting of listed options may be seen in Figure 11–3.

Who Buys and Who Sells Options and Why?

The most basic reason for buying a call option is in anticipation of an increase in the price of the underlying stock. If the stock goes up the call will go up and may be sold at a profit, before the cessation of trading in that series, in the secondary market. Or the call may be exercised with the holder of the call acquiring the underlying stock.

The excitement of buying options comes from their leverage effect. Through the use of options the buyers aim to make $1,000 do the work of $10,000. To achieve this leverage the buyers take a risk. They face the possibility of losing the entire amount of the premium they pay for the option against that of participating in the potential capital gain from the stock, without buying the stock itself.

The call buyers hope the stock will rise and their option price will rise with it. If the stock goes down, they stand to lose their whole premium, but that might be less than they would have lost by owning the stock outright and they would have tied up less capital. If the stock goes up, their percentage return on investment can be considerably higher than if they had bought the stock outright.

For example, on February 15, XYZ common stock is selling for $40 a share and an October 40 call can be purchased for $500 (100 shares at $5 per share). On April 15, XYZ is selling at $46 a share and the October 40 call is trading at $750. The call buyer is now able to sell the option at the higher premium and take the profit. The option is not exercised but sold. And the leverage is as follows:

	Call	Stock
Bought February 15	$500	$4,000
Sold April 15	750	4,600
Profit (before transaction costs)	250	600
Percent return on investment (not annualized)	50%	15%

The option buyer risks losing the whole investment rather quickly if expectations are wrong. He may, though, be able to resell the option in the secondary market before cessation of trading in that series and recover part of the cost. Or had he purchased the stock directly for $4,000 and it declined substantially, he could incur a loss

of more than $500 if he sold. He has a chance, of course, of recouping ground if he holds the stock and it later appreciates in value.

Writers of options, on the other hand, seek two ends—additional income from their portfolios and a hedge against a possible decline in the price of the stock they own. If the underlying stock remains stable or declines the option sold may not be exercised and the writer may retain the premium income. If the stock declines then the premium income helps reduce the loss on the stock. For example, assume that the stock of ABC Corp. is selling at 50. An owner of 100 ABC decides to write an option on the stock for a premium of $4 per share, receiving $400. That premium is determined by a variety of factors: supply and demand, the amount of time remaining in the option, and the market's evaluation of the outlook for the underlying stock. The asset (the stock) was used to produce immediate income ($400). If the price of the stock declines the option may expire worthless and the writer will have a premium to offset the stock's loss in value up to $4 a share. If, on the other hand, the stock rises and the option is exercised by the buyer, the option writer will have sold the stock for $54 a share.

Just as the buyers of an option may usually sell the option at any time prior to the expiration, the writers of an option may usually "buy in" an option they have previously written (assuming, of course, that the option has not yet been exercised). This offsetting transaction—known as a closing purchase—terminates their obligation to deliver the stock. Their profit or loss is the difference between the premium of the option initially sold and the premium cost of the option later purchased. For example, if they were to write an ABC option when the premium was $400 (for 100 shares) and later buy back an identical offsetting option at a time when the premium had declined to $200, their profit would be $200 less commissions.

The ability of the option writer to terminate the obligation to deliver the stock, by "buying in" an offsetting option, in no way affects the buyer's right to exercise the option purchased. The reason is that the OCC (Options Clearing Corporation) acts as the buyer to every seller and seller to every buyer. There is no continuing relationship between original buyer and seller. This feature helps to assure the financial integrity of all options bought and sold on the registered exchanges (CBOE, AMEX, PBW).

The point should, however, be indelibly recorded in the mind of every option writer that an option can be exercised and the writer called on to deliver the stock (at the exercise price) at any time prior to expiration regardless of the current price of the stock. The decision whether to exercise and when to exercise, is entirely up to the buyer (holder) of the option. Indeed, although it is not customary, there are circumstances under which options are exercised "early"; that is, days,

weeks, and even months prior to expiration. For instance, a situation in which the option premium happened to be less than the tangible value of the option (the market price of the stock minus the option's exercise price) would make the purchase of the option attractive to an arbitrageur. Such a trader would make a "short" sale of the underlying stock and cover the short position by buying and exercising the option, thereby realizing a "locked-in" profit.

Early exercise could also result from an option holder's desire to acquire rights to a cash dividend. Unless an exercise notice is assigned prior to an ex-dividend date for an ordinary cash dividend, the option writer retains all such dividends. In contrast to the older conventional option market, listed option striking prices are not reduced to compensate for the payment of cash dividends. Finally, an option may be exercised early if the option holder wishes to acquire the stock at the earliest possible date. For example, an investor anticipating a cash flow at a future date may have bought the option simply to establish a maximum purchase cost for the stock. Then, when he has cash at hand, he exercises the option, without regard to its remaining time value. Still another investor might exercise early to establish a longer holding period for tax purposes. Thus, it bears repeating: The writer of an option should clearly understand that he or she may be called upon to deliver the stock at the exercise price at any time during the life of the option.

Covered writing is the most common strategy. It involves writing calls against a long position in the underlying common stock in one's portfolio. The covered writer is long the underlying stock or convertible security such as warrants, convertible bonds, convertible preferreds or a listed option of the same class. He or she is willing to forego possible appreciation in the underlying issue in return for payment of the premium.

Several observers have argued that covered option writing is a particularly attractive technique for tax free institutional investors. Institutional investors have, however, intuitively shied away from covered option writing on the belief that such activity was either too speculative or inappropriate. Recently, however, a new attitude on the part of several regulatory agencies has created a heightened level of interest in the benefits which may be derived from option writing. For example, the Administration of National Banks has accepted the position that bank trust departments "could safely engage in writing call options on securities held in inventory subject to the prudent-man rule under the present state of the law."[26] New York State's

---

[26] Administration of National Banks, Washington, D.C.: Trust Banking Circular, no. 2, July 2, 1974.

Insurance Department, in late 1974, changed a ruling prohibiting licensed insurance companies from dealing in options on common stocks by noting, "The sale of exchange-traded call options through an exchange, on stock which is already owned by an insurer, provides the insurer with a conservative money management tool by which it can minimize the risk inherent in the ownership of stock."[27] Several other states have adopted a similar position.

Despite these new "endorsements," institutional investors, particularly pension funds, were reluctant to engage in covered option writing due to a peculiarity of the tax laws. Premium income received on expired options was, until September 1976, considered "unrelated" business income and is, therefore, taxable even if received by otherwise tax-free accounts, such as pension funds and endowment trusts. It was not just the tax liability that limited institutional covered option writing activity, but the fear that once part of the income flow became taxable, legislators would seek to tax as income other receipts of the trust, such as capital gains. New legislation adding income from options to the list of exclusions from taxable unrelated business income was passed in 1976. Option activity does not now endanger the tax-exempt status of non-profit institutions, such as pension funds, charitable foundations, endowment funds, and others.

The *uncovered* call writer also hopes to realize income from the writing of an option, but without the security of the underlying stock. The uncovered writer is, however, required to maintain margin with his or her broker. As in the case of the covered writer the maximum profit is the premium (less transaction costs). Large risks, however, are involved. These stem from the possibility of a sharp rise in the market price of the underlying stock above the exercise price, leading to the exercise of the option. An uncovered (naked) option sale is not unlike a short sale of the underlying stock. An uncovered writer stands to lose the amount by which the current market price of the underlying stock exceeds the exercise price (which theoretically can be without limit) less the amount of the premium (plus transactions costs).

Uncovered options should be written only by individuals who fully understand the substantial risks and are willing and financially able to assume them. It should be remembered, of course, that an uncovered writer, like the covered writer, may usually cancel the obligation at any time, prior to being assigned an exercise notice, by executing a closing purchase transaction. The profit or loss will depend, of course, on the difference between the cost of such closing transaction and the net proceeds from the original writing transaction. An uncovered

[27] Insurance Department of the State of New York, Regulation no. 72 (11 New York 174), December 11, 1974.

writer may also, during the life of the option, buy the underlying stock, thereby becoming a covered writer.

Choosing the Option to Write

There are conservative strategies in writing options, aggressive strategies and speculative strategies. Even within the framework of a conservative strategy, an investor has opportunities to tailor an option writing program to individual investment goals. One such area is in the selection of which options to write: an option with a nearby expiration or with a more distant expiration. Another decision to be made is whether to purchase an option whose exercise price is below the current market value of the stock, called an *"in-the-money"* option, or one whose exercise price is above the current market value of the stock, an *"out-of-the-money"* option. Other things being equal, the premium is generally higher for an "in-the-money" option, reflecting the fact that it has an immediate, tangible value.

The investor may have a choice of writing options with different exercise prices and, of course, different premiums and with three different expiration dates. For example, in early May, QED stock is acquired at the current price of $50 a share. In choosing an option to write, the investor may have the following alternatives:

Market Value of QED Stock: $50 per Share

	Premium†		
Option	July	October	January
QED 60 (out-of-the-money)	$1	$3	*
QED 50 (at-the-money)	$4	$6	$ 8
QED 45 (in-the-money)	$7	$9	$11

* No option offered.
† Cost per share.

You are clearly confronted with a wide range of choices—from a QED/July/60 with a premium of only $1 to a QED/January/45 with a premium of $11. The latter's substantially higher premium is due to the facts that: (*a*) it currently has a tangible value of $5 and (*b*) it has an added time value of six additional months during which it may be exercised. Since the QED/July/60 is currently $10 out of the money (with the stock selling at $50), its only value is its time value of $1.

Investors may choose from among these options depending upon their objectives. For example, if investors wish to improve the yield of their stock by earning option premium income but are anxious

to minimize the possibility of having the stock called away from them, they might write a QED/July/60 at a premium of $1. For each option written, they receive premium income of $100. Of all options currently offered, it is the least likely to be exercised. First, because its exercise price is well above the current stock price, and second, because of its early expiration. Or, as another example, an investor is "neutral" about the outlook for QED stock, having no feeling as to whether the price will increase or decrease, but is willing to sell the stock at a profit of $6 a share. The investor therefore writes a QED/Oct./50 option at a premium of $6. If the stock goes up and the call is exercised, the $6 premium gives him an effective price of $56. On the other hand, if the stock declines, he is protected against a loss unless the stock is below $44 at expiration.

Or, a third possibility, an investor believes the outlook for QED stock, at least through next January, is very bearish for the near future but wants to maintain his position long run. Instead of selling his stock he then decides to write a QED/Jan./45 option at a premium of $11. If he is correct in his expectation of a decline in stock prices, he does not incur a net loss unless the stock drops below $39 at expiration in January. Even if he is wrong about prices, and the option is exercised, he still has a profit of $6 (a $45 exercise price + $11 premium = $56).

Choosing the Option to Buy

Option prices generally move in the same direction as their underlying stock prices, but often move sharply and erratically. Buyers of options include investors and speculators who seek to increase their leverage and/or limit the risk of equity ownership in case the stock falls instead of rising. Buyers of call options include short sellers, who are buying relatively inexpensive insurance against short stock rising rather than falling. Buyers of options also include converters, who are selling stocks short and issuing puts from their riskless position. Buyers of options are arbitrageurs, who are buying "underpriced" options and selling "overpriced" options in varying proportions and seek only to profit from short-lived aberrations in the market which they expect will eventually adjust to more normal price relationships no matter which way the underlying stock moves. The expectations of these various participants on the buy side range from high-risk, large gains to low-risk, small gains.

For example, suppose a speculator last July 31 had become impressed with prospects for Digital Equipment (DEC) common. Instead of buying 100 shares of DEC for $11,025 (110¼ a share) he bought a DEC October 100 call for $15⅝ ($1,562.50)![28] With DEC at

---

[28] An October 100 call entitled this speculator to buy 100 shares of DEC common at $100 a share on or before October 24, 1975.

110¼, the option had a tangible value of $1,025 (market price of $11,025 minus exercise price of $10,000). Thus, this option buyer paid a premium of $537.50 over and above the option's tangible value for the right to acquire the stock at any time over the ensuing 12 weeks. By October 24 (expiration date), DEC common had increased in price to 129½, or by 17.5 percent. The October 100 call, however, had soared to 31¼ (up 100 percent). The speculator "closed out" his position by selling the call, netting a percentage return nearly six times that on the common.

Not all call options are bought with the intention of reselling them. Every option holder has the privilege—at any time prior to expiration—of exercising the option and calling for delivery of the stock. The mechanics are simple: the holders merely notify their broker that they wish to exercise the option and deliver a check to cover the cost of the stock plus commissions.

Exercising is normally to the buyer's advantage, however, only if the market value of the underlying stock is above the exercise price of the option. And even then, it may be more advantageous to sell the option than to exercise it, in order to minimize commissions. For example, the ABC Corporation July 50 option is bought at a premium of $5 a share. At expiration, the stock is selling for $58 a share and the option premium is $8. By selling the option, the commission is $25. But if the option is exercised and the stock resold, there is a commission when the stock is bought and again when it is sold. Assume a commission of $80 for each transaction, then:

Sale of Option		**Exercise of Option**	
Cost of option	$500	Cost of option	$ 500
Proceeds from sale of		Cost of stock	5,000
option	800	Sale of stock	5,800
Gain	$300	Gain	$ 300
Less $25 commission on		Less $25 commission on	
purchase and $25		option purchase, $80	
commission on sale	50	commission on both stock	
		purchase and stock sale ...	185
Net gain	$250	Net gain	$ 115

The decision to sell or exercise an option may also be influenced by the tax treatment of profits and losses. While these can be of considerable importance, we do not discuss them because the changing tax rulings might make obsolete our discussion in a short time.[29] As the

[29] See *Tax Considerations in Using CBOE Options*, the Chicago Board Options Exchange, February 1975. For a free copy write to the Chicago Board Options Exchange, La Salle at Jackson, Chicago, Illinois 60604. See also Robert J. Cirino, "Options: Pension Funds Prepare for the Green Light," *Institutional Investor*, August 1976, p. 45.

above example clearly illustrates, lower call option commissions—compared with stock commissions—can be an important consideration in the total investment decision. Indeed, the fact that an option on 100 shares of stock involves a considerably smaller commission than the commission charged on the purchase of 100 shares of the stock is a major advantage of options for many investors.

Complex Option Strategies

Option traders have developed a series of involved and sophisticated techniques[30] to take advantage of anticipated market movements in the price of the underlying common stock. Most of these are sufficiently complex so that only investors or speculators well versed in the nuances of option trading techniques can expect to use them with any degree of consistent success. For example, the strategy of variable option hedging requires that traders combine, in any ratio they decide, the writing of both covered and uncovered options on the same underlying common stock. An option trader who is modestly bearish may decide to sell three calls for each 200 shares held long in the portfolio. A more aggressive option writer, convinced of a downside move, might sell three calls for each 100 shares held long. Writing two or three options against 100 shares held in the portfolio provides two or three times as much premium income as writing one option. Variable hedging can mean increased cash flow and also increased downside protection. But it also means additional risk. During a period of declining prices, the investor may use successive options "walking down" in an effort to conserve capital. Should the market reverse itself and begin to move up, the same investor can reverse the strategy and begin "walking up."

Option spreading is the simultaneous purchase and sale of options within the same class of options. The options may be either at the same striking prices with different expiration months, or at different striking prices with the same or different expiration months. The spread is the dollar difference between the buy and sell premiums. If the cost of the purchased option is more than the proceeds of the option sold, the spread is expressed as a "debit." If the reverse is true, the spread is termed a "credit." If the costs and proceeds are equal, the spread is "even money."

---

[30] See, *The Versatile Option*, American Stock Exchange (New York: 1975). A free copy may be obtained by writing to the American Stock Exchange, Inc., 86 Trinity Place, New York, New York 10006. You can also write for *Option Writing Strategies*, and *Understanding Options*, both published by the Chicago Board Options Exchange, LaSalle at Jackson, Chicago, Illinois 60604. There is no charge for these useful booklets. See also *The Merrill Lynch Guide to Writing Options*. For a free copy write to Merrill Lynch, Pierce, Fenner & Smith, Inc., One Liberty Plaza, 165 Broadway, New York, New York 10006.

According to the American Stock Exchange, "Spreading is essentially a hedging strategy that is used to reduce, but not eliminate, risk in the trading of options."[31] Obviously, an option spreader's potential profit is lowered by the same amount that reduces risk.

The type of spread and the strike price will be based upon expectations for the price of the underlying stock over a specified period of time. The basic premise upon which an option spreader operates is that the dollar difference between premiums received for selling an option, and the cost of buying one, will change in his or her favor, and thereby create a profit.

Before describing specific and somewhat complex, option strategies it is important to point out a noticeable pattern in the general relationship between premiums on near-term option contracts relative to premiums on longer-term contracts for the same stock. Usually, these premium relationships are *not* directly proportional to the time remaining until expiration. That is, premiums for six-month and nine-month option contracts are usually less than two and three times the premium for the three-month options.

A "calendar spread" is the simultaneous purchase and sale of options within the same class with different expiration dates. Such spreads are also referred to as "time" or "horizontal" spreads. For example, a time or calendar spread is formed when an option trader sells a call of the nearest maturity and simultaneously buys one of the next expiration month. The exercise price of both sides of the spread will be identical. Consider, for example, that on May 26 with two months left in the July series of options, IBM common stock is trading at $250 with the following prices for the various call options:

	July	October	January
IBM 240	17⅜	25	31½
IBM 260	5⅞	13	18½
IBM 280	1⅜	5⅝	10¼

An option trader seeking to develop a time or calendar spread would sell an IBM July 280 contract at 1⅜ and buy the IBM October 280 at 5⅝, creating a 4¼ point debit spread. A spread such as this, will be widest when the stock price and exercise price are equal at expiration.

Another common spread is the "price," or "vertical" spread. This is the simultaneous purchase and sale of options within the same class with the same expiration date but with different striking prices.

In a rising market, option traders can attempt to capitalize on upward stock price movements with predetermined downside risk by

---

[31] "Spreading Strategies," American Stock Exchange, 1975, p. 3.

engaging in "bull-spreading." A "bull spread" is created when an option contract is purchased at a lower striking price than the contract sold, with both contracts due to expire at the same time. The higher striking price contract is sold to reduce the exposure required to establish the long, or bullish, position. Invested in this manner, the option trader will benefit, point for point, from any upward movement in the price of the underlying common stock until the higher striking price is reached. Once the stock sells above the higher striking price no further gain will be realized.

Let's consider the following stock price and option contract conditions:[32]

Underlying Stock	Striking Price	Option Premiums October	Last Stock Price
CMF	40	4	42
CMF	45	1¾	42

An investor, bullish on CMF, may decide to buy the October CMF contract at 4. In order to hedge this bullish position, however, an October 45 contract is sold at 1¾, for a 2¼ debit. By hedging in this manner, risk is reduced from $400 to $225 (4 minus 1¾). At the same time, profit is limited to $275 (less commissions).

This is in contrast to the unhedged purchase of the October 40 call, which theoretically could increase ten-fold or more if the underlying stock rose from $42 to $80 or more. The actual premiums are not as important to the spreader's strategy as the spread between them.

As in the calendar spread, the investor would anticipate the spread widening. This would occur, typically, if the stock moved up a few points. For instance, if the stock should climb to $45 a share or more before October expiration, the October 40 would intrinsically be worth 5 points more than the October 45. Therefore, shortly before expiration, the spread could be closed at approximately a 5 point difference, resulting in a $275 profit ($500 credit less $225 debit), less transaction costs. In effect, the investor bought the 5 point interval between $40 and $45 for $225.

On the other hand, an investor who is bearish on CMF at 42 can execute the opposite, or "bear," spread. In other words, the October 40 contract at 4 is sold and the October 45 contract at 1¾ is purchased at a 2¼ credit. By hedging in this manner, rather than simply writing an *uncovered* October 40 call, risk (which is theoretically unlimited in an uncovered position) is reduced to 2¾ and, at the same time, profit potential reduced from $400 to $225. If the stock declines to $40 or below as the expiration date approaches, the option trader would profit by the entire 2¼ points, pretax, less whatever small time

---

[32] Abstracted from "Spreading Strategies," American Stock Exchange, 1975, p. 6.

value remains in the October 40 and less transaction costs. If the stock climbs to $45 or above by expiration, the extent of pretax loss would be approximately 2¾ points, plus transaction costs. In effect, the 5 point interval is sold between $40 and $45 for $225.

One of the more intriguing option strategy maneuvers is known as a "butterfly spread" which involves buying option contracts in the middle (in terms of either striking price or time) and selling contracts on each side, or conversely selling options in the middle and buying contracts on each side. Here is how a "butterfly spread" (hedge) works:[33]

Assume Burrough's (BUR) common stock closes at a price of 96¼ on April 30, and call option contracts are priced as follows:

BUR
July   80s @ 17⅛
July   90s @ 12⅛
July 100s @   7⅛

The hedge-option player executes a bullish spread and a bearish spread simultaneously by buying a July 100 (@7⅛), and a July 80 (@17⅛), the two "outside" calls, and sells two "inside" July 90s (@12⅛).

The two outside option contracts cost $2,425 (2 × 12⅛), and the hedge option player receives the same amount as the sale of the two inside contracts, putting up $1,000 in a margin account as required by NYSE regulations.

If the stock closes at the end of July at 80 or below, or at 100 or above, the buy and sell contracts offset each other. If the stock closes on July 30 at prices anywhere between 81 and 99, the option spread creates a profit. For example, at a price of 94, there is a loss of $800 on the sell side, but a profit of $1,400 as realized on the long side (ex commissions) producing a net profit of $600.

We should point out, however, that there is more to this game than just simple arithmetic. Frequently, it is not possible to buy and sell option contracts at prices which create a non-risk spread position, such as the one just discussed. Also, commission costs are relatively expensive if only a small number of call option contracts are bought and sold.

Premiums

The size of premium an investor should be willing to pay for an option depends, essentially, on the probabilities attached to changes in the price of the underlying stock during the life of the option. For example, suppose that he is considering purchasing a six months' call at the current price of, say $50, and his expectations are as shown in Table 11–2.

The probability weighted, or "expected," price is $54. Therefore, a call on this stock with a premium of $500 is most likely to produce a

---

[33] Based on an example from William G. Shepherd, "Inside Wall Street," *Business Week*, May 5, 1975, p. 78.

TABLE 11–2
Calculation of "Expected Value" of a Stock

Price within 6 Months	Probability (percent)	Price × Probability
$70	0.05	$ 3.50
65	0.10	6.50
60	0.15	9.00
55	0.25	13.75
50	0.25	12.50
45	0.15	6.75
40	0.05	2.00
	1.00	$54.00

loss and is not attractive. On the other hand, if one could find a call on the same stock, exercisable 5 points *below* the market (i.e., at $45), a profit could be expected as long as the premium did not exceed about $800.

Some of the most important factors influencing option premiums are:

1. Puts are usually cheaper than calls because there is less buyer demand for them (investors are more often bulls than bears). Likewise, calls are more expensive in bull than in bear markets; and puts are more expensive in bear than in bull markets.

2. Options on active, highly volatile, stocks usually cost more than on inactive or stable stocks because there is more opportunity for the buyers of such options to make a profit sometime during the option period. For a similar reason, long option periods cost more than shorter term options.

3. The higher the price of the stock, the lower the percentage premium on the option, other things being equal.

4. Option prices seem responsive to changes in interest rates; they have been higher in recent years of very high interest rates than, say, a decade ago.

GLOSSARY OF OPTION TERMS

Call. An option contract that entitles the holder to buy a number of shares of the underlying security at a stated price on or before a fixed expiration date.

Class of Options. Options contracts of the same type (call or put) covering the same underlying security.

Clearing Member. A member of an exchange who has become a clearing member of the Options Clearing Corporation.

Closing Purchase Transaction. A transaction in which an investor who has previously written an option intends to liquidate his or her posi-

tion as a writer. This is accomplished by "purchasing" in a closing purchase transaction an option having the same terms as the option previously written. Such a transaction has the effect, upon payment of the premium, of canceling the investor's preexisting position as a writer, instead of resulting in the issuance of an option to the investor.

Closing Sale Transaction. A transaction in which an investor who has previously purchased an option intends to liquidate his or her position as a holder. This is accomplished by "selling" in a closing sale transaction an option having the same terms as the option previously purchased. Such a transaction has the effect of liquidating the investor's preexisting position as a holder of the option, instead of resulting in the investor's assuming the obligation of a writer.

Contract. A call or put issued by the Options Clearing Corporation.

Covered Option. An option in which the seller (or writer) owns the underlying security, as opposed to uncovered (or naked), where the option is written against cash or other margin.

Covered Writer. The writer of an option who owns the underlying stock.

Exchange Traded Option. A call option traded on an exchange, which gives the holder the right to buy the number of shares or other units of the underlying security covered by the option from the Options Clearing Corporation at the stated exercise price prior to its expiration on a fixed expiration date. The designation of an option includes the underlying security, the expiration month and the exercise price (e.g., "XYZ July 50" means an option covering a unit of trading [typically 100 shares] of XYZ stock which may be purchased at $50 per share until the option expires on the expiration date in July.)

Exercise Notice. A notice issued by the Option Clearing Corporation obligating a customer to deliver the securities covered by the option against payment of the exercise price.

Exercise Price. The price per unit at which the holder of an option may purchase the underlying security upon exercise. The exercise price is sometimes called the "striking price."

Expiration Date. The last day on which an option may be exercised. (Holders of options should determine from their brokers the time limit for instructing the broker to exercise an option, so that the expiration deadline, when an exercise notice must be received *at the Options Clearing Corporation*, may be met.)

In-the-Money. Call option in which the striking price is below the market price of the underlying stock.

Intrinsic Value. The difference between the market value of the underlying stock and the striking price of the option (but not less than zero).

Long Position. A situation in which the number of calls in a given series of options that have been bought in an account exceeds the number which have been sold, as opposed to a short position, in which the number of calls sold exceeds the number bought.

Open Interest. The number of outstanding contracts in the exchange market, or in a particular class or series.

Opening Purchase Transaction. A transaction in which an investor intends to become the holder of an option.

Opening Sale Transaction. A transaction in which an investor intends to become the writer of an option.

Options Clearing Corporation. The issuer of all options contracts on the exchanges on which listed options are traded.

Out-of-the-Money. A call option in which the striking price is above the market price of the underlying stock.

Premium. The aggregate price of an option agreed upon between the buyer and writer or their agents in a transaction on the floor of an exchange.

Put. An option contract that entitles the holder to sell a number of shares of the underlying stock at a stated price on or before a fixed expiration date.

Secondary Market. A function of listed option exchanges that enables investors to buy and sell options just as they buy and sell securities on the New York Stock Exchange or the American Stock Exchange. This function provides the liquidity which enables option writers to "buy back" their options. "Buying back" liquidates the option writer's position, freeing him from his obligation.

Short Position. See long position.

Spread. A strategy which involves writing one option in a given security at a given price for a certain expiration date and buying an option on the same security at a different price and/or with a different expiration date.

Striking Price (or Exercise Price). The price per share at which the option buyer may buy, in the case of a call, or sell, in the case of a put, 100 shares of the underlying stock. On option exchanges, the exercise price is set in advance and does not change during the life of the option. If the underlying stock's price changes appreciably, new exercise prices will be introduced for trading to more closely reflect the price of the underlying stock.

Uncovered Writer. The writer of an option who does not own the underlying stock.

Underlying Security. The security subject to being purchased upon the exercise of an option.

Underlying Stock. The stock subject to purchase upon exercise of the option.

Unit of Trading. The number of units of the underlying security designated by the Options Clearing Corporation as the subject of a single option. In the absence of any other designation, the unit of trading for a common stock is 100 shares.

Variable Hedge. A strategy which involves writing one covered option and one or more uncovered options.

HEDGING

Convertibles and options are of investment interest not only in their own right, but also as part of so-called hedge transactions. In a hedge, the underlying common stock is bought or sold short, and an *opposite* position is taken via convertibles or options on the stock. The purpose of this opposing position is to limit the dollar loss if the position in the stock turns out to be an error. Some examples will make this clearer.

A "convertible hedge" refers to a transaction in which a bearish investor buys a convertible and simultaneously sells short the common stock into which it may be converted. If the stock declines in price, as anticipated, the price of the convertible declines less than proportionately (he hopes). He then sells the convertible at a loss, buys common at the depressed price, and covers his short sale at a greater profit than the loss on the convertible. If he is wrong about the market, and a rise in the stock's price confronts him with a potential loss on the covering of the short sale, he has two alternatives. If the price of the convertible has risen, he can sell it at a profit which offsets the short-sale loss in whole or in part. Indeed, the price rise of the convertible may exceed that of the stock, resulting in a net profit. At the very worst, if the price of the convertible has not risen, he can exercise his conversion privilege and use the shares received to cover the short sale. His maximum loss will be the difference between the cost of the convertible and the proceeds of the short sale, namely the "premium" which he paid over conversion value. Thus, the main purpose of a "convertible hedge" is the profit from a declining stock market at a predeterminable risk.

Alternatively, a bearish investor can hedge a short-sale by purchasing a six-months' call. If the stock goes down, as he anticipates, he will not exercise the call. He will have a profit on his short sale, reduced by the amount of the call premium. If the stock goes up, he will lose on his short sale, but his loss is limited to the amount of the call premium since the loss on the short sale will be offset by the profit on the call.

Similarly, if the investor is bullish rather than bearish, he can buy the stock and also buy a put. If the stock rises, he will not exercise the put. He will have a profit on his long position in the stock, reduced by the amount of the put premium. If the stock goes down, he will lose on his long position, but his loss is limited to the amount of the put premium since the loss on the long position will be offset by the profit on the put.

Warrants also can be used in hedging by shorting stock and purchasing warrants. However, the mathematics involved in deciding how many warrants to buy is quite complicated, and the risk/reward trade-off is more uncertain because of the larger element of unpredictability in warrant price behavior than in convertibles or in calls. In any event,

it is clear that hedging transactions are for the sophisticated investor only.

SPECIAL SITUATIONS

For the sophisticated investor, special situations also offer considerable attraction. They afford the opportunity for capital gains because of some special development either within the company or in the external environment affecting the company. The development, if it occurs, will ensure the gain regardless of the general trend of the market. Narrowly defined, the true special situation has a mathematically predictable gain, like buying a $10 bill for only $7.50. More broadly and more usually, a special situation may work out to a calculable gain if certain developments come to pass. It also includes calculation of downside risk if the developments anticipated do not materialize.

True Special Situations

In the more limited sense of the term, special situations may arise from:

Liquidations. (In a complete liquidation the company disposes of its assets and distributes the proceeds to its shareholders.)

Residual Stubs. (These are certificates of participation or liquidation certificates, or certificates of beneficial interest, representing a residual interest in a company. They usually arise out of liquidations.)

Tenders. (An offer by a corporation to buy back its own shares. Or an offer by an outsider, interested in acquiring control, to buy up shares, usually at a price above the market.)

Spin-Offs. (A corporate divestiture of a division or a subsidiary by distributing shares in the new corporate entity to existing shareholders of the divesting company.)

Appraisals. (Court determination of the fair value of a dissenting shareholder's stock which the dissenter refuses to exchange in a merger or acquisition.)

Oversubscriptions. (These arise in rights offerings when shareholders who have exercised their rights are additionally offered an opportunity to buy remaining unsubscribed shares.)

Mergers and Acquisitions. (A merger usually involves an exchange of shares and a pooling of interests.)

Hedges and Arbitrages. (Out of mergers and acquisitions frequently arises the opportunity to profit by arbitrage and to minimize losses by hedging.)

Reorganizations. (When a company undergoes reorganization certain of its securities bought at panic prices may subsequently emerge from the reorganization at higher values.)

Recapitalizations. (Administrative changes in the capital structure of a corporation may involve a realignment of relationships among the company's securities with attendant profit possibilities.)

True special situations have three distinguishing characteristics:

1. Some unique development is occurring which makes this particular security attractive apart from general industry, economic, or security market conditions.
2. This development is usually noncontinuing in nature. If not seized upon when it appears, the specific opportunity may be lost. The security may continue to be a worthwhile purchase but not as a "special situation."
3. The situation is usually amenable to measurement of expected gains and calculation of probable risks.

   Some Examples. Two simple illustrations cited by *Business Week* are as follows:

1. Liquidation
   Hidden Value Corporation was preparing to sell all its assets.

The sales price per share would yield	$10.00
On liquidation, it could claim a tax refund of	4.40
Making a total sure value of	$14.40
But the stock was then selling for	11.00
So the buyer could count on a net profit of	$ 3.40

2. Merger
   Attractive Company was about to merge with High-Powered Company.

Shareholders of Attractive were due to get one share of High-Powered common worth	$26.00
Plus 4/50 of a share of High-Powered preferred (selling at $44 a share)	3.50
Making a total sum value of	$29.50
Attractive Co. stock was selling for	25.75
So the buyer could make a profit of	$ 3.75

Not all mergers, of course, present special situation possibilities. There must exist a chance to purchase shares of the company to be acquired at a discount from their ultimate exchange value in terms of the acquiring company's stock to be received. Even where the desired

discount is to be found, it may quickly be narrowed or wiped out by market action. Thus, as in all investments, timing is an important factor in the merger-acquisition special situation. Moreover, this type of special situation is not devoid of risk.

In a study of "merger-hedges," Dr. John Shelton points to two risks: (1) the merger may never be completed; and (2) the merger may be completed only after such a long delay that the profit represents an unsatisfactory return for the length of time the money was tied up. Of 402 merger or buy-out proposals studied, occurring during the five-year period 1958–62, only 41 were deemed suitable for the arbitrage procedure. Of the 41, 8 were not completed,[34] and a 9th resulted in a loss because the company on the short side of the hedge paid large dividends during the pendency period.

Dr. Shelton concluded:

Merger-hedges, if properly screened, appear to offer a satisfactory rate of return in view of the limited risk associated with them. They may not appeal to many investors either because the actual profit spread (typically about 3% to 4% after transaction costs) may seem too small to justify the effort if consideration is not given to the rather fast turnover of the capital, or because the operation requires fairly close scrutiny of the securities markets. This study indicates that the professional would have to sift through about ten potential mergers to find one that is suitable for hedging. . . . Finally, the merger-hedge appears to be a special situation that offers moderately good rewards for moderately low risk.

In a study of the overall effects of mergers, Gort and Hogarty concluded that:

a. Mergers, on the average, have an approximately neutral effect on the aggregate net worth of firms that participate in them.
b. The shareholders of *acquiring* firms *lose* on the average.
c. The shareholders of *acquired* firms *gain* on the average.[35]

Block studied completed mergers in relation to the gains in the prices of acquired companies' stock over varying time periods. He found that in the month prior to the announcement of the merger, prices of the shares of the acquired company rose, on the average, 17 percent, indicating that in this period, either the acquiring company was making substantial stock purchases, or that some investors were benefiting from inside information, or both.[36]

---

[34] In a 1969 study, Value Line found that 162 mergers were completed and 86 were called off (*More Profit and Less Risk: Convertible Securities and Warrants* [New York: Arnold Bernhard & Co., 1970], p. 92).

[35] Michael Gort and Thomas F. Hogarty, "New Evidence on Mergers," *The Journal of Law and Economics*, April 1970.

[36] Stanley B. Block, "The Effect of Mergers and Acquisitions on the Market Value of Common Stock," *Journal of Finance*, December 1968.

Also, after the announcement, if the merger is actually consummated, the shares of the acquired company tend to rise. For example, one week before the announcement of the acquisition of Scientific Data Systems, Inc. by Xerox, the former's stock rose $15.25 per share (from $86.75 to $102). Xerox sold at $268. The acquisition announcement stated that one share of Xerox would be exchanged for two shares of Scientific Data Systems, a premium of about 35 percent. The day after the board of director approved, Scientific Data stock sold for $111 a share, Xerox for $254.375. By the time the stockholders approved Scientific Data sold for $124.50. While there was a possibility that the Department of Justice might have moved against the merger, an investor who bought Scientific Data one week before the announcement and sold it the day of approval, some 15 weeks later, would have realized a gain of about 60 percent. He could have cemented his gain by a merger hedge, buying 200 shares of Scientific Data and concurrently selling 100 shares of Xerox short.[37]

Reorganizations. Reorganizations are also traditional special situations. In the case of a company facing reorganization, the old securities will be greatly depressed in value. Through careful financial analysis, workout values can be approximated for some classes of securities. Two trading procedures can then be utilized. Either the selected depressed securities can be purchased and held and in due course exchanged for new securities issued under the plan of reorganization, or a hedge operation can be undertaken. This is accomplished by buying the old securities and then subsequently selling on a "when, as, and if issued" basis, the new securities to be received in exchange. This is predicated, of course, on the assumption that the market value of the new securities to be received in the exchange will be greater than the cost of the old securities purchased at very depressed prices. This occurs often in reorganizations but not inevitably or invariably, and thus careful financial evaluation of pro forma balance sheets and income accounts in reorganization plans is essential. It is not an area for amateurs.

The Spin-Off. Another traditional special situation is the spin-off. This occurs when a company distributes the stock of one or more of its subsidiaries to the shareholders of the parent company. Since the shareholders of the parent company in effect own the subsidiaries controlled by the parent, the shares of the subsidiaries are usually not sold but rather distributed free of any additional charge. They are "spun off." In a spin-off special situation one and one do not add up to two—but to more. That is, the sum of the parts is equal to more than the whole.

---

[37] See Maurece Schiller and Martin Benis, "Special Situations," *Financial Analyst's Handbook*, vol. 1 (Homewood, Ill.: Dow Jones-Irwin, Inc., 1975), chap. 16, p. 451.

When J. Ray McDermott distributed 0.88 shares of Transocean for each share of McDermott, its stock was selling for $32 per share. Some months later McDermott stock sold for $36 and Transocean for $16 a share. Thus an investor realized a gain of over 60 percent from this divestiture in less than one year.[38]

The Broader Special Situation

In contrast to the precise calculations involved in traditional special situations, the broader sense of the concept, as used by many investment advisory services and stock brokerage houses, includes the following:

Hidden Earnings.
Court Orders and Litigation.
New Technological Developments.
Changing Government Regulations or Tax Rulings.
New Management.
Comeback Situations.
New Markets.

Several investment advisory firms have special situation services. This is true of *Forbes,* and Value Line. In the view of Arnold Bernhard "a special situation refers to some security in which an extraordinary, nonrecurring corporate development is taking place—a development which can reasonably be expected to enhance the value of the security in question irrespective of the trend of the market as a whole."

The broader special situation concept is illustrated by:

a. Polaroid's introduction of the camera capable of developing prints in seconds after the picture is snapped, sent the stock soaring from 10 to a high of 149½, adjusted for numerous stock splits.

b. Xerox Corporation's stock was selling around $5 a share (adjusted for subsequent stock splits), and its sales were at the $30 million mark, when the company introduced the 914 Copier. This new machine was the first offered commercially, and it revolutionized and expanded the market. Within a little more than five years, sales had expanded by 13 times, and the stock price appreciated over 50 times. On an adjusted basis the stock rose from 1⅞ to 171⅞.

c. Burroughs was a stodgy maker of adding machines and electromechanical accounting equipment up until it transformed itself into a highly successful producer of electronic data processing and electronic accounting machines. Earnings rose almost 700 percent in five years, and the stock rose from 5¾ to 126⅜.

---

[38] See Schiller and Benis, "Special Situations," p. 455.

d. St. Joe Minerals was misunderstood. The Street thought of it as a lead and zinc company, which it was. But there was also, as *Forbes Special Situation Service* pointed out, a big new commitment to energy. In early 1974, SJO bought Massey Coal for $56 million of SJO stock. Massey's operating income in 1973 was $9 million, in 1974 it was over $43 million. *Forbes* recommended SJO on October 18, 1974 at 35 (17½ adjusted for a 2-for-1 stock split). The stock doubled in less than a year. Mapco, another energy play, recommended by *Forbes,* went from 17½ on July 19, 1974 to 50½ in 1975. Followers of the *Forbes* Service had a 70 percent gain in the first six months.

SUGGESTED READINGS

Ansbacher, Max G. *The New Options Market.* New York: Walker Publishing Co., 1975.

Black, Fischer. "Fact and Fantasy in the Use of Options." *Financial Analysts Journal,* July/August 1975.

———, and Scholes, Myron. "The Valuation of Option Contracts and a Test of Market Efficiency." *Journal of Finance,* May 1972.

———, and Scholes, Myron. "The Pricing of Options and Corporate Liabilities." *The Journal of Political Economy,* May/June 1973.

Brealey, Richard A. *Security Prices in a Competitive Market,* Cambridge, Mass.: M.I.T. Press, 1971.

Fried, Sidney. *Fortune Building in the 70's with Common Stock Warrants and Low Priced Stock.* New York: RHM Associates, 1975.

Gastineau, Gary L. *The Stock Options Manual.* New York: McGraw-Hill Book Co., 1975.

Hettenhouse, G. W., and Puglisi, D. J. "Investor Experience with Options." *Financial Analysts Journal,* July/August 1975.

Leibowitz, Martin L. "Analysis of Convertible Bonds," *Financial Analyst's Handbook,* vol. I. Homewood, Ill.: Dow Jones-Irwin, Inc., 1975, chap. 10.

Malkiel, Burton G., and Quandt, Richard E. *Strategies and Rational Decisions in the Securities Option Market.* Cambridge, Mass.: M.I.T. Press, 1969.

The Merrill Lynch Guide to Writing Options. For a free copy write to Merrill Lynch, Pierce, Fenner & Smith, Inc., One Liberty Plaza, 165 Broadway, New York, N.Y. 10006.

Merton, Robert G. "Theory of Rational Option Pricing." *Bell Journal of Economics and Management Science,* Spring 1973.

Noddings, Thomas C. The Dow Jones-Irwin *Guide to Convertible Securities.* Homewood, Ill.: Dow Jones-Irwin, Inc., 1973.

Noddings, Thomas C., and Zazove, Earl. *CBOE Call Options: Your Daily Guide to Portfolio Strategy.* Homewood, Ill.: Dow Jones-Irwin, Inc., 1975.

Option Writing Strategies. A free copy may be obtained from the Chicago Board Options Exchange, LaSalle at Jackson, Chicago, Illinois 60604.

Platnick, Kenneth B. *The Option Game*. New York: CommuniConcepts, 1975.

Reback, Robert. "Risk and Return in Option Trading." *Financial Analysts Journal*, July/August 1975.

Rosen, Lawrence R. *How to Trade Put and Call Options*. Homewood, Ill.: Dow Jones-Irwin, Inc., 1974.

Schiller, Maurece, and Benis, Martin. "Special Situations," *Financial Analyst's Handbook*. vol. I. Homewood, Ill.: Dow Jones-Irwin, Inc., 1975, chap. 16.

Shelton, John P. "The Relation of the Price of a Warrant to the Price of Its Associated Stock," (in two parts), *Financial Analysts Journal*, May/June and July/August 1967.

Soldofsky, Robert M. "Performance of Convertibles." *Financial Analysts Journal*, March/April 1971.

Turov, Daniel. "Dividend Paying Stocks and Their Warrants." *Financial Analysts Journal*, March/April 1973.

———. "Warrants and Options," *Financial Analyst's Handbook*. vol. I. Homewood, Ill.: Dow Jones-Irwin, Inc., 1975, chap. 17.

Understanding Options. A free copy may be obtained from the Chicago Board Options Exchange, LaSalle at Jackson, Chicago, Illinois 60604.

The Versatile Option. New York: American Stock Exchange. 1975. A free copy may be obtained by writing to the American Stock Exchange, Inc., at 86 Trinity Place, New York, N.Y. 10006.

REVIEW QUESTIONS AND PROBLEMS

1. What considerations may lead a corporation to issue convertible securities rather than straight bonds, preferred stock, or common stock?

2. Explain the significance of the conversion parity price of the common stock into which a senior security is convertible.

3. What is the significance of the call price of a convertible security (a) from the issuer's viewpoint, and (b) from the investor's viewpoint?

4. What is the significance of (a) the current yield, and (b) the yield to maturity in the analysis of a convertible debenture?

5. Under what circumstances are convertible securities, in general, likely to *decline* in price?

6. Describe the determinants of changes in the market price of a warrant.

7. What are the essential features and advantages of the new exchange traded option, as compared to the older traditional put and call option?

8. In what ways can call options be used by (a) long-term investors, and (b) short-term traders?

9. Distinguish between the broader and the narrower concepts of the term "special situation."

10. In what way can an analysis of corporate *managements* enable one to uncover special-situation opportunities?

RESEARCH PROJECTS

1. Review the history of American Telephone & Telegraph's use of convertibles and warrants.
2. Select a convertible security from the daily quotation sheets and analyze its investment attractiveness.
3. Select a warrant from the daily quotation sheets and analyze its investment attractiveness.
4. Select a call option from the daily quotation sheets and analyze its investment attractiveness.
5. Illustrate how a recent merger gave rise to a special situation opportunity.

C.F.A. QUESTION

1. *From Exam I, 1974*

Todd Hammer, a security analyst in the trust investment department of Nutmeg National Bank, learned that Xacta Corporation had called for redemption of its $20 par value convertible preferred stock on October 1, 1974 at par plus accrued dividends. The annual dividend of $1.20 had been paid regularly, quarterly on the first of January, April, October and December. Each preferred share is convertible into two common shares until June 30, 1974.

The preferred stock is currently selling at $30 and the common stock at $15. A statistical analysis of Xacta's preferred stock is shown on page 494.

The common stock is estimated to earn $0.75 a share this year, and its indicated annual dividend rate at present is $0.45 a share.

a. Discuss the implications of (1) continuing to hold the preferred stock and (2) converting the preferred stock.

Hammer decided he should replace the shares of Xacta Corporation convertible preferred stock in accounts he managed with another convertible preferred stock. His search for a suitable replacement narrowed down to the convertible preferred stocks of Yerba Corporation and Zorro Corporation. In his opinion, both corporations had equally good prospects. A factual description of the two issues is given in the following paragraphs and a statistical comparison is also shown.

Yerba Corporation's $3.00 preferred stock is convertible share-for-share into common at any time until June 30, 1982, and is noncallable until 1977. The preferred stock is selling at $50 and the common at $45½. The common stock is estimated to earn $4.50 a share this year and its indicated annual dividend rate is $2.50 a share at present.

Zorro Corporation's $2.68 preferred stock is convertible into two common shares until June 30, 1976 and into 1.8 common shares thereafter until June 30, 1982. It is noncallable until 1978. The preferred stock is selling at $44 and

the common at $20. The common stock is estimated to earn $1.80 a share this year and its indicated annual dividend rate is $1.00 a share at present.

	Xacta	Yerba	Zorro
Current market price, preferred	30	50	44
Current market price, common	15	45½	20
Premium over conversion value	0	10%	10%*
			22%†
Preferred dividend	$1.20	$3.00	$2.68
Preferred yield	4.0%	6.0%	6.1%
Common dividend	$0.45	$2.50	$1.00
Common yield	3.0%	5.5%	5.0%
P/E ratio	20.0	10.0	11.1

* Based on conversion ratio of 2 to 1 until 6/30/76.
† Based on conversion ratio of 1.8 to 1 after 6/30/76.

b. Select the better convertible preferred stock issue—that of Yerba or Zorro—to satisfy Mr. Hammer's request for a combination of capital appreciation and current income. Discuss fully.

Appendix to Part II

Summary of Widely Used Financial Ratios

As will be evident from the chapters on security valuation, investment analysts make use of a large number of financial ratios. It may be convenient for the reader to have the most common ratios brought together in one section which can serve as a "checklist" when attempting a comprehensive analysis of a company's financial statements. That is the purpose of this appendix.

We present the appendix with some trepidation, however, because we fear the reader may take it as a suggestion that investments can be appraised mechanistically. Such an impression would be a serious error, not taking into account either the quality of a company's management, the validity of its accounting procedures, or the fact that the past record is useful mainly as a basis for focusing upon those critical variables which may *change* in the future.

Having sounded this word of caution, we proceed with the summary of financial ratios. An attempt has been made to group the ratios in a sequence which might be followed by an analyst. That is, an analyst normally would begin with an examination of a company's historical rates of growth of sales and earnings, both in absolute terms and in relation to the growth rates of other companies and of the economy. Next would come an effort to understand the key sources of past earnings growth: profit margin on sales, utilization of assets, and financial policies. The growth analysis would be followed by an appraisal of the company's financial strength, particularly its ability to service its debts and to generate the funds needed to carry out its operating programs. Finally, the prices of its securities would be examined in various perspectives in preparation for a decision to buy or sell.

495

I. HISTORICAL GROWTH RATES

To gain an overview of the historical development of a company, it is helpful to calculate the growth rates of its sales, earnings, book value, and stock price over an extended period of time. Preferably, the beginning and ending years of the time period should be at approximately the same stage of the general business cycle or of the particular industry's own cycle, if different from the general cycle. These growth rates should be compared with those of other companies in the same industry, and with the growth rates of broad economic aggregates such as gross national product and total corporate profits.

Since mergers and acquisitions can seriously distort trends in the *dollar totals* of a company's sales and earnings, it is desirable to express these amounts in *per share* terms. This will require adjustment for stock splits and stock dividends, and will take into account the existence of "common stock equivalents." Per share calculation procedures were described in Chapter 4.

Growth rates of the following items should be of particular interest:

1. Sales
    (Note: If data are available, sales growth should be calculated for each major product line, and unit growth should be distinguished from price growth.)
2. Operating Income, equal to
        Sales minus:
            Cost of Goods Sold
            Selling, General, and Administrative Expenses
            Depreciation, Amortization, and Depletion
    (Note: Some analysts define operating income as being *before* depreciation.)
3. Net Available for Common, equal to
        Net Income minus Preferred Dividends
    (Note: Net income usually is taken before extraordinary items; this is the familiar "earnings per share" amount.)
4. Cash Flow, equal to
        Net Available for Common plus Depreciation and Deferred Tax Charge
    (Note: While "Cash Flow" is a misnomer for this figure, it can be very useful analytically.)
5. Dividends on Common Stock
6. Stockholders' Equity (also known as Book Value), equal to
        Tangible Assets minus Liabilities and Preferred Stock Liquidation Value
    (Note: Preferred stock is, technically, equity, but it is excluded from equity in the ratios described in this Appendix.)

7.   Averge Price of Common Stock, equal to
     Mean of Annual High and Low Price

II. DETERMINANTS OF EARNINGS GROWTH

There are many ways to gain insight into the sources of a company's earnings growth. The approach followed in this text is based upon the widely utilized methods developed by the Du Pont Corporation. This approach focuses on *profit margins* and *turnover of operating assets*. The interaction of margin and turnover produces a rate of *return on operating assets*. Depending on the degree of *leverage* introduced into a company's capital structure, the *return on equity* will be greater than the return on assets. Finally, given the return on equity, a company's earnings growth (aside from mergers and acquisitions) will depend on whether it pays out most of its earnings as dividends to stockholders or whether it reinvests most of its earnings in additional assets.

All of the ratios listed in this section should be studied both "temporally" and "cross-sectionally." Temporal analysis refers to a study of the ratios over a period of time. Cross-sectional analysis refers to a comparison of the ratios for different companies at the same point in time.

    A.   Profit Margin Analysis.   This involves not only measuring the margins, but also examining each major component of costs to determine why the margin is high or low, rising or falling. The most significant ratios are:

1.   Operating Margin, equal to
     Operating Income as a percentage of Sales
2.   Pretax Margin, equal to
     Net Income Before Taxes as a percentage of Sales
3.   Net Profit Margin, equal to
     Net Available for Common as a percentage of Sales
4.   Expense ratios, which express each of the following expenses as a percentage of Sales
     a.   Labor costs. (Note: This ratio often is supplemented by a study of sales per employee and wages per employee.)
     b.   Other costs of goods sold (mainly materials and direct overhead).
     c.   Selling, general, and administrative expense. (Note: Research and development outlays often are separately analyzed.)
     d.   Depreciation, amortization, and depletion. (Note: This item often is expressed as a percentage of average gross plant.)
5.   Tax Rate, equal to
     Income taxes as a percentage of net income before taxes

    B.   Turnover Analysis.   This involves an examination of the intensity of utilization of each major class of asset, as well as of total operat-

ing assets. In addition, various "capital turnover" ratios are common. The key ratios are:

1. Asset Turnover, equal to Sales divided by each of the following:
    a. Cash
    b. Accounts Receivable
    c. Inventory
    d. Current Assets $(a + b + c)$
    e. Working Capital $(d -$ Current Liabilities$)$
    f. Gross Plant
    g. Net Plant
    h. Total Operating Assets $(d + g)$
2. Capital Turnover, equal to
    Sales divided by the sum of Long-Term Debt, Preferred Stock, and Stockholders' Equity
3. Equity Turnover, equal to
    Sales divided by Stockholders' Equity

C. Rate of Return. The rate of return measures the relationship of earnings to either assets or capital. There are several rate of return measures upon which analysts focus attention, as follows:

1. Return on Operating Assets, equal to
    Operating Income as a percentage of Operating Assets

    (Note: This ratio is the product of the Operating Margin multiplied by the Turnover of Operating Assets; that is,

    $$\frac{\text{Operating Income}}{\text{Sales}} \times \frac{\text{Sales}}{\text{Operating Assets}}.$$

2. Return on Total Assets, equal to
    Earnings before Interest and Taxes (known as EBIT) as a percentage of Total Assets
    (Note: This ratio adds to the return on operating assets a company's net nonoperating income, before interest and taxes, and its nonoperating assets.)
3. Pretax Return on Total Capital, equal to
    EBIT as a percentage of the sum of Long-Term Debt, Preferred Stock, and Stockholders' Equity
    [Note: The *after-tax* return on total capital would use as the earnings amount the sum of (a) net available for common, (b) preferred dividends, and (c) (interest $\times$ [$1.0 -$ tax rate]).]
4. Return on Stockholders' Equity, equal to
    Net Available for Common as a percentage of Stockholders' Equity
    (Note: The difference between pretax return on total capital and

return on equity reflects the tax rate and the degree of financial leverage.)

D. Financial Policy. This impacts earnings growth in two ways. One major feature of financial policy is "leverage," or the degree to which a company uses borrowed funds as opposed to equity. Leverage enables the return on assets (if higher than the interest rate on borrowed funds) to be translated into an even higher rate of return on stockholders' equity. Similarly, growth of return on assets becomes magnified into a higher growth of return on equity. Of course, leverage also poses significant risks, because it has a reverse impact on stockholders' well-being if return on assets is low or declining.

A second major feature of financial policy is a company's dividend policy. Given a positive rate of return on equity, every dollar of earnings retained in the business, rather than paid out as dividends to common stockholders, will generate incremental earnings per share in succeeding years. Indeed, as was demonstrated in Chapter 7, a company's "internal growth rate" (the growth potential of earnings per share exclusive of additional issuance of common stock) is equal to the product of its rate of return on equity multiplied by its earnings retention rate.

The key measures of a company's leverage policy are as follows:

1. Total Leverage, equal to
   Total Assets divided by Stockholders' Equity
   (Note: This measure is referred to as total leverage because it reflects the portion of assets financed by all funds other than common equity—that is, short-term debt [notes and accounts payable], long-term debt, and preferred stock.)

2. Debt-to-Capital, equal to
   Long-Term Debt plus Preferred Stock as a percentage of Total Capital
   (Note: This ratio considers only long-term leverage. Preferred stock is considered a form of borrowed capital. Definitions of terms will be elaborated below.)

3. Debt-to-Equity, equal to
   Long-Term Debt plus Preferred Stock as a percentage of Stockholders' Equity
   (Note: This concept is identical to debt-to-capital, but expresses the relationship a bit differently.)

4. Debt to Tangible Assets, equal to
   Total Liabilities plus Preferred Stock as a percentage of Total Assets excluding Intangibles.
   (Note: This measure is related to total leverage, and permits a division of debt into long-term and short-term portions, with each portion expressed as a percentage of tangible assets.)

In all of the leverage measures, the following definitions are generally applicable:

a. Long-term debt should include the capitalized value of long-term lease obligations as well as many of the other off-balance sheet liabilities discussed in Chapter 4.

b. Preferred stock should be taken at the liquidation value stated in the contract, if different from par.

c. Minority interests generally should be treated as "other liabilities."

d. Intangibles should be deducted from assets and stockholders' equity, unless the analyst believes they have realizable value.

e. Deferred tax liabilities may be treated as either long-term debt, "other liabilities," or stockholders' equity, depending on the analyst's views regarding the likelihood that they will have to be paid.

The key measures of a company's dividend policy are:

1. Payout Ratio, equal to
   Common Dividends as a percentage of Net Available for Common
   (Note: As a supplement, dividends may be expressed as a percentage of "cash flow.")
2. Retention Rate, equal to
   100 percent minus the Payout Ratio

III. MEASURES OF FINANCIAL STRENGTH

Generally, the ratios enumerated below are measures of credit quality and, therefore, are of greatest interest to bond and preferred stock investors. But they are by no means insignificant for common stock investors. For if a company's credit-worthiness deteriorates, there are negative implications for owners as well as for creditors. The key ratios on which analysts focus have to do with fixed charge coverage, leverage, and liquidity. Since leverage already has been covered above, only the coverage and liquidity ratios will be itemized here.

A. *Coverage Ratios.* Coverage ratios are designed to measure the relationship between a company's earnings and its obligations to pay interest, preferred stock dividends, and any sinking-fund obligations. The principal ratios are:

1. Fixed charge coverage, equal to
   Earnings before Interest and Taxes (EBIT) divided by Interest

(Note: Interest should include relevant long-term lease obligations.)

2. Coverage of Interest and Sinking Funds, equal to
   Earnings before Interest, Taxes, *and Depreciation* divided by Interest plus Sinking Fund Requirements
   (Note: The assumption is that depreciation bears a relationship to sinking-fund requirements.)

3. Coverage of Interest and Preferred Dividends, equal to
   EBIT divided by Interest plus [Preferred Dividends $\div$ (1.0 − Tax rate)]
   (Note: The preferred dividend [not tax-deductible] is adjusted upward to make it comparable to interest [tax-deductible].)

4. Alternative Fixed Charge Coverage, equal to
   EBIT as a percentage of the Principal Amount of Long-Term Debt or of Debt plus Preferred Stock
   (Note: This alternative measure is used to compare companies whose debt was issued at different times and, as a result, bears very different coupon rates of interest. The concept is that since the debt probably will be refunded from time to time, the coupon rates may be less relevant than the principal amounts.)

B. Liquidity Measures. These measures are needed because a company may be generating a lot of "bookkeeping earnings," but may be "cash poor." The most widely used ratios are:

1. Current Ratio, equal to
   Current Assets divided by Current liabilities

2. Acid Test (or Quick Asset) Ratio, equal to
   Sum of Cash (and equivalents) plus Accounts Receivable divided by Current Liabilities

3. Cash Ratio
   Cash (and equivalents) divided by Current Liabilities

4. Working Capital-to-Sales, equal to
   (Current Assets minus Current Liabilities) as a percentage of Sales

5. Cash Flow-to-Debt, equal to
   Cash Flow as a percentage of Principal Amount of Debt

6. Receivables Collection Period, equal to
   Average Receivables divided by Average Daily Sales

7. Days to Sell Inventory, equal to
   Average Inventory divided by Average Daily Cost of Goods Sold

8. Internal Funding of Capital Expenditures, equal to
   Capital Expenditures as a percentage of the sum of Retained Earnings plus Depreciation

IV. MEASURES OF STOCK AND BOND PRICES

It is meaningless to compare the prices of different securities, or of the same security over time, in absolute dollar-and-cents terms. The fact that stock X sells for, say, $50 per share, while stock Y sells for $200 per share, in no way implies that stock Y is "dearer" than stock X. It is necessary to relate price to earnings, or dividends, or interest rate, or book value—in other words, to relate price to a fundamental determinant of value. The key measures are:

1. Price/Earnings Ratio, equal to
    Price divided by Net Available for Common per Share
    (Note: The earnings figure used in the denominator is usually either the sum of the latest four quarters or the analyst's estimate of earnings for the current year. However, if current earnings are greatly influenced by unusual factors, an attempt should be made to determine a "normalized" earnings amount.)
2. Relative P/E, equal to
    Price/Earnings Ratio of a particular stock expressed as a percentage of the Price/Earnings Ratio of a broad market index such as the S&P Index.
3. Price/Book Value, equal to
    Price divided by Stockholders' Equity per Share
    (Note: This ratio is used mainly in appraising the stocks of financial companies and in mergers and acquisitions.)
4. Current Yield, equal to
    Annual Dividend Rate on Stock (common or preferred) as a percentage of Price, or Annual Coupon Rate on Bond as a percentage of Price
5. Yield to Maturity, equal to
    Discount Rate which equates Price with Future Interest and Principal Payments
    (Note: This yield is most readily determined from a set of yield tables. However, it usually can be approximated by applying the following formula:

$$\frac{\text{Coupon Rate} \pm (\text{Discount or Premium} \div \text{Years to Maturity})}{\tfrac{1}{2} \, (\text{Price of Bond} + \text{Par Value})}$$

PART III

INVESTMENT TIMING

INTRODUCTION TO PART III

Investment decisions usually are classified under two broad headings: "selection" and "timing." Selection deals with the question: *What* to buy or sell—bonds or stocks; which bonds; which stocks? Timing deals with the question: *When* to buy or sell—now or wait? As a practical matter, of course, these two categories are not mutually exclusive. The question of what to buy or sell is not made in a time vacuum. The real question is: *What* to do with my capital *now?* Granting the interlocking nature of selection and timing, however, it is useful to differentiate between them conceptually.

The traditional textbook approach to both the selection and timing aspects of investment has been that of "security analysis," or "evaluation." In Chapter 5 of this text, for example, it was shown that the goal of common stock evaluation is to determine the approximate trend line around which actual stock prices can be expected to fluctuate. At any given time, according to this approach, common stock analysts should have a reasonably clear idea whether stocks generally, and individual stocks in particular, seem underpriced or overpriced. This enables them to come to grips with both the what and when questions. For example, they may seek to buy issues which are relatively most underpriced, at a time when the market in general seems underpriced.

Value analysts assume that underpriced and overpriced situations ultimately will come into better balance. But they typically make little or no effort to predict when the corrective price movement will occur. Their reasons for ignoring efforts to predict are several. First, they argue that it is not possible to make predictions about turning points of prices with a better than chance probability of being accurate. (As will be described in Chapter 15, this argument is supported by believers in the "efficient markets hypothesis," who also doubt, however, that

"value analysis" can be effective.) Second, they point out that investors confront "a market of stocks rather than a stock market." By this they mean that efforts to predict the turning points of, say, the Dow Jones Industrial Average are rather futile, since an average can go up or down but there is great disparity in the price movement of the individual component stocks of the average. Furthermore, they note with regard to attempts to predict the averages, most downturns during the postwar period have amounted to only some 10–20 percent. Certainly one cannot expect to be prescient enough to sell at the very peaks and buy back at the troughs. Assuming that even a good forecaster will make his or her sales at least 3–5 percent below the peaks, and that repurchases will be made 3–5 percent above the troughs, and making allowance for brokerage commissions and taxes of several percent on combined sale-repurchase transactions, the average price decline of 10–20 percent doesn't leave much, if anything, for profit. Moreover, there are very real dangers of being "whipsawed" by selling in anticipation of a price decline which fails to occur.

So strong is the antipathy of many value analysts toward price prediction efforts outside of the value context that it seems important to comment on the logic of their position. In the first place, it is hoped that the following chapters will demonstrate that predictive tools are available which can produce better than chance results if utilized properly. It will not be argued that these tools are at all perfect or that they can be employed with little effort. But neither are the tools of security valuation perfect or easy to utilize.

The claim that the stock market is "selective"—i.e., that individual stock prices do not all move in tandem—is quite correct. But inappropriate implications seem to have been drawn from this observation. Major upward and downward swings of "the averages" usually do reflect the overall tone of the market rather well, as is shown in the accompanying tabulation. The tabulation indicates that when the averages fall, stocks in most industries fall also. Likewise, when the averages rise, the majority of stock groups rise also.

"Selectivity" means that in a bull market different stocks rise by very different percentage amounts, and in a bear market they fall by very different amounts. Nor do all stocks make their highs and lows at the same time. Therefore, the investor's attention should not be focused exclusively on the averages. But neither should the averages be ignored. For once a major trend in the averages gets under way, it is extremely difficult to select the issues that will resist the trend. The true significance of the existence of disparate price movements among different stocks would seem to be that value analysis and price forecasting approaches should be considered powerful allies rather than opposing philosophies.

Industry Group Price Changes during Bear Markets*

	Peak Month†	6/48	1/53	7/56	7/59	12/61	1/66	12/68	1/73
	Trough Month†	6/49	9/53	12/57	10/60	6/62	10/66	5/70	12/74
Percent Change S&P Composite ..		−17	−11	−17	−10	−23	−17	−28	−43
Percent Change S&P Industrials ..		−18	−12	−17	−11	−23	−18	−28	−44
No. of groups with price changes of:									
+10.1% and over		2	1	8	18	0	1	0	4
+ .1 to +10.0%		4	6	9	13	0	5	2	2
0 to −10.0		20	37	13	12	8	9	3	4
−10.1 to −20.0		18	29	24	12	23	25	18	3
−20.1 and over		39	10	31	33	57	55	74	76

Industry Group Price Changes during Bull Markets*

	Trough Month†	6/49	9/53	12/57	10/60	6/62	10/66	5/70
	Peak Month†	1/53	7/56	7/59	12/61	1/66	12/68	1/73
Percent Change S&P Composite ...		+87	+110	+48	+34	+68	+38	+56
Percent Change S&P Industrials ...		+93	+125	+48	+33	+70	+41	+59
No. of groups with price changes of:								
+100.1% and over		21	29	11	4	24	28	18
+ 50.1 to +100.0%		26	20	38	21	29	29	33
+ 25.1 to + 50.0		20	21	29	32	19	24	26
0 to + 25.0		14	12	8	27	12	13	19
− .1 to − 10.0		2	1	1	4	0	1	2
− 10.1 to − 20.0		0	1	0	0	1	0	5
− 20.0 and over		0	0	0	0	2	0	2

* The industry groups covered in the analysis are as classified by Standard & Poor's. Excluded are various "composites"—for example, Food Composite, Machinery Composite—and also various redundant groupings—for example, Autos, ex. G.M. The number of groups has changed over the years.

† The peak and trough dates are based on monthly average prices of the S&P stock price indexes. Daily highs and lows may not have taken place in precisely those months. For example, the 1974 daily low occurred in October, although the low month was December.

The argument that the mildness of postwar bear markets reduces the importance of timing also has flaws. First, as the value analysts themselves admit, "selectivity" means that some stocks may have quite severe downturns even when the averages decline only moderately. Second, venturesome investors can enhance the rewards of correct forecasts of downturns by *short* selling over and above their sales of existing holdings. Third, although most postwar bear markets have been milder than in the prewar period (e.g., stocks declined 40 percent in 1920–21, 80 percent in 1929–32, and 40 percent in 1937), the severity of the 1969–70 and 1973–74 drops should give pause to those who feel certain that major collapses are rare occurrences. And the difficulty is that the early warning signals prior to major collapses are not really different from the warning signals prior to moderate downturns. In other words, it can be argued that it pays to sell (or at least to stop

buying) even in anticipation of a moderate downturn, as insurance against the possibility that the downturn will be very sharp.

The opportunity to improve investment yield by improving one's timing is greater during the more volatile type of stock market experienced in the past decade, and quite possibly to be experienced in the future, than was the case in the 1950–65 period. But even if price-value divergences once again become short-lived and mild, the position that only "in-and-out traders" should attempt to forecast these swings and act accordingly is unconvincing. Merely consider the impact of an extra 1 percent per annum rate of return on the results of a lifetime investment program. If an individual of 35 invests $1,000 a year in a cross-section of common stocks which produce an annual rate of return of, say, 8 percent in dividends plus capital appreciation, upon retirement at age 65 a portfolio worth $122,000 will have been accumulated. If, through more appropriate timing of investments, the annual rate of return can be raised from 8 percent to 9 percent, at retirement the portfolio will be worth $148,000, a 20 percent advantage.

Finally, a psychological observation is in order. Focusing on long-term value is supposed to enable investors to weather the cyclical storms of the capital markets—to enable them to avoid being overwhelmed emotionally by cyclical swings. Unfortunately, human beings are not as strong-willed as they should be for their own good. Even institutional investors, who are professionally trained and in an eminent position to take a long-term view of things, have a tendency to get carried away by the market's gyrations. It is only too common for members of bank and insurance company investment committees to change their minds about "values" because of the incessant pronouncements of the ticker tape. Would they not have a better frame of reference if they understood the causes of divergences from value, as well as the causes of value itself?

In the chapters which follow, two basic approaches to the problem of forecasting turning points of security prices are examined. One approach—the "fundamental" approach described in Chapter 12—relates security price changes to general business cycle developments and to the economic cycles of specific industries. The other approach—the "technical" approach described in Chapter 13—focuses attention on internal developments within the securities markets themselves.

Chapter 12

Business Cycle Analysis

> Better is one fore thought than two after.
> ———————————— *Erasmus*

This chapter is divided into two sections. The first section surveys the relationships between stock prices, interest rates, and the broad movements of economic activity which are referred to as the business cycle. The survey suggests that an ability to anticipate forthcoming changes in business conditions can be used to improve the timing of security purchases and sales.

The second section of the chapter follows logically from the first. If economic forecasting can be helpful to the investor, how should the investor go about making or using such forecasts? Obviously, in a single section of a single chapter we cannot present all there is know about the subject of economic forecasting. But we can encourage familiarity with some of the most useful tools of the forecaster.

CAPITAL MARKET INFLUENCES OF BUSINESS CYCLES

Impact on Stock Prices

1947–1965. Figure 12–1 compares Standard and Poor's Industrial Stock Price Index with the Federal Reserve Board Index of Industrial Production from 1947 through 1965. Examination of the chart reveals that:

1. Both series exhibited uptrends, with stock prices rising more steeply than production.

2. There were five extended reversals in the stock price uptrend. In 1948–49, prices declined 18 percent; in 1953, they declined 12

FIGURE 12–1
Stock Prices and Industrial Production, 1947–1965

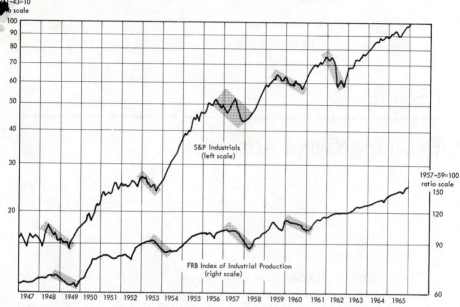

percent; in 1956–57, 17 percent; in 1959–60, 11 percent; and in 1962, 23 percent. (All percentages are based on *monthly average* prices at the beginning and end of the reversal periods. See tabulation in Introduction to Part III for the monthly dates used.)

3. Four of these five stock price reversals began several months prior to extended periods of decline in industrial production, and ended shortly before the start of renewed advances in production. The 1962 stock price decline did not precede an actual slump in industrial production, but rather a seven-month period of no growth. The end of the stock price decline occurred a few months prior to a strong resumption of growth.

1966–1975. Figure 12–2 compares stock prices and industrial production from 1966 to 1975. Some differences during this period may be noted versus the relationships described above, but the overall picture leads to similar conclusions.

1. Both stock prices and industrial production had exhibited strong uptrends from 1947 to 1965. During the 1966–75 period, on the other hand, stock prices churned violently up and down, with no real trend. But this pattern did not occur in isolation. It seemed to reflect the slower and more volatile growth path of industrial production.

2. Industrial production staged a "mini-recession" from the fall of

FIGURE 12–2
Stock Prices and Industrial Production, 1966–1975

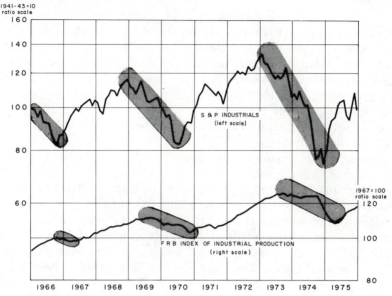

1966 to the spring of 1967. But the associated stock price decline began earlier than would be expected on the basis of prior postwar experience—fully nine months before the slowdown in industrial production began. Moreover, a renewed bull market started up in late 1966, just when industrial production started down. Although this timing sequence was unusual compared with earlier precedent, it seems clear that the 1966 bear market *was* related to forthcoming economic difficulties. If one recollects that during the early months of 1966 there was a "credit crunch," which led many observers to anticipate a recession, the tie between stock price cycles and the overall business cycle becomes obvious.

3. The 1969–70 bear market lends further support to the notion of a connection between stock price cycles and business cycles. The bear market again began early in relation to economic developments— about nine months prior to the start of a general recession (and again in conjunction with a "credit crunch"). Stock prices hit bottom in May 1970, about six months prior to the economic recovery, then "bounced along the bottom" through July 1970, and turned up vigorously in August, about three months before the end of the recession.

4. The most recent bear market, in 1973–74, was the deepest and longest since the 1930s. It is more than a coincidence that the nation (and, indeed the world) suffered the worst economic setback since

the Great Depression during a period overlapping this stock market collapse.

The stock market decline of 1973–74 occurred in two phases. After peaking in January 1973, it declined about 12 percent (monthly average basis) to August 1973. It then rallied in September and October, but in November, when the Arab oil embargo hit, the market plunged again and continued downward for another year, finally hitting bottom in December 1974. The total decline from January 1973 to December 1974 was 44 percent.

What was happening to industrial production at this time? It had started to flatten out in July 1973, six months after the stock price peak, and from July to November rose at an annual rate of only 2 percent—not a recession, but a marked economic slowdown. After the embargo, industrial production moved horizontally until September 1974. It then began a full-fledged decline which did not end until April 1975, four months after the stock price trough and a year-and-a-half after the production peak. Measuring from the November 1973 peak to the April 1975 trough, industrial production declined over 15 percent. This compares with a 2 percent decline during the 1966–67 mini-recession, and 8 percent during the 1969–70 recession.

Conclusion.   This evidence suggests strongly that an ability to foresee business cycle turning points several months in advance should improve one's ability to foresee major turning points in the general level of stock prices. The evidence does not imply that *every* bear market *must* be accompanied by an economic recession, or vice versa. However, the tendency for this relationship to exist has been so pronounced, and the lead-lag relationship between the stock market and the business cycle has been so persistent, that if a recession or a pronounced retardation of economic growth appears to lie ahead, the investor should consider the odds to be high that it will be preceded by a significant stock market downturn some months in advance.

It is essential to stress the fact that stock price peaks and troughs typically have *preceded* turning points of general business activity. Untutored investors invariably are surprised when, in the midst of rather dreary business news, stock prices rise, and in the midst of prosperity, stock prices fall. But such is the nature of the stock market.

Several hypotheses have been offered to explain the stock market's apparent forecasting ability. One is that investors in aggregate have good foresight, and that they act on the basis of what they think is *going to happen* to business activity rather than on the basis of what they currently see happening. Another argument is that investors act on the basis of current rather than anticipated future developments, but that the chief current indicators they watch—corporate profits and profit margins—tend to turn in advance of general business activity.

Therefore, profit-oriented investors coincidentally bid stock prices up and drive them down in advance of general business activity. Yet a third theory is that stock price reversals help *cause* subsequent economic reversals by affecting consumer and business confidence and spending decisions. Finally, various monetary explanations for the stock price lead have been offered, as will be noted in later sections. Perhaps the truth lies closest to a combination of all these hypothesis.[1]

From the General to the Particular. Since an ability to foresee business cycle turning points normally would improve one's ability to foresee major turning points in the stock market as a whole, would it also improve one's ability to select the particular stocks to be most affected by the change in overall trend? The answer to this question is "sometimes yes, sometimes no." The relative price changes of indi-

FIGURE 12–3
Relative Production versus Relative Stock Prices: Consumer Durables, Business Capital Goods, and Construction

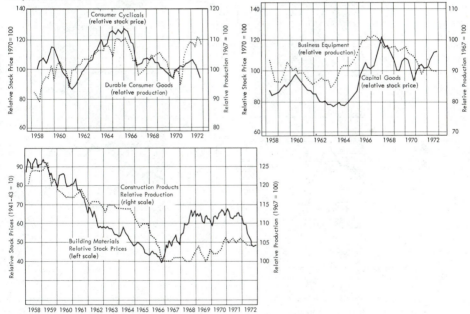

Source: William D. Witter Inc.

---

[1] The recent literature on the subject includes G. H. Moore, "Stock Prices and the Business Cycle," *The Journal of Portfolio Management*, Spring 1975; R. J. Rogalski and J. D. Vinso, *Stock Returns, Money Supply and the Direction of Causality*, Working Paper No. 7–75 (Philadelphia: Rodney L. White Center for Financial Research, University of Pennsylvania); and B. Bosworth, "The Stock Market and the Economy," *Brookings Papers on Economic Activity*, No. 2–1975.

vidual stocks over short periods of time reflect many factors. These factors include relative changes in company sales, earnings, and dividends, but they also include the degree to which different stocks had been overpriced or underpriced prior to the turning point of the general market. To the extent that accurate forecasts of the overall economy can improve forecasts of relative changes in the prosperity of different industries, forecasts of relative price changes of stocks in different industries should be improved. Examples of this statement are contained in Figures 12–3 to 12–6.

The first set of three charts (Figure 12–3) covers years prior to the severe stock market decline of 1973–74. The charts reveal a fairly close relationship between the relative production in three major sectors of

FIGURE 12–4
Copper Prices, Earnings, and Stock Prices

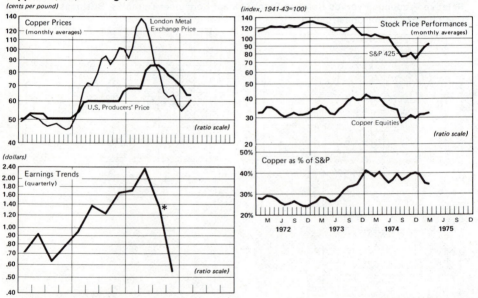

* Reflects strike in July and August.

Not terribly surprising, over a long period of years there has been a fairly close correlation in the fluctuations in the price of copper, earnings of copper companies, and the price performance of copper shares. The top left chart displays the more recent relationships that have existed. The mid-1974 industry strike, as well as government price controls earlier in the year and their subsequent demise, distorted the relationships a bit. Moreover, since the Standard & Poor's Indices are weighted by share capitalization, Kennecott represents almost 40 percent of the copper price index, and interest in this equity for some time has focused more on its ownership of Peabody Coal rather than on copper fundamentals. Therefore the S&P copper index appears to have performed somewhat better than would have been expected by observing copper prices or quarterly earnings trends. Nevertheless, the coincident patterns are still evident.

Source: Loeb, Rhoades & Co.

FIGURE 12–5

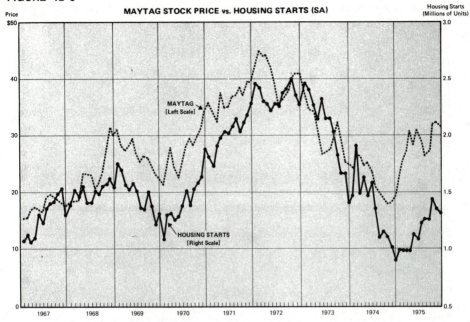

MAYTAG STOCK PRICE vs. HOUSING STARTS (SA)

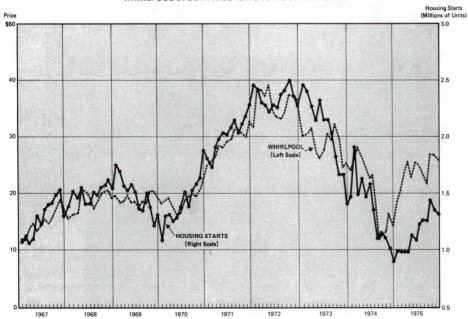

WHIRLPOOL STOCK PRICE vs. HOUSING STARTS (SA)

Note: End-of-month prices.
Source: White, Weld & Co., Inc.

FIGURE 12–6

Consumer Economic Indicators and Their Relationship to Retail Stock Prices

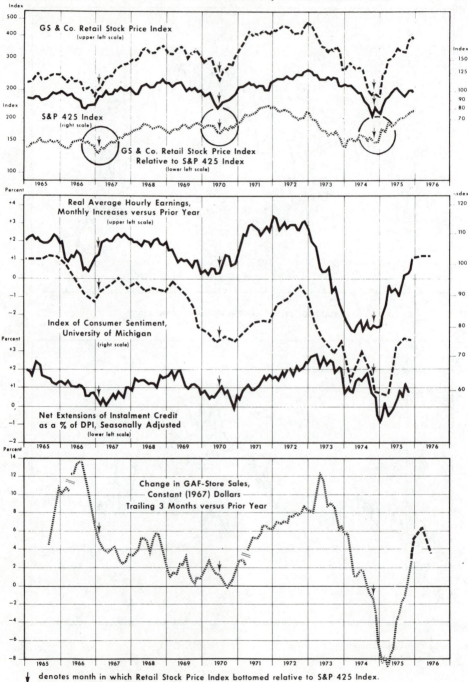

↓ denotes month in which Retail Stock Price Index bottomed relative to S&P 425 Index.

Source: Goldman Sachs & Co.

the economy—consumer durable goods, business capital goods, and construction—and the relative price movement of the common stocks of companies operating in those economic sectors. (Relative production data are composites of Federal Reserve Board production indexes for each sector, expressed as a percentage of the aggregate FRB Industrial Production Index. Relative stock prices are composites of the appropriate Standard & Poor's industry group price indexes, expressed as a percentage of the aggregate S&P Stock Price Index.)

Few industry groups withstood the 1973–74 bear market. However, as can be seen in the right hand panel of Figure 12–4, one industry whose stocks held up reasonably well was the copper industry. The left panels of the chart, and the accompanying commentary, suggest that the reason was a tremendous surge in the price of raw copper, which became reflected in the earnings of copper companies.

Figure 12–5 is another illustration of the close relationship between the stock prices of companies in a major economic sector and an index of the direction of business activity in that sector. In this case, the prices of the individual companies' stocks are traced, rather than a composite group price. Specifically, the stock prices of Maytag Co. and Whirlpool Corp.—two leading producers of washers, dryers, and other "white goods"—are shown to be intimately tied to new housing starts.

Figure 12–6 is an example of a more eclectic approach to the relationship between developments in a particular sector of the economy and the behavior of stock prices of companies operating in that sector. Here, the analyst is concerned with timing the troughs of relative prices of retail stocks. Rather than focus on a single measure of retail activity, the analyst traces the behavior of four different aspects of the retailing process: the real earnings of consumers, their "sentiment," their use of installment credit, and, finally, their actual purchases of general merchandise, apparel, and furniture (GAF).

Impact on the Level of Bond Yields

1952–1965. Figure 12–7 compares the movements from 1952 through 1965 of yields on long-term U.S. government bonds and Moody's Aaa corporate bonds with the FRB index of industrial production. Data prior to 1952 are not shown because the bond market was "pegged" by the monetary authorities until spring 1951, and interest rates were not freely responsive to economic forces.

As with stock prices, the timing of interest rate cycles was rather closely related to the upturns and downturns of general economic activity. However, there was one notable difference between the two relationships. Whereas stock prices typically turned well ahead of production, interest rates typically turned at about the same time as

FIGURE 12–7
Bond Yields and Industrial Production, 1952–1965

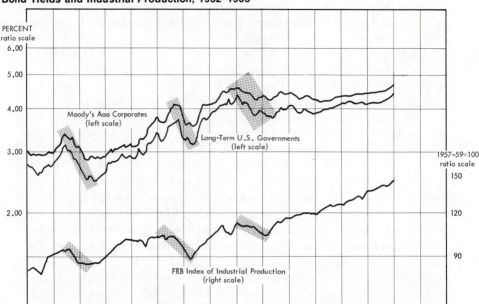

production. Thus, the best time to buy bonds was when the peak of economic activity had been reached, not before. Bond prices then were at their lowest point (interest rates were highest). The best time to sell bonds was when a new economic advance began following a recession. At such time, bond prices usually were highest (interest rates lowest).

1966–1975. Although the relationship between stock price cycles and business cycles in recent years has conformed fairly well to the traditional pattern, this has been much less true of bond yield behavior.[2] In the past, as noted above, peaks and troughs of bond yields corresponded fairly closely to peaks and troughs of industrial production. Let us consider, in this context, the movement of bond yields during the "mini-recession" of 1966–67, the recession of 1969–70, and the major economic downturn of 1974–75.

As shown in Figure 12–8, prior to the onset of the mini-recession in the fall of 1966, yields on new issues[3] of high-grade corporate bonds

---

[2] An interesting article on the subject is P. Cagan, "The Recent Cyclical Movements of Interest Rates in Historical Perspective," *Business Economics*, January 1972.

[3] Figure 12–7 illustrated yields on bonds already outstanding rather than on new issues because good data on new issue yields are not available for earlier years.

FIGURE 12–8
Bond Yields and Industrial Production, 1966–1975

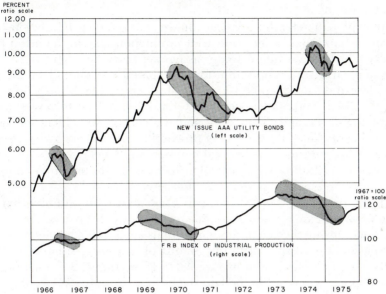

had risen to a postwar high of almost 6 percent. As industrial production slipped, bond yields declined about 0.75 percent over a three-month period. Before industrial production turned up again, however, the rise of bond yields resumed, and by the summer of 1967 bond yields once more were setting new highs.

By the time the recession of 1969–70 began, high-grade corporate bond yields had reached the 8 percent level. While industrial production declined during the fall of 1969, bond yields *rose* another 0.5 percent. And as the recession cumulated in the first half of 1970, bond yields continued to rise and passed the 9 percent level. It was not until late 1970 that such yields began to decline. Once the decline began, however, it continued (with a notable reversal in the second quarter of 1971, to be discussed below) despite the fact that industrial production had resumed an uptrend. By the end of 1971, high-grade bond yields had reached a 7.25–7.50 percent level, and they were still at that level in the summer of 1972 although a vigorous economic expansion was in progress.

The same pattern recurred in 1974 and 1975. Bond yields rose to unprecedented heights well after the point at which economic activity had peaked. And when interest rates finally turned down, they continued in that direction well beyond the point at which a renewed economic expansion had gotten under way. Early in 1976 (not shown

in Figure 12–8), bond yields dropped to significantly lower levels than had been reached in 1975, despite the fact that economic activity was improving steadily.

An explanation for this atypical, almost *countercyclical*, relationship between bond yields and industrial production may be found in the theory which views interest rates as having two components—a "real rate of return" and a premium for anticipated inflation. (This theory was described in Chapter 10.) Most students of the subject believe that the "real" corporate bond yield tends to be fairly stable over time, fluctuating in a range of about 3–4 percent, with some tendency toward procyclicality—i.e., to rise during prosperity and fall during recession. Since it is doubtful that this real component of bond yields became countercyclical after 1965, attention focuses on the inflation component. And here a change does seem to have occurred.

In the past, recessions have been associated with a diminution of inflationary pressures, and economic recoveries with an acceleration of inflation. During the economic contractions since 1965, however, inflation has not diminished with the coming of recession, either in fact or in the expectations of the marketplace. If anything, the inflationary expectations generated in the late stages of prosperity have continued to spiral upward after the economy has peaked out, thus explaining the soaring level of bond yields in the face of declining industrial production. Only in the late stages of recessions have investors foreseen diminished inflationary pressures, an attitude which has tended to persist beyond the economic trough and carried bond yields down until the point when investors realized that they had been duped once again into thinking that the inflation cancer had been cured.

An excellent illustration of the influence of inflationary expectations on interest rates was provided in the early 1970s. By late 1970, the inflationary spiral seemed to be easing, and bond yields began to drop. But fears of renewed inflation gripped the market again in the spring of 1971, and a sharp upward movement of bond yields took place. The renewed inflation psychology was a major cause of the national program of economic controls announced on August 15, 1971. The controls program was at least partially successful in dampening inflation expectations, and this was reflected in lower bond yields side-by-side with rising industrial production, until the end of 1972.

Again in 1974, in the midst of severe recession, bond yields rose sharply because of rampant inflation fears. In 1975, each month's price index announcements by the Department of Labor were eagerly awaited by the bond market. When the announcements were favorable (slower inflation), interest rates softened. When the announcements were grim (faster inflation), interest rates rose.

Conclusion.   It should be clear from the preceding account, that to forecast peaks and troughs of bond yields it is no longer sufficient to

concentrate mainly on forecasting industrial production. One must also try to forecast the rate of inflation and inflation expectations. And as we shall emphasize later in this chapter, economists' tools for making such forecasts are by no means as good as their tools for forecasting real output.

Impact on Yield Curves and Yield Spreads

As discussed in Chapter 10, the term structure of interest rates refers to the relationship at a given point in time, between bonds of very similar quality but of different maturity. A pictorial representation of the term structure of rates is known as a "yield curve." Figure 12–9 is a

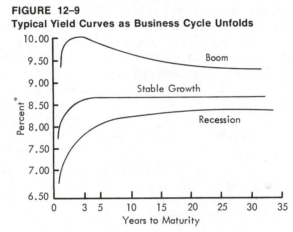

FIGURE 12–9
Typical Yield Curves as Business Cycle Unfolds

* The interest rate levels are merely illustrative.

schematic diagram of the typical behavior of yield curves (especially of U.S. government obligations, but also of corporate bonds[4]) during recession-recovery-boom periods. The bottom curve tends to occur in the midst of a recession, the middle curve during a recovery phase which might be labeled "normal prosperity," and the top curve during months of very high business and financial activity.

Note that when the *level* of rates rises as the tempo of business activity speeds up, the shape of the yield curve takes on certain characteristics. These characteristics can be outlined as follows:

1. Up to maturities of about three years—the "short end" of the yield curve—longer term securities tend to have higher yields than shorter term securities whether the level of the yield curve is high or

---

[4] The yield curve of tax-exempts seldom departs from an upward slope.

low. This is the area of the maturity spectrum in which investors seek to satisfy their liquidity needs. The shorter the maturity, the greater the liquidity, the greater the demand from liquidity-seeking investors, and therefore the lower the yield. The upward slope of the yield curve within this maturity range reflects the increments in interest which borrowers have to pay to persuade lenders (investors) to accept lesser degrees of liquidity. Since demands for liquidity tend to be higher in recessions than in booms, the slope is steepest during recessions.

2.   From 3 years to about 20 years, that is, between the boundaries of relatively short-term and relatively long-term securities, the yield curve gradually changes shape as the level of rates rises. The curve moves from "upward sloping," to "flat," to "downward sloping." Downward sloping means that longer term securities tend to have lower yields than shorter term securities. In Chapter 10, it was shown that this change in shape can be explained by reference to the expectations of the marketplace regarding future levels of interest rates. If rates are low and expected to rise, lenders prefer short maturities and borrowers prefer long maturities. This leads to an upward sloping curve. The reverse occurs when rates are high and expected to fall. And when the concensus expectation is that future rates will be similar to current rates, the curve tends to flatten. Market participants, in other words, are relatively indifferent to maturity under such conditions.

3.   Beyond maturities of about 20–25 years, yield usually does not change significantly as maturity is extended. That is, the "long end" of the yield curve typically is rather "flat" regardless of level. It appears to be a matter of relative indifference to both borrowers and lenders whether a maturity is 25, 30, or 40 years.

4.   Yield volatility is inversely related to maturity. When the general level of rates rises or falls, short-term rates change much more sharply than long-term rates. (On the other hand, as demonstrated in Chapter 10, *price* volatility is *directly* related to maturity so far as effects of changes in the level of interest rates are concerned.)

The business cycle can have a significant effect on the interrelationships of yields on securities of different types and quality as well as on securities of different maturity. There is a general tendency for yield spreads on different types of long-term fixed-income investments to narrow during the major portion of prosperity periods and to widen as the prosperity reaches a peak and the economy turns down. As an economic advance progresses, investors' confidence in the nation's ability to avoid a severe recession is bolstered. They are, therefore, increasingly reluctant to pay relatively high prices (accept low yields) for high-quality securities, and increasingly willing to raise their bid prices for lower quality issues relative to high-quality issues. If inter-

est rates on both types of securities rise, those of highest quality and lowest yield will tend to have the most rapid increases, and yield spreads therefore will narrow. Conversely, as the boom ends and turns into recession, investors' confidence tends to wane and high quality becomes more important to them. If fixed-income securities of most quality grades are characterized by declining interest rates, those of highest quality will tend to decline most rapidly in yield, and yield spreads will widen.

Care must be taken, however, not to make an interpretation of changing yield spreads too lender oriented. While shifts in investor confidence have a powerful effect on yield spreads, changes in borrowing also are important and may work in an opposite direction. For example, a major reason for a widening rather than a continued narrowing of yield spreads between corporate bonds and government bonds as a boom period nears a peak may be a very heavy volume of corporate bond flotations to finance plant and equipment expenditures. If this heavy corporate financing occurs when Treasury financing diminishes due to favorable budgetary conditions, corporate bond yields will rise faster than governments and the yield spread will widen.

A cyclical yield spread pattern has been observable not only in comparisons of yields on different types of fixed-income investments, but also in comparisons of common stock dividend yields with bond yields. As has been shown, stock prices usually rise during most of the prosperity phase of the business cycle. At the same time, dividend payments usually rise also, but at a slower rate. Consequently, dividend yields on stocks fall rather steadily during prosperity. Accompanying the declining trend of dividend yields, typically, has been a rising trend of bond yields.

The changing spread between stock and bond yields as the economic advances progresses—stock yields falling and bond yields rising—gradually begins to draw income-minded investors away from stocks and into bonds. In addition, capital-gains-minded investors begin selling stocks as corporate profit margins narrow and economic recession begins to threaten. The proceeds of these sales either are put into the bank or into fixed-income securities. The shifting of funds out of the stock market weakens stock prices prior to the peak of business activity, but dividends are still high or rising. Therefore, stock yields begin to reverse their downward movement prior to the business peak.

Eventually the economy reaches a peak and turns down. Interest rates ultimately move down as well. Dividends reach a plateau or decline, but stock prices decline faster, and stock yields therefore rise. The yield spread thus becomes gradually less favorable to bond investment. Income seekers begin switching back into stocks, and bar-

gain hunters do likewise in anticipation of eventual recovery. The expansion process begins anew shortly thereafter.

BUSINESS CYCLE FORECASTING

A Business Cycle Chronology

For more than 50 years, the National Bureau of Economic Research, a private nonprofit organization, has sponsored the research efforts of America's leading students of the business cycle. Among the products of their efforts are techniques for measuring economic fluctuations and identifying major turning points of overall economic activity. Focusing on the period since the end of World War I, and omitting the years of the Great Depression and World War II, Table 12–1 presents a

TABLE 12–1
A Calendar of Major Economic Expansions and Contractions, 1920–1929, 1946–1975

Dates of Turning Points			Duration, in Months, of:	
Peak	Trough	Peak	Contractions	Expansions
Jan. 1920	July 1921	May 1923	18	22
May 1923	July 1924	Oct. 1926	14	27
Oct. 1926	Nov. 1927	Aug. 1929	13	21
Nov. 1948	Oct. 1949	July 1953	11	45
July 1953	May 1954	Aug. 1957	10	39
Aug. 1957	April 1958	April 1960	8	24
April 1960	Feb. 1961	Dec. 1969	10	106
Dec. 1969	Nov. 1970	Nov. 1973*	11	36
Nov. 1973*	April 1975*		17	
		Median: 11		31

* Tentative.
Source: U.S. Department of Commerce, *Business Conditions Digest* and *55th Annual Report* of the National Bureau of Economic Research, p. 28.

chronology of American business cycles, based on the National Bureau's identification system.

Examination of the table suggests that the "average business cycle" consists of an expansion lasting about two-and-one-half years and a contraction lasting about a year. But even though the table excludes the atypical years of world war and catastrophic depression, considerable diversity of duration remains. These findings suggest that the timing of American business cycles has not been consistent enough to warrant purely calendar-oriented judgments as to the probability of a peak or trough occurring at any given time.

Moreover, the National Bureau itself has become quite humble about its dating of business cycles. For example, in a recent "President's Report," Dr. John R. Meyer, head of the National Bureau, wrote:[5]

. . . considerable disagreement exists among traditional cycle analysts in the United States about whether the starting date of the current U.S. recession should be placed at November 1973 or August 1974.

Indeed, the National Bureau has been reassessing its basic business cycle classification framework. As Meyer puts it:[6]

Declines in absolute measures of output have become increasingly rare in the market economies of Europe, Japan, and North America. . . . Perhaps the most formal recognition of this new awareness about cyclical phenomena is the definition of so-called growth cycles, in which a declining *rate* of growth, rather than an *absolute* decline, defines an economic retardation or recession. . . . It is less than fully edifying under modern business cycle conditions to adhere to a two-phase scheme that differentiates only between recessions and periods of nonrecession. . . . A four-phase classification scheme might suit modern cyclical circumstances better. . . . These four cyclical stages might be defined as: Recession, Recovery, Demand-pull inflation, Stagflation.

Notwithstanding all of these caveats against trying to forecast a business cycle turning point simply by reference to the elapsed calendar time since the prior turning point, practicing economists do find it helpful to use historical analogies in their work. For example, in November 1975, Dr. Irwin Kellner, economist for Manufacturers Hanover Trust Company, introduced his economic forecast for 1976 with a discussion of the prior recession. In his comments he presented several pairs of charts (see Figure 12–10 for excerpts) which traced the path taken by various economic indicators during each postwar recession. The pairs of charts were based on two different assumptions as to when the latest recession had begun: first quarter of 1974 (one quarter later than the NBER's tentative dating), or third quarter of 1974 (in line with the NBER's alternative dating). Kellner noted that the first assumption made the latest recession look much more severe than earlier postwar recessions, while the second assumption made it look rather typical. For various reasons, Kellner argued that the second assumption was more plausible, and since the recession was, therefore, a "typical" one, he was led to predict a normal type of recovery. Thus,

---

[5] *55th Annual Report* of the National Bureau of Economic Research (New York, September 1975), p. 5.

[6] Ibid., pp. 1–2. Also see Ilse Mintz, "U.S. Growth Cycles," *Explorations in Economic Research*, Summer 1974; and J. R. Meyer and D. H. Weinberg, "On the Classification of Economic Fluctuations," *Explorations in Economic Research*, Spring 1975.

FIGURE 12–10
Two Perspectives on the 1974–1975 Recession

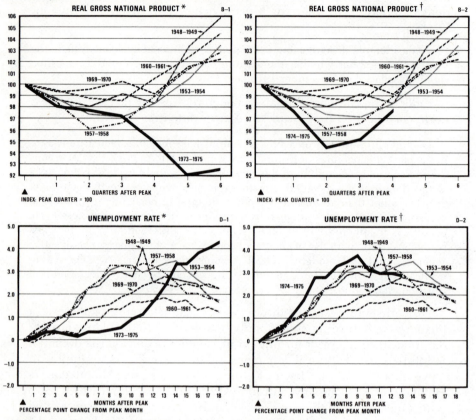

* Assume peak at first quarter, 1974.
† Assume peak at third quarter, 1974.
Source: Irwin W. Kellner, *Economic Forecast for 1976* (New York: Manufacturers Hanover Trust Co.),
November 1975.

one way to start an economic forecast is to see if the timing sequence of
current economic developments resembles that of past stages of the
business cycle. The more the present resembles the past, the more
likely is the forecaster to assume that the future also will be similar to
historical precedent.

Leading Economic Indicators

It is a common observation that no two business cycles are exactly
alike. Indeed, most modern business economists have become increasingly impressed with the almost endless variety of the cyclical fluctuations they are trying to forecast. Nevertheless, the unique aspects of

each individual cycle usually fit into a common framework which has been referred to as "the cumulative process" or "the self-generating cycle." The essential characteristics of this framework can be described briefly.

If we break into a cycle as revival is beginning, we find business sales and inventories at a depressed level and considerable excess plant capacity. As sales begin to rise and profit expectations improve, business leaders start planning for production increases. They expand working hours, and gradually rehire previously laid-off workers. This increases employee incomes and stimulates personal consumption expenditures. With sales and profits rising, the managers begin to expand and modernize production facilities. These purchases from the capital goods industries create still more jobs and incomes and more consumption by workers in those industries. And so the expansion *cumulates*.

Workers, machines, and materials eventually are being utilized at capacity, and demand exerts upward pressure on prices and wages. Business leaders go increasingly into debt to finance expanding inventories, receivables, and fixed assets. Interest rates rise. Soon costs are rising faster than prices, and profit margins deteriorate. This coincides with the gradual realization that productive capacity has outstripped potential sales. Business executives become uneasy and pull in their reins. They reduce their orders for heavy equipment, cut back on the rate of inventory accumulation, repay loans, lay off marginal personnel, and even sell some of their personal common stock holdings. Caution spreads as incomes are reduced. Consumers postpone purchases of durable goods, business executives slash inventories sharply, and the cumulative process is at work in a downward direction.

As the downturn continues, credit terms ease and interest rates fall. The monetary authorities usually reinforce the ease. Housing construction often picks up as reduced mortgage rates, lowered down payments, and extended maturities bring monthly carrying charges to a level which buyers are willing to undertake despite the recessionary atmosphere. Government spending acts as a strong prop to the economy. The stock market, after a sizeable shake-out, stabilizes and begins to move up. Soon consumers realize that the worst is over and begin to unloosen their purse strings. A new revival is in the making.

It should be clear from this brief "physiology of a business cycle" that fluctuations of the whole of economic activity reflect fluctuations of the economy's many parts. Moreover, while the parts tend to move in unison, there is also observable a sequence. When one part changes direction, it pushes another part, which pushes still another. It is logical, therefore, that if we wish to predict turning points of the whole

economy, we should try to isolate and study those parts which usually turn *before* the whole.

The search for "leading," "coincident," and "lagging" indicators of general economic activity has been one of the major continuing projects of the National Bureau of Economic Research. In its most recent reappraisal of the indicators,[7] the NBER has selected 12 "leaders" which come closest to meeting ideal characteristics, such as smoothness of movement from month to month, and consistency and logic of relationship to the general business cycle. These 12 are identified in Table 12–2, which also shows the median number of months by which

TABLE 12–2
Leading Indicators of Economic Activity

	Median Lead (in months)	
	Peak	Trough
1. Average hours in workweek of manufacturing production workers	12	2
2. Layoffs of manufacturing workers (per 1,000)	11	1
3. New orders of consumer products (in constant dollars)	6	1
4. Vendor performance (i.e., percent of companies reporting slower deliveries)	6	5
5. Net new business formations	11	2
6. Permits to build new private housing units	13	8
7. Contracts for new plant and equipment (in constant dollars)	9	2
8. Change in business inventories on hand and on order (in constant dollars)	5	4
9. Common stock prices (S&P 500)	9	4
10. Change in wholesale prices of industrial raw materials	15	5
11. Money supply (in constant dollars)	10	8
12. Change in total liquid assets	6½	6
Average lead of 12 indicators	9½	4

Source: *Business Conditions Digest,* May 1975, p. xv.

the indicator historically has turned in advance of general economic peaks and troughs.

Professional economists carefully study the monthly movements of these indicators, as well as dozens of others. Their effort is facilitated by the Department of Commerce, which publishes charts and data on a wide variety of economic indicators in a monthly publication, *Business Conditions Digest*. Figure 12–11 contains a key to help read the

---

[7] V. Zarnowitz and C. Boschan, "Cyclical Indicators: An Evaluation and New Leading Index," *Business Conditions Digest,* May 1975; and "New Composite Indexes of Coincident and Lagging Indicators," *Business Conditions Digest,* November 1975.

FIGURE 12–11
How to Read Charts in Figures 12–12 and 12–13

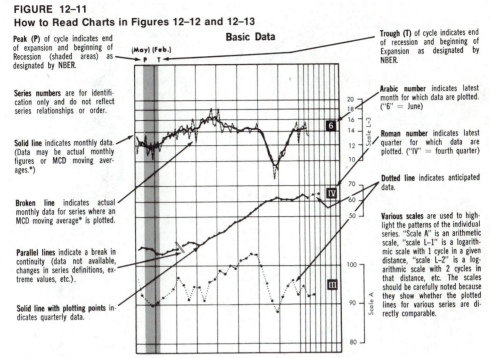

Peak (P) of cycle indicates end of expansion and beginning of Recession (shaded areas) as designated by NBER.

(May) (Feb.)

Basic Data

Trough (T) of cycle indicates end of recession and beginning of Expansion as designated by NBER.

Series numbers are for identification only and do not reflect series relationships or order.

Arabic number indicates latest month for which data are plotted. ("6" = June)

Solid line indicates monthly data. (Data may be actual monthly figures or MCD moving averages.*)

Roman number indicates latest quarter for which data are plotted. ("IV" = fourth quarter)

Broken line indicates actual monthly data for series where an MCD moving average* is plotted.

Dotted line indicates anticipated data.

Parallel lines indicate a break in continuity (data not available, changes in series definitions, extreme values, etc.).

Various scales are used to highlight the patterns of the individual series. "Scale A" is an arithmetic scale, "scale L–1" is a logarithmic scale with 1 cycle in a given distance, "scale L–2" is a logarithmic scale with 2 cycles in that distance, etc. The scales should be carefully noted because they show whether the plotted lines for various series are directly comparable.

Solid line with plotting points indicates quarterly data.

Source: U.S. Department of Commerce, *Business Conditions Digest*, November 1975, p. 4.

charts, and Figure 12–12 shows the postwar behavior of each of the 12 leading indicators noted above.

As a valuable supplement to the individual indicators, there is a composite index which combines the leading indicators into a single statistical series. There also are composites of the coincident and lagging indicators. The latter are used as checks on the validity of turns in the leading index. That is, if the leading indicator index seems to have turned down, that fact should be confirmed by subsequent downturns of, first, the coincident index, and next, the lagging index. Figure 12–13 displays these composite indexes.

Of course, the investor cannot wait until all the confirming signals have been given before taking action to sell or buy stocks and bonds. It will be too late. But if quick action is taken, say, by selling stocks when the composite *leading* index looks like it is turning down,[8] but the

---

[8] We do not mean to imply that stocks should be sold just because a single economic indicator turns down. Indeed, the whole thrust of this and the next chapter is that a variety of factors should be reviewed and action should be taken when a consensus emerges. Nevertheless, it must be emphasized that if you wait until "all the evidence is in hand," the market's move will have passed you by.

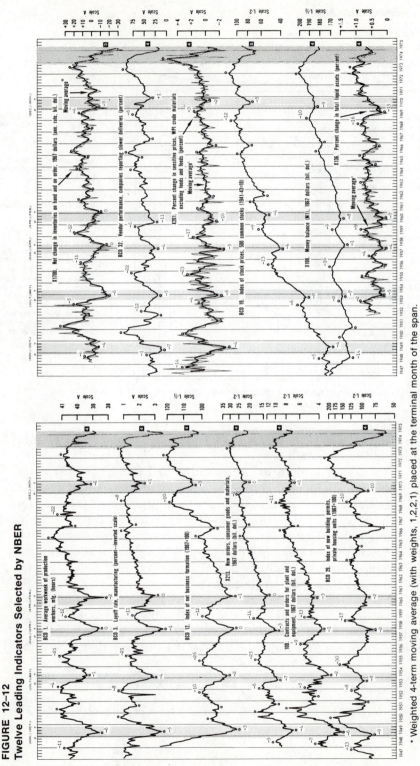

FIGURE 12–12
Twelve Leading Indicators Selected by NBER

* Weighted 4-term moving average (with weights, 1,2,2,1) placed at the terminal month of the span.

Note: Circles entered on the chart indicate specific turning points; numbers indicate length of leads (–) and lags (+) in months from reference turning dates.

Shading for 1973–75 recession was not in original but has been added for greater perspective.

Source: U.S. Department of Commerce, *Business Conditions Digest*, May 1975, pp. xi–xii.

FIGURE 12–13
Composite Indexes of NBER Indicators

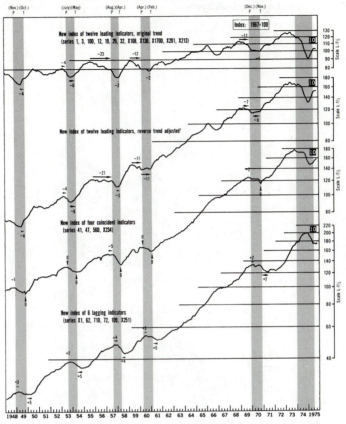

* Numbers entered on the chart indicate length of leads (−) and lags (+) in months from reference turning dates. Reverse trend adjusted index of 12 leaders contains the same trend as the index of 5 coincident indicators.

Note: Shading for 1973–75 recession was not in original but has been added for greater perspective.

Source: U.S. Department of Commerce, *Business Conditions Digest,* November 1975, p. 37.

composite *coincident* index subsequently fails to turn down, the investor would be well advised to conclude that a mistake has been made and should buy back into stocks.

It may be noted also that most economists are of the opinion that the leading indicators are useful mainly in forecasting the *direction* of the economy but not the *magnitude* of change. However, there is some evidence in Figure 12–14 that this negative view may be unwarranted. This chart is a scatter diagram of year-to-year changes in real GNP versus the prior December-to-December changes in the composite

FIGURE 12–14
Percent Change in Real GNP versus Leading Indicators*

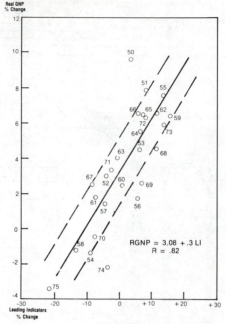

* Percent change in leading indicators is the year-to-year change in December of the preceding year.
  Source: William D. Witter, Inc. *Economic Review*, July 21, 1975.

index of leading indicators. The diagram suggests that large moves in the leading index have been associated with subsequent large moves in real GNP.

Monetary Indicators. Among the NBER's selected list of leading indicators is the "real" money supply (i.e., demand deposits plus currency held by the nonbank public, deflated by a price index). The influence of money on economic activity is at the center of a good deal of dispute among economists. Some view money as a prime mover of the economy, as a causal factor of business cycles. Others see money as a sort of lubricating oil—a good supply is necessary to keep the economic engine running, but it doesn't cause movement by itself.

In addition to their theoretical disputes, economists also argue about the empirical evidence. For example, the research staff of the Federal Reserve Bank of St. Louis has argued in numerous articles in that bank's monthly *Review* that:

1. Short-term accelerations and decelerations of monetary growth are followed by accelerations and decelerations of economic output.

2. But these changes in output are only temporary. In the longer run, the trend rate of growth of money directly impacts the rate of inflation but it does not shape the course of real output.

Critics of monetarism take issue with the statistical procedures leading to these conclusions, including importantly the definition of money supply.[9] The critics allege that monetarists select from a variety of so-called monetary aggregates whichever ones prove the particular case they are trying to make. For example, it will be noted that the NBER chose to include a *constant dollar* money supply series in its list of leading indicators whereas most traditional monetary analysis has been in terms of *current dollar* data. The point of the critics was well-articulated recently by *Business Week* magazine:[10]

M_1 is growing far more slowly than M_2. The narrowly defined money supply measure, M_1, includes only currency and checking accounts in commercial banks; M_2 in addition includes time deposits in the commercial banks. In the final quarter of 1975, M_1 probably grew no more than 2.5 percent, down from 7.1 percent in the third quarter and 8.9 percent in the quarter before that. Growth of M_2 has also slowed, but far less—to 6.5 percent in the fourth quarter, compared with 10.8 percent in the third quarter and 11.6 percent in the second. Those economists for whom M_1 is the forecasting touchstone, therefore, see the possibility of a substantial business slowdown. Those who believe in M_2 are far less worried.

The growth of the monetary base—basically the bank reserves that are the raw material for money creation—has not slowed at all. The probable 7.7 percent growth rate for the fourth quarter is a shade above that of the second and third quarters. Base-watchers, therefore, see no business slowdown.

None of the money growth numbers is solid. They all may be revised upward when the Fed issues its customary revision sometime in January. There is, indeed, a belief among economists that deposits at banks that do not belong to the Federal Reserve System, mainly country banks, are growing faster than those of member banks. These deposits get directly counted in the money supply infrequently, and there is a good chance that these deposits have been growing faster in the hinterlands than in the big cities.

In the face of these conflicting views, perhaps the best advice that can be given to analysts and investors is to examine several monetary series rather than any single one. This should improve the investor's awareness of the overall direction of monetary trends. It should be noted also that the near-term monetary targets of the Federal Reserve

---

[9] On a more theoretical plane, the critics argue that "velocity"—i.e., the relationship between GNP and money supply—is unstable, whereas the monetarists argue that it is relatively stable.

[10] *Business Week*, January 19, 1976, p. 12.

System's "Open Market Committee" are published in summary form every month, with a one-month lag. Since May 1975, moreover, the chairman of the Federal Reserve Board has been revealing the Fed's longer range targets for money supply growth (defined in several ways) in testimony before Congress. These statements are subjected to intensive scrutiny and commentary by Wall Street firms.

Anticipation Surveys.   The economic and monetary indicators discussed thus far all are measures of what might be called accomplished facts—orders *placed,* hours *worked,* prices of *transactions,* changes in *existing* money supply, and so forth. In addition to these accomplished facts, economists have available for analysis a group of surveys of spending *intentions* of business leaders and consumers. These surveys are conducted by various governmental and private organizations, and the investor should be familiar with at least some of them.

Probably the most widely used group of surveys are those relating to business spending for plant and equipment. In October each year, the economists of McGraw-Hill, Inc. conduct a survey of business capital expenditure plans for the year ahead. The results are published in *Business Week* during the month of November. In December, the Department of Commerce publishes (in the *Survey of Current Business*) an estimate of capital spending in the first quarter of the coming year based on a survey conducted through government auspices. By March, the Department of Commerce has run another survey, this time covering expectations for the first and second quarters and for the full year. In April, McGraw-Hill publishes the results of a follow-up to their October survey, and in June and September, Commerce provides estimates for the current and succeeding quarters based on still more surveys. In addition to this abundance of data, the Conference Board compiles a quarterly record of budgetary appropriations for future capital spending by the boards of directors of America's largest corporations. These findings are discussed and interpreted in the Conference Board's monthly publication, the *Record.*

Since capital spending plays such an important role in our economy (many economists believe it is the single most important generating factor in the business cycle), a successful forecast of such spending obviously is desirable. While the surveys do not have a perfect record, use of the data usually results in a correct forecast of the direction of capital spending, although not necessarily in a correct forecast of magnitude.

During recent years, consumers have joined business executives as objects of economic surveyors' attentions. While no one claims that consumers "plan" their future spending in the same sense as business leaders do, it seems reasonable to hypothesize that families "talk things over" some time prior to purchasing major items such as au-

tomobiles, houses, home furnishings and appliances, and perhaps even some nondurables such as clothing. Surely "impulse buying" cannot be the only driving force behind consumer spending, particularly on expensive durable goods. Although consumer spending intentions are subject to swift revisions due to unexpected changes in employment conditions, fluctuations in purchases of consumer durables are such a key element in the business cycle that all available evidence should be brought to the fore in an attempt to forecast these fluctuations.

Since 1952, the Survey Research Center of the University of Michigan has conducted several nationwide surveys each year in an attempt to determine changes in consumer attitudes and in their intentions to purchase durable goods. The findings are made public via books and press conferences. Other organizations, notably the Bureau of the Census and the Conference Board have built upon the work of the Survey Research Center but have taken issue with the Center's emphasis on attitudes as distinguished from intentions. A much debated question among economists is whether attitude data really add significantly to the forecasting potential of intentions data.[11]

It may seem as if there is no efficient way to organize this mass of survey data, monetary data, and other leading indicators in such a way as to derive an overview of what is developing in the nation's economy and a forecast of what is to come. But there is. Economists approach the problem by utilizing what is known as a "GNP model."

The GNP Model

The word "model" in the context of economic forecasting often refers to a complex set of mathematical equations.[12] But it also may be used simply to convey an impression of *structure*. The gross national product (GNP) is a framework within which economic information may be arranged in an orderly fashion. Analysts can bring to bear whatever amount of mathematics they desire in their attempt to gain insight from this information.

Gross national product, simply defined, is the market value of the nation's output of goods and services. Its measurement can be approached from either of two directions: (*a*) by adding up the incomes generated by the economy—wages, salaries, profits, interest, and rent;

[11] The most recent book by the pioneer in this field is George Katona, *Psychological Economics* (Elsevier, 1975).

[12] See, for example, B. G. Hickman, ed., *Econometric Models of Cyclical Behavior.* 2 vols. (New York: National Bureau of Economic Research, 1972). Also, M. Evans, "Econometric Models," in W. F. Butler et al., *Methods and Techniques of Business Forecasting* (Englewood Cliffs, N.J., Prentice Hall, 1974).

or (*b*) by adding up the expenditures of consumers, businesses, and governments (plus net exports). For short-term forecasting purposes, the expenditure approach is more useful than the income approach. What one does is to forecast each major expenditure component of GNP, add up the component forecasts, and thus forecast the movement of aggregate economic activity as measured by GNP. This is why GNP model building is often referred to as "sector analysis."

GNP data are compiled by the Department of Commerce every quarter (on a seasonally adjusted annual rate basis), and are published in most complete detail in the *Survey of Current Business*. The data are revised frequently as new information becomes available, and the analyst must be careful to work with the most up-to-date statistics. Extensive revisions usually are published in each July issue of the *Survey*, and historical data running back to 1939 on a quarterly basis and to 1929 on an annual basis have been published in a supplement entitled *The National Income and Product Accounts of the United States, 1929–1965: Statistical Tables*. Detailed descriptive material on the conceptual underpinnings of national income accounting have been published in supplementary volumes entitled *National Income* and *U.S. Income and Output*.[13] An analytically convenient statement of the U.S. GNP accounts is shown in Table 12–3.

TABLE 12–3
Major Components of Gross National Product, 1975
(in billions of dollars)

Personal consumption expenditures		
Durable goods	$132	
Nondurable goods and services	841	
Total		$ 973
Gross private domestic investment		
Residential construction (including farm)	51	
Business capital spending	147	
Business inventory accumulation	− 14	
Total		184
Government purchases of goods and services		
Federal	124	
State and local	215	
Total		339
Net exports of goods and services		20
Gross national product		$1,516

Source: *Survey of Current Business*, August 1976.

---

[13] See also *The Economic Accounts of the United States–Retrospect and Prospect*. Part II of the July 1971 *Survey of Current Business*.

As noted previously, the economic forecasters' tasks are to enter the numbers they believe are most realistic for each calendar quarter of the period they are forecasting. To do this, they make use of any and every piece of evidence they think is pertinent. The latter point should be stressed. Sector analysis permits a maximum degree of analytical flexibility and ingenuity. As one analyst has put it, a GNP model has "a ravenous appetite for any data, evidence or insight concerning the current situation and outlook."

Achieving Internal Consistency in a Forecast.   Since investment timing depends more on a proper forecast of the *direction* than of the *magnitude* of economic change, it may seem unnecessary to attempt quantitative forecasts of the GNP sectors. Quantification is desirable, however. In the first place, without quantification the significance of each component of the economic outlook cannot be assessed properly. For example, a decline in defense spending may be foreseen and a rise in residential construction may be foreseen. But without an estimate of the magnitude of the change in each sector, the analyst cannot determine direction of change of the two sectors *combined*.

Furthermore, the various GNP sectors are interrelated. For example, consumer spending for durable goods such as furniture and appliances is related to purchases of homes; these expenditures affect saving; saving affects business investment; business investment affects consumer incomes, thereby affecting consumer spending. The circles go on and on. Since the major economic sectors are so fundamentally interrelated, an overall forecast based on a summation of individual sector forecasts must be internally consistent. The sectors must be in reasonable proportion to the whole and to each other— reasonable in the sense of conforming to the analyst's theory of business cycles and reasonable in the light of past empirical relationships. The only way to achieve internal consistency is to quantify.

With regard to internal consistency, it also must be recognized that the entire discussion thus far has been in terms of the expenditure, or demand, components of gross national product. Forecasters cannot rest easy, however, until they compare estimates of national spending with some measures of *supply* potential—that is, with some measures of national productive capacity. They must try to determine what their projections of gross national product imply for the rate of employment, for example. Can the projected demand for goods and services in fact be supplied by the available labor force? Or will the need for labor become so intense that production bottlenecks will result? On the other hand, does the projected demand fall far short of the productive capacity of the economy, leaving a high degree of slack in labor utilization? Similarly, what are the implications for plant and equipment adequacy?

If the forecast's implied rate of utilization of physical and human resources is very high, the forecasters may consider either scaling down their projections or maintaining their projections but adding a substantial price increase factor. On the other hand, if a preliminary forecast indicates that gross national product will be far below the economy's productive capacity, the forecasters must consider the possibility of federal government measures designed to take up the slack.[14]

Price versus Output.   Perhaps the most difficult aspect of economic forecasting, especially since 1965, has been the decomposition of a GNP forecast into its "real" and price components. For example, analysis of the forecasts of the President's Council of Economic Advisers and of private economists reveals a rather good "batting average" on forecasts of real output, both in direction and magnitude, but a very poor record on price forecasts.[15] Few economists have correctly foreseen the enormous inflationary spiral which has plagued the United States, Europe, and Japan during the past decade.

One approach to price forecasting is that of the monetarists, who believe that the price trend, at least in the long run, is a function of the trend rate of growth in money supply relative to the capacity for growth in real output. But, as noted earlier, there are many critics of this view. Moreover, even if it is correct, it leaves open two serious problems: (1) we do not know how to forecast the growth of money, and (2) long-run trends do not tell us much about the shorter run developments we are concerned with in investment timing.

Another approach, which appears more promising, begins with the recognition that the broadest price index—the so-called GNP deflator—can be decomposed as follows:

	Approximate Weighting
Private sector unit labor costs	45%
Government sector wage costs	20
Raw materials and other costs	30
Profits per unit	5

Utilizing this analytical framework, in late 1975, the New York investment firm of William D. Witter, Inc. predicted that in 1976 the

---

[14] In considering such measures, however, the analyst should bear in mind that many scholars have reached a conclusion similar to that reached by D. M. Bechter, in his study, "Federal Government Purchases of Goods and Services," *Federal Reserve Bank of Kansas City, Review,* November 1975, p. 10. He wrote: "Federal purchases more often than not have changed in ways that aggravate the business cycle."

[15] G. H. Moore, "Economic Forecasting—How Good a Track Record?" *The Morgan Guaranty Survey,* January 1975.

GNP deflator would rise by 5.3 percent. This figure was derived as follows:

1. Based on a study of trends in wage settlements of key industries, average wage gains in 1976 were expected to be about 8 percent. Offsetting this wage gain was·an expected productivity gain of about 4.5 percent (based on analogies with historical changes in productivity at similar stages of the business cycle). Therefore, unit labor costs were expected to rise 3.5 percent (8.0 − 4.5).

2. Government wage gains were predicted to be somewhat higher than in the private sector, about 9 percent versus 8 percent. Moreover, in national income accounting there are assumed to be no productivity gains in government.

3. Changes in materials and other costs are estimated on the basis of what the Witter firm refers to as the Pressure Index. This index represents percentage changes in the ratio of manufacturing and trade sales to inventories. When the ratio rises, sales are rising in relation to inventory stockpiles, putting upward pressure on prices; and vice versa when the ratio falls. Empirical evidence supporting this argument is shown in Figure 12–15. With this type of analysis, materials and other costs were predicted to rise 5 percent in 1976.

4. Profit margins per unit of output typically rise in the early stages of economic recovery, then flatten and fall as the prosperity ripens and then turns into recession. Given this pattern, the firm predicted a 10 percent rise in 1976 profit margins.

5. Putting its component forecasts together, the result was:

(a)	(b)	(c)	(b × c)
	Predicted		Contribution to Price
Factor	Change	Weight	Change
Unit labor costs	3.5%	.45	1.5%
Government wages	9.0	.20	1.8
Materials and other costs	5.0	.30	1.5
Profit margins	10.0	.04	0.5
		.05	5.3

If GNP is forecast to change by X percent and a broad-based price index is forecast to change by Y percent, then "real GNP" can be forecast to change by a percentage roughly equal to X minus Y. A valuable by-product of a real GNP forecast is a forecast of the Federal Reserve Board Index of Industrial Production. In the first part of this chapter, stock prices and interest rates were compared with the FRB index. This is a monthly rather than a quarterly series, is based upon

FIGURE 12–15
Relationship between Price Changes and
"Pressure Index"

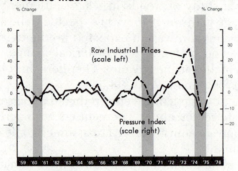

Source: William D. Witter, Inc.

physical output rather than current dollar data, and is highly sensitive to the supply and demand forces which have a strong influence on capital market conditions.

Most economists forecast the FRB index two ways and then reconcile the two forecasts. First, they build up a forecast of the aggregate FRB index by forecasting the individual components—manufactured durables, manufactured nondurables, mining, and utility output. The factors entering these forecasts are similar to those entering the forecast of the individual GNP sectors. Second, they translate their forecast of *real* GNP into a forecast of the FRB index. Figure 12–16 shows

FIGURE 12–16
Relationship between Industrial Production and Real GNP

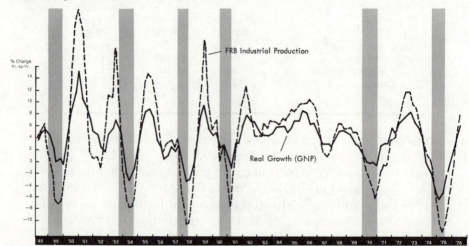

Source: William D. Witter, Inc.

that the timing relationship between real GNP and the FRB index has been quite close, with the FRB index tending to be more volatile.

Sources and Uses of Funds Model

Closely allied to the GNP model is an analytical structure which is widely used in interest rate forecasting. It is known as sources and uses of funds analysis. The object of sources and uses of funds analysis is to quantify the individual supply and demand forces at work in the money and capital markets, and thereby to determine whether the balance of forces lies in the direction of higher or lower interest rates. For example, Table 12–4 shows the major components of sources and uses of investment funds, based on data contained in Federal Reserve

TABLE 12–4
Net Demand and Supply for Funds (billions of dollars)

	1969	1970	1971	1972	1973	1974	1975E
NET DEMAND							
Mortgages—privately financed .	$23.3	$19.8	$ 40.6	$ 60.6	$ 62.8	$ 40.9	$ 40
Residential	16.1	12.6	28.5	43.2	41.4	24.5	30
Other	7.2	7.2	12.1	17.4	21.4	16.4	10
Corporate issues	15.4	25.5	30.2	23.1	16.6	23.8	38
Bonds	12.0	19.8	18.8	12.2	9.2	19.7	28
Equity....................	3.4	5.7	11.4	10.9	7.4	4.1	8
Government issues—							
privately financed	11.2	27.3	38.2	37.6	33.7	45.6	92
Federal	− 5.5	7.9	17.3	13.5	− 1.6	6.8	70
Budget agency	− 2.3	0.0	− 0.5	3.5	2.0	0.0	− 1
Sponsored agency	9.1	8.2	3.8	6.2	19.6	21.4	7
State and local	9.9	11.2	17.6	14.4	13.7	17.4	16
Total Long-Term	49.9	72.6	109.0	121.3	113.1	110.3	168
Bank loans, N.E.C.	17.6	5.8	12.4	28.5	52.1	39.5	− 10
Consumer credit	10.5	6.0	11.2	19.2	22.9	9.6	6
Open-market paper and other ..	12.5	1.5	11.4	1.5	3.8	14.9	7
Total Short-Term	40.6	13.3	35.0	49.2	78.8	64.0	3
Total Net Demand	90.5	84.9	144.0	170.5	191.9	174.3	171
NET SUPPLY							
Banks.......................	18.2	31.1	50.6	70.5	86.6	64.6	35
Financial Intermediaries	37.3	44.0	73.4	85.6	72.4	68.0	110
Pension and insurance	22.6	26.9	31.6	34.7	37.0	41.0	49
S&L's	9.9	11.6	29.2	36.4	27.1	21.0	41
Other*.....................	4.8	5.5	12.6	14.5	8.3	6.0	21
Nonfinancial corporations	2.5	− 2.3	7.0	2.6	7.9	7.5	17
Foreign	1.3	11.0	27.3	10.7	3.5	12.1	17
Total Institutional	$59.3	$87.8	$158.3	$169.4	$170.4	$152.2	$172
Residual (household and							
others)	31.2	− 2.9	− 14.3	1.1	21.5	22.1	− 3

* Includes discrepancies.
Source: William D. Witter, Inc.

Flow-of-Funds tabulations. These tabulations are updated quarterly in the *Federal Reserve Bulletin*.

Since, by definition, sources and uses of funds must always balance, it may be wondered how such tabulations can be useful in forecasting interest rates. After all, changes in interest rates, like changes in any prices, come about because of *imbalances* in supply and demand. Unsatisfied demands for funds pull interest rates upward, and pressures of excess supplies push them down.

Admittedly, it would be very helpful to have statistics on ex ante sources and uses of funds, which would reveal such imbalances. But even a balanced ex post framework can be useful. In the first place, as analysts attempt to forecast the various components of the sources and use statement—as they try to strike a balance between the forecast supplies and demands—they develop a "feel" for the ex ante gap between supply and demand. Another clue to the probable direction of interest rate changes is the magnitude of "noninstitutional sources of funds"[16] which the forecaster envisions in estimating forthcoming sources and uses of investment funds.

Institutional investors are under considerable pressure to commit their funds whether interest rates are high or low. Therefore, when demands for funds are expected to be low relative to the available

FIGURE 12–17
Residual Sources of Funds and Interest Rate Cycles

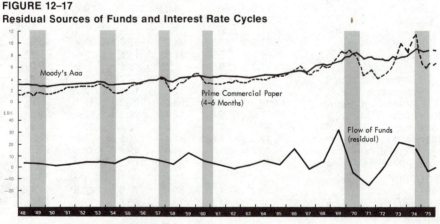

Source: William D. Witter, Inc.

---

[16] For an extensive discussion of the subject, see W. C. Freund and E. D. Zinbarg, "Forecasting Interest Rates," in M. E. Polakoff, ed., *Financial Institutions and Markets* (Boston: Houghton Mifflin Co., 1970). Although Table 12–4 and Figure 12–17 treat "noninstitutional" sources of funds as representing mainly *U.S. individual investors*, the work here cited includes nonfinancial corporations and foreigners as noninstitutional sources.

institutional supply, interest rates usually can be expected to decline. But when demands are forecast to rise rapidly relative to institutional supply, they cannot be met unless funds are forthcoming from other sources, such as individuals. In order to entice these noninstitutional funds (frequently referred to as "residual" sources of funds) into the capital markets, higher interest rates can be expected. Of course, as stressed earlier in this chapter, the interpretation of any set of data such as these must be conditioned by the forecaster's beliefs about inflation and inflationary expectations. But the relationship between "residual" sources of funds and interest rate changes has been consistent enough (see Figure 12–17) to be of great use to the bond market analyst.

Summary

Historical precedent, as outlined in the first part of this chapter, suggests various investment strategies which may be employed profitably if investors develop an ability to forecast major economic turning points about four to six months in advance—or if they rely on the counsel of others who have such an ability. (Of course, many investors will adopt a "buy-and-hold" strategy which ignores cyclical swings.) The precise implementation of these strategies depends on how aggressive, self-confident, *and flexible* an investor is. For example, large institutional investors are much less flexible than individual investors, as will be described in Chapter 14. Nevertheless, the general nature of the strategies may be indicated.

1. If investors suspect that the prosperity phase of the business cycle is coming to an end but are not yet firmly convinced of the fact, they might continue buying common stocks but confine purchases to companies whose sales are likely to be least vulnerable to recession and whose stocks' price-earnings ratios still seem relatively attractive. (See Chapters 15 to 17 for a discussion of formal attempts to quantify the volatility characteristics of different stocks.)

2. When investors become convinced that a recession lies shortly ahead, even though the stock market is still strong, they should have the courage to stop making new common stock commitments. Investable funds should be kept liquid at this stage, however—i.e., in bank time deposits or in short-term securities. Long-term bond investments probably are not yet appropriate, since interest rates are likely still to be rising. But the typical flat or downward-sloping shape of the yield curve at such times suggests that a good rate of return will be secured even on liquid investments.

3. When stock prices begin to weaken, in their classical lead relationship to general economic activity, it is time to institute quickly a

net selling program with regard to common stocks. In particular, stocks of highly cyclical companies and stocks whose price-earnings ratios have risen to unrealistic levels should be eliminated from the portfolio. Proceeds from these sales still should be kept in liquid form.

4. When the recession gets under way, and stock prices are falling rapidly, interest rates are likely to be at a peak, and liquid funds should be shifted into high-quality bonds of long maturity. These are likely to appreciate most in value when the cyclical decline in interest rates takes place.

5. In the midst of the recession, yield spreads between high-quality and lower quality bonds, and between bonds and mortgages, may become relatively wide. Income-oriented investors often find it worthwhile to shift funds from high-quality bonds to these higher yielding investments at such times.

6. When investors perceive the forthcoming end of the recession, a renewed stock buying program is in order—particularly the stocks of cyclical and "glamour-growth" companies which probably were severely depressed during the bear market. Profits on long-maturity bonds can be realized through sales, although some further rise in bond prices can be anticipated, with the proceeds of the sales to be invested in common stocks.[17]

It must be recognized, of course, that the "business cycle approach" to investment timing has faults as well as virtues. First, since many full-time professional economists have only mediocre forecasting records, investors who are not economists cannot be expected to do very well in forecasting on their own—or in evaluating the forecasts of professionals. Second, even a consistent record of perfect six-month forecasts is unlikely to result in consistently correct investment timing. For although the timing relationships among stock price, interest rate, and business cycle turning points have been reasonably stable, they have not been, and doubtless will not in the future be, unchanging. Consequently, many investors supplement business cycle analysis with the tools of "technical analysis" described in the next chapter.

SUGGESTED READINGS

Butler, William; Kavesh, Robert; and Platt, Robert. *Methods and Techniques of Business Forecasting.* Englewood Cliffs, N.J.: Prentice-Hall, Inc., 1974.

Council of Economic Advisers. *Economic Report of the President.* Washington, D.C.: U.S. Government Printing Office, annually.

---

[17] All of these investment operations, of course, should take place within an overall policy framework regarding the appropriate percentages of total assets to be allocated to stocks versus fixed income investments. This latter aspect of investment policy is discussed in Part IV of the text.

"Economic Analysis and Timing," *Financial Analyst's Handbook*, vol. I, part V. Homewood, Ill.: Dow Jones-Irwin, Inc., 1975.

Federal Reserve Board of Governors. *Introduction to Flow of Funds*. Washington, D.C., 1975.

Hickman, Bert G. *Econometric Models of Cyclical Behavior*. 2 vols. New York: National Bureau of Economic Research, 1972.

Katona, George. *Psychological Economics*. Elsevier, 1975.

Kendrick, John W. *Economic Accounts and Their Uses*. New York: McGraw-Hill Book Co., 1972.

Meigs, A. James. *Money Matters*. New York: Harper & Row, Publishers, 1972.

"The National Income and Product Accounts of the United States: Revised Estimates, 1929–74," *Survey of Current Business*, January 1976.

Sommers, Albert T. (ed.) *Answers to Inflation and Recession: Economic Policies for a Modern Society*. New York: The Conference Board, 1975.

Sprinkel, Beryl W. *Money and Markets: A Monetarist View*. Homewood, Ill.: Dow Jones-Irwin, Inc., 1971.

Zarnowitz, Victor (ed.). *The Business Cycle Today*. New York: National Bureau of Economic Research, 1972.

———, and Boschan, Charlotte. "Cyclical Indicators: An Evaluation and New Leading Indexes." *Business Conditions Digest*, May 1975.

REVIEW QUESTIONS AND PROBLEMS

1. Describe the timing relationships which have existed between business cycles and stock prices.

2. Describe the timing relationships which have existed between business cycles and interest rates.

3. What is the rationale of the leading indicator approach to economic forecasting?

4. Describe six leading indicators which have been identified by the National Bureau of Economic Research.

5. In what way can monetary statistics be useful and in what way misleading in business forecasting?

6. What kinds of anticipations data are available to the forecaster?

7. How is the national income accounting framework used in economic forecasting?

8. What problems exist in decomposing a GNP forecast into its "real" and price components?

9. Compare and contrast sources and uses of funds data with national income data: (*a*) in concept, and (*b*) in application.

10. In your own investment program, how would you utilize forecasts of (*a*) total GNP, (*b*) specific components of GNP?

RESEARCH PROJECTS

1. Using as many as possible of the techniques described in Chapter 12, prepare a six-month forecast of GNP, industrial production, and the consumer price index.
2. Contrast sources and uses of funds data during a low-interest rate period and a high-interest rate period.
3. Have the relationships among stock prices, interest rates, yield curves, and yield spreads during the past year or two conformed with expectations based on the historical record of such relationships?
4. Prepare a paper which considers the possible impact on stock prices of a lengthy period of federal price and wage controls.
5. Can you find some illustrations, in addition to those given in Chapter 12, of a close relationship between the stock price behavior of a specific industry group and the cyclical behavior of that industry's production or sales?

C.F.A. QUESTIONS

1. *From Exam III, 1975*

In Sidney Homer's 1966 article, "Techniques for Forecasting Interest Rate Trends," he proposed a four-step procedure for the analysis of cyclical interest rate trends:

a. The selection of a tentative economic model for the year ahead.
b. A judgment on the effect of this economic model on: (1) commodity prices and (2) employment.
c. The construction of a corresponding financial model estimating the supply and demand for credit which is implicit in the economic model.
d. An estimate of the effect of steps (*a*), (*b*), and (*c*) above on monetary and fiscal policy.

In the light of recent events and as reviewed by the latest *Economic Report of the President*, list and discuss, carefully, the major difficulties that may be faced today in forecasting interest rates over the next twelve months by the procedures proposed by Mr. Homer.

2. *From Exam I, 1976*

In your Economic readings the "cumulative process" of business cycles was described as how the various sectors of the economy react to changes in economic conditions to produce revivals and recessions in aggregate economic activity.

Congress, alarmed by the continuing high levels of unemployment, passes over the President's veto a public works program totaling $30 billion. This program creates a net addition to government spending with no offsetting increase in taxes or decrease in other previously scheduled government spending.

a. Assuming that the economy is in the *initial* stages of an economic recovery indicate the sectors of the economy and the components of GNP
that would be most *immediately* affected and describe their reaction.
b. Describe how the changes in these sectors would spread changes in employment, money, interest rates, and prices to other parts of the economy
and indicate the impact on total GNP.
c. Assume that before any of the changes in the economy occurred your
portfolio was as follows: 60 percent common stocks, 30 percent bonds, and
10 percent cash equivalents. Based on the above economic changes, describe and justify any adjustment you would make in this three-way distribution of your portfolio.

Chapter 13

Technical Analysis

> There is nothing so disastrous as a rational investment policy
> in an irrational world.
> ———————————————————*John Maynard Keynes*

The business cycle approach to common stock timing deals with factors outside the stock market itself—for example, industrial production and money supply. The technical approach, on the other hand, seeks to improve the basis of timing decisions by studying phenomena which are an integral part of the market mechanism—for example, prices and volume of trading. For this reason, technical analysis is often referred to as internal analysis or market analysis.

Technical analysts study internal stock market data in an attempt to gain insight into what economists call the "supply and demand schedules" for a stock or for the stock market as a whole. They do this by looking for recurring patterns of price movement or recurring interrelationships between stock price movements and other market data. Since price movements reflect the opinions of millions of different people about everything having a bearing on stocks, it is unlikely that "technicians" can know in all cases *why* the discovered patterns occur. They may try to learn why—including in this effort an examination of relevant external information in addition to internal data—but the probability remains that many patterns and relationships will be unexplainable. Nevertheless, if the patterns are known to recur consistently, it seems sensible to take advantage of this knowledge even though the explanations remain unknown. After all, physicians do not know why aspirin works as well as it does, but they prescribe it nonetheless.

Technical analysts who are intellectually honest will be quick to

admit that they have no hope of discovering foolproof methods of forecasting stock prices. Mistakes are bound to be made, often severe mistakes. But they also will argue that as long as their methods improve the *probabilities* of investment success, as long as they reduce the margin of error, they are worthy of serious consideration.

It should be noted that technical analysis is not a new, or even recent development. In fact, it is considered by many to be the original form of investment analysis, dating back to the late 1800s. It came into widespread use before the period of extensive and fully disclosed financial information, which in turn enabled the practice of so-called fundamental research to develop. Its principal purpose was to help market technicians monitor the actions of informed investors. Many of the techniques used today have been utilized for over 50 years, although the use of computers has given rise to substantial modification of established methods.

Despite its age, technical analysis has been enjoying a renaissance on Wall Street. According to *Fortune,* one of the interesting events of the recent past has been the revived popularity of technical analysis.[1] Interestingly, much of the new demand for technical market analysis has come from institutional investors, presumably the most sophisticated.[2]

Most technicians explain their present popularity, again according to *Fortune,* by noting that many professional investors were hurt badly by the advice they were getting from fundamentalists in 1973–74. The trouble with this explanation is that the technicians were just as wrong in 1973–74.[3] Whatever the case, technical analysis and technicians are riding higher than they have in years.

The purpose of this chapter is to examine the validity of the technicians' claims that they have methods which "work." Obviously, each and every technical tool cannot be examined, just as all of the methods of analyzing the business cycle could not be covered in the previous chapter. But the reader will be exposed to some of the most widely used technical tools. We shall try to point out the basic strengths and weaknesses of each tool and in doing so to note whether it is applicable to an analysis of the market as a whole, of individual securities, or of both.

For the sake of convenience, we have divided our discussion into

---

[1] A. F. Ehrbar, "Technical Analysts Refuse to Die," *Fortune,* August 1975, p. 99.

[2] It has been reported, for example, that nine out of the ten largest commercial banks either have their own technical analysts working in their trust departments or have procedures for monitoring the recommendations of other technicians. Of the 290 investment managers of all types surveyed by *Pensions & Investments,* 176 claimed directly or implied that they used market timing techniques in managing portfolios.

[3] Ehrbar, "Technical Analysts Refuse to Die," p. 99.

three sections: general market analysis, contrary opinion, and price charts and stock selection techniques. Some of the subjects in each naturally overlap into other sections. For example, security credit is discussed as part of the theory of contrary opinion, but could just as accurately be considered an element in general market supply-demand analysis. Similarly, Dow theory is covered under "price charts," because the philosophy underlying Dow theory is applicable to the study of individual stocks as well as to the overall market, but it could just as well have been a part of the market analysis section.

GENERAL MARKET ANALYSIS

General market analysis covers a very long list of tools and techniques designed to determine the basic, general trend of stock prices. Technicians, and in fact most investors, consider it easier to select "up" stocks, i.e., stocks which are expected to rise in price, if the general trend is favorable (bullish) as opposed to unfavorable (bearish). As we shall show in later chapters, new advances in portfolio theory also support this conclusion.

Breadth of Market

Breadth of market analysis is one of the most popular techniques used to study major turning points of the market as a whole. It is based on a theory of the nature of stock market cycles. Bull markets are viewed as being long drawn-out affairs during which individual stocks reach peaks gradually, with the number of individual peaks accelerating as the market averages (for example, the Dow Jones Industrials) rise toward a turning point. Bear markets, on the other hand, are viewed as concentrated collapses of a large number of stocks in a short period of time. Accordingly, to detect a condition of internal market weakness before it is generally recognized that a bull market tide has turned, evidence is sought to determine whether large numbers of stocks are falling while the averages rise. And to detect the approaching end of a bear market, technical analysts consider how widespread the selling pressure is. In short, what is being examined is the dispersion of a general price rise or decline; thus the phrase "breadth of market."

There are many ways of measuring breadth of market. The easiest to apply, and probably the most widely used, is a daily cumulation of the net number of advancing or declining issues on the New York Stock Exchange. The daily newspapers publish a table showing the number of issues traded on the previous day, the number which advanced in price, the number which declined, and the number which were unchanged. If the declines are subtracted from the advances, a net positive or negative figure results (described as net advances or

net declines). For example, a week's market activity might produce the following data.

	Number of Issues Traded	Advances	Declines	Unchanged	Net Advances or Declines
Monday	1,301	530	535	236	− 5
Tuesday	1,310	464	597	249	−133
Wednesday	1,323	303	739	281	−436
Thursday	1,295	607	453	235	+154
Friday	1,308	807	241	260	+566

The next step is to cumulate the net advances and net declines, thus constructing a measure of a breadth. Cumulation simply means the successive addition of a series of numbers. In the above example, cumulation of the final column of data would produce the following:

Breadth of Market

Monday	− 5
Tuesday	−138
Wednesday	−574
Thursday	−420
Friday	+146

The cumulation is continued ad infinitum. Obviously, over a period of many years of generally rising stock prices the absolute *level* of the breadth measure can become very high. Moreover, if different analysts begin their cumulations on different days, the levels of their breadth series will differ. However, breadth analysis focuses on *change* rather than on level, and the change during any given time period will be the same no matter what the original starting date of the cumulation.

Having measured breadth, the next step is to chart it in conjunction with one of the market averages, such as the Dow Jones Industrials. Normally, breadth and the DJI will move in tandem. What the analyst must be wary of during a bull market is an extended divergence of the two lines—that is, a breadth line which declines to successive new lows while the DJI makes new highs. Such a divergence indicates that an increasing number of issues are turning down while the "blue chips," which weigh heavily in the DJI and in most other market averages, continue to rise. According to the theory underlying breadth analysis, this suggests an approaching peak in the averages and a major downturn of stock prices generally.[4]

---

[4] It should be stressed that this theory of the nature of bull markets suggests that they usually end "not with a bang but a whimper." It is a contradiction of the thesis that bull markets typically end with a "speculative blowoff." According to breadth theory, the prices of low-quality and speculative stocks, together with volume of trading, reach a blowoff stage before the market averages hit a peak, and then settle down while better quality stocks move up somewhat further in price. Finally, when the better quality stocks turn down, the whole price structure deteriorates.

Anthony Tabell, a leading stock market technician, explains the general concept by citing an old Wall Street notion that "the 30 Dow Industrials are the generals in an army and all the other stocks are the troops. When the generals lead and the troops follow, everything's all right. But when the troops don't follow, you've got trouble."[5]

This theory has considerable historical validity. Price-breadth divergences preceded the major market downturns of 1929, 1936–37, 1948–49, 1956–57, 1960, and 1962. On the other hand, the 1953 stock price decline was not preceded by a price-breadth divergence. Moreover, there often may be room for differing interpretations of the movement in breadth. For example, looking at Figure 13–1, some ob-

FIGURE 13–1
Stock Prices and Breadth of Market

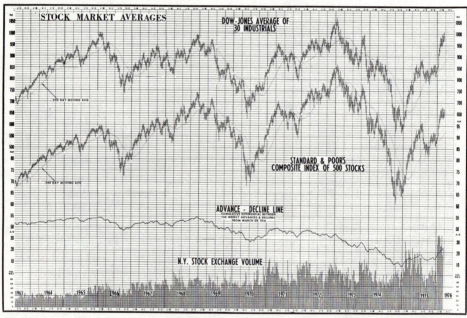

Source: Trendline's *Current Market Perspectives,* March 1976, p. 7.

servers claim that the 1966 stock market downturn was preceded by at least a mild price-breadth divergence, since breadth in January 1966 was little different from its level in May 1965, while the market averages were at record highs. However, others counter that this really wasn't a divergence since breadth did not make a series of *new lows* during the intervening months.

[5] William G. Shepard, "Inside Wall Street," *Business Week,* May 5, 1975, p. 78.

Breadth of market was not very helpful in timing some recent general market downturns. The advance-decline line shown in Figure 13-1 "topped out" coincident with, rather than ahead of, the 1968 peaks in both the DJI and S&P 500. Furthermore, from April 1971 throughout 1972 the advance-decline line was in a general downtrend but the broad market averages were able to record successive new highs despite the deterioration in breadth. Market breadth deteriorated even further in conjunction with the 1973–74 bear market, reaching a low in December 1974, when the market averages also bottomed. Since then, breadth improved as the market averages moved higher.

Overall, the evidence suggests that breadth of market may be a useful advance indicator of major stock price declines but that, like any other indicator, it is by no means infallible.

Once the market has entered its declining phase, breadth also can be useful in detecting an impending recovery. It will be recalled that a major premise of breadth analysis is that large numbers of stocks tumble in price in a short period of time during bear markets. Therefore, the end of a bear market is likely to be near when all anxious and panicky investors rush to sell out at once. Evidence of a so-called selling climax may be obtained by examining the movement of breadth in conjunction with prices and the volume of trading. Typically, for a number of weeks during the latter stages of a bear market the cumulative net advance-decline line will fall by several thousand, the Dow Jones Industrials will fall several percent, and trading volume will be substantially higher than in previous weeks. Prices will not necessarily begin rising immediately after such a selling climax— indeed, they typically bump along the bottom for a few months—but the worst is usually over.[6]

A relatively recent development in market breadth technique has been the extension of the general concept to the analysis of individual securities, made possible largely through the use of computers. Muller & Company provide a "net volume" service covering 1,500 individual stocks to institutional investors, notes that:

[its analysis] is based on the simple theory that every transaction that takes place on the floor of the exchange reflects the supply and demand factors present at the time of the transaction. If a security trades at a price no different from the previous transaction, supply and demand are in balance. If the transaction occurs at an up-tick however, demand is evident and at that instant buyers are willing to bid higher for the stock. If the reverse occurs we know

---

[6] Professional stock traders frequently wait to see if there is a second big "bump" before they resume buying. This second bump, if it occurs, may be on relatively light volume.

the seller desires to get out of the stock and drops his price to attract a buyer; selling pressure is predominant and the down-tick is registered.[7]

Net volume measures the difference between up-ticks and down-ticks. It is calculated in the same general manner as the advance-decline index. That is, for example, if a given issue trades 80,000 shares in a day, with 40,000 traded on plus-ticks, 30,000 on minus-ticks, and the balance at no change in price, the net volume difference at the end of the day is 10,000 shares traded on plus-ticks. The objective is to spot any patterns of divergence between the price trend of a stock and its net volume. When such divergences occur, a reversal of the price trend is considered likely. A disparity between falling price and a rising net volume line, leads to the conclusion that accumulation is taking place. The reverse holds true when the combination is a rising price and a weak or falling net volume line. Figure 13–2 illustrates the concept quite clearly.

FIGURE 13–2
Example of Net Volume and Stock Price Trends—U.S. Steel Corp.

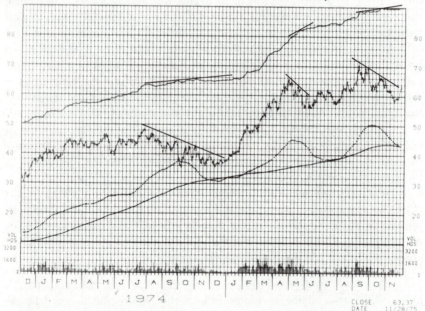

Note: Two relative strength lines are plotted below the chart of daily prices. These are arrived at by dividing the daily closing price of the particular issue by the daily closing of the NYSE composite index. The resulting ratio is stored in the computer and, along with the preceeding 29 days' ratios, used to compute a 30-day moving average which is plotted on the chart as a dotted line. A 150-day moving average is also computed and plotted as a solid line. These are referred to as the "short-term" and "long-term" relative strength, respectively. These three lines are used in concert to mark the beginning and end of significant moves in issue prices.
Source: Muller & Company.

---

[7] "Net Volume Studies," Muller and Company, 1975.

Volume of Trading

In May 1901, Charles Dow wrote "Great activity means great movement whenever the normal balance between buyers and sellers is violently disturbed."[8] Since then, and quite probably before, technicians have followed volume data closely in order to gain perspective as to the general health and trend of the market.

There are many ways to measure volume trends, and technicians delight in creating new ones as a means of gaining some proprietary knowledge. However, the basic rule is quite simple—price tends to follow volume. Moreover, as Smilen and Safian (two well-known, and respected market analysts) have noted:

Stock prices traditionally tend to rise easily on relatively little volume in the early phase of an important advance, indicating that the path of least resistance is up, and to require steadily more volume as the move ages, until a stalemate is reached at the point of reversal, with heavy volume and negligible net progress made by prices. This is the prototype of the pattern we would expect to see. While there are exceptions to it, these departures often tell us as much about the nature of the market at the time as conformity would.[9]

Given these generalizations, volume of trading data may provide a useful indicator of the end of a *bull* market. Volume has a tendency to fall in advance of major declines in the stock price averages, as shown in Figure 13–3. Volume data also can help in detecting the end of a *bear* market, since, as noted earlier, volume rises sharply during selling climaxes.

In fact, Figure 13–3 indicates that the volume-price characteristics of the four market cycles from 1956 through 1962 were remarkably similar. In each cycle, volume and price experienced a steady buildup until the midpoint of the cycle. Then, volume peaked and declined to a relatively low level until the next cycle began. In other words, for most of the postwar period, new volume highs were always accompanied by new highs in price.

Starting in 1965, again referring to Figure 13–3, changes in the price-volume relationship developed. Prices failed to show any further significant increase despite a persistent uptrend in volume. Peaks in volume no longer led peaks in price, but coincided with them. Finally,. volume trends became highly erratic.

Viewing these trends, Stone & Mead conclude "There is absolutely no precedent in the volume-price relationships that have developed

---

[8] Harry D. Schultz, "Bear Markets: How to Survive and Make Money in Them" (Englewood Cliffs, N.J.: Prentice-Hall, Inc., 1966), p. 88.

[9] Smilen and Safian, Inc., "Comprehensive Technical Service for Institutional Investors," 1971, p. 14-A.

FIGURE 13-3. Stock Prices and Volume of Trading, 1956–1975

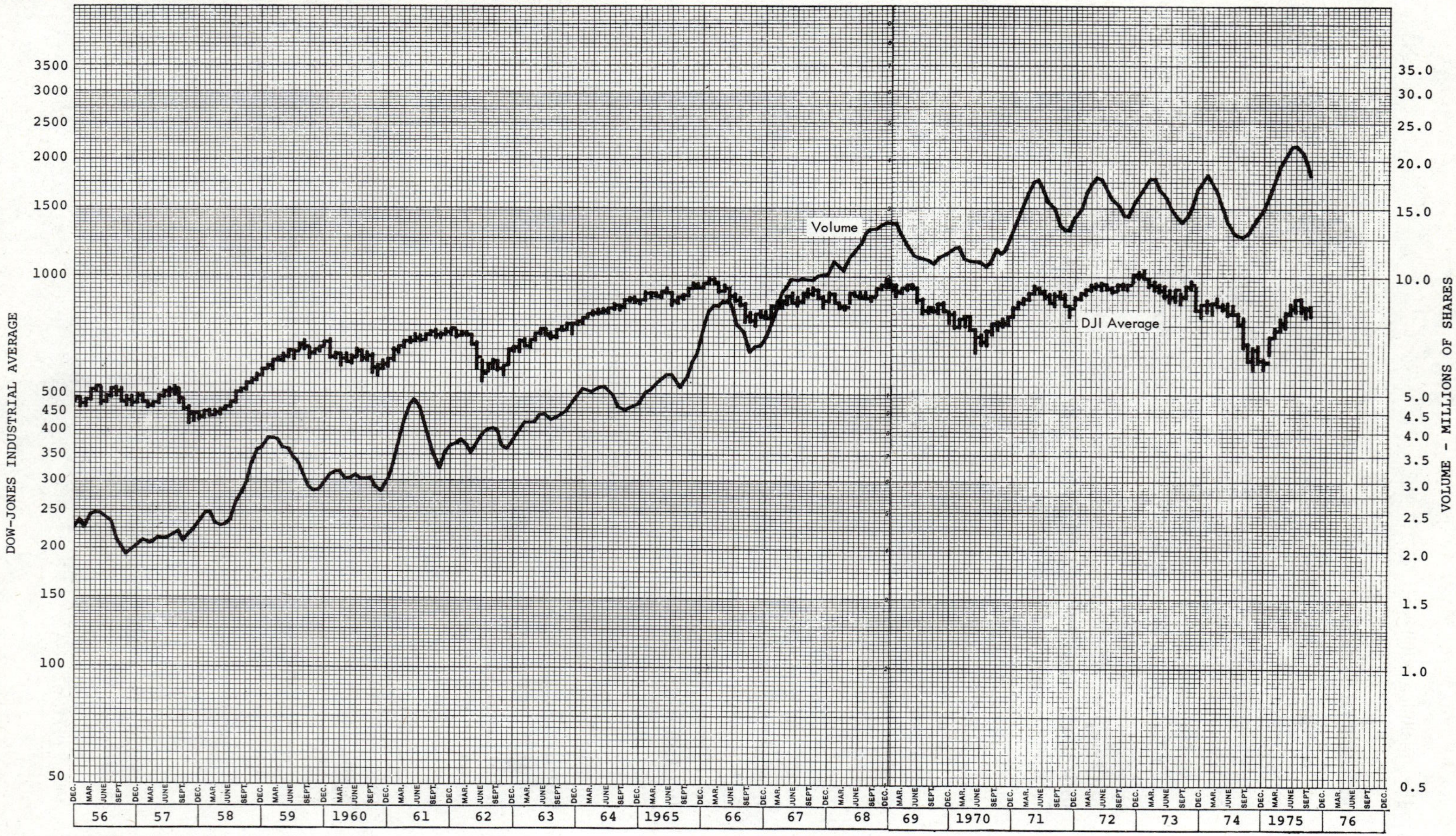

Source: Stone & Mead, Inc.

since 1965. To the best of our knowledge, no other bear market in history has been accompanied by rising rather than falling volume."[10]

A third application of volume data is in the study of individual stocks. Prices obviously do not move steadily in the same direction every day. Even if a stock's price is in a major uptrend, it frequently will decline. It does not move up like an arrow, but zigzags up. Many technical analysts believe that if the volume of trading in a stock rises on the days when its price rises during the course of this zigzag movement, and then falls off when price recedes temporarily, the overall pattern is bullish. On the other hand, if volume rises when price falls, and falls when price rises, the overall pattern is believed to have bearish connotations (unless the volume rise and price decline are of such magnitude as to suggest a selling climax).

The idea behind this application of volume data to the analysis of individual stocks is that volume of trading varies directly with the intensity of emotion on the part of stock buyers and sellers. When anxious buyers outnumber anxious sellers, they bid aggressively and push prices up on heavy volume. When anxious sellers come to dominate events, they offer stock in increasing volume at markdowns in price. Volume therefore becomes a clue to shifts in the supply and demand schedules for a stock. This theory has not been subjected to much formal testing, but our general impression is that it is essentially correct. One possible reason for its validity is that unusual volume may reflect the activity of large traders who may possess information or interpretations not yet generally known or appreciated. A collection of studies gathered by Perry Wysong, who publishes a market letter based on insider trading activity, indicates that insiders *really do know* what they are doing.[11]

In recent years, substantial trading activity has been conducted in the third and fourth markets, where volume data have been less available publicly than for listed dealings. Many technicians have feared that continued development away from recorded and reported transactions would obsolete established technical tools predicated on volume analysis. However, the SEC's emphasis on development of a central market should permit the practice of volume analysis in its traditional form.

---

[10] Stone & Mead, Inc., "Long-Term Technical Trends," October 1975, p. 22. Stone & Mead offer two possible explanations for recent volume developments. The first is the shifting supply-demand relationships for common stocks in the postwar period, moving from a position of overdemand and undersupply to one of oversupply and underdemand. The second explanation centers around the increased institutionalization of the market, and the shift in emphasis on the part of the institutions from a long-term buy and hold strategy to an approach that can only be characterized as trading.

[11] See Perry Wysong, "How You Can Use the Wall Street Insiders" (Fort Lauderdale, Fla.: Wilton House, 1972). The market letter is called "Consensus of Insiders," P.O. Box 10247, Ft. Lauderdale, Fla. 33305.

Supply–Demand Analysis

Supply–demand analysis is a technical tool which has been developed largely because of an increase in the availability of information covering the flow of funds into security markets. Generally speaking, it seeks to measure imbalances between new stock offerings and anticipated investment demand for common stocks. An excess of offerings relative to demand will tend to depress stock prices, and vice versa. In this regard, the approach is very similar to the "sources and uses of funds" technique described in Chapter 12 to forecast interest rates.

Table 13–1 summarizes the general elements utilized by most

TABLE 13–1
Summary of Common Stock Supply and Demand Elements (in billions of dollars)

	Annual Net Issuance and Net Purchases						
	1970	1971	1972	1973	1974	1975e	1976p
Gross new cash offerings:							
Public utilities	3.0	4.2	5.0	4.7	4.0	6.3	7.1
Communication	0.1	1.6	1.1	1.4	0.2	1.0	0.9
Railroads	0.0	0.0	0.0	0.0	0.0	0.0	0.0
Other transportation	0.0	0.5	0.2	0.0	0.0	0.0	0.3
Manufacturing	1.3	2.1	1.8	0.7	0.5	1.8	4.3
Mining	1.8	1.1	1.3	0.8	0.7	1.0	0.9
Financial and real estate	1.6	2.2	2.1	2.9	0.6	0.5	0.7
Commercial and miscellaneous	0.8	1.3	1.6	0.6	0.3	0.5	0.8
Total cash offerings	8.6	13.0	13.1	11.1	6.3	11.1	15.0
Adjustments for delayed delivery, etc.	−1.1	−1.1	−1.0	−3.0	−1.0	−1.0	−1.0
Plus stock options and all other sales	0.8	1.2	1.3	2.1	2.1	2.5	2.7
Less cash retirements	2.2	1.2	2.2	2.7	3.0	3.1	3.0
Plus conversions of bonds	0.8	1.6	1.8	1.6	0.5	0.9	1.0
Less (merger) exchanges into bonds	0.1	0.0	0.0	0.0	0.6	0.1	0.2
Net issuance	6.8	13.5	13.0	9.1	4.3	10.3	14.5
Ownership:							
Mutual savings banks	0.3	0.5	0.6	0.4	0.3	0.2	0.2
Life insurance companies	2.0	3.7	3.7	3.5	2.2	2.0	2.4
Fire and casualty companies	1.2	2.6	3.2	2.2	−1.4	−0.4	0.5
Private Noninsured pension funds ..	4.6	8.9	7.3	5.3	2.3	5.6	6.0
State and local retirement funds ...	2.1	3.2	3.5	3.9	3.5	2.5	2.9
Open-end mutual funds	1.2	0.4	−1.8	−2.3	−0.5	−0.9	−0.5
Total Nonbank investing institutions	11.4	19.3	16.5	13.0	6.4	9.0	11.5
Foreigners	0.7	0.8	2.3	2.8	0.5	4.0	5.5
Residual: Individuals and miscellaneous	−5.3	−6.6	−5.8	−6.7	−2.6	−2.7	−2.5
Total ownership	6.8	13.5	13.0	9.1	4.3	10.3	14.5

Source: Salomon Bros., *Supply & Demand for Credit in 1976.*

analysts. These will be examined more closely below. It should be borne in mind that, *after the fact* (ex post), supply and demand must be in balance. What the analyst seeks to determine is whether there are imbalances *before the fact* (ex ante). Some of the items in Table 13–1 are composites, subject to further breakdown, and require substantial analysis beyond the mere listing of a reported figure. For example, the change in stock demands by individuals cannot be measured directly. It appears in the table as a "residual" item. But it can be studied indirectly by analyzing, for example, odd-lot trading trends and short interest activity (both of which are described later in this chapter). The supply side, predominantly new corporate offerings for cash, is particularly complex.

A forecast of new offerings basically relates to the anticipated needs of corporations to finance capital spending plans through new equity, as opposed to increasing debt or from internally generated sources. This, in turn, requires an analysis of corporate liquidity, the profits outlook, dividend policies, capital spending plans, and many other factors. However, despite the complexity, careful scrutiny of the basic factors can lead to meaningful conclusions. For example, Figure 13–4 graphically summarizes the major elements affecting corporate offerings. Between 1955 and 1965, retained corporate cash flow just about equaled capital expenditures, and even exceeded annual spending in a number of years. After 1965, gaps of various proportions developed, indicating a growing need for greater external funds. At the same time, corporate debt levels had also increased. As a result, new equity offerings increased substantially during most of the subsequent years (see Table 13–1). In fact, gross cash offerings of common stock doubled from 1969 to 1972, while the net impact of equity issues actually tripled, from \$4.3 billion in 1969 to \$13 billion in 1972. The flood of new shares abated in the weaker market of 1973 but was still more than double the 1969 level.[12]

Despite the sharp increase in supply during the past few years, net purchases by institutional investors have substantially exceeded net new issues. The difference has been largely made up by public liquidation of holdings, as depicted in Figure 13–5. There is some reason to believe that these patterns may be about to reverse themselves. That is, institutional investors are not likely to change the stock-bond ratios of their portfolios, while individual investors are in good position to increase their purchase of equity securities.[13] But supply–

---

[12] See Peter Bernstein, "The Supply and Demand for Equities: Opportunity or Disaster?" *Market Letter* (New York: Peter L. Bernstein, Inc., April 1, 1975), for an analysis of supply-demand forecasts covering the 1976–80 period.

[13] Charles H. Mott, "The Outlook for the U.S. Equity Market," Baker, Weeks & Co., October 28, 1975 for a recent discussion of these possibilities.

FIGURE 13–4
Long-Term Investment and Cash Flow
(nonfinancial corporations)

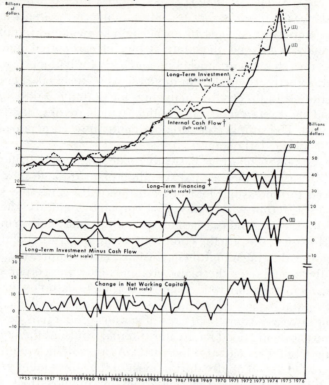

* Business fixed investment plus direct foreign investment.
† Depreciation plus retained earnings including inventory profits.
‡ Stocks, bonds, and mortgages.
§ Change in current assets less change in current liabilities.
Source: Goldman, Sachs & Co.

demand analysis is concerned less with long-term trends than with short-term departures from trend. These are by no means easy to trace, much less to predict.

One problem is that data are still largely incomplete and untimely for several important investor categories, including bank trust departments, foundations, and educational endowments. Second, there is the dynamic aspect of investor psychology to contend with. Buyers can quickly become sellers, and vice versa, thereby distorting supply–demand calculations. Finally, it is not clear that, even if one can predict what the ultimate supply–demand numbers will be, one can properly infer stock price movements from the data. For example, Goldman Sachs has noted that there is no correlation between changes

FIGURE 13–5
Net New Issues and Net Purchases of Corporate Equities
(billions of dollars)   *(billions of dollars)*

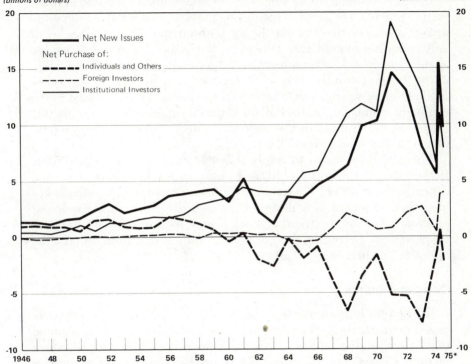

* To 1975: Seasonally adjusted annual rates.
Source: Loeb, Rhoades & Co.

in the magnitude of "excess" institutional demand (institutional purchases less new issues) and the rate at which the market capitalizes earnings.[14] Dr. William C. Freund, vice president and chief economist of the New York Stock Exchange points out that "there is simply no consistent relationship between stock prices and net demand from institutional investors."[15] Nonetheless, as Goldman Sachs has also noted, "Market-watchers generally view institutional purchasing power with the attitude of the more the better in the belief that if other considerations are equal, institutional buying pressure may lead to higher market prices. Conversely, fear that there will be a shortage of institutional funds available for equity investment causes great concern about the future course of the market."[16]

---

[14] Richard B. Worley, "Factors Affecting the Supply and Demand for Common Stocks—A Countrary View," in Goldman, Sachs & Co., *Economic Comments*, October 25, 1971, p. 6.

[15] William C. Freund, "What Bad New Era For Stocks?" *Fortune*, April 1972, p. 50.

[16] Goldman, Sachs & Co., *Economic Comments*, p. 8.

THEORY OF CONTRARY OPINION

Contrary opinion in the stock market is actually an attitude or intellectual process, not a tool of technical analysis. Further, it is difficult to define *precisely* the general theory without the use of ludicrous or silly-sounding statements. However, the *general* concept is to "go against the crowd." Humphrey Neill, generally considered the father of the theory, put it this way—"When everyone thinks alike, everyone is likely to be wrong," or "The crowd is usually wrong, at least in the timing of events."[17] Leslie Pollack stated it differently, by noting that "It is not the opinion of the majority, but the action of the minority which makes stock prices."[18]

This does not mean to imply that the majority is *always* wrong. Rather, that the majority is *likely* to be wrong when there is no real difference of opinion. Therefore, technicians have developed a series of tools and techniques designed to measure the status of popular opinion regarding the trend of stock prices, to determine when popular opinion is becoming "too uniform," and, at that time, to take the opposite position in the market.

Odd-Lot Trading

Odd-lot trading (transactions involving less than 100 shares)[19] is engaged in primarily by the proverbial "man in the street." It is assumed that by examining odd-lot trading data in conjunction with the stock market price averages a useful composite picture of popular opinion can be obtained.

The general thesis of odd-lot trading analysis was formulated by Garfield A. Drew in 1940. He believed basically that the general public was not sufficiently sophisticated to compete with professional investors due to a lack of knowledge and the inability to develop an emotional detachment from investment decisions. Over the years since, odd-lot analysis has become one of the most popular, but widely misunderstood, elements of contrary opinion technique.

---

[17] Over the years, Humphrey B. Neill has expressed these views many times, many ways, in many places. His most recent collection of thoughts and suggestions on contrary thinking are contained in *The Ruminator* (Caldwell, Ida.: Caxton Printers, Ltd., 1975).

Martin Zweig, one of the newer market technicians, holds the view "whenever non-professional investors become significantly one-sided in their expectations about the future course of stock prices, the market will move in the direction opposite to that which is anticipated by the masses." To the support this contention he has published a comprehensive analysis on the tools of contrary opinion. See Martin Zweig, "Investor Expectations: Why They Are the Key to Stock Market Trends," *The Zweig Forecast,* (New York: Zweig Securities Advisory, Inc., 1975).

[18] Leslie M. Pollack, "Technical Analysis: A Basic Approach," Reynolds & Co., p. 3.

[19] Aggregate odd-lot trading data are published in the newspapers on a daily and weekly basis.

Most analysts of odd-lot data place primary emphasis upon the ratio of odd-lot selling volume to odd-lot buying volume. Usually volume is expressed in number of shares rather than dollar amounts, although dollar amounts are published in the monthly SEC *Statistical Bulletin* and are used by some analysts. Some analysts also use ratios of odd-lot short sales to total odd-lot sales, and total odd-lot volume (purchases plus sales) to round-lot volume on the New York Stock Exchange. But these latter ratios can be viewed chiefly as devices to confirm the indications of the sales-to-purchases ratio, rather than as indicators in their own right.

The general theory is that sophisticated investors should begin to consider selling when the public markedly increases its buying relative to its selling, and vice versa. The underlying assumption is that small investors buy most heavily at market tops, and sell most heavily at the bottom. They seem to reverse Wall Street's golden adage—"buy low—sell high." Much of the historical data supports this theory of the small investor's behavior. The perverse timing of the odd-lotter is usually reflected in the sales-to-purchases ratio diverging in direction from the market just as the latter is reaching a peak or trough. But there also have been periods when the small investor's behavior has been quite astute, particularly in recent years.

The Cleveland Trust Company has provided commentary on this point. Calling attention to the period 1966–74 covered in Figure 13–6, they noted that "near every Dow Jones Industrial Average peak, odd-lot sales increase faster than purchases, and near every Dow Jones Industrial trough, purchases rise more than sales. Thus, overall, small investors have bought more at troughs and sold more at peaks, contrary to an old adage that the small investor is invariably wrong."[20]

The contemporary value of tracking changes in odd-lot activity patterns has been recently questioned since the small investor has steadily reduced participation in the market, while, at the same time, institutions have become an increasingly dominant force. Nevertheless, Becker Securities Corporation, among others, believes that odd-lot indicators are as valid as ever for two principal reasons. First, odd-lot statistics are not analyzed to determine the small investors' potential market impact, but rather their existing psychology. The only requirement for this determination is the availability of data on a numerically representative sample of this type of investor, and, while diminishing, there are still enough less-than-100 share investors to meet this requirement. Second, by determining the prevailing market psychology of the odd-lotter an insight into the feelings of many institutional portfolios managers is obtained.[21]

---

[20] *Business Bulletin*, Cleveland Trust Company, November 1974, p. 4.

[21] Donald D. Hahn, "Stock Market Comments," Becker Securities Corporation, Members New York Stock Exchange, April 1974, p. 2.

FIGURE 13–6
Odd-Lot Trading and Industrial Stock Prices

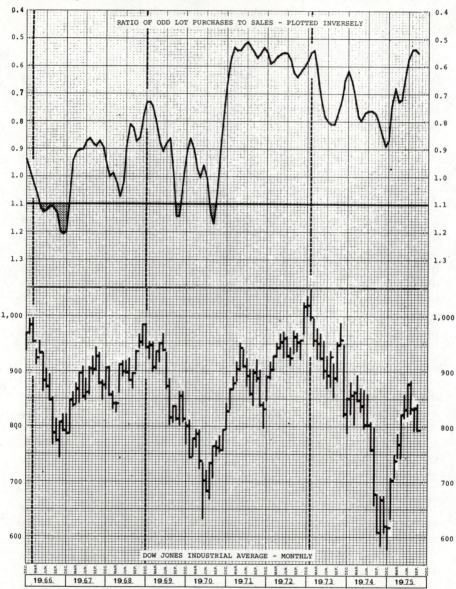

Source: Stone & Mead, Inc.

Thus while the odd-lotter may have become increasingly astute in timing purchases and sales, technical analysts still consider their timing to be sufficiently wrong to have some predictive value.

Short Selling

Short selling activity is another widely used barometer of changes in investor sentiment. Short sales are made by people who expect stock prices to decline. From the technical analyst's point of view, it makes no difference whether short sellers are right or wrong. The fact is that most short sales eventually must be covered by purchases.[22] Therefore, an increase in the outstanding (meaning uncovered) short interest generally means an increased potential demand for stock. A reduction in the short interest generally means a reduced potential demand.

Actually, the short-interest ratio is more closely followed than the number of shares sold short. This is a ratio derived by dividing the latest reported short-interest position by some current volume figure, usually the daily average of the preceding month. Historically, this ratio for the aggregate of all stocks on the New York Stock Exchange has moved within a range of around 1.0 to 1.75. Technicians generally believe that a low ratio is bearish and a high ratio a positive harbinger of future market action. Penetrations of the short-interest ratio normal "band" are designated as sell and buy signals. Most, though not all, of the time, these "signals" have been justified by subsequent market price movements.[23] Short-interest ratios of 2.0 or higher were associated with important market lows of 1962, 1966, and 1970. The 1974 market low was "bracketed" by relatively high short-interest ratios both several months before and after the fact. At the extreme bottom of the market, the short-interest ratio was actually fairly low, as can be seen in Figure 13–7.

---

[22] Short sales "against the box," or in "arbitrage" operations, need not be covered by subsequent purchases. Short sales against the box are made by people who already own the stock. In the usual case, they have capital gains or losses, which they want to realize immediately, but they do not wish to record the gain or loss on the current tax return. By selling short, they can realize the gain or loss now, but transfer it to a following year for taxation. Arbitrage short sales are made by people who own bonds or warrants convertible into the stock sold short. If prices rise after the short sale, they can cover by converting their bonds or warrants instead of buying stock in the open market.

[23] A recent study of the short-interest ratio concluded that it did in fact prove to be an excellent tool for forecasting the future direction of the market. See Thomas J. Kerrigan, "The Short-Interest Ratio and Its Component Parts," *Financial Analysts Journal*, November/December 1974. A contrary view of the same data was expressed by William L. Goff in a letter to the editor published in the *Financial Analysts Journal*, March/April 1975.

FIGURE 13-7
Short-Interest Ratio versus Dow Jones Industrial Averages

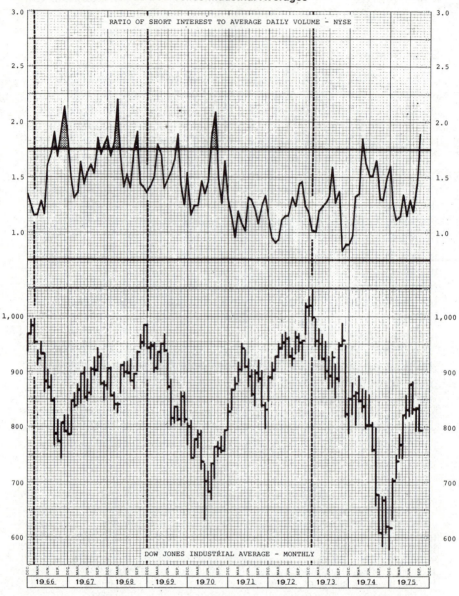

Source: Stone & Mead, Inc.

The data needed to calculate short-interest ratios are readily available. The New York and American Stock Exchanges make public, around the 20th of each month, aggregate short-interest figures plus a detailed list of all issues in which a sizable short-interest existed as of the middle of the month or which showed a sizable increase in short interest from the previous month. These data are published in whole or part by the financial press. Volume of trading data, of course, are published daily, and can be averaged by the analyst. Thus, when trying to judge whether the time is ripe to purchase or sell a stock, it may be helpful to record its short interest outstanding each month relative to the average daily trading volume for the month. When this ratio rises steadily, it implies that a larger and larger percentage of future trading activity is likely to be represented by anxious buyers, the short coverers. A steady decline in the ratio implies that the price cushion to be had from the short sellers is deflating. Of course, a high short interest should lead investors to double-check the underlying value of the stock. They should try to ascertain whether the short sellers have discovered some critical condition which makes the stock fundamentally unattractive at existing prices.

Some technicians believe that the general character of short-interest activity may have changed in recent years, reflecting the increase in the number of arbitrage situations and the growth of hedge funds. Hedge funds are portfolios, such as mutual funds or private partnerships, which continuously maintain a short position as part of their overall investment strategy. As a result of this suspicion, increased attention is now being directed toward some of the smaller components of total short interest (which are published daily or weekly in the financial press).

One such element which has fascinated market technicians is the trend of odd-lot short sales. The odd-lot short seller is sometimes considered as possibly the least astute, if not dumbest, of all investors. In essence, the true amateur, who can be counted upon to be *always* wrong in behavior. Donald Hahn of Becker Securities Corporation put it this way:

unlike his odd-lot counterpart dealing on the long side of the market, the small investor who is "shorting" tends to be both emotional and short-term oriented. For these reasons his market activities are almost always unsuccessful. When the odd-lot short seller is exceptionally bearish the monthly plot moves to high levels (4% or more). On the other hand, wide spread bullishness is suggested when the odd-lot short ratio[24] falls to minimal amounts (less than 1% for at least several consecutive months). A useful forecasting device is to observe these odd-lot selling patterns and then act in a contrary manner.[25]

[24] Considered as the ratio of odd-lot short selling to total odd-lot sales.

[25] Hahn, "Stock Market Comments," April 1974, p. 3.

All things considered, changes in odd-lot short selling activity is construed by many as one of the better gauges of public sentiment. For example, the odd-lot short sales ratio reached approximate monthly levels of 6.2 percent, 7 percent, and 4 percent at the primary market bottoms of 1962, 1966, and 1970, respectively.[26] On the other hand, one of the major technical abnormalities of the 1973–74 bear market was the failure of odd-lot short sales to build up more sharply than it did, given the severity of the decline.

Although this indicator has been more spectacular in identifying market bottoms, a low level (near 0.5 percent) which lasts for a period of several months usually signals the top area of a major bull market.[27] Figure 13–8, which also shows a 12-month moving average of odd-lot short sales as a percentage of total odd-lot sales, seems to confirm these observations.

FIGURE 13–8
Dow Jones Industrials versus Odd-Lot Short Sales Ratio, 1964–1975

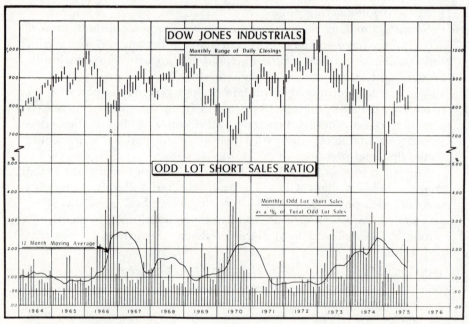

Source: Drexel Burnham & Co., Inc.

---

[26] Ibid.

[27] Indicator Digest "The Directory of Indicators" Palisades Park, N.J., 1974, p. 6.

Specialists' Sentiment

Another interesting component of short-interest activity is the trading behavior of "specialists" on the floor of the New York Stock Exchange; also known as the "informed minority." The short selling of this group, unlike aggregate or odd-lot short selling, is interpreted in a direct rather than a contrary fashion. That is, whereas a high level of aggregate short interest is considered bullish, a high specialist short interest is considered bearish because specialists represent "smart money" and if they are bearish enough to take a large short position we'd better be wary. Likewise, if they cover most of their short sales, we can adopt a similar bullish stance.

Several market technicians have constructed a simple index to gauge specialist sentiment. It is the number of shares sold short by specialists on the floor of the Exchange expressed as a percent of the total shares sold short. Thus, if the specialists sell 1.5 million shares short in a particular week during which the volume of total short selling is 3 million shares, the figure is 50 percent. According to John G. Goode of Davis, Skaggs & Co., "When specialist's short sales reach or exceed 65% of all short sales, it has usually been time to adopt a more conservative approach to the market. When specialist's short sales have fallen to 40% or less, this has usually meant that it is time to become more aggressive in accumulating equities."[28]

As an example, in the fall of 1968 the ratio rose to 68 percent, while in early 1972 it reached 62 percent—both times preceding major tops. In mid-1970, just about when a market bottom was forming, specialist short selling dropped close to 40 percent. Again in late 1974, when a major bottom was unfolding, the specialist short-selling ratio once again approached the 40 percent level. (See Figure 13–9.)

Mutual Fund Cash Positions

One of the newer tools in the technician's extensive kit is the analysis of changes in mutual fund aggregate cash positions. This is measured by the percentage of total mutual fund assets held in cash or equivalents, as reported monthly by the Investment Company Institute. Significant changes in this figure are taken by some to reflect overall institutional portfolio management thinking, and not just that of the mutual funds, although this correspondence of views has never been documented due to the lack of consistent and frequent reporting

---

[28] John G. Goode, "Technical Indicators and Market Statistics," Davis, Skaggs & Co., Inc., June 2, 1974, p. 8.

FIGURE 13–9
NYSE Specialists' Short Sales versus the DJIA, 1968–1975

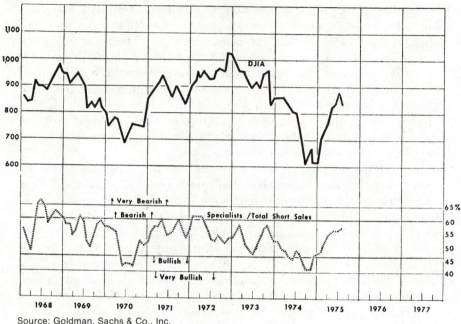

Source: Goldman, Sachs & Co., Inc.

by other segments of the institutional market. In any event, it is believed that, as a general rule, the greater the cash position of the funds, the more bullish the market outlook because when the uninvested funds are put back into the market, stock prices will be driven up. Similarly, the lower the cash position, the more bearish the outlook is believed to be.

Data on mutual fund cash goes back to 1955, and for most of this period has proven to be a useful indicator of future market conditions. A ratio of about 10 percent has usually been bullish, but it is important to note that there appears to be a rising secular trend taking place. For example, the mutual fund cash ratio approximated 9.5 percent at the 1966 market bottom, 11.9 percent at the 1970 bottom, and reached nearly 14 percent in 1974.[29] By comparison, in 1962 an increase to 7 percent, which at that time was regarded as a relatively high level, provided a good buy signal.

Bearish signals have been rendered when the level of available buying power falls to about the 5 to 5.5 percent area. This happened in mid-1965 and late 1967, in late 1968, and in 1974.

---

[29] Indicator Digest, "Directory of Indicators," p. 32.

FIGURE 13–10
Mutual Fund Cash Ratio versus Dow Jones Industrial Averages, 1966–1975

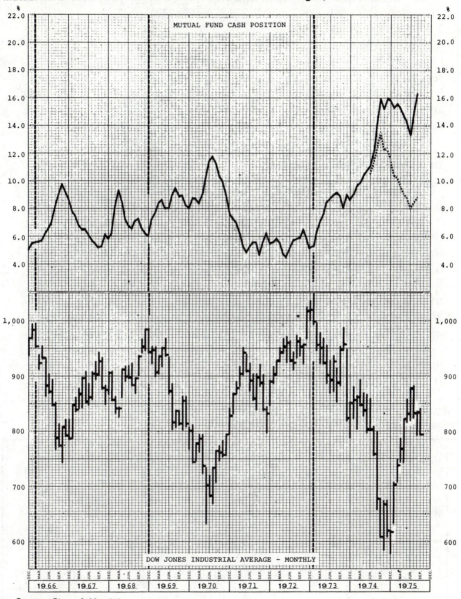

Source: Stone & Mead, Inc.

Since mid-1974, the reported cash position of mutual funds includes money market funds, which are discussed in Chapter 14. To reflect this distortion, the cash ratio—ex the money funds—is shown in Figure 13–10 with a broken line.

Historically, then, institutions, or at least mutual funds, appear to have acted in a fashion generally attributed to amateurs—that is, reaching a fully invested position at the top of a market cycle, and having the most reserve buying power at the bottom. It is understandable, in view of this evidence, why some technicians refer to the mutual fund cash position as the "Institutional Odd-Lot Ratio."

Investment Advisory Opinion

One of the more interesting contrary opinion indexes has been created by *Investors Intelligence*, an investment advisory service which summarizes the opinions and recommendations of other market letter writers for its subscribers. *Investors Intelligence* began in 1963 to monitor the market trend opinions of a large number of leading investment advisory services, and has found a correlation between the bearish sentiment of the services covered and the Dow Jones Industrial Averages. Typically, the investment services as a group tend to be least bearish at market tops and most bearish at market bottoms. More specifically, when the Bearish Sentiment Index (ratio of services bearish relative to the number of services expressing an opinion) approaches 10 percent, the Dow Jones Industrial Average is usually ready to reverse its trend from bullish to bearish; and, conversely,

FIGURE 13–11
Investment Services Opinion and the Stock Market, 1963–1975

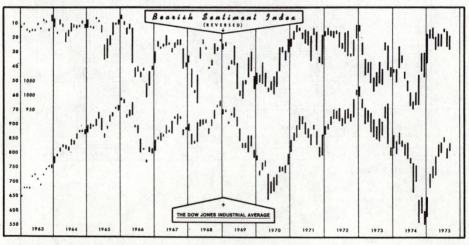

Source: *Investors Intelligence.*

when the Bearish Sentiment Index goes above 60 percent, the Dow Jones Industrial Average is ready to reverse its trend from bearish to bullish. This is true, according to *Investors Intelligence*, because most of the investment advisory services are trend followers instead of trend anticipators, and this lends itself to contrary opinion—when they are least bearish, the market should go down and when they are most bearish, the market should go up.[30] Figure 13–11 shows the correlation between the Bearish Sentiment Index and the Dow Jones Industrial Averages for the 1963–75 period.

Other Speculative Indexes

When investors sell stock without concurrently purchasing an equal dollar amount of some other stock, they have one of two options regarding the proceeds of the sale. If they intend to reinvest the funds in the foreseeable future, they are likely to leave the funds with the broker, who credits their accounts with an appropriate sum. But since they receive no interest on credit balances, they will withdraw the proceeds in cash if they do not foresee a reinvestment opportunity.

Each month, the New York Stock Exchange reports the amount of outstanding credit balances at brokerage houses.[31] (The figures are published in the newspapers, in the *Federal Reserve Bulletin*, and in other media.) As with the mutual fund cash ratio, when this amount rises steadily, it means that strong potential buying support is building up. That is, sellers of stock are neither reinvesting immediately nor withdrawing the sales proceeds in cash. They are keeping funds ready for reinvestment.

Credit balances tend to build up during the major part of a bull market. Apparently the owners of these balances are waiting for a market setback to step in and buy. Like that of the odd-lotters, however, their sentiment usually tends to change at the wrong time. For this reason, analysis of credit balance activity is regarded as another tool of contrary opinion thinking. As the market moves up toward its peak, they begin their reinvestment, and credit balances decline.[32] A decline of credit balances—which represents the diminution of potential buying support—typically has preceded major stock price de-

---

[30] A. W. Cohen, "A Contrary Opinion Indicator," *Investors Intelligence*, October 23, 1975, p. 1.

[31] Credit balances are reported for both cash and margin accounts, based on a sample of member firms generally accounting for approximately 98 percent of all balances. On September 30, 1975 credit balances in cash accounts amounted to $1.5 billion, about three times margin account credit balances of $470 million.

[32] The decline of credit balances might also reflect transfers of funds to bank accounts, as the owners of the balances get tired of waiting for an opportunity to reinvest. However, the fact that the market keeps rising suggests that most of the balances are actually being reinvested.

clines, although the lead times have been erratic. Martin E. Zweig has compiled a long-term record of credit balance movements and has concluded that it is possible to determine shifts which are useful indications of pending downward market movements.[33]

Two other widely used "speculation" indices are the changing relationships between New York Stock Exchange and American Stock Exchange prices and volume. The theory is that institutions rarely trade heavily in American Stock Exchange securities. So, great activity in them means frenzied public speculation. Another hypothesis behind these measurements is that "activity on the American surges forward relative to that of the Big Board when the public becomes enamoured with stocks, jumping into the market buying issues that they can afford—the low priced stocks which are found in plentiful supply on the American Stock Exchange."[34]

According to Stone & Mead, the danger point on the volume ratio index—when speculation appears to be getting out of hand—is about the 50 percent level,[35] that is, when the volume on the American Stock Exchange exceeds 50 percent of the volume on the New York Stock Exchange. Peaks above 50 percent have normally been very

FIGURE 13–12
Ratio of ASE Volume to NYSE Volume, 1927–1975

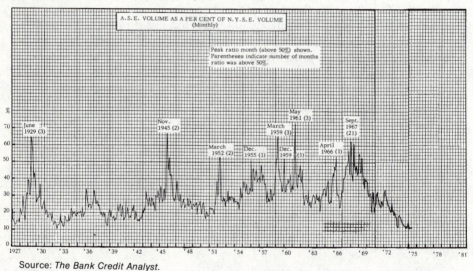

Source: *The Bank Credit Analyst.*

---

[33] See Martin E. Zweig, "New Sell Signal?" *Barron's*, October 13, 1975.

[34] Indicator Digest, *Directory of Indicators*, p. 26.

[35] Stone & Mead, Inc., "Long-Term Technical Trends," Boston, Mass., October 1975, p. 18.

sharp and have preceded major market declines by about 6–12 months. The five moves above 50 percent from mid-1967 to mid-1969 were unprecedented and indicated that the market had been in one of the greatest speculative periods in history. John Train has calculated this indicator back to the 1930s, and notes that it has never given a false signal, although it does not always call every turn. When it does signal a major top, according to John Train, one should always take it very seriously.[36]

On the other hand, at market troughs, the ratio falls to levels of 15 to 25 percent. Only at extremes does it touch the 10 percent level. This has happened on two occasions; in the summer of 1932 and in January 1975. It is also interesting to note that the index touched 12½ in 1927 prior to the run-up in the Dow to its 1929 top.[37] Figure 13–12 supports these conclusions.

PRICE CHARTS AND STOCK SELECTION TECHNIQUES

Dow Theory

Charles H. Dow is generally recognized as the father, if not the grandfather of technical analysis. His theories have been used for many years as a means of estimating the general trend of the market. Dow summarized his basic beliefs in three short sentences in an editorial published December 19, 1900 in *The Wall Street Journal,* the newspaper of which he was editor.[38] He stated that "The market is always to be considered as having three movements, all going at the same time. The first is the narrow movement from day to day. The second is the short swing, running from two weeks to a month or more; the third is the main movement, covering at least 4 years in its duration."[39] The trick, of course, is how to measure and determine each of these movements, assuming some validity of the general premise. Dow suggested a method in a series of *The Wall Street Journal* editorials, often commenting on the proper interpretation of each development.[40] Today, there are many versions of the Dow theory—perhaps as

---

[36] John Train, *Dance of the Money Bees* (New York: Harper & Row, Publishers, 1974), p. 67.

[37] *The Bank Credit Analyst,* "Stock Market and Business Forecast," September 1975, p. 35.

[38] Dow originally intended his index of stock prices to serve as a barometer of business trends, not a stock market timing tool.

[39] William Peter Hamilton, *The Stock Market Barometer* (New York: republished by Richard Russell Associates, 1960), p. 30.

[40] The Hamilton book noted above contains several of these in their entirety, and makes for interesting reading.

many versions as there are analysts who profess to use it. Therefore, it is unlikely that any description of the technique would command unanimous acceptance of what it *is*, must less how well it works. Nevertheless, aside from certain relatively unimportant details, what seem to be its essential characteristics can be outlined briefly.

As a major ("primary") uptrend of the market averages proceeds, there are numerous intermediate ("secondary") downward reactions, each of which retraces a substantial proportion of the preceding rise. After each reaction, price recovers and goes on to surpass the previous high. Dow theorists keep on the alert for a recovery which falls short of the previous high. If, following such an abortive recovery, a downward reaction pierces the low point of the last previous reaction, evidence is at hand that the market has gone into a major ("primary") downtrend. This is illustrated schematically in Figure 13–13.

FIGURE 13–13
Schematic Diagram of a "Dow Theory" Bear
Market Signal

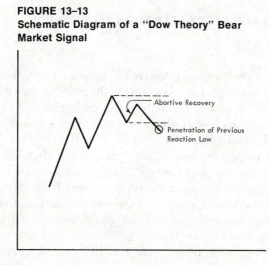

Most Dow theorists do not consider a signal of a new primary downtrend to be valid unless the pattern of "descending tops and bottoms" just described occurs in both the Industrial and the Transportation averages.[41] Since the Industrials and Transportations usually

---

[41] The Transportation average used to include only railroads. The insistence on the "confirmation" of a signal by both the Industrial and Railroad averages originally was based on the idea that the Industrials reflect productive processes and the Railroads distributive processes. To have a healthy economy, both types of activities have to be sound. In recent times, the declining importance of railroads in the economy caused many critics to question the significance of railroad stock prices as a barometer. Even before the change to a more comprehensive Transportation average, however, some technicians argued that railroad stock prices, if not a barometer of economic affairs, are at least a barometer of *speculation* in the stock market and therefore are of legitimate interest.

will not form the pattern simultaneously, the market may have a very sizable decline before a confirmed sell signal is given. Herein lies the principal failing of the technique. In shallow bear markets, the signal usually comes shortly before the downtrend is about to reverse itself. Even this would not be too bad if the Dow theory promptly called the bottom of the market. A few percent saved is better than nothing. But to get a signal of a renewed uptrend the whole pattern previously described must repeat itself in reverse. That is, the Industrials and Transportations must each trace out a pattern of *ascending* bottoms and tops. By the time they do, the investor who has acted upon the signals is likely to have been whipsawed.

Figure 13–14 shows how a "Dow" theorist would interpret the action of the market in late 1974 and early 1975.

FIGURE 13–14
The Dow Theory Flashes a Bear Signal

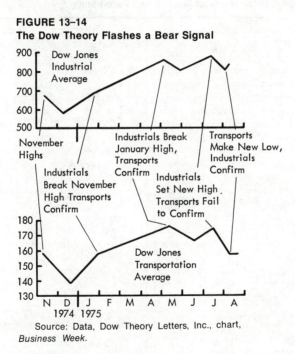

Source: Data, Dow Theory Letters, Inc., chart, *Business Week*.

Price Chart Patterns

The Dow theory deals with the market as a whole. But the underlying principle of ascending and descending tops and bottoms as symptoms of primary trend reversals also is applied to individual securities. Technical analysts keep hundreds of price charts on stocks in which they have an interest.

Since individual stocks have much more extensive cyclical swings in price than the market averages, it might be that a Dow-type ap-

proach produces generally favorable results. The trouble is that we simply have no statistically significant method of appraising the technique. For in addition to ascending and descending tops and bottoms, which are often referred to as "channels" and which are amenable to reasonably precise definitions, technicians refer to "heads and shoulders" formations, "triangles," "rectangles," "flags and pennants," and a host of other configurations with equally exotic names but with quite imprecise definitions (see Figure 13–15). A half-dozen analysts looking at the same chart will rarely give anything near a unanimous interpretation. We therefore end up testing the performance of the *particular analyst* rather than the *method*.

FIGURE 13–15
Graphic Illustrations of Major Chart Formations

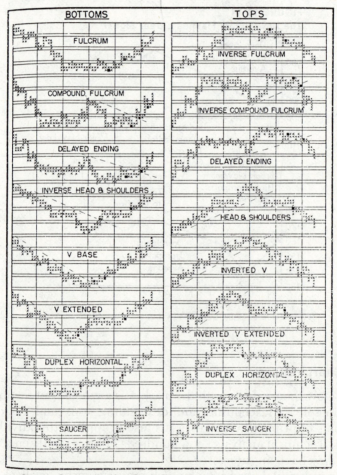

Source: *Commodity Year Book*. Reproduced with special permission of the Commodity Research Bureau, Inc.

Of course, somewhat the same comments can be made with regard to intrinsic value analysis. Given the same "fundamental" information, numerous evaluations are possible. But the lack of clarity seems particularly troublesome in price chart reading.[42]

Bar Charts

Technicians utilize three basic types of price charts: line charts, bar charts, and point-and-figure charts. On both line and bar charts the horizontal axis represents time—days, weeks, or months—and the vertical axis represents price. On a line chart, the closing prices of successive time periods are connected by straight lines. On a bar chart, vertical lines are drawn at each time period, with the top and bottom of each bar plotted at the high and low prices for the period. A small horizontal line is drawn across the bar at the closing price level. Bar charts of various market averages are published regularly in the financial sections of the newspapers. Most such charts include a vertical scale at the bottom of the chart against which are drawn bars representing the volume of trading during each time period. Figure 13–16

FIGURE 13–16
Illustrative Bar Charts of Stock Prices

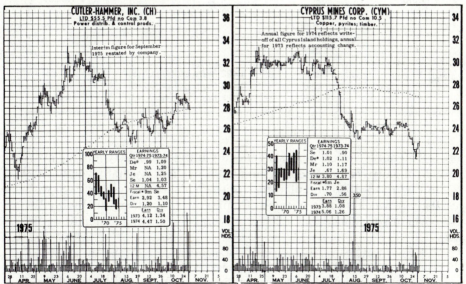

Source: Trendline Corp., *Daily Basis Stock Charts.*

---

[42] A study which attempts to define rigorously the specification of various patterns, detect their existence and measure performance after breakouts finds "no evidence of profitable forecasting ability." See Robert A. Levy, "The Predictive Significance of Five Point Chart Patterns," *Journal of Business,* July 1971.

contains examples of this type of chart, each of which also shows a 200-day moving average of the daily closing price of the stock together with summary data on earnings, dividends, and capital structure.

Moving Averages

Many technical analysts believe that a reversal in a major uptrend of the price of an individual stock, or of the market in general, can be detected in advance, or at least confirmed shortly after its occurrence, by studying the movement of current prices in relation to a long-term moving average of prices. A moving average is designed to reveal the underlying direction and rate of change of a highly volatile series of numbers.[43] It is constructed by averaging a portion of the series and then successively adding the next number of the series to the numbers previously averaged, dropping the first number, and securing a new average. For example, we could construct a five-day moving average of the daily closings of the Dow Jones Industrials as shown in Table 13–2.

TABLE 13–2
Five-Day Moving Average

Trading Day	DJI	Five-Day Moving Total	Five-Day Moving Average
1	900		
2	902		
3	899		
4	894		
5	897	4,492 (sum of items 1–5)	898.4
6	896	4,488 (sum of items 2–6)	897.6
7	898	4,484 (sum of items 3–7)	896.8

Veteran technical analysts generally utilize a 200-day moving average of daily closing prices in their work,[44] which is usually graphed (as in Figure 13–16) on regular stock price charts for easy comparison with daily or weekly price changes. Frankly, we have been unable to discover any evidence that a 200-day average—covering about 40 weeks

---

[43] Rates of change can also be analyzed by other procedures, ranging all the way from simple year-to-year percentage changes to sophisticated methods involving calculus.

[44] Many technicians take a short cut and use only one price a week for 30 or 40 weeks to construct a 200-day moving average. The Trendline chart service, a division of Standard & Poor's, for example, computes its 200-day moving average by adding the closing price of 30 consecutive Thursdays, and dividing by 30. Each week, the new figure is added, and the one for 30 weeks earlier is dropped. The resultant moving average thus actually covers approximately 150 trading days.

of trading—produces any better results than some other long-term average, say 250 days (covering a year of trading). Be that as it may, the 200-day moving average is a usable technical tool, and is usually interpreted as follows:[45]

Buy signals:
1. If the 200-day average line flattens out or advances following a decline, and the daily price of the stock penetrates that average line on the upside.
2. If the stock price is above the 200-day line and declines toward it, but fails to go through and instead turns up again.

Sell signals:
1. If the average line flattens out or declines following a rise, and the daily stock price penetrates that line on the downside.
2. If the stock price is below the average line and rises toward it, but fails to go through and instead turns down again.

Point-and-Figure Charting

Of all the techniques described thus far in this chapter, not one attempts to forecast how far a price swing will carry. They all have sought to answer such questions as: Are we in a major uptrend or downtrend? Is the trend about to reverse itself? Point-and-figure analysts ask these questions and one more: What price is likely to be achieved by a particular stock or by the market averages?

A point-and-figure chart is quite different in concept and design from a line or bar chart. First, there is no time scale on such a chart—only a vertical price scale. Second, plots are made on the chart only when price moves up or down by a predetermined amount—typically 1 or 2 points in the case of medium-priced stocks, ½ point in the case of low-priced stocks, and 3 or 5 points for high-priced stocks. In addition to these differences, a point-and-figure chart provides no volume data unless the analysts work out some intricate schemes of their own, such as making their plots in different colors to represent different volumes. Most point-and-figure chartists take volume into account only indirectly.

The purpose of point-and-figure charting is to show a compressed picture of *significant* price changes. The analyst decides in advance that all movements of, say, ⅞ of a point or less will be considered as

---

[45] See the latest edition of *Encyclopedia of Stock Market Techniques* (Larchmont, N.Y.: Investors Intelligence). However, some years ago a test of moving averages, with negative conclusions as to profitability, was reported in J. C. Van Horne and G. G. C. Parker, "The Random-Walk Theory: An Empirical Test," *Financial Analysts Journal*, November/December 1967.

irrelevant. Thus, if price changes by ½ during a given day, no entry
will be made on the chart. On the other hand, if price changes by 3
points in one day, three entries will be made on a 1-point chart. If time
and facilities are limited, the analyst may work only with closing
prices, but most serious chartists work with intraday prices as revealed
by the ticker tape.

To illustrate the point-and-figure method of charting prices, let us
assume that we are constructing a 1-point chart of a particular stock on
the basis of the following closing prices (ignoring, for the sake of
simplicity, any other intraday price changes):

December 29	....	45
January 2	....	46⅛
January 3	....	45¾
January 4	....	48⅛
January 5	....	46½
January 8	....	45⅞
January 9	....	47⅛

There are a few simple rules to follow:

1. Put an X in the appropriate box each time the price rises to or
   through a round number, and a O each time it falls to or through a
   round number.
2. Do not allow gaps. If successive closing prices are, say, 45 and 47,
   make entries for 45, 46, and 47.
3. Move to a new column each time the *direction* of price *reverses*,
   except if there is only one entry in a column at the time of reversal.

Figure 13–17 is the resulting point-and-figure chart for these data.
The first entry of a new month (46 for January 2, in this example) is
designated by a number (1 through 12) instead of by an X or O, in
order to give some idea of time for future reference. The new year also
is indicated for this reason. There is no entry for January 3, because
price did not change by a sufficient amount. Two entries (47 and 48)
are made for January 4, as price went through two round numbers
beyond the previous entry. The January 5 entry (47) calls for a new
column because the direction of price reversed by more than a point
from the previous entry (48)—and so forth.

Point-and-figure analysts examine their charts to discover areas of
"congestion," also called "upside resistance areas," "downside support areas," "tops," "bases," "lateral trends," and so forth. Essentially,
these are extended narrow horizontal bands of price fluctuation, indicating a standoff between relative supply and demand pressures.
Point-and-figure charting technique, by condensing many months of
price fluctuation within a limited space, is uniquely designed to reveal

FIGURE 13–17
Illustration of Point-and-Figure Method of Charting

50					
49					
48	X				
47	X	O	X		
46	1	O			
45	X				

197X

such congestion areas. Since a breakout of price from a congestion area very often seems to be symptomatic of a new trend, point-and-figure technique can be said to have merit in making detection easy. Figure 13–18 illustrates upside and downside breakouts from congestion areas. But at this stage the point-and-figure chartists broaden their scope and thereby call into question the value of their techniques.

Having detected what appears to be a new trend, the point-and-figure chartist measures the width of the band of congestion by counting horizontally the number of columns covered. If the price breakout has indicated an uptrend, the "horizontal count" is added to the price level of the congestion area, and the resulting price is said to be the level toward which the new uptrend is heading. In a downtrend, the horizontal count is subtracted from the price level of the congestion area to determine the likely stopping point of the decline.

The reader may wonder why on earth price potentials so established should be reliable. It is a fact that most point-and-figure analysts haven't the vaguest notion why, although a few have tried to give an explanation.[46] But explanation or no, they all claim that the technique produces good results on balance. Pressed for some proof of this claim, however, they respond unsatisfactorily.

Indeed, the proof or disproof of the claim is an extremely difficult task. In the first place, several price potentials can be read from the

---

[46] For example, see David L. Markstein, *How to Chart Your Way to Stock Market Profits* (New York: Arco, 1972).

FIGURE 13–18
Point-and-Figure Upside and Downside Breakouts

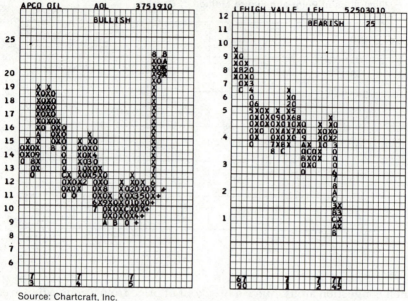

Source: Chartcraft, Inc.

same chart, depending on which price level is chosen for the horizontal count. In most cases, the choice of level is not clear-cut, and analysts use several levels to arrive at a range of possibilities. This complicates the problem of testing the accuracy of the technique. Further complicating testing is the fact that a 1-point chart often produces quite different target prices from a 3-point chart, and many stocks are equally adaptable to either type of chart.

Even more troublesome is the meaning of the price potential which is read from the chart. First, it is not made clear whether the price is a *minimum* or an *absolute* goal. Suppose price rises 50 percent beyond an indicated upside potential. Was the indicated potential right or wrong? Second, how long do we have to wait before deciding whether it was right or wrong? Bear in mind that no time dimension is attached to the reading of the chart. Because of these ambiguities, we are obliged to regard point-and-figure technique, as well as bar chart technique, as unproven.

Relative Strength

One technical tool which deals exclusively with the forecasting of individual stock prices (and industry groups), rather than the aggregate market, is so-called relative strength analysis. The method is to

compute ratios of individual stock prices to an index of "the market," or to an appropriate industry group price index, and ratios of industry group price indexes to the overall market index. For example, suppose that we are analyzing Eli Lilly & Co. We could investigate the relative strength of the company's common stock as follows:

1. Obtain a record of the monthly average price of Lilly common stock (the means of the monthly high and low prices are usually adequate). There are numerous sources of such data—for example, *The Bank and Quotation Record*. Set these data up in column (1) of a work sheet, as shown in Table 13–3.

TABLE 13–3
Work Sheet for Relative Strength Analysis

	(1) Mean Price*	(2) S&P Drugs	(3) S&P Ind.	(4) Lilly/ Drugs	(5) Lilly/ Market	(6) Drugs/ Market
August 1975	65	202.1	103.84	32.2	62.6	194.6
September 1975	57	177.6	96.07	32.1	59.3	184.9

* Average of high and low price.

2. In columns (2) and (3) of the work sheet, list the monthly averages of Standard & Poor's Drug Price Index and S&P Industrial Stock Price Index (or Composite Price Index). Historical data are available in Standard & Poor's *Security Price Index Record*, and current data appear in the weekly *Outlook*.

3. Divide column (1) by column (2), column (1) by column (3), and column (2) by column (3), and plot the resulting ratios on a graph.

Several institutional research firms prepare just such output for a wide variety of industries and stocks on a monthly basis, although some vary slightly in format from our illustration. For example, Figure 13–19 is from Mitchell, Hutchins, Inc., and includes relative price-earnings ratios and relative earnings along with relative price trends. The top panel covers their own ethical drug group composite (Abbott Labs, Eli Lilly, Merck, and Upjohn), while the bottom panel indicates the same relative information for Eli Lilly alone.

These graphs indicate, among other things, how Eli Lilly has fluctuated relative to the market, and how a cross section of drug stocks have also moved relative to the market. The Mitchell, Hutchins service does not include a graph indicating how Eli Lilly has fluctuated relative to the drug group, as we calculated in our example. However, they provide some other useful information on the trend of relative earnings and relative price-earnings ratios. This enables the detection of disparities between relative price and relative earnings performance.

FIGURE 13–19
Example of Relative Strength Charts

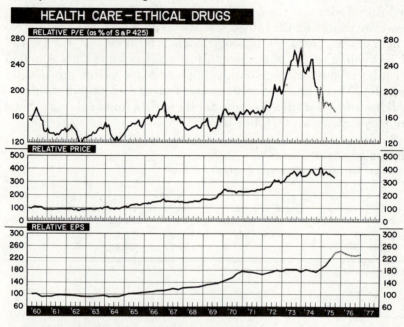

HEALTH CARE – ETHICAL DRUGS

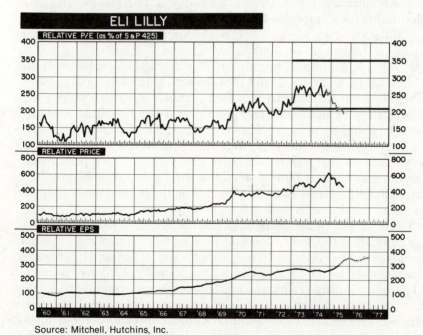

ELI LILLY

Source: Mitchell, Hutchins, Inc.

A rising relative price line (for example, Eli Lilly relative to the market during 1974) means that the numerator of the ratio is outperforming the denominator—rising faster or falling slower. A falling ratio (for example, as the drug group displayed in 1975 relative to the market) means that the numerator is not doing as well as the denominator—it is rising slower or falling faster.

Knowledge of whether a stock or industry group is outperforming or doing worse than the market may have forecasting value. Some portfolio managers even pursue a "relative strength" investment philosophy which is essentially predicated on the theory that strong (relative) stocks and groups will get stronger, and weak stocks and groups will get weaker. In other words, according to Richard Hubman of Marine Midland Bank, who conducted a study which demonstrated the benefits of following relative strength trends, "The probabilities favor a stock [or group] continuing its [relative] trend."[47]

Robert J. Farrell of Merrill Lynch lends support to the general theory by noting "historical studies show that any industry group underperforming the market in the first six months of a bull market is statistically unlikely to have a superior [relative] performance at a later stage of the cycle."[48]

On the other hand, some technicians believe that there is a difference between relative strength during a decline and relative strength during an advance. A group outperforming a major stock average in a general advance may be expending its energy and be about to reverse itself. During a decline, however, we may often get a clue to future leadership by observing those groups (or stocks) which are resisting the decline relatively.

Of course, these are only general tendencies, not invariable rules. However, the tendencies are strong enough to suggest that by coupling relative strength analysis to techniques for analyzing overall market trends and turning points, investors should be able significantly to improve their results. Additionally, a change in relative price action of an industry or stock often reflects some new fundamental development. Thus, a monitoring of relative price behavior can also serve to indicate areas requiring new or additional basic research.

The use of relative strength techniques by institutional investors has increased markedly over the past few years, aided in large measure by the ability of computers to utilize screening techniques and filter systems (discussed further in Chapter 18). Consequently, many large investors now spot the same relative price change at the same time, and this may have enhanced stock price volatility.

[47] William G. Shepard, "Wall Street," Business Week, May 18, 1974, p. 65.

[48] Robert J. Farrell, "Group Performance: Automobiles," Market Analysis Report, Merrill Lynch, Pierce, Fenner and Smith, Inc., September 1975, p. 3

CRITIQUE AND CONCLUSIONS

Readers of investment texts usually are led to think to stock market technicians in much the same way as scientists think of astrologers. To be perfectly candid, there are some understandable grounds for this attitude. The field of technical analysis has attracted large numbers of self-styled "professionals" who might be better classified as crackpots, or even charlatans.

Thus, we can understand the characterization of technical analysis as "crystal-ball gazing." But we consider this characterization to be rather unfortunate, for it casts aside the good with the bad. The more scholarly and sophisticated technical analysts use their tools with a proper sense of proportion. Typically, they use technical analysis as a guide to further study. If a stock looks attractive to them on technical grounds they probe into its "fundamentals." While their decisions may be more heavily influenced by technical considerations, they are certainly not unmindful of earnings growth, of "values," or of the impact of business cycles.

The honest technical analysts know that their approaches will not solve all investment problems. But they also know that no other single approach will either. They believe their tools can reduce the margin of error.

Moreover, while no single technical indicator can be expected to "work" every time, a useful picture may emerge when one follows several indicators which appear to be reasonably reliable, particularly in conjunction with the various economic indicators which have been discussed. Indeed, just as a diffusion index of a large number of economic indicators can be created, so too can a composite index of many technical indicators be constructed. A major advantage of a composite index is its stability, or infrequency of giving new signals. Hopefully, this lessens the chance of a whipsaw.

There are several commercial investment services which publish such a composite index on a subscription basis. Figure 13–20 shows the buy and sell signals that would have been given since 1965 by a composite of 12 technical indicators prepared by *Indicator Digest*. While we do not necessarily endorse the particular choice of indicators on which the chart is based, or the assigned weights,[49] the results are quite intriguing.

Technical analysis may be on the threshold of new discoveries. Economic statisticians are becoming increasingly interested in the subject of price fluctuations in the stock market. They have been inves-

---

[49] Since the interpretation of whether any particular component of the composite is favorable or unfavorable involves subjective judgments, the method is not as "scientific" as it appears at first glance.

FIGURE 13–20
Indicator Digest **Composite Index**

Source: *Indicator Digest,* October 3, 1975, p. 5.

tigating the so-called random-walk hypothesis. The hypothesis, which is discussed in detail in Chapter 15, states that stock prices respond quickly to new information as it becomes available and that new items of information enter the marketplace in random fashion. Therefore prices also move in random fashion. Specifically, periodic changes in price—hourly, daily, weekly, or monthly—are independent of the price changes during equivalent preceding periods.

The random-walk hypothesis does not deny the possibility of forecasting stock prices. It accepts the principle that investment analysts who can forecast company earnings and dividends accurately should do a fairly good job of forecasting stock prices. What it denies is that the analysis of *past data,* particularly past market price data, can produce better-than-chance price change forecasts.

Most of the statistical investigations of the random-walk hypothesis

confirm the belief that successive price changes are generally statistically independent. In our opinion, however, this fact does not necessarily warrant a conclusion that technical analyses of the type which have been described in this chapter are useless as methods of predicting future price movements. Several additional avenues of research appear to be called for. Among them are the following:

1. While successive changes in *absolute* prices may be independent, successive changes in *relative* prices may not be. For example, if a particular stock's price shows the sequence 50, 49½, 49, 49½, the direction of change is down, down, up. But suppose that at the same time the S&P Industrial Stock Price Index moves as follows: 90, 90.5, 91, 92.5. *Relative to the market,* the stock's price action is down, down, down, a different sequence from that revealed by absolute price data. Since the concept of relative strength plays so important a role in technical analysis, as indicated earlier in this chapter, it would be helpful if students of the random-walk hypothesis would apply some of their tests (serial correlation, analysis of runs, spectral analysis, etc.) to relative price behavior.

2. Price patterns may become significant when interpreted *in conjunction with* other technical phenomena such as volume of trading, and short selling. Furthermore, it may be that a statistical combination of technical and "fundamental" data will produce better clues to the future than either one used independently. Work done by Standard & Poor's Corporation and elsewhere suggests that past rates of change of profits offer good clues to subsequent stock price changes. This implies that there is a significant time lag between the market's receipt of fundamental information and the ultimate price response to that information. If so, statistical investigations of the interaction of technical and fundamental data may prove to be very fruitful.

3. Specific technical theories should be tested directly, as a supplement to the indirect approach which has characterized most of the research to date. Essentially, this involves (*a*) establishing trading decision rules which incorporate the premises of a technical theory, (*b*) simulating investment transactions based on these decision rules, and (*c*) observing whether these transactions produce better results, on average, than some sort of random investment policy. Such investigations may well prove that, say, the search for patterns of ascending or descending price tops or bottoms is a waste of time if the analyst is trying to predict future prices. But a proof obtained in this manner probably would be more convincing to investment practitioners than a demonstration that any given period's price change is statistically independent of an equivalent previous period's price change.

We would conclude this chapter by suggesting that the key imped-

iment to investment success is inflexibility of approach. There is no method which is appropriate under all situations. Thus let the intelligent investor discard unjustified biases and consider the possibility of using any and all methods from which there is a theoretical or empirical reason to expect assistance.

SUGGESTED READINGS

Dines, James. "How the Average Investor Can Use Technical Analysis for Stock Profits." New York: Dines Chart Corporation, 1974.

Edwards, R. D., and Magee, John, Jr. *Technical Analysis of Stock Trends.* Springfield, Mass.: Stock Trend Service, latest edition.

Indicator Digest, "The Directory of Indicators." Palisades Park, N.J., latest edition.

Investors Intelligence, Inc. *Encyclopedia of Stock Market Techniques.* Larchmont, N.Y., latest edition.

Jiler, William L. *How Charts Can Help You in the Stock Market.* New York: Commodity Research Publications Corp., latest edition.

Markstein, David L. *How to Chart Your Way to Stock Market Profits.* New York: Arco, 1972.

Neill, Humphrey B. *The Ruminator.* Caldwell, Ida.: Caxton Printers, Ltd., 1975.

Schultz, Harry D. *Panics and Crashes and How You Can Make Money out of Them.* New Rochelle, N.Y.: Arlington House, Inc., 1972.

Shaw, Alan R. "Technical Analysis," *Financial Analyst's Handbook,* vol. I. Homewood, Ill.: Dow Jones-Irwin, Inc., 1975, chap. 34.

REVIEW QUESTIONS AND PROBLEMS

1. Why is technical analysis referred to as "internal" or "market" analysis?
2. Describe the rationale behind the use of the following technical tools: (a) breadth of the market, and (b) volume of trading.
3. Why have some analysts feared that volume of trading data would become a less reliable technical tool?
4. What is the purpose of relative strength analysis?
5. Describe the concept of "odd-lot" analysis.
6. What is the general principle behind the "theory of contrary opinion"?
7. Explain the utilization of the "specialists'" index.
8. Describe how each of the following is used in technical analysis: (a) point and figure charts and (b) bar charts.
9. What does an abortive recovery after a brief decline tell a Dow theorist?
10. Why is a composite index a better tool than a single indicator?

RESEARCH PROJECTS

1. Prepare a statement explaining how technical analysis can be used to supplement a fundamental research effort. Document your position with examples of the current technical position of the market, and for three individual issues.

2. Prepare a supply/demand forecast for common stocks covering the next calendar year. Explain the assumptions behind each estimate.

3. Develop a profile of current "contrary opinion" thinking.

4. What are the current technical signals being given by:
   a. Odd-Lot Trading activity
   b. Dow Theory
   c. Breadth of the market
   d. Short-interest ratio
   e. Mutual fund cash position

5. Contrast and compare the current fundamental and technical position of two issues contained in the Dow Jones Industrial Average.

PART IV

PORTFOLIO MANAGEMENT

INTRODUCTION TO PART IV

Portfolio management is the art of handling a pool of funds so that it not only preserves its original worth but also over time appreciates in value and yields an adequate return, consistent with the level of risk assumed.

Practicing portfolio managers, in their pursuit of this all too often elusive goal, employ a wide variety of investment philosophies and procedures. In fact, it has been frequently noted that there are perhaps as many methods of managing a portfolio as there are portfolio managers.

Some portfolio managers predicate the ebb and flow of their investments on business cycle analysis or the identification of technical trends, as we discussed in Part III. Others structure their equity portfolios to resemble closely the composition of a market index, such as the Standard & Poor's Composite, placing special emphasis on those industrial sectors believed to be particularly attractive—while at the same time limiting or eliminating those considered less attractive. Still others confine their efforts almost entirely to individual stock selection techniques.

Whatever the case, portfolio managers have not typically practiced integrated decision making—that is, a system of procedures that incorporates an explicit determination of the specific objectives of the particular portfolio under management, establishes a framework for asset selection and distribution, provides for the realignment of holdings as conditions change, and monitors performance in an objective manner. Instead, portfolio management both by amateur individuals and professional institutions has traditionally been practiced as if it were divisible into a variety of unrelated activities. For lack of any governing

591

agreement about portfolio objectives, common stock investments have been made independent of bond investments, and those in turn independent of mortgage, real estate, and other investment decisions. As a result, portfolio managers sometimes fail to develop an understanding of the impact their investment results, good or bad, will have on the owners of the portfolio.

These shortcomings have not gone unnoticed. There is now a widening recognition that a haphazard approach to portfolio planning fails to reward investors sufficiently. As Keith Ambachtscheer so accurately observed, "the notion that portfolio management concerns itself only with selecting 'good' stocks or bonds is fading."[1] Institutional investors and Wall Street research firms alike are now expending great energy in attempting to provide an "integrated" portfolio management service.

A variety of new views on the "proper" organizational relationship of the component activities of portfolio management has emerged. Two such "schematics" appear in Exhibits A and B. They are not the

EXHIBIT A
Schematic Diagrams of an Investment Decision-Making Process

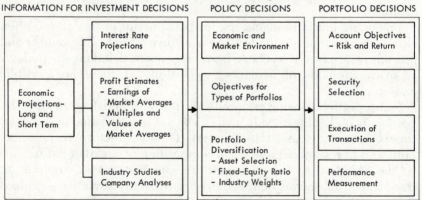

Source: Edmund A. Mennis, "An Integrated Approach to Portfolio Management," *Financial Analyst's Handbook,* vol. 1 (Homewood, Ill.: Dow Jones-Irwin, Inc., 1975), chap. 42, p. 1208.

final word as to how one should look at the portfolio decision-making process; rather, they represent two different efforts to define better the relationship of the various parts to the whole.

Looking at these "schematics," it will become readily apparent that each of the items listed not only call for difficult decisions, but are to a

---

[1] Keith Ambachtsheer, "The Portfolio Management Process," *The Portfolio Management Services Letter* (Toronto: Canavest House Limited, January 1974).

EXHIBIT B

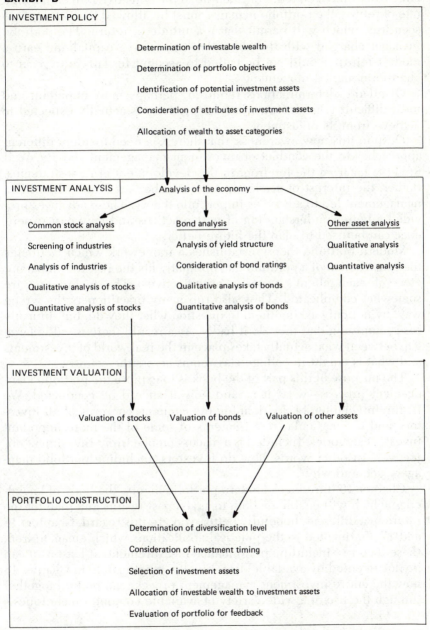

Source: Keith V. Smith and David K. Eiteman, *Essentials of Investing* (Homewood, Ill.: Richard D. Irwin, Inc., 1974), p. 12.

large extent interrelated. For example, if the objective is to earn a high rate of return, the portfolio manager must be allowed to diversify into securities which will permit that magnitude of return. The portfolio manager charged with the obligation to preserve capital and earn a modest return should not be called to account for failure to react to short-term market movements.

Of all the determinations required, perhaps most important and most difficult is to decide what the portfolio is actually expected to achieve from its investments.

Despite this new awareness, that there is a need to adopt different approaches to the conduct of investment management activity, Wall Street is far from the forefront in the development of new strategies. Rather, the interest of academic critics of the "art form" of portfolio management led to advances in portfolio theory. These advances provided a better understanding of past practices and how past experience can be used to plan the future better.

Modern portfolio theory establishes a framework which facilitates the construction of a portfolio that optimally fits the risk-return parameters of each client's investment objectives. The techniques are somewhat complicated. They also rub many practitioners the wrong way, by not only asking them to question what they do, but, in many cases, implying that they do it badly. As a result, there is still a large gap between what actually takes place in the real world of investments and what is taught in college classrooms across the country.

The purpose of this part of the book is to explore the portfolio management process—what it is, and how it should be conducted. We begin, in Chapter 14, by defining the common concerns of all investors, and the particular requirements of some of the more important investor categories. Included is a discussion of current investment objectives. In other words, how do investors, including portfolio managers, act, and why?

Chapter 15 introduces modern portfolio theory, the body of knowledge which will enable us both to assess past results and plan for the future in a different, hopefully better, way. In this regard, Chapters 16 and 17 are devoted to the practical applications which emanate from these theories, including performance measurement, at least as it can be documented by available data. Finally, we illustrate in Chapter 18 how the entire investment management process can be tied together through the use of a wide variety of available computer techniques.

Chapter 14

Portfolio Management Objectives and Practices

> Those who cannot remember the past are
> condemned to repeat it.
> —————————— *George Santayana*

Investment objectives cannot be set in a vacuum. They must reflect both investment market conditions and the particular requirements and constraints of the investor. To illustrate this point, Professor Scott Bauman, of the C.F.A. Institute, recently presented a matrix (Figure 14–1) of different classes or types of portfolios (column 1) together with a dozen variables (columns 2 through 13) which influence the way a portfolio should be constructed.

Each matrix cell contains a letter symbol which is defined in the legend at the bottom of the figure. Bauman was reluctant to present such a matrix because he recognized that no two investors are alike, even within a given class. His letter ratings are intended to represent the proper performance influence for a *majority* of portfolio accounts within a given class, rather than for all of them. Even so, the ratings (A, B, and C) are loosely defined, many matrix cells have two ratings (such as A–B or B–C), and many cells have a wide range of possible ratings (where D is used). In spite of its shortcomings, however, the matrix does highlight the fact that portfolio decisions reflect both broad risk/return considerations and the specific needs of particular investors. We turn, first, to the broad considerations.

FIGURE 14–1

Matrix of Portfolio Performance Requirements: Variables Which Affect the Flexibility or Restrictiveness of Investment Goals and Performance, by Class of Portfolio

(1)	(2)	(3)	(4)	(5)
			Risk of Principal	
	Maximize Rate of Return	Generous Invest-ment Income	Impair-ment	Vola-tility
Class of Portfolio				
I. Individual/Family				
1. Advisory account	A–B	D	D	D
2. Management account	A–B	D	D	D
3. No-load mutual fund	A–B	D	D	D
4. Load mutual fund	D	D	D	D
5. (Conventional) closed-end fund	B	D	D	D
6. Revocable living trust	D	D	A–B	A–B
7. Irrevocable trusts and estates	B–C	D	A–B	A–B
II. Formal Retirement Funds— Accumulation Phase				
1. Deferred fixed annuity	C	B	A	A
2. Trusteed pension	A–B	C	B–C	D
3. Profit sharing fund	A–B	C	A–B	D
4. Deferred variable annuity	A–B	C	A	D
III. Retirement Funds— Distribution Phase				
1. Immediate fixed annuity	A–B	A–B	A	A
2. Trusteed pension	A–B	C	A–B	A–B
3. Profit sharing fund	A–B	C	A	A–B
4. Immediate variable annuity	A–B	C	A	A–B
5. Mutual funds	A–B	D	A	A–B
IV. Other				
1. Property and casualty	B–C	B	A–B	A–B
2. Foundations, endowments, and charitable trusts	D	D	A–B	D

Legend: Degree of importance or of concern:
  A—relatively demanding.
  B—moderately demanding or moderately tolerant.
  C—quite tolerant or less restrictive.
  D—wide range of possible differences among portfolios in the same class.

Risk and Return: Objectives in Conflict

Generally speaking, all rational investors would like to:

1. Preserve principal and have it available at any time (i.e., maintain liquidity).
2. Maximize the rate of return[1] on investment, net of taxes and inflation.

---

[1] Historically, rate of return was broken down into two parts, income and capital gains and losses. More recently, investors have accepted the concept of *total* return.

| (6) Emotional Tolerance toward Risk | (7) Market-ability Need | (8)(9) Investment Management | | (10)(11)(12) Constraints | | | (13) Invest-ment Environ-ment |
		Tenure	Profi-ciency	Fee and Cost Structure	Legal or Fiduciary	Tax	
D	D	D	A–B	D	C	D	A–B
D	D	D	D	C	C	D	A–B
D	A–B	D	A–B	D	C	C	A–B
D	A–B	D	A–B	D	C	C	A–B
D	C	D	D	D	C	C	A–B
A–B	A–B	B–C	D	A	A	D	B–C
A–B	D	C	B–C	A	A	D	B–C
A	C	C	C	C	A	B	C
B–C	C	A–B	A–B	B–C	C	C	A–B
D	C	A–B	A–B	B–C	C	C	A–B
B–C	C	B–C	B–C	B–C	C	C	A–B
A	A–B	C	C	C	A	C	C
A–B	A–B	A–B	A–B	B–C	C	C	A–B
A–B	A–B	A–B	A–B	B–C	C	C	A–B
A–B	A–B	B–C	B–C	B–C	C	C	A–B
D	A	D	D	D	C	C	A–B
A–B	B	A–B	A–B	C	B	A	B–C
D	D	D	B–C	D	C	C	D

Source: W. Scott Bauman, *Performance Objectives of Investors,* Occasional Paper No. 2 (Charlottesville, Va.: Financial Analysts Research Foundation, 1975), p. 52.

One of the better descriptions of the "total return" concept was provided by the Trustees of Princeton University: "We believe that the objective of investment policy should be to obtain the highest possible total rate of return—defined to reflect changes in capital values as well as dividend and interest income—consistent, of course, with adequate concern that the risk level assumed is not inconsistent with the need to preserve the corpus of the fund. If this objective is accepted, it follows that the composition of the portfolio must be determined by actual and expected conditions in money and capital markets and by the prospects for various securities and other possible types of investment—not by the relative importance of interest and dividend income on the one hand and capital gains on the other. It is the size of the total return, not its form, which matters." See *The Definition of Endowment Income,* a report of a special faculty administration committee, Princeton University, February 1970, p. 2. We should point out, however, that many investors still continue the traditional distinction between income and capital gains, as Figure 14–1 above clearly indicates.

Unfortunately, these admirable twin objectives conflict with each other. It is a central tenet of finance that the greater the assurance that principal will be preserved from loss, the lower the *anticipated* rate of return. Conversely, the higher the *expected* return, the greater the possibility of loss.

As we shall soon see, there is substantial evidence documenting a *long-run* tendency for actual (ex post) returns on investment and anticipated (ex ante) risk of principal to vary directly. But the data also show that over shorter periods of time there is frequently an inverse relationship; with less risky investments actually earning more than risky ones. Therein lies the dilemma. The undertaking of increased investment risk does not inherently guarantee a higher return than a less risky position. If it did, it wouldn't be called "risky."[2]

Thus, in both the setting of their objectives and in making actual portfolio decisions, investors must engage in a compromise, or trade-off, between the desire to preserve capital and maintain liquidity on the one hand, and to maximize anticipated total return on the other. Peter Bernstein summarized the point:

> The search for capital gain is never assured of success, so it inevitably involves risk of loss of capital; assured income is seldom available with opportunities for capital gain; high income is frequently associated with high risk. Consequently, when the time horizon is short or when the investor has to face cash withdrawals from the portfolio, we lean toward those assets with greatest certainty of income and capital value; while when the time horizon stretches out into the future and when the investor is adding to rather than withdrawing principal, we can live more comfortably with uncertainty.[3]

In order to grapple with the concept of a risk/return trade-off more effectively, investors should view their alternatives as being represented by a spectrum such as that shown in Figure 14–2. At one extreme are the "safest" investments with the lowest anticipated returns available in the marketplace. These include U.S. Treasury bills, bank certificates of deposit, commercial paper, and the like. At the other extreme lie the high risks and highest anticipated returns, usually associated with venture capital, real estate development activities, works of art, stamps, coins, and so on. In between, where most investors operate most of the time, are fixed-income securities, real estate mortgages, common stocks, and other media. Of course, anticipated returns vary within each asset category. It is not unlikely that a particular security in a relatively low-risk investment category could provide

---

[2] Definitions of risk vary, let alone its measurement. The subject occupies the central theme of Chapter 15. For the moment, consider that risk is related to the prospect that future asset values will be less than expected.

[3] Peter L. Bernstein, "Management of Individual Portfolios," *Financial Analyst's Handbook*, vol. I (Homewood, Ill.: Dow Jones-Irwin, Inc., 1975), chap. 47. p. 1374.

FIGURE 14–2
The Spectrum of Anticipated Investment Returns and Risks

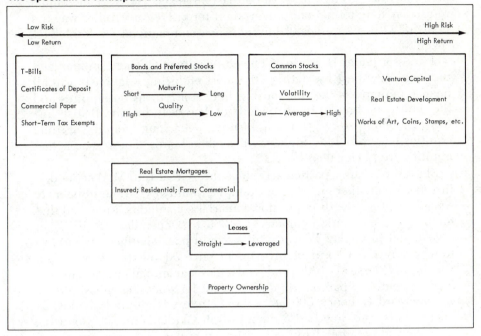

a higher anticipated return than another particular security in a higher risk category. A low-quality bond, for example, might provide a higher total return than a high-quality common stock.

Stocks versus Bonds. The investor's risk-return trade-off is usually discussed in terms of the relative rates of return provided by the stock market versus fixed-income securities. Over the years, extensive research efforts have documented the proposition that stocks, over the *long run,* do in fact provide higher total returns. In other words, higher actual returns are related to higher anticipated risk.

Roger G. Ibbotson, of the University of Chicago, and Rex A. Sinquefield, trust investment officer at the American National Bank and Trust Company in Chicago, recently completed an extensive study.[4] During the measurement period (1926–74), common stocks returned an arithmetic average annual rate of 10.9 percent, compared with 3.7 percent for corporate bonds and 2.3 percent for Treasury bills. The difference between the rate of return on stocks and T-bills, 8.6 percent, is sometimes considered as the "risk" premium earned from the

---

[4] Roger G. Ibbotson and Rex A. Sinquefield, "Stocks, Bonds, Bills, and Inflation: Year-by-Year Historical Returns (1926–1974)," *The Journal of Business,* The University of Chicago, January 1976.

decision to invest in common stocks. The study showed that the risk premium was positive in 31 of the past 48 years. The average annual return on long-term bonds over short-term Treasury bills, was 1.4 percent. Other significant findings are summarized in Table 1–3 (page 8).

Professor James H. Lorie of The University of Chicago summarized the *long* view best by stating "the most enduring relationship in all finance perhaps, is the relationship between returns on equities and the returns on bonds. In all periods of American history, British history, French history, German history, over long periods of time equities have provided higher returns than bonds. The reason is that equities are riskier than bonds."[5]

Short-run returns, particularly since the "Great Bull Market" ended in 1968, are another matter. For example, a study by Dreher, Rogers & Associates, Inc.,[6] leading pension actuarial consultants, indicated that for the ten-year period January 1, 1966 to December 31, 1975, an investment in 90-day Treasury bills would have significantly outperformed any other form of investment covered by the study. More specifically, Treasury bills produced a ten-year annual rate of return of 5.66 percent, compared with 3.28 percent for stocks, as measured by the Standard & Poor's 500 Stock Price Index. High-grade bonds, as measured by the Standard & Poor's High Grade Corporate Bond Index, showed an annualized rate of return of only 1.34 percent. Comparisons for some shorter time periods, as shown in Table 14–1, reveal even greater distortions of the traditional relationships between relative rates of return.

Commenting on the similar findings of an earlier study, Dreher, Rogers noted that "these results, which show the highest rate of return for "risk-free" investments and a negative differential between the returns on common stock and fixed income portfolios, are extreme examples of the volatility inherent in common stock investments and the reverse leverage bearing on fixed income portfolios at times when interest rates are rising."[7]

It should also be noted that inflation rates for most of the measurement period substantially exceeded anticipations, prompting renewed interest in the relationships between inflation, interest rates, and the returns earned by different investment categories.

---

[5] James H. Lorie, "Rates of Return during Inflation," *The Renaissance of Value* (Charlottesville, Va.: Financial Analysts Research Foundation, 1974), p. 22.

[6] *1976 Survey of Investment Performance* (New York: Dreher, Rogers & Associates, Inc., 1976).

[7] *1975 Survey of Investment Performance* (New York: Dreher, Rogers & Associates, Inc., 1975), p. 8.

TABLE 14–1
Annualized Rates of Return for Market Indicators

	Cumulative Periods through December 31, 1975			
	1 Year since 1/1/75	3 Years since 1/1/73	5 Years since 1/1/71	10 Years since 1/1/66
S&P Composite Stock Index*	37.34	− 4.82	3.25	3.28
S&P Ind. Stock Index*	37.20	− 5.17	3.53	3.63
New York Stock Exchange Index*	37.45	− 5.95	2.48	2.90
Dow Jones Industrial Average*	45.03	− 1.42	4.53	2.74
American Stock Exchange Index	38.40	−10.05	−3.37	2.88
Value Line Average	44.34	−14.74	−7.36	−6.27
S&P High-Grade Corporate Bond Index*	8.01	1.54	3.76	1.34
Salomon Bros. High-Grade Long-Term* Corporate Bond Index ...	14.63	3.68	5.83	—
Kuhn Loeb Bond Index*	16.90	3.74	—	—
90-Day Treasury Bill Portfolio*	5.80	6.89	5.81	5.66

* Including dividends or interest.
Source: Dreher, Rogers & Associates, Inc., New York, 1976.

Other Assets. Unfortunately, there has been little research conducted on the relative rates of return from assets other than stocks and bonds. One of the few available studies[8] covering mortgage investing indicates that returns on a FHS insured mortgage portfolio exceeded AAA bond returns by 0.8 percent per annum between 1969 and 1973 and by 1.2 percent from 1964 through 1973. (See Table 14–2.) Although strictly comparable data are not available, yields on commercial and industrial mortgages (as opposed to residential) were generally another 50 to 100 basis points higher. It should be noted, however, that commercial and industrial mortgages are considered more risky than residential mortgages. Moreover, bond.returns have tended to exceed mortgage returns in more recent years, so definitive conclusions about bond/mortgage risk-return trade-offs are not possible.

For several years, The Prudential Insurance Company has offered retirement funds an opportunity to invest in the equity ownership of real property on a commingled basis. This unique vehicle, known as PRISA (The Prudential Property Investment Separate Account) is ac-

---

[8] Kenneth T. Rosen, "The Role of Pension Funds in Housing Finance," *Working Paper No. 35* (Cambridge, Mass.: Joint Center for Urban Studies of the Massachusetts Institute of Technology and Harvard University, June 1975), p. 42.

TABLE 14-2
Relative Rates of Return

	1964–1973	1969–1973
Bank regular equity (stock)	5.2%	– .2%
Insurance company separate		
equity (stock) accounts	4.7	–1.3
Mutual funds—long-term growth	7.3	–2.1
Standard & Poor's 500	6.0	2.0
Mortgage portfolio (FHA insured)	5.8	7.0
AAA bonds................................	4.6	6.2

Source: Joint Center for Urban Studies, MIT/Harvard.

tually a mutual fund devoted to diversified real estate equity investment. Table 14–3 compares the value of PRISA units, reflecting the
appraised value of property held, with a stock and bond index, for the
period July 31, 1970 to December 31, 1975.

Before making any comparison of rates of return, it is important to
point out that the S&P 500 Price Index does not include any dividend
return for the measurement period. Therefore, to make comparisons
more meaningful, we have arbitrarily added approximately 3 percent a
year to the change in stock prices in order to gain a better perspective
of relative "total" returns.

It is apparent from Table 14–3 that equity real estate investment, as
measured by PRISA unit value changes, substantially exceeded stock
market rewards over the measurement period. The Salomon Brothers
Bond Index provided a slightly greater total return. However, an interesting feature of PRISA unit value changes is the constant period-
to-period increase exhibited since inception. In no period was the unit
value lower than in the preceding one.

Whether stock returns will be higher than bond or other investment
returns in the future depends, of course, on a wide variety of factors.
Even if they do, ex post, investors must decide whether the ex ante
"risk" is justified by whatever higher returns are expected. This "risk-
return" decision is a difficult one. The starting point is, or at least
should be, a careful understanding of the needs and constraints of
a portfolio. Therefore, we now turn our attention to the specific objectives of the major investor categories, beginning with the individual.

THE INDIVIDUAL AS AN INVESTOR

Portfolio objectives of the individual investor are influenced by a
wide variety of factors but the two most important are (a) stage in the
life cycle, and (b) psychological makeup or capacity to withstand the
stress and tensions of risk.

TABLE 14–3

Real Estate Equity versus Stocks and Bonds, July 31, 1970–December 31, 1975

Date	PRISA Unit Value	S&P 500	Salomon Bros. Bond Index
July 31, 1970	$1,012.60	78.05	92.57
September 30, 1970	1,026.86	84.21	98.69
December 31, 1970	1,047.20	92.15	104.89
March 31, 1971	1,057.58	100.31	110.38
June 30, 1971	1,066.94	99.70	108.78
September 30, 1971	1,080.60	98.34	115.75
December 31, 1971	1,102.35	102.09	118.14
March 31, 1972	1,114.52	107.20	121.67
June 30, 1972	1,129.96	107.14	124.38
September 30,1972	1,149.36	110.55	124.80
December 31, 1972	1,167.69	118.05	129.60
March 31, 1973	1,184.76	111.52	129.15
June 30, 1973	1,208.61	104.26	130.02
September 30, 1973	1,251.16	108.43	127.52
December 31, 1973	1,275.17	97.55	132.20
March 31, 1974	1,298.30	93.98	130.44
June 30, 1974	1,328.12	86.00	123.43
September 30, 1974	1,360.32	63.54	114.24
December 31, 1974	1,387.79	68.56	128.01
March 30, 1975	1,409.62	83.36	136.46
June 30, 1975	1,447.84	95.19	133.80
September 30, 1975	1,477.63	83.87	135.04
December 31, 1975	1,502.45	90.19	139.48
Percent Change July 31, 1970 to December 31, 1975	48.4%	15.5%	50.6%
Dividend adjustment (3%) ·········		18.0	
		33.5%	

Source: The Prudential Insurance Co. of America; Standard & Poor's Corporation; and Salomon Brothers.

Consider three key stages in the life cycle: (a) *the young family;* (b) *the family at midstream;* (c) *on the verge of retirement—the older family.*

The Young Family

"Thrift is a wonderful virtue, especially in ancestor," someone once said. Naturally *a young family* which has inherited a substantial estate has no financial problem. It has merely an investment problem, probably requiring investment counseling. But for the average family, Mark Twain's quip holds true: "The first half of life consists of the capacity to enjoy without the chance; the last half consists of the chance without the capacity."

The head of the average family between 25 and 30 years of age is married and has one child. Income ranges from about $8,000 to $20,000 per annum approximately. The largest single expenditure for the young American family is on housing. For many families it may be the largest single purchase and the biggest investment of a lifetime. How much to pay for a house and how to finance it is likely to be the first major investment problem for the young family. Generally, experts suggest that one should pay between two and two-and-one-half times annual take-home pay for a house. Thus, if take-home pay is about $15,000 per year, the family can pay from $30,000 to $37,500 for a house, according to this rule of thumb. (Unfortunately, the dilemma of the modern young family is that the average cost of a new house is now about $45,000.) Another useful concept for quick calculation is the "1 percent" rule. Total monthly operating costs will approximate 1 percent of the purchase price of the house. Thus a $30,000 home will absorb and require a $300-a-month housing expense.

Most young families go into debt to finance a house, a car, furniture, and so on. But even these families manage to accumulate some assets—the equity in paying off the mortgage, contributions to a retirement or pension plan, and so forth. While debts usually exceed assets at first, in time, with financial progress, this position tends to reverse, with assets exceeding debts. Some young families are, however, able to accumulate small surpluses from the outset. When this is the case they usually are utilized in the following order of priority: (*a*) savings account, (*b*) life insurance, and (*c*) investments.

Every young family needs an emergency fund to fall back upon in the event of trouble, such as loss of job or serious illness in the family. A good rule of thumb to follow is that the emergency fund, the savings account, should be built up until it amounts to at least three and preferably six months take-home pay.

After savings, family protection via life insurance is next in order. The quickest way for a young family to build an estate is via life insurance.

There are only three basic types of policies: (*a*) *term*, which is temporary protection, (*b*) *whole life*, which is lifetime protection with some savings, (*c*) *endowment*, which is mostly savings with protection until the endowment matures.

The initial need for the young family usually is for maximum protection at minimum cost. This is provided by term insurance. Term insurance provides temporary protection for a given period of time. It pays off only if you die within the given period which may be one year, five years, ten years. Term insurance is the lowest premium life insurance because it provides only temporary protection. It may not require any payment by the insurance company and does not as a rule build

any cash value. For an expenditure of $125–$150 a year, a young head of family can build an immediate estate of $25,000 for the protection of dependents.

If the young family can achieve an additional surplus for investment, what are its alternatives? Two considerations tend to predominate. First, the family can look forward to 40 to 50 years of ability to earn income, accumulate surpluses, and invest them. This prospect provides it with a risk-taking capacity that otherwise would be absent. Second, if the past is any indicator of the future, the purchasing power of the dollar will continue to decline. Both of these considerations suggest investment in common stocks for the young family, since stock investment, has, over the long run, in this century, been an effective hedge against inflation and it tends to provide a substantial total return, combining dividend accumulation and capital gain.

A high degree of speculative risk is usually unwise for the young family since it is new at investment and probably would be quite distressed by the loss of a significant share of its hard-earned initial accumulation. But the overall risk of common stocks is quite tolerable. Over time, there will, of course, be setbacks either in corporate earnings or in the securities market as a whole, but, in the longer run, quality shares tend to rise, as dividends and earnings grow. At this stage of life, time is the one thing the family has in abundance!

Young investors usually build a portfolio one stock at a time or buy mutual fund shares. Generally, individual stocks are selected from a list of blue chips, or established growth stocks, provided by many brokerage firms.

The Investor at Midstream

The average business or professional person is probably moving into the prime of life from 40 to 50. Although earnings are perhaps not at the highest level that will be attained, they find themselves in these years with greater financial mobility than previously. Generally the house is paid for, or almost so, insurance programs are well under way, and a comfortable cash balance is available in the bank for any emergency which may arise. The investor is financially more mature and sophisticated. It is during this period that funds can be used more aggressively. The whole gamut of investment possibilities may be considered. These include a speculative capital gains portfolio, or trading in performance stocks—the market favorites of the time—or moving into cyclical stocks at the appropriate stage of the business cycle. The investor can buy on margin to enhance profitability, sell short, look into special situations, consider convertible bonds or warrants, or trade in options. The switching from stocks to bonds to take

advantage of interest rate trends can also be undertaken. In light of their tax position, they can consider tax-exempt state and municipal bonds, tax-sheltered investments, oil and gas royalties, real estate, or stock gifts to children.

Investors are also in a better position to know their own psychological makeup at this stage of their career. The capacity to take risks varies among individuals. Some, aiming at preservation of capital, perhaps painfully accumulated, are content with a low-anticipated return involving little risk. Others, confident of their earning capacity and their ability to replace any losses, will aim at higher returns commensurate with higher risks. The utility curves of investors represent the demand side of the investment market.

Attempts have been made to analyze the utility preferences and the risk-return trade-off preferences of investors. Such an analysis suggests that investors have different investment preferences, that these desires internally conflict within a given portfolio, and that these preferences must be compromised in order to devise a portfolio which is optimal to a given investor. For example, an investor's preferences for return and for risk conflict in a very basic way. How this conflict is compromised depends on his requirements; these may be expressed graphically as a utility curve or an indifference curve, sometimes called a utility preference function. The framework of utility analysis is a very useful and systematic way to conceptualize the portfolio performance objectives and constraints of a given investor.[9]

An individual investor may have a utility curve which is (a) *linear,* (b) *concave,* or (c) *convex,* depending on the risk willing to be assumed and/or the return sought. As Figure 14–3(a) shows, the *linear* risk-return trade-off is typical of an individual who is willing to invest at any level of risk, provided that the investment offers a proportional or corresponding amount of return. As Bauman notes: "He is equally indifferent to holding either a very safe portfolio or a very risky portfolio as long as the difference in size of the potential returns from the two different portfolios is proportional to the difference in the size of the risks from the two portfolios."

The *concave* functional trade-off, shown in Figure 14–3(b), is typical of risk-oriented investors. They are willing to assume disproportionately greater amounts of risk if they can obtain some incremental return potentially. This function is characteristic of speculators, who find the possibility, however remote, of very substantial returns, compensation for the excitement of large risks.

But most individual investors are believed to be risk averters and the *convex* curve shown in Figure 14–3(c) describes their utility curve

_____
[9] W. Scott Bauman, *Performance Objectives of Investors: A Basic Introduction,* Occasional Paper Number 2 (Charlottesville, Va.: The Financial Analysts Research Foundation, 1975), p. 14.

FIGURE 14-3
Portfolio Utility Preference Functions

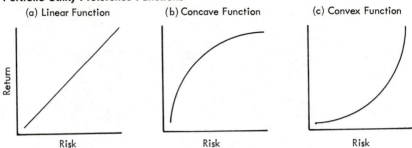

Source: W. Scott Bauman, *Performance Objectives of Investors: A Basic Introduction,* Occasional Paper Number 2 (Charlottesville, Va.: Financial Analysts Research Foundation, 1975), p. 15.

or risk-return trade-off. Each additional increment of income or wealth is of less utility, so the theory goes, than the preceeding increment. These individuals may be willing to undertake additional risk but only for proportionately greater increments in expected return.

Unfortunately, we know very little about the actual investment behavior and portfolio activity of individuals. One recent study found that U.S. individuals owned over $700 billion in stock. Of this total, $460 billion was held in listed stock, $50 billion in mutual fund shares, $35 billion in unlisted bank and insurance company stock, and $190 billion in direct holdings of other traded and privately held unlisted stock. The holdings were quite concentrated. The 1 percent of U.S. families (including single individuals) with the largest personal income accounted for 47 percent of dividend income received and 51 percent of the market value of stock owned by all families, while the 10 percent of families with the largest income accounted for 71 percent of dividend income and 74 percent of market value.[10]

This study found that "a surprisingly high proportion of the portfolios held by individuals was dominated by a very small number of issues; thus the portfolios were not well diversified. This finding applies to all income groups." The implications of lack of diversification will be explored in the following chapters.

Another study, based on a questionaire sent to individual investors, asked, among other questions: "What annual percentage rate of return, before taxes, do you think is attainable on a regular basis from invest-

---

[10] See Marshall E. Blume, Jean Crockett, and Irwin Friend, "Stock Ownership in the United States: Characteristics and Trends, *Survey of Current Business,* November 1974; see also Marshall E. Blume and Irwin Friend, "The Asset Structure of Individual Portfolios and Some Implications for Utility Functions," *Journal of Finance,* May 1975.

ments in common stocks, with moderate skill and understanding on the investor's part?"

The answers were:

Average Annual Return	Percent
0– 5%	20%
6–10	49
11–15	20
16–20	7
21–25	2
Above 25	2

The median response, obviously, lies in the "6–10 percent" category, while the mean worked out to 9.3 percent.[11]

This study portrays the individual investor as, primarily, a "fundamental analyst" who perceives himself or herself to hold a well-balanced and diversified portfolio. He or she invests predominantly for the long run and capital appreciation is the primary concern. Amusingly, the responses suggest that roughly half the sample spends less than five hours a month, and less than $15 a year, on collecting the information for and making the decisions about the securities in its portfolios. The authors conclude: "Over all, therefore, the picture is one of an individual who is far from preoccupied with managing his portfolio and who gets most of his information from public sources— but who has shopped around reasonably carefully for a brokerage firm to work with, and who is willing at least to try some of the more exotic investment vehicles in search of an edge."

The Older Investor

As the individual investor moves along in years to the verge of retirement, we would expect the desire for risk aversion to become greater. For the investor between 55 and 65 it makes less sense to take speculative chances in the pursuit of capital gains and high returns. Since the prime earning years are about over, there is no time left to rebuild capital and recoup possible speculative losses. Presumably, then, the investor on the eve of retirement will want to shift the portfolio to provide income to augment social security and other possible retirement benefits. The objective becomes mainly the highest

---

[11] Ronald C. Lease, Wilbur G. Lewellen, and Gary G. Schlarbaum, "The Individual Investor: Attributes and Attitudes," *Journal of Finance*, May 1974; see also H. Kent Baker and John Haslem, "The Impact of Investors' Socioeconomic Characteristics on Risk and Return Preferences," *Journal of Business Research*, October 1974; and Richard A. Cohn, Wilbur G. Lewellen, Ronald C. Lease, and Gary G. Schlarbaum, "Individual Investor Risk Aversion and Investment Portfolio Composition," *Journal of Finance*, May 1975.

income commensurate with safety, rather than speculative or even long-term capital gains.

Of course, individuals differ greatly in financial status, especially at this stage of life. In some cases financial planning undertaken in productive years will now pay off by adequately supplementing social security, insurance, and pension income. Previous success in achieving substantial capital appreciation may make the difference between a lean retirement and an ample one. Recipients of substantial deferred compensation and large pensions may face no problem at all. In fact, in some cases, because of a change in tax and insurance status, a person may be as well off in retirement as he or she was when actively employed.

But for the average older family the most pressing investment problem is having an accumulation which does not yield enough to live on comfortably, especially in an inflationary environment. This presents a very difficult investment dilemma. An accumulation of $100,000 or $200,000 which seemed ample when the family was living on the salary of the breadwinner, becomes much less adequate when one has to rely on the income from the fund to live on for 15 or more years of retirement, with an inflation rate of 5 percent to 6 percent per annum. This is the preeminent problem of investing for retirement.

Many experts believe that the only way to resolve the problem is to cannibalize the accumulated fund. The retired family should not plan to leave an estate. It should plan to use up its accumulated resources over its remaining lifetime. It can do this by means of annuities, fixed, variable, or balanced, or by a mutual fund withdrawal plan. These programs have merit for yet another reason. With age comes a certain weariness of attention to investment trends and detail. In all probability, investing at this stage of the life cycle is better turned over to the institutional professional, who devotes full time and attention to these matters.

THE INSTITUTIONAL INVESTORS

Institutional investment behavior reflects factors such as:

1. The nature of an institution's obligations to its clients—its "reason for being."
2. Legal regulations applicable to its investments.
3. Taxation of its investment income.
4. Intangible considerations such as the psychology of its clients and of its own personnel.

These factors influence each institution's investment objectives with regard to current income, capital gains, marketability, liquidity,

and safety. The institution then attempts to balance these objectives—which are often in conflict—in the management of its portfolio.

Regretably, institutional investment behavior also reflects a sometimes unhealthy competition among institutions. Instead of making investment decisions designed solely to serve their clients' real long-run needs, institutional portfolio managers often seek to achieve the best relative performance on a short-term basis. Both of these aspects of institutional portfolio management will be reviewed in the pages which follow.[12]

Investment Companies

While mutual funds represent one of the alternative investment opportunities for the individual investor, the importance of this group of institutions extends far beyond that function. To begin with, literally all phases of their activity fall under some form of governmental regulation and supervision. Consequently, much more is known of investment company portfolio activity (and performance) than of any other group of institutional investors. Second, and perhaps because of this visibility, investment companies have in the past been the pacesetters of many new investment trends and practices. Third, unlike most other investing institutions, the managers of investment companies have been free to promote, often via aggressive selling techniques and accompanied by much publicity, new portfolios designed to serve whatever the popular demand requested. As such, investment company development over the years closely mirrors the changing focus of overall investment concern. While no longer the largest segment of institutional demand, it is clear that they warrant our initial attention.

Open-End versus Closed-End. An investment company sells its own securities to the public and invests the proceeds in accordance with a stated objective—income, capital gain, or both. The Investment Company Act of 1940 defines an investment company as one with over 40 percent of its assets in securities other than U.S. government obligations or majority-owned subsidiaries other than investment company subsidiaries. Historically, only two general types of investment com-

---

[12] We have omitted a discussion of the investment activities of commercial banks, mutual savings banks, and savings and loan associations. This omission does not reflect any lack of importance of these institutions in the money and capital markets. Rather, it reflects the fact that their major investments—short-maturity securities in the case of commercial banks, and mortgages in the case of mutual savings banks and savings and loan associations—are largely tangential to the main topic of this book, namely common stock and long-term bond investments. For an extensive analysis of bank investments (other than the investments of bank trust departments, which *are* treated in this chapter), see the first edition of this text, Chapter 18. Also see B. J. Fabbri, *Commercial Bank Investments in the Postwar Period* (New York: Salomon Brothers, September 1975).

panies have been of any significance—closed-end and open-end "managed" companies. So-called unit investment trusts (which invest in a fixed list of securities and are, therefore, "unmanaged") and "face-amount certificate companies" (whose investments are similar to time deposits in a bank) have been relatively unimportant in terms of assets controlled. Recently, however, unit trusts have gained in popularity as a means of offering investors participation in portfolios of fixed-income securities designed to provide a high level of interest income over a specified period of time. This type of organizational structure is particularly well suited for municipal bond portfolios since it is the only way of passing through tax-free income to the unit holder.[13]

The distinguishing feature of a closed-end company is that its own securities—stocks and bonds[14]—are traded in the open market like any other corporate issues. Thus, the value of its common stock, at any given time, may be above or below the value at that time of the securities held in its investment portfolio (the so-called net asset value). Moreover, unless the company offers a new security issue to the public, which is an infrequent occurrence, its capitalization remains static.

In sharp contrast, an open-end company—popularly referred to as a "mutual fund,"—continuously offers new shares for sale and always stands ready to redeem existing shares in cash at the stockholder's request.[15] Sales and repurchases are executed by the funds at the current net asset value per share, which is recalculated daily. (The arithmetic is to obtain the current market value of each security in the portfolio, sum up, subtract any outstanding liabilities, and divide the resulting figure by the number of outstanding shares of the fund's own common stock.)

Growth Patterns. At the end of 1975, the combined assets of open-end and closed-end investment companies were about $55 billion, down about 20 percent from the record peak of $69 billion at the end of 1972. Approximately 88 percent of the total was comprised of

---

[13] Merrill Lynch, Pierce, Fenner & Smith, Inc., for example, periodically offer monthly unit trusts of both tax-exempt (Municipal Investment Trust) and taxable (Corporate Income Fund) income portfolios. Wiesenberger's *Investment Companies 1975* estimates that approximately $730 million of assets were registered as unit trusts on December 31, 1974. Legislation is pending which would extend tax-free pass-through treatment to open-end funds as well.

[14] Closed-end companies may sell bonds and preferred stocks within specified legal limits (asset coverage of 300 percent is required on debt; 200 percent on preferred stock). On the other hand, open-end companies organized since 1940 may not have any senior securities in their capital structure, although short-term debt may be undertaken if the fund's statement of policy permits.

[15] A few funds redeem at all times but sell new shares only occasionally. Some funds have adopted the policy of discontinuing the sale of new shares after a certain size is attained, although existing shareholders do not lose their right of redemption.

556 mutual funds, and the balance consisted of a much smaller number of closed-end companies.[16] By comparison, total industry assets at the end of 1946 were $2.2 billion, divided roughly 60 percent–40 percent between the two groups. Most of the growth of closed-end assets during this period came from rising prices of stocks in the companies' portfolios, while only about half of the open-end growth was derived from price appreciation with the balance from the marketing of new shares.

A major factor responsible for the rapid growth of mutual fund assets during the 1950–70 period was the ability of management companies to organize and market new funds with specific investment objectives designed to accommodate particular investor demands. In fact, such activity closely mirrors the changing nature of general investment attitudes.

For example, during the early postwar period there were only two general types of mutual funds—common stock funds and balanced funds. Common stock funds at that time were essentially designed to offer investors, particularly the smaller ones, an alternative to direct common stock ownership. Through the commingling of assets, individual investors were able to obtain an interest in a diversified portfolio of high quality, essentially conservative common stocks, under the full-time supervision of professional management at relatively low cost.

Balanced funds were considered to offer a broader investment package representing a portfolio composed of both stocks and bonds. The basic principle was that the proportion of the portfolio invested in each type of security would be shifted according to the manager's view of potential risk and return.

Wiesenberger's *Investment Companies* manual reports that as recently as ten years ago, diversified common stock funds accounted for 60 percent of all mutual fund assets, and balanced funds 24 percent. Specialized funds and income funds accounted for 9 percent and 3 percent, respectively.[17] In contrast, at the end of 1975 diversified common stock funds represented almost 70 percent of all mutual fund assets, while the share held in balanced portfolios had declined to less than 10 percent. More significantly, diversified common stock funds could no longer be lumped into a single group as they had been until the mid-1960s. Rather, it was necessary to subdivide the common stock category into three different classifications in accordance with their relative capital gains orientation. Table 14–4 indicates a more complete mutual fund industry classification covering both size and type of the fund.

---

[16] Wiesenberger Services, Inc., *Investment Companies* (New York, 1975), p. 11.
[17] Ibid., p. 50.

TABLE 14–4
Classification of Mutual Funds by Size and Type (as of December 31, 1975)

	Number of Funds	Combined Assets ($000)	Percent of Total
Size of Fund:			
Over $1 billion	7	$10,764,800	22.1
$500 million–$1 billion	14	9,745,800	20.0
$300 million–$500 million	18	6,473,200	13.3
$100 million–$300 million	69	11,930,200	24.5
$50 million–$100 million	59	3,981,800	8.2
$10 million–50 million	197	4,967,700	10.2
$1 million–10 million	157	699,800	1.4
Under $1 million	35	143,000	0.3
Total	556	$48,706,300	100.0
Type of Fund:			
Common stock:			
Maximum capital gain	119	$4,570,500	9.4
Growth	153	14,238,000	29.2
Growth and income	95	14,706,300	30.2
Specialized	17	295,800	0.6
Balanced	20	4,408,300	9.1
Income	97	5,905,900	12.1
Bond & pfd stock	8	449,700	0.9
Money market	34	3,493,800	7.2
Tax-free exchange	12	638,000	1.3
Total	556	$48,706,300	100.0

Source: Wiesenberger Services, Inc., *Investment Companies* (New York, 1976), p. A-40.

The changing complexion of mutual fund assets reflects more than the long-term shift of investor emphasis from safety of principal and income to capital growth. It also documents a basic mutual fund marketing belief that it is easier to sell a new product than an old one. As a result, most mutual fund management companies have adopted over the years the "family of funds concept," by sponsoring a series of different funds designed to meet a variety of portfolio requirements.

Another factor stimulating mutual fund development was the expectation of above-average investment performance. Greed acted as a stimulant to mutual fund sales, most notably during the late 1960s, a period many consider to be the vintage years of mutual fund development. This was the "performance period," the years in which "go-go"[18] investment techniques proliferated and "go-go" investment

---

[18] According to John Brooks, *The Go-Go Years* (New York, Weybright and Talley 1973), p. 127: "The term 'go-go' came to designate a method of operating in the stock market—a method that was, to be sure, free, fast, and lively, and certainly in some cases attended by joy, merriment, and hubbub. The method was characterized by rapid in-and-out trading of huge blocks of stock, with an eye to large profits taken very quickly, and the term was used specifically to apply to the operation of certain mutual funds, none of which had previously operated in anything like such a free, fast or lively manner."

managers achieved the type of fame usually reserved for movie stars.[19] Whether these investment heroes, and their predecessors, did as much for their clients as they did for themselves is questionable.

The Performance Aftermath. In retrospect, the performance years turned out to be, at best, a mixed blessing for the mutual fund industry. The gain experienced by the better performing funds created an atmosphere of excessive expectation as to reasonable long-term investment returns. This overexuberance as to the rewards to be derived from the ownership of a "go-go" common stock portfolio led in turn to an extended period of disappointment. A contributing factor was the unfavorable experience of most of the highly publicized, highly merchandised performance funds which were, in fact, among the poorer performers in the following years.

Investor disenchantment with mutual funds led to a sharp turn in the subsequent growth and development of the industry. Most, if not all, of the well-known, well-established funds experienced increasing difficulty in developing a net new sales flow, and many of the smaller ones merged to form larger portfolios.

As the figures in Table 14–5 demonstrate, "investors became in-

TABLE 14–5
Sales and Redemptions by Investment Objective (millions of dollars)

Investment Objective	Sales		Redemptions		Net Sales	
	1973	1974	1973	1974	1973	1974
Growth	$2,422.1	$1,465.9	$2,652.8	$1,456.2	$ (230.7)	$ 9.7
Growth and income	1,212.5	902.1	2,012.5	1,223.6	(800.0)	(321.5)
Balanced	244.5	223.9	544.6	365.4	(300.1)	(141.5)
Income	476.8	472.3	439.7	326.3	37.1	146.0
Money market	3.4	2,256.5	1.5	565.5	1.9	1,691.0
Total	$4,359.3	$5,320.7	$5,651.1	$3,937.0	$(1,291.8)	$1,383.7

Source: Investment Company Institute, *Mutual Funds Forum*, February 1975.

creasingly risk averse as stock prices fell and interest rates rose. For example, sales of growth funds, traditionally heavily invested in volatile common stocks, fell about 40 percent in 1974. The sales of growth and income funds, which are somewhat less volatile, declined 26 percent, while the sales of balanced and income funds fell only 8.4 percent and 0.9 percent, respectively. These latter two types of funds

---

[19] See also 'Adam Smith,' *The Money Game* (New York: Random House, 1967); "Fred Alger: Portrait of a Star," *Institutional Investor*, February 1968; Charles Raw, Bruce Page, and Godfrey Hodgson, *Do You Sincerely Want To Be Rich?* (New York: The Viking Press, 1971); and Robert A. Hutchison, "The Looting of I.O.S." *Fortune*, March 1973.

place more emphasis on current income than capital gains—a product ingredient that appeared to be reasonably in tune with investor preferences in the highly unstable market environment of 1974."[20] In fact, it was precisely these investment preferences that enabled mutual fund management companies to create another new product—"money market" funds, invested in short-term credit instruments—which prevented an even further erosion of industry assets.

Investment Policies. Assuming that management chooses to operate a "diversified" portfolio,[21] a decision must be made whether to include both stocks and bonds in varying proportions, or whether to invest exclusively in either bonds and preferred stocks, on the one hand, or predominantly in common stocks, on the other. If the company chooses to run a common stock fund, it has several further alternatives:

1. It may follow a policy of buying stocks in a broad cross section of the American economy.
2. It may invest in so-called growth stocks.
3. It may specialize in the securities of a particular industry or group of industries.

Whatever investment policies are chosen must be stated in general terms in a registration statement filed with the SEC. This statement of policy also must appear in the company's prospectuses and may not be changed without consent of the stockholders. It should be noted that there has been much agitation on the part of public agencies and others to require the policy statement to be more specific than traditionally has been the case. Such requirements are opposed by investment company managers on the grounds that they need a rather flexible framework within which to operate in order to carry out their job most

---

[20] Investment Company Institute, *Mutual Funds Forum*, February 1975, p. 2.

[21] In order to be classified as diversified, a mutual fund may not invest, with respect to 75 percent of its total assets, more than 5 percent of its total assets in the securities of any one company nor hold more than 10 percent of the outstanding voting securities of any company. A company choosing to be classified as nondiversified has no limitation on the amount of assets it may have invested in the securities of any company. However, in order to qualify for the special flow-through tax treatment permitted investment companies under the Internal Revenue Code, (whereby the company itself pays taxes only on *retained* income) a nondiversified company must be at least 50 percent diversified throughout its taxable year. This means that, with respect to 50 percent of its assets, it may not invest more than 5 percent of total assets in any one company nor hold more than 10 percent of the outstanding voting securities of any one company. In order to change its classification from diversified to nondiversified, a company must receive the consent of a majority of its shareholders. A company may, however, change its classification from nondiversified to diversified without shareholder approval. In recent years, a number of newer mutual funds have chosen "nondiversified" status in order to provide somewhat more freedom over their portfolio; however, they are under no compulsion to take advantage of it.

FIGURE 14–4
Illustrative Mutual Fund Statements of Policy

A CONSERVATIVE BALANCED FUND—
WELLINGTON FUND

Wellington Fund is designed to provide conservative investors with a prudent investment program with the following objectives:

a. Conservation of principal.
b. Reasonable income return.
c. Profits without undue risk.

Wellington Management Company, the investment manager for the Fund, endeavors to achieve these objectives for the Fund through a balanced and diversified program of investing in bonds, preferred stocks and common stocks.

The bonds and preferred stocks are held for relative stability of income and principal, while the common stocks are held for possible growth of capital and income. The amount invested in each class of securities is varied from time to time, depending upon an interpretation of business, economic and market conditions. The Certificate of Incorporation and By-Laws of the Fund place no limit on portfolio turnover or upon the percentage of the Fund's assets which may be invested in common stocks, bonds or preferred stocks. However, the present intention of management is that generally the Fund will have not more than 75% of its assets in common stocks.

Such a balanced investment program is an attempt to reduce the inherent market risks of investing. However, these risks can never be eliminated and the program cannot assure attainment of the objectives of the Fund. The Fund does not invest to control other companies nor concentrate its investments in a particular industry or group of industries.

efficiently under conditions of constant economic change. A sample mutual fund policy statement is presented in Figure 14–4.

Pension Funds

Pension fund assets represent the nation's largest and fastest growing aggregation of institutional capital. Total pension fund assets (on a book value basis) at the end of 1975 were estimated by the Securities and Exchange Commission at $407.1 billion, up from $262 billion at the end of 1970, $108 billion at the end of 1960, and only $41 billion in 1950.

Of the total amount, approximately 53 percent ($214.6 billion) consisted of private pension fund reserves, with the remaining 47 percent

($192.5 billion) representing various governmental agency (state, local, and federal organizations) employee retirement plan assets. Of this amount, Federal Old Age and Survivors Insurance Funds (OASI) amounted to approximately $37 billion.

Within the private sector, noninsured funds represented 68 percent ($145 billion) of the total, and insured reserves ($69 billion) the remaining 32 percent. In 1960, the relationship between these two classifications, which are defined in the next section, was roughly 64–36 percent, and approximately 50–50 percent in 1950.

Noninsured Private Pension Funds

A pension fund can be broadly defined as a plan established and maintained by an employer primarily to provide for the systematic payment of benefits to employees after their retirement. As such, pension fund assets represent a pool of capital being set aside for the specific purpose of meeting *future* liability payments. There are two general methods of providing for such future distribution: through insured pension fund reserves or by the maintenance of a noninsured program.

Under the traditional insured plan, pension obligations are funded by premium payments made by the sponsoring company to a life insurance company. The life insurance company in turn guarantees that it will make specified annuity payments in the future.[22] The insurance company then seeks to maximize its return on the investment of the premiums within constraints provided by the various statutes which govern its investment activity. Traditional insured plans are more prevalent for small companies, or for programs containing relatively few employee participants. For larger companies, recent years have witnessed the development and rapid growth of so-called deposit administration plans, which are similar in nature to the noninsured plans described below yet are managed by life insurance companies.

Under noninsured private pension plans, company contributions are usually paid into a trust fund at a bank or trust company. The trustee then holds and invests the accumulated contributions, making benefit payments to the plan's participants in accordance with the specific provisions of the program. It is important to note that a trustee's investment powers are governed exclusively by the precise terms

---

[22] Edward H. Friend pointed out in an excellent article on changing pension fund definitions that, "the overall cost of a pension plan is *never* guaranteed although *insured plans* provide full guarantees with respect to the cost of *individual benefit units*." See Edward H. Friend, "A 1972 Critique on Funding Media for Pension Plans," *Journal of Accounting*, August 1972, p. 29.

of the trust agreement. The most common terms are, in order of popularity:

a. The trustee is given relatively complete discretion to invest the assets as he or she believes most appropriate. This type of arrangement applies both to the trustee who also acts as investment manager, and to those nontrustee investment advisors selected solely for the purpose of portfolio decision making.

b. The trustee is given discretion within certain prescribed limits, such as the maximum percentage of assets that may be invested in common stocks, maximum concentration of assets in any one industry or any one company, and limitations on the holding of foreign securities, or private placements. This form of control is gaining rapidly in. popularity and is particularly prevalent among newly selected, independent, nonbank portfolio managers.

c. Investments may be made only with the approval of a designated co-trustee, usually a senior company executive.

d. Investments are made at the direction of the company, with or without the advice of outside counsel. The trustee in this case acts merely as a custodial agent. Some very large companies have been notably successful following this "internal management" approach. General Electric, General Tire, and Bethelem Steel are included in this category.[23]

The ability to "tailor" the utilization of a variety of different investment manager relationships, and to impose a wide variety of portfolio restrictions, is an important reason for the diminishing use of traditional insured plans. However, the burden of responsibility for meeting benefit obligations is thus shifted to the sponsoring company from the life insurance company. Many company managements in the past felt that the elimination of this responsibility was worth the sacrifice of investment flexibility; but today this attitude is found mainly among smaller companies rather than among giant corporations.

Factors Influencing Investment Policies.   There are four major factors which influence pension fund investment policies:

1.   All income and capital gain of pension fund investments are tax exempt while in the hands of the trustee.[24]

2.   Until recently, there have been no legal restrictions on pension fund investing other than the usual fiduciary principle that a trustee

---

[23] Since the IRS requires pension funds to be outside employer control, some interesting questions arise when company executives act as trustees of their company's pension plan. Under federal fiduciary law, individual trustees are *personally* liable for the funds under their control.

[24] However, under certain circumstances the IRS may rule that the trust is actually operating a business concern via its investment, and such "unrelated business income" would be taxable.

must deal at arm's length with the trust, making no personal profit from its operation other than the regular service fee. In addition, the Commissioner of Internal Revenue has had the power to restrict the investment of pension trust assets in the securities of the employer corporation if he has good reason to believe that the trust is being used as a captive source of funds for the corporation—i.e., if purchase of the securities cannot be defended on their own investment-worthiness.[25] In 1974, the general fiduciary principles were made much more concrete by their incorporation in the Employee Retirement Income Security Act (ERISA). This act has had a profound impact on the attitudes of pension fund investment managers and will be discussed below.

3. The manager is usually relatively unhampered by liquidity considerations until a pension plan is quite old. The average plan which is funded in reasonably orderly fashion takes 30 or more years to "mature"—i.e., to reach the stage where benefit payments and expenses equal contributions and investment income. Plans of strong, growing companies may not mature at any time in the visible future. As long as cash inflow exceeds outgo, there is no danger of having to liquidate securities in a bear market.

It is important to note, however, in connection with this latter point, that far too many trustees blithely assume that scheduled employer contributions will, in fact, be made. A company may very well suspend contributions, temporarily during an economic recession or permanently if it goes out of business or for some other reason, and trustees should consider the probabilities of this occurring when they determine the extent to which they can invest in volatile, illiquid, high-risk types of securities or mortgages. At the least, it is probably good policy to keep sufficient funds in relatively safe investments to assure payments to existing pensioners.

4. There is usually a strong incentive for the investment manager to try to maximize investment return and thereby reduce the employer's cost. For the employer, after all, is usually the one who chooses the plan's investment manager. With regard to cost, several observations are in order.

  a. Actuarial Assumptions. The level of annual contributions re-

---

[25] The Employee Retirement Income Security Act of 1974 (P. L. 93–406) places limitations on investments in employer stock; however, Employee Stock Ownership Trusts (ESOTs) are exempted from such limitations so long as the plan specifically provides for such holdings. For more details on this interesting and controversial corporate financing technique, see Robert Frisch, *The Magic of ESOT: The Fabulous New Instrument of Corporate Finance* (Rockville Centre, N.Y.: Farnsworth Publishing Company, Inc., 1975); Jack Hofert, "Employee Stock Ownership Trusts," *The Tax Magazine*, May 1975, p. 305–13; and Mayer Siegel, "Employee Stock Ownership Plans Raise Questions Concerning Potential Applications, Public Policy," *The New York Law Journal*, September 22, 1975, p. 22–24.

quired to cover the cost of a company's employee retirement plan are normally determined through the efforts of a competent pension actuary. This important determination is predicated on a careful consideration of the particular characteristics which describe the group of employees to be covered by the company's pension benefit formula. Without offering a complete listing, actuaries review such factors as the size of the labor force, the nature of employee turnover, expected mortality rates, anticipated salary adjustments, the length of the funding period, and perhaps most important, the assumed rate of investment return on pension fund portfolio assets. After incorporating an allowance for administrative expenses, the actuary estimates the probable net costs of the pension plan to the sponsoring company. The accuracy of this estimate will depend, of course, on the accuracy of the assumptions referred to.

Relatively small changes in any of these assumed variables can produce a significant difference in annual funding requirements, and consequently in the company's net income for the period. For example, actuaries estimate that just lowering the retirement age from 65 to 60 will increase a company's contribution cost by 50 percent if the investment yield is not increased. It is also generally assumed that an increase of 1 percent in the assumed rate of return on portfolio assets can reduce the annual contributions by 25 percent. Differing rates of employee turnover estimates can also change the level of annual contribution.

Actuarial assumptions are not permanent calculations but are frequently adjusted to reflect both the actual investment experience and changes in assumed financial market conditions. In fact, companies have been significantly increasing their expectation as to the future return on portfolio assets. Part of this trend can be attributed to the higher interest rate levels which have persisted for many years. Another factor is the changed mix of portfolio assets, from fixed-income securities to common stocks, which are assumed to produce higher rates of return than bonds. As a result, "the so-called 'actuarial assumption' about the average compound long-term rate of return on these assets has suddenly emerged from technical obscurity to take on an important role in the strategic management of corporate pension funds."[26]

b. Increasing Cost Pressures. Continued labor union pressure to increase retirement income levels has reached a point which now places pension fund decisions among the foremost of corporate considerations.

---

[26] Charles D. Ellis, "Caution on Pension ROI Assumptions," *Harvard Business Review*, July-August 1972, p. 6.

Charles Ellis, who has conducted several extensive surveys on pension fund management, has noted that the typical corporation has more money in its pension fund than in any operating division. He estimates that the country's top 625 corporations together put more money into their pension funds each year than they spend on new plant and equipment.

Business Week recently conducted a study covering companies with annual sales of more than $500 million, for which pension fund data were available, and determined that this group carried a total unfunded pension liability of close to $30 billion and a shortfall of more than $16 billion in the funding of currently *vested* benefits.[27] A corporation's unfunded vested liability is simply a measure of the difference between funds actually contributed to the pension account, and the present value of what the company would have to pay out in the form of employee benefits if the plan were liquidated at the time of the calculation. Since most corporations expect to remain in business, the more critical measure of pension liability, according to *Business Week*, is total unfunded costs, not just the currently vested portion. For the entire 200 companies included in the survey, unfunded costs amounted to 16 percent of common equity.

Investment Policies. It should be clear from the above that, at least until ERISA, the investment managers of a pension fund have had more flexibility than virtually any other type of investor, individual or institutional. They have been relatively unfettered by law. Their relative lack of liquidity needs has enabled them to seek higher yields in off-the-beaten-path investment media. Tax exemption has permitted them to do this without distinguishing between current income and capital gain. It also has allowed them to switch out of overpriced investments and into undervalued situations without regard to tax consequences. If they felt unable to "time" cyclical turning points, their steady fund inflow enabled them simply to dollar average. It also permitted them to restructure their portfolios by reallocating the investment of new fund inflows without being forced to sell existing holdings if doing so would upset prices.

Pension trustees became increasingly aggressive in their investment policies with the passage of time. Twenty-five years ago, when the pension movement was in its infancy, safety dominated the thinking in the field, and investments were confined largely to government bonds and Aaa-to-A rated corporate bonds. Slowly, but steadily, it began to be recognized that pension trusts were ideally suited to undertake common stock investments because of the long-term nature of their liabilities and their slight liquidity needs.

---

[27] "When Pension Liabilities Dampen Profits," *Business Week*, June 16, 1975, p. 80.

Figure 14–5 is an example of a pension fund investment policy statement typical of these trends. The trend toward common stock investment accelerated until, today, the "typical" corporate pension trust has 60 percent (down from almost 70 percent at the end of 1972) of its assets, at market value, in common stock and most of the balance in corporate bonds. This is shown in Table 14–6, which also reveals

TABLE 14–6
Market Value of Assets of Private Noninsured Pension Funds (millions of dollars)

Market Value	1965	1970	1975
Cash and deposits	900	1,800	2,962
U.S. Government securities	2,900	3,000	11,097
Corporate and other bonds	21,900	24,900	34,519
Preferred stock	800	1,600	892
Common stock...................	40,000	65,500	87,669
Own company	4,400	6,000	n.a.
Other companies	35,600	59,400	n.a.
Mortgages	3,400	3,500*	2,139
Other assets	3,000	4,400*	6,341
Total assets	72,900	104,700	145,622

* Revised.
n.a. = Not available.
Note: Includes deferred profit sharing funds and pension funds of corporations, unions, multiemployer groups, and nonprofit organizations. Figures may not add to totals because of rounding.
Source: Securities Exchange Commission, *Statistical Bulletin,* vol. 34, no. 4, April 1976.

that government bonds comprise about 5 percent of assets, and mortgages about the same proportion. Preferred stocks and state and local government bonds are relatively unattractive to these tax-exempt institutions. The category labeled "other assets" mostly represents direct investments in real estate.

A frequent criticism of pension fund investment policies is that the one third of assets which are invested in fixed-income securities are too high in average quality. They should be more similar, it is argued, to life insurance investments which, as will be described later, include more lower quality corporate bonds and more mortgages. In response to this criticism, pension fund managers usually argue that higher quality fixed-income securities are needed to balance the relatively high common stock proportions and that many pension funds are not large enough to be able to diversify in the broad manner called for when lower quality bonds and mortgages are purchased. To this defense the critics reply, in turn, that the safety of diversification could be provided through specialized "common trust funds" in which the

FIGURE 14–5
Investment Policy Statement of a Pension Fund

POLICY

It is our policy to invest the pension fund for total return. We seek the greatest return consistent with the fiduciary character of the fund and the need of annuitants for timely payment of benefits.

Equity investments, not limited to common stocks, will normally be the principal investment medium, and we expect common stocks to make up 75 percent to 85 percent of the fund.

We maintain a contingency reserve of fixed-income securities with relatively high liquidity. This would cover cash demands on the fund for three years in event retirement plan contributions were interrupted.

OBJECTIVES

We want the pension fund to earn 10 percent per year compounded over each five-year period.

We believe the equity trust funds should also outperform the market in the long run. For each five-year period we aim for superiority of not less than the smaller of: 25 percent of the S&P 500 total return or two percentage points of return (10 percent when the index earns 8 percent).

The absolute target is more important to us than the relative goal. Equity portfolios should grow with rising markets, but we would trade market superiority for the 10 percent cumulative rate of return.

We prefer consistency of investment yield. If equity funds earn the same over five years, we prefer the one whose interim results were less volatile. We hope to do at least as well as the market when it goes down, and better than the market when the drop is severe.

Ideally, the best performing managers should be responsible for the largest asset pools. To reach this state we shall make periodic transfers of principal assets from lower performing to better performing managers.

GUIDELINES

Subject to the following guidelines, portfolio managers have full discretion in investment decision.

1. Diversification.   Each portfolio should hold at least 15 issues, and no more than 10 percent of the fund at cost should be invested in any one issue.
2. Parent Company Securities.   Pension fund portfolios should not hold securities of The Parent Company or its subsidiaries.
3. Marketable securities.   Investments are normally limited to marketable securities. Exceptions should be cleared with trustees.

Source: The Conference Board, *Financial Management of Corporate Pension Plans*, p. 35.

fixed-income assets of smaller pension trusts could be pooled.[28] Barring this, there is always available the alternative of placing the fixed-income portion of a pension trust's assets with a life insurance company under a so-called split-funding arrangement—although this may not be acceptable to a commercial bank trustee from a competitive point of view.

In our opinion, the pension fund critics have the better of the argument. While we feel, as noted earlier, that safety is particularly important in situations where there is a significant possibility of contributions being terminated, we feel that the employment of common trust funds and insurance company facilities can help provide such safety. Indeed, even without resorting to these methods, over the years, pension trustees could have significantly increased earnings on fixed-income investments without sacrificing safety, by the simple device of purchasing government-insured mortgages. Pension trustees have only recently showed some interest in real estate investments[29] and were notably slow in getting into private placements in their bond operations.

Changing Objectives and New Constraints. In late 1974, Congress passed the Employee Retirement Income Security Act of 1974, now popularly referred to as ERISA. Many believe that passage of this comprehensive and complex legislation ushered in a new series of investment constraints for corporate pension fund trustees, and perhaps other institutional investor categories.[30]

The bill creates, for the first time, a uniform federal standard for fiduciary conduct relating specifically to the establishment and maintenance of corporate employee benefit plans. The overall purpose of this lengthy legislation is to assure that pension plans are financed and

---

[28] Common trust funds are widely used for investing smaller trust fund assets in common stocks. Also, commingled accounts have been utilized for the specific purpose of investing a portion of a fund's assets in small, speculative growth company stocks, in real estate, and in other specialized media.

[29] It is noteworthy that in the relatively small number of pension plans where labor unions play an important role in investment administration, mortgages represent a much more substantial share of assets than is typical of noninsured plans. It is not clear, however, whether this is due to labor's greater recognition of the investment merits of mortgages or to its greater awareness of the social welfare aspects of mortgage financing.

[30] Numerous summaries and interpretations have been published on ERISA, covering either the entire bill, or selected aspects important to investment managers. See, for example, Neil A. Burger, "Pension Reform Law Details Fiduciary Responsibility," *Pensions and Investments,* November 18, 1974; "Pension Reform: A Summary," *Pensions and Investments,* September 9, 1974; Erica H. Steinberger, "Fiduciary Responsibilities in Employee Benefit Plans," *New York Law Journal,* January 28, 1975; and the November 1974 issue of *Pension and Welfare News,* which included a complete text of ERISA, running 64 pages, and a variety of articles commenting on different portions of the legislation.

managed in a manner guaranteeing employees their benefits, and certain provisions are likely to change the portfolio behavior of this important institutional group.[31]

From an investment management viewpoint,[32] the major provisions of ERISA can be summarized briefly as follows:

Section	Area of Activity	Language of the Bill
404	Fiduciary conduct	Fiduciaries must act with the care, skill, prudence and diligence under the circumstances then prevailing that a prudent man acting in a like capacity and familiar with such matters would use in the conduct of an enterprise of a like character and with like aims.
404	Diversification of investments	Investments must be diversified so as to minimize the risk of large losses, unless it is clearly prudent not to do so.
409a	Personal liability	A fiduciary of a plan, which includes investment managers, is *personally* liable to make good to the plan any losses resulting from the breach of responsibility.
302	Valuation of securities	Value of portfolio assets must be based on reasonable actuarial method which takes into account the fair market value of portfolio investments. However, issues of indebtedness (bonds) not in default *may* be valued on an amortized basis running from cost at purchase to par value at maturity or earliest call date.

Each of the provisions noted above have contributed to the reassessment of only recently accepted investment management practice. In many cases, the recognition of personal liability has prompted indepth investigations by many trustees as to just how their pension portfolios were actually being managed. Frequently, their findings do little to remove the fear of "imprudence" and the threat of extensive personal liability.

---

[31] Much of the impetus for ERISA can be traced directly to the circumstances surrounding the closing of Studebaker Corporation's auto facilities in 1963. Studebaker's pension plan had been in effect only since 1950, and had not had adequate time to accumulate sufficient assets to cover all of its retirement liabilities. When the plants closed in December 1963, pension fund assets amounted to $24 million, and of that amount $21.7 million was required to purchase annuities for workers who had already retired or who qualified for a pension. As a result, the plan was able to provide only 15 cents on the dollar to those employees (4,500 in number), ages 40–59, who had 11 years or more of service. While not the largest plan ever to be terminated, publicity at the time prompted President Kennedy to appoint a Committee on Corporate Pension Funds to look into the matter, and the effects of its findings resulted in the enactment of ERISA and are just beginning to be felt.

[32] ERISA also includes extensive provisions covering the vesting and funding of corporate pension plans. For further detail on these provisions, which are likely to accelerate pension fund cost pressures, see the various citations in footnote 30.

Current trust law, under the Prudent Man Rule,[33] focuses solely on the risk of loss, and on minimizing such risk on each security in a portfolio rather than on the portfolio as a whole. Risk, under the rule, is viewed apart from the return that a risky investment may contribute to the total portfolio. A recent New York State Court of Appeals decision[34] clearly reaffirmed this principle by ruling that each particular security in a portfolio must, *individually,* meet the prudent test and that an overall increase in the total value of the portfolio will not excuse a single imprudent investment.

Furthermore, the prudent man rule as applied in most states distinguishes between speculation and investment, and emphasizes the conservation of capital. State courts have required that fiduciaries invest for the production of reasonable income and the preservation of capital, with the latter taking priority. For this reason, state prudent man rules do not regard a high rate of return as adequate justification for higher risk. It is also interesting to note that judicial decisions have stressed the preservation of capital and not the preservation of purchasing power. The distinction is an important one in an inflationary environment. These delineations will become clearer when we discuss modern portfolio theory in the next chapter.

If future court decisions follow the precedent of trust law in interpreting the "prudent man" provision of ERISA, fiduciaries and portfolio managers may have to restrict their range of investment to the most conservative, and most conventionally accepted choices. On the other hand, Section 404 of ERISA also states that courts are expected to bear in mind the special nature and purpose of employee plans when they interpret such rulings. To say the least, the matter is still very unclear, and probably will not be decided, through the courts, for some time to come. In the meantime, many are opting for the side of conservatism, thereby hopefully preventing their actions from becoming test cases.

To cite two examples of such opting for conservatism, the bond-stock mix within many pension portfolios has shifted back toward more bonds, less stock. Also, the list of equity holdings has been in many cases narrowed, in favor of the larger, more well-established

---

[33] The Prudent Man Rule was first articulated in 1830 by the Supreme Court of Massachusetts, *Harvard College* v. *Amory*, 26 Mass. (9 Pick) 446, and contained the following wording: "All that can be required of a trustee to invest is that he shall conduct himself faithfully and exercise a sound discretion. He is to observe how men of prudence, discretion and intelligence manage their own affairs, not in regard to speculation, but in regard to the permanent disposition of their funds, considering the probable income, as well as the probable safety of the capital invested."

[34] *Matter of Bank of New York*, 43 A.D. 2d 105 (App. Div. 1st Dept. 1973). Discussed in *New York Law Journal*, January 15, 1975. See also M. Rollin Pelton, *Reflections on the Pension Reform Act of 1974 and The Prudent Man Rule* (Cottonwood, Ariz.: Bridge Trading Company, 1975), and F. C. McLaughlin, "Investing as a Prudent Expert," *Financial Executive*, June 1975.

companies at the expense of the smaller, less seasoned ones. At the same time, the level of diversification has been increased; i.e., the percentage of the total portfolio concentrated in the top 10, or top 20 holdings, has been reduced.

The shift back to bonds results from several factors and deserves further comment. With current returns on fixed-income securities exceeding most actuarial assumptions, the fear that total returns may fall short of requirements, thereby necessitating an increase in company funding costs, is reduced, especially since comparable returns from stocks are much less assured, and were not achieved from 1965 through 1976. Further, Section 302 of ERISA, noted above, gives fixed-income securities an added appeal that goes beyond the investment merits of the case. Bonds can be evaluated at cost while common stocks, generally speaking, must be evaluated at market value. Thus, as the *Institutional Investor* recently noted, "Corporate executives are equating *ERISA* with increasing their bond portfolios to about 35 to 40 percent of total assets. It doesn't even matter, really, if it's an attractive investment move. It's safe. It's diversification."[35] It would be unfortunate, at least to our way of thinking, if this type of decision making perpetuates itself, and investment decisions become a function of minimizing legal concerns as opposed to representing the product of an organized risk-return analysis.

To be sure, ERISA concerns are not the only factors prompting a reassessment of portfolio policies. At the end of 1974, for the first time since 1955, the market value of all pension fund assets dropped below the book value. This negative spread, which for some companies was quite severe, produced a profound psychological impact on many trustees.

Many now believe that trusteed pension assets, despite a long time horizon and limited liquidity demands, can no longer tolerate significant negative fluctuations in the market value of portfolios. Perhaps it's the newness of ERISA, and its attendant responsibilities, which are still unfamiliar and unclear. Perhaps it's a "knee-jerk" reaction to a prolonged bear market, during which time achievements fell far short of expectations. Only time will tell.

Some of the changes on the horizon, however, may well be for the better. As Martin E. Segal & Company, Inc., recently pointed out "possibly the greatest long-term changes in the investment management picture will be in the philosophy of investment management, the way its objectives are perceived, the way its performance is measured and evaluated."[36]

There is already some evidence that this assessment will prove ac-

---

[35] Sandra Kazinetz, "ERISA: A Boost for Bond Managers," *Institutional Investor*, August 1975, p. 57.

[36] Martin E. Segal & Company, Inc., *Newsletter*, July 1975.

curate. The provisions of ERISA affect different pension plans in different ways. Pension fund trustees are beginning to recognize that their particular needs find difficulty in being serviced effectively when portfolios are managed by large organizations responsible for hundreds, and often thousands of clients all with different objectives. To rectify this problem, trustees are slowly drifting away from granting total discretion to their managers by establishing new constraints and restrictions on investment selections. In some cases, direct control of the portfolio has been returned to the sponsoring organization through the hiring of an internal portfolio manager. Maximization of total return is now rarely established as the investment objective irrespective of risk tolerance levels.

Deferred Profit Sharing Plans

Many employers do not wish to commit themselves to the fixed obligations entailed by standard pension plans, but prefer to make contributions to an employee pension trust in relation to annual profits—for example, some percent of total profits or some percent of profits over and above a specified level. This arrangement—known as a deferred profit sharing plan—may also be used to supplement standard pension plans. That is, the company may have two plans running simultaneously. As with a standard pension plan, employees pay no income tax on the employer's contribution until they receive a cash benefit—either in the form of a monthly annuity or a lump-sum payment (in the latter case, they pay a capital gains tax rather than regular income tax).[37] Similarly, funds in the trust are invested *tax free*. The law limits annual contributions to 15 percent of a company's total wages and salaries.

In several respects, the investment problems of a deferred profit sharing plan trustee are different from those inherent in standard pension plans. The major differences are as follows:

1. Since the employer's contributions are based on profits, the profit sharing trust's cash flow is far more uncertain in both timing and magnitude. The uncertainty is magnified by the choice given the employee at retirement to either take a lump-sum payment or an annuity.

2. High investment income does not reduce the employer's costs, because these costs are a function of the profits earned by the business. Moreover, investment losses are borne directly by the employee.

---

[37] Under both standard pension plans and deferred profit sharing plans, there are a broad variety of provisions regarding the employee's rights in the event of resignation or death before retirement. Many deferred profit sharing plans also permit an employee to choose whether to take a share of the company's contribution on a regular annual basis—in effect, a regularly taxed bonus—or whether to let it accumulate and earn interest tax free in a retirement trust.

3.   The employer's motive in establishing a deferred profit sharing plan may be only in part a desire to provide employees with a retirement income. The employer may, in addition, see the plan as an incentive device; if the employees know that higher profits mean higher contributions (up to the legal limits), they presumably have an incentive to work harder and more efficiently.[38]

The first two factors cited suggest a more conservative investment policy for deferred profit sharing trusts than for standard pension trusts. Since cash flow is uncertain, liquidity needs are greater. With regard to common stock investments, cash flow is not only uncertain— it is perverse. Net cash inflow tends to rise, along with the employer's profits, during periods of good business when, presumably, stock prices also tend to be high; and it tends to fall when stock prices are relatively low. An aggressive common stock program thrives on precisely the opposite cash inflow pattern—up when prices are low, down when prices are high. Moreover, since the employer's contributions are not reduced by good investment results, there is less incentive than under a standard pension plan for a trustee to strive for maximum investment income. The diminution of this incentive is reinforced by the knowledge that poor investment results directly injure the employee-beneficiaries.

While these factors suggest a conservative investment policy, if a deferred profit sharing plan is being used by the employer largely as an employee incentive device, a daring and imaginative investment policy may be advisable. Indeed, purchase of the employer's own stock may be called for to provide a triple-barreled incentive: hard work means higher profits, which result in (1) higher contributions, (2) higher dividends on the stock held in the trust fund, and (3) higher prices on the stock. Of course, such a program also places the employees in triple jeopardy.

Which of the two approaches should be emphasized in managing a deferred profit sharing plan is probably not for the investment manager to determine. The basic philosophy is more the responsibility of the employer. Under some plans, the choice is given to the employees themselves. They are permitted to specify whether they want their share of the fund to be invested in (a) high-quality bonds, (b) a balanced portfolio of bonds and common stocks, (c) an all-stock portfolio, or (d) the employer's stock. The choice may be a once-and-for-all proposition or may be periodically changeable; if changeable, the new choice may be applicable to new contributions only or to existing funds as well.

Data on the actual investment of all deferred profit sharing trusts

---

[38] Whether or not the employees actually view the plan in this light is a matter of debate among students of labor relations.

are not available separate from data on standard pension plans. They are included in the figures and references used elsewhere in this chapter.

Pension Plans of State and Local Governments

Generally speaking, state and local employee retirement systems are established and operated under relatively complex statutes which precisely dictate most aspects of both administrative and investment policy.[39] From an investment point of view, the most noteworthy feature of this large, and rapidly growing, collection of funds has been their history of mismanagement. Trustees in this area have been much slower than others in moving away from government bonds and into corporates. Traditionally, these types of pension trusts have invested a large percentage of total assets in low-yielding, tax-exempt bonds, particularly issues of the sponsoring governmental unit.[40] Perhaps more importantly, common stockholdings, in the aggregate, are still far below the levels of most corporate pension funds.[41] Table 14–7 indicates the changing complexion of state and local pension fund portfolios. It is also of interest to note that ten state and municipal funds now have assets of more than $2 billion each.

There are several explanations for this traditionally peculiar investment behavior, some of which are understandable but most of which seem outmoded:

1. Many trustees have been shackled by obsolete state laws regulating the handling of public funds.

2. The trustees are usually elected or appointed public officials rather than professional fund managers, and they have been reluctant to incur the costs of hiring professionals.

---

[39] On July 31, 1975 a new bill, H.R. 9155, was introduced in the House of Representatives which, if passed, would affect public employee pension funds the same way ERISA affected private pension plans. As of this writing, the bill was still in committee.

[40] It is interesting to comment on the investment practices of New York City retirement funds in this regard. From 1921–61, the New York City retirement funds invested heavily in New York City bonds, with the proportion of these bonds in the portfolio reaching a high point in 1961, when the city retirement funds' holding of the city's obligations totaled nearly $2 billion, some 66 percent of their holdings. From then on, retirement funds sharply reduced their holding of New York City bonds, to a low 7 percent of assets at the end of 1973. But, in 1975, when New York City faced the specter of bankrupcy, trustees of both New York City and New York State employee retirement funds were called upon from a variety of directions to begin, once again, to purchase large quantities of new bonds. Part of the new argument was that available yields exceeded those of corporate securities. See Louis M. Kohlmeier, "Conflicts of Interest: State and Local Pension Fund Asset Management," *Report to the Twentieth Century Fund Steering Committee on Conflicts of Interest in the Securities Markets* (New York: The Twentieth Century Fund, 1976).

[41] While this may have been an enviable position during the 1973–74 bear market, common stock commitments had increased steadily just prior to the decline, but long after "performance" opportunities evaporated.

TABLE 14–7
Assets of State and Local Government Retirement Funds, Book Value, End of Year
(billions of dollars)

	1959	1965	1970	1973	1974	1975
Cash and deposits	0.2	0.3	0.6	1.0	0.9	0.6
U.S. government securities	5.6	7.6	6.7	4.6	5.4	6.9
State and local government securities	4.3	2.6	2.0	1.4	0.8	1.9
Corporate and other bonds....................	6.0	17.2	33.9	49.4	57.6	65.1
Common and preferred stock	0.3	1.6	8.1	18.6	22.1	24.7
Mortgages	1.0	3.7	6.8	6.6	7.0	7.2
Total assets	17.4	33.2	58.1	81.6	93.8	106.5

Source: Flow of Funds Section, Board of Governors of the Federal Reserve System.

3.   Private pension plans, for the most part, are private matters, but public plans are subject to examination by political partisans. This sort of atmosphere is not conducive to aggressive investment management.

4.   There is a temptation to relieve strained government budgets by using pension funds as a captive buyer of the employing-government's bonds, despite their relatively low yields.

5.   Most governmental pension plans require substantial employee contributions in addition to those of the employer. Therefore, errors have a more severe impact on the welfare of state and local government employees than of corporate employees, suggesting a more conservative investment philosophy.

It is encouraging to note that to an increasing degree public pension plans are now being more effectively managed. Figure 14–6 showing the investment objectives and policies of the state of Nevada, is a good example of this change. In other cases, state laws are being updated, and the use of professional investment consultants has sharply increased. As a result, common stock purchases have accelerated, and state and local funds have developed into a major class of equity buyers. A U.S. Department of Commerce study[42] covering the 100 largest public employee retirement systems found that on March 31, 1975 common stock amounted to 21.6 percent of portfolio holdings, up from only 11.6 percent in March 1970. The single most important factor behind this trend is the continued liberalization of state laws that have in the past severely limited the percentage of portfolio assets that could be held in equity commitments.

---

[42] U.S. Department of Commerce, "Holdings of Selected Public Employee Retirement Systems," *Governments Quarterly Report*, June 1975.

FIGURE 14–6

Investment Objectives and Policies of the State of Nevada

Objective

The BOARD's objective is to produce an annual total investment return from this fund sufficient to pay the difference between employee/employer contributions and the total cost of current retirement benefits, present benefits earned by the members, and the interest on the unfunded liability. It is realized that this objective cannot be achieved in a brief period of time.

Policies

A. Are intended to establish what the BOARD considers to be in compliance with the prudent man rule.
B. Allocation:
    1. Up to 40 percent in common stock.
    2. Up to 80 percent in bonds.
    3. Up to 10 percent in real estate and real estate related investments.
    4. Up to 5 percent in convertible bonds, preferred stock, and convertible preferred stock.
    5. The residue in cash equivalents.
C. Bonds:
    1. The bond portfolio, exclusive of convertibles and preferred stock, shall be invested within the following ranges:
        a. 10 percent to 35 percent in AAA.
        b. 10 percent to 45 percent in AA.
        c. 10 percent to 50 percent in A.
        d. 0 percent to 10 percent in BAA.
        Note: The BOARD will always use the lowest of the Moody's and Standard & Poor's ratings.
    2. A bond trade is a related trade of an equal number of bonds on the same day. No bond trade shall be made unless it improves the bond portfolio. The bonds received will assume the book value of the bonds sold, with equivalent adjustment for take out or pay up. Yield to maturity should be figured on the bonds to be sold and purchased. Any pay up on a bond trade must also be compared to a current AAA bond of a similar type. Any other purchase or sale of bonds must immediately reflect the profit or loss in the income.
    3. No municipal bonds may be purchased without prior BOARD approval.
    4. The BOARD shall establish written objectives, criteria and procedures for bond trades which shall be provided to COUNSEL and each firm on the dealer list, together with a list of bond holdings which shall be updated quarterly.

FIGURE 14-6 (continued)

D. Common Stock:
  1. No stock may be purchased that is not currently paying a cash dividend. A currently held stock must be sold within a reasonable time if it ceases to pay a dividend.
  2. An evaluation, preliminary investment decision and staff notification shall be made by the COUNSEL at any time that the daily closing price of a common stock shows a 15 percent loss from the previous calendar quarter close.
  3. An evaluation, preliminary investment decision and staff notification shall be made by the COUNSEL at any time that the daily closing price of a common stock appreciates 20 percent above the previous calendar quarter close.
  4. A preliminary investment decision consists of a sell, hold, or additional purchase applying either in whole or in part to the original investment.
E. Convertible Bonds, Preferred Stocks, and Convertible Preferred Stocks:
  1. Convertible bonds shall be rated at least BA by Moody's and BB by Standard & Poor's.
  2. Convertible and nonconvertible preferred stocks shall be rated at least A by both services.

Source: State of Nevada, Public Employees Retirement System, March 15, 1976.

Despite this "average" increase, many state and local pension funds still maintain relatively small equity portfolios. For example, a survey by *Pension and Welfare News*[43] indicates that four state public employee retirement portfolios had less than 10 percent common stock, and six between 11 percent and 20 percent of the total portfolio. On the other hand, several states have developed relatively high levels of common stock concentration, and would seem to be pursuing investment policies and objectives every bit as aggressive as their corporate counterparts.

LIFE INSURANCE COMPANIES

The Nature of Life Insurance

During the early years of the life insurance business, premiums on policies were calculated on an annual cost basis. Each year an increas-

[43] "Stock Holdings of State Retirement Systems," *Pension and Welfare News*, August 1974, p. 13.

ing premium would be required in accordance with the advancing age of the insureds and the corresponding greater chances of his or her dying. This, in effect, was one-year term insurance, renewed each year. Experience proved, however, that this type of arrangement often caused difficulty in the middle and later years of the insureds' lives, when the financial burden became intolerably heavy or their health deteriorated and made them uninsurable.

To correct the defects of annual cost individual insurance,[44] a method was devised under which constant annual premiums would be levied on multiyear policies. The premium on any given policy would be higher than necessary to cover mortality risks in the early years of coverage. The excess would be built up as a reserve, and invested in income-producing assets to be employed during the later years of coverage, when the premium would be lower than warranted by the then higher mortality risks.

Numerous variations on the general idea of "level premium" insurance were devised, thus stimulating the industry's shift from an annual cost premium basis to a level premium basis. It was this shift (together with the successful marketing of retirement annuity policies) which gave rise to large-scale investment activities. Under the old basis, if all the actuarial calculations were correct, annual income equaled annual outgo, leaving nothing to be invested other than, perhaps, capital, surplus, and contingency reserves. Under the new basis, a reserve for investment was deliberately established.

In modern life insurance, premiums are made up of three components: (1) the cost of pure insurance (protection against mortality risks), plus (2) a charge to cover the company's selling and operating expenses (including profit if a stockholder-owned company), minus (3) an assumed rate of return on the investment of excess premiums during the early years of policies. (Some policies, like endowments, have a fourth premium component which provides for an extra savings element.) Bearing in mind the three key components of life insurance premiums, it becomes obvious that the success of a life insurance company depends on three factors: (1) accurate calculations of mortality risks, (2) success in minimizing operating expenses, and (3) success in earning at least as high a rate of return on reserves as is assumed in the premium calculation. These factors apply whether the company is a mutual or a stockholder-owned organization (the former account for only 10 percent of the number of companies but 70 percent of the assets), except that mutuals pay dividends to policyholders when premiums prove to be higher than necessary to meet obligations.[45]

---

[44] Group coverage still employs the annual cost concept.

[45] Some stockholder-owned companies issue "participating" policies, which pay dividends.

Investment Objectives

The objectives of life insurance investment are not at all clear-cut. The immediate goal, of course, is implied by our discussion of the nature of life insurance—it is to earn, at a minimum, the rate of return assumed in calculating premiums. Beyond that, however, there is great room for differing viewpoints. Let us detail why this is so.

Factors Suggesting Conservative Investments. Several aspects of the life insurance business suggest that a quite conservative investment policy is advisable. In the first place, public policy places great emphasis on the safety of life company assets. Regulation of life insurance companies is diffused among the individual state legislatures and insurance commissions. However, there are many common characteristics among the different state regulations, and these characteristics are remarkably similar to the major regulations imposed on the investments of commercial banks and savings banks. This similarity suggests that from the point of view of public policy the investment portfolio of a life insurance company is in the nature of a trust fund and should be handled in accordance with conservative fiduciary principles. Chief among the regulations to which we refer are:

1. Relative freedom to invest any proportion of assets in U.S. government, state, or municipal securities, high-grade corporate bonds, or federally insured mortgages.

2. Limitation of conventional mortgage investments to a specified percentage of assets and to a specified maximum loan/value ratio.

3. Requirement that companies set aside annually larger reserves on low-quality bonds and preferred stocks than on higher quality issues. (Quality tests are prescribed by the National Association of Insurance Commissioners.) These more stringent reserve requirements will reduce dividend-paying ability unless interest income is sufficiently higher on low-quality issues to offset their impact. In addition, the bonds and preferred stocks of companies in poor financial condition must be marked down to market value on the owning company's balance sheet, thus cutting into valuation reserves, or even into surplus. Bonds and preferred stock "in good standing," on the other hand, may be valued at cost.

4. Strict limitation on equity investments. New York law is among the most strict in this regard, and since companies wishing to do business in New York must "substantially comply" with that state's law, it tends to set the standard. For example, New York limits common stock ownership to the lesser of 10 percent of assets (at cost) or 100 percent of surplus.[46] Although the limit is based on cost values, common stock

---

[46] This limitation does not apply to segregated pension fund accounts, which may be invested entirely in common stocks.

must be carried on the balance sheet at market values. Realized and unrealized appreciation must be set aside in a reserve account, unavailable for dividends, until the reserve reaches one third of the common stock portfolio's market value. In addition, 1 percent of the value of the stock has to be set aside annually until the maximum reserve is reached. (Realized and unrealized capital losses are charged against this reserve.)

It is not difficult to understand why public policy puts so much emphasis on safety. Confidence in the ability of life insurance companies to pay death and annuity benefits as they fall due is vital to the financial well-being of the community. With capital, surplus, and contingency reserves equal to only 8–9 percent of the industry's assets, there is not much margin for severe losses on investments. Moreover, life insurance and annuity benefits are payable for the most part in fixed dollar amounts. Aside from the impact of inflation on its operating expenses, therefore, the need for a life insurance company to take the risks involved in equity investments in order to hedge against inflation is limited.

Factors Suggesting Aggressive Investment Policies.   Proponents of more aggressive investment policies stress the minimal liquidity needs of life insurance companies. They point out that even at the very depth of the Great Depression, in 1932 and 1933, most life insurance companies had cash inflow far in excess of cash outflow, and the need to liquidate assets in a depressed market was negligible. All that companies really had to do was sit tight and not panic, and ultimately most investment values were restored.

The liquidity needs of a life insurance company are minimal for several reasons. Most of the industry's business consists of whole-life, multiyear term, and annuity policies. Therefore, liabilities are long term in nature. In addition, the demand for insurance is constantly growing. Unless a company's sales effort is dreadfully unsuccessful, premiums from new policies going on the books should exceed premiums terminated due to death, lapse, surrender, and so forth, and total premiums should exceed total benefits and operating expenses. Finally, much built-in liquidity is provided by amortization and prepayments of bonds and mortgages. Indeed, this turnover of assets provides almost as much cash inflow as the net increase in the industry's assets.

A few qualifications to the absence of liquidity needs should be made. (1) Young companies often operate at deficits because sales commissions absorb much of the initial premium income. (2) Companies which are too small to diversify their operations geographically are exposed to calamitous developments and need more liquidity than

larger companies. (3) Companies whose business is heavily in group life and other short-term insurance may not be able to build up as much cash reserves as companies with a large portion of whole life insurance and annuity business. (4) Since cash surrender values are payable on demand, either upon termination of policies or as policy loans, there is some need for liquidity especially during periods of very "tight money," when the low-interest-rate policy loan becomes a very convenient source of funds for policyholders. (The drain on liquidity during periods of tight money frequently is compounded by a slowdown in housing activity and a consequent reduction of mortgage loan prepayments.) (5) While actual operating requirements may not dictate distress sales of investments, state insurance regulations demand that securities in default be marked down in price and that properties acquired in mortgage foreclosures be sold within a specified number of years (five, for example).

Despite these qualifications, it is generally valid to argue that life insurance companies have little need for liquidity and that this suggests an aggressive investment policy. But lack of liquidity needs is not the only argument for an aggressive policy. Companies which take the easy way out, and invest merely to achieve minimum required rates of return, can be accused of depriving their policyholders of the lowest possible cost of insurance. In view of the quasi-public nature of the life insurance business, do not the companies owe it to their policyholders to strive for the maximum return consistent with the degree of safety needed, thereby enabling the cost of insurance to be minimized? Indeed, even from a selfish point of view, such a policy would seem wise. For in a highly competitive business like life insurance and annuities (especially pension plans), a company which can reduce insurance costs should be able to compete more effectively.

A final factor influencing life insurance investment policies is taxation. The income tax status of the industry has shifted gradually from being a relatively inconsequential investment factor to one which is taking on increasing importance. Life insurance taxation is extremely complex, but, at the risk of oversimplifying, its main features can be outlined as follows: (1) Investment income, net of investment expenses, is divided into two portions. One portion represents earnings required to maintain actuarial soundness and earnings paid out in the form of *policyholder* dividends. The other portion represents earnings transferred to surplus (or paid to stockholders). Only the latter portion is taxed. (2) The tax rate is a progressive one, rising as the level of interest rates rises. (3) The combined impact of these two factors produces an *average* tax rate on *aggregate* net investment income of only some 14 percent, only some 4 percentage points higher than in 1959,

when the current tax law was enacted. But the *marginal* tax rate on *incremental* investment income has risen sharply since then, as the level of interest rates has risen, and now approaches 35 percent.

A 35 percent marginal tax rate makes investments with tax preferences more significant now than in the past. Such tax-sheltered investments include preferred stocks (because of the dividend credit), municipal bonds (which are, in fact, not totally tax exempt because of the peculiarities of life company taxation, but which are taxed at a marginal rate of about 20 percent), and capital gains vehicles (because such gains carry a lower tax rate and may, in fact, not be taxed at all if offset by capital losses).

Investment Policies

It is apparent, on the basis of the preceding discussion, that we have in a life insurance company the peculiar situation of an investing institution which is fully capable of taking substantial investment risks, but which may not feel under great pressure to do so and which, in fact, is discouraged by law from doing so. The end result of these conflicting influences has been what one might expect—a compromise. Life insurance company investments, as a whole, have not been particularly bold and imaginative; but neither has the industry "played it safe."

Private Placement Debt.   The life insurance industry is one of the most important creditors of American industry, holding about one third of the long-term nonmortgage debt of domestic corporations. These investments, plus some foreign issues, accounted for about 37 percent of the life insurance industry's $280 billion of assets in 1975. The great majority of these investments are made by the private placement (also known as direct placement) technique, whereby corporations sell their notes to a single financial institution or to a small group of institutions, rather than by the traditional underwritten public offering technique. Private placements were described at length in Chapter 9.

In negotiating the terms of their private placement investments, life insurance companies have placed heavy emphasis on limitations of the borrower's right to refund the issue at lower interest rates. The reason life insurance companies are so anxious to have nonrefundability clauses in their bond investments is simple to understand. If interest rates were to drop sharply from the relatively high levels they have attained in recent years, borrowers who have unlimited call privileges would have little hesitation in calling their outstanding issues and refunding at more favorable rates. Insurers, however, could not increase premiums on existing policies, nor could they recoup the entire

reduction in income through increased premiums on newly written policies. And curtailment of dividends is a step they would be most hesitant to take. Therefore, they try to assure themselves of continuing high income by demanding nonrefundability.

While there are no publicly available data on the quality distribution of life insurance company private placement holdings, trade association compilations indicate that their average quality is approximately equivalent to Moody's Baa/Standard & Poor's BBB. This medium quality represents a compromise between the regulatory emphasis on safety and the competitive desire to exploit the industry's natural risk-taking ability. The major life insurance companies are large enough to be able to diversify broadly, and the risks inherent in any individual investment tend to be offset through the diversification process. Another step taken to reduce risk has been to shorten loan maturities (the typical maturity of life company private placements is about 15 years) and require fairly rapid amortization (which brings the typical "average life" down to 10–12 years). This leaves less time for a borrowing company's product to become obsolete or for it to get into trouble in some other way.

Mortgages. The search for yield improvement has caused life insurance companies to alternate their emphasis on mortgage lending versus private placements. During the postwar period until the mid-60s, for example, interest rates on mortgages were substantially higher than on bonds. Accordingly, from 1950 through 1965 life companies added a larger amount of mortgages than corporate bonds (mainly private placements) to the portfolio—$44 billion of mortgages versus $35 billion of corporate bonds. From 1965 to 1970, corporate bond and mortgage yields were fairly similar, and the life companies added about $15 billion of each to their portfolios. But then bond yields soared ahead of mortgage yields, and between 1970 and 1974 life companies made net investments of $27 billion in corporate bonds, with only $12 billion going into mortgages. Moreover, their mortgage activity after the mid-1960s was channeled progressively away from home mortgages and toward higher yielding (especially after taking expenses into account) commercial and industrial mortgages, which often provide a type of equity participation through percentage overrides based on gross rentals of the mortgaged properties.

Precise quality comparisons between private placement debt and mortgages are not feasible. In general, however, most observers believe that the life insurance industry's mortgage portfolio, which presently represents about 33 percent of total assets, has about the same overall medium-grade quality as the industry's private placement portfolio (37 percent of assets). Thus, we have further evidence of a compromise between safety and risk-taking, coupled with an aggres-

sive effort to shift funds to the highest yielding markets within the medium-grade portion of the quality spectrum.

Other Investments.   The 30 percent of life insurance company assets not invested in private placements and mortgages is distributed approximately as follows:

	Percent
Fixed-Income Investments	
U.S. and foreign government securities	3
Tax-exempt (state and local government) securities	2
Preferred stock	3
Policy loans	9
Total	17
Equity Investments*	
Common stock	5
Real estate	3
Total	8
Receivables, etc...	5

* Excludes equity participation features of bonds and mortgages.

Of particular interest is the common stock percentage. Of the total, approximately half is now represented by the common stock portion of the investments behind the industry's ordinary insurance and annuity liabilities. The balance represents so-called separate accounts maintained for pension funds which do not wish to be constrained by the legal regulations restricting ordinary insurance and annuity investments. These accounts are the most rapidly growing segment of life insurance equity investments. They are managed in much the same way as bank trustees manage the common stocks in their pension accounts. Some are growth stock oriented, while some are invested mainly in the stocks of a wide cross section of large industrial corporations. (Variable annuity premiums also are invested through these separate accounts.)

PROPERTY AND CASUALTY INSURANCE COMPANIES

Property and casualty insurance is written by many-different types of organizations. Stockholder-owned companies account for only about one quarter of the number of organizations in the business, but do two thirds or more of the volume. Mutual companies account for almost three quarters of the number, but account for only about one quarter of the volume. (Note that the situation is precisely the opposite in the life insurance industry, where mutuals are in the minority in number but do the bulk of the business.) Both mutual and stock companies compete with state workmen's compensation funds, nonprofit

hospital-medical associations, and life insurance companies writing various types of sickness and accident insurance.

Property and casualty insurance companies are controlled by state governmental authorities in several ways, perhaps the most important being the establishment of maximum premium rates on various policy lines. Premiums are determined in the following manner. Statistical data are gathered which show industry claim-payment experience, by line of insurance, during the past three to five years, on a national, state, and county basis. To these claim data are added allowances for operating expenses, contingencies, and a margin for profit. On the basis of this information, the state insurance commissions calculate maximum premiums. Generally, no allowance is made, in setting these premiums, for income earned on the investment of any surplus or reserves.

Since investment earnings usually are not taken into account in calculating premiums, a property and casualty insurance company is, in a very real sense, two separate organizations—an insurance company and a diversified balanced closed-end investment company.[47] There is no specific investment income goal which must be met to keep the insurance end of the business sound. However, to the extent that underwriting activities are unsuccessful, the soundness of the total company depends on the soundness of the investment portfolio. Thus, the two parts of a property and casualty company are interdependent. When risks of loss are increased in one part, they must ordinarily be reduced in the other.[48] Good investment management, therefore, facilitates the achievement of a proper balance between the two parts of the business.

Legal Restrictions on Investments. The legal regulation of property and casualty insurance company investments is relatively lenient. In New York State, for example, the following regulations are most significant:

1. Since policyholders receive a discount for paying premiums in advance—for example, a three-year policy may be fully paid with a lump sum equal to 2½ years' premiums—the premium income of most companies contains a large "unearned" element. In New York, at least 50 percent of unearned premiums plus 50 percent of the portion of earned premiums which is set aside as a reserve for payment of losses must be invested in high-grade bonds and mortgages.

2. The balance of a company's funds may be invested in a wide

---

[47] It is not an investment company in the legal context of the Investment Company Act of 1940, however.

[48] An opposing argument is presented in Y. Kahane and D. Nye, "A Portfolio Approach to the Property-Liability Insurance Industry," *The Journal of Risk and Insurance*, December 1975.

variety of bonds, stocks, mortgages, or real estate. There are a few requirements dealing with quality and diversification; however, these are easily satisfied.

3. Stocks—preferred and common—must be carried at year-end market values, other assets at cost. As will be seen shortly, this is a crucial factor.

Liquidity Needs. It is much more difficult for a property and casualty insurance company to forecast cash inflow and outflow than for a life insurance company. Liquidity requirements are, therefore, considerably greater. As a result, U.S. government securities often represent 15–20 percent of the assets of property and casualty companies. This compares with only a few percent for life companies. Of the governments held, between one half and two thirds have maturities of less than five years, and within this segment a policy of spaced maturities is usually followed, so that some issues are always nearing maturity. Liquidity consciousness has discouraged these companies from entering the mortgage market to any considerable extent.

Taxation. Both stock and mutual property and casualty insurance companies are taxed like other business corporations with regard to investment income: (1) They are subject to an income tax rate of 48 percent on net interest income. (2) The same rate applies to net dividend income—but after an 85 percent credit, so that the rate is really only 7 percent. Long-term capital gains are taxed at the prevailing preferential rate.

These tax factors make state and local government bonds highly attractive to property and casualty companies in comparison with corporate bonds.[49] Since dividend income is taxed leniently, preferred stock is also often preferable to corporate bonds and mortgages. Convertible preferreds may be particularly appealing. Obviously, common stock investment also takes place with taxation prominently in mind, because dividends and capital gains receive favored treatment.

Common Stock Investment Policies. The most crucial aspect of fire and casualty company portfolio management is determining the proportion of total assets to be invested in common stock—or, more accurately, the proportion of capital and surplus to be so invested, since policy reserves and unearned premiums are largely invested in fixed-income securities. We have seen that investment policy must complement insurance policy. If insurance risks are great, investment risks must be reduced, and vice versa. Common stock is the investment medium carrying the most risk, since stock prices are very volatile and the law requires stocks to be carried at market value.

---

[49] However, companies with large underwriting loss carry-forwards may not find tax-exempts so attractive. For them, higher coupon rates may be desirable, even if taxable, since the underwriting losses can act as an offset against the interest income.

When we speak of risk exposure in any business, the first thing that comes to mind is the capital position of the business in relation to those phases of its operations that carry a high degree of risk. Traditionally, the degree of risk exposure in the insurance part of a fire and casualty company is measured by the ratio of annual premium volume to capital and surplus. (Some analysts use "premiums written" in the numerator of the ratio, others use "premiums earned"; for old, established companies the two figures are usually quite similar.) Investment risk is measured by the ratio of common stockholdings to capital and surplus. To illustrate the significance of these ratios, let us refer, first, to an extreme example, and then to a more realistic case.

Suppose that a company has annual premium volume of five times capital and surplus. Obviously, if in any one year a 20 percent loss is suffered—that is, if claim payments and operating expenses equaled 120 percent of premium income—capital and surplus would be wiped out. Of course, a 20 percent loss is extremely severe. But a 10 percent loss is not improbable, and two consecutive years of 10 percent insurance losses would also wipe out capital and surplus.[50] If, under such circumstances, the company had common stocks in its portfolio, and the stock market declined during the period, the stocks would have to be marked down on the books, and the company would become insolvent. The stated value of assets would be less than stated liabilities. Therefore, it is axiomatic that a company with an insurance exposure ratio of 5 to 1 could not afford to have any investment exposure.

Now, an insurance exposure ratio of 5 to 1 is virtually unheard of, because the risks are simply too great. As a more realistic example, let us assume the following facts: At the end of year X, a company has capital and surplus of $100 million, and common stock investments of an equal amount, at market value. Normal premium volume for the company is $150 million. Thus, its insurance exposure ratio is 1.5 and investment exposure is 1.0. Next, assume that during year X + 1, an underwriting loss of 6 percent is suffered, and on top of this the stock market declines 25 percent (measured from December 31st of year X to December 31st of year X + 1).

A 6 percent loss on premium volume of $150 million is $9 million, and a 25 percent markdown of a $100 million stock portfolio is equal to $25 million. In other words, capital and surplus is reduced by $34 million, to $66 million. If new premium volume continues at the $150 million level, the new insurance exposure ratio is 150/66, or almost 2.3. Investment exposure is 75/66, or 1.1. At this point, the company

---

[50] Because of the possibility of large underwriting losses, property and casualty insurance companies typically have a ratio of capital and surplus to policy liabilities which is several times larger than that of life insurance companies.

would prudently have to consider switching out of common stocks and into safer investments, because another such year would bring it to perilous straits. Another $9 million underwriting loss combined with a $19 million writedown of common stock (25 percent of $75 million) would reduce capital and surplus to $38 million and raise the company's insurance exposure ratio to a totally unacceptable level of almost 4.0.

Selling stocks after a 25 percent price decline is a questionable action, because the odds probably would be high that a turnaround is in the offing. Nevertheless, prudence would suggest such action, because a continued price decline would have unacceptable consequences. The moral of the example, therefore, is that an investment exposure ratio of 1.0 is probably too high for a company whose insurance exposure ratio is 1.5. Unfortunately, many insurers forgot this moral in the early 1970s, and found themselves in dire straits during the ensuing bear market.[51] Considerations other than the absolute insurance exposure ratio are also important in the determination of common stock investment policy. The most important of these other considerations are:

1. If premium quality is high, more investment risk is justified at a given insurance exposure ratio than if premium quality is poor. Two companies may write the same amount of business, but one may show consistently greater underwriting profits than the other. Premium quality is related to such factors as type of business underwritten (auto lines, for example, are generally more risky than fire), geographic diversification of risks, and extent of reinsurance.

2. The trend of the insurance exposure ratio may be as important as its level. Young companies, which are rapidly expanding their volume of activity, usually have rising insurance exposure ratios because their capital and surplus expands less rapidly than sales. The opposite may be true of older companies with stable or declining sales. Other things being equal, the latter companies can follow a more aggressive investment policy than the former.

3. Identical investment exposure ratios do not necessarily signify identical risks. One company may stress stocks in relatively stable industries while another may put more emphasis on growth stocks or highly cyclical stocks. Furthermore, the stockholdings of many fire and casualty companies contain a large segment which is not a security investment in the usual sense of the word. Rather, it represents the ownership of subsidiary and affiliated insurance companies.

Over and above these influences on investment policy is the general business philosophy of a particular company's management. Consider,

---

[51] Lynn Brenner, "Insurers Flunking Finance," *Journal of Commerce*, July 28, 1975, p. 8.

for example, the two leading auto insurance companies: State Farm, a mutual company, and Allstate, a subsidiary of Sears, Roebuck. Both companies are similar in size (between \$3.5 and \$4 billion of assets in 1975) and similar in premiums written (\$2.3 billion). State Farm is almost exclusively concentrated in auto lines, while Allstate writes other lines as well; but Allstate is, nevertheless, predominantly an auto insurer (about 70 percent of premiums). Despite these similarities in operating circumstances, the investment policies of the two companies are very different, as shown by the asset distribution in Table 14–8—differences which can only be explained by basic managerial attitudes.

TABLE 14–8
Asset Distribution of State Farm Mutual and Allstate Insurance, December 31, 1974

	State Farm	Allstate
U.S. Treasury and agency bonds	45%	27%
Tax-exempt bonds	26	17
Corporate bonds and preferred stocks	2	8
Fixed-income investments	73	52
Common Stocks:		
Of subsidiaries	10	2
Other	9	29
Real estate	3	3
Receivables	5	14

Source: Moody's *Bank and Finance Manual.*

NONPROFIT ORGANIZATIONS

The investment management activities of nonprofit institutions[52] are an often overlooked segment of the institutional investor market, despite their significant size, rapid growth rate, and serious portfolio problems. The combination of historically conservative investment policies, inflationary pressures, and accelerating demands for greater investment income have placed these institutions in particularly difficult positions. The need for current income is usually not best served by the same securities offering the greatest long-term growth potential. Consequently, trustees of these nonprofit portfolios have, in recent years, developed new attitudes and policies designed to rectify their characteristic somnolence and blunt the criticism of an increasing horde of detractors.

---

[52] Generally considered to include charitable, religious, educational, civic, social and eleemosynary organizations exempt from federal taxation under Section 5 of the Internal Revenue Code.

For example, the results of a recent study covering 383 colleges and universities and 66 foundations revealed that 40 percent of the educational institutions and 30 percent of the foundations now include proportionately more growth stocks in their portfolios than they did three years ago.[53]

Figure 14–7 contains a good example of the contemporary thinking governing the investment objectives of nonprofit organizations. Notice the inclusion of "social concern" as part of the stated investment philosophy.

Perhaps the clearest reflections of the changed attitudes relating to the management of endowment funds can be found in new legislation, either proposed or actually adopted. The most important is the Uniform Management of Institutional Funds Act, which was approved in August 1972 by the National Conference of Commissioners on Uniform State Laws and recommended by the Conference for enactment in all states.

The act in essence endorses the "total return" concept of measuring portfolio returns, and allows trustees to spend a "prudent" portion of capital gains, either realized or unrealized. Historically, trustees have confined their spending to income actually received, and were reluctant to spend capital gains, even if they were substantial.

Much of the impetus for these changed attitudes can be traced to the efforts of the Ford Foundation, which is itself responsible for a $1.7 billion portfolio.[54] In a study designed to stimulate educational endowment trustees to accept a more aggressive investment posture, an advisory committee on endowment management to the Ford Foundation noted, "The record of most American colleges and universities in increasing the value of their endowments through investment management has not been good."[55] Many endowment trustees have since responded to the challenge. In fact, several leading endowment trusts are known to be pursuing investment objectives (in terms of total return) every bit as aggressive as the most ambitious corporate pension funds, and through the utilization of the same basic techniques; that is, splitting the management of portfolio assets, encouraging competition between the managers, granting full investment discretion, allowing high levels of portfolio turnover, and perhaps most significant, chang-

---

[53] William L. Cary and Craig B. Bright, "The Developing Law of Endowment Funds: 'The Law and the Lore' Revisited," Report to the Ford Foundation, *Educational Endowment Series*, February 1974, p. 10.

[54] We should also point out that the urgings of the Ford Foundation were not the only factors at work. The spectacular performance achieved by "growth stock" portfolios during the middle and late 1960's was also a major stimulant.

[55] Report to the Ford Foundation, *Managing Educational Endowments*, August 1969, p. 3.

In common with the management of many other private pools of capital such as pension funds, trust funds, and endowment funds; Loren D. Ross, the Foundation's Investment Manager emphasizes maximum investment productivity. This is the greatest possible overall rate of return that can be earned by exercising ordinary business care and prudence, and which is consistent with the Foundation's particular requirements. The Foundation, for example, needs a regular flow of interest and dividends (augmented sometimes by portions of specified principal funds) to fulfill its operating purpose. Income must also be sufficient to absorb excise tax payments stemming from the Tax Reform Act of 1969 and to enable the Foundation's activities to expand in the future.

Growth in the Foundation's capital funds over the long-term is necessary to provide increased income; to overcome erosion in real value due to inflation; and to allow greater capacity to absorb investment risks. The Foundation's investment philosophy does not ignore or avoid investment risks. On the contrary, it is aware of their potential severity and frequency and thus encourages the Investment Manager to compare potential gains with concomitant risks of loss as well as to anticipate and minimize short-run and long-term fluctuations in values of holdings whenever feasible. There is a related long-term goal to define levels of risk that are appropriate or acceptable for the Foundation's investments. The investment philosophy also encourages a flexible stance with regard to changing interest rate levels and therefore does not set any fixed percentage of assets for investment in either fixed income securities or in common stocks, since income, capital appreciation, and risks must all be balanced.

* * * * *

In the view of Russell Sage Foundation and also from society's broader perspective, there is a social concern that relates to the managements and activities of corporations. There are social criteria, first, as to how the managers of certain companies (whose bonds or stocks represent otherwise suitable investment possibilities) recognize their political and social responsibilities. Second, there are social judgments as to what these managers are doing constructively within their corporate framework to meet human needs and to ameliorate many kinds of current social problems, such as pollution, discrimination, unsafe conditions, and urban blight.

This social concern is consistent with investment criteria, in the sense of what management is accomplishing with its resources—to paraphrase the classic economic formula of land, labor, and capital—materials, people, and capital. In this case, the focus is on and for people: as people themselves, as well as in their social, economic, and political roles as customers, employees, creditors, and shareholders comprising society at large.

Source: Russell Sage Foundation.

ing managers when performance fails to achieve the desired results. One leading university employs eight different managers for its $175 million endowment fund, and seeks a minimum average return of 12 percent per annum.

We should point out, however, that these "new" investment attitudes have not, as yet, produced their designed goals. In fact, quite the contrary. Because of historically high common stock positions, and in many cases "growth" stock oriented, the bear market of 1973–74 created severe damage to the value of endowment and foundation portfolios. Late in 1974 *The Economist* reported that the Carnegie Foundation suffered a decline of 40 percent of its asset value, the Rockefeller Foundation one third, while other major foundations—Mott, Kettering, Duke, and Luce among them—lost as much as 50 percent of their market value.[56] In response, trustees, in many cases, drastically reduced or suspended long-cherished grant programs and some publicly contemplated going out of existence if the market did not recover. Commenting upon the squeeze created by rising expenditures and declining investment returns, Roger Kennedy of the Ford Foundation put this perspective on his investment management problem, "We have been like a mutual fund in redemption to the tune of $20 million or more a month in recent years."[57]

Endowments and Foundations

The two most important categories of nonprofit portfolios are college and university endowment funds and private foundations. That is not to say that other types of nonprofit organizations do not possess substantial portfolios. For example, the United Methodist Church has an endowment fund of over $400 million, The Metropolitan Museum of Art (New York) has one of over $150 million and several other museums and hospitals are endowed with investment portfolios exceeding $50 million in assets.

Endowment Funds. A college or university endowment is a perpetual fund whose investment income usually is used to supplement operating revenues of the school. Increases in educational expenses have generally outpaced the growth of endowment assets and the portion of operating expenses supported by investment income is today much lower than it used to be. However, many universities still depend upon their endowment return to prevent their budgets from run-

---

[56] *The Economist,* September 28, 1974, p. 48.

[57] Roger G. Kennedy "What Happened at the Ford Foundation?" *Journal of Portfolio Management,* Spring 1975, p. 52. See also Burton G. Malkiel and Paul B. Firstenberg, *Managing Risk in an Uncertain Era: An Analysis for Endowed Institutions* (Princeton, N.J.: Princeton University, 1976).

ning at a deficit. Furthermore, it has been estimated that a quarter of all private colleges and universities are using some portion of their endowment capital, in addition to investment income, to meet operating expenses.[58]

Total endowment funds are estimated at $15 billion,[59] with the ten largest universities accounting for over 30 percent of the total. This degree of concentration should not be viewed as surprising, as the ten largest mutual funds also accounted for 30 percent of total mutual fund assets at the end of 1974.

Historically, endowment funds have been managed to provide high current income and preservation of capital. More recently, many endowment fund trustees have embraced the Ford Foundation's position of "maximizing" total investment return.

Figure 14–8 summarizes the University of Rochester's investment

FIGURE 14–8
An Example of Endowment Objectives—University of Rochester

> The Board of Trustees adopted what we refer to as the "5 Percent Policy" at the June 1970 meeting. Beginning with our fiscal year ended June 30, 1971, the Endowment Fund contribution to the University's cash flow will equal 5 percent of a moving average of the market values of the endowment as of December 31 of each of the preceding five years. Obviously this decision required a complete review of our investment policy.
>
> Historically, our policy attempted to balance current income, growth of income, and principal growth. The record shows that these goals were achieved via a balance of growth stocks, fixed-income investments, and convertible securities. The "5 Percent Policy" obviously relates to a "Total Return" concept, a phrase which has become quite popular in recent years. Thus, if we have a negative flow of funds on the order of 5 percent and continuing inflation of around 4 percent, we must have an annual compound rate of return of 9 percent just to stand still and maintain the purchasing power of the Endowment Fund.
>
> The Investment Committee's best judgment for investment policy at this time is a greater portfolio emphasis on common stocks and principal growth.

Source: *Investment Report*, University of Rochester, December 31, 1971, p. 5.

objectives and at the same time provides an example of how endowment trustees are attempting to integrate investment management with the university's budget problems.

---

[58] James C. Crimmins, "Our Friends in Non-Profit Land Say a Major Financial Crisis Is Under Way," *Institutional Investor*, August 1972, p. 35.

[59] Estimated by the *Money Market Directory*, 1975.

Foundations. Foundations are nonprofit organizations established to contribute to the common welfare through social, educational, religious, or charitable activities. There are five basic types of foundations, the most important of which are the general-purpose ones.[60] This type of organization conducts its activities in a wide variety of fields, and usually derives its initial funds from very wealthy individuals.

Once again, we find the assets relatively concentrated. The ten largest foundations in the list account for about 35 percent of all foundation assets listed in the latest edition of the *Foundation Directory*. Table 14–9 indicates the growth in foundation assets which has taken

TABLE 14–9
Changes in Number and Assets of Foundations with Assets of $1 Million or More

Date*	Number of Foundations	Assets (billions)
Edition 1 (1958)	780	$10.7
Edition 2 (1962)	1,023	13.4
Edition 3 (1965)	1,464	18.6
Edition 4 (1969)	2,172	23.9
Edition 5 (1972)	2,504	31.5

* Date approximate; reporting years varied.
Source: *Foundation Directory*, 5th ed. (New York: Foundation Center, Columbia University Press, 1975).

place since 1958 as measured by the *Foundation Directory* at different publication dates.

The single most interesting investment characteristic of the large general-purpose foundations is that they were usually established by means of a large block of stock of a company in which the donor was one of the founders. In many cases, the desire to avoid burdensome capital gains and estate taxation without losing effective control was as important a motivating desire as the promotion of charitable intentions.

Portfolio diversification of foundation assets has been generally slow over the years, although the pace has picked up recently. This is largely due to some of the provisions of the 1969 Tax Reform Act, which makes it difficult for largely "one-stock" portfolios to escape taxation.[61]

---

[60] The other classifications are special purpose, company sponsored, community and family. For further definitions and details, see *Philanthropic Foundations in the United States*, published by the Foundation Center, 888 Seventh Avenue, New York, N.Y.

[61] Sections 4940–4942 of the Tax Reform Act of 1969.

BANK TRUST DEPARTMENTS

Commercial bank trust departments control the largest pool of private investment funds in the United States. At the end of 1974, total trust department assets of all insured commercial banks amounted to $325 billion, with much of this amount concentrated in a relatively small number of bank trust departments. As Table 14–10 indicates, 60

TABLE 14–10
Distribution of Commercial Bank Trust Department Assets

	Number of Trust Departments	Percent of Number	Assets ($ millions)	Percent of Total Trust Dept. Assets	Percent of Total Trust Dept. Accounts	Average Size of Account ($ thousands)
Under $10 million	2,805	70.1	5,271	1.6	9.5	41.4
$10 to $25 million	418	10.5	6,748	2.1	7.9	64.2
$25 to $100 million	454	11.4	22,846	7.0	18.3	93.5
$100 to $500 million	222	5.5	47,418	14.6	24.5	144.9
$500 million to $1 billion	40	1.0	27,460	8.4	9.1	224.7
$1 billion and over	60	1.5	215,582	66.3	30.7	524.5
	3,999	100.0	325,325	100.0	100.0	243.3

Source: Federal Deposit Insurance Corporation, 1974.

bank trust departments, less than 2 percent of the total number, held over $215 billion in trust assets, over 66 percent of all trust department assets in the country.[62]

Asset control is even more concentrated than these numbers would suggest. For example, the ten largest trust departments, six of them in New York, held over $117 billion in assets at the end of 1974, about 36 percent of the total. These trust departments, and others of very large size, are frequently referred to as the "dinosaurs" of the investment management community, a term used to infer an inflexibility of movement with regard to portfolio decisions because of their size. In actual practice, some of these large trust departments have demonstrated a greater willingness, and ability, to adopt to new investment trends than many portfolios of much smaller size.[63]

---

[62] It is also interesting to notice the dramatic increase in average account size that parallels the increase in trust asset size. This relationship reflects both the larger size of accounts and the greater proportion of investment advisory and employee benefit fund business that usually associates with larger trust departments.

[63] See, for example, John Carson Parker, "Behind the Top-Tier Sell-Off," *Business Week*, September 15, 1975, p. 82; Charles J. Elia, "Banks Switch to Cyclicals in Second Period Signaling Basic Change in Investment Thrust," *The Wall Street Journal*, September 5, 1975, p. 27.

Bank trust departments administer a wide variety of client accounts. The services performed by the bank vary in accordance with the type of account and the degree of investment discretion granted in the management of investment portfolios.[64] Over the years, the composition of bank trust department assets has changed dramatically. Prior to World War II, bank trust activity was largely concentrated in the administration and management of estate and personal trust accounts. During the last 20 years, the investment supervision of employee benefit plans, both corporate and public employee, has grown much more rapidly than any other type of bank trust business, and now exceeds, particularly for the larger banks, personal trust and estate business.[65]

Most bank trust departments, especially the larger ones, conduct their portfolio management activities through the use of approved lists; i.e., lists of securities which may be purchased or held by the trust department's various accounts. Approved lists, some of them quite lengthy, are frequently coded or classified so that portfolio managers who actually make the buy-and-sell decisions, can track changes in enthusiasm for securities on the list. Codes are also used to delineate which securities are considered appropriate for different types of accounts, such as those seeking maximum capital gains, income, and safety of capital. Usually, an investment committee, which sets overall policy in terms of cash reserves, industry concentration, and often individual stock selection choices, is responsible for changing the approved list.

Over the past few years, it has become rather common practice, especially in the larger trust departments, to allow the managers responsible for large, performance-oriented portfolios substantial discretion to deviate from approved list selections and to use their own judgment when making portfolio decisions. Such practices raise the question whether all of the trust departments' accounts receive the same treatment, or whether some accounts receive preference in terms of reaction time to new information, portfolio manager capability, equitable allotment of security transactions, and so on.[66]

---

[64] A short, excellent history of bank trust development is contained in Edward S. Herman's "Conflicts of Interest: Commercial Bank Trust Departments" *Report to The Twentieth Century Fund Steering Committee on Conflicts of Interest in the Securities Markets* (New York: Twentieth Century Fund 1975), p. 7–25.

[65] See Edna E. Ehrlich, "The Function and Investment Policies of Personal Trust Departments," *Monthly Review, Federal Reserve Bank of New York*, October 1972, p. 255–70.

[66] See Edward S. Herman and Carl F. Safanda, "Allocating Investment Information," *Financial Analysts Journal*, January–February 1973, for a detailed discussion of the possible conflicts inherent in the handling of new investment information in a bank trust department.

Bank Common Trust Funds. Most bank trust departments operate commingled pooled equity funds, very much similar to an open-end mutual fund, but open only to customers of the bank. The original purpose of these fund portfolios was to reduce costs and provide diversification for smaller clients. More recently, trust departments have been aggressive in establishing single-purpose funds which could be used by portfolio managers to achieve a specific investment objective for some portion of the funds under their supervision. By mixing investments in a number of funds, each with a different purpose, portfolio managers could presumably construct a portfolio designed to achieve the specific investment objectives sought by the client. The Morgan Guaranty Trust Company, for example, sponsors 12 commingled funds, and together these funds hold more than one fourth of the total assets of all employee benefit trusts managed by the bank. Table

TABLE 14–11
Commingled Pension Trust Funds Managed by Trust and Investment Division (market value in millions, December 31, 1975)

Type of Investment	Number of Participating Trusts	Market Value (% of total employee benefit trust assets)
Equity funds:		
Common stocks of larger companies	352	$ 439 (3.27)
Common stocks of medium-sized companies	591	672 (5.01)
Common stocks of smaller companies	590	526 (3.92)
Equities in foreign companies	534	77 (0.57)
Fixed-income securities with equity features	465	312 (2.32)
Real estate-related equities and securities with equity features	466	141 (1.05)
Fixed-income funds:		
Publicly traded corporate bonds*	392	87 (0.65)
Directly placed corporate securities†	311	47 (0.35)
Demand and short-term notes‡	673	532 (3.96)
Short-term investments§	502	348 (2.59)
Intermediate-term securities	509	380 (2.83)
Directly placed mortgages and real property	321	331 (2.47)
Directly placed medium-term corporate debt obligations	463	244 (1.82)
Total commingled pension trust funds		$3,964‖(29.52)

* Name changed from Bonds.
† Fund established October 1, 1975 by allocation from Bonds fund.
‡ Includes $130 million representing participations held by other commingled pension trust funds.
§ Includes $42 million representing participations held by other commingled pension trust funds.
‖ After deduction of amounts cited in notes ‡ and §.
Appraised value used for assets without market quotations.
Source: Morgan Guaranty Trust Company of New York, "Report of the Trust and Investment Division," 1975, p. 7.

14–11 is a listing of Morgan Guaranty Trust Company's commingled funds along with the market value at year-end 1975.

Conclusion

We have attempted to compare and contrast the investment objectives of a variety of institutions and individuals, and to trace the investment management processes which tend to develop from the pursuit of these objectives. The results are probably disappointing since there appears to be no unifying theme of analysis and decision making. Portfolio managers have not brought to bear on their problems many meaningful decision techniques consistent with their large responsibilities. Academic critics have noted this deficiency in the real world of finance and have moved to supplement traditional methods of investing with a framework of theoretic analysis which they maintain can be applied in practice with positive, beneficial results. It is to these theoretic developments of the last two decades, to the attempts to apply them in practice, and to the measurement of their results that we now turn in the next several chapters.

SUGGESTED READINGS

Investment Objectives

Bauman, W. Scott. *Performance Objectives of Investors* Occasional Paper No. 2. Charlottesville, Va., *Financial Analysts Research Foundation*, 1975.

Lorie, James H., and Hamilton, Mary T. "New Focus for Investment Counselling to Pension and Endowment Portfolios—Long Range Risk Policy." *Financial Analysts Journal*, July/August 1973.

McDonald, John G. "Investment Objectives: Diversification, Risk and Exposure to Surprise." *Financial Analysts Journal*, March/April 1975.

O'Brien, John W. "Investment Objectives, Policy and Risk." *The Journal of Portfolio Management*, Summer 1975.

Tepper, Irwin. "Optimal Financial Strategies for Trusteed Pension Plans." *Journal of Financial and Quantitative Analysis*, June 1974.

Rates of Return on Investments

Cagan, Phillip. "Common Stock Values and Inflation—The Historical Record of Many Countries." *National Bureau Report Supplement* New York: National Bureau of Economic Research, Inc., March 1974.

Holmes, John Russell. "100 Years of Investment Experience with Common Stocks." *Financial Analysts Journal*, November/December 1974.

Ibbotson, Roger G., and Sinquefield, Rex A. "Stocks, Bonds, Bills and Infla-tion." *Journal of Business*, University of Chicago, January 1976.

Reilly, Frank K. "Companies and Common Stocks as Inflation Hedges." *Bulletin 1975–2*. New York: Center for the Study of Financial Institutions, New York University, 1975.

Sharpe, William F. "Bonds versus Stocks." *Financial Analysts Journal*, November/December 1973.

Individual Portfolio Management

Barnes, John. *Who Will Get Your Money?* New York: William Morrow & Co., 1972.

Cohen, Jerome B. *Personal Finance: Principles and Case Problems*, 5th ed. Homewood, Ill.: Richard D. Irwin, Inc., 1975.

Institute of Chartered Financial Analysts. "Portfolio Management," in *1973 Supplementary Readings in Financial Analysis*. Homewood, Ill.: Richard D. Irwin, Inc., 1973.

Lyons, John T. (ed.) *Personal Financial Planning For Executives*. New York: American Management Association, 1970.

Sauvain, Harry C. *Investment Management*. 4th ed. Englewood Cliffs, N.J.: Prentice-Hall, Inc., 1973.

Schreiber, Irving (ed.). *How to Use Tax Shelters Today*. Greenvale, N.Y.: Panel Publishers, 1973.

Slovic, Paul. "Human Judgment and Investment Decision Making." *Journal of Finance*, September 1972.

Widicus, Wilbur W., and Stitzel, Thomas E. *Personal Investing*. Rev. ed. Homewood, Ill.: Richard D. Irwin, Inc., 1976.

Investment Companies

Brooks, John. *The Go-Go Years*. New York: Weybright & Talley, 1973.

Forbes magazine. Annual survey of mutual fund performance (usually ap-pearing in the mid-August issue).

Friend, Irwin; Blume, Marshall; and Crockett, Jean. *Mutual Funds and Other Institutional Investors*. A Twentieth Century Fund Study. New York: McGraw-Hill Book Co., 1970.

Investment Company Institute. *Mutual Fund Fact Book*. Washington, D.C., (annually).

Tomlinson, Lucile (ed.). *How to Start, Operate and Manage Mutual Funds*. New York: Presidents Publishing House, Inc., 1971.

Wiesenberger Services, Inc. *Investment Companies*. New York, annual.

Pension Funds

'Bagehot, Walter.' "Risk in Corporate Pension Funds." *Financial Analysts Journal*, January/February 1972.

Brooks, John. *Conflicts of Interest: Corporate Pension Fund Asset Management*. New York: The Twentieth Century Fund, 1975.

The Conference Board. "Financial Management of Company Pension Plans," New York, 1973.

Kohlmeier, Louis M. *Conflicts of Interest: State and Local Pension Fund Asset Management. New York: The Twentieth Century Fund, 1975*.

Regan, Patrick J. "Potential Corporate Liabilities under ERISA." *Financial Analysts Journal*, March/April 1976.

Tucker, J. Richard. *State and Local Pension Funds*. Washington, D.C.: Securities Industry Association, 1972.

Insurance Companies

Alfred M. Best & Co. *Best's Fire and Casualty Aggregates and Averages*. (Annual.)

Bishop, George A. *Capital Formation through Life Insurance: A Study in the Growth of Life Insurance Services and Investment Activities*. Homewood, Ill.: Richard D. Irwin, Inc., 1976.

Institute of Life Insurance. *Life Insurance Fact Book*. (Annual.)

Journal of Risk and Insurance. (Quarterly).

Property and Liability Insurance Investment Management. C.F.A. Monograph Series, No. 5. Homewood, Ill.: Richard D. Irwin, Inc., 1971.

Shapiro, Eli, and Wolf, Charles R. *The Role of Private Placements in Corporate Finance*. Boston: Division of Research, Graduate School of Business Administration, Harvard University, Soldiers Field Station, 1972.

Bank and Trust Companies

Beazer, William F. *Optimization of Bank Portfolios*. Lexington, Mass.: Lexington Books, D. C. Heath & Co., 1975.

Bradley, Stephen P., and Crane, Dwight B. *Management of Bank Portfolios*. New York: John Wiley & Sons, Inc., 1975.

Ehrlich, Edna. "The Functions and Investment Policies of Personal Trust Departments," *Monthly Review*, Federal Reserve Bank of New York, October 1972, pp. 255–70.

———. "The Functions and Investment Policies of Personal Trust Departments—Part II," *Monthly Review*, Federal Reserve Bank of New York, January 1973, p. 12–19.

Federal Deposit Insurance Corporation. "Trust Assets of Insured Commercial Banks," Washington, D.C. annually.

Fiske, Heidi. "The Banks Fight Back," *Institutional Investor*, April 1972.

Herman, Edward S. *Conflicts of Interest: Commercial Bank Trust Departments*. New York: The Twentieth Century Fund, 1975.

Herman, Edward S., and Safanda, Carl F. "Allocating Investment Information." *Financial Analysts Journal*, January/February 1973.

Hester, Donald D., and Pierce, James L. *Bank Management and Portfolio Behavior.* Cowles Foundation Monograph 25. New Haven: Yale University Press, 1975.

Nonprofit Institutions

Advisory Committee on Endowment Management. *Managing Educational Endowments,* 2d ed. New York: Ford Foundation, 1972.

————. "Managing Educational Endowments," Report to the Ford Foundation, *The Educational Endowment Series,* July 1972.

Cary, William L., and Bright, Craig B. "The Developing Law of Endowment Funds: 'The Law and the Lore' Revisited." Report to the Ford Foundation, *Educational Endowment Series,* February 1974.

Ennis, Richard M., and Williamson, J. Peter. "Spending Policy for Educational Endowments, A Research and Publication Report of *The Common Fund,* January 1976.

Kennedy, Roger G. "What Happened at the Ford Foundation?" *The Journal of Portfolio Management,* Spring 1975.

————. "Endowment Funds: Income, Growth, and Total Return." *The Journal of Portfolio Management,* Fall 1974.

————. "Twentieth Century Fund Task Force on College and University Endowment Policy." (background paper) *Funds for the Future.* New York: McGraw-Hill Book Co., 1975.

Malkiel, Burton, G., and Firstenberg, Paul B. *Managing Risk in an Uncertain Era: An Analysis for Endowed Institutions.* Princeton, N.J.: Princeton University, 1976.

REVIEW QUESTIONS AND PROBLEMS

1. Define the portfolio management decision-making process in your own terms.
2. Describe the risk-return "trade-off" in your own language.
3. What is the long-term record of return on stocks versus bonds? How does the more recent experience differ? Why?
4. How do the problems of individual portfolio management differ from those of institutional portfolio management? What alternatives are open to an individual who does not have time to manage his or her own individual portfolio?
5. What factors primarily determine the investment objectives of a pension fund?
6. How have ERISA concerns affected pension fund investment attitudes?
7. How do the investment objectives of a profit sharing plan and pension fund differ?
8. What are the important determinants of investment policy for a fire and casualty company? How do they differ from a life insurance company?

9. Why have state and local employee retirement funds been slow to accept common stock investing?

10. In addition to insurance companies and pension funds, what other types of institutional investors are active participants in the stock market? Describe their investment policies.

RESEARCH PROJECTS

1. Select a mutual fund that has an asset value of over $500 million and trace the changing nature of portfolio composition since 1960. Have these changes consistently mirrored the investment objectives stated in the prospectus?

2. Visit or communicate with a corporate pension fund executive and determine how and why its investment objectives have changed over the past ten years. What has been its average annual return over this period?

3. Select a major life insurance company and a major fire and casualty company. Compare the changes that have taken place in their investment policies over the past five years.

4. Select two major nonprofit organizations. Compare and contrast their investment policies and performance over the past ten years.

5. Describe the present versus the historic relationship of growth stocks to cyclical stocks in terms of price-earnings ratios. Which would you choose on a total return basis for each of the following institutions:
   a. A fully funded pension plan.
   b. An educational endowment institution.
   c. A profit sharing plan.
   d. A public employee retirement system.

C.F.A. QUESTIONS

1. *From Exam III, 1975*

Following is the *Summary* of Peter L. Bernstein's article, "What Rate of Return Can You 'Reasonably' Expect?"

> Both the improving economic environment and the below-average rate of return over the past five years suggest that *at best* common stocks should provide a total return of more than the 6.5% rate of 1967–72 but probably no more than 9.5% over the next five years and an average of something around 8% over the longer run; the returns of 9% or more suggested by the Fisher-Lorie study are probably irrelevant to current analysis.
>
> Performance data for relatively sophisticated portfolio managers, however, offer little hope that investors will be able to achieve results consistently better than the performance of the market as a whole, and that goals set at or below market rates of return are much more likely to be realistic than efforts to outperform the market.

Relative to realizable investment objectives in the current environment for common stocks, the yield available on long-term high-grade bonds is much more attractive than it would appear to have been in the past. Stocks are likely to provide significantly higher returns than bonds only under optimistic assumptions as to the environment if interest rates go higher than they are now, or as to the capitalization rates for corporate earning power under unusually favorable economic conditions.

Answer each question below separately listing your reasons 1, 2, 3, etc.

State specific reasons that would tend to support agreement and state specific reasons that would tend to support disagreement with the statements that:

a. Common stocks will provide a total return averaging not more than 8 percent over the longer run.
b. Stocks are likely to provide significantly higher returns than bonds *only* under optimistic assumption.

2. *From Exam I, 1975*

The Ancient Brotherhood of Railroad Firemen has a pension fund with a book value of $100 million. Additions to the portfolio are currently being made from annual net cash inflow. The fund has been managed for many years by a committee of the Brotherhood. None of the committee members has had any formal training or experience in either security analysis or portfolio management. They have relied largely on security salesmen for advice.

The committee now recognizes that the members of The Ancient Brotherhood of Railroad Firemen are in a profession that will die with them. In five years the majority of the Brotherhood will have retired and most will be dead within 25 years. In view of these circumstances, the committee feels that the portfolio is not as well structured as it should be and has approached you to seek your help as a professional investment counselor.

The percentage structure of the portfolio at market value is now:

15% Recently issued long-term premium bonds with ten-year call protection.
10   Medium-term bonds.
15   Tax-free municipal bonds.
15   Growth stocks.
15   Cyclical stocks—principally companies mining or producing natural resources considered to be in scarce supply.
15   Preferred stocks.
5   Short-term notes.
10   Residential real estate mortgage loans—average maturity of 15 years.
100%

Comment on the suitability of this portfolio given the circumstances of the Brotherhood. Suggest portfolio changes you think are appropriate.

Chapter 15

Portfolio Theory I: Major Tenets

> These are sweeping changes, and those who are committed to
> traditional theories and practices naturally resist them.
> — *B. F. Skinner*

In recent years, portfolio management techniques have entered a critical and innovative phase of activity. Faced with increasing pressure for higher rates of return, with advances in performance measurement technique, and with the glare of academic inquiry, portfolio managers are being forced to develop new decision-making procedures.

The Historical Setting

These developments reflect the historic inability of those concerned with investment analysis, portfolio decision making, and performance evaluation to express quantitatively their views concerning risk and its relationship to investment return. Past returns could not be compared through the use of a generally accepted common denominator of "risk." And the future uncertainty of expected return could not be expressed with any degree of quantitative assurance.

The lack of a quantitative risk dimension created widespread confusion as to what had actually been accomplished in a portfolio management sense. Mutual fund management companies, for example, compared their results to the broad market averages as a yardstick, but made no allowance for portfolio objectives, management techniques, the variability or volatility of return, or the "risk" exposure. During the 1950s and through most of the 1960s it often was easy to achieve higher returns than the stock market averages by adopting an aggres-

sive attitude toward maximizing capital gains, with minimal regard for the consequences of such policies during a bear market. It has been more recently recognized that the *apparent* achievement of portfolio managers during this period did not necessarily reflect their real capabilities, but merely their willingness to take high risks.

As for future anticipations, it was increasingly recognized that the problem of uncertainty was only being qualitatively assessed, with most managers nurturing fuzzy notions as to broad, generalized stock classifications such as conservative, defensive, growth, income, and speculative.

Thus, deficiencies in the investment environment created an excellent opportunity for the academic community to attempt to apply formal analytical techniques to very practical types of problems. The availability of mutual fund data on a continuous basis for an extended period of time facilitated the effort. The result was a significant body of new thought concerning the usefulness of widely employed investment decision-making practices—a body of thought now described under the general heading of "Modern Portfolio Theory" or "Capital Asset Pricing Theory."

Modern portfolio theory treats risk for the first time in quantitative terms. It focuses attention beyond the traditional exhaustive analysis and evaluation of individual security issues, and to the problem of overall portfolio composition predicated on explicit risk-reward parameters and on the identification and quantification of client objectives.

These techniques and theories have been slow to evolve and to gain acceptance by practitioners. Several reasons are apparent, not the least of which is the traditional inability of academic critics to communicate effectively with practicing professionals. Suspicion and lack of understanding, and the personal fear of recognizing how ineffective results actually have been, further reduced practitioners' willingness to accept the benefits which can be provided by these techniques. And, of course, the theories themselves are continually being challenged and revised, so that practitioners are reluctant to implement new ideas which may become obsolete quite rapidly.

Nevertheless, the attempt to introduce scientific tools and techniques to the long-established conduct of investment management shows signs of success. Available theory is no longer in its infancy, and substantial practical implications—both as to performance measurement and portfolio balancing techniques—have already received significant acceptance.

The purpose of this chapter is to explore the development of modern portfolio theory and its implications for the evaluation of professional investors' performance. The presentation relies importantly on

the works of others, not to serve as a review of available literature, but to portray the painstaking development of theory over time, commencing with largely academic concerns which found little acceptance at first, and culminating in quasi-regulatory endorsement and the growing application by professional portfolio managers and their clients.

MODERN PORTFOLIO THEORY

Markowitz and "the Efficient Frontier"

The basic elements of modern portfolio theory emanate from a series of propositions concerning rational investor behavior set forth by Dr. Harry M. Markowitz briefly in 1952, and later in a complete monograph sponsored by the Cowles Foundation.[1]

Essentially, the Markowitz model provided a theoretical framework for the systematic selection of optimum portfolios, once the level of "risk" willing to be assumed by the investor was established. Markowitz applied the complex mathematics of quadratic programming to the question of how most effectively to diversify portfolio holdings, given a free choice among hundreds of individual securities, and provided that certain basic information could be supplied by either security analysts or portfolio managers. In so directing the focus, Markowitz, and others following the same line of reasoning, recognized the function of portfolio management as one of composition, and not individual stock selection—as it is more commonly practiced. Decisions as to individual security additions to and deletions from an existing portfolio are then predicated on the effect such a maneuver has on the delicate diversification balance.

The central theme of Markowitz's work is that investors conduct themselves in a rational manner which reflects their inherent aversion to absorbing increased risk without compensation by an adequate increase in expected return. As such, it was stated that for any given "expected" rate of return (where the expected return is the mean of a probability distribution), most investors will prefer a portfolio containing minimum expected deviation of returns around the mean over a determined period of time. Thus, it can be seen that risk was defined by Markowitz (and others) as the uncertainty,[2] or variability, of expected returns, marking a major effort to quantify investment risk for

---

[1] Harry M. Markowitz, *Portfolio Selection—Efficient Diversification of Investments* (New Haven, Conn.: Yale University Press, 1959).

[2] Risk and uncertainty are used synonymously, although some would argue that a situation of risk exists if an investor is willing to base actions on probability distributions; otherwise there is only certainty and uncertainty. William F. Sharpe, *Portfolio Theory and Capital Markets* (New York: McGraw-Hill Book Co., 1970), p. 25. More will be said about risk versus uncertainty at a later point.

portfolio planning purposes. The use of variance as a measure of risk also forces the investor to consider a fixed time horizon for investment calculations.[3]

For example, if Portfolio "A" is expected to yield (in 2 chances out of 3) 10 percent plus or minus 2 percent (i.e., it may yield as much as 12 percent or as little as 8 percent during the period), it is more desirable than Portfolio "B," whose expected yield is the same 10 percent, but plus or minus a range of 4 percent.[4]

Starting with this conception of risk, and the investor's aversion to risk, Markowitz observed that investors try to minimize the deviations from the expected portfolio rate of return by "diversifying" their portfolios, holding either different types of securities and/or securities of different companies. But he importantly pointed out that simply holding different issues would not significantly reduce the variability of the portfolio's expected rate of return if the income and market prices of these different issues contained a high degree of positive "covariance." That is, if the timing, direction, and magnitude of their fluctuations were similar. Effective diversification is only achieved if the portfolio is composed of securities that do not fluctuate in a similar fashion, so that the variability of the portfolio's rate of return becomes significantly less than the variability of the individual components of the portfolio.

This important principle can be more easily understood by considering a simple two-stock portfolio, with equal amounts invested in each issue. Let us first assume that both securities are perfectly, and positively, correlated with respect to their price movements. When one moves up, the other does the same in exactly the same proportion; and a similar relationship exists on the downside. For the sake of simplicity, let us also assume that each security fluctuates in a perpetual up and down pattern of equal dimensions, as exhibited in Chart A, Figure 15–1. In this case, therefore, the variance of portfolio return will be the same as the variance in the return of either, or both, of the two securities. Consequently, combining the two into a portfolio does not reduce the variance in total return.

Now, let's assume that the two securities are negatively related to each other. When one moves up, the other moves down in exactly the same proportion, and vice versa, as exhibited in Chart B, Figure 15–1. By combining these two issues into a portfolio, variance in the portfolio's return is completely eliminated.

---

[3] Jerome L. Valentine, *Investment Analysis and Capital Market Theory*, Occasional Paper No. 1 (Charlottesville, Va.: The Financial Analysts Research Foundation, 1975), p. 25.

[4] In this case, as in Markowitz's presentation, the variability is expressed in terms of the familiar standard deviation. Others have used different measures of variability, such as the mean absolute deviation.

FIGURE 15–1

Chart A
Positive Correlation of Returns

Chart B
Negative Correlation of Returns

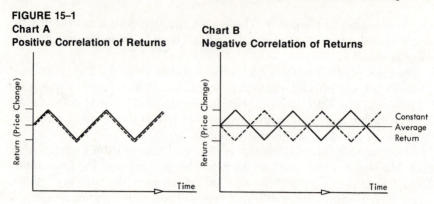

We can now formulate a general rule for our two-stock portfolio models. When the correlation of price movement between the two securities is not highly positive, the variance in the portfolio's return is less than if the portfolio was composed of only one security.[5]

Obviously, practical problems go far beyond the consideration of two-stock portfolios. Therefore, this basic principle must be expanded to include all of the possible portfolio combinations available for selection. For each portfolio considered, it is necessary to calculate the expected return, and the expected variance in this return, over the time period under review. The range of resulting combinations will, at least conceptually, lie at any point of the graph shown in Figure 15–2. In reality, most portfolios would lie in a region beneath the heavy line indicated as the "efficient frontier."

Portfolios falling beneath this border of "efficiency," fail to represent the optimal level of diversification which can be achieved through a different distribution of holdings.

Portfolio A is inefficient because portfolio B produces the same expected return but at a lower risk level, while portfolio C has the same degree of risk but affords a higher expected return.

In general, portfolios that lie in the middle region of the curve are usually highly diversified, while those at the extremes are much less so. For example, at point D the greatest possible expected return would usually be associated with total investment in the one security expected to produce the maximum return.

Thus, an optimum, or efficient portfolio can be defined as one providing the highest possible expected return given a predetermined risk level willing to be assumed by the decision-making investor. Con-

[5] The mathematical proof behind this proposition can be found in many texts. One of the most easily understandable explanations has been presented by Professor William J. Baumol, in *Portfolio Theory: The Selection of Asset Combinations* (New York: McCaleb, Seiler Publishing Company, 1970).

FIGURE 15-2
The Efficient Frontier

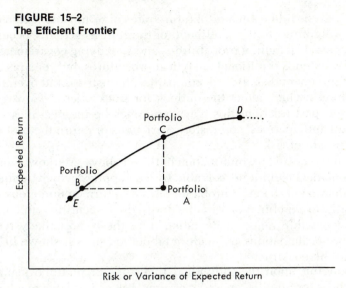

Risk or Variance of Expected Return

versely, all other portfolios possessing the same or less risk, would produce a lower anticipated return.

In order to determine the composition of "efficient portfolios," portfolio planners require the following knowledge:

1. Projections of the expected rate of return, including both current income and capital gain or loss, to be earned on each security that might be considered for inclusion in the portfolio.
2. Estimates of the possible range of error of each rate of return projection—for example, 15 percent plus or minus 8 percent.
3. An indication of the interrelationships (covariances) of the error ranges among securities. That is, if something happens to cause security A's rate of return to be, say 2 percent, higher than the "most probable" projection, what is the likelihood that the return on security B will be similarly higher than its most probable return? What about securities C, D, E, and so forth?
4. An indication of any constraints placed upon the portfolio manager, such as maximum percentage of the portfolio to be invested in any one security, and minimum number of different securities to be included in the portfolio.

Thus, the application of modern portfolio theory begins with judgments concerning individual securities, and how their price changes relate to each other over time. These judgments must be predicated on reasonable expectations of future, uncertain developments. The security analyst and portfolio manager must translate their investment re-

search analysis into estimates of future rates of return and assign probability weightings to the likelihood of the returns actually occurring. The process of assigning probabilities and specifying covariances substantially extends traditional analytical procedures, but remains based on the fundamental analysis of companies, industries, and overall economic forces which affect the outlook for stock prices.[6] However, as seen later, past relationships may sometimes be the best measure of uncertain anticipations, and historic variations of return the best available estimate of risk.[7]

Given the necessary information outlined above, Markowitz offered a mathematical technique, solvable by a computer,[8] which permits the determination of the most probable rates of return on numerous possible portfolio combinations of the individual securities and the associated possible range of deviation from these most likely returns. Once these calculations are made, a tabulation such as shown in Table 15–1 can be constructed.

Depending upon the individual investor's or portfolio manager's willingness (or unwillingness) to assume risk as it relates to a level of return, either portfolio 1, 2, . . ., or 100 would be considered optimum. Different investors and portfolio managers, obviously, will reach different decisions as to which of the various portfolios is best suited to reflect their risk/return preferences. However, Markowitz would argue that portfolio 4 is clearly better than portfolio 5, since both have a mean expected return of 10 percent but the former is "less risky"—has a lower variance—than the latter.

It should be at once recognized that an efficient portfolio, once constructed, will not retain its optimum status for long, due to the basic nature of fluctuating stock prices. Thus, the computer program must be rerun and a new, efficient portfolio composition determined at each review period. High-speed computer capability also enables investors to rerun the program utilizing different assumptions regarding expected returns, variances, and covariances of various combinations of individual securities.

---

[6] See Jack Clark Francis and Stephen H. Archer, *Portfolio Analysis* (Englewood Cliffs, N.J.: Prentice-Hall, Inc., 1971), p. 17; who further noted that "efficient portfolios generated by portfolio analysis are no better than the statistical inputs on which they are based," p. 47. Also Franco Modigliani and Gerald A. Pogue, "An Introduction to Risk and Return: Concepts and Evidence," *Financial Analyst's Handbook*, vol. I (Homewood, Ill.: Dow Jones-Irwin, Inc., 1975), chap. 44.

[7] If analysts simply provide the same projections that could have been calculated using the past returns from the stock in question, they are not providing additional useful information. See Valentine, *Investment Analysis and Capital Market Theory*, p. 28.

[8] IBM first offered a computer program for the solution of Markowitz' portfolio models in 1962, and since then modifications have been made available to investors incorporating the basic concepts explained above.

TABLE 15–1
Estimated Returns of Alternative Portfolios

Portfolio	Expected Average Rate of Return	Expected Standard Deviation	Expected Range of Returns at Two Standard Deviation* Level	
			Lowest	Highest
1	4%	¼%	3½%	4½%
2	6	1½	3	9
3	8	2¾	2½	13½
4	10	4	2	18
5	10	5	0	20
.	.	.	.	.
.	.	.	.	.
.	.	.	.	.
100	20	15	−10	50

*The user can choose any number of standard deviations, and the results will vary accordingly.

As we shall see in a later chapter, several services are currently available to institutional investors which incorporate these basic theories in a manner readily usable by portfolio managers. Such utilization provides a better understanding of the implications surrounding alternative portfolio structures. Which portfolio composition is actually chosen depends importantly upon the investor's attitude toward risk versus return, and to a lesser degree upon the costs associated with altering the existing portfolio structure. But perhaps most significantly, investors availing themselves of these techniques can begin the process of quantifying the consequences of alternative strategies, and at the same time become obliged to document investment goals and constraints, and to make more explicit their ideas concerning the future but uncertain prospects of different securities.

Critique. Several criticisms were made of the Markowitz approach, both from theoretical and practical points of view. One criticism has to do with the assumption that rational investors are actually risk averters. In the illustration previously cited, it was pointed out that Markowitz's theory considered portfolio 4, with a minimum return of 2 percent, a maximum of 18 percent, and a mean of 10 percent, to be superior to portfolio 5, with a minimum of 0 percent, a maximum of 20 percent, and the same 10 percent mean as portfolio 4. But the question is whether or not this necessarily represents a rational choice. Why would it be irrational for an investor to be willing to chance a zero return in exchange for the possibility of a 20 percent return.

A closely related question, and one that should be kept in mind as we further develop the theoretical understanding of quantitative portfolio techniques, is whether variance as such is the most appropriate measure of risk. Most of the work stimulated by Markowitz uses short-term price volatility to determine whether the expected rate of return from a security should be assigned a high or low expected variance. But if an investor has limited liquidity constraints, and is truly a long-term holder, then price volatility per se does not really pose a risk. Rather, in this case, the question of concern is one of ultimate price realization and not interim volatility.

There were (and still are) some very practical obstacles that restricted the use and development of the techniques suggested by the Markowitz model. An obvious drawback was that practicing investment managers were unable to understand the conceptual mathematics involved and became immediately suspicious that an academic approach to portfolio management was essentially unsound. Second, while security analysts and portfolio managers are accustomed to thinking about expected rates of return, they are much less comfortable in assessing the possible ranges of error in their expectations, and are generally totally unaccustomed to estimating covariances among securities.

Another limitation in the use of the Markowitz model is that each time a change in the existing portfolio comes under consideration, the entire population of possible securities must be reevaluated in order to preserve the desired risk-return balance. This, in turn, requires a large number of mathematical calculations. Markowitz himself pointed this out by observing that "an analysis of 100 securities requires 100 expected returns, 100 variances, and almost 5,000 covariances."[9] He then suggested a simpler procedure—relating the returns on each security to the returns on an overall index of market prices, and thereby implicitly relating the returns on each security to each other security. As we shall see later, it was precisely this simplification that led to the practical application of the underlying theory.

Even more significant than the voluminous mathematical computations required to apply the Markowitz technique, is that the portfolio alterations required to achieve constant portfolio efficiency may be so numerous that they can give rise to large, uneconomic transaction costs. This could be true even if portfolio managers reviewed their holdings less often than daily or weekly.

Despite these shortcomings, Markowitz's contribution to contemporary portfolio theory cannot be minimized. The presentation of his

---

[9] Markowitz, *Portfolio Selection*, p. 96. See also, Lawrence Fisher, "Using Modern Portfolio Theory to Maintain an Efficiently Diversified Portfolio," *Financial Analysts Journal*, May/June 1975, p. 75.

technique was a stimulating statement of portfolio selection theory and the benefits that could be derived from efficient diversification. It should not be considered as a package of guidelines immediately transferable for use by practicing portfolio managers.

Second, Markowitz forced others to consider that some measure of risk, and not just the expected rate of return, should be considered when dealing with investment decisions. Finally, given the fundamental propositions, others became attracted to the theory and began to adjust the basic framework so that practical application could be more readily considered.[10]

Capital Asset Pricing Theory

The presentation of portfolio theory by Markowitz was followed by a period of active academic concern dealing with the underlying implications for the security market pricing mechanism, and shortly gave rise to a cohesive body of thought now known as capital asset pricing theory, also referred to as capital market theory.[11] This theory details the character of the market's pricing mechanism when all investors act as if they are governed by the principles of risk aversion and the desire to optimize portfolio composition through effective diversification.

In general terms, the following assumptions, best detailed by William F. Sharpe,[12] provide the framework for the application of portfolio diversification techniques, and the foundation for comparative portfolio measurement procedures.

1. Investors are risk averse in that they will prefer the smaller variance at comparable levels of return, and the greater return at the same level of variance.[13]

2. Investors as a group view the risk-return relationship for individual securities over similar time periods (i.e., they have similar "investment horizons").

3. Investors seek to optimize their portfolios through efficient diversification.

---

[10] Markowitz's work had another interesting and stimulative impact. It gave rise to a better understanding of how high-speed electronic computers could be utilized in investment decision-making applications, and created a sense of urgency with regard to the development of data banks composed of stock price information heretofore only inefficiently available to curious historians.

[11] For an excellent summary of capital market theory and a thorough bibliography of research, see Michael C. Jensen, "Capital Markets Theory and Evidence," *The Bell Journal of Economics and Management Science*, Autumn 1972, p. 357–98.

[12] Sharpe, *Portfolio Theory and Capital Markets*, p. 77–78. See also Franco Modigliani and Gerald A. Pogue, "An Introduction to Risk and Return," chapter 44.

[13] For a classic article on this subject, see Milton Friedman and Leonard J. Savage, "The Utility Analysis of Choices Involving Risk," *Journal of Political Economy*, August 1948, pp. 279–304.

4.   Investors hold similar views as to the variance, risk, or distribution of future returns.

5.   Investors are able to lend or borrow unlimited funds at the prevailing risk-free rate (e.g., taken as 91-day Treasury bills).

6.   Securities are also assumed to be perfectly divisible, and an investor able to commit any desired amount of funds without affecting the price or the rate of return associated with each and any investment.[14]

It is immediately apparent that many of these assumptions do not coincide with the actual state of the working-day security market pricing mechanism. However, it is not necessary for every assumption to serve as an exact description for every circumstance. It is rather more important that the general theory represent a reasonable approximation of real-world investor activity and of the market's pricing behavior.[15] As such, the price of an individual security, and of the market as a whole, is seen at any point in time as being the composite view of interested investors, balanced to reflect differences in existing opinions, views, and preferences. While these differences may be large on occasion, security prices are seen as being basically in equilibrium. That is, each security, and the market as a whole, is seen as being, on balance, priced "fairly" in relation to the risk associated with its ownership.

Given this equilibrium assumption, rational investors should develop their desired portfolio positions by adjusting the risk element of their investments. Higher returns can be expected by increasing risk; and lowering of the risk element reduces the expected return. But capital asset pricing theory departs somewhat from the Markowitz presentation at this point. Whereas the Markowitz scheme adjusts risk by moving up or down the efficient frontier of *alternative portfolios of different individual securities,* risk is adjusted under capital asset pricing theory by borrowing or lending against *a single optimal risky portfolio.* This portfolio, moreover, because of equilibrium assumptions, is the *entire market.* The concept is presented graphically in Figure 15–3, which will be reviewed in detail.

As with Markowitz, expected investment return is measured on the vertical axis, while the horizontal axis indicates the risk (estimated variability of the return).

A key tenet of capital asset pricing theory is shown in Figure 15–3. Point M represents the expected return and the variability (risk) for the

---

[14] Some observers also consider transaction costs at zero, and tax consequences unimportant, but these are lesser considerations.

[15] Sharpe himself noted that the proper test of a theory is not the realism of its assumptions, but the acceptability of its implications.

FIGURE 15–3
The Capital Market Line

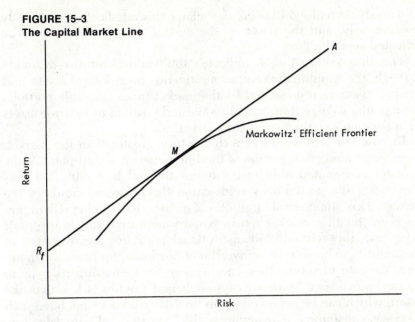

market as a whole—the complete universe of risky investments available for purchase, with each issue weighted in proportion to its share of the total market value of all risky investments. Since it is virtually impossible to calculate precisely this universe of risky investments at any given point in time, it is much more practical to use a "proxy" for the market universe. The Standard & Poor's 500 Stock Price Index has been most frequently used, although the choice is certainly not limited to this selection.[16]

The important concept to recognize is that the market, or its surrogate stock price index, is seen in capital asset pricing theory as the ultimate limit of efficient diversification which can be contained in a portfolio of risky investments. It is, in this sense, the optimal risky portfolio. As such, market risk cannot be further reduced through additional diversification. Market risk is contained in every security and every portfolio. It reflects the responsiveness of price level changes in each security to overall market movements.

The point R_f in Figure 15–3 is the rate of return available from investment in a risk-free asset during the period under consideration.[17]

---

[16] If it were feasible, a price index of all risky assets (stocks, bonds, real estate, options, and so on) should be devised. Sharpe has noted that such a comprehensive portfolio index could well turn out to be less risky than an index representing the price movement of New York Stock Exchange common stocks.

[17] The asset has zero risk in the sense of assured rate of return. Other risks, such as loss of purchasing power, are not considered in this context.

Obviously, in real-world every day affairs, this rate fluctuates virtually continuously, and the point on the vertical axis would have to be adjusted accordingly.

The line segment R_fM indicates the various returns available through the combination of commitments in risk-free assets and "risky" assets as represented by the market index. Possible portfolio combinations range from a totally invested position in risk-free assets to one which exactly mirrors the market.

In order to achieve an expected return greater than the market, some point along that portion of the line between M and point A, the investor is assumed able to borrow at the risk-free rate, and thus "leverage" the portfolio by reinvesting the borrowed funds in the market. This "theoretical" portfolio of greater than market risk to produce greater than market return is not practically available to most investors, since virtually all institutional portfolios are restricted in their ability to borrow for reinvestment purposes. Presumably, therefore, the rate of return they can achieve by increasing risk via an upward move on a Markowitz-type efficient frontier is less than the return which can be achieved by an investor who does not have such leverage constraints. Furthermore, the "constrained" investor sacrifices diversification in the move up on the efficient frontier. Most individual investors have also tended to forego the leveraging of their portfolios by borrowing, although—as has been noted—capital asset pricing theory suggests that they would be better off by considering such practice.[18]

Random Walk and Efficient Markets

One should immediately question at this point why daily stock market trading activity (over 30 million shares per day in early 1976 on the New York Stock Exchange alone)[19] is actually so hectic if the market mechanism even approximates a condition of price equilibrium. The answers most often given are, first, that investors' risk/return preferences are constantly changing, which gives rise to a frequent need to adjust the composition of their holdings to reflect these changes. Second, different investors are continually revising their anticipations about the expected risk and return associated with the holding of particular securities in response to new events. These new events are held to occur in a random fashion, a tenet of another and related aspect of modern portfolio theory, namely, the random-walk theory of stock price movements.

The random-walk hypothesis of stock price movement is based on

---

[18] Douglas A. Love, "The Use and Abuse of Leverage," *Financial Analysts Journal*, March/April 1975.

[19] *New York Stock Exchange Fact Book*, 1975 issue, p. 6.

the assumption that the security trading mechanism represents an "efficient" marketplace. In essence, the market is said to be characterized by the presence of a large number of rational, profit-seeking, risk-averting investors who compete freely with each other in their efforts to predict the future value of individual securities. Information significant enough to affect any security's future value is held to be quickly available to knowledgeable investors.[20] As a result, new information affecting a stock's value becomes quickly reflected in the price of the issue. Consequently, a new investment decision, made after the information becomes widely known, is believed to carry the risk/reward potential of a randomly selected purchase (or sale). This is because the next piece of information is believed to bear no necessary relationship to the prior information. That is, new information is believed to enter the marketplace in random fashion.

This general premise flies in the face of what many professional investors consider their greatest strength—the ability to benefit from quick action taken after some new important event occurs which substantially affects the value of a particular stock, or occasionally the market as a whole. Most professionals still accept what can be considered the "sociology of information recognition." This is a principle indicating that the movement of new information and its proper interpretation flows from the intelligent, well-informed and understanding sophisticated segments of the market, who do tend to act quickly to the lesser informed, slower moving elements at the other end of the spectrum.[21] This, in turn, is believed to cause a sequence of interim stock price movements to develop, which reflects the accompanying gradual discounting of new information as it moves through the investor system.

Benjamin Graham, widely regarded as the dean of security analysts, recently put a different perspective on the market's response to new information.

To establish the right price for a stock, the market must have adequate information, but it by no means follows that if the market has this information it will thereupon establish the right price. The market's evaluation of the same data can vary over a wide range, dependent upon bullish enthusiasm, concentrated speculative interest, and similar influences, or bearish disillusionment. Knowledge is only one ingredient on arriving at a stock's proper price. The other ingredient, fully as important as information, is sound judgment.[22]

---

[20] This is certainly the intent of SEC rules and regulations covering the release of important information.

[21] See Arthur Zeikel, "The Random Walk and Murphy's Law," *The Journal of Portfolio Management*, Fall 1974.

[22] Benjamin Graham, "The Renaissance of Value," *Proceedings of a Seminar on the Economy, Interest Rates, Portfolio Management, and Bonds vs. Common Stocks* (Charlottesville, Va.: The Financial Analysts Research Foundation, 1974), p. 10.

Nevertheless, actual stock prices are considered—by random-walk definition—to reflect at any point in time past events, along with those considered likely to take place. In other words, in the efficient market model, at any point in time, the actual price of a security is the best composite investor estimate of its real value.[23] Obviously, the true, or intrinsic value of a risky investment can never be precisely determined. If it could, uncertainty and risk would thereby be eliminated and a certainty of return substituted in its place. Furthermore, the market mechanism and the model of its efficiency accommodates the disagreements which do arise among investors. However, the interaction of a large number of buyers and sellers—acting with a knowledge base ranging from extremely well informed to complete ignorance—works in a manner which prices stocks at a level reflecting their investment value at any point in time. If this were not the case, the significant discrepancies were allowed to exist for any length of time—either of an overvalued or undervalued nature—knowledgeable investors would be able to recognize these differences in price as compared to value, and profit from the spread—which is exactly what professional investors claim to be able to do but on which the evidence casts doubt (see Chapter 16).

There has been no evidence submitted that securities are in fact often *systematically* overvalued or undervalued. On the contrary, the validity of the basic premise that successive price changes are independent has been supported by a growing amount of research effort in recent years, encompassing two different types of analysis. The first, and most prominent, has been the direct statistical testing of price changes over time.

Quite interestingly, the earliest record of the notion that fluctuations in stock price movements could be statistically explained only in terms of a random walk was presented by a French Mathematician in 1900.[24] Bachelier concluded that past price patterns (for commodities) provided no basis for predicting future price changes. The basic concept remained largely unexplored until the early 1950s. Since that time, innumerable regression studies, analysis of runs, and similar tests, have been carried out to determine whether or not stock price

---

[23] Putting the matter in still other words, random-walk proponents see stock prices as moving randomly around an earning-power-related trend line. Forecast the earnings level and you can forecast the price level, they believe; but you cannot forecast the timing of the swings around that level by analyzing past data. It is worth noting that from an economic point of view a random walk of stock prices around an earnings-related trend line is highly desirable. Such movement implies that rational processes are basically determining stock prices, thus improving the chances that capital is allocated "efficiently."

[24] L. J. B. A. Bachelier, *Théorie de la Speculation* (Paris: Gauthier Villars, 1900).

movements are independent of previous price changes.[25] Perhaps the best summary of such research was presented by Eugene Fama in an exhaustive paper entitled, "The Behavior of Stock Market Prices."[26] After reviewing most of the important work, Fama concluded that the evidence is "against important dependence" in successive price changes.

The second, and more recent approach to testing the random-walk hypothesis is less direct. It involves the use of various mechanical trading rules or other decision-making guidelines considered largely "technical" in nature. The basis for such an analysis is relatively obvious. If changes in stock prices occur in a random manner, then mechanical trading rules or predetermined decision-making guidelines should provide no profit beyond that of a random selection.

An excellent survey of the more important work in this area was contained in an article entitled, "The Random-Walk Hypothesis and Technical Analysis."[27] The author efficiently summarizes the major studies concerning random walk and the effectiveness of mechanical trading rules, such as: if the daily closing price of a particular security moves up at least X percent, buy and hold the security until its price moves down at least X percent from a subsequent high, at which time simultaneously sell and go short. The short position should be maintained until the daily closing price rises at least X percent above a subsequent low at which time one covers, and buys again. Moves less than X percent in either direction are ignored. The basic premise is quite simple. A stock that is moving up will keep moving up, and vice versa, until the move is reversed by an X percent price change. The research suggests that no form of mechanical trading rule will produce profits significantly greater than random selection.

In sum, the random-walk theory presents an important challenge to both the fundamental and technical techniques described in previous chapters. It might be well to note again that fundamentalists try to

---

[25] It is interesting to note that little testing has been conducted to determine the efficiency of other security markets, such as the bond market. One of the few studies available concluded, "the average 6–10 week lag in complete price adjustment subsequent to a rating change implies an inefficient 'bond' market slow to assimilate newly relevant information." See Steven Katz, "The Price Adjustment Process of Bonds to Rating Reclassifications: A Test of Bond Market Efficiency," *The Journal of Finance*, May 1974. For a different view, see: George J. Benston, "Interest Rates Are a Random Walk Too," *Fortune*, August 1976.

[26] Eugene F. Fama, "The Behavior of Stock Market Prices," *Journal of Business*, January 1965 and "Random Walks in Stock Market Prices," *Financial Analysts Journal*, September/October 1965. For a summary of more recent tests, which confirm earlier findings, see Charles D. Kuehner, "Efficient Markets and Random Walk," *Financial Analyst's Handbook*, vol. I (Homewood, Ill.: Dow Jones-Irwin, Inc., 1975), chap. 43.

[27] George Pinches, "The Random Walk Hypothesis and Technical Analysis," *Financial Analysts Journal*, March 1970, p. 104.

predict price changes through the analysis and interpretation of new developments or basic trends such as changes in profits and market share, which affect the value of the underlying common stock. Technicians, on the other hand, believe that predictions can be made by carefully observing stock price and volume movements of one sort or another.

To the chartist, or technician, the threat is simple. If the random-walk hypothesis does, in fact, describe reality, perusing past price data with the hope of identifying future value points is a worthless effort.

The concern of those following a "fundamental" investment analysis approach is somewhat more involved. As noted, the random-walk theory holds that stock prices at any point in time represent the best estimate of intrinsic or basic value. Therefore, additional research efforts of a fundamental nature are of value only when such undertakings can uncover new information which is not part of the body of knowledge or anticipations forming prevailing market prices. Unfortunately, "most analysts are usually capable of knowing only what is generally known."[28] In making this observation, Professor Lorie further suggests that security analysis should be carried out by fewer, more highly paid persons who seek insights in unconventional ways or can follow companies and industries for which their education and experience gives them a reasonable hope of superior understanding.[29]

Therefore, readers should not completely doubt the value of applying the basic research tools and techniques explored in earlier chapters, even though this doubt will probably increase when considering some of the commentary in this and the following chapters. The random-walk hypothesis does not deny the possibility of accurately predicting future stock price changes. It clearly accepts the principle that if investment research techniques can lead to accurate forecasts of future company earnings they should result in better price forecasts.

Furthermore, it still appears reasonable to believe that every industry, company, and economic sector responds to a different set of critical factors. Any sound analytical approach requires that these factors be identified and followed on a consistent basis. Changes in these elements alter the profits outlook and immediately begin to affect investment expectations. And random-walk theory notwithstanding, it is doubtful that all interested investors react in a manner which totally and immediately assesses new developments as they occur.[30] Opportunities to "move faster than one's competitors" probably do arise.

---

[28] James H. Lorie, "Four Cornerstones of a New Investment Policy," *Institutional Investor*, November 1971, p. 48.

[29] Zeikel, "Random Walk and Murphy's Law," p. 21.

[30] The implication that most, if not all, analysts cannot make an unusual profit from their efforts does not mean that all analysts are failing to perform a valuable service for

Several observers have concluded that there are trends in stock prices once the "move" is taken as the unit under study (e.g., 5 percent) rather than the week or the month. This would suggest that while stock price changes over adjacent time periods can be considered statistically independent of one another, there is reason to believe that good news is often followed by more good news and the converse is also true.[31]

Finally, the effective application of portfolio theory rests on judgments which pertain to the estimating of *relative* future stock price relationships.[32] This vital information can be often best obtained from a careful understanding of a business, and those vital factors which shape its success or failure.

Whichever view is correct, at this point the link between the random-walk hypothesis and portfolio theory can be closed. New value-changing events are assumed to occur in an unpredictable and random fashion. The efficiency of the marketplace is such that investors as a group rapidly translate the new information into a new price which fully reflects its expected impact. A new state of equilibrium is then established. Given these assumptions, there is no apparent advantage to be gained by most investors in their search for improperly valued securities or in the hope of forecasting new events which may be expected eventually to change stock prices. In essence, the situation greatly simplifies many investors' problems, since they are now free to be concerned with the question of portfolio composition and the establishment of an investment position which reflects their risk/return preferences.

MEASURING INVESTMENT RETURNS AND RISKS

Investment Return Components

Now that we have established the framework of a rational investment environment, and developed the assumptions of the capital asset pricing model, we can move to consider the central question of risk and return.

---

society. They *are* the engines responsible for the efficiency in the market, and as such do, collectively, perform a needed and valuable service to society as a whole. See Valentine, *Investment Analysis and Capital Market Theory*, p. 18; also Jack L. Treynor, "Some Second Thoughts about Keynes Beauty Contest," *Financial Analysts Journal*, May/June 1974, p. 14.

[31] This view can also be reinforced by a casual perusal of long-term stock price charts, such as those exhibited in Chapter 13. See also Frederick C. Klein and John A. Prestbo, *News and the Market* (Chicago: Henry Regnery Company, 1974).

[32] It is important to point out that random walk studies have been almost entirely concerned with absolute, not relative, stock price changes.

It is helpful to begin this part of our discussion[33] by reflecting once again on just what constitutes an investment rate of return.[34] Three key elements can be conceptually identified: (1) the "pure interest rate," (2) a premium for lack of marketability, and (3) a premium for risk.

1.   The "pure interest rate," often referred to as the "risk-free rate," is included in the return on all investments at any given time, and, in turn, has two components: "real" and "price." The "real" component of the pure interest rate reflects (a) the expected growth in the productivity of the economy (the higher the expected growth rate of "real GNP," the higher the pure interest rate tends to be); and (b) people's reluctance to save (the more reluctant they are to postpone present consumption, the higher the pure interest rate tends to be).

The "price" component of the pure interest rate reflects the expected rate of inflation (the higher the anticipated rate of inflation, the higher the pure interest rate tends to be).

The U.S. Treasury 91-day bill rate is perhaps the closest approximation we have to the pure interest rate at any given time, although its sensitivity to such factors as short-term international capital movements makes it less than ideal as a measure.

2.   Over and above the pure interest component, the return on most investments includes some *premium for lack of marketability*. This component is highest for investment media having a low degree of marketability, such as real estate or common stocks of small companies trading over-the-counter.

There are two reasons why investors demand an increased rate of return as marketability worsens: (a) many investors fear that they may have to sell their investment quickly in order to raise cash for operating purposes; therefore, they must be offered a satisfactory incentive to reduce marketability; (b) even large institutional investors, such as corporate pension funds, which do not usually have emergency needs for working capital, prefer to be able to sell investments quickly in order to correct portfolio management mistakes or to take advantage of new information.

The question of institutional portfolio liquidity has come under increasing concern in recent years, accompanying the growth in institutional portfolio concentration. In fact, a few years ago the SEC went so far as to suggest[35] that institutional holders (mutual funds) arbitrarily reduce the carrying value of large, hard to market holdings in their

---

[33] Much of the material in this and the following sections has been presented by E. D. Zinbarg, in "Modern Approaches to Investment Risk," *The Financial Executive*, February 1973.

[34] Rate of return is defined as the change in a security's price, plus dividend, interest, and other distribution income during the measurement period, divided by the price at the beginning of the period.

[35] Securities and Exchange Commission, *Statement on the Future Structure of the Securities Markets*, February 4, 1972.

portfolios, below current market prices, a process identified as "hair-cutting." No suggested guidelines as to the size of the "haircut" were recommended, but the thought was that such a practice "would result in a better balance between the propensity to accumulate large blocks and the expectation of instant liquidity."[36]

3. Finally, in addition to the pure interest rate plus a premium for lack of marketability, an investment should be expected to produce a higher average rate of return as its "riskiness" increases. Note that we say "should be expected to produce" rather than "will produce." For if we could be sure that a risky investment "will produce" a higher rate of return than a less risky investment, it would be rather foolish to refer to the higher yielding investment as "risky." The ability to discuss this third component of rate of return (the risk premium) in quantitative terms is perhaps the principal contribution afforded by modern portfolio theory.

Investment Risk

We have established that modern portfolio theory rests on, among other things, the investor's concern over the relationship between risk and return. We have not, as yet, however, precisely defined how to measure risk. There is still substantial controversy over exactly how investment risk is to be measured, and the techniques described below are not likely to represent the final solution.

Most students of the subject agree that investment risk is related to changes in the value of the investment under consideration—changes either in the actual market value, if there is an active market in existence, or in an imputed value if there is no active market. The reason for this linkage of risk to value change, or price fluctuation, is that such fluctuations reflect investors' uncertainty about the future. That is, current price change when investors change their ideas about probable future prices (whether for logical or for purely emotional reasons). Therefore, investments whose future prices are highly uncertain are the object of frequent revaluation by the investment community, and their current prices change frequently as a result. Less risk is generally associated with decisions where expected return is more predictable, and conversely greater risk is associated with decisions surrounding less confident expectations.

This line of reasoning carries with it an implication that the term "uncertainty" is synonymous with "risk." The pairing has led to the

---

[36] This unusual suggestion ignored the other side of the coin. That is, whether under some market conditions, so-called illiquid portfolio positions should be benefited by some premium value over prevailing prices to reflect the inability of others to duplicate the holding, without substantially increasing the market price of the stock. This has been referred to as "scarcity value."

use of price fluctuation per se as the best measure of risk. However, this definition is not without its ambiguity.

For example, consider first Chart 1 in Figure 15–4. The horizontal axis of this chart represents time, measured in days, weeks, quarters, or years (more will be said about the time interval at a later point). The vertical axis, labeled "rate of return," represents primarily the percentage change in the price of an investment during the time interval on the horizontal axis. But in addition to price change, rate of return includes any interest or dividend income received during the time interval, thus better representing the change in "value" during the period. The returns on two investments are shown on the chart. Note that the *average* return over all the time intervals is identical for the two investments, but that the return on B has a wider range of variation around the average than A. Presumably, most people would agree that in this example B was more risky than A because it was so much more erratic and a holder might have had to sell during one of the downthrusts.

Next consider Chart 2, Figure 15–4. Although the return on B is again very erratic relative to A, its average return is much higher and even its lowest returns are higher than A's highest returns. Presumably, most people would find it difficult to refer to B as more risky than A despite its very erratic behavior. B may be more "uncertain," but common sense tells us it is not more "risky."

Charts 3, 4 and 5, Figure 15–4, illustrate more complex cases than 1 and 2. In 3, as in 2, the average return on B is much higher than on A. Case 3 differs from case 2, however, in two respects. First, the highly variable nature of B causes its return often to be lower than that of A. Moreover, note that there has been drawn onto 3 a horizontal line at a return equal to zero. Points below this line, therefore, represent losses. It will be seen that the return on B not only is often below that of A, but often represents an actual loss of principal, whereas A does not produce any losses. Surely, a commonsense definition of risk must make reference to the losses produced by an investment and not merely to the variability of its returns.

Chart 4 is identical to 3, except that the term "loss" is defined more strictly. Clearly, investors can assure themselves of a minimal rate of return, without any fear of loss of principal, merely by putting their funds into Treasury bills and regularly rolling them over at maturity. Therefore, a loss can be said to occur whenever the return on an asset is lower than this "pure interest rate," even if the return is greater than zero.[37] Economists refer to such shortfalls as "opportunity losses."

---

[37] For the sake of simplicity, the pure interest rate is drawn as a constant—i.e., a horizontal line. In fact, of course, the Treasury bill rate is not constant. Thus, the standard against which returns on various assets are to be judged is itself a fluctuating standard.

FIGURE 15–4
Various Aspects of Risk

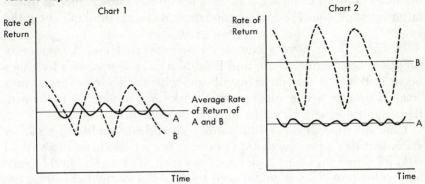

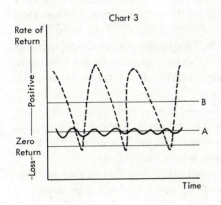

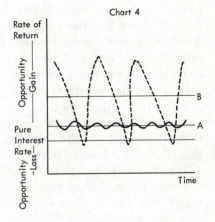

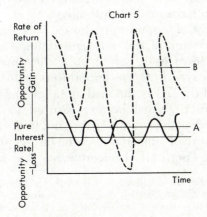

While the typical investor probably is more sensitive to absolute losses than to opportunity losses, a more widespread understanding of the latter concept would prevent a good deal of sloppy thinking about the subject.

In Chart 5 we have a complex case indeed. Here, A frequently produces opportunity losses and B seldom does. But when a loss does occur in B it is of very large magnitude, whereas A's losses are always small. Common sense suggests that "risk" has something to do with the magnitude, as well as the mere existence, of losses.

Consideration of these illustrations should make clear the earlier statement that price fluctuation per se is not an adequate measure of risk. As shown in Chart 2, the returns on an asset can be highly variable yet common sense might well rebel at the thought of calling the asset risky since it may consistently produce much better returns than alternative investments. A better term to describe high variability (which can be measured by the standard deviation of period-to-period returns about the average return) is "uncertainty." The term "risk" would be better reserved to refer to the frequency and average value of opportunity losses. The more frequent the opportunity losses, the more risky the investment. The larger the magnitude of these losses, the more risky the investment.

Admittedly, this working definition of risk is not without its own ambiguity. It does not clarify whether, in Chart 5, Figure 15–4, A or B is the riskier investment. A produces more frequent opportunity losses than B, but B's losses are much larger when they occur.

Perhaps empirical research will eventually reveal that this conflict is more apparent than real, because frequency and average value of losses may be highly correlated. If not, some synthesis of the two concepts is needed. But frequency and average value of opportunity losses would appear to be more meaningful and more concrete definitions of risk than have existed in the past.

The frequency of opportunity losses is a function of the ratio, $(\overline{r - r_0})/s$.[38] The terms of this ratio are defined as follows: r is the asset's rate of return each period; r_0 is the pure interest rate each period; therefore, $r - r_0$ is the opportunity gain or opportunity loss each period and $(\overline{r - r_0})$ is the arithmetic average of such gains and losses over the full time span being measured; s is the standard deviation of the individual opportunity gains and losses around the average. Since s is a measure of "uncertainty," the ratio represents the "average opportunity gains per unit of uncertainty." The higher this ratio the

---

[38] This assumes that the distribution of returns typically encountered in the stock market approximates the familiar bell-shaped or "normal" curve. In that case, the area under any portion of the curve can be calculated as a function of the number of standard deviations away from the mean.

lower the frequency of opportunity losses for the particular asset (or portfolio if we are measuring portfolio returns rather than returns on individual assets).

While the *frequency* of opportunity losses is a function of this straight-forward ratio, the *average value* of the losses is a function not only of the relationship between the numerator and denominator of the ratio but also of the absolute amount of each figure. For example, (10 percent/16 percent) will produce the same frequency of losses as (5 percent/8 percent), but the average loss will be of greater magnitude in the former case.

The importance of being able to state that risk is a function of the average return versus the standard deviation of returns will become evident in the next section. There it will be shown that both $(\overline{r - r_0})$ and s can be further subdivided into a component attributable to the movements of the overall market and a component attributable to the specific security. This subdivision, in turn, has important implications for portfolio theory.

Market Risk versus Specific Risk

In presenting the capital asset pricing theory, Sharpe also advanced the practical utilization of the Markowitz model an important step forward. Rather than measuring the covariance of every pair of securities under consideration for possible investment, he built upon Markowitz's suggestion that each security's price movement could be related to a common broad-based stock price index, such as the Standard & Poor's 500 Stock Price Index. By relating each security to a common base, each would implicitly be related to other securities.[39] This immediately reduced the number of calculations involved in determining efficient portfolios, and vastly simplified the practical application of the basic theory.

Sharpe further indicated that this approach could separate risk into two distinct elements.[40] The first, identified as the "market risk" (also called systematic or nondiversifiable risk), is that portion of a stock price (or portfolio) movement which can be attributed to movement of the market as a whole. The second element of risk is that portion of

---

[39] Jack Treynor, an early and important contributor to the development of capital asset pricing theory, made similar suggestions. We shall return to his contributions in the next chapter. See Jack L. Treynor, "How to Rate Management of Investment Funds," *Harvard Business Review*, January–February 1965.

[40] Sharpe (*Portfolio Theory and Capital Markets*, p. 83) defined risk in the traditional manner, as variance (or its square root, standard deviation). We have previously shown that risk might be better defined in terms of the *interaction* between standard deviation and average return. In either case, however, the separation of risk into two distinct elements is feasible and desirable.

price movement unique to the specific asset, and is defined (for reasons to be discussed below) as nonsystematic or diversifiable risk. This, in turn, might be further subdivided into some part attributable to industry characteristics and the balance distinct to the issuing company itself.[41]

Obviously, not all companies are positioned to respond to broad market movements with the same degree of sensitivity. Important market events change the value of some companies more than others. This may reflect the relative degree of financial, operating or earnings leverage; comparative capitalization rates (price/earnings ratios); competitive industry conditions; patterns of earnings instability (or stability); or endless other considerations.

Whatever the case, we can measure this "sensitivity-to-market" relationship. Figure 15–5 illustrates the procedure for partitioning the return on a common stock into its two basic elements—a market component and a specific stock component.

FIGURE 15–5
Measurement of Market Sensitivity

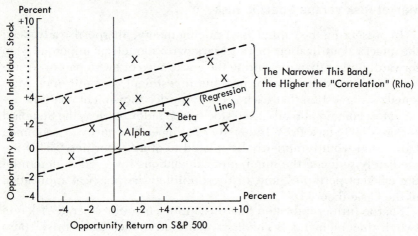

Assume that we are measuring returns (net of the pure interest rate) monthly for a one-year period, recognizing that any other base and interim period can be considered as well. Each X on the chart represents a particular month's gain or loss on the stock (measured on the vertical axis) and the corresponding gain or loss on the "market" during the same month (measured on the horizontal axis and using the S&P 500 Index as representative of the overall market).

[41] Large-scale merger activity in recent years has blurred traditional industry classification of companies, and it might be better to deemphasize the industry element of diversifiable risk.

Using standard statistical techniques, a least squares "regression line" is drawn through the 12 monthly observations. This regression line is a quantitative description of the relationship between the returns on the stock and the returns on the market. It provides the following information:

1. Beta is the "slope" of the regression line, the amount of vertical movement (stock return) per unit of horizontal movement (market return). If the slope were at a 45° angle, beta would be 1.0, meaning that *on average* every 1 percent opportunity return on the market was associated during this period of time with a 1 percent opportunity return on the stock. A shallower slope, would be represented by a beta of less than 1.0. Suppose that it worked out to 0.8. This would mean that, *on average*, a 1 percent opportunity return on the market was associated with a return on the stock of 0.8 percent. Likewise, a steeper slope—a beta of say 1.4—would mean an average relationship of 1.4 percent on the stock per 1 percent on the market. Note that the beta relationship applies to negative as well as to positive returns; that is, it indicates what will happen to the stock, *on average*, if the overall market *declines*. High-beta stocks are said to be highly "volatile," and low-beta stocks are said to be very "stable." Thus, beta measures the market component of a stock's returns.

2. Alpha is the "intercept" of the regression line, the point at which the line crosses the vertical axis and zero on the horizontal axis. It represents the amount of return produced by the stock, *on average*, independent of the return on the market. It measures the specific component of a stock's returns.

    Suppose, for example, that alpha is 1 percent and beta is 1.5. If, in this case, the market's opportunity return for a particular month was, say, 2 percent, the most likely return on the stock that month would be 4 percent. The 4 percent is derived as follows: a 2 percent market return is, *on average*, associated with a 3 percent stock return (2 percent multiplied by the 1.5 beta equals 3 percent); in addition, and independent of the market, the stock tends to produce a return of 1 percent; thus 3 percent plus 1 percent equals 4 percent. Alphas can be positive, negative, or zero. (Beta can be negative as well; that is, a stock could rise when the market falls, and vice versa, but this is highly unusual).[42]

---

[42] It is widely believed that gold stocks react contra to a down market, especially when such a movement is caused by concern over international monetary conditions. In a recent listing of betas for 5,148 securities, not one was shown to have a negative beta; three New York Stock Exchange gold mining stocks had an average beta of .169, which is very low. This is why it can be said that market risk is not diversifiable. The only feasible way to hedge against market risk, in the absence of many negative-beta stocks, would be to sell short. See Edward A. Dyl, "Negative Betas: The Attraction of Selling Short," *The Journal of Portfolio Management*, Spring 1975.

3. In the preceding paragraphs, the words "on average" were stressed. This is because the relationship between the returns on the stock and the returns on the market is not perfectly consistent in each and every month. If it was, all of the Xs would fall on the line of regression. But, clearly, they do not. Indeed, none do in this case. The line of regression merely represents the average relationship. As described in the Appendix to Chapter 5, statisticians have a measure of the extent to which the individual observations deviate from the line of average relationship. It is called "rho," the correlation coefficient, or rho-squared, the coefficient of determination.[43]

Rho is equal to 100 percent when all the observations fall on the line of regression. This would mean that all of the variability in the return on the stock is explained by the returns on the market. As the observations deviate from the line, rho declines. A total absence of any (linear) relationship between the stock's returns and the market's returns would be indicated by a rho of zero percent.

At this point, modern analysts take a giant step. They recognize that any one stock can have a substantial positive or negative alpha, and can have a fairly low rho. But they argue that as we combine many stocks into a portfolio—i.e., as we "diversify"—the relationship between the portfolio's opportunity returns and the market's opportunity returns becomes much closer than the relationship between the returns on any individual stock in that portfolio and the returns on the market. In other words, rho moves toward 100 percent. Moreover, they argue, the positive alphas of some of the individual stocks in the portfolio tend to be offset by the negative alphas of other stocks in the portfolio. As a result, the alpha of the total diversified portfolio tends toward zero.

At a later point, some questions will be raised about the assumption that portfolio alphas tend toward zero. However, once this assumption is made, together with the less questionable assumption that portfolio rhos tend toward 100 percent, it becomes clear that the opportunity return on a portfolio is essentially a function of the portfolio's beta times whatever "the market's" opportunity return happens to be. Beta becomes the most important determinant of the portfolio's opportunity return, given the movement of the market (which the portfolio manager cannot control).

---

[43] In the Appendix to Chapter 5, rho was described as expressing the relationship between (1) the standard error of estimate of a regression of Y against X, and (2) the variance of Y. Another way of describing rho is as an expression of the relationship between (1) the covariance of X and Y, and (2) the product of the standard deviations of X and Y. See Jerome L. Valentine and Edmund A. Mennis, *Quantitative Techniques for Financial Analysis* (Homewood, Ill.: Richard D. Irwin, Inc., 1971), p. 85–87.

In addition, it can be shown that the standard deviation of a portfolio's opportunity returns over time is a function of the portfolio's beta and the standard deviation of the market's opportunity returns.

Thus the argument has progressed as follows:

1. Risk refers to the frequency and average value of opportunity losses.
2. The frequency and average value of opportunity losses are functions of average opportunity returns and the standard deviation of period-to-period returns about the average.
3. The dominant factors explaining the average return and the standard deviation of returns for an individual asset, *insofar as the asset is viewed as a component of a portfolio*, are the asset's beta and the behavior of "the market."
4. Since the behavior of the market is outside the control of the portfolio manager, the contribution of an individual asset to the total risk of a portfolio is measured by the beta of that asset.
5. The comparative risks of alternative well-diversified portfolios can be measured by comparing their betas.

A growing number of "beta" measurement services, which offer calculated coefficients on virtually every widely traded security, are presently available to institutional investors. It is worthwhile to present some samples of such material.

However, it is necessary to note at this point that the concepts and techniques just discussed, and illustrated by these available services, are not universally accepted. This is true of both practicing portfolio managers and academicians. Despite the growing incorporation of these general principles into actual investment management practices (to be discussed in Chapter 17), the general methodology underlying capital asset pricing analysis is viewed by some observers with basic distrust. More precisely, substantial skepticism exists as to whether the two components of a stock's price movement, alpha and beta, can, in actual practice, be separated. There is no question that it can be done *statistically,* but whether the statistics truly measure what they are supposed to measure is a subject of debate. We shall consider the arguments in this debate at a later point.

We have chosen for illustration pages from Merrill Lynch, Pierce, Fenner & Smith's Security Risk Evaluation Service and The Value Line Investment Survey, two widely used beta sources available to institutional portfolio managers in return for brokerage commissions (Figure 15–6).[44]

Merrill Lynch calculates its betas by using linear regression tech-

---

[44] The Value Line Service is available to individual investors for a fairly modest fee.

FIGURE 15–6
a. Merrill Lynch, Pierce, Fenner & Smith Inc.—Market Sensitivity Statistics*

TKR SYMB	SECURITY NAME	07/75 CLOSE PRICE	BETA	ALPHA	R-SQR	RESID DEV-N	STD.ERR. STD OF BETA	STD.ERR. OF ALPHA	ADJUSTED BETA	NUMBER OF OBSERV
ABI	AM BUSINESS PRODS IN	10.750	1.25	2.39	.19	12.20	.32	1.58	1.17	60
AC	AMERICAN CAN CO	29.375	.54	-.55	.21	5.13	.13	.66	.70	60
ACT!	AMER CENTY MTG INV	2.000	1.92	-2.41	.17	20.35	.53	2.63	1.61	60
ACM7	AMER CENTY MTG I.W .	.250	2.18	-3.59	.15	25.79	.73	3.84	1.78	45
ACN	AMERN CHAIN & CABLE	16.250	1.10	-.66	.44	6.03	.16	.78	1.06	60
GCM	AMERN COMWLTH FINL C	4.500	1.81	1.21	.16	19.91	.52	2.58	1.54	60
AMCS	AMER COMMTY SYS INC	.625	.74	-.43	.02	36.46	1.12	6.71	.83	30
ACA	AMER CONSUMER INDS	5.250	.27	-.37	.00	8.84	.30	1.14	.52	60
AHM1	AMER CONTL HOMES INC	2.250	1.76	-.46	.11	24.94	.70	3.76	1.51	44
ACIN	AMERN CONTROLLED IND	5.250	.12	-.07	.03	10.49	.31	1.90	.42	31
ACY	AMERICAN CYANAMID CO	25.250	1.04	-.37	.42	5.99	.16	.78	1.03	60
ADC	AMERICAN DISTILLING	8.000	1.50	-1.09	.34	10.24	.27	1.32	1.33	60
ADT	AMERICAN DIST TELEG	23.375	1.64	.14	.39	9.94	.26	1.29	1.42	60
ADV	AMERICAN DUALVES.F .	4.375	1.45	-.89	.45	7.92	.21	1.02	1.30	60
AEP	AMERICAN ELEC PWR IN	19.750	.77	-.39	.27	6.12	.16	.79	.85	60

*BASED ON S&P 500 INDEX, USING STRAIGHT REGRESSION

b. Value Line Investment Survey—Summary of Advices and Index

NAME OF STOCK	Ticker Symbol	Recent Price	Performance Rank	Rank for Safety	Beta	Estimated Range of 3-5 yr. average prices 1978-80	Current P/E Ratio	Est'd Yield next 12 mos.	Est'd Earns. 12 mos. 9-30-76	Est'd Div'd next mos.	Qtr. Ended	Earns. Per Sh.	Year Ago	Qtr. Ended	Latest Div'd	Year Ago
955 AMER.CAN	AC	33	3	2	.75	48– 66 (45-100%)	6.9	7.3%	4.75	2.40	3/31	◆.96	.82	6/30	.55	.55
1987 AMER.CEN.MTG.INV.	ACT	1¾	3	5	1.15	4– 8(150-400%)	NMF	NIL	d2.75	NIL	12/31	d1.05	d2.41	3/31	NIL	NIL
1440 AMER. CHAIN & CABLE						ACQUIRED BY BABCOCK&WILCOX LTD.OF LONDON										
557 AMER.CYANAMID	ACY	25	4	2	1.10	48– 64 (90-155%)	8.1	6.0%	3.10	1.50	3/31	◆.76	.81	3/31	.375	.375
343 AMER. DISTILLING	ADC	9¼	3	4	.70	20– 32(120-250%)	8.3	NIL	1.10	NIL	12/31	.36	.13	3/31	NIL	.125
354 AMER. DIST. TELEGRAPH	ADT	24	3	3	1.10	36– 54 (50-125%)	10.3	2.8%	2.33	.66	12/31	.60	.57	3/31	▲.16	.13
2001 AMER. DUALVEST (CAP.)	ADV	6¼	2	4	1.30	11– 17 (75-170%)	NMF	NIL	NMF	NIL	12/31	6.05(q)	3.67(q)	3/31	NIL	NIL
706 AMER. ELEC. POWER	AEP	23	▼4	2	.80	35– 47 (50-105%)	8.6	8.7%	2.67	2.00(c)	12/31	.57	.54	3/31	.50	.50
1819 AMER.EXPRESS	(OTC) AEXP	32	4	3	1.50	70–156(120-230%)	12.6	3.1%	2.54	1.00	12/31	.54	.50	6/30	.20	.20
1125 AMER.FAMILY CORP.	AFL	13	2	4	1.30	34– 56(160-330%)	6.3	2.2%	2.06	.29	12/31	.47	.38	3/31	.07	.06

▲ Arrow indicates the direction of a change. When it appears with the Latest Dividend, the arrow signals that a change in the regular payment rate has occurred in the latest quarter. For Performance Rank, Estimated Range of 3- to 5-year average prices 1978-80, or Estimated Earnings 12 months to 9-30-76, the arrow indicates a change since the preceding week. When a diamond ◆ (indicating a new figure) appears alongside the latest quarterly earnings results, the rank change probably was primarily caused by the earnings report. In other cases, the change is due to the dynamics of the ranking system and could simply be the result of the improvement or weakening of other stocks.
◆ New figure this week.
(a) Excludes distribution of capital gains, if any.
(b) Canadian Funds.
(c) Dividends estimated partly exempt from ordinary income tax.
d Deficit.
(e) All data adjusted for announced stock split or stock dividend.
(f) The estimate may reflect a probable increase or decrease. If a

dividend boost or cut is possible but not probable, two figures are shown; the first is the most likely.
(g) Dividends subject to Canadian withholding tax for non-residents.
(h) Rank removed due to merger involvement.
(j) Trading suspended.
(k) 12 months. (r) 9 months. (p) 6 months.
(q) Asset value. (r) Estimates.
(s) Rank removed due to outstanding exchange offer.
N Negative figure. NA Not available.
NC Not comparable. NMF No meaningful figure.

niques based upon five years of monthly return information, using the Standard & Poor's Stock Price Index as a proxy for the market. Its betas are adjusted for a "regression" bias, which has a tendency to overestimate high beta stocks and underestimate low-beta stocks.

Betas presented by Value Line are derived from a least squares regression analysis between weekly percent changes in the price of a stock and weekly percent changes in the New York Stock Exchange index over a period of five years. Where five years of data are not available, a smaller time period is used, but never less than two years.

Other services may, and do, choose different periods and present somewhat different coefficients for the same securities. Obviously, one can choose whatever period for measurement desired, although evidence suggests that the longer the base time period used, the greater the amount of variance that will be explained by general market movements. In other words, the rho increases as the time period lengthens. (Some people mistakenly believe that a high rho implies an alpha near zero. This is a failure to recognize that rho measures only

the degree to which the points lie close to the regression line—i.e., the variance of Y is explained by the variance of X. It says nothing about the alpha, which is a "constant" and merely sets the *level* of the regression line.)

This lack of conformity has created some confusion for investors seriously interested in using such statistics in portfolio planning or stock selection procedures. The problem arises because the use of different base periods results in the calculation of different beta coefficients for the same security. For example, a beta coefficient might be derived from weekly observations over a three-year period (approximately 150 data pairs) or from monthly data observations over 12 years (144 pairs). However, it is doubtful that the beta coefficient (or the alpha and rho) in each case would be the same.

To illustrate this point, we have abstracted the beta coefficients for each of the 30 Dow Jones Industrial stocks from four different beta services (see Table 15–2). Notice the relatively wide discrepancies which appear for several of the individual issues and the differences in the average beta for all 30 stocks. For instance, Bethlehem Steel has a beta range of .88 (Datagraphs) to 1.16 (Merrill Lynch). In the first case, the stock would be considered less sensitive to general market movements than in the second, where it appears to be one of the slightly volatile components of the average. Several stocks appear in both the Merrill Lynch and Value Line pages selected for Figure 15–6. Just for fun, compare their respective beta values.

Betas and Basics. Another argument used by some practitioners as an excuse to reject betas as a measure of risk is the claim that beta relates only to relative stock price movements and not to the fundamental business and financial features of the company. This argument prompted several researchers to investigate the relationship of betas to fundamental security analysis considerations.

Professors Beaver, Kettler, and Scholes conducted the first important study by determining the relationship between accounting and market measures of risk. Their findings strongly suggests that accounting measures of risk[45] such as dividend payout ratios, capitalization ratios, and asset size are in fact impounded in market price risk measures. More to the point, they also concluded that "a strategy of selecting and ranking portfolios according to the accounting risk measures is essentially equivalent to the strategy of ranking these same portfolios according to the market determined risk measures."[46]

---

[45] The use of such relationships as a measure of risk is justified on the premise that they explain, or at least account for, the uncertainty associated with the earnings (or return) pattern exhibited by the company (or common stock).

[46] William Beaver, Paul Kettler, and Myron Scholes, "The Association between Market Determined and Accounting Determined Risk Measures," *The Accounting Review*, October 1970.

TABLE 15–2
Example of Differences in Calculated Betas

	Value Line	University of Pennsylvania	Datagraphs	Merrill Lynch
Allied Chemical	1.10	1.14	1.26	1.09
Aluminum Co.	1.05	0.64	0.83	0.68
American Brands	0.85	0.71	0.71	0.87
American Can	0.80	0.58	0.41	0.54
Amer. Tel. & Tel.	0.75	0.67	0.60	0.62
Anaconda	1.20	1.17	0.83	1.25
Bethlehem Steel	1.05	1.11	0.88	1.16
Chrysler	1.25	1.38	1.22	1.30
Du Pont	1.00	0.58	1.06	0.84
Eastman Kodak	1.10	0.90	1.33	1.02
Esmark	0.95	0.82	1.02	0.89
Exxon	0.95	0.68	0.90	0.81
General Electric	1.10	1.17	1.19	1.29
General Foods	0.95	0.93	0.95	1.00
General Motors	1.05	0.82	0.82	0.86
Goodyear	1.10	1.01	0.95	1.07
Int'l Harvester	1.05	0.87	1.06	0.94
Int'l Nickel	0.90	n.c.	0.86	1.01
Int'l Paper	1.10	0.98	1.02	1.00
Johns-Manville	1.00	0.86	0.88	0.91
Owens Illinois	0.90	1.09	1.11	1.06
Procter & Gamble	1.00	1.04	0.80	0.85
Sears, Roebuck	1.10	0.99	1.14	1.02
Standard Oil, Calif.	1.05	0.86	0.95	1.03
Texaco	0.95	0.82	0.79	0.88
Union Carbide	1.15	1.20	1.19	1.25
United Technologies	0.95	0.94	0.77	0.92
U.S. Steel	1.05	0.90	0.82	0.96
Westinghouse Elec.	1.15	0.76	1.02	0.89
Woolworth	1.05	1.00	0.98	1.02
Average	1.02	0.92	0.95	0.97

n.c. = Not calculated: averages for 29 issues.
Sources: The Value Line Investment Survey; University of Pennsylvania; William O'Neil's Datagraphs; Merrill Lynch, Pierce, Fenner & Smith's Security Risk Evaluation.

These same conclusions were confirmed by several later studies[47] including one which related common stock systematic risk (beta) to

[47] Barr Rosenberg and James Guy "Predication of Beta From Investment Fundamentals" *Financial Analysts Journal*, July/August 1976, p. 62–70. See also Uri Ben-Zion and Sol S. Shalit, "Size, Leverage, and Dividend Record as Determinants of Equity Risk," *Journal of Finance*, September 1975; Carl J. Schwendiman and George E. Pinches, "An Analysis of Alternative Measures of Investment Risk," *Journal of Finance*, March 1975; William J. Breen and Eugene M. Lerner, "Corporate Financial Strategies and Market Measures of Risk and Return," *Journal of Finance*, May 1973; Barr Rosenberg and Walt McKibben, "The Prediction of Systematic and Specific Risk in Common Stocks," *Journal of Financial and Quantitative Analysis*, March 1973.

corporate bond ratings. In this case, increasing beta values were consistently associated with decreasing bond quality ratings as shown in Table 15–3.

TABLE 15–3
Common Stock Betas and Bond Quality Ratings

Bond Quality Rating	Common Stock Beta
Aaa	.593
Aa	.674
A	.816
Baa	1.046
Ba	1.160
B	1.430

Source: Carl J. Schwendiman and George E. Pinches, "An Analysis of Alternative Measures of Investment Risk," *Journal of Finance*, March 1975, p. 197.

Thus, it turns out that the same economic determinants that cause a stock to be risky in the ordinary sense of the word also cause it to be high in systematic risk, that is, high in beta.[48] It is therefore safe to conclude that beta calculations are a legitimate portrayer of investment risk, at least relatively, if not precisely. Furthermore, there is evidence that professional investors' *perception* of risk is quite in accord with the statistical measures of risk we have been discussing.[49]

Portfolio Risk

Perusal of the sample page from Merrill Lynch's Security Risk Evaluation immediately indicates that individual issues can carry both positive and negative alpha coefficients. At the same time, market movements explain varying proportions of individual stock price changes. We have already indicated that the statistical reliability of these specific stock calculations (the rho coefficients) tends to be limited. Research studies have shown that, in the general case, the market influence accounts for between 20 percent and 30 percent of an individual stock's price change over time, while company and industry factors; i.e., specific risk, contribute the remainder.[50] However, the process of combining several (or many) individual issues into a

---

[48] William L. Fouse, William W. Jahnke, and Barr Rosenberg, "Is Beta Phlogiston?" *Financial Analysts Journal*, January/February 1974.

[49] J. G. McDonald and R. E. Stehle, "How Do Institutional Investors Perceive Risk?" *The Journal of Portfolio Management*, Fall 1975.

[50] Merrill Lynch, Pierce, Fenner & Smith Inc., *Investment Performance Analysis*, July 1975, Appendix D.

portfolio—thereby diversifying holdings[51]—has the effect of increasing the proportion of variance explained by general market price changes. That is, the coefficient rho is increased, and the reliability of portfolio betas is substantially greater than of stock betas.

Merrill Lynch notes on this point, "In a typical, diversified investment portfolio of thirty or more common stocks, diversification eliminates so much of the specific risk that roughly 85–95 percent of all the risk (in the portfolio) is market risk and only 5–15 percent is specific risk."[52]

Diversification reduces the nonmarket element of portfolio risk. As the process continues, the positive variations in returns caused by the specific elements of some of the holdings tend to be offset by the negative specific variations in returns of other holdings. At the point where the volatility of portfolio holdings exactly mirrors that of the market index (rho equals 100 percent), any change in the overall price level will be reflected in portfolio values in proportion to the beta coefficient of the portfolio. (It should be remembered that the portfolio can still have a positive or a negative alpha coefficient despite this relationship.) Although perfect correlation between portfolio returns and market returns is rarely the case, the variability of the market's returns will explain more than 85 percent of the variability in most portfolio returns.

At these levels of relationship between the portfolio and the market, much of the nonmarket risk associated with individual security price movements is eliminated. Consequently, as noted earlier, the return and price variance of the portfolio then becomes essentially a function of the portfolio's beta coefficient multiplied by the market's opportunity return and variance over a given time period.

It should be noted that the market sensitivity of a portfolio (its beta coefficient) can be derived either by regressing portfolio returns against market returns or, alternatively, by calculating the weighted average of the market sensitivities of its component securities, using the relative values as weights. The two procedures often produce somewhat different results because the latter takes the portfolio composition at a specific point in time where as the former reflects a changing composition. An example of the latter procedure is shown in Table 15–4.

---

[51] James H. Lorie recently noted, "Before the development of the modern theory of investment, investors relied on either of two homilies for guidance in diversifying their portfolios. The first is 'don't put all of your eggs in one basket!' The second is, 'put all your eggs in one basket and watch it carefully." These homilies, according to Lorie, suffer from obvious deficiencies, including but not limited to the facts that they are contradictory and have no precise operating meaning. See James H. Lorie, "Diversification: Old and New," *The Journal of Portfolio Management*, Winter 1975, p. 25.

[52] Merrill Lynch, Pierce, Fenner & Smith Inc., *Investment Performance Analysis*, Appendix D.

TABLE 15–4
Calculation of a Portfolio's Estimated Market Sensitivity

Security	Current Market Price per Share	Number of Shares in Portfolio	Current Market Value	Percent of Portfolio	Estimated Market Sensitivity	Portfolio Weight times Market Sensitivity
ABC	$13.00	1,000	$13,000	.325	.80	.26
DEF	50.00	300	15,000	.375	1.20	.45
GHI	30.00	400	12,000	.300	1.30	.39
			$40,000	1.000		1.10*

* Portfolio estimated market sensitivity.

Regardless of the method of calculation, it is argued that the portfolio's beta becomes a measure of "risk" relative to the market, and the beta coefficient of alternative portfolios can be used to measure their comparative "riskiness." As a result, Sharpe's "market line" can be relabeled as shown in Figure 15–7.

FIGURE 15–7
The Shift from Total Variance to Beta as a Measure of Risk

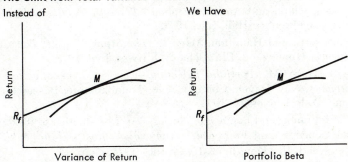

Concluding Comments

The major lines of thought presented in this chapter are:
1. Markowitz's *Efficient Frontier* is a risk/return trade-off curve. This is a set of alternative portfolios each of which is most "efficient" in that it provides maximum expected return at its level of risk. The investor's own risk attitude dictates precisely what point on the curve is best for him or her.
2. Sharpe's *Efficient Market* concept builds upon the random-walk hypothesis regarding stock price movement. This hypothesis views the security trading mechanism as a highly efficient processor of new information, which enters the marketplace in random fashion. In this type of environment, Sharpe argues, the market itself represents

the optimal risky portfolio. Consequently, the investor's risk attitudes should be reflected by borrowing or lending against this optimal risky portfolio rather than by creating different risky portfolios for different investors.

3. The next major development in *capital asset pricing* theory was to move from total variance to "beta" as the principal measure of risk. Beta reflects that part of a portfolio's returns, and variation in returns, which is attributable to the overall movement of the market rather than to any unique characteristics of the portfolio.

SUGGESTED READINGS

Blume, Marshall E. "On the Assessment of Risk." *Journal of Finance,* March 1971.

Brealey, Richard A. *An Introduction to Risk and Return from Common Stocks.* Cambridge, Mass.: M.I.T. Press, 1969.

Fama, Eugene F. "Efficient Capital Markets: A Review of Theory and Empirical Work," *Journal of Finance,* May 1970.

The Financial Analysts Research Foundation. "Is Financial Analysis Useless?" *The Proceedings of a Seminar on the Efficient Capital Market and Random Walk Hypotheses,* Charlottesville, Va., 1975.

Francis, Jack Clark, and Archer, Stephen. *Portfolio Analysis.* Englewood Cliffs, N.J.: Prentice-Hall, Inc., 1971.

Lorie, James H., and Hamilton, Mary T. *The Stock Market: Theories and Evidence.* Homewood, Ill.: Richard D. Irwin, Inc., 1973.

Markowitz, Harry M. *Portfolio Selection—Efficient Diversification of Investments.* New Haven, Conn.: Cowles Foundation for Research in Economics, Yale University, 1959.

Modigliani, Franco, and Pogue, Gerald A. "An Introduction to Risk and Return: Concepts and Evidence," *Financial Analyst's Handbook,* vol. I. Homewood, Ill.: Dow Jones-Irwin, Inc., 1975, chap. 44.

Sharpe, William F. *Portfolio Theory and Capital Markets.* New York: McGraw-Hill Book Co., 1970.

Valentine, Jerome L. *Financial Analysis and Capital Market Theory.* Charlottesville, Va.: Financial Analysts Research Foundation, 1974.

REVIEW QUESTIONS AND PROBLEMS

1. What are the basic ingredients of the Markowitz theory?
2. What are the contributions attributed to the Markowitz theory? What are some of the criticisms?
3. What conditions generally characterize the capital asset pricing theory?
4. What is the random-walk hypothesis? Do you agree with it? Why? Why not?

5. How does the capital asset pricing theory measure risk?
6. What do alpha, beta, and rho represent in terms of capital asset pricing theory?
7. Describe portfolio diversification in terms of modern portfolio theory.
8. What are the basic elements of investment return?
9. What is the difference between market risk and specific risk?
10. Describe the relationship between corporate "fundamentals" and beta. Why do you think this relationship exists?

RESEARCH PROJECTS

1. Calculate the "beta" of a large mutual fund portfolio, and see how it compares with the investment objectives of the fund as stated in its prospectus.
2. Communicate with one of the "beta" services and ascertain the alpha and beta coefficients for each of the 30 Dow Jones Industrial stocks. Indicate how and why these differ from those in the text on page 690.
3. Create an efficient frontier for a five stock portfolio using any of the Dow Jones Industrial issues.
4. Determine the "market lines" during recent peak and trough periods of stock prices. Are the slopes of the lines what you would have expected? Explain any differences.
5. Select five leading companies in different industries and calculate various "fundamental measures of risk" (e.g., debt/equity ratio). Compare these measures with the betas of the companies' stocks and discuss similarities and differences.

C.F.A. QUESTIONS

1. *From Exam II, 1975*

In his book, *An Introduction to Risk and Return from Common Stocks*, Brealey points out that portfolio risk is a function of three different factors:

1. The riskiness of each individual holding.
2. The number of holdings.
3. The degree to which the risks are independent of each other.

Review these concepts as they apply to a trust account with a current market value of $1 million. Of this amount, half is in fixed-income securities, and the remainder is divided equally among ten stocks: American Telephone & Telegraph, Bethlehem Steel, Exxon, General Foods, General Motors, International Business Machines, Mobil, Sears Roebuck, Texaco, and Xerox.

2. *From Exam III, 1974*

Suppose a market index (Standard and Poor's 425 Industrials) is likely to produce an annual average return of about 9 percent over a long period of

time. Year-to-year fluctuations might range between +30 percent and −20 percent. Assume risk-free investment opportunities will average 5 percent. A fund wishes to strive for a return that is 11 percent "better than the market" over the long term, or 10 percent per year $(0.09 \times 1.11 = 0.10)$.

a. Calculate the average beta level for the portfolio that would be required to meet the 10 percent per year goal.
b. Assume the following conditions in a given year: (1) portfolio beta level of 1.5, (2) market index decline of 15 percent, and (3) risk free rate of 4 percent. Calculate the expected return for the fund under these conditions.

Chapter 16

Portfolio Theory II: Measuring Investment Performance

> Is it not strange that desire should so
> many years outlive performance?
> ———————*William Shakespeare*

Capital asset pricing theorists argue that their view of the world provides an improved ability to measure the performance of competing investment managers. For, if the beta coefficient of a portfolio is used as a measure of its relative risk, the actual rate of return earned by the portfolio can be compared to hypothetical rates of return from portfolios of similar risk. This provides insight as to whether or not investment managers have selected commitments which outperform "unmanaged" portfolios of similar risk. In addition, by observing whether portfolio managers periodically *change* the risk orientation of their portfolios, it becomes possible to separate performance results into the portion derived from stock selection capability and the portion derived from the effectiveness of timing decisions.

Measurement Procedures

Figure 16–1 illustrates the so-called "market line" by which capital market theorists represent the risk and return levels of hypothetical unmanaged portfolios. It is assumed that the time horizon is one year, that the risk-free rate was 5 percent, and that the S&P 500 Index

FIGURE 16–1

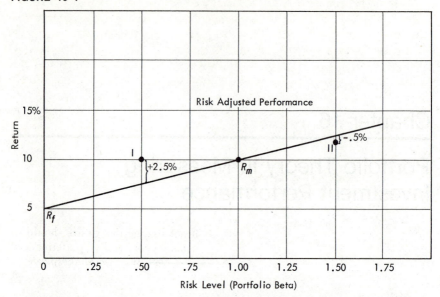

Risk Adjusted Performance

Risk Level (Portfolio Beta)

produced a total return of 10 percent during the year.[1] Also shown on the figure are the one-year returns of two assumed "real-life" portfolios, one (I) with a beta of 0.50 and a return of 10 percent, and the other (II) with a beta of 1.5 and a return of 12 percent.

The market line formula for calculating expected portfolio return is:

$$R_p = R_f + B(R_m - R_f)$$

Where

R_p = Return of the portfolio.
R_f = Return of risk-free investment during the measurement period.
B = Portfolio beta coefficient.
R_m = Return of the market during the measurement period.

---

[1] The market line indicates hypothetical returns of unmanaged portfolios by conceiving of a portfolio manager who borrows (or lends) at the risk free rate and reinvests in a market index. The following represents the technique in tabular form.

Portfolio Beta	Percent Invested in Risk-Free Assets		Percent Invested in Market Index
0.0		100%	0%
0.25	*lending*	75	25
0.50		50	50
0.75		25	75
1.00		0	100
1.25	*borrowing*	−25	125
1.50		−50	150

Therefore, portfolio I should have returned 7.5 percent [5% + 0.5 (10% − 5%)], but actually returned 10 percent. Its risk-adjusted performance can be considered plus 2.5 percent, the difference between the actual return and the estimated return.

Portfolio II, on the other hand, which had a beta coefficient of 1.5, and should have returned 12.5 percent [5% + 1.5 (10% − 5%)], achieved a 12 percent rate of return. Its risk-adjusted performance is −0.5 percent.

The same technique can be applied when the market index declines. In both rising and falling markets, we can consider portfolio returns lying above the market line as representing "better than market" risk-adjusted performance, while those lying below represent "less than market" achievement, on a risk-adjusted basis. In other words, the distance between actual returns and the market line can be used to measure risk-adjusted performance and to compare portfolios with different risk levels developed by actual portfolio decisions (although the observer should be cognizant that these may have been different from prescribed investment objectives). The technique provides a framework for trustees and others to compare the results of different managers, and for managers to compare the results of different portfolios under their supervision, which may be managed with varying investment guidelines.[2]

It should be noted, however, that there are other dimensions to portfolio evaluation. It is quite clear that, in absolute terms, portfolio II earned 2 percentage points more than portfolio I, and over a few years the difference of such achievement compounds dramatically. Perhaps the best judgment that can be made is that the difference in performance achievement of portfolio II versus I was not commensurate with the risk level undertaken to achieve the superior results. But we should not ignore one manager's willingness to assume a higher risk level in the quest for higher returns. This, of course, assumes that the higher beta portfolio was constructed as the result of conscious planning, and was not the accidental product of some other stock selection policy. It would do no real good to make note of a manager's willingness to assume a higher risk level if he backed into such a position without serious forethought.

Internal versus Time-Weighted Rate of Return. In order to apply the measurement technique just described, it is necessary first to calculate a portfolio's periodic rate of return. This often is a complicated

---

[2] It is also significant to point out that the SEC has endorsed these general market line procedures for the calculation of risk-adjusted performance. See Securities and Exchange Commission, *Institutional Investor Study Report* (Washington, D.C.: U.S. Government Printing Office, 1971), vol. I, p. 408.

procedure, however, because most individuals and institutions, other than mutual funds, do not express their assets in terms of unit values whose percentage change can be simply calculated. Therefore, pension fund trustees, and others whose portfolios experience periodic cash flow changes, employ two different rate of return calculations. One is designed to measure portfolio earnings, and the other to measure the effectiveness of investment management decisions.

The first method, the internal rate of return (or dollar weighted rate of return), provides an indication of the performance of the fund itself, but not necessarily the performance of the fund manager. This arises because some factors that influence the performance of a fund are not under the control of the fund manager. The most important factor is the timing and amount of cash flows to and from the portfolio.

The internal rate of return is the compound interest rate which equates all of the cash flows of the fund with the terminal value of the fund. It allows trustees and corporate officials to determine whether or not the return on invested assets is adequate to meet the requirements of the fund—such as the actuarial assumption of a pension fund or of a life insurance company, or the expenditure program of a university endowment fund.

The second method, called the time-weighted rate of return, is insensitive to the timing and amount of cash flows. It is equivalent to the return which would be calculated on the basis of unit values. Therefore, it can be used to measure the comparative performance of different investment managers. According to the Bank Administration Institute (BAI), which did a pioneering study of performance measurement techniques,[3] "The time-weighted rate of return is computed ideally by dividing the interval under study into subintervals whose boundaries are the dates of cash flows into and out of the fund and by computing the internal rate of return for each subinterval. The time-weighted rate of return is the average of the rates for these subintervals, with each rate having a weight proportional to the length of time in its corresponding subinterval." The calculation requires (a) the value of the fund at the beginning and the end of the period being evaluated, (b) the date and amount of each cash flow, and (c) the value of the fund at the date of each cash flow.

The BAI recommended calculating the time-weighted rate of return at the end of each calendar quarter by making precise valuations of the fund's assets at these times and whenever there is a cash flow equal to more than 10 percent of total assets. Calendar quarters were suggested to facilitate interfund comparisons.

---

[3] Bank Administration Institute, *Measuring the Investment Performance of Pension Funds* (Park Ridge, Ill., 1968).

As an aside, it may be noted that the BAI study recommended that "risk" be measured by the "mean absolute deviation" rather than the more familiar variance or standard deviation. The derivation of this calculation is illustrated below.

Assume that a pension fund (or other) portfolio's rate of return for 197X consisted of the following four quarterly results

Quarter Ended	Actual Return
March 31, 197X	+ 5.0%
June 30, 197X	− 3.0
September 30, 197X	+12.0
December 31, 197X	+ 6.0
Average Quarterly Return (20% ÷ 4)	5.0%

The mean absolute deviation would be calculated as follows:

Quarter Ended	Actual Return	Average Quarterly Return	Absolute Deviation
March 31, 197X	+ 5.0%	5.0%	0%
June 30, 197X	− 3.0	5.0	8.0
September 30, 197X	+12.0	5.0	7.0
December 31, 197X	+ 6.0	5.0	1.0
			16.0%
Mean Absolute Deviation = (16.0% ÷ 4) = ...			4.0%

Illustrations. A number of commercial services have been developed to measure portfolio performance, including the services offered to institutional clients by Merrill Lynch, Pierce, Fenner & Smith Inc., Becker Securities, Wertheim & Co., Inc., and Computer Directions Advisors Inc. Since the basic idea behind most of these is similar, we have chosen only one—the Merrill Lynch service—as an example.

The Merrill Lynch service begins by calculating the excess return, or return in excess of the Treasury bill rate, earned by both the portfolio and the market (Standard & Poor's 500) during the measurement period.[4] A scatter diagram (Figure 16–2) is prepared, on which the market's excess return is plotted on the horizontal axis and the portfolio's excess return is plotted on the vertical axis. A line of regression, or *characteristic line*, is then fitted to the data. The slope of the line measures the average sensitivity of the portfolio to changes in market levels—the beta coefficient (1.17 in the illustration). The diversification factor (95 percent) indicates the closeness of the relationship

---

[4] The report actually contains several separate sections covering the analysis of fixed-income securities, equities, cash, and the total portfolio. For our example we have chosen to discuss only the equities section of a typical report. The portfolio returns are, of course, "time-weighted" in cases where cash flows exist and there are no unit values.

FIGURE 16–2
Characteristic Line of Excess Returns

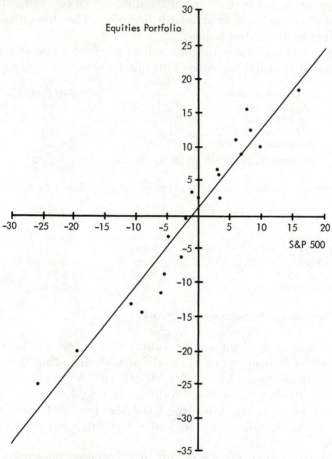

Market sensitivity = 1.17
Average differential return = 1.2%
Annual equivalent = 4.6%
Percent of portfolio fluctuations explained by market movement = 95%
Source: Merrill Lynch, Pierce, Fenner & Smith Inc.

between movement in the portfolio and movement in the market. It is the coefficient of determination (r^2) described in Chapter 15.

The intercept, or alpha, of the characteristic line (the point where it crosses the vertical axis) measures the expected return for the portfolio when the market's excess return is zero (in the example, it is 1.2 percent quarterly, or 4.6 percent expressed on an annual basis). It is also used as a measure of a manager's "performance," i.e., the average gain achieved by the portfolio once the impact of risk policy (beta) and the behavior of the market have been eliminated. The higher this number, the better. A measure near zero indicates that management's skill

neither significantly enhanced nor detracted from the portfolio's return.

This first phase of the analysis thus summarizes the portfolio results for the full period being measured. The next step is to examine each quarter's results separately. This is accomplished by calculating the difference each quarter between the fund's actual return and the return which would have been achieved by an unmanaged fund of equivalent risk. The calculations are shown in Table 16–1. Consider, for example, the first quarter of 1970.

TABLE 16–1
Analysis of Portfolio Returns (all data are percentages)

Quarter Ended	(1) S&P 500 Return	(2) Treasury Bill Return	(3) Return Due to Market	(4) Differ- ential Return	(5) Total Equities Return
3/1970	− 1.8	2.1	− 2.4	− 2.2	− 4.6
6/1970	−18.0	1.6	−21.3	2.4	−18.9
9/1970	16.9	1.6	19.5	0.2	19.7
12/1970	10.4	1.5	11.9	−0.7	11.2
3/1971	9.7	1.2	11.1	5.1	16.2
6/1971	0.2	0.9	0.0	3.7	3.7
9/1971	− 0.6	1.3	− 0.9	1.6	0.7
12/1971	4.6	1.2	5.2	−1.6	3.6
3/1972	5.8	0.9	6.6	4.9	11.5
6/1972	0.7	1.0	0.6	2.5	3.2
9/1972	3.9	1.0	4.4	2.2	6.7
12/1972	7.6	1.2	8.6	1.2	9.8
3/1973	− 4.9	1.3	− 5.9	−2.1	− 8.0
6/1973	− 5.8	1.7	− 7.0	−3.4	−10.4
9/1973	4.8	2.0	5.3	2.9	8.2
12/1973	− 9.2	1.8	−11.0	−0.7	−11.7
3/1974	− 2.8	1.9	− 3.6	2.0	− 1.7
6/1974	− 7.6	2.1	− 9.2	−3.5	−12.7
9/1974	−25.2	2.0	−29.7	6.1	−23.6
12/1974	9.4	1.6	10.7	3.0	13.7

Source: Merrill Lynch, Pierce, Fenner & Smith Inc.

The S&P 500 produced a return of −1.8 percent (column 1). The return of an unmanaged fund with beta 1.17 and a risk-free rate of 2.1 percent would be −2.46 percent, derived as follows:

$$R_p = R_f + B(R_m - R_f)$$
$$= 2.1 + 1.17(-1.8 - 2.1)$$
$$= 2.1 - 4.56$$
$$= -2.46 \text{ (which has been rounded down to } -2.4 \text{ in column 3)}$$

Since the fund actually earned −4.6 percent (column 5), the differential is −2.2 percent (column 4). The differential was due to the total impact of both stock selection decisions and management's variation of the fund's beta around the average level of 1.17. The average differential return for the 20-quarter period was 1.2 percent, which is another way of expressing the alpha.

In those instances where sufficient data are available, the typical Merrill Lynch performance report contains a quarter-by-quarter measurement of the portfolio's beta. This shows whether there was any attempt to vary the portfolio's market sensitivity in an effort to capitalize upon expected bull or bear movements of the market. If the beta for any quarter was roughly the same as the average beta for the full period, the differential return for that quarter can be attributed to the specific stocks selected by the portfolio manager and the proportions held in each stock.

Subject to a number of caveats to be discussed at a later point, the measurement of investment results in the general manner suggested by the Merrill Lynch and similar "performance" systems permits both managers and their clients to answer better the following important questions:

Did the manager actually follow the preestablished policies in terms of acceptable risk levels?

Were the returns achieved equal to, better or worse than the returns attributable to the risk level assumed?

Were the results of portfolio decisions achieved via timing (a conscious shifting of the beta level) or by superior stock selection capabilities?

Perhaps most importantly, the original investment objectives and policies can be reassessed as to whether or not they were sound to begin with. Were the objectives attainable? Were the policies consistent with the objectives? Could the desired return have been achieved with lower risk levels?

Performance Review of Professional Investment Management

Many observers have applied risk-adjusted performance measurement techniques to the assessment of professional investment management capability. The original focus of most of these studies centered upon the open-end mutual funds. Until very recently, mutual funds were the only financial institutions for which complete and documented records were readily available. In fact, even at this writing,

performance data for other institutional investor categories are still largely incomplete, although there is now sufficient information available upon which reasonably sound conclusions can be based. However, mutual fund results can still be considered a good proxy for all of professional investment management. First of all, there are a lot of them, which eliminates the distortion that may be created by the unique performance of a few organizations. In the same vein, mutual funds have for many years "competed" in a performance sense, and this has stimulated the use of competent, highly compensated investment managers. Mutual funds generally have been aggressive in their pursuit of superior investment results. Consequently, we can assume that during most of the measurement periods they were in fact "trying harder," and it is therefore very worthwhile to see what capital market theorists have concluded regarding the mutual funds' ability to "beat the market." At the same time, we will introduce and comment upon the performance of other institutional categories when we can.

We will not discuss every aspect of every study. However, we recognize the interest and importance generally attached to these investment performance analyses. For this reason, Figure 16–3 provides a reference listing of portfolio performance studies for the interested reader. For convenience, the text will refer to these studies by number.

Diversification. It is important to establish, first, whether or not mutual fund and other institutional portfolios are, according to capital asset pricing theory, reasonably well diversified with respect to the overall market. That is, how does the variation of fund returns relate to that of the market? What is the typical rho?

Merrill Lynch (6) notes that approximately 90 percent of a typical institutional portfolio's fluctuations is caused by general market activity, with an additional 10 percent of total risk resulting from the remaining specific and industry effects. However, the range of movement explained by the market was relatively wide for the portfolios surveyed.

McDonald (9) points out that the greater the differencing interval over which fund and market returns are calculated, the larger is the percentage of variation in fund returns explained by the market return. For example, he found that the mean value of r^2 for his sample of 123 funds,[5] based on monthly returns, was 0.593. Sharpe, using quarterly

---

[5] As we pointed out in Chapter 15, rho is equal to 100 percent when all the observations relating portfolio returns to the market fall on the line of regression. As the observations deviate from the line, rho declines. Some of the studies cited use r^2, instead of r, as a measure of variability. As a result, the "numbers" look much lower, but convey the same information; i.e., a rho of .80 produces a r^2 of .64, and so on.

FIGURE 16–3
Reference List of Portfolio Performance Studies

Author and Source	Data Base and Time Period of Study
1. *Mutual Fund Performance Review,* Computer Directions Advisors Inc., August 31, 1975.	Monthly risk-adjusted performance service covering 390 mutual funds by investment objective, size and various time periods.
2. Friend, Irwin; Blume, Marshall; and Crockett, Jean. *Mutual Funds and Other Institutional Investors.* New York: McGraw-Hill, 1970.	136 mutual funds, 1960–1968.
3. Gentry, James A. "Capital Market Line Theory, Insurance Company Portfolio Performance, and Empirical Anomalies," *Quarterly Review of Economics and Business,* Spring 1975, pp. 8–16.	32 life insurance company and 34 property and liability insurance company portfolios, 1956–1969.
4. *Hanson Investment Performance Survey,* 1966–1975, A. S. Hansen, Inc., 1976.	341 bank pooled trust funds, 54 insurance company separate accounts, 307 mutual funds, and selected market averages, 1966–1975.
5. *Institutional Investor Study Report of the Securities and Exchange Commission.* Washington, D.C.: U.S. Government Printing Office, 1971, vol. 2, pp. 325–47.	Two groups of mutual funds, one containing 125 and the other 236, 1960–1969, and for the five-year periods January 1960–December 1964, and January 1965–December 1969.
6. *Investment Performance Analysis,* Merrill Lynch, Pierce, Fenner & Smith Inc., Comparative Survey 1970–1974, April 1975.	Performance report covering retirement funds, bank commingled equity portfolios, and mutual funds.
7. Jensen, Michael. "Risk, the Pricing of Capital Assets and the Evaluation of Investment Portfolios," *The Journal of Business,* April 1969, pp. 167–247.	115 mutual funds, 1955–1964, with some data covering 1945–1964.
8. Jensen, Michael. "The Performance of Mutual Funds in the Period 1945–1964," *The Journal of Finance,* May 1968, pp. 389–419.	Same as above.

FIGURE 16–3 *(continued)*

9. McDonald, John G. "Objectives and Performance of Mutual Funds, 1960–1969," *Journal of Financial and Quantitative Analysis*, June 1974, pp. 311–33.
    123 mutual funds, 1960–1969.

10. Schlarbaum, Gary G. "The Investment Performance of the Common Stock Portfolios of Property-Liability Insurance Companies," *Journal of Financial and Quantitative Analysis*, January 1974, pp. 89–106.
    20 property-liability companies, 1958–1967.

11. Sharpe, William F. "Mutual Fund Performance," *The Journal of Business*, January 1966, pp. 119–38.
    34 mutual funds, 1954–1963.

12. Treynor, Jack L., and Mazuy, Kay K. "Can Mutual Funds Outguess the Market?" *Harvard Business Review*, July–August 1966, pp. 131–36.
    57 mutual funds, 1953–1962.

13. Treynor, Jack L. "How to Rate Management of Investment Funds," *Harvard Business Review*, January–February 1965, pp. 63–75.
    20 mutual funds, 1953–1962.

14. Mutual Fund Performance Monthly, Wiesenberger Services, Inc.
    Monthly mutual fund performance report covering over 300 mutual funds listed in various ways for ten-year, five-year, and year-to-date periods.

15. Williamson, J. Peter. "Funds For the Future," Twentieth Century Fund Task Force Report on College and University Endowment Policy, New York: McGraw-Hill, 1975.
    79 unidentified endowment funds, ten years ending June 30, 1974.

16. Williamson, J. Peter. "Performance Measurement and Investment Objectives for Educational Endowment Funds," New York: The Common Fund, 1972.
    36 unidentified endowment funds, ten years ending June 30, 1971.

returns, calculated an average r^2 value of 0.785 for 100 mutual funds.[6] Jensen (7), using annual data, reported an average r^2 of 0.852 for his sample of 115 mutual funds. McDonald (9) draws the implication that only about 60 percent of any *month's* return of the average mutual fund is likely to be attributable to the market factor, whereas about 85 percent of any *year's* return of the average fund's return is likely to be attributable to the market.

Diversification also appears to be a function of portfolio size. Table 16–2, prepared from data presented by CDA's (1) performance report indicates that there is a tendency for diversification to increase with the size of the portfolio.

TABLE 16–2
Mutual Fund Diversification and Portfolio Size

Category	Size	r^2
Aggressive growth	0–25 million $	69
	25–100	77
	100–250	83
	250–500	79
Growth	0–25	74
	25–100	83
	100–250	88
	250–500	89
	Over 500	92
Growth and income	0–25	81
	25–100	86
	100–250	89
	250–500	84
	Over 500	91
Income	0–25	62
	25–100	68
	100–250	66
	Over 500	84
Balanced	0–25	78
	25–100	87
	100–250	88
	250–500	94
	Over 500	95

Source: Computer Directions Advisors, Inc.

Gentry (3), using annual data, found that the mean coefficient of correlation (r) for both 32 life insurance company portfolios and 34 property and liability insurance company portfolios was 0.82.

Another good nonmutual fund portfolio performance study was conducted by Professor J. Peter Williamson of Dartmouth College (16)

---

[6] Based on an unpublished finding reported in John G. McDonald, "Objectives and Performance of Mutual Funds, 1960–1969," *Journal of Financial and Quantitative Analysis,* January 1974, p. 313.

and covered 36 endowment funds for the ten-year period ending June 30, 1971. Only six of the endowment portfolios had coefficients of correlation (rho) with the market below 0.9, and only one of these was below 0.8.

Thus, most of the available evidence suggests that professionally managed portfolios are fairly well diversified relative to the market, at least if rho is used as the measure of diversification. From this evidence, capital market theorists have concluded that knowledge of a portfolio's beta should enable one to make rather good predictions of the portfolio's rate of return, conditional on knowledge of overall market returns. As we shall soon show, this conclusion is open to a good deal of question. Nevertheless, we shall proceed for the time being as if the conclusion were valid.

Risk and Investment Intentions. It will probably come as no surprise to learn that all of the available studies reveal a strong relationship between a mutual fund's stated investment objective and its volatility, or beta coefficient.[7] For example, the SEC study (5) of data from the 1960s indicated that funds having more aggressive, capital gains oriented objectives consistently tended to display higher volatility measures than did funds having more conservative investment objectives. This conclusion can still be supported with current statistics. For example, it is readily observable in Table 16–3 that beta coeffi-

TABLE 16–3
Mutual Fund Beta Coefficients

Investment Objective	Number of Funds	10-Year Period 7/1/65– 6/30/75	5-Year Period 7/1/70– 6/30/75	Year-to Date 1/1/75– 6/30/75	1974	1973
Maximum capital gain	107	1.20	1.09	.84	.76	1.04
Long-term growth	102	1.02	1.00	.84	.77	.93
Growth and current income	71	.95	.93	.77	.71	.85
Balanced funds	19	.73	.71	.56	.50	.57
Income—stock funds	9	.75	.68	.51	.49	.57
Income—flexible policy	31	.67	.60	.39	.35	.40

Source: Mutual Fund Performance Monthly, Wiesenberger Services, Inc.

---

[7] Studies of the betas of other institutional groups are not too useful in testing the relationship between beta and investment objective. For example, Gentry (3) found that the average beta value for 32 life insurance company portfolios was 0.898, while 34 property and liability portfolios were found to be slightly less risky, having an average beta of 0.776. Schlarbaum (10) also found that property and liability insurance company portfolios carried less than market risk. The average beta coefficient of his 20 portfolio sample was 0.8, with only 2 portfolios having a beta value of over 0.9. But the investment objectives of these institutions are not stated anywhere. Thus, we might infer from the betas that insurance company portfolio managers have been very risk averse, but we really don't know.

cients increase as the investment objective becomes more ambitious. It is also interesting to look at the risk reduction which took place in the more aggressive categories between 1973 and 1974.

Computer Directions Advisors calculates that the beta for 95 bank commingled common stock funds was 0.95. On the other hand, eighteen bank trust funds identified as "aggressive growth" equity were found to have a beta value of 1.14.

Performance Review. We can at this point conclude that mutual fund portfolios appear to be fairly diversified and carry market risks in accordance with their stated investment objectives. Now the question is to determine whether the returns produced by the managers of these portfolios have been better or worse than might have been predicted from a knowledge of these characteristics.

Interest in this vital question led to the development of several "single-index" measures which incorporate both risk and return in a single statistic. This was accomplished by calculating the ratio of a fund's average return for a period (net of the risk-free rate) to its beta, or to the standard deviation of its intraperiod returns. Thus, the single index was purported to be a measure of "reward per unit of risk" and to permit a more meaningful ranking of the performance of different funds than the more traditional direct comparison of absolute rates of return.

The pioneering effort in this area was produced by Jack L. Treynor in his study (13) of 20 mutual funds during the period 1953–62. Using the concepts described above, Treynor concluded that 8 funds did better than their risk characteristics would have suggested and 12 did worse. Sharpe, in his study (11) of 34 mutual funds during the period 1954–63, concluded that 11 did better and 23 did worse.

Michael Jensen, in a landmark study (7), departed from the single-index ratio approach. He measured the difference between the portfolio return and the return which would have been earned by a hypothetical portfolio of equal risk, where the hypothetical portfolio consists of a combination of "the market" and lending or borrowing, i.e., the approach described at the beginning of this chapter. Jensen concluded that 39 funds did "better than expected" and 76 did worse.

The SEC's *Institutional Investor Study Report* (5) used Jensen's measure of "differential return" to determine whether or not mutual funds outperformed the market, on a risk-adjusted basis. Somewhat different conclusions were reached by the SEC than by Jensen. Looking at a 125 fund sample, mutual funds outperformed the market at every risk level during the full ten-year period of study—although in most cases by admittedly very small amounts. For example, the 44 funds in the 0.8–1.0 beta classification had a performance superiority of 0.066 percent per month, or 0.792 percent per year, less than 1 percent.

One of the more important performance findings of the SEC's report concerned the question of consistency. There was none. During the first five-year period, 1960–64, the least volatile funds tended to have the best performance, while during the second period, 1965–69, the more volatile funds had the superior performance. As a result, good performance during the first five-year period tended to be associated on average with poor performance during the second five-year period, since the mutual funds in the study demonstrated no pattern of changing their volatility from one period to the next. Later studies confirm a lack of consistency in terms of superior performance.

Friend, Blume, and Crockett took another approach. In their study (2), instead of the hypothetical portfolios being combinations of "the market" plus lending or borrowing, the hypothetical portfolios consisted entirely of stocks selected at random from among stocks with betas equivalent to the betas of the funds whose results were being measured. For example, if a fund had a beta of 1.2, the hypothetical yardstick portfolio was created by randomly selecting from stocks with betas of about 1.2. This seemed more realistic than to use as a yardstick a hypothetical 20 percent leveraged market portfolio, since few real-world professionally managed funds undertake such leveraged positions.

Mutual funds were divided into three groups, according to their risk class, or beta coefficient. Three sets of random portfolios were compared with actual fund returns for the 1960–68 period. The first of these portfolios was created from all stocks listed on the New York Stock Exchange, with an equal dollar amount theoretically invested in each stock chosen. The second set held the probability of any listed stock being selected proportionate to the aggregate market value of the shares outstanding. The logic behind this criterion was that a large company (with a large capitalization) would be a more likely mutual fund holding than a small one. Once selected, an equal amount was assumed to be invested in each portfolio holding. The third set of portfolios assumed equal probability of any stock being selected, but instead of equal investments in each stock the amount invested in each stock was proportionate to its market value. In this case, it was assumed that mutual funds were more likely to hold large amounts of the stocks of large companies and lesser amounts of small ones.

Mutual funds in the two highest risk classes were found to have outperformed the second and third sets of randomly selected portfolios, in some cases by significant margins. Random portfolios did better in the other comparisons. All in all, the funds did not fare too badly, a rather different conclusion than in most of the previously discussed studies. Since the Friend-Blume-Crockett study attempted to replicate "real-world conditions," whereas the other studies were

based essentially on capital market theory, a question arises whether the theory, as commonly interpreted, has some significant flaws—a possibility which we have been hinting and to which we will return shortly.

Turning to more recent years, Wiesenberger's performance study (14) ranked 320 mutual funds by their "alpha" coefficient for the ten- and five-year periods ending December 31, 1974. For the ten-year period, 188, or 59 percent of the 320 funds, exhibited a negative value. For the five-year period, 232 mutual funds (72 percent of the total) had zero or negative values, indicating that the ability to "beat the market" declined in recent years.[8]

CDA's performance studies (1) also calculate the alpha coefficient designed to measure risk-adjusted performance. Table 16–4 is a sum-

TABLE 16–4
Risk-Adjusted Performance

Category	Number of Portfolios	R^2	Beta	Alpha
Bank				
Common stock	95	88	.95	−.31
Aggressive growth	18	85	1.14	−.82
Insurance company-				
Common stock	27	84	.99	−.15
Mutual fund				
Aggressive growth	103	78	1.08	−.64
Growth	110	89	1.06	−.41
Growth and income ...	85	89	.91	.02
Income	40	71	.56	−.02
Bond and preferred	14	45	.32	−.12
Bond	20	93	.68	−.29
Total industry	390	85	.91	−.21

Source: Computer Directions Advisors, Inc.

mary of alpha coefficients by institutional category for the 36 months ended August 31, 1975. The only group with a positive risk-adjusted performance (and very minute, at that) is in the mutual fund "growth and income" category. All the others in Table 16–4 exhibit negative risk adjusted performance.

Merrill Lynch (6) also calculated portfolio alpha's for the equity segment of retirement fund portfolios and for the total portfolios of

---

[8] The number one "alpha-ranked" fund in both periods, International Investors, achieved the lofty and outstanding risk-adjusted performance of +176 percent and +154.4 percent, for the ten- and five-year periods, with portfolio beta values of *only* 0.33 and 0.38, respectively. It should be pointed out that in recent years International Investors has followed a policy of concentrating its portfolio in gold mining and securities which have low betas.

bank commingled equity funds and mutual funds in the 1970–74 period. The mean average annual alpha for these three categories, 1970 through 1974, was −1.2 percent, −1.5 percent, −2.0 percent, respectively, again indicating below-market performance.

Schlarbaum (10) created bench-mark portfolios of comparable risk in order to evaluate properly the performance of his insurance company portfolio sample. Two sets of random portfolios were selected from a sample of 757 common stocks, which represented all of the stocks held in the portfolios of the property and liability companies at any time during the measurement period, and for which 20 years of annual return data were available. Schlarbaum compared the actual returns with those generated by the random sample and concluded that the returns earned by the insurance company portfolios were significantly lower than those earned by random portfolios of equivalent risk.[9]

With few exceptions—e.g., the Friend, Blume, and Crockett study (2)—the consensus view of researchers is that practicing portfolio managers simply do not outperform the market over any but very short time periods, on a "risk-adjusted" basis. What about on an absolute, unadjusted basis?

Since most institutional investors usually maintain less than market risk in their total portfolios (stocks plus whatever cash is available for investment), and we have already explored the difficulty of developing positive alphas from good stock selection or timing, it is not surprising to find that the same unfavorable comparisons exist on a straight rate of return basis. That is, institutional portfolio returns, unadjusted for risk, also fail to match those of the broad market averages.

For example, a study by A. S. Hansen, Inc. (4), summarized in Table 16–5, shows that very few groups of investors significantly outperformed the stock market during the ten-year period 1966–75. Of 65 bank regular equity funds studied, only four outperformed the S&P 500 by 1 percent or more in the ten-year period, and 85 percent of the funds failed to match or exceed the 3.3 percent market rate of return. Insurance company equity separate accounts did worse, with 17 of 18 portfolios returning less than the market. Mutual funds, on the other hand, did much better before adjusting for risk. The Hansen study also found no consistency of performance among the funds on a year-to-year or on a market cycle basis. That is, funds ranking high in terms of relative performance during one measurement period failed to repeat their superior showing in subsequent periods.

---

[9] Gary G. Schlarbaum, "The Investment Performance of the Common Stock Portfolios of Property-Liability Insurance Companies," *Journal of Financial and Quantitative Analysis*, January 1974.

TABLE 16–5
Institutional Portfolio Returns against the Market, 1966–1975

Type of Fund	Number of Funds	Average Annual Rate of Return
Bank regular equity	65	1.9
Bank special equity	4	1.0
Bank fixed income	52	3.7
Insurance company equity	18	1.4
Mutual fund:		
Maximum capital gain	11	0.0
Long-term growth, income secondary	30	3.2
Mutual: Growth and current income	38	3.8
Mutual fund income: Common stock	3	3.9
S&P 500		3.3

Source: A. S. Hansen Seventh Annual Investment Performance Survey.

Some Questions about Capital Market Theory

Confronted with so much evidence that professional investment management does not succeed, two reactions are possible. First, one may take the evidence as confirmation of the efficient market hypothesis. That is, since the market is efficient, those who try to "beat it" by trying to sell overvalued issues and buy undervalued ones, or by switching out of stocks and into cash, then back again, will merely generate a lot of transaction costs which reduce rate of return. It is better to pick an overall level of volatility (beta), buy a large number of stocks with an average volatility at the desired level, and then hold to a steady course.

A second reaction, however, may be as follows. Most institutional portfolios, knowingly or by accident, *do maintain* a fairly steady beta level. And most *do* have quite a large number of stocks in their portfolio. Is it really the transaction costs that are causing them to do poorly, or is it possible that there are some flaws in the measurement framework which create an appearance of poor performance which is not fully justified by the reality?

To consider these two reactions, let's first review the key premises of capital asset pricing theory. It is argued that (*a*) historic variability of return represents an accurate assessment of, or proxy for, investment risk; (*b*) the past pattern of variance (of return) will tend to prevail in the future; and (*c*) the anticipated or ex ante rate of return derived from observing the past variance will approximate, if not equal, the realized or ex post return of a well-diversified portfolio. Stated in other terms, modern theory separates risk and return into market-related (beta) and specific (alpha) components. It is argued that the alphas of diversified portfolios tend toward zero and the rhos toward 100 percent. That

being the case, risk is measured by beta and the relationship between risk and return is assumed to be linear. When the overall market rises, return is expected to rise proportionately to a portfolio's beta. Likewise, when the overall market falls, return is expected to fall proportionately to a portfolio's beta.

Two critical pieces of empirical evidence are needed to support this theory. First, evidence must be presented that beta coefficients are, by their nature, stable over time; i.e., that a stable beta can be expected to be maintained *without active management*. Second, evidence must be offered which links realized, ex post, investment returns with historic beta calculations. Many investigations have been conducted in recent years in the search for evidence of this nature, and we can review briefly several of the most interesting of these.

Stability of Beta.   Every study we are aware of suggests that the betas of individual stocks are *not* very stable over time. For example, an analysis of the betas of 800 issues was published by the private banking firm of Brown Brothers Harriman & Co.[10] It was found that when later betas are regressed against earlier betas (e.g., the betas of 1966 versus the betas of 1963–65), the resulting correlation coefficient is rather low (about 60 percent).

Marshall Blume, author of several studies on the stability of beta and the relationship of risk and return, has also provided evidence that betas tend to regress toward the overall mean beta of one (1.0). That is, securities with estimated betas greater than one (1.0) in one period have betas greater than 1.0 in a future period, but the future beta tends to be closer to 1.0, and vice versa for low-beta stocks.[11]

Beta instability is not limited to individual issues, but seems to be characteristic of industry groups as well. Research conducted by Jerome L. Valentine reveals substantial shifts in industry betas over successive five-year periods (see Table 16–6). Viewing these patterns of instability, Valentine concluded: "with betas apparently changing frequently, they cannot provide highly accurate projections of future returns on individual companies or industries."[12]

However, even though individual stock and industry betas seem to change a good deal over time, there is substantial evidence that the betas of unmanaged *portfolios* of stocks remain *relatively* stable from period to period. Further, the larger the number of portfolio issues, the

---

[10] *A Study of the Usefulness of Beta Analysis in the Management of Common Stock Portfolios,* Brown Brothers Harriman & Co., November 1972.

[11] Marshall E. Blume, "Betas and Their Regression Tendencies," *Journal of Finance,* June 1975.

[12] Jerome L. Valentine "Investment Analysis and Capital Market Theory," *Occasional Paper No. 1* (Charlottesville, Va.: The Financial Analysts Research Foundation, 1975), p. 34.

TABLE 16–6
Industry Beta Values over Time

	1951–55	1956–60	1961–65	1966–70
Aerospace	.96247	.66585	.72409	1.31815
Agricultural machinery	.78687	.90875	.81422	1.14613
Aluminum	1.18617	1.60756	1.13980	1.21376
Apparel manufacturing	.50733	.47428	1.23344	1.52437
Auto parts and accessories	.87577	1.03116	.84302	1.17786
Autos	1.21383	1.00899	.87593	1.00869
Auto tires and rubber goods	1.18350	1.20016	1.16497	.97226
Auto trucks and parts	.96299	1.24551	1.21358	1.24255
Biscuit bakers	.34377	.18935	.76037	.68711
Bituminous coal	1.02612	1.14341	1.11203	.80200
Bread and cake bakers	.35396	.35301	.93734	1.91074
Brewers	.18364	.56817	.74847	1.03782
Business and office equipment	1.12362	1.12134	1.44912	1.09700
Canned foods	.65238	.55939	1.04155	1.01861
Cement	1.01518	.87642	.82306	1.53511
Chemicals	1.06482	1.04785	.94006	.85256
Cigarettes	.29077	.23970	1.29410	.55432
Confectionery	.35793	.35514	1.04756	.59934
Construction and material handling machinery	1.14771	1.18300	.91518	1.19976
Copper	1.17911	.97515	.94643	1.08206
Corn refiners	.32177	.44286	1.02606	.93091
Crude oil producers	.69844	1.03158	1.12971	.95093
Dairy products	.40212	.35200	.98700	1.04501
Department stores	.60589	.53718	.66176	1.21765
Distillers	.74801	.79331	.86246	.90287
Drugs	.54110	1.05861	1.29238	.95521
Electrical equipment	.96542	1.25540	1.04542	1.19990
Electrical household appliances	.76593	1.01648	.91009	1.15041
Electronics	.90328	1.31251	1.55722	1.56784
Food chain stores	.38349	.51301	1.00418	.73317
Gold mining	.54291	.63910	.06125	.07090
Heating and plumbing	.64976	.86583	.95464	1.27624
Home furnishings	.45473	.76023	1.18308	1.60301
Industrial machinery	.81678	1.18670	1.03285	1.33398
Integrated domestic oil companies	.79546	1.09107	.82772	.96288
Integrated international oil companies	1.05360	.98599	.70443	.73875
Lead and zinc	.91563	.99167	1.07584	.72259

Source: Jerome L. Valentine, "Investment Analysis and Capital Market Theory," *Occasional Paper No. 1* (Charlottesville, Va.: The Financial Research Foundation, 1975), p. 34.

greater the stability. For example, Blume examined the behavior of portfolios comprised of New York Stock Exchange stocks ranked by their beta coefficients over six different time periods from 1933 to 1968. The number of securities in each portfolio varied from 1 to 50, with additional analysis performed on portfolios with 100 securities. The correlations between the betas of adjacent periods are summarized in Table 16–7. Observe, for example, the association of beta

TABLE 16–7
Correlation Coefficients of Betas for Portfolios of N Securities

Number of Securities per Portfolio	7/26–6/33 and 7/33–6/40	7/33–6/40 and 7/40–6/47	7/40–6/47 and 7/47–6/54	7/47–6/54 and 7/54–6/61	7/54–6/61 and 7/61–6/68
1	0.63	0.62	0.59	0.65	0.60
2	0.71	0.76	0.72	0.76	0.73
4	0.80	0.85	0.81	0.84	0.84
7	0.86	0.91	0.88	0.87	0.88
10	0.89	0.94	0.90	0.92	0.92
20	0.93	0.97	0.95	0.95	0.97
35	0.96	0.98	0.95	0.97	0.97
50	0.98	0.99	0.98	0.98	0.98

Source: Abstracted from Marshall Blume, "On the Assessment of Risk," *Journal of Finance*, March 1971, p. 7.

coefficients for the period July 1926 to June 1933 with the subsequently measured period, July 1933 to June 1940. The correlation varied from 0.63 for a single-security portfolio to 0.98 for one comprised of 50 securities. This pattern of increasing correlation as the number or portfolio securities increases persists for all of the periods in the study, and led Blume to conclude that "at least as measured by the correlation coefficients, naïvely extrapolated assessments of future risk for larger portfolios are remarkably accurate, whereas extrapolated assessments of future risk for individual securities and smaller portfolios are of some, but limited value in forecasting the future."[13] Subsequent studies confirm this conclusion.[14]

Rate of Return versus Beta. On balance, the beta stability of *unmanaged portfolios* has been substantially documented. However, the relationship between a portfolio's beta and its subsequent rate of return is not at all as clear. For instance, Black, Jensen and Scholes[15] analyzed portfolio returns for different beta levels covering the period 1926 to 1966 and found the results inconsistent with the capital asset pricing model. High-beta securities earned less on average over the 35-year period than that predicted by the model. At the same time, low-beta securities earned more.

---

[13] Marshall E. Blume, "On the Assessment of Risk," *Journal of Finance*, March 1971, p. 7.

[14] See Michael Jensen, "Tests of Capital Market Theory and Implications of the Evidence" (Charlottesville, Va.: The Financial Research Foundation, 1975). Robert A. Levy, "On the Short-Term Stationarity of Beta Coefficients," *Financial Analysts Journal*, November/December 1971; and Marshall E. Blume, "Betas and Their Regression Tendencies," *Journal of Finance*, June 1975.

[15] Fisher Black, Michael C. Jensen, and Myron Scholes, "The Capital Asset Pricing Model: Some Empirical Tests," *Working Paper*, Series No. F7030, University of Rochester, November 1970.

These findings were substantially supported by a study conducted by Marshall Blume and Irwin Friend, who noted:

There is no necessary euphoria in investing in high-risk stocks over the long run even though they may have higher *expected* rates of return. From 1928 through 1968, high-risk stocks for the market as a whole tended to yield less than low-risk stocks. In other words, there is no guarantee that high-risk stocks will yield bigger returns in any single period—no matter how long—even though their *expected* returns may be greater.[16]

The figures in Table 16–8, taken from the Blume and Friend study, indicate that higher risk strategies do not dominate lower risk strategies for investors in the aggregate. That is, for value-weighted buy-and-hold strategies, the returns realized over the 40-year measurement period were, if anything, negatively related to risk. For example, one dollar invested in stocks of the lowest risk would have increased $32.74 while the same dollar in stocks of the highest risk would have increased to only $26.65.[17]

TABLE 16–8
Risk and Return, July 1928–June 1968
(ending value per $ invested)

Risk Class	Dollar Value
Low	$32.74
2	27.24
3	51.66
4	55.88
5	43.74
6	43.76
7	42.63
8	46.50
9	42.27
High	26.65

Source: *The Review of Economics and Statistics,* August 1974.

Another study, by Robert A. Levy,[18] sought answers to the following questions: (1) Is there any correlation between historical beta coefficients and future stock performance? (2) Will portfolios with high historical betas outperform the averages over an ensuing market advance?

---

[16] Marshall E. Blume and Irwin Friend, "Risk, Investment Strategy and the Long-Run Rates of Return," *The Review of Economics and Statistics,* August 1974, p. 259. (Emphasis added.)

[17] Ibid., p. 268.

[18] Robert A. Levy, "Beta Coefficients as Predictors of Return," *Financial Analysts Journal,* January/February, 1974.

(3) Will portfolios with low historical betas successfully resist a market setback?

Looking first at the relationship between individual stock returns and beta, Levy calculated, for the nine years shown in Table 16–9,

TABLE 16–9
Beta and Individual Stock Returns

Beta Coefficient for 52 Weeks Ended	Returns for 52 Weeks Ended	Correlation Coefficient	S&P 500 Percent Change
12/29/61	12/28/62	−.18	− 9.0
12/28/62	12/27/63	−.10	22.0
12/27/63	12/25/64	−.04	16.5
12/25/64	12/24/65	.21	12.9
12/24/65	12/23/66	.14	− 8.6
12/23/66	12/22/67	.10	20.6
12/22/67	12/20/68	−.07	15.2
12/20/68	12/19/69	−.13	−11.3
12/19/69	12/18/70	−.29	2.5

Source: *Financial Analysts Journal,* January/February 1974, p. 62.

beta coefficients and returns for each of 500 stocks. The beta coefficients for each year were used to predict returns for the next one—that is, nine cross-sectional regressions of return against prior year's beta were performed. The results were mixed.

Only during four of the nine test periods (1961–62, 1964–65, 1966–67, and 1968–69) was the correlation coefficient both significant and with the same sign as the direction of the market. These four observations support the hypothesis that high-beta stocks will do better than the market in bullish years and low-beta stocks will do worse. In two periods, 1962–63 and 1965–66, the correlation was significant and the sign violated the hypothesis. In 1969–70, significant correlation was exhibited when none was anticipated because the market's movement was nominal. In two cases, 1963–64 and 1967–68, the coefficient of correlation was insignificant.[19]

Next, Levy grouped the individual securities into ten portfolios of 50 securities each. Portfolios were constructed by ranking the 500 securities by their historical beta coefficient, from lowest to highest. The first portfolio consisted of those securities with the 50 lowest betas; the second with the next 50, and so on. Then assuming equal dollar investment in every security, each portfolio's performance, i.e., return, was calculated for the ensuing year. Once again, the results were mixed. Results for four of the measurement periods

---

[19] Ibid., p. 62.

support the hypothesis (that high-beta portfolios do better in rising markets and low-beta portfolios do worse); two of the periods support an opposite hypothesis; two periods show insignificant performance difference; and one period shows negatively significant correlation during a flat market.

To get another perspective of the relationship between risk and return, Levy also identified all swings in the S&P 500 exceeding 15 percent or more during the test period. Six such swings were identified. Using the same 50-stock portfolios, beta coefficients for the six 52-week periods immediately preceding the six primary market moves were then calculated, and matched against subsequent returns. Without exception, the beta coefficients, according to Levy, served as excellent predictors of return during the three primary bear markets. The results for the bull markets were ambiguous.

Gerald D. Levitz, of Brown Brothers Harriman, contends that risk and return for portfolios with betas falling within the range of 0.80 and 1.50, where most institutional portfolio managers operate, are not correlated to any discernible degree. Rather, the pattern of correlation between risk and return is created by portfolios with extreme beta values. For example, the coefficients of determination in the top portion of Table 16–10 confirm that during three recent periods of significant movement in the S&P 500, the test portfolios with nonextreme beta values exhibited almost no statistically significant relationship between return and estimated market risk. At best, 20 percent of the differences in return were explained by differences in estimated mar-

TABLE 16–10
Risk and Return Correlation for Portfolios of Different Beta

Test Period and S&P 500 Performance	Number of Stocks in Each Portfolio	Number of Test Portfolios	Coefficient of Determination
Betas of .80 to 1.50			
10/66–9/67	30	11	0.13
+28%	40	8	0.13
2/69–5/70	30	15	0.19
−29%	40	11	0.20
2/71–1/72	30	16	0.00
+12%	40	12	0.08
Extreme Beta Values			
10/66–9/67	30	8	0.81
+28%	40	6	0.79
2/69–5/70	30	7	0.87
−29%	40	6	0.87
2/71–1/72	30	8	0.88
+12%	40	6	0.97

Source: *Financial Analysts Journal*, January/February 1974, p. 59.

ket risk. On the other hand, the figures in the lower portion of Table 16–10 show that the differences in return between portfolios with very high- and very low-beta values were largely explained by the differences in risk.[20]

These findings were corroborated by A. G. Becker's Funds Evaluation Service, which measures the historical investment performance of actual institutional portfolios. Looking at the rate of return over the time periods 1962 to 1972 and 1966 to 1972, A. G. Becker found virtually no correlation with beta in either time period.[21]

Some recent research puts still another perspective on the inadequacy of beta in explaining difference in portfolio returns. James L. Farrell, Jr., suggests that when portfolios are concentrated in one or more of four homogeneous stock groupings, the expected relationship between risk and return is distorted.[22] For example, Table 16–11

TABLE 16–11
Portfolio Construction, Beta Values and Total Return

Stock Sector	S&P 500	Affiliated Fund	T. Rowe Price
Growth	39.8%	10.5%	80.2%
Cyclical	24.0	57.5	8.7
Stable	20.0	18.0	4.1
Oil	16.2	14.0	7.0
Total	100.0%	100.0%	100.0%
Portfolio Beta	1.00	1.09	1.11
Fund performance (12/31/72 to 7/31/74)	−29%	−16%	−42%

Source: *Financial Analysts Journal*, May/June 1975.

shows the weightings of the four groupings of growth, cyclical, stable and oil stocks in the S&P 500 along with the portfolio structure of two large mutual funds—Affiliated and T. Rowe Price Growth. It also shows the betas, calculated on the basis of monthly data over the 1969 to 1973 period, along with the total return performance of the two funds and the S&P 500 between December 31, 1972 and July 31, 1974.

Notice that Affiliated Fund was heavily weighted (approximately twice as heavily) relative to the market in the cyclical group while T.

[20] Gerald D. Levitz, "Market Risk and the Management of Institutional Equity Portfolios," *Financial Analysts Journal*, January/February 1974.

[21] Mike Edesess, "Beta and Return Correlation," *Financial Analysts Journal*, May/June 1974, p. 90.

[22] James L. Farrell, Jr., "Homogeneous Stock Groupings," *Financial Analysts Journal*, May/June 1975.

Rowe Price was heavily weighted (again approximately twice as heavily) relative to the market in the growth group. Both funds had approximately the same beta. However, the performance of the two funds was substantially different over the measurement period. The S&P 500 declined 29 percent, while Affiliated was down 16 percent and T. Rowe Price was down 42 percent.

Perhaps the most important implication of Farrell's research is that apparent diversification is not the same as actual diversification. That is, while both Affiliated Fund and T. Rowe Price had a large *number* of holdings, they were concentrated in different market segments. As a result, their betas were poor predictors of their performance.

Implications of the Findings. We have presented evidence which supports the theoretical proposition that the betas of unmanaged portfolios remain fairly stable from period to period. But the evidence does not fully support the proposition that the rates of return on unmanaged portfolios are highly correlated with the betas of those portfolios. This finding calls into some question the performance measurements of real-life portfolios described earlier in this chapter.

It is clear that some limitations must exist in capital market theory. One aspect of the theory which has come into serious question is the assumption that all investors can borrow or lend unlimited sums at equal rates of interest (the risk-free rate). In the real world, this assumption simply is untenable. It produces unrealistic estimates of the returns on hypothetical portfolios consisting of the market plus borrowing or lending. And since these are the estimated returns which actual portfolios are predicted to achieve, the predictions obviously will be wrong to some extent.[23]

Furthermore, it is possible that risk-oriented investors tend to exaggerate in their minds the opportunity for gain from high-risk stocks. Certainly, the speed with which "hot new issues" frequently are distributed, despite the high mortality rate of new companies, suggests that this may be so. If it is so, then the prices of high-risk stocks may, in general, be "too high"—i.e., investors may "overpay" for them—thus causing ultimate realized returns to be incommensurate with the risks involved.

Third, many portfolios are mixtures of common stocks and fixed-income securities. To calculate a beta for such a hybrid portfolio on the basis of its periodic net asset values is to treat stocks and bonds as if they were both a part of the same risk spectrum. While it is certainly convenient to think of them this way, there are growing reasons for

---

[23] See Irwin Friend and Marshall Blume, "Measurement of Portfolio Performance under Uncertainty," *American Economic Review*, September 1970.

believing that, in an inflationary world, they may not be.[24] If they are not, then performance measurements of balanced funds must separate the stock and bond components rather than treat them in combined fashion.[25]

Finally, it would appear that the theoretical use of rho to measure diversification simply is inadequate. Diversification is supposed to result in the specific positive returns of some stocks canceling out the specific negative returns of other stocks in a portfolio. That is, some stocks will have positive alphas and some negative alphas, but a diversified *portfolio* is supposed to have a *net alpha of zero*. Since there is ample evidence that many portfolios have high rhos but at the same time have significantly *nonzero alphas,* we must conclude that a high rho is not synonymous with high "diversification.[26]

Other Questions. We have indicated throughout our presentation that different researchers have used different base periods for calculating the beta coefficient. The lack of conformity gives rise to significantly different measures of beta for the same stock. This poses the interesting question: Is there an appropriate, or preferred, time interval for measuring beta?

One suggestion frequently offered to resolve this problem is to relate the base period for measurement to the investor's time horizon. For example, betas calculated on a daily basis for a relatively short period of time, say three to six months, might be of limited value to a long-term investor who generally maintains a holding period of more than a year. On the other hand, such a calculation could be of value to a short-term investor because it would reflect the stock's sensitivity to the most recent market movement.

Others argue that the measurement period should be quite short, say no more than quarterly as opposed to a year or longer, even for investors with long-time horizons. The reason behind this suggestion is that short measurement intervals may enable portfolio managers to observe whether a beta is in the process of changing. If the managers are attempting to maintain a long-term risk level equivalent to a given value of beta, they should be tracking their portfolios frequently and making adjustments if betas begin to drift away from their target levels.

But short-time intervals for measuring beta give rise to serious

---

[24] John B. Long, Jr., "Stock Prices, Inflation, and the Term Structure of Interest Rates," *Journal of Financial Economics*, July 1974.

[25] See M. Blume and I. Friend, "A New Look at the Capital Asset Pricing Model," *Journal of Finance*, March 1973. The Appendix to this chapter describes some newly developed bond performance measurement techniques.

[26] An (unpublished) paper treating this subject at greater length is available from D. A. Love Associates, 350 Fifth Avenue, New York, N.Y.

statistical problems. If the basic file (data bank) of returns data from which beta is calculated is on a monthly basis, as is common, then quarterly calculations would have to depend on only three observations. This is hardly reliable statistically. On the other hand, if, in order to overcome this problem, the calculation is based on daily returns data (approximately 60 per quarter), a great deal of so-called noise is introduced, and statistical reliability is again doubtful. Thus, the question of the optimal time period for measuring beta may remain unanswered.

Another open question, referred to above, is: What are the risks of bonds, mortgages, and real estate in relation to common stocks: For example, are "triple-A" bonds really less risky than "A" bonds and, if so, how much less risky? How does one compare the risks of stocks and bonds in the presence of inflation? And, is real estate a good equity substitute for common stock?[27] There are two serious obstacles to efforts to answer these questions within the framework of capital market theory.[28]

First, there are simply no large-scale price data banks available on investment assets other than common stocks. Second, even such fragmentary price data as are available do not provide very useful rate of return data because most assets other than common stocks are not readily marketable in large quantities. Therefore, some portion of their rate of return is, presumably, a "premium for lack of marketability," as discussed in Chapter 15. Yet there is no accepted measure of marketability which can be used to estimate the size of this premium.

The lack of a good measure of marketability is also an obstacle to progress in common stock risk/return analysis. Obviously, some stocks are more marketable than others, small portfolios are more marketable than large portfolios, a 100 share holding is more marketable than a 100,000 share holding of the same stock. Thus, comparisons of the returns against the betas of different stocks or different portfolios may be quite muddied up by differences in their marketability.[29]

There is still another consideration that tends to blur the precision of performance measurement comparisons predicated on capital asset pricing theorems. As we have already indicated, market line performance measures assume that portfolios with a zero beta would exactly earn the risk-free rate over the measurement period. However, recent

[27] This is becoming a particularly relevant question since corporate pension funds and other institutional investors are devoting an increasing portion of their assets to real estate investments.

[28] An attempt to cope with the bond problem is contained in John S. Bildersee, "Some New Bond Indexes," *Journal of Business*, October 1975.

[29] For evidence that return is related to marketability as well as to risk, see William L. Fouse, "Risk and Liquidity: The Keys to Stock Price Behavior," *Financial Analysts Journal*, May/June 1976.

findings indicate that hypothetical portfolios with zero beta (i.e., portfolios totally insensitive to general stock market volatility) frequently earn returns that differ substantially from the risk-free rate, sometimes higher, sometimes lower.[30] Why this should be is quite unclear, but it suggests that performance measurement based on the market line concept may be misleading.

Conclusion

We have shown in this chapter that capital asset pricing theory created an improved ability to measure the performance of competing investment managers. Observers, applying these measurement techniques to the historical rates of return of institutional portfolios, have accumulated a great deal of evidence suggesting that professional investment managers have not, with any degree of consistency, outperformed the market on a risk-adjusted basis. On the other hand, evidence has also been accumulated to suggest that the relationship between risk, at least as measured by beta, and realized return is not as strong as portfolio theory argues. Therefore, conclusions with regard to the performance of professional portfolio managers must be arrived at with care.

SUGGESTED READINGS

Bildersee, John S. "Some New Bond Indexes." *The Journal of Business,* October 1975.

Blume, Marshall E. "Betas and Their Regression Tendencies." *Journal of Finance,* June 1975.

Blume, Marshall E., and Friend, Irwin. "Risk, Investment Strategy and the Long-Run Rates of Return." *The Review of Economics and Statistics,* August 1974.

Levitz, Gerald D. "Market Risk and the Management of Institutional Equity Portfolios." *Financial Analysts Journal,* January/February 1974.

Levy, Robert A. "Beta Coefficients as Predictors of Return." *Financial Analysts Journal,* January/February 1974.

Modigliani, Franco, and Pogue, Gerald A. "An Introduction to Risk and Return. Concepts and Evidence." Two part article, *Financial Analysts Journal,* March/April 1974 and May/June 1974.

―――. "Alternative Investment Performance Fee Arrangements and Implications for SEC Regulatory Policy." *The Bell Journal of Economics,* Spring 1975.

---

[30] See Franco Modigliani and Gerald A. Pogue, "An Introduction to Risk and Return: Concepts and Evidence," *Financial Analyst's Handbook,* vol. I (Homewood, Ill.: Dow Jones-Irwin, Inc., 1975), chap. 44, particularly pages 1318–40.

Valentine, Jerome L., C.F.A. "Investment Analysis and Capital Market Theory." *Occasional Paper Number 1.* Charlottesville, Va.: The Financial Analysts Research Foundation, 1975.

APPENDIX: MEASURING BOND
PORTFOLIO PERFORMANCE

As we have noted, many institutional investors have adopted a more aggressive attitude toward the management of fixed-income securities. Generally speaking, the goal is to augment the interest income which would be earned under a buy-and-hold strategy by actively trading debt securities in order to profit from interest rate changes or from disparities in value that develop from time to time between the various sectors of the market and occasionally between securities of similar character. While the term "active bond management" still means different things to different people, one thing is clear. The primary focus of many fixed-income portfolio managers is now more the maximization of total return over relatively short-term periods than it is holding bonds for their yield to maturity.

Accompanying this performance-oriented focus is a need to measure the results of the increased bond portfolio turnover. Unfortunately, the creation of adequate standards by which to judge the investment performance of bond portfolio managers is even more complicated than it is for equity portfolios. Several problems contribute to this difficulty. First, the yield data published by the leading financial services, such as Dow Jones, Moody's, and Standard & Poor's, cover too few issues to represent accurately the entire market. In addition, the data are considered by many to be based on inaccurate prices.

Most bond issues are not listed on any of the major exchanges and trade in the over-the-counter market. This means that true transaction prices are not centrally recorded. Even for those bonds that are listed, many are relatively inactively traded. Some issues can go for weeks, or even longer, without being traded. In these instances, current prices are not available, and the last sale prices are likely to be quite inaccurate if interest rates have changed since the trade date. Moreover, trading on the exchanges is frequently limited to odd-lot transactions and prices do not reflect the impact of larger size institutional orders. Prices of a small listed transaction and an over-the-counter institutional trade in the same issue often differ greatly. In addition to the pricing problem, bond risk theory is still in the formative stage.

Despite these shortcomings, the creation of several new bond indices in recent years has greatly improved the ability to make comparisons of bond portfolio total rates of return on an absolute basis. The

two most prominent indices are published, at each month end, by Salomon Brothers and Kuhn, Loeb & Co., each of which employ a different methodology.

Kuhn, Loeb & Co. has overcome the pricing problem by designing a computer program which calculates the "theoretical prices" of corporate bonds. In addition to the standard factors used in pricing bonds—coupon, maturity, and rating—the program also incorporates such information as sinking fund data, call protection, amount outstanding, and various credit data. These basic factors are modified at each month-end to reflect changes in the yield curve and shifting spreads between various market sectors.[31] The computerized price is verified, where possible, by comparison with actual market quotations. U.S. government and agency prices are obtained from actual quotations.

The *Kuhn Loeb Bond Index* includes both price changes and interest income for about 4,000 publicly traded, nonconvertible, domestic corporate bonds rated BBB or higher. There are also various subindexes that permit the measurement of trends within maturity, rating, and industry classifications. The indexes are weighted by the total market value of each issue. This means that larger, more widely held issues, have a proportionately greater effect on the index. Figure A16–1 is an example of the monthly *Kuhn Loeb Bond Index* report.

The *Kuhn Loeb Long-Term Corporate Bond Index* is comprised of the same issues as the *Kuhn Loeb Bond Index* except that a minimum maturity of 20 years is specified. As of December 31, 1975, over 1,525 issues were included in the index.

The *Kuhn Loeb U.S. Government/Agency Bond Index* is comprised of all publicly issued domestic debt of the U.S. government or any agency thereof, quasi-federal corporation debt or corporate debt guaranteed by the U.S. government. U.S. Treasury bills and all other debt maturing in less than a year are omitted. As of December 31, 1975, over 375 issues were included in the index.

Using a different approach, Salomon Brothers has also developed a package of bond indexes designed to approximate the rates of return which have been provided by the entire high-grade, long-term corporate bond market over various time spans.[32]

The composition of Salomon Brothers' market-weighted indexes

---

[31] For a detailed discussion of the computerized technique employed to price each bond, see Arthur D. Lipson, "The Kuhn Loeb Bond Index," *Technical Comments Regarding the Analytical Methodology and Pricing Procedure* (New York: Kuhn, Loeb & Co., 1973).

[32] Martin L. Leibowitz and Richard I. Johannesen, Jr., "Introducing the Salomon Brothers Total Performance Index for the High-Grade Long-term Corporate Bond Market," (New York: Salomon Brothers, November 1973).

FIGURE A16-1
The Kuhn Loeb Bond Index

Last Twelve Months ending December 31, 1975 using December 31, 1974 as a base of 100.0

	Industrial	Utility	Financial	Aaa	Aa	A	Baa	Total
Price Index	106.1 6.1%	108.6 8.6%	105.2 5.2%	105.7 5.7%	106.1 6.1%	108.4 8.4%	112.9 12.9%	107.5 7.5%
% Coupon Income				8.1%	8.3%	8.8%	9.8%	8.5%
Coupon Reinvested	9.3%	9.7%	9.1%	8.8%	9.1%	9.9%	11.4%	9.5%
Total Return Index	115.4 15.4%	118.3 18.3%	114.3 14.3%	114.6 14.6%	115.2 15.2%	118.3 18.3%	124.4 24.4%	116.9 16.9%

Last Three Months ending December 31, 1975 using September 30, 1975 as a base of 100.0

	Industrial	Utility	Financial	Aaa	Aa	A	Baa	Total
Price Index	105.9 5.9%	106.2 6.2%	104.0 4.0%	106.5 6.5%	105.9 5.9%	105.6 5.6%	104.4 4.4%	105.8 5.8%
% Coupon Income				2.0%	2.1%	2.2%	2.4%	2.2%
Coupon Reinvested	2.1%	2.2%	2.2%	2.1%	2.2%	2.3%	2.5%	2.3%
Total Return Index	108.2 8.2%	108.5 8.5%	106.1 6.1%	108.7 8.7%	108.0 8.0%	107.9 7.9%	106.9 6.9%	108.1 8.1%

Last Month ending December 31, 1975 using November 30, 1975 as a base of 100.0

	Industrial	Utility	Financial	Aaa	Aa	A	Baa	Total
Price Index	102.9 2.9%	103.1 3.1%	101.5 1.5%	103.5 3.5%	103.0 3.0%	102.4 2.4%	101.7 1.7%	102.8 2.8%
% Coupon Income								
Coupon Reinvested	.7%	.7%	.7%	.7%	.7%	.7%	.8%	.7%
Total Return Index	103.6 3.6%	103.8 3.8%	102.2 2.2%	104.2 4.2%	103.7 3.7%	103.2 3.2%	102.5 2.5%	103.5 3.5%

	Industrial	Utility	Financial	Aaa	Aa	A	Baa	Total
Number of Issues	757	2,815	388	537	1,117	1,609	697	3,960
Principal Amount	51,886	106,962	22,766	53,549	47,570	56,826	23,669	181,614
Total Market Value	47,707	89,264	20,512	47,262	41,787	49,931	18,502	157,484
% of Total Market	30	57	13	30	27	32	12	100
Average Price	91.95	83.45	90.10	88.26	87.85	87.87	78.17	86.71
Average Coupon	7.65	7.02	7.39	6.94	7.13	7.56	7.41	7.24
Average Maturity	18.45	20.86	11.49	22.25	18.14	17.37	16.26	18.91
Average Yield to Maturity	8.65	9.15	9.00	8.39	8.71	9.20	10.49	8.98

Source: Kuhn, Loeb & Co., January 15, 1976.

FIGURE A16–2
High-Grade Corporate Bond Total Rate-of-Return Index

Total Rate of Return for Composite Corporate Bond Portfolio
Over Various Holding Periods

Holding Period Covered		Principal Return	Coupon Return	Principal + Coupon Return	Reinvestment Return	Total Return
Month	-Feb. 1976	-0.07	0.68	0.61	0.00	0.61
Last 3 Months	-Dec.'75-Feb. '76	4.90	2.10	7.00	0.04	7.04
Year to Date	-Jan.-Feb. '76	1.13	1.37	2.50	0.00	2.50
Last 12 Months	-Mar. '75-Feb. '76	0.92	7.88	8.80	0.61	9.41
Quarterly	-4th Qtr. '75	7.07	2.10	9.17	0.06	9.22
	3rd Qtr. '75	-5.25	1.99	-3.26	-0.03	-3.29
	2nd Qtr. '75	1.54	2.02	3.55	0.05	3.60
	1st Qtr. '75	2.71	2.07	4.78	-0.02	4.75

Note: The adjusted average price index for the Composite Portfolio (January 1, 1969 = 100) as of Mar. 1, 1976 = 87.48. (This figure is now shown as a principal value index. Back data on request.). The cumulative return index of the Composite Portfolio (January 1, 1969 = 100) as of Mar. 1, 1976 = 149.30.

Cumulative Change in Market Value of Rate of Return Index
(Including Reinvestment) January 1, 1969 = 100

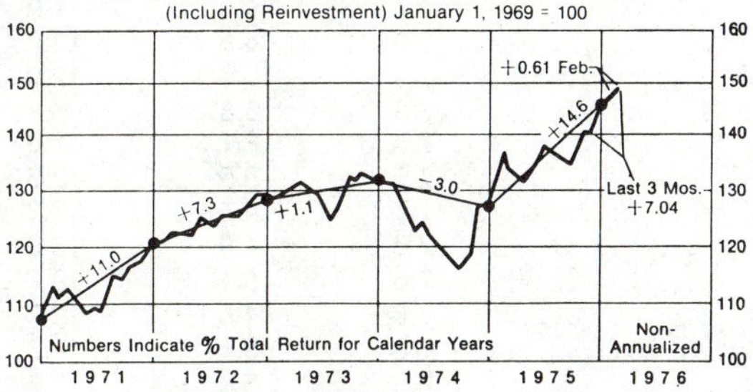

TABLE II

Comparison of Total Rates of Return for Composite Portfolio
and Selected Component AA Rated Coupon Groups

Holding Period Covered		Composite Portfolio	Util. 4⅝-¾	Util. 5⅞-6½	Util. 7½-⅞	Ind. 7½-⅞	Util. 8½-9⅛
Month	-Feb. 1976	0.61	1.77	0.69	0.49	0.87	0.53
Last 3 Months	-Dec. '75-Feb. '76	7.04	7.74	7.74	9.31	6.86	7.89
Year to Date	-Jan.-Feb. '76	2.50	3.70	3.05	3.51	2.34	3.12
Last 12 Months	-Mar. '75-Feb. '76	9.41	10.18	10.91	10.99	9.59	9.52
Quarterly	-4th Qtr. '75	9.22	9.12	9.51	10.02	9.63	8.58
	3rd Qtr. '75	-3.29	-3.52	-3.85	-3.79	-2.41	-2.80
	2nd Qtr. '75	3.60	3.79	4.10	4.07	2.97	3.60
	1st Qtr. '75	4.75	6.29	5.28	5.54	4.07	4.19

TABLE III

Incremental Relative Return by Sector
(Based on Table II)

Holding Period Covered		Total Return for Composite Portfolio	Sector Returns as Increments Above the Composite Portfolio Return				
			Util. 4⅝-¾	Util. 5⅞-6½	Util. 7½-⅞	Ind. 7½-⅞	Util. 8½-9⅛
Month	-Feb. 1976	0.61	+1.16	+0.08	-0.12	+0.26	-0.08
Last 3 Months	-Dec. '75-Feb. '76	7.04	+0.70	+0.70	+2.27	-0.15	+0.85
Year to Date	-Jan.-Feb. '76	2.50	+1.20	+0.55	+1.01	-0.16	+0.62
Last 12 Months	-Mar. '75-Feb. '76	9.41	+0.77	+1.50	+1.58	+0.18	+0.11
Quarterly	-4th Qtr. '75	9.22	-0.10	+0.29	+0.80	+0.41	-0.64
	3rd Qtr. '75	-3.29	-0.23	-0.56	-0.50	+0.88	+0.49
	2nd Qtr. '75	3.60	+0.19	+0.50	+0.47	-0.63	0.00
	1st Qtr. '75	4.75	+1.54	+0.53	+0.79	-0.68	-0.56

Source: Salomon Brothers, February 1976.

FIGURE A16–3
Bank Commingled Bond Fund Performance

Bank	5 Years	3 Years	1 Year	Size ($ million)
Seattle 1st	8.9%	5.5%	14.7%	7
U.S. Trust	8.9	8.3	12.0	105
St. Louis Union	8.7	6.6	14.9	127
Morgan (l.t.)	8.7	5.2	13.3	86
American Fletcher	8.5	7.6	12.7	50
First Pennsylvania	8.5	4.0	14.5	29
First Minneapolis	8.4	6.7	12.7	40
Harris	8.4	6.9	13.4	481
Chemical	8.4	5.8	14.7	183
Citizens & Southern	8.2	6.4	11.7	48
Mfrs. Hanover	8.1	5.1	12.7	65
Irving Trust	8.0	6.0	11.0	20
Wachovia	8.0	4.5	13.6	36
Northern Trust	7.9	5.9	12.9	69
Bankers Trust (i.t.)	7.8	6.8	6.8	45
United of Denver	7.8	3.1	11.9	7
Mercantile Safe	7.7	6.5	12.6	17
Provident National	7.7	4.4	13.3	25
Continental II.	7.6	4.9	13.9	89
Mellon	7.6	5.1	12.7	35
National Shawmut	7.6	4.5	12.7	30
Bank of America	7.5	3.8	11.8	50
Old Kent	7.5	5.9	9.6	38
Valley National (Phoenix)	7.4	5.4	8.3	8
Citibank	7.2	4.5	11.8	565
First of Boston	7.1	3.9	10.1	42
Girard	7.1	2.3	14.4	34
Detroit Bank & Trust	7.0	4.8	11.4	31
Crocker National	7.0	5.4	13.1	10
Wells Fargo	7.0	4.8	11.4	40

has changed from time to time. At present, they reflect the returns of all publicly offered AAA and AA[33] utility and industrial bonds outstanding as of December 31, 1975, with a maturity of 1988 or longer and having at least $25 million par value. The bonds are actually priced individually by traders at Salomon Brothers rather than by a mathematical formula. Figure A16–2 is an example of Salomon's monthly report.

Most recent studies of bond portfolio performance now compare the managers' investment results with at least one of these indexes. For example, a recent study by *Pensions and Investments*[34] indicates that 56 of 67 bond funds managed by bank trust departments equaled or bet-

---

[33] For the purpose of constructing their index, Salomon Brothers defined the high grade corporate bond market as consisting of issues rated AA or better.

[34] Michael Clowes, "Fixed Income Did Better," *Pensions and Investments*, March 15, 1976.

FIGURE A16-3 (continued)

Bank	5 Years	3 Years	1 Year	Size ($ million)
First Bartlesville	6.8 %	3.6 %	11.7%	1
First Kentucky	6.7	4.6	13.3	19
Marine Midland (N.Y.)	6.6	3.4	10.9	11
Mercantile Trust	6.6	4.1	11.9	16
Rainier National...................	6.6	4.0	11.5	6
Bank of Southwest.................	6.6	5.8	11.1	4
United Missouri	6.5	4.3	12.2	13
First of Oregon	6.5	2.9	12.3	8
First of Chicago	6.5	4.5	13.2	161
Northwestern National..............	6.5	2.6	14.2	33
First in Dallas....................	6.5	4.1	10.7	48
Trust Co. of Georgia	6.5	4.1	11.4	19
Philadelphia National	6.5	4.3	11.4	26
First of Cincinnati................	6.5	4.8	11.5	16
Lloyds Bank	6.4	3.8	17.9	7
Fidelity Bank (Pa.)	6.3	3.9	11.3	15
Bankers Trust (l.t.)	6.3	3.9	11.1	46
Bank of California	6.3	4.4	12.9	4
Fidelity Union (N.J.)	6.2	5.0	12.3	3
Lincoln 1st (Rochester)	6.2	2.2	14.2	11
Mfrs. of Detroit	6.2	3.6	14.8	6
Equitable Trust	6.1	4.2	14.7	5
Republic National	6.1	4.4	10.0	69
Wilmington Trust	6.0	4.2	12.5	7
R.I. Hospital Trust	6.0	4.0	15.0	17
Cleveland Trust	6.0	2.5	15.9	15
Salomon Bros. Bond Index	6.0	4.0	14.6	—
American National (Chicago)	5.8	4.8	11.7	10
Chicago Title & Trust	5.8	3.0	11.7	4
Industrial National (R.I.)	5.8	4.4	11.0	10
LaSalle National	5.8	3.1	13.5	18
Marine National	5.8	3.2	13.0	8
Mercantile of Dallas...............	5.8	3.5	12.1	31
First of Tulsa	5.6	3.6	11.8	13
United California	5.5	3.4	11.0	8
N.C. National Bank	5.5	4.5	12.6	25
Central Trust	5.2	2.4	14.0	21
Maryland National	4.1	0.5	13.3	7

Source: *Pensions and Investments*, March 15, 1976.

tered the Salomon Brothers' bond index, which had a five-year compound annual rate of return of 6 percent during the period 1971 through 1975. Over the three-year period, 1973 to 1975, 48 of 70 funds equaled or bettered the Salomon Brothers index, which had a return of 4 percent. In the last year of the study, 1975, only ten banks were able to produce a better return than the Salomon Brothers' index. Figure A16-3 is a listing of the bank commingled bond funds in the study, ranked in order of performance.

REVIEW QUESTIONS AND PROBLEMS

1. What is meant by risk-adjusted performance? How is it calculated?
2. What is the purpose of using risk-adjusted performance measures? What are some of the specific questions attempted to be answered by these techniques?
3. What is meant by the term "single-index" performance measurement?
4. Describe the difference between the internal rate of return and the time-weighted rate of return. Which is better suited to measure a manager's performance? Why?
5. How can betas be used to assess timing decisions?
6. What does a performance review of professional investment management show?
7. Does available evidence support the conclusion that "high risk earns a high return"?
8. Are betas stable over time? Should they be expected to change? Why?
9. What effect can the use of different base periods have on the beta coefficient? Why?
10. Discuss the shortcomings of modern portfolio theory.

RESEARCH PROJECTS

1. Calculate the quarterly risk-adjusted performance for a large mutual fund for the last five years. Comment on whether or not the fund "outperformed" the market.
2. Determine the degree of diversification currently maintained by any two large mutual funds.
3. Using the available risk-adjusted performance data explain the difference in the ten-year performance among the following funds: Dreyfus Fund; Fidelity Trend Fund; Massachusetts Investors Growth Stock Fund; and T. Rowe-Price Growth Stock Fund.
4. Using published data, determine how mutual fund risk and return were related last year.
5. Compare the performance of five closed-end bond funds with the Salomon Brothers and Kuhn Loeb indexes for last year. Interview one of the bond management companies and determine what accounts for their better or worse performance.

C.F.A. QUESTIONS

1. *From Exam III, 1975*

In their article, "An Introduction to Risk and Return," Modigliani and Pogue discussed measurement of investment portfolio performance. Shown in the exhibit, the line AD is the "Market Line," the line BE is the "Empirical Line," the point C identifies the position of the "Market Index," and the Xs identify the positions of investment portfolios.

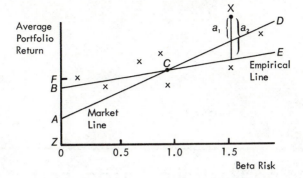

a. Identify what is measured by the distances on the Return scale noted as:
   1. AZ
   2. BZ
   3. FZ
b. Identify the circumstances in which it is preferable to measure the investment performance of an individual portfolio, X, by the distance (a_1) rather than by the distance (a_2).
c. The slope of the Market Line is greater than the slope of the Empirical Line. Discuss the implications concerning the relationship of risk and return in the context of the capital asset pricing model.

2. *From Exam III, 1973*

The trust department of Inner City Bank has decided to monitor the investment performance of its portfolio managers due to a recent increase in the number of performance-related complaints from clients. As director of portfolio management of the bank, you are reviewing two performance measurement techniques proposed by a committee established to investigate the problem and to recommend solutions. A basic stumbling block has arisen because the bank's clients require portfolios with a diversity of investment objectives.

One group has proposed that the portfolio performance be measured by comparing portfolio performance with the performance achieved by the market as a whole. In its opinion, this approach should be sufficient since most investors normally relate their portfolio's performance to that of the general market.

An opposing body of opinion—led by several "beta theorists"—argues that the general market approach does not adequately take into account the degree of risk assumed by portfolio managers in achieving performance.

a. Describe how the beta theorists might take investment risk into consideration by outlining a possible portfolio performance measurement technique.
b. Discuss briefly some of the weaknesses of the measurement technique described in (a) above.
c. Without using either the "beta technique" or the general market approach, outline another approach to the measurement of performance.

Chapter 17

Integrating Portfolio Theory and Management

> Progress is impossible without change, and those
> who cannot change their minds cannot change anything.
> —————————————— *George Bernard Shaw*

The previous two chapters described the major tenets of capital asset pricing theory, the concept of risk-adjusted performance measurement, and some criticisms of modern portfolio theory. We turn in this chapter to a consideration of the feasibility of integrating the strong points of the theory with actual portfolio management practice. The focus of our discussion is on three important phases of the investment decision making process: (1) clarifying investment objectives; (2) determining an appropriate strategy for achieving these objectives; and (3) adopting operating tactics to carry out the broad strategy.

Clarifying Investment Objectives

As was emphasized in Chapter 14, determining one's objectives should be the first step in the development of any soundly conceived investment program. For without first determining the final purpose of investing, it will be impossible to judge effectively the success of investment decisions or the appropriateness of the particular strategies employed. Unfortunately, both individual and institutional investors have found it difficult to articulate their investment objectives with precision or consistency. Capital asset pricing theory can be very helpful in this regard.

For example, a corporate pension plan outlined its investment objectives as follows:[1]

The investment objective of the Trust is to attain maximum growth of assets and income consistent with overall quality investments and preservation of capital. The manager of the assets should select investments in a diversified portfolio, primarily consisting of investment grade common stocks, convertible securities, preferred stocks and bonds.

At the same time, the company seeks a minimum total annual rate of return for the equity related segment of 25% above the Standard & Poor's 500 Composite Index. We are cognizant of the fact that such an objective entails more volatility than the overall market. However, if the asset manager's professional expertise foresees a major decline or unfavorable market environment, it will be acceptable and desirable to reduce the market volatility, and the Committee will expect at least 15% superior performance on the downside, related to the S&P Composite Index. The following table illustrates our expectations for the equity related segment of the portfolio in relation to the time weighted rate of return of the S&P 500 for any given year.

Investment Expectations
(annual percent change)

S&P 500	Trust Fund
+30	+37.5
+20	+25.0
+10	+12.5
0	+ 2.5
−10	− 8.5
−20	−17.0
−30	−25.5

These are not atypical desires. But are they reasonable? The authors of the statement acknowledge that the objective of 25 percent above-average return entails above-average volatility, and then proceed to demand superior performance in both bull and bear markets. Capital asset pricing theory highlights the inconsistency of such all-too-frequent statements of objectives, as will be shown below.

Figure 17–1 illustrates expected returns in terms of various levels of risk, as expressed by the beta coefficient of the portfolio. A portfolio carrying a beta of 1.0 would represent the market as measured by, say, the Standard & Poor's Stock Price Index. The graph assumes that the average rate of return on the S&P 500 (appreciation plus dividend income) will be 10 percent per annum, that periodic bear markets will produce negative market returns of 10 percent during those bear market years, and that the average risk-free rate will be 5 percent. Using

---

[1] This statement is abstracted from an actual set of instructions sent by a relatively large company (which we are not at liberty to identify) to a number of investment management organizations who were competing for a portion of its pension fund and profit sharing trust assets.

FIGURE 17–1

A Framework for Establishing Long-Term Investment Objectives

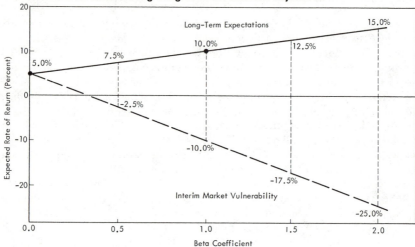

the "market line" concept, Figure 17–1 illustrates the expected rate of return of a portfolio with beta other than 1.0.

Let us consider in this context the set of investment objectives described above. The trustees demand a return of 12.5 percent during a year when the market returns 10 percent. In order to achieve this level of return, Figure 17–1 indicates that the portfolio beta coefficient will have to be 1.5. (To simplify the discussion, it is assumed for the moment that alpha is zero.) Even if one does not accept the notion that there is a clear linear relationship between beta and rate of return, surely the implication of the market line is that the portfolio required to achieve the upside objective represents a position significantly "more risky than the market." Moreover, the portfolio probably would violate the desire for a "diversified portfolio" of "quality investments," with "preservation of capital." This incompatibility of objectives stands out when we consider the portfolio results during a bear market.

The investment manager is being asked to achieve a loss of only 8.5 percent when the market declines 10 percent. Does our market line model, even if we recognize its imperfections, accommodate these expectations? Clearly it does not. We can see, in Figure 17–1, that under the assumptions of our model, a portfolio with a beta of 1.5 can be expected to generate a return of −17.5 percent when the market declines 10 percent (and the risk-free rate is 5 percent).

In order for the portfolio to achieve a return of −8.5 percent when

the market return is -10 percent, the beta would have to be reduced from 1.5 to 0.9. This is derived as follows:

$$R_p = R_f + B(R_m - R_f)$$
$$-8.5\% = 5\% + B(-10\% - 5\%)$$
$$-13.5\% = B(-15\%)$$
$$B = \frac{-13.5\%}{-15\%}$$
$$B = 0.9$$

It would appear rather utopian, however, to expect portfolio managers to forecast a bear market long enough in advance, and be willing to incur the high transaction costs involved, to shift the beta of their portfolios from 1.5 to 0.9. And it would appear equally utopian, in view of the evidence provided in Chapter 16, to expect portfolio managers to be so expert at security selection that a sufficient alpha can be achieved to offset the results of having an inappropriate beta.

Thus, the "market line" concept can be used to clarify investment objectives and to indicate what a set of objectives implies in terms of market timing (adjustment of beta) and the ability to secure gains (alphas) from the astute selection of undervalued securities. This greater degree of understanding on the part of both client and investment manager can provide the basis for a better relationship than generally exists. Let us next explore the process by which modern portfolio theory can be applied to selecting strategies for achieving the desired objectives.

Selecting Efficient Strategies

Once objectives are classified in capital asset pricing terms, managers must determine how most efficiently to distribute portfolio assets. Few investment managers, operating in the traditional intuitive

FIGURE 17–2
Alternative Points on the Efficient Frontier

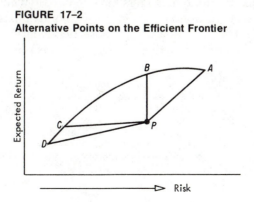

manner, achieve portfolios which lie on the "efficient frontier" described in Chapter 15. More often than not, a portfolio will be at some interior point P of Figure 17–2. (The illustration relates to a portfolio manager who is unable to employ leverage to raise the risk level.)

Through the use of portfolio optimization mathematics, given certain information inputs to be described below, the portfolio manager can determine what actions would be necessary to shift from point P to any one of four (or more) points on the efficient frontier:[2]

At point A he would minimize portfolio risk at the maximum level of expected return which his universe of securities is capable of providing.

At point B he would maximize the portfolio's expected return at the *existing level of risk*.

At point C he would minimize portfolio risk at the *existing level of expected return*.

At point D he would maximize the portfolio's expected return at the minimum risk level which his universe of securities is capable of providing.

In determining the investment composition required to arrive at these points on the efficient frontier, most of the available computer programs allow for the inclusion of a variety of portfolio constraints. The most important of these involves the predetermination of some maximum or minimum level of commitment (in terms of a percentage of total portfolio value) for any one class of security, any one issue, or any one industry classification. This type of constraint can be critical because many investment organizations (e.g., mutual funds) have legally mandated diversification requirements. Moreover, most applications of the capital asset pricing model assume a high degree of diversification.

The concept of efficient frontiers can be readily applied to the problem of asset mix. Portfolio managers have to decide whether they want to run an all-stock portfolio or a portfolio of bonds mixed with stocks. Within the bond sector, they may choose between short-maturity issues and long maturities. Other choices may also be required (e.g.,

---

[2] It is not necessary for each investment management organization to develop and maintain its own complicated programming and computer capability to make these determinations. There are available to most institutional investors a variety of service firms which will perform quantitative portfolio analysis on a regular basis. Frequently, this can be arranged through a New York Stock Exchange firm which will accept commissions as payment. The examples used in this section are based upon a Portfolio Optimization Model developed by Philadelphia Investment Company, 1617 JFK Blvd., Philadelphia, Pennsylvania.

whether or not to purchase real estate)[3] but to keep the illustration simple, we shall deal here with only three asset categories: common stocks, long-term bonds and U.S. Treasury bills.

Table 17–1 shows the simulated returns of various efficient and inefficient portfolio combinations that incorporate average return forecasts of 10 percent for common stocks (as measured by the S&P 500), 7 percent for long-term corporate bonds (as measured by the Salomon Brothers Index), and 5 percent for Treasury bills.[4] The assumed standard deviation of one-year returns is 20 percent for stocks, 8 percent for bonds, and 1.5 percent for T-bills. Covariance assumptions are based on 1956–75 experience, as shown in Table 17–2, along with data for a longer time period. (These risk/return/covariance assumptions are used merely to illustrate the process; alternative forecasts can easily be incorporated into computer programs.)

The high and low return columns in Table 17–1 delineate the expected range of each portfolio's annual compound rate of return at the 90 percent probability level. That is, there is only a 5 percent chance that the portfolio returns will exceed the high values, and only a 5 percent chance that the returns will be less than the low values.

The portfolios are ranked in order of return, and it is clear that risk and return are positively correlated. Also, the higher the expected return the greater the proportion of common stock in the portfolio. Table 17–3 compares portfolio number 5 with number 50. Portfolio 5 is primarily a common stock portfolio (80 percent of total assets) and has an expected annual compound rate of return of 9.20 percent. Over a five-year period the rate of return may be as high as 21.84 percent or as low as −2.13 percent. The range of returns (high to low) is about 24 percentage points. On a ten-year basis, the return range narrows to about 17 percentage points.

Portfolio 50 is much more conservative, composed of only 10 percent common stock, 50 percent bonds, and 40 percent Treasury bills. The expected rate of return is 6.50 percent per annum, almost 3 per-

---

[3] In 1976 it was difficult to determine accurately from available data the variance of real estate equity returns and the covariances with other asset categories. For this reason, real estate equity has not been considered as one of the investment alternatives in our discussion. However, perusal of available data suggests, at least to us, that investment in real estate equity ought to be considered for a significant portion of most institutional portfolios. See, for example, Stephen E. Roulac, "Can Real Estate Returns Outperform Common Stocks?" *The Journal of Portfolio Management*, Winter 1976.

[4] This section draws heavily on the research work of Stewart Zobian and Myra Drucker of the Philadelphia Investment Company. We are very grateful for their permission to use their work to illustrate these important concepts. A good article on the subject is Rodger F. Smith and Thomas M. Richards, "Asset Mix and Investment Strategy," *Financial Analysts Journal*, March/April 1976.

TABLE 17–1
Simulation of Portfolio Returns

Portfolio Number	Portfolio Mix† Stocks	Bonds	Bills	Expected Return	Risk	5-year Annual Return High	Low	10-year Annual Return High	Low
1*	1.00	0.00	0.00	10.00	20.00	25.79	−3.81	20.94	0.05
2*	0.90	0.10	0.00	9.70	18.14	24.01	−2.96	19.64	0.59
3*	0.90	0.00	0.10	9.50	17.92	23.62	−3.00	19.30	0.50
4*	0.80	0.20	0.00	9.40	16.32	22.27	−2.11	18.35	1.13
5*	0.80	0.10	0.10	9.20	16.06	21.84	−2.13	18.00	1.06
6*	0.70	0.30	0.00	9.10	14.57	20.58	−1.29	17.10	1.65
7	0.80	0.00	0.20	9.00	15.84	21.45	−2.17	17.66	0.97
8*	0.70	0.20	0.10	8.90	14.26	20.12	−1.27	16.72	1.60
9*	0.60	0.40	0.00	8.80	12.89	18.95	−0.48	15.88	2.15
10	0.70	0.10	0.20	8.70	13.99	19.69	−1.28	16.36	1.54
11*	0.60	0.30	0.10	8.60	12.52	18.44	−0.43	15.47	2.14
12	0.70	0.00	0.30	8.50	13.77	19.30	−1.32	16.03	1.46
13*	0.50	0.50	0.00	8.50	11.33	17.41	0.26	14.73	2.61
14	0.60	0.20	0.20	8.40	12.20	17.98	−0.40	15.09	2.10
15*	0.50	0.40	0.10	8.30	10.89	16.86	0.37	14.28	2.63
16	0.60	0.10	0.30	8.20	11.92	17.54	−0.40	14.73	2.04
17*	0.40	0.60	0.00	8.20	9.95	16.02	0.91	13.67	2.99
18	0.50	0.30	0.20	8.10	10.49	16.33	0.45	13.86	2.63
19	0.60	0.00	0.40	8.00	11.69	17.15	−0.44	14.39	1.96
20*	0.40	0.50	0.10	8.00	9.42	15.39	1.08	13.18	3.06
21	0.50	0.20	0.30	7.90	10.15	15.85	0.49	13.46	2.61
22*	0.30	0.70	0.00	7.90	8.82	14.82	1.40	12.75	3.26
23	0.40	0.40	0.20	7.80	8.93	14.80	1.23	12.70	3.11
24	0.50	0.10	0.40	7.70	9.85	15.41	0.51	13.09	2.56
25*	0.30	0.60	0.10	7.70	8.19	14.12	1.64	12.20	3.38
26	0.40	0.30	0.30	7.60	8.49	14.25	1.34	12.26	3.13
27*	0.20	0.80	0.00	7.60	8.06	13.91	1.64	12.03	3.35
28	0.50	0.00	0.50	7.50	9.62	15.01	0.48	12.76	2.48
29*	0.30	0.50	0.20	7.50	7.59	13.44	1.87	11.67	3.49
30	0.40	0.20	0.40	7.40	8.11	13.74	1.41	11.85	3.13
31*	0.20	0.70	0.10	7.40	7.33	13.14	1.95	11.43	3.52
32*	0.30	0.40	0.30	7.30	7.04	12.81	2.06	11.17	3.57
33	0.10	0.90	0.00	7.30	7.77	13.37	1.55	11.56	3.20

* Portfolio is efficient.
† Mix values are arbitrarily fixed at integer multiples of 10 percent (0.10); e.g. 20 percent, 70 percent, and so on.

cent lower than for portfolio 5, but the range of probable returns is only 7 percentage points for five-year periods and only 5 percentage points for ten-year periods. Stated another way, the risk factor, variance in expected annual return, is only 4.65 percent for portfolio 50 as compared with 16.06 percent for portfolio 5. Thus, for a 40 percent increase in expected return (9.20 percent versus 6.50 percent), investors must be willing to assume almost four times the risk.

Armed with this information, let's assume that a pension fund trus-

TABLE 17–1 (continued)

Portfolio Number	Portfolio Mix† Stocks	Bonds	Bills	Expected Return	Risk	5-year Annual Return High	Low	10-year Annual Return High	Low
34	0.40	0.10	0.50	7.20	7.80	13.29	1.44	11.47	3.09
35*	0.20	0.60	0.20	7.20	6.62	12.38	2.26	10.83	3.68
36*	0.30	0.30	0.40	7.10	6.54	12.21	2.22	10.69	3.63
37	0.10	0.80	0.10	7.10	6.97	12.54	1.92	10.92	3.41
38	0.40	0.00	0.60	7.00	7.56	12.89	1.41	11.13	3.02
39*	0.20	0.50	0.30	7.00	5.94	11.64	2.55	10.26	3.84
40	0.00	1.00	0.00	7.00	8.00	13.23	1.11	11.37	2.80
41	0.30	0.20	0.50	6.90	6.11	11.67	2.34	10.25	3.65
42	0.10	0.70	0.20	6.90	6.19	11.73	2.28	10.29	3.61
43*	0.20	0.40	0.40	6.80	5.30	10.94	2.82	9.71	3.97
44	0.00	0.90	0.10	6.80	7.20	12.40	1.48	10.73	3.01
45	0.30	0.10	0.60	6.70	5.76	11.19	2.39	9.85	3.64
46	0.10	0.60	0.30	6.70	5.41	10.92	2.64	9.66	3.82
47*	0.20	0.30	0.50	6.60	4.70	10.26	3.06	9.18	4.08
48	0.00	0.80	0.20	6.60	6.41	11.58	1.84	10.10	3.21
49	0.30	0.00	0.70	6.50	5.51	10.79	2.38	9.51	3.57
50*	0.10	0.50	0.40	6.50	4.65	10.12	3.00	9.05	4.01
51*	0.20	0.20	0.60	6.40	4.19	9.66	3.24	8.70	4.15
52	0.00	0.70	0.30	6.40	5.62	10.77	2.21	9.47	3.42
53*	0.10	0.40	0.50	6.30	3.90	9.33	3.35	8.44	4.21
54*	0.20	0.10	0.70	6.20	3.78	9.14	3.34	8.27	4.17
55	0.00	0.60	0.40	6.20	4.84	9.96	2.57	8.84	3.62
56*	0.10	0.30	0.60	6.10	3.19	8.58	3.68	7.85	4.38
57	0.20	0.00	0.80	6.00	3.51	8.72	3.34	7.92	4.11
58	0.00	0.50	0.50	6.00	4.07	9.16	2.93	8.22	3.82
59*	0.10	0.20	0.70	5.90	2.54	7.87	3.96	7.29	4.53
60	0.00	0.40	0.60	5.80	3.33	8.38	3.28	7.62	4.01
61*	0.10	0.10	0.80	5.70	2.01	7.26	4.16	6.80	4.61
62	0.00	0.30	0.70	5.60	2.63	7.64	3.60	7.04	4.18
63*	0.10	0.00	0.90	5.50	1.72	6.83	4.18	6.44	4.57
64	0.00	0.20	0.80	5.40	2.01	6.95	3.87	6.50	4.31
65*	0.00	0.10	0.90	5.20	1.57	6.41	4.00	6.06	4.35
66*	0.00	0.00	1.00	5.00	1.50	6.16	3.86	5.82	4.19

Source: Philadelphia Investment Company.

tee desires to earn 7.5 percent—consisting of the fund's actuarial rate of 4.5 percent plus another 3 percent to accelerate the funding of past service liabilities without increasing company contributions. The optimum 7.5 percent return portfolio under our capital market assumptions would be number 29 in Table 17–1. The asset mix would be 30 percent stocks, 50 percent bonds, and 20 percent T-bills.

It would have to be understood by the trustee that during a "bull market," this portfolio's return would most likely be lower than the general market's and lower than portfolios more heavily invested in

TABLE 17–2
Correlation Coefficients of One-Year Returns (50 years 1926–1975: upper value; 20 years 1956–1975: lower value)

	Common Stock	Corporate Bonds	Treasury Bills
Common stock	1.000	0.170	−0.167
	1.000	0.155	−0.532
Corporate bonds........	0.170	1.000	−0.087
	0.155	1.000	0.007
Treasury bills	−0.167	−0.087	1.000
	−0.532	0.007	1.000

Source: Philadelphia Investment Company.

common stocks. In other words, while the objective would be achieved, "relative performance" would be poor.[5] Conversely, during a "bear market," relative performance would be much better.

TABLE 17–3
Portfolio Comparisons

Portfolio Number	Portfolio Mix			Expected		5 Year Annual Returns		10 Year Annual Returns	
	Stocks	Bonds	Bills	Return	Risk	High	Low	High	Low
5	.80	.10	.10	9.20	16.06	21.84	−2.13	18.00	1.06
50	.10	.50	.40	6.50	4.65	10.12	3.00	9.05	4.01

Source: Table 17–1.

Simulation Models. One of the major difficulties usually facing trustees and others responsible for choosing among alternative "efficient investment strategies" is their limited direct experience with the impact of economic adversity on the flow of funds under their guardianship. And they have still less direct experience with the interaction of high-risk investments and internally-generated cash flows under adverse conditions. Accordingly, their notions of appropriate risk limits are based primarily upon intuition rather than evidence and experience.

---

[5] Pension fund officers, according to a recent Institutional Investor survey, still believe the best measurement of their managers' performance is comparison with that of other managers. In other words, relative performance is considered more important than absolute returns. See "How Pension Funds Monitor the Performance of Their Outside Managers," *Institutional Investor*, May 1976, p. 65. A nonconformist view which holds that a conservative all-bond strategy makes good sense for a pension fund will be found in Paul J. Johnson, "Cutting the Ticker Tape Umbilical Cord," *The Journal of Portfolio Management*, Winter 1976.

FIGURE 17–3
Flowchart Diagrams of Pension Fund Investment Planning Models

THE MONTE CARLO SIMULATION PROCESS

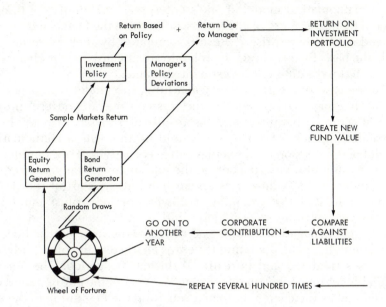

PENSION SIMULATION MODEL

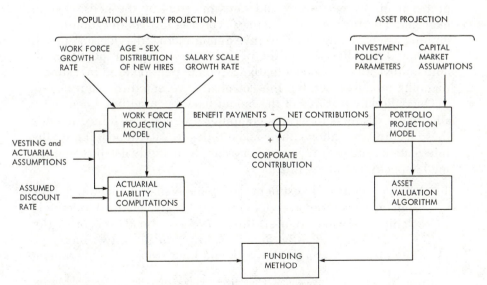

Source: Wilshire Associates Incorporated.

Recently, financial planning models have been developed which allow trustees and portfolio managers to "simulate" the experience they lack. The process, according to John O'Brien, "consists of building a mathematical model of one's enterprise and simulating the impact of the uncertainty of alternative policies on the financial demands placed on that enterprise."[6] Results generated by such exercises provide the basis for assessing the probable advantages and disadvantages associated with different investment strategies.

In the case of a corporate pension fund, the model would pull together the major components of the trustee's overall concern: projection of actuarial liabilities and the results of a variety of possible investment policies. The first step would be to create a mathematical model of the pension fund's actual pattern of activity. For example, the market value of invested assets at the end of any given year is equal, essentially, to the value of assets on hand at the start of the period being simulated (for example, a 25-year period), plus: employer-employee contributions, dividend and interest income, and capital gains (realized and unrealized) during the period, minus: benefits paid under the plan, operating expenses charged to the plan, and capital losses (realized and unrealized) during the period. The amount available for new investments during any year of the entire period can be defined as the change in total assets from the beginning to the end of that year, exclusive of capital gains and losses, plus the turnover of assets which were on hand at the beginning of the year. Turnover includes mandatory amortization payments by borrowers, optional prepayments by borrowers, and sales of assets by the pension fund manager. The investment "strategy" consists of the allocation of beginning assets among different investment media, the decision to sell assets, and the allocation of the periodic amounts made newly available for investment. Conceptually, corporate pension fund investment planning models resemble the flowcharts presented in Figure 17–3.

Once the key features of the model have been outlined conceptually, the next step is to write a computer program which incorporates these features but allows their magnitudes to vary depending on the information sought by the user. For example, a highly flexible program might specify the following:

1. A dozen different investment media are available, including three common stock categories (for example, highly volatile, moderately volatile, and fairly stable), three corporate bond categories (for example Aaa-A, Baa-Ba, and B or lower quality), two mortgage categories (for example, low risk and high risk), U.S. government

---

[6] John W. O'Brien, "Investment Objectives, Policy and Risk," *The Journal of Portfolio Management*, Summer 1975, p. 32.

bonds, real estate equity, preferred stock, and an "all other" composite.

2. Annual interest rates, default rates (loss of interest), and capital gain and loss rates on these investment media are specified as a function of general level of economic activity in each year of the simulation period, plus a random variable which can be generated by the computer. The precise mathematical functions utilized are based on a study of historical experience plus judgment regarding future conditions. (The functions can be changed in successive runnings of the program but are held constant throughout any given 25-year simulation.)

3. The general level of economic activity in each year is specified by the user each time the program is run. Likewise the rates of amortization and optional prepayment are specified for each investment category where such rates are applicable. These factors can all be changed in successive runs.

4. The stream of employer-employee contributions are specified as a joint function of initial actuarial estimates, the level of economic activity, cumulative capital gains or losses, and a random variable.

5. Benefit payments are specified as a function of initial actuarial estimates plus a random variable.

6. Operating expenses are assumed to be a constant percentage of asset value at the end of each year.

7. At the start of each simulation run the user specifies:

   a. The percentage of beginning assets to be allocated to each investment category.

   b. The percentage of new investments to be allocated to each category.

   c. A formula timing plan for the sale of portions of each investment category. This plan can be as simple or as complex as desired. It could also be geared to alter the allocations of new investment funds *within* the simulation period.

A computer program such as outlined above could be run hundreds of times. In each run some aspects would be held constant and some would be changed. The output of each run would be 25 income statements and balance sheets for the pension fund. Assuming that each component of the program bears some semblance to reality, pension fund managers could gain great insight into the consequences of a given investment strategy under different economic conditions and of the consequences of different investment strategies under similar economic conditions. They would also learn a good deal about the impact on income and assets of changes in assumptions regarding investment maturities, interest rates, loss rates, and so forth.

The simulation approach can be illustrated by abstracting from an actual study prepared by Wilshire Associates Incorporated[7] to help the corporate executives of a leading enterprise examine the impact of alternative investment policies on the expected level of benefit programs. It is also interesting and relevant to point out that the analysis incorporates "market line" theory in determining the possible impact of investment strategy on pension costs.

The capital market assumptions used in the Wilshire Associates study, based on extensive analysis of historical data together with estimates of economic variables such as growth of real GNP and inflation rates, are as follows:

	Percent
Equity market return	12.0
Standard deviation of equity returns	18.0
Bond market return	8.5
Bond market standard deviation	12.0
Risk-free rate	7.0

In addition, Wilshire made assumptions regarding the investment policy alternatives which would be available to the investment manager. Four alternative policies, which were established in consultation with the corporate manager of the pension fund, are summarized below. They range from a relatively low risk policy of 50 percent equities (policy A) to a higher risk policy of nearly all equities (policy D) (see Table 17–4).

Using these assumptions together with data covering contributions,

TABLE 17–4
Policy Alternatives

Policy	Percent Equities	Per-cent Bonds	Per-cent Cash	Equity Beta	Equity R^2	Ex-pected Return*	Man-agement Fee
A	50%	45%	5%	1.20	85%	10.7%	.5
B	65	30	5	1.20	85	11.4	.5
C	85	10	5	1.20	85	12.3	.5
D	95	0	5	1.20	85	12.7	.5

*Expected return is the weighted average of the capital market assumptions shown previously. For example, under policy A, the expected return of 10.7 percent is arrived at by adding 50 percent of the expected return of a 1.2 beta portfolio where the market return is expected to be 12 percent; 45 percent of a 8.5 percent expected bond market return; and 5 percent of an expected risk-free return of 7 percent.

[7] Wilshire Associates Incorporated, 100 Wilshire Boulevard, Santa Monica, California 90401, conducts research for institutional investors and managers of institutional portfolios.

forfeitures, benefit plan changes, salary increases, and so on, projections were made of the benefits, expressed as a percentage of final pay, which could be expected to be covered by the various investment policies. Some of these projections are shown in Figure 17–4.

FIGURE 17–4
Annual Retirement Benefit as a Percent of Final Pay for Average Retiring Participant—Tenth Year

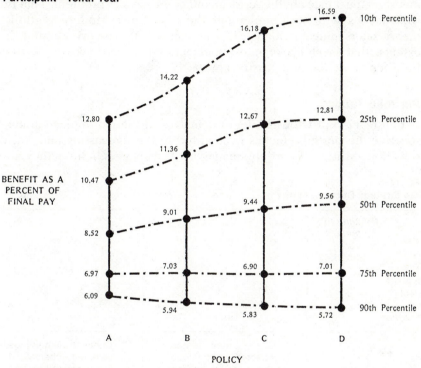

Source: Wilshire Associates Incorporated.

The chart shown in Figure 17–4 indicates the most likely result (50th percentile), together with a range of less likely alternative outcomes, for participants retiring in 10 years. An unlikely (one chance in ten) adverse outcome is labeled "90th percentile" and an unlikely positive outcome is labeled "10th percentile."

It can be seen from the results that the average participant retiring ten years from the date of the study is most likely to have a retirement benefit ranging from 8.5 to 9.5 percent of final pay depending on which investment policy is implemented. The adverse outcome ranges from 6.1 to 5.7 percent of final pay. It is seen that while the most risky investment alternative (policy D) provides a larger expected

benefit, it also leads to the possibility of producing an inferior result under adverse circumstances.

Used in this manner, simulation techniques, combined with capital asset pricing theory, can be instrumental in helping corporate officials and their portfolio managers, better understand the implications of their investment policies.

Once objectives and broad strategies as to asset mix are determined, investors must face another critical and controversial problem. That is, what tactics will best implement the strategies? Modern portfolio theory offers much guidance in this context, the theory arguing, in essence, that the choice of investment tactics narrows down to selecting between an *active* or a *passive* approach.

Portfolio Tactics

Figure 17–5 provides a "decision matrix" designed to place in perspective the portfolio tactics best suited to the forecasting and stock selection abilities of portfolio managers. If managers believe they are

FIGURE 17–5
Portfolio Strategy Decision Matrix

Ability to Select Undervalued Securities \ Ability to Forecast Overall Market	Good	Poor
Good	1. Concentrate holdings in selected undervalued securities rather than diversify broadly. 2. Shift beta above and below desired long-term average, based on market forecasts.	1. Concentrate holdings in selected undervalued securities rather than diversify broadly. 2. Keep beta stable at desired long-term average.
Poor	1. Hold a broadly diversified list of securities. 2. Shift beta above and below desired long-term average, based on market forecasts.	1. Hold a broadly diversified list of securities. 2. Keep beta stable at desired long-term average.

Source: Adapted from Keith Ambachtsheer, "Portfolio Theory and the Security Analyst," *Financial Analysts Journal*, November/December 1972, p. 33.

good market forecasters, they should vary their portfolios' betas quite often, in line with their forecasts. If they believe they are good stock selectors, they should depart from the principle of broad diversification. If they are doubtful that they possess a high degree of either ability, they should concentrate on determining the most appropriate overall risk level for their clients and should proceed to create broadly diversified portfolios with constant beta levels that conform to their risk appraisals.

Active Portfolio Management. This term represents what most investment professionals try to do to earn their living. It is the attempt to profit from stock selection, market timing, or both. In capital asset pricing terms, it is an attempt to achieve investment returns that differ from those implied by the market line.

According to Russell J. Morrison, two considerations are necessary for success in active portfolio management.[8] First, one must have a good idea of how others view alternative investments. Second, one must disagree with the concensus—disagree as to direction or disagree as to amplitude of price movement. Thus, the task of the active portfolio manager is not to forecast returns accurately, but to forecast *more accurately* than the market. Moreover, the difference in expectations must be of sufficient magnitude to cover transaction costs and to allow for the error factor.

Active managers consider the holding period for portfolio securities to be temporary. Once the difference in expectation disappears, either because the market's perception changes or because the manager is proven wrong, portfolio holdings are replaced by others which are believed to offer better returns than expected by the market. Active portfolio management requires either: (*a*) concentration in a fairly small number of issues with continuous reassessment of alternatives; or (*b*) moving in and out of well-diversified portfolios. Unfortunately, as was shown in the previous chapter, historical evidence suggests that most professional portfolio managers are not very successful in these efforts.

Charles D. Ellis, in an award winning *Financial Analysts Journal* article, recently put a new perspective on the difficulty of outperforming the market by solving "a simple but distressing equation."[9]

Assume:

a. Equities will return an average 9 percent rate of return.

b. Average turnover of 30 percent per annum.

---

[8] Russell J. Morrison, "Speculation: Its Nature and Implications for Portfolio Management," *Financial Analysts Journal*, January/February 1976.

[9] Charles D. Ellis, "The Loser's Game," *Financial Analysts Journal*, July/August 1975, p. 19.

c. Average costs—dealer spreads plus commissions—on institutional transactions are 3 percent of the principal value involved.
d. Management and custody fees total 0.20 percent.
e. The goal of the manager is to outperform the averages by 20 percent.

Solve for $X\%$: $(X)(9) - [.30(3 + 3)] - (0.20) = (1.20)(9)$

$$X = \frac{1.8 + 0.20 + 10.8}{9}$$

$$X = \frac{12.8}{9}$$

$$X = 142\%.$$

In plain language, according to Ellis, the manager who intends to deliver *net* returns of 20 percent better than the market must earn a gross return before fees and transaction costs (liquidity tolls) that is more than 40 percent better than the market. If this sounds absurd, he points out, the same equation can be solved to show that the active manager must beat the market *gross* by 22 percent just to come out even with the market. In other words, for institutional investors to perform as well as, *but no better than,* the S&P 500, they must be sufficiently astute and skillful to "outdo" the market by 22 percent.

Ellis suggests four rules for those who are determined to win the "Loser's Game" despite the odds against them.

First, be sure you are playing your own game. Know your policies very well and play according to them all the time.

Second, keep it simple. Make fewer and perhaps better investment decisions. Simplify the professional investment management problem. Try to do a few things unusually well.

Third, concentrate on your defenses. Almost all of the information in the investment management business is oriented toward purchase decisions. The competition in making purchase decisions is too good. It's too hard to outperform the other fellow in buying. Concentrate on selling instead.

Fourth, don't take it personally. The game is tougher than it looks, and lots of players accustomed to winning (other games) will lose at trying to beat the market.

Passive Portfolio Management. Unfortunately, most players do not follow these, or their own, rules very well and there is now a serious trend toward *passive* portfolio management. This term implies the creation of a well-diversified portfolio at some predetermined risk level, usually not much different from 1.0 beta, and holding it relatively unchanged for the long run. Index funds, which will be discussed shortly, are one form of passive portfolio management.

Passive portfolios are characterized by very low turnover, hence

minimum transaction costs, reduced management expenses, and low levels of specific risk. Managers of such portfolios regard "new" investment information as containing little or no worthwhile value. That is, acting on such information, by changing the composition of portfolio holdings, is believed unlikely to produce any extra return.

Jack Treynor, editor of the *Financial Analysts Journal* recently pointed out that:

. . . most traditional portfolios contain an *active* part and a *passive* part. Most purchases [for active portfolios] are based on expectations of abnormal return, and enter the *active* part. But once the market comes around to the investor's point of view, or the investor comes around to the market's point of view, that expectation disappears. Rarely, however, does the investor sell an asset as soon as this point of "reconciliation" is reached. Assets held beyond this point comprise the *passive* part of the portfolio."[10]

Efficient Frontier Revisited. Whether one chooses to run an active or a passive portfolio, or a bit of each, the efficient frontier concept can be applied. That is, a passive portfolio manager assumes that every individual security is "correctly priced" on the basis of available information. Active managers assume that they are "smarter than the market." In the former case, the risk/reward forecasts made by portfolio managers for each security being contemplated for purchase will be the "concensus forecast." In the latter case, portfolio managers will overlay their own judgments on the concensus. Either way, the forecasts can be entered into a computer program which will generate efficient frontiers based on those forecasts.

To illustrate, the Philadelphia Investment Company has been kind enough to calculate an efficient frontier for a "blue chip" stock portfolio of a leading New York City bank. The risk/reward parameters used in the calculation assume a rate of return for the overall market of 15 percent, and individual stock alphas and betas equivalent to those actually recorded during a recent 12-month period. A constraint was applied which limited any one holding to 5 percent of the portfolio.

Figure 17–6 presents the efficient frontier thus calculated, and identifies the "points of optimization" A, B, C, and D referred to earlier in the Portfolio Strategy section. Figure 17–6 also shows the position of the original portfolio (P), and the market portfolio (M). Point E represents the same issues in the original portfolio, but with equal weighting given to each issue.

Table 17–5 summarizes the expected returns, betas, correlation coefficients, and issue count of the various portfolios. The portfolio designed to maximize return, for example, (portfolio A) has an expected return of 27.1 percent and a beta, or risk level, of 1.5. The original

---

[10] Jack L. Treynor, "Index Funds and Active Portfolio Management," *Financial Analysts Journal*, May/June 1976, p. 18.

FIGURE 17–6
Calculated Efficient Frontier of Portfolio Stocks

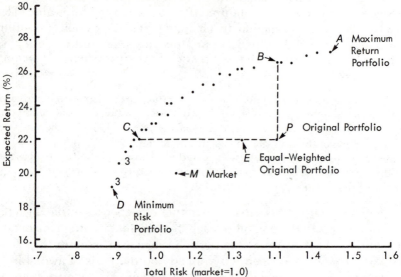

Note: The numeral 3 refers to three portfolios having the same risk/reward parameters.
Source: Philadelphia Investment Company

portfolio (*P*) has an expected return of 21.9 percent and a beta level of 1.3. Thus, by increasing beta .2, expected return is increased 5.2 percent over the forecast period.

Looking at Table 17–6, which details the composition of the various portfolios, we can see that portfolio *A* consists simply of the 20 issues

TABLE 17–5
Quantitative Characteristics of Alternative Efficient Stock Portfolios

	Original P	Efficient Portfolios				Equal Weighted E	Market* X
		A	B	C	D		
Return (percent)							
Market	18.0	19.8	17.7	13.3	12.4	17.2	15.0
Nonmarket (alpha) ..	.6	2.9	3.4	3.8	2.8	.9	—
Dividend	3.3	4.4	5.2	4.8	4.1	3.8	4.0
Total	21.9	27.1	26.3	21.9	19.3	21.9	19.0
Risk (Market = 1.0)							
Beta	1.2	1.3	1.2	.9	.8	1.1	1.0
Total†	1.3	1.5	1.3	1.0	.9	1.2	1.0
Market correlation (percent)	81%	79%	79%	87%	90%	85%	100%
Issue count	44	20	22	21	23	44	500

* S&P 500 Composite.
† Relative standard deviation of periodic return.

TABLE 17–6
Composition of Model Portfolios

	Expected Return*	Total Risk†	Original P	A	B	C	D
					Efficient Portfolios		
1. Virginia Elec & Pwr	36.9	2.0	1.14	5.00	5.00	5.00	—
2. Gen Tel & Elec	30.7	1.6	2.17	5.00	5.00	5.00	—
3. Beatrice Foods	28.9	2.2	3.02	5.00	4.51	—	—
4. Coca Cola	28.9	2.0	2.91	5.00	5.00	—	—
5. Federated Dept. Stores	28.2	1.6	1.73	5.00	5.00	5.00	5.00
6. First Bank SYS	27.6	1.9	2.35	5.00	5.00	—	—
7. Gen. Electric	27.5	1.6	2.81	5.00	5.00	5.00	.06
8. Whirlpool	27.3	2.5	2.28	5.00	5.00	—	—
9. Eastman Kodak	26.9	1.8	4.34	5.00	5.00	1.34	—
10. Oklahoma Gas & Elec	26.9	2.1	1.94	5.00	4.99	—	—
11. Hewlett-Packard	26.5	2.3	2.48	5.00	3.27	—	—
12. FMC	26.4	1.9	.99	5.00	5.00	5.00	5.00
13. Middle South Utils	25.9	1.6	.59	5.00	5.00	5.00	5.00
14. American Express	25.8	2.1	1.56	5.00	—	—	—
15. Continental Tel.	25.7	1.9	.52	5.00	5.00	—	.01
16. Northern Ind. Pub. Svc	25.5	1.6	.94	5.00	5.00	5.00	5.00
17. Chesebrough Ponds	25.1	2.1	3.85	5.00	—	—	—
18. Sears, Roebuck	24.4	1.5	1.90	5.00	4.30	—	4.47
19. Emerson Elec..............	24.0	1.8	.46	5.00	—	—	—
20. Intl Business Machines	23.6	1.8	10.68	5.00	5.00	4.70	.46
21. Armstrong Cork	23.0	2.2	2.80	—	—	—	—
22. Xerox	22.8	2.6	3.34	—	—	—	—
23. Mobil Oil	22.7	1.3	1.84	—	5.00	5.00	5.00
24. Texas Utils	21.1	2.0	2.31	—	—	—	—
25. Travelers	20.4	2.0	1.13	—	—	—	—
26. Exxon	20.3	1.2	4.31	—	5.00	5.00	5.00
27. Caterpillar Tractor	20.3	1.3	.71	—	2.30	5.00	5.00
28. Southern Cal. Edison	19.8	1.2	1.08	—	5.00	5.00	5.00
29. Minnesota Mng & Mfg	19.4	1.9	1.98	—	—	—	—
30. American Tel & Tel	18.3	.9	2.20	—	—	5.00	5.00
31. Moore Ltd	18.0	1.3	2.02	—	—	3.96	5.00
32. Kresge	17.9	1.3	2.21	—	—	5.00	5.00
33. Gen. Mills	17.9	1.2	.85	—	—	5.00	5.00
34. Merck	16.7	1.6	4.37	—	—	—	5.00
35. AMP	16.5	2.1	2.03	—	—	—	—
36. Ralston Purina	16.4	1.1	1.59	—	—	5.00	5.00
37. Du Pont	16.4	1.5	1.01	—	.63	5.00	5.00
38. Morgan JP	14.9	1.7	2.19	—	—	—	—
39. Procter & Gamble	14.7	1.1	1.66	—	—	—	5.00
40. Black & Decker	14.2	2.3	1.11	—	—	—	—
41. Johnson & Johnson	13.9	1.5	3.81	—	—	—	5.00
42. Philip Morris	12.3	1.5	4.02	—	—	5.00	5.00
43. Alcan Aluminum	11.2	1.4	.13	—	—	5.00	5.00
44. Eli Lilly	10.2	1.8	2.55	—	—	—	—

* Forecast period: One year.
† Relative standard deviation of periodic return.

with the highest expected return, each weighted with 5 percent of the portfolio's assets. It is also interesting to note that portfolio A has a coefficient of determination (r^2) of 79 percent as against 81 percent for the original portfolio.

It is easy to see what happens as we move around the efficient frontier, from portfolio A to portfolio D. The beta coefficient decreases, as does the expected return. On the other hand, alpha and dividend income jump around without exhibiting any discernible pattern. Also, the correlation with the market increases as risk decreases, even though the number of issues in all cases is about the same. Overall, we can conclude that *if the risk/reward assumptions incorporated in the computer run are accurate*—an admittedly big "if"—the existing portfolio P is quite inefficient. For instance, the beta coefficient of portfolio P(1.3) is equal to that of portfolio B, but the expected return (21.9 percent) is equal only to that of the much less risky portfolio C.

Of course, the risk/reward assumptions were made quite mechanistically on the basis of historical price behavior. For example, consider the six utility issues included in the original bank portfolio. Table 17–7

TABLE 17–7
Expected Returns for Six Utility Stocks

		Expected Return (percent)			
	Beta	Market	Nonmarket	Dividend	Total
Virginia Elec & Pwr	1.20	17.94	10.23	8.74	36.91
Oklahoma Gas & Elec	1.16	17.36	2.88	6.62	26.86
Middle South Utils	.93	13.95	2.55	9.43	25.93
Northern Ind Pub Svc	.79	11.86	5.67	7.94	25.47
Texas Utils	1.00	14.95	—	6.16	21.11
Southern Cal Edison	.68	10.20	.81	8.78	19.79
Equities Market*	1.00	15.00	—	4.00	19.00

* Standard & Poor's 500 Composite.
Source: Philadelphia Investment Company.

shows for each issue: (*a*) the general market influence, beta; (*b*) the nonmarket, specific influence, alpha; (*c*) the dividend yield; and (*d*) the total expected return.[11]

Presumably, knowledgeable utility analysts would be able to account for most of the indicated differences among the betas by documenting differences in financial leverage and economic sensitivity of service areas. But even if they cannot, they might accept as reasonable

---

[11] We have eliminated from this discussion and example treatment of the risk-free rate as a part of total return. Also, expected return departs from our discussion in the previous chapters by separating price change from the dividend portion of total return.

forecasts betas calculated from recent history. On the other hand, the nonmarket returns (alphas) represent an area where investment analysts might make an important contribution to the portfolio optimization process. For example, the differences in alphas in Table 17–6 could be a result of several current events: favorable rate case decisions, uneven recovery from very depressed recent stock price levels, anticipated dividend increases, and so on. Active portfolio managers would expect utility analysts to be a much better source of estimated future alpha returns than a simple extension of past alphas into the forecast period. Virginia Electric & Power, for example, probably would not be expected to sustain its historically high level of alpha, +10.23 percent. The utility analyst would be consulted for this judgment.

Furthermore, in the example just cited, the optimization universe consisted only of existing holdings of portfolio P. Obviously, a portfolio manager has available a much wider population of stocks from which to choose. For example, many organizations provide managers with a "buy" list, or approved list, and any issue so listed can be selected for purchase. Issues on such a list, but not present in a portfolio, can also be submitted for inclusion as alternative choices in creating a portfolio to be positioned on the efficient frontier. In these cases, the model will create the best portfolio, at any point, from among all the issues entered into the program.

In addition to reviewing a variety of alternative strategies with different lists of securities, the same model allows an assessment of the impact of different market movements or different investment time horizons on the portfolio's estimated return. In other words, an investment manager can estimate portfolio performance under a number of possible future market environments during a number of different time periods.

Index Funds. Portfolio managers to whom the concept of passive management has appeal are turning increasingly to the use of "index" funds to control both portfolio risk and/or guarantee market performance.[12]

An index fund is a portfolio designed to mirror the movement of a selected broad market index by holding commitments in the same proportions as those which comprise the index itself. For example, if IBM accounts for 7 percent of the S&P 500, and the desire is to match

---

[12] To a large extent, index funds appear to represent a natural extension of the random-walk hypothesis and the acceptance of capital market theory. However, the concept is far from new. For example, Scottish trusts in the last century essentially tried to create portfolios that represented the universe of available investments and did not attempt to "pick winners." The same was true of trusts in the United States prior to the growth of mutual funds.

the S&P 500, then the portfolio would have put 7 percent of its assets in IBM, and so on. Once the portfolio is established, it need not be disturbed except to accommodate cash flows (in and out), to reinvest dividend income, and to adjust for issues added to, or deleted from, the market index.[13]

An index fund, by definition, has a beta of 1.0. Beta can be adjusted down or up from 1.0 by adding risk-free assets to the portfolio or leveraging it. However, the most popular motivation for index portfolios, at least to date, is the desire to "match the market" over long periods of time with at least some portion of a portfolio's assets.

Impetus behind the acceptance of index funds by some institutional investors emanates from a variety of sources. For one, expenses are substantially reduced, since transaction costs, once the portfolio is established, are minimal and there is no need for extensive security analysis or portfolio management staffs.[14] Batterymarch Financial Management Corporation, which manages an index fund, has estimated that the annual cost (management fee, brokerage commissions and custodial fees) of a $500 million fund under conventional management would be equal to 0.55 percent of the fund's assets; the corresponding figure for a Batterymarch index fund of the same size would be only 0.06 percent of the fund's assets. Even if an index fund had only $25 million in assets, the estimated annual cost would be only 0.18 percent of the fund's assets, still a low charge and plainly a reasonable one for trustees not in a position to create their own market portfolios.

Recently, some research into investment trust law has developed other arguments in favor of the use of index funds by pension trustees. Professors John H. Langbein and Richard A. Posner have taken a careful look at "the extent to which a trustee may invest in a market fund without thereby violating the legal standards that govern the investment of trust assets."[15] The question, they point out, is a particularly timely one in view of the new pension reform law, ERISA.

In the past, some observers have argued that the legal regulations

---

[13] For example, on June 30, 1976 the composition of the S&P 500 was substantially changed. The industrial component was reduced from 425 to 400 issues, the utility component reduced from 60 to 40 issues, and a new finance subsector introduced consisting of banks and insurance companies.

[14] This is not to say that index fund managers are relieved of the concern to follow closely the securities in their portfolios. Rather, research and portfolio management efforts can be directed toward nontraditional areas which require less labor resources, such as seeking to exclude potential bankruptcy candidates from the portfolio, developing a better understanding of the appropriate investment objectives for the portfolio, or refining estimates of the market's expected return.

[15] John H. Langbein and Richard A. Posner, "Market Funds and Trust-Investment Law," *American Bar Foundation Research Journal*, 1975, p. 2.

governing trust and fiduciary responsibilities are largely incompatible with modern portfolio theory. That is, trust law in general has focused on the merits of investing in each individual security, rather than focusing on the portfolio as a whole.[16] Langbein and Posner argue otherwise. In fact, they conclude their study by warning fiduciaries that they cannot play safe by ignoring modern theory and continuing uncritically to put trust money into old-fashioned, managed portfolios. They make their case even stronger by a further warning that:

When market funds have become available in sufficient variety and their experience bears out their prospects, courts may one day conclude that it is imprudent for trustees to fail to use such vehicles. Their advantages seem decisive: at any given risk/return level, diversification is maximized and investment costs minimized. A trustee who declines to procure such advantages for the beneficiaries of his trust may in the future find his conduct difficult to justify.[17]

Whatever the soundness of such legal arguments, the increasing use of index funds reflects, more than anything else, dissatisfaction over the performance of conventionally managed portfolios. Despite the evidence that this dissatisfaction has considerable justification, most professional portfolio managers, quite naturally, reject the use of index funds to improve performance. The basis for most of their rejection, unfortunately, reflects more their selfish interest than intellectual substance. There is one objection, however, deserving of comment, namely that if more and more investors adopt the index approach, the market will lose the very efficiency which gave rise to the concept. Then, according to those who hold this view, the index fund strategy would lose out to those who could profit from stock selection and timing maneuvers. Langbein and Posner anticipated this line of attack, and pointed out:

. . . there is little danger that even if all trustees adopted the passive strategy, which is not likely, that strategy would fail. There would still be many other investors, they would continue to search out under-valued stocks to buy and over-valued stocks to sell, and their activities would make it unnecessary and unprofitable for trustees to do any picking.[18]

Apparent versus Actual Diversification. Some advocates of index funds suggest that a carefully selected sample of stocks can provide almost the same diversification as would be obtained by owning all of

---

[16] See, for example, "The Regulation of Risky Investment," *Harvard Law Review*, January 1970. Also, Martin Lipton, "An Analysis: Prudent Man Test in Investments," *New York Law Journal*, January 15, 1975.

[17] Langbein and Posner, "Market Funds and Trust Investment Law," p. 30.

[18] Ibid., p. 18.

the stocks included in the index. For example, Lorie states that about 90 percent of the market's movement can generally be achieved by holding only about 32 stocks.[19] Beyond that point, Lorie says, substantial increases in portfolio size are required for any additional significant reduction in nonmarket variation. For example, to increase the 90 percent to 95 percent, 64 stocks are needed. In other words, doubling the number of issues from 32 to 64 raises the diversification level only 5 percent.

A graphic illustration prepared by Sharpe is perhaps even more revealing. Figure 17–7 indicates that the impact of diversification in-

FIGURE 17–7
Effect of Diversification on Nonmarket Risk

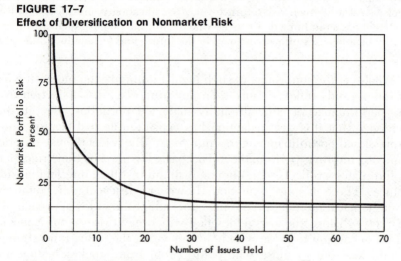

Source: *Financial Analysts Journal,* January/February 1972, p. 77.

creases with the number of holdings at a rapidly decreasing rate, becoming asymptotic at approximately the level of 35 holdings. Notice that the increase in diversification achieved by moving from a 32 to a 64 issue portfolio is not even noticeable.

Viewed in this perspective, most large (and even most small) portfolios would seem to contain far too many securities.[20] However, it should be recognized that the term "diversification" can have different definitions. It can mean, for example, developing a portfolio which has

---

[19] James H. Lorie, "Diversification: Old and New," *The Journal of Portfolio Management,* Winter 1975.

[20] This applies even to mutual funds registered as diversified investment trusts where regulatory requirements restrict most holdings to less than 5 percent of total assets and no more than 10 percent of the voting stock of any one issue.

Most employee pension trusts are governed by more liberal guidelines, and 8 percent of total assets is often allowed as a maximum portfolio position.

SUGGESTED READINGS

x, Fischer. "The Investment Policy Spectrum: Individuals, Endowment Funds and Pension Funds." *Financial Analysts Journal*, January/February 1976.

, Charles D. "The Loser's Game." *Financial Analysts Journal*, July–August 1975.

ll, James L., Jr. "Homogeneous Stock Groupings: Implications for Portfolio Management." *Financial Analysts Journal*, May/June 1975.

, Roger, and Wolman, William. *The Beat Inflation Strategy*. New York: Simon & Schuster, 1975.

bein, John H., and Posner, Richard A. "Market Funds and Trust-Investment Law." *American Bar Foundation Research Journal*, 1975.

onald, John G. "Investment Objectives: Diversification, Risk and Exposure to Surprise." *Financial Analysts Journal*, March/April 1975.

iel, Burton G., and Firstenberg, Paul B. *Managing Risk in an Uncertain Era*. Princeton, N.J.: Princeton University, 1976.

ien, John W. "Investment Objectives, Policy and Risk." *The Journal of Portfolio Management*, Summer 1975.

nberg, Barr, and Guy, James. "Beta and Investment Fundamentals." *Financial Analysts Journal*, May/June 1976.

pe, William F. "Likely Gains from Market Timing." *Financial Analysts Journal*, March/April 1975.

h, Rodger F., and Richards, Thomas M. "Asset Mix and Investment Strategy." *Financial Analysts Journal*, March/April 1976.

nor, Jack L., and Black, Fischer. "How to Use Security Analysis to Improve Portfolio Selection." *Journal of Business*, January 1973.

iamson, J. Peter. *Funds for the Future*. Report of the Twentieth Century Fund Task Force on College and University Endowment Policy. New York: McGraw-Hill Book Co., 1975.

REVIEW QUESTIONS AND PROBLEMS

How can capital asset pricing theory be helpful in establishing the investment objectives of a portfolio?

What is the purpose of "portfolio balancing"?

How can traditional security analysis techniques be used to supplement portfolio balancing efforts?

Under what conditions would a portfolio manager intentionally seek to create an "undiversified" portfolio?

What are some of the problems associated with trying to create a diversified, high-risk position for a large portfolio? Discuss an alternative approach.

Define the difference between active and passive portfolio management. Which would you choose? Why?

a high degree of correlation between its own returns and that of the general market index. In this case, the variability of portfolio return would be substantially explained by price movements in a broad market index. Such a portfolio condition could be accomplished with a portfolio containing relatively few issues. As we have indicated, some 30 to 60 randomly selected issues would just about achieve this objective.

On the other hand, some observers contend that diversification implies a portfolio with a high degree of "conditional predictability"—that is, a portfolio whose return can be predicted with a relatively high degree of certainty, once given an estimate of the market's overall price change during a specifically defined period. Such a portfolio not only would have to have a predetermined "beta" level which can be regarded with a high degree of confidence; *it would require a near zero alpha*. To satisfy this definition, 50 or even 100 issues might be too few. For example, studies show that a portfolio of the 50 stocks of the Standard & Poor's 500 which have the largest market values (and with allocation of funds among included stocks proportional to market values) produces returns that can easily differ from returns for the entire 500 stocks by as much as 4.5 percentage points per year. Portfolios of 100 stocks could easily differ by as much as 3.0 percentage points.[21]

Still another consideration is that the effect of adding additional stocks varies with the *level* of portfolio risk. Studies have shown that there is a significantly higher level of nonmarket risk present in high beta stocks than in low beta stocks. Therefore, a larger number of issues is required in a high-risk portfolio to achieve the same level of diversification as in a low-risk portfolio. According to one researcher, for example, the diversification achieved by a low beta portfolio of five securities cannot be matched by a high beta portfolio containing as many as 25 securities.[22]

Portfolio managers also have some reason to be concerned over factors other than just the number of securities in a portfolio. Many studies indicate that efforts to establish efficient portfolio diversification must contend with factors other than general market influences. For example, Farrell sought to determine whether the price volatility of stocks conforms to "classes," such as growth stocks, cyclical issues, and stable or defensive investments. Table 17–8 summarizes the important findings of his study[23] and shows a matrix of correlation coeffi-

---

[21] Lorie, p. 28.

[22] Robert C. Klemkosky and John D. Martin, "The Effect of Market Risk on Portfolio Diversification," *Journal of Finance*, March 1975.

[23] James L. Farrell, Jr., "Homogeneous Stock Groupings," *Financial Analysts Journal*, May/June 1975.

TABLE 17–8
Correlation Coefficients of Stock Groupings

Growth Stocks	Growth Index Cor. Coef.	Stable Index Cor. Coef.	Cyclical Index Cor. Coef.	Oil Index Cor. Coef.
1. Ampex	0.49	-.01	-.02	-.12
2. Avon	0.45	0.10	-.17	-.21
3. Int'l Flavors & Fragrances	0.37	-.06	-.11	-.09
4. Chesebrough-Pond's	0.34	0.02	-.07	-.07
5. Baxter Labs	0.47	-.03	-.14	-.22
6. Becton-Dickinson	0.39	0.10	-.07	-.12
7. Eastman Kodak	0.36	-.04	-.13	-.16
8. Polaroid	0.60	-.01	-.05	-.14
9. Minnesota Mining	0.38	-.00	-.07	-.15
10. AMP	0.57	0.03	-.19	-.11
11. Texas Instruments	0.50	-.34	0.15	-.08
12. Hewlett-Packard	0.53	-.06	-.13	-.06
13. Perkin-Elmer	0.64	-.15	-.14	-.12
14. Burroughs	0.53	-.21	-.03	-.25
15. IBM	0.45	0.06	-.41	-.34
16. Honeywell	0.26	-.07	-.07	-.34
17. Nat'l Cash Register	0.34	0.01	-.19	-.27
18. Xerox	0.44	-.05	-.16	-.24
19. Nalco	0.27	.12	0.07	-.18
20. Maryland Cup	0.39	-.05	0.11	-.10
21. Harcourt, Brace	0.40	0.04	-.01	-.17
22. Corning Glass	0.55	-.02	-.37	-.08
23. Motorola	0.50	-.21	0.07	-.22
24. Zenith	0.38	-.11	0.06	-.26
25. International Telephone	0.42	0.02	-.10	-.12
26. UAL, Inc.	0.44	-.16	0.18	-.15
27. Pan American	0.40	-.23	0.21	-.13
28. United Aircraft	0.39	-.21	0.09	-.10
29. TRW	0.25	-.12	-.05	-.16
30. Trane	0.48	0.02	0.20	-.29
31. Merck	0.24	0.04	-.13	-.08
Stable Stocks				
32. Sears	0.02	0.20	-.12	-.11
33. Federated Department Stores	0.04	0.23	-.19	-.08
34. Reynolds	-.04	0.29	0.06	-.13
35. Coca-Cola	0.12	0.38	-.07	-.17
36. Procter and Gamble	0.01	0.35	-.05	-.10
37. General Foods	-.05	0.55	-.04	-.12
38. Quaker Oats	-.08	0.37	-.04	-.01
39. Kraftco	-.21	0.39	-.13	0.06
40. National Biscuit	0.02	0.37	-.13	0.01
41. CPC International	-.04	0.38	-.06	0.09
42. Gillette	0.18	0.23	-.08	-.06
43. American Home Products	0.05	0.25	-.07	-.12
44. C.I.T.	-.08	0.34	0.09	-.11
45. Hershey	0.02	0.39	0.11	-.04
46. Campbell	0.02	0.33	0.00	-.13
47. Kellogg	-.05	0.31	0.00	-.12
48. Household Finance	-.03	0.49	-.05	-.06
49. Chase Manhattan Bank	-.25	0.46	-.01	0.12
50. Northwest Bancorp.	-.08	0.44	0.03	0.01
51. Transamerica	-.27	0.44	0.01	0.11

Growth Stocks	Growth Index Cor. Coef.	Stable Index Cor. Coef.	Cyclical Index Cor. Coef.	Oil Index Cor. Coef.
52. Florida Power	0.09	0.37	-.05	0.10
53. Virginia Electric	-.14	0.47	-.04	0.03
54. Central & Southwest	-.14	0.47	-.02	0.09
55. American Electric Power	-.31	0.47	-.10	0.24
56. Columbia Gas	-.21	0.45	0.03	0.08
Cyclical Stocks				
57. Bethlehem Steel	-.18	-.06	0.44	-.09
58. Continental Can	-.12	-.05	0.40	0.02
59. International Harvester	-.10	-.08	0.45	0.01
60. National Lead	-.11	-.03	0.47	0.13
61. Burlington	0.09	-.16	0.25	-.24
62. Borg-Warner	-.07	0.03	0.32	-.27
63. International Paper	-.17	0.01	0.29	-.07
64. Babcock & Wilcox	0.08	-.04	0.25	0.05
65. Weyerhauser	0.00	-.12	0.32	-.06
66. Goodyear	-.21	0.08	0.25	-.17
67. Pullman	-.09	-.12	0.48	-.07
68. National Steel	-.04	-.02	0.45	-.22
69. Johns-Manville	-.16	-.03	0.47	-.06
70. Kennecott	-.06	-.05	0.39	0.02
71. Gardner-Denver	-.23	-.03	0.51	-.04
72. American Can	0.01	0.03	0.36	0.00
73. Square D	-.10	0.01	0.31	0.05
74. Clark Equipment	0.10	0.06	0.48	-.13
75. Eaton, Yale & Towne	-.16	0.00	0.38	-.08
76. Mohasco	0.02	-.12	0.25	0.00
77. Consolidated Freightways	0.04	-.09	0.44	-.17
78. Georgia-Pacific	0.05	0.08	0.29	0.06
79. Otis Elevator	0.07	0.19	0.42	-.17
80. Sunbeam	0.00	-.09	0.28	0.01
81. American Smelting & Refining	-.09	0.02	0.30	0.05
82. Timken	-.24	-.11	0.41	-.05
83. Alcoa	0.00	-.05	0.26	-.21
84. Ingersoll Rand	-.05	-.09	0.49	-.14
85. Joy Mfg.	0.05	0.06	0.46	-.12
86. American Standard	-.05	-.08	0.28	-.02
87. Rohm & Haas	-.01	-.03	0.34	-.12
88. American Metal Climax	0.00	0.13	0.41	-.02
89. Monsanto	-.21	-.11	0.34	-.09
90. Caterpillar	0.00	-.12	0.39	-.08
91. Cincinnati Milling	0.03	-.13	0.44	-.02
92. Deere	0.04	-.03	0.24	-.14
Oil Stocks				
93. Standard of California	-.30	-.04	-.10	0.66
94. Union Oil	0.00	0.02	-.07	0.54
95. Mobil	-.32	-.00	-.13	0.74
96. Jersey Standard	-.51	-.13	-.12	0.68
97. Shell Oil	-.13	-.03	-.04	0.48
98. Gulf Oil	-.22	-.06	-.22	0.64
99. Standard	-.23	-.04	-.12	0.73
100. Texaco	-.35	0.06	-.19	0.65

Source: *Financial Analysts Journal*, May/June 1975, p. 56.

cients of 100 individual stocks with each of four indexes: growth, cyclical, stable, and oil stocks. Each stock in the sample was positively correlated with the index of its own class at a statistically significant level (correlations of 0.19 or higher occur by chance only one time in 20). Only six stocks (Gillette, Otis, UAL, Pan Am, Trane, and American Electric Power) showed significantly positive correlation with an index other than the one to which it was assigned, and in each of these cases the stock was more highly correlated with its own index than with any other.

Viewing these data, Farrell notes, "It is hard to avoid t[...] that growth, cyclical, stable and oil stocks do in f[...] homogeneous groupings."[24] More to the point, these [...] stock groupings can be thought of as representing four di[...] markets. Therefore, when constructing a diversified port[...] portant for managers to compare the weightings in th[...] *sibly other* groupings,[25] to that of the general marke[...] giving consideration simply to the number of individua[...] included.

Conclusion

The questions that were raised in Chapter 16 sugg[...] ern portfolio theory is far from perfect as it now stan[...] have shown in this chapter, it should not be dismiss[...] irrelevant, or uninteresting. Rather, it should be appre[...] viding a framework within which all participants in t[...] process—clients, portfolio managers, researchers, [...] students—can gain a better understanding of the proce[...]

We would be the first to admit that it still remain[...] portfolio assets can be most effectively distributed a[...] stocks, real estate, bonds, mortgages, and risk-free in[...] remain doubtful that portfolio performance has been [...] fined or measured. But we believe that the participant[...] ment process are now able to engage in a more produ[...] than ever before.

---

[24] Ibid., p. 56. If various homogeneous stock groupings are though[...] different equity markets, some theoreticians have suggested that e[...] function of a "multi-index" equation instead of the "single-index[...] instead of:

$$R_p = R_f + B(R_m - R_f)$$

where R_m represents the overall market (e.g., the S&P Composite I[...] for estimating return would be written:

$$R_p = R_f + B_1(R_{m1} - R_f) + B_2(R_{m2} - R_f) + B_3(R_{m3} - R_f)$$

with the subscripts representing the different homogeneous group[...] stable, etc.). See James L. Farrell, Jr. "The Multi-Index Model an[...] Analysis," *Occasional Paper No. 4* (Charlottesville, Va.: The Financi[...] Foundation, 1976).

[25] One other "grouping" which might be considered is the c[...] foreign companies. See: Gary L. Bergstrom, "A New Route to [...] Lower Risks," *The Journal of Portfolio Management*, Fall 1975. [...] Solnik, "Why Not Diversify Internationally Rather Than Dome[...] *Analysts Journal*, July/August 1974.

a high degree of correlation between its own returns and that of the general market index. In this case, the variability of portfolio return would be substantially explained by price movements in a broad market index. Such a portfolio condition could be accomplished with a portfolio containing relatively few issues. As we have indicated, some 30 to 60 randomly selected issues would just about achieve this objective.

On the other hand, some observers contend that diversification implies a portfolio with a high degree of "conditional predictability"—that is, a portfolio whose return can be predicted with a relatively high degree of certainty, once given an estimate of the market's overall price change during a specifically defined period. Such a portfolio not only would have to have a predetermined "beta" level which can be regarded with a high degree of confidence; it would require a near zero alpha. To satisfy this definition, 50 or even 100 issues might be too few. For example, studies show that a portfolio of the 50 stocks of the Standard & Poor's 500 which have the largest market values (and with allocation of funds among included stocks proportional to market values) produces returns that can easily differ from returns for the entire 500 stocks by as much as 4.5 percentage points per year. Portfolios of 100 stocks could easily differ by as much as 3.0 percentage points.[21]

Still another consideration is that the effect of adding additional stocks varies with the *level* of portfolio risk. Studies have shown that there is a significantly higher level of nonmarket risk present in high beta stocks than in low beta stocks. Therefore, a larger number of issues is required in a high-risk portfolio to achieve the same level of diversification as in a low-risk portfolio. According to one researcher, for example, the diversification achieved by a low beta portfolio of five securities cannot be matched by a high beta portfolio containing as many as 25 securities.[22]

Portfolio managers also have some reason to be concerned over factors other than just the number of securities in a portfolio. Many studies indicate that efforts to establish efficient portfolio diversification must contend with factors other than general market influences. For example, Farrell sought to determine whether the price volatility of stocks conforms to "classes," such as growth stocks, cyclical issues, and stable or defensive investments. Table 17–8 summarizes the important findings of his study[23] and shows a matrix of correlation coeffi-

[21] Lorie, p. 28.

[22] Robert C. Klemkosky and John D. Martin, "The Effect of Market Risk on Portfolio Diversification," *Journal of Finance*, March 1975.

[23] James L. Farrell, Jr., "Homogeneous Stock Groupings," *Financial Analysts Journal*, May/June 1975.

TABLE 17–8
Correlation Coefficients of Stock Groupings

Growth Stocks	Growth Index Cor. Coef.	Stable Index Cor. Coef.	Cyclical Index Cor. Coef.	Oil Index Cor. Coef.	Growth Stocks	Growth Index Cor. Coef.	Stable Index Cor. Coef.	Cyclical Index Cor. Coef.	Oil Index Cor. Coef.
1. Ampex	0.49	−.01	−.02	−.12	52. Florida Power	0.09	0.37	−.05	0.10
2. Avon	0.45	0.10	−.17	−.21	53. Virginia Electric	−.14	0.47	−.04	0.03
3. Int'l Flavors & Fragrances	0.37	−.06	−.11	−.09	54. Central & Southwest	−.14	0.47	−.02	0.09
4. Chesebrough-Pond's	0.34	0.02	−.07	−.07	55. American Electric Power	−.31	0.47	−.10	0.24
5. Baxter Labs	0.47	−.03	−.14	−.22	56. Columbia Gas	−.21	0.45	0.03	0.08
6. Becton-Dickinson	0.39	0.10	−.07	−.12					
7. Eastman Kodak	0.36	−.04	−.13	−.16	Cyclical Stocks				
8. Polaroid	0.60	−.01	−.05	−.14	57. Bethlehem Steel	−.18	−.06	0.44	−.09
9. Minnesota Mining	0.38	−.00	−.07	−.15	58. Continental Can	−.12	−.05	0.40	0.02
10. AMP	0.57	0.03	−.19	−.11	59. International Harvester	−.10	−.08	0.45	0.01
11. Texas Instruments	0.50	−.34	0.15	−.08	60. National Lead	−.11	−.03	0.47	0.13
12. Hewlett-Packard	0.53	−.06	−.13	−.06	61. Burlington	0.09	−.16	0.25	−.24
13. Perkin-Elmer	0.64	−.15	−.14	−.12	62. Borg-Warner	−.07	0.03	0.32	−.27
14. Burroughs	0.53	−.21	−.03	−.25	63. International Paper	−.17	0.01	0.29	−.07
15. IBM	0.45	0.06	−.41	−.34	64. Babcock & Wilcox	0.08	−.04	0.25	0.05
16. Honeywell	0.26	−.07	−.07	−.34	65. Weyerhauser	0.00	−.12	0.32	−.06
17. Nat'l Cash Register	0.34	0.01	−.19	−.27	66. Goodyear	−.21	0.08	0.25	−.17
18. Xerox	0.44	−.05	−.16	−.24	67. Pullman	−.09	−.12	0.48	−.07
19. Nalco	0.27	.12	0.07	−.18	68. National Steel	−.04	−.02	0.45	−.22
20. Maryland Cup	0.39	−.05	0.11	−.10	69. Johns-Manville	−.16	−.03	0.47	−.06
21. Harcourt, Brace	0.40	0.04	−.01	−.17	70. Kennecott	−.06	−.05	0.39	0.02
22. Corning Glass	0.55	−.02	−.37	−.08	71. Gardner-Denver	−.23	−.03	0.51	−.04
23. Motorola	0.50	−.21	0.07	−.22	72. American Can	0.01	0.03	0.36	0.00
24. Zenith	0.38	−.11	0.06	−.26	73. Square D	−.10	0.01	0.31	0.05
25. International Telephone	0.42	0.02	−.10	−.12	74. Clark Equipment	0.10	0.06	0.48	−.13
26. UAL, Inc.	0.44	−.16	0.18	−.15	75. Eaton, Yale & Towne	−.16	0.00	0.38	−.08
27. Pan American	0.40	−.23	0.21	−.13	76. Mohasco	0.02	−.12	0.25	0.00
28. United Aircraft	0.39	−.21	0.09	−.10	77. Consolidated Freightways	0.04	−.09	0.44	−.17
29. TRW	0.25	−.12	−.05	−.16	78. Georgia-Pacific	0.05	0.08	0.29	0.06
30. Trane	0.48	0.02	0.20	−.29	79. Otis Elevator	0.07	0.19	0.42	−.17
31. Merck	0.24	0.04	−.13	−.08	80. Sunbeam	0.00	−.09	0.28	0.01
					81. American Smelting				
Stable Stocks					& Refining	−.09	0.02	0.30	0.05
32. Sears	0.02	0.20	−.12	−.11	82. Timken	−.24	−.11	0.41	−.05
33. Federated Department					83. Alcoa	0.00	−.05	0.26	−.21
Stores	0.04	0.23	−.19	−.08	84. Ingersoll Rand	−.05	−.09	0.49	−.14
34. Reynolds	−.04	0.29	0.06	−.13	85. Joy Mfg.	0.05	0.06	0.46	−.12
35. Coca-Cola	0.12	0.38	−.07	−.17	86. American Standard	−.05	−.08	0.28	−.02
36. Procter and Gamble	0.01	0.35	−.05	−.10	87. Rohm & Haas	−.01	−.03	0.34	−.12
37. General Foods	−.05	0.55	−.04	−.12	88. American Metal Climax	0.00	0.13	0.41	−.02
38. Quaker Oats	−.08	0.37	−.04	−.01	89. Monsanto	−.21	−.11	0.34	−.09
39. Kraftco	−.21	0.39	−.13	0.06	90. Caterpillar	0.00	−.12	0.39	−.08
40. National Biscuit	0.02	0.37	−.13	0.01	91. Cincinnati Milling	0.03	−.13	0.44	−.02
41. CPC International	−.04	0.38	−.06	0.09	92. Deere	0.04	−.03	0.24	−.14
42. Gillette	0.18	0.23	−.08	−.06					
43. American Home Products	0.05	0.25	−.07	−.12	Oil Stocks				
44. C.I.T.	−.08	0.34	0.09	−.11	93. Standard of California	−.30	−.04	−.10	0.66
45. Hershey	0.02	0.39	0.11	−.04	94. Union Oil	0.00	0.02	−.07	0.54
46. Campbell	0.02	0.33	0.00	−.13	95. Mobil	−.32	−.00	−.13	0.74
47. Kellogg	−.05	0.31	0.00	−.12	96. Jersey Standard	−.51	−.13	−.12	0.68
48. Household Finance	−.03	0.49	−.05	−.06	97. Shell Oil	−.13	−.03	−.04	0.48
49. Chase Manhattan Bank	−.25	0.46	−.01	0.12	98. Gulf Oil	−.22	−.06	−.22	0.64
50. Northwest Bancorp.	−.08	0.44	0.03	0.01	99. Standard	−.23	−.04	−.12	0.73
51. Transamerica	−.27	0.44	0.01	0.11	100. Texaco	−.35	0.06	−.19	0.65

Source: *Financial Analysts Journal,* May/June 1975, p. 56.

cients of 100 individual stocks with each of four indexes: growth, cyclical, stable, and oil stocks. Each stock in the sample was positively correlated with the index of its own class at a statistically significant level (correlations of 0.19 or higher occur by chance only one time in 20). Only six stocks (Gillette, Otis, UAL, Pan Am, Trane, and American Electric Power) showed significantly positive correlation with an index other than the one to which it was assigned, and in each of these cases the stock was more highly correlated with its own index than with any other.

Viewing these data, Farrell notes, "It is hard to avoid the conclusion that growth, cyclical, stable and oil stocks do in fact represent homogeneous groupings."[24] More to the point, these homogeneous stock groupings can be thought of as representing four different equity markets. Therefore, when constructing a diversified portfolio, it is important for managers to compare the weightings in these, *and possibly other* groupings,[25] to that of the general market, as well as giving consideration simply to the number of individual issues to be included.

Conclusion

The questions that were raised in Chapter 16 suggest that modern portfolio theory is far from perfect as it now stands. But, as we have shown in this chapter, it should not be dismissed as useless, irrelevant, or uninteresting. Rather, it should be appreciated for providing a framework within which all participants in the investment process—clients, portfolio managers, researchers, professors and students—can gain a better understanding of the process.

We would be the first to admit that it still remains unclear how portfolio assets can be most effectively distributed among common stocks, real estate, bonds, mortgages, and risk-free investments. We remain doubtful that portfolio performance has been adequately defined or measured. But we believe that the participants in the investment process are now able to engage in a more productive dialogue than ever before.

---

[24] Ibid., p. 56. If various homogeneous stock groupings are thought of as representing different equity markets, some theoreticians have suggested that expected return is a function of a "multi-index" equation instead of the "single-index" formula. That is, instead of:

$$R_p = R_f + B\ (R_m - R_f)$$

where R_m represents the overall market (e.g., the S&P Composite Index), the equation for estimating return would be written:

$$R_p = R_f + B_1\ (R_{m1} - R_f) + B_2\ (R_{m2} - R_f) + B_3\ (R_{m3} - R_f)\ .\ .\ .,$$

with the subscripts representing the different homogeneous groupings (e.g., cyclical, stable, etc.). See James L. Farrell, Jr. "The Multi-Index Model and Practical Portfolio Analysis," *Occasional Paper No. 4* (Charlottesville, Va.: The Financial Analysts Research Foundation, 1976).

[25] One other "grouping" which might be considered is the category of issues of foreign companies. See: Gary L. Bergstrom, "A New Route to Higher Returns and Lower Risks," *The Journal of Portfolio Management*, Fall 1975. See also, Bruno H. Solnik, "Why Not Diversify Internationally Rather Than Domestically?" *Financial Analysts Journal*, July/August 1974.

SUGGESTED READINGS

Black, Fischer. "The Investment Policy Spectrum: Individuals, Endowment Funds and Pension Funds." *Financial Analysts Journal,* January/February 1976.

Ellis, Charles D. "The Loser's Game." *Financial Analysts Journal,* July–August 1975.

Farrell, James L., Jr. "Homogeneous Stock Groupings: Implications for Portfolio Management." *Financial Analysts Journal,* May/June 1975.

Klein, Roger, and Wolman, William. *The Beat Inflation Strategy.* New York: Simon & Schuster, 1975.

Langbein, John H., and Posner, Richard A. "Market Funds and Trust-Investment Law." *American Bar Foundation Research Journal,* 1975.

McDonald, John G. "Investment Objectives: Diversification, Risk and Exposure to Surprise." *Financial Analysts Journal,* March/April 1975.

Malkiel, Burton G., and Firstenberg, Paul B. *Managing Risk in an Uncertain Era.* Princeton, N.J.: Princeton University, 1976.

O'Brien, John W. "Investment Objectives, Policy and Risk." *The Journal of Portfolio Management,* Summer 1975.

Rosenberg, Barr, and Guy, James. "Beta and Investment Fundamentals." *Financial Analysts Journal,* May/June 1976.

Sharpe, William F. "Likely Gains from Market Timing." *Financial Analysts Journal,* March/April 1975.

Smith, Rodger F., and Richards, Thomas M. "Asset Mix and Investment Strategy." *Financial Analysts Journal,* March/April 1976.

Treynor, Jack L., and Black, Fischer. "How to Use Security Analysis to Improve Portfolio Selection." *Journal of Business,* January 1973.

Williamson, J. Peter. *Funds for the Future.* Report of the Twentieth Century Fund Task Force on College and University Endowment Policy. New York: McGraw-Hill Book Co., 1975.

REVIEW QUESTIONS AND PROBLEMS

1. How can capital asset pricing theory be helpful in establishing the investment objectives of a portfolio?

2. What is the purpose of "portfolio balancing"?

3. How can traditional security analysis techniques be used to supplement portfolio balancing efforts?

4. Under what conditions would a portfolio manager intentionally seek to create an "undiversified" portfolio?

5. What are some of the problems associated with trying to create a diversified, high-risk position for a large portfolio? Discuss an alternative approach.

6. Define the difference between active and passive portfolio management. Which would you choose? Why?

of stored historical data, DRI users can program their telephone-coupled terminal to utilize a series of prepared routines to expedite analytical tasks such as regression equations and seasonal adjustments of raw data.

Summing up, we believe that computer-oriented investment analysis programs can be undertaken with relatively modest increases in an organization's research budget. It would seem, therefore, that financial organizations which do not undertake such programs must fail to do so because they do not appreciate the potential advantages to be gained. The purpose of this chapter is to show how computer techniques can be integrated into the daily activities of investment managers. These activities have been grouped, for convenience, under the following headings:

1. Economic and Industry Analysis
2. Security Analysis
3. Monitoring Portfolio Activity

ECONOMIC AND INDUSTRY ANALYSIS

We have expressed the opinion in this book that the chances of investment success can be enhanced significantly if the investor develops an ability to foresee major turning points in general economic activity a number of months in advance.[1] Admittedly, such an ability is largely intuitive. Nevertheless, a solid core of quantitative analysis is helpful, if not indispensable. Many aspects of the process of economic forecasting are ideally suited to computer application. Among those that stand out are the analysis of "economic indicators," econometric model building, and the determination of how different companies and industries are affected by changing economic conditions.

The pioneering work of Julius Shiskin, formerly at the Bureau of the Census and now at the Department of Labor, best illustrates the application of computers to the analysis of the so-called leading, coincident, and lagging indicators. These indicators are statistical series which become available each month or quarter and which provide important insight into the ebb and flow of aggregate economic activity (see Chapter 12 for illustrations). The Census Bureau prepares a monthly publication called *Business Conditions Digest*, which presents the indi-

---

[1] Edmund A. Mennis argues that economic projections are the foundation of any effective investment management process. See Edmund A. Mennis, "An Integrated Approach to Portfolio Management," *Financial Analyst's Handbook*, vol. I (Homewood, Ill.: Dow Jones-Irwin, Inc., 1975), chap. 42. See also Roy E. Moor, "The Use of Economics in Investment Analysis," *Financial Analysts Journal*, November/December 1971, and "The Fundamentalist's Chart Book or What's Relevant?" Becker Securities Corp., August 1973.

cators in various perspectives. All data are seasonally adjusted; series with highly irregular patterns of movement are smoothed with appropriate moving averages; all series are listed and charted; directions of change and incidence of new highs and lows for each series are shown; special charts compare the movements of selected indicators in the latest leg of the business cycle with their movements in corresponding phases of previous cycles; and various "diffusion indexes" are presented. Virtually all of this data manipulation and charting is done with electronic equipment.

For many years there has been a need to supplement *Business Conditions Digest* with a compendium of leading, coincident, and lagging indicators of *specific industry* trends. The raw data for such a systematic compendium has been available for some time in hundreds of different files and in such central files as that of Data Resources, Inc. Recently, several Wall Street research firms have devoted substantial effort to determining how changing economic conditions influence specific industries, and even specific companies. Becker Securities Corporation, members of the New York Stock Exchange, has been in the forefront of developing these kinds of analytical tools, and recently introduced a new service to institutional clients, called *Sector Analysis.* This service is designed to determine and to quantify the influences of the economic environment upon the market, companies, or industries in which the investment community is interested.

According to Becker Securities, Sector Analysis is a form of fundamental research which relates external economic factors to the fundamental changes in the particular sector of the economy, or in an individual stock. For example, a recent report analyzed the effects of the economic environment on the automobile industry and isolated the critical variables affecting automobile stock price movements. It indicated that the single most relevant factor for the investment community to examine is relative unit domestic auto sales, defined as domestic automobile sales relative to GNP in constant dollars. This was determined by regression analysis of many alternative variables.

Figure 18–1 illustrates the relationship between relative auto stock prices (S&P auto stock price index divided by S&P 500 stock price index) and relative unit domestic auto sales on an annual basis from 1952 to 1974. Declining lines indicate underperformance; rising lines, superior performance; and horizontal movements, equal performance. For example, from 1965 to 1974, stock prices of the auto group underperformed the S&P 500 in every year except 1970 and 1971, as shown by a declining line in every year except those two.

In addition to identifying relative unit sales as the key influence on relative auto stock prices, the report examined in detail the factors that

FIGURE 18–1
Relative Auto Stock Price versus Relative Domestic Auto Sales*

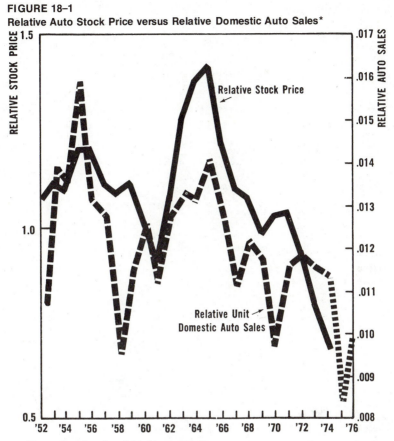

*Domestic auto sales divided by real GNP.
Source: Becker Securities Corporation.

affect automobile industry earnings. These are shown in Figure 18–2, which is designed to show how each economic factor influences particular items in the auto industry income statement. The right side of Figure 18–2 indicates the economic factors, and the arrows show the direction of influence. The left side traces the influences which are internal to the industry.

The Becker service is but one illustration of the fact that over the past few years, widespread computer availability has fostered a substantial expansion of interest in economic model building. Many institutional research firms now employ their own economist, whose economic outlook and overview largely determines the focus of research activity. Quite a few large institutional investors, such as mutual funds, insurance companies, and a few investment advisors,

FIGURE 18–2
Auto Industry Flowchart

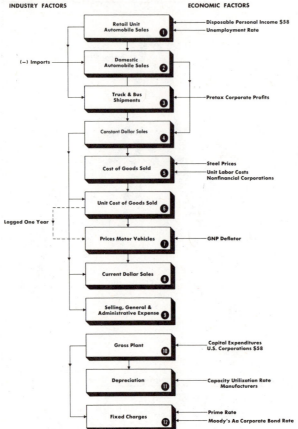

Source: Becker Securities Corporation.

follow a similar approach in their attempt to improve market timing and portfolio planning.

Some of the economic models used by these "investment" economists are relatively simple, depending upon logic and simple regression techniques rather than sophisticated econometric tools. Others are quite complicated. For example, the DRI model (which is part of the Data Resources Inc. information service described earlier) includes an input/output matrix designed to weigh the GNP demand component effect on 81 industries. These calculations are then fed into a set of equations which estimate the Federal Reserve Board production indexes for 41 industries, and into other equations which estimate sales, profits, taxes, dividends, and capacity utilization

estimates for all the industries (25) for which the FTC-SEC publish data.[2] Figure 18–3 shows a typical computer printout covering the overall economic forecasts from the DRI model. Figure 18–4 shows examples of the detailed industry forecast of profits before tax on an industry by industry basis.

FIGURE 18–3
Data Resources Quarterly Forecast of the U.S. Economy (billions of dollars—SAAR)

DATA RESOURCES FORECAST OF THE U.S. ECONOMY
(Billions of Dollars - SAAR)
CONTROL 12/31

	Quarters								Years			
	75:4	76:1	76:2	76:3	76:4	77:1	77:2	77:3	77:4	75	76	77	78

GNP AND ITS COMPONENTS

Total Consumption	989.6	1014.4	1041.8	1072.6	1103.1	1129.7	1158.3	1189.0	1219.5	952.5	1058.0	1174.2	1276.6
Business Fixed Investment	146.4	150.7	155.6	160.5	166.6	172.9	179.7	184.6	189.5	144.9	158.3	181.7	198.1
Residential Construction	46.0	51.2	56.5	62.0	66.4	70.2	74.0	77.1	79.0	39.7	59.0	75.1	79.2
Inventory Investment	-0.1	2.6	6.7	9.8	12.6	14.5	15.3	15.7	17.8	-14.0	7.9	15.8	10.3
Net Exports	16.1	14.0	12.9	10.7	8.3	7.2	7.2	8.1	7.6	13.5	11.5	7.5	13.8
Total Federal	134.2	136.3	138.5	140.1	146.1	147.5	149.1	150.5	156.5	129.9	140.2	150.9	163.4
State and Local	218.2	223.2	228.3	233.8	239.8	245.6	251.4	257.4	263.7	211.5	231.3	254.5	280.6
Gross National Product	1550.3	1592.4	1640.3	1689.4	1742.9	1787.5	1835.1	1882.3	1933.7	1478.1	1666.2	1859.7	2022.0
Real GNP (1958 dollars)	817.7	827.8	840.3	853.0	865.7	875.9	886.9	896.6	906.3	797.5	846.7	891.4	910.7

PRICES AND WAGES --- ANNUAL RATES OF CHANGE

Implicit Price Deflator	7.8	6.0	6.1	5.9	6.8	5.5	5.7	6.0	6.7	8.8	6.2	6.0	6.4
Consumer Price Index	7.1	5.9	6.4	6.3	6.4	6.1	6.2	6.3	6.4	9.2	6.6	6.3	6.3
Wholesale Price Index	10.6	3.1	5.8	7.2	8.1	7.2	7.2	7.3	7.5	9.3	6.5	7.3	6.5
Adj. Avg. Hourly Earnings Index	8.7	8.6	8.8	8.7	8.7	8.4	8.2	8.1	8.0	8.9	8.6	8.4	7.9

PRODUCTION AND OTHER KEY MEASURES

Industrial Production (67=1)	1.168	1.197	1.233	1.267	1.301	1.328	1.348	1.363	1.380	1.133	1.249	1.355	1.373
Annual Rate of Change	9.7	10.0	12.7	11.5	11.3	8.6	6.0	4.7	4.9	-8.9	10.3	8.4	1.4
Housing Starts(mil. units)	1.409	1.533	1.632	1.739	1.796	1.837	1.883	1.885	1.878	1.182	1.675	1.871	1.731
Ret. Unit Car Sales-Total	9.3	9.5	9.7	9.9	10.1	10.4	10.6	10.9	11.1	8.7	9.8	10.7	11.2
Unemployment Rate (percent)	8.3	7.9	7.6	7.4	7.1	6.9	6.7	6.6	6.4	8.5	7.5	6.6	6.7
Federal Budget Surplus (NIA)	-64.0	-59.6	-55.7	-53.5	-49.0	-43.2	-38.2	-37.1	-34.6	-72.2	-54.4	-38.3	-37.2
Capacity Utilization - Manufacturing	0.701	0.713	0.730	0.745	0.759	0.768	0.772	0.772	0.772	0.686	0.737	0.771	0.762

MONEY AND INTEREST RATES

Money Supply (M1)	296.2	301.7	307.6	313.6	320.8	326.6	332.7	339.2	346.1	290.6	310.9	336.1	358.1
Annual Rate of Change	2.8	7.7	8.0	8.1	9.4	7.5	7.6	8.1	8.3	4.3	7.0	8.1	6.5
New AA Corp. Utility Rate (%)	9.51	9.20	9.32	9.45	9.48	9.50	9.55	9.61	9.67	9.46	9.36	9.58	9.50
New High-grade Corp.Bond Rate (%)	8.92	8.76	8.94	9.10	9.14	9.17	9.23	9.28	9.34	8.99	8.90	9.25	9.17
Federal Funds Rate (%)	5.40	5.66	6.15	6.76	7.23	7.60	8.10	8.34	8.62	5.82	6.45	8.16	7.16
Prime Rate (%)	7.49	7.51	7.70	8.01	8.30	8.57	8.93	9.13	9.35	7.84	7.88	8.99	8.48

INCOMES

Personal Income	1290.9	1323.7	1361.3	1405.4	1446.2	1478.5	1515.9	1558.6	1600.9	1240.0	1384.1	1538.5	1680.8
Real Disposable Income	618.5	624.3	632.6	643.4	652.0	656.9	663.7	672.9	680.9	610.3	638.1	668.6	687.4
Saving Rate (percent)	8.3	8.3	8.4	8.6	8.6	8.4	8.4	8.5	8.6	8.6	8.5	8.5	8.7
Profits before Tax	148.7	148.7	154.6	163.6	171.4	173.7	177.1	181.0	185.0	124.5	159.6	179.2	177.9
Profits after Tax	91.2	91.1	94.8	100.3	105.1	106.5	108.5	110.9	113.4	76.6	97.8	109.8	108.6
Four Qtr. Percent Change	14.7	46.3	34.8	21.4	15.3	16.8	14.5	10.6	7.9	-9.9	27.7	12.3	-1.1

DETAILS OF REAL GNP --- ANNUAL RATES OF CHANGE

Gross National Product	4.6	5.0	6.2	6.2	6.1	4.8	5.1	4.5	4.4	-2.9	6.2	5.3	2.2
Total Consumption	2.6	4.3	4.9	6.1	5.5	4.1	4.6	5.0	4.5	0.7	4.8	4.9	2.7
Business Fixed Investment	0.9	5.1	7.6	7.3	9.1	9.9	10.6	4.9	3.7	-13.6	3.3	8.4	2.4
Equipment	4.4	5.6	10.0	10.3	13.1	14.6	16.6	8.9	6.1	-15.4	5.3	12.6	3.4
Nonresidential Construction	-7.1	4.1	1.6	-0.1	-0.9	-2.1	-4.9	-6.0	-3.4	-8.9	-1.7	-2.5	-0.6
Residential Construction	55.4	45.0	33.5	27.1	19.3	13.7	11.1	6.2	2.9	-21.1	38.1	15.1	-2.1
Exports	12.0	1.9	4.5	3.7	4.0	8.5	8.8	7.5	4.8	-8.0	5.4	6.5	5.5
Imports	7.5	11.0	10.8	12.4	8.9	10.0	7.5	6.5	3.7	-15.2	10.1	8.8	2.6
Federal Government	-5.0	1.7	2.4	1.2	2.3	0.1	0.6	-0.1	0.6	2.9	1.1	0.9	0.5
State and Local	3.4	2.0	2.0	2.2	2.5	2.0	2.0	2.2	2.4	1.8	2.3	2.2	2.4

SAAR = Seasonally adjusted annual rates.
Source: Data Resources, Inc.

The DRI economic information system, as well as several others now available to institutional investors, is designed to allow subscribers to utilize a "top-down" approach to industry and company analysis. That is, to use a forecast of aggregate business and financial conditions to determine the impact of these conditions on a particular

---

[2] *Industry Analysis with the DRI System*, Data Resources, Inc., 29 Hartwell Avenue, Lexington, Mass. 02173. Also see the Appendix to Chapter 6, in which the application of input/output technique to sales forecasting is discussed.

FIGURE 18–4
Industry Highlights: Profits before Tax

| | BILLIONS OF DOLLARS | | | | | | | PERCENTAGE CHANGES | | | | | | |
| | HISTORY | | | FORECAST | | | | HISTORY | | | | FORECAST | | |
	74	75	76	77	78	79	80	61-75	75	76	77	78	79	80
FOOD & PRODUCTS	7.89	9.17	10.93	11.30	11.67	12.20	12.70	10.3	16.2	19.2	3.3	3.3	4.6	4.1
TOBACCO MANUFACTURES	1.35	1.67	2.26	2.36	2.45	2.66	2.74	6.5	23.8	35.0	4.6	3.6	8.7	3.1
TEXTILE MILL PRODUCTS	1.47	1.00	1.48	1.94	2.10	2.12	2.64	6.0	-32.3	48.9	30.9	8.1	0.8	24.5
PAPER & PRODUCTS	1.70	2.74	3.32	3.84	3.58	3.91	4.26	11.3	-27.5	21.0	15.7	-6.7	9.0	8.5
CHEMICALS & PRODUCTS	11.47	10.72	15.22	17.13	18.24	20.37	24.28	8.7	-6.5	41.9	12.5	6.5	11.7	19.2
BASIC CHEMICALS	5.61	4.63	6.45	7.45	8.57	10.25	12.21	8.3	-17.6	39.4	15.4	15.1	19.5	19.1
DRUGS & MEDICINES	2.33	2.55	2.93	3.13	3.31	3.59	4.11	9.7	9.7	14.8	7.0	5.8	8.4	14.4
PETROLEUM & PRODUCTS	17.48	13.43	15.40	17.77	21.00	23.40	26.32	11.4	-23.2	14.7	15.4	18.6	11.0	12.5
RUBBER & PLASTICS PRODS	2.24	1.31	2.02	2.73	2.85	3.59	4.65	9.3	-41.4	53.0	35.0	4.6	26.0	29.5
STONE, CLAY & GLASS	1.92	1.76	2.48	2.87	2.86	3.17	3.53	5.0	-8.5	41.1	15.7	-0.2	10.6	11.5
PRIMARY IRON & STEEL	5.30	3.28	4.77	5.57	5.77	6.47	7.36	12.1	-39.1	45.6	16.7	3.6	12.2	13.7
NONFERROUS METALS	3.11	1.21	1.96	2.67	2.66	2.85	3.35	13.1	-61.1	61.6	36.4	-0.4	7.3	17.4
FABRICATED METAL PRODS	4.94	4.51	5.62	6.36	6.63	7.53	8.90	13.1	-8.5	24.6	13.2	4.2	13.6	18.1
NON-ELECTRICAL MACHINERY	9.34	10.14	12.29	13.46	14.05	15.51	18.00	13.3	8.5	21.2	9.5	4.4	10.4	16.0
ELECTRICAL MACHINERY	5.24	4.54	5.58	7.06	7.26	7.61	8.17	7.9	-13.2	22.8	26.5	2.9	4.8	7.3
MOTOR VEHICLES & PARTS	3.01	3.46	7.13	7.55	7.69	7.81	7.98	11.6	14.9	106.2	5.9	1.8	1.6	2.2
AIRCRAFT & PARTS	1.46	1.51	1.74	2.05	2.03	2.23	2.57	10.8	3.4	15.3	17.8	-1.1	9.8	15.2
INSTRUMENTS	3.16	2.92	3.56	3.91	4.03	4.54	5.40	14.0	-7.5	21.9	9.7	3.0	12.5	19.0
INDUSTRIES ABOVE	83.25	73.38	95.77	108.57	114.96	125.97	142.84	8.7	-11.9	30.5	13.4	5.9	9.6	13.4
ALL INDUSTRIES	140.72	124.46	155.75	173.64	172.57	187.09	219.34	7.3	-11.6	25.1	11.5	-0.6	8.4	17.2

Source: Data Resources, Inc.

economic sector, industry, or company. Subscribers are also able to make comparisons of estimated industry profitability under a variety of alternative economic forecasts.

Many investment groups have found that the use of a "top-down" approach to the forecasting of individual industry and company sales and earnings improves the consistency of estimates made by various members working in different areas. That is, each participant in the forecasting process starts out with the same assumptions governing the "macro-" economic outlook.

The institutional research firm of Cyrus J. Lawrence Inc., for example, provides its clients with a variety of computer-based reports designed to ensure consistency between an overall economic forecast and specific industry and company projections.[3] Interestingly, the "top-down" macroeconomic forecast is put together from the "ground up." That is, each analyst feeds into a computer model of the economy estimates covering those critical variables which will affect the outlook for his or her own particular area of expertise. Then, each of these estimates are checked for consistency against historic economic relationships stored in the computer data base. Research reports on specific industries show a comparison between estimates generated by the econometric model and by the analysts, as shown in Figure 18–5. Portfolio managers are usually interested in exploring the differences, and generally ignore similarities.

In recent years, projections of interest rates have been undertaken by most, if not all, investment decision making organizations. Frequently, the decision to invest in common stocks, buy bonds (long

---

[3] For a complete description of this entire computer-based research service, see Cyrus J. Lawrence Inc., "Company and Industry Econometric Research," *Portfolio Strategy Service*, July 17, 1975.

FIGURE 18–5
Comparison of Economic Estimates with Analyst Estimates

1976 Cyrus J. Lawrence Chemical Analysts'
Estimates (January 14, 1976)

	1976 EPS	1976/1975 – Percent Change
Allied Chemical (DAP)	$5.50	53%
American Cyanamid (JEB)	3.40	6
Celeanese (JEB)	6.50	110
Dow (DAP)	8.00	23
DuPont (JEB)	9.00	89
Hercules (DAP)	2.50	257
Monsanto (JEB)	10.90	39
Stauffer (DAP)	11.75	29
Union Carbide (DAP)	8.50	37
Weighted Average	$7.12	42%

The 42% gain in EPS compares to the following CJL model results for operating earnings translated down to net income.

1976 Cyrus J. Lawrence Chemical Model Estimates:
Operating Income versus Net Income

Based on Cyrus J. Lawrence Outlook of January 1976 (Implies 6% Volume Gain)	1976/1975 Percent Change – Operating Income	1976/1975 Percent Change Net Income
I. Strong Prices	27%	36%
II. Moderate Prices	11	10
III. Flat Prices	0	–9
Based on a 10 Percent Volume Gain		
I. Strong Prices	33%	47%
II. Moderate Prices	17	19
III. Flat Prices	6	–2

Cyrus J. Lawrence chemical companies' earnings per share estimates made by Jon E. Browning (JEB) and Donald A. Pattison (DAP). These estimates assume an average annual price increase of 8 percent (JEB) and 10 percent (DAP) and a volume increase for the industry of around 10 percent.

Source: Special Econometric Study, Chemical Profits for 1976, *Portfolio Strategy Service,* Cyrus J. Lawrence, Inc., February 3, 1976.

maturity or short), or keep funds in cash equivalents rests largely on the interest rate forecast. Therefore, it is not surprising that very specialized computer-based services have become available to fill this important need.

SECURITY ANALYSIS

Screening

A very large proportion of the time spent by most security analysts and portfolio managers is in the nature of routine paper work. Most of this work is designed to screen out from the thousands of stocks and bonds available to investors a few dozen which, at a given moment of time, are deserving of intensive study for the purpose of determining whether to buy, hold, or sell. Electronic computers can be utilized in the screening process to relieve highly trained and well-paid personnel from much of this routine work, thus freeing their time for more creative endeavors. Furthermore, the speed and accuracy of the computer can be expected to do a more efficient screening job on a larger list of securities than humans can.

The basis of much of the current screening effort is the Compustat® data tapes, leased and maintained by Investors Management Sciences, Inc. (IMS), a division of Standard & Poor's Corporation. Table 18–1 summarizes the raw data files currently available on Compustat tapes.

IMS also offers a screening service based upon the Compustat data. Several illustrations of the use of this service are shown in Figure 18–6. The top portion presents a ten-year history of specified financial ratios for an individual company. The user in this case wanted a printout of the same ratios for 50 companies in a variety of industries. The bottom portion is part of a study which compared General Foods Corp. with 18 other food companies. The particular printout shown here relates to the ratio of sales to average net plant. Other ratios were also compared. The report also calculated an 18-company composite ratio, by which the analyst could compare General Foods to the rest of its industry.

In addition to IMS, several other organizations now offer investors screening services based on Compustat data. The Boston Company Investment Research and Technology, Inc., for example, provides subscribers with a continuous monitoring of a large number of "fixed" screens. A fixed screen is a periodic review of the data base using the same screening criteria each time. Table 18–2 summarizes the criteria used—for example, there are five *growth* criteria, three *profitability* criteria, and so on. Figure 18–7 is from the "steady growth" screen. This report shows companies that have achieved a sales and earnings

TABLE 18–1
Compustat Data Coverage

Available Tapes	Approximate Number of Companies	Number of Time Periods	Number of Data Items for Each Time Period	Data Content						
				Complete Balance Sheet	Complete Income Account	Partial Income Account	Price and Related Data	Production Information	Source and Application of Funds	Restated
Industrial annual										
Listed stocks	2,700	20	122	X	X		X		X	X
Primary companies	900	20	122	X	X		X		X	X
Supplementary										
companies	900	20	122	X	X		X		X	X
Tertiary companies	900	20	122	X	X		X		X	X
Nonlisted stocks	900	15	60	X	X		X			
Canadian	400	15	60	X	X		X			
Industrial quarterly										
Listed stocks	2,700	40	26	X	X	X	X			
Utility										
Annual	155	20	90	X	X		X	X		
Quarterly	155	48	98	X	X		X	X		
Bank										
Annual	115	15	221	X	X		X			
Quarterly	115	15	141	X	X		X			

X indicates coverage.

All data items have been collected from annual and quarterly reports to shareholders, reports filed with the SEC and other government agencies, and personal contacts with companies. Files are updated daily as source documents become available. Extensive computerized validity checks applied to raw data ensure accuracy.

Compustat® uses standardized accounting definitions developed in cooperation with major public accounting firms. Changes are made when necessary so as to be in complete agreement with recommendations of the Financial Accounting Standards Board. This continuing process assures uniform comparability.

Source: Investors Management Sciences, Inc.

FIGURE 18–6
Compustat Data Screen

AMERICAN HOME PRODUCTS CORP   12

	1974	1973	1972	1971	1970	1969	1968	1967	1966	1965
P/E – HI	31.50	39.00	37.65	32.87	28.21	30.72	30.82	29.56	24.90	29.19
P/E – LOW	18.40	29.10	26.54	24.48	19.89	22.28	23.12	19.64	16.85	20.93
P/E – AVG	25.00	34.05	32.10	28.67	24.05	26.50	26.97	24.60	20.87	25.06
EARNINGS PER SHARE	1.42	1.25	1.08	0.95	0.86	0.78	0.73	0.68	0.61	0.52
9 YR EPS GROWTH RATE	11.10	11.22	11.18	11.19	10.94	10.43	9.62	8.76	7.88	7.85
3 YR EPS GROWTH RATE	14.36	13.41	11.44	9.36	8.05	8.56	12.11	15.53	14.49	10.23
INDEX OF AVG P/E 67-67=100	101.63	138.42	130.48	116.55	97.77	107.71	109.63	100.00	84.85	101.87
DIVIDENDS PAID PER SHARE	0.78	0.63	0.59	0.57	0.52	0.47	0.42	0.38	0.33	0.32
INDEX OF DIVIDENDS PER SH 67-67=100	202.70	163.13	153.74	147.83	134.78	121.74	108.70	100.00	86.84	84.21
DIVIDEND PAYOUT RATIO	0.55	0.50	0.55	0.59	0.60	0.60	0.57	0.57	0.53	0.61
INDEX OF DIVIDEND PAYOUT 67-67=100	96.59	88.31	96.32	104.93	106.46	105.61	100.75	100.00	92.98	107.02
A/T RETURN ON TOT INVESTED CAPITAL	28.47	28.59	26.06	25.44	25.92	26.06	25.09	24.20	24.68	24.73

Industry Analysis Screen

SALES/AVERAGE NET PLANT

		1974	1973	1972	1971	1970	1969	1968	1967	1966	1965
GENERAL FOODS CORP	03	3.71	3.11	2.78	2.66	2.76	2.84	3.01	3.18	3.40	3.46
GENERAL MILLS INC	05	3.66	3.68	3.26	2.79	2.55	2.65	2.57	2.23	2.39	2.39
KELLOGG CO	12	2.87	2.72	2.48	2.56	2.52	2.54	2.51	2.60	2.63	2.50
PILLSBURY CO	05	2.95	2.83	2.80	2.74	2.87	3.30	3.66	4.17	4.53	4.38
STANDARD BRANDS INC	12	3.88	3.42	3.03	2.90	3.00	3.00	3.04	3.52	3.75	3.45
BEATRICE FOODS CO	02	5.93	5.74	5.28	5.28	5.06	5.53	6.60	6.31	6.41	6.72
BORDEN INC	12	3.95	3.39	3.16	3.09	2.89	2.91	2.80	2.76	3.06	3.41
KRAFTCO CORP	12	5.85	5.08	4.74	4.74	4.84	4.84	4.68	4.54	4.51	4.06
PET INC	03	3.93	3.57	3.10	3.18	3.09	3.23	3.55	3.42	3.79	4.26
DEL MONTE CORP	05	4.20	3.63	3.42	3.21	3.03	2.85	2.90	3.00	2.85	2.93
GREEN GIANT CO	03	3.92	3.80	3.65	3.23	3.05	2.68	2.71	3.14	3.57	3.74
HEINZ (H.J.) CO	04	3.76	3.54	3.14	3.10	2.73	2.55	2.46	2.41	2.39	2.38
RALSTON PURINA CO	09	3.69	3.43	2.84	2.95	3.04	3.19	3.56	4.39	4.53	4.11
CPC INTL INC	12	3.38	2.64	2.23	2.14	2.06	1.96	1.96	1.97	2.04	2.08
WARD FOODS INC	12	6.09	4.80	4.06	3.96	4.13	4.67	5.26	6.24	6.10	6.14
NABISCO INC	12	3.15	2.92	3.01	3.10	2.81	2.49	2.76	2.94	3.17	3.12
HERSHEY FOODS CORP	12	2.75	2.45	2.51	2.74	2.77	2.75	2.79	2.52	2.66	2.78
COCA-COLA CO	12	3.01	2.73	2.57	2.52	2.51	2.39	2.41	2.54	2.80	2.83
PEPSICO INC	12	3.36	3.16	2.96	2.79	2.83	2.75	3.02	2.79	2.98	3.65
COMPANY COMPOSITE		3.88	3.49	3.18	3.09	3.02	3.02	3.10	3.16	3.31	3.32

Source: Investors Management Sciences, Inc.

increase of at least 5 percent, each year, for at least five years in a row. The companies are listed in descending order on a basis of "years of steady growth." An interesting feature of the Boston Company Investment Research and Technology service is that each screen category is accompanied by a chart which illustrates the comparative performance of those companies meeting the screen test against the S&P 500 Stock Index.

Merrill Lynch provides a "flexible" screening service that enables portfolio managers to search for issues that meet specific requirements. Figure 18–8 shows how *Qwick Qwery*, the Merrill Lynch service, works when a portfolio manager requests an alphabetical list of securities from the 1,800 company data bank meeting four distinct criteria. Normally the computer would screen for all four criteria[4] simultaneously and produce only a final report, Step 4. We are showing each step separately to demonstrate how the universe diminishes as each screen is added. *Qwick Qwery* currently contains 60 basic items of balance sheet and income data that can be combined in a great many ways, producing an almost infinite variety of screening ratios.

---

[4] The full *Qwick Qwery* data base covers 3,600 companies and the number of items for each company is being expanded from 60 to 120.

FIGURE 18–7
Sample Page from a Steady Growth Screen

TKR	COMPANY	PRICE 11/17	EST EPS 1975	P/E RATIO	DAILY VOLUME ($MIL)	5-YR GROWTH SALES	5-YR GROWTH EPS	SUST GROWTH	YRS OF STEADY GROWTH
NCH	NATIONAL CHEMSEARCH	37	1.60	23.4	0.31	23.0	24.0	21.7	10
MO	PHILIP MORRIS INC	55	3.45	15.8	3.12	12.9	14.8	19.3	10
BETZ	BETZ LABS INC	37	1.26	29.6	0.45	23.0	21.3	15.7	10
BGH	BURROUGHS CORP	84	4.07	20.6	3.72	14.3	17.4	8.5	10
MOB	MOBIL OIL CORP	47	7.53	6.2	1.95	23.9	17.0	5.6	10
MCD	MCDONALDS CORP	58	2.12	27.2	3.41	31.7	30.3	27.1	9
ALB	ALCON LABS INC	23	NA	NA	0.13	15.7	17.7	12.6	9
SEVN	SEVEN UP CO	35	1.76	19.8	0.39	16.1	14.3	16.6	8
BKO	BAKER OIL TOOLS INC	48	3.22	15.0	0.79	29.1	22.9	12.1	8
GPC	GENUINE PARTS CO	36	1.76	20.3	0.22	12.5	13.5	11.7	8
*VET	VETCO OFFSHORE INDS	28	2.76	10.2	0.62	49.7	47.1	27.8	7
BDG	BANDAG INC	28	1.63	17.2	0.42	39.6	34.8	34.1	7
FM	FRANKLIN MINT CORP	30	2.20	13.6	0.64	31.9	32.9	30.5	7
LOWE	LOWES CO	41	1.17	35.0	0.44	NA	NA	24.5	7
MAS	MASCO CORP	50	2.49	20.3	0.51	32.1	25.5	24.2	7
PST	PETRIE STORES CORP	71	3.20	22.3	0.21	17.3	22.3	19.3	7
DOV	DOVER CORP	46	5.15	8.9	0.18	19.1	17.0	17.9	7
KSF	QUAKER ST OIL REFNG	18	1.76	10.1	0.15	18.5	16.6	14.6	7
*FICE	FRIENDLY ICE CREAM	25	1.18	21.6	0.17	21.8	17.5	13.7	7
AMB	AMERICAN BRANDS INC	36	5.16	7.0	0.41	11.3	4.5	13.4	7
PFE	PFIZER INC	30	2.09	14.3	1.53	14.4	10.6	10.7	7
APD	AIR PRODS & CHEMS	62	4.02	15.5	1.21	20.4	28.9	10.0	7
HNG	HOUSTON NAT GAS CORP	50	3.97	12.6	0.88	27.2	27.4	9.6	7
PEP	PEPSICO INC	74	4.25	17.5	1.02	15.9	10.6	9.6	7
WLA	WARNER LAMBERT CO	36	2.18	16.5	1.19	11.2	11.2	9.0	7
XRX	XEROX CORP	53	4.11	12.8	6.58	18.6	14.8	16.7	14
CCK	CROWN CORK & SEAL	20	2.50	7.9	0.23	15.5	14.2	15.7	14
TAN	TANDY CORP	49	4.38	11.3	0.94	17.3	25.8	13.1	14
ARA	ARA SVCS INC	45	3.47	12.9	0.38	12.6	10.0	11.5	14
*CGT	CONSUMERS GAS CO	12	NA	NA	0.10	15.9	8.5	7.1	14
TXO	TEXAS OIL & GAS CORP	13	2.05	6.2	0.39	46.1	33.0	NA	14
AUD	AUTOMATIC DATA PROCE	60	2.23	26.8	0.46	27.0	21.9	23.9	13
SBP	STANDARD BRANDS PAIN	42	1.69	25.2	0.24	16.6	17.1	16.1	13
AHP	AMERICAN HOME PRODS	35	1.59	22.2	2.85	11.4	12.8	15.2	13
LZ	LUBRIZOL CORP	41	2.67	15.3	0.86	18.9	21.0	13.9	13
BDK	BLACK & DECKER MFG	23	0.92	25.1	1.24	22.9	14.3	10.7	13
LDG	LONGS DRUG STORES	71	2.57	27.5	0.16	17.7	16.1	18.3	12
MDTR	MEDTRONIC INC	36	1.60	22.3	0.44	NA	NA	16.3	12
ODRL	OCEAN DRILLING &	28	2.98	9.6	0.30	NA	NA	10.3	12
FBKS	FIRST BK SYS INC	47	4.25	11.1	0.42	18.4	7.9	NA	12
SGP	SCHERING PLOUGH CORP	56	2.55	21.9	2.22	14.9	22.5	19.7	11
TPAX	TAMPAX INC	36	2.84	12.7	0.83	12.7	12.1	18.3	11
DELX	DE LUXE CHECK PRINTE	28	1.86	14.9	0.50	NA	NA	15.4	11
*PTO	PETROLANE INC	23	NA	NA	0.13	22.2	17.4	15.1	11
JNJ	JOHNSON & JOHNSON	93	3.24	28.6	2.74	16.8	14.8	14.6	11
MHS	MARRIOTT CORP	15	0.77	19.5	0.39	18.9	13.2	12.8	11
MALL	MALLINCKRODT INC	42	1.96	21.4	0.55	NA	NA	10.3	11
NOB	NORTHWEST BANCORPORA	46	4.82	9.6	0.21	17.8	10.0	NA	11
JPM	MORGAN J P & CO INC	53	5.11	10.5	1.91	28.3	13.1	NA	11
MKC	MARION LABS INC	16	0.91	17.4	0.24	19.6	18.8	28.1	10

*New this month.
Source: The Boston Company Investment Research and Technology, Inc.

TABLE 18–2
Contents of a "Fixed" Screen Investment Service

Growth:
Steady Growth (sales and earnings)
  The companies appearing in this screen have turned in significant gains in sales and earnings of at least 5 percent every year for at least five years in a row. Qualifiers have been ranked by number of years of steady growth.
Steady Growth (dividends and earnings)
  The companies passing this screen have increased both dividends and earnings for at least ten years in a row. Qualifiers are ranked by market value.
High Sustainable Growth
  Companies with sustainable growth rates in excess of 12.5 percent per annum.
High-Trend Growth
  Companies passing this screen have sales and earnings trend growth rates above 12.5 percent measured over the last five years. A geometric mean of the two growth rates is used to order the list.
Good Earnings Stability
  To determine earnings stability, a five-year log-linear trend line is fitted to a moving four-quarter sum of earnings. The percentage deviation of earnings from the trend value, disregarding sign, is then averaged over the latest five-year period. Typically average deviations less than 5 percent indicate good earnings stability. The range from 5 percent to 25 percent includes companies of average stability, while values above 25 percent are associated with very erratic earnings records.

  To qualify for this screen, the five-year average deviation from earnings must be less than 3 percent.
Profitability:
High Margin
  Companies on this screen must show a pretax margin exceeding 20 percent for the latest four quarters.
High Profitability
  Companies passing this screen must show a retained return on equity, averaged over the latest three years, of at least 12.5 percent.
Improving Profitability
  Companies passing this screen must show successive increases in return on equity for the past four years.
Projected Value:
High Rate of Return Based on Historical Price/Earnings Ratio
  Companies on this screen are ranked on the basis of total annual rate of return, assuming future growth at the long-term sustainable growth rate and a valuation consistent with their historical median price/earnings. A price/earnings adjustment over a three-year period is assumed. To qualify a company must have a minimum rate of return of 25 percent.
High Rate of Return Based on Sustainable Growth Price/Earnings
  Companies selected by this screen are those which show the highest rate of return assuming a price/earnings valuation consistent with their long-term sustainable growth rate. A target price/earnings of 8.0 plus 1.5 times the sustainable growth rate is assumed,

TABLE 18–2 *(continued)*

with the price/earnings adjustment amortized over a three-year period. Current yield and the sustainable growth rate are also factors in the rate of return computation.

Accelerating Earnings

Companies passing this screen must show successively larger percentage increases in earnings for the latest four quarters in a row. Qualifiers are generally experiencing earnings turnarounds or responding to particularly favorable industry developments.

Increasing Estimated Earnings

Companies whose estimated earnings are undergoing upward adjustments may generally be expected to outperform the market. This screen selects companies for which the current median estimate is at least 10 percent above the median value last month.

Recent Results:

Large Sales Increase

Companies on this screen are ranked in order of largest percentage increase in sales over the latest four quarters. An increase of at least 20 percent is required to qualify.

Large Earnings Increase

Companies on this screen must show an increase in earnings over the latest four quarters of at least 40 percent. Qualifiers are generally recovering from previously depressed earnings or achieving large sales increases.

Large Margin Increase

This screen limits selections to companies showing an increase in pretax margin of at least 2 percentage points compared to the year ago level.

Miscellaneous:

Largest Market Value

This screen features the 50 companies with largest current market value. Together they represent about half the total market value of the entire New York Stock Exchange list.

High Yield

The selections of this screen must show a dividend yield exceeding 6 percent.

Low Price/Earnings

This screen ranks companies by lowest price/earnings, based on estimated earnings. To qualify, the price/earnings must be below 8. Many low-priced stocks are included in the list.

Low Price/Book Value

This screen ranks companies in order of the lowest ratio of price to book value. The companies generally have low price/earnings ratios and low sustainable growth rates.

High Volume

This screen lists the companies which have shown the highest turnover, measured by the ratio of trading volume to total shares outstanding, over the past 50 weeks. This list includes many "special situations" and stocks with highly volatile price and earnings records. Note that high volume tends to occur during a dramatic increase in price.

Source: The Boston Company Investment Research and Technology, Inc.

FIGURE 18–8
Qwick Qwery
STEP 1

The manager's first criterion is that the list include only stocks that show an increase in earnings per share every quarter for the last eight quarters. The computer scans all of the industrial companies and screens out those stocks that fail to qualify. The print-out includes 376 companies out of the list of 1800. (Note that we are reproducing only the first page of the print-out.) The eight columns of figures in the center of the print-out shows the percentage increase in earnings for each successive quarter.

EPS QUARTERLY INCREASING
LAST 8 QUARTERS THRU 3RD QUARTER 1973
EPS ARE FULLY DILUTED EXCLUDING EXTRAORDINARY CHARGES

COMPANY NAME	MKT VAL 11/30 $MM	PCT CHGE 71Q4/70Q4 EPS DIL	PCT CHGE 72Q1/71Q1 EPS DIL	PCT CHGE 72Q2/71Q2 EPS DIL	PCT CHGE 72Q3/71Q3 EPS DIL	PCT CHGE 72Q4/71Q4 EPS DIL	PCT CHGE 73Q1/72Q1 EPS DIL	PCT CHGE 73Q2/72Q2 EPS DIL	PCT CHGE 73Q3/72Q3 EPS DIL	PRICE EARNS 11/30	YLD	% ABOVE / BELOW BK VALU
A C F INDS INC	220.8	33.8	11.1	40.4	33.3	8.0	45.6	46.2	22.4	9.1	6.1	17.0
A T O INC	40.2	47.1	216.7	21.1	27.3	40.0	31.6	65.2	57.1	4.9	2.7	-18.3
AAV COS	7.0	3.8	66.7	25.0	15.4	22.2	15.0	16.7	16.7	4.3	3.7	13.2
AIR PRODUCTS & CHEMI	564.8	36.7	2.0	11.2	5.0	12.7	29.7	24.8	56.7	23.5	0.5	214.4
AIRPAX ELECTRONICS	4.4	150.0	70.0	16.5	120.0	219.0	113.5	110.0	8.5	4.4	0.0	-22.4
ALCON LABORATORIES	199.9	24.4	23.5	10.0	20.0	23.5	21.4	15.2	20.0	40.0	0.5	610.1
ALLIED MAINTENANCE	59.2	14.3	7.1	12.5	12.4	17.0	14.4	15.6	10.0	12.8	2.4	146.9
AMERICAN BROADCASTIN	376.7	86.8	132.4	110.7	167.7	76.1	44.3	49.2	39.8	8.4	3.6	56.9
AMERICAN DISTRICT TE	222.3	10.0	10.8	5.0	12.2	13.6	7.3	9.5	8.7	21.4	1.2	177.7
AMERICAN EXPRESS	3158.4	10.4	36.8	12.5	23.4	11.0	24.0	25.6	25.5	21.6	1.2	311.0
AMERICAN HOME PRODUC	6420.9	10.8	13.5	12.7	13.0	13.9	14.3	18.3	17.2	32.9	1.6	1052.8
AMERICAN HOSPITAL SU	1368.8	50.0	37.5	31.6	8.7	3.7	13.6	8.0	16.0	35.0	0.7	291.4
AMERICAN MFG CO	42.8	178.9	21.7	51.0	40.8	0.6	22.6	36.6	50.0	4.7	5.3	-41.9
AMERICAN STERILIZER	89.4	21.2	12.0	10.5	15.4	10.0	17.9	14.3	13.3	13.8	2.5	65.1
AMETEK INC	67.2	22.7	36.8	57.1	36.0	29.6	50.0	39.4	44.1	7.8	6.3	39.1
AMF INC	380.2	19.0	30.9	35.8	34.6	7.2	5.6	8.3	4.3	6.7	6.0	68.3
AMFAC INC	157.5	5.9	12.5	7.0	16.7	14.6	2.4	10.9	11.1	6.0	4.7	-23.4
AMP INC	1643.5	14.9	17.8	45.8	42.9	42.6	54.7	28.6	45.7	38.0	0.6	906.6
AMPCO PITTSBURGH COR	23.0	50.0	81.8	12.5	216.7	66.7	80.0	100.0	73.7	5.3	5.1	-38.3
ANSUL CO	19.2	9.0	12.0	36.0	102.8	37.1	197.1	44.8	33.3	6.4	0.0	7.1
APL CORP	12.2	4.7	6.9	12.1	10.5	11.1	6.5	10.8	7.1	3.3	0.0	-33.0
ARISTAR INC	40.5	2.6	3.4	130.8	26.1	27.5	23.3	30.0	6.9	5.5	7.9	-35.1
ARIZ-COLO LAND & CAT	54.0	1300.0	375.0	78.6	3.8	32.1	84.2	68.0	-29.6	10.1	0.5	150.9
ARMCO STEEL CORP	570.6	63.6	46.7	11.5	130.8	83.3	68.2	69.0	33.3	6.1	6.2	-44.4
ASPRO INC	6.8	5.0	25.0	1.8	51.7	152.0	42.8	47.3	41.9	3.7	7.3	-36.1
AUGAT INC	70.0	38.0	50.0	35.0	35.7	37.0	16.7	33.3	26.3	26.4	0.4	713.1
AVNET INC	98.1	8.0	25.0	68.8	23.1	25.9	32.0	63.0	31.2	4.4	4.1	2.0
AVON PRODUCTS	4663.7	12.8	11.5	27.8	17.9	8.0	20.7	8.7	4.3	35.3	1.7	1128.4
BAKER INDS INC	110.6	50.0	57.9	27.8	30.0	30.0	30.0	21.7	11.5	16.7	0.9	269.3
BANDAG INC	338.3	60.7	50.0	35.9	36.0	36.7	44.0	37.9	35.3	34.8	0.0	1139.6
BARRY WRIGHT CORP	9.1	1700.0	160.0	150.0	81.8	22.2	76.9	8.0	15.0	5.8	5.8	-38.3
BECKMAN INSTRUMENTS	114.4	3.7	25.9	46.9	18.5	21.4	20.6	25.5	21.9	18.4	1.6	51.6
BEECH AIRCRAFT CORP	52.2	13.1	40.5	42.1	71.2	73.1	54.7	34.7	11.7	5.3	6.7	7.3
BELL & HOWELL CO	136.3	63.9	30.2	14.7	16.3	22.0	28.6	14.1	3.2	7.2	3.5	-17.7
BENDIX CORP	428.0	25.0	35.1	45.2	44.7	30.8	28.6	22.2	1.6	6.3	6.1	-15.3
BERKEY PHOTO INC	45.0	92.9	83.3	68.4	33.3	44.4	72.7	18.8	29.5	6.0	0.5	2.3
BETZ LABORATORIES IN	311.8	31.6	28.6	45.5	21.4	12.0	25.9	12.5	23.5	56.2	0.5	924.6

STEP 2

Next the portfolio manager asks that we screen all stocks with dividend yields of less than 3%. The result: 201 more stocks are dropped out of the list leaving a total of 175. The yields appear in the next to last column in the print-out. Note that 15 stocks have been eliminated on the first page alone.

EPS QUARTERLY INCREASING
LAST 8 QUARTERS THRU 3RD QUARTER 1973
YIELD 3% OR BETTER
EPS ARE FULLY DILUTED EXCLUDING EXTRAORDINARY CHARGES

COMPANY NAME	MKT VAL 11/30 $MM	PCT CHGE 71Q4/70Q4 EPS DIL	PCT CHGE 72Q1/71Q1 EPS DIL	PCT CHGE 72Q2/71Q2 EPS DIL	PCT CHGE 72Q3/71Q3 EPS DIL	PCT CHGE 72Q4/71Q4 EPS DIL	PCT CHGE 73Q1/72Q1 EPS DIL	PCT CHGE 73Q2/72Q2 EPS DIL	PCT CHGE 73Q3/72Q3 EPS DIL	PRICE EARNS 11/30	YLD	% ABOVE / BELOW BK VALU
A C F INDS INC	220.8	33.8	11.1	40.4	33.3	8.0	45.6	46.2	22.4	9.1	6.1	17.0
AAV COS	7.0	3.8	66.7	25.0	15.4	22.2	15.0	16.7	16.7	4.3	3.7	13.2
AMERICAN BROADCASTIN	376.7	86.8	132.4	110.7	167.7	76.1	44.3	49.2	39.8	8.4	3.6	56.9
AMERICAN MFG CO	42.8	178.9	21.7	51.0	40.8	0.6	22.6	36.6	50.0	4.7	5.3	-41.9
AMETEK INC	67.2	22.7	36.8	57.1	36.0	29.6	50.0	39.4	44.1	7.8	6.3	39.1
AMF INC	380.2	19.0	30.9	35.8	34.6	7.2	5.6	8.3	4.3	6.7	6.0	68.3
AMFAC INC	157.5	5.9	12.5	7.0	16.7	14.6	2.4	10.9	11.1	6.0	4.7	-23.4
AMPCO PITTSBURGH COR	23.0	50.0	81.8	12.5	216.7	66.7	80.0	100.0	73.7	5.3	5.1	-38.3
ARISTAR INC	40.5	2.6	3.4	130.8	26.1	27.5	23.3	30.0	6.9	5.5	7.9	-35.1
ARMCO STEEL CORP	570.6	63.6	46.7	11.5	130.8	83.3	68.2	69.0	33.3	6.1	6.2	-44.4
ASPRO INC	6.8	5.0	25.0	1.8	51.7	152.0	42.8	47.3	41.9	3.7	7.3	-36.1
AVNET INC	98.1	8.0	25.0	68.8	23.1	25.9	32.0	63.0	31.2	4.4	4.1	2.0
BARRY WRIGHT CORP	9.1	1700.0	160.0	150.0	81.8	22.2	76.9	8.0	15.0	5.8	5.8	-38.3
BEECH AIRCRAFT CORP	52.2	13.1	40.5	42.1	71.2	73.1	54.7	34.7	11.7	5.3	6.7	7.3
BELL & HOWELL CO	136.3	63.9	30.2	14.7	16.3	22.0	28.6	14.1	3.2	7.2	3.5	-17.7
BENDIX CORP	428.0	25.0	35.1	45.2	44.7	30.8	28.6	22.2	1.6	6.3	6.1	-15.3
BLISS & LAUGHLIN IND	43.1	4.3	42.9	9.8	77.8	39.6	67.5	23.7	32.9	5.2	7.3	4.1
BORDEN INC	647.1	16.7	9.3	5.3	3.9	8.2	4.3	10.0	7.5	9.0	5.7	7.8
BORG-WARNER CORP	370.3	12.8	26.0	29.7	27.9	15.9	36.5	15.7	21.8	5.4	7.1	-38.6
BRIGGS & STRATTON	300.1	40.5	68.5	65.4	20.9	37.2	18.7	1.2	15.4	10.9	4.5	234.8
BROADWAY HALE STORES	391.5	8.6	20.2	8.3	3.4	10.5	9.5	44.2	40.0	11.5	3.4	104.8
BROWN GROUP INC	166.5	6.1	9.1	2.8	17.0	12.6	2.8	12.2	12.7	6.9	7.2	3.0
BURNDY CORP	68.6	176.9	44.8	22.2	10.0	2.8	26.2	29.5	25.0	12.1	3.0	51.9
CARBORUNDUM CO	146.9	13.3	15.2	26.4	14.6	23.5	39.6	31.3	27.3	7.3	4.0	-18.8
CARLISLE CORP	33.8	60.7	24.3	66.7	31.2	40.0	47.8	27.3	45.2	5.5	4.8	10.9
CARPENTER TECHNOLOGY	105.8	750.0	110.7	78.3	450.0	352.9	83.1	37.8	100.0	6.9	5.2	3.1
CARRIER CORP	336.0	100.0	81.3	22.9	10.2	12.5	29.3	24.6	10.8	8.5	3.7	13.4
CENTRAL TELEPHONE & UTILS	388.8	8.6	2.2	7.5	16.1	7.9	4.3	14.0	19.4	11.5	5.2	77.5
CESSNA AIRCRAFT CO	92.5	38.1	47.8	107.4	141.7	95.5	128.5	46.2	6.8	4.3	6.5	-11.6
CHAMPION INTL CORP	449.9	36.8	54.5	28.6	10.3	42.3	58.8	68.9	34.9	6.3	5.7	0.1
CHAMPION SPARK PLUG	653.2	15.2	5.3	20.3	4.7	25.0	10.1	20.8	34.3	14.2	3.0	226.6

FIGURE 18–8 (continued)

STEP 3

The portfolio manager then asks that we screen out all stocks selling for more than ten times earnings. This reduced the total from 175 to 144 issues. The price/earnings column is the third from last on the print-out.

EPS QUARTERLY INCREASING
LAST 8 QUARTERS THRU 3RD QUARTER 1973
P/E LESS THAN 10X
YIELD 3% OR BETTER
EPS ARE FULLY DILUTED EXCLUDING EXTRAORDINARY CHARGES

COMPANY NAME	MKT VAL 11/30 $MM	PCT CHGE 71Q4/70Q4 EPS DIL	PCT CHGE 72Q1/71Q1 EPS DIL	PCT CHGE 72Q2/71Q2 EPS DIL	PCT CHGE 72Q3/71Q3 EPS DIL	PCT CHGE 72Q4/71Q4 EPS DIL	PCT CHGE 73Q1/72Q1 EPS DIL	PCT CHGE 73Q2/72Q2 EPS DIL	PCT CHGE 73Q3/72Q3 EPS DIL	PRICE EARNS 11/30	YLD	% ABOVE /BELOW BK VALU
A C F INDS INC	220.8	33.8	11.1	40.4	33.3	8.0	45.6	46.2	22.4	9.1	6.1	17.0
AAV COS	7.0	3.8	66.7	25.0	15.4	22.2	15.0	16.7	16.7	4.3	3.7	13.2
AMERICAN BROADCASTIN	376.7	86.8	132.4	110.7	167.7	76.1	44.3	49.2	39.8	8.4	3.6	56.9
AMERICAN MFG CO	42.8	178.9	21.7	51.0	40.8	0.6	22.6	36.6	50.0	4.7	5.3	39.1
AMETEK INC	67.2	22.7	36.8	57.1	36.0	29.6	50.0	39.4	44.1	7.8	6.3	39.1
AMF INC	380.2	19.0	30.9	35.8	34.6	7.2	5.6	8.3	4.3	6.7	6.0	68.3
AMFAC INC	157.5	5.9	12.5	7.0	16.7	14.6	2.4	10.9	11.1	6.0	4.7	-23.4
AMPCO PITTSBURGH COR	23.0	50.0	81.8	12.5	216.7	66.7	80.0	100.0	73.7	5.3	5.1	-38.3
ARISTAR INC	40.5	2.6	3.4	130.8	26.1	27.5	23.3	30.0	6.9	5.5	7.9	-35.1
ARMCO STEEL CORP	570.6	63.6	46.7	11.5	130.8	83.3	68.2	69.0	33.3	6.1	6.2	-44.4
ASPRO INC	6.8	5.0	25.0	1.8	51.7	152.0	42.8	47.3	41.9	3.7	7.3	-36.1
AVNET INC	98.1	8.0	25.0	68.8	23.1	25.9	32.0	63.0	31.2	4.4	4.1	-2.0
BARRY WRIGHT CORP	9.1	1700.0	160.0	150.0	81.8	22.2	76.9	8.0	15.0	5.8	5.8	-38.3
BEECH AIRCRAFT CORP	52.2	13.1	40.5	42.1	71.2	73.1	54.7	34.7	11.7	5.3	6.7	7.3
BELL & HOWELL CO	136.3	63.9	30.2	14.7	16.3	22.0	28.6	14.1	3.2	7.2	3.5	-17.7
BENDIX CORP	428.0	25.0	35.1	45.2	44.7	30.8	28.6	22.2	1.6	6.3	6.1	-15.3
BLISS & LAUGHLIN IND	43.1	4.3	42.9	9.8	77.8	39.6	67.5	23.7	32.9	5.2	7.3	-4.1
BORDEN INC	647.1	16.7	9.3	5.3	3.9	8.2	4.3	10.0	7.5	9.0	5.7	7.8
BORG-WARNER CORP	370.3	12.8	26.0	29.7	27.9	15.9	36.5	15.7	21.8	5.4	7.1	-38.6
BROWN GROUP INC	166.5	6.1	9.1	2.8	17.0	12.6	2.8	12.2	12.7	6.9	7.2	-3.0
CARBORUNDUM CO	146.9	13.3	15.2	26.4	14.6	23.5	39.6	31.3	27.3	7.3	4.0	-18.8
CARLISLE CORP	33.8	60.7	24.3	66.7	31.2	40.0	47.8	27.3	45.2	5.5	4.8	10.9
CARPENTER TECHNOLOGY	105.8	750.0	110.7	78.3	450.0	352.9	83.1	37.8	100.0	6.9	5.2	3.1
CARRIER CORP	336.0	100.0	81.3	22.9	10.2	12.5	29.3	24.6	10.8	8.5	3.7	13.4
CESSNA AIRCRAFT CO	92.5	38.1	47.8	107.4	141.7	95.5	128.5	46.2	6.8	4.3	6.5	-11.6
CHAMPION INTL CORP	449.9	36.8	54.5	28.6	10.3	42.3	58.8	68.9	34.9	6.3	5.7	0.1
CHEMETRON CORP	58.5	158.8	194.4	585.7	50.0	20.5	18.9	31.3	28.2	6.3	7.0	-64.2
CHLORIDE CONNREX COR	12.7	170.0	67.9	138.3	15.8	10.0	13.8	38.5	30.0	5.7	6.8	-8.0
CHROMALLOY AMERICAN	103.5	30.4	6.9	23.1	29.7	56.7	19.4	14.6	14.6	4.8	6.8	-17.3
COLE NATIONAL CORP	19.4	92.6	70.0	36.7	36.4	42.3	23.5	22.0	26.7	5.1	5.6	33.3
COLUMBIA BRDCSTING S	781.1	45.7	94.7	27.1	9.6	28.7	40.5	15.5	13.9	8.6	5.2	118.3
CONRAC CORP	18.4	55.6	31.0	30.3	19.4	23.8	18.4	16.3	23.3	7.3	4.1	55.7
COPELAND CORP	77.3	8.5	30.4	22.7	24.1	37.7	30.7	18.5	13.4	7.8	3.8	82.9
COPPERWELD CORP	52.1	100.0	25.8	28.0	117.9	39.0	37.2	31.2	21.3	4.5	7.5	-20.8
CTS CORP	61.5	61.8	97.1	67.4	63.0	47.3	34.3	39.6	34.0	5.0	3.2	19.7

STEP 4

Finally, the portfolio manager asks that the list include only stocks selling under book value. Again the computer scans and screens. The result: 61 additional stocks are eliminated leaving a total of 83. By providing us with four basic criteria, we were able to reduce a cumbersome list of 1800 stocks to a small manageable universe from which carefully analyzed selection can be made.

EPS QUARTERLY INCREASING
LAST 8 QUARTERS THRU 3RD QUARTER 1973
P/E LESS THAN 10X
YIELD 3% OR BETTER
SELLING BELOW BOOK VALUE
EPS ARE FULLY DILUTED EXCLUDING EXTRAORDINARY CHARGES

COMPANY NAME	MKT VAL 11/30 $MM	PCT CHGE 71Q4/70Q4 EPS DIL	PCT CHGE 72Q1/71Q1 EPS DIL	PCT CHGE 72Q2/71Q2 EPS DIL	PCT CHGE 72Q3/71Q3 EPS DIL	PCT CHGE 72Q4/71Q4 EPS DIL	PCT CHGE 73Q1/72Q1 EPS DIL	PCT CHGE 73Q2/72Q2 EPS DIL	PCT CHGE 73Q3/72Q3 EPS DIL	PRICE EARNS 11/30	YLD	% ABOVE /BELOW BK VALU
AMERICAN MFG CO	42.8	178.9	21.7	51.0	40.8	0.6	22.6	36.6	50.0	4.7	5.3	-41.9
AMFAC INC	157.5	5.9	12.5	7.0	16.7	14.6	2.4	10.9	11.1	6.0	4.7	-23.4
AMPCO PITTSBURGH COR	23.0	50.0	81.8	12.5	216.7	66.7	80.0	100.0	73.7	5.3	5.1	-38.3
ARISTAR INC	40.5	2.6	3.4	130.8	26.1	27.5	23.3	30.0	6.9	5.5	7.9	-35.1
ARMCO STEEL CORP	570.6	63.6	46.7	11.5	130.8	83.3	68.2	69.0	33.3	6.1	6.2	-44.4
ASPRO INC	6.8	5.0	25.0	1.8	51.7	152.0	42.8	47.3	41.9	3.7	7.3	-36.1
AVNET INC	98.1	8.0	25.0	68.8	23.1	25.9	32.0	63.0	31.2	4.4	4.1	-2.0
BARRY WRIGHT CORP	9.1	1700.0	160.0	150.0	81.8	22.2	76.9	8.0	15.0	5.8	5.8	-38.3
BELL & HOWELL CO	136.3	63.9	30.2	14.7	16.3	22.0	28.6	14.1	3.2	7.2	3.5	-17.7
BENDIX CORP	428.0	25.0	35.1	45.2	44.7	30.8	28.6	22.2	1.6	6.3	6.1	-15.3
BLISS & LAUGHLIN IND	43.1	4.3	42.9	9.8	77.8	39.6	67.5	23.7	32.9	5.2	7.3	-4.1
BORG-WARNER CORP	370.3	12.8	26.0	29.7	27.9	15.9	36.5	15.7	21.8	5.4	7.1	-38.6
BROWN GROUP INC	166.5	6.1	9.1	2.8	17.0	12.6	2.8	12.2	12.7	6.9	7.2	-3.0
CARBORUNDUM CO	146.9	13.3	15.2	26.4	14.6	23.5	39.6	31.3	27.3	7.3	4.0	-18.8
CESSNA AIRCRAFT CO	92.5	38.1	47.8	107.4	141.7	95.5	128.5	46.2	6.8	4.3	6.5	-11.6
CHEMETRON CORP	58.5	158.8	194.4	585.7	50.0	20.5	18.9	31.3	28.2	6.3	7.0	-64.2
CHLORIDE CONNREX COR	12.7	170.0	67.9	138.3	15.8	10.0	13.8	38.5	30.0	5.7	6.8	-8.0
CHROMALLOY AMERICAN	103.5	30.4	6.9	23.1	29.7	56.7	19.4	14.6	14.6	4.8	6.8	-17.3
COPPERWELD CORP	52.1	100.0	25.8	28.0	117.9	39.0	37.2	31.2	21.3	4.5	7.5	-20.8
DANA CORP	290.0	146.7	95.0	31.1	21.3	35.1	33.3	27.8	17.6	5.2	6.3	-3.8
DEL MONTE CORP	211.5	28.1	2.4	3.1	8.1	9.8	11.6	15.2	45.0	7.4	6.9	-13.2
DENNISON MFG CO	55.4	50.0	8.0	10.8	29.9	30.4	20.4	15.3	20.7	5.6	4.7	-20.2
DI GIORGIO CORP	46.7	2000.0	30.0	10.8	16.1	9.5	15.4	14.6	2.8	5.6	8.1	-24.4
DIVERSIFIED MTG INVE	128.9	16.7	10.5	11.9	13.1	11.1	14.3	10.6	5.8	6.1	16.3	-11.9
EATON CORP	412.7	56.5	53.2	23.5	19.0	1.0	26.3	43.0	27.5	5.1	7.5	-6.5
ESQUIRE INC	12.9	16.7	100.0	71.4	40.0	4.8	7.7	54.2	38.1	4.1	5.4	-28.9
EVANS PRODUCTS CO	191.8	42.3	36.3	37.8	31.6	44.0	31.4	21.7	8.2	6.1	3.5	-16.1
FABERGE CORP	47.7	43.6	5.3	5.9	31.8	12.5	10.0	5.6	27.6	5.6	5.1	-41.1
FIRESTONE TIRE & RUB	863.4	23.6	23.3	5.5	15.7	38.2	21.6	29.3	28.8	5.5	6.6	-30.8
FORD MOTOR CO	4182.7	38.6	50.3	43.5	9.6	16.5	42.8	40.5	1.1	3.9	7.6	-24.5
FRUEHAUF CORP	183.8	35.0	56.4	100.0	8.2	9.9	36.1	15.4	32.1	5.8	8.6	-23.5
GAMBLE SKOGMO	117.0	28.6	10.8	77.8	13.8	12.7	12.2	56.3	48.5	5.4	5.0	-53.6
GULF & WESTERN INDS	421.3	11.0	30.5	22.7	46.0	8.6	24.7	34.6	22.8	5.2	3.0	-20.8
HARSCO CORP (DELI)	117.1	5.4	10.0	8.5	20.4	8.5	22.7	22.0	4.4	5.9	7.3	-23.4

Source: Merrill Lynch, Pierce, Fenner & Smith Inc.

Improvement of Screening Filters. Just as the computer can be used efficiently in the actual screening process, which consists of putting hundreds of companies through filters and extracting a shorter list of companies worthy of more intensive study, it also can be used to help improve the underlying nature of the filters themselves. Essentially, what is done is to hypothesize various characteristics of a stock which may cause its price to improve more than the prices of stocks in general. Then the computer is programmed to search for these characteristics in past data records of many stocks, isolate the stocks which have exhibited these characteristics, and trace the price performance of these selected stocks in comparison with those not selected. One finding of this type of research has been that companies with *accelerating* earnings growth rates have been excellent candidates for further common stock analysis. Another is that stockholder rewards are directly related to a company's return on invested capital.[5] In fact, Faulkner, Dawkins and Sullivan, Inc., a leading institutional research firm, decided to reorient the direction of its research effort after extensive computer screening indicated that high rates of return on equity offer the investor the greatest opportunity for profit.[6]

Along these lines, it is interesting to take note of William O'Neil's effort to identify the common characteristics of those stocks which produced the best results in the marketplace during various time periods over the last 20 years. These are summarized in Table 18–3. While it would be difficult to create a list of stocks possessing all of these at the same time, utilization of computer screening techniques can isolate those with a sufficient number to warrant a closer look via traditional security analysis techniques.

Security Evaluation I: Common Stock

Having screened out a group of stocks "for further analysis," the computer has many applications in this further analysis, and particularly in evaluation procedures. In common stock analysis, evaluation consists essentially of making projections of the growth and stability of sales, earnings, and dividends, and then applying capitalization factors to derive measures of intrinsic value. Computers can make an important contribution to both the projection and the capitalization efforts of the analyst.

Projection. In our opinion, a major source of error in making *short-term* forecasts of corporate operating results is the tendency of

---

[5] Peter L. Bernstein, "Advice to Managers: Watch Earnings, Not the Ticker Tape," *Harvard Business Review*, January–February 1973.

[6] John D. Connolly, *The Mechanics of Stockholder Return* (New York: Faulkner, Dawkins & Sullivan, Inc., April 25, 1974).

TABLE 18–3
Common Characteristics of the Best Performing Stocks

1. Major increases in quarterly earnings per share were the dominant reason behind the success of almost all of the greatest winners.
2. Seventy percent of the examples had already reported increases of 20 percent or more in earnings for the quarter prior to their large price increase.
3. The average percent increase in quarterly earnings reported, and showing before the move, exceeded 70 percent.
4. The minority that did not show a major earnings increase prior to their big move usually did so in the following quarter.
5. The average earnings increase shown in the following quarter exceeded 90 percent.
6. The percent increase in earnings was 2 to 3 times more important than the price-earnings ratio as a cause of price increases.
7. Many stocks were selling at low P/Es and many were selling at high P/Es. The average P/E was approximately 23 at the stock's early emerging stage and most continued on to expand their P-Es to higher levels. The average P/E for the Dow Jones at the same point was 16. With the exception of cyclical stocks, it appeared that low P/Es were due to bear markets and high P/Es were due to bull markets and that P/Es were more of an effect or result than a basic cause of moves.
8. More than half of the examples were a result of group or industry moves that occurred due to changes within an industry.
9. Only 3 percent of the companies that produced real results had over 20 million shares outstanding during the period of their success.
10. The outstanding leaders throughout one complete bull market were not usually the leaders in the next bull market unless they began late in the past cycle. Many new names led the way in each new cycle.
11. The majority of stocks were not necessarily "growth stocks" (at least in the prior five years). Many could be classified as mediocre companies where an important change had occurred; i.e., new products or new management.
12. Most of the outstanding successes showed a period of greater relative strength than the general market before their major move occurred.
13. Important volume indications at a few key points occurred prior to the movement of many of the examples.
14. Most of the major moves were preceded by correction and consolidation areas as well as general market corrections in many cases.
15. The average time period movements lasted from their emerging stage until the peak was 17 months.

Source: William O'Neil & Co., Inc.

security analysts to compare the data of each quarter with the same
quarter a year earlier. This technique can produce very misleading
impressions of current developments during periods of cyclical fluctuation. Much more informative is a comparison of each quarter with the
immediately preceding quarters, after having adjusted each quarter's
data for normal seasonal variations. Without the availability of a computer, seasonal adjustment is a laborious and time-consuming statistical procedure. With a computer, hundreds of series of data can be put
onto punched cards or magnetic tape and seasonally adjusted quickly
and accurately.

A program can also be written to take in the seasonally adjusted data
and calculate quarter-to-quarter percentage changes. For even greater
perspective, the computer can be programmed to calculate ratios of
any one company's results to those of any other company, or to all
other companies. Not only can the ratios be automatically calculated,
moreover, but relatively inexpensive equipment is available which
can mechanically chart the results in almost any format desired by the
analyst.

With regard to intercompany or interindustry comparisons, the technique of input-output analysis was discussed in Chapter 6. As noted
there, presently available input-output tables show the sales of each of
scores of industries to each other industry. This results in many
thousands of entries on the table. Probably the only efficient way to
utilize the treasure-house of material thus made available is via
computers.

The long-term projection of corporate growth and stability characteristics obviously involves much qualitative analysis. But it is equally
obvious that the beginning point of most such analyses is a quantitative determination of past rates of change. However, one of the problems in determining past rates of change is that there is no single best
measure. Different rates will result by varying the starting and stopping dates of the historical record being used. Trend lines can be
either arithmetic or logarithmic, linear or curved. If curved, a number
of different mathematical formulas may produce a number of strikingly
different results. Or the analyst may wish to try a moving average
procedure, or an advanced averaging technique such as "exponential
smoothing." With the help of a computer, analysts need not confine themselves to one or two trend-fitting methods, chosen on an a
priori basis and applied across the board to all companies. Rather,
analysts can experiment with many different methods under many
different circumstances, and perhaps end up with a better qualitative
as well as quantitative "feel" for the data. Finally, as noted earlier,
computers provide sophisticated security analysts with the ability to
break away from the elementary ratio and percentage change type of

calculations and to experiment with more advanced econometric approaches to forecasting.

Capitalization. In Chapter 5 we discussed at some length the theory that a common stock's value is equal to the present worth of its future dividends. A long-term projection of the dividend stream of a company is discounted at an appropriate rate, and the present values of each future dividend are summed to derive the stock's theoretical value. Several ingenious books of tables have been published in recent years to assist the analyst who wishes to make such calculations. These tables show how many dollars can be paid per dollar of today's dividends or earnings (the capitalization rate, or "multiplier") given various assumptions as to growth and discount rates. The tables are unique in that they do not require the growth or discount rates to remain constant throughout the period being forecasted. However, the number of dimensions that can be conveniently encompassed in a series of tables is necessarily quite limited. By utilizing computers, on the other hand, analysts need not be at all restricted in making discount calculations.

For example, a computer program could be written to allow the user to specify any or all of the following conditions:

1. Changing growth rates of earnings for any number of spans of years during the projection period.
2. Changing dividend payout ratios.
3. An ultimate date of sale of the stock, with an assumed price-earnings ratio or dividend yield at the time of sale.
4. Changing discount rates for different time spans of the projection period.

The discounting approach to stock valuation is designed to tell the analyst what price a dollar of current earnings or dividends should command under varying assumptions about future conditions. In Chapter 5 we applied this approach to the evaluation of the market as a whole (specifically to the evaluation of Standard & Poor's Industrial Stock Price Index). However, in dealing with the evaluation of individual stocks, we followed a different approach. Here the question asked was not what price a dollar of earnings *should* be worth, but rather what price investors have actually been willing to pay for, say, a 1 percent above-average (or below-average) expected growth rate of earning power and how this price is affected by differences in dividend policy, sales stability, leverage, and so forth.

To attempt a thorough answer to the latter type of question it is necessary to analyze hundreds of different stocks over a period of many years. Such an analysis is feasible only with the assistance of computers. Just measuring the variables is a task of enormous com-

plexity, not to mention the analysis once the measurements have been made.

Security Evaluation II: Bonds

As indicated in Chapter 9, bond quality evaluation traditionally has consisted mostly of a retrospective calculation of various financial ratios, and a qualitative attempt to determine whether these ratios are indicative of a debtor's ability to meet its obligations in the future. Application of computers to the task of ratio calculation has been covered, in effect, in the section on screening. The qualitative aspect of the ratio analysis does not seem particularly amenable to computer assistance. However, recent theoretical discussions of debt-servicing ability focus on the analysis and forecasting of the entire cash flow network of debtor corporations. Here, the applicability of computers is outstanding.

First, the computer can be used to help determine past interrelationships among the major cash flow items, especially the relationships of various expense and balance sheet categories to sales. Second, since the likelihood is that the interrelationships will not prove to have been stable over time, a relatively large number of net changes in cash balances can be envisioned at any hypothesized future sales level. When many different future sales levels are hypothesized, the number of possible net changes in cash is greatly expanded. A computer is an ideal tool for calculating the impact on cash of numerous assumed interrelationships of cash flow items. Moreover, the bond analyst is interested not only in the *range* of possible cash changes but also in the *probabilities* of these changes occurring.[7] Admittedly, the analyst must employ a good deal of subjective judgment when assigning probabilities to each individual component of the cash flow forecast. However, once these have been assigned, the task of calculating the joint and cumulative probabilities is straightforward and simple for a computer, but extremely tedious to do manually.

The application of computers to bond analysis does not stop at forecasting the borrower's debt-servicing ability. Computers are clearly applicable to bond pricing problems. One pricing area where computers have been fairly widely used is in bidding for municipal bond underwriting awards. Municipal bonds are issued in serial form, and each serial maturity can carry a different coupon, price, and yield. Since the number of possible combinations is astronomical, computers can perform yeoman service in spelling out alternatives. Likewise,

---

[7] For an extensive discussion of how probability analysis can actually be applied to the problem of cash flow projections, see the revised edition of this text, Chapter 9, pp. 393–404.

investors in corporate bonds can use the computer to calculate the yields that would result under different assumptions regarding defaults, refunding calls, and reinvestment alternatives at the time of call. Commercial banks and other investors in U.S. government bonds use computers to advantage in analyzing the probable yield gains available in advance refunding offerings and in tax-motivated "swap" transactions (i.e., sale of one security and simultaneous purchase of another).[8]

TECHNICAL ANALYSIS OF STOCK PRICES

Of all the controversies alluded to in this book, one of the most heated involves the question of whether past movements of stock prices, and related *internal* market developments, can be used as indicators of future stock prices. In Chapter 13, we illustrated the usefulness—and also the shortcomings—of breadth-of-market concepts and of such statistics as volume of trading and short selling. However, we indicated that several techniques suffer from a lack of adequate supporting evidence. Chief among these "unproven" techniques is the attribution of forecasting ability to various price patterns, such as "ascending or descending tops and bottoms," "congestion areas," and penetration of long-term moving averages.

In our opinion, the availability of electronic computers makes it possible to test thoroughly the validity of most price-pattern theories. Precise definitions of each theory can first be spelled out. If, as in most cases, the theories are ambiguous, alternative definitions can be established. The definitions, moreover, can be elaborate enough to include data supplementary to price—for example, volume of trading or even earnings per share. After establishing the definitions, computer programs can be written which will act as filters through which the price history of hundreds of stocks can be run. For each theory it can then be determined (a) how many times the particular pattern occurred, and (b) how many times the appearance of the pattern was followed by the price behavior indicated in the theory.

We would be surprised if studies of this type revealed that in a large proportion of cases the appearance of well-defined price patterns is followed by the hypothesized price behavior.[9] Indeed, a finding of this nature would make "value analysis" relatively unimportant. But even if the proportion is not large, as long as it is statistically significant it would be relatively useful information. For the price-pattern filter could then be incorporated in a screening process, such as those dis-

---

[8] IBM has made available some prepackaged programs along these lines.

[9] See Robert A. Levy, "The Predictive Significance of Five-Point Chart Patterns," *The Journal of Business*, July 1971.

FIGURE 18-9. A Complex Computer-Produced Chart and Information Detail

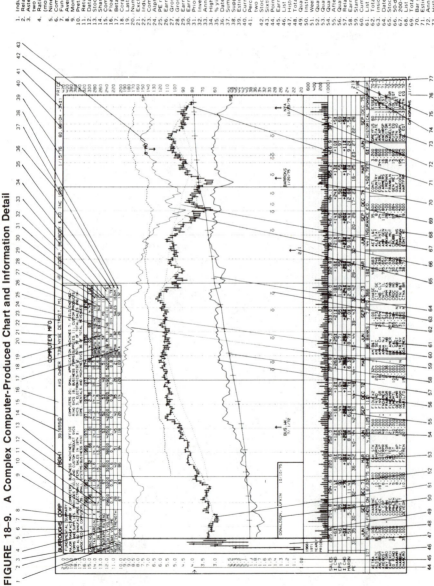

1. Industry group rank (most recent week on right)
2. Relative strength of stock (most recent week on right)
3. Asterisk indicates earnings reported within last two weeks
4. Ratio of daily up-volume to daily down-volume (most recent week on right)
5. Nine-year earnings record
6. Fundamental summary
7. Fundamental summary
8. Average daily volume (most recent week on right)
9. Month fiscal year ends (December blank)
10. Pretax profit margin percentage
11. Return on equity percentage
12. Datagraph rating (most recent week on right)
13. Stock symbol
14. Shares outstanding (in thousands)
15. Company has convertible issue when indicator shown
16. Floating supply
17. Floating supply
18. Corporate debt as percentage of equity
19. Last quarter earnings % change
20. Number of shares held by average owner
21. Exchange where traded
22. Industry group
23. Company headquarters
24. Alpha value
25. P/E rate for five years prior to start of graph
26. Earnings estimate and % change
27. Growth rate for latest five year period
28. Growth rate for five years prior to start of graph
29. Earnings stability factor — 5 to 10 years ago
30. Earnings stability factor
31. Prior quarter earnings % change
32. Investment banker
33. Annual dividend (indicated)
34. High-low price ranges — 5 to 10 years ago
35. % yield (indicated)
36. Date of incorporation
37. Sum of last four quarters sales
38. Supply-demand ratio this week
39. Estimated date of next earnings report
40. Current closing price
41. Percent change from highest price within last two years
42. Stock price scale
43. Sixth month pointer
44. Pointer indicating sum of last four quarters earnings
45. Earnings per share scale
46. Historic yearly price range
47. Quarterly price range
48. Quarterly price range
49. Stock price scale
50. Institutional brokerage reports during last three months
51. Weekly high, low and closing prices
52. Quarterly % change in sales versus a year ago
53. Quarterly earnings per share
54. Quarterly % change in earnings versus a year ago
55. After tax profit margin
56. Quarterly price-earnings ratio range
57. Relative strength line (stock relative to S&P 500)
58. Earnings plotted on running 12 month basis
59. Standard & Poor's 500 line
60. Cumulative tic volume line
61. List of bank sponsorship
62. Total bank sponsorship
63. Weekly high, low and closing prices
64. Date earnings actually reported
65. Stock split or dividend
66. 50-day moving average of price
67. 200-day moving average of price
68. List of insurance company sponsorship
69. Total insurance company sponsorship
70. Bar graph of total weekly volume
71. Estimated earnings line
72. Announcement or news pertaining to security
73. Historical sponsorship by selected growth funds
74. Current price-earnings ratio?
75. Price-earnings ratio on estimated future earnings
76. Date of publication
77. Weekly volume scale (in thousands)

HOW TO READ SERVICE DETAIL

1. **INDUSTRY GROUP RANK** is derived by calculating the percentage price change for the past six months of each stock in a particular group, and then averaging these individual percentage changes for an overall industry group average. These averages are then put in order from the smallest and numbered so that the group with the largest positive change is number 1, etc. This ranking indicates investor favor regarding next largest is number 2, etc. This ranking indicates investor favor regarding

2. **RELATIVE STRENGTH OF EACH STOCK** is the result of calculating price changes over the last six months, and arranged in order of price change and assigned a percentile rank from 99 to 1. The number 99, 98, 97, etc. indicates the most recent relative strength on the basis of time weighted price changes. This number indicates relative investor favor regarding individual stocks.

3. **NINE-YEAR EARNINGS RECORD** shows reported primary earnings (excluding extraordinary items) for each of the last nine years.

4. **THE FUNDAMENTAL SUMMARY** is a description of recent corporate activity with emphasis on product or service, operating locale, research and development, management changes, and stocking figures.

...

(Source: William O'Neil & Co., Inc.)

cussed earlier, and could help analysts zero in on the relatively small number of stocks that are worthy of intensive study at any given point in time.

Computers can also be utilized in other aspects of technical analysis. For example, it has been noted repeatedly that charts of various types are indispensable tools of the trade. Tens of thousands of man-hours are consumed each year on Wall Street to prepare price-volume charts, point-and-figure charts, and relative-strength charts. Yet much of this work could be executed mechanically, more accurately and at lower cost. Even very complex charts can be done mechanically.

In fact Figure 18–9 from William O'Neil's Datagraph service, represents an example of one of the most ambitious computer-based information tools available to institutional investors on a continuous basis. The weekly report, covering virtually every New York Stock Exchange and American Stock Exchange issue, is received each Monday morning, weighs almost five pounds, and contains 50 items of information on each chart—all generated from a computer which stores information. Figure 18–9 details and interprets each item of standard information. In addition, the service contains summary tables which rank all of the issues by various criteria, such as relative strength, alpha coefficients, earnings growth rates, and many others.

Yet another area of computer-oriented investigation of stock price behavior could be an analysis of price "covariance" to aid investors in applying the principle of diversification. One does not achieve the risk-spreading objectives of diversification by purchasing many different security issues if the prices of these issues tend to move up and down simultaneously and by similar magnitudes. Computers can be put to work in an attempt to gain insight into the interrelationship of general market price movements, industry price movements, and individual security price movements. For example, several researchers have successfully applied the statistical technique of factor analysis to this problem, making extensive use of computers in their work.

MONITORING PORTFOLIO ACTIVITY

Over the past few years, a variety of new services has been developed to help portfolio managers, trustees and others, better monitor investment activity. We have discussed several aspects of computer-based performance reports in Chapter 16. In this section, a number of additional features of such reports will be reviewed and illustrated.

Investment Management Sciences, a Standard & Poor's subsidiary, provides institutional investors with a service called *Portfolio Insight*

which provides a weekly report arranged in the following major sections:

I. Portfolio changes for week.
II. Schedule of investments and time-weighted rate of return.
III. Portfolio summary and five largest equity investments.
IV. Performance of equity investments sold.
V. Relative portfolio performance.

Section I of *Portfolio Insight* summarizes all the portfolio transactions that have taken place for the prior week, as well as listing dividend and estimated earnings changes. The report contains the following specific information:

A. Changes in cash, contributions, and interest and dividends.
B. Changes in equity and fixed-income investments.
C. Announced changes in dividend rate.
D. Reported interim earnings per share compared with year ago.

Figure 18–10 is an example of *Portfolio Insight*. Section II provides managers with some basic data regarding the composition of portfolio investments. For example, securities are classified into four major groups—cash and cash equivalents, fixed-income investments, convertible securities, and equities. Data given for each position includes: the size of the position; the unit cost; current unit value; total dollar cost; total market value; annualized income; and current yield. The price performance of each position is indicated on a year-to-date basis and includes the last quarter performance on a risk-adjusted basis.

Section III, the Weekly portfolio summary, shows the equity portion of the portfolio decomposed as to economic, cyclicality, and quality representation. The report also shows both the S&P 500 and DJIA dissected in a similar manner. Thus, portfolio managers can quickly compare the structure of their portfolio with the composition of these broader market indexes.

The final two sections of the weekly report, not shown, provide a summary of performance for those securities sold and shows the relative portfolio performance against other funds of a similar nature.

De Marche Associates' *Diversification Monitor* shows how different managers have structured their equity portfolios in terms of quality, growth, and economic orientation. These comparisons utilize standard definitions to minimize the impact of different managers using different meanings for the same investment terminology. The report provides trustees and portfolio administrators with an objective basis for comparing investment managers by monitoring their respective strategies and measuring the impact of each decision on the portfolio. Perhaps more importantly, *Diversification Monitor* is a tool by which portfolios

FIGURE 18–10
Portfolio Insight

Section II Schedule of Investments and Time–Weighted Rate of Return

INVESTMENTS	UNITS	UNT CST	CUR UNT PRC	TOT $ COST	MARKET VALUE $ AMT	%TOT	---INCOME--- $ AMT	YLD	---TOT G/L--- $ AMT	%	---YTD G/L--- $ AMT	%	BETA COEF	--% QTR RET-- MKT SEL TOT

CASH & EQUIVALENTS
```
ST INVESTMENTS
  COMML PAPER              771,421    771,421 12    92,571 12.0
  TOTAL                    771,421    771,421 12    92,571 12.0
```

EQUITIES
```
AUTOMOTIVE
  FORD MOTOR   4,938 41 35  200,000   173,447  3  15,802  9.1  -26,553 -13  -26,542 -13 1.2 -2 -3 -5
  GEN MOTORS   4,336 46 35  200,000   152,302  2  21,246 13.9  -47,698 -24  -47,696 -24 1.1 -2  1 -1
  TOTAL                     400,000   325,749  5  37,048 11.4  -74,251 -19  -74,238 -19 1.1 -2 -1 -3

BANK & BANK H.
  BANKERS TR   4,036 49 31  196,490   124,612  2  12,108  9.7  -71,878 -37  -71,836 -37 1.2 -2  6  4
  CITICORP     4,371 46 22  200,000    97,801  1   3,497  3.6 -102,199 -51 -102,172 -51 0.6 -1 -1 -2
  FST CHICAGO  5,682 35 17  200,000    98,725  1   5,114  5.2 -101,275 -51 -101,213 -51 1.6 -3  2 -1
  TOTAL                     596,490   321,138  5  20,719  6.5 -275,352 -46 -275,221 -46 1.1 -2  3  1

BUILDING
  OWENS-CORNG  4,078 50 29  204,716   118,772  2   3,589  3.0  -85,944 -42  -85,944 -42 0.9 -2  1 -0

CHEMICALS
  DUPONT E.I.  1,262 158 95  199,106  119,575  2   7,257  6.1  -79,531 -40  -79,531 -40 1.1 -2 -10 -12
  HERCULES     8,695  36 29  315,491  254,329  4   6,956  2.7  -61,162 -19  -61,159 -19 1.1 -2  3  1
  MONSANTO     3,669  55 45  200,000  166,022  2   8,806  5.3  -33,978 -17  -33,939 -17 1.4 -3  4  1
  TOTAL                     714,597   539,926  8  23,019  4.3 -174,671 -24 -174,629 -24 1.1 -2 -0 -2

COMMUNICATIONS
  AM BRDCSTNG  6,451 23 17  150,000   108,054  2   5,161  4.8  -41,946 -28  -41,932 -28 1.3 -2  7  5
  KNIGHT NEWS  8,040 25 19  200,000   148,740  2   2,573  1.7  -51,260 -26  -51,255 -26 2.0 -4 -17 -21
```

Section III Weekly Portfolio Summary

PORTFOLIO ECONOMIC STRUCTURE

-----CATEGORY-----	TOTAL COST	MKT VALUE	---% EQ WTG--- PORT	500	DJI	% YLD	--TOT G/L--- $ AMT	%	---YTD--- %GL	%TOT	BETA COEF	--% QTR RET-- MKT	SEL	TOT	-- % -- WK G/L
CASH & EQUIVALENTS	422,540	422,540				6.0	0	0							
FIXED INCOME INVESTMENTS	434,440	420,875				8.0	-13,565	-3	1	0			-1		-1
CONSUMER-DUR			12	15											
CONS NONDUR(X DRG)	909,640	856,375	19	11	18	3.5	-53,265	-6	6	5	1.2	4	-3	1	0
CONS NONDUR(DRG)	126,400	130,000	3	7	0	3.7	3,600	3	31	3	1.1	4	2	6	6
ENERGY	920,580	768,625	17	15	11	6.8	-151,955	-17	16	11	1.0	3	2	5	1
FINANCIAL			1	0											
HOUSING RELATED	317,830	660,450	15	3	1	2.1	342,620	108	55	24	.5	2	14	16	1
MFG DUR(X OFF EQUP)	553,650	364,250	8	12	17	3.6	-189,400	-34	77	16	2.2	8	-20	-13	0
MFG DUR(OFF EQP)	142,350	105,250	2	10	0	5.7	-37,100	-26	17	2	.9	3	-6	-3	0
MFG NONDURABLES	550,390	726,500	16	6	23	5.2	176,110	32	36	20	1.4	5	-2	2	-2
MINING	567,960	510,000	11	2	4	5.9	-57,960	-10	48	17	1.5	5	7	12	13
RETAIL TRADE				5	6										
SERVICES				2	0										
TRANSPORTATION	219,460	188,125	4	2	0	6.7	-31,335	-14	-2	100	.6	2	-2	0	2
UTILITIES	234,030	226,395	5	12	4	7.0	-7,635	-3	8	2	.6	2	-4	-2	-1
BANKS				0	0										

PORTFOLIO CYCLICALITY STRUCTURE

-----CATEGORY-----	TOTAL COST	MKT VALUE	---% EQ WTG--- PORT	500	DJI	% YLD	--TOT G/L--- $ AMT	%	---YTD--- %GL	%TOT	BETA COEF	--% QTR RET-- MKT	SEL	TOT	-- % -- WK G/L
QUALITY GROWTH	921,250	878,750	19	38	21	2.9	-42,500	-5	4	4	1.1	4	-3	0	-0
AGGRESSIVE GROWTH	553,650	364,250	8	5	0	3.6	-189,400	-34	77	17	2.2	8	-20	-13	0
CYCLICAL GROWTH	2,337,830	2,569,700	57	33	37	4.8	231,870	10	32	64	1.0	4	4	8	3
CYCLICAL	495,530	496,875	11	7	25	8.0	1,345	0	35	13	1.3	5	-0	4	-0
INCOME	234,030	226,395	5	17	17	7.0	-7,635	-3	8	2	.6	2	-4	-2	-1
SPECIAL SITUATIONS				0	0										

PORTFOLIO QUALITY STRUCTURE

-----CATEGORY-----	TOTAL COST	MKT VALUE	---% EQ WTG--- PORT	500	DJI	% YLD	--TOT G/L--- $ AMT	%	---YTD--- %GL	%TOT	BETA COEF	--% QTR RET-- MKT	SEL	TOT	-- % -- WK G/L
QUALITY RATING A	142,350	105,250	2	25	15	5.7	-37,100	-26	17	2	.9	3	-6	-3	0
QUALITY RATING B	737,830	597,875	13	7	5	7.5	-139,955	-19	21	11	1.0	3	-1	3	3
QUALITY RATING C			15	10											
QUALITY RATING D	543,180	527,145	12	27	33	5.3	-16,035	-3	11	5	.8	3	2	5	-1
QUALITY RATING E	1,916,040	1,935,700	43	18	37	4.4	19,660	1	46	63	1.2	4	1	6	5
UNRATED	1,202,890	1,370,000	30	0	0	3.8	167,110	14	15	19	1.3	4	-3	1	-1
S&P 500		86.3				4.7			26					4	3
DJIA		808.4				5.6			31					5	2

Source: Investors Management Sciences, Inc.

can be monitored to ensure that the strategy expressed by investment managers is actually implemented. In other words, the report is designed to document the actual follow-through of investment decision making.

Figure 18–11 shows the equity diversification of the portfolio under

FIGURE 18–13
Investment Research Data for a Particular Security

```
PTA ASSET NUMBER    *51-0041
INTERMED PRODUCTS & SERVICES

RECOMMENDATION STATUS                12-MONTH TARGETS              24-MONTH TARGETS
                                        LOW  MP  HI                  LOW  MP  HI
ANALYST
REC AS OF 12/21/71      III      P/E    26   36  39        P/E      26   36  39
PRICE ON ABOVE DATE      33      PRICE  38   52  57        PRICE    43   59  64
                                 RETURN 11   53  66        RETURN   15   34  40
CURRENT PRICE, PE, YIELD

PRICE AS OF  7/17    69.701      CALENDAR YEAR EARNINGS HISTORY (DECEMBER FY)
P/E ON 75 MP EPS        49
P/E ON 76 MP EPS        44            MAR   JUN  SEP  DEC  -------YEAR-------
INDICATED DIVIDEND    1.250            1     2    3    4   LOW   MP    HIGH
INDICATED CUR YIELD   1.79%
                                 75                        1.50  1.55  1.65
QUALITY                          74    .31                 1.35  1.40  1.45
                                 73    .28  .33  .33  .33        1.27
INSTITUTIONAL QUALITY    D       72    .24  .26  .27  .29        1.06
MARKETABILITY            E
QUALITY OF MANAGEMENT    A
FINANCIAL CAPABILITY     B
INDUSTRY POSITION        C       CALENDAR YEAR PRICE & P/E HISTORY

EARNINGS AND PROFITABILITY                ---PRICE---    ----P/E----
                                          LOW   HIGH     LOW   HIGH
CURRENT NORMAL EPS     1.40      74 YTD   33    40       22E   28E
PROJ BASIC EPS GROWTH  13.0%     1973     34    40       25    30
HIST 10-YR EPS GROWTH  10.6%     1972     35    45       26    34
EARNINGS STABILITY     B17.17    1971     32    43       29    40
RETURN ON EQUITY       B 23.8    1970     23    33       25    36
STABILITY OF R.O.E.    C 2.90
                                 FIVE-YR AVG ABSOLUTE    25    35
                                 FIVE-YR AVG RELATIVE    94    83

PRICE AS OF  7/17    69.701      PTA ASSET NUMBER: *51-0041    CUSIP: 604059-10
INDICATED DIVIDEND    1.250
INDICATED CUR YIELD   1.79%      SCHEME 1: CONSUMER STAPLES

BETA AS OF  4/31      4.620      SCHEME 2: PREDIC MOD GROWTH (UNDER 7%)
STANDARD ERROR OF BETA 1.472     SCHEME 3: MODERATE GROWTH
CORRELATION COEFFICIENT .730
TOTAL VOLATILITY COEFF. 7.131            TOT SHRS--M   VALUE--M  ACCTS  PCT

STOCK SPLIT FACTOR    2.000      SHRS OUT    113,092   7,882,625
EX-DATE             JUNE 20      PIM ACCOUNTS    187     13,048   243  2.69
PAYABLE DATE        JUNE 21                        2        163     4   .03
                                                118      8,283   102  1.70
                                                 66      4,601   137   .94
```

Source: Bank of America, NT & SA.

FIGURE 18–11
Diversification Monitor: Equity Portfolio Diversification

Quality of Companies Owned	Historical Earnings Growth Rate of Companies Owned				
	Stable Growth				
	10 Percent or Better	6–10 Percent	0–6 Percent	Variable Growth	Quality Totals
A. Superior	5.9%	5.6%	6.7%	11.8%	30.0%
B. Above average	8.9	9.3	2.4	21.3	41.9
C. Average	6.3	0.0	1.8	15.1	23.2
D. Acceptable	0.0	0.0	1.4	3.5	4.9
Growth Totals	21.1%	14.9%	12.3%	51.7%	100.0%

Weighting of Companies Owned by Economic Orientation to:	ABC Corporation	Comparative Weighting of S&P 500 Index
Interest rates	20.0%	12.8%
Consumer spending	26.1	23.9
Basic industry	32.3	25.8
Energy	7.8	16.8
Technology	13.8	20.7
Economic Totals	100.0%	100.0%

Note: Individual common stocks represented 96.2 percent of the total equity portfolio as of 12/31/75. Mutual funds represented 3.5 percent and are not rated in the diversification mix shown above.

Source: De Marche Associates, February 1976.

review by classifying each holding in terms of quality, historical earnings, growth rate and by economic orientation. Another part of *Diversification Monitor,* not shown, compares the impact on performance of the portfolio manager's security selection to that which would have occurred if the weightings were equal to the S&P 500 Stock Price Index.

THE WAVE OF THE FUTURE

One of the exciting new developments regarding computer applications and the investment management process is the creation of integrated, or total, information systems that combine all, or at least most, of the various services discussed separately. Thus far only a very few of the largest bank trust departments have installed such data processing capability, but it is more than likely that smaller size management organizations will soon begin similar efforts.

Index Systems, Inc., for example, now offers an on-line, completely integrated Portfolio Management System (PMS) that enables invest-

ment managers to retrieve portfolio and investment research information instantaneously at their desks, and then evaluate that information with the aid of a number of powerful, computer-based tools. To accomplish this, the manager uses a desk-side computer terminal to communicate with a centralized computer system and information bank. PMS uses time-shared computer techniques enabling many managers to use the system simultaneously. Managers may develop and apply their own criteria to the execution of portfolio strategy.

The major features of the Portfolio Management System are separated into three primary groups: portfolio information functions, research information functions, and investment decision aids which support a "management by exception" approach.

The information retrieval portion of the system enables portfolio managers easily to get and display the relevant investment information stored in the computer. For example, Figure 18–12 is a list of all accounts managed by a particular manager, showing the current market value of major components of the account.[10] The printout shown in Figure 18–12 contains other data which is usually of interest to on-line portfolio managers. In addition to listing the market value of each of the managers' accounts, the report shows, reading across the columns on the top, the number of stocks in the portfolio; the composition of the portfolio by major asset category; the amount of common stock held in each of six basic stock classifications, the amount of uninvested funds in the portfolio, net realized capital gains since the beginning of the year, (POW) the level of investment discretion granted by the account (on a scale of one to nine), the investment objective of the account, the risk or beta level of common stock holdings, the total return or performance on a trailing 12-month basis, and the date of the latest transaction.

Other data which can be quickly obtained are the current holdings in a single account, valued at the close of the previous day's trading, and showing purchase cost where such data are available, all recent trades in an account, customer and legal background of the account, all portfolios holding a specified security, and all portfolios not holding a specified security.

In addition, managers may rank the information in any of the displays so that they may quickly and efficiently identify portfolios or securities in exceptional positions that demand their further attention and action. For example, they might rank their list of accounts by the value of uninvested cash. The system will accept their requests and provide this information within seconds.

___

[10] The format and sample data shown for illustration are from the version of PMS developed by Index Systems, Inc. for Bank of America, NT & SA.

FIGURE 18–12
List of Accounts Managed by a Particular Manager

ACCOUNT	TOTAL MKT VAL (000)	NO CS	PCT. OF TOTAL COMMON	FIX	CONVER	C/E	GROUP PERCENT OF COMMON STOCK A	B	C	D	E	F	UN-INV 000	NET CAP GAIN (000)	POW	OBJ	RISK
4233-0	650	-	-	-	-	100	-	-	-	-	-	-	-	37	0	3	
1140-0	521	-	-	-	-	100	-	-	-	-	-	-	-	47	0	2	
4660-0	883	12	48	-.	-	52	33	7	46	-	-	13	-	37	2	1	
1882-0	345	7	54	-	-	46	51	-	49	-	-	-	NEG	47	9	3	
4948-0	252	12	58	-	-	42	30	-	64	-	-	7	-	36	9	3	
2966-0	924	13	54	-	-	42	33	8	40	-	8	10	1	55	9	N	
3487-0	70,237	25	31	39	-	28	17	13	42	6	7	15	2047	41	1	1	
2714-0	1,287	14	61	-	-	27	32	13	32	-	8	14	NEG	46	6	2	
3325-0	814	13	49	24	-	27	30	10	43	-	8	10	1	43	9	1	
2935-0	585	13	75	-	-	25	36	7	40	-	7	10	-	45	0	4	
1665-0	355	12	75	-	-	25	26	10	9	11	14	31	-	44	9	1	
3327-0	2,384	14	51	21	7	20	29	15	39	-	7	11	10	43	9	2	
2862-0	221	13	78	-	-	19	31	12	38	-	7	12	-	45	6	3	
4202-0	98	9	82	-	-	18	37	9	42	-	-	12	-	31	6	4	
3922-0	1,216	14	51	32	-	17	28	13	42	-	7	11	2	38	2	1	
3494-0	2,912	13	83	-	-	17	31	14	37	-	8	10	5	41	9	2	
2616-0	1,436	13	58	26	-	15	34	10	37	-	7	11	5	46	2	1	
4502-0	311	13	87	-	-	13	31	7	43	-	7	11	-	37	2	4	
4692-3	653	12	34	53	-	13	31	6	28	6	8	21	-	43	6	2	
3659-0	260	12	82	-	-	11	33	9	46	-	-	12	-	40	9	1	
0666-0	701	13	56	34	-	10	26	15	42	-	5	11	-	37	8	4	
1740-0	453	14	71	-	-	8	39	5	27	7	9	13	34	43	9	4	
4232-0	4,103	21	52	8	5	7	38	13	37	-	6	5	-	36	9	2	
4147-0	495	11	95	-	-	5	25	8	34	-	14	20	-	32	5	2	
2000-0	64	5	68	28	-	4	27	23	44	-	6	-	-	41	6	3	
1438-0	997	11	61	-	-	3	19	6	48	-	10	17	-	44	9	4	
3927-0	113	9	67	-	-	1	32	11	12	-	14	32	-	34	9	1	
3928-0	129	8	59	-	-	1	22	7	12	-	16	43	-	34	9	2	
1998-0	283	-	-	-	-	-	-	-	-	-	-	-	-	47	9	4	
1721-0	398	11	85	-	-	-	45	10	25	7	9	3	-	43	9	2	
1722-0	124	6	78	-	-	-	15	33	42	-	10	-	-	43	9	3	
4216-0	396	19	100	-	-	-	22	11	53	-	4	10	-	55	1	N	

A = Consumer staples.
B = Consumer cyclicals.
C = Intermediate process.
D = Capital goods companies.
E = Financial stocks.
F = Utilities.
Source: Bank of America, NT & SA.

The portfolio manager, in reviewing a portfolio, needs to k the composition of the portfolio in terms of holdings, cost, v yield, as well as the investment potential of the securities h account.

Managers using the PMS system may request reports on i portfolios or graphic plots, incorporating investment researc help identify potential buy or sell candidates among the holdings. Managers can integrate investment research d portfolio holdings data, using total portfolio measures to an compare accounts. Measures such as average portfolio price ratio and average earnings growth rate, which are difficult to manually, are available instantaneously.

In addition, PMS maintains a historical record of stock pri ings, and other relevant information for any selected group such as an organization's approved "buy" list. Figure 18–13 s investment research data stored in the computer for a particu

rity. An interesting feature of the information available from this report is the "target level" calculations contained in the body of the middle of the computer printout. These "target levels" represent analysts' low, most probable, and high price-earnings estimates for the security based on their own earnings expectations, for the coming 12- and 24-month periods. The target boxes also show the price at which the security would sell assuming both the price-earnings ratio and earnings estimates are achieved, along with the total return which would be produced by the stock. Earnings estimates appear in the box labeled "Calendar Year Earnings History."

A graph comparing changes in the prices of two securities can be used to analyze the potential of a switch from one security to the other. Earnings growth rates, price-earnings ratios, and so on can be compared to similar values for an appropriate index, such as the S&P 500. Individual portfolio performance and other aggregate measures may also be analyzed and compared with similar values for a market index, in either a graphical or tabular report format.

The PMS system also has several features designed to facilitate comparisons between accounts. Managers can create tabular lists of accounts, ordered by any desired account characteristic, or graphic displays highlighting various aggregate account measures, they may easily scan long lists of accounts to identify exceptional situations.

For example, a manager can define a group of accounts similar in investment objectives and constraints. A report showing selected aggregate measures of these accounts can be used to identify those which are currently exposed to unduly high risks and require remedial action. Either graphic or tabular displays can be used for this purpose.

The computer also stores programs which allow managers to create a model or "simulated" portfolio. Using this capability, portfolio managers can create simulated portfolios which reflect a desired portfolio structure and which can then be compared to the real portfolios in order to identify variances from the desired structure. This type of capability can also be used to conduct a "pro forma" analysis of trade programs.

For example, a manager can ask to see all those portfolios whose two-year performance is 5 percent less than the S&P 500 and with an average portfolio price-earnings ratio greater than that of the S&P. Using these PMS functions, portfolio managers can quickly focus on those accounts requiring their immediate attention. They can then evaluate the impact of any decisions they might make. The implications of this "management-by-exception" approach are obvious: a manager can direct more accounts effectively and make more efficient use of the time spent on each account.

Conclusion

It is easy to see that most of the important new advances in security analysis and portfolio management techniques discussed in this book would not have been possible without computer capability. Looking ahead, the computer can be expected to play a continued and important role in the effort:

1. To build upon and refine established procedures, carrying them out faster, with greater accuracy and with increased comprehensiveness.

2. To solve problems which investment people have been aware of but which have heretofore been insoluble because of the sheer size and complexity of the necessary data manipulation.

3. To facilitate original research which leads to a better understanding of security price determination, thereby focusing the attention of analysts and portfolio managers on the most critical variables.

SUGGESTED READINGS

Berton, Lee. "Investing by Computer: Can You Beat the Market?" *Financial World,* July 17, 1974.

Fairbanks, Ralph W., Jr. "New Computer Techniques Help Manage Investment Portfolios," *The Spectator,* February 1972.

Hobman, Richard J. "Setting Investment Policy in an ERISA Environment." *The Journal of Portfolio Management,* Fall 1975.

Laurie, Edward J. *Modern Computer Concepts.* Cincinnati, O.: Southwestern Publishing Co., 1970.

Lorie, James H., and Hamilton, Mary T. "New Focus for Investment Counselling to Pension and Endowment Portfolios—Long Range Risk Policy." *Financial Analysts Journal,* July/August 1973.

McLaughlin, Frank C. "Using Simulation to Chart the Way." *Pension World,* September 1975.

Mlynarczyk, Francis A., Jr. "Computers and Financial Data," *Financial Analyst's Handbook,* vol. I. Homewood, Ill.: Dow Jones-Irwin, Inc., 1975, chap. 40.

O'Brien, John W. "Investment Objectives, Policy and Risk." *The Journal of Portfolio Management,* Summer 1975.

Valentine, Jerome L., and Mennis, Edmund A. "The Computer and Programming," Chap. 14 and "Computer Usage," Chap. 15, in *Quantitative Techniques for Financial Analysis.* C.F.A. Research Foundation. Homewood, Ill.: Richard D. Irwin, Inc., 1971.

Williamson, J. Peter. *"Computerized Approaches to Bond Switching."* *Financial Analysts Journal,* July/August 1970.

Williamson, J. Peter, and Downes, David H. *Manuals for Computer Programs in Finance and Investments.* 3d ed. Hanover, N.H.: The Amos Tuck School of Business Administration, Dartmouth College, 1973.

REVIEW QUESTIONS AND PROBLEMS

1. In the investment process how has the computer been used for screening?

2. What uses are being made currently and can be made in the future of Standard & Poor's Compustat tapes?

3. What are the advantages and disadvantages of using a "fixed" screen instead of a flexible one?

4. How can the computer be used in the process of common stock evaluation?

5. What are the major roles which the computer has to play in bond analysis compared with common stock analysis.

6. How may the computer be used to analyze investment timing?

7. What are the essential elements of a bond evaluation program?

8. Describe and explain how the computer has been used in determining portfolio strategy.

9. How can computer programming be utilized to assess the impact of alternative investment strategies for a pension plan?

10. To what additional areas and additional problems in investment analysis and portfolio management do you envisage computer techniques will be applied? Explain.

RESEARCH PROJECTS

1. Select an investment institution and investigate its present use of computer techniques in its investment activity. Assess the effectiveness of current operations. How can they be improved?

2. Devise a computer screen to identify "growth" stocks. Explain the choice of criteria included and excluded.

3. Outline the steps of a computer program designed to adjust seasonally and calculate quarter-to-quarter percentage changes of corporate sales and earnings.

4. Outline the steps of a computer program designed to determine the advantage of "swapping" a convertible bond holding into the underlying common stock, and vice versa. Test the program with three specific convertible issues.

5. Obtain a computer-generated economic model for the next calendar year and use it as the basis for a "top down" approach to industry and stock selection. Which industries and stocks appear attractive for investment based on the model's conclusion? Which ones should be avoided?

INDEX

Index

A

B

*This book has been set in 10 and 9 point
Caledonia, leaded 2 points. Part and chapter
numbers and titles are in 18 point Helvetica
Medium. The size of the type page is 27 by
45½ picas.*